DOS 5
Principles with Practice

Carolyn Z. Gillay
Saddleback College

FRANKLIN, BEEDLE & ASSOCIATES, INC.
8536 S. W. St. Helens Drive, Suite D
Wilsonville, Oregon 97070
(503) 682 - 7668

Publisher	**James F. Leisy, Jr.**
Manuscript Editor	**Sheryl Rose**
Design and Production	**Bill DeRouchey**
Keyboarding and Corrections	**Lisa Cannon**
Cover Design	**Neo Nova**
Book Manufacturing	**Malloy Lithography (Ann Arbor, MI)**

Rights and Permissions
Franklin, Beedle & Associates Incorporated
8536 SW St. Helens Drive, Suite D
Wilsonville, Oregon 97070

Library of Congress Cataloging-in-Publication Data

Gillay, Carolyn Z.
DOS 5 principles with practice / by Carolyn Z. Gillay.
832 p. cm.
Includes index.
ISBN 0-938661-39-6
1. Operating systems (Computers) 2. PC-DOS (Computer file) 3. MS -DOS (Computer file) I. Title.
QA76.76.O63G543 1992
005.4'46--dc20 92-13663
CIP

Dedication:

To my Mother, Emily Gillay Markiw, who is a wonderful role model and who keeps me supplied with ideas, love, and encouragement.

C.Z.G.

Related books from ...

FRANKLIN, BEEDLE, AND ASSOCIATES INCORPORATED

DOS 5 Fundamentals
by Carolyn Z. Gillay

From DOS through Windows
by Carolyn Z. Gillay

Windows: Principles with Practice
by Carolyn Z. Gillay

PC/MS DOS Fundamentals
by Carolyn Z. Gillay

Word for Windows
by Jane Troop and Dale Craig

WordPerfect for Windows
by Jane Troop and Dale Craig

WordPerfect 5.1: Word Processing to Desktop Publishing
by Jane Troop and Dale Craig

WordPerfect 5.1 Exercise Book
by Jane Troop, Sarah J. Stackhouse, and Esther S. Kelder

Desktop Publishing withWordPerfect
by Jane Troop and Dale Craig

Macintosh and You: The Basics
by Patricia Sullivan

Works for Students
by Patti D. Nogales

AppleWorks for Students
by Patti D. Nogales

Introduction to the Personal Computer
by Keith Carver and June Carver

Brief Contents

Preface

DOS 5: Principles with Practice is for Beginning to Advanced Computer Users

This book assumes no prior experience with computers, software, or PC/MS DOS. It is intended to be used as the core textbook for a course which focuses exclusively on PC/MS DOS. It is appropriate for use in a beginning through advanced sequence of DOS courses. Or, it may also be used for the PC/MS-DOS portion of an operating system course on operating systems for students studying programming. It leads the student from a basic to the sophisticated use of DOS. Each chapter has challenge questions for the advanced student that follows general questions for the beginning student. Thus, the advanced student can be challenged without sacrificing the concerns of the beginning student.

MS-DOS Version 5.0 Focus, but Compatible with Earlier Versions

This textbook was written to focus specifically on DOS 5.0. However, earlier versions of DOS are not eliminated. All versions of DOS 2.0 through 5.0 are included. The core commands that are common to all versions of DOS are covered and can be used in any DOS environment. New features and the DOS 5.0 specific commands are so indicated.

Covers Hard Disk Management Concepts

Today, most students and schools use system configurations that include hard disks. Students are anxious to learn hard disk management. Although the student uses the hard disk, for the most part, all activities are written to floppy disks, not the laboratory hard disks. The text is designed so that the student may work at home or the office without compromising the integrity of the assignments.

The primary tool for understanding hard disks is subdirectories. Subdirectories are introduced early and included with commands and exercises so that students are comfortable using paths and directories prior to covering them in depth in Chapter 9. Furthermore, Chapter 10 goes beyond the use and understanding of subdirectory commands with a practical approach to principles and practices of organizing a hard disk. The student uses the ACTIVITIES disk that comes with the text to accomplish a real-life example of organizing a disk. Thus, the instructor and laboratory environment do not need to be concerned with students writing to the hard disks or network disks.

Step Through Approach that Demystifies DOS

Each PC/MS DOS command covered in this book is presented in a careful student-oriented step-by-step approach. Interspersed within the steps are the reasons for and results of each action. At the end of each chapter are application assignments which allow the student to apply his knowledge independently and prove mastery of the subject area through critical thinking skills. In addition, each command is presented in a syntactically correct manner so that, when students complete the course, they will be able to use computer manuals because they will be able to read syntax diagrams. Thus, no matter what changes are made to DOS in the future, students will be able to use any new commands. This skill also transfers to the use of application packages.

ACTIVITIES Disk with Toy Programs and Data Files Accompanies the Book

The most difficult part of teaching DOS to students is the esoteric nature of operating systems. Although students find the material interesting, the question that I repeatedly get is, "What good is DOS? It doesn't do anything." If an instructor attempts to use a complex application program such as WordPerfect, the time is spent teaching the application and not DOS. Thus, there are two toy applications (provided on the student Activities Disk) that the student works with: a simple database, ADDRESS, and a simple spreadsheet, SS. The student has the opportunity to load an application program and prewritten data files, as well as to create simple data files. This experience highlights the differences between data files and program files, and how to use DOS commands to manipulate those files.

Intermediate and Advanced DOS Concepts Covered

At Saddleback College, I teach the DOS course as a beginning eight/nine week class and as an intermediate eight/nine week class. The first nine chapters are used for the beginning DOS class, the second nine chapters are used for the intermediate class. The value of EDIT new to DOS 5.0 is covered in the same thorough step-by-step methodology. Batch files are covered including loading application software with batch files, creating menu systems and writing an `AUTOEXEC.BAT` file. Many computer users—the students—need to customize their system installation, so special attention has been paid to the implementation of `CONFIG.SYS`. Again, care is taken so that the students boot off a floppy disk with the `CONFIG.SYS` file so as not to harm the computer laboratory environment.

Since so many questions arise concerning memory management, the different kinds of memory are discussed. The more sophisticated user will learn to take advantage of pipes, filters and redirection as well as to write useful batch files with these tools. BACKUP, RESTORE and installing DOS to the hard disk have been treated outside the main body of the text in the Appendices. These are powerful commands and their presentation is left to the discretion of the instructor.

Coverage of MS-DOS Shell, PC Tools, Norton Utilities, and Windows

Since the shell environment is becoming increasingly more important, a chapter is included on MS-DOS Shell as well as an introduction to Windows. The student can compare and contrast the virtues of Windows to DOS Shell. In addition, the student gets first hand experience with a look at two of the better known DOS utility programs—PC Tools and Norton Utilities as well as comparing and contrasting recovering a deleted file in both of these utility programs as well as the new UNDELETE command in DOS 5.0.

Self-Mastery Approach

Each chapter includes a chapter summary, key terms and application assignments that can be assigned as homework. Each assigned problem can stand alone, so the instructor has great latitude in the use of this material. These assignments help to reinforce the materials in the chapter as well as develop problem solving abilities of students. In addition, shrink-wrapped with the book is a Study Guide with paper and pencil exercises including true/false, completion, matching, multiple choice, responding to commands and writing commands questions for every chapter. Answers to half of the questions are included with the study guide while answers to the second half are in the Instructor's Manual.

Built-in Reference Tools

The book is useful as a reference to PC/MS DOS commands. The first Appendix includes a means to make a single working DOS booting disk out of the many disks that come with DOS 3.3, 4.0, and 5.0. This feature is particularly useful for those students working at home or at the office. The rest of the Appendices include a tutorial for using BACKUP and RESTORE, as well as installing DOS to the hard disk and partitioning it. Also within the Appendices are explanations of bits and bytes, the SYS command, special keys in DOS and EDIT, commands within EDIT and EDLIN, device drivers, system configuration commands, batch file commands, and a DOS command summary.

Supplementary Material

An Instructor's Manual is available to the teacher upon adoption of this book for the classroom. It includes:

— A syllabus for both eight/nine-week and sixteen/seventeen week courses.
— Teaching suggestions for each chapter.
— Answers to all the application assignments and Study Guide questions.
— Tests and transparency masters for each chapter.
— Midterms and final exams.

Conventions Used in this Text

Special keys found on the keyboard are denoted by angle brackets in this text. For example:

<Enter>	means the key labeled "Enter" or ↵.
<Shift>	means the key labeled "Shift" or ⇧.
<Backspace>	means the key labeled "Backspace" or ←.
<Ctrl>	means the key labeled "Ctrl".
<Alt>	means the key labeled "Alt".
<Esc>	means the key labeled "Esc".
<Pause>	means the key labeled "Pause".
<PrtSc>	means the key labeled "PrtSc" or "Print Screen".
<NumLock>	means the key labeled "Num Lock".
<Tab>	means the key labeled "Tab".
<Plus>	means the key labeled with the plus symbol (+).
<Minus>	means the key labeled with the minus symbol (-).
<Spacebar>	means the long bar at the bottom of the keyboard.

In addition, there are four directional arrow keys. On older keyboards, they are part of the numeric keypad on the right side of the keyboard. On newer keyboards, they are a separate key group. They are:

<Up arrow>	means the key labeled ↑.
<Down arrow>	means the key labeled ↓.
<Left arrow>	means the key labeled ←.
<Right arrow>	means the key labeled →.

Multiple key combinations will be connected with plus symbols. For example:

<Ctrl>+C	means to press and hold down the <Ctrl> key and then simultaneously press the letter C.

Certain conventions have been followed in the text to allow you to follow the instructions easily. The major points are displayed below.

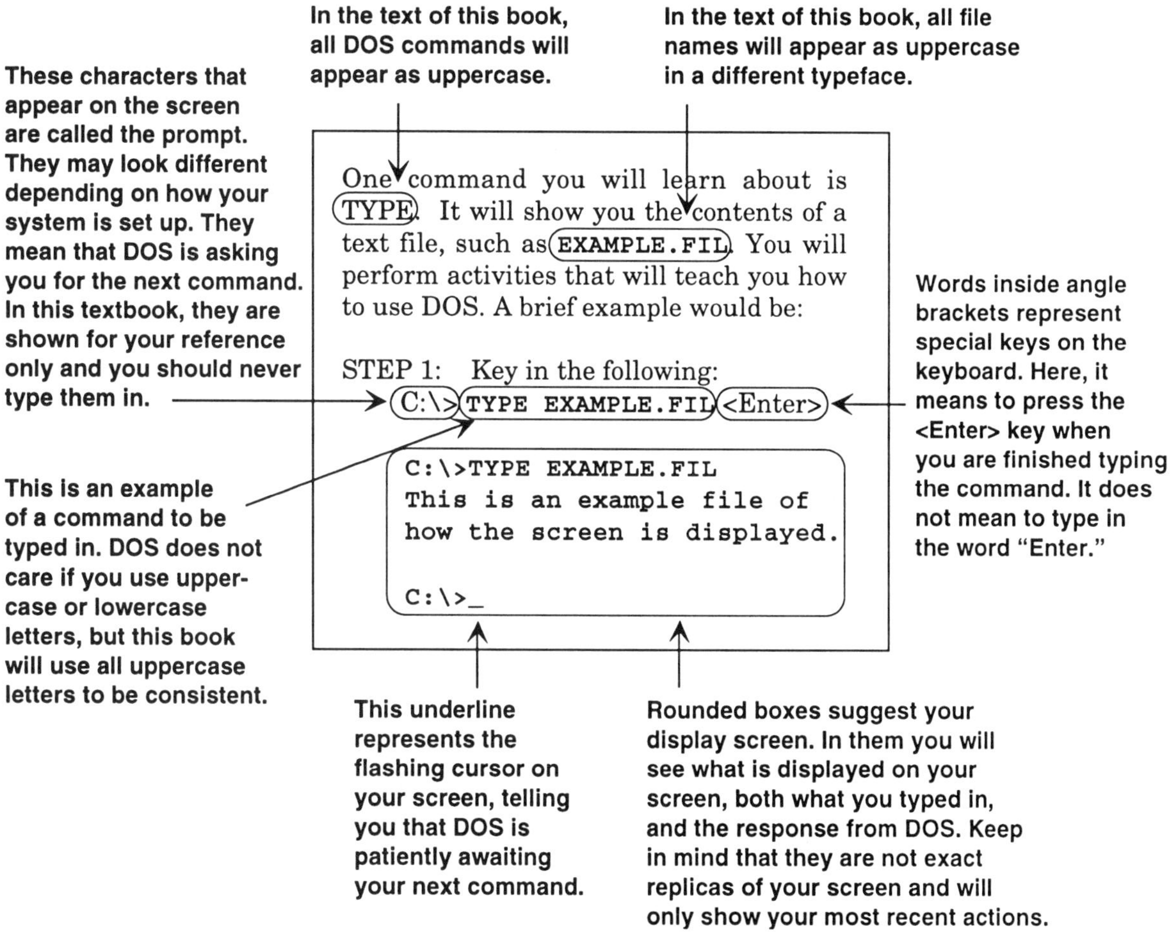

In the text of this book, all DOS commands will appear as uppercase.

In the text of this book, all file names will appear as uppercase in a different typeface.

These characters that appear on the screen are called the prompt. They may look different depending on how your system is set up. They mean that DOS is asking you for the next command. In this textbook, they are shown for your reference only and you should never type them in.

One command you will learn about is TYPE. It will show you the contents of a text file, such as EXAMPLE.FIL. You will perform activities that will teach you how to use DOS. A brief example would be:

STEP 1: Key in the following:

C:\>TYPE EXAMPLE.FIL<Enter>

```
C:\>TYPE EXAMPLE.FIL
This is an example file of
how the screen is displayed.

C:\>_
```

Words inside angle brackets represent special keys on the keyboard. Here, it means to press the <Enter> key when you are finished typing the command. It does not mean to type in the word "Enter."

This is an example of a command to be typed in. DOS does not care if you use upper-case or lowercase letters, but this book will use all uppercase letters to be consistent.

This underline represents the flashing cursor on your screen, telling you that DOS is patiently awaiting your next command.

Rounded boxes suggest your display screen. In them you will see what is displayed on your screen, both what you typed in, and the response from DOS. Keep in mind that they are not exact replicas of your screen and will only show your most recent actions.

Acknowledgements

A project of this scope is difficult to successfully complete without the contributions of many individuals. Thank you to all who have contributed. A special thanks to:

Steven Tuttle, my son, for working through each activity and exercise in the book and for reminding me that physical activities and exercise are equally as important as mental activities.

Sonia Maurdeff, my niece, for working through each activity and exercise in the book as well as assisting with the glossary.

Nick Markiw, my brother, for creating some of the utilities used in the book as well as letting me know of every new hardware innovation.

Mark Potter, for writing the toy database and spreadsheet applications included in this book.

Indigo Brude, who, like magic, always seems to appear in my life when I need her most.

The "Family," *Sophie Nyles*, *Nick Babchuk*, *Walter Babchuk*, and *Nick Markiw*, *Sr.*, for always believing in me and encouraging me in all I do.

A heartfelt thanks to my sister, *Kathryn Maurdeff*, who with her professional experience in education, helped and assisted greatly in preparing questions when I just could not think of any more.

To the students at Saddleback College—and at the different workshops I have given, who have taken the DOS course and provided me with many insights. And who also have loved DOS so much that they have demanded and gotten an advanced DOS class at Saddleback College.

To my colleagues in the Computer Information Management Department at Saddleback College who are always encouraging me, with a special thanks to the administrators who have been so supportive—*Pat Sullivan*, Department Chair, *Marly Bergerud*, Dean of Business Science, and *Don Busche*, Dean of Vocational Education.

California Business Education Association and *National Business Education Association* for providing a forum in which to present ideas on the teaching of DOS, as well as inviting me to make presentations sharing my experiences.

Jim Leisy, my publisher, for being absolutely wonderful, patient, understanding and cooperative, even when I was most harried. And a special thanks to *Ann*, *Stephen* and *Eric* who also put up with me.

And a special heartfelt thanks and gratitude to *Bill DeRouchey* who suffered with me, created wonderful drawings that clarified my words, and let me make changes at the 11th hour. And thanks as well to all at FBA, who are great to me—*Charles*, *Scott*, *Samantha*, *Lisa*, *Sean* and *Christina*.

And how could I do this if it were not for my wonderful husband, *Frank Panezich*, who does it all—is supportive, patient, offers suggestions, edits materials (if you want to write books, always marry an English teacher) and has become far more computer literate than he ever wanted to be. And above all, who I have the most fun with no matter what we are doing—even writing books.

Thank you to the following teachers for reading and critiqueing the manuscript. In addition, I appreciated their willingness to share insights and experiences in teaching DOS courses.

W. L. Barry, Jr.	El Paso Community College
William Beidler	University of Southern Mississippi
David Blossom	Career Development Institute
Joseph Dean	El Centro College
Nick Newell	Northeast Mississippi Community College
Angelina Rayne	Colorado Training Institute
Wesley Scruggs	Brazosport College
Pat Tillman	Grayson County College

Special thanks to Microsoft Corporation for their help during the development of this textbook. The technical staff was extremely cooperative in providing answers to my questions. Thank you to the following individuals, for supplying beta copies and updated information on DOS: *Christy Gersich*, *Ellen Mosner*, *Tanya D. van Dam*, and *Arlene Wagar* (Waggener Edstrom).

Table of Contents

Chapter 1

Microcomputer Systems
Hardware, Software, and the Operating System

Chapter 2

Getting Started with DOS
Booting the System, Using the Keyboard, Using DISKCOPY and DISKCOMP

Chapter 3

Command Syntax

Using the DIR Command with Parameters and Wildcards

Chapter 4

Disks and Formatting

Chapter 5

Using Internal Commands
COPY and TYPE

Chapter 6

Expanding the Use of the COPY Command

Chapter 7

Using ERASE, DEL, and RENAME

Chapter 8

Informational Commands
CHKDSK, ATTRIB, COMP, FC, VER, and LABEL

Chapter 9

Subdirectories

Chapter 10

Organizing the Hard Disk

Chapter 11

EDIT, The Text Editor

Chapter 12

Introduction to Batch Files

Chapter 14

Configuring the System

Chapter 15

Managing Devices with PRINT and MODE

Chapter 16

Using Shells: MS-DOS Shell

Chapter 17

Utility Programs: Norton Utilities and PC Tools

Chapter 18

Windows

Appendices

Chapter 1

Microcomputer Systems
Hardware, Software, and the Operating System

After completing this chapter you will be able to:

1. Categorize the types of computers in use today.
2. Name the hardware components of a computer and explain the purpose of each component.
3. Explain how a CPU functions.
4. List and explain the functions of the various peripheral input and output devices of a computer.
5. Compare and contrast RAM and ROM.
6. Explain how the use of adapter boards increases the capabilities of the computer.
7. Explain what external storage devices are.
8. Name and explain how the different types of floppy disks function.
9. Explain how the hard disk functions.
10. Explain how and why a disk is divided.
11. Explain how disk drives derive their names.
12. Explain how disk drives write information to and read information from a disk.
13. Explain how the capacity of a disk is measured.
14. Compare and contrast system software and application software.
15. Explain the functions of an operating system.

Chapter Overview

It is impossible to live in today's society without being affected by the widespread use of computers. They are used by the government, found in almost every sector of the business world, prevalent in schools, and will soon be as common as television sets in the home. The computer software available today makes it possible to use computers for sophisticated scientific applications such as nuclear and atomic physics, for general business purposes such as payroll and banking functions, for specialized applications in engineering and industrial research, for teaching basic skills to children, for record keeping and accounting in small businesses, and for word processing, entertainment, and record keeping in the home. The list of the many ways to utilize computer technology is endless.

To use a computer and run application packages (programs that can be used with a microcomputer), one must first understand how the operating system of a computer works and how to use the operating system software that comes with the computer. The operating system of a computer takes care of the mandatory functions for computer operations and allows the computer to run application programs. Since **DOS** (Disk Operating System) is the major microcomputer operating system in use today, this text is devoted to teaching the concepts of the operating system in general and DOS operations in particular.

1.0 An Introduction to Computers

The desire to automate repetitive calculations, as well as complex ones, is very old. For hundreds of years, the Chinese have automated their business transactions with a wooden calculator called an abacus. English mathematician Charles Babbage invented a mechanical calculator in the middle of the last century. A little over forty years ago, a professor at Iowa State University, John Atanasoff, designed the first known workable electronic computer to store and calculate student grades.

Today's personal computers, at the most basic level, are calculators, but this definition is very narrow. Now, we use these machines to handle accounting chores (spreadsheets), to write books (word processing), to organize and retrieve information (data bases), and to design automobiles (computer-aided design), all very high-level processes.

1.1 Categories of Computers

Computers are divided into categories based on a variety of factors such as size, processing speed, information storage capacity, and cost. In the ever-changing technical world, these classifications are not absolute. Technical lines blur the categories. For instance, some microcomputers today exceed the capabilities of mainframes manufactured five years ago. Table 1.1 shows the major categories of computers.

Table 1.1 Computer Types

Computer	Applications
Supercomputer: Very large computer	Used most often in sophisticated scientific applications such as nuclear physics, atomic physics, and seismology.
Mainframe: Large computer	General-purpose business machines. Typical applications include accounting, payroll, banking and airline reservations.
Minicomputer: Small mainframe	Specialized applications such as engineering and industrial research.
Microcomputer: Small, general-purpose, computers	Applications include word processing, accounting for a small business, time and record keeping for attorneys, and medical accounting.

1.2 Computer Components

All computers operate the same way, regardless of their category. Information is input, processed, and stored, and the results are output. Figure 1.1 is a graphic representation of this process.

The figure shows the physical components of a computer system, referred to as **hardware**. All computer systems, large or small, have these basic components. However, hardware by itself can do nothing. A computer system needs a program called **software**. Software is a set of detailed instructions that tell the hardware what operations to perform.

Data, in its simplest form, are related or unrelated numbers, words, or facts that when arranged in a particular way provide information. For example, if you wanted to add 2 plus 3 using a computer, you would need the hardware to do the work. Next, you would need the software instructions to tell the computer how to add. Then, you would have to input the data, the numbers 2 and 3, so that the program would know what was to be processed. Last, you would have to enter the appropriate software instructions so that the addition can occur.

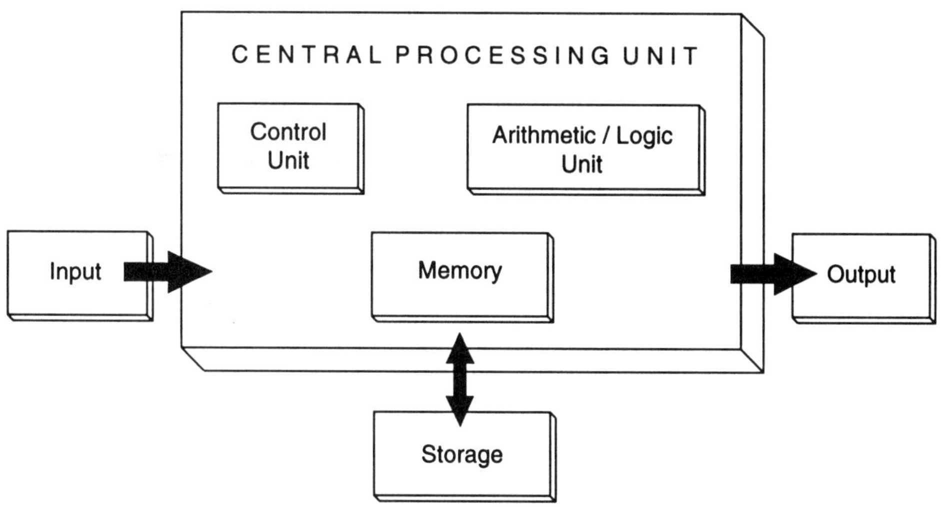

Figure 1.1 Components of a Computer System

1.3 Microcomputer Hardware Components

This text is devoted to **microcomputers**. Microcomputers, which may be called micros, personal computers, home computers, laptops, PCs, or desktop computers, are comprised of hardware components. In other words, a complete microcomputer system has several parts, much like a stereo system. The basic components of a complete system, also called the **system configuration**, include an input device (typically a keyboard) for entering data and programs; a system unit that houses the electronic circuitry for storing and processing data and programs (CPU, adapter cards, ROM, and RAM); a visual display unit (a monitor); an external storage unit that stores data and programs on disks (disk drives); and a printer for producing a printed version of the results. Figure 1.2 represents a typical microcomputer system.

Figure 1.2
A Typical Microcomputer System

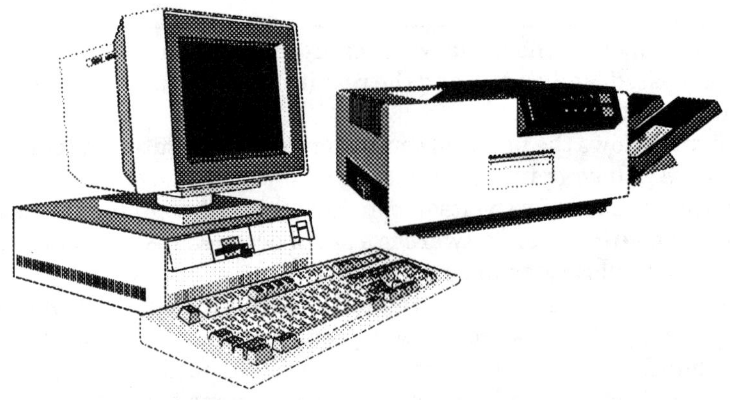

1.4 The System Unit

Figure 1.3
The System Unit

The system unit, as shown in Figure 1.3, is the "black box" that houses the electronic and mechanical parts of the computer. If the outer case were removed and the unit were opened, it would look like the diagram in Figure 1.4.

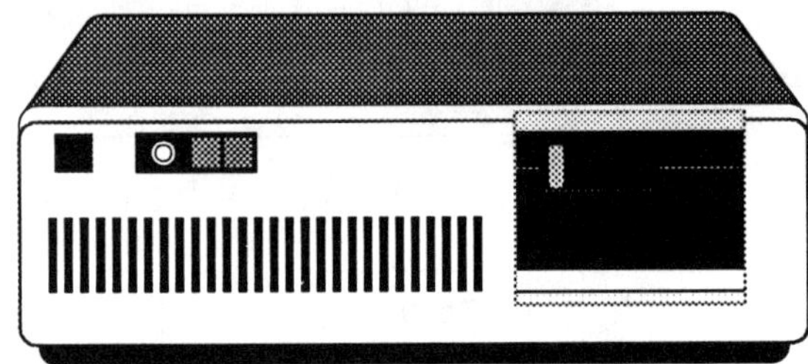

Figure 1.4
Inside the System Unit

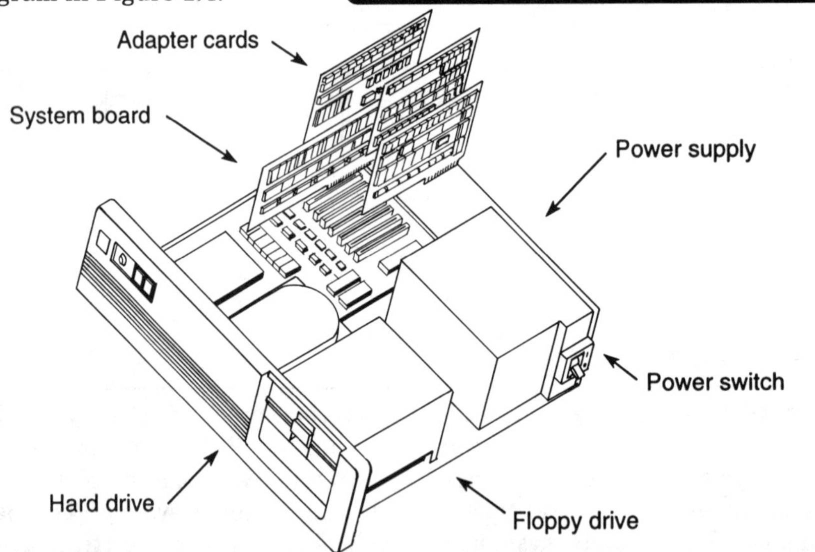

The system unit has some mechanical parts, such as the power supply (to get power to the computer) and the disk drives. In addition, it contains many printed electronic circuit boards, also called cards or **adapter cards**. One of these is a special printed circuit board called the system board or the "motherboard." Attached to the system board is the microprocessor chip that is the central processing unit or **CPU**, the Random Access Memory, and the Read-Only Memory.

1.5 Central Processing Unit

The **central processing unit**, most commonly referred to as the **CPU**, is the brain of the computer and is composed of transistors on a silicon chip. It comprehends and carries out instructions sent to it by a program and directs the activity of the computer. It is comprised of two parts, the control unit and the arithmetic/logic unit (ALU). The **control unit** is responsible for directing and coordinating program (software) instructions. It does not actually execute the instructions but directs the other parts of the system to carry them out. The **ALU** performs the arithmetic functions: addition, subtraction, multiplication, and division and the logical functions which, in most cases, are comparisons. Programs are designed to take action based on these comparisons.

1.6 Random Access Memory

Random Access Memory (**RAM**) is the workspace of the computer, often referred to as main **memory**. The terms RAM and memory are used interchangeably. Physically, RAM is contained in many electrical circuits. However, a computer's memory is not like a person's memory. RAM is not a permanent record of anything. RAM is the place where the programs and data are placed while the computer is working. Computer memory is temporary (volatile) and useful only while the computer is on.

1.7 Read-only Memory

Read-Only Memory (**ROM**) holds permanently stored programs installed by the manufacturer of the specific computer. ROM is also made from electronic circuits. "Read only" means exactly what it says. The CPU can only read the instructions from ROM; it cannot write, erase, or alter the contents of ROM in any way. ROM is nonvolatile, which means that when you turn off the computer, none of the information stored on ROM is lost. Actually, ROM has programs etched on it; it is a program-on-a-chip. Here, however, is where the terms hardware and software get somewhat blurred. ROM is hardware because it is a chip. However, it is also software because it contains instructions. Hence, ROM is sometimes called **firmware**, halfway between hardware and software. Nearly all computers use ROM to hold start-up programs, including the instructions for loading the operating system into RAM. Most ROM is located on the system board, but some ROM can also be located on adapter boards.

1.8 Adapter Cards

Adapter boards, really printed circuit boards called **adapter cards**, are installed in the system unit when purchased or later as an addition. Adapter cards allow the user to add more RAM, use a special video display, or utilize a modem or a mouse. These items are considered **peripheral devices**. The locations inside the computer where these adapter cards are installed are called **expansion slots**. How many options you can install depends on how many slots you have. For instance, an IBM PS/2 model 55SX has three slots whereas an IBM PS/2 model 80 has seven.

1.9 What a Computer Does

The preceding configuration sounds complex, but in principle it is fairly simple. For example, I want to fill out a credit application, an activity analogous to what a computer can do. I have a brain and can follow instructions. The computer has a brain, the CPU, and it can follow instructions. However, I need some instructions so that I can fill out the credit application correctly. The computer also needs instructions to follow. For me the instructions are called directions; for the computer the instructions are called programs.

When I want to complete the application, I need a place to work. I choose a desk. The computer also needs a place to work. It uses memory. I place my program on the desk. The computer places its program in memory (RAM). I also need some information to fill out the credit form such as my name, address, income, and debts. I gather this information and place it on the desk. The computer also needs information to fill out its form. This information is called data, which it also gathers and places in RAM.

Now the computer and I are ready to work. I read the first instruction. So does the computer. The first instruction asks how much is my monthly income? I get my salary stubs and on a piece of scratch paper, I write down the information. The computer does the same thing. The CPU reads the first instruction in the program. It then reads the piece of data it needs and writes it to a "scratch pad" in RAM.

I read the next instruction. It asks, how much is my rent? I get the amount from my canceled check and write it on the scratch pad. The computer does the same thing. The CPU reads the next instruction, gets the amount, and writes it in the "scratch pad" in RAM. I read the next instruction, which says to subtract. The computer does the same. I keep reading instructions until there are no more instructions and I have completed the activity. The computer does the same.

If I have more than one credit application to fill out, I start all over again. I read the first instruction, get the data, and complete the form. This process is exactly what the computer does. However, the computer does it much faster than I do. If, for instance, it takes me an hour to fill out one form, the computer can fill out 200 forms in an hour. There is one major difference between a CPU and my brain. I can be creative, take shortcuts, or not follow instructions exactly. The computer cannot think on its own. It must have instructions, and it must follow them *exactly*.

1.10 Peripherals: Input Devices

We have been illustrating what goes on in the "box," but how do program and data get into RAM? This process is done with input devices. The most common input device is the typewriterlike keyboard attached to the system unit by means of a cable. By keying in instructions and data, you communicate with the computer, which places the information into RAM. Thus, instead of writing down my monthly salary, I would key it in. There are other input devices such as a **light pen**, which has a light-sensitive cell. When the tip of the pen comes in contact with the monitor, it identifies a point on the screen. You can use the light pen to draw or enter data. **Scanners**, such as those in grocery stores, allow a clerk to wave an item across an electrosensitive plate, and the plate reads the magnetic price code. Touch-sensitive display screens allow the user to touch the screen with a finger to input data. A **mouse** is a hand-held device that is moved around on a flat surface, allowing the user to move information on the screen.

1.11 Peripherals: Output Devices

In addition to getting information into the "box," you also want to get it out of the box. You may want to see what you keyed in on the monitor, or you might want to have a "hard" copy of the data printed. These processes are known as output or where information is written to. Thus, you "read" information in and you "write" information out, commonly known as I/O for input and output.

1.12 Output Devices: Monitors

A **monitor**, also called a terminal, display screen, screen, cathode ray tube (CRT), or video display tube (VDT), looks like a television. The CPU writes information to the screen where it is displayed. Thus, when I key in my monthly salary, it is written to the screen so I can see what I keyed in.

The monitors themselves come in two basic types, monochrome and color. Monochrome monitors display in one color. The user can choose the color: green characters on a black screen, amber characters on a black screen, etc. Color monitors obviously display in color. Most monitors display 80 characters across the screen and 25 lines down the screen. However, other types of monitors display an entire page. The clarity or resolution of what is displayed is measured in picture elements or pixels. **Pixels** are little dots that light up and connect to form images on the screen. The more pixels, the sharper the image.

Information written to the screen by the CPU needs a special kind of circuit board—a video display adapter which controls the monitor. In the early days of computing, the most popular adapters were the monochrome adapter and the color graphics adapter (CGA), which can display up to 16 colors. However, there was a trade-off. If you used the monochrome adapter you got good resolution of characters. If, however, you wanted color, you lost the sharp resolution of characters. Thus, today people prefer the enhanced graphics adapter (EGA) that can paint up to 64 colors. Some now have even better adapters, the video graphics array (VGA), which can paint up to 256 colors. Today, there is even Super VGA. All of these generate sharp characters.

1.13 Output Devices: Printers

Not only do I want to see my credit application written to the screen, but I also want a copy of it so I can mail it to the store where I applied for credit. Thus, I want to use the most common output device, the **printer**. A printer is attached to the system unit with a cable. The printer allows the user to have a **hard copy** (unchangeable because it is on paper) of information. The two major types of printers are **impact** and **nonimpact**.

An impact printer works like a typewriter. The element strikes some kind of ribbon, which in turn strikes the paper and leaves a mark. A **dot-matrix** printer, the most common type, forms characters by selecting dots from a grid pattern on a movable print head and permits printing in any style of letters and graphics (pictures). A dot-matrix printer operates from 80 characters per second (cps) to over 200. There are also impact printers that have elements on which the letters are already formed. The most well-known element printer is a **daisy-wheel**, which is considered a letter-quality impact printer. It operates from 12 cps to 55 cps. A dot-matrix impact printer tends to be faster, less expensive, and more versatile than a daisy-wheel printer, but its output does not have the "finished" quality of that produced by a daisy-wheel printer. However, once again technology has done some wonderful things. You can purchase a dot-matrix printer that has what is called NLQ or near letter quality. It gives a better output, usually because of the number of pins in the print head. For example, a nine-pin printer creates acceptable copy by going over the characters twice. A 24-pin printer, since it has more pins, gives an even sharper resolution and also prints twice. A dot-matrix printer in NLQ prints more slowly than in draft mode. However, it does give you nearly the quality of a daisy-wheel printer.

Nonimpact printers include **thermal printers** that burn images into paper using a dot-matrix grid. Some thermal printers heat the ribbon and melt ink onto the paper. **Ink-jet** printers spray drops of ink to shape characters. However, the most recent news in printers is the **laser printer**. Also a nonimpact device, this printer uses a laser beam instructed by the computer to form characters with powdered toner fused to the page by heat, like a photocopying machine. This printer produces high-quality character and graphic images. Laser printers operate noiselessly at speeds up to 300 cps (eight pages or more per minute).

1.14 Modems

I also have another choice. I can transmit my credit application over telephone lines. I can do this if I have a device called a **modem** (**mod**ulator/**dem**odulator). A modem translates the digital signals of the computer to the analog signals that travel over phone lines. The party on the other end must also have a modem that translates the analog signals back into digital signals. In addition, the computer needs special instructions, a communication program, so that this activity can occur.

1.15 Disks and Disk Drives

Previously, I mentioned that RAM (memory) is volatile and disappears when the power is turned off. Thus, when I finished my credit application and turned off the computer everything in RAM disappeared. If I come back tomorrow and want to fill out another credit application, I would have to key in the same information again. In addition, I have another problem. How does that set of instructions, the program, get into RAM? I do not want to have to write the instructions to tell the computer what to do every time I use the computer. In fact, I do not want to write the program at all. I want to purchase a program someone else wrote.

This problem is handled with **secondary** or **external storage media**, which are actually magnetic media that store data and programs in the form of magnetic impulses. Such media include floppy disks, hard disks, tape, magnetic cards, and tape cartridges. In the microcomputer world, the most common secondary storage media are **floppy disks** and **hard disks**.

Floppy disks serve a dual purpose. First, disks provide a permanent way to hold data. When power is turned off, the disk retains what has been recorded on it. Second, floppy disks are transportable. Programs or data developed on one computer can be used by another merely by inserting the disk. If it were not for this capability, programs such as the operating system or other application packages could not be used. Each time you wanted to do some work, you would have to write your own instructions.

Storing information on a disk is equivalent to storing information in a file cabinet. Like a file cabinet, disks store information in disk files. When the computer needs the information, it goes to the disk, opens a file, "reads" the information from the disk file into RAM, and works on it. When the computer is finished working on that file, it closes the file and returns ("writes") it back to the disk. Thus, once I have purchased a credit program and once I have entered my salary, name and address, and other such repetitive information, the next time I want to use my computer, I can just tell the computer to "read" the program where the instructions are located and to "read" my credit file into RAM. Now, all I have to do is key in any changes that have occurred since the last time I used it. The program will do any calculations necessary to the new data I entered into my credit file and thus can generate the new credit report.

1.16 Capacity Measurement: Bits and Bytes

In order to do work, I want to know how big my desk is and how much my file cabinets hold. I can measure my desk in feet and my file cabinets in drawers. However, how do I measure the capacity of RAM (memory) or a disk (storage)? A computer does not understand actual words, letters, or numbers. A computer is made primarily of switches. All it can do is turn a switch on or off: 0 represents an off state and 1 represents an on state. A **bit** (from **b**inary dig**it**) is the smallest unit a computer can recognize. However, while a bit may be meaningful to a computer, it is not meaningful to human beings. So bits are combined in meaningful groups, much as letters of the alphabet are combined to make words. The most common grouping is eight bits, called a **byte**. Thus, a byte can be thought of as one character.

Computer capacities like RAM and ROM are measured in bytes, typically in thousands of bytes or kilobytes. Since a computer is binary, it works in powers of 2. A **kilobyte** is 2 to the 10th power (2^{10} or 1024) and K or KB is the symbol for 1024 bytes. If your computer has 64 KB of memory, its actual memory size is 64 times 1024 or 65,536 bytes. For simplification, KB is rounded off to 1000, so that 64 KB of memory means 64,000 bytes. You should know the capacity of your computer's memory because it determines how big a program and/or data the computer will hold. For instance, if you have a 64 KB computer and a program that requires 256 KB, your computer does not have the capacity to hold that program.

Disk capacity is also measured in bytes. A single-sided 5 1/4-inch disk holds 180 KB of data (180,000 bytes); a double-sided 5 1/4-inch disk holds 360 KB (360,000 bytes); a 3 1/2-inch double-density disk holds 720 KB. Because high-density and hard disks hold so much more information, they are measured in millions of bytes or **megabytes** (M or MB). A 5 1/4-inch high-density holds 1.2 MB; a 3 1/2-inch high-density disk holds 1.44 MB. Hard disks vary in size ranging from 20 MB to over 300 MB. Today, most people consider a 60 MB hard disk typical; it has a capacity of approximately 60 million bytes. However, most computer users, when referring to megabytes, use the term **meg**. A hard disk with 60 million bytes would be referred to as a "60 meg hard disk."

1.17 Minifloppy Disks

Floppy disks come in several sizes: 8-inch, 5 1/4-inch, and 3 1/2-inch. The 8-inch disk is rarely used today. The standard size has been the 5 1/4-inch floppy, but now the 3 1/2-inch floppy is becoming the standard. The 5 1/4-inch floppy disk, technically known as a **minifloppy** diskette, is a circular piece of plastic, polyurethane, or Mylar covered with magnetic oxide (see Figure 1.5). It is always inside a relatively rigid nonremovable protective jacket with a lined inner surface. Like a phonograph record, the disk has a hole (called a hub) in the center so that it can fit on the disk drive's spindle. The disk drive spins the disk to find information on it or to write information to it. Once the disk is locked into the disk drive, it spins at about 300 revolutions per minute. The disk has an exposed opening called the **head slot** where data is written to and read from. Here is where the disk drive's magnetic heads actually touch the surface of the disk. There is also a cutout on the side of the disk known as a **write-protect notch**, which can be covered with a write-protect tab. If a disk is write-protected, with the notch covered, the programs and data on the disk cannot be written over, so

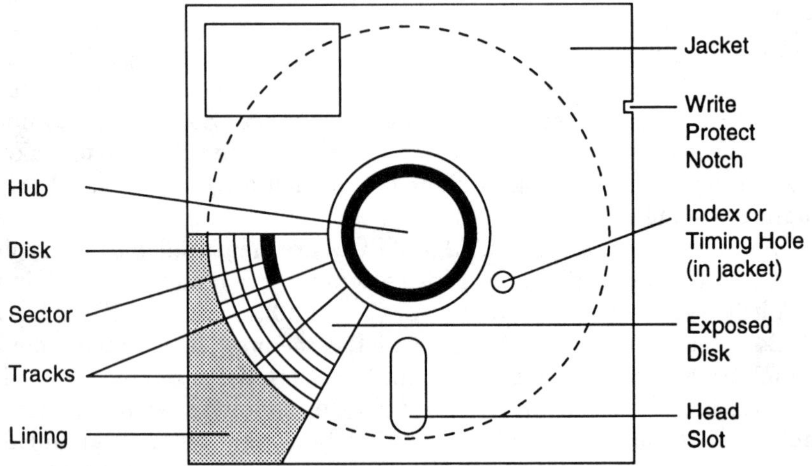

Figure 1.5 A Minifloppy 5 1/4-Inch Disk

the original data and programs can never be lost. If the write-protect notch is not covered, data can be read from the disk as well as written to it. Some disks, like the original DOS System Disk, have no notch and therefore can never be written on. These disks are write-protected and can only be read.

There is a small hole in the jacket near the center of the disk called the index or timing hole. If you rotated the plastic disk, you could find a small hole in the actual disk itself. The disk drive uses this hole to indicate where a circle has begun and ended, to help determine where information is stored on the disk. A disk with only one hole is considered **soft-sectored**; if it has many holes, it is considered **hard-sectored**. Most personal computers use a soft-sectored disk that indicates the first sector and track.

A 5 1/4-inch disk comes in two formats, double-density and high-density. The type of format you use depends on what kind of disk drive you have. A 5 1/4-inch double-sided, double-density disk can store approximately 360 KB, whereas a 5 1/4-inch double-sided, high-density disk can store 1.2 MB worth of information. Usually, a high-density disk is referred to as a **high-capacity disk**. There are also some older sizes—the 8-inch and the 5 1/4-inch single-sided, double-density disks, but neither is commonly used today.

1.18 Microfloppy Disks

The IBM PS/2 family, portable, and laptop computers are using a new disk format technically called a **microfloppy disk**. In principle, these 3 1/2-inch disks work the same way that the 5 1/4-inch disks do, except that they are smaller and are enclosed in a rigid plastic shell. In addition, each disk has a shutter that covers the read/write head. The computer's disk drive opens the shutter only when it needs access. When the disk is not in the drive, the shutter is closed. This disk does not use an index or timing hole; this function is performed by the sector notch next to the disk drive's spindle. The write-protect notch can be either a built-in slider or a breakaway tab. The 3 1/2-inch disk also comes in two formats. A 3 1/2-inch double-sided, double-density disk can store approximately 720 KB whereas a 3 1/2-inch double-sided, high-density disk can store 1.44 MB worth of information. There is also a newer size, the 3 1/2-inch high-density disk that handles 2.88 MB of information. Figure 1.6 shows the 3 1/2-inch disk.

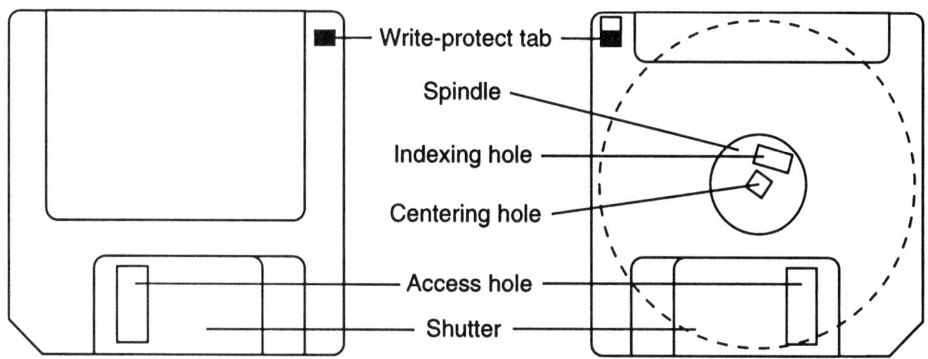

Figure 1.6 A Microfloppy 3 1/2-Inch Disk

1.19 Fixed Disks

A fixed disk drive, known as a **hard disk**, a Winchester disk, or a hard drive, is a nonremovable disk that is usually permanently installed in the system unit (see Figure 1.7). A hard disk holds much more information than a removable floppy disk. If a floppy disk can be compared to a file cabinet that holds data and programs, a hard disk can be compared to a room full of file cabinets. Both floppy disks and hard disks hold data and programs, but a hard disk simply holds a lot more.

A hard disk is composed of two or more rigid platters, usually made of aluminum and coated with oxide, which allow data to be encoded magnetically. Both the platters and the read/write heads are permanently sealed inside a box; the user cannot touch or see the drive or disks. These platters are affixed to a spindle that rotates at about 3600 RPM, although this speed can vary, depending on the type of hard disk. This speed makes it much faster than a standard floppy disk drive. The rapidly spinning disks in the sealed box create air pressure that lifts the recording heads above the surface of the platters. As the platters spin, the read/write heads float on a cushion of air.

Because the hard disk rotates faster than a floppy disk and because the head floats above the surface, the hard disk can store much more data and access it much more quickly than a floppy disk. Today, a common hard disk storage capacity is 40 megabytes, with 60 MB or 110 MB not uncommon. Obviously, hard disks hold much more information than floppy disks.

Figure 1.7
A Hard Disk

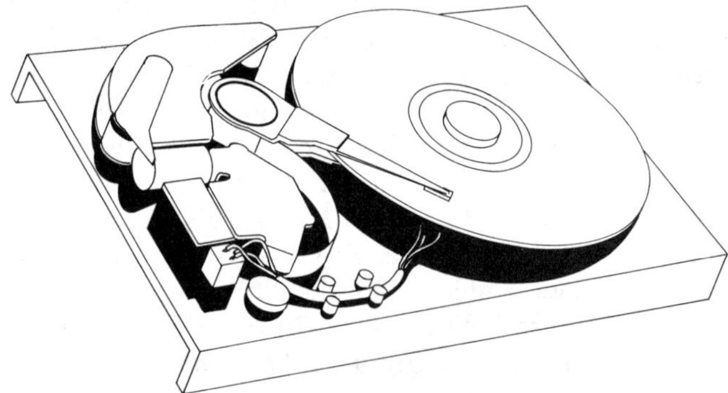

1.20 Dividing the Disk

In the paper world, my file cabinets do not have paper randomly thrown into them. Instead, I organize my file cabinets with hanging folders and file folders. A disk must also be organized and have a structure.

A disk's structure is essentially the same whether it is a hard disk or a floppy disk. Disks are organized or divided into numbered tracks and sectors so that the computer can locate information. The disk itself is much like a file cabinet with numbered file dividers. Data is recorded on the surface of a disk in a series of concentric circles known as **tracks**, similar to a record's grooves. Each track on the disk is a separate circle divided into **sectors**. The amount of data that can be stored on a disk depends on the density of the disk—the number of tracks and the size of the sectors. Since a hard disk is comprised of several platters, it has an additional measurement, a **cylinder**. Two or more platters are stacked on top of one another with the tracks aligned. If you connect any one track through all the platters, you have a cylinder (see Figure 1.8).

A **cluster** is the basic unit of disk storage. Whenever a computer reads or writes to a disk, it always reads and writes a full cluster, regardless of the space the data needs. Clusters are always made from adjacent sectors, from one sector to eight sectors or more. The location and number of sectors per cluster are determined by the software in a process known as **formatting**.

A disk is a random access medium, which does not mean that the data and/or programs are randomly arranged on the disk. It means that the head of the disk drive, which reads the disk, does not have to read all the information on the disk to get a specific item. The CPU can instruct the head of the disk drive to go directly to the track and sector that holds the specific item of information.

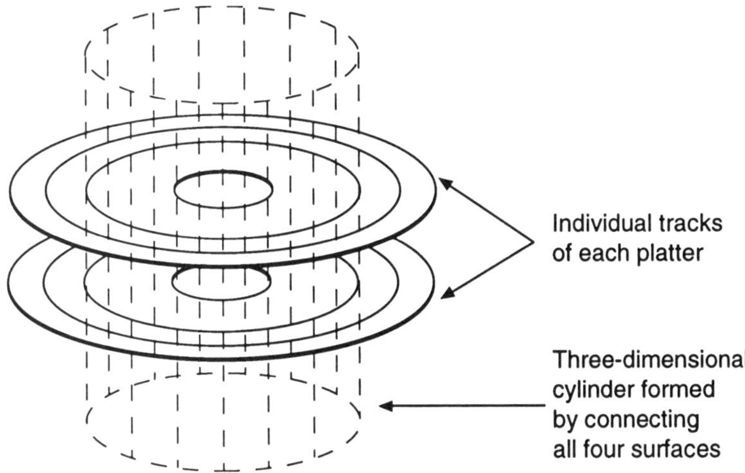

Figure 1.8
Hard Disk Cylinders

1.21 Disk Drives

Now that I have disks to store my data and programs, I need a way to get that information off the disks into memory and from memory to the disks. Thus, I have **disk drives**. A disk drive is used to write information to and from a disk. If a disk contains the information I wish to use, it is the disk drive that "plays" it back. All disk drives have read/write heads which read and write information back and forth between RAM and the disk, much like the ones on tape or video recorders. Floppy disks have one head; most hard disks have more than one. In addition, all disk drives have a means of spinning the disk. Since a hard disk is sealed, all the mechanics of the spinning are internal. The user never interacts directly with the hard disk, or, in other words, never has to "change the tape." The user just accesses different parts of the disk. The mechanics are different with a floppy disk drive because the user does have to interact with the disk drive to "change tapes" (disks) in order to "play" different information.

A floppy disk drive is the device that holds a floppy disk. The user inserts the floppy disk into the disk drive (see Figure 1.9). The hub of the disk fits onto the hub mechanism, which grabs the disk. When the disk drive door is shut, the disk is secured to the hub mechanism. The jacket remains stationary while the floppy disk rotates. The disk drive head reads and writes information back and forth between RAM and the disk through the exposed head slot. Some floppy disk drives are single-sided, which means that they can only read and write to one side of a disk. Others are double-sided, which means that they can read and write to both sides of a disk. Another type of floppy disk drive is known as a high-capacity or high-density floppy disk drive. It can not only read and write to both sides of a disk but the disk can also accept more information than a standard disk because more data can be packed on the high-capacity disk, nearly four times more than the storage capacity of a standard floppy disk.

Figure 1.9
A Floppy Disk Drive

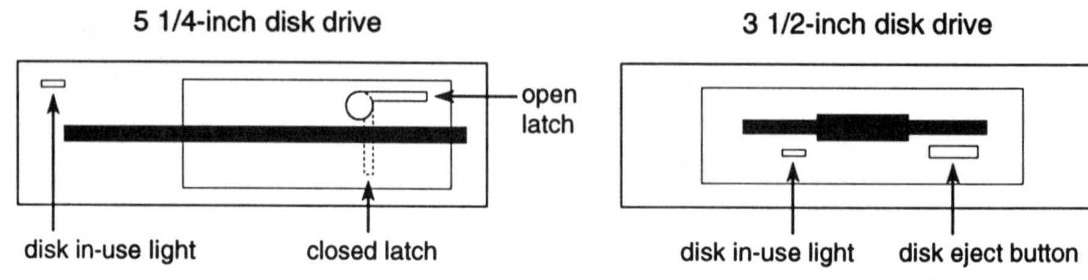

1.22 Device Names

A disk drive, which comes in a variety of sizes and door configurations, is an example of a device name. A **device** is a place for the computer to send information (write) or a place from which to receive information (read). Disk drives are not the only devices that the system uses. However, in order for the operating system to know which device it is supposed to be communicating with at any given time, every device is given a specific and unique name by the system. Disk drives are given one-letter names followed by a colon. You must determine the configuration of disk drives you have on your microcomputer. Some common configurations are illustrated in Figure 1.10.

Figure 1.10
Disk Drive Configurations

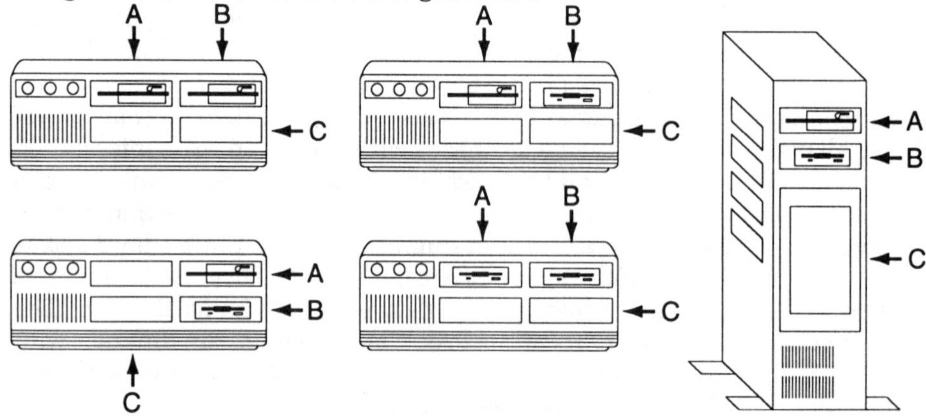

Floppy disk drives have doors, which are either shut or latched, into which the user inserts a floppy disk. The first floppy disk drive (either the one on top in a half-height configuration or the one on the left in a two-floppy configuration) is always known as Drive A or A:. The second floppy disk drive (either the one on the bottom or the one on the right) is always known as Drive B or B:. The sealed hard disk inside the system unit is always known as Drive C or C:. Any other drives are lettered alphabetically, using the letters D: through Z:. Device names, which are also known as reserved names, cannot be used for any other purpose.

1.23 Software

To this point, we have been discussing primarily hardware. However, software is what makes a computer useful. In fact, without software, hardware has no use. You can think of hardware as a box to run software. Software is the step-by-step instructions that tell the computer what to do. These instructions are called **programs**. Programs need to be installed or **"loaded"** into RAM, where the CPU executes them. The total execution of a program is called "running" the program. Programs usually come stored on disks. The program is read into memory from the floppy disk or hard disk. Software can also be divided into categories. The most common division is system software and application software.

Application software, as its name suggests, is a set of instructions, a complete program, that directs the computer to solve a particular problem. Application software solves problems, handles information, and is user-oriented. Application software may also be called packages, off-the-shelf software, or canned software. You may have heard of application software by brand names such as WordPerfect or Lotus. For example, it would be useful to purchase a payroll package to run the payroll on the computer. All you would have to do would be to key in the information needed by the program, such as hours worked and rate of pay, and the package would have the instructions needed to complete the calculations and print the paychecks. There are thousands of commercially available application packages. The reason most people purchase a computer is the availability of application programs.

System software is also a set of instructions or programs. These programs coordinate the operations of all the various hardware components. System software is usually supplied by the computer manufacturer because it is necessary to run application software. System software is always computer-oriented rather than user-oriented. It takes care of what the computer needs so the computer can run application software (see Table 1.2).

Table 1.2 Application and System Software

Application Software	System Software
Solves problems	Coordinates operation of hardware
Handles information	Necessary to run application software
User-oriented	Computer-oriented

System software is also divided into three categories: operating systems, system utilities, and programming language processors (see Table 1.3).

The **operating system** supervises the processing of application programs and all the input/output of the computer. Running a computer is somewhat analogous to producing a concert. The hardware is like the musicians and their instruments. They do not change. The application software is like the score the musicians play, anything from Ludwig van Beethoven to Paul McCartney. The computer hardware can "play" any application software from accounting to a game. Like the conductor who tells the violins or trumpets when to play and how loudly, the operating system makes the computer work. It is the first and most important program on the computer and *must* be loaded into memory before any other program. Working with the operating system is known as being at the **system level**.

Typically, operating systems are comprised of several important programs. These include a program that transfers data to and from the disk and into and out of memory and performs other disk-related tasks. Another important program handles hardware-specific tasks. These programs check such things as whether a key has been pressed and, if it has, encodes it so that the computer can read it and then decodes it so that it can be written to the screen. It encodes and decodes from bits and bytes into letters and words. The operating system also includes a **command processor**, which has some built-in commands known as **internal** or **resident commands**, available as long as the power is on. These internal commands allow the user to manage disk files at the system level and to perform such activities as looking into the **directory** of a specific disk. In addition, the command processor allows the user to instruct the computer to load a system utility or an application package into RAM.

System utilities are special programs stored on an operating system disk. However, system utilities are not necessary to run the computer. They are only loaded and executed when the user needs them. Also known as **external** or **transient commands**, system utilities do useful tasks such as formatting a disk or giving statistical information about a disk. A system utility program formats a disk with the proper tracks and sectors so that it is a readable single-sided or double-sided disk.

Programming language processors are programs that support the use of a programming language on a computer system. They are tools for the development of application packages. Programmers who wish to write step-by-step instructions that tell the computer what to do use these programming language processors.

The term operating system is generic. Brand names for microcomputer operating systems include CP/M, Unix, Xenix, Apple-DOS, TRS-DOS, and UCSD-P. However, the standard operating system for microcomputers today is **DOS**, pronounced *dahs*. DOS, which stands for disk operating system, was developed and is owned by Microsoft Corporation. Their version is known as **MS-DOS**. It is licensed to computer manufacturers who tailor it to their specific hardware. MS-DOS runs on the majority of personal computers in use today. In addition, Microsoft also supports the IBM personal computer with a version of DOS known as **PC-DOS**. PC-DOS is also tailored to specific IBM hardware. PC-DOS and MS-DOS work exactly the same and have virtually identical commands.

Table 1.3
System Software

Operating System	System Utilities	Programming Language Processors
Handles input/output of computer	Enhances usefulness of computer	Supports use of programming languages
Manages computer resources	Adds capabilities	
Enables the running of application software		

If you are going to use a computer and run application packages, first you are going to need to know how to use the operating system. Since DOS is the major microcomputer operating system in use today, this text is devoted to teaching the concepts of the operating system in general and DOS operations in particular.

Most people who use a computer are really interested in application software. They want programs that are easy to use. However, in order to use the applications, the user must know the operating system. The operating system is the most important program loaded into the computer. Operating systems typically have programs stored as system files that take care of the mandatory functions that a computer needs to operate. When you purchase a computer, you also purchase the operating system software. It is a manual with several disks. On these disks are the programs that comprise the system software and the system utilities.

1.24 Operating System Fundamentals

DOS is a program that is always working. No computer can work unless it has an operating system in RAM. When you boot the system, you are loading the system software or operating system programs into RAM. This is what DOS is all about. DOS is comprised of three parts: the programs that handle input and output to peripherals and files; the command processor; and the utility programs. However, the utility programs are not a mandatory part of the operating system.

Some of the software is built into the hardware. When you turn on the power to the computer, or "power up," the computer would not know what to do if there were no programs or sets of instructions. The first necessity is to communicate with the computer using peripheral devices. When you key in a character on the keyboard, that character moves to the CPU and RAM; this is input. When a character is displayed (written) to the monitor or the printer, it moves from the CPU and RAM; this is output. Input and output take place within the CPU, memory, and the different peripherals. **BIOS** (Basic Input/Output System) routines or programs provide some of the control for the input/output (I/O) devices.

Where is BIOS? It is actually found in two places. First, it is built into the hardware of the microcomputer on the system board in a read-only memory chip called **ROM-BIOS** (Read-Only Memory—Basic Input/Output System). This ROM-BIOS chip is abbreviated to RIOS, pronounced *RYE-ose*. This ROM-BIOS, a built-in part of the computer, deals with the specific computer brand hardware. BIOS programs provide the interface between the hardware and DOS.

Thus, when you turn on the computer, the power goes first to the ROM-BIOS. One of the things this programmed chip does is execute the power on self-diagnostic test (POST) routine programs. This routine simply means that this is the first set of instructions to be followed, so the program checks the RAM and equipment attached to the computer. Thus, before getting started, the user knows whether or not there is a hardware failure. Once the self-test is completed successfully, the next job or program to execute is loading the operating system.

Loading the operating system entails ROM-BIOS checking to see if a disk drive is installed. The program then checks to see if there is a disk in Drive A. If there is no disk in Drive A and if there is a hard disk, the program will check Drive C. It is looking for the DOS System Disk. A DOS System Disk has a special program on it called the **boot record**. If ROM-BIOS does not find the boot record or if there is something wrong with the boot record, control is turned over to the BASIC interpreter (on an IBM Personal Computer) or you will get an error message telling you something is wrong. If the program does find the proper boot record, it reads the record from the DOS disk into RAM and turns control over to this program. The boot record is also a program that executes; its job is to read into RAM the rest of the operating system, in essence, pulling the system up by its **bootstraps**. Thus, one "**boots**" the computer instead of merely turning it on.

The purpose of the operating system files that are loaded into RAM is to manage the resources and primary functions of the computer. The application program can then concentrate on doing its job, such as word processing, without having to worry about how the document gets from the keyboard to RAM and from RAM to the screen. The operating system takes care of those critical functions. This whole process can be considered analogous to driving an automobile. Most of us use our cars to get from point A to point B. We would not like it if every time we wanted to drive, we first had to open the hood and attach the proper cables to the battery and to all the other parts that are necessary to start the engine. The operating system is the engine of the computer that lets the user run the application in the same manner as a person driving a car to the store.

There is an operating system file that extends the capability of ROM-BIOS to manage input/output handling, known as device handling. The main job of the boot record for DOS is to load the **hidden system file** called `IO.SYS`, which is stored at a predefined location on the DOS System Disk. (In IBM PC-DOS this file, called `IBMBIO.COM`, serves the same function.) The term hidden system file means that it is hidden from the user but resident in RAM. When the user asks to have the files on the disk displayed on the screen, any file that is marked hidden will not be shown. The boot record reads this file into memory, and it remains there until the computer is turned off.

In addition, any errors in ROM-BIOS can be corrected by making changes in the programs in `IO.SYS`, rather than having to install a new ROM chip inside the system unit. `IO.SYS` can also handle the addition of new peripheral devices, such as a hard disk, a new printer, or a display screen. It tells the computer that these devices exist and how to handle the I/O without making major changes. It extends the capability of RIOS to handle the input and output between the CPU and the peripheral devices.

The next program loaded into RAM is stored on the DOS System Disk in a file called `MSDOS.SYS`. (In IBM PC-DOS, this file is called `IBMDOS.COM` and serves the same function.) `MSDOS.SYS` is the hidden system file that handles most of the disk routines, known as high-level interface. This program deals with intermediate-level input-output routines such as reading what is input from the keyboard or writing output to the screen. In addition, `MSDOS.SYS` handles disk operations and takes care of reading and writing to a disk, including opening and closing files on a disk, searching the table of contents or directory of a disk, deleting files, reading and writing data, or placing and retrieving information on the disks. Thus the first part of the DOS operating system is the two hidden files `IO.SYS` and `MSDOS.SYS` (or `IBMBIO.COM` and `IBMDOS.COM` in IBM PC-DOS).

The last program to be loaded into RAM is stored on the DOS System Disk in a file called `COMMAND.COM`. This program is not a hidden file like `IO.SYS` and `MSDOS.SYS`. Also known as the command processor, it is the second major part of DOS. It is what the user actually communicates and interacts with. When you key in something on the keyboard, `COMMAND.COM` reads what you key in and decides what to do with it; this is why it is called the **command processor** or **command interpreter**. It processes or interprets what you have keyed in. However, you cannot just key in anything. `COMMAND.COM` is looking for specific predefined instructions to execute.

Inside `COMMAND.COM` are built-in commands or subroutines, also called **internal** or **resident commands**. Once you have loaded DOS, these internal commands remain in memory until you turn off the power. You do not need to have the DOS System Disk in any drive to "call" or run these programs; that is why they are called internal commands. These internal commands are programs that are routines for functions regularly used in file management such as finding out what is on a disk using the DIR command; deleting a file from a disk with the ERASE command; or changing the name of a file with the RENAME command. These commands or programs are listed in a table. When you key in a command name, `COMMAND.COM` looks it up in the table for a match. When it finds a match, it can run the program.

Utility programs, also called **external** or **transient commands** because they are not resident in RAM, make up the third part of DOS. These utility programs reside in program files located on the DOS System Disk. When you wish to use one of these utilities, you key in the command name at the keyboard.

COMMAND.COM looks for it in the table. If it cannot find a match, it must go to the disk and look for a match. When it finds a match on the appropriate disk, it loads that program into RAM and executes it. The utility programs must be on the disk that DOS reads for DOS to be able to locate them. Thus, the program is only loaded when you need it; it is transient because it is not retained in RAM unless you have called it. COMMAND.COM can recognize a program because the program will have a file name with the file extension .COM, .EXE, or .BAT.

Remember that although external commands or utilities are handy programs, they are not mandatory for running the operating system. Any program, including an application program, is external and stored as a file on a disk.

Thus, the MS-DOS operating system is comprised of two hidden files, IO.SYS and MSDOS.SYS (called IBMBIO.COM and IBMDOS.COM in IBM PC-DOS), and the file COMMAND.COM. These files are loaded into memory when you place the DOS System Disk in the drive and boot up the system or boot off the hard disk. The programs remain in RAM until you turn off the computer.

To recap, the operating system is comprised of the following:

RIOS	ROM-BIOS (Read-Only Memory—Basic Input/Output System), a preprogrammed chip that handles the start-up routines and loads the operating system.
BOOT	The bootstrap routine that loads the remainder of DOS into memory.
IO.SYS (IBMBIO.COM)	A hidden system file that is loaded into RAM and manages the basic input and output devices or peripherals.
MSDOS.SYS (IBMDOS.COM)	A hidden system file that is loaded into RAM and manages the disks.
COMMAND.COM	The command processor that interprets what is keyed in and contains the subroutines or internal commands.

In general, using the operating system, particularly the two hidden files, is transparent to the user, which means that the work is being done but the user does not see the operating activities, just the results. In other words, the first two system files take care of the tedious but vital routines such as moving information to and from disks. However, the user actually interfaces with COMMAND.COM, the third system file.

Figure 1.11 illustrates the operation of the command processor. When DOS lets you know that it is ready to do some work, it displays a signal on the screen. The signal is called the prompt. When the prompt is displayed on the screen, the command processor has finished running one program or command and is waiting for the next. When the user keys in something on the keyboard, the command processor tries to follow the instructions. It is looking for a program to execute. Some built-in internal or resident commands are listed in a table within the command processor. These are routines for commonly used functions such as displaying the table of contents or copying a file. These internal commands are always available after DOS is loaded because they are in RAM (memory). The command processor does not have to go to the disk to find these programs. Some major internal commands are DIR, ERASE, TYPE, RENAME, and COPY. Even though these are programs, the internal commands are not listed when you do a directory display.

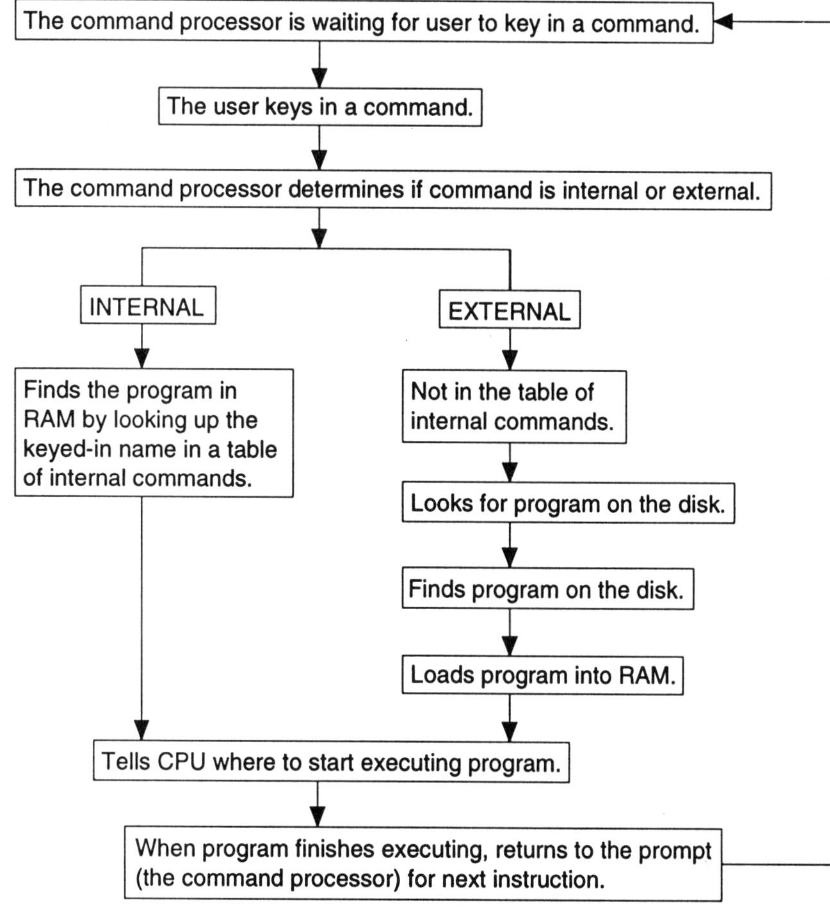

Figure 1.11 Operation of the Command Processor

If the command processor does not find the command internally, it goes to the disk in the disk drive to locate and load the program. Hence, these commands are called external or transient because they are outside of memory, reside on a disk, and are only loaded and executed when the user requests them. All programs are stored as files on a disk. These files have a two-part name, the file name and the file extension. External programs are stored on a disk with a file extension of `.EXE`, `.COM`, or `.BAT`. All application programs are external. There is a special group of external programs or external commands that comes with DOS called utility programs. These are not a mandatory part of the operating system but, as you will learn later, are very useful.

If what was keyed in does not match the preceding scenario, DOS returns an error message, "Bad command or file not found." The message means that DOS could not find a matching program in RAM or on the disk and, therefore, could not act on the command. Remember, a computer has a limited vocabulary. You have to speak its language; it does not speak yours.

Chapter Summary

1. All computers function in the same way. Data is input, processed, and stored, and the results are output.
2. Hardware components include the system unit, the monitor, the keyboard, and the printer.
3. The central processing unit is the brain of the computer and can comprehend and carry out instructions sent to it by a program.
4. Random Access Memory (RAM) is the work space of the computer. RAM is volatile and is only there when the computer has power.
5. Read-Only Memory (ROM) is a chip with programs written on it. ROM is not volatile. It usually holds the start-up routines of the computer.
6. Adapter cards are printed circuit boards that allow the user to add various peripheral devices.
7. Floppy and hard disks are a means of permanent storage for data and programs. A floppy disk is a piece of plastic inside a jacket. Floppy disks come in two popular sizes, 5 1/4-inch or minifloppy and 3 1/2-inch or microfloppy. They also come in two capacities, double-sided, double-density and high-capacity. A hard disk is made of rigid platters that are permanently sealed inside a box.
8. All disks are divided into numbered tracks and sectors so that the computer can locate needed information.
9. A floppy disk drive is the device where a floppy disk is inserted so that the computer can read or write to the inserted disk.
10. Disk drives have reserved names made of a letter of the alphabet followed by a colon. The left-hand or top disk drive is known as Drive A or A:. The first hard disk drive is known as Drive C or C:.
11. A byte represents a single character. The capacity of RAM, ROM, and disks is measured in bytes, usually thousands of bytes or kilobytes (KB). The capacity of hard disks or high-capacity floppy disks are measured in millions of bytes or megabytes (MB), often referred to as meg.
12. Peripherals are different devices that are attached to the system unit. The most common input device is a keyboard. The common output devices are the monitor and the printer.
13. Software is the step-by-step instructions that tell the computer what to do.

These instructions are called programs. Programs are loaded into RAM where the CPU executes each instruction. Programs are referred to as "running" or "executing."

14. Programs are stored on disks and loaded into RAM.
15. Software is divided into application software and system software.
16. Application software solves problems, handles information, and is user-oriented.
17. System software coordinates the operation of the hardware, is mandatory for running application software, and is computer-oriented.
18. An operating system is comprised of programs called system software that perform the functions necessary to control the operations of the computer. The operating system tells the computer what to do and interfaces with the user.
19. ROM-BIOS (Read-Only Memory—Basic Input/Output System) is a chip that is built into the hardware of the system unit. Its job is to run self-diagnostics and load the boot record (which loads the rest of the operating system), the software that primarily deals with input/output devices, the software that primarily deals with writing to and from disks, and the command processor or interpreter (which processes what the user keys in).
20. On an MS-DOS system disk, the system files have specific names. The software that deals with input/output devices is stored as a hidden file called `IO.SYS`. The software that deals with reading from and writing to the disks is stored as a hidden file called **`MSDOS.SYS`**. The command interpreter is stored as a file called **`COMMAND.COM`** and is not hidden from the user. On an IBM PC-DOS system disk, the system files also have specific names. One hidden file is called **`IBMBIO.COM`** and the other is called **`IBMDOS.COM`**. The command interpreter is stored as a file called **`COMMAND.COM`** and is not hidden from the user.
21. Internal commands are programs loaded with the operating system in `COMMAND.COM`. They remain in memory until the power is turned off.
22. External commands are stored on a disk and must be loaded into memory each time they are used. External commands are transient and do not remain in memory after they are executed.
23. The external commands that come with DOS are also known as system utilities.
24. Booting the system is more than powering up the system; it means loading the operating system.
25. Application packages are external to the computer and must be loaded in order to be executed.

Key Terms

Adapter cards
ALU
Application software
BIOS
Bit
Boot
Boot record
Bootstraps
Byte
Cluster
COMMAND.COM
Command interpreter
Command processor
Control Unit
CPU
Cylinder
Daisy-wheel printer
Data
Device
Directory
Disk drives
DOS
Dot-matrix printer
Expansion slots
External commands
Firmware
Floppy disks
Formatting
Hard copy
Hard disk
Hard sectored
Hardware
Head slot
Hidden system file
High-capacity disk
IBMBIO.COM
IBMDOS.COM
Impact printer
Ink-jet printer
Internal commands
IO.SYS
Kilobyte (KB)
Laser printer
Light pen
Loaded
Meg
Megabyte (MB)
Memory
Microcomputer
Microfloppy disk
Minifloppy disk
Modem
Monitor
Mouse
MS-DOS
MSDOS.SYS
Nonimpact printer
Operating system
PC-DOS
Peripheral device
Pixels
Printer
Programming language processors
Programs
RAM
Resident commands
ROM
ROM-BIOS
Scanners
Sectors
Soft sectored
Software
System level
System software
System utilities
Thermal printers
Tracks
Transient commands
Write-protect notch

Discussion Questions

1. Define hardware.
2. Define RIOS.
3. What is meant by the system configuration?
4. Describe a typical microcomputer configuration.
5. Define DOS.
6. Why is an operating system important?
7. What files comprise DOS? What is the purpose of each file?
8. Where is DOS stored for use by the computer?
9. Can application packages run without an operating system?
10. What is an internal command?
11. What is an external command?
12. What purpose do disks serve?
13. How many types of disks are there? Describe them.
14. What is the difference between a hard disk and a floppy disk?
15. What are tracks and sectors? Where are they found?

Chapter 2

Getting Started with DOS

Booting the System, Using the Keyboard, Using DISKCOPY and DISKCOMP

After completing this chapter you will be able to:

1. Define DOS.
2. Identify the system configuration of your computer.
3. Explain what DOS version numbers are.
4. Explain the need and procedure for booting and rebooting the system.
5. Describe three kinds of keyboard keys and explain the purpose of each set of keys.
6. List and explain the importance of the three types of computer files.
7. Identify, use, and describe the functions performed by the <Backspace>, <Esc>, <NumLock>, <Ctrl>, <PrtSc>, and <Shift> keys.
8. Cancel a command.
9. Explain the purpose of and procedure for utilizing the DATE and TIME commands.
10. Make a copy of the DOS System Disk and verify that it is an exact copy of the master DOS System Disk.
11. Make a copy of the ACTIVITIES disk that accompanies this book and verify that it is an exact copy of the master ACTIVITIES disk.
12. Correctly end a work session with the computer.

Chapter Overview

Most people who use computers are really interested in application software. They want programs that are easy to use and can help them solve specific problems. However, before you can utilize application software you must first know how to use the operating system. No computer can work unless it has an operating system in RAM. DOS, which is the major microcomputer operating system in use today on IBM and IBM-compatible microcomputers, takes care of the mandatory functions for computer operations such as handling the input and output of the computer, managing the computer resources, and running the application software. It enables the user to communicate with the computer.

In this chapter you will learn how to load the operating system into the computer, familiarize yourself with the keyboard, learn some basic commands, make a system disk or an ACTIVITIES disk to use in future activities and verify that these copies are exact copies of the original disks.

2.0 What is DOS?

The operating system is a software program. Although there are many different operating system "brand names," the major operating system in use today on IBM and IBM-compatible microcomputers is DOS, either PC-DOS or MS-DOS. MS-DOS was developed by Microsoft and licensed to IBM, which called it IBM PC-DOS. Other computer manufacturers also licensed DOS from Microsoft but call their versions MS-DOS. If you have an IBM microcomputer you are probably using PC-DOS, and if you have a compatible that operates like an IBM, you are probably using MS-DOS. However, both PC-DOS and MS-DOS are virtually identical and function in the same way. Thus, this text focuses exclusively on DOS, regardless if it is PC-DOS or MS-DOS.

You cannot use most other software programs without first loading DOS into memory or RAM. Furthermore, DOS is in charge of the hardware components of the computer. You, the user, communicate what you want your computer to do through DOS **commands**, which are instructions that DOS understands. These commands are usually English words such as COPY or PRINT.

2.1 Versions of DOS

Note to users using DOS 3.3, 4.0, or 5.0 for the first time

DOS was first released for the IBM PC in 1981. However, in the computer world, things change very rapidly. Today there is new technology such as the hard disk and the 3 1/2-inch floppy disk. In order for DOS to take advantage of new technology, new versions of DOS are released by Microsoft and IBM. These new upgrades also have what is known as **enhancements**. Enhancements simply mean more commands. In addition, new versions fix problems in older versions of DOS. This is known as fixing bugs. To keep track of these **versions**, they are assigned version numbers. DOS 1.0 was the first version, and DOS 5.0 is the most recent version.

This text is applicable to any version of DOS 2.0 or above. If a command is only available in 4.0 or 5.0, it will be indicated. The early versions of DOS came complete on one disk. DOS 3.3 came on two 5 1/4-inch disks (or one 3 1/2-inch disk); DOS 4.0 came on five 5 1/4-inch disks (or two 3 1/2-inch disks) and DOS 5.0 comes on six 5 1/4-inch disks (or three 3 1/2-inch disks). Users who have earlier versions of DOS can use the original system disk. However, users who have DOS 3.3, 4.0, or 5.0 should refer to Appendix A so that they can make a single system disk.

2.2 Identifying Your System Configuration Using DOS

All microcomputers come with disk drives of two basic types, the floppy disk drive and the hard or fixed disk drive. In the past, microcomputers had only one floppy drive. Today, however, most computer systems are configured in one of the three following ways:

Two floppy disk drives.
One hard disk drive and one floppy disk drive.
One hard disk drive and two floppy disk drives.

The floppy disk drives can be any combination of the 5 1/4 360 KB, the 5 1/4 1.2 MB high-capacity, the 3 1/2 720 KB, and the 3 1/2 1.44 MB high-capacity disk drives. High-capacity disk drives are also known as high-density disk drives. In order to follow the text, you must know which system configuration you have.

2.3 Booting the System

You must know how to get the programs from the DOS System Disk to memory or RAM so that you can use the computer. This process is known as **booting the system**. The following activity allows you to have your first hands-on experience with the microcomputer using the DOS System Disk. You are going to load DOS or boot the system. Although you will be using the hard disk for most of this textbook, it is still important to be able to boot from a floppy disk. When you first install DOS or other software on the hard disk, you begin with a floppy disk. In addition, if something goes wrong with the hard disk, you need to be able to start the computer with a floppy disk.

If you are using a two-disk computer system with no hard disk, treat Drive C as Drive A and Drive A as Drive B. Be sure to follow the instructions exactly for your system configuration. For this textbook, the hard disk configuration is comprised of one hard disk and one 5 1/4-inch 1.2 MB disk drive.

Materials Needed

1. A microcomputer
2. Master DOS System Disk, version 2.0 or higher
   (If you or your instructor have not already done so, see Appendix A to create a single master DOS System Disk from the original system disks for DOS 3.3, 4.0, or 5.0.)
3. Since laboratory procedures will vary, check with your instructor whether or not you are to boot your system with a floppy disk.

Activity 2.4 Booting the System: Cold Start

STEP 1: Check to see if the monitor has a separate on/off switch. If it does, turn on the monitor.

STEP 2: Get the disk labeled DOS. If the master DOS System Disk is in a paper envelope or plastic case, remove it.

STEP 3: The master DOS System Disk should have a label. It also has an exposed opening where you can see the actual plastic disk. This opening is called the head slot, where the magnetic head reads and writes information to the disk. If it is a 3 1/2-inch disk, the head slot is covered with a metal shield. Never put your fingers on this area because the oil from your fingers could prevent the disk from being read properly. The DOS System Disk must be placed in Drive A. Look at Figure 2.1 to identify Drive A.

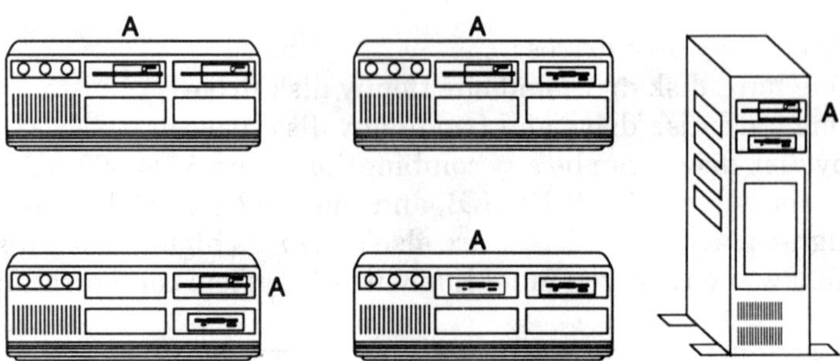

Figure 2.1
Identifying Drive A

STEP 4: To insert a 5 1/4-inch disk properly into the disk drive, hold it label side up, with the head slot facing away from you and toward the floppy disk drive. The write-protect notch should be facing left. If you have a 3 1/2-inch disk, hold it label side up with the metal shutter facing away from you and toward the floppy disk drive. The write-protect notch should be facing left. See Figure 2.2 to correctly insert the disk.

Figure 2.2
Inserting the Disk

STEP 5: Gently lift the latch or door of Drive A on the system unit. Usually with 3 1/2-inch disk drives you do not have a door to open. Instead, there is a slot into which you slip the disk until it clicks. Insert the master DOS System Disk, label up, into Drive A. Shut or latch the drive door for a 5 1/4-inch disk drive. For the 3 1/2-inch disk drive, gently push the disk in the drive until you hear a click.

STEP 6: Power on the computer by locating the power switch and lifting it. Often, it is a red switch. On an IBM PC the switch is located on the right-hand side on the back of the system unit. On an IBM PS/2 the switch is located on the front of the system unit.

WHAT'S HAPPENING? The system checks itself in the diagnostic routine. You see a blinking horizontal line called the **cursor** displayed on the screen. (Cursor is a Latin word for runner.) After the system checkout is complete, the computer reads DOS into RAM from the master DOS System Disk: the two hidden files, `IO.SYS` and `MSDOS.SYS` (`IBMBIO.COM` and `IBMDOS.COM` in PC-DOS), and the other system file, `COMMAND.COM`. The computer boots DOS from the master DOS System Disk. When this happens, the disk drive makes a brief buzzing noise and a light on the drive flashes on, letting you know that the system is reading the disk. The computer beeps. If the boot is successful, the screen displays the following prompt:

```
Current date is Thur 06-11-92
Enter new date (mm-dd-yy):_
```

STEP 7: Note: You must enter the date in the format displayed, mm-dd-yy (month-day-year). You can also use the slash to separate the numbers as in mm/dd/yy or a period as in mm.dd.yy. You must use numbers only, not alphabetic characters. Most newer computers have a built-in clock so that the date is already current. When this is true, you do not need to enter the date. However, here, for the experience you will need later, you will enter the date, even if it is the correct date. Enter the current date and press the <Enter> key, the wide key located towards the right side of the keyboard and labeled "Enter" and/or ◄┘.

```
Current time is 0:00:16:25
Enter new time:_
```

STEP 8: Do not be concerned if the time displayed is different from what is shown above. Newer computers will have the correct time. Some computer clocks are 24-hour clocks, i.e., 1:00 p.m. is 13:00. You can always enter the time on a 24-hour basis. Entering the hours and minutes is sufficient. Enter the current time and press <Enter>.

```
Microsoft(R) MS-DOS(R) Version 5.00
         (C)Copyright Microsoft Corp 1981-1991.

A>_
```

WHAT'S HAPPENING? You have successfully booted the system. After you entered the date and time prompt correctly the `A>` appeared on the screen. The `A>`, known as the A **prompt**, is the drive that the system reads from to get the operating system into memory. If you have a different version of DOS, the screen display will be slightly different.

2.5 Rebooting the System

Rebooting the system means reloading the operating system from the disk. Usually, you reboot the system because there is a problem, much like a reset button on a home appliance. When you reboot, everything that is in memory disappears and DOS is again read into memory from the master DOS System Disk. The only difference between rebooting and booting is that when you reboot you do not have to turn on the power to the computer by pressing the on switch. Some microcomputers have a reset key, making the rebooting process a one-key step. Most often, during a reboot the self-diagnostic routine is not run.

Activity 2.6 Rebooting the System: Warm Start

STEP 1: On the keyboard locate the keys labeled <Ctrl>, <Alt>, and <Del>.

STEP 2: To reboot the computer, hold down the <Ctrl> key, then press the <Alt> key and the <Del> key simultaneously. If your computer has a reset button, press it instead.

```
Current date is Sat 11-23-1991
Enter new date (mm-dd-yy):_
```

WHAT'S HAPPENING? This activity is intentionally made awkward so you do not reboot accidentally, because rebooting erases everything in RAM (memory). When you pressed the three keys, the system went to the master DOS System Disk in Drive A and read the operating system into RAM. In this example, the computer has a built-in clock and the correct date is displayed. However, you can still key in the date.

STEP 3: At the date prompt, key in the invalidly formatted date shown below:
`May 7, 1992` <Enter>

```
Invalid date
Enter new date (mm-dd-yy):_
```

WHAT'S HAPPENING? The operating system must have information entered in the proper format. Like all programs, the operating system has steps that must be followed. If you do not follow the format, the computer cannot recognize the information and will reject it. That is why you got the error message "Invalid date" with an opportunity to correct the error.

STEP 4: Key in the current date in the proper format. Press <Enter>.

```
Current time is 8:28:37.15p
Enter new time:_
```

STEP 5: At the time prompt key in the invalid formatted time shown below:
`75:00 am` <Enter>

```
Current time is 8:28:37.15p
Enter new time: 75:00am

Invalid time
Enter new time:_
```

WHAT'S HAPPENING? Not only must information be entered in the proper format, but it must also be correct information. The system knows that there is no such time as 75:00 and, thus, will not process the information.

STEP 6: Key in the correct time and press <Enter>.

```
Microsoft(R) MS-DOS(R) Version 5.00
         (C) Copyright Microsoft Corp 1981-1991.

A>_
```

WHAT'S HAPPENING? Now that you entered a valid date and time, you see the **A>** prompt displayed on the screen. You rebooted the system and again loaded the operating system from the master DOS System Disk in Drive A. DOS was read into RAM or memory from the disk that you inserted into Drive A. It is much like using a turntable (the disk drive) to play a record (the master DOS System Disk).

2.7 Overview of Files and Disks

Each time you turn off the computer, whatever was in memory (RAM), programs or data, is gone. The memory is temporary. You need a way to store this information permanently. In the microcomputer world, the primary way to save data and programs permanently is to store them on a disk. After you have booted your computer, DOS reads the programs or data it needs from the disk back into its memory. However, in order for DOS to find this information, it has to have a way of organizing it, which it does by keeping programs and data in files on the disk. Just as you organize your written work in files, DOS organizes computer information in **disk files**.

A disk file is much like a file folder stored in a file cabinet. The file cabinet is the floppy disk or the hard disk. A file consists of related information stored on the disk in a "file folder" with a unique name. All information with which a computer works is contained and stored in files on the disk. Thus, an analogy might be:

A file cabinet is equivalent to a box of disks or a hard disk. A file drawer is equivalent to one disk. A file folder is equivalent to one file on the disk. A name on a file folder is equivalent to a file name of a disk file. (See Figure 2.3.)

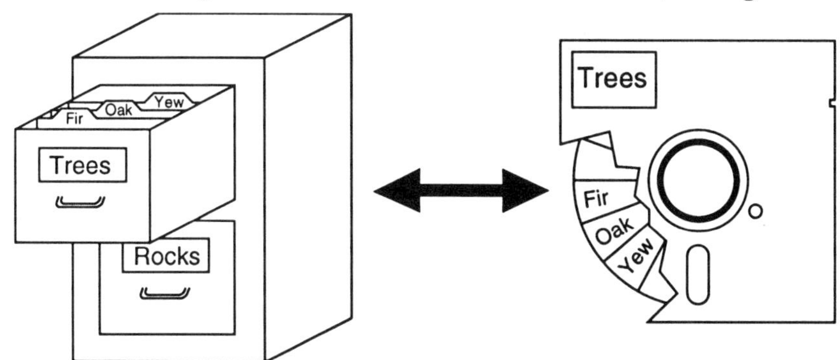

Figure 2.3
Disks and Files

If the computer did not have the ability to store information permanently on disk, all the work you did would be lost every time you turned off the computer.

2.8 File Names and File Types

Because computers must follow very specific rules, there is a specific format for file names. Technically, a **file name** is called the **file specification**. The first rule is that the file specification must be unique. Second, the file specification is broken into two parts, a file name and a **file extension**. The file name typically describes or identifies the file, and the file extension typically identifies the kind of data in the file. Since the term file specification is rather awkward, most people simply refer to the file name, meaning both the file name and its extension.

There are three major types of computer files—text files, data files, and program files. A **text file** is one that contains information that you can read on the screen. Some application programs generate text files. **Data files** are those files that contain information generated usually from an application program. Most often, only an application program can use the data file directly. **Program files** are application programs that allow the user to solve some type of specific problem, such as a payroll program that would allow the user to create and maintain a payroll system for a company.

2.9 What is a Command?

DOS commands are programs, but a program is the series of instructions that tell the computer what to do. A program is stored in a file on a disk. In order for a program to be used, the instructions must be placed in memory and followed by the computer. This process is known as **executing a program**. When you wish to use a program or a command, you must first load the program into memory. You load or call the program first by knowing the name of the program that is stored as a file on a disk, and second by getting the file into memory by keying in the file name or the command. DOS responds by opening the file on the disk, reading the contents of the file from the disk into memory, and executing or running the program.

2.10 The DIR Command

When you booted the system by placing the master DOS System Disk in Drive A and powering on the computer, you loaded the operating system into RAM or memory. The system programs that reside or are stored on the master DOS System Disk are read into RAM. You are going to be using the operating system commands, those programs that you call by keying in the command name and pressing <Enter>. The command then executes or runs.

Certain commands, known as internal commands or resident commands, always remain in memory for you to use until you turn off the computer. The other commands, known as external or transient commands, reside only on the DOS System Disk and must be read into RAM each time you key in the command name. When using external commands, you will find that, if the DOS System Disk is not in the drive or you are not logged into the DOS subdirectory where the computer looks, the command or program will not be found and, therefore, cannot be run.

The master DOS System Disk is in Drive A. How do you know what files are on the disk? There is an internal command called DIR for directory. This command was loaded into memory when you booted the system and is part of the file called **COMMAND.COM**. When you key in DIR, you are asking DOS to run the program. The purpose of this command is to display on the screen the names of all the files located on the disk in Drive A, in other words, the table of contents for the disk. The DIR command is the first DOS internal command you will use.

Activity 2.11 Using the DIR Command

STEP 1: The master DOS System Disk should be in Drive A. The **A>** prompt should be displayed on the screen.

Note: Remember, when you see the notation <Enter>, it means to press the <Enter> key located towards the right side and labeled "Enter" and/or ◄—┘.

STEP 2: Key in the following:

A>DIR <Enter>

```
Directory of A:\

COMMAND   COM   47845   04-09-91   5:00a
APPEND    EXE   10774   04-09-91   5:00a
ASSIGN    COM    6399   04-09-91   5:00a
CHKDSK    EXE   16200   04-09-91   5:00a
COMP      EXE   14282   04-09-91   5:00a
DISKCOMP  COM   10652   04-09-91   5:00a
DISKCOPY  COM   11793   04-09-91   5:00a
FIND      EXE    6770   04-09-91   5:00a
FORMAT    COM   32911   04-09-91   5:00a
JOIN      EXE   17870   04-09-91   5:00a
LABEL     EXE    9390   04-09-91   5:00a
MODE      COM   23537   04-09-91   5:00a
MORE      COM    2618   04-09-91   5:00a
PRINT     EXE   15656   04-09-91   5:00a
RAMDRIVE  SYS    5873   04-09-91   5:00a
SORT      EXE    6938   04-09-91   5:00a
SUBST     EXE   18478   04-09-91   5:00a
TREE      COM    6901   04-09-91   5:00a
XCOPY     EXE   15804   04-09-91   5:00a
       19 file(s)      280691 bytes
                         1024 bytes free
A>_
```

Note: Shown here is the screen display of the MS-DOS version 5.0 directory as created in Appendix A. Your screen display will be different if you are using another version of DOS. It is all right if more files are displayed. Earlier versions of DOS could fit on one disk. Just be sure you have the master DOS System Disk in Drive A. The number of bytes and the date created will also vary, but this is not significant. If you are using a version of IBM PC-DOS, some file extensions will be different. The **.COM** file extension is often used in IBM PC-DOS rather than the **.EXE** file extension found in MS-DOS.

WHAT'S HAPPENING? You see text moving vertically on the screen. This movement is known as **scrolling**, the result of executing the DIR command. DOS is displaying, or listing, all the files on the disk in Drive A and stops scrolling when the list ends. The DIR command displays the files on the disk in Drive A, and it also gives information about the files. Look at the top line of the screen. You see the following:

```
COMMAND   COM   47845   04-09-91   5:00a
```

COMMAND is the name of the file. COM is the file extension. (COMMAND.COM is the file specification.) Next is the number 47845, the size of the file in bytes; the date, 04-09-91; and the time, 5:00a. The date and time indicate either when this file was created or when it was last modified. Now look at the bottom line of the display shown on the previous page. The line states: 19 file(s) 280691 bytes and 1024 bytes free. This line indicates the total number of files on the disk—19. The next number—280691 bytes—indicates how much room the files take up on the disk. This is new in DOS 5.0. The next number—1024—indicates how much room is left in bytes, so you will know if you have room on this disk for more files. On the disk with only 1024 bytes free, there is not much room for more files.

All the files listed on the disk are programs or commands that you will learn to use. All the file names scrolled are external commands from the master DOS System Disk.

2.12 The Keyboard

The keyboard on a microcomputer is similar to a typewriter keyboard but has at least 40 additional keys, many with symbols rather than alphabetic characters. Generally, the keyboard can be broken down into four categories:

1. **Alphanumeric keys**. These keys, located in the center of the keyboard, are the standard typewriter keys. They consist of the letters of the alphabet and Arabic numerals.
2. **Function keys**. Keys labeled F1, F2, etc., located on the left side or across the top of the keyboard, are known as function keys. These keys are program-dependent which means that their functions are dependent on the software used.
3. **Directional keys**. These keys, located between the alphanumeric keys and the number pad, are the cursor keys. These keys are also program-dependent and when used allow you to move the cursor in the direction of the arrows. Directly next to the directional keys are keys that are labeled Insert, Home, Page Up, Delete, End, and Page Down. These keys are also program-dependent. Older PC keyboards do not have separate directional keys or separate labeled keys. Instead, these keys are located on the numeric key pad.
4. **Numeric keys**. These keys, located to the right of the directional keys, are known as the number or numeric pad. Numeric keys can be used in two ways: like a calculator keypad or with the directional arrows and other commands.

The directional arrows in combination with other commands are program-dependent. The user must activate the mode desired (numeric keypad or directional arrows) with the <NumLock> key which acts as a toggle switch. A **toggle switch** acts like an on/off switch. Press the <NumLock> key once and the numbers are turned on. Press the <NumLock> key again and the numbers are turned off. Other toggle keys will be discussed later.

The following activity will familiarize you with some of the special keys and features of a computer keyboard. Figure 2.4 shows some of the major types of keyboards used today. Identify the keyboard used with your system so that you can locate the appropriate keys.

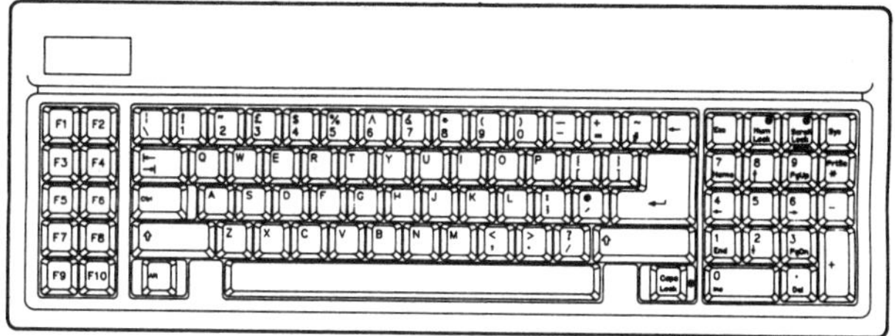

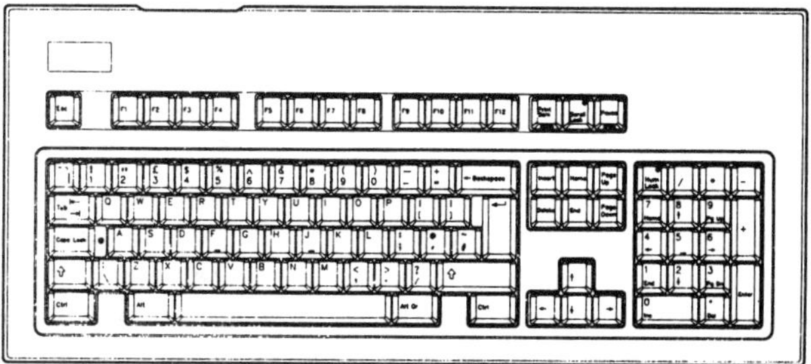

Figure 2.4 Various Keyboard Layouts

2.13 The Backspace Key

The <Backspace>, the key labeled <— Backspace or just with the symbol <— on it, allows you to erase characters you have keyed in prior to pressing <Enter>.

Activity 2.14 Correcting Typographical Errors Using the Backspace Key

STEP 1: Key in the following:

```
A>The quick brown fox
```

STEP 2: Press the <Backspace> key until you reach the A prompt (`A>`). As you see, each time you press this key, you delete a character.

2.15 The Escape Key

Esc is an abbreviation for Escape. Look for the key labeled Esc. When you press this key, it cancels a line you have keyed in, provided you have not yet pressed <Enter>. After you press the <Esc> key and DOS has eliminated the line of text, the line still appears on the screen. All DOS does is wait for you to key in something else.

Activity 2.16 Using the Escape Key

STEP 1: Key in the following:

```
A>The quick brown fox
```

STEP 2: To erase this line, you could repeatedly press the <Backspace> key. However, you can use the <Esc> key to cancel the line instead. Press the <Esc> key.

```
A>The quick brown fox\
```

WHAT'S HAPPENING? DOS displayed a backslash (\) to show you that the line you keyed in was canceled. DOS then moved the cursor to the beginning of the next line. The **A>** is not shown where the cursor is blinking. The blinking indicates that DOS is ready for you to key in another command. DOS is ignoring the line you had keyed in.

STEP 3: Press <Enter>. DOS again displays the **A>** on the next line.

```
A>The quick brown fox\

A>_
```

2.17 The Shift Key

The <Shift> key is labeled Shift with an up arrow symbol (⇧) or just the up arrow symbol. This key allows the user to shift to uppercase letters and special characters such as the * above the number 8 key. There are usually two <Shift> keys, one on either side of the alphabet keys. To activate, you need only press one <Shift> key.

Activity 2.18 Using the Shift Key

STEP 1: Press the letter m.

```
A>m_
```

STEP 2: Hold down the <Shift> key and press the letter m.

```
A>mM_
```

STEP 3: Press either <Backspace> or <Esc> to delete the letters.

2.19 The Shift Key and Print Screen Keys

Look for the key labeled <PrtSc> or <Print Screen>, which means print the screen. If you want to print what is displayed on the screen, hold down <Shift> and press the <PrtSc> key. This procedure gives you a hard copy or printed version of what the screen displays, like a "snapshot" of the screen at a specific moment in time. Be sure to turn on the printer before you begin this exercise. Many of the newer computers only require you to press <PrtSc>; you do not have to press <Shift> first.

Activity 2.20 Using the Shift Key and the Print Screen Key

STEP 1: Key in the following:

A>DIR <Enter>

STEP 2: Wait until the table of contents has stopped scrolling. Hold the <Shift> key down and then press the <PrtSc> key. Press only <PrtSc> if that is how your system works.

WHAT'S HAPPENING? You should see the cursor moving along the screen. At the same time, you should see that the printer is printing what is displayed on the screen.

Activity 2.21 Printing with a Laser Printer

Special note to users with laser printers:

If you have a laser printer, it is much harder to print the screen. Some laser printers will let you print the screen by following these steps:

STEP 1: Press <Shift>+<PrtSc> or just <PrtSc>.

STEP 2: Go to the printer (when the ready light stops blinking) and turn <On Line> off.

STEP 3: Press <Form Feed> on the printer.

STEP 4: After you have a hard copy, press <On Line> on the printer to place the printer back online.

2.22 The Control Key and Print Screen Key

Look for the key labeled <Ctrl>, the Control key. It has many functions depending on what combinations of keys are used. Pressing the Control key has no meaning by itself. However, when used with another key, it "triggers" a meaning for that key. When you see the notation <Ctrl>, ^, or Control key, it means to hold down the Control key with another specified key. For example, <Ctrl>+C or ^C is computer notation for pressing the control key and another key, the letter C. Do not type or key in the word Control, <Ctrl>, or ^. In the last example, when you printed the screen, you could only get what was displayed on the screen. The files that scrolled by were not printed. If, however, you hold down the <Ctrl> key and the <PrtSc> key, DOS will print everything as it is displayed. Be sure the printer is turned on.

Note: If you have a laser printer, you will not be able to do this activity.

Activity 2.23

Using the Control Key and the Print Screen Key

STEP 1: Press the <Ctrl> key. While pressing the <Ctrl> key, press the <PrtSc> key.

STEP 2: Key in the following:

A>**DIR** <Enter>

WHAT'S HAPPENING? As the directory is displayed, it is also being printed. The table of contents or the directory is displayed much more slowly than when you use the DIR command by itself because DOS waits until a line is printed before going on to the next line. Pressing <Ctrl>+<PrtSc> creates what is known as a toggle switch, much like a light switch. In one position the light is turned on; in the other position the light is turned off. You have turned on the printing function and it will stay turned on, printing *everything* you key in and display on the screen, until you turn it off. To turn off a toggle switch, simply press the same keys again.

STEP 3: Press the <Ctrl> key. While pressing the <Ctrl> key, press the <PrtSc> key.

2.24

Freezing the Display

You have already seen that when you use the DIR command, the display scrolls by so quickly on the screen that it is very difficult to read. There is a way to stop displays from rapidly scrolling on the screen. DOS allows you to read a long display by temporarily halting the scrolling procedure. How you do it depends on what kind of computer you have. Once again you use the <Ctrl> key, but now you use it in conjunction with a key labeled <NumLock>. Locate the key with <NumLock> on it. (Other computers have a key labeled <Pause>; all you need to do is press <Pause>. Nearly every kind of computer will let you use <Ctrl>+S for freezing the display.)

Activity 2.25

Using the Control Key and NumLock Key, the Pause Key, and the Control Key and the S Key

STEP 1: Key in the following:

A>**DIR** <Enter>

STEP 2: Press the <Ctrl> key. While pressing the <Ctrl> key, press the <NumLock> key.

WHAT'S HAPPENING? Pressing these keys halts or "freezes" the display on the screen. If this did not freeze the display, repeat Step 1 but press the <Pause> key for Step 2. The display stops and the cursor remains blinking when you press these two keys. To continue scrolling, press any key.

STEP 3: Press any key.

STEP 4: Key in the following:
A>DIR <Enter>

STEP 5: Press the <Ctrl> key. While pressing the <Ctrl> key, press the S key.

WHAT'S HAPPENING? Pressing these keys halts or "freezes" the display on the screen. The display stops with a blinking cursor set when you pressed these two keys. To continue scrolling, press any key.

STEP 6: Press any key.

2.26 Cancelling a Command

If you keyed in a command and pressed <Enter>, but you either made an error or changed your mind about executing the command, you can cancel the command or cause it to stop executing. This command, however, is not the same as <Esc>, which is used prior to pressing <Enter>. To cancel a command after you have pressed <Enter>, press the <Ctrl> key in conjunction with the <Break> key or the letter C. Look for the key labeled <Break>. It is often paired with the <Scroll Lock> key or the <Pause> key.

Activity 2.27 Using DIR and Cancelling a Command

STEP 1: Key in the following:
A>DIR <Enter>

STEP 2: As soon as the directory starts displaying on the screen, hold the <Ctrl> key down. While holding down the <Ctrl> key, press the <Break> key.

WHAT'S HAPPENING? DOS stops running or executing the DIR command. You are returned to the A> prompt. You interrupted or stopped the program or the command from running and, therefore, you see only a partial directory display. At the point where you pressed the <Ctrl> key and the <Break> key, you see ^C displayed on your screen. <Ctrl>+C has the same function and meaning as <Ctrl>+<Break>.

STEP 3: Key in the following:
A>DIR <Enter>

STEP 4: As soon as the directory starts displaying on the screen, hold the <Ctrl> key down and then simultaneously press the letter C.

WHAT'S HAPPENING? This worked exactly like <Ctrl>+<Break>. DOS ceased executing the program or the DIR command and returned you to the A> prompt, ready for another command.

2.28

The CLS, DATE, and TIME Commands

So far, the only internal command you have been working with is the DIR command. There are many other internal commands. The next three commands that will be demonstrated are minor but useful internal commands.

2.29

The CLS Command

Your screen is filled with the display of the directory and other commands that you have keyed in. You may want to have a "fresh" screen, with nothing displayed except the **A>** prompt and the cursor in its "home" position (the upper left-hand corner of the screen). The internal command CLS clears or "refreshes" the screen. Whatever is displayed on the screen will go away, as if you erased a blackboard. The command erases the screen, not your files.

Activity 2.30

Using the CLS Command

STEP 1: Key in the following:
A>**CLS** <Enter>

```
A>_
```

WHAT'S HAPPENING? The screen is now cleared, and the **A>** is back in the upper left-hand corner.

2.31

The DATE and TIME Commands

You used the DATE and TIME commands each time you booted up the system and entered the date and time in response to the DATE/TIME prompts. The date and time that are entered are known as the **system date** and the **system time**. The system date and time are the date and time the computer uses when it opens and closes files (last date/time accessed) or when another program asks for the date and time. Newer computers have a built-in clock. Older computer systems may have an "add-on" built-in clock. You add it after you purchase the computer system. It is simply a built-in 24-hour battery-operated clock that sets the date and time automatically when you boot the system so that you never see the DATE/TIME prompts when you start. However, regardless of whether you entered the date and time when you booted the system or whether you have an automatic clock, you can change or check the system date and system time whenever you wish by using the internal DATE and TIME commands.

Activity 2.32

Using the DATE and TIME Commands

STEP 1: Key in the following:
A>**DATE** <Enter>

```
Current date is Mon 11-23-1992
Enter new date (mm-dd-yy):
```

WHAT'S HAPPENING? The date displayed on your screen is the one you entered when you booted the system, not the above example. This prompt appears exactly like the one you saw when you first booted the system. If you did not wish to change the date, you would just press <Enter>, retaining the date displayed and returning you to the **A>**. However, if you do want to change the date, you respond to the prompt.

STEP 2: Key in the following:
12-31-99 <Enter>

```
A>_
```

WHAT'S HAPPENING? You did change the date, and we will examine this change in a moment. You can also change the time in the same fashion with the TIME command.

STEP 3: Key in the following:
A>**TIME** <Enter>

```
Current time is 10:44:14.42
Enter new time:_
```

WHAT'S HAPPENING? The time displayed on your screen is the current time, not the above example. This prompt is exactly like the one you saw when you first booted the system. If you did not wish to change the time, you would just press <Enter>, retaining the time displayed and returning you to the **A>**. However, if you do want to change the time, you respond to the prompt.

STEP 4: Key in the following:
23:59:59 <Enter>

WHAT'S HAPPENING? You have just reset the computer clock with the DATE and TIME commands. These are internal commands. How do you know the system date and time have been changed? You can check by keying in the commands.

STEP 5: Key in the following:
A>**DATE** <Enter>

```
Current date is Sat 01-01-2000
Enter new date (mm-dd-yy):_
```

STEP 6: Press <Enter>.

STEP 7: Key in the following:
A>**TIME** <Enter>

```
Current time is 12:01:16.25a
Enter new time:_
```

STEP 8: Press <Enter>.

WHAT'S HAPPENING? Your time display numbers may be slightly different. What have you done? You have changed the system date and time. You entered the date of December 31, 1999 (12-31-99), prior to changing the time. The date now displayed is Sunday, January 1, 2000. How did that happen? Why is the displayed date different from the keyed-in date? After you entered the date of 12/31/99, you entered the time of 11:59 p.m. (23:59:59). When you set the time or clock, it runs until you turn off the power. Seconds went by; the time rolled over past midnight, and when you are past midnight, you are into a new day. Hence, the day "rolled over" from December 31, 1999 to January 1, 2000. In other words, DOS is keeping the date and time current based on the information you gave.

The day of the week is displayed in the date. You can play around with DATE and TIME commands. For instance, you can find the day of your birthday in any future year by using the DATE command.

STEP 9: Key in the following:
A>**DATE** <Enter>

```
Current date is Sat 1-01-2000
Enter new date (mm-dd-yy):_
```

STEP 10: At the prompt on the screen—date (mm-dd-yy)—key in your birthdate for 1995. In the example below, I will use my birthday, 5-7-95. Key in the following:
5-07-95 <Enter>

STEP 11: Key in the following:
A>**DATE** <Enter>

```
Current date is Sun 5-07-1995
Enter new date (mm-dd-yy):_
```

WHAT'S HAPPENING? The screen display shows you the exact day of your birthday in 1995. In this case, my birthday will fall on a Sunday in 1995. If you wish to see or change the system date or time, use the DATE command and the TIME command.

STEP 12: Use the DATE and TIME commands to enter the current date and time.

2.33 Making a System Disk: DISKCOPY (When Legal)

IMPORTANT NOTE: IT IS ILLEGAL TO MAKE A COPY OF A PROGRAM THAT YOU DID NOT PURCHASE AND DO NOT OWN. DOS IS A PROGRAM. IF YOU ARE AT HOME OR THE OFFICE AND HAVE PURCHASED YOUR COPY OF DOS, YOU MAY PROCEED WITH ACTIVITY 2.34. ALSO NOTE THAT WITH DOS 3.3, 4.0, AND 5.0, YOU ARE WORKING WITH AN INCOMPLETE VERSION OF DOS THAT IS ON THE FLOPPY DISK. (SEE APPENDIX A FOR HOW TO MAKE A SINGLE COPY OF THE DOS SYSTEM DISK.) IF YOU ARE IN A COMPUTER LAB, CHECK WITH YOUR INSTRUCTOR ON THE PROCEDURES IN YOUR SPECIFIC LAB.

You are now going to make a working copy of the master DOS System Disk. You will work from a copy of the master DOS System Disk so that if anything happens, you can go back to the original master DOS System Disk to make another copy. Whenever possible, always work from a copy, never the original. This copy of the master DOS System Disk will be used for all future exercises. In addition, you should always have a bootable copy of DOS on a floppy disk so that you can boot from the floppy disk instead of the hard disk in case anything happens and you cannot access the hard disk.

You are going to use your first external program, called DISKCOPY. It is stored as a file called `DISKCOPY.COM` on the master DOS System Disk. It does exactly what it says: it copies all the information from one disk to another. However, the disks must be compatible. That is, you must copy a 5 1/4 360 KB disk to a 5 1/4 360 KB disk, or a 5 1/4 1.2 MB disk to a 5 1/4 1.2 MB disk, or a 3 1/2 720 KB disk to a 3 1/2 720 KB disk, or a 3 1/2 1.44 MB disk to a 3 1/2 1.44 MB disk. Since DISKCOPY makes an identical copy, you must use the same type of disk. You can *never* use the DISKCOPY command to copy from a hard disk to a floppy disk or from a floppy disk to a hard disk.

Note 1: The master DOS System Disk should be in Drive A. The `A>` prompt should be displayed on the screen. If you do not have the `A>`, boot or reboot the system.

Note 2: Hard disk users, please follow the instructions precisely. Be sure your screen looks like the sample, especially the prompt. You do not want `C>` displayed, only `A>`.

Activity 2.34 Using DISKCOPY to Make a System Disk (When Legal)

STEP 1: Get a blank disk and a blank label. On the label write DOS SYSTEM DISK. Put the label on the blank disk, label side up. If the disk has no label, you can determine which is "label side up" by placing the disk on a flat surface with the read/write area facing away from you and the write-protect notch at the left. Here is the side on which to place the label. If you ever need to write on a label that is already affixed to the disk, be sure to use only a felt-tip pen and write very gently.

STEP 2: The master DOS System Disk is in Drive A with the disk drive door closed or latched.

STEP 3: Key in the following:
A>**DISKCOPY A: A:** <Enter>

```
Insert SOURCE diskette in drive A:
Press any key to continue. . . . . _
```

WHAT'S HAPPENING? By keying in DISKCOPY, you are asking the command processor to find a program called DISKCOPY. It first looked in the internal table of commands. When it could not find a match, it went to the disk in Drive A and found the program, loaded it into memory, and started executing it. This program has some prompts, which are simply instructions to follow. The program asks you to put the SOURCE disk that you wish to copy in Drive A. In this case, the master DOS System Disk, which you want to copy, already is in Drive A. Since you have only one floppy disk drive, you are going to have to swap disks when prompted. You keyed in two disk drive letters, A and A, to make sure that you do not accidentally copy the hard disk. You are telling DOS to make a copy from the disk in Drive A to the disk in Drive A. To make the copy or begin executing the command DISKCOPY, press any key. This instruction literally means any key on the keyboard. Typically, you use <Enter>.

STEP 4: Press <Enter>.

```
Copying 40 tracks
9 sectors per track, 2 side(s)
```

WHAT'S HAPPENING? Track and sector numbers will vary depending on the type of disk used. The DISKCOPY command tells DOS to copy everything on the disk in Drive A (the SOURCE) to RAM. While this program is doing the copying, the cursor is flashing on the screen. When the command is completed or the program is finished executing (copying), you will need to take another step. You see the following prompt:

```
Insert TARGET diskette in drive A:
Press any key to continue . . . . . _
```

WHAT'S HAPPENING? This prompt tells you to remove the SOURCE disk from Drive A and insert the blank or TARGET disk in Drive A so DOS has a place to copy the information.

STEP 5: Remove the master DOS System Disk from Drive A. Insert the blank disk into Drive A. Close or latch the drive door. Press <Enter>.

WHAT'S HAPPENING? Again, you see the flashing cursor. Now, whatever was copied into RAM is being copied or written to the blank disk in Drive A. If you do not have a 360 KB floppy disk drive, you will receive the following prompt:

```
Insert SOURCE diskette in drive A:
Press any key to continue. . . . . _
```

Because you do not have enough memory (RAM) to capture all of the master DOS System Disk in one transfer, you will have to swap disks back and forth in drive A until the transfer is completed. The instructions will tell you to remove the TARGET diskette from Drive A and insert the SOURCE diskette (master DOS System Disk) into Drive A. Therefore, you remove the target disk from Drive A, insert the master DOS System disk back into Drive A, and press <Enter> until you see the message "Insert TARGET diskette in drive A." You continue to swap disks until you get the following screen display.

```
Volume Serial Number is 1DE2-136A
Copy another diskette (Y/N)?_
```

WHAT'S HAPPENING? The prompt tells you that the program has finished executing and asks you a question. Do you want to execute this program again to make another copy of a disk? In this case, you do not wish to make another copy so you key in the letter n for no. The Volume Serial Number, by the way, changes with each DISKCOPY command and is only seen in DOS 4.0 or above.

STEP 6: Key in the letter n.

```
A>_
```

WHAT'S HAPPENING? You are returned to the `A>`. DOS is ready for a new command.

2.35 Making a Copy of the Activities Disk

You are now going to make a working copy of the ACTIVITIES disk. You will work from a copy of the ACTIVITIES disk so that if anything happens, you can go back to the original ACTIVITIES disk to make another copy. Whenever possible, always work from a copy, never the original. This copy of the ACTIVITIES disk will be used in all future exercises. It is legal to make a copy for your personal use only.

In order to make a copy of the ACTIVITIES disk with the DISKCOPY command, the TARGET disk must be in the same format as the ACTIVITIES disk.

Note 1: The master DOS System Disk should be in Drive A. The `A>` prompt should be displayed on the screen. If you do not have the `A>`, boot or reboot the system.

Note 2: Hard disk users, please follow the instructions precisely. Be sure your screen looks like the sample, especially the prompt. You do not want **C>** displayed, only **A>**.

Note 3: If you have a 5 1/4-inch ACTIVITIES disk, which is 360 KB, your blank disk must also be 360 KB. If you have a 3 1/2-inch ACTIVITIES disk, which is 720 KB, your blank disk must also be 720 KB.

Activity 2.36

Using DISKCOPY to Make a Copy of the Activities Disk

STEP 1: Get a blank disk and a blank label. On the label write: ACTIVITIES DISK—WORKING COPY. Put the label on the blank disk, label side up.

STEP 2: The master DOS System Disk is in Drive A.

STEP 3: Key in the following:

A>**DISKCOPY A: A:** <Enter>

```
Insert SOURCE diskette in drive A:
Press any key to continue. . . . . _
```

WHAT'S HAPPENING? By keying in **DISKCOPY**, you are asking the command processor to find a program called DISKCOPY. However, you *do not want* to press <Enter> yet. What you want to copy, the SOURCE, is the ACTIVITIES disk, not the DOS System Disk in Drive A. If you pressed <Enter> now, you would get a copy of the DOS System Disk.

STEP 4: Remove the DOS System Disk from Drive A. Insert the ACTIVITIES disk in Drive A.

STEP 5: Press <Enter>.

```
Copying 40 tracks
9 sectors per track, 2 side(s)
```

WHAT'S HAPPENING? Track and sector numbers will vary depending on the type of disk used. The DISKCOPY command tells DOS to copy everything on the disk in Drive A (the SOURCE) to RAM. While this program is doing the copying, the cursor flashes on the screen. When the command is completed or the program is finished executing (copying), you will need to take another step. You see the following prompt:

```
Insert TARGET diskette in drive A:
Press any key to continue. . . . . _
```

WHAT'S HAPPENING? This prompt tells you to remove the SOURCE disk from Drive A and insert the blank or TARGET disk in Drive A so DOS has a place to copy the information.

STEP 6: Remove the ACTIVITIES disk from Drive A. Insert the blank disk labeled ACTIVITIES DISK—WORKING COPY into Drive A. Press <Enter>.

WHAT'S HAPPENING? Again, you see the flashing cursor. Now, whatever was copied into RAM is being copied or written to the blank disk in Drive A. If you do not have a 360 KB floppy disk drive, you will receive the following prompt:

```
Insert SOURCE diskette in drive A:
Press any key to continue. . . . . _
```

Because you do not have enough memory (RAM) to capture all of the master ACTIVITIES Disk in one transfer, you will have to swap disks back and forth in Drive A until the transfer is completed. The instructions will tell you to remove the TARGET disk from Drive A and insert the SOURCE diskette (master ACTIVITIES disk) into Drive A. You remove the target disk from Drive A, insert the master ACTIVITIES disk back into Drive A, and press <Enter> until you see the message "Insert TARGET diskette in drive A." You continue to swap disks until you get the following screen display.

```
Volume Serial Number is 1DE2-136A
Copy another diskette (Y/N)?_
```

WHAT'S HAPPENING? The prompt tells you that the program has finished executing and asks you a question. Do you want to execute this program again to make another copy of a disk? In this case, you do not wish to make another copy so you key in the letter n for no. The Volume Serial Number, by the way, changes with each DISKCOPY command and is only seen in DOS 4.0 or above.

STEP 7: Key in the letter n.

```
Insert disk with \COMMAND.COM in drive A
Press any key to continue. . . . . _
```

WHAT'S HAPPENING? The ACTIVITIES disk does not have a copy of the command processor, the file called `COMMAND.COM`. In order to carry out your next command, DOS must have access to `COMMAND.COM`.

STEP 8: Remove the ACTIVITIES disk from Drive A. Insert the DOS System Disk in Drive A. Press <Enter>.

```
A>_
```

WHAT'S HAPPENING? You are returned to the `A>`. DOS is ready for a new command.

2.37 Verifying the Copy with DISKCOMP

How do you know that the disks were copied correctly? One way to confirm this is to use another command, DISKCOMP. DISKCOMP is stored as a file called **DISKCOMP.COM** on the master DOS System Disk. This external command does exactly what it says. It compares two disks track by track and sector by sector, making sure that the two disks are absolutely identical. However, to compare two disks, the disks must be compatible. That is, you must compare a 5 1/4 360 KB disk to a 5 1/4 360 KB disk, a 5 1/4 1.2 MB disk to a 5 1/4 1.2 MB disk, a 3 1/2 720 KB disk to a 3 1/2 720 KB disk, or a 3 1/2 1.44 MB disk to a 3 1/2 1.44 MB disk. Since DISKCOMP is comparing identical disks, you must use the same type of disk. You can never use the DISKCOMP command to compare a hard disk and a floppy disk.

Note: Hard disk users, please follow the instructions precisely. Be sure your screen looks like the sample, especially the prompt. You do not want **C>** displayed, only **A>**.

Activity 2.38 Verifying the Copy of the Activities Disk with DISKCOMP

STEP 1: Place the master DOS System Disk in Drive A.

STEP 2: Key in the following:
A>**DISKCOMP A: A:** <Enter>

```
Insert FIRST diskette in drive A:
Press any key to continue. . . . . _
```

STEP 3: Remove the master DOS System Disk from Drive A and place the master ACTIVITIES disk in Drive A. Press <Enter>.

```
Comparing 40 tracks
9 sectors per track, 2 side(s)
```

WHAT'S HAPPENING? Track and sector numbers will vary depending on the type of disk used. By keying in **DISKCOMP**, you are asking the command processor to find a program called DISKCOMP. It first looked in the table of commands. When it could not find a match (since DISKCOMP is external), it went to the disk in Drive A, found and loaded the program into memory, and began executing it. Its job is to verify that the two disks are alike. Since you want to compare the master ACTIVITIES disk to the copy, you had to remove the master DOS System Disk and insert the master ACTIVITIES disk in Drive A. This command is only used with floppy disks, since you cannot compare a hard disk and a floppy disk. DISKCOMP read the disk in Drive A into RAM. Now it needs another disk to complete the comparison. Do not do anything until you see the following prompt displayed on the screen:

```
Insert SECOND diskette in drive A:
Press any key to continue. . . . . _
```

STEP 4: Remove the master ACTIVITIES disk from Drive A. Insert the working copy of the ACTIVITIES disk you made, the disk that you wish to compare to the original. Press <Enter>.

WHAT'S HAPPENING? Again, you see the flashing cursor while the program is working. It is comparing the original disk to the copy. It read into memory whatever was on the second diskette and is checking it against the original. If you do not have a 360 KB floppy disk, you will receive the following prompt:

```
Insert FIRST diskette in drive A:
Press any key to continue . . . _
```

This prompt tells you to remove the disk in Drive A and insert the master ACTIVITIES disk in Drive A. You continue to swap disks until you see the following screen display:

```
Compare OK
Compare another diskette (Y/N)?_
```

WHAT'S HAPPENING? The DISKCOMP command told you that it checked the disks and found that they are exactly the same (Compare OK). It also asks you a question. Do you want to compare any more disks? Since you do not, you press n.

STEP 5: Press n.

```
Insert disk with \COMMAND.COM in drive A
Press any key to continue. . . . . _
```

WHAT'S HAPPENING? The ACTIVITIES disk does not have a copy of the command processor, the file called **COMMAND.COM**. In order to carry out your next command, DOS must have access to **COMMAND.COM**.

STEP 6: Remove the ACTIVITIES disk from Drive A. Insert the DOS System Disk in Drive A. Press <Enter>.

```
A>_
```

WHAT'S HAPPENING? You are returned to the **A>**. DOS is ready for a new command.

WHAT TO DO WHEN IT DOESN'T WORK If you get beeps from the computer and the following screen display ("n" represents any numerical value):

```
Compare error on side n, track n
```

Press the <Ctrl> key and the <Break> key simultaneously to return to Step 1 and repeat the steps.

2.39

How to End the Work Session

You can stop working with the computer any time you wish. Since your programs are stored on disks, you will not lose them. Whatever is in RAM or memory will go into the byte bucket, i.e. disappear, but that does not affect what is on your disk any more than when you turn off your tape deck; you do not lose what is on the tape. The only thing you need to be cautious about is the disk drive light. When the disk drive light is on, it indicates that the head is reading or writing to the disk. Removing the disk at this time is the equivalent of taking a record off the turntable without first removing the needle.

Activity 2.40

Ending the Work Session

STEP 1: Be sure no disk drive lights are on.

STEP 2: Remove any disks that are in the disk drives. Place the floppy disks in their envelopes.

STEP 3: Turn off the printer, the monitor, and the system unit.

Chapter Summary

1. An operating system is a software program that is required in order to run application software and to oversee the hardware components of the computer system.
2. DOS is the major operating system in use today on IBM and IBM compatible microcomputers.
3. PC-DOS and MS-DOS are functionally the same. PC-DOS usually runs on an IBM PC and MS-DOS usually runs on an IBM-compatible PC.
4. DOS is released in different version numbers. New versions of DOS allow it to take advantage of new technology, to add new commands, and to fix bugs.
5. All microcomputers come with disk drives. There are two basic types of disk drives, the floppy disk drive and the hard disk drive.
6. Most computer systems are configured in one of three ways; two floppy disk drives, one floppy disk drive and one hard disk drive, or one hard disk drive and two floppy disk drives.
7. Booting the system, also known as a cold start, means inserting the DOS System Disk in Drive A and powering on the system. This loads the operating system into memory and executes the self-diagnostic test routine.
8. Rebooting, also known as a warm start, involves pressing the <Ctrl>, <Alt>, and <Del> keys, erasing everything from memory and reloading the operating system from the disk. Rebooting does not execute the self-diagnostic test routine.
9. Internal commands are programs loaded with the operating system in `COMMAND.COM`. They remain in memory until the power is turned off.
10. External commands are stored on a disk and must be loaded into memory each time they are used. They are transient and do not remain in memory after being executed.

11. Programs, data and text are stored on disks as files. The formal name is file specification, which includes the file name and file extension.
12. A command is a program. A program is the set of instructions telling the computer what to do.
13. Programs (commands) must be loaded into memory in order to be executed.
14. To load a program into memory, the user keys in the command name at the system prompt.
15. The DIR command is an internal command that displays the table of contents or directory of a disk.
16. The <Backspace> key deletes characters to the left.
17. The <Esc> key ignores what was previously keyed in.
18. The <Shift> key shifts letters to uppercase.
19. The <PrtSc> key and <Shift> key when held down together print the screen. Newer computers only require you to press the <Print Screen> key.
20. The <Ctrl> key and the <PrtSc> key when held down together toggle the printer on or off, when using a dot-matrix printer.
21. A toggle switch is like a light switch. In one position, the function is turned on. By pressing the same toggle switch the function is turned off.
22. The <NumLock> key and the <Ctrl> key when held down together freeze the screen display on older computers. Newer computers use the <Pause> key. Both older and newer computers can use <Ctrl>+S.
23. The <Ctrl> key and the <Break> key or the <Ctrl> key and the letter C when held down together cancel a command.
24. Minor internal commands include CLS, DATE, and TIME.
25. CLS clears the screen.
26. DATE and TIME allow you to look at and/or change the system date and system time.
27. DISKCOPY is an external command that makes an identical copy of any disk, track for track, sector for sector. It was used to make a working copy of the master DOS System Disk and the ACTIVITIES disk but can be used to make exact copies of any two floppy disks that have the same format.
28. DISKCOMP is an external command that compares two disks, track for track, sector for sector. It was used to verify that the copy of the master ACTIVITIES disk that was made was correct but can be used to verify any two floppy disks that have the same format.
29. When using DISKCOPY or DISKCOMP, the disks must be the same format.
30. To end a work session with the computer, remove any disks and turn off the monitor, printer, and system unit.

Key Terms

Alphanumeric keys
Application software
Booting the system
Commands
Cursor
Data files
Directional keys
Disk files
Enhancements
Executing a program
File extension
File name
File specification
Function keys
Numeric keys
Operating system
Program files
Prompt
Rebooting
Scrolling
System date
System time
Text files
Toggle switch
Version

Discussion Questions

1. What is an operating system?
2. Define system configuration.
3. How would you boot the system?
4. Why is it necessary to boot the system?
5. Compare and contrast two kinds of disk drives.
6. Describe a disk file.
7. What is a file specification?
8. Identify three types of files.
9. What is the difference between a command and a program?
10. Compare and contrast internal and external commands.
11. What is the purpose of the DIR command?
12. Name the four parts of a keyboard.
13. How do you correct typographical errors?
14. What is the purpose of the <Esc> key?
15. What is a toggle switch?
16. Name one way to print the screen.
17. Describe one way to stop the screen from scrolling.
18. How can you cancel a command after you have pressed <Enter>?
19. How must you enter the date when using the DATE command?
20. How must you enter the time when using the TIME command?
21. What is the purpose of the DISKCOPY command?
22. Identity one characteristic of memory.
23. Identify one concern when using DISKCOPY.
24. What is the purpose of the DISKCOMP command?
25. How do you end the work session when using a computer?

Chapter 3

Command Syntax

Using the DIR Command with Parameters and Wildcards

After completing this chapter you will be able to:

1. Define command syntax.
2. Read a syntax diagram and be able to name and explain what each part signifies.
3. Explain what parameters are and how they are used.
4. Explain the purpose and use of the DIR command.
5. Use both fixed and variable parameters with the DIR command.
6. Define prompts and explain how they are used.
7. Define defaults and explain how they affect computer commands.
8. Change the default.
9. Explain what subdirectories (paths) are and use them with the DIR command.
10. Be able to boot off the hard disk.
11. Define global specifications, identify the symbols for global specifications, and use them with the DIR command.
12. Be able to use the online help feature.
13. Print (make a hard copy) what is on the screen.

Chapter Overview

To communicate with any computer it is necessary to learn the computer's language, to follow its syntax, and to use punctuation marks the computer understands. As in mastering a new language, new vocabulary words must be learned, the word order (syntax) must be determined, and the method of separating statements into syntactic units must be understood. The computer has a very limited use of language so it is exceedingly important to be precise when speaking to it.

In this chapter, you will learn some basic computer commands, the syntax or order of these commands, and where the commands begin and end. You will learn how to make your commands more specific, how to use wildcards to affect a command, and how to determine which disk you want to write to or read from. You will also learn how to use the online help feature, which is new in DOS 5.0.

3.0 Command Syntax

All languages have rules or conventions for speaking or writing. The **syntax** or order of a language is important. For example, in English the noun (person, place, or thing) is followed by the verb (the action). In another language, however, the syntax or order might be different: first the verb, followed by the noun. When you learn a language, you learn its syntax.

Computers also communicate with language, but you must speak the computer's language and follow its syntax exactly because the computer has a very limited understanding of language. You cannot just key in any word and expect the computer to understand. Anything you key in must be a recognized word (which is a program the computer executes) the computer understands. Not only must you use the computer's vocabulary, but you must also use the proper syntax. In other words, you must have the proper vocabulary and the proper order or syntax of the vocabulary. The computer cannot guess what you mean. For example, if I said, "Going I store," people would still understand. But if I key in an incorrect word or put correct words in the wrong order, the computer will respond with a message, "Bad command or file name." This statement is the computer equivalent of "I do not understand."

In computer language, the command can be compared to a verb, the action you wish to take. In Chapter 2, you used the command DIR. In other words, when you keyed in DIR, you were asking DOS to take an action: run the program called DIR that lets you see the table of contents or the directory of a disk.

3.1 What are Parameters?

A **parameter** is information that you want a command to have. Some commands require parameters, while other commands let you add them when needed. Some parameters are variable. A **variable parameter** is one to which you supply the value. This process is similar to a math formula. For instance, $x + y = z$ is a simple formula. You can plug in whatever values you wish for x and y. If $x = 1$ and $y = 2$, you know the value of z. These values can change or are variable so that x can equal 5 and y can equal 3 or any other numerical value you wish to use. You can also have $z = 10$, $x = 5$, and mathematically establish the value of y. No matter what numbers x, y, or z are, you will be able to establish the value of each.

Other parameters are fixed. For instance, if the formula now reads $x + 5 = z$, then the x is the variable parameter and the 5 is the fixed value. You can change the value of x but not the value of 5.

When you are working with DOS commands, you are allowed to add one or more qualifiers or modifiers to the command to make it more specific. These qualifiers are the parameters. This process is the same in English. If I give my son my Visa card and tell him, "Go buy," I have given him an open-ended statement—he can buy anything (making him one happy guy). However, if I add a qualifier, "Go buy shoes," I have limited what he can do. This pattern is precisely what parameters do to a command.

3.2 Reading a Syntax Diagram

DOS is like a foreign language. How do you know what the commands are, what the syntax is, and what the parameters are? The DOS Reference Manuals provide **syntax diagrams** that explain the commands. The command syntax diagrams tell you how to enter the command with its optional or mandatory parameters. However, you need to be able to interpret these syntax diagrams. These syntax diagrams can also be found in other software applications.

You have used the DIR command. The following is a brief example of the formal command syntax diagram:

DIR [*drive:*][*path*][*filename*] [/P] [/W]

The first entry is the command name. You may only use this name. You cannot substitute another word such as DIRECTORY. The only word that will work is DIR. Then, you have items that follow the command. In this case, everything is in brackets except DIR, indicating that the command DIR needs no parameters to execute. Thus, all the parameters (all the items in brackets) are optional. Whenever you see brackets, you know you can choose whether or not to include parameters.

3.3 Using Fixed Parameters with the DIR Command

DIR is one of the commands with **optional parameters**. Prior to DOS 5.0, DIR had only two modifiers or **fixed parameters** that allowed you to control the way the operating system displayed the table of contents on the disk: /W for "wide display" and /P for "pause display." DOS 5.0 includes many new parameters. In the DIR command syntax diagram, the /W and the /P were in brackets. You never key in the brackets, only the / (forward slash), also known as a **switch**, and the W or P.

When you key in DIR and the files scroll by, they move so quickly that you cannot read them. In the previous chapter, you learned that you could halt the display by pressing the <Ctrl> and <NumLock> keys. However, there is a more efficient way to solve this problem by using the /P parameter. The /P parameter will display one screen of information at a time. It will also give you a prompt that you must respond to before it will display another screenful of information.

Note 1: From now on, unless otherwise specified, the DOS System Disk refers to the working copy of the DOS disk you made in the previous chapter by using the DISKCOPY command. Remember, you are working with *your* working copy, not the original.

Note 2: Be sure you *know* what your computer laboratory procedures are.

Note 3: From this point on in the text, you will be booting off Drive C. There are certain system considerations that need to be discussed so that you can more easily follow the text. If you have a hard disk system (one hard disk drive and one floppy disk drive), the hard disk is designated as C: and the floppy disk drive is A:. Typically, DOS has already been copied to your hard drive. This process is usually done at the time of purchase or when you upgrade to a new version of

DOS. Thus, when you boot the system, you do not need to insert the DOS System Disk into Drive A. The system boots from the disk in Drive C because that is where the operating system files are. For the remainder of this text, it is assumed that Drive C is where the operating system and utility files are located.

Activity 3.4

How to Use Fixed Parameters with the DIR Command

STEP 1: Boot from the hard disk.

STEP 2: Insert the DOS System Disk in Drive A.

STEP 3: Key in the following:
C>**A:** <Enter>

WHAT'S HAPPENING? The default drive is now Drive A.

STEP 4: Key in the following:
A>**DIR /P** <Enter>

```
    Volume in drive A has no label
    Volume Serial Number is 1AF4-1342
    Directory of A:\

COMMAND   COM   47845   04-09-91   5:00a
APPEND    EXE   10774   04-09-91   5:00a
ASSIGN    COM    6399   04-09-91   5:00a
CHKDSK    EXE   16200   04-09-91   5:00a
COMP      EXE   14282   04-09-91   5:00a
DISKCOMP  COM   10652   04-09-91   5:00a
DISKCOPY  COM   11793   04-09-91   5:00a
FIND      EXE    6770   04-09-91   5:00a
FORMAT    COM   32911   04-09-91   5:00a
JOIN      EXE   17870   04-09-91   5:00a
LABEL     EXE    9390   04-09-91   5:00a
MODE      COM   23537   04-09-91   5:00a
MORE      COM    2618   04-09-91   5:00a
PRINT     EXE   15656   04-09-91   5:00a
RAMDRIVE  SYS    5873   04-09-91   5:00a
SORT      EXE    6938   04-09-91   5:00a
SUBST     EXE   18478   04-09-91   5:00a
TREE      COM    6901   04-09-91   5:00a
XCOPY     EXE   15804   04-09-91   5:00a
Press any key to continue. . . . . _
```

WHAT'S HAPPENING? You keyed in the command DIR followed by a slash / and the parameter P. The slash, which must be included, is known as a **delimiter** or switch and is used to separate characters. The slash is the signal to the DIR command that there are additional instructions. P, the parameter that tells the program what to do, is the additional information. The slash and P stop the directory from scrolling. Thus, /P told the DIR command to fill the screen and then pause until the user takes some action. The message at the bottom of the screen tells you to press any key.

STEP 5: Press <Enter>.

```
(continuing A:\)
        19 file(s)     280691 bytes
                         1024 bytes free

A>_
```

WHAT'S HAPPENING? When you pressed <Enter> or any key, the display continued scrolling. Since there was only one more screen, it returned you to the system prompt. There is another way to display the files on the screen. You may use the /W parameter which displays the directory in a wide format.

STEP 6: Key in the following:
A>DIR /W <Enter>

```
A>DIR /W

   Volume in drive A has no label
   Volume Serial Number is 1AF4-1342
   Directory of A:\

COMMAND.COM    APPEND.EXE     ASSIGN.COM   CHKDSK.EXE   COMP.EXE
DISKCOMP.COM   DISKCOPY.COM   FIND.EXE     FORMAT.COM   JOIN.EXE
LABEL.EXE      MODE.COM       MORE.COM     PRINT.EXE    RAMDRIVE.SYS
SORT.EXE       SUBST.EXE      TREE.COM     XCOPY.EXE
      19 file(s)     280691 bytes
                       1024 bytes free

A>_
```

WHAT'S HAPPENING? The directory display is now spread across the screen, five files wide. In addition, all you see is the file specification—the file name and extension. You do not see the file size, date, or time, but you still see the total number of files and the number of bytes free. Thus, the /W parameter allows you to see all the files at one time and side by side.

3.5 Using File Names as Variable Parameters

In the previous activities, you used the DIR command with two different optional fixed parameters, /P and /W. These optional fixed parameters have specific meanings. There is another parameter you can use with the DIR command: the name of the file.

Files are formally called file specifications. A file specification is broken into two parts, the file name and the file extension. The words **file** or file name really mean the file specification, the file name and file extension. In this case, the files are already named. However, DOS has rules or naming conventions for the files that need names. These are:

1. All files on one disk or one subdirectory must have unique names.
2. File names are mandatory. All files must have file names that may be less than but no more than eight characters. Typically, file names reflect the subject of the file, for example, **EMPLOYEE**, **TAXES**.
3. File extensions are optional. An extension may be less than but not more than three characters. Typically, file extensions refer to the type of data in the file, for example, **.TXT** (text), **.DAT** (data), **.DBF** (database), **.WKS** (spreadsheet).
4. Any alphanumeric character can be used in a file name or file extension, except the following:

<space> . " / \ [ ] : ; ¦ < > + = , * ?

When you key in the DIR command, you get the entire table of contents or directory. Usually, you do not care about all the files. Most often, you are only interested in whether or not one specific file is located or stored on the disk. If you use one of the parameters, /P or /W, you still have to look through all the files. You can locate a specific file quickly by using only the file name. Simply give the DIR command specific information about what file you seek. Looking at the syntax diagram:

DIR [*drive:*][*path*][*filename*] [/P] [/W]

The *filename*, indicated above in brackets, is a variable optional parameter. You may include a file name, but DOS does not know what file you are looking for. You must plug in the value or the name of the file you are looking for [*filename*], much like the *x* in the formula discussed earlier. In some syntax diagrams, you will see [*filename*[*.ext*]]. The *.ext* is in brackets because it is part of the file name syntax. A file may not have an extension, but if it does have an extension, you must include it.

Activity 3.6

Using File Names as Variable Parameters with the DIR Command

Note: The DOS System Disk should be in Drive A with the **A>** displayed.

STEP 1: Key in the following:
A>**CLS** <Enter>

STEP 2: Key in the following:
A>**DIR** <Enter>

WHAT'S HAPPENING? First you cleared the screen by using the internal command CLS. Then, you keyed in DIR and the entire table of contents of the disk in Drive A was displayed on the screen.

```
   Directory of A:\

COMMAND   COM   47845   04-09-91   5:00a
APPEND    EXE   10774   04-09-91   5:00a
ASSIGN    COM    6399   04-09-91   5:00a
CHKDSK    EXE   16200   04-09-91   5:00a
COMP      EXE   14282   04-09-91   5:00a
DISKCOMP  COM   10652   04-09-91   5:00a
DISKCOPY  COM   11793   04-09-91   5:00a
FIND      EXE    6770   04-09-91   5:00a
FORMAT    COM   32911   04-09-91   5:00a
JOIN      EXE   17870   04-09-91   5:00a
LABEL     EXE    9390   04-09-91   5:00a
MODE      COM   23537   04-09-91   5:00a
MORE      COM    2618   04-09-91   5:00a
PRINT     EXE   15656   04-09-91   5:00a
RAMDRIVE  SYS    5873   04-09-91   5:00a
SORT      EXE    6938   04-09-91   5:00a
SUBST     EXE   18478   04-09-91   5:00a
TREE      COM    6901   04-09-91   5:00a
XCOPY     EXE   15804   04-09-91   5:00a
       19 file(s)    280691 bytes
                       1024 bytes free

A>_
```

WHAT'S HAPPENING? You are looking at all the file specifications on the disk in Drive A. You see the file names and, separated by some spaces, the file extensions. The other information is the size in bytes and the date and time the files were last updated.

STEP 3: Key in the following:
A>CLS <Enter>

STEP 4: Key in the following:
A>DIR DISKCOPY.COM <Enter>

```
A>DIR DISKCOPY.COM

   Volume in drive A has no label
   Volume Serial Number is 1AF4-1342
   Directory of A:\

DISKCOPY  COM   11793   04-09-91   5:00a
        1 file(s)     11793 bytes
                       1024 bytes free

A>_
```

WHAT'S HAPPENING? You asked the operating system a question. Does the table of contents on the disk in Drive A (DIR) have a specific file (DISKCOPY.COM)?

DIR is the command; DISKCOPY.COM is the variable parameter. You substituted DISKCOPY.COM for the [*filename*[.*ext*]]. You did not key in the brackets, but when you entered DISKCOPY and COM, you separated the file name from the file extension with a period, called a **dot**. The dot must be entered between DISKCOPY and COM because it separates the file name from the file extension. The dot, a delimiter, tells DOS that the file name is over and the file extension is about to begin. The DIR program will search the entire list of files on the disk in Drive A to find an exact match for DISKCOPY.COM. DOS answered your question with the screen display. DOS is telling you that, yes, a file called DISKCOPY.COM is on the disk in Drive A. The file name is DISKCOPY. The file extension is COM. The file size is 11793. The date and time are 04-09-91 and 5:00a. It is also telling you that there is only one file with that name.

DOS is not case sensitive. You can key in information in either uppercase or lowercase letters. Most people use lowercase letters because it is easier. However, in this textbook for the sake of clarity, commands and file names will be in uppercase letters, and the file names will be in a different printing style.

Actually, DISKCOPY.COM is a file and a command (program). In Chapter 2, you used it as a program by keying in the command name, DISKCOPY. In that instance, DOS not only found the program, but it also loaded it into memory and executed the program. The "work" of DISKCOPY was to make an exact copy of a disk. In this example, you are using DISKCOPY.COM as a file. The command or program you are running is DIR. You are not asking to execute the program DISKCOPY.COM; you are asking DIR if it has a file called DISKCOPY.COM on the disk. DISKCOPY copies the whole file cabinet while DISKCOPY.COM is one of the file folders within the cabinet. When you locate the folder, you now know where the folder is, but you do not yet know what is in the folder.

STEP 5: Key in the following:
A>DIR FORMAT.COM <Enter>

```
A>DIR FORMAT.COM

   Volume in drive A has no label
   Volume Serial Number is 1AF4-1342
   Directory of A:\

FORMAT     COM   32911    04-09-91   5:00a
        1 file(s)     32911 bytes
                       1024 bytes free

A>_
```

WHAT'S HAPPENING? This command tells you that DOS did find the file FORMAT.COM on the disk in Drive A. Furthermore, FORMAT.COM is the variable parameter. You substituted FORMAT.COM for [*filename*[.*ext*]]. If there were no file by that name, you would get the answer "File not found."

STEP 6: Key in the following:
A>**DIR NOFILE.EXT** <Enter>

```
A>DIR NOFILE.EXT

   Volume in drive A has no label
   Volume Serial Number is 1AF4-1342
   Directory of A:\

File not found

A>_
```

WHAT'S HAPPENING? "File not found" is both a system message and an error message. DOS is telling you that it looked through the entire list of files on the disk in Drive A and could not find a "match" or the file called **NOFILE.EXT**. This message is the equivalent of going to your file cabinet and not locating the folder called **NOFILE.EXT**. You cannot "open" this folder because it is not in this file cabinet.

3.7 Drives as Device Names

You have become familiar with seeing the **A>** or A prompt. What is the A **prompt**? **A>** indicates the disk drive or the device where the floppy disk is "playing." A disk drive is an example of a **device name**. A device is a place to send information (write) or a place from which to receive information (read). Disk drives have assigned names so that DOS knows which disk drive to read from or write to. Disk drive names are the letters of the alphabet followed by a colon. The first floppy disk drive is called A:. The first hard disk drive is called C:. A second floppy drive is called B:. If you have one hard disk drive and one floppy disk drive, the floppy disk drive is A:. The hard disk drive is still C:. Disk drives are not the only places where the system sends or receives information. Other common devices are the keyboard, the printer, and the monitor.

3.8 Defaults

In addition to understanding device names, it is also important to understand the concept of **defaults**. Computers must have very specific instructions for everything they do. However, there are implied instructions that the system "falls back to" or defaults to in the absence of other instructions. If you do not specify what you want, the system will make the assumption for you. For example, when the **A>** is displayed on the screen it is called the A prompt, but it is also the **default drive**. In other words, the prompt that is displayed on the screen is the default drive. When you want any activity to occur but do not specify where you want it to happen, the system assumes that you must mean that the activity will occur on the default drive, the **A>** that is displayed on the screen.

When you key in **DIR** at the **A>**, how does DOS know that you are asking for the system to give you a table of contents of the disk in Drive A? It knows for two reasons. First, when a specific direction is given, DOS must have a specific place to look. Second, the **A>** prompt, or default drive, is displayed on the screen. Since you did not specify which disk you wanted DOS to see, it made the assumption (programmed in by the programmer) that since you did not give any instructions to the contrary, you must mean that you want the table of contents or directory listing for the default drive or the disk in Drive A.

The prompt displayed on the screen can also be known as the **designated drive** or the **logged drive**. All commands, if given no other specific instructions to the contrary, assume that all activities must take place or default to the prompt on the screen.

Activity 3.9 Working with Defaults

Note: You will have the DOS System Disk in Drive A and the **A>** displayed.

STEP 1: Key in the following:
A>**DIR** <Enter>

```
   Directory of A:\

COMMAND   COM   47845   04-09-91  5:00a
APPEND    EXE   10774   04-09-91  5:00a
ASSIGN    COM    6399   04-09-91  5:00a
CHKDSK    EXE   16200   04-09-91  5:00a
COMP      EXE   14282   04-09-91  5:00a
DISKCOMP  COM   10652   04-09-91  5:00a
DISKCOPY  COM   11793   04-09-91  5:00a
FIND      EXE    6770   04-09-91  5:00a
FORMAT    COM   32911   04-09-91  5:00a
JOIN      EXE   17870   04-09-91  5:00a
LABEL     EXE    9390   04-09-91  5:00a
MODE      COM   23537   04-09-91  5:00a
MORE      COM    2618   04-09-91  5:00a
PRINT     EXE   15656   04-09-91  5:00a
RAMDRIVE  SYS    5873   04-09-91  5:00a
SORT      EXE    6938   04-09-91  5:00a
SUBST     EXE   18478   04-09-91  5:00a
TREE      COM    6901   04-09-91  5:00a
XCOPY     EXE   15804   04-09-91  5:00a
       19 file(s)    280691 bytes
                       1024 bytes free

A>_
```

WHAT'S HAPPENING? Displayed on the screen is the result of the DIR command you asked DOS to execute. Since you did not specify which disk drive DOS should look into, it assumed or defaulted to the disk in Drive A. Review the syntax diagram: DIR [*drive:*][*path*][*filename*] [/P] [/W]. The syntax diagram has [*drive:*], which is another optional variable parameter. You substitute the letter of the drive you wish DOS to look into.

STEP 2: Key in the following:
A>**DIR A:** <Enter>

```
   Directory of A:\

COMMAND  COM   47845   04-09-91  5:00a
APPEND   EXE   10774   04-09-91  5:00a
ASSIGN   COM    6399   04-09-91  5:00a
CHKDSK   EXE   16200   04-09-91  5:00a
COMP     EXE   14282   04-09-91  5:00a
DISKCOMP COM   10652   04-09-91  5:00a
DISKCOPY COM   11793   04-09-91  5:00a
FIND     EXE    6770   04-09-91  5:00a
FORMAT   COM   32911   04-09-91  5:00a
JOIN     EXE   17870   04-09-91  5:00a
LABEL    EXE    9390   04-09-91  5:00a
MODE     COM   23537   04-09-91  5:00a
MORE     COM    2618   04-09-91  5:00a
PRINT    EXE   15656   04-09-91  5:00a
RAMDRIVE SYS    5873   04-09-91  5:00a
SORT     EXE    6938   04-09-91  5:00a
SUBST    EXE   18478   04-09-91  5:00a
TREE     COM    6901   04-09-91  5:00a
XCOPY    EXE   15804   04-09-91  5:00a
       19 file(s)     280691 bytes
                        1024 bytes free

A>_
```

WHAT'S HAPPENING? You substituted A: for the variable optional parameter, [*drive:*]. You did specify A:. The display, however, is the same as DIR without specifying the A:. Since **A>** is the default drive, it is unnecessary to key in **A:** but not wrong to do so. However, what if you want to see what files are on the disk in Drive C or, if you have it, Drive B? You must tell DOS to look on the drive you are interested in, the disk in Drive B or the disk in Drive C. In other words, you must be specific when telling DOS on which drive to look.

STEP 3: Key in the following:
A>**C:** <Enter>

```
A>C:

C>_
```

WHAT'S HAPPENING? You have changed the default drive to the hard disk, Drive C.

STEP 4: Remove the DOS System Disk from Drive A. Get the disk labeled ACTIVITIES DISK—WORKING COPY that you made in Chapter 2. From now on, ACTIVITIES disk will refer to this working copy, not the original that came with the book, unless otherwise stated. Insert it into Drive A. Be sure to close the drive door.

STEP 5: Key in the following:
C>**DIR A:** <Enter>

```
FEB       99        74   11-23-92   7:05a
MAR       99        70   11-23-92   7:06a
APR       99        71   11-23-92   7:07a
FILE2     CZG       18   12-06-92  10:15a
FILE3     CZG       18   12-06-92  10:15a
FILE2     FP        18   12-06-92  10:15a
FILE3     FP        18   12-06-92  10:15a
FILE4     FP        18   12-06-92  10:15a
FILE2     SWT       18   12-06-92  10:15a
FILE3     SWT       18   12-06-92  10:16a
RIGHT     RED       25   05-07-92  11:15a
MIDDLE    RED       28   05-07-92  11:15a
LEFT      RED       24   05-07-92  11:15a
RIGHT     UP        25   05-07-92  11:15a
DRESS     UP        25   05-07-92  11:15a
MIDDLE    UP        28   05-07-92  11:16a
BLUE      JAZ       18   10-12-92   9:00p
GREEN     JAZ       18   10-12-92   9:00p
FRIENDS           3162   10-12-92   9:00p
BUSINESS          1622   10-12-92   9:00p
TEST         <DIR>       11-16-93   7:05a
       73 file(s)        44643 bytes
                         64512 bytes free

C>_
```

WHAT'S HAPPENING? The display of files scrolled by quickly. The display of files is completely different from the one you have been observing. Because you keyed in **DIR** and a drive letter, **A:**, you told DOS, "I want a display of the directory (DIR), but this time I don't want you to display the files on the default drive. I want you to look only on the ACTIVITIES disk." The ACTIVITIES disk is in Drive A. As long as you tell DOS on which disk drive to look, you can work with any drive you wish. Again, you substituted A: in the syntax diagram, [*drive:*]. If you are not specific, DOS always defaults to the disk drive shown on the screen (**A>** or **B>** or **C>**).

STEP 6: Key in the following:
C>**DIR HELLO.TXT** <Enter>

```
C>DIR HELLO.TXT

   Volume in drive C is MS-DOS_5
   Volume Serial Number is 16CB-59F8
   Directory of C:\

File not found

C>_
```

STEP 7: Key in the following:
C>**DIR A:HELLO.TXT** <Enter>

```
C>DIR A:HELLO.TXT

   Volume in drive A is ACTIVITIES
   Volume Serial Number is 0ED4-161B
   Directory of A:\

HELLO     TXT      52   11-23-92   7:07a
        1 file(s)          52 bytes
                        64512 bytes free

C>_
```

WHAT'S HAPPENING? In Step 6, you asked DOS to look on the default drive for a file called **HELLO.TXT**. The default drive is Drive C. The prompt displayed on the screen, **C>**, is the default drive. Since you did not specify which drive to look on for the file called **HELLO.TXT**, the default drive was assumed. DOS could not find the **HELLO.TXT** file on the default drive so it responded with "File not found." DOS is not smart enough to say, "Oh, this file is not on the disk in the default drive. Let me go check the ACTIVITIES disk in a different disk drive." DOS followed your instructions exactly.

In Step 7, you were specific. You made the same request: "Look for a file called **HELLO.TXT**." However, first of all, you told DOS what disk drive to look into—**A:HELLO.TXT**. The drive designator (**A:**) preceded the file name (**HELLO.TXT**) because you always tell DOS which "file cabinet" to look in (the disk drive) before you tell it which "folder" you want (**HELLO.TXT**). By looking at the syntax diagram, you can see that you can combine optional variable parameters. You gave DIR [*drive:*][*path*][*filename*[.*ext*]][/P][/W] some specific values—**DIR A:HELLO.TXT**. **A:** was substituted for the [*drive:*] and **HELLO.TXT** was substituted for [*filename*]. So far, you have used the optional variable parameters [*drive:*] and [*filename*] and the optional fixed parameters [/P] and [/W]. You have not used [*path*].

3.10 A Brief Introduction to Subdirectories, the Path

Subdirectories are used primarily but not exclusively with hard disks. Because hard disks, which range in capacity from 10 million bytes to over 100 million bytes, are so large in capacity, they are more difficult to manage. The quantity of files that can be stored on them is enormous. In general, users like to have similar files grouped together. Subdirectories allow a disk to be divided into smaller, more manageable portions.

Furthermore, subdirectories can also be used on floppy disks. If you think of a disk as a file cabinet, a subdirectory can be thought of as a drawer in the file cabinet. These file cabinet drawers (subdirectories) also hold disk files. Just as disk drives have a name, such as A: or B: or C:, subdirectories must also have names so DOS will know where to look. Since subdirectories are part of a disk, their names cannot be letters of the alphabet. Letters of the alphabet are reserved for disk drives. Every disk comes with one subdirectory that is named for you by DOS. This subdirectory is called the root directory and is indicated by the backslash (\). However, all other subdirectories on a disk have names. These names are not letters; they are text names, such as `UTILITY` or `SAMPLE` or any other name you choose (see Figure 3.1).

The subdirectory name is referred to as the **path** name. The way you tell DOS to look in a subdirectory on a disk is to tell it the path name. In essence, you are telling DOS to be more specific and not just go to the file cabinet (the disk) but go to a drawer (subdirectory) in the file cabinet.

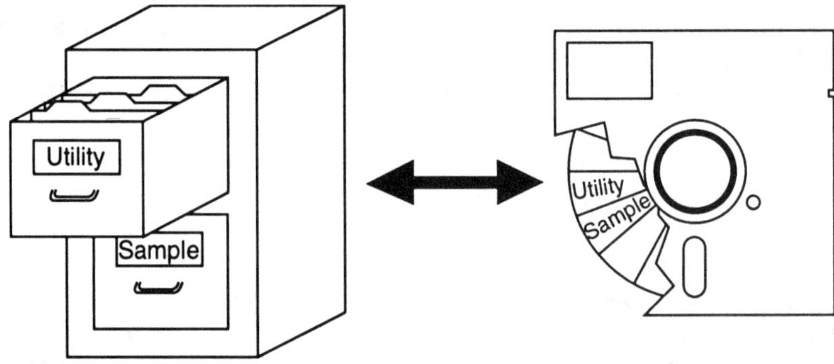

Figure 3.1 File Cabinets and Subdirectories

Activity 3.11 Using Path with the DIR Command

STEP 1: The ACTIVITIES disk is in Drive A. The `C>` is displayed as the default drive.

STEP 2: Key in the following:
C>**DIR A:** <Enter>

```
FEB      99     74   11-23-92   7:05a
MAR      99     70   11-23-92   7:06a
APR      99     71   11-23-92   7:07a
FILE2    CZG    18   12-06-92  10:15a
FILE3    CZG    18   12-06-92  10:15a
FILE2    FP     18   12-06-92  10:15a
```

```
FILE3      FP        18   12-06-92 10:15a
FILE4      FP        18   12-06-92 10:15a
FILE2      SWT       18   12-06-92 10:15a
FILE3      SWT       18   12-06-92 10:16a
RIGHT      RED       25   05-07-92 11:15a
MIDDLE     RED       28   05-07-92 11:15a
LEFT       RED       24   05-07-92 11:15a
RIGHT      UP        25   05-07-92 11:15a
DRESS      UP        25   05-07-92 11:15a
MIDDLE     UP        28   05-07-92 11:16a
BLUE       JAZ       18   10-12-92  9:00p
GREEN      JAZ       18   10-12-92  9:00p
FRIENDS            3162   10-12-92  9:00p
BUSINESS           1622   10-12-92  9:00p
TEST          <DIR>       11-16-93  7:05a
       73 file(s)         44643 bytes
                          64512 bytes free

C>_
```

WHAT'S HAPPENING? On the screen display there is one entry, **TEST** with **<DIR>** following its name. The **<DIR>** indicates that this is a subdirectory. **TEST** is a path name. How do you know what files are inside this subdirectory? Look at the syntax diagram: DIR [*drive:*][*path*][*filename*[*.ext*]][/P][/W]. You will plug in the correct drive letter for [*drive:*] and plug in the desired subdirectory name for [*path*].

STEP 3: Key in the following:
C>**DIR A:\TEST** <Enter>

```
C>DIR A:\TEST

   Volume in drive A is ACTIVITIES
   Volume Serial Number is 0ED4-161B
   Directory of A:\TEST

.             <DIR>       11-16-93  7:05a
..            <DIR>       11-16-93  7:05a
NEW        FIL       31   11-16-93  7:05a
SAMPLE     FIL       23   11-16-93  7:05a
        4 file(s)            54 bytes
                          64512 bytes free

C>_
```

WHAT'S HAPPENING? You keyed in the command you wanted to execute, the drive letter you were interested in, the backslash, and finally the name of the subdirectory. The backslash indicates the root directory. The screen display shows you only what files are in the subdirectory (file drawer) called **TEST**. The third line of the display ("Directory of A:\TEST") tells you what subdirectory you are looking in. What if you wanted to look for a specific file in a subdirectory? Once again, look at the syntax diagram: DIR [*drive:*][*path*][*filename*[.*ext*]] [/P] [/W]. You will substitute the drive letter, the path name, and the file name you wish to see. You must use the backslash as a delimiter to separate the path name from the file name so that DOS knows which is which.

STEP 4: Key in the following:
C>**DIR A:\TEST\NEW.FIL** <Enter>

```
C>DIR A:\TEST\NEW.FIL

   Volume in drive A is ACTIVITIES
   Volume Serial Number is 0ED4-161B
   Directory of A:\TEST

NEW        FIL       31    11-16-93   7:05a
        1 file(s)             31 bytes
                           64512 bytes free

C>_
```

WHAT'S HAPPENING? You keyed in the command you wanted to execute, the drive letter you were interested in, the first backslash indicating the root directory, the name of the subdirectory, then a backslash used as a delimiter, and finally the name of the file. The screen display shows you only the file called **NEW.FIL** located on the ACTIVITIES disk in the subdirectory **TEST**.

3.12 Changing Default Drives

Since you are always going to be working on a specific drive, instead of keying in the drive letter every time, you can override or change the default drive so that DOS will be able to assume that the drive displayed on the screen is the default drive.

In addition, if the hard disk has been set up with subdirectories, which is usually true, refer to your installation documentation or consult your instructor to see where the DOS utility programs are located. You will need to log into the proper subdirectory where the DOS utility programs are located to follow the rest of this text. If the DOS files are in a subdirectory, you will have to know the name of that subdirectory, and you will have to issue another command at this point to locate the DOS utility programs. With **C>** as the default drive, the command could be **CD \BIN** or **CD \DOS**. The actual name or subdirectory where the DOS utility programs are located is machine-specific. If you do not know where the DOS programs are located, use the DIR command and look on the screen for something like:

```
DOS        <DIR>        11-23-92   1:03p
```
or
```
BIN        <DIR>        11-23-92   1:03p
```

Once you have logged into the **DOS** subdirectory, there may be another difference. The way your prompt looks can vary—it could look like **C:\DOS>** or **C:\BIN>** or other displays depending on the setup of your hard disk. Initially, in this text **C>** will indicate that you are logged into the hard disk and subdirectory with the DOS utility programs. In later activities **C:\DOS>** will indicate the **DOS** subdirectory. What you are actually doing is changing the logged or default drive so that you will be using the hard disk as the DOS System Disk. Here is where the DOS utility programs are located. In addition, this text will assume that the DOS files are in a subdirectory called **DOS**. If your system is set up differently, you will need to substitute the proper path name for **\DOS**.

Activity 3.13 Changing the Default Drive

STEP 1: Insert the ACTIVITIES disk into Drive A. The **C>** should be displayed on the screen.

```
C>_
```

WHAT'S HAPPENING? Drive C is the default drive. In your system, the prompt may be displayed as **C:\>**. The \ tells you that you are in the root directory of C.

STEP 2: Key in the following:
C>**A:** <Enter>

```
A>_
```

WHAT'S HAPPENING? Devices have specific reserved names. The name of the hard disk drive is C:. The name of the first floppy disk drive (the one on the left or on top) is A:. The name of the second floppy disk drive, if you have one (the one on the right or bottom) is B:. If you have more disk drives, each has a lettered name. By keying in a letter followed by a colon, you are telling DOS that you want to change your work area to the designated drive that you keyed in. Thus, when you keyed in A:, you changed the work area from the hard disk, Drive C, to the floppy disk in Drive A. You have now made A: the default drive. The assumption DOS will make is that all files and work will come from the disk in Drive A. It will not look at the hard disk, Drive C, unless you specifically tell it to.

STEP 3: Key in the following:
A>**DIR** <Enter>

```
FEB      99     74   11-23-92   7:05a
MAR      99     70   11-23-92   7:06a
APR      99     71   11-23-92   7:07a
FILE2    CZG    18   12-06-92  10:15a
FILE3    CZG    18   12-06-92  10:15a
FILE2    FP     18   12-06-92  10:15a
```

```
FILE3      FP        18   12-06-92 10:15a
FILE4      FP        18   12-06-92 10:15a
FILE2      SWT       18   12-06-92 10:15a
FILE3      SWT       18   12-06-92 10:16a
RIGHT      RED       25   05-07-92 11:15a
MIDDLE     RED       28   05-07-92 11:15a
LEFT       RED       24   05-07-92 11:15a
RIGHT      UP        25   05-07-92 11:15a
DRESS      UP        25   05-07-92 11:15a
MIDDLE     UP        28   05-07-92 11:16a
BLUE       JAZ       18   10-12-92  9:00p
GREEN      JAZ       18   10-12-92  9:00p
FRIENDS            3162   10-12-92  9:00p
BUSINESS           1622   10-12-92  9:00p
TEST           <DIR>      11-16-93  7:05a
       73 file(s)         44643 bytes
                          64512 bytes free

A>_
```

WHAT'S HAPPENING? DOS does not display the directory of the hard disk. It displays the directory of the ACTIVITIES disk in Drive A. You have changed the assumption or default, and since you did not specify which drive you wanted, DOS "defaulted" to the displayed prompt and showed the directory of the ACTIVITIES disk. Since the default is now `A>`, if you wish to locate any information on any other disk, you must specify the parameters and include the letter of the drive where the file is located. For instance, in a prior activity, you asked DOS to find a file called `DISKCOPY.COM` (`DIR DISKCOPY.COM`). You did not include a drive designator in front of the file name because the file was on the default disk drive where the DOS system files were. If you now want to locate that same file, you need to specify on what drive it is located.

STEP 4: Key in the following:
A>`DIR DISKCOPY.COM` <Enter>

```
A>DIR DISKCOPY.COM

   Volume in drive A is ACTIVITIES
   Volume Serial Number is 0ED4-161B
   Directory of A:\

File not found

A>_
```

WHAT'S HAPPENING? Because the default is the drive with the ACTIVITIES disk, DOS looked for this file only on the ACTIVITIES disk in Drive A. You must be aware of where you are (what the default drive and subdirectory are) and where your files are located.

STEP 5: Key in the following:

A>**DIR C:\DOS\DISKCOPY.COM** <Enter>

Note: If the DOS utility programs are in a subdirectory other than **DOS**, you must substitute its name for **DOS**. If the **\DOS** subdirectory was called **\BIN**, the above command would be keyed in as:

A>**DIR C:\BIN\DISKCOPY.COM**

```
A>DIR C:\DOS\DISKCOPY.COM

   Volume in drive C is MS-DOS_5
   Volume Serial Number is 16CB-59F8
   Directory of C:\DOS

DISKCOPY  COM   11793   04-09-91   5:00a
        1 file(s)        11793 bytes
                       8824832 bytes free

A>_
```

WHAT'S HAPPENING? In this case, because you specified the drive and subdirectory as well as the file name, DOS knew where to look and located the file. You asked DOS not only to look on Drive C but more specifically to look on Drive C in the subdirectory called **\DOS** for the file called **DISKCOPY.COM**.

3.14 Global File Specifications: Wildcards, the ? and the *

Using the DIR command and a file specification, you can find one specific file that matches what you keyed in. Every time you wish to locate a file, you can key in the entire file specification. Often, however, you wish to work with a group of files that have similar names or a group of files whose names you do not know. DOS has a "shorthand" system that allows you to operate on a group of files rather than a single file. This system is formally called **global file specifications**; informally, it is called using **wildcards**. Conceptually they are similar to playing cards, where the joker can stand for another card of your choice. In DOS the question mark (?) and the asterisk (*) are the wildcards. These symbols can stand for unknowns. The * represents or substitutes for a group of characters; the ? represents or substitutes for a single character. Many commands allow you to use global file specifications. You will use the DIR command to demonstrate the use of wildcards.

Activity 3.15 DIR and Wildcards

Note: The **A>** is displayed and the ACTIVITIES disk is in Drive A. Because it is easier to work when you know both the default drive and subdirectory, you are going to change the way the prompt looks with a command. This process will be explained fully in a later chapter.

STEP 1: Key in the following:
A>**C:** <Enter>

STEP 2: Key in the following:
C>**PROMPT pg** <Enter>

```
C>PROMPT $p$g

C:\>_
```

WHAT'S HAPPENING? You can now see that you are in the root directory of Drive C.

STEP 3: Key in the following:
C:\>**CD \DOS** <Enter>

Remember that if the DOS utility programs are in a subdirectory with a different name, you will have to substitute your subdirectory name for **\DOS**, i.e., **CD \BIN**.

WHAT'S HAPPENING? You have changed the default directory to where the DOS utility programs are located. If you wanted to locate a file and all you remembered about the file name was that it began with the letter M and was located on the default drive and subdirectory, you could not find that file. You have insufficient information.

STEP 4: Key in the following:
C:\DOS>**DIR M** <Enter>

```
C:\DOS>DIR M

   Volume in drive C is MS-DOS_5
   Volume Serial Number is 16CB-59F8
   Directory of C:\DOS

File not found

C:\DOS>_
```

WHAT'S HAPPENING? First, note how the prompt, instead of merely reflecting **C>** or Drive C, now also reflects the subdirectory **\DOS** and shows **C:\DOS>**. Changing the prompt does not change the way it works. You can still key in any command. When you keyed in **DIR M**, you were correct, but only somewhat. You first entered the work you wanted done, or the command DIR. You did not need to enter the drive letter. DOS assumed both the default drive and default subdirectory. However, DOS specifically looked for a file called **M**. There was no file called **M**; that was simply the first letter of the file. You could find out what files you have that begin with M by using the wildcard symbol * to represent all other characters.

STEP 5: Key in the following:
C:\DOS>**DIR M*.*** <Enter>

```
C:\DOS>DIR M*.*

   Volume in drive C is MS-DOS_5
   Volume Serial Number is 16CB-59F8
   Directory of C:\DOS

MODE      COM   23537   04-09-91  5:00a
MEM       EXE   39818   04-09-91  5:00a
MIRROR    COM   18169   04-09-91  5:00a
MSHERC    COM    6934   04-09-91  5:00a
MONEY     BAS   46225   04-09-91  5:00a
MORE      COM    2618   04-09-91  5:00a
        6 file(s)      137301 bytes
                      8845312 bytes free

C:\DOS>_
```

WHAT'S HAPPENING? Your screen display in this activity could be different from what appears in the example because files in the **DOS** subdirectory can vary.

In this example, you asked DOS what files that begin with the letter M were located on the disk in the default drive and default subdirectory. You did not know anything else about the file names or even how many files you might have that begin with the letter M. You represented any and all characters following the letter M with the asterisk, separated the file name from the file extension with a period, and represented all the characters in the file extension with the second asterisk. Thus, **M***.* (called M, star dot star) means all the files that start with the letter M, can have any or no characters following the letter M, and can have any or no file extension. Now, DOS could look for a match. Although you might have keyed in a lowercase **m**, DOS returns uppercase **M** because all file names are stored in uppercase letters. The first file DOS found that had the **M** you specified was **MODE.COM**. DOS could display this file because the * following the **M** matched **ODE**. Remember, the * represents any group of letters. The second * representing the file extension matched **.COM** because, again, the * represents any group of characters. The second file DOS found that had the **M** you specified was **MEM.EXE**. DOS could display this file because the * following the **M** matched **EM**. Remember, the * represents any group of letters. The second * representing the file extension matched **.EXE** because, again, the * represents any group of characters. The rest of the files match **M***.* for the same reasons. You could have more or fewer files depending on how your system is set up.

There are other ways of requesting information using the *. Let us say that all you know about a group of files on the disk in the default drive is that the group has a file extension of **.SYS** in common. You could display these files on the screen using wildcards.

STEP 6: Key in the following:
C:\DOS>DIR *.SYS <Enter>

```
C:\DOS>DIR *.SYS

   Volume in drive C is MS-DOS_5
   Volume Serial Number is 16CB-59F8
   Directory of C:\DOS

EGA       SYS    4885   04-09-91  5:00a
COUNTRY   SYS   17069   04-09-91  5:00a
DISPLAY   SYS   15792   04-09-91  5:00a
HIMEM     SYS   11552   04-09-91  5:00a
KEYBOARD  SYS   34697   04-09-91  5:00a
ANSI      SYS    9029   04-09-91  5:00a
RAMDRIVE  SYS    5873   04-09-91  5:00a
SMARTDRV  SYS    8335   04-09-91  5:00a
DRIVER    SYS    5409   04-09-91  5:00a
PRINTER   SYS   18804   04-09-91  5:00a
       10 file(s)      131445 bytes
                      8833024 bytes free

C:\DOS>_
```

WHAT'S HAPPENING? In response to your query, DIR *.SYS, the above screen display answered. The * represented any file name, but all the files must have .SYS as a file extension. Again, the number of files displayed may vary, depending on what is in the DOS subdirectory. The next activities will demonstrate the differences between the * and the ?.

STEP 7: Key in the following:
C:\DOS>DIR A:*.TXT <Enter>

```
C:\DOS>DIR A:*.TXT

   Volume in drive A is ACTIVITIES
   Volume Serial Number is 0ED4-161B
   Directory of A:\

EXERCISE  TXT     316   11-23-92  7:03a
JANUARY   TXT      72   11-23-92  7:04a
FEBRUARY  TXT      74   11-23-92  7:05a
MARCH     TXT      70   11-23-92  7:06a
APRIL     TXT      71   11-23-92  7:07a
HELLO     TXT      52   11-23-92  7:07a
TEST      TXT      64   11-23-92  7:07a
BYE       TXT      44   11-23-92  7:07a
GOODBYE   TXT      33   11-23-92  7:07a
        9 file(s)          796 bytes
                         64512 bytes free

C:\DOS>_
```

WHAT'S HAPPENING? You asked DOS what files had an extension of **.TXT** and were located on the ACTIVITIES disk. You did not know anything about the file names, only the file extension. DOS searched the table of contents in Drive A since you placed an **A:** prior to the ***.TXT**. The command found nine files that matched ***.TXT**. Now, how does the question mark differ from the asterisk?

STEP 8: Key in the following:
C:\DOS>**DIR A:?????.TXT** <Enter>

```
C:\DOS>DIR A:?????.TXT

   Volume in drive A is ACTIVITIES
   Volume Serial Number is 0ED4-161B
   Directory of A:\

MARCH      TXT      70   11-23-92   7:06a
APRIL      TXT      71   11-23-92   7:07a
HELLO      TXT      52   11-23-92   7:07a
TEST       TXT      64   11-23-92   7:07a
BYE        TXT      44   11-23-92   7:07a
          5 file(s)          301 bytes
                           64512 bytes free

C:\DOS>_
```

WHAT'S HAPPENING? This time you asked your question a little differently. You still asked for any file that had the file extension of **.TXT**. However, instead of "any number of characters," you used the ? five times. To DOS, this means look for any file name that starts with any letter and that has a file name no longer than five characters. It can be less than five characters but no more than five. Thus, the ????? represented five characters. You then separated the file name from the file extension with a period saying any file extension that had **.TXT** was fine. This time only five files matched your request. Note how the above screen display differs from the screen display in Step 7. This time you do not see the files called **EXERCISE.TXT**, **JANUARY.TXT**, or **FEBRUARY.TXT** displayed on the screen. Those file names were longer than five characters. However, files such as **TEXT.TXT** and **BYE.TXT** were displayed even though they did not have five-character file names, because their names had less than five. Remember, ????? means five characters *or less*. Let's try this again.

STEP 9: Key in the following:
C:\DOS>**DIR A:????.TXT** <Enter>

```
C:\DOS>DIR A:????.TXT

   Volume in drive A is ACTIVITIES
   Volume Serial Number is 0ED4-161B
   Directory of A:\
```

```
TEST      TXT       64   11-23-92   7:07a
BYE       TXT       44   11-23-92   7:07a
        2 file(s)          108 bytes
                         64512 bytes free

C:\DOS>_
```

WHAT'S HAPPENING? This time you asked DOS for any file name that used four characters or less in length, that had a file extension, **.TXT**, and that was located on the ACTIVITIES disk in Drive A. You separated the file name and file extension with a period. Note the differences in the screen displays. Using the ????.**TXT** only displayed two files that met the specification. The * is most commonly used. In fact, ????????.??? is the same as *.*. However, there are occasions when the ? is extremely useful.

STEP 10: Key in the following:
C:\DOS>**DIR A:EXP*.*** <Enter>

```
C:\DOS>DIR A:EXP*.*

   Volume in drive A is ACTIVITIES
   Volume Serial Number is 0ED4-161B
   Directory of A:\

EXP92JAN  DAT      303   11-23-92   7:01a
EXP92FEB  DAT      297   11-23-92   7:01a
EXP92MAR  DAT      301   11-23-92   7:04a
EXP93JAN  DAT      303   11-23-92   7:05a
EXP93FEB  DAT      304   11-23-92   7:05a
EXP93MAR  DAT      303   11-23-92   7:06a
EXP94JAN  DAT      303   11-23-92   7:07a
EXP94FEB  DAT      305   11-23-92   7:08a
EXP94MAR  DAT      301   11-23-92   7:09a
        9 file(s)         2720 bytes
                         64512 bytes free

C:\DOS>_
```

WHAT'S HAPPENING? This time your request to DOS was to show you all the files (DIR) located on the ACTIVITIES disk (Drive A) that start with the letters **EXP**, and that's all you know (**EXP***.*). The *.* following the **EXP** represented the rest of the file name and the file extension. Here are some budget files. **EXP** means expenses, followed by the year (**92**, **93**, or **94**), followed by the month (**JAN**uary, **FEB**ruary, or **MAR**ch). The file extension is **.DAT**, meaning that there is data in these files; they are not programs. However, often you are not interested in all the files. You only want some of them. A typical example would be that you want to know what expense files you have on the ACTIVITIES disk for the year 1992.

STEP 11: Key in the following:
C:\DOS>**DIR A:EXP92*.*** <Enter>

```
C:\DOS\DIR A:EXP92*.*

   Volume in drive A is ACTIVITIES
   Volume Serial Number is 0ED4-161B
   Directory of A:\

EXP92JAN  DAT     303   11-23-92   7:01a
EXP92FEB  DAT     297   11-23-92   7:01a
EXP92MAR  DAT     301   11-23-92   7:04a
        3 file(s)          901 bytes
                         64512 bytes free

C:\DOS>_
```

WHAT'S HAPPENING? Here you asked for all the files (DIR) on the ACTIVITIES disk in Drive A that were expense files for 1992 (**EXP92**). The rest of the file names were represented by *.*. On your screen display you got only the 1992 files. However, suppose your interest is in all the files for all the months of January. You no longer care which year, only which month.

STEP 12: Key in the following:
C:\DOS>**DIR A:EXP*JAN.*** <Enter>

```
C:\DOS>DIR A:EXP*JAN.*

   Volume in drive A is ACTIVITIES
   Volume Serial Number is 0ED4-161B
   Directory of A:\

EXP92JAN  DAT     303   11-23-92   7:01a
EXP92FEB  DAT     297   11-23-92   7:01a
EXP92MAR  DAT     301   11-23-92   7:04a
EXP93JAN  DAT     303   11-23-92   7:05a
EXP93FEB  DAT     304   11-23-92   7:05a
EXP93MAR  DAT     303   11-23-92   7:06a
EXP94JAN  DAT     303   11-23-92   7:07a
EXP94FEB  DAT     305   11-23-92   7:08a
EXP94MAR  DAT     301   11-23-92   7:09a
        9 file(s)         2720 bytes
                         64512 bytes free

C:\DOS>_
```

WHAT'S HAPPENING? This display is not quite what you wanted. This display looks exactly like the display following Step 10 when you asked for **DIR A:EXP***.*. Why weren't only the **JAN** files displayed? The reason is that when you state your request as **DIR A:EXP*JAN.***, everything in the file name segment after the first * is ignored. Hence, the DIR command picked up all the files with **EXP** and ignored your specific **JAN**. Now, the question mark becomes useful.

STEP 13: Key in the following:
C:\DOS>**DIR A:EXP??JAN.*** <Enter>

```
C:\DOS>DIR A:EXP??JAN.*

   Volume in drive A is ACTIVITIES
   Volume Serial Number is 0ED4-161B
   Directory of A:\

EXP92JAN  DAT     303   11-23-92   7:01a
EXP93JAN  DAT     303   11-23-92   7:05a
EXP94JAN  DAT     303   11-23-92   7:07a
        3 file(s)          909 bytes
                         64512 bytes free

C:\DOS>_
```

WHAT'S HAPPENING? This time the ? was critical. It acted as a place holder. You asked for a file name that specifically started with **EXP** and ended with **JAN**. The middle two characters, represented by ??, could be any two characters but they must be alphanumeric. The **92**, **93**, and **94** matched ?? because any character could have been there as long as there was something in that place in the file name. The program could have displayed a file called **EXPxxJAN.TXT** since the **xx** would match the ??.

Activity 3.16 Printing the Screen

You can print whatever is displayed on the screen at any time by using the <Shift> key (the ⇧ key) in conjunction with the <PrtSc> key. Some computers do not require you to press the <Shift> key. These computers only require that you press the <PrtSc> key.

STEP 1: To print the screen display, first be sure the printer is turned on.

STEP 2: Press the <Shift> key. While pressing the <Shift> key, press the <PrtSc> key. If you have a newer system, you need only press the <PrtSc> key. For laser printers, refer to Chapter 2, Activity 2.21.

WHAT'S HAPPENING? You see what is displayed on the screen printed by the printer. Remember that, if the <Shift>+<PrtSc> key combination does not work, just press the <PrtSc> key.

3.17 Getting Help: DOS 5.0 Only

As you begin to use DOS commands, their name, purpose, and proper syntax become familiar. Initially, however, these commands are new to users. Prior to DOS 5.0, the only way to become familiar with a command or to check the proper syntax was to locate the command in the manual. The reference manual that comes with DOS or with any software package is called **documentation**. The completeness of the documentation can vary from software package to software package. The documentation that comes with DOS consists of at least the installation instructions and a command reference manual, which is a list of commands with a brief description and syntax for each. Regardless of what version of DOS you have, you can always use the manuals. However, with DOS 5.0, a new feature was introduced called **online help**. Rather than going to the documentation, you can request immediate help from the screen. When you key in **HELP**, you will see a list of all the DOS commands with their purpose and syntax. In addition, if you know a specific command, you can request help for that command by keying in the help command or the command with /?.

Activity 3.18 Using HELP

Note: The **C:\DOS>** will be displayed and the ACTIVITIES disk will be in Drive A. To follow the text, key in **PROMPT pg**. Then, key in **CD \DOS** to make **\DOS** the default subdirectory. Remember, if the DOS files are in a subdirectory with a different name, you will have to substitute your subdirectory name for **\DOS**, i.e., **CD \BIN**.

STEP 1: Key in the following:
C:\DOS>**HELP** <Enter>

```
For more information on a specific command, type HELP command-name.
APPEND   Allows programs to open data files in specified directories as
         if they were in the current directory.
ASSIGN   Redirects requests for disk operations on one drive to a
         different drive.
ATTRIB   Displays or changes file attributes.
BACKUP   Backs up one or more files from one disk to another.
BREAK    Sets or clears extended CTRL+C checking.
CALL     Calls one batch program from another.
CD       Displays the name of or changes the current directory.
CHCP     Displays or sets the active code page number.
CHDIR    Displays the name of or changes the current directory.
CHKDSK   Checks a disk and displays a status report.
CLS      Clears the screen.
COMMAND  Starts a new instance of the MS-DOS command interpreter.
COMP     Compares the contents of two files or sets of files.
COPY     Copies one or more files to another location.
CTTY     Changes the terminal device used to control your system.
DATE     Displays or sets the date.
DEBUG    Runs Debug, a program testing and editing tool.
```

```
DEL      Deletes one or more files.
DIR      Displays a list of files and subdirectories in a directory.
DISKCOMP Compares the contents of two floppy disks.
---More---_
```

WHAT'S HAPPENING? Displayed on the screen is an alphabetical list of DOS commands. Locate DIR on the screen. You see that it defines the purpose of DIR: to display a list of files and subdirectories.

STEP 2: Press <Enter> until you have returned to the **C:\DOS>** prompt.

STEP 3: Key in the following:
C:\DOS>**HELP DIR** <Enter>

```
Displays a list of files and subdirectories in a directory.

DIR [drive:][path][filename] [/P] [/W] [/A[[:]attributes]]
  [/O[[:]sortorder]] [/S] [/B] [/L]

  [drive:][path][filename]
              Specifies drive, directory, and/or files to list.
  /P          Pauses after each screenful of information.
  /W          Uses wide list format.
  /A          Displays files with specified attributes.
  attributes   D Directories                R  Read-only files
               H Hidden files               A  Files ready for archiving
               S System files               -  Prefix meaning "not"
  /O          List by files in sorted order.
  sortorder    N By name (alphabetic)       S  By size (smallest first)
               E By extension (alphabetic)  D  By date & time (earliest first)
               G Group directories first    -  Prefix to reverse order
  /S          Displays files in specified directory and all subdirectories.
  /B          Uses bare format (no heading information or summary).
  /L          Uses lowercase.

Switches may be preset in the DIRCMD environment variable. Override
preset switches by prefixing any switch with - (hyphen) --for example, /-W.

C:\DOS>_
```

WHAT'S HAPPENING? You see a brief description of what the command does, including its syntax. You see what the parameters do to the command. In DOS 5.0, the DIR command has many more parameters than earlier versions of DOS.

STEP 4: Key in the following:
C:\DOS>**DIR /?** <Enter>

```
Displays a list of files and subdirectories in a directory.

DIR [drive:][path][filename] [/P] [/W] [/A[[:]attributes]]
  [/O[[:]sortorder]] [/S] [/B] [/L]
```

```
  [drive:][path][filename]
              Specifies drive, directory, and/or files to list.
  /P          Pauses after each screenful of information.
  /W          Uses wide list format.
  /A          Displays files with specified attributes.
  attributes   D Directories              R Read-only files
               H Hidden files             A Files ready for archiving
               S System files             - Prefix meaning "not"
  /O          List by files in sorted order.
  sortorder    N By name (alphabetic)     S By size (smallest first)
               E By extension (alphabetic) D By date & time (earliest first)
               G Group directories first  - Prefix to reverse order
  /S          Displays files in specified directory and all subdirectories.
  /B          Uses bare format (no heading information or summary).
  /L          Uses lowercase.

Switches may be preset in the DIRCMD environment variable. Override
preset switches by prefixing any switch with - (hyphen) --for example, /-W.

C:\DOS>_
```

WHAT'S HAPPENING? The command followed by a /? will also provide help. You can use help to refresh your memory about a command and its syntax. Let's try a new parameter, /O for sort order, followed by N for name sort order. We will sort the files in alphabetical order by file name on the ACTIVITIES disk.

STEP 5: Key in the following:
C:\DOS>**DIR A:/ON** <Enter>

```
MUSIC     MOV     225   11-23-92  7:10a
OTHER     MOV     211   11-23-92  7:12a
PERSONAL  FIL    2306   11-23-92  7:14a
RIGHT     RED      25   05-07-92 11:15a
RIGHT     UP       25   05-07-92 11:15a
SAMPLE      <DIR>       05-14-92 11:03a
STEVEN    FIL      45   11-23-92  7:13a
TEST      TXT      64   11-23-92  7:07a
TEST        <DIR>       11-16-93  7:05a
UTILS       <DIR>       12-06-92 10:00a
WILD1     XXX      63   05-07-93  9:03a
WILD2     YYY      63   05-07-93  9:03a
WILD3     ZZZ      63   05-07-93  9:03a
WILDONE   DOS     180   05-07-93  9:02a
WILDONE            92   05-07-93  9:04a
WILDTHR   DOS     180   05-07-93  9:03a
WILDTWO   DOS     181   05-07-93  9:03a
Y         FIL       4   05-14-92 11:00a
YOURA     LAB      39   05-14-92 11:00a
YOURB     LAB      44   05-14-92 11:00a
YOURC     LAB      41   05-14-92 11:00a
           73 file(s)   44643 bytes
                        64512 bytes free

C:\DOS>_
```

WHAT'S HAPPENING? The files scrolled by quickly, but they were in alphabetical order, from A to Z. You used the / to indicate a parameter, the O for order, and the N for name order. By using another switch or delimiter, you can sort the files in reverse alphabetical order.

STEP 6: Key in the following:
C:\DOS>`DIR A:/O-N` <Enter>

```
EXP93JAN  DAT       303    11-23-92  7:05a
EXP93FEB  DAT       304    11-23-92  7:05a
EXP92MAR  DAT       301    11-23-92  7:04a
EXP92JAN  DAT       303    11-23-92  7:01a
EXP92FEB  DAT       297    11-23-92  7:01a
EXERCISE  TXT       316    11-23-92  7:03a
EMPLOYEE  ONE        52    05-07-93  9:00a
EMPLOYEE  TWO        53    05-07-93  9:00a
EMPLOYEE  THREE      53    05-07-93  9:00a
DRESS     UP         25    05-07-92 11:15a
DRAMA     MOV       221    11-23-92  7:11a
DATA         <DIR>         11-23-92 10:15a
CAROLYN   FIL        46    11-23-92  7:13a
BYE       TXT        44    11-23-92  7:07a
BUSINESS           1622    10-12-92  9:00p
BLUE      JAZ        18    10-12-92  9:00p
APRIL     TXT        71    11-23-92  7:07a
APR       TMP        71    11-23-92  7:07a
APR       NEW        71    11-23-92  7:07a
APR       99         71    11-23-92  7:07a
ADDRESS   EXE     30960    01-15-88  4:10p
         73 file(s)        44643 bytes
                           64512 bytes free

C:\DOS>_
```

WHAT'S HAPPENING? Again, the files scrolled by quickly, but they were in reverse alphabetical order, from Z to A. Thus, by using the parameter /O-N, O for order, - for reverse, and N for name, you could accomplish your task.

STEP 7: Key in the following:
C:\DOS>`CD \` <Enter>

Chapter Summary

1. Command syntax means using the correct command and the proper order for keying in commands.
2. A parameter is some piece of information that you want a command to have. It allows a command to be specific.
3. A delimiter indicates where parts of a command begin or end. It is similar to punctuation marks in English.

4. Some commands require parameters. They are called mandatory parameters. Other commands allow parameters, but these are called optional parameters.
5. A variable parameter is one that requires the user to supply a value. A fixed parameter has its value determined by DOS.
6. A syntax diagram is a graphic representation of a command and its syntax.
7. The DIR command is an internal command that displays the table of contents or a directory of a disk.
8. The basic syntax diagram for DIR is:

   DIR [*drive:*][*path*][*filename*] [/P] [/W]
9. DIR has five parameters in all versions of DOS, /P to stop the display from scrolling, /W to have a wide display of only file names and extensions, *drive* that allows you to specify on what drive to look for a file, *path* that allows you to search a specific subdirectory, and *filename* that allows you to search the directory for specific files.
10. The syntax for DIR in DOS 5.0 is:

    DIR [*drive:*][*path*][*filename*] [/P] [/W] [/A[[:]*attributes*]]
    [/O[[:]*sortorder*]] [/S] [/B] [/L]
11. If you have DOS 5.0, you have many more parameters to choose from. One of these is O for sort order. It must be followed by the sort order you wish the directory in. Any item you want sorted in reverse must be preceded by a hyphen.
12. A file specification has two parts, the file name and the file extension. The file name may be no longer than eight characters. The file extension may be no longer than three characters. A file name is mandatory; however, a file extension is optional. If you use a file extension, separate it from the file name by a period, called a dot.
13. A valid file name contains legal characters, most often alphanumeric characters. It cannot contain illegal characters.
14. Every device attached to the computer has a reserved, specific, and unique name so that the operating system knows what it is communicating with. Disk drives are designated by a letter followed by a colon, as in A:.
15. Defaults are implied instructions the operating system falls back to when no specific instructions are given.
16. A subdirectory allows a disk to be divided into areas that can hold files. Subdirectories are named by the user, except the root directory whose name is \. The subdirectory name is the path name.
17. The system prompt displayed on the screen is the default drive.
18. To change the prompt so that it displays the subdirectory name, key in `PROMPT $p$g`.
19. You can change the default drive and default subdirectory.
20. To change the default drive, you key in the drive letter followed by a colon as in A: or B:.
21. To change the default subdirectory, you key in `CD` followed by the subdirectory name such as `CD \PROG` or `CD \DOS`.

22. The subdirectory that contains the DOS utility programs is often called `\DOS`. It may sometimes be called `\BIN` or `\PROG`.
23. You can look for files on drives and subdirectories other than the default if you tell DOS where to look by prefacing the file names with a drive designator and/or path name.
24. If the file is in a subdirectory, the file name must be prefaced by the drive designator and followed by the subdirectory name. A user must include the subdirectory name in the command, as in `C:\DOS\FILENAME`.
25. Global file specifications (*, ?) or wildcards allow the user to substitute a wildcard for an unknown.
26. The ? represents one character in a file name; the * matches a group of characters.
27. The screen display may be printed by pressing the <Shift> key and the <PrtSc> key. If you have a newer computer you may only need to press the <PrtSc> key.
28. DOS 5.0 includes an online help feature.
29. To use the online help, the user keys in HELP *command-name* or *command-name* /?.
30. In DOS 5.0, the DIR command allows you to sort the directory listing by use of the parameter /O followed by the sort order letter you are interested in. For instance, to sort by size, you would key in `DIR /OS`.

Key Terms

Command syntax
Default
Default drive
Delimiter
Designated drive
Device names
Documentation
Dot
File
Fixed parameters
Global file specifications
Logged drive
Online help
Optional parameters
Parameters
Path
Prompt
Subdirectories
Switch
Syntax
Syntax diagram
Variable parameters
Wildcards

Discussion Questions

1. Define command syntax. Why is syntax important when using a computer?
2. How would you use a syntax diagram? Why is the diagram important?
3. Define parameters.
4. What is the difference between variable and fixed parameters?
5. Name two parameters that can be used with the DIR command. Explain why you would use the parameters.
6. Explain defaults.
7. Define default drive.
8. Define default subdirectory.
9. What is the difference between default drive and designated or logged drive?
10. How can you tell which drive is the default drive?

11. How can you change the default drive? Why would you change it?
12. How can you tell which directory is the default subdirectory?
13. How can you change the default subdirectory? Why would you change it?
14. What does `A>` mean?
15. What does `C:\DOS>` mean?
16. Define file specification.
17. What is the difference between a file name and a file extension?
18. What are the file naming rules?
19. How do you separate a file name from a file extension?
20. Define global file specifications.
21. How are wildcards used?
22. Define delimiters. Give an example of a delimiter.
23. The syntax diagram for DIR is:
    DIR [*drive:*][*path*][*filename*] [/P] [/W]
    Identify each item in this diagram and explain its purpose.
24. How would you print the screen display?
25. If you have DOS 5.0, how would you get on-line help if you forgot the parameters for the DIR command?

Application Assignments

Note: The following activities use the <Shift> and <PrtSc> keys to get the output to the printer. Be sure the printer is turned on. If you have a newer system you need only press <PrtSc>. For laser printers refer to Chapter 2, Activity 2.21.

1. Clear the screen. Find all the files on the ACTIVITIES disk that have the file extension `.NEW`. Display the file names on the screen. Print the screen.
2. Clear the screen. Find the file in the `\DOS` subdirectory called **`APPEND.EXE`**. Display the file name on the screen. Print the screen.
3. Clear the screen. Find the file on the ACTIVITIES disk called **`BYE.TXT`**. Display the file name on the screen. Print the screen.
4. Clear the screen. Do a wide display of the `\DOS` directory in the hard disk. Print the screen.
5. Clear the screen. Find all the files in the `\DOS` subdirectory that begin with the letter C. Display these file names on the screen. Print this screen.
6. Clear the screen. Find all the files in the `\DOS` subdirectory that begin with the letter C, whose file names have five characters or less and have any file extension. Display the file names on the screen. Print the screen.
7. Clear the screen. Do a wide display of the ACTIVITIES disk. Print the screen.
8. Clear the screen. Do a directory display of the ACTIVITIES disk. The screen will scroll. Wait until it has stopped scrolling. Print only the last screen displayed.
9. Change the default drive to where the ACTIVITIES disk is located. The prompt of the default directory will be on the screen. Print the screen.

10. While the default drive is A, find all the files in the `\DOS` subdirectory that begin with the letter `F` and have a file extension of `.EXE`. Display these file names. Print the screen.
11. Without booting or rebooting the system, display the system date. Print the screen.
12. Without booting or rebooting the system, display the system time.

Challenge Assignments

13. Clear the screen. Find all the files on the ACTIVITIES disk in the subdirectory `UTILS` that have the file extension `.EXE`. Display the file names on the screen. Print the screen.
14. Clear the screen. Find all the files on the ACTIVITIES disk in the subdirectory `DATA` that begin with the letter `T` and have any file name and any file extension. Display these file names. Print the screen.
15. Clear the screen. Find all the files on the ACTIVITIES disk in the subdirectory `DATA` that begin with the letter `T`, whose total file name is four characters or less and have any file extension. Display these file names. Print the screen.
16. Clear the screen. Display all the files on the ACTIVITIES disk in the `UTILS` subdirectory by file name in alphabetical order. Print the screen.
17. Clear the screen. Arrange all the files on the ACTIVITIES disk in the `DATA` subdirectory by file size from the largest to smallest. Print the last screen.
18. Get on-line help for the DISKCOPY command. Print the screen.

Chapter 4

Disks and Formatting

After completing this chapter you will be able to:

1. Explain the need for formatting disks.
2. Describe the structure of a disk.
3. Name and explain the purpose of each section of a disk.
4. Define formatting.
5. Explain the difference between internal and external commands.
6. Explain the difference between FORMAT as a command and as a file.
7. List and explain the steps in formatting a floppy disk.
8. Format a floppy disk.
9. Format a floppy disk with a system and volume label.
10. Explain the difference between bootable and nonbootable disks.
11. Electronically label your disk using the VOL command.
12. Use the /U and /Q parameters in DOS 5.0.
13. Explain how to format a 360 KB disk in a 1.2 MB high-capacity disk drive.
14. Explain how to format a 720 KB disk in a 1.44 MB high-capacity disk drive.

Chapter Overview

Each computer has a unique way of recording information so that the user can read from and write to the disk. So far the disks that you used with this text were disks that were prepared or disks that you copied. As you work with the computer you will want to prepare disks to store program and data files. In order to do this, you will need to purchase new disks. These disks cannot be used until they are prepared for use with your specific computer. The process of preparing a disk so that it will be compatible with a computer is known as formatting the disk. In this chapter you will learn how a disk is structured, how DOS uses disks, and how to format and electronically label a disk.

4.0 Why Format a Disk?

The only floppy disks you have used to this point are the DOS System Disk and the ACTIVITIES disk. These disks were prepared for you. However, as you work with computers, you will want to store program and data files on disks. When you buy disks, most are not ready to be used. The reason for this is that the disk manufacturer does not know which computer you are going to use. It could be an IBM or IBM clone, or it could be an Apple. Each computer has a specific way of recording information so that the operating system can read from the disk and write to the disk. This process of preparing the disk for use is known as **formatting**. You use one of the DOS commands to prepare a disk for use, the DOS utility program called FORMAT.

In addition, disks that have been used but have information that is no longer needed can be "erased" or reprepared with the FORMAT command. All disks must be formatted, including hard disks. However, since formatting eliminates what is on the disk, this text deals only with formatting floppy disks.

4.1 Structure of a Disk

Formatting a disk means that the physical layout of the disk is defined so that, when information is stored, there is an appropriate location on the disk for that information. Each disk is divided into tracks (concentric circles on the disk, similar to the grooves on a record), and each track is divided into sectors, a block of 512 bytes. A cluster is the smallest unit of disk space that DOS will work with. On a 5 1/4-inch single-sided disk one sector is a cluster; on a 5 1/4- or 3 1/2-inch double-sided disk two sectors equal one cluster; on a 5 1/4- or 3 1/2-inch high-capacity disk one sector equals one cluster. The number of sectors that make up a cluster can vary on a hard disk, although usually four sectors make up a cluster. A hard disk is divided in the same way as a floppy disk; however, hard disks also use cylinders. A hard disk is comprised of two or more platters stacked on each other. If you connected a track through all four surfaces of the disks, you would have a cylinder (see Figure 4.1).

Figure 4.1 Cylinders of a Hard Disk

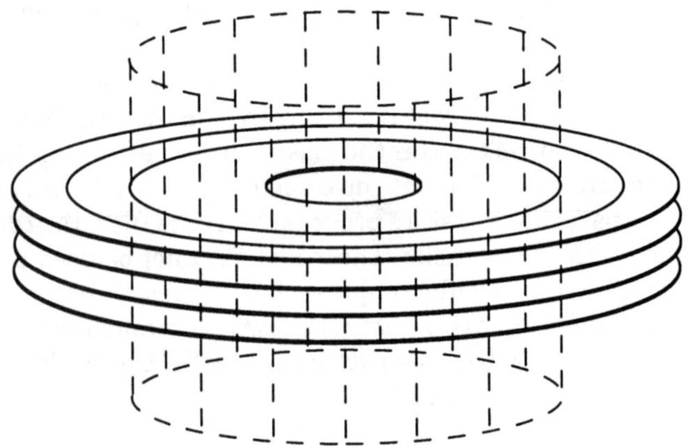

Formatting also determines how many sides of the disk will be used and the media type. The formatting process determines the amount of information that can be stored on the disk. Formatting determines the size of the tracks and sectors and establishes a framework for DOS to work in. Part of the formatting process is to assign a number to each disk side, track, and sector so that every space on the disk is accounted for. This process is similar to assigning zip codes to different geographical areas, so that any place in the country is immediately identifiable. In addition, through the use of the FORMAT command, DOS sets up the boot record, the file allocation table (FAT), the directory, and the data sectors for each disk. Although the size of each portion can vary, the order of the sections is always the same. The boot record, the FAT, and the directory, always located in the first sectors, control how the files are stored on a disk. The data sectors are where the data or files are actually stored.

Boot Record

The boot record, located on side 0, track 0, sector 1, includes the bootstrap routine that DOS uses to load the system files, but only if it is a system disk. All disks have a boot record that indicates which version of DOS was used to format the disk, the number of sectors on the disk, the number of sectors per cluster, the size of the FAT, and the root directory. The boot record also establishes the disk's media type (360 KB, 720 KB, etc.) so that the disk can be properly identified.

File Allocation Table (FAT)

Following the boot record are several sectors reserved for the **file allocation table** (FAT). The FAT is a map of the disk which is connected to the file names in the directory table and is made up of entries that correspond to every cluster on the disk. The FAT entries include information about which clusters contain data being used, which cluster represents the last cluster in a file's chain, which clusters are marked as "bad" or unusable, and which clusters are available for data. Since most data files are greater than one cluster in length, the FAT entry also records the number of the next cluster that a file occupies. The FAT keeps linking these clusters until it finds an end-of-file marker, indicating that there is no more data in the file. The FAT tells DOS which sectors on the disk actually have the data and points to those locations. It is the record of the disk's format, and, since it is used to control the entire disk, two copies of the FAT are kept on the disk in case one is damaged. The FAT can occupy as many sectors as it needs to map out the disk.

Directory

Next on the disk are the **directory sectors**. When you ask for the DIR, the information that is displayed on the screen comes from these directory sectors. The directory stores information in a table about every file, including the file name, the file extension, and the file attributes. A file can be marked by the following attributes: (1) read-only, which means the file normally cannot be erased; (2) hidden status, which means that a file will not be displayed when you issue the DIR command; (3) system status, which typically marks the file as the system files, `IO.SYS` and `MSDOS.SYS` (`IBMBIO.COM` and `IBMDOS.COM` for IBM PC-DOS); (4) volume label; (5) subdirectory status, if needed; (6) archive status, which is set when the file is opened and closed and is used by some backup and restore utilities. Further information about the files in the directory table include the time and date of creation/update, the file's starting cluster entry in the FAT or the FAT address, and the file size in bytes. The DOS directory does not say where a specific file is located on a disk; instead, it points to an entry in the FAT. Thus, the directory table keeps track of what the files are, and the FAT keeps track of where the files are located.

Data Sectors

The rest of the disk, and its largest part, is used for storing the files or data. As far as DOS is concerned, all files, programs, and data are just chains of bytes laid out in sequence. Space is allocated to files on an as-needed basis, one cluster at a time. When a file is written to a disk, DOS begins writing to the first available cluster. It writes in adjacent or contiguous clusters if possible, but if any adjacent sectors are already in use (allocated by FAT), DOS skips to the next available space (unallocated). Thus, a file can be noncontiguous, or physically scattered over the disk.

To analogize this process, imagine a self-storage facility. It is comprised of storage bins that hold things (data). The front office that manages the self-storage facility does not care what is stored in the bins. The front office just has to know how many bins there are, where they are located, and if anything is in them. The front office has a map of all its numbered storage bins (FAT). The bins are numbered so that the front office knows where the bins are physically located. The other piece of information the front office needs is a list of all the people who have rented any of the bins (directory). Thus, I walk in and say I want the boxes stored for Gillay. The first thing the front office does is look up Gillay in their list (directory) to be sure that they have stored my boxes. In this case, they find the name Gillay so that they know I have rented at least one bin. Besides my name, the directory list points to another list. It says go to the map (FAT), starting with bin 2. The front office goes to the map (FAT) and sees that storage bin 2 is linked to storage bin 3 which is linked to storage bin 4. Storage bin 4 has no links. Now the front office knows that Gillay has bins 2, 3, and 4 full of boxes. The front office can send someone (rotate the disk) to bins 2, 3, and 4 to retrieve the boxes. To look at this graphically, see Figure 4.2.

Figure 4.2
Storing Files

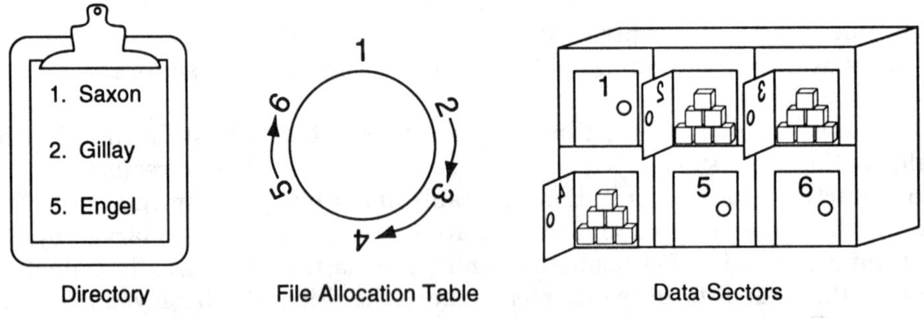

4.2 Formatting a Floppy Disk

A new disk must be formatted so that the operating system can read from the disk and write to it. In addition, the FORMAT command can be used to erase a disk completely, if it contains information you no longer want. However, you must be very careful when using the FORMAT command. Formatting deletes or eliminates *everything* on a disk, and the data cannot be recovered. In DOS 5.0, there is a little more protection, and under the right circumstances you can recover data from a formatted disk. However, it is still extremely wise to be cautious with the FORMAT command. Although the format routine can be used on a hard disk, you must be very careful because FORMAT does not distinguish between a floppy disk and a hard disk. It will format any disk, including the hard disk, and this means that everything stored on a hard disk would be gone, both programs and data. Thus, in the next activity, you will only be formatting floppy disks. If you are going to be working in a computer laboratory, please familiarize yourself with the proper laboratory procedures so that a computer tragedy does not occur.

4.3 Clarifying Procedural Assumptions

1. **DOS** subdirectory. You will boot off Drive C. Do not place the DOS System Disk in Drive A; simply power on the computer. You should then get the **C>**. Next, change the prompt to **PROMPT pg**. You will also have to log into the subdirectory that has the DOS utility programs, as in **CD \DOS**, and your prompt should then read **C:\DOS>**. If your DOS programs are in a different subdirectory, such as **\BIN**, you will have to substitute **CD \BIN** for **CD \DOS**. Whenever the **DOS** subdirectory is referred to, it means the **DOS** subdirectory on Drive C or whatever drive or subdirectory holds the DOS utility programs. Furthermore, in later chapters you will need to log into the **\JUNK** subdirectory on Drive C. The preceding steps apply except that you key in **CD \JUNK**.
2. A blank or new disk. Whenever a new or blank disk is referred to, you may use a brand-new disk or an old disk with information on it. However, it is assumed that if there is information on the disk, you no longer want it, because it will be written over in the format process.

Activity 4.4 Formatting a Disk

WARNING: Never format an application disk you have purchased or a disk that has data you wish to keep. Also, if you have a hard disk/fixed disk, you must be *exceedingly* careful. *Never, never* key in C>**FORMAT** or C>**FORMAT C:**. If you did, you would *completely* erase, forever, all the information on the hard disk.

STEP 1: Key in the following:
C>**PROMPT pg** <Enter>

STEP 2: Key in the following:
C:\>**CD \DOS** <Enter>

```
C>PROMPT $p$g

C:\>CD \DOS

C:\DOS>
```

WHAT'S HAPPENING? You are logged into the **\DOS** subdirectory. The **C:\DOS>** should be displayed because you changed the way the prompt looks.

To format a disk, you use the FORMAT command. FORMAT is an external command located in the **DOS** subdirectory. The **C:\DOS>** prompt which represents the default drive and subdirectory should be displayed on the screen. You do not have a disk in Drive A yet. The default drive in this situation becomes a very important concept. Whenever you key in a command and/or file name, the operating system looks only for that command and/or file on the default drive and in the default subdirectory, unless you tell it otherwise. Remember that the prompt on the screen represents the default drive and subdirectory. When the operating system looks for an external command and/or file, it will only look on the default Drive C and in the default subdirectory **\DOS** for the command or file that you keyed in. You can tell DOS to look or do something on a different disk drive or different subdirectory, but you must specify that disk drive and/or subdirectory. In this case, you are looking for the command FORMAT. You can see whether or not this command, which is stored as a file called **FORMAT.COM**, is located on the disk in the default drive and in the default subdirectory.

STEP 3: Key in the following:
C:\DOS>**DIR FORMAT.COM** <Enter>

```
C:\DOS>DIR FORMAT.COM

   Volume in drive C is MS-DOS_5
   Volume Serial Number is 16D1-68D4
   Directory of C:\DOS

FORMAT    COM   32911    04-09-91   5:00a
        1 file(s)        32911 bytes
                       9240576 bytes free

C:\DOS>_
```

WHAT'S HAPPENING? The screen display tells you that the FORMAT command, stored as the file named **FORMAT.COM**, is located on the default drive, Drive C. In addition, since your DOS utility programs are in a subdirectory, you will not only be in Drive C but also in a subdirectory called **\DOS**. The command used was DIR. To use, execute, or run the FORMAT program, you key in the name of the command.

STEP 4: Key in the following (be sure to use A:):
C:\DOS>**FORMAT A:** <Enter>

```
C:\DOS>FORMAT A:
Insert new diskette for drive A:
and press ENTER when ready . . . _
```

WHAT'S HAPPENING? This command differs from Step 3. Here, you called the program by keying in the name of the command. FORMAT is the command that tells the system what work you want it to do. The A: tells the system where the disk that you want formatted is located (in Drive A). If you did not specify a lettered drive, A:, B:, or C:, the operating system would format the default drive. Since the default drive is C, and C is the hard disk, FORMAT will erase everything on the hard disk. You *never* want this to happen.

In addition, you are getting a message or prompt that tells you what to do. Before you get involved in the following activity, it is exceedingly important that you know what kind of disk drive you have so that you can choose the correct disk with the correct format. If you have a 5 1/4-inch disk 360 KB disk drive, use a 360 KB double-sided, double-density disk. DO NOT USE A HIGH-CAPACITY DISK. If you have a 5 1/4-inch 1.2 MB high-capacity disk drive, use a 1.2 MB, high-capacity disk. DO NOT USE A 360 KB DISK. If you have a 3 1/2-inch 720 KB disk drive, use a 720 KB double-sided, double-density disk. DO NOT USE A 1.44 MB HIGH-CAPACITY DISK. If you have a 3 1/2-inch high-capacity 1.44 MB disk drive, use a 1.44 MB disk. DO NOT USE A 720 KB DISK.

Get the blank disk out and prepare a label for the disk. Write your name and the words DATA DISK on the label. Place the label on the disk. Open the door to Drive A (the left-hand drive door or top drive door), insert the new disk into Drive A, label side up, and shut the drive door. Be sure that this disk is blank. Everything on it will be eliminated after <Enter> is pressed. **The following response will depend on what version of DOS you are using:** either 5.0, 4.0, 3.3, or 3.2 and below. Locate the screen display for your version of DOS.

STEP 5: Press <Enter>.

DOS 5.0

```
Checking existing disk format.
Formatting 360K
100 percent of disk formatted
```

WHAT'S HAPPENING? The light on the floppy disk drive is glowing, indicating that some activity is taking place on the disk you are formatting. DOS 5.0 is smarter than earlier versions of DOS. The FORMAT command now checks to see what format the disk is. If you are not using a brand-new disk, you will also get the following additional message.

```
Checking existing disk format.
Saving UNFORMAT information
Formatting 360K
100 percent of disk formatted
```

The message "Saving UNFORMAT information" is protecting you so that if you want to unformat the disk, DOS will save a picture of the disk as it used to be. The message "nn percent of disk being formatted" tells you that DOS 5.0 is formatting the disk. The nn represents a number which will change as the disk is being formatted until it reaches 100 percent. Do not do anything until you see the following message displayed on the screen. DOS version 5.0 users will then do Step 6.

DOS 4.0

```
100 percent of disk formatted
```

WHAT'S HAPPENING? The light on the floppy disk drive is glowing, indicating that some activity is taking place on the disk you are formatting. The message "nn percent of disk being formatted" tells you that DOS 4.0 is formatting the disk. The nn represents a number which will change as the disk is being formatted. Do not do anything until you see the following message displayed on the screen. DOS version 4.0 users will then do Step 6.

DOS 3.3

```
Head:     1     Cylinder:     39
```

WHAT'S HAPPENING? The light on the floppy disk drive is glowing, indicating that some activity is taking place on the disk you are formatting. The message "Head: n Cylinder: n" tells you that DOS 3.3 is formatting the disk. The n represents a number and will change as the disk is being formatted. Do not do anything until you see the following message displayed on the screen. Look for the screen display for your version of DOS. DOS version 3.3 users will skip Step 6 because it is applicable only to DOS 4.0 and DOS 5.0 users.

DOS 3.2 and below

```
Formatting . . . . .
```

WHAT'S HAPPENING? The light on the floppy disk drive is glowing, indicating that some activity is taking place on the disk you are formatting. "Formatting..." is a message telling you that DOS is carrying out the command that you keyed in. Do not do anything until you see the following message displayed on the screen. Look for the screen display for your version of DOS. DOS version 3.2 and below users will skip Step 5 because it is applicable only to DOS 4.0 and DOS 5.0 users.

DOS 4.0 and DOS 5.0

```
Format complete.

Volume label (11 characters, ENTER for none)?_
```

WHAT'S HAPPENING? DOS 4.0 and DOS 5.0 automatically ask for a volume label. However, you are not going to place a volume label on the disk.

STEP 6: Press <Enter>.

```
362496 bytes total disk space
362496 bytes available on disk

 1024 bytes in each allocation unit.
   354 allocation units available on disk.

Volume Serial Number is 0E69_1DD6

Format another (Y/N)?_
```

```
Format complete

     362496 bytes total disk space
     362496 bytes available on disk

Format another (Y/N)?_
```

DOS 3.3 and below

STEP 7: Press n. Press <Enter>.

WHAT'S HAPPENING? The command called FORMAT was executed. You formatted the disk in Drive A. The version of DOS does not matter. If you have either a high-capacity 5 1/4- or 3 1/2-inch disk, you will have more bytes available. The disk was formatted in all cases. DOS can now can read and write to this disk because it has set up the tracks and sectors, FAT, directory, and data sectors as needed.

Activity 4.5 Understanding Internal/External Commands

Note: You are logged into the `\DOS` subdirectory on Drive C and have the `C:\DOS>` displayed. The disk just formatted is in Drive A.

STEP 1: Key in the following:
C:\DOS>**DIR A:** <Enter>

```
C:\DOS>DIR A:

   Volume in drive A has no label
   Volume Serial Number is 0E69-1DD6
   Directory of A:\

File not found

C:\DOS>_
```

WHAT'S HAPPENING? You asked DOS to display a table of contents for the DATA disk located in Drive A. You just completed formatting this disk. You get a message, "File not found." There are no files on this disk because formatting only prepares the disk for files; it does not place any files on the disk.

STEP 2: Key in the following:
C:\DOS>**A:** <Enter>

STEP 3: Key in the following:
A:\>**DIR** <Enter>

```
C:\DOS>A:

A:\>DIR
```

```
   Volume in drive A has no label
   Volume Serial Number is 0E69-1DD6
   Directory of A:\

File not found

A:\>_
```

WHAT'S HAPPENING? You changed the default to the drive that has the DATA disk in it, which means that DOS will look for programs only on the disk in Drive A. DOS did not show you any of the files on any other drive. It only looked on the default drive. The internal command, DIR, did work or execute. It displayed the directory or table of contents for the default drive, which is "File not found."

STEP 4: Key in the following (include the semicolon after the word **PATH**):
A:\>**PATH;** <Enter>

STEP 5: Key in the following:
A:\>**FORMAT A:** <Enter>

```
A:\>FORMAT A:
Bad command or file name

A:\>_
```

WHAT'S HAPPENING? The system message tells you that there are no files on the DATA disk just formatted. Thus, when DOS went to the DATA disk to find the external command of FORMAT, so that this command could be loaded into memory and executed, it found no file by that name. In fact, it found no files. The message tells you that DOS could not do what you asked because it could not locate the file on the DATA disk. DOS is not smart enough to check any other disk.

Here we have an excellent opportunity to illustrate the difference between internal and external commands. DIR, an internal command, worked regardless of which drive was the default, because internal commands are kept in memory once the system is booted. FORMAT, an external command, did not load or work because DOS had to go to the disk to find the command.

STEP 6: Key in the following:
A:\>**C:** <Enter>

```
A:\>C:

C:\DOS>_
```

WHAT'S HAPPENING? You changed the default drive back to Drive C. Since you were last in the subdirectory **DOS** when you changed drives, DOS remembered where you were and took you back to the last subdirectory you were in.

STEP 7: Key in the following:
C:\DOS>CD \ <Enter>

```
C:\DOS>CD \

C:\>_
```

WHAT'S HAPPENING? A wise thing to do when you finish working is to return to the root directory. The root directory is *always* the backslash (\).

4.6 Formatting a Disk with a Volume Label

There are also parameters other than the disk drive letter that can be used with the FORMAT command. The partial syntax for the FORMAT command is:

FORMAT *drive:*[/S][/V][/4][/N:*xx*][/T:*yy*]

In DOS version 3.3 and above, the *drive:* or drive letter is mandatory. It *must* be included. This mandatory drive letter prohibits you from accidentally formatting the disk in the default drive. Earlier versions of DOS do not require a drive letter. The /S, /V, and /4 are all fixed parameters. The /N and /T must be used together. The *xx* and *yy* represent specific capacity. /F:*size* also represents specific capacity. You indicate an option by first using a switch (the slash /).

In DOS 5.0, there are more parameters than in earlier versions of DOS. The syntax for FORMAT looks like the following:

FORMAT *drive:* [/V[:*label*]] [/Q] [/U] [/F:*size*] [/B ¦ /S]
FORMAT *drive:* [/V[:*label*]] [/Q] [/U] [/T:*tracks* /N:*sectors*] [/B ¦ /S]
FORMAT *drive:* [/V[:*label*]] [/Q] [/U] [/1] [/4] [/B ¦ /S]
FORMAT *drive:* [/Q] [/U] [/1] [/4] [/8] [/B ¦ /S]

There are some differences in the way the FORMAT command works in DOS 5.0. If you do not specify, DOS will make a mirror image so that the disk can be "unformatted." The /U parameter performs an unconditional format so that a disk cannot be unformatted. The /Q parameter performs a quick format which does not check for bad sectors on the disk.

However, in this case, the option you are going to use is placing a **volume label** on the disk you are formatting. A volume label is an electronic name. You are naming your disk. It is very much like labeling a file drawer so you know what it contains. The switch is /V, which tells the **FORMAT** command that not only is it to format a disk, but it is also going to allow you to place a volume label on the disk. Whenever you format a disk using DOS 4.0 or 5.0 it automatically asks you for a volume label.

Activity 4.7 Formatting a Disk with a Volume Label and Using the VOL Command

Note: The DATA disk is in Drive A. The screen displays are those of DOS 5.0. Refer to Activity 4.4 for screen displays of earlier versions of DOS.

STEP 1: Key in the following:
C:\>CD \DOS <Enter>

```
C:\>CD \DOS

C:\DOS>_
```

WHAT'S HAPPENING? You made `\DOS` the default subdirectory.

STEP 2: Key in the following:
C:\DOS>**FORMAT A:/V** <Enter>

```
C:\DOS>FORMAT A:/V
Insert new diskette for drive A:
and press ENTER when ready . . . _
```

STEP 3: You should have the DATA disk in Drive A. Press <Enter>.

```
100 percent of disk formatted
```

WHAT'S HAPPENING? You have begun the process of formatting the DATA disk. The message is the same for all versions of DOS. Do not do anything until the following is displayed:

```
Format complete.
Volume label (11 characters, ENTER for none)?_
```

WHAT'S HAPPENING? DOS first asks you a question: "Do you want to place a volume label on this disk?" It then gives you the rule, which is that a volume label can be less than but no more than 11 characters. If you have a label already and do not want a volume label on this disk, press <Enter> ("ENTER for none"). However, in this instance, you do want a volume label.

STEP 4: Key in the following after the question mark:
SAMPLE DATA <Enter>

```
Format complete.

Volume label (11 characters, ENTER for none)? SAMPLE DATA

     362496 bytes total disk space
     362496 bytes available on disk

       1024 bytes in each allocation unit
        354 allocation units available on disk.

Volume Serial Number is 0D18-1EEF

Format another (Y/N)?_
```

STEP 5: Key in the following:
N <Enter>

```
Format another (Y/N)?N

C:\DOS>_
```

WHAT'S HAPPENING? Since you formatted your disk again, you have a different volume serial number. You named your disk SAMPLE DATA because this disk is where you are going to enter samples. Whenever you use a volume label, make it as meaningful as possible so that you do not have to look at all the files on the disk to know what is on the disk. A meaningful name (labels) might be DOS 5.0, telling you that this disk is your DOS System Disk, or INCOMETAXES for a disk that contains your income tax data. There are two ways to see your volume label.

STEP 6: Key in the following:
C:\DOS>**DIR A:** <Enter>

```
C:\DOS>DIR A:

   Volume in drive A is SAMPLE DATA
   Volume Serial Number is 0D18-1EEF
   Directory of A:\

File not found

C:\DOS>_
```

WHAT'S HAPPENING? In earlier directory displays, the message read "Volume in drive N has no label." N represents the letter of the drive where the disk is located. You can see displayed the label you entered, SAMPLE DATA. There is a command specifically for the volume label. It is VOL, an internal command, which allows you to look at the volume label on any disk or check to see if there is a label. By using this command, you can quickly see what is on a disk without having to run the directory command. The syntax is:

VOL [*d:*]

STEP 7: Key in the following:
C:\DOS>**VOL** <Enter>

```
C:\DOS>VOL

   Volume in drive C is MS-DOS_5
   Volume Serial Number is 16D1-68D4

C:\DOS>_
```

WHAT'S HAPPENING? The volume label on your hard disk may well be different depending on whether a volume label was entered when the hard disk was formatted. If no volume label was placed on the hard disk drive, you will see a negative answer—"Volume in drive C has no label." When you used the VOL command, DOS only looked on Drive C, the default drive. To look at the volume label on Drive A, you must specifically request that DOS look on Drive A by giving VOL another parameter, the variable parameter [*d:*] where *d:* represents the drive letter.

STEP 8: Key in the following:
C:\DOS>**VOL A:** <Enter>

```
C:\DOS>VOL A:

   Volume in drive A is SAMPLE DATA
   Volume Serial Number is 0D18-1EEF

C:\DOS>_
```

WHAT'S HAPPENING? Here you placed a volume label on the DATA disk. As you can see, if a volume label is meaningful, it can help you know what files are on the disk. It is much like labeling a file cabinet drawer, so that when you are looking for a file you do not have to open every drawer to know what is in the file cabinet.

Note: Sometimes you may get a message like the following, particularly if you are using a used disk:

```
Drive A error. The boot sector for this
drive is incompatible with the MIRROR command.
There was an error creating the format recovery file.
This disk cannot be unformatted.
Proceed with Format (Y/N)?_
```

This message just means that the disk cannot be unformatted because it has been used for other data. Since you have no valuable information on this disk, go ahead and key in Y for Yes—Proceed.

4.8 Bootable and Nonbootable Disks

You have learned that in order to use a new disk, you must first prepare the disk with the FORMAT command. In addition, you have learned to place an electronic label on your disk with the volume (/V) parameter. There is another major parameter you can use with the FORMAT command. This parameter or option allows you to place the operating system on a disk, making it **bootable**. What is a bootable disk? We have learned that in order for a computer to work, an operating system must be resident in memory. The computer has that operating system in memory because you booted the system from the hard disk which has the system files on it. This allowed the system to read the operating system files into memory. These critical files on the disk, the actual operating system, are comprised of two hidden system files, `IO.SYS` and `MSDOS.SYS` (`IBMBIO.COM` and `IBMDOS.COM` if you have IBM PC-DOS), and the nonhidden file `COMMAND.COM`. Since the hard disk is already bootable, why would you want to make a floppy disk bootable? Sometimes, you do not need all the utility programs. In fact, with

DOS 3.3 and above, you cannot get all the utility files on one disk. You may have to set up a DOS System Disk for your laptop computer when there is no hard disk. You will see later that you will want to copy application programs to a disk. You do not want to load DOS as a separate disk first; you want the ability to boot from the disk that contains your application. Another reason is that you always want one floppy disk that you can boot from in case you have a hard disk problem.

In the last activity, you formatted a disk with a volume label of SAMPLE DATA, but you did not put an operating system on the disk, making it a **nonbootable** or nonsystem disk. The following activity will show you what happens with a nonsystem disk.

Activity 4.9 Trying to Boot with a Nonsystem Disk

STEP 1: Be sure that the disk that you formatted in the previous activity is in Drive A and that the drive door is shut.

STEP 2: The disk, labeled with your name and DATA DISK, is in Drive A. Refer to this disk from now on as the DATA disk.

STEP 3: Reboot the system. To reboot the system, hold down the <Ctrl> key, the <Alt> key, and the <Del> key simultaneously.

```
Non-system disk or disk error
Replace and press any key when ready_
```

WHAT'S HAPPENING? When you rebooted the system, you eliminated anything that was in memory. The system went through its start-up routine and went to the disk in Drive A, looking for the boot record to load `IO.SYS`, `MSDOS.SYS`, and `COMMAND.COM`. Since the DATA disk did not have these system files stored on it, the computer could not locate them. Since there are no system files on the DATA disk in Drive A and, hence, no files to load into memory, nothing happened. The boot record displayed the "disk error" message.

STEP 4: Open the door to Drive A or press the disk eject button.

STEP 5: Press any key, per the instructions on the screen.

STEP 6: You may see the date prompt. Enter the correct date and then enter the correct time at the prompt.

```
C>_
```

WHAT'S HAPPENING? You have successfully booted the system. Opening the drive door is the equivalent of having nothing in the drive. When you rebooted the system, the start-up routine went to the disk in Drive A looking for the system files. Since there was no disk in Drive A (the door was open), the system looked on the hard disk and found the files `IO.SYS`, `MSDOS.SYS`, and `COMMAND.COM` on the hard drive. It could load these files into memory and thus boot the system.

STEP 7: Close the drive door.

Activity 4.10 Formatting a Data Disk with an Operating System and a Volume Label

Note: You have booted off the hard disk. The **C>** is displayed and the DATA disk is in Drive A. To follow the text, key in **PROMPT pg**. Remember that if the DOS utility programs are in a subdirectory with a different name, you will have to substitute your subdirectory name for **\DOS**, i.e., **CD \BIN**.

STEP 1: Key in the following:
C:\>**CD \DOS** <Enter>

WHAT'S HAPPENING? You made the **\DOS** subdirectory the default.

STEP 2: Key in the following:
C:\DOS>**FORMAT A:/S/V** <Enter>

```
C:\DOS>FORMAT A:/S/V
Insert new diskette for drive A:
and press ENTER when ready . . . _
```

WHAT'S HAPPENING? You are asking that the program called FORMAT be loaded into memory and executed, which means the DATA disk is going to be formatted again. In addition, the fixed /S parameter, per the syntax (FORMAT *drive*: [/S]), is telling the FORMAT command that you not only want the DATA disk to be formatted but that you also want the operating system entered on this disk so that your DATA disk will be bootable. The /S parameter will copy the hidden files **IO.SYS** and **MSDOS.SYS** to the DATA disk as well as the file named **COMMAND.COM**. The /V label will allow you to place a volume label on the disk. If you have DOS 4.0 or 5.0, you do not need to include the /V parameter because these versions of DOS will ask you for a volume label.

STEP 3: Confirm/insert the DATA disk in Drive A.

STEP 4: Press <Enter>.

```
n percent of disk formatted
```

WHAT'S HAPPENING? The message displayed tells you that the program is executing. Do not do anything until you see the following screen display:

```
Checking existing disk format.
Saving UNFORMAT information.
Verifying 360K
Format complete.
System transferred

Volume label (11 characters, ENTER for none)?_
```

STEP 5: Key in the following:
SAMPLE DATA <Enter>

```
Volume label (11 characters, ENTER for none)? SAMPLE DATA

     362496 bytes total disk space
     119808 bytes used by system
     242688 bytes available on disk

       1024 bytes in each allocation unit.
        237 allocation units available on disk.

Volume Serial Number is 4141-17CE

Format another (Y/N)?_
```

STEP 6: Key in the following:
N <Enter>

```
Format another (Y/N)?N

C:\DOS>_
```

WHAT'S HAPPENING? The DATA disk was formatted. However, because you added the fixed parameter /S, the operating system was transferred. The "**System transferred**" message on the screen tells you that the two hidden files and COMMAND.COM are now residing on the DATA disk. In addition, 119808 bytes are taken up by the system, so you have only 242688 bytes left for data on a 360 KB disk. If you had any unusable sectors, they would be reported at this time. You used SAMPLE DATA for your volume label. Again, if you have a version of DOS above 4.0, you did not need to include the /V parameter to be prompted for a volume label.

STEP 7: Be sure the Drive A door is shut. Then, to reboot the system, press the <Ctrl>, <Alt>, and <Del> keys.

WHAT'S HAPPENING? The DATA disk booted the system. You did not get the message "Non-system disk or disk error" as you did in Activity 4.9. You know you booted the system when you got the date prompt.

STEP 8: Enter the correct date and time.

```
A>_
```

STEP 9: Key in the following:
A>**FORMAT A:** <Enter>

```
A>FORMAT A:
Bad command or file name

A>_
```

WHAT'S HAPPENING? This message appeared because FORMAT is an external command or utility and is not on the disk in Drive A. When you formatted the DATA disk, you transferred the operating system to the disk. The operating system only consists of **IO.SYS**, **MSDOS.SYS**, and **COMMAND.COM** and does not include the utility programs or external commands. The system files are mandatory for operating the system. The utilities or external commands, although extremely useful, do not need to be on the disk for you to use the computer.

STEP 10: Key in the following:
A>**DIR** <Enter>

```
A>DIR

   Volume in drive A is SAMPLE DATA
   Volume Serial Number is 0C2F-16EC
   Directory of A:\

COMMAND   COM   47845   04-09-91   5:00a
        1 file(s)       47845 bytes
                       242688 bytes free

A>_
```

WHAT'S HAPPENING? This command executed because DIR is an internal command, always resident in memory after the operating system is booted and loaded into memory. You do not see **FORMAT.COM** or any other file on this directory, because the operating system could not find it when you keyed in the FORMAT command in Step 8.

You have formatted this disk with the operating system and a volume label. However, should a disk be bootable and have a label, particularly if it is a disk that is only going to be used for data? This decision is for the user. Unless you need to boot off the floppy disk, you do not need to place an operating system on the disk. When you place the operating system on the disk, you lose 119808 bytes for data. You should, however, have one floppy disk that is bootable so that if you have a problem and cannot boot off the hard disk, you can boot off the floppy disk. Furthermore, volume labels can be very useful and do not require much space.

STEP 11: Open the drive door to Drive A. Reboot the system, entering the date and time, if necessary.

STEP 12: Key in the following:
C>**PROMPT pg** <Enter>

STEP 12: Key in the following:
C:\>**CD \DOS** <Enter>

```
C>PROMPT $p$g

C:\>CD \DOS

C:\DOS>_
```

WHAT'S HAPPENING? You rebooted the system from Drive C, changed the prompt so that you can see the default drive and default subdirectory displayed on the screen, and changed the default subdirectory to the **DOS** subdirectory so that you can have access to the DOS utility programs.

4.11 Formatting a Disk Using /Q and /U DOS 5.0

The FORMAT command in DOS 5.0 has some interesting features. One of the things that happens with the new FORMAT command is that it has become less dangerous. When you format a disk, you can "unformat" it because when you use the FORMAT command without any parameters, it empties the file allocation table and root directory, copies them to an unused portion of the disk, and saves them in a file called **MIRORSAV.FIL**. This information saving process was not available in earlier versions of DOS. In versions of DOS before 5.0, formatting destroyed all data. One warning, however: Even with DOS 5.0, once you begin writing new data to the disk, the disk can no longer be "unformatted," and the old data is lost. If you want to clear the disk completely like older versions of DOS did with the FORMAT command, you must use the /U parameter, which lets you format the disk unconditionally so that no data can be recovered.

Another new feature of DOS 5.0 is the /Q parameter which stands for "quick" format. However, it only works on a disk that has been previously formatted. It does clear the FAT and the root directory when it prepares a disk for new files, but in order to clear the disk rapidly, /Q will not check for bad sectors on a disk.

Activity 4.12 Using the /Q and /U Parameters DOS 5.0

Note: The **C:\DOS>** is displayed and the DATA disk is in Drive A.

STEP 1: Key in the following:
C:\DOS>**FORMAT A:/Q** <Enter>

```
C:\DOS>FORMAT A:/Q
Insert new diskette for drive A:
and press ENTER when ready . . . _
```

WHAT'S HAPPENING? It is asking you for the disk to format.

STEP 2: Be sure the DATA disk is in Drive A and the drive door is shut. Then press <Enter>.

```
Checking existing data format.
Saving UNFORMAT information.
Quickformatting 360K
Format complete.

Volume Label (11 characters, ENTER for none)?_
```

WHAT'S HAPPENING? DOS is asking you for a volume label. Notice how fast the formatting occurred.

STEP 3: Press <Enter>.

```
     362496 bytes in each allocation unit
     262496 bytes available on disk.

        1024 bytes in each allocation unit
         354 bytes available on disk

Volume Serial Number is 1068-18DD

Quickformat another (Y/N)?_
```

WHAT'S HAPPENING? The FORMAT command wants to know if you have any more disks to quick format.

STEP 4: Press N and <Enter>.

```
Quickformat another (Y/N)?N

C:\DOS>_
```

WHAT'S HAPPENING? You have returned to the system prompt. When you use the next parameter, /U for unconditional formatting, you are indeed formatting the disk so that the information on the disk cannot be recovered.

STEP 5: Be sure the DATA disk is in Drive A. Key in the following:
C:\DOS>**FORMAT A:/U** <Enter>

```
C:\DOS>FORMAT A:/U
Insert new diskette for drive A:
and press ENTER when ready . . . _
```

STEP 6: Press <Enter>.

```
Formatting 360K
Format complete.

Volume label (11 characters, ENTER for none)?_
```

STEP 7: Press <Enter>.

```
    362496 bytes total disk space
    362496 bytes available on disk

      1024 bytes in each allocation unit.
       354 allocation units available on disk.

Volume Serial Number is 3F56-18F3

Format another (Y/N)?_
```

STEP 8: Press N and <Enter>.

```
Format another (Y/N)?N

C:\DOS>_
```

WHAT'S HAPPENING? You have unconditionally formatted the DATA disk in Drive A, which is the most drastic form of formatting in DOS 5.0. This disk is no longer unformattable.

STEP 9: Key in the following:
C:\DOS>CD \ <Enter>

```
C:\DOS>CD \

C:\>_
```

WHAT'S HAPPENING? You have returned to the root directory of the hard disk.

4.13 The 5 1/4-inch High-capacity Disk

If you have an IBM PC AT, an AT compatible, an IBM PS/2, or a similar type of computer, you probably have what is called a high-capacity disk drive, which can use a 5 1/4-inch disk, called a high-capacity disk or a high-density disk. This type of disk stores much more information than a standard 360 KB floppy disk. In fact, it stores 1.2 MB. Thus, if you have been using this high-capacity disk drive with the FORMAT command, the message from the FORMAT command would indicate that you had 12135952 bytes free. DOS knows that this number of bytes indicates a high-capacity disk and will format it in the high-capacity mode, unless you tell it otherwise. If you use a DS/DD (double-sided/double-density) 360 KB disk in a high-capacity drive, DOS will format the disk as a high-capacity disk. Because a DS/DD was not designed as a DS/HD (double-sided/high density) disk, it does not have as many magnetic particles. Thus, the last screen will show many bytes as "bad sectors."

If you have a high-capacity disk drive and use only high-capacity disks, you will have no problems. However, if you have both a double-sided disk drive and high-capacity 5 1/4-inch disk drive, the 360 KB and the 1.2 MB, or if you want to exchange data files with someone who has a 360 KB drive, you will have some major problems. A high-capacity drive can read a disk that has been formatted in a 360 KB drive. However, a 360 KB disk drive can never read or write to a disk that has been formatted as a 1.2 MB high-capacity disk. Furthermore, if a high-capacity disk drive writes to a disk that has been formatted in a 360 KB disk drive, the 360 KB disk drive may not be able to read that disk. The tough part of this situation is that there is no way to tell by looking at a disk drive whether it is a 360 KB or a 1.2 MB disk drive. Presumably, you know when you purchase your computer what kind of disk drives you have. The best way to tell what kind of disk drive you have is to execute the FORMAT command and see how many bytes you have on the disk.

However, two fixed parameters, the /4 parameter and the /N:*xx*/T:*yy*, can help. You only use these parameters if you have a high-capacity drive and wish to format a disk as if it were a 360 KB disk so it can be written to and read from on a 360 KB drive. However, using the parameters is no guarantee. The command information states that even using the /4 parameter "may not be read reliably or written in a 360 KB drive." Enter the command as:

C:\DOS>**FORMAT A:/4**

If you wanted to place a system and a volume label on the disk, enter the command as:

C:\DOS>**FORMAT A:/S/V/4**

Remember that if you have a version of DOS greater than 4.0, you do not need to include the /V parameter because the FORMAT command will always ask you for a volume label. A more reliable parameter is /N:*xx*/T:*yy*. Although these are two parameters, they must be used together. The N represents the number of sectors per track, and the /T represents the number of tracks. Since a 360 KB disk has 40 tracks and 9 sectors per track, enter the command as:

C:\DOS>**FORMAT A:/N:9/T:40**

If you want to place a system and a volume label on the disk, enter the command as:

C:\DOS>**FORMAT A:/N:9/T:40/S/V**

DOS 4.0 and above has a much easier parameter to remember: /F:*size*. You simply state the format size you wish. Enter the command as:

C:\DOS>**FORMAT A:/F:360**

If you want to place a system and a volume label on the disk, enter the command as:

C:\DOS>**FORMAT A:/S/F:360**

4.14 The 3 1/2-inch High-capacity Disk

If you have an IBM PS/2 or similar type of newer computer, you probably have a 3 1/2-inch disk drive. This drive can come in two flavors, the standard 720 KB and the 1.44 MB high-capacity disk drive. The high-capacity disk drive also takes a 3 1/2-inch disk. However, it is also called a high-capacity disk and stores much more information than a standard 720 KB floppy disk. In fact, it stores 1.44 MB.

Thus, if you have been using this high-capacity disk drive with the FORMAT command, the message from the FORMAT command would indicate that you had 1457664 bytes free. DOS knows that it is a high-capacity disk drive and will format a disk in the high-capacity mode unless you tell it otherwise. If you use a DS/DD (double-sided, double-density) 720 KB disk in a high-capacity drive, DOS will format the disk as a high-capacity disk. Because a DS/DD was not designed as an MF/2HD (Micro floppy/double-sided, high-density), it does not have as many magnetic particles on it. Thus, the last screen will show many bytes as "bad sectors."

If you only use a high-capacity disk drive and high-capacity disks, you will have no problems. However, if you have both a double-sided disk drive and high-capacity 3 1/2-inch disk drives, the 720 KB and the 1.44 MB, or if you want to exchange data files with someone who has a 720 KB drive, you will have some major problems. A high-capacity drive can read a disk that has been formatted in a 720 KB drive. However, a 720 KB disk drive can never read or write to a disk that has been formatted as a 1.44 MB high-capacity disk. Furthermore, if a high-capacity disk drive writes to a disk that has been formatted in a 720 KB disk drive, the 720 KB disk drive may not be able to read the disk. Some computer manufacturers, such as IBM, indicate that the disk drive is a high-capacity disk drive by printing 1.44 on the switch. Most computer manufacturers do not. Presumably, you know when you purchase your computer what kind of disk drives you have. The way to tell what kind of disk drive you have is to execute the FORMAT command and see how many bytes you have on the disk.

However, although you may not use the /4 parameter with the 3 1/2-inch disk drive, you may use /N:*xx*/T:*yy* to resolve this problem. Again, you only use these parameters if you have a high capacity drive and wish to format a disk as if it were a 720 KB disk so it can be written to and read from on a 720 KB drive. However, using these parameters is no guarantee. Although these are two parameters, they must be used together. The N represents the number of sectors per track and the /T represents the number of tracks. Since a 720 KB disk has 80 tracks and 9 sectors per track, enter the command as:

C:\DOS>**FORMAT A:/N:9/T:80**

If you want to place a system and a volume label on the disk, enter the command as:

C:\DOS>**FORMAT A:/S/N:9/T:80**

DOS 4.0 and above has a much easier parameter to remember: /F:*size*. You simply state the format size you wish. Enter the command as:

C:\DOS>**FORMAT A:/F:720**

If you want to place a system and a volume label on the disk, enter the command as:

C:\DOS>**FORMAT A:/S/F:720**

If you want to format the new size high-capacity disk drive, 2.88 MB, as a 1.44 MB disk, enter the command as:

C:\DOS>**FORMAT A:/F:1.44**

Chapter Summary

1. Disks that are purchased are not ready to use. They must first be prepared for use.
2. Each computer has its own specific way of recording information on a disk.
3. The command processor is stored as a file called **COMMAND.COM**. It processes what the user keys in. When you boot the system, this file is one of the operating system files placed in memory. **COMMAND.COM** has internal commands that are resident in memory until the computer is turned off.
4. Disks are the means to store data and programs permanently.
5. All disks must be formatted by a utility program stored as a file called **FORMAT.COM** so that DOS can read and write data and programs to them.
6. Disks that have information on them can be formatted again.
7. If a disk has files on it, formatting the disk will remove all those files.
8. Since the FORMAT command removes all data, formatting a hard disk can be dangerous.
9. Formatting a disk means that the physical layout of the disk is defined to determine how the information is stored on the disk so that DOS can locate what is stored.
10. DOS uses sections of a disk, be it a hard disk or a floppy disk. A disk is divided into concentric circles called tracks. Each track is divided into sectors. The number of tracks, sectors, and sides of a disk determine the capacity of the disk. A hard disk uses the concept of cylinders, which divides the disk vertically.
11. The smallest unit that DOS will read from or write to is a cluster. A cluster is made up of one or more sectors depending on the kind of disk.
12. Each disk has a directory and file allocation table (FAT). The number of files that a disk can hold is based on the size of the directory.
13. When formatted, all disks have a boot record, a FAT, a directory, and data sectors.
14. A boot record has either the bootstrap routine to load DOS if it is a system disk or a message indicating that it is not a system disk.
15. The FAT (file allocation table) is a map of every track and sector on the disk and tells DOS where files are on the disk.
16. The directory has information about the files including the file name and the file's starting cluster entry in the FAT. The directory also keeps track of the file attributes.
17. The data sectors are where files are actually stored.
18. Files are chains of bytes laid out in sequence.
19. DOS writes files to a disk at the first available cluster, if possible in adjacent or contiguous clusters. If the adjacent clusters are already in use, DOS skips to the next available space or noncontiguous cluster.
20. A disk is formatted with the FORMAT command, an external utility program. Parameters for the FORMAT command include the letter of the disk drive to format, /V to place a volume label on a disk, /4 to format a 360 KB disk in a high-capacity disk drive, and /S to place the operating system files

on the disk. In addition, if you are using high-capacity disks (the 1.2 MB 5 1/4-inch or the 1.44 MB 3 1/2-inch), you may use /N:*xx*/T:*yy* to format the disks so they may be read in a lower capacity disk drive. If you are using DOS 4.0 or above, you may use the /F:*size* parameter.

21. The syntax of the FORMAT command is:
    FORMAT *drive:*[/V:*label*][/S][/4][/N:*xx*/T:*yy*]
22. In DOS 5.0, there are many more parameters with the FORMAT command. The syntax is:
    FORMAT *drive:* [/V[:*label*]] [/Q] [/U] [/F:*size*] [/B ¦ /S]
    FORMAT *drive:* [/V[:*label*]] [/Q] [/U] [/T:*tracks* /N:*sectors*] [/B ¦ /S]
    FORMAT *drive:* [/V[:*label*]] [/Q] [/U] [/1] [/4] [/B ¦ /S]
    FORMAT *drive:* [/Q] [/U] [/1] [/4] [/8] [/B ¦ /S]
23. There are also some differences in the way that the FORMAT command works in DOS 5.0. If you do not specify, DOS will make a mirror image so that the disk can be "unformatted."
24. The /U parameter performs an unconditional format so that a disk cannot be unformatted.
25. The /Q parameter performs a quick format that does not check for bad sectors on a disk. In addition, it can only be used on a disk that has been previously formatted.

Key Terms

Bootable disk
Directory sectors
File allocation table (FAT)
Formatting
Nonbootable disk
"System transferred"
Volume label

Discussion Questions

1. What are the three system files that make up the operating system?
2. What purpose do disks serve?
3. Why must you format a disk?
4. Define tracks, sectors, clusters, and cylinders.
5. What determines the size of the sectors on a disk?
6. Define the FAT. How is it used?
7. What information is in the directory sectors?
8. Define file attributes. Give at least two examples of file attributes.
9. What is a volume label?
10. What command allows you to see the volume label?
11. Why is FORMAT a dangerous command?
12. What does FORMAT /S do to a disk?
13. What is a bootable disk?
14. Define internal commands. What is another name for these commands?
15. Define external commands. What is another name for these commands?
16. Is `FORMAT.COM` part of the operating system?
17. Explain the message, "Bad command or file name."

18. What can you do when you see the message, "Bad command or file name?"
19. Who determines whether or not a disk is formatted with a system and/or a volume label, and why?
20. When a disk is formatted with no parameters, what files are on the disk?
21. What is a high-density disk? When is it used?
22. Define the four types of floppy disks. Where may they be used?
23. Can you use a 1.2 MB 5 1/4-inch disk in a 360 KB drive? Why or why not?
24. What can you do to use a 1.44 MB disk in a 720 KB disk drive?
25. What does FORMAT /4 do to a disk?
26. How does the FORMAT command in DOS 5.0 differ from previous versions?
27. What is the difference between the /Q and /U parameters?
28. When would you want to use the /Q parameter? The /U parameter?
29. What does "unformat" mean?
30. How does DOS 5.0 accomplish an unformat?

Application Assignments

Remember, be very careful in using the FORMAT command. Never issue the command C>`FORMAT C:` or C>`FORMAT`.

1. Format the DATA disk (the disk that is in Drive A). Put a volume label on the DATA disk. The volume label will be DATA DISK. When you have finished formatting the DATA disk, use the directory command to display what is on the DATA disk. Print the screen.
2. Clear the screen. Display the volume label of Drive C. Do not use the DIR command to display the volume label. Print the screen.

Challenge Assignments

3. Format the DATA disk again (the disk that is in Drive A). Put an operating system and a volume label on the DATA disk. The volume label is MY DISK. When you have finished formatting the DATA disk, use the directory command to display what is on the DATA disk. Print the screen.
4. Format the DATA disk again. Place only a volume label on the DATA disk. The volume label is DATA DISK. Display the volume label but do not use the DIR command. Print the screen.

The following challenge assignments are for those who have high-capacity drives.

5. Format the DATA disk as a 720 KB or 360 KB disk, depending on what kind of drive you have. Put a volume label on the DATA disk. The volume label is LOWDISK. When you have finished formatting the DATA disk, use the directory command to display what is on the DATA disk. Print the screen.
6. DOS 5.0—Format the DATA disk again but use the quick format. Add the volume label DATA DISK. Print the screen displays of the use of the quick format parameter.
7. DOS 5.0—Format the DATA disk again but use the unconditional format. Add the volume label DATA DISK. Print the screen with the unconditional format parameter command.

Chapter 5

Using Internal Commands
COPY and TYPE

After completing this chapter you will be able to:

1. List and explain the three major reasons for learning DOS.
2. Explain the difference between application program files and data files.
3. Load and use an application program.
4. List the file-naming rules.
5. Write and explain the syntax for the COPY and TYPE commands.
6. Copy a file on the same disk using the COPY command.
7. Create dummy files.
8. Explain what dummy files are and how they are used.
9. Display a text file using the TYPE command.
10. Create and display a dummy file using the COPY and TYPE commands.
11. Use the COPY command to make additional files on the same disk.
12. Copy additional files on the same disk but to a different subdirectory.
13. Explain when and how to use wildcards with the COPY command.
14. Use wildcards with the COPY command to copy files on the same disk to a different subdirectory.
15. Print a file using the COPY command.

Chapter Overview

As you construct new files, you should know how to name, manage, and manipulate them. Specific rules must be adhered to when you choose a unique name for a file. It may be advantageous to know how to change a file name as information in a file is altered, to delete a file from a disk if the file is no longer needed, or to take a quick peek inside a file to see if the file contains the information you seek. It may be necessary to transfer files within the disk, from one disk to another, or from one device to another. DOS has several internal commands that will make it easy to manage and manipulate the files that you create.

In this chapter you will review the rules used to create unique names for files and learn some essential internal commands that will help you manage and manipulate your files. You will also create some dummy files so that you can have some experience in naming, managing, and manipulating files.

5.0 Why DOS?

So far, you have used DOS commands to prepare a disk for use (FORMAT), to copy a disk (DISKCOPY), to compare the copies (DISKCOMP), and to see what files are on a disk (DIR). In addition, you are able to set the time and date (DATE and TIME) and clear the screen (CLS). Each of these commands is useful, but no one buys a computer to use DOS. A person purchases a computer to assist in doing work, and the way one does work on a computer is by the purchase and use of application programs. The three major categories of application programs include **word processors** to make writing easier, **spreadsheets** to manage budgets and do financial projections, and **databases** to manage and manipulate a collection of data. Each program has its own instructions which must be learned. If this is true, why are you learning DOS, the disk operating system?

There are three reasons for learning DOS. First and foremost, you cannot run an application program without first loading DOS. DOS is the manager of the system, supervising the hardware and software components allowing you to load and execute the specific application package. Application programs run under the supervision of DOS.

The second reason for learning DOS is that application programs are stored as files on disks and usually generate data files. DOS has a variety of commands that allow you to manage and manipulate these files. DOS does not deal with the details of the files but with the entire files.

The third reason for learning DOS is that it allows you to install and manage special hardware devices such as a mouse. You might want to use a mouse to make your work easier. The program that makes the mouse work is stored on a disk. Without a place to store the file called `MOUSE.COM`, the mouse would not work. If DOS doesn't know about the mouse file, you have no mouse, only a piece of plastic.

5.1 Program Files, Data Files, and DOS

On the ACTIVITIES disk there is an application program called ADDRESS. The purpose of this program is to assist you in your understanding of how DOS works in the "real world." You are going to use DOS to load this program, look at files, and generate files. The DOS commands help you understand how DOS works in conjunction with the various types of files. A program file (application program) is a file that you load from a disk into memory. The program is what actually does the work. It provides the computer instructions to the system. DOS is the means by which a program is loaded into memory. DOS then turns control over to the application program. But when the application program needs to interface with the hardware, such as when it wants to write a character to the screen, the application program tells DOS what to write and DOS does the labor of the actual writing to the screen.

The application program is the set of instructions that tell the computer what to do, but usually that is not enough. With an application program, you also want to produce results, or data. Data are also stored in files that usually can only be used by the specific application program. However, DOS is the means by which the data files are loaded into memory so that the application program can use the data. This cooperative effort among DOS, the application program, and the data files is the true work of DOS. An operating system takes care of all these tedious but necessary tasks. You, the user, do not directly interface with DOS at this level. There is another component: the commands that DOS provides. Commands are also programs. These DOS commands allow you to interface directly with DOS and manage the various files.

ADDRESS is a simple application program that works much like a Rolodex. It is a database that allows you to keep track of names, addresses, and phone numbers.

Activity 5.2 Using DIR to Locate the ADDRESS Program and the Data File FRIENDS

Note: It is assumed that you have booted off the hard disk. Remember, the Drive A door must be open until after you boot the system. The **C>** is displayed and the ACTIVITIES disk is in Drive A. Key in **PROMPT pg**.

STEP 1: Key in the following:
C:\>**A:** <Enter>

```
C:\>A:

A:\>_
```

WHAT'S HAPPENING? You changed the default drive to the ACTIVITIES disk where the ADDRESS program is located.

STEP 2: Key in the following:
A:\>**DIR ADDRESS.EXE** <Enter>

```
A:\>DIR ADDRESS.EXE

   Volume in drive A is ACTIVITIES
   Volume Serial Number is 0ED4-161B
   Directory of A:\

ADDRESS   EXE   30960   01-15-88  4:10p
        1 file(s)       30960 bytes
                        64512 bytes free

A:\>_
```

WHAT'S HAPPENING? You used the DIR command to see if the file called **ADDRESS.EXE** is on the ACTIVITIES disk. DIR is the command; **ADDRESS.EXE** is the file name of the program. All the DIR command does is allow you to see if the file is on the disk. DIR does not let you use the program; it just lets you see if it is on the disk. The name of the file is **ADDRESS**. The name of the extension is **.EXE**. The **.EXE** file extension has a special meaning: executable code. This extension lets DOS know the file is a program. Both file extensions, **.EXE** and **.COM**, always indicate programs to DOS.

STEP 3: Key in the following:
A:\>**DIR FRIENDS** <Enter>

```
A:\>DIR FRIENDS

   Volume in drive A is ACTIVITIES
   Volume Serial Number is 0ED4-161B
   Directory of A:\

FRIENDS          3162   10-12-92  9:00p
         1 file(s)       3162 bytes
                        64512 bytes free

A:\>_
```

WHAT'S HAPPENING? You used the DIR command to see if the file called **FRIENDS** is on the ACTIVITIES disk. DIR is the command; **FRIENDS** is the file name and it is a data file. All the DIR command does is allow you to see if the file is on the disk. DIR does not let you use the data; it just lets you see if it is there on the disk. The name of the file is **FRIENDS**. It does not have a file extension.

5.3 An Application Program and Data File

In the above activity, you used the DOS command DIR to see if there were two files on the disk, **ADDRESS.EXE** and **FRIENDS**. All DIR did was let you know that these files exist. To make use of these files, you have to load them into memory. The next activity will show you how to do this.

Activity 5.4 Using an Application Program and Data File

Note: The **A:\>** is displayed (hard disk booted) and the ACTIVITIES disk is in Drive A.

STEP 1: Key in the following:
A:\>**FRIENDS** <Enter>

```
A:\>FRIENDS
Bad command of file name

A:\>_
```

WHAT'S HAPPENING? The file called **FRIENDS** is a data file. It is not a program, so it does not have a program file extension, **.EXE** or **.COM**. DOS cannot execute a data file. Only a program can be loaded into memory and executed.

STEP 2: Key in the following:
A:\>**ADDRESS** <Enter>

```
Enter the name of the data file:_
```

WHAT'S HAPPENING? Because **ADDRESS** is a file with an **.EXE** file extension, DOS knew what to do. It took an image copy of the program from the disk and loaded it into memory. DOS then turned control over to the ADDRESS program. ADDRESS has its own commands and instructions. ADDRESS is asking you to enter the name of the data file.

STEP 3: Key in the following:
FRIENDS <Enter>

```
Enter the name of the data file: FRIENDS
 The data file is being read.
 Press any key to continue
```

WHAT'S HAPPENING? You directly interfaced with DOS when you keyed in the command ADDRESS and by doing so loaded the program. DOS turned control over to the ADDRESS program. The ADDRESS program then prompted you for a data file name. You responded to the prompt by keying in the name of the data file, **FRIENDS**. Then the ADDRESS program directly interfaced with DOS. It asked DOS for the file **FRIENDS**, which DOS copied off the disk into RAM. Then ADDRESS again took control.

STEP 4: Press <Enter>.

```
The number of entries currently in the database is: 20
 Select an option by pressing a function key:
   F1   Find an entry.
   F2   Add an entry.
   F3   Edit an entry.
   F4   Delete an entry.
   F5   Print all (or part) of the data file.
   F6   Sort data file.
   F7   Save changes.
   F8   Exit to DOS.
_
```

WHAT'S HAPPENING? This list is a **menu-driven program**. It is called a menu-driven program because the screen display gives you choices, like a menu. You choose the option you want by pressing the appropriate function key. This simple database program is essentially a list of names and addresses. You can look at the file (F1), add a new name (F2), make changes to a name or address (F3), eliminate a name (F4), print the list (F5), be able to sort the list (F6), be able to save any changes that you make (F7), and exit back to DOS, also called exiting to the system level (F8). There are 20 names and addresses currently in the database.

STEP 5: Press the F1 key.

```
Define search field:
  F1  Last name.
  F2  First name.
  F3  Home phone number.
  F4  Work phone number.
  F5  City.
  F6  Cancel request and return to main menu.
_
```

WHAT'S HAPPENING? This program took you to another menu. This prompt (Define search field) is asking you how you want to look at the information, by last name, first name, home phone, work phone, or city. You select the option you want by pressing the appropriate function key.

STEP 6: Press the F1 key.

```
Enter last name search key. All names that start with this key will be listed.
Press <ENTER> to list all entries.
_
```

STEP 7: Press <Enter>.

```
First name: Nick                        Last name: Babchuk
Street address: 45 White
City: Lincoln                 State: NE             Zip code: 68502
Home phone number: (402) 384-8888    Work phone number: (    )
General notes: Birthday: May 6.



Press <ENTER> for next record (if there is one).
Press F1 to exit to main menu.

There are 19 records to view after this one.
_
```

WHAT'S HAPPENING? You are looking at the first entry (record) in this file. The information in this record is the data. The prompts at the bottom of the screen tell you how to find more records (Press <Enter>) or return to the main menu (Press F1 to exit). By pressing <Enter>, you can "thumb" through the data in this file.

STEP 8: To see other entries in this file, press <Enter>. Then, press the F1 key to return to the main menu.

```
The number of entries currently in the database is: 20
 Select an option by pressing a function key:
   F1     Find an entry.
   F2     Add an entry.
   F3     Edit an entry.
   F4     Delete an entry.
   F5     Print all (or part) of the data file.
   F6     Sort data file.
   F7     Save changes.
   F8     Exit to DOS.
_
```

STEP 9: Press the F8 key.

```
    A:\>_
```

WHAT'S HAPPENING? You exited the program ADDRESS and returned to the system prompt. You are now at the DOS system level. Thus, you used DOS to load the application program ADDRESS. You then loaded and perused the data file `FRIENDS`. You followed the instructions of the menu-driven program ADDRESS. Then you exited the program ADDRESS with one keystroke (F8) and returned to the DOS system level.

5.5 Managing Your Files with Internal Commands

Several major internal commands will help manage your files on disks: DIR, COPY, RENAME, DEL, and TYPE. These commands are internal, meaning that once you have booted the system, you no longer need to have the DOS System Disk in any drive, nor do you need to be logged into the `DOS` subdirectory. The commands deal only with files as a whole; you are not working with the contents of the files, just manipulating the files. The commands allow you to see what files you have (DIR), move files from here to there (COPY), change their names (RENAME), throw files away (DEL), and take a quick peek at what is inside a file (TYPE). The following activities in this chapter will show you how to use the COPY and TYPE commands.

5.6 The COPY Command

COPY, one of the most frequently used internal commands, is used to copy files from one place to another. COPY does exactly what it says—it takes an original **source file**, makes an identical copy of that file, and places the copy where you want it to go. In a sense, it is similar to a photocopy machine. You place your original on the copy plate, press the appropriate button, and receive a copy of your original document. Nothing has happened to your document. If it has a smudge on it, so does your copy. The same thing is true with the COPY command.

It makes an exact copy of the file, and the original file remains the same. Copying a file does not alter the original file in any way.

Why might you want to copy files? You might want to copy a file from one disk to another. For example, you might create an inventory of all your household goods for your homeowner's insurance policy. It would be stored as a file on your disk. If your home burned down, so would your disk with your inventory file. Thus, it makes sense to copy this file onto another disk and store it somewhere else, perhaps in a safe-deposit box.

You might want to make a second copy of an existing file on the same disk. Why would you want to do this? One of the advantages of computers is that you can minimize your labor. For instance, you are very interested in a particular political issue and wish to send letters to your government representatives expressing your views. The content of the letter is going to be the same, but the addresses will be different. One letter is for your senators, one for your representative, and one for the President. The letter you write is stored as a file on your disk. Rather than having to rekey or retype each letter, you can make copies of the letter, changing just the address block and the salutation.

You might want to copy a file to a device. One of the most common devices is the printer. You can copy a file to the printer to get a hard copy. In the above example, you were going to mail a letter, not a disk, to your representative. Therefore, you needed a hard copy of the file; in other words, you copied the file from the disk to the printer. Indeed, the COPY command is useful.

You have been using the ADDRESS program. You might wish to make another copy of it, in case something happens to the original. You have also been working with the **FRIENDS** data file. You might like to have another copy, a backup copy, so that if anything goes wrong, you still have another copy to work with.

COPY has a very specific syntax. Its partial syntax is always:

COPY [*d:*][*path*]*filename*[*.ext*] [*d:*][*path*]*filename*[*.ext*]

or conceptually:

COPY *source destination*

COPY is the command or the work you want the system to do. The source is *what* you want copied, your original. The destination is *where* you want it copied. In the formal syntax, the variables are as follows: [*d:*] stands for the drive letter where the file is located; [*path*] is the subdirectory where the file is located, and *filename*[*.ext*] is the name of the file you wish to copy. COPY, source file name, and a **destination file** name are mandatory. Drive and path do not need to be specified if you are using the default drive and subdirectories.

5.7 Review of File-Naming Rules

To name a file, you must follow the DOS file-naming rules. The file specification is comprised of two parts, the file name and the file extension. The file-naming rules are as follows:

1. Every file on one disk must have a unique name.

2. Every file must have a name that is no longer than eight characters.
3. File extensions are optional, but an extension cannot be longer than three characters.
4. All alphanumeric characters can be used in file names and file extensions except the following illegal or forbidden characters:

   <space> . " / \ [ ] : ; ¦ < > + = , * ?

Activity 5.8 Making Copies of Files on the Same Disk

Note: The **A:\>** is displayed (hard disk booted) and the ACTIVITIES disk is in Drive A.

STEP 1: Key in the following:

A:\>**DIR ADD*.*** <Enter>

```
A:\>DIR ADD*.*

   Volume in drive A is ACTIVITIES
   Volume Serial Number is 0ED4-161B
   Directory of A:\

ADDRESS   EXE   30960   01-15-88  4:10p
        1 file(s)       30960 bytes
                        64512 bytes free

A:\>_
```

WHAT'S HAPPENING? You have one copy of the program file, **ADDRESS.EXE**. You are going to make an identical copy of it with the COPY command.

STEP 2: Key in the following:

A:\>**COPY ADDRESS.EXE ADD.BAC** <Enter>

```
A:\>COPY ADDRESS.EXE ADD.BAC
         1 file(s) copied

A:\>_
```

WHAT'S HAPPENING? Following the syntax diagram, COPY is the command. **ADDRESS.EXE** is the source file or what you want to copy. **ADD.BAC** is the destination file name. Each file followed the file-naming rules; each is a unique name no longer than eight characters with no illegal characters. Each file extension is no longer than three characters with no illegal characters. You used a period to separate the file name from the file extension. The period is *not* part of the file specification. It is a delimiter telling DOS that you are done with the file name; get ready for the file extension. Thus, **ADDRESS** is the source file name and **.EXE** is the source file extension. **ADD** is the destination file name and **.BAC** is the destination file extension. You did not need to substitute the drive letter or path name in either the source or destination file. DOS always assumes the default drive and subdirectory, unless you tell it otherwise. The default drive is the disk in Drive A. The default subdirectory is the root directory.

STEP 3: Key in the following:
A:\>DIR ADD*.* <Enter>

```
A:\>DIR ADD*.*

   Volume in drive A is ACTIVITIES
   Volume Serial Number is 0ED4-161B
   Directory of A:\

ADDRESS   EXE   30960    01-15-88   4:10p
ADD       BAC   30960    01-15-88   4:10p
               2 file(s)    61920 bytes
                            32768 bytes free

A:\>_
```

WHAT'S HAPPENING? You now have two copies of the ADDRESS program, one called **ADDRESS.EXE** and another called **ADD.BAC**. When you made a copy of the **ADDRESS.EXE** file, the date and time remained the same in the copy.

STEP 4: Key in the following:
A:\>DIR FRI*.* <Enter>

```
A:\>DIR FRI*.*

   Volume in drive A is ACTIVITIES
   Volume Serial Number is 0ED4-161B
   Directory of A:\

FRIENDS   EXE    3162    10-12-92   9:00p
               1 file(s)     3162 bytes
                            32768 bytes free

A:\>_
```

WHAT'S HAPPENING? You have one copy of the data file **FRIENDS**. You are going to make an identical copy of it with the COPY command.

STEP 5: Key in the following:
A:\>COPY FRIENDS FRIEN.BAC <Enter>

```
A:\>COPY FRIENDS FRIEN.BAC
        1 file(s) copied

A:\>_
```

WHAT'S HAPPENING? Following the syntax diagram, COPY is the command. **FRIENDS** is the source file or what you want to copy. **FRIEN.BAC** is the destination file name. Each file followed the file-naming rules; each is a unique name no longer than eight characters with no illegal characters. The source file does not have an extension, but you placed an extension on the destination that was no longer than three characters with no illegal characters. You used a period to separate the file name from the file extension. The period is not part of the file specification. It is a delimiter telling DOS that you're done with the file name; get ready for the file extension. You did not need to substitute the drive letter or path name in either the source or destination file. DOS always assumes the default drive and subdirectory, unless you tell it otherwise. The default drive is the disk in Drive A. The default subdirectory is the root directory.

STEP 6: Key in the following:
A:\>**DIR FRI*.*** <Enter>

```
A:\>DIR FRI*.*

   Volume in drive A is ACTIVITIES
   Volume Serial Number is 0ED4-161B
   Directory of A:\

FRIENDS             3162   10-12-92   9:00p
FRIEN      BAC      3162   10-12-92   9:00p
         2 file(s)          6324 bytes
                           28672 bytes free

A:\>_
```

WHAT'S HAPPENING? You now have two copies of the **FRIENDS** data file. One is called **FRIENDS** and another is called **FRIEN.BAC**.

5.9 Creating Text Files Using the COPY Command

The files that you have been working with were program files supplied by DOS or by the disk included with this textbook. There are also data files on the disk included with this textbook. You can create or make up your own text files with your own data without having to use an application program. These are not going to be program files. They are known as text files, text being data or information that you key in. One of the ways to make or create a file is to use the COPY command.

Presently, you do not have any "original files" that you created. In this example, the source—what you want to copy—is going to be a device. The device you are going to use is the console or **CON**, the device name. CON means that the source is going to be whatever you enter on the keyboard and display on the monitor. The destination is going to be a file that you will place on your DATA disk. You are going to name this file, which is analogous to making a file folder and pasting a name or label on the outside of the folder. The contents, what is inside the file, will be what you key in at the console.

Activity 5.10

How to Create a Text File Using the COPY Command

Note: You are going to create or name a file based on the file-naming rules and then key in data for that file. Please key in exactly what is shown below. If you make an error keying in data, you can use the <Backspace> key to delete it. Once you advance a line by pressing <Enter>, you cannot go back to correct any typing errors. However, in this text typographical errors are not that important. This is not a class in typing.

STEP 1: Key in the following:
A:\>**C:** <Enter>

STEP 2: Key in the following:
C:\>**CD \DOS** <Enter>

```
A:\>C:

C:\>CD \DOS

C:\DOS>_
```

STEP 3: Remove the ACTIVITIES disk from Drive A. Place the disk labeled DATA DISK or a new, blank disk in Drive A. Be sure that the disk you use is in the same format as your disk drive.

STEP 4: Key in the following:
C:\DOS>**FORMAT A:** <Enter>

```
C:\DOS>FORMAT A:
Insert new diskette for drive A:
and press ENTER when ready . . .
```

STEP 5: Press <Enter>.

```
Checking existing disk format.
Saving UNFORMAT information.
Verifying 360K
Format complete.

Volume label (11 characters, ENTER for none)_?
```

STEP 6: Key in the following:
DATA DISK <Enter>

```
Volume label (11 characters, ENTER for none)DATA DISK

    362496 bytes total disk space
    362496 bytes available on disk

       1024 bytes in each allocation unit.
        354 allocation units available on disk.
```

```
Volume Serial Number is 3839-0EC8

Format another (Y/N)?_
```

STEP 7: Key in the following:
N <Enter>

```
Format another (Y/N)?N

C:\DOS>_
```

WHAT'S HAPPENING? You formatted the DATA disk with a volume label to prepare the disk for files.

STEP 8: Key in the following:
C:\DOS>**DIR A:** <Enter>

```
C:\DOS>DIR A:

   Volume in drive A is DATA DISK
   Volume Serial Number is 3839-0EC8
   Directory of A:\

File not found

C:\DOS>_
```

WHAT'S HAPPENING? The newly formatted DATA disk has no files on it, but it is ready to receive files.

STEP 9: Key in the following:
C:\DOS>**COPY CON A:EXERCISE.TXT** <Enter>

WHAT'S HAPPENING? COPY is the command. CON is the source from which the data will come. CON is a device name, meaning that everything that is keyed in from the keyboard and displayed on the screen will be entered into that file. The designated drive with the file name is the destination. In this case the A: tells DOS that you want this file placed on the DATA disk in Drive A. The name of the file is **EXERCISE**. It is a unique name, no longer than eight characters with no illegal characters, and **.TXT** is the file extension, no longer than three characters with no illegal characters. You used a period to separate the file name from the file extension. The period is not part of the file specification. It is a delimiter telling DOS that you're done with the file name; get ready for the file extension. Once you press <Enter>, you see the cursor blinking directly below the command line. DOS is waiting for you to key in something. <Enter> at the end of a line means to press the <Enter> key, like a carriage return moving you to the next line.

STEP 10: Key in the following:

Today's date <Enter>
<Enter>
This activity is a practice exercise in creating or <Enter>
making a text file with EXERCISE as the <Enter>
file name and TXT as the selected file <Enter>
extension. All the data, starting with <Enter>
the date is the data or text that is <Enter>
going to be inside the "file folder" named <Enter>
EXERCISE.TXT. <Enter>
<Enter>
Your name <Enter>

WHAT'S HAPPENING? You have just keyed in some data that is going to go into this file. However, you need to tell DOS that you are finished keying in data. DOS has no way of knowing that you are done unless you tell it so. At this point, nothing has yet been written to the DATA disk. The way you tell DOS that you are ready to write this file to the disk is to give it a signal. The signal is to press the <Ctrl> key and hold down the letter Z on the keyboard. The computer notation for this signal is either <Ctrl>+Z or ^Z. Remember, you hold down the Control key and the letter Z. Do not type or key in the word "Control." Your cursor should be under the first letter in your first name.

STEP 11: Do the following:

Press <Ctrl>+Z. Press <Enter>.

```
C:\DOS>COPY CON A:EXERCISE.TXT
November 23, 1992

This activity is a practice exercise in creating or
making a text file with EXERCISE as the
file name and TXT as the selected file
extension. All the data, starting with
the date is the data or text that is
going to be inside the "file folder" named
EXERCISE.TXT

Carolyn Z. Gillay
^Z
        1 file(s) copied

C:\DOS>_
```

WHAT'S HAPPENING? The date and name in your file will differ, obviously, from the example. There is a message, "1 file(s) copied." Here is what happened when you pressed <Ctrl>+Z and then <Enter>. DOS wrote the file you created to the DATA disk. The prompt is displayed, **C:\DOS>**. Even though **C:\DOS>** is the prompt, the file **EXERCISE.TXT** was written to the DATA disk, not the default drive and subdirectory. DOS is ready for your next command. How do you know that the file you just created was written to the DATA disk?

STEP 12: Key in the following:
C:\DOS>**DIR A:** <Enter>

```
C:\DOS>DIR A:

   Volume in drive A is DATA DISK
   Volume Serial Number is 3839-0EC8
   Directory of A:\

EXERCISE  TXT     313   11-23-92  7:05a
        1 file (s)        313 bytes
                       361472 bytes free

C:\DOS>_
```

WHAT'S HAPPENING? The bytes, date, and time in your display will vary. Using the DIR command, you now know that there is a file called **EXERCISE.TXT** located on the DATA disk. Remember that the DATA disk is in Drive A. The display does not tell you the contents of the file. It only says that there is a "file folder" named **EXERCISE.TXT** on the DATA disk.

5.11 The TYPE Command

The DIR command allowed you to determine that, indeed, there is a "file folder" named **EXERCISE.TXT** on the DATA disk. Using the DIR command is like opening your file drawer (the disk) and looking at the labels on the file folders. DIR does not show you what is in the file folder. An internal command called TYPE opens the file folder and places the contents on the screen. The TYPE command displays the file on the screen without stopping (scrolling). If the file is longer than one full screen, you can stop the scrolling by pressing <Ctrl>+<NumLock> or, if your computer has it, the <Pause> key.

TYPE has a syntax. It is:

TYPE [*drive:*][*path*]*filename*[*.ext*]

TYPE is the command or the work you want the system to do. The brackets [ ] indicate that what is between the brackets is optional. You do not key in the brackets, only what is inside them. [*drive:*] represents the drive letter. You do not key in "drive:." You must substitute the drive letter where the file is located (A:, B:, or C:). Another name for the drive letter is designated disk drive. This letter tells DOS on which disk drive to look for the information. [*path*] is the name of the subdirectory where the file is located. You do not key in "path" but substitute the name of the path or subdirectory name, as in **\DOS**. The file name is mandatory. If the file has an extension, it must be included as part of the file name. You substitute the file name you are interested in. You do not key in "filename.ext."

filename is the parameter that the TYPE command expects. You can only display one file at a time on the screen. You may not use wildcards or global file specifications with the TYPE command. In addition, the file must be a text file to be readable.

Activity 5.12 Displaying Files Using the TYPE Command

Note: The **C:\DOS>** is displayed and the DATA disk is in Drive A.

STEP 1: Key in the following:
C:\DOS>**TYPE** <Enter>

```
C:\DOS>TYPE
Required parameter missing

C:\DOS>_
```

WHAT'S HAPPENING? The message displayed on the screen is telling you that TYPE does not know what to do. DOS is asking you, "TYPE" or display what? Since you did not give a file name as the parameter the syntax mandates, the TYPE command cannot show the contents of this file. If you have a version of DOS earlier than DOS 4.0, the message could say, "Invalid number of parameters."

STEP 2: Key in the following:
C:\DOS>**TYPE MORE.COM** <Enter>

```
C:\DOS>TYPE MORE.COM
_º.s_¥,|L-!_*.s.|L-!-+@ Ä+áä+u._.óù.+ D+. |..ì.¢.-!r.ì>¢.Ç}
..u.ïE.óù.|.-.ê&ÿ.3_|>-!+. |E-!ï2|0+. |@-!n|:| .ï||?-!
+u.- ï+ï_<

C:\DOS>_
```

WHAT'S HAPPENING? What you see displayed on the screen is, indeed, the contents of a file named **MORE.COM**. It is a program or executable code, but it is in machine language and not meaningful to you. This should demonstrate to you that a program is not readable and is not a text file. Programs or executable code are recognized by their file extensions. If you see the file extension **.EXE**, **.COM**, or **.SYS**, it tells you that the file is a program. **EXE** stands for executable code. **COM** stands for command file. **SYS** stands for system file. However, the TYPE command will do whatever you ask, even if it means displaying nonsense. Remember, a file must be a text file to be readable.

Another name for a text file is an **ASCII** file, pronounced as-key. ASCII is an acronym for American Standard Code for Information Interchange. ASCII is a code that translates the bits of information into "human" readable letters. All you need to remember is that an ASCII file is a readable text file. You can see the text file you just created by using the TYPE command, the drive designator or disk drive where the file is located, and the file name.

STEP 3: Key in the following:
C:\DOS>**TYPE A:EXERCISE.TXT** <Enter>

```
C:\DOS>TYPE A:EXERCISE.TXT
November 23, 1992

This activity is a practice exercise in creating or
making a text file with EXERCISE as the
file name and TXT as the selected file
extension. All the data, starting with
the date is the data or text that is
going to be inside the "file folder" named
EXERCISE.TXT

Carolyn Z. Gillay

C:\DOS>_
```

WHAT'S HAPPENING? In this case, the above is a text file and, thus, you can read it. Using the TYPE command, you "opened" your file folder, **EXERCISE.TXT** and saw the contents displayed on the screen. You needed to include the drive designator, A: in front of the file name **EXERCISE.TXT** because that told DOS which disk drive to select. Had you not included the drive designator, DOS would have looked for the file **EXERCISE.TXT** on the default Drive C: and in the default subdirectory **\DOS**. Since the file was not on the default drive, you would have received a "File not found" message. After DOS has executed the TYPE command, it returns to the system prompt, ready for the next command.

5.13 Dummy Files

You are going to create some **dummy files**. "Dummy" means that these files have no particular meaning. You can use these files as examples of file management techniques. The concept of dummy files and/or dummy data is common in data processing. Often data processing professionals wish to test different portions of systems or programs. For instance, if you were writing a program about employee benefits, rather than looking at every employee, you would create dummy files and data in order to have a smaller representative sample that is manageable and easily tested. The following activities allow you to do the same. Following the instructions, you create or make up the file names and contents using the COPY command. You then display the contents of the file on the screen with the TYPE command.

Activity 5.14

Creating and Displaying Dummy Files with the COPY and TYPE Commands

Note 1: The **C:\DOS>** is displayed and the DATA disk is in Drive A.

Note 2: Remember that <Ctrl>+Z means holding down the Control key and then pressing the letter Z on the keyboard. Do not key in the word "Control." However, there is an easier way to get the <Ctrl>+Z. You can press function key F6. The F6 key is <Ctrl>+Z.

STEP 1: Key in the following:
C:\DOS>**CD ** <Enter>

STEP 2: Key in the following:
C:\\>**A:** <Enter>

```
C:\DOS>CD \

C:\>A:

A:\>_
```

WHAT'S HAPPENING? You changed the default drive so that all activities will automatically occur or default to the DATA disk. The DATA disk is in Drive A.

STEP 3: Key in the following:
A:\\>**COPY CON JANUARY.TXT** <Enter>
This is my January file. <Enter>
It is my first dummy file. <Enter>
This is file 1. <Enter>
<Ctrl>+Z <Enter>

```
A:\>COPY CON JANUARY.TXT
This is my January file.
It is my first dummy file.
This is file 1.
^Z
        1 file(s) copied

A:\>_
```

WHAT'S HAPPENING? What you are doing here is telling DOS what work you want to do by keying in the command (COPY). The source or what you want copied is going to come from what you key in on the keyboard and will be displayed on the screen (the source is CON). The destination is going to be a file that will be copied to the DATA disk. The file will be named **JANUARY.TXT** (the destination is **JANUARY.TXT**), with **JANUARY** as the file name and **TXT** as the file extension. You used a period as a delimiter separating the file name from the file extension. There are no spaces between the delimiter and the file name and extension. You did not need to specify the letter of the drive or the path name prior to the file name. DOS will automatically write the file **JANUARY.TXT** to the default drive (Drive A) and default subdirectory (the root directory \), unless told otherwise.

STEP 4: Key in the following:
A:\>**DIR** <Enter>

```
A:\>DIR

   Volume in drive A is DATA DISK
   Volume Serial Number is 3839-0EC8
   Directory of A:\

EXERCISE  TXT     313   11-23-92   7:05a
JANUARY   TXT      71   11-23-92   7:05a
         2 file(s)        384 bytes
                       360448 bytes free

A:\>_
```

WHAT'S HAPPENING? You should see the name of the new file you just created, **JANUARY.TXT**, listed in the directory or table of contents. Do not worry if the time and date are different. That time and date reflect when you created the file. In addition, the bytes can vary because if you enter even one extra letter or space, the number of bytes will change. The directory listing just presents the name of the file, like a file folder label. It does not indicate the contents or the inside of the file folder. If you want to see what is inside the folder, you can display the contents of the file called **JANUARY.TXT** on the screen by using the TYPE command.

STEP 5: Key in the following:
A:\>**TYPE JANUARY.TXT** <Enter>

```
A:\>TYPE JANUARY.TXT
This is my January file.
It is my first dummy file.
This is file 1.

A:\>_
```

WHAT'S HAPPENING? The TYPE command displayed the contents of the file on the screen, or what is inside the file called **JANUARY.TXT**. Now you are going to create more files.

Note: Each time you press the F6 key or <Ctrl>+Z, you get a message on the screen saying "1 file(s) copied," indicating that the file you created was written to the DATA disk.

STEP 6: Key in the following:
A:\>**COPY CON FEBRUARY.TXT** <Enter>
This is my February file. <Enter>

It is my second dummy file. <Enter>
This is file 2. <Enter>
<Ctrl>+Z <Enter>

```
1 file(s) copied
```

STEP 7: Key in the following:
A:\>**COPY CON MARCH.TXT** <Enter>
This is my March file. <Enter>
It is my third dummy file. <Enter>
This is file 3. <Enter>
<Ctrl>+Z <Enter>

```
1 file(s) copied
```

STEP 8: Key in the following:
A:\>**COPY CON APRIL.TXT** <Enter>
This is my April file. <Enter>
It is my fourth dummy file. <Enter>
This is file 4. <Enter>
<Ctrl>+Z <Enter>

```
1 file(s) copied
```

STEP 9: Key in the following:
A:\>**DIR** <Enter>

```
A:\>DIR

   Volume in drive A is DATA DISK
   Volume Serial Number is 3839-0EC8
   Directory of A:\

EXERCISE TXT     313   11-23-92  7:05a
JANUARY  TXT      71   11-23-92  7:05a
FEBRUARY TXT      73   11-23-92  7:10a
MARCH    TXT      69   11-23-92  7:11a
APRIL    TXT      70   11-23-92  7:11a
        5 file(s)          596 bytes
                        357376 bytes free

A:\>_
```

WHAT'S HAPPENING? The directory display tells you that you have added four "file folders" to the DATA disk. The directory display only tells you that the files are on the disk. It does not tell you what, if anything, is inside the file folders. If you want to look at the inside of the files to see the contents, you must use the TYPE command.

STEP 10: Key in the following:
A:\>**TYPE MARCH.TXT** <Enter>

```
A:\>TYPE MARCH.TXT
This is my March file.
It is my third dummy file.
This is file 3.

A:\>_
```

WHAT'S HAPPENING? With this command, **TYPE MARCH.TXT**, you told DOS to display on the screen the contents of the file named **MARCH.TXT**. You can only display one file at a time. If you want to look at your other files, you need to use the TYPE command again, followed by the name of the file.

5.15 Making Additional Files on the Same Disk

You often want to have extra copies of files on the same disk. A copy is exactly that—it is identical to the original. Often, you may wish to make copies of files created when you use other software application packages. You choose to make copies because you want to leave your original files intact. Then, if you err, you will still have your originals. For instance, if you created an extensive client list with a database management package and needed to update it, rather than working on the original file, you could rekey in the entire client list. If you made a mistake, you would still have your original list. However, an easier method would be to copy the client list, stored as a file, to a new file with a new name and make changes to the new file. When you make a copy of a file on the same disk, you must give it a different name. Every file name on a disk must be unique.

Activity 5.16 Using the COPY Command to Make Additional Files on the Same Disk

Note: The DATA disk is in Drive A. The **A:\>** is displayed.

STEP 1: Key in the following:
A:\>**COPY MARCH.TXT MARCH.TXT** <Enter>

```
A:\>COPY MARCH.TXT MARCH.TXT
File cannot be copied onto itself
         0 file(s) copied

A:\>_
```

WHAT'S HAPPENING? You must give new files on the same disk different names. Just as you would not label two file folders the same in a file drawer, you would not label two disk files the same.

STEP 2: Key in the following:
A:\>**COPY JANUARY.TXT JAN.TMP** <Enter>

```
A:\>COPY JANUARY.TXT JAN.TMP
         1 file(s) copied

A:\>_
```

WHAT'S HAPPENING? Here, you are making a copy of the contents of the file on the DATA disk called **JANUARY.TXT**, copying the contents to the DATA disk, and calling this new file **JAN.TMP**. You could have keyed in A>**COPY A:\JANUARY.TXT A:\JAN.TMP**. Either is correct, but it is not necessary to specify the disk drive since the default drive is assumed. Nor is it necessary to specify the path or subdirectory because the root directory (\) is the default subdirectory.

STEP 3: Key in the following:
A:\>**TYPE JAN.TMP** <Enter>

```
A:\>TYPE JAN.TMP
This is my January file.
It is my first dummy file.
This is file 1.

A:\>_
```

STEP 4: Key in the following:
A:\>**TYPE JANUARY.TXT** <Enter>

```
A:\>TYPE JANUARY.TXT
This is my January file.
It is my first dummy file.
This is file 1.

A:\>_
```

WHAT'S HAPPENING? The contents of each file are identical even though the file names are different. The COPY command does nothing to the original; the contents of the original file remain the same. As far as DOS is concerned, what makes a file different is its unique file name. To DOS, **JANUARY.TXT** and **JAN.TMP** are unique, separate files.

STEP 5: Key in the following:
A:\>**COPY FEBRUARY.TXT FEB.TMP** <Enter>

```
        1 file(s) copied
```

STEP 6: Key in the following:
A:\>**COPY MARCH.TXT MAR.TMP** <Enter>

```
        1 file(s) copied
```

STEP 7: Key in the following:
A:\>**COPY APRIL.TXT APR.TMP** <Enter>

```
        1 file(s) copied
```

STEP 8: Key in the following:
A:\>**DIR** <Enter>

```
A:\>DIR

   Volume in drive A is DATA DISK
   Volume Serial Number is 3839-0EC8
   Directory of A:\

EXERCISE TXT     313   11-23-92   7:05a
JANUARY  TXT      71   11-23-92   7:05a
FEBRUARY TXT      73   11-23-92   7:10a
MARCH    TXT      69   11-23-92   7:11a
APRIL    TXT      70   11-23-92   7:11a
JAN      TMP      71   11-23-92   7:05a
FEB      TMP      73   11-23-92   7:10a
MAR      TMP      69   11-23-92   7:11a
APR      TMP      70   11-23-92   7:11a
         9 file(s)        879 bytes
                       353280 bytes free

A:\>_
```

WHAT'S HAPPENING? You had four files with the extension **.TXT**. You still have those files, but, in addition, you now have four more files that you just copied or "created" with the extension **.TMP**. DOS keeps track of all these files.

5.17 Making Additional Files on the Same Disk but in a Different Subdirectory

You often want to have extra copies of files on the same disk but in a different subdirectory. You may want to keep your backup files in the same file cabinet (disk) but in a different drawer (subdirectory). Thus, you can group similar files together. When you make a copy of a file on the same disk, in a different subdirectory, it may have the same file name. Every file on a disk must have a unique name. However, if it is in a subdirectory, even though the file name is the same, the path name makes the file name unique.

Activity 5.18 Using the COPY Command to Make Additional Files on the Same Disk but in Different Subdirectories

Note: The DATA disk is in Drive A. The **A:\>** is displayed.

STEP 1: Key in the following:
A:\>**MD \CLASS** <Enter>

```
A:\>MD \CLASS

A:\>_
```

WHAT'S HAPPENING? You created a subdirectory called **CLASS** on the DATA disk. MD, which means Make Directory, is the command to create a place for additional files. The backslash (\) is the name of the root directory. **CLASS** is the name of the subdirectory. The only reserved name for a directory is the \. You can use any name for the subdirectory you create, provided that you follow the DOS file-naming rules. **CLASS** is like a drawer in the file cabinet called DATA disk.

STEP 2: Key in the following:
A:\>**DIR** <Enter>

```
A:\>DIR

   Volume in drive A is DATA DISK
   Volume Serial Number is 3839-0EC8
   Directory of A:\

EXERCISE TXT      313   11-23-92  7:05a
JANUARY  TXT       71   11-23-92  7:05a
FEBRUARY TXT       73   11-23-92  7:10a
MARCH    TXT       69   11-23-92  7:11a
APRIL    TXT       70   11-23-92  7:11a
JAN      TMP       71   11-23-92  7:05a
FEB      TMP       73   11-23-92  7:10a
MAR      TMP       69   11-23-92  7:11a
APR      TMP       70   11-23-92  7:11a
CLASS       <DIR>       11-23-92  7:46a
        10 file(s)        879 bytes
                       352256 bytes free

A:\>_
```

WHAT'S HAPPENING? The directory display shows the subdirectory called **CLASS**. You know it is a subdirectory because it has **<DIR>** following the file name. To see what is inside the file cabinet, you must use the path name. The syntax is:

DIR [*drive:*][*path*][*filename*[*.ext*]]

You do not need to include the drive letter since the default drive is where the DATA disk is. You do need to include the path name. The path name is the subdirectory name, **CLASS**.

STEP 3: Key in the following:
A:\>**DIR \CLASS** <Enter>

```
A:\>DIR \CLASS

   Volume in drive A is DATA DISK
   Volume Serial Number is 3839-0EC8
   Directory of A:\CLASS

.               <DIR>     11-23-92  7:46a
..              <DIR>     11-23-92  7:46a
      2 file(s)                0 bytes
                          352256 bytes free

A:\>_
```

WHAT'S HAPPENING? This directory listing is not for the root directory. DOS tells you what you are looking at. The third line of the display says "Directory of A:\CLASS" telling you that you are looking in the file drawer called **CLASS** on the DATA disk. There is nothing yet in this drawer. Then what are the . and .. ? The . tells DOS that this is a subdirectory. The .. is a shorthand name for the directory above **CLASS**, the root (\). How do you copy a file into this subdirectory? You do this by following the syntax:

COPY [*drive:*][*path*]*filename*[*.ext*] [*drive:*][*path*]*filename*[*.ext*]

You must include the command, COPY. Since the DATA disk is the default drive, you do not need to include the drive letter. You do include the path name and the source file name. The same is true with the destination file. You do not need to include the drive letter, but you must include the path name and the file name.

STEP 4: Key in the following:
A:\>**COPY \JAN.TMP \CLASS\JAN.PAR** <Enter>

```
        1 file(s) copied
```

WHAT'S HAPPENING? You copied the source file, **JAN.TMP**, from the root directory on the DATA disk, to the destination, the subdirectory **CLASS** and gave the destination file a new name, **JAN.PAR**. By looking at the syntax diagram, you can follow how you substituted the values you wanted:

```
COPY  [drive:][path]filename[.ext]  [drive:][path]filename[.ext]
COPY           \    JAN    .TMP            \CLASS \JAN   .PAR
```

In the destination syntax what is the second backslash? The first backslash is the name of the root directory. The second backslash is used as a delimiter between the subdirectory name and the file name. This delimiter tells DOS that the subdirectory name is over and the file name is to begin. Backslashes are used as delimiters separating subdirectory and file names.

STEP 5: Key in the following:
A:\>**DIR \CLASS** <Enter>

```
A:\>DIR \CLASS

   Volume in drive A is DATA DISK
   Volume Serial Number is 3839-0EC8
   Directory of A:\CLASS

.             <DIR>     11-23-92   7:46a
..            <DIR>     11-23-92   7:46a
JAN      PAR       71   11-23-92   7:05a
        3 file(s)          71 bytes
                       351232 bytes free

A:\>_
```

WHAT'S HAPPENING? You copied the file **JAN.TMP** from the root directory to the subdirectory **CLASS** on the DATA disk. You gave the copy a new file name, **JAN.PAR**. Are the files the same? You can use the TYPE command to compare the contents visually. Again, since you want to look at the contents of two files in different subdirectories, you must follow the TYPE syntax:

TYPE [*drive:*][*path*]*filename*[*.ext*]

STEP 6: Key in the following:
A:\>**TYPE JAN.TMP** <Enter>

STEP 7: Key in the following:
A:\>**TYPE \CLASS\JAN.PAR** <Enter>

```
A:\>TYPE JAN.TMP
This is my January file.
It is my first dummy file.
This is file 1.

A:\>TYPE \CLASS\JAN.PAR
This is my January file.
It is my first dummy file.
This is file 1.

A:\>_
```

WHAT'S HAPPENING? The contents of the files are the same, even though they are in different subdirectories.

5.19 Using Wildcards with the COPY Command

In Chapter 3, you used global file specifications or wildcards (* and ?) with the DIR command so that you could display a group of files. You can also use the wildcards to copy files on the same drive. In Activity 5.16 you copied one file at a time, for example, **COPY JANUARY.TXT JAN.TMP**. You then proceeded to key in a command line for each file you wanted copied. Since the files had their file extension, **.TXT**, in common, instead of having to key in each source file and destination file, you could have used the wildcards to key in the command line.

Activity 5.20 Using Wildcards with the COPY Command to Copy Files on the Same Disk Drive

Note: The DATA disk is in Drive A. The **A:\>** is displayed.

STEP 1: Key in the following:
A:\>**COPY *.TMP *.NEW** <Enter>

```
A:\>COPY *.TMP *.NEW
JAN.TMP
FEB.TMP
MAR.TMP
APR.TMP
          4 file(s) copied

A:\>_
```

WHAT'S HAPPENING? As each file is copied, it is displayed on the screen. Your command line says COPY any file on the DATA disk that has the file extension **.TMP**, regardless of its file name, to a new set of files that will have the same file name but a different extension, **.NEW**. The * represented any file name. DOS knew that you were referring to file extensions because you preceded the file extension with the delimiter, the period. These files will be copied onto the DATA disk. You could have keyed in A>**COPY A:*.TXT A:*.NEW**. Once again, it is unnecessary to specify the designated drive (default drive) and subdirectory. Since you did not tell it otherwise, DOS assumed the default drive and default subdirectory.

STEP 2: Key in the following:
A:\>**DIR *.TMP** <Enter>

STEP 3: Key in the following:
A:\>**DIR *.NEW** <Enter>

```
A:\>DIR *.TMP

   Volume in drive A is DATA DISK
   Volume Serial Number is 3839-0EC8
   Directory of A:\

JAN       TMP      71   11-23-92   7:05a
FEB       TMP      73   11-23-92   7:10a
MAR       TMP      69   11-23-92   7:11a
APR       TMP      70   11-23-92   7:11a
         4 file(s)        283 bytes
                       347136 bytes free
```

```
A:\>DIR *.NEW

   Volume in drive A is DATA DISK
   Volume Serial Number is 3839-0EC8
   Directory of A:\

JAN        NEW       71    11-23-92   7:05a
FEB        NEW       73    11-23-92   7:10a
MAR        NEW       69    11-23-92   7:11a
APR        NEW       70    11-23-92   7:11a
          4 file(s)          283 bytes
                          347136 bytes free

A:\>_
```

WHAT'S HAPPENING? You keyed in two separate commands, **DIR *.TMP** and **DIR *.NEW**. You used the wildcards to display the **.NEW** files and the **.TMP** files instead of displaying the entire directory. You also used the wildcard * to make copies of the **.TMP** files. The file names are identical, but the extensions are different. You successfully copied the four files with the extension **.TMP** to four new files with the extension **.NEW**. However, the directory display merely shows that the files are there. To see that the contents of the original files and copied files are the same, you may use the TYPE command.

STEP 4: Key in the following:
A:\>**TYPE FEB.TMP** <Enter>

STEP 5: Key in the following:
A:\>**TYPE FEB.NEW** <Enter>

```
A:\>TYPE FEB.TMP
This is my February file.
It is my second dummy file.
This is file 2.

A:\>TYPE FEB.NEW
This is my February file.
It is my second dummy file.
This is file 2.

A:\>_
```

WHAT'S HAPPENING? The file contents are identical even though the file names are different. To display the two files, you keyed in two command lines, **TYPE FEB.TMP** and then **TYPE FEB.NEW**. Why not use wildcards with the TYPE command? You cannot use wildcards with the TYPE command because the syntax of the TYPE command is TYPE *filename* and TYPE can only display *one* file at a time.

STEP 6: Key in the following:
A:\>**TYPE *.NEW** <Enter>

```
A:\>TYPE *.NEW
Invalid filename or file not found

A:\>_
```

WHAT'S HAPPENING? The message displayed on the screen tells you that the TYPE command was literally looking for a file called ***.NEW**. You have no files by that name (file not found) and, furthermore, it is an invalid file name because the * cannot be used when naming a file.

5.21 Using Wildcards with the COPY Command and Subdirectories

You can also use the wildcards to copy files on the same drive to a different subdirectory.

Activity 5.22 Using Wildcards with the COPY Command to Copy Files on the Same Disk Drive to a Different Subdirectory

Note: The DATA disk is in Drive A. The **A:\>** is displayed.

STEP 1: Key in the following:
A:\>**COPY *.TMP \CLASS*.PAR** <Enter>

```
A:\>COPY *.TMP \CLASS\*.PAR
JAN.TMP
FEB.TMP
MAR.TMP
APR.TMP
        4 file(s) copied

A:\>_
```

WHAT'S HAPPENING? As each file is copied, it is displayed on the screen. Your command line says COPY any file on the DATA disk in the default root directory that has the file extension **.TMP**, regardless of its file name, to a new set of files that will have the same file name but a different extension, **.PAR**. These files will be copied onto the DATA disk and into the subdirectory called **CLASS**. You could have keyed in A:\>**COPY A:*.TXT A:\CLASS*.PAR**. Once again, for the source files (***.TXT**), it is unnecessary to specify the designated drive (default drive) and subdirectory. Since you did not tell it otherwise, DOS assumed the default drive and default subdirectory. However, for the destination, you had to include the subdirectory name, **CLASS**; otherwise, DOS would have assumed the default subdirectory.

STEP 2: Key in the following:
A:\>**DIR *.TMP** <Enter>

STEP 3: Key in the following:
A:\>**DIR \CLASS*.PAR** <Enter>

```
A:\>DIR *.TMP

   Volume in drive A is DATA DISK
   Volume Serial Number is 3839-0EC8
   Directory of A:\

JAN      TMP       71   11-23-92   7:05a
FEB      TMP       73   11-23-92   7:10a
MAR      TMP       69   11-23-92   7:11a
APR      TMP       70   11-23-92   7:11a
         4 file(s)        283 bytes
                       344064 bytes free

A:\>DIR \CLASS\*.PAR

   Volume in drive A is DATA DISK
   Volume Serial Number is 3839-0EC8
   Directory of A:\

JAN      PAR       71   11-23-92   7:05a
FEB      PAR       73   11-23-92   7:10a
MAR      PAR       69   11-23-92   7:11a
APR      PAR       70   11-23-92   7:11a
         4 file(s)        283 bytes
                       344064 bytes free

A:\>_
```

WHAT'S HAPPENING? You keyed in two separate commands, **DIR *.TMP** and **DIR \CLASS*.PAR**. You used the wildcards to display the **.PAR** files in the subdirectory **CLASS** and the **.TMP** files in the root directory. You also used the wildcard * to make copies of the **.TMP** files. The file names are identical, but the extensions are different. The files were copied to the subdirectory **CLASS**. You successfully copied the four files with the extension **.TMP** to four new files with the extension **.PAR** to the subdirectory **CLASS**. However, the directory display merely shows that the files are there. To see that the contents of the original files and copied files are the same, you may use the TYPE command. Remember, you must specify the subdirectory where the ***.PAR** files are located.

STEP 4: Key in the following:
A:\>**TYPE FEB.TMP** <Enter>

STEP 5: Key in the following:
A:\>**TYPE \CLASS\FEB.PAR** <Enter>

```
A:\>TYPE FEB.TMP
This is my February file.
It is my second dummy file.
This is file 2.

A:\>TYPE \CLASS\FEB.PAR
This is my February file.
It is my second dummy file.
This is file 2.

A:\>_
```

WHAT'S HAPPENING? The file contents are identical even though the file names are different and the files are in a different subdirectory. To display the two files, you keyed in two command lines, **TYPE FEB.TMP** and then **TYPE \CLASS\FEB.PAR**.

5.23 Printing Files Using the COPY Command

You have used COPY with a device (CON) as the source. COPY is the command, and CON is the source used to create dummy text files. You have also been using the COPY command to copy or make additional files on the same disk. You have used the TYPE command to display the contents of the text files that you created. So far, the only way you could get a hard copy of the contents of your file has been to use the <Shift> and <PrtSc> keys, but this method of printing has several disadvantages. When you use the <Shift> and <PrtSc> keys, you get *everything* that is displayed on the screen or monitor—the prompts, the commands, as well as the contents of the file. So far, your text files have been very short and have fit entirely on the screen, but what if the contents of the file were longer than the number of lines available on your screen? You would continually have to freeze the screen with the <Ctrl>+<NumLock> keys and have the contents of your file printed in sections, which is neither efficient nor attractive. There is an easier way to send or copy the contents of your file to the printer. As you copied from a device, the console, you can also copy to a device; in this case the device is the printer. Since the printer is a device, it has a reserved name: PRN for printer. You can also use LPT1 for Line Printer 1. If you use LPT1, be sure to key in the letter L, the letter P, the letter T, and the number 1. You cannot use the letter l ("ell") as the number 1.

Activity 5.24 Using the COPY Command to Print Files

Note: The DATA disk is in Drive A. The **A:\>** is displayed.

STEP 1: Turn on the printer.

STEP 2: Key in the following:
A:\>**COPY JANUARY.TXT PRN** <Enter>

Note: Laser printer users: You must take some extra steps to get the hard copy.

STEP 1: Take the printer offline by pushing the <On Line> button (the online light should turn off).
STEP 2: Press <Form Feed> (FF).
STEP 3: Push the <On Line> button to put the printer back online (the online light should turn back on).

WHAT'S HAPPENING? Even though you are using a device, the syntax remains the same. COPY is the command, the work you want done. **JANUARY.TXT** is the source, the file you want copied. You do not need to enter a drive designator in front of the file name because DOS will assume the default. (If, however, you wanted to copy a file to the printer from a subdirectory, you would need to include the path name.) PRN is the device name for the printer. The printer is the destination, where you want the contents of the file to go. As soon as you press <Enter>, you should hear/see the printer begin to print. The hard copy or output is at the printer. Your screen displays the message "1 file(s) copied." You see on the printed paper the following words:

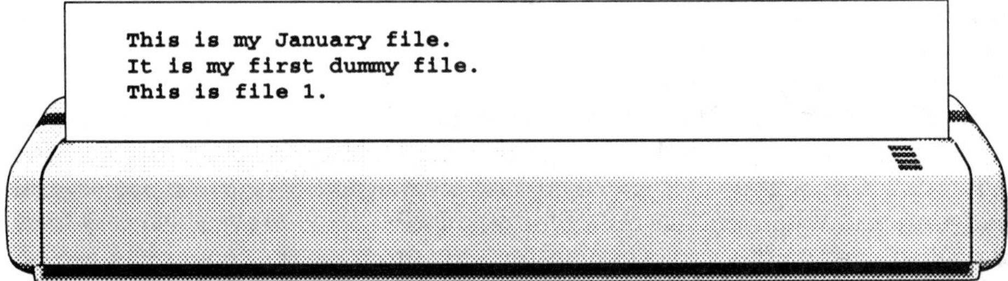
This is my January file.
It is my first dummy file.
This is file 1.

WHAT'S HAPPENING? Neither the file name nor the command line is printed, only the contents of the file or what is inside the "file folder." You can use an alternate device name that is synonymous with PRN, called LPT1. Again, remember that it is the letter L, the letter P, the letter T, and the number 1. DOS is very particular about device names. Only LPT1 is correct. Do not substitute the lowercase letter l for the number 1.

STEP 3: Key in the following:
A:\>**COPY MARCH.TXT LPT1** <Enter>

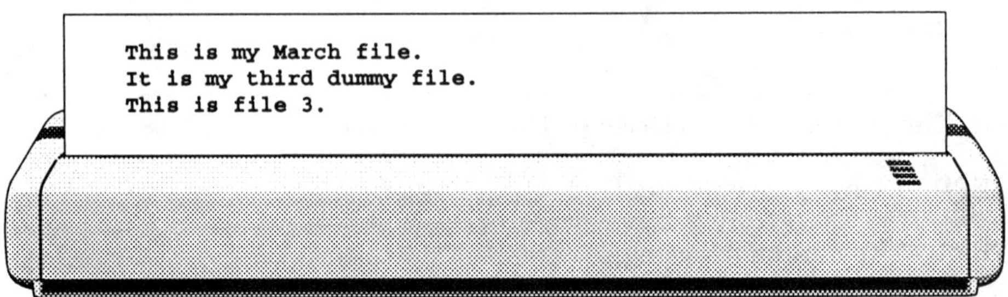
This is my March file.
It is my third dummy file.
This is file 3.

WHAT'S HAPPENING? As you can see, DOS executed the command whether you used PRN or LPT1 as the destination. You cannot use the TYPE command to print files because **TYPE JANUARY.TXT PRN** would be incorrect syntax. TYPE expects only one parameter. It is used for displaying text on the monitor, not for starting the printer.

5.25 Printing Files Using the COPY Command and Wildcards

You can also use wildcards when using COPY to print similarly named files. This procedure allows you to use one command line to print several files.

Activity 5.26 Using the COPY Command and Wildcards to Print Files

Note: The DATA disk is in Drive A. The **A:\>** is displayed.

STEP 1: Key in the following:
A:\>**COPY *.TMP PRN** <Enter>

```
A:\>COPY *.TMP PRN
JAN.TMP
FEB.TMP
MAR.TMP
APR.TMP
         1 file(s) copied

A:\>_
```

```
This is my January file.
It is my first dummy file.
This is file 1.
This is my February file.
It is my second dummy file.
This is file 2.
This is my March file.
It is my third dummy file.
This is file 3.
This is my April file.
It is my fourth dummy file.
This is file 4.
```

WHAT'S HAPPENING? The hard copy or printout wrote the contents, one file right after another with no differentiation among the files. The printout does not print the file names, only the contents of the files. You actually printed the contents of four different files. As they were printed, the file names appeared on the screen. The reason the screen display only showed one file copied was that you gave only one destination, the printer.

Note: Your screen display and printout can vary if you create the files in a different order. When you use a wildcard, DOS finds the files on a first-come, first-served basis.

Chapter Summary

1. One of the major reasons people buy computers is for application programs that assist people in different tasks.
2. Application software can also be called application packages, programs, and application programs.
3. The three major categories of application software are word processing, spreadsheets, and database managers.
4. DOS is system software.
5. Application software usually generates data. Both application software and data are stored as disk files.
6. The three major reasons for learning DOS are first, DOS must be loaded before any other software can be used. Second, DOS has commands that allow the user to manage the disk files. Third, DOS allows the user to install and manage other types of hardware devices.
7. A program file is loaded from the disk into memory and provides instructions that tell the computer what to do.
8. Programs usually generate data stored as files on the disk. Usually, only the program can use the data file.
9. DOS is the means by which the program and data are loaded into memory.
10. Another component of DOS are the commands that allow the user to manage and manipulate program and data files.
11. A data file without the application program cannot be used by itself.
12. A menu-driven program is one that presents choices to the user who selects the options, much like selecting something from a menu in a restaurant.
13. The internal commands DIR, COPY, and TYPE allow you to manage the files on a disk.
14. The file extensions `.EXE` (executable code) and `.COM` (command file) tell DOS that the file is a program.
15. DIR allows you to display the names of files on any disk on the screen. The syntax is:

    DIR [*drive:*][*path*][*filename*[*.ext*]][/P][/W]
16. TYPE allows you to display the contents of a file on the screen. The syntax is:

    TYPE [*drive:*][*path*]*filename*
17. COPY allows you to copy files selectively. You can copy files on the same disk; copy (create) files from a device, CON; and copy files to a device, PRN.
18. The syntax of the copy command is:

    COPY [*d:*][*path*][*filename*[*.ext*]] [*d:*][*path*][*filename*[*.ext*]]

A simple way to remember the COPY syntax is
COPY *source destination.*
Source is what you want to copy. *Destination* is where you want it copied.

19. The COPY command never changes the source file.
20. When you name files, you must follow the DOS file-naming rules. Every file must have a unique file name that does not exceed eight characters. A file extension is optional but, if included, must not exceed three characters. File names usually refer to what is in the file, and file extensions usually refer to the type of data in the file. Some application programs assign file extensions.
21. When naming files, it is best to stick with alphanumeric characters. Certain characters are illegal, such as the colon : and the <Space>.
22. A dummy file is a file usually created for test purposes. A dummy text file can be created using the COPY CON *filename.ext* command, which creates a "file folder." Any text data keyed in after that becomes the contents of that file.
23. When copying a file to a subdirectory, you must include the path name. The path name and the file name are separated by the backslash. The backslash is used as a delimiter. The one exception is that the root directory's name is \ or backslash.
24. Wildcards may be used with the COPY command. Wildcards may not be used with the TYPE command.
25. Files must have unique names on the same drive and subdirectory, but those files that are copied to a subdirectory may have identical names because the path makes those file names unique.

Key Terms

ASCII
CON
Database management programs
Destination file
Dummy files
Menu-driven program
Source file
Spreadsheet programs
Word processing programs

Discussion Questions

1. What is the difference between program files and data files?
2. Name two major reasons why DOS is used.
3. What tells DOS that a file on a disk is a program?
4. What is the maximum number of characters that may be used when naming a file? A file extension?
5. What command will allow you to see the file names on your disk?
6. How can you create a text file?
7. How can you print your file? What are the advantages/disadvantages of each method?
8. What command allows you to see the contents of your file displayed on the screen?
9. What is the syntax for the DIR command?
10. What is the syntax for the COPY command?

11. What is the syntax for the TYPE command?
12. What makes internal commands significant?
13. What are the major internal commands?
14. What is a path? How is it used?
15. Can you use wildcards with the COPY command? If yes, why would you use a wildcard?
16. Can you use wildcards with the DIR command? If yes, why would you use a wildcard?
17. Can you use wildcards with the TYPE command? If yes, why would you use a wildcard?
18. What are some examples of legal file names?
19. What are some characters that you cannot use in to name files?
20. Must file names be unique on a disk? Why or why not?
21. Is a file extension mandatory when naming a file?
22. Can you use the TYPE command to get a hard copy of a text file?
23. Can files with the extension **.EXE** or **.COM** be displayed on the screen with the TYPE command? What kind of display will you get?
24. Give two reasons for making a copy of a file on the same disk.
25. Name two major categories of application software.

Application Assignments

Note: Change the prompt by keying in **PROMPT pg**. The DATA disk in Drive A. The **A:\>** is displayed.

1. Create a text file to be placed on the DATA disk. Name it **HOMEWORK.DAT**. The contents of the file are as follows:

```
Today's date

I am learning how to create a text file. I am using
the console as my source. When I key in data, it is similar
to typing a document. When I am done keying in data,
I will tell DOS that I am done by pressing Ctrl+Z.
DOS will then write this file to the DATA disk.

Your name
```

   a. After you have finished creating this file, clear the screen. Then, display the contents of this file, **HOMEWORK.DAT**, on the screen. Print the screen.
   b. Print only the contents of the file **HOMEWORK.DAT**. Do not use the <Shift> and <PrtSc> keys.
2. Clear the screen. Do a directory display of the DATA disk to display the file names. If the screen is scrolling, wait until the last screen is displayed. Print this screen.
3. For the following assignment:
   a. Create three text files on the DATA disk using the COPY CON command

and the contents as shown below:

File name	Contents
`NAME.FIL`	Your name
`RESIDENC.FIL`	The city, state and zip code where you live.
`BIRTH.FIL`	The date of your birthday and your astrological sign.

b. Use the DIR command to display only the files you just created. Print this screen.
c. Display the contents of the file **NAME.FIL** on the screen. Print this screen.
d. Copy the contents of the file **RESIDENC.FIL** to the printer. Do not use the <Shift> and <PrtSc> keys.
e. Make copies of all the files with **.FIL** as an extension on the DATA disk. The file names will be the same, but the file extensions will now be **.OLD**. Use a wildcard. You will end up with three new files with **.OLD** as the file extension. Use the DIR command to display only the file names with **.OLD** as an extension on the DATA disk. Print this screen.
f. Copy the contents of all the files with **.FIL** as an extension to the printer. Do not use the <Shift> and <PrtSc> keys. Use a wildcard.
g. Make a copy of **NAME.FIL**. Call the new file **TESTING**. Use the DIR command to display only the **TESTING** file name on the screen. Print this screen.
h. Create a subdirectory on the DATA disk called **FILES**. Copy all the files with an extension of **.FIL** to this subdirectory. Do a directory display of the **FILES** subdirectory. Print this screen.

4. For the following assignment:
   a. Create three text files on the DATA disk using the COPY CON command and the contents as shown below:

File name	Contents
`BOOK.DBF`	The author and title of two of your favorite books.
`MOVIE.DBF`	The name of two of your favorite movies.
`TV.DBF`	The name of two of your favorite TV shows and the name of one of the characters in each show.

   b. Use the DIR command to display only the files you just created. Print this screen.
   c. Display the contents of the file **BOOK.DBF** on the screen. Print this screen.
   d. Copy the contents of the file **MOVIE.DBF** to the printer. Do not use the <Shift> and <PrtSc> keys.
   e. Make copies of all the files with **.DBF** as an extension on the DATA disk. The file names will be the same, but the file extensions will now be **.BAC**. Use a wildcard. You will end up with three new files with **.BAC** as the file

extension. Use the DIR command to display only the file names with **.BAC** as an extension on the DATA disk. Print this screen.

f. Copy the contents of all the files with **.DBF** as an extension to the printer. Do not use the <Shift> and <PrtSc> keys. Use a wildcard.

g. Make a copy of the **TV.DBF** file. Call the new file **DISKFILE**. Use the DIR command to display only the **DISKFILE** file name on the screen. Print this screen.

h. Create a subdirectory on the DATA disk called **DATA**. Copy all the files with an extension of **.DBF** to this subdirectory. Do a directory display of the **DATA** subdirectory. Print this screen.

Challenge Assignment

5. Place the ACTIVITIES disk in Drive A. Load the ADDRESS program. When it asks you to enter the name of the data file, key in **MYPHONE** and press <Enter>. Then follow the prompts on the screen to get to the main menu. Once you are at the main menu, press the F2 key to "Add an Entry." You will be presented with a screen that allows you to enter data. Key in the names and addresses of five people. When you finish entering the names and addresses, press the F4 key, which will take you back to the main menu. Press the F8 key, which exits to DOS. The message will say, "Do you wish to save changes before exiting?" Press Y.

   a. Use the DIR command to display the file name, **MYPHONE**. Print the screen.
   b. Display the contents of **MYPHONE** on the screen. Print this screen.
   c. Copy **MYPHONE** to the subdirectory **TEST** on the ACTIVITIES disk, keeping the file name the same. Display the file name in the subdirectory **TEST**. Print the screen.
   d. Copy **MYPHONE** to the subdirectory **TEST** on the ACTIVITIES disk, but call it **LIST** when you copy it. Display the file name, **LIST**, in the subdirectory **TEST**. Print the screen.

Chapter 6

Expanding the Use of the COPY Command

After completing this chapter you will be able to:

1. Copy a file to another disk.
2. Create a subdirectory.
3. Copy a file to another disk and keep the same file name.
4. Copy files to another disk with a new file name.
5. Make a subdirectory on another disk and copy files to that disk and subdirectory with the same file name.
6. Copy files from one disk and subdirectory to another disk and subdirectory with different file names.
7. Overwrite a file using the COPY command.
8. Use wildcards with the COPY command to copy files to another disk.
9. Use wildcards with the COPY command to copy files to different drives and subdirectories.
10. Use wildcards to copy data files to another disk and subdirectory.
11. Use the COPY command to verify that a file has been copied correctly.
12. Combine the contents of two or more files using the COPY command.

Chapter Overview

The COPY command is one of the most used commands. You used it in the last chapter to make copies of files. However, there are many more uses for the COPY command. It can be used to make backup copies, to copy files to another disk or another subdirectory with the same name or with a file name change, to overwrite files, to combine the contents of two or more files, and to verify that a file has been copied correctly.

In this chapter you will continue to explore how and when to use the COPY command and to use wildcards with the COPY command. You will continue learning about subdirectories, while learning how to reinforce the use of the DIR and TYPE commands. Lastly you will learn how and when to overwrite files.

6.0 Copying Files to Another Disk

The COPY command, introduced in Chapter 5, is an internal command. It is always there to use once you have booted the system. Internal commands remain in memory even if the DOS System Disk is not in any drive and even if you are not logged into the \DOS subdirectory. Internal commands remain resident in memory until you turn off the computer.

COPY is one of the most used internal commands. In Chapter 5, you used COPY to make duplicate copies of files. You also used wildcards to make copies of files and to create some text files. In this chapter you are going to explore the other uses of the COPY command. The important point to remember is that the syntax *always* is:

COPY *source destination*

or, in a syntax diagram:

COPY [*drive:*][*path*]*filename* [*drive:*][*path*]*filename*[*.ext*]

The latest abbreviated syntax diagram is:

COPY *source* [*destination*]

source	Specifies the file or files to be copied
destination	Specifies the directory and/or filename for the new file(s)

When using any command, you must first enter the command to tell the system what work is to be done. Then you enter any mandatory parameters that the command requires. The mandatory parameters for the COPY command are the *source* (what you want to copy) and the *destination* (where you want the source copied to). You do not key in the brackets, only what is inside the brackets. Do not key in *drive:*, which indicates the designated drive or drive specifier because *drive:* is a variable parameter. You must substitute the letter of the drive you want.

Often you wish to copy files to another disk in order to make backup copies, copy a program file (external command) to another disk, or share data files with an associate. The following activities will demonstrate how to copy files from one disk to another.

You can specify not only which drive [*drive:*] a file is on but also what path [*path*] the COPY command should follow. The path is a variable parameter. Paths are used most commonly with hard disks or with high-capacity disks. You substitute the specific path name you are seeking for the word [*path*]. However, you do not key in the brackets or the word "path."

6.1 A Brief Introduction to Subdirectories and Paths

A hard disk can be compared to a large office building under construction. Part of the completion process is to divide the large, open area into many separate offices. Life would be very difficult if there were no offices in this building. If you went into an office building for an appointment with an accounting firm, you would have to stop at every desk to ask if it were the accounting firm you sought.

A hard disk is divided into subdirectories as a building is divided into offices. The user does not have to look at every file on the hard disk to find a group of related files. Instead, all the accounting data files and programs for your company would be placed into a subdirectory named **ACCOUNTING**. To carry this analogy further, it would be very difficult to find a specific office without a guide. You really do not want to wander from office to office looking for an accounting firm. Thus, when you walk into the office building, you usually go to the building directory to locate the room number of the office you seek. The directory is a list that indicates where the specific office is located. The term path serves the same function for a disk. You don't have to "wander" from subdirectory to subdirectory. You can tell DOS specifically where the "office" is by means of the path.

Just as an office building can add new offices or remove existing offices, a user can both make and remove subdirectories with the special commands MD and RD. However, as in an office building, putting a sign on the door saying "Jones Accounting Firm" does not mean there is anything in that office yet. The accountants have to move in. The same is true for subdirectories. Creating subdirectories means creating an "office" where files can be placed. A subdirectory is created by the command MD (make directory), but until you copy files into the subdirectory, it is just a shell.

In addition, in an office building, you are not limited to looking at a list of the offices. You can physically visit any office. Again, the same is true with subdirectories. Just as you can change the default drive, you can also change the default subdirectory by means of the CD command (current or change directory). Thus, you can physically place your arena of work in the specific subdirectory so that it becomes the default subdirectory.

The command for creating a subdirectory is MD. The syntax is:

MD [*drive:*]*path*

The drive is optional, but the path name is mandatory. You substitute the letter of the drive on which you wish to create a subdirectory. You then follow that with the name of the subdirectory (path). The subdirectory can be any name you wish, but it must follow the DOS file-naming rules. Usually, subdirectories do not have file extensions.

To ensure that you will be able to follow the text, the remainder of the text assumes that a subdirectory called **C:\JUNK** has been installed on the hard disk and that all the directories and files have been copied from the ACTIVITIES disk to the **C:\JUNK** subdirectory on the hard disk. Since many of the activities in the text involve using the **C:\JUNK** subdirectory, the creation of this subdirectory will eliminate floppy disk swapping. If you are not working in a laboratory environment or if the **C:\JUNK** subdirectory has not been set up for you, please refer to Special Section 6.18 and Special Activity 6.19 at the end of this chapter for the instructions to create **C:\JUNK** and copy the files and subdirectories to the hard disk.

Activity 6.2

Copying Files to Another Disk and Keeping the Same File Name

Note: Key in **PROMPT pg**. The **C:\>** is displayed.

STEP 1: Key in the following:
C:\>**CD \JUNK** <Enter>

```
C:\>CD \JUNK

C:\JUNK>_
```

WHAT'S HAPPENING? Drive C is still the default drive, but you have now made JUNK the default subdirectory. Just as you can change default drives, you can also change default subdirectories. The command is CD and the syntax is CD [*drive:*][*path*]. Since both optional parameters are not required, CD with no parameters shows you what the default subdirectory is. CD followed by the path name changes the default subdirectory.

STEP 2: Insert the disk labeled DATA disk in Drive A.

WHAT'S HAPPENING? The work you want to do now is to copy files from one disk to another. Since COPY is an internal command, you do not need the DOS System Disk in the drive, nor do you need to be logged into the DOS subdirectory. The internal commands are in memory or RAM until you turn off the computer. In order to copy files from one disk to another, you have to place the disks in the disk drives so that you can access the files you want to copy. In other words, you are setting up the work activity area. You want to copy files from the subdirectory C:\JUNK, which has all the ACTIVITIES disk files. The destination will be the DATA disk. For this activity the \JUNK subdirectory is where you are logged in; \JUNK should be the current default subdirectory. The COPY command must be able to locate the files before it can copy them.

STEP 3: Key in the following:
C:\JUNK>**DIR HELLO.TXT** <Enter>

```
C:\JUNK>DIR HELLO.TXT

   Volume in drive C is MS-DOS_5
   Volume Serial Number is 16D1-68D4
   Directory of C:\JUNK

HELLO     TXT      52   11-23-92   7:07a
        1 file(s)          52 bytes
                      9187328 bytes free

C:\JUNK>_
```

WHAT'S HAPPENING? You asked DOS to see if you had a file called HELLO.TXT in the \JUNK subdirectory, which is the default drive and subdirectory, and DOS confirmed that the file you want to copy is there.

STEP 4: Key in the following:
C:\JUNK>**DIR A:HELLO.TXT** <Enter>

```
C:\JUNK>DIR A:HELLO.TXT

   Volume in drive A is DATA DISK
   Volume Serial Number is 3839-0EC8
   Directory of A:\

File not found

C:\JUNK>_
```

WHAT'S HAPPENING? You asked DOS to look for the file on the DATA disk. DOS told you there is no file by that name on the DATA disk. Preceding the file name, **HELLO.TXT**, you had to place a drive letter so that DOS would know on which disk drive to look.

STEP 5: Key in the following:
C:\JUNK>**COPY HELLO.TXT A:** <Enter>

```
C:\JUNK>COPY HELLO.TXT A:
        1 file(s) copied

C:\JUNK>_
```

WHAT'S HAPPENING? You said COPY (the command or the work you wanted done) the source (the file named **HELLO** with the file extension of **.TXT**, located on the hard disk in the **\JUNK** subdirectory) to the destination (the DATA disk). Since you did not supply a file name, how did DOS know what name to give the file on the DATA disk? The answer has to do with default values or assumptions. The command you keyed in is a "shorthand" version of the syntax for the COPY command. The "longhand" version or complete command would look like the following:

COPY C:\JUNK\HELLO.TXT A:\HELLO.TXT

DOS makes certain assumptions when you do not key in all the information. You must always key in the command; in this case, the command is COPY. You must always key in a source. The source is C:, the physical disk drive. In addition, DOS also needs the path or subdirectory of **\JUNK**. This specification tells DOS where to look for this file. However, you did not need to include **C:\JUNK**. Since you gave DOS no other instructions, it assumes or defaults to where you are logged in, which is **C:\JUNK**. It is looking for the file called **HELLO.TXT** on the default drive in the default subdirectory. You must always have a destination or where you want the file copied to. Your destination in this case is the DATA disk in Drive A.

You did not have to follow the drive designator letter with the root directory (\) because the assumption or default the COPY command makes is that if you do not indicate the subdirectory you want, DOS will use the destination default subdirectory. You did not need to include the destination file name or file specification, if you wish to keep the same file name. DOS assumes that the destination file name will be the same as the source file name, unless you tell it otherwise. However, the process is different when copying a file from the same disk and the same subdirectory. On the same disk and subdirectory, files may not have the same file specification—each file has to have a unique name. However, since you are going to a different disk, you can use the same file name.

STEP 6: Key in the following:
C:\JUNK>**DIR A:HELLO.TXT** <Enter>

```
C:\JUNK>DIR A:HELLO.TXT

   Volume in drive A is DATA DISK
   Volume Serial Number is 3839-0EC8
   Directory of A:\

HELLO       TXT       52    11-23-92   7:07a
         1 file(s)           52 bytes
                         319488 bytes free

C:\JUNK>_
```

WHAT'S HAPPENING? By using the DIR command, you verified that the file called **HELLO.TXT** was copied to the root directory of the DATA disk. You can use the TYPE command to see if the contents of **HELLO.TXT** located in **C:\JUNK** and on **A:** are identical.

STEP 7: Key in the following:
C:\JUNK>**TYPE HELLO.TXT** <Enter>

STEP 8: Key in the following:
C:\JUNK>**TYPE A:HELLO.TXT** <Enter>

```
C:\JUNK>TYPE HELLO.TXT
HELLO, EVERYONE.
HOW ARE YOU?
ISN'T THIS FUN???

C:\JUNK>TYPE A:HELLO.TXT
HELLO, EVERYONE.
HOW ARE YOU?
ISN'T THIS FUN???

C:\JUNK>_
```

WHAT'S HAPPENING? As you can see, you successfully copied the file called **HELLO.TXT** from the hard disk in the **\JUNK** subdirectory to the DATA disk. The file names are the same and the contents of the two files are identical.

Activity 6.3 Copying Files to Another Disk with Another File Name

STEP 1: You should be logged into the subdirectory **C:\JUNK**. You can be sure by keying in C:\>**CD \JUNK**. The DATA disk should be in Drive A.

STEP 2: Key in the following:
C:\JUNK>**COPY HELLO.TXT A:HI.TXT** <Enter>

```
C:\JUNK>COPY HELLO.TXT A:HI.TXT
        1 file(s) copied

C:\JUNK>_
```

WHAT'S HAPPENING? The syntax of the COPY command has not changed. You said COPY (the command or the work you wanted done) the source (the file named **HELLO** with the file extension of **.TXT**, located on the hard disk) to the destination (the DATA disk), followed by the "new" file name, **HI.TXT**. Since you assigned a new file name, **HI.TXT**, DOS used it. The only default value DOS used was the one that assumed **HELLO.TXT** was located on the hard disk in the **\JUNK** subdirectory. DOS did not use any default value for the new file name on the DATA disk because you supplied the file name you wanted DOS to use, in this case, **HI.TXT**. Remember, a computer follows your instructions. It only uses default values when you do not tell it what to do. You now have two files on the DATA disk in the root directory with the same file contents but different file names, **HELLO.TXT** and **HI.TXT**. DOS does not know that the file contents are identical.

STEP 3: Key in the following:
C:\JUNK>**TYPE A:HELLO.TXT** <Enter>

STEP 4: Key in the following:
C:\JUNK>**TYPE A:HI.TXT** <Enter>

```
C:\JUNK>TYPE A:HELLO.TXT
HELLO, EVERYONE.
HOW ARE YOU?
ISN'T THIS FUN???

C:\JUNK>TYPE A:HI.TXT
HELLO, EVERYONE.
HOW ARE YOU?
ISN'T THIS FUN???

C:\JUNK>_
```

WHAT'S HAPPENING? The contents of the file are identical; only the file names are different. You used the correct syntax, COPY *source destination*. As you can see, you can either let the system use default values, or you can provide the values you want.

6.4 Working with Subdirectories on Other Disks

Subdirectories can be created on any disk. Files can be copied to any disk and any subdirectory as long as you give DOS the proper instructions, telling DOS specifically where the source file is located, including both the drive and subdirectory, and giving the destination, including both the drive and subdirectory. If you do not include the drive or path in either the source or destination, DOS will always assume the default.

Activity 6.5 How to Make a Subdirectory on and Copy Files to Another Disk and Subdirectory while Keeping the Same File Name

STEP 1: You should be logged into the subdirectory **C:\JUNK**. You can be sure by keying in C:\JUNK>**CD \JUNK**. The DATA disk should be in Drive A. Again, be sure that you follow the instructions exactly, including the disk drives and backslashes.

STEP 2: Key in the following:
C:\JUNK>**MD A:\USERS** <Enter>

```
C:\JUNK>MD A:\USERS

C:\JUNK>_
```

WHAT'S HAPPENING? You created a subdirectory on the DATA disk under the root directory called **USERS**, like a "divider" in a file drawer. There are no files in this subdirectory yet. You can verify this by using the DIR command.

STEP 3: Key in the following:
C:\JUNK>**DIR A:\USERS** <Enter>

```
C:\JUNK>DIR A:\USERS

   Volume in drive A is DATA DISK
   Volume Serial Number is 3839-0EC8
   Directory of A:\USERS

.              <DIR>     05-07-93 10:05a
..             <DIR>     05-07-93 10:05a
        2 file(s)             0 bytes
                         317440 bytes free

C:\JUNK>_
```

WHAT'S HAPPENING? There are no files in this new subdirectory on the DATA disk. The two entries, **. <DIR>** and **.. <DIR>**, are subdirectory entries.

STEP 4: Key in the following:
C:\JUNK>**COPY ADDRESS.EXE A:\USERS** <Enter>

```
C:\JUNK>COPY ADDRESS.EXE A:\USERS
        1 file(s) copied

C:\JUNK>_
```

WHAT'S HAPPENING? You said COPY the source file, **ADDRESS.EXE** from the subdirectory **\JUNK** on the hard disk to the subdirectory called **USERS** on the DATA disk. You used the shorthand version, letting DOS use the default assumptions. The longhand version would be:

COPY C:\JUNK\ADDRESS.EXE A:\USERS\ADDRESS.EXE

You did need the command COPY, but you did not need the default source drive because DOS assumed the default drive, C:. You did not need to include the default subdirectory because DOS assumed the default subdirectory, **\JUNK**. However, when you entered the destination, you did need the drive designator, A:. Otherwise DOS would have assumed the default for the destination drive. You also needed to include the destination subdirectory, **USERS**. If you had not included that parameter, DOS would have assumed the default subdirectory, the root directory on the DATA disk. Since you did not give a destination file name, DOS assumed you wanted the file called **ADDRESS.EXE**.

STEP 5: Key in the following:

C:\JUNK>**DIR A:\USERS** <Enter>

```
C:\JUNK>DIR A:\USERS

   Volume in drive A is DATA DISK
   Volume Serial Number is 3839-0EC8
   Directory of A:\USERS

.             <DIR>      05-07-93 10:05a
..            <DIR>      05-07-93 10:05a
ADDRESS  EXE  30960      01-15-88  4:10p
        3 file(s)        30960 bytes
                        285696 bytes free

C:\JUNK>_
```

WHAT'S HAPPENING? You successfully copied the file called **ADDRESS.EXE** from the **\JUNK** subdirectory on the hard disk to the DATA disk in the subdirectory **USERS**.

6.6 Copying Files between Disks and Subdirectories while Changing File Names

Files can be copied from any disk and subdirectory to any other disk and subdirectory as long as you give DOS the proper instructions, telling DOS specifically where the source file is located, including both the drive and subdirectory, and giving it the destination, including both the drive and subdirectory. If you do not include the drive or path in either the source or destination, DOS always assumes the default.

Activity 6.7

How to Copy Files between Disks and Subdirectories while Changing File Names

Note: The **C:\JUNK>** should be displayed. The DATA disk is in Drive A.

STEP 1: Key in the following:
C:\JUNK>**COPY DATA\TEA.TAX A:\USERS\TEA.TIM** <Enter>

```
C:\JUNK>COPY  DATA\TEA.TAX  A:\USERS\TEA.TIM
        1 file(s) copied

C:\JUNK>_
```

WHAT'S HAPPENING? You copied the file called **TEA.TAX** from the hard disk (**\JUNK** subdirectory) from the subdirectory **DATA** to the DATA disk subdirectory **USERS**, and you gave it a new name on the DATA disk, **TEA.TIM**. There is something very significant about how the command was keyed in. If you look at the longhand syntax, you can see what is mandatory to key in and what is assumed.

COPY	[*d:*] [*path*] *filename* [*.ext*]	[*d:*] [*path*] *filename* [*.ext*]
COPY	**C:\JUNK\DATA\ TEA .TAX**	**A:\ USERS\ TEA .TIM**

For the source, you did not need to key in **C:\JUNK**. Since the default drive is C: and the default subdirectory is **JUNK**, DOS assumed the default. You did not need the \ following **JUNK** because that is the delimiter that would separate **JUNK** from **DATA**. However, you did have to key in the second subdirectory name, **DATA**, and key in the next backslash because it is needed as a delimiter between the subdirectory name, **DATA**, and the file name, **TEA.TAX**. The tricky thing here is that if you had keyed in **COPY \DATA\TEA.TAX**, DOS would have gone to the root directory. There is no subdirectory called **DATA** in the root directory. **DATA** is only under the subdirectory **JUNK**. A simple rule of thumb to follow is that the first backslash *always* means the root directory. Any other backslash is a delimiter. The destination needed to have the **A:** to tell DOS which drive to write the file to. DOS did not need the first backslash because it assumed the root as the default. However, it did need the second backslash between the subdirectory name, **USERS**, and the destination file name, **TEA.TIM**, as a delimiter between the directory name and the file name.

STEP 2: Key in the following:
C:\JUNK>**DIR A:\USERS** <Enter>

```
C:\JUNK>DIR A:\USERS

    Volume in drive A is DATA DISK
    Volume Serial Number is 3839-0EC8
    Directory of A:\USERS
```

```
.            <DIR>        05-07-93 10:05a
..           <DIR>        05-07-93 10:05a
ADDRESS   EXE   30960     01-15-88  4:10p
TEA       TIM      51     11-23-92 10:15a
         4 file(s)        31011 bytes
                         284672 bytes free

C:\JUNK>_
```

WHAT'S HAPPENING? You successfully copied the file called **TEA.TAX** from the **\JUNK** subdirectory on the hard disk to the DATA disk in the subdirectory **USERS** and you gave it a new name, **TEA.TIM**.

6.8 How to Overwrite Files with the COPY Command

When you made copies of files, you gave the files on the same disk and in the same subdirectory unique names. One of the reasons for doing this is that, when you tried to use the same file name on the same disk, you got an error message, "File cannot be copied onto itself, 0 file(s) copied." DOS would not permit you to make that error. However, the rule of unique file names is only true if the files are on the same disk and subdirectory. If you are using more than one disk or more than one subdirectory, DOS will let you use the same file name. There have been no problems so far because, when you copied the source file from one disk to the destination file on another disk, it was a new file on the destination disk. However, if you already had a file on the destination disk with the same file name, DOS would not give you the error message saying, "File cannot be copied onto itself, 0 file(s) copied." It would merely *overwrite* the destination file with the contents of the source file. **Overwrite** means just what it says; it writes over or replaces what used to be in that file. Hence, if the contents of the source file are different from the contents of the destination file, the destination and source file will now have not only the same file name but also the same file contents. The previous contents of the destination file will be gone. Overwriting also happens on the same disk when the destination filename already exists. The same rules apply to subdirectories. See Figure 6.1 for a graphic representation of this.

A:THIS.FIL
This data will overwrite any data in the destination file.

B:THIS.FIL
This data will be replaced by the data in the source file.

BEFORE

C:\>COPY A:THIS.FIL B:

A:THIS.FIL
This data will overwrite any data in the destination file.

B:THIS.FIL
This data will overwrite any data in the destination file.

AFTER

Figure 6.1 Overwriting Files

This process seems dangerous because you could lose the data in a file. You may wonder why DOS does not protect you against this error as it does when you try to copy a file with the same name on the same disk and subdirectory. The programmers who wrote DOS do not protect you because to DOS it is not an error. In working with computers, typically, you do want to overwrite files.

Data, or what is inside a file, changes all the time. For example, if you have a customer list stored as a file named **CUSTOMER.LST** on a disk, the information in the file or (the data) changes as you add customers, delete customers, and update information about customers. When you have completed your work for the day, you want to **backup** your file or copy it to another disk, because you are working with it on a daily basis. Thus, you have a file called **CUSTOMER.LST** on your source disk and a file called **CUSTOMER.LST** on your destination disk. Since **CUSTOMER.LST** is a clearly descriptive file name, you really do not want to create a new file name every time you copy the file to the destination disk because creating new file names and then tracking current files can be time-consuming and confusing. In addition, as you can see, if you are working with a file on a daily basis, you could end up with hundreds of file names. In reality, you do not care about last week's or yesterday's customer information, or the old file; you care about the current version and its backup file. Thus, when copying a file for backup purposes, you do want the source file to overwrite the destination file. To demonstrate how this process works, you are going to create a file on the DATA disk and overwrite it with a file from the hard disk that has the same file name.

Activity 6.9 Overwriting Files Using the COPY Command

Note: The **C:\JUNK>** is displayed. The DATA disk is in Drive A. Remember that <Ctrl>+Z means holding down the <Control> key while pressing the letter Z. The easier way is simply to press the <F6> key.

STEP 1: Key in the following:

```
C:\JUNK>COPY CON A:TEST.TXT <Enter>
The contents of this <Enter>
file will be replaced <Enter>
by the contents of the <Enter>
file created on the <Enter>
ACTIVITIES disk. <Enter>
<Ctrl>+Z <Enter>
```

WHAT'S HAPPENING? You have created a text file with COPY as the command, CON as the source, and **TEST.TXT** as the destination. The file **TEST.TXT**, however, was written to the DATA disk.

STEP 2: Key in the following:

```
C:\JUNK>TYPE TEST.TXT <Enter>
```

STEP 3: Key in the following:

```
C:\JUNK>TYPE A:TEST.TXT <Enter>
```

```
C:\JUNK>TYPE TEST.TXT
This is a test file.
It will show how to
overwrite a file.
```

```
C:\JUNK>TYPE A:TEST.TXT
The contents of this
file will be replaced
by the contents of the
file created on the
ACTIVITIES disk.

C:\JUNK>_
```

WHAT'S HAPPENING? The contents of the files are different, even though the file names are the same.

STEP 4: Key in the following:
C:\JUNK>**COPY TEST.TXT TEST.TXT** <Enter>

```
C:\JUNK>COPY TEST.TXT TEST.TXT
File cannot be copied onto itself
        0 file(s) copied

C:\JUNK>_
```

WHAT'S HAPPENING? You tried to make a copy of a file with the same file name on the same disk in the same disk drive and in the same subdirectory. DOS will not let you overwrite the file on the same disk. You already have a file called **TEST.TXT** in the **\JUNK** subdirectory on the hard disk. Now you are going to copy the file with the same name from one disk to another.

STEP 5: Key in the following:
C:\JUNK>**COPY TEST.TXT A:TEST.TXT** <Enter>

```
C:\JUNK>COPY TEST.TXT A:TEST.TXT
        1 file(s) copied

C:\JUNK>_
```

WHAT'S HAPPENING? You could have written the command as **COPY TEST.TXT A:**. You did not need to key in **A:TEST.TXT**. COPY is the command; **C:\JUNK\TEST.TXT** is the source, but since you are in the **C:\JUNK** subdirectory, DOS defaults to **C:\JUNK**; **A:** is the destination, and DOS assumes that the file name is **TEST.TXT**, since you did not specify otherwise.

This time you did not get an error message. The file **TEST.TXT** was successfully copied from the hard disk to the DATA disk. But what about the contents of the file? The files still have the same name. Did anything change?

STEP 6: Key in the following:
C:\JUNK>**TYPE TEST.TXT** <Enter>

STEP 7: Key in the following:
C:\JUNK>**TYPE A:TEST.TXT** <Enter>

```
C:\JUNK>TYPE TEST.TXT
This is a test file.
It will show how to
overwrite a file.

C:\JUNK>TYPE A:TEST.TXT
This is a test file.
It will show how to
overwrite a file.

C:\JUNK>_
```

WHAT'S HAPPENING? The file contents are identical. What used to be inside the file called **TEST.TXT** located on the DATA disk has been overwritten or replaced (gone forever) by the contents of the file called **TEST.TXT** located in the **\JUNK** subdirectory on the hard disk. You should be aware of how this procedure works so that you do not overwrite a file accidentally.

Overwriting also occurs on the same disk or subdirectory if the source file and destination file have different names.

STEP 8: Key in the following:
C:\JUNK>**TYPE A:TEST.TXT** <Enter>

STEP 9: Key in the following:
C:\JUNK>**TYPE A:HI.TXT** <Enter>

```
C:\JUNK>TYPE A:TEST.TXT
This is a test file.
It will show how to
overwrite a file.

C:\JUNK>TYPE A:HI.TXT
HELLO, EVERYONE.
HOW ARE YOU?
ISN'T THIS FUN???

C:\JUNK>_
```

WHAT'S HAPPENING? You have displayed two separate files on the screen, **HI.TXT** and **TEST.TXT**, which are on the DATA disk. The file names and file contents are different.

STEP 10: Key in the following:
C:\JUNK>**COPY A:TEST.TXT A:HI.TXT** <Enter>

```
C:\JUNK>COPY A:TEST.TXT A:HI.TXT
        1 file(s) copied

C:\JUNK>_
```

WHAT'S HAPPENING? You did not get an error message telling you that you already had an existing file called **HI.TXT**. DOS just overwrote the contents of **HI.TXT** with the contents of **TEST.TXT**. You can prove that this occurred by using the TYPE command.

STEP 11: Key in the following:
C:\JUNK>**TYPE A:TEST.TXT** <Enter>

STEP 12: Key in the following:
C:\JUNK>**TYPE A:HI.TXT** <Enter>

```
C:\JUNK>TYPE A:TEST.TXT
This is a test file.
It will show how to
overwrite a file.

C:\JUNK>TYPE A:HI.TXT
This is a test file.
It will show how to
overwrite a file.

C:\JUNK>_
```

WHAT'S HAPPENING? The contents of the existing file **HI.TXT** was overwritten by the content of the file **TEST.TXT**. Overwriting files is the norm. You do not overwrite when the source file and the destination file on the same disk and same subdirectory have *exactly* the same file specification. This process works the same when dealing with subdirectories.

STEP 13: Key in the following:
C:\JUNK>**TYPE A:TEST.TXT** <Enter>

STEP 14: Key in the following:
C:\JUNK>**TYPE A:\USERS\TEA.TIM** <Enter>

```
C:\JUNK>TYPE A:TEST.TXT
This is a test file.
It will show how to
overwrite a file.

C:\JUNK>TYPE A:\USERS\TEA.TIM
This is a file that was
written as a test file.

C:\JUNK>_
```

WHAT'S HAPPENING? The files have different names, different contents, and are in different subdirectories.

STEP 15: Key in the following:
C:\JUNK>**COPY A:\TEST.TXT A:\USERS\TEA.TIM** <Enter>

```
C:\JUNK>COPY A:\TEST.TXT A:\USERS\TEA.TIM
        1 file(s) copied

C:\JUNK>_
```

WHAT'S HAPPENING? DOS has overwritten the contents of the file **TEA.TIM**, located in the subdirectory **USERS** on the DATA disk with the contents of the file called **TEST.TXT** located in the root directory on the DATA disk. You can prove this occurred by using the TYPE command.

STEP 16: Key in the following:
C:\JUNK>**TYPE A:\TEST.TXT** <Enter>

STEP 17: Key in the following:
C:\JUNK>**TYPE A:\USERS\TEA.TIM** <Enter>

```
C:\JUNK>TYPE A:\TEST.TXT
This is a test file.
It will show how to
overwrite a file.

C:\JUNK>TYPE A:\USERS\TEA.TIM
This is a test file.
It will show how to
overwrite a file.

C:\JUNK>_
```

WHAT'S HAPPENING? The contents of the two files are identical. You did overwrite the destination file with the contents of the source file.

6.10 Using Wildcards to Copy Files to Different Drives

In this chapter, in order to copy files from one disk to another, you had to key in each file name as a source and each drive designator and file name as a destination. This process can become very tedious, particularly when you wish to copy a group of files. Usually, you work with groups of files. There is a shortcut you can take, using the global file specifications (wildcards) of * or ? that you used to copy files on the same disk in Chapter 5. Rather than having to key in the entire file name, you look for a common denominator so that you can copy the files as a group. You use the drive designator (A: or B: or C:) so that the COPY command knows which disk drive to look on for the files to copy and if you are in a subdirectory, you include the path name (the source) and the disk drive the files are going to be copied to (the destination).

Activity 6.11 Using Wildcards to Copy Data Files to Another Disk

Note: The **C:\JUNK>** is displayed. The DATA disk is in Drive A.

STEP 1: Key in the following:
C:\JUNK>**DIR *.DOS** <Enter>

```
C:\JUNK>DIR *.DOS

   Volume in drive C is MS-DOS_5
   Volume Serial Number is 16D1-68D4
   Directory of C:\JUNK

WILDONE  DOS     180   05-07-93  9:02a
WILDTWO  DOS     181   05-07-93  9:03a
WILDTHR  DOS     180   05-07-93  9:03a
        3 file(s)        541 bytes
                     9451520 bytes free

C:\JUNK>_
```

WHAT'S HAPPENING? Since global file specifications are so inclusive or "global," before you initiate any activity, it is always a good idea to verify the files you are really going to use with the parameters. DIR is a good test command to use because all DIR does is display the files you have selected. Files are not affected by just displaying their file names on the screen. If you are worried about overwriting files on the destination disk, it is a good idea to use the DIR command on the DATA disk.

STEP 2: Key in the following:
C:\JUNK>**DIR A:*.DOS** <Enter>

```
C:\JUNK>DIR A:*.DOS

   Volume in drive A is DATA DISK
   Volume Serial Number is 3839-0EC8
   Directory of A:\

File not found

C:\JUNK>_
```

WHAT'S HAPPENING? You have verified which files you are going to select to copy, and you have verified that there are no files by those names on the DATA disk. Now you can do the work.

STEP 3: Key in the following:
C:\JUNK>**COPY *.DOS A:** <Enter>

```
C:\JUNK>COPY *.DOS A:
WILDONE.DOS
WILDTWO.DOS
WILDTHR.DOS
        3 file(s) copied

C:\JUNK>_
```

WHAT'S HAPPENING? You asked DOS to copy the contents of all the files with any file name and the file extension of **.DOS** in the **\JUNK** subdirectory on the hard disk to the DATA disk in the root directory. You want all the file names on the DATA disk to be the same as they are on the hard disk. As the files are found on the hard disk and copied to the DATA disk, you will see their names displayed on the screen, one file at a time.

Note: If the file names appear in a different order on the screen, there is no problem. The order of files on the screen is determined by the order DOS found on the source disk. The order will not affect the outcome of the COPY command. All the files with a **.DOS** extension on the hard disk remain there; you are simply making copies of these files on the DATA disk, which is no different from keying in C:\JUNK>**COPY WILDONE.DOS A:**, then C:\JUNK>**COPY WILDTWO.DOS A:**, and C:\JUNK>**COPY WILDTHR.DOS A:**. Wildcards save keystrokes. Now, were the files copied?

STEP 4: Key in the following:
C:\JUNK>**DIR *.DOS** <Enter>

STEP 5: Key in the following:
C:\JUNK>**DIR A:*.DOS** <Enter>

```
C:\JUNK>DIR *.DOS

   Volume in drive C is MS-DOS_5
   Volume Serial Number is 16D1-68D4
   Directory of C:\JUNK

WILDONE   DOS      180   05-07-93   9:02a
WILDTWO   DOS      181   05-07-93   9:03a
WILDTHR   DOS      180   05-07-93   9:03a
        3 file(s)          541 bytes
                       9451520 bytes free

C:\JUNK>DIR A:*.DOS

   Volume in drive A is DATA DISK
   Volume Serial Number is 3839-0EC8
   Directory of A:\

WILDONE   DOS      180   05-07-93   9:02a
WILDTWO   DOS      181   05-07-93   9:03a
WILDTHR   DOS      180   05-07-93   9:03a
        3 file(s)          541 bytes
                        280576 bytes free

C:\JUNK>_
```

WHAT'S HAPPENING? By doing a directory display of the specified files, you now know that the ***.DOS** files are still in the **\JUNK** subdirectory on the hard disk and you have copies of these files on the DATA disk. Furthermore, you can also use combinations of the ? and the *.

STEP 6: Key in the following:

C:\JUNK>`COPY WILD?.* A:` <Enter>

```
C:\JUNK>COPY WILD?.* A:
WILD1.XXX
WILD2.YYY
WILD3.ZZZ
        3 file(s) copied

C:\JUNK>_
```

WHAT'S HAPPENING? Again, do not be concerned if the files do not appear on the screen in the exact order shown here. You copied a different set of files. `WILD?.*` is completely different from `*.DOS`, even though all the `*.DOS` files started with the word `WILD`. You asked DOS to copy all the files that had names starting with `WILD` but were only five characters in length (`WILD?`). That is why the `WILDONE`, `WILDTWO`, and `WILDTHR` files were not selected. Their file names were longer than five characters. The * represented any file extension which is why you could get files that had extensions of `.XXX`, `.YYY`, and `.ZZZ`.

STEP 7: Key in the following:

C:\JUNK>`COPY W*.* A:` <Enter>

```
C:\JUNK>COPY W*.* A:
WILDONE.DOS
WILDTWO.DOS
WILDTHR.DOS
WILD1.XXX
WILD2.YYY
WILD3.ZZZ
WILDONE
        7 file(s) copied

C:\JUNK>_
```

WHAT'S HAPPENING? You copied all the files in the `\JUNK` subdirectory on the hard disk that started with the letter `W` and had any file name and any or no file extension. The file called `WILDONE` had no file extension. You did overwrite files, but that was your intent. You can also use wildcards to copy files and change the file names on the destination disk.

STEP 8: Key in the following:

C:\JUNK>`COPY *.DOS A:*.AAA` <Enter>

```
C:\JUNK>COPY *.DOS A:*.AAA
WILDONE.DOS
WILDTWO.DOS
WILDTHR.DOS
        3 file(s) copied

C:\JUNK>_
```

WHAT'S HAPPENING? In this example, you created three more files on the DATA disk that do not have the **.DOS** extension (the source). Instead, all the new files have the file extension of **.AAA**.

STEP 9: Key in the following:
C:\JUNK>**DIR A:W*.*** <Enter>

```
C:\JUNK>DIR A:W*.*

   Volume in drive A is DATA DISK
   Volume Serial Number is 3839-0EC8
   Directory of A:\

WILDONE  DOS      180   05-07-93  9:02a
WILDTWO  DOS      181   05-07-93  9:03a
WILDTHR  DOS      180   05-07-93  9:03a
WILD1    XXX       63   05-07-93  9:03a
WILD2    YYY       63   05-07-93  9:03a
WILD3    ZZZ       63   05-07-93  9:03a
WILDONE            92   05-07-93  9:04a
WILDONE  AAA      180   05-07-93  9:02a
WILDTWO  AAA      181   05-07-93  9:03a
WILDTHR  AAA      180   05-07-93  9:03a
       10 file(s)        1363 bytes
                       273408 bytes free

C:\JUNK>_
```

WHAT'S HAPPENING? You successfully copied the files named ***.DOS** from the **\JUNK** subdirectory on the hard disk. On the directory display of the DATA disk you have three new **WILD** files with the **.AAA** file extension. Not only did you copy the ***.DOS** files from the **\JUNK** subdirectory, but, as you copied them to the DATA disk, you also changed the file names but not the file contents.

6.12 Using Wildcards to Copy Files to Different Drives and Subdirectories

The COPY command does not change when you copy to subdirectories on different drives. You must, however, remember to include the correct path.

Activity 6.13 Using Wildcards to Copy Data Files to Another Disk and Subdirectory

Note: The **C:\JUNK>** is displayed. The DATA disk is in Drive A.

STEP 1: Key in the following:
C:\JUNK>**COPY *.DOS A:\USERS** <Enter>

```
C:\JUNK>COPY *.DOS A:\USERS
WILDONE.DOS
WILDTWO.DOS
WILDTHR.DOS
        3 file(s) copied

C:\JUNK>_
```

WHAT'S HAPPENING? You asked DOS to copy the contents of all the files with any file name and the file extension of **.DOS** from the hard disk in the subdirectory **\JUNK** to the subdirectory called **USERS** on the DATA disk. You want all the file names on the DATA disk to be the same as they were in the **\JUNK** subdirectory. As the files are found in the **\JUNK** subdirectory and copied to the DATA disk, you will see their names displayed on the screen, one file at a time. Now, were the files copied?

STEP 2: Key in the following:
C:\JUNK>**DIR *.DOS** <Enter>

STEP 3: Key in the following:
C:\JUNK>**DIR A:\USERS*.DOS** <Enter>

```
C:\JUNK>DIR *.DOS

   Volume in drive A is MS-DOS_5
   Volume Serial Number is 16D1-68D4
   Directory of C:\JUNK

WILDONE   DOS     180   05-07-93  9:02a
WILDTWO   DOS     181   05-07-93  9:03a
WILDTHR   DOS     180   05-07-93  9:03a
        3 file(s)          541 bytes
                       9453568 bytes free

C:\JUNK>DIR A:\USERS\*.DOS

   Volume in drive A is DATA DISK
   Volume Serial Number is 3839-0EC8
   Directory of A:\USERS

WILDONE   DOS     180   05-07-93  9:02a
WILDTWO   DOS     181   05-07-93  9:03a
WILDTHR   DOS     180   05-07-93  9:03a
        3 file(s)          541 bytes
                        270336 bytes free

C:\JUNK>_
```

WHAT'S HAPPENING? By doing a directory display of the specified files, you know that the ***.DOS** files are still in the **\JUNK** subdirectory on Drive C and you now have more copies of these files on the DATA disk located in the subdirectory called **USERS**.

6.14 Combining Text Files with the COPY Command

Sometimes it is useful to combine the contents of two or more text files, known as concatenation of files. **Concatenation** means to link together. You might wish to concatenate if you have several short documents that would be easier to work with if they were combined into one file. When you combine files, nothing happens to the original files; they remain intact. You just create another new file from the original files. The syntax never changes. It is always COPY *source destination*. Look at the full syntax diagram:

COPY [/A ¦ /B] *source* [/A ¦ /B] [+ *source* [/A ¦ /B] [+ ...]] [*destination* [/A ¦ /B]] [/V]

The /A indicates an ASCII file, whereas a /B indicates a binary file. However, you can see that you can have multiple source files connected by the plus sign. If you want to append files to each other or concatenate them, you can have only one destination file.

Activity 6.15 Combining the Contents of the Files Using the COPY Command

STEP 1: You should be logged into the subdirectory **C:\JUNK**. You can be sure by keying in C>**CD \JUNK**. The DATA disk should be in Drive A.

WHAT'S HAPPENING? You may have noticed that this text often has you change the default drive, and/or reiterate which disk is in which drive, and/or reiterate which subdirectory is the default. Is this necessary? Yes and no. Obviously, as long as you follow the syntax, you can choose to have any drive as the default drive and any subdirectory as the default subdirectory. However, there are reasons for changing the default drive and subdirectory. One is to simplify the instructional process. More importantly, when you work with computers, it is best to train yourself to follow certain patterns in order to minimize careless errors. A good pattern to follow is to go from left to right, or from Drive A to Drive B, or from Drive C to Drive A. The important thing is to be consistent.

A computer will do exactly what you tell it to do and will do it quickly. What sophisticated computer users find is that they get into trouble very quickly by being too sure they know what they are doing. More than one user has overwritten or deleted files that should not have been overwritten or deleted, simply by not paying attention to the default drive and/or default subdirectory.

The default drive and the default subdirectory are very important. It is very important to know which disk is which. Pay attention to the prompt; it tells where the activity is occurring. It is easy to tell which is the default drive because the prompt on the screen tells you what drive you are in. You have been changing or customizing the prompt to display the default subdirectory. Without the customized prompt, it is not so easy to tell what the default subdirectory is. One way to see what subdirectory you are in is to key in CD. CD by itself will display the default subdirectory.

STEP 2: Key in the following:
C:\JUNK>**CD** <Enter>

```
C:\JUNK>CD
C:\JUNK

C:\JUNK>_
```

WHAT'S HAPPENING? CD with no parameters means "current directory." Keying in **CD** showed you what subdirectory you were in. You have C: as the default drive and the **JUNK** subdirectory as the default subdirectory. Your prompt showed you both the default drive and default subdirectory, but you can always use CD alone to verify the default subdirectory.

STEP 3: Key in the following:
C:\JUNK>**TYPE EMPLOYEE.ONE** <Enter>

STEP 4: Key in the following:
C:\JUNK>**TYPE EMPLOYEE.THR** <Enter>

```
C:\JUNK>TYPE EMPLOYEE.ONE
This is employee file one.
It is the first file.

C:\JUNK>TYPE EMPLOYEE.THR
This is employee file three.
It is the third file.

C:\JUNK>_
```

WHAT'S HAPPENING? You have displayed the contents of two files on the screen. Each file is unique with different file names and different file contents. You are going to place the contents of these two files into a new file that will consist of the contents of the first file, **EMPLOYEE.ONE**, followed by the contents of the second file, **EMPLOYEE.THR**. The new file will reside on the DATA disk. The command line is one line. There is one space between **EMPLOYEE.THR** and **A:JOINED.SAM**. Be sure to include the **A:** prior to **JOINED.SAM**. If you do not, the file **JOINED.SAM** will be written to the default drive and default subdirectory—**C:\JUNK**.

STEP 5: Key in the following:
C:\JUNK>**COPY EMPLOYEE.ONE + EMPLOYEE.THR A:JOINED.SAM** <Enter>

```
C:\JUNK>COPY EMPLOYEE.ONE + EMPLOYEE.THR A:JOINED.SAM
EMPLOYEE.ONE
EMPLOYEE.THR
        1 file(s) copied

C:\JUNK>_
```

WHAT'S HAPPENING? The message says "1 file(s) copied." It seems as if you have too many parameters because the syntax is COPY *source destination*. However, you are still following the correct syntax for the COPY command. You are making one destination file out of two source files. What you did here was to say COPY (the command) the contents of the file called **EMPLOYEE.ONE** and the contents of the file called **EMPLOYEE.THR** (*source*) to a new file called **JOINED.SAM** that will reside on the DATA disk (*destination*). The + (plus sign) told DOS that the source had more to it than just one file. It also told DOS that you were joining files. The destination file is the last file name on the command line that does not have a plus sign in front. Look at Step 5 and note that **A:JOINED.SAM** has a space in front of it, not a plus sign, making **A:JOINED.SAM** the destination.

STEP 6: Key in the following:
C:\JUNK>**TYPE A:JOINED.SAM** <Enter>

```
C:\JUNK>TYPE A:JOINED.SAM
This is employee file one.
It is the first file.
This is employee file three.
It is the third file.

C:\JUNK>_
```

WHAT'S HAPPENING? The contents of the file **JOINED.SAM** consist of the contents of the file **EMPLOYEE.ONE**, followed immediately by the contents of the file **EMPLOYEE.THR**. The contents in **JOINED.SAM** do not show any file names. You do not know where one file ended and the next began. **JOINED.SAM** is a new file, but you did not destroy or in any way alter the two original source files, **EMPLOYEE.ONE** or **EMPLOYEE.THR**. You can prove this by using the TYPE command.

STEP 7: Key in the following:
C:\JUNK>**TYPE EMPLOYEE.ONE** <Enter>

STEP 8: Key in the following:
C:\JUNK>**TYPE EMPLOYEE.THR** <Enter>

```
C:\JUNK>TYPE EMPLOYEE.ONE
This is employee file one.
It is the first file.

C:\JUNK>TYPE EMPLOYEE.THR
This is employee file three.
It is the third file.

C:\JUNK>_
```

WHAT'S HAPPENING? As you can see, the source files remain unchanged. You merely created a third file from the contents of two files. You can join many files with the plus sign. However, you can also use wildcards to join files, which eliminates the need to key in all the file names. If you wanted to join all the files with a **.TMP** file extension and place them into a new file called **MONTHS.SAM**, located on the DATA disk, you would have to key in

COPY JAN.TMP + FEB.TMP + MAR.TMP + APR.TMP A:MONTHS.SAM

You can save many keystrokes by using wildcards. Again, be sure to include the **A:** preceding the **MONTHS.SAM**.

STEP 9: Key in the following:

C:\JUNK>**COPY *.TMP A:MONTHS.SAM** <Enter>

```
C:\JUNK>COPY *.TMP A:MONTHS.SAM
JAN.TMP
FEB.TMP
MAR.TMP
APR.TMP
        1 file(s) copied

C:\JUNK>_
```

WHAT'S HAPPENING? Using the wildcard has the same effect as keying in all the file names and connecting the source files with plus signs. DOS found each file with a **.TMP** file extension and wrote the contents of those files to a new file called **MONTHS.SAM**. However, there is a risk in using wildcards. When you use a wildcard, DOS does the order of selection based on the order of the files on the disk, and you have no way of knowing what that order is. In fact, your display could be different if you created the files in a different order or if you did not follow all the text instructions precisely in the order given. Remember, if you must have files copied in a specific order, the plus sign will order the files the way you specify. If you use a wildcard, DOS will select the order the files are copied.

STEP 10: Key in the following:

C:\JUNK>**TYPE A:MONTHS.SAM** <Enter>

```
C:\JUNK>TYPE A:MONTHS.SAM
This is my January file.
It is my first dummy file.
This is file 1.
This is my February file.
It is my second dummy file.
This is file 2.
This is my March file.
It is my third dummy file.
This is file 3.
This is my April file.
It is my fourth dummy file.
This is file 4.

C:\JUNK>_
```

WHAT'S HAPPENING? As you can see, you joined together the contents of all the **.TMP** files into a new file called **MONTHS.SAM**. Your original **.TMP** files remain as they were. If your display is not exactly like the display above, do not be concerned. DOS selected the files based on how the hard disk has been set up.

You can also concatenate files from different drives or different subdirectories, provided you use the drive designator and the path in front of the file name. For example, if you wanted to combine a file from the disk in Drive A and a file from the disk in Drive B, you would write the command as A>**COPY FILE.ONE + B:FILE.TWO FILE.THR**. The source in this example is **FILE.ONE**, located on the disk in Drive A, but since the default drive is A you did not need to place **A:** in front of **FILE.ONE**. The other source file connected by the + is **B:FILE.TWO**. You would need to include the **B:** in front of **FILE.TWO** because otherwise DOS would look for **FILE.TWO** only on the disk in Drive A, the default. The destination file is going to be on Drive A since no other drive was specified. The destination file will be called **FILE.THR**.

If you wanted to combine a file from a subdirectory called **JUNK** on Drive C and a file in Drive A, you would write the command as A>**COPY FILE.ONE + C:\JUNK\FILE.TWO FILE.THR**. The source in this example is **FILE.ONE**, located on the disk in Drive A, but, since the default drive is A, you did not need to place **A:** in front of **FILE.ONE**. The other source file connected by the + is **C:\JUNK\FILE.TWO**, located on Drive C in the subdirectory **\JUNK**. You need to include the **C:\JUNK** in front of **FILE.TWO** because otherwise DOS would look for **FILE.TWO** only on Drive A, the default. The destination file, **FILE.THR** is going to be on Drive A because no other drive or subdirectory was specified.

One other important point about concatenation. It can only be used with ASCII files. You cannot concatenate program files or data files that have been generated by program files.

6.16 Understanding VERIFY when Using the COPY Command

There is another parameter you can use for the COPY command, /V for **verify**. When this parameter is added to the COPY command, the command checks to ensure that the sectors written to the destination disk are recorded correctly. Errors when written to a destination disk are rare. However, if you have a critical file or program that you wish to double-check, you can use this option. Verify does cause the COPY command to run slowly because of the additional work. The /V is only effective during the duration of the COPY command.

Activity 6.17 Using VERIFY with the COPY Command

Note: The **C:\JUNK>** is displayed. The DATA disk is in Drive A.

STEP 1: Key in the following:
C:\JUNK>**COPY A:JOINED.SAM A:\USERS\GOOD.SAM /V** <Enter>

```
C:\JUNK>COPY A:JOINED.SAM A:\USERS\GOOD.SAM /V
        1 file(s) copied

C:\JUNK>_
```

WHAT'S HAPPENING? You copied the file called **JOINED.SAM** (*source*) located on the DATA disk in the root directory to a new file called **GOOD.SAM** (*destination*) on the DATA disk but in the subdirectory called **USERS**. The COPY command not only copied the source file **JOINED.SAM**, but, as it copied, the /V parameter also verified that the destination file **GOOD.SAM** was correctly copied. You can prove these files are the same by using the TYPE command.

STEP 2: Key in the following:
C:\JUNK>**TYPE A:JOINED.SAM** <Enter>

STEP 3: Key in the following:
C:\JUNK>**TYPE A:\USERS\GOOD.SAM** <Enter>

```
C:\JUNK>TYPE A:JOINED.SAM
This is employee file one.
It is the first file.
This is employee file three.
It is the third file.

C:\JUNK>TYPE A:\USERS\GOOD.SAM
This is employee file one.
It is the first file.
This is employee file three.
It is the third file.

C:\JUNK>_
```

WHAT'S HAPPENING? The files are the same. The /V parameter verified that as the file was copied, it was copied correctly.

STEP 4: Key in the following:
C:\JUNK>**CD ** <Enter>

```
C:\JUNK>CD \

C:\>_
```

WHAT'S HAPPENING? You have returned to the root directory of C:.

Special Section 6.18 Setting up C:\JUNK

To ensure that you will be able to follow the instructions in the text, the following activity will set up a subdirectory on the hard disk and then copy the files from the ACTIVITIES disk into the hard disk subdirectory. Since many of the activities in the chapter involve copying files from the ACTIVITIES disk to the DATA disk, creating a subdirectory will also eliminate floppy disk swapping for you. *Do not do this activity if the* **C:\JUNK** *subdirectory is already set up on your hard disk.*

Special Activity 6.19

Setting Up a Subdirectory on the Hard Disk

STEP 1: Be sure the system is booted with the **C:\>** on the screen. Insert the ACTIVITIES disk in Drive A. Use the ACTIVITIES disk that came with the textbook, not your working copy.

STEP 2: Key in the following:
C:\>**MD \JUNK** <Enter>

```
C:\>MD \JUNK

C:\>_
```

WHAT'S HAPPENING? With the **MD \JUNK** command, you created a subdirectory on the hard disk called **\JUNK**. This is an area or shell on the hard disk. It is like creating a new file cabinet called **\JUNK**. It is empty. There are no files in **\JUNK** yet, but you now have a place to put files. **\JUNK** was selected as a name for the subdirectory because it is highly unlikely that this subdirectory name will conflict with any other subdirectory on the hard disk. You are now going to "fill" the shell with all the files on the ACTIVITIES disk. But first, you are going to move to the **JUNK** subdirectory with the CD command.

STEP 3: Key in the following:
C:\>**CD \JUNK** <Enter>

```
C:\>CD \JUNK

C:\JUNK>_
```

WHAT'S HAPPENING? Drive C is still the default drive, but you have now made **JUNK** the default subdirectory. Be sure to follow the instructions exactly, including the backslashes.

STEP 4: Key in the following:
C:\JUNK>**COPY A:*.* \JUNK** <Enter>

```
A:\YOURC.LAB
A:\JAN.99
A:\FEB.99
A:\MAR.99
A:\APR.99
A:\FILE2.CZG
A:\FILE3.CZG
A:\FILE2.FP
A:\FILE3.FP
A:\FILE4.FP
A:\FILE2.SWT
A:\FILE3.SWT
A:\RIGHT.RED
```

```
A:\MIDDLE.RED
A:\LEFT.RED
A:\RIGHT.UP
A:\DRESS.UP
A:\MIDDLE.UP
A:\BLUE.JAZ
A:\GREEN.JAZ
A:\FRIENDS
A:\BUSINESS
        69 file(s) copied

C:\JUNK>_
```

WHAT'S HAPPENING? Many files went scrolling by and what appears is the last screenful of files. The syntax of the COPY command was followed. COPY is the work you want to do. **A:*.*** is the source or what you want copied. A: is the physical disk drive you want DOS to look on. \ is the root directory. *.* means you want *every* file on the ACTIVITIES disk to be copied to the subdirectory **JUNK** on Drive C. As each file was found on the ACTIVITIES disk in Drive A, it was listed on the screen, until the COPY command found every file. The destination is the subdirectory **\JUNK** of Drive C. Just as a disk drive has a name, like A: or B:, the name of the subdirectory is **C:\JUNK**. All the files that were on the ACTIVITIES disk in the root directory are now also on the hard disk subdirectory called **\JUNK**. However, the ACTIVITIES disk also has subdirectories. The previous command copied only those files from the root directory, as you specified, to the subdirectory **JUNK**. To copy the files from the subdirectories on the ACTIVITIES disk, you need to specify where they are. In addition, you need to create the subdirectories on the hard disk under the subdirectory **JUNK**.

STEP 5: Key in the following:
C:\JUNK>**MD \JUNK\UTILS** <Enter>

STEP 6: Key in the following:
C:\JUNK>**MD \JUNK\DATA** <Enter>

STEP 7: Key in the following:
C:\JUNK>**MD \JUNK\SAMPLE** <Enter>

STEP 8: Key in the following:
C:\JUNK>**MD \JUNK\SAMPLE\EQUIP** <Enter>

STEP 9: Key in the following:
C:\JUNK>**MD \JUNK\SAMPLE\TENNIS** <Enter>

STEP 10: Key in the following:
C:\JUNK>**MD \JUNK\TEST** <Enter>

```
C:\JUNK>MD \JUNK\UTILS

C:\JUNK>MD \JUNK\DATA

C:\JUNK>MD \JUNK\SAMPLE

C:\JUNK>MD \JUNK\SAMPLE\EQUIP

C:\JUNK>MD \JUNK\SAMPLE\TENNIS

C:\JUNK>MD \JUNK\TEST

C:\JUNK>_
```

WHAT'S HAPPENING? You created four subdirectories called **UTILS**, **DATA**, **SAMPLE**, and **TEST**. However, each of these subdirectories was in reality created under the subdirectory called **JUNK**. That is why **\JUNK** preceded these names. A subdirectory can have subdirectories of its own. When you created **EQUIP** and **TENNIS**, these two subdirectories were under the main subdirectory **JUNK** and then under the subdirectory **SAMPLE**. If a hard disk is like a file cabinet and a subdirectory is like a file drawer, these further divisions are like putting dividers in that file drawer. Each can hold files. Thus, going to the file cabinet, opening the file drawer, and then going to the particular divider is like following the path. Now that you have set up the subdirectories, you need to copy the files, using the proper COPY syntax.

STEP 11: Key in the following:
C:\JUNK>**COPY A:\UTILS*.* \JUNK\UTILS** <Enter>

STEP 12: Key in the following:
C:\JUNK>**COPY A:\DATA*.* \JUNK\DATA** <Enter>

STEP 13: Key in the following:
C:\JUNK>**COPY A:\SAMPLE*.* \JUNK\SAMPLE** <Enter>

STEP 14: Key in the following:
C:\JUNK>**COPY A:\SAMPLE\EQUIP*.* \JUNK\SAMPLE\EQUIP** <Enter>

STEP 15: Key in the following:
C:\JUNK>**COPY A:\TEST*.* \JUNK\TEST** <Enter>

```
A:\DATA\DRAMA.TV
A:\DATA\COMEDY.TV
        11 file(s) copied

C:\JUNK>COPY A:\SAMPLE\*.* \JUNK\SAMPLE\
A:\SAMPLE\BASKETBL.TMS
A:\SAMPLE\PRO.TMS
A:\SAMPLE\COLLEGE.TMS
```

```
A:\SAMPLE\AMERICAN.TMS
A:\SAMPLE\NATIONAL.TMS
         5 file(s) copied

C:\JUNK>COPY A:\SAMPLE\EQUIP\*.* \JUNK\SAMPLE\EQUIP
A:\SAMPLE\EQUIP\BASEBALL.EQP
A:\SAMPLE\EQUIP\FOOTBALL.EQP
         2 file(s) copied

C:\JUNK>COPY A:\TEST\*.* \JUNK\TEST
A:\TEST\NEW.FIL
A:\TEST\SAMPLE.FIL
         2 file(s) copied

C:\JUNK>_
```

WHAT'S HAPPENING? As you keyed in each command, DOS went to the disk in Drive A and to the subdirectory you specified and found all the files (*.*). These were the source files. Each file was listed as it was copied to the destination. The destination was Drive C, the subdirectory JUNK and then the appropriate sub-subdirectory. Now that you have successfully copied all the files from the ACTIVITIES disk to the \JUNK subdirectory on the hard disk, you are going to use the hard disk instead of the ACTIVITIES disk. So that you can eliminate keying in \JUNK, the path name, each time you want the ACTIVITIES files, you are going to change the default subdirectory to the \JUNK subdirectory. Just as you can change default drives, you can also change default subdirectories. The command is CD and the syntax is: CD [*drive:*][*path*].

Since both the optional parameters are in brackets, parameters are not required. CD with no parameter shows you what the default subdirectory is. CD followed by a variable parameter changes the default subdirectory.

STEP 16: Key in the following:
C:\JUNK>CD <Enter>

```
C:\JUNK>CD
C:\JUNK

C:\JUNK>_
```

WHAT'S HAPPENING? When you keyed in CD \JUNK in Step 3, you logged into the subdirectory \JUNK. This step was the equivalent of changing logged drives. The default is now C:\JUNK. CD followed by \JUNK changed the default subdirectory to JUNK. CD by itself showed you the default drive and subdirectory. Since you have copied all the files from the ACTIVITIES disk to the subdirectory \JUNK on the hard disk and made \JUNK the default directory, you no longer need to have the ACTIVITIES disk in Drive A. The directory \JUNK is the functional equivalent of the ACTIVITIES disk. Because you changed the prompt with the command PROMPT pg, your prompt, instead of simply being C>, displays as

C:\JUNK>. By changing the prompt, you now can see the default subdirectory instead of always having to key in CD by itself to see where you are.

STEP 17: Key in the following:
C:\JUNK>**CD ** <Enter>

```
C:\JUNK>CD \

C:\>_
```

WHAT'S HAPPENING? You returned to the root directory of C:. You may now proceed with Activity 6.2 on page 154.

Chapter Summary

1. The syntax of the COPY command is:
   COPY [*d:*][*path*]*filename*[*.ext*] [*d:*][*path*]*filename*[*.ext*][/V]
   d: represents any lettered drive. *path* represents any subdirectory location. Because *d:* and *path* are enclosed in brackets, they are optional parameters. Substitute the needed values for the variable parameters. The full syntax of the COPY command is:
   COPY [/A ¦ /B] *source* [/A ¦ /B] [+ *source* [/A ¦ /B] [+ ...]] [*destination* [/A ¦ /B]] [/V]
2. The syntax of the TYPE command is:
   TYPE [*drive:*][*path*]*filename*
3. With the TYPE command you must have one parameter, the file name. You *cannot* use wildcards with the TYPE command.
4. A subdirectory is a means to divide a hard disk into manageable portions. A subdirectory has a name the user selects, called the path. To locate a file in a subdirectory, you use the path name, also the subdirectory's name.
5. The command to create a subdirectory is MD, which means "make directory." The syntax is: MD [*drive:*]*path*.
6. The command to display the current subdirectory is CD. The command to change the subdirectory is CD *path*.
7. The root directory's name is \.
8. You can copy files from one disk to another if you provide the disk drive letter and/or path for the source file and the destination file so DOS knows where to read the file and where to write the file. If you do not provide the disk drive letter or the path name, DOS will *always* assume the default. The default is usually indicated by the prompt displayed on the screen. To see the default subdirectory, key in **CD**.
9. Wildcards can be used to copy files to different disks and subdirectories, provided that the proper path, disk drive letter, and subdirectory name are supplied to DOS.
10. When using wildcards to copy files, first use the DIR command with the wildcard specifications to be sure you know the files selected will be copied.
11. When using wildcards to copy files, you can also use the DIR command to see if there are any files on the destination drive/subdirectory by the same name.

12. If you use *.* with a command, it will find all the files. Thus, DIR *.* will display all the files on the default drive. COPY *.* B: would copy all the files on the default drive to B:.
13. Overwriting files with the COPY command is the process whereby the content of the source file copies over the content of the destination file. You cannot overwrite a file when there is already a file with the identical name on the same disk and/or subdirectory.
14. Concatenation means combining the contents of files using the COPY command. The syntax is still COPY *source destination*. The source files are connected by a plus sign, and there is only one destination file.
15. COPY *source destination* /V is a parameter that verifies that the destination files are copied properly.

Key Terms

Backup file
Concatenation
Default subdirectory
Overwrite
Verify

Discussion Questions

1. Explain what a subdirectory is.
2. What purpose do subdirectories serve?
3. What is a path? How is it used?
4. The syntax of the COPY command is:

   COPY [*d:*][*path*]*source*[*.fil*] [*d:*][*path*]*destination*[*.fil*][/V]

   What do the brackets mean? What does *d:* mean? Is *d:* keyed in? What does *path* mean? Is *path* keyed in? What does /V mean? Which are optional parameters? Which are mandatory parameters?
5. How would you write a command line to create a text file called **LEFT.ONE** on the disk in Drive B?
6. Your default drive is A. How would you write a command line to copy a file called **OLD.TXT**, located on the disk in Drive A, to the disk in Drive B without changing the file name?
7. Your default drive is A. How would you write a command line to copy a file called **OLD.TXT**, located on the disk in Drive A, to the disk in Drive B, changing the file name to **NEW.TXT**?
8. The default drive is A:. How would you write a command line to copy a file called **ADDRESS.TXT**, located on Drive C: in a subdirectory called **PERSONAL**, to the disk in Drive A:?
9. You have a group of files located on Drive C that have the file extension **.TXT**. You want to copy these files to a disk in Drive A. How would you do it?
10. The default drive is C. The default subdirectory is **DATA**. You want to copy all the files with the file extension **.TMP** to a subdirectory on Drive C called **BACKUP**. How would you accomplish this task?

11. The default drive is A. You want to create a subdirectory on the disk in Drive C, under the root directory called **SAMPLES**. How would you do this?
12. The prompt displayed on the screen is **C>**. What command could you use to find out what the default subdirectory is?
13. The prompt displayed on the screen is **C>**. What command could you use to change the default subdirectory to **SAMPLES**?
14. How would you combine the contents of two files?
15. What is the most efficient way to combine the contents of several files?
16. What does overwriting of files mean?
17. Why or why not should a computer user be aware of the overwriting of files?
18. Why would you want to make one or more additional files and copy them to another disk?
19. Why would you want to make a copy of a file on the same disk?
20. What parameter allows you to verify that a file has been copied correctly?
21. Under what circumstances would you verify copying a file?
22. Before you use wildcards to make copies of files, is there anything you should do first? Why?
23. Why is the default drive an important concept?
24. Why is the default subdirectory an important concept?
25. Why would you want to concatenate files?
26. Subdirectories are used primarily on a hard drive. Why?
27. If you are copying files from one disk to another and do not provide the disk drive letter or the path name, what will happen?
28. How can the user determine what the default subdirectory is?
29. When do you not need to designate the source drive when copying files from one disk to another?
30. What would happen if you tried to copy a file from one disk to another and the destination disk already had a file with the same name?

Application Assignments

Note 1: Remember that the ACTIVITIES disk files are in the subdirectory **\JUNK** on the hard disk. The path name would therefore be **C:\JUNK**. When the assignments refer to **\JUNK**, use the subdirectory **JUNK** on the hard disk.

Note 2: If you did not do all the activities in the chapter and/or all the application assignments, you could be missing files and/or subdirectories. If you are, create the appropriate subdirectories on the DATA disk and/or copy the necessary files from the **\JUNK** subdirectory to the DATA disk.

1. For the following assignment:
   a. Copy all the files that have a file extension of **.LAB** from **\JUNK** to the root directory of the DATA disk. Keep the file names the same on the DATA disk.
   b. Do a directory display of all the file names on the DATA disk that have a file extension of **.LAB**.
   c. Print the screen.

2. For the following assignment:
   a. Copy all the files that have a file extension of **.LAB** from **\JUNK** to the root directory of the DATA disk. Keep the file names the same on the DATA disk but change the file extension to **.EEE**.
   b. Use the DIR command to display on the screen only those files that have an **.EEE** extension on the DATA disk.
   c. Print the screen.
3. For the following assignment, you are going to concatenate some files. Be sure you have a subdirectory called **USERS** on the DATA disk. If you do not have this subdirectory on the DATA disk, create it now.
   a. Find all the files in **\JUNK** that have the file extension **.TMP**. Put the contents of these files into a new file on the DATA disk called **TOGETHER.ACE** that will be located in the subdirectory called **USERS**.
   b. Print the contents of this new file. Do not use the <Shift> and <PrtSc> keys.
4. For the following assignment, if you have not copied all the files that have the file extension **.LAB** from **\JUNK** to the root directory of the DATA disk, do so now. Be sure you have a subdirectory called **USERS** on the DATA disk. If you do not have this subdirectory on the DATA disk, create it now.
   a. Copy the all the files with a **.LAB** extension in the root directory of the DATA disk to the subdirectory called **USERS** on the DATA disk.
   b. Display only the **.LAB** file names on the DATA disk in the **USERS** subdirectory by using the DIR command.
   c. Print the screen.
5. For the following assignment:
   a. Find all the files in **\JUNK** that have the file extension **.TMP**. Copy these files to the root directory of the DATA disk. Keep the file name the same but make the file extensions **.HHH**.
   b. Do a directory display of only the **.HHH** file names on the DATA disk.
   c. Print the screen with only the file names displayed.
6. For the following assignment:
   a. Find all the files in **\JUNK** that have **.MOV** as a file extension. Place the contents of these files into one new file on the DATA disk in the root directory called **MOVIES.LST**.
   b. Print the contents of the file called **MOVIES.LST**. You do not want the file name but the contents of the file. Do not use the <Shift> and <PrtSc> keys.
7. For the following assignment:
   a. Create a text file on the DATA disk using the COPY CON command and the contents as shown below:

File name	**Contents**
EXTRA.ABC	This is a sample file.

   b. Overwrite the file named **EXTRA.ABC** with the contents of the file called **BLUE.JAZ** located in **\JUNK**.

c. Use the TYPE command to display the contents of **EXTRA.ABC** on the screen after you have overwritten it.
d. Print the screen.

8. For the following assignment:
   a. Copy all the files that have **.FIL** as a file extension from **\JUNK** to the DATA disk.
   b. Use the DIR command to locate any files that have **.FIL** as a file extension on the directory of the DATA disk and display the file names on the screen.
   c. Print the screen. If you have more files with an extension of **.FIL** than were copied from **\JUNK**, display all the files on DATA disk that have **.FIL** as an extension, not just the files you copied.

Challenge Assignments

9. For the following assignment:
   a. On the DATA disk, create a subdirectory called **SERIES**.
   b. Then:
      (1) Copy all the files under **\JUNK\DATA** that have **.TV** as a file extension to the DATA disk in the subdirectory **SERIES**.
      (2) Display the file names from the DATA disk on the screen.
      (3) Print this screen.
   c. Then:
      (1) On the DATA disk, in the subdirectory **SERIES**, concatenate all the files with the **.TV** extension into a new file that will be called **TELEV.SER** and will be written to the DATA disk in the subdirectory **SERIES**.
      (2) Print the contents of this file. Do not use the <Shift>+<PrtSc> keys.
10. For the following assignment:
   a. On the DATA disk, if you have not already done so, create a subdirectory called **SERIES**.
   b. Then:
      (1) Change the default subdirectory to **SERIES** on the DATA disk.
      (2) Prove that this is the default subdirectory.
      (3) Print this screen.
   c. Then:
      (1) Copy all the files in the subdirectory called **\JUNK\DATA** that have **.MAK** as a file extension to the DATA disk in the subdirectory **SERIES**.
      (2) Display the file names on the screen.
      (3) Print the screen.
   d. Then:
      (1) On the DATA disk, with the subdirectory **SERIES** being the default subdirectory, concatenate all the files with the **.MAK** extension into a new file that will be called **AUTOMOB.ILE** and that will be written to the DATA disk in the default subdirectory.
      (2) Print the contents of this file. Do not use the <Shift>+<PrtSc> keys.

Chapter 7

Using ERASE, DEL, and RENAME

After completing this chapter you will be able to:

1. Explain why it is necessary to delete files from a disk.
2. Use the ERASE or DEL command to erase individual files on the same disk.
3. Use the ERASE or DEL command to erase individual files on the same disk in different subdirectories.
4. Explain when and how to use wildcards with the ERASE or DEL command.
5. Use the ERASE or DEL command to erase a file on a disk in another drive and subdirectory.
6. Explain and use the /P parameter with the DEL command when using a version of DOS above 4.0.
7. Change the names of files using the RENAME command.
8. Change the names of files on the same drive and subdirectory using the RENAME command with wildcards.
9. Use wildcards with the RENAME command to change file names on different drives and subdirectories.
10. Explain the importance of backing up data.
11. Back up a data disk using the DISKCOPY command.
12. Back up files using the COPY command.

Chapter Overview

Typically, when working with computers the number of files on a disk increases dramatically. The more files and/or disks you have, the harder it is to manage them. It becomes increasingly difficult to keep track of what disks have which files and which files are needed. In addition, as new data is keyed into existing files the name given to the file may no longer be appropriate. It is also important to be able to make a copy of an entire disk or specific files so that data is not lost due to a power failure or surge or because a disk goes bad.

In this chapter you will continue to work with internal commands that help you manage and manipulate your files. This chapter will focus on the DEL and ERASE commands, which allow you to delete files you no longer need or want, and the RENAME command, which is used to rename files. You will also learn why and how to back up specific files or an entire disk so that you do not lose important data.

7.0 Eliminating Files with the ERASE and DEL Commands

In the various activities completed previously, you have created many files. Some have been copies of other files, both data and program files, and some you created as text files with the COPY CON *filename.ext* command. The DATA disk began as a disk absent of files. As you have been working, the number of files on the disk has increased dramatically, typical when working with computers. There is a kind of Murphy's Law that says you create as many files as you have disk space. However, you do not want to keep files forever. The more files and/or disks you have, the harder it is to keep track of what disks have which files and which files are the ones you need. If you have floppy disks, you end up with many floppies, and if you have a hard disk, you end up with many subdirectories and many files. Often, you're not quite sure what files are where. Looking at a floppy disk tells little because a floppy disk's information is magnetically encoded, and if you have a hard disk, you cannot even look at it because it is sealed. Thus, keeping only the files you need on your disk will decrease the number of files you have to manage.

Logic should tell you that, if you can copy and create files, you should be able to eliminate files by deleting or erasing them. You can do these tasks with the ERASE or the DEL command. These commands are internal, always resident in memory. You do need to be careful with these commands. Once you press <Enter> after the ERASE or DEL command, the file is gone forever. DOS does not ask you if this is really the file you want to get rid of; it simply obeys your instructions. DEL and ERASE do not remove hidden files, nor do they remove files with a read-only attribute.

A deleted file cannot be recovered except by certain special utility programs, but they are chancy. Technically, what happens when you delete a file is that DOS does not actually remove the file from the disk physically. Instead, it replaces the first character of the file name with a special byte that marks the file as deleted in the directory table. It then "zeroes" out the file entry from the FAT (File Allocation Table). The FAT "unallocates" the space that the data in the file occupied, even though, in fact, the data is still on the disk. When you create the next file, DOS sees that there is available space in the directory table and FAT and assigns the new file to that space. DOS then overwrites the old file with the new file. Special utility programs such as Norton Utilities or the new UNDELETE command in DOS 5.0 can occasionally help you recover deleted files, particularly if you realize immediately that you have inadvertently erased a file. However, once a file is overwritten by new data, nothing can recover the previous data. It is gone forever. When you use the DOS ERASE or DEL command, you cannot recover deleted files. There is no utility on the DOS System Disk or DOS subdirectory that allows you to retrieve erased files except on versions of DOS 5.0 and special utility programs.

The internal command to expunge files is either ERASE or DEL. Is there a difference between these two commands? No. Both ERASE and DEL work precisely the same. The syntax of the command is:

DEL [*drive:*][*path*]*filename* [/P]
or ERASE [*drive:*][*path*]*filename* [/P]

The /P parameter is only available in DOS 4.0 or above. ERASE is spelled out and DEL is an abbreviation for delete. You can neither abbreviate ERASE as ERA, nor can you spell DELETE for DEL. The commands must be used as they are specified. Most computer users key in DEL instead of ERASE for the simple reason that DEL has fewer characters. Computer users are big on saving keystrokes.

Activity 7.1 Using the ERASE and DEL Commands with Individual Files on the Same Disk

Note: The `C:\>` is displayed and the DATA disk is in Drive A. Key in `PROMPT $p$g`.

STEP 1: Be sure the DATA disk is in Drive A. Key in the following:
C:\>**A:** <Enter>

```
C:\>A:

A:\>_
```

WHAT'S HAPPENING? You changed the default drive to A. The work you wish to do is to erase or delete files. Since DEL and ERASE are internal commands, when you booted the system from Drive C, you installed the operating system in memory. DEL and ERASE are commands in RAM. They will remain there until you turn off the power.

Note: You have the DATA disk in Drive A with the `A:\>` displayed. The following activities assume you have copied the files from the `\JUNK` subdirectory that had a `.DOS` file extension. When you copied them from the `\JUNK` subdirectory to the DATA disk, you changed the file extension to `.AAA`—C:\JUNK>`COPY *.DOS A:*.AAA`. If you have not done so, copy these files now.

STEP 2: Key in the following:
A:\>**DIR WILDONE.AAA** <Enter>

```
A:\>DIR WILDONE.AAA

   Volume in drive A is DATA DISK
   Volume Serial Number is 3839-0EC8
   Directory of A:\

WILDONE  AAA     180   05-07-93  9:02a
        1 file(s)        180 bytes
                      236544 bytes free

A:\>_
```

WHAT'S HAPPENING? You are asking DOS if the file called **WILDONE.AAA** is located on the DATA disk. This file is on the disk.

STEP 3: Key in the following:
A:\>**ERASE WILDONE.AAA** <Enter>

```
A:\>ERASE WILDONE.AAA

A:\>_
```

WHAT'S HAPPENING? You are asking DOS to ERASE the file called **WILDONE.AAA**, located on the DATA disk. You did not need to include the drive letter A: because DOS assumed the default and looked only for the file called **WILDONE.AAA** on Drive A:, the default drive. However, it appears that nothing happened. All you got on the screen was the system prompt.

STEP 4: Key in the following:
A:\>**DIR WILDONE.AAA** <Enter>

```
A:\>DIR WILDONE.AAA

   Volume in drive A is DATA DISK
   Volume Serial Number is 3839-0EC8
   Directory of A:\

File not found

A:\>_
```

WHAT'S HAPPENING? Although the file was there in Step 2, now the file is gone. You now know that DOS executed the ERASE command and removed the file called **WILDONE.AAA**. It is no longer on the DATA disk.

STEP 5: Key in the following:
A:\>**DIR WILDTWO.AAA** <Enter>

```
A:\>DIR WILDTWO.AAA

   Volume in drive A is DATA DISK
   Volume Serial Number is 3839-0EC8
   Directory of A:\

WILDTWO   AAA     181   05-07-93   9:03a
        1 file(s)          181 bytes
                        237568 bytes free

A:\>_
```

WHAT'S HAPPENING? The screen display indicates that the file named **WILDTWO.AAA** is on the DATA disk. Before you delete a file, it is always a good practice to verify that the file is on the disk and that you really want to remove it.

STEP 6: Key in the following:
A:\>**DEL WILDTWO.AAA** <Enter>

```
A:\>DEL WILDTWO.AAA

A:\>_
```

WHAT'S HAPPENING? The system prompt is displayed on the screen, indicating that the file was deleted. Deletion can be verified by using the DIR command.

STEP 7: Key in the following:
A:\>**DIR WILDTWO.AAA** <Enter>

```
A:\>DIR WILDTWO.AAA

   Volume in drive A is DATA DISK
   Volume Serial Number is 3839-0EC8
   Directory of A:\

File not found

A:\>_
```

WHAT'S HAPPENING? The file called **WILDTWO.AAA** is gone from the DATA disk. As you can see, the ERASE command and the DEL command do exactly the same thing. What if the file you want to erase is not on the disk?

STEP 8: Key in the following:
A:\>**DEL NOFILE.XXX** <Enter>

```
A:\>DEL NOFILE.XXX
File not found

A:\>_
```

WHAT'S HAPPENING? In order for DOS to execute the command DEL, it must be able to find the file to delete. Here, the file was not found.

STEP 9: Key in the following:
A:\>**DEL** <Enter>

```
A:\>DEL
Required parameter missing

A:\>_
```

WHAT'S HAPPENING? Not only must DOS find the file, it must also have a file to find. Remember, the syntax is DEL *filename*. The "Required parameter missing" message is the computer equivalent of "Get rid of what file?" Unless you tell DOS precisely what to do, it will not know what to do. If you are using DOS 3.3 or below, the message is "Invalid number of parameters." It means the same as the 4.0 and 5.0 messages. However, the new message is more explicit—"Required parameter missing." One of the things that happen when software is upgraded is that corrections are made. The old message does not give you as much information as the new message.

Activity 7.2

Using the ERASE and DEL Commands with Individual Files on the Same Disk in Different Subdirectories

Note: You have the DATA disk in Drive A with the **A:\>** displayed. The following activities assume that you have created a subdirectory called **JUNK** on the hard disk and have copied all the files from the ACTIVITIES disk to the subdirectory called **JUNK** on the hard disk. If you have not done so, see Chapter 6, Special Activity 6.19 and follow those instructions.

STEP 1: Key in the following:
A:\>**MD TRIP** <Enter>

```
A:\>MD TRIP

A:\>_
```

WHAT'S HAPPENING? You have created another subdirectory on the DATA disk called **TRIP**.

STEP 2: Key in the following:
A:\>**COPY C:\JUNK*.99 \TRIP** <Enter>

STEP 3: Key in the following:
A:\>**COPY C:\JUNK*.JAZ \TRIP** <Enter>

```
A:\>COPY C:\JUNK\*.99 \TRIP
C:\JUNK\JAN.99
C:\JUNK\FEB.99
C:\JUNK\MAR.99
C:\JUNK\APR.99
        4 file(s) copied

A:\>COPY C:\JUNK\*.JAZ \TRIP
C:\JUNK\BLUE.JAZ
C:\JUNK\GREEN.JAZ
        2 file(s) copied

A:\>_
```

WHAT'S HAPPENING? You copied files from the **\JUNK** subdirectory on Drive C to the subdirectory called **TRIP** on the DATA disk. You used the COPY command. You had to specify where the source files are located, which was **C:\JUNK**. However, for the destination of these files, since the default drive is A, the default is assumed, and you did not have to specify the destination drive. The default subdirectory is the root (\); thus, you did not need to include it in the destination. However, if you had not included the name of the subdirectory, **TRIP**, where you wanted the files copied, DOS would have assumed the default and copied the files to the root directory. The longhand version of the command is A:\>**COPY C:\JUNK*.99 A:\TRIP*.99**.

STEP 4: Key in the following:
A:\>**DIR TRIP\JAN.99** <Enter>

```
A:\>DIR TRIP\JAN.99

   Volume in drive A is DATA DISK
   Volume Serial Number is 3839-0EC8
   Directory of A:\TRIP

JAN      99       72   11-23-92   7:04a
        1 file(s)          72 bytes
                       231424 bytes free

A:\>_
```

WHAT'S HAPPENING? The file is there. You successfully copied it.

STEP 5: Key in the following:
A:\>**DEL TRIP\JAN.99** <Enter>

```
A:\>DEL TRIP\JAN.99

A:\>_
```

WHAT'S HAPPENING? You had to provide the proper syntax, which is where the **JAN.99** file is located. It was located in the subdirectory **TRIP** under the root directory on the DATA disk. Since the default drive is A, you did not need to include the drive letter because it is the default drive. Since the default subdirectory is the root (\); the \ is assumed and does not need to be keyed in. However, the \ between the subdirectory **TRIP** and the file name **JAN.99** does need to be keyed in. In this case the \ is used as a delimiter between the subdirectory name and the file name. Has the file been deleted?

STEP 6: Key in the following:
A:\>**DIR TRIP\JAN.99** <Enter>

```
A:\>DIR TRIP\JAN.99

   Volume in drive A is DATA DISK
   Volume Serial Number is 3839-0EC8
   Directory of A:\TRIP

File not found

A:\>_
```

WHAT'S HAPPENING? The file called **JAN.99** is gone from the subdirectory called **TRIP** on the DATA disk. Look at the display. The third line, "Directory of A:\TRIP", tells you that DOS looked only in the subdirectory called **TRIP**.

7.3 Using Wildcards with the DEL Command

You have been erasing or deleting individual files one file at a time. Often, however, you want to erase many files to clean up your disk. It is tedious to erase many files one at a time. Just as you can use the global file specifications with the DIR and COPY commands, you can also use the wildcards with the ERASE or DEL command. These allow you to erase a group of files with a one-line command. However, be *exceedingly careful* when using wildcards with the DEL command. Once again, the strength of wildcards is also their weakness. Global means *global*. You can eliminate a group of files very quickly. If you are not careful you could erase files you want to keep. In fact, you probably will some day. "Oh no, not *those* files gone." However, this does not mean you should not use wildcards. They are far too useful. Just be careful.

Activity 7.4 Using the ERASE and DEL Commands with Wildcards on the Same Disk

Note: You have the DATA disk in Drive A with the **A:\>** displayed.

STEP 1: Key in the following:
A:\>**COPY C:\JUNK*.TMP** <Enter>

```
A:\>COPY C:\JUNK\*.TMP
C:\JUNK\JAN.TMP
C:\JUNK\FEB.TMP
C:\JUNK\MAR.TMP
C:\JUNK\APR.TMP
        4 file(s) copied

A:\>_
```

WHAT'S HAPPENING? You copied all the files with a **.TMP** extension from the **\JUNK** subdirectory on Drive C to the root directory of the DATA disk.

STEP 2: Key in the following:
A:\>**DIR *.TMP** <Enter>

```
A:\>DIR *.TMP

   Volume in drive A is DATA DISK
   Volume Serial Number is 3839-0EC8
   Directory of A:\

JAN      TMP      72   11-23-92   7:04a
FEB      TMP      74   11-23-92   7:04a
MAR      TMP      70   11-23-92   7:04a
APR      TMP      71   11-23-92   7:04a
        4 file(s)         287 bytes
                       232448 bytes free

A:\>_
```

WHAT'S HAPPENING? You should see four files that have **.TMP** as a file extension displayed on the screen. You just copied them to the DATA disk. However, prior to a global erase, it is *always* wise to key in DIR with the global file specification you are going to use. This process allows you to confirm visually that you are not going to erase a file you want to retain.

STEP 3: Key in the following:
A:\>**DEL *.TMP** <Enter>

```
A:\>DEL *.TMP

A:\>_
```

WHAT'S HAPPENING? You asked DOS to erase or delete *every* file on the DATA disk that has any file name and has the file extension **.TMP**. Only the system prompt appears on the screen. The DEL command executed, erasing those ***.TMP** files quickly and permanently. To verify this, use the DIR command.

STEP 4: Key in the following:
A:\>**DIR *.TMP** <Enter>

```
A:\>DIR *.TMP

   Volume in drive A is DATA DISK
   Volume Serial Number is 3839-0EC8
   Directory of A:\

File not found

A:\>_
```

WHAT'S HAPPENING? Those ***.TMP** files are, indeed, gone from root directory on the DATA disk and, therefore, not recoverable except by a special UNDELETE command found only in DOS 5.0. Again, let it be emphasized that before you use a wildcard to delete groups of files, you should use the DIR command to see what files you are going to delete. For instance, if you had a file called **TEST.TMP** that you had forgotten about, the directory display would include it as follows:

```
A:\>DIR *.TMP

   Volume in drive A is DATA DISK
   Volume Serial Number is 3839-0EC8
   Directory of A:\

JAN      TMP      72   11-23-92   7:04a
FEB      TMP      74   11-23-92   7:04a
MAR      TMP      70   11-23-92   7:04a
APR      TMP      71   11-23-92   7:04a
TEST     TMP     110   11-23-92   7:10a
        5 file(s)         397 bytes
                       232448 bytes free
```

Using the DIR command with the wildcards and the DEL command will let you display on the screen all the files that have been selected by ***.TMP**, which includes the **TEST.TMP** file that you did not want to erase. If you had keyed in **DEL *.TMP**, all those **.TMP** files would have been deleted. Remember, the computer does not come back and tell you, "Oh, by the way, **TEST.TMP** is also included with the ***.TMP** files; did you want to erase that file?" The DEL command simply eliminates all the **.TMP** files because that is what you told it to do. You can also use wildcards when files are in a subdirectory.

STEP 5: Key in the following:
A:\>**DIR TRIP*.99** <Enter>

```
A:\>DIR TRIP\*.99

   Volume in drive A is DATA DISK
   Volume Serial Number is 3839-0EC8
   Directory of A:\TRIP

FEB        99         74    11-23-92   7:05a
MAR        99         70    11-23-92   7:06a
APR        99         71    11-23-92   7:07a
         3 file(s)             215 bytes
                            236544 bytes free

A:\>_
```

WHAT'S HAPPENING? There are three files with the extension **.99** on the DATA disk in the subdirectory **TRIP**. The DEL command works the same way, but you must be sure to include the path name.

STEP 6: Key in the following:
A:\>**DEL TRIP*.99** <Enter>

```
A:\>DEL TRIP\*.99

A:\>_
```

WHAT'S HAPPENING? You asked DOS to erase or delete *every* file on the DATA disk in the subdirectory **TRIP** that has any file name and has the file extension **.99**. Only the system prompt appears on the screen. The DEL command executed, erasing those ***.99** files quickly and permanently. To verify this, you can use the DIR command.

STEP 7: Key in the following:
A:\>**DIR TRIP*.99** <Enter>

```
A:\>DIR TRIP\*.99

   Volume in drive A is DATA DISK
   Volume Serial Number is 3839-0EC8
   Directory of A:\TRIP

File not found

A:\>_
```

WHAT'S HAPPENING? The files are indeed gone.

7.5 Using the ERASE and DEL Commands on Another Drive and Subdirectory

Using the DEL command to eliminate files works exactly the same on other drives and subdirectories, with or without wildcards, as it did in the previous activities. The syntax of the command remains DEL [*drive:*][*path*]*filename*. The only difference is that you must specify which disk drive and which subdirectory DOS is going to look on. Once again, DOS follows your instructions exactly as keyed in; it does not check with you to see if you are deleting the correct file. One of the most common mistakes computer users make is placing the drive designator or subdirectory in the wrong place, completely changing the instructions. Again, the syntax of the command is:

DEL [*drive:*][*path*]*filename.ext*

DEL is the command. *drive:* represents the designated drive. *path* represents any subdirectory. *filename.ext* represents the name of the file you wish to delete. For example, if the file you want to delete is on Drive A, you would substitute A: for *drive:*. If the file you want to delete is on Drive C, you would substitute C: for the *drive:*. If the path name was **\DOS**, you would substitute **\DOS** for *path*. *filename.ext* is the name of the file—the file specification. For example, if the default drive is **A>** and you want to delete a file on the disk in Drive B called **GONE.FIL**, a common error is to key in the command as:

A>**DEL GONE.FIL B:**

This sequence is *wrong* because you did not use the proper syntax, DEL *d:filename.ext*. The command should have been keyed in as:

A>**DEL B:GONE.FIL**.

Not only is the command wrong, but it is also illogical, the equivalent of sending someone to throw away a file folder and not telling that person which file cabinet. What are the results of incorrectly keying in the command? It depends on the version of DOS that you have. If you have a version prior to 3.3, DOS will delete the file on the disk in Drive A, the default drive, and will not pay attention to the B:, because it is in the wrong place. If you have DOS 4.0 or above, it will tell you that you have too many parameters. Remember to be aware of the default drive and the path syntax.

Activity 7.6

Using the ERASE and DEL Commands on Another Disk and Subdirectory

Note: The DATA disk is in Drive A and the **A:\>** is displayed.

STEP 1: Key in the following:
A:\>**C:** <Enter>

STEP 2: Key in the following:
C:\>**CD \JUNK** <Enter>

```
A:\>C:

C:\>CD \JUNK

C:\JUNK>_
```

WHAT'S HAPPENING? You changed the default subdirectory from the root of the disk in Drive C to the **\JUNK** subdirectory. The purpose of this activity is to have two identically named files on different drives.

STEP 3: Key in the following:
C:\JUNK>**DIR HELLO.TXT** <Enter>

```
C:\JUNK>DIR HELLO.TXT

   Volume in drive C is MS-DOS_5
   Volume Serial Number is 16D1-68D4
   Directory of C:\JUNK

HELLO     TXT      52   11-23-92   7:07a
        1 file(s)          52 bytes
                      9306112 bytes free

C:\JUNK>_
```

STEP 4: Key in the following:
C:\JUNK>**DIR A:HELLO.TXT** <Enter>

```
C:\JUNK>DIR A:HELLO.TXT

   Volume in drive A is DATA DISK
   Volume Serial Number is 3839-0EC8
   Directory of A:\

HELLO     TXT      52   11-23-92   7:07a
        1 file(s)          52 bytes
                       239616 bytes free

C:\JUNK>_
```

Note: If you do not have the file **HELLO.TXT** on the DATA disk, copy it to the DATA disk from the **\JUNK** subdirectory on Drive C.

WHAT'S HAPPENING? You have two files called **HELLO.TXT**. One file is on the hard disk in the subdirectory **\JUNK** in Drive C. The other file is on the DATA disk in Drive A. You want to delete the file on the DATA disk, not on the hard disk.

STEP 5: Key in the following:
C:\JUNK>**DEL A:HELLO.TXT** <Enter>

```
C:\JUNK>DEL A:HELLO.TXT

C:\JUNK>_
```

WHAT'S HAPPENING? You asked DOS to erase the file on the DATA disk called **HELLO.TXT**. The file should be gone from the DATA disk, but the file called **HELLO.TXT** on the hard disk (Drive C, subdirectory **\JUNK**) should still be there.

STEP 6: Key in the following:
C:\JUNK>**DIR HELLO.TXT** <Enter>

STEP 7: Key in the following:
C:\JUNK>**DIR A:HELLO.TXT** <Enter>

```
C:\JUNK>DIR HELLO.TXT

   Volume in drive C is MS-DOS_5
   Volume Serial Number is 16D1-68D4
   Directory of C:\JUNK

HELLO    TXT      52   11-23-92   7:07a
        1 file(s)          52 bytes
                      9306112 bytes free

C:\JUNK>DIR A:HELLO.TXT

   Volume in drive A is DATA DISK
   Volume Serial Number is 3839-0EC8
   Directory of A:\

File not found

C:\JUNK>_
```

WHAT'S HAPPENING? The file called **HELLO.TXT** is still on the hard disk in the subdirectory **\JUNK** on Drive C, but the file called **HELLO.TXT** on the DATA disk is gone.

STEP 8: Key in the following:
C:\JUNK>**DIR A:\TRIP\BLUE.JAZ** <Enter>

```
C:\JUNK>DIR A:\TRIP\BLUE.JAZ

   Volume in drive A is DATA DISK
   Volume Serial Number is 3839-0EC8
   Directory of A:\TRIP

BLUE      JAZ      18   10-12-92   9:00a
        1 file(s)          18 bytes
                       240640 bytes free

C:\JUNK>_
```

WHAT'S HAPPENING? There is a file called **BLUE.JAZ** in the subdirectory **TRIP** on the DATA disk. To delete this file, you once again follow the syntax of the DEL command, substituting the values you want for the variable parameters.

STEP 9: Key in the following:
C:\JUNK>**DEL A:\TRIP\BLUE.JAZ** <Enter>

```
C:\JUNK>DEL A:\TRIP\BLUE.JAZ

C:\JUNK>_
```

WHAT'S HAPPENING? The syntax is DEL [*drive:*][*path*]*filename*[*.ext*]. You substituted the drive letter of the DATA disk for the [*drive:*]. You then substituted **TRIP** for the [*path*]. You did not need to key in the first backslash because the root directory is the default. DOS assumed you meant the root directory of the DATA disk because you did not otherwise specify. However, to be on the safe side, you included the \ for the root directory. You then substituted **BLUE.JAZ** for the [*filename*[*.ext*]. The second backslash was necessary because you need a delimiter between the file name and the subdirectory name. This backslash is just like the period that you used to separate the filename from the file extension. Is the file gone?

STEP 10: Key in the following:
C:\JUNK>**DIR A:\TRIP\BLUE.JAZ** <Enter>

```
C:\JUNK>DIR A:\TRIP\BLUE.JAZ

   Volume in drive A is DATA DISK
   Volume Serial Number is 3839-0EC8
   Directory of A:\TRIP

File not found

C:\JUNK>_
```

WHAT'S HAPPENING? The file **BLUE.JAZ** from the directory **TRIP** on the DATA disk is gone.

7.7 The /P Parameter with the DEL Command

One of the things that happens with new versions of software is that enhancements are often included. This is true with DOS 4.0 and 5.0. The problem with earlier versions of the DEL command was that there was no way to change your choices. DOS simply erased the file. With the new versions of DOS, you can ask DOS to confirm with you prior to deleting the file. The syntax is:

DOS 4.0 and 5.0

DEL [*drive:*][*path*]*filename* [/P]
or ERASE [*drive:*][*path*]*filename* [/P]

The last statement, /P, is an optional fixed parameter. Its purpose is to display each file name with a message to verify that you really want to delete this file. You can think of the P standing for "prompt you for an answer." This parameter is particularly useful when using wildcards. You cannot accidentally eliminate a file. This feature, however, is only available in DOS 4.0 or 5.0.

Activity 7.8 Using the /P with the DEL Command

DOS 4.0 and 5.0

Note: The **C:\JUNK>** is displayed. The DATA disk is in Drive A.

STEP 1: Key in the following:
C:\JUNK>**COPY *.99 A:\TRIP** <Enter>

```
C:\JUNK>COPY *.99 A:\TRIP
JAN.99
FEB.99
MAR.99
APR.99
        4 file(s) copied

C:\JUNK>_
```

WHAT'S HAPPENING? You copied files from **\JUNK** on the hard disk to the subdirectory called **TRIP** on the DATA disk. Next, you will verify that those files are there.

STEP 2: Key in the following:
C:\JUNK>**DIR A:\TRIP** <Enter>

```
C:\JUNK>DIR A:\TRIP

   Volume in drive A is DATA DISK
   Volume Serial Number is 3839-0EC8
   Directory of A:\TRIP

.           <DIR>       06-17-92   9:00p
..          <DIR>       06-17-92   9:00p
```

```
JAN        99        72    11-23-92   7:04p
FEB        99        74    11-23-92   7:05p
MAR        99        70    11-23-92   7:06p
APR        99        71    11-23-92   7:07p
GREEN      JAZ       18    10-12-92   9:00p
         7 file(s)            305 bytes
                           237568 bytes free

C:\JUNK>_
```

WHAT'S HAPPENING? The files you just copied are in the subdirectory **\TRIP** on the DATA disk. In addition, the file called **GREEN.JAZ** is also in that subdirectory. Next you are going to delete some of the **.99** files selectively.

STEP 3: Key in the following:
C:\JUNK>**DEL A:\TRIP*.99 /P** <Enter>

```
C:\JUNK>DEL A:\TRIP\*.99 /P

A:\TRIP\JAN.99,     Delete (Y/N)?_
```

WHAT'S HAPPENING? The /P parameter, when included in the command line, prompts you asking if you want to delete the file called **JAN.99** in the subdirectory **TRIP** on the DATA disk.

STEP 4: Key in the following:
Y

```
C:\JUNK>DEL A:\TRIP\*.99 /P

A:\TRIP\JAN.99,     Delete (Y/N)?Y
A:\TRIP\FEB.99,     Delete (Y/N)?_
```

WHAT'S HAPPENING? DOS found the next file and asked if you want to delete the file called **FEB.99**.

STEP 5: Key in the following:
N

```
C:\JUNK>DEL A:\TRIP\*.99 /P

A:\TRIP\JAN.99,     Delete (Y/N)?Y
A:\TRIP\FEB.99,     Delete (Y/N)?N
A:\TRIP\MAR.99,     Delete (Y/N)?_
```

WHAT'S HAPPENING? DOS found the next file and asked if you want to delete the file called **MAR.99**.

STEP 6: Key in the following:
Y

```
C:\JUNK>DEL A:\TRIP\*.99 /P

A:\TRIP\JAN.99,    Delete (Y/N)?Y
A:\TRIP\FEB.99,    Delete (Y/N)?N
A:\TRIP\MAR.99,    Delete (Y/N)?Y
A:\TRIP\APR.99,    Delete (Y/N)?_
```

WHAT'S HAPPENING? DOS found the next file and asked you if you want to delete the file called **APR.99**.

STEP 7: Key in the following:
N

```
C:\JUNK>DEL A:\TRIP\*.99 /P

A:\TRIP\JAN.99,    Delete (Y/N)?Y
A:\TRIP\FEB.99,    Delete (Y/N)?N
A:\TRIP\MAR.99,    Delete (Y/N)?Y
A:\TRIP\APR.99,    Delete (Y/N)?N

C:\JUNK>_
```

WHAT'S HAPPENING? DOS returned you to the system prompt because there were no more files with the extension **.99** on the DATA disk in the subdirectory **TRIP**. You were able to delete files selectively. You deleted the files **JAN.99** and **MAR.99** but kept the files **FEB.99** and **APR.99**. You can verify this by using the DIR command.

STEP 8: Key in the following:
C:\JUNK>**DIR A:\TRIP** <Enter>

```
C:\JUNK>DIR A:\TRIP

   Volume in drive A is DATA DISK
   Volume Serial Number is 3839-0EC8
   Directory of A:\TRIP

.            <DIR>      06-17-92   9:00p
..           <DIR>      06-17-92   9:00p
FEB        99       74  11-23-92   7:05p
APR        99       71  11-23-92   7:07p
GREEN      JAZ      18  10-12-92   9:00p
        5 file(s)         163 bytes
                       239616 bytes free

C:\JUNK>_
```

WHAT'S HAPPENING? You did retain the files **FEB.99** and **APR.99** but deleted **JAN.99** and **MAR.99**. The file **GREEN.JAZ** was not deleted because it did not have the file extension **.99**.

7.9 Changing the Names of Files with the RENAME Command

Often, when you are working with files, you find that you want to change a file name. For example, you may wish to change the name of a file to indicate an older version. COPY would not work because you would overwrite the file. In addition, COPY creates an additional file—you would have a source file and a destination file. You might also think of a more descriptive file name. As the contents of a file change, the old name may no longer reflect the contents. Sometimes, the reason is that you made a typographical error when you first named the file. DOS supplies a way to change existing file names using the RENAME command, an internal command. RENAME does exactly what it says; it changes the name of a file, similar to relabeling a file folder. The contents of the file do not change, only the name of the file folder. Using RENAME is different from copying a file. When copying a file, you retain the original and make a copy; you start with one file and end with two. With the RENAME command you start with one file under one name and end up with the same file under a new name. The syntax for this command is:

RENAME [*drive:*][*path*] *filename1* *filename2*
or REN [*drive:*][*path*] *filename1* *filename2*

Note: You cannot specify a new drive or path for your destination file.

The RENAME command has two forms, RENAME or REN, with exactly the same syntax. Most computer users choose REN, simply because it has fewer keystrokes. The syntax is the command, REN; the first parameter, or the old file name; and the second parameter, or the new file name, from left to right.

Activity 7.10 Using the RENAME Command with Individual Files on the Same Disk

Note: The **C:\JUNK>** is displayed. The DATA disk is in Drive A.

STEP 1: Key in the following:
C:\JUNK>**CD ** <Enter>

STEP 2: Key in the following:
C:\>**A:** <Enter>

```
C:\JUNK>CD \

C:\>A:

A:\>_
```

WHAT'S HAPPENING? You first changed the default directory to the root directory on the hard disk. You then changed the default drive to A.

STEP 3: Key in the following:
A:\>**COPY C:\JUNK\DATA*.TV** <Enter>

```
A:\>COPY C:\JUNK\DATA\*.TV
C:\JUNK\DATA\DRAMA.TV
C:\JUNK\DATA\COMEDY.TV
        2 file(s) copied

A:\>_
```

WHAT'S HAPPENING? You copied two files from the hard disk subdirectory **\JUNK\DATA** to the root directory of the DATA disk.

STEP 4: Key in the following:
A:\>**TYPE COMEDY.TV** <Enter>

```
A:\>TYPE COMEDY.TV
COMEDY TELEVISION SERIES

Cheers
Family Ties
SOAP
Head of the Class
Perfect Strangers
I Love Lucy
Roseanne
TAXI
The Mary Tyler Moore Show
The Wonder Years

A:\>_
```

WHAT'S HAPPENING? You are displaying the contents of the file called **COMEDY.TV** located in the root directory on the DATA disk. You opened the file folder called **COMEDY.TV** and looked inside.

STEP 5: Key in the following:
A:\>**REN COMEDY.TV COMEDY.TV** <Enter>

```
A:\>REN COMEDY.TV COMEDY.TV
Duplicate file name or file not found

A:\>_
```

WHAT'S HAPPENING? The message tells you that two files on the same disk and same subdirectory cannot have the same name ("Duplicate file name"), or that DOS could not find a file called **COMEDY.TV** ("file not found"). In this example, the broken rule is "Duplicate file name." You already have a file on the DATA disk called **COMEDY.TV**.

STEP 6: Key in the following:
A:\>**REN COMEDY.TV FUNNY.TV** <Enter>

```
A:\>REN COMEDY.TV FUNNY.TV

A:\>_
```

WHAT'S HAPPENING? Using the command REN, you asked DOS to change the name of the file called **COMEDY.TV** to a new file name—**FUNNY.TV**. Since the default is the DATA disk and the default subdirectory the root, DOS will only look on the root directory of the DATA disk for the file called **COMEDY.TV**. Once you pressed <Enter>, you got back only the system prompt. Did anything happen?

STEP 7: Key in the following:
A:\>**DIR COMEDY.TV** <Enter>

```
A:\>DIR COMEDY.TV

   Volume in drive A is DATA DISK
   Volume Serial Number is 3839-0EC8
   Directory of A:\

File not found

A:\>_
```

WHAT'S HAPPENING? Once you have renamed a file, it no longer exists under its old file name.

STEP 8: Key in the following:
A:\>**DIR FUNNY.TV** <Enter>

```
A:\>DIR FUNNY.TV

   Volume in drive A is DATA DISK
   Volume Serial Number is 3839-0EC8
   Directory of A:\

FUNNY    TV       170    11-23-92 10:17a
        1 file(s)          170 bytes
                        237568 bytes free

A:\>_
```

WHAT'S HAPPENING? The above display demonstrates that the file called **FUNNY.TV** is on the DATA disk in the root directory. You know that the file named **COMEDY.TV** is no longer on the DATA disk. Are the contents of the file **FUNNY.TV** the same as the contents of the file that was named **COMEDY.TV**?

STEP 9: Key in the following:
A:\>**TYPE FUNNY.TV** <Enter>

```
A:\>TYPE FUNNY.TV
COMEDY TELEVISION SERIES

Cheers
Family Ties
SOAP
Head of the Class
Perfect Strangers
I Love Lucy
Roseanne
TAXI
The Mary Tyler Moore Show
The Wonder Years

A:\>_
```

WHAT'S HAPPENING? As you can see, you changed the file name from **COMEDY.TV** to **FUNNY.TV**, but the contents of the file did not change. This process does not change when a file is in a subdirectory. You just have to follow the syntax:

REN [*drive:*][*path*]*oldfile.ext newfile.ext.*

In Activity 7.2, you copied the files with a **.JAZ** extension to the subdirectory called **TRIP**. Although you deleted the file called **BLUE.JAZ**, you still have a file called **GREEN.JAZ** on the DATA disk in the subdirectory **TRIP**.

STEP 10: Key in the following:
A:\>**DIR TRIP\GREEN.JAZ** <Enter>

```
A:\>DIR TRIP\GREEN.JAZ

   Volume in drive A is DATA DISK
   Volume Serial Number is 3839-0EC8
   Directory of A:\TRIP

GREEN     JAZ      18   10-12-92   9:00p
         1 file(s)          18 bytes
                        237568 bytes free

A:\>_
```

WHAT'S HAPPENING? The file called **GREEN.JAZ** is in the subdirectory called **TRIP** on the DATA disk. Using REN is different from using COPY. The COPY syntax requires that you place the path name in front of the source file and destination file. You are dealing with two files; thus, each file could be in a separate location. This situation is not true with REN. You are dealing only with one file and are only changing the file folder name. You are not moving the file; thus, the path name is only placed in front of the source file.

STEP 11: Key in the following:
A:\>**REN TRIP\GREEN.JAZ TRIP\RED.JAZ** <Enter>

```
A:\>REN TRIP\GREEN.JAZ TRIP\RED.JAZ
Invalid filename or file not found

A:\>_
```

WHAT'S HAPPENING? The message is really not very descriptive. "Invalid filename" really refers to the **TRIP\RED.JAZ. TRIP\RED.JAZ**, the portion that is incorrect. It is incorrect because you do not place a drive or subdirectory preceding the new filename.

STEP 12: Key in the following:
A:\>**REN TRIP\GREEN.JAZ RED.JAZ** <Enter>

```
A:\>REN TRIP\GREEN.JAZ RED.JAZ

A:\>_
```

WHAT'S HAPPENING? You received no error message, indicating that this command was executed. You will confirm that the file name was changed from **GREEN.JAZ** to **RED.JAZ** using the DIR command.

STEP 13: Key in the following:
A:\>**DIR TRIP*.JAZ** <Enter>

```
A:\>DIR TRIP\*.JAZ

   Volume in drive A is DATA DISK
   Volume Serial Number is 3839-0EC8
   Directory of A:\TRIP

RED      JAZ      18   10-12-92   9:00p
        1 file(s)          18 bytes
                       237568 bytes free

A:\>_
```

WHAT'S HAPPENING? There is only one file with a **.JAZ** extension in the subdirectory **TRIP** on the DATA disk, but it is now called **RED.JAZ** instead of **GREEN.JAZ**.

7.11 Using RENAME with Wildcards on the Same Drive and Subdirectory

When you wish to change the names of a group of files, you can use the REN or RENAME command with the wildcards, ? and *, allowing you to change many file names with a one-line command. The wildcards or global file specifications are so "global" that, prior to renaming files, it is wise to do a directory display with the wildcards you want to use so that you can see what files are going to be renamed. You do not want to rename a file accidentally. Once a file is renamed, you cannot find the file under its old name, *ever*. This rule has caused havoc for users because it seems as if the file is lost. The file is still on the disk, but you cannot find it unless you know the new name.

Activity 7.12 Using RENAME with Wildcards on the Same Drive and Same Subdirectory and Different Subdirectories

Note: The DATA disk is in Drive A. The **A:\>** is displayed. This activity assumes you have files on the DATA disk with the file extension **.NEW**. If you do not, you may copy them from **\JUNK** to the DATA disk.

STEP 1: Key in the following:
A:\>**DIR *.NEW** <Enter>

```
A:\>DIR *.NEW

   Volume in drive A is DATA DISK
   Volume Serial Number is 3839-0EC8
   Directory of A:\

JAN      NEW      71   11-23-92   7:05a
FEB      NEW      73   11-23-92   7:10a
MAR      NEW      69   11-23-92   7:11a
APR      NEW      70   11-23-92   7:11a
        4 file(s)        283 bytes
                      237568 bytes free

A:\>_
```

WHAT'S HAPPENING? You have four files with the extension **.NEW**. Your objective is to retain these four files, keep their file names, and change the file extension from **.NEW** to **.BUD**. You could rename these files one at a time, **REN JAN.NEW JAN.BUD**, then **REN FEB.NEW FEB.BUD**, then **REN MAR.NEW MAR.BUD** and **REN APR.NEW APR.BUD**. However, this repetition becomes very tiresome. Using the wildcards will allow you to rename these four files at one time.

STEP 2: Key in the following:
A:\>**REN *.NEW *.BUD** <Enter>

```
A:\>REN *.NEW *.BUD

A:\>_
```

WHAT'S HAPPENING? All that is displayed is the system prompt. Was the work done? Are the files renamed? To verify that you did rename these files, you can use the DIR command.

STEP 3: Key in the following:
A:\>**DIR *.NEW** <Enter>

```
A:\>DIR *.NEW

   Volume in drive A is DATA DISK
   Volume Serial Number is 3839-0EC8
   Directory of A:\

File not found

A:\>_
```

WHAT'S HAPPENING? Files with the extension **.NEW** no longer exist on the DATA disk.

STEP 4: Key in the following:
A:\>**DIR *.BUD** <Enter>

```
A:\>DIR *.BUD

   Volume in drive A is DATA DISK
   Volume Serial Number is 3839-0EC8
   Directory of A:\

JAN      BUD      71   11-23-92   7:05a
FEB      BUD      73   11-23-92   7:10a
MAR      BUD      69   11-23-92   7:11a
APR      BUD      70   11-23-92   7:11a
        4 file(s)        283 bytes
                      237568 bytes free

A:\>_
```

WHAT'S HAPPENING? With the REN command and the use of the wildcards, you renamed four files with one command. You can also use wildcards with subdirectories. In Activity 7.2, you created a subdirectory called **TRIP** on the DATA disk. If you have not done this, do so now.

STEP 5: Key in the following:
A:\>**COPY *.BUD \TRIP** <Enter>

```
A:\>COPY *.BUD \TRIP
JAN.BUD
FEB.BUD
MAR.BUD
APR.BUD
        4 file(s) copied

A:\>_
```

WHAT'S HAPPENING? You copied files with the **.BUD** extension from the root directory of the DATA disk to a subdirectory called **TRIP** on the DATA disk. You created the **.BUD** files in the root directory in Activity 7.12.

STEP 6: Key in the following:
A:\>**REN TRIP*.BUD *.PEN** <Enter>

STEP 7: Key in the following:
A:\>**DIR TRIP*.BUD** <Enter>

STEP 8: Key in the following:
A:\>**DIR TRIP*.PEN** <Enter>

```
A:\>REN TRIP\*.BUD *.PEN

A:\>DIR TRIP\*.BUD

   Volume in drive A is DATA DISK
   Volume Serial Number is 3839-0EC8
   Directory of A:\TRIP

File not found

A:\>DIR TRIP\*.PEN

   Volume in drive A is DATA DISK
   Volume Serial Number is 3839-0EC8
   Directory of A:\TRIP

JAN      PEN      71   11-23-92   7:05a
FEB      PEN      73   11-23-92   7:10a
MAR      PEN      69   11-23-92   7:11a
APR      PEN      70   11-23-92   7:11a
        4 file(s)        283 bytes
                      237568 bytes free

A:\>_
```

WHAT'S HAPPENING? You successfully renamed all the files with the **.BUD** extension in the subdirectory **TRIP** on the DATA disk to a new set of files with the same file name but with the file extension of **.PEN**.

7.13 Using RENAME on Different Drives and Subdirectories

Since REN is an internal command, you can use it at any time, for any file, in any drive and in any subdirectory. If you wish to rename a file on a different drive, you must specify on which drive the old file is located. If you want it renamed in a different subdirectory as well, you must specify in which subdirectory the file is located. In the syntax of REN *oldfile.ext newfile.ext*, DOS looks only for *oldfile.ext* on the designated drive and subdirectory. If you do not preface *oldfile.ext* with a drive letter, DOS only looks on the default drive. When you key in the command **REN B:OLDFILE.EXT NEWFILE.EXT**, DOS will look only on the disk in Drive B for the file called **OLDFILE.EXT**. If a subdirectory is involved, you must also include the subdirectory, so the command would read:

REN C:\JUNK\OLDFILE.EXT NEWFILE.EXT.

In addition, there is a substantial difference between the COPY command and the REN command. With the COPY command, you can copy a file from one disk to another disk, ending up with two identical files on different disks. You cannot do this with the REN command because it only changes the names of files on one disk at a time. Remember, with REN you are changing the name of an existing file on a specific disk. REN finds a file on the designated disk and renames it. The REN command cannot and does not move a file from one disk to another. For example, if you had a file cabinet (disk), and in this cabinet you had a file folder called *oldfile* (file) that you renamed *newfile*, that folder is still in the same file cabinet. It does not jump to another file cabinet by the mere act of changing the name. That is how REN works.

Activity 7.14 How to Use RENAME on Different Drives and Subdirectories

Note: The **A:\>** is displayed. The DATA disk is in Drive A.

STEP 1: Key in the following:
A:\>**C:** <Enter>

STEP 2: Key in the following:
C:\>**CD \JUNK** <Enter>

```
A:\>C:

C:\>CD \JUNK

C:\JUNK>_
```

WHAT'S HAPPENING? You have changed the default drive to C: and have logged into the **\JUNK** subdirectory.

STEP 3: Key in the following:
C:\JUNK>**DIR A:APRIL.TXT** <Enter>

```
C:\JUNK>DIR A:APRIL.TXT

   Volume in drive A is DATA DISK
   Volume Serial Number is 3839-0EC8
   Directory of A:\

APRIL     TXT       70    11-23-92   7:11a
        1 file(s)             70 bytes
                          233472 bytes free

C:\JUNK>_
```

Note: If you do not have **APRIL.TXT** on the DATA disk, copy it now to the DATA disk from **\JUNK**.

WHAT'S HAPPENING? The directory display tells you that the file called **APRIL.TXT** does exist on the DATA disk.

STEP 4: Key in the following:
C:\JUNK>**TYPE A:APRIL.TXT** <Enter>

```
C:\JUNK>TYPE A:APRIL.TXT
This is my April file.
It is my fourth dummy file.
This is file 4.

C:\JUNK>_
```

WHAT'S HAPPENING You used the TYPE command to see the contents of the file called **APRIL.TXT** located on the DATA disk.

STEP 5: Key in the following:
C:\JUNK>**REN A:APRIL.TXT A:APR.TST** <Enter>

```
C:\JUNK>REN A:APRIL.TXT A:APR.TST
Invalid parameter

C:\JUNK>_
```

WHAT'S HAPPENING? The syntax of this command is:
REN *[drive:][path]oldfile.ext newfile.ext*

Since DOS knows you cannot change a file name on any other disk except where the original file is located, it will not allow you to put a drive designator before the new file name.

STEP 6: Key in the following:
C:\JUNK>**REN A:APRIL.TXT APR.TST** <Enter>

```
C:\JUNK>REN A:APRIL.TXT APR.TST

C:\JUNK>_
```

WHAT'S HAPPENING? You see no messages because the syntax is correct. DOS could find the file called **APRIL.TXT** on the DATA disk. You requested that DOS change the name of the file on the DATA disk called **APRIL.TXT** to a new file name **APR.TST**.

STEP 7: Key in the following:
C:\JUNK>**DIR APRIL.TXT** <Enter>

STEP 8: Key in the following:
C:\JUNK>**DIR A:APRIL.TXT** <Enter>

```
C:\JUNK>DIR APRIL.TXT

   Volume in drive C is MS-DOS_5
   Volume Serial Number is 16D1-68D4
   Directory of C:\JUNK
```

```
APRIL     TXT      71   11-23-92  7:07a
       1 file(s)          71 bytes
                     8675328 bytes free

C:\JUNK>DIR A:APRIL.TXT

   Volume in drive A is DATA DISK
   Volume Serial Number is 3839-0EC8
   Directory of A:\

File not found

C:\JUNK>_
```

WHAT'S HAPPENING? You did not rename the file **APRIL.TXT** on the hard disk, only the one on the DATA disk. You got the message "File not found" on the DATA disk because the file no longer exists under the file name **A:APRIL.TXT**.

STEP 9: Key in the following:
C:\JUNK>**DIR A:APR.TST** <Enter>

```
C:\JUNK>DIR A:APR.TST

   Volume in drive C is DATA DISK
   Volume Serial Number is 3839-0EC8
   Directory of A:\

APR       TST      70   11-23-92  7:11a
       1 file(s)          70 bytes
                      233472 bytes free

C:\JUNK>_
```

WHAT'S HAPPENING? You successfully renamed the file on the DATA disk from **APRIL.TXT** to **APR.TST**. Does the file **APR.TST** have the same contents as **APRIL.TXT**? It should, because renaming changes only the file name, not the contents. To verify this, you can use the TYPE command.

STEP 10: Key in the following:
C:\JUNK>**TYPE A:APR.TST** <Enter>

```
C:\JUNK>TYPE A:APR.TST
This is my April file.
It is my fourth dummy file.
This is file 4.

C:\JUNK>_
```

WHAT'S HAPPENING? If you check the screen display following Step 4, you will see that the file contents are identical. REN works the same way with subdirectories on other drives. In Activity 7.12, you copied the files with the **.BUD** extension to the subdirectory **TRIP** on the DATA disk; you then renamed them with the same file name but with the **.PEN** file extension.

STEP 11: Key in the following:
C:\JUNK>**DIR A:\TRIP*.PEN** <Enter>

```
C:\JUNK>DIR A:\TRIP\*.PEN

   Volume in drive A is DATA DISK
   Volume Serial Number is 3839-0EC8
   Directory of A:\TRIP

JAN      PEN      71   11-23-92   7:05a
FEB      PEN      73   11-23-92   7:10a
MAR      PEN      69   11-23-92   7:11a
APR      PEN      70   11-23-92   7:11a
        4 file(s)        283 bytes
                      233472 bytes free

C:\JUNK>_
```

WHAT'S HAPPENING? The files are there in the subdirectory **TRIP** on the DATA disk.

STEP 12: Key in the following:
C:\JUNK>**REN A:\TRIP*.PEN *.INK** <Enter>

```
C:\JUNK>REN A:\TRIP\*.PEN *.INK

C:\JUNK>_
```

WHAT'S HAPPENING? Once again, all that appears is the system prompt. Notice how you placed only the drive and path in front of the file names that you wanted to change (the old file names). These files can only be renamed on the DATA disk in the subdirectory **TRIP**. The REN command does not move files; it only changes the file names.

STEP 13: Key in the following:
C:\JUNK>**DIR A:\TRIP*.PEN** <Enter>

STEP 14: Key in the following:
C:\JUNK>**DIR A:\TRIP*.INK** <Enter>

```
C:\JUNK>DIR A:\TRIP\*.PEN

   Volume in drive A is DATA DISK
   Volume Serial Number is 3839-0EC8
   Directory of A:\TRIP

File not found

C:\JUNK>DIR A:\TRIP\*.INK

   Volume in drive A is DATA DISK
   Volume Serial Number is 3839-0EC8
   Directory of A:\TRIP
```

```
JAN      INK      71   11-23-92   7:05a
FEB      INK      73   11-23-92   7:10a
MAR      INK      69   11-23-92   7:11a
APR      INK      70   11-23-92   7:11a
       4 file(s)          283 bytes
                       233472 bytes free

C:\JUNK>_
```

WHAT'S HAPPENING? You successfully renamed all the **.PEN** files in the subdirectory **TRIP** on the DATA disk. These files no longer exist with the **.PEN** file extension.

7.15 Backing Up Your DATA Disk

You should get into the habit of *always* backing up your data files so that, if something happens to the original data, you will have a copy of the original material. In data-processing circles, this habit is called **Disaster and Recovery Planning**. It means exactly what it says. If there is a disaster—fire, flood, power surge, theft, head crash, coffee spilled on a disk—what is your plan to recover your programs and data? Nowadays, the term that is used is **Business Resumption Plan**, to cover more than data processing and include the entire business spectrum. However, backing up programs on application disks can be tricky, especially on **copy-protected** disks (which means you cannot back them up with regular DOS commands). You should never back up your program or software application disks until you understand how the application programs work. All application software comes with documentation that instructs you how to back up the specific application program disk you own. Backing up a hard disk is a special circumstance, using special DOS commands. You cannot and should not back up the hard drive using the techniques that will be described here because the contents of a hard disk will not fit on one floppy disk.

However, you can and should back up all the data on any data disk with the following techniques. There are three ways to back up data files. One way is to back up the entire data disk. You will get all the files and all the subdirectories. You use the DISKCOPY command, which makes an identical copy of a disk, track for track and sector for sector. However, remember that DISKCOPY cannot be used to back up the hard disk.

You can also use the COPY command to back up specific files. Later, we will discuss the third method, using the XCOPY command.

Typically, a data disk is backed up at the end of every work session so that you can keep your data and files current. It is very important to acquire a regular backup routine so that it becomes an automatic process. In general, most people make a point of backing up their data files regularly. Usually, since people have purchased application software, they are not so worried about backing up the programs. If something happens to the hard disk, the user can recover and reinstall the programs from the floppy disks. However, the data that the user created is unrecoverable, unless the user has backed up the data.

Activity 7.16 Backing Up the DATA Disk Using the DISKCOPY Command

STEP 1: You should have the **C:\JUNK>** displayed and the DATA disk in Drive A. The default subdirectory is **\JUNK**. You need to log into the **\DOS** subdirectory with the DOS utility programs. The DATA disk is in Drive A and has the files you have been creating and using. You are going to be backing up the DATA disk, not the DOS System Disk, ACTIVITIES disk or the hard disk.

STEP 2: Get a blank disk, one that has not been used or one that has data on it that you no longer want. Write BACKUP DATA DISK on the label.

Note: Remember that when using DISKCOPY, the media types must be the same. If the DATA disk is a 360 KB, you must use a blank 360 KB disk as the backup disk. If the DATA disk is a 1.2 MB, you must use a blank 1.2 MB disk as the backup disk. If the DATA disk is a 720 KB disk, you must use a blank 720 KB disk as the backup disk. If the DATA disk is a 1.44 MB disk, you must use a blank 1.44 MB disk as the backup disk.

STEP 3: Key in the following:
C:\JUNK>**CD \DOS** <Enter>

Note: If the subdirectory name that has the DOS utility programs in it has a different subdirectory name, use that as the path name, i.e. **CD \BIN**.

```
C:\JUNK>CD \DOS

C:\DOS>_
```

WHAT'S HAPPENING? You have changed the default subdirectory to the place where the DOS utility programs are. Remember, you are not going to use DISKCOPY to copy the hard disk or Drive C.

STEP 4: Key in the following:
C:\DOS>**DISKCOPY A: A:** <Enter>

```
Insert SOURCE diskette in drive A:

Press any key to continue . . . . .
```

WHAT'S HAPPENING? You are asked to put the SOURCE disk that you wish to copy in Drive A. In this case, the DATA disk, which you want to copy, is already in Drive A. Since you are using only one floppy disk drive, you are going to have to swap disks when prompted. You keyed in two disk drives, A and A, to ensure that you do not accidentally copy the hard disk. You are telling DOS to make a copy from the disk in Drive A to the disk in Drive A.

STEP 5: Press <Enter>.

```
Copying 40 tracks
9 sectors per track, 2 side(s)
```

WHAT'S HAPPENING? The number of tracks and sectors will vary depending on the disk media type. The DISKCOPY command tells DOS to copy everything on the disk in Drive A (the SOURCE) to RAM. While this program is doing the copying, the cursor flashes on the screen. When the command is completed or the program is finished executing (copying), you need to take another step. You receive the following prompt:

```
Insert TARGET diskette in drive A:

Press any key to continue . . . . .
```

WHAT'S HAPPENING? This prompt tells you to remove the SOURCE disk from Drive A and insert the blank or TARGET disk in Drive A so DOS has a place to copy the information.

STEP 6: Remove your original DATA disk from Drive A. Insert the blank disk labeled BACKUP DATA DISK into Drive A. The BACKUP DATA DISK is your target disk. Close or latch the drive door. Press <Enter>.

WHAT'S HAPPENING? Again, you see the flashing cursor. Now, whatever was copied into RAM is being copied or written to the blank disk in Drive A. Remember, if you do not have a 360 KB floppy disk drive, you will receive the following prompt:

```
Insert SOURCE diskette in drive A:

Press any key to continue...
```

This prompt tells you to remove the TARGET disk from Drive A and insert the original DATA disk back into Drive A. You then remove the target disk from Drive A and insert the original DATA disk back into Drive A and press <Enter> until you get the message "Insert TARGET diskette in drive A." You continue to swap disks until you get the following screen display:

```
Volume Serial Number is 1DE2-136A

Copy another diskette (Y/N)?_
```

WHAT'S HAPPENING? The prompt tells you that the program has finished executing and now asks you a question. Do you want to execute this program again to make another copy of a disk? In this case, you do not wish to make another copy so you key in N. The Volume Serial Number, by the way, changes with each DISKCOPY command and is only seen in DOS 4.0 or above.

STEP 7: Press n.

```
C:\DOS>_
```

WHAT'S HAPPENING? DOS has completed the DISKCOPY program. You now have two copies of the DATA disk, the original and the backup. At the end of each work session, you should follow these steps to back up your DATA disk. You do not need a new backup disk each time. Keep using the same disk over and over. You are merely keeping current by today's date; you do not need an archival or historical record of each day's work. Some organizations, however, such as banks or the IRS, may need to recreate such records so they will have not only a Disaster and Recovery Plan but also **archival data** or **archival backup**.

STEP 8: Remove the disk labeled BACKUP DATA DISK and keep it in a safe place until you need it again to make another backup.

STEP 9: Key in the following:
C:\DOS>CD \ <Enter>

7.17 Backing Up Files with the COPY Command

The following material is informational and meant only to be read. It is not an activity. Using the DISKCOPY command backs up an entire disk. Often, however, you only need to back up files or you want to back up files from the hard disk to a floppy disk. Remember that you can also use the COPY command to back up specific files at any time. The syntax does not change. It is:

COPY [*drive:*][*path*]*source.fil* [*drive:*][*path*]*destination.fil*

COPY is the command. *drive:* represents the disk drive designator where the file is located. *path* is the subdirectory. *source.fil* is the name of the file that you wish to copy—the source. *drive:* represents the disk drive designator where you want the file copied to. *destination.fil* is the name of the file to be copied—the destination.

There is also a way to back up all files with one COPY command. Be sure that the destination disk is already formatted, because COPY does not format a new disk as DISKCOPY does.

It is easier to use this command with two floppy disk drives. In addition, the disk media types do not have to be identical. For example, you can copy from a 5 1/4-inch 360 KB disk to a 3 1/2-inch 1.44 MB disk. Place the source disk in Drive A and the destination disk in Drive B. Key in:

A>COPY *.* B:

A> is the default drive. COPY is the command. *.* means every file with every file extension, the first * represents any file name, the second represents any file extension. DOS goes to the source disk to find each file. As it copies the source file, it lists the file name on the screen. B: represents the destination disk. Since you give no file names following B:, DOS assumes that you want the same file name on the destination disk. If there is a file with the same name on the destination disk, DOS overwrites it. If you want to back up files from a hard disk, you can also use this command to copy the files in the individual subdirectories, if there are not too many files to fit on a floppy disk. DOS 5.0 tells you how many bytes are in a subdirectory when you use the DIR command. For instance, look at the following display:

```
C:\JUNK>DIR *.TMP

   Volume in drive C is MS-DOS_5
   Volume Serial Number is 16D1-68D4
   Directory of C:\JUNK

JAN        TMP        72    11-23-92   7:04a
FEB        TMP        74    11-23-92   7:05a
MAR        TMP        70    11-23-92   7:06a
APR        TMP        71    11-23-92   7:07a
         4 file(s)            287 bytes
                          8671232 bytes free
```

After 4 file(s), the number is 287. This tells you that these four files only require 287 bytes and will easily fit on a floppy disk. On the other hand, if you get a display like the one that follows:

```
EDITOR     PIF       545    03-12-91 11:47p
LOTUS      PIF       545    03-12-91 11:47p
123        PIF       545    05-01-90  3:00a
WP         PIF       545    03-12-91 11:47p
_DEFAULT   PIF       545    03-12-91 11:47p
EXPAND     EXE     18377    05-01-90  3:00a
EDITO0     PIF       545    03-12-91 11:55p
LINK       PIF       545    03-12-91 11:55p
LOTU0      PIF       545    03-12-91 11:55p
W0         PIF       545    03-12-91 11:55p
WINFILE    INI       200    06-24-91 10:41p
ENTPACK    INI       389    06-25-91  2:24a
WEPBINXZ   EXE     69680    03-12-91 11:58p
WEP        GRP      5943    03-30-91  3:43a
WIN        TST      1628    03-13-91 12:57p
WIN        WRD      1685    03-15-91  6:57p
WGLIB      EXE     11992    06-08-90 11:37a
WIN        INI      3065    06-24-91 10:21p
WINHELP    BMK        63    03-15-91  9:56p
WINGRAB    EXE     19024    06-08-90  1:07p
WIN386     SWP 4194304    06-25-91 10:37p
        98 file(s)     7509674 bytes
                       8671232 bytes free
```

The number is now 98 file(s) that occupy 7.5 KB, which will not fit on a single floppy disk. However, if the files will fit on a floppy disk, you could use the COPY command. Thus, if you wanted to back up the subdirectory `\JUNK`, the command would be keyed in as: C>**COPY C:\JUNK*.* A:**

The wildcard, *.*, is the most global of the global file specifications. It means *all* the files since all file names match it. *.* can be used with any command that accepts the use of wildcards. However, be careful with this wildcard because every file means *every* file. Also, this command would not copy any of the subdirectories within the **\JUNK** subdirectory. You would have to key in another command such as: C:\JUNK>**COPY \JUNK\SAMPLE*.* A:**

If you are copying from a hard disk to a floppy disk, you must be very careful not to key in C:\>**COPY *.* B:** or C:\>**COPY *.* A:**. You *cannot* and *must not* copy all the files from a hard disk to a floppy disk with the COPY command. There are too many files on the hard disk, and they will not fit on a single floppy disk. Other programs such as BACKUP and RESTORE are designed to back up a hard disk. See Appendix D for further information on these commands.

Chapter Summary

1. DEL or ERASE eliminates files.
2. Deleting files helps to manage the data on the disk.
3. The syntax for the DEL and ERASE commands are:
   ERASE [*drive:*][*path*]*filename.ext*
   or DEL [*drive:*][*path*]*filename.ext*
4. Wildcards can be used with DEL or ERASE.
5. DEL or ERASE do not eliminate the data on the disk, only the entry in the directory table.
6. In DOS, prior to version 5.0, there is no way to recover a deleted file. The entry in the FAT is freed up when you delete a file, and thus the next time DOS writes to the disk, it uses that area and overwrites the data.
7. Once a file has been deleted, it cannot be recovered except with special utility programs such as UNDELETE.
8. Before you use wildcards with DEL or ERASE, it is wise to use the DIR command to see what is going to be erased.
9. DOS 4.0 and above has a special parameter, /P, which prompts you to confirm whether or not you wish to delete a file.
10. The /P parameter in DOS 4.0 and above is an example of an enhancement in a new release of software.
11. You can change the names of files with the RENAME or REN command.
12. The syntax for renaming files is:
    REN [*drive:*][*path*]*oldfile.ext* *newfile.ext*
    or RENAME [*drive:*][*path*]*oldfile.ext* *newfile.ext*
13. Renaming can only be done on one drive or subdirectory. RENAME does not move files.
14. Renaming just changes the file name; it does not change the contents of the file.
15. With the REN command, you start with one file and end up with the same file with a new name. It is not like the COPY command, where you start with one file and end up with two, the original and the copy.

16. Wildcards can be used with the REN command.
17. Before you use wildcards with the REN command, it is wise to use the DIR command to see what files are going to be affected by the renaming.
18. Once a file is renamed, it cannot be found under the old name.
19. It is wise to make backup copies of data files so that if something happens, you have another source to recover from.
20. You can back up a disk with the DISKCOPY command or you can back up files on your disk using the COPY command. *.* allows you to back up all the files.

Key Terms

Business Resumption Plan
Copy-protected
Disaster and Recovery Plan

Discussion Questions

1. What is the syntax of the DEL command?
2. What is the purpose of the DEL command?
3. What is the difference between DEL and ERASE?
4. What is the new parameter that can be used with the DEL command in DOS 4.0 and above? What is the purpose of this parameter?
5. What is an enhancement?
6. Why might you want to get rid of files on a disk?
7. What is the syntax of the REN command?
8. What is the difference between REN and RENAME?
9. Why would you want to change the name of a file?
10. What process would you use to make a backup copy of an entire data disk?
11. How can you create text files on a disk?
12. Why do you make backup copies of disks?
13. What does *.* represent?
14. If you keyed in: A>`DEL FILE.ONE` and got the message "Bad command or file name," what could be wrong and what steps could you take to solve this problem?
15. If you keyed in: A>`REN B:FILE.ONE C:FILE.TWO` and got the message "Invalid parameter," what could be wrong and what steps could you take to solve this problem?
16. If you keyed in: A>`DEL B:*.TXT`, what would happen?
17. If you keyed in: A>`REN *.TWO *.FIL`, what would happen to all the files with the extension `.TWO`?
18. If you keyed in: A>`DEL MYFILE.TXT B:`, what would happen?
19. If you keyed in: C>`REN \BOOK\*.OLD *.NEW`, what would happen?
20. If you keyed in: A>`DEL C:\BOOK\MYFILE.TXT`, what would happen?

21. Give two reasons why you would want to delete files from a disk.
22. When would you use wildcards with the ERASE or DEL commands?
23. What is the danger in using wildcards with the DEL command?
24. What would happen when you key in ERASE *.*?
25. What is the difference between the RENAME and COPY commands?
26. If you are using the REN command and get the message "duplicate file name or file not found" what does it mean?
27. How can you change the names of a group of files with a one-line command?
28. What process would you use to back up specific files?
29. What process could you use to back up a subdirectory?
30. Why would you not copy all the files from a hard disk to a floppy disk with the DISKCOPY command?

Application Assignments

If you do not have the files on the DATA disk for the questions below, you can copy them from \JUNK to the DATA disk. All activities occur on the DATA disk in the root directory unless otherwise stated.

1. For the following assignment:
   a. Rename the file **YOURA.LAB** to **NOFILE.XYZ**.
   b. Using the DIR command, locate the file called **YOURA.LAB**.
   c. Using the DIR command, locate the file called **NOFILE.XYZ**.
   d. Print the screen that displays the result of these commands.
   e. Rename **NOFILE.XYZ** to **YOURA.LAB**.
2. For the following assignment:
   a. Rename the file **YOURB.LAB** to to **NOTHING.XYZ**.
   b. Using the DIR command, locate the file called **YOURB.LAB**.
   c. Using the DIR command, locate the file called **NOTHING.XYZ**.
   d. Print the screen that displays the results of these commands.
   e. Rename **NOTHING.XYZ** to **YOURB.LAB**.
3. For the following assignment:
   a. Complete these steps:
      (1) Rename all the files that have a file extension of **.DOS** to the same file name but with **.WG** as the file extension. Use a wildcard.
      (2) Display the names of these new files with the **.WG** file extensions.
      (3) Print the screen that displays the results.
   b. Complete these steps:
      (1) Make copies of all the **.WG** files on the DATA disk with the same file name but with the file extension of **.RRR**.
      (2) Make copies of all the **.WG** files on the DATA disk with the same file name but with the file extension of **.MMM**.
      (3) Display the names of these copies with **.RRR** and the **.MMM** file extensions.
      (4) Print the screen that displays the results of these commands.

c. Complete these steps:
   (1) Concatenate all the files with a file extension of **.MMM** and call the new file **PLUSFILE.TTT**.
   (2) Print **PLUSFILE.TTT**. Do not use the <Shift> and <PrtSc> keys.
d. Complete these steps:
   (1) Rename all the files with the **.WG** extension with the same file name but with the extension **.DOS**.
   (2) Display the names of these files with the **.WG** extensions.
   (3) Display the names of these files with **.DOS** extensions.
   (4) Print the screen that displays the results of these commands.
e. Delete the file **PLUSFILE.TTT**. Print the screen to prove that it is gone.
f. Delete the files with the **.MMM** and **.RRR** file extensions and print the screen to prove they are gone.
g. **Challenge Assignment**: If you do not have a subdirectory on the DATA disk called **SERIES**, create this directory now. Next, copy all the files with the extension **.TV** from the subdirectory **C:\JUNK\DATA** to the subdirectory **SERIES** on the DATA disk.
   (1) In the **SERIES** subdirectory, change the name of the **.TV** files. Have the file names be the same but with the extension **.VCR**.
   (2) Display the names of these files with the **.VCR** extensions, and print the screen that displays the results of these commands.
   (3) Eliminate all the files with the **.VCR** extension in the **SERIES** subdirectory. Print the screen to prove that they are gone.

4. For the following assignment:
   a. Copy all the files from the **\JUNK** directory that have the file extension **.TMP** to the DATA disk.
   b. Complete these steps:
      (1) Rename all the files on the DATA disk that have a file extension of **.TMP** to the same file name but with **.FDP** as the file extension. Use a wildcard.
      (2) Display the names of these new files with the **.FDP** file extensions.
      (3) Print the screen that displays the results of these commands.
   c. Complete these steps:
      (1) Make copies of all the **.FDP** files on the DATA disk with the same file name but the file extension of **.PPP**.
      (2) Make copies of all the **.FDP** files on the DATA disk with the same file name but with the file extension of **.FFF**.
      (3) Display the names of these copies with **.PPP** and the **.FFF** file extensions.
      (4) Print the screen that displays the results of these commands.
   d. Complete these steps:
      (1) Concatenate all the files on the DATA disk with a file extension of **.PPP**. Call the new file **HOME.RUN**.
      (2) Print **HOME.RUN**. Do not use the <Shift> and <PrtSc> keys.

   e. Complete these steps:
      (1) Rename all the files on the DATA disk that have a file extension of **.FDP** to the same file name but with **.TMP** as the file extension. Use a wildcard.
      (2) Display the names of these files with the **.TMP** file extensions and print the screen that displays the results of these commands.
   f. Delete the file **HOME.RUN**. Print the screen to prove that it is gone.
   g. Delete the files with the **.PPP** and the **.FFF** extensions and print the screen to prove they are gone.
   h. If you do not have a subdirectory on the DATA disk called **CLASS**, make this directory now.
      (1) Copy the files with the **.NEW** extension from **\JUNK** to the subdirectory **CLASS** on the DATA disk.
      (2) In the **CLASS** subdirectory, change the names of the **.NEW** files. Have the file names the same but with the extension **.OLD**.
      (3) Display the names of these files with the **.OLD** extensions and print the screen that displays the results of these commands.
      (4) Eliminate all the files with the **.OLD** extensions in the **CLASS** subdirectory. Print the screen to prove that they are gone.

5. For the following assignment:
   a. Delete all the files with the file extension of **.EEE** created in the Application Assignment 2.a in Chapter 6.
   b. Delete the file called **HI.TXT** created in Activity 6.4.
   c. Do a wide directory display and print the screen of the wide display.
   d. **Challenge Assignment**: Display all the files in the root directory in a wide display, alphabetically by file name. Print this screen. Note: You must have DOS 5.0 to complete this assignment.

6. For the following assignment all the work will be done in the root directory of the DATA disk. If you do not already have a subdirectory called **SERIES** on the DATA disk, make this directory now. Then, copy all the files with **.MAK** as an extension from the **C:\JUNK\DATA** subdirectory to the **SERIES** subdirectory keeping the file names the same.
   a. Complete these steps:
      (1) From the root directory of the DATA disk, rename all the files with a **.MAK** extension in the **SERIES** subdirectory to the file extension **.CAR**.
      (2) Print the screen with the command line that you used to accomplish this task.
   b. Complete these steps:
      (1) From the root directory of the DATA disk, concatenate all the files with the file extension **.CAR** to a new file called **AUTOS.FIL**. The **AUTOS.FIL** will be in the **SERIES** subdirectory.
      (2) Print **AUTOS.FIL**. Do not use <Shift> and <PrtSc>.

c. Complete these steps:
   (1) From the root directory of the DATA disk delete the file called **AUTOS.FIL**.
   (2) Print the screen with the command line that you used to accomplish this task.
d. Complete these steps:
   (1) From the root directory of the DATA disk, rename all the files with a **.CAR** extension in the **SERIES** subdirectory to the file extension **.MAK**.
   (2) Print the screen with the command line that you used to accomplish this task.

Chapter

Informational Commands
CHKDSK, ATTRIB, COMP, FC, VER, and LABEL

After completing this chapter you will be able to:

1. Use the CHKDSK command to elicit statistical information about disks and memory.
2. Interpret the statistical information obtained by using the CHKDSK command.
3. Use the COPY and CHKDSK commands to demonstrate the use and relationship of internal and external commands.
4. Explain and use the verbose parameter with the CHKDSK command.
5. Explain the difference between contiguous and noncontiguous files.
6. Use the CHKDSK command to see if files are contiguous or noncontiguous.
7. Explain when and how to use the /F parameter with the CHKDSK command.
8. Explain file attributes.
9. Use the ATTRIB command to view or change file attributes.
10. Use the COMP and FC commands to compare files.
11. Use wildcards with the FC and COMP commands.
12. Explain version numbers and how they are determined.
13. Use the VER command to determine what version of DOS is loaded into memory.
14. Change the volume label of a disk using the LABEL command.

Chapter Overview

The operating system has the ability to monitor itself and convey information to the user. By using different commands, the user can discover how much room is left on a disk for new files, if there are any bad spots on the disk, if a disk is a system disk, and if files are being stored efficiently on a disk. The user can discover if files are alike, what the file attributes are, and what version of DOS is in memory.

In this chapter you will learn to use the CHKDSK command to obtain statistical information about a disk, to use the ATTRIB command to set and change file attributes, to use the COMP and FC commands to get information about files, to use the VER command to see which version of DOS is in memory, and to use the LABEL command so you can change the volume label on a disk.

8.0 Checking a Disk and Memory

There is information about your disks you often need. You need to know how much room is left on the disk so that you can add a new file. You want to know if there are any bad spots on a disk, which can mean the loss of a file. Bad spots can come from a variety of sources such as a mishandled disk or a manufacturing defect. You want to know if a disk has the operating system on it or if it is a system disk. Using the DIR command would not help you because the system files are hidden and do not display on the screen. Occasionally, you might want to know if the files are being stored efficiently on a disk. Maybe you installed extended memory and want to be sure that it is being used, or you may have installed such RAM-resident programs as SideKick and GOfor and want to know how much RAM you have for a program.

None of these tasks can be accomplished by merely looking at a disk or at memory, but you can find out by using a utility program called the CHKDSK command, an external command located in the \DOS subdirectory. In addition to showing the system files, which let you know that a disk is a system disk, CHKDSK also gives other statistical information about a disk and about computer memory as well. The CHKDSK command analyzes the directory on a disk, making sure that the directory entries match the location and lengths of files with the File Allocation Table on the default drive (or designated drive). It makes sure that all the directories are readable. After checking the disk, CHKDSK reports any errors and gives information about the disk's total capacity—how many files are on a disk and how much space is taken. CHKDSK establishes the space left on the disk for additional files and displays the size of the computer's memory in terms of bytes. Thus, the command supplies a disk and memory status report. You should run the CHKDSK command occasionally for each disk to ensure that your file structures have integrity.

In DOS versions 3.0 and above CHKDSK allows you to correct some problems. Thus, this command makes sure that every entry in the directory points to a valid location in the FAT and that the length in the directory matches the disk space that the FAT allocated to the specific file.

CHKDSK informs you of errors. The two kinds of errors are **cross-linked** files and **lost clusters**. Cross-linked files means that two files claim the same sectors in the File Allocation Table. Different files cannot share clusters. Lost clusters indicates sectors that have no directory entry and are "orphans," not belonging to any file that DOS knows about.

The syntax is:

CHKDSK [*drive:*][[*path*]*filename*] [/F] [/V]

Note: The **C:\>** is displayed on the screen. The DATA disk is in Drive A. Remember that if your DOS utility programs are in a subdirectory such as **\BIN** you key in **CD \BIN**. Be sure to change the prompt to **PROMPT pg**.

STEP 1: Key in the following:
C:\>**CD \DOS** <Enter>

STEP 2: Key in the following:
C:\DOS>**DIR CHKDSK.EXE** <Enter>

```
C:\>CD \DOS

C:\DOS>DIR CHKDSK.EXE

   Volume in drive C is MS-DOS_5
   Volume Serial Number is 16D1-68D4
   Directory of C:\DOS

CHKDSK    EXE   16200   04-09-91  5:00a
        1 file(s)        16200 bytes
                       8667136 bytes free

C:\DOS>_
```

WHAT'S HAPPENING? The DIR command told you that the program **CHKDSK.EXE** is stored as a file in the **\DOS** subdirectory. CHKDSK is an external command. In order to execute or run this program, DOS has to be able to find it on a disk and load it into memory. By keying in **DIR CHKDSK.EXE**, you have verified that the file is on the disk. However, to execute the command or program, you have to load it into memory or call it. In some versions of DOS, **CHKDSK.EXE** is called **CHKDSK.COM**.

STEP 3: Key in the following:
C:\DOS>**CHKDSK** <Enter>

```
C:\DOS>CHKDSK

Volume MS-DOS_5     created 06-10-1991 8:43p
Volume Serial Number is 16D1-68D4

  68100096 bytes total disk space
     73728 bytes in 2 hidden files
    129024 bytes in 51 directories
  59039744 bytes in 1461 user files
     16384 bytes in bad sectors
   8841216 bytes available on disk

      2048 bytes in each allocation unit
     33252 total allocation units on disk
      4317 available allocation units on disk

    655360 total bytes memory
    565744 bytes free

C:\DOS>_
```

WHAT'S HAPPENING? Do not worry if you do not see the same numbers displayed on your screen. These numbers are related to how the disk was formatted, the size of the hard drive, and how much internal memory is installed in a specific computer. What is important is what the status report is telling you. Let us look at this example, line for line.

The first line on the screen tells you that the disk in Drive C has "68100096 bytes total disk space." This number is the entire capacity of a specific disk. Suppose you have a two-drawer filing cabinet. No matter what you do, the filing cabinet will only hold two drawers full of files.

The second line on the screen display indicates that you have "73728 bytes in two hidden files." You may have a display that says you have three hidden files. What are hidden files? On Drive C, which you booted from, these hidden files are `IO.SYS` (`IBMBIO.COM` for PC-DOS) and `MSDOS.SYS` (`IBMDOS.COM` for PC-DOS). The hidden files message informs you that this is a system disk. If you have a third hidden file, it is a volume label that is stored as a hidden file in some versions of DOS. Usually, the later the version of DOS, the larger the amount of space taken by the system files because, as a program gets more powerful, it gets larger. Other application programs can also create hidden system files.

In this example, you are looking at a disk with subdirectories. The next line says "129024 bytes in 51 directories," which tells you that on this disk there are 51 subdirectories that take up 129024 bytes. This number is just for the entries for the subdirectories themselves. If there are no subdirectories on your disk, there will be no information about them.

The fourth line (third line if you have no subdirectories) on the screen display tells you that you have "59039744 bytes in 1461 user files." A user file is any file that is stored on the disk. It does not have to be a file that you, the user, created. In this example in addition to system files, Drive C contains many other files.

Sometimes you will have a fifth line indicating, as in this example, how many bad sectors a disk may have. Having bad sectors is not uncommon on hard disks. In this example, there are "16384 bytes in bad sectors." Since this is a 60 MB hard disk, you need not be concerned.

The sixth line on the screen display, "8841216 bytes available on disk," establishes how much room remains on the disk in Drive C for new files or information. What does this mean to you? A byte is one character. It can be the letter b, the letter c, the number 3, or the punctuation mark ?. To give you a rough idea of what byte means, a page of a printed novel contains about 3000 bytes. Thus, a disk with a total capacity of 360,000 bytes could hold or store a maximum of about 120 pages of a novel. If you had a 20 MB or 20 meg hard disk (one megabyte means one million bytes) it would hold approximately 20,000,000 bytes or 6,667 pages of text, and if the average novel has about 400 pages, you could store about sixteen and a half books. You can see why people like the capacity of hard disks. Imagine the numbers with a 40 MB hard disk (33 books) or a 100 MB hard disk (83 books). This approximation, however, is not entirely accurate because it does not take into account that often information is stored in such a way as to be compressed. However, it does give you an idea of the disk capacity in "human terms." As you work with computers, you become accustomed to thinking in bytes. From these lines of statistics you have information about a disk in terms of bytes.

After these lines of information, there are two blank lines. If you have a version of DOS that is less than 4.0, you do not see the next lines of information. In this example, the line will say "2048 bytes in each allocation unit."

The smallest unit that DOS actually reads is a cluster. A cluster is made up of sectors. The number of sectors that make up a cluster vary depending on the type of disk. On a 360 KB floppy disk, a cluster is made up of two sectors (512 x 2 = 1024), and on most hard disks, like the one used in this textbook, a cluster is made up of 4 sectors (512 x 4 = 2048). The next line, "33252 total allocation units on disk," indicates the total number of clusters available. If you multiply 33252 x 2048, you get 68,100,096 bytes or the capacity of this hard disk, a 60 MB hard disk. The next line, "4317 available allocation units on disk," tells you how much room is available on the disk by cluster.

Whatever version of DOS you have, after all these numerical lines on the display screen, there are two blank lines. Then, the next two lines of information appear. This second group of numbers discloses the internal memory or RAM of the particular personal computer you are using. Memory and disk space are measured in bytes. Bytes are expressed in the context of the binary numbering system, as 2^0, 2^1, 2^2, and so on. Rather than being stated individually, bytes are grouped in kilobytes (KB). One kilobyte is 2^{10} or 1024. The odd 24 per thousand is dropped to simplify calculations. For all practical purposes the value of KB is equal to 1000. Thus, 64 KB technically speaking would be 64 x 1024 = 65536. In user terms, 64 KB is translated as 64,000 bytes, even though a 64 KB memory would actually have room for 65,536 bytes. Some common internal memory sizes are shown in Table 8.1.

Table 8.1 Computer Memory Sizes

System memory	Actual Number of Bytes
64 KB	65,536
128 KB	131,072
256 KB	262,144
512 KB	524,288
640 KB	655,360

When a specific computer, regardless of its different disk drive, has "655360 bytes total memory," it is a 640 KB machine. Remember that memory refers to the work space of a computer, the place where programs and data are held while they are processed. If a computer has 655,360 bytes of total memory, why are there only "565744 bytes free"? Free means that you have only 565744 bytes available for data and programs. You must have an operating system installed in RAM or memory to be able to use the computer, and some of the bytes were used. When you booted the system and loaded the operating system, you loaded it into memory where the bytes remain resident.

STEP 4: Key in the following:
C:\DOS>**CHKDSK A:** <Enter>

```
C:\DOS>CHKDSK A:

Volume DATA DISK      created 11-23-1992 7:00a
Volume Serial Number is 3839-0EC8

    362496 bytes total disk space
      6144 bytes in 6 directories
    120832 bytes in 86 user files
    235520 bytes available on disk

      1024 bytes in each allocation unit
       354 total allocation units on disk
       230 available allocation units on disk

    655360 total bytes memory
    565744 bytes free

C:\DOS>_
```

WHAT'S HAPPENING? In Step 3, CHKDSK checked out the disk on the default drive, Drive C. Since you wanted to know about the status of the DATA disk, located in Drive A, you had to ask specifically for that information by telling DOS which disk to check. In other words, you added a parameter (the parameter A:). This display looks similar to the first screen display. You have "362496 total disk space" because this is a 360 KB disk (360 x 1024 = 368640, rounded off to 360 KB). If you had formatted this disk with an operating system, you would have seen the two hidden files. Since you did not format the disk with an operating system and/or volume label, you did not see this information. If you have another capacity disk such as a 720 KB disk, you would have more space available. User files and bytes available will vary based on what is on the DATA disk. The last two lines displayed on the screen do not change, because you are still using the same computer and the amount of internal memory or RAM on a specific computer does not vary. However, the statistical information about the disk does change because you asked for information about a different disk. If you placed another disk in Drive A, you would get different information about files and the bytes remaining on the disk.

8.2 Understanding Internal and External Commands

In previous chapters, you used the major internal commands: DIR, COPY, RENAME, DEL, and TYPE. You also used some minor internal commands: CLS, DATE, and TIME. All of these commands are installed in RAM when you boot the system. If you change the default subdirectory from the **\DOS** subdirectory you still have access to and use of an internal command because it is resident in memory for as long as the computer is on. External commands, however, have to be found on a disk and loaded into memory before they can be used. If DOS cannot find the external command on a disk, it gives you the message "Bad command or file name." You have used a few external commands, among them FORMAT, DISKCOPY, and DISKCOMP. CHKDSK is also an external command. The next activity will demonstrate the use and relationship of internal and external commands.

Activity 8.3 Using the COPY and CHKDSK Commands to Understand External and Internal Commands

Note: The `C:\DOS>` is displayed and the DATA disk is in Drive A.

STEP 1: Key in the following:
C:\DOS>**CHKDSK** <Enter>

```
C:\DOS>CHKDSK

Volume MS-DOS_5      created 06-10-1991 8:43p
Volume Serial Number is 16D1-68D4

  68100096 bytes total disk space
     73728 bytes in 2 hidden files
    129024 bytes in 51 directories
  59162624 bytes in 1462 user files
     16384 bytes in bad sectors
   8718336 bytes available on disk

      2048 bytes in each allocation unit
     33252 total allocation units on disk
      4257 available allocation units on disk

    655360 total bytes memory
    565744 bytes free

C:\DOS>_
```

WHAT'S HAPPENING? The CHKDSK command is located in the `\DOS` subdirectory on Drive C. To execute or run the program, you keyed in CHKDSK at the system prompt. DOS first looked in memory for this command. Since CHKDSK is not an internal command, DOS could not find the program in RAM. It went to the default disk and subdirectory, located the program, loaded it into memory, and executed the program, giving you the above results.

STEP 2: Key in the following:
C:\DOS>**A:** <Enter>

```
C:\DOS>A:

A:\>_
```

WHAT'S HAPPENING? You have changed the default drive to Drive A, where the DATA disk is located.

STEP 3: Key in the following:
A:\>**PATH ;** <Enter>

STEP 4: Key in the following:
A:\>**CHKDSK** <Enter>

```
A:\>PATH ;

A:\>CHKDSK
Bad command or file name

A:\>_
```

WHAT'S HAPPENING? Since you keyed in CHKDSK at the system prompt, you are treating it as a program. DOS looked in memory for the CHKDSK program. Since it is an external command, DOS could not locate it. DOS, then, went to the disk in the default drive, Drive A. However, CHKDSK is not stored as a file on the DATA disk. DOS is not smart enough to go to any other disk to locate and load the CHKDSK program. It simply told you that it could not find the command or program you keyed in, which is why you got the message "Bad command or file name." How can you solve the problem? One thing you could do is change the default drive back to where the CHKDSK program is located and key in **CHKDSK A:**.

Often, however, you do not wish to change the default drive constantly just to use a command. The syntax of the **CHKDSK.EXE** (or **CHKDSK.COM** in some versions of DOS) is:

[*drive:*][*path*]CHKDSK [*drive:*][*path*]

The [*drive:*][*path*] in front of CHKDSK tells you that you may insert the drive and/or subdirectory where the CHKDSK command is located and DOS will know where to find the command. The drive and path after CHKDSK tells CHKDSK which drive and path you wish to check.

STEP 5: Key in the following:
A:\>**C:\DOS\CHKDSK** <Enter>

```
A:\>C:\DOS\CHKDSK

Volume DATA DISK      created 11-23-1992 7:00a
Volume Serial Number is 3839-0EC8

    362496 bytes total disk space
      6144 bytes in 6 directories
    120832 bytes in 86 user files
    235520 bytes available on disk

      1024 bytes in each allocation unit
       354 total allocation units on disk
       230 available allocation units on disk

    655360 total bytes memory
    565744 bytes free

A:\>_
```

WHAT'S HAPPENING? DOS displayed what you asked. There is also another alternative. You can copy the file **CHKDSK.EXE** from the disk in Drive C to the disk in Drive A so that when DOS looks for the CHKDSK program on Drive A, it will find it, load it, and execute it.

STEP 6: Key in the following:
A:\>**COPY C:\DOS\CHKDSK.EXE** <Enter>

```
A:\>COPY C:\DOS\CHKDSK.EXE
        1 file(s) copied

A:\>_
```

WHAT'S HAPPENING? You are using the internal command COPY. Since COPY is an internal command, it does not matter which drive is the default drive. COPY is resident in memory and, thus, can execute. You still followed the proper COPY syntax, COPY *source destination*. COPY is the command. The source is **C:\DOS\CHKDSK.EXE**. (In some versions of DOS, the file is **CHKDSK.COM**.) You had to place C: in front of the file name because you want DOS to go to the hard disk, which is Drive C, to find the file. So that, DOS would go to the correct subdirectory to locate the file, **\DOS** had to follow **C:**. Now, the CHKDSK command is being treated as a file called **CHKDSK.EXE** stored on the hard disk, Drive C, in the subdirectory **\DOS**. The destination is implied. Since no drive was specified, the default (A:) takes precedence, and since no file name was specified, the old file name takes precedence. The longhand version of the command is:
A:\>**COPY C:\DOS\CHKDSK.EXE A:\CHKDSK.EXE**

Usually, on a hard disk, the DOS utility programs are stored in a subdirectory. The subdirectory name can vary, depending on who named it. A popular name for the DOS files is **\DOS** used in this text.

STEP 7: Key in the following:
A:\>**CHKDSK** <Enter>

```
A:\>CHKDSK

Volume DATA DISK     created 11-23-1992 7:00a
Volume Serial Number is 3839-0EC8

    362496 bytes total disk space
      6144 bytes in 6 directories
    137216 bytes in 87 user files
    219136 bytes available on disk

      1024 bytes in each allocation unit
       354 total allocation units on disk
       214 available allocation units on disk

    655360 total bytes memory
    565744 bytes free

A:\>_
```

WHAT'S HAPPENING? You did not get an error message, "Bad command or file name," because you copied the file called **CHKDSK.EXE** to the DATA disk in the default drive, Drive A. When you keyed in **CHKDSK** at the system prompt, DOS still could not find the program in memory because CHKDSK is not an internal command, but it could find it on the default disk. Once DOS found the **CHKDSK.EXE** file, it could load the CHKDSK program into memory and run the CHKDSK command.

8.4 The Verbose Parameter with the CHKDSK Command

The CHKDSK command has an exceedingly useful parameter, /V, known as running in **verbose** mode. This parameter, in conjunction with the CHKDSK command, not only gives the usual status report but also lists every file on the disk, including hidden files. An important thing to remember about parameters is that they are associated with specific commands and perform specific tasks for those commands. The same parameter does not do the same thing with other commands. For instance, you have used /V with both the COPY and the FORMAT commands. However, for the COPY command, /V means to verify a file as it is copied. When /V is used with the FORMAT command, it means put a volume label on the disk. However, when you use /V with the CHKDSK command, it displays all the files on the disk.

Activity 8.5 Using the /V Parameter with the CHKDSK Command

Note 1: The **A:\>** is displayed and the DATA disk is in Drive A.

Note 2: When you key in Step 2, the screen display scrolls by very quickly. There is a way to stop a screen from scrolling by "freezing the display." Simply hold the <Ctrl> key down and press the <NumLock> key. This procedure freezes the screen display. After you press <Enter> in Step 2, immediately press the <Ctrl> key and the <NumLock> key. If it fails to stop scrolling and the screen scrolls by too quickly, you can key in the command again. If your computer has a <Pause> key, you may use that key or you may use <Ctrl>+S keys.

STEP 1: Key in the following:
A:\>**CHKDSK /V** <Enter>

STEP 2: Hold down the <Ctrl> key and press the <NumLock> key. If you have a <Pause> key, press that instead.

```
A:\>CHKDSK /V

Volume DATA DISK   created 11-23-1992 7:00a
Volume Serial Number is 3839-0EC8
Directory A:\
A:\EXERCISE.TXT
A:\JANUARY.TXT
A:\FEBRUARY.TXT
A:\MARCH.TXT
A:\APR.TST
A:\DRAMA.TV
```

```
A:\FUNNY.TV
A:\JAN.TMP
A:\FEB.TMP
Directory A:\CLASS
A:\CLASS\JAN.PAR
A:\CLASS\FEB.PAR
A:\CLASS\MAR.PAR
A:\CLASS\APR.PAR
A:\JAN.BUD
A:\FEB.BUD
A:\MAR.BUD
```

WHAT'S HAPPENING? Your display might be slightly different, depending on where you pressed the <Ctrl> and <NumLock> keys or the <Pause> key and what files you have on the DATA disk. This display shows you all the files on the disk, including the subdirectories and the files in the subdirectories.

STEP 3: To continue the display and "unfreeze" the screen, press any key.

```
A:\EXTRA.ABC
A:\CAROLYN.FIL
A:\FRANK.FIL
A:\STEVEN.FIL
A:\PERSONAL.FIL
A:\Y.FIL
Directory A:\SERIES
A:\SERIES\TELEV.SER
A:\SERIES\OLDAUTO.MAK
A:\SERIES\NEWAUTO.MAK
A:\SERIES\AUTOMOB.ILE

    362496 bytes total disk space
      6144 bytes in 6 directories
    136192 bytes in 86 user files
    220160 bytes available on disk

      1024 bytes in each allocation unit
       354 total allocation units on disk
       214 available allocation units on disk

    651264 total bytes memory
    565744 bytes free

A:\>_
```

WHAT'S HAPPENING? When you pressed any key, you allowed the command to continue executing, so the display continued scrolling. You also got the statistical and memory information at the end of the display for all the files on the disk. You do not have to change default drives if you wish to use the command on other than the default drive. All you need to do is to specify another drive and use the /V parameter. For instance, you could key in A>**CHKDSK B:/V** or A>**CHKDSK C:/V**.

STEP 4: This step will scroll by very quickly, so as soon as you press <Enter>, hold down the <Ctrl> key and press the <NumLock> key. If you have a <Pause> key, press that instead. Key in the following:
A:\>**CHKDSK C: /V** <Enter>

```
Directory C:\
C:\IO.SYS
C:\MSDOS.SYS
C:\COMMAND.COM
```

WHAT'S HAPPENING? Your display will be different, depending on where you pressed the <Ctrl> and <NumLock> keys or the <Pause> key and what files you have on the hard disk. The important files to note are at the top of the display, **IO.SYS** and **MSDOS.SYS** (**IBMBIO.COM** and **IBMDOS.COM** if you have PC-DOS). These are the two hidden system files that you have never seen displayed on the screen with the DIR command. This tells you absolutely that this is a system or bootable disk.

STEP 5: Press any key to continue the display.

```
      2048 bytes in each allocation unit
     33252 total allocation units on disk
     10078 available allocation units on disk

    655360 total bytes memory
    565744 bytes free

A:\>_
```

WHAT'S HAPPENING? Since the screen displays *all* the files on the hard disk, the actual scrolling will take some time to finish, but once it does stop, you have returned to the system prompt.

8.6 Contiguous and Noncontiguous Files or Fragmented Files

Contiguous means being in contact or touching. What does this have to do with files? As far as DOS is concerned, data is a string of bytes that DOS keeps track of by grouping it into a file. In order to manage the storing and retrieving of the files, DOS divides a disk into numbered blocks called sectors. Sectors are then grouped into clusters. A cluster is the smallest unit that DOS will deal with. A cluster is always a set of contiguous sectors. Clusters on a 360 KB floppy disk are made of two 512-byte sectors. The number of sectors that make up a cluster on a hard disk varies depending on the size of the hard disk and the version of DOS being used. However, it is usually four sectors. Most often, a file full of information will take up more space on a disk than one cluster. Thus, DOS has to keep track of the location of all the parts of the file that are on the disk. It does so by means of the directory and the FAT.

The FAT (File Allocation Table) keeps a record of the cluster numbers each file occupies. As DOS begins to write files on a new disk, it makes an entry in the disk's directory for that file and updates the FAT with the cluster numbers used to store that file. DOS writes the data to the disk based on the next empty cluster. As DOS begins to write the file to a disk, it writes the information in adjacent clusters. As a matter of fact, DOS wants all the file information to be next to each other and thus, tries to write to adjacent clusters because it is easier to retrieve or store information when it is together. When this occurs, the file is considered to be **contiguous**. For example, if you began writing a letter to your United States senator, it would be stored on your disk in the manner shown in Figure 8.1.

The clusters with nothing in them are simply empty spaces on the disk. Now, you decide to write a letter to your mother. DOS writes this new file to the next adjacent sector, which would begin with cluster 4 as shown in Figure 8.2.

These two files, SENATOR and MOTHER, are contiguous. Each part of each file follows on the disk. Now, you decide to add a comment to your senator letter, making the SENATOR file bigger. When DOS goes to write the letter to the disk, it looks for the next empty cluster, which is cluster 7. It would appear as shown in Figure 8.3.

The parts of the file named SENATOR are separated, making this file **noncontiguous** or **fragmented**. The process becomes more complicated as you add and delete files. For example, if you delete the file SENATOR, the FAT marks clusters 1, 2, 3, 7 and 8 as available even though the data actually remains on the disk. You then decide to develop a PHONE file, shown in Figure 8.4.

Next, you decide to write a letter to your friend Joe, to write a letter to your friend Mary, to add to the PHONE file and to add to the letter to your mother. The disk would look like Figure 8.5.

Thus, the parts of these files are broken up and are no longer stored in adjacent clusters. They are now known as **noncontiguous** or **fragmented files**. If the disk is comprised of noncontiguous files, it can be called a **fragmented disk**. DOS will take longer to read noncontiguous files because the read/write heads must move around the disk to find all the parts of a file. You can see if files are contiguous or noncontiguous by using another parameter with the CHKDSK command.

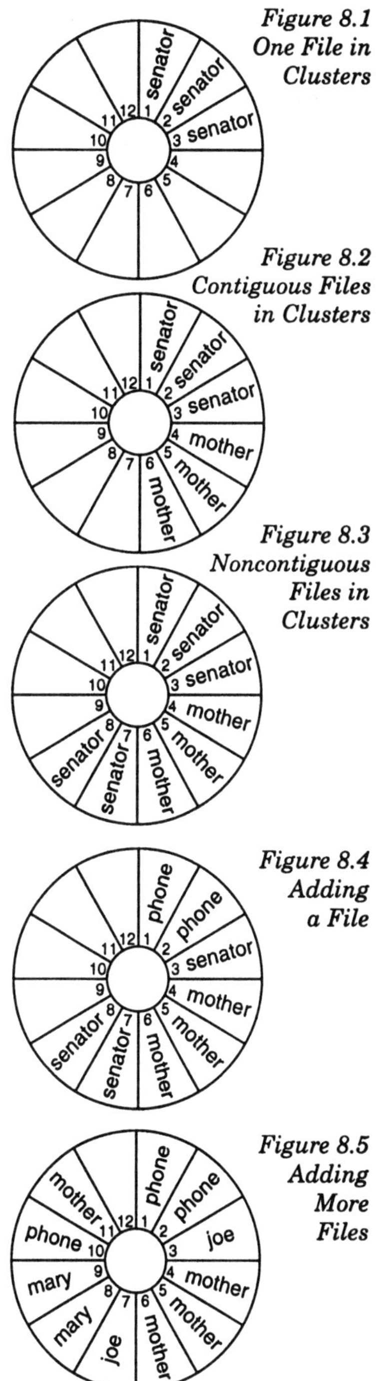

Figure 8.1 One File in Clusters

Figure 8.2 Contiguous Files in Clusters

Figure 8.3 Noncontiguous Files in Clusters

Figure 8.4 Adding a File

Figure 8.5 Adding More Files

Activity 8.7 Using the CHKDSK Command to See if Files are Contiguous

Note: The DATA disk is in Drive A. The **A:\>** is displayed.

STEP 1: Key in the following:
A:\>**CHKDSK MARCH.TXT** <Enter>

```
A:\>CHKDSK MARCH.TXT

Volume DATA DISK      created 11-23-1992 7:00a
Volume Serial Number is 3839-0EC8

    362496 bytes total disk space
      6144 bytes in 6 directories
    137216 bytes in 87 user files
    219136 bytes available on disk

      1024 bytes in each allocation unit
       354 total allocation units on disk
       214 available allocation units on disk

    655360 total bytes memory
    565744 bytes free

All specified file(s) are contiguous

A:\>_
```

WHAT'S HAPPENING? The screen display supplies all the statistical information about the DATA disk and about memory. In addition, the last line states, "All specified file(s) are contiguous." By adding the parameter of the file name **MARCH.TXT** after the CHKDSK command, you asked DOS not only to check the disk but also to look at the file **MARCH.TXT** to see if all the parts of this specific file are next to one another on the DATA disk. Are they contiguous? The message said, "Yes."

STEP 2: Key in the following:
A:\>**CHKDSK *.TXT** <Enter>

```
A:\>CHKDSK *.TXT

Volume DATA DISK      created 11-23-1992 7:00a
Volume Serial Number is 3839-0EC8

    362496 bytes total disk space
      6144 bytes in 6 directories
    137216 bytes in 87 user files
    219136 bytes available on disk

      1024 bytes in each allocation unit
       354 total allocation units on disk
       214 available allocation units on disk
```

```
     655360 total bytes memory
     565744 bytes free

All specified file(s) are contiguous

A:\>_
```

WHAT'S HAPPENING? The command asked CHKDSK not only to give you the usual statistical information but also to see if all the files that have **.TXT** as an extension are contiguous. By using wildcards, you can check a group of files with a common denominator. In this case, the common denominator is the file extension **.TXT**. The message displayed on the screen said, "Yes." All the files with the extension **.TXT** are contiguous.

STEP 3: Key in the following:
A:\>**CHKDSK *.*** <Enter>

```
A:\>CHKDSK *.*

Volume DATA DISK     created 11-23-1992 7:00a
Volume Serial Number is 3839-0EC8

     362496 bytes total disk space
       6144 bytes in 6 directories
     137216 bytes in 87 user files
     219136 bytes available on disk

       1024 bytes in each allocation unit
        354 total allocation units on disk
        214 available allocation units on disk

     655360 total bytes memory
     565744 bytes free

A:\CHKDSK.EXE Contains 6 non-contiguous blocks

A:\>_
```

WHAT'S HAPPENING? On this screen display, the file **CHKDSK.EXE** shows as "noncontiguous" with six blocks of the file not together. Your screen display may vary. It may not show the same files as noncontiguous. You may have more noncontiguous files, or you may have none. If you have no fragmented files, you would have received the message, "All specified file(s) are contiguous." The point is that the CHKDSK command, followed by star dot star (*.*), checked every file in the root directory on the DATA disk to see if all the files were contiguous. The *.* represents all files in the root directory.

STEP 4: Key in the following:
A:\>**CHKDSK \CLASS*.*** <Enter>

```
A:\>CHKDSK \CLASS\*.*

Volume DATA DISK      created 11-23-1992 7:00a
Volume Serial Number is 3839-0EC8

    362496 bytes total disk space
      6144 bytes in 6 directories
    137216 bytes in 87 user files
    219136 bytes available on disk

      1024 bytes in each allocation unit
       354 total allocation units on disk
       214 available allocation units on disk

    655360 total bytes memory
    565744 bytes free

 All specified file(s) are contiguous

A:\>_
```

WHAT'S HAPPENING? You are seeing if all the files in the subdirectory **CLASS** are contiguous. If a subdirectory had any noncontiguous files, the screen display would look as follows:

```
Volume DATA DISK      created 11-23-1992 7:00a
Volume Serial Number is 3839-0EC8

    362496 bytes total disk space
      6144 bytes in 6 directories
    137216 bytes in 87 user files
    219136 bytes available on disk

      1024 bytes in each allocation unit
       354 total allocation units on disk
       214 available allocation units on disk

    655360 total bytes memory
    565744 bytes free

A:\CLASS\FILE2    Contains 2 non-contiguous blocks
A:\CLASS\FILE3    Contains 1 non-contiguous blocks
A:\CLASS\FILE4    Contains 3 non-contiguous blocks

A:\>_
```

WHAT'S HAPPENING? What difference does it make if files are contiguous or not? It matters to the extent that noncontiguous files or a fragmented disk can slow performance. In other words, if a file is contiguous, DOS can find all its parts quickly, minimizing the amount of time the head needs to read and write to the disk. If files are noncontiguous, DOS has to look for all the parts of the file, causing the read/write heads to fly about the disk. Furthermore, the longer the disk is used, the more fragmented it becomes, slowing its performance. However, there is a way to solve the problem with a floppy-based system—format a new disk. Place the newly formatted disk in Drive B, the old, fragmented disk in Drive A, and key in A>**COPY *.* B:**. As DOS executes the command, it finds the first file, including all the associated clusters, on the disk in Drive A and copies that file contiguously to the disk in Drive B. Then, it goes to the second file and so on. Remember, the disk in Drive B must be newly formatted. Furthermore, you do *not* use the DISKCOPY command. DISKCOPY makes an identical, track for track, cluster for cluster, sector for sector version of an old disk. You want to make your newly formatted disk a contiguous copy of the old, noncontiguous disk.

Where you notice a big decline in performance is on a hard drive system. This is not so easy to fix. You cannot use the C:\>**COPY *.* A:** command. You need to back up the hard disk, using the special hard disk BACKUP command. Then, you need to reformat the hard disk—not a task to be taken lightly—and then restore all the programs with the special hard disk RESTORE command. However, that would not really solve the long-term problem because as you continue to work with the hard disk you are again making the hard disk noncontiguous.

The solution most hard disk users opt for is to purchase a special type of utility program that is not present in the DOS system, an optimization program that rearranges the storage on the hard disk so that each file is stored in sequentially numbered clusters. Norton's Utilities and PC Tools include optimization programs. These special programs make all the files contiguous by reading clusters into memory and then writing the clusters back to the hard disk contiguously.

8.8 Using the /F Parameter with CHKDSK

The File Allocation Table (FAT) and directory work in conjunction. Every file has an entry in the directory table. The file entry in the directory table points to the first starting cluster in the FAT. If the file is longer than one cluster, which it usually is, the File Allocation Table has a pointer that leads it to the next cluster and the next cluster and so on. These pointers **chain** all the data together in a file. If the chain is broken (a lost pointer), the disk ends up with "lost clusters," which means that these clusters are marked as used in the FAT and not available for new data. However, since these lost clusters belong to no file, they cannot be retrieved. The data becomes useless. Thus, you lose space on the disk. This phenomenon occurs for a variety of reasons. The most common reason is that a user does not exit a program properly, interrupting the process, and hence the data will not be properly written to the disk. Other times power failures or power surges are the cause.

If one of these events happens, when you execute the CHKDSK command, you will get a message, "xx lost allocation units found in yy chains. Convert lost chains to files (Y/N)?" What this message means is that DOS will turn these lost clusters into files with the file name **FILE000*n*.CHK** (where *n* is a number such as 1, 2 or 3). However, you cannot convert these lost clusters into files unless you used CHKDSK with the /F parameter. Thus, should you get the preceding message, you would key in CHKDSK /F and answer Y. Then, when the process is completed, you can use the TYPE command to see if there may be data that you need to recover. Usually, the data is useless so you simply delete these files (**DEL *.CHK**) to free up disk space.

8.9 File Attributes and the ATTRIB Command

In the directory table, DOS keeps track of the file name, the file extension, the size of the file, the date and time the file was last modified and a pointer to the File Allocation Table. Each file, in addition, has an "attribute" bit that is reported for each file. These **file attributes** give information about a file. These attributes include whether a file is a system file, a hidden file, whether or not the file is read-only, and an archive bit.

The **system attribute** is a special signal to DOS that the file is a system file. This bit is usually reserved for the DOS system files, but some application programs may set a bit to indicate that a particular program is a system file. The **hidden attribute** means that when you use the DIR command, the file name is not displayed. You have seen this with the `IO.SYS` and `MSDOS.SYS` files that have only been displayed when you used CHKDSK with /V parameter. When a file is marked as read-only, it means exactly that. A user can only read the file, not modify or delete it. Sometimes, application programs will mark a file with a **read-only attribute** bit so that a user cannot delete the file. Last, the archive attribute is used to indicate the backup history (archive status) of a file. When you create or modify a file, an **archive bit** is turned on or set. When you use certain DOS commands such as XCOPY or BACKUP, these commands, with the proper parameters, allow you to choose to copy only files that have been modified since the last time you copied them. Then these commands will reset (turn off or clear) the archive bit.

DOS has a command that allows you to manipulate file attributes. It is called the ATTRIB command. You can view, set, and reset all the file attributes for one file or many files. Prior to DOS 5.0, you could only set the archive bit and the read-only bit, but DOS 5.0 also allows you to mark files as hidden or system files. The ATTRIB command is an external command. The syntax for the ATTRIB command is:

ATTRIB [+R ¦ -R] [+A ¦ -A] [+S ¦ -S] [+H ¦ -H] [[*drive:*][*path*]*filename*] [/S]

When you see a parameter in brackets, as you know, it is an optional parameter. When you see a parameter displayed as [+R ¦ -R], the bar acts like a toggle switch. The parameter can be one thing or the other, not both—the choices are mutually exclusive. Thus, you can set a file with +R *or* -R but not both at the same time. The parameters are as follows:

- \+ Sets an attribute.
- \- Clears an attribute.
- R Read-only file attribute.
- A Archive file attribute.
- S System file attribute.
- H Hidden file attribute.
- /S Processes files in all directories in the specified path.

In the next activity, you are going to work with the R and H parameters

Note: The **A:\>** is displayed and the DATA disk is in Drive A. If specific files are not on your DATA disk, you can copy them from **\JUNK** to the DATA disk.

STEP 1: Key in the following:
A:\>**C:** <Enter>

STEP 2: Key in the following:
C:\>**CD \DOS** <Enter>

```
A:\>C:

C:\>CD \DOS

C:\DOS>_
```

WHAT'S HAPPENING? You made **C:\DOS** the default drive and subdirectory.

STEP 3: Key in the following:
C:\DOS>**ATTRIB A:*.*** <Enter>

```
  A        A:\WILDTHR.DOS
  A        A:\WILD1.XXX
  A        A:\WILD2.YYY
  A        A:\WILD3.ZZZ
  A        A:\WILDONE
  A        A:\APR.TMP
  A        A:\WILDTHR.AAA
  A        A:\JOINED.SAM
  A        A:\MONTHS.SAM
  A        A:\NOFILE.XYZ
  A        A:\NOTHING.XYZ
  A        A:\YOURC.LAB
  A        A:\JAN.KKK
  A        A:\FEB.KKK
  A        A:\MAR.KKK
  A        A:\APR.KKK
  A        A:\MOVIES.LST
  A        A:\EXTRA.ABC
  A        A:\CAROLYN.FIL
  A        A:\FRANK.FIL
  A        A:\STEVEN.FIL
  A        A:\PERSONAL.FIL
  A        A:\Y.FIL

C:\DOS>_
```

WHAT'S HAPPENING? You asked the ATTRIB command to show you the attributes of all the files in the root directory of the DATA disk. The only file attribute that these files have is that the A or archive bit is set. These files have not been copied with BACKUP or XCOPY.

STEP 4: Key in the following:
C:\DOS>**ATTRIB C:*.*** <Enter>

```
C:\DOS>ATTRIB C:\*.*
       SH C:\IO.SYS
       SH C:\MSDOS.SYS
  A         C:\COMMAND.COM
  A         C:\AUTOEXEC.WRK
  A         C:\TREEINFO.NCD
  A         C:\CONFIG.BOO
  A         C:\AUTOEXEC.CZG
  A         C:\AUTOEXEC.OLD
  A         C:\HIMEM.SYS
  A         C:\CONFIG.BAK
  A         C:\CONFIG.OLD
  A         C:\CONFIG.SYS
  A         C:\AUTOEXEC.BAK
  A         C:\SFINSTAL.DIR
  A         C:\AUTOEXEC.BAT
  A         C:\CONFIG.WIN
        R   C:\WINA20.386
  A         C:\CONFIG.WRK

C:\DOS>_
```

WHAT'S HAPPENING? Here you are looking at the files in the root directory of C: where the DOS system files are kept. Your display will be different depending on what files are in your root directory. Also, if you are using a network, you may not be able to access the root directory of the network drive. If you cannot access the root directory of C: on your system, just look at the above example. In the above example, you can see that **IO.SYS** and **MSDOS.SYS** are marked with an S for system attribute and H for hidden attribute. In addition, the file called **WINA20.386** is marked as a read-only file. In addition to using the ATTRIB command to view file attributes, you can use it to change file attributes.

STEP 5: Key in the following:
C:\DOS>**ATTRIB +R A:\STEVEN.FIL** <Enter>

```
C:\DOS>ATTRIB +R A:\STEVEN.FIL

C:\DOS>_
```

WHAT'S HAPPENING? You asked the ATTRIB command to make **STEVEN.FIL** a read-only file.

STEP 6: Key in the following:
C:\DOS>**ATTRIB A:\STEVEN.FIL** <Enter>

```
C:\DOS>ATTRIB A:\STEVEN.FIL
  A    R  A:\STEVEN.FIL

C:\DOS>_
```

WHAT'S HAPPENING? Now **STEVEN.FIL** is marked as a read-only file.

STEP 7: Key in the following:
C:\DOS>**DEL A:\STEVEN.FIL** <Enter>

```
C:\DOS>DEL A:\STEVEN.FIL
Access denied

C:\DOS>_
```

WHAT'S HAPPENING? This file, since it is marked as read-only, cannot be deleted. You can also protect against other kinds of file destruction.

STEP 8: Key in the following:
C:\DOS>**TYPE A:\STEVEN.FIL** <Enter>

```
C:\DOS>TYPE  A:\STEVEN.FIL
Hi, my name is Steven.
What is your name?

C:\DOS>_
```

WHAT'S HAPPENING? You see displayed the contents of **STEVEN.FIL** on the DATA disk.

STEP 9: Key in the following:
C:\DOS>**COPY CON A:\STEVEN.FIL** <Enter>
This is a test. <Enter>
<Ctrl>+Z <Enter>

```
C:\DOS>COPY CON A:\STEVEN.FIL
This is a test.
^Z
Access denied  - A:\STEVEN.FIL
         0 file(s) copied

C:\DOS>_
```

WHAT'S HAPPENING? Once again, with the read-only attribute, you are protected from accidentally overwriting the file. However, other operations do not work the same. If you rename the file it keeps the same file attributes, but if you copy the file it no longer has the read-only attribute.

STEP 10: Key in the following:
C:\DOS>**REN A:\STEVEN.FIL THIS.ONE** <Enter>

STEP 11: Key in the following:
C:\DOS>**ATTRIB A:\THIS.ONE** <Enter>

```
C:\DOS>REN A:\STEVEN.FIL THIS.ONE

C:\DOS>ATTRIB A:\THIS.ONE
  A    R  A:\THIS.ONE

C:\DOS>_
```

WHAT'S HAPPENING? Even though you renamed **STEVEN.FIL** to **THIS.ONE**, **THIS.ONE** retained the same file attributes that **STEVEN.FIL** had. However, things change when you copy a file.

STEP 12: Key in the following:
C:\DOS>**COPY A:\THIS.ONE A:\STEVEN.FIL** <Enter>

STEP 13: Key in the following:
C:\DOS>**ATTRIB A:\STEVEN.FIL** <Enter>

STEP 14: Key in the following:
C:\DOS>**ATTRIB A:\THIS.ONE** <Enter>

```
C:\DOS>COPY A:\THIS.ONE A:\STEVEN.FIL
        1 file(s) copied

C:\DOS>ATTRIB A:\STEVEN.FIL
  A       A:\STEVEN.FIL

C:\DOS>ATTRIB A:\THIS.ONE
  A    R  A:\THIS.ONE

C:\DOS>_
```

WHAT'S HAPPENING? When you copied **THIS.ONE**, which had a read-only file attribute, to a new file called **STEVEN.FIL**, it did indeed copy it, but although **THIS.ONE** still is read-only, the new file **STEVEN.FIL** is not. Thus, setting the read-only attribute is really most valuable for protecting you against accidental erasures of a file, not for any particular security reason. In addition, if you mark a file read-only, you could not edit it in a word processing program. You can also hide a file from the casual observer. This feature became available in DOS 5.0.

STEP 15: Key in the following:
C:\DOS>**ATTRIB +H A:\THIS.ONE** <Enter>

STEP 16: Key in the following:
C:\DOS>**DIR A:\THIS.ONE** <Enter>

```
C:\DOS>ATTRIB +H A:\THIS.ONE

C:\DOS>DIR A:\THIS.ONE

   Volume in drive A is DATA DISK
   Volume Serial Number is 3839-0EC8
   Directory of A:\

File not found

C:\DOS>_
```

WHAT'S HAPPENING? You did indeed hide the file with the +H parameter, **THIS.ONE**, from view. The problem with hiding files is that you can hide them all too well. You can forget that you had the file or what the name was. Also, if you cannot find the file, neither can most application programs. DOS 5.0 gives a new parameter to the DIR command, /A, which will show you all the files, including the hidden ones.

STEP 17: Key in the following:
C:\DOS>**DIR /A A:\THIS.ONE** <Enter>

```
C:\DOS>DIR /A  A:\THIS.ONE

   Volume in drive A is DATA DISK
   Volume Serial Number is 3839-0EC8
   Directory of A:\

THIS      ONE      45   11-23-92  7:13a
         1 file(s)         45 bytes
                       218112 bytes free

C:\DOS>_
```

WHAT'S HAPPENING? As you can see, with the new /A parameter for DIR in DOS 5.0, you can even find hidden files. You have been setting file attributes with the plus sign (+). You can "unset" file attributes with the minus (-) sign. You can delete several file attributes with a one-line command, but there must be a space between each parameter so follow the spacing of the command line carefully.

STEP 18: Key in the following:
C:\DOS>**ATTRIB -H -R A:\THIS.ONE** <Enter>

STEP 19: Key in the following:
C:\DOS>**ATTRIB A:\THIS.ONE** <Enter>

```
C:\DOS>ATTRIB -H -R  A:\THIS.ONE

C:\DOS>ATTRIB A:\THIS.ONE
  A       A:\THIS.ONE

C:\DOS>_
```

WHAT'S HAPPENING? You made **THIS.ONE** neither hidden nor read-only. You can also use the ATTRIB command on a subdirectory and/or on a group of files in a subdirectory.

STEP 20: Key in the following:
C:\DOS>**ATTRIB A:\SERIES** <Enter>

STEP 21: Key in the following:
C:\DOS>**ATTRIB A:\SERIES*.*** <Enter>

```
C:\DOS>ATTRIB A:\SERIES
           A:\SERIES

C:\DOS>ATTRIB A:\SERIES\*.*
  A        A:\SERIES\TELEV.SER
  A        A:\SERIES\OLDAUTO.MAK
  A        A:\SERIES\NEWAUTO.MAK
  A        A:\SERIES\AUTOMOB.ILE

C:\DOS>_
```

WHAT'S HAPPENING? Neither the subdirectory **SERIES** nor the files in it are read-only files. (Note: If you do not have this subdirectory on the DATA disk, create it now. Then copy the files with a **.MAK** file extension from **C:\JUNK\DATA**.)

STEP 22: Key in the following:
C:\DOS>**ATTRIB +R A:\SERIES** <Enter>

STEP 23: Key in the following:
C:\DOS>**ATTRIB +R A:\SERIES*.*** <Enter>

STEP 24: Key in the following:
C:\DOS>**ATTRIB A:\SERIES** <Enter>

STEP 25: Key in the following:
C:\DOS>**ATTRIB A:\SERIES*.*** <Enter>

```
C:\DOS>ATTRIB +R A:\SERIES

C:\DOS>ATTRIB +R A:\SERIES\*.*

C:\DOS>ATTRIB A:\SERIES
      R   A:\SERIES

C:\DOS>ATTRIB A:\SERIES\*.*
  A      R  A:\SERIES\TELEV.SER
  A      R  A:\SERIES\OLDAUTO.MAK
  A      R  A:\SERIES\NEWAUTO.MAK
  A      R  A:\SERIES\AUTOMOB.ILE

C:\DOS>_
```

WHAT'S HAPPENING? You made both the subdirectory **SERIES** and all the files in the **SERIES** subdirectory read-only.

STEP 26: Key in the following:
C:\DOS>**ATTRIB -R A:\SERIES** <Enter>

STEP 27: Key in the following:
C:\DOS>**ATTRIB -R A:\SERIES*.*** <Enter>

STEP 28: Key in the following:
C:\DOS>**ATTRIB A:\SERIES** <Enter>

STEP 29: Key in the following:
C:\DOS>**ATTRIB A:\SERIES*.*** <Enter>

```
C:\DOS>ATTRIB -R A:\SERIES

C:\DOS>ATTRIB -R A:\SERIES\*.*

C:\DOS>ATTRIB A:\SERIES
          A:\SERIES

C:\DOS>ATTRIB A:\SERIES\*.*
  A       A:\SERIES\TELEV.SER
  A       A:\SERIES\OLDAUTO.MAK
  A       A:\SERIES\NEWAUTO.MAK
  A       A:\SERIES\AUTOMOB.ILE

C:\DOS>_
```

WHAT'S HAPPENING? You made the **SERIES** subdirectory and the files in the **SERIES** subdirectory so that they are no longer read-only. If you had files in subdirectories beneath the subdirectory **SERIES** that you wanted to assign attributes to, you could key in the command as **ATTRIB +R \SERIES*.* /S**. In this instance, the /S parameter would make all the files in the **SERIES** subdirectory read-only and any files in any subdirectory beneath **SERIES** also read-only. The ability to make files read-only can be helpful to protect any important files from being accidentally deleted.

8.11 Comparing Files

In the preceding activities, you made copies of many files. As you may have noticed, the number of files on the disk continues to grow. The more files you have, the harder it is to remember which file is which. Many times you will want to know if two files with different names or two files with the same name might have the same contents. One method of checking the contents is to use the TYPE command with each file name (TYPE *filename.ext*) and compare the contents visually on the screen. Another way is to send the contents of each file to the printer and compare the contents of these files visually (COPY *filename.ext* PRN). Neither process is too difficult when dealing with the dummy files you have created, because the contents of these files have been brief, but brevity is *not* the norm for files.

Usually, file contents are extensive, and either one of these visual checks would be time-consuming. In addition, it would be very easy to miss small differences. Also, many programs are in binary format, the "nonsense characters," and there is no way to compare these files visually. It would be useful to have a command that would allow you to compare files quickly. You have already used the DISKCOMP command. DISKCOMP compares an entire disk, track for track, sector for sector. As the name DISKCOMP implies, the command compares disks, not files. There are also file compare commands. Depending on which version of DOS you have, you could have the COMP or FC for (file compare) commands. In later releases of DOS, you get both the COMP command and the FC command. The COMP command has fewer options than the FC command.

Both COMP and FC are external commands. Both COMP and FC allow you to compare the contents of any two files very quickly. DOS does the work for you and compares the files to see if they are identical. If you compare files that are different or have been modified, even by one character, you will get an error message. FC and COMP differ in that COMP, after finding ten errors, stops reporting on the files. FC, when it finds a difference, resynchronizes the files. This means if it finds one character difference, such as a space, FC then attempts to see if the files return to being the same. The COMP command prompts you for input where the FC command does not. In general, use COMP when you expect the files to be the same and FC when you expect the files to be different.

The syntax for the COMP command is as follows:

COMP [*data1*] [*data2*] [/D] [/A] [/L] [/N=*number*] [/C]

The parameters are as follows:

data1 Specifies location and name(s) of first file(s) to compare.
data2 Specifies location and name(s) of second files to compare.
/D Displays differences in decimal format. This is the default setting.
/A Displays differences in ASCII characters.
/L Displays line numbers for differences.
/N=*number* Compares only the first specified number of lines in each file.
/C Disregards case of ASCII letters when comparing files.

The syntax for the FC command is as follows:

FC [/A] [/C] [/L] [/LB*n*] [/N] [/T] [/W] [/*nnnn*] [*drive1:*][*path1*]*filename1* [*drive2:*][*path2*]*filename2*

If you wish to compare binary files, such as application programs, use the following syntax:

FC /B [*drive1:*][*path1*]*filename1* [*drive2:*][*path2*]*filename2*

The parameters are as follows:

/A Displays only first and last lines for each set of differences.
/B Performs a binary comparison.

/C Disregards the case of letters.
/L Compares files as ASCII text.
/LB*n* Sets the maximum consecutive mismatches to the specified number of lines.
/N Displays the line numbers on an ASCII comparison.
/T Does not expand tabs to spaces.
/W Compresses white space (tabs and spaces) for comparison.
/*nnnn* Specifies the number of consecutive lines that must match after a mismatch.

In the next activity, you will work with both the COMP command and the FC command. If you have a version of DOS that does not include both commands, do only the portions of the activities that correspond to the command that you have for you specific version of DOS.

Activity 8.12 Using the COMP and FC Commands to Compare Different Files

Note: The **C:\DOS>** is displayed and the DATA disk is in Drive A.

STEP 1: Remove the DATA disk from Drive A. Insert the ACTIVITIES disk in Drive A.

STEP 2: Key in the following:
C:\DOS>**TYPE A:\APRIL.TXT** <Enter>

STEP 3: Key in the following:
C:\DOS>**TYPE A:\WILDTWO.DOS** <Enter>

```
C:\DOS>TYPE A:\APRIL.TXT
This is my April file.
It is my fourth dummy file.
This is file 4.

C:\DOS>TYPE A:\WILDTWO.DOS
This is a file created to demonstrate how to
use wildcards.  Wildcards allow me to copy a
group of files using the wildcards symbols, * and ?.
It is the second wildcard file.

C:\DOS>_
```

WHAT'S HAPPENING? The file names are different, and the file contents are different. Remember, COMP compares the contents of the files. COMP is an external command. However, you are logged into the **\DOS** subdirectory and DOS can find the COMP command.

STEP 4: Key in the following:
C:\DOS>**COMP A:\APRIL.TXT A:\WILDTWO.DOS** <Enter>

```
C:\DOS>COMP A:\APRIL.TXT A:\WILDTWO.DOS
Comparing A:\APRIL.TXT and A:\WILDTWO.DOS . . .
Files are different sizes

Compare more files (Y/N) ? _
```

WHAT'S HAPPENING? You are asking DOS to compare the contents of two files located on the ACTIVITIES disk. The first file name is **APRIL.TXT**. You want to compare the contents of this file with the contents of a second file called **WILDTWO.DOS**. Because both files are located on Drive A, you had to specify the disk drive for each file. Then, you pressed <Enter> to execute the COMP command. However, the message is telling you that the two files you asked COMP to compare, **APRIL.TXT** and **WILDTWO.DOS**, are different sizes. If they are different sizes, the files cannot be the same and there is no point in continuing. The COMP command will go no further.

STEP 5: Key in the following:
N <Enter>

```
C:\DOS>COMP A:\APRIL.TXT A:\WILDTWO.DOS
Comparing A:\APRIL.TXT and A:\WILDTWO.DOS . . .
Files are different sizes

Compare more files (Y/N) ? N

C:\DOS>_
```

WHAT'S HAPPENING? You are returned to the system prompt. However, what if you were interested in the differences between the two files? Here you can use the FC command. Even though the FC is an external command, you can use it because you are logged into the **\DOS** subdirectory, but you must remember to preface the file names with the drive letter.

STEP 6: Key in the following:
C:\DOS>**FC A:\APRIL.TXT A:\WILDTWO.DOS** <Enter>

```
C:\DOS>FC A:\APRIL.TXT A:\WILDTWO.DOS
Comparing files A:\APRIL.TXT and A:\WILDTWO.DOS
***** A:\APRIL.TXT
This is my April file.
It is my fourth dummy file.
This is file 4.
***** A:\WILDTWO.DOS
This is a file created to demonstrate how to
use wildcards.  Wildcards allow me to copy a
group of files using the wildcards symbols, * and ?.
It is the second wildcard file.
*****

C:\DOS>_
```

WHAT'S HAPPENING? The FC command literally showed you each file on the screen. You can see that the files are different.

Activity 8.13 Using the COMP and FC Commands to Compare Identical and Nonidentical Files

Note: The **C:\DOS>** is displayed and the ACTIVITIES disk is in Drive A.

STEP 1: Key in the following:
C:\DOS>**TYPE A:\APRIL.TXT** <Enter>

STEP 2: Key in the following:
C:\DOS>**TYPE A:\APR.99** <Enter>

```
C:\DOS>TYPE A:\APRIL.TXT
This is my April file.
It is my fourth dummy file.
This is file 4.

C:\DOS>TYPE A:\APR.99
This is my April file.
It is my fourth dummy file.
This is file 4.

C:\DOS>_
```

WHAT'S HAPPENING? The file names are different, but the file contents are identical. COMP compares the contents of the files.

STEP 3: Key in the following:
C:\DOS>**COMP A:\APRIL.TXT A:\APR.99** <Enter>

```
C:\DOS>COMP A:\APRIL.TXT A:\APR.99
Comparing A:\APRIL.TXT and A:\APR.99 . . .
Files compare OK

Compare more files (Y/N) ? _
```

WHAT'S HAPPENING? The COMP command first determined that the files were the same size. It compared the two files character by character and found them identical: "Files compare ok."

STEP 4: Key in the following:
N <Enter>

```
C:\DOS>COMP A:\APRIL.TXT A:\APR.99
Comparing A:\APRIL.TXT and A:\APR.99 . . .
Files compare OK

Compare more files (Y/N) ? N

C:\DOS>_
```

WHAT'S HAPPENING? You have returned to the system prompt. How does the FC command compare identical files?

STEP 5: Key in the following:
C:\DOS>**FC A:\APRIL.TXT A:\APR.99** <Enter>

```
C:\DOS>FC A:\APRIL.TXT A:\APR.99
Comparing files A:\APRIL.TXT and A:\APR.99
FC: no differences encountered

C:\DOS>_
```

WHAT'S HAPPENING? FC also says that the two files are identical, but with a slightly different message. However, what if the files were the same size but had different contents?

STEP 6: Key in the following:
C:\DOS>**TYPE A:\FILE2.CZG** <Enter>

STEP 7: Key in the following:
C:\DOS>**TYPE A:\FILE3.CZG** <Enter>

```
C:\DOS>TYPE A:\FILE2.CZG
This is file 2.

C:\DOS>TYPE A:\FILE3.CZG
This is file 3.

C:\DOS>_
```

WHAT'S HAPPENING? These two files are nearly identical, except that one has the number 3 and the other has the number 2.

STEP 8: Key in the following:
C:\DOS>**COMP A:\FILE2.CZG A:\FILE3.CZG** <Enter>

```
C:\DOS>COMP A:\FILE2.CZG A:\FILE3.CZG
Comparing A:\FILE2.CZG and A:\FILE3.CZG . . .
Compare error at OFFSET D
file1 = 32
file2 = 33

Compare more files (Y/N) ? _
```

STEP 9: Key in the following:
N <Enter>

```
Compare more files (Y/N) ? N

C:\DOS>_
```

WHAT'S HAPPENING? The N returned you to the system prompt, but prior to returning to the system prompt, a message was displayed on the screen. The message disclosed that the files were identical in size. However, when the COMP command checked each character in each file, it found only two differences, and it told you where the differences were located. It is telling you this in the hexadecimal, base-16 number system. Do not worry. You do not need to know hexadecimal numbers. There are utility programs such as PC Tools and Norton Utilities that let you enter and make changes at the byte level, but that process goes beyond the scope of this text. What is important is that the message tells you the files are not the same, even though the only difference is that **FILE2.CZG** has a number 2 and **FILE3.CZG** has a number 3. COMP literally compares character to character. However, this information would be more useful if you could see it in a text format, or what is called ASCII (American Standard Code for Information Interchange). ASCII is a code used for transmitting text data between computers and devices. Each character has its own numerical equivalent in ASCII, but for our purposes, ASCII is what we as human beings recognize. The COMP command has a parameter, the /A switch, which displays the differences in ASCII or characters.

STEP 10: Key in the following:
C:\DOS>**COMP /A A:\FILE2.CZG A:\FILE3.CZG** <Enter>

```
C:\DOS>COMP /A A:\FILE2.CZG A:\FILE3.CZG
Comparing A:\FILE2.CZG and A:\FILE3.CZG . . . .
Compare error at OFFSET D
file1 = 2
file2 = 3

Compare more files (Y/N) ? _
```

WHAT'S HAPPENING? The message tells you what the actual differences are between the two files.

STEP 11: Key in the following:
N <Enter>

```
Compare more files (Y/N) ? N

C:\DOS>_
```

WHAT'S HAPPENING? You have returned to the system prompt. The FC command will display the contents of both files on the screen.

STEP 12: Key in the following:
C:\DOS>**FC A:\FILE2.CZG A:\FILE3.CZG** <Enter>

```
C:\DOS>FC A:\FILE2.CZG A:\FILE3.CZG
Comparing files A:\FILE2.CZG and A:\FILE3.CZG
***** A:\FILE2.CZG
This is file 2.
***** A:\FILE3.CZG
This is file 3.
*****

C:\DOS>_
```

WHAT'S HAPPENING? The files' contents are displayed, showing you the lines that differ. You have been comparing text files, but the COMP and FC commands will compare any two files, even binary or program files. There are two program files on the ACTIVITIES disk in the subdirectory **UTILS**. The file names are **ROB.EXE** and **DEMOS.EXE**. Are these files identical? Since the two commands work similarly, we will test only the FC command.

STEP 13: Key in the following:
C:\DOS>**FC A:\UTILS\DEMOS.EXE A:\UTILS\ROB.EXE** <Enter>

```
C:\DOS>FC A:\UTILS\DEMOS.EXE A:\UTILS\ROB.EXE
Comparing files A:\UTILS\DEMOS.EXE and
A:\UTILS\ROB.EXE
FC: no difference encountered

C:\DOS>_
```

WHAT'S HAPPENING? The two program files are identical.

Activity 8.14 Using the COMP and FC Commands with Wildcards

Note: The **C:\DOS>** is displayed and the ACTIVITIES disk is in Drive A.

STEP 1: Key in the following:
C:\DOS>**COMP A:*.FP A:*.SWT** <Enter>

```
C:\DOS>COMP A:\*.FP A:\*.SWT
Comparing A:\FILE2.FP and A:\FILE2.SWT . . .
Files compare OK

Comparing A:\FILE3.FP and A:\FILE3.SWT . . .
Files compare OK

Comparing A:\FILE4.FP and A:\FILE4.SWT . . .
Can't find/open file:  A:\FILE4.SWT
Compare more files (Y/N) ? _
```

STEP 2: To return to the system prompt, key in the following:
N <Enter>

```
Compare more files (Y/N) ? N

C:\DOS>_
```

WHAT'S HAPPENING? You have three files with the **.FP** extension, **FILE2.FP**, **FILE3.FP**, and **FILE4.FP**. Beginning at the top, you are asking DOS to take **FILE2.FP**, find a file that has an identical file name with the extension **.SWT** (**FILE2.SWT**), and compare the two files (**FILE2.FP** and **FILE2.SWT**). When the comparison is complete, DOS will go to the next file, **FILE3.FP**, and do the same (**COMP FILE3.FP FILE3.SWT**). DOS carries out the instructions. However, when it gets to **FILE4.FP**, it cannot find a corresponding file, **FILE4.SWT**. Therefore, DOS cannot compare these files ("Can't find/open file: A:\FILE4.SWT"). Since the files that did compare are identical, you get the message "Files compare ok." By keying in N, you returned to the system prompt. FC works much the same way.

STEP 3: Key in the following:
C:\DOS>**FC A:*.FP A:*.SWT** <Enter>

```
C:\DOS>FC A:\*.FP A:\*.SWT
Comparing files A:\FILE2.FP and A:\FILE2.SWT
FC: no differences encountered

Comparing files A:\FILE3.FP and A:\FILE3.SWT
FC: no differences encountered

Comparing files A:\FILE4.FP and A:\FILE4.SWT
FC: cannot open A:\FILE4.SWT - No such file or directory

C:\DOS>_
```

WHAT'S HAPPENING? The process works almost the same. With FC, however, you do not need to key in N to return to the system prompt. COMP allows you to enter more files to compare. FC simply returns you to the system prompt.

8.15 Understanding Version Numbers

These is a common numbering scheme relating to revisions that is used with almost all software programs. Software is often revised in order to add more commands (called enhancements), to repair errors in the programs (**bugs** or **fixes**), or to incorporate the new advances in hardware. To keep track of these versions or **releases**, they are numbered. (Another name for them is **upgrades**.) If you have version 1.0, you have an early version. If you have 3.2, you have a later release. You must know which release or version of software you are working with so that you know what commands are available. In addition, application software packages often require a certain version of DOS. When you purchase a software package, it is not merely comprised of disks; it also comes with what is known as documentation or the instructions for the package. One section, called System Requirements, will specify how much memory you need to run the package, as well as the needed version of DOS.

Although it is system software, DOS is still software that has been revised several times and will be revised in the future. DOS releases typically are associated with new hardware advances. These are summarized in Table 8.2 and Table 8.3. The first version was numbered 1.0. The numbering scheme means that if the number preceding the decimal changes, there were major changes or enhancements. If the number following the decimal changes, only minor changes were made. Thus, the differences between DOS 3.1 and 3.2 are minor. However, the differences between DOS 1.0 and 5.0 are significant. DOS is downwardly compatible but not upwardly compatible, which means that if you are using DOS version 3.3, it can read disks created under DOS version 2.1. However, if you are using DOS 2.1, it may not be able to read a disk created under DOS version 3.3, and the new commands available under version 3.3 would not be available to users of version 2.1.

However, since DOS is generally tied to hardware advances, it is not quite that simple. For instance, you could boot a new computer such as an IBM-PS/2 Model 80 with a 110 MB hard drive with DOS 3.3. However, DOS 3.3 did not expect disk drives to be larger than 32 MB, so DOS 3.3 would not recognize the 110 MB hard drive as one hard drive. That drive would have to be partitioned to create smaller, logical drives. DOS 5.0, however, does recognize large hard drives and you would not have to do anything special to be able to read or write to the large hard drive. The good news is that the knowledge you learn, even on an early version of DOS, is transferable. In other words, the DIR command works the same in DOS 2.1 as it does in DOS 5.0. The only difference is that in DOS 5.0, you have many more enhancements or additional parameters making the DIR command more powerful.

You can see that it is important to know which version of DOS was loaded into memory. All external DOS commands work correctly only when they are used with the same version of DOS. In other words, if you booted with DOS version 2.1 and then placed a version 3.3 disk in the drive to run the CHKDSK command, an external program available under both versions, you would get an error message saying "Incorrect DOS version." DOS has an internal command, VER, to verify which version is loaded into memory.

There are also some differences in the way that DOS was marketed. Prior to DOS 5.0, Microsoft licensed DOS to different computer manufacturers who fit DOS to their specific computers. You could not go into a software store and purchase or upgrade to a new version of MS-DOS. You could, however, purchase a new version of IBM PC-DOS in any software store. IBM PC-DOS was licensed from Microsoft. However, with MS-DOS 5.0, Microsoft for the first time is making MS-DOS available as an upgrade through software, hardware and computer retail outlets. Microsoft has made MS-DOS 5.0 the most generic of operating systems with the least expectations of any problems. It was extensively beta-tested. **Beta-test** means that Microsoft gave out copies of DOS 5.0 to many different users with many different pieces of hardware so that DOS could be tested in real-life situations. Thus, besides all the significant new features in MS-DOS 5.0 and because of all the testing, there are minimal problems with MS-DOS 5.0.

Date	Version	Changes
1981	1.0	Original version of DOS
1981	1.1	Support for double-sided disks
1983	2.0	Support for hard disks and subdirectories
1983	2.1	Fixes
1984	3.0	Support for 1.2 MB high-capacity disk
		Support for larger hard disks
1985	3.1	Support for networks
1985	3.2	Support for 3 1/2-inch disks
1987	3.3	Support for the PS/2 family
		Support for 3 1/2, 1.4 MB high-capacity disk
1988	4.0	Support for hard disk larger than 32 MB
		Introduces DOS Shell
1989	4.01	Fixes
1991	5.0	Ability to load DOS in high memory
		Full-screen editor
		On-line help and command line editor
		Disk and file recovery tools

Table 8.2 Versions of IBM PC-DOS

Date	Version	Changes
1981	1.0	Original version of DOS
1982	1.25	Support for double-sided disks
1983	2.0	Support for hard disks and subdirectories
1983	2.01	Support for international symbols
1983	2.11	Fixes
1983	2.25	Supports extended character set
1984	3.0	Support for 1.2 MB high-capacity disk
		Support for larger hard disks
1984	3.1	Support for networks
1986	3.2	Support for 3 1/2-inch disks
1987	3.3	Support for 3 1/2, 1.44 MB high-capacity disk
1988	4.0	Support for hard disk larger than 32 MB
		Introduces DOS Shell
1989	4.01	Fixes
1991	5.0	Ability to load DOS in high memory
		Full-screen editor
		On-line help and command line editor
		Disk and file recovery tools

Table 8.3 Versions of MS-DOS

8.16 The VER Command

So that you know which version of DOS is installed on your computer, DOS supplies an internal command called VER. VER tells you what version of DOS you are using. The syntax is:

```
VER
```

Activity 8.17 Using the VER Command

STEP 1: Key in the following:
C:\DOS>**VER** <Enter>

```
C:\DOS>VER

MS-DOS Version 5.00

C:\DOS>_
```

WHAT'S HAPPENING? The version of DOS in this specific computer's memory is 5.0. If you have a different version of DOS, it will appear here. Remember that the version shown is the version of DOS you booted from. Even if you place a DOS 3.3 System Disk into Drive A of this computer, the version of DOS that is running is DOS 5.0. The only way that could change is if you rebooted the system with the DOS 3.3 disk in Drive A. Then, DOS 3.3 would be installed into memory.

8.18 Understanding the LABEL Command

You have been able to change the names of files with the RENAME command. When you formatted your disk in Chapter 4, you put a volume label on your DATA disk: DATA DISK. Often, the contents of your data disk change, so you need a new volume label to reflect that change. You cannot use the RENAME command because the volume label is stored as a hidden file. You do not want to reformat the disk to place a new volume label on it when you have data on the disk. There is another way to change the volume label, by using DOS version 3.0 or above. Prior to 3.0, there was no way to change the volume label. However, later releases of DOS offer an external command called LABEL. The syntax for the label command is:

LABEL [*drive:*][*label*]

The bracketed parameters represent an option, which means that LABEL, when used without parameters, assumes the default drive. For instance, A>**LABEL** assumes you want to change the volume label on the disk in Drive A, since A: is the default. *drive:* is a parameter that allows you to specify on which disk you want to change the volume label. For instance, A>**LABEL B:** allows you to change the volume label on the disk in Drive B, and A>**LABEL C:** allows you to change the label on Drive C.

Activity 8.19 Using the LABEL Command

Note: The **C:\DOS>** is displayed and the ACTIVITIES disk is in Drive A.

STEP 1: Key in the following:
C:\DOS>**LABEL A:** <Enter>

```
C:\DOS>LABEL A:
Volume in drive A is ACTIVITIES
Volume Serial Number is 0ED4-161B
Volume label (11 characters, ENTER for none)?_
```

WHAT'S HAPPENING? You are not asking DOS to look at the volume label as you have with the VOL command; you are asking DOS to allow you to change the label on the ACTIVITIES disk. This message is identical to the one that you saw when you formatted the disk with the FORMAT /V command.

STEP 2: Press <Enter>.

```
C:\DOS>LABEL A:
Volume in drive A is ACTIVITIES
Volume Serial Number is 0ED4-161B
Volume label (11 characters, ENTER for none)?

Delete current volume label (Y/N)?_
```

WHAT'S HAPPENING? You pressed <Enter> for no; you do not want to place a volume label on the disk. Now you get a new question that is different from using FORMAT A:/V. This is a "used disk," and there already is a volume label. When you pressed <Enter>, the LABEL command gave you the option of retaining the current volume label on the ACTIVITIES disk or deleting the volume label completely. You are going to delete the volume label from this disk.

STEP 3: Key in the following:
Y <Enter>

```
Delete current volume label (Y/N)? Y

C:\DOS>_
```

WHAT'S HAPPENING? You just deleted the volume label, ACTIVITIES. To verify that the label is gone, you can use the internal command, VOL, to display the label on the ACTIVITIES disk.

STEP 4: Key in the following:
C:\DOS>**VOL A:** <Enter>

```
C:\DOS VOL A:

 Volume in drive A has no label
 Volume Serial Number is 0ED4-161B

C:\DOS>_
```

WHAT'S HAPPENING? You displayed, not changed, the volume label on the ACTIVITIES disk, proving that there is no longer a volume label on the ACTIVITIES disk. You did indeed delete the volume label from the ACTIVITIES disk.

STEP 5: Key in the following:
C:\DOS>**LABEL A:ACTIVITIES** <Enter>

```
C:\DOS>LABEL A:ACTIVITIES

C:\DOS>_
```

WHAT'S HAPPENING? The system prompt is displayed. Because you followed the command with the new volume label, you did not need to wait for the prompt in order to enter the new label. You can use the VOL command to verify that the volume label was changed.

STEP 6: Key in the following:
C:\DOS>VOL A: <Enter>

```
C:\DOS> VOL A:

 Volume in drive A is ACTIVITIES
 Volume Serial Number is 0ED4-161B

C:\DOS>_
```

WHAT'S HAPPENING? You successfully changed the label of the disk. Remember, the VOL command *displays* the volume label and is an internal command. LABEL is an external command and lets you *change* the volume label.

STEP 7: Key in the following:
C:\DOS>CD \ <Enter>

WHAT'S HAPPENING? You have returned to the root directory of Drive C.

Chapter Summary

1. The CHKDSK command allows you to get statistical information about disks and memory.
2. CHKDSK will tell you whether or not the disk has hidden files, how much room is left on the disk in bytes, how many files are on the disk, if there are any bad spots on the disk, how much total memory is in the computer, and how much memory is available.
3. Files that are contiguous have been written to the disk in adjacent sectors. Noncontiguous files are those that have been written to the disk in nonadjacent sectors. This is also known as a fragmented disk. It can slow the access time to a file. Using a file parameter with the CHKDSK command will verify whether or not the specified files are contiguous.
4. Clusters are made up of sectors. Clusters are the smallest unit written to on a disk. The amount of sectors in a cluster can vary. Clusters on a double-sided disk are made of two 512-byte sectors. The number of sectors that make up a cluster on a hard disk can vary.
5. If you use the /V parameter with the CHKDSK command, it not only checks the disk but also lists all the files on that disk.
6. If you use the /F parameter with the CHKDSK command, it not only checks the disk but also writes any lost sectors to files that have the .CHK file

extension. You can then delete these files and free up disk space.
7. File attributes are tracked by DOS in the directory table.
8. There are four file attributes that DOS tracks: whether a file is a system file, a hidden file, a read-only file, and the archive status of a file.
9. The ATTRIB command allows you to manipulate file attributes.
10. You may compare file contents with file compare commands. Some versions of DOS have the FC command, others have the COMP command. DOS 5.0 includes both commands.
11. The COMP command compares the contents of files. Both text and program files can be compared. If you wish to see file differences in ASCII, you must use the /A parameter.
12. The FC command also compares the contents of files.
13. The COMP command only compares files that are identical in length, whereas FC will compare any two files.
14. ASCII (American Standard Code for Information Interchange) is an acronym that essentially indicates that a file is an unformatted text file readable with the TYPE command.
15. Software is released under a version number. This is for the purpose of fixing problems or adding enhancements. The higher the number, the later the release. These are also known as upgrades.
16. DOS has had several releases. The most current is version 5.0. For the first time, Microsoft is offering a generic version of DOS to be sold in retail outlets.
17. To find out what version is in memory, you can use the VER command, an internal command.
18. With version 3.0 or above, you can change the volume label of a disk using the LABEL command. Earlier releases of DOS did not have this command.

Key Terms

Archive bit
Beta-test
Bug
Chain
Contiguous
Cross-linked files
File attributes
Fixes
Fragmented disks
Fragmented files
Hidden attribute
Lost clusters
Noncontiguous
Read-only attributes
Releases
System attribute
Upgrade
Verbose

Discussion Questions

1. What does the CHKDSK command do? Why should you use it?
2. What is a fragmented disk?
3. How can you tell whether files are contiguous? Why does it matter if files are contiguous?
4. What does linked or chained files mean?
5. What is the verbose mode? What does it show the user?
6. With the CHKDSK command, what does the /F parameter do? When should you use it? Do any other commands have an /F parameter? If so, what do they do?

7. What are file attributes?
8. What does the ATTRIB command do?
9. Name two parameters for the ATTRIB command and describe their purposes.
10. What effect does a file marked read-only have for a user?
11. What effect does a file marked hidden have for a user?
12. What does the COMP command do?
13. What does the FC command do?
14. What are the differences between the FC and COMP commands, if any?
15. Look at the following screen display:

```
362496 bytes total disk space
 38192 bytes in two hidden files
262144 bytes in 36 user files
 61440 bytes available on disk

655360 bytes total memory
618272 bytes free
```

    What are the hidden files? What are the user files?
16. Why are you interested in the version number of DOS that you are using? How would you find out what version number you are using?
17. What is the difference between the VOL and LABEL commands?
18. When would you use the CHKDSK command?
19. How would you use the ATTRIB command?
20. Why can you not use the DIR command with no parameters to see if a disk is a system disk?
21. Explain two types of errors that can be found on a disk.
22. What is the syntax for CHKDSK?
23. What is the syntax for ATTRIB?
24. What is the verbose mode and how is it used?
25. Why would you add the parameter of the file name after the CHKDSK command?
26. What is a lost cluster?
27. What are linked or chained files?
28. Give the syntax of the COMP command.
29. Explain two ways to see if the contents of two files are identical.
30. What is the difference between DISKCOMP and COMP?
31. What is the latest release of DOS?
32. Why would you be interested in upgrading to a new version of DOS?
33. How are version numbers used with software?
34. Give the syntax for the LABEL command.
35. Explain the difference between hidden and user files.

Application Assignments

Note: The **C:\DOS>** is displayed and the ACTIVITIES disk is in Drive A.

1. For the following assignment:
   a. Display the volume label of the ACTIVITIES disk. Do not use the LABEL command.
   b. Print the screen.
2. For the following assignment:
   a. Check the status of the ACTIVITIES disk.
   b. Print the screen.
3. For the following assignment:
   a. Check to see if all the files in the root directory with the extension **.DAT** on the ACTIVITIES disk are contiguous.
   b. Print the screen.
4. For the following assignment:
   a. Use the verbose mode with the CHKDSK command on the ACTIVITIES disk.
   b. When the display has stopped scrolling, print the screen.
5. For the following assignment:
   a. On the ACTIVITIES disk, compare the files **RIGHT.RED** and **DRESS.UP**.
   b. When the command has completed executing and the results of the comparison are on the screen, print the screen.
6. For the following assignment:
   a. On the ACTIVITIES disk, compare all the files with the extension **.RED** to all the files with the extension **.UP**. Use a wildcard.
   b. When the command has completed executing and the results of the comparison are on the screen, print the screen.
7. For the following assignment:
   a. Using the FC command, compare the files **FILE2.FP** and **FILE3.SWT**.
   b. Print the screen that displays the differences.
8. For the following assignment:
   a. Compare the files **EXP92JAN.DAT** and **EXP93JAN.DAT**.
   b. Print the results.
   c. Which command did you use and why did you use it?

Note: Please remove the ACTIVITIES disk from Drive A. Insert the DATA disk in Drive A. The **C:\DOS>** continues to be the default drive and subdirectory, unless otherwise specified. If the requested files are not on the DATA disk, they may be copied from **\JUNK** or a subdirectory under **\JUNK**.

9. For the following assignment:
   a. Copy the file **DRAMA.TV** to a new file called **GRAVE.TV**.
   b. Make the file **GRAVE.TV** read-only.
   c. Prove that you cannot eliminate **GRAVE.TV** and print the screen.
   d. Take what steps you need to make **GRAVE.TV** readable.
   e. Delete the file called **GRAVE.TV**.

   f. Prove that **GRAVE.TV** is no longer on the DATA disk. Print the screen.

10. For the following assignment:
    a. Make all the files that have a **.FIL** extension read-only.
    b. Prove that you cannot eliminate **FRANK.FIL** and print the screen.
    c. Make all the files that have a **.FIL** file extension not read-only.
    d. Display the file attributes of the files that have **.FIL** as a file extension. Print the screen.
11. For the following assignment:
    a. Make all the files that have a file extension **.TV** hidden files.
    b. Prove that they are hidden and print the screen.
    c. Using the DIR command show the hidden files with the **.TV** extension and print the screen.
    d. "Unhide" the **.TV** files.
    e. Prove that the files are no longer hidden and print the screen.
12. For the following assignment:
    a. Display the volume label of the DATA disk.
    b. Print the screen.
    c. Change the volume label on the DATA disk from DATA DISK to LESSONS.
    d. Display the new volume label.
    e. Print the screen.
    f. Change the volume label on the DATA disk from LESSONS to DATA DISK.
    g. Display the new volume label.
    h. Print the screen.
13. For the following assignment:
    a. Copy the file **BLUE.JAZ** and **GREEN.JAZ** to the DATA disk from **\JUNK**.
    b. Compare these two files on the DATA Disk.
    c. After the command has executed and the results of the comparison are on the screen, print the screen.
    d. Compare these files again, but display the output in an ASCII mode. Print the screen.
14. For the following assignment:
    a. Check to see if all the files in the root directory on the DATA disk are contiguous.
    b. Print the screen.
15. For the following assignment:
    a. Display the version number of DOS you are using.
    b. Print the screen.

Challenge Assignments

Note: The assignments will occur on the DATA disk. If you do not have the appropriate subdirectories, you will need to create them and copy files into them.

16. For the following assignment:
    a. See if all the files in subdirectory **SERIES** are contiguous.
    b. Print the screen.
17. For the following assignment:
    a. Make all the files in the subdirectory **USERS** hidden files.
    b. Prove that they are hidden files and print the screen.
    c. "Unhide" the files in the **USERS** subdirectory.
    d. Prove that they are now no longer hidden and print the screen.
    e. Hide the subdirectory **USERS**.
    f. Prove that it is a hidden subdirectory and print the screen.
    g. "Unhide" the subdirectory **USERS**.
    h. Prove that it is no longer hidden and print the screen.
    i. Make the **USERS** subdirectory read-only.
    j. Prove that the **USERS** subdirectory is a read-only subdirectory and print the screen.
    k. Make the **USERS** subdirectory readable.
    l. Prove that it is readable and print the screen.
18. For the following assignment:
    a. Compare the files **WILDONE.DOS** and **WILDTHR.DOS** in the subdirectory **USERS**.
    b. Print the screen.
    c. Compare the files **WILDONE.DOS** and **WILDTWO.DOS** in the subdirectory **USERS**.
    d. Print the screen.
19. For the following assignment:
    a. Compare all the files with a **.LAB** extension to all the files with a **.DOS** extension in the **USERS** subdirectory.
    b. Print the screen.
    c. Compare the files with a **.LAB** extension in the subdirectory **USERS** to all the files in the root directory that have a **.LAB** file extension.
    d. Print the screen.
20. For the following assignment:
    a. Eliminate any lost clusters on the DATA disk.
    b. Print the screens to demonstrate how you did this.

9 Chapter

Subdirectories

After completing this chapter you will be able to:

1. Explain the hierarchical filing system of a tree-structured directory.
2. Explain what a root directory is, how it is created, and what its limitations are.
3. Explain what subdirectories are and how they are named, created, and used.
4. Create subdirectories using the MD command.
5. Display the default directory using the CD command.
6. Change directories using the CD command.
7. Use the COPY command to copy files from one directory to another.
8. Use the PROMPT command with metastrings to change the prompt to reflect the default drive and subdirectory.
9. Explain the purpose and use of subdirectory markers.
10. Identify the commands that can be used with subdirectories.
11. Use subdirectory markers with commands.
12. List the steps to remove a directory.
13. Use the RD command to eliminate a directory.
14. Set and use the PATH command for DOS to search for executable files.
15. Use the PATH command to cancel currently set path(s).
16. Use the TREE command to see the structure of a disk.

Chapter Overview

The directory of a disk contains a list of the files stored on that disk. In previous chapters, the directories that were used contained a small number of files, and it was fairly easy to locate a specific file. But a disk is capable of containing hundreds or even thousands of files. When a directory contains over a thousand files it becomes much more difficult to locate a specific file.

The main directory that is used to find files is automatically created when a disk is formatted. It is called the root directory, but it is limited in the number of entries it can contain. Also, there is no particular method by which files are listed in the root directory. To solve these problems a further means of organizing files was developed—subdirectories.

Subdirectories are files that contain lists of files that have been grouped together under one heading. Subdirectories can contain any number of entries—limited only by the available disk space. These subdirectories can be added whenever new files are created and deleted whenever the subdirectory and the files within it are no longer needed. Thus, creating, using, and deleting subdirectories makes it possible to manage large numbers of files efficiently.

In this chapter you will learn the subdirectory commands, learn to create and use subdirectories, copy files to other directories, erase or rename files within subdirectories, and, when necessary, remove a subdirectory.

9.0 The Hierarchical Filing System or Tree-structured Directories

Every disk must be formatted before it can be used. When you format a disk, a directory known as the **root directory** is always created automatically. Every disk must have a root directory so that files can be located on the disk. The directory is the area of the disk that contains information about what is stored there. However, there is a limit to the number of files or entries that can be placed in the root directory of a disk. A 5 1/4-inch single-sided disk has a maximum of 64 entries. Both the 5 1/4-inch and the 3 1/2-inch double-sided disks have maximums of 112 entries. A 5 1/4-inch or a 3 1/2-inch high-capacity disk have a maximum of 224 entries, and a hard disk has a maximum of 512 entries.

For a 360 KB floppy disk, 112 directory entries is usually sufficient. However, if you have many small files, 112 file entries are not sufficient. In addition, scrolling through 112 entries looking for a specific file is time-consuming. Even high-capacity floppy disks with 224 entries and hard disks with 512 entries is not enough. Normally, people work more efficiently when they logically group files and programs together, for example, placing all accounting programs and accounting files together. DOS version 2.0 and above gives you the capability of "fooling" the system so that you can create as many file entries as you need. The only limitation is the size or capacity of the disk.

This capability is known as the hierarchical or **tree-structured** filing system. In this system the directory has not only entries for files but also entries for other directories called subdirectories, which can contain any number of entries.

The root directory is represented by a backslash. (Do not confuse the backslash \ with the slash /.) All directories other than the root directory are technically called subdirectories, yet the terms directory and subdirectory are used interchangeably. Unlike the root directory, the subdirectories are not limited to a specific number of files. Subdirectories may have subdirectories of their own. The subdirectories divide the disk into different areas that can be treated like completely separate disks. The directory structure of a disk is like an inverted tree with the root directory at the top and the subdirectories branching off from the root. It is much like a family tree, especially because of the dependent nature of subdirectories. For instance, the example on the left in Figure 9.1 is a family tree showing a mother who has two children; the one on the right is a root directory with two subdirectories. The two subdirectories will contain all the files and programs that have to do with sales and accounting.

Figure 9.1
A Directory Is Like a Family Tree

A child can have only one biological mother, but a child can become a parent and have children. Those children can also become parents and have children. Likewise, accounting can be a **"child"** of the root directory but also a **"parent"** to subdirectories beneath it (see Figure 9.2).

Figure 9.2
Hierarchical Structure of a Directory

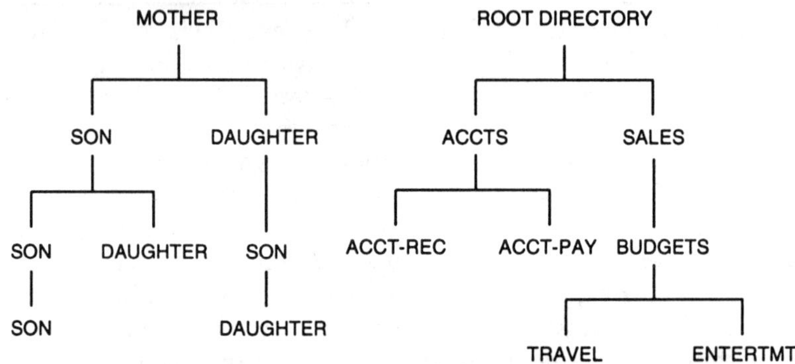

The children are dependent on the parent above. Each subdirectory is listed in its parent directory but not in any directory above the parent. Note the absolute **hierarchical structure**. You cannot skip a subdirectory any more than you can have a grandfather with a grandson and no father in between. You move around in the directories via the path that tells DOS where to go for a particular file.

Think of a disk as a building. When a structure is built, it has a finite size, which is also true of a disk. You can have a 1.44 MB floppy disk or a 80 MB hard disk. The size is fixed. You cannot make it larger or smaller, but you can divide it into rooms. However, you have to get inside. To open the door you need a drive letter. Once inside, you are in a big room called the root directory and its name is backslash (\). Thus, the structure could look like Figure 9.3.

Figure 9.3
Root Directory as a Building

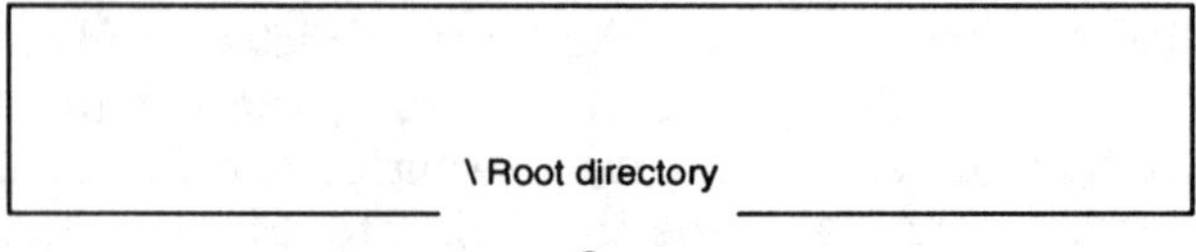

Since it is difficult to find things when they are scattered about a large room, you want to put up walls (subdirectories) so that like things can be grouped together. When the walls go up, the root directory becomes the main lobby—backslash (\). In the rooms (subdirectories) you plan to have games, names and addresses in phone books, and the DOS commands. You post a sign indicating what you plan to put inside each room (see Figure 9.4).

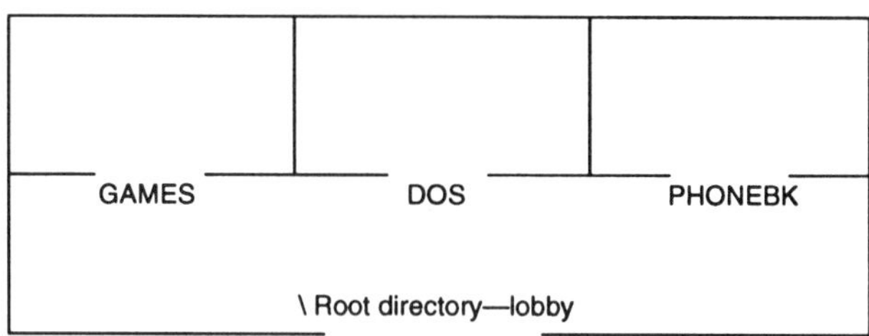

Figure 9.4 Subdirectories as Subrooms

Each room is off the main lobby, the \. You cannot go from the **GAMES** room to the **PHONEBK** room without first going through the main lobby (\). Furthermore, the lobby (\) only sees the entry ways to the rooms. It does not know what is in the rooms, only that there are rooms (subdirectories). In addition, each room can be further divided (see Figure 9.5).

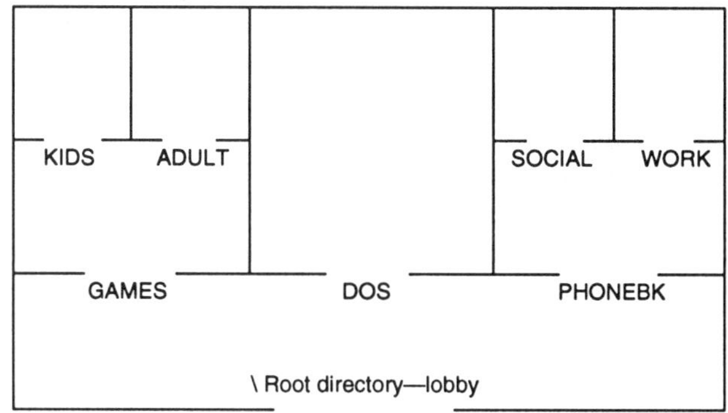

Figure 9.5 More Subdirectories

Each new room (subdirectory) is off another room (subdirectory). The **GAMES** room, for example, now has two new rooms—**KIDS** and **ADULTS**. The **GAMES** room (subdirectory) now becomes a lobby. You can get to the **KIDS** and **ADULT** rooms (subdirectories) only through the **GAMES** lobby. Furthermore, in order to get to the **GAMES** room, you must pass through the main lobby \ (root directory).

The **GAMES** lobby knows that there are two new rooms but does not know what is inside each. The main lobby (\) knows the **GAMES** room but does not know what is inside **GAMES**. The **KIDS** and **ADULT** rooms know only the **GAMES** lobby.

The same relationship exists for all other new rooms (subdirectories). A subdirectory knows only its parent lobby and any children it may create. There are no shortcuts. If you are in the **KIDS** room and wish to go the **SOCIAL** room, you must return to the **GAMES** lobby, then you must pass through the main lobby (root directory) to the **PHONEBK** lobby. Only then can you enter the **SOCIAL** room.

A room does not have to be subdivided, but each room could be subdivided.

GAMES is subdivided, while DOS is not. Remember, you are not changing the size of the structure; you are merely organizing it. Presently, these rooms have nothing in them, but they are ready to receive something. That something is files or many files (see Figure 9.6).

Figure 9.6 Files in Subdirectories

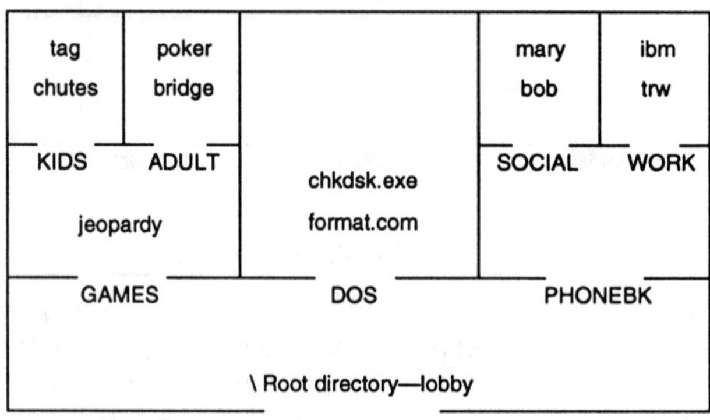

You have now placed file cabinets in your room and filled them with files. Thus, using subdirectories is like setting up and using a file cabinet. In some way a subdirectory is acting as if it were a floppy disk. Subdirectories are a place to put files, just like a floppy disk. When you use subdirectories, you can change your work area, much like using another file cabinet or another room. Subdirectories have names that you choose. The only exception is the root directory, which is created when you format the disk and is always known as backslash (\).

Subdirectories follow the same naming conventions as files: a maximum of eight characters for the file name, a period, and a maximum of three characters for a file extension. Usually, subdirectory names do not have extensions. Although DOS treats subdirectories as files, the subdirectories themselves cannot be manipulated with the standard file manipulation commands like COPY or DEL.

Table 9.1 lists the directory management commands.

Table 9.1 Directory Management Commands

Command	Function
CHDIR or CD	Change the directory
MKDIR or MD	Make or create a directory
RMDIR or RD	Remove or erase a directory
PATH	Define the search path(s)
PROMPT	Changes the look of the prompt to identify what subdirectory is the default
TREE	Allows you to see the structure of the disk

9.1 Creating Subdirectories

When you create a subdirectory, you are setting up an area where files can be stored. There is nothing in the subdirectory initially. The internal MD command creates a subdirectory much like setting up a separate disk. When you format a disk, you are preparing it to hold files. When you set up a subdirectory, you are also preparing it to hold files. The syntax of the command is:

MD [*drive:*]*path*
or MKDIR [*drive:*]*path*

In the following activity, you will create two subdirectories under the root directory on the DATA disk. These subdirectories will be for two classes, one in political science and the other in physical education.

Activity 9.2 How to Create Subdirectories

Note: The DATA disk is in Drive A. The default drive is Drive A. The **A:\>** is displayed.

STEP 1: Key in the following:
A:\>**MD POLY-SCI** <Enter>

STEP 2: Key in the following:
A:\>**MD PHYS-ED** <Enter>

```
A:\>MD POLY-SCI

A:\>MD PHYS-ED

A:\>_
```

WHAT'S HAPPENING? You created two subdirectories called **POLY-SCI** and **PHYS-ED** under the root directory on the DATA disk. **POLY-SCI** will hold all the files that involve classes in political science, and **PHYS-ED** will hold files that involve classes in physical education. Although you have created the subdirectories to hold the files, they are now "empty" file cabinets. When you used the MD command, all you saw on the screen was the system prompt. How do you know that you created subdirectories? You can see the subdirectories you just created by using the DIR command.

STEP 3: Key in the following:
A:\>**DIR P*.*** <Enter>

```
A:\>DIR P*.*

   Volume in drive A is DATA DISK
   Volume Serial Number is 3839-0EC8
   Directory of A:\

PERSONAL FIL    2306   11-23-92  7:14a
POLY-SCI      <DIR>    11-16-93  9:47p
```

```
PHYS-ED        <DIR>     11-16-93   9:47p
        3 file(s)          2306 bytes
                         216064 bytes free

A:\>_
```

WHAT'S HAPPENING? The DIR command selected anything that began with **P**, which included the file **PERSONAL.FIL** and then the two subdirectory files you just created. It is the **<DIR>** after each file name that indicates a subdirectory. **POLY-SCI** and **PHYS-ED** are subdirectories. **PERSONAL.FIL** is not. It is also important to note that the \ following the "Directory of A:\" that appears on the screen indicates the root directory of the disk.

What if you wanted to see only the directories? If you have DOS 5.0, you have that option. One of the parameters in the new DIR command is /A for attributes. The attribute you are interested in is D for directories only. If you look at the complete syntax diagram, it indicates the /A followed by a list of the attributes you can request. The D is for directories:

DIR [*drive:*][*path*][*filename*] [/P] [/W] [/A[[:]attributes]]

/A	Displays files with specified attributes			
attributes	D	Directories	R	Read-only files
	H	Hidden files	A	Files ready for archiving
	S	System files	-	Prefix meaning "not"

STEP 4: Key in the following:
A:\>**DIR /AD** <Enter>

```
A:\>DIR /AD

   Volume in drive A is DATA DISK
   Volume Serial Number is 3839-0EC8
   Directory of A:\

CLASS          <DIR>     11-23-92   7:46a
FILES          <DIR>     12-06-92   9:03a
DATA           <DIR>     12-06-92   9:05a
USERS          <DIR>     05-07-93  10:05a
TRIP           <DIR>     06-17-92   9:00p
SERIES         <DIR>     05-14-92   3:10p
POLY-SCI       <DIR>     11-16-93   9:47p
PHYS-ED        <DIR>     11-16-93   9:47p
        8 file(s)             0 bytes
                         216064 bytes free

A:\>_
```

WHAT'S HAPPENING? You see displayed only the directories on the DATA disk. The above command listed the directories. But what if you wish to see what files are inside the directory? Since **POLY-SCI** is a subdirectory, not just a file, you can display the contents of the directory with the DIR command. Remember, the terms directory and subdirectory are used interchangeably by most users. The truth though is that there is only one directory—the root directory. Although others may be called directories, they are really subdirectories. Again, the abbreviated syntax of the DIR command is: DIR [*drive:*][*path*]. [*path*] is an optional variable parameter. You use the subdirectory name for *path*.

STEP 5: Key in the following:
A:\>**DIR POLY-SCI** <Enter>

```
A:\>DIR POLY-SCI

   Volume in drive A is DATA DISK
   Volume Serial Number is 3839-0EC8
   Directory of A:\POLY-SCI

.             <DIR>      11-16-93  9:47p
..            <DIR>      11-16-93  9:47p
        2 file(s)             0 bytes
                         216064 bytes free

A:\>_
```

WHAT'S HAPPENING? The directory line, "Directory of A:\POLY-SCI" is telling you the path. You are looking from the root directory into the subdirectory called **POLY-SCI**. Even though you just created the subdirectory **POLY-SCI**, it seems to have two subdirectories in it already, . (one period, also called "the dot") and .. (two periods, also called "the double dot") followed by **<DIR>**. Every subdirectory, except the root directory, *always* has two named subdirectories. The subdirectory named . is another name or abbreviation for **POLY-SCI**. The subdirectory name .. is an abbreviation for the parent directory, in this case the root directory \.

STEP 6: Key in the following:
A:\>**DIR PHYS-ED** <Enter>

```
A:\>DIR PHYS-ED

   Volume in drive A is DATA DISK
   Volume Serial Number is 3839-0EC8
   Directory of A:\PHYS-ED

.          <DIR>         11-16-93  9:47p
..         <DIR>         11-16-93  9:47p
        2 file(s)             0 bytes
                         216064 bytes free

A:\>_
```

WHAT'S HAPPENING? The line that reads "Directory of A:\PHYS-ED" is telling you the path. You are looking from the root directory into the subdirectory called **PHYS-ED**, the same way you looked when you asked for a directory on another drive. If, for instance, you asked for a directory of the disk in Drive B that line would have read "Directory of B:\." If you had asked for a directory of Drive C, that line would have read "Directory of C:\." It tells you not only what drive but also what subdirectory is on the screen.

9.3 The Current Directory

Just as DOS keeps track of the default drive with **A>** or **B>** or **C>**, it also keeps track of the **current** or default directory. When you boot the system, the default drive is the drive where you loaded DOS, and the default directory is the root directory of the current drive. You can change the directory just as you can change the drive designator. Doing so makes a specific subdirectory the default. In previous chapters you used the CD command to change the default directory to the **\DOS** subdirectory on the hard disk. It was important to have that as the default subdirectory so that you could use the DOS external commands.

The change directory (CHDIR or CD) command has two purposes. If you key in CD with no parameters, DOS displays the name of the current default directory. If you include a parameter, the name of a directory after the CD, it changes the default directory to the directory that you requested and make that directory the default. This process is similar to changing drives by keying in the desired drive letter followed by a colon, i.e., A:, B:, C:. The syntax is:

CD [*drive:*][*path*]
or CHDIR [*drive:*][*path*]

Activity 9.4 Using the CD Command

Note: The DATA disk is in Drive A. The default drive is Drive A. The **A:\>** is displayed.

STEP 1: Key in the following:
A:\>**CD** <Enter>

```
A:\>CD
A:\

A:\>_
```

WHAT'S HAPPENING? This display tells you that you are in the root directory of the DATA disk and that any command you enter will apply to this root directory, which is also the default directory. You can also change the default subdirectory by using the CD command. You are going to change the default subdirectory from the root to the subdirectory called **POLY-SCI**.

STEP 2: Key in the following:
A:\>**CD POLY-SCI** <Enter>

STEP 3: Key in the following:
A:\POLY-SCI>**CD** <Enter>

```
A:\>CD POLY-SCI

A:\POLY-SCI>CD
A:\POLY-SCI

A:\POLY-SCI>_
```

WHAT'S HAPPENING? In Step 2, CD followed by the name of the subdirectory, **POLY-SCI**, changed the default from the root directory to the subdirectory, **POLY-SCI**. Since you changed the way the prompt looked, the prompt now says **A:\POLY-SCI>**. However, you can always confirm that you changed the default directory by keying in CD. CD with no parameters always displays the default drive and default subdirectory. When you keyed in **CD**, it displayed **A:\POLY-SCI**. This display tells you that you are in the subdirectory **\POLY-SCI** on the DATA disk in Drive A and indicates that any command you enter with no parameters will apply to this default subdirectory. You can think of the command this way: CD with no parameters shows you the current directory; CD followed by a subdirectory name changes the subdirectory. CD cannot be used to change drives.

STEP 4: Key in the following:
A:\POLY-SCI>**DIR** <Enter>

```
A:\POLY-SCI>DIR

   Volume in drive A is DATA DISK
   Volume Serial Number is 3839-0EC8
   Directory of A:\POLY-SCI

.           <DIR>        11-16-93   9:47p
..          <DIR>        11-16-93   9:47p
        2 file(s)             0 bytes
                        216064 bytes free

A:\POLY-SCI>_
```

WHAT'S HAPPENING? You are displaying the default directory, but the default is now the directory of **\POLY-SCI** rather than the root directory. Thus, when you use a command, it always assumes the default drive and default subdirectory unless you specify another drive and/or subdirectory.

9.5 Using Subdirectories

The DATA disk is structured as shown in Figure 9.7. You can use each of these directories as if it were a separate disk, but instead of a lettered drive, you must give the path name. The path tells DOS what route to follow when looking for files. You can use any DOS command. You can copy files, delete files, display files, and rename files. Remember that as long as you follow the syntax, you can use any DOS command with subdirectories. The next activity will demonstrate the use of the COPY command with subdirectories. You are going to copy a file to the root directory and then make copies in various subdirectories.

Figure 9.7 Structure of the DATA Disk

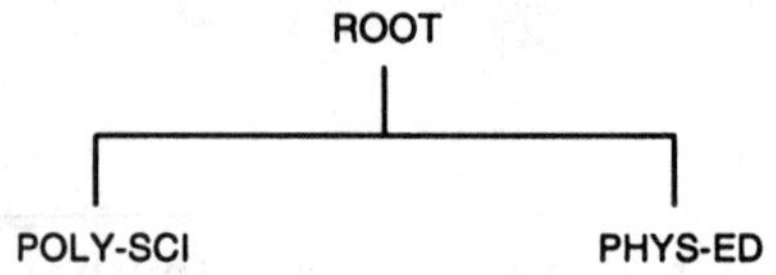

Activity 9.6

Copying From One Directory to Another

Note: The DATA disk is in Drive A. The default drive is Drive A. The default subdirectory is **POLY-SCI**. The **A:\POLY-SCI>** is displayed. To be sure you are in the correct subdirectory, you can key in **CD A:\POLY-SCI**.

STEP 1: Key in the following:
A:\POLY-SCI>**COPY C:\JUNK\BYE.TXT ** <Enter>

```
A:\POLY-SCI>COPY C:\JUNK\BYE.TXT \
        1 file(s) copied

A:\POLY-SCI>_
```

WHAT'S HAPPENING? It is very important to include the second backslash. The syntax for the COPY command remains the same:

COPY [*drive:*][*path*]*source* [*drive:*][*path*]*destination*

You keyed in the command, COPY. Then, you keyed in the source file, **C:\JUNK\BYE.TXT**. The destination was the root directory on the DATA disk, \. You wanted the file to have the same name, so you did not need to key in a destination file name. You keyed in the \ or backslash to indicate that you wanted that file written to the root directory. Since the default directory is now **POLY-SCI**, had you not included the \, the file would have been written to the default subdirectory, **POLY-SCI**. Again, this file contains dummy data. It is a file you are going to use to explore the use of commands with subdirectories.

STEP 2: Key in the following:
A:\POLY-SCI>**DIR BYE.TXT** <Enter>

STEP 3: Key in the following:
A:\POLY-SCI>**DIR \BYE.TXT** <Enter>

```
A:\POLY-SCI>DIR BYE.TXT

   Volume in drive A is DATA DISK
   Volume Serial Number is 3839-0EC8
   Directory of A:\POLY-SCI

File not found

A:\POLY-SCI>DIR \BYE.TXT
```

```
   Volume in drive A is DATA DISK
   Volume Serial Number is 3839-0EC8
   Directory of A:\

BYE      TXT      44   11-23-92  7:07a
        1 file(s)          44 bytes
                       215040 bytes free

A:\POLY-SCI>_
```

WHAT'S HAPPENING? In the first command, when you requested the file **BYE.TXT**, you did not specify which directory the file was in, so the command displayed the contents of the default directory, **POLY-SCI**. There are no files in this directory, certainly not **BYE.TXT**. In the next command you specified the \ followed by the file name, **BYE.TXT**. Since that was where the file was, DOS could locate it. Since a subdirectory can be treated as if it were a separate disk, you can copy from one directory to another. The COPY syntax is the same, but you must include the subdirectory name or the path.

STEP 4: Key in the following:
A:\POLY-SCI>**COPY \BYE.TXT CLASS.NAM** <Enter>

```
A:\POLY-SCI>COPY \BYE.TXT CLASS.NAM
        1 file(s) copied

A:\POLY-SCI>_
```

WHAT'S HAPPENING? You just copied the file called **BYE.TXT** located on the DATA disk in the root directory (\). You copied it to a new file called **CLASS.NAM** located in the subdirectory **POLY-SCI**. Since you did not specify otherwise, DOS assumed you wanted the file copied to the subdirectory you are currently in. The longhand version of the command would be:

A:\POLY-SCI>**COPY A:\BYE.TXT A:\POLY-SCI\CLASS.NAM**

All you needed to key in for the destination was **CLASS.NAM**. The drive letter and subdirectory, **A:\POLY-SCI**, was assumed because it is the default.

STEP 5: Key in the following:
A:\POLY-SCI>**DIR** <Enter>

```
A:\POLY-SCI>DIR

   Volume in drive A is DATA DISK
   Volume Serial Number is 3839-0EC8
   Directory of A:\POLY-SCI

.             <DIR>      11-16-93  9:47p
..            <DIR>      11-16-93  9:47p
CLASS    NAM      44     11-23-92  7:07a
        3 file(s)           44 bytes
                        214016 bytes free

A:\POLY-SCI>_
```

WHAT'S HAPPENING? You are looking at the directory for the subdirectory, **POLY-SCI**. The file called **BYE.TXT** has been copied to the subdirectory but is now called **CLASS.NAM**.

STEP 6: Key in the following:
A:\POLY-SCI>**DIR \CLASS.NAM** <Enter>

```
A:\POLY-SCI>DIR \CLASS.NAM

   Volume in drive A is DATA DISK
   Volume Serial Number is 3839-0EC8
   Directory of A:\

File not found

A:\POLY-SCI>_
```

WHAT'S HAPPENING? The file called **CLASS.NAM** does not appear in the root directory. It is only found inside the subdirectory, **POLY-SCI**. You can copy a file with the same name to another disk. You can also copy a file with the same name to another subdirectory.

STEP 7: Key in the following:
A:\POLY-SCI>**COPY CLASS.NAM \PHYS-ED** <Enter>

```
A:\POLY-SCI>COPY CLASS.NAM \PHYS-ED
        1 file(s) copied

A:\POLY-SCI>_
```

WHAT'S HAPPENING? The COPY syntax remained the same: the command, COPY; the source, **CLASS.NAM** from the default subdirectory, **POLY-SCI**; the destination, the subdirectory **\PHYS-ED**. That is, you were copying the file to the subdirectory **\PHYS-ED** while maintaining the same file name. There are now two files with the same name on the disk but in different directories. Had you not used "computer shorthand," you would have keyed in what is shown in Figure 9.8. (Do not key it in. This is an illustration and the spacing is incorrect.)

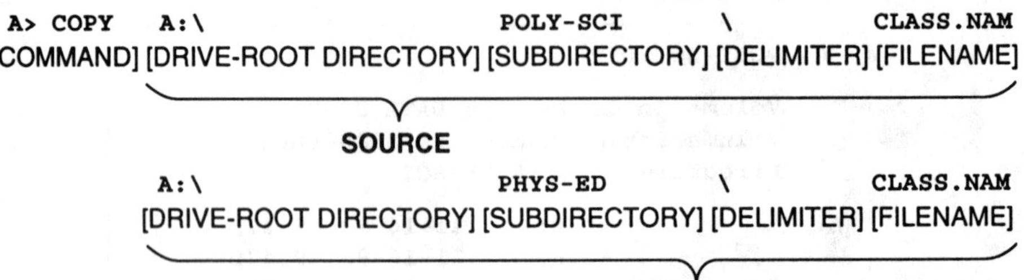

Figure 9.8 COPY Command Syntax

Figure 9.8 shows the path that the COPY command follows. The search path leads to the specified area of the tree that contains the requested files. The path is the list of names of the directories starting with the root directory, continuing through all the subdirectories that lead through the areas of the tree, and ending with the directory that has the file you seek. The directory names in a path are separated by the backslash. The first backslash always means the root directory. Any other backslash is a delimiter.

STEP 8: Key in the following:
A:\POLY-SCI>**DIR** <Enter>

STEP 9: Key in the following:
A:\POLY-SCI>**DIR \PHYS-ED** <Enter>

```
A:\POLY-SCI>DIR

   Volume in drive A is DATA DISK
   Volume Serial Number is 3839-0EC8
   Directory of A:\POLY-SCI

.            <DIR>     11-16-93   9:47p
..           <DIR>     11-16-93   9:47p
CLASS    NAM       44  11-23-92   7:07a
        3 file(s)          44 bytes
                       212992 bytes free

A:\POLY-SCI>DIR \PHYS-ED

   Volume in drive A is DATA DISK
   Volume Serial Number is 3839-0EC8
   Directory of A:\PHYS-ED

.            <DIR>     11-16-93   9:47p
..           <DIR>     11-16-93   9:47p
CLASS    NAM       44  11-23-92   7:07a
        3 file(s)          44 bytes
                       212992 bytes free

A:\POLY-SCI>_
```

WHAT'S HAPPENING? Each subdirectory has a file with the same name, **CLASS.NAM**. This occurrence supposedly violates the unique file name for each disk, but these files names *are* unique. One file name is actually **A:\POLY-SCI\CLASS.NAM**, and the other is **A:\PHYS-ED\CLASS.NAM**. This is the same idea as **A:\CLASS.NAM** or **B:\CLASS.NAM** or **C:\CLASS.NAM**. Any DOS internal command will work the same way as long as you use the proper syntax and specify where you are and where you are going.

9.7 Adding Subdirectories

You are going to add additional subdirectories to the tree structure so that the levels will look like those in Figure 9.9. To create these additional subdirectories, you use the MD or make directory command (MKDIR or MD). The command syntax allows these parameters: MD [*drive:*]*path*.

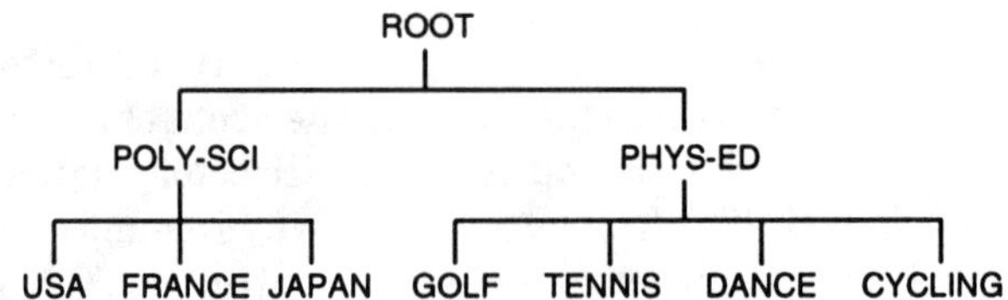

Figure 9.9 Directory with Subdirectories

The *drive:* is the letter of the drive that contains the disk on which the subdirectory is to be created (such as A: or B: or C:). If you omit the drive designator, DOS creates the subdirectory on the default or current drive. The *path* is the path name of the directory in which the subdirectory is to be created. If you omit the path name, the subdirectory is created in the default or current subdirectory.

Activity 9.8 Creating More Subdirectories

Note: The DATA disk is in Drive A. The default drive is Drive A. The default subdirectory is **POLY-SCI**. The **A:\POLY-SCI>** is displayed.

STEP 1: Key in the following:
A:\POLY-SCI>**CD** <Enter>

```
A:\POLY-SCI>CD
A:\POLY-SCI

A:\POLY-SCI>_
```

WHAT'S HAPPENING? You confirmed that the default directory is **POLY-SCI**. To create three subdirectories under **POLY-SCI**, you will use the MD command along with the subdirectory names. The subdirectories will be called **USA**, **JAPAN**, and **FRANCE**.

STEP 2: Key in the following:
A:\POLY-SCI>**MD USA** <Enter>

STEP 3: Key in the following:
A:\POLY-SCI>**MD JAPAN** <Enter>

STEP 4: Key in the following:
A:\POLY-SCI>**MD FRANCE** <Enter>

STEP 5: Key in the following:
A:\POLY-SCI>**DIR** <Enter>

```
A:\POLY-SCI>MD USA

A:\POLY-SCI>MD JAPAN

A:\POLY-SCI>MD FRANCE
```

```
A:\POLY-SCI>DIR

   Volume in drive A is DATA DISK
   Volume Serial Number is 3839-0EC8
   Directory of A:\POLY-SCI

.              <DIR>     11-16-93  9:47p
..             <DIR>     11-16-93  9:47p
CLASS     NAM       44   11-23-92  7:07a
USA            <DIR>     11-16-93 10:03p
JAPAN          <DIR>     11-16-93 10:03p
FRANCE         <DIR>     11-16-93 10:03p
       6 file(s)            44 bytes
                        209920 bytes free

A:\POLY-SCI>_
```

WHAT'S HAPPENING? The file **CLASS.NAM** is displayed as well as the three subdirectories you just created. Remember, there are no files in the newly created subdirectories. You have made "rooms" for files. You can create subdirectories wherever you wish as long as the proper path is included.

STEP 6: Key in the following:
A:\POLY-SCI>**MD \PHYS-ED\TENNIS** <Enter>

```
A:\POLY-SCI>MD \PHYS-ED\TENNIS

A:\POLY-SCI>_
```

WHAT'S HAPPENING? Since the default or "current" directory at this time is **POLY-SCI**, you first had to tell DOS to return to the root (\) and then go to the subdirectory called **PHYS-ED**. Thus, the path is **\PHYS-ED**. You had to tell DOS what the new subdirectory under **PHYS-ED** would be called, **TENNIS**. The second backslash (**\PHYS-ED\TENNIS**) is a delimiter separating the first subdirectory name from the second subdirectory name. Only the first backslash indicates the root. Any other backslash is a delimiter. This statement is always true. The MD command does not change the current or default directory. You can verify that you created the subdirectory **TENNIS** in the subdirectory **\PHYS-ED** by using the DIR command with the path name.

STEP 7: Key in the following:
A:\POLY-SCI>**DIR \PHYS-ED** <Enter>

```
A:\POLY-SCI>DIR \PHYS-ED

   Volume in drive A is DATA DISK
   Volume Serial Number is 3839-0EC8
   Directory of A:\PHYS-ED

.              <DIR>     11-16-93  9:47p
..             <DIR>     11-16-93  9:47p
```

```
CLASS     NAM      44    11-23-92   7:07a
TENNIS         <DIR>     11-16-93 10:10p
        4 file(s)            44 bytes
                         208896 bytes free

A:\POLY-SCI>_
```

WHAT'S HAPPENING? The subdirectory **PHYS-ED** is displayed with the **TENNIS** subdirectory listed. It was very important to key in the backslash in **\PHYS-ED** in order to tell DOS to go up to the root and then down to the subdirectory **PHYS-ED**. If you had not included the \ and had only keyed in **DIR PHYS-ED**, DOS would have given you a "File not found" message because DOS would have looked only below **POLY-SCI**. **PHYS-ED** is under the root directory, not under the subdirectory **POLY-SCI**.

9.9 Knowing the Default Directory

Since DOS always uses default values unless you specify otherwise, knowing the default is very important. Recognizing the default drive is easy because the screen displays the prompt or disk drive letter, **A>** or **B>** or **C>**. Knowing the default subdirectory is not so easy. You can always key in the CD command, which will display the default or current drive and directory you are in, but it would be easier if you could display the default subdirectory as well as the default drive on the screen. You can do this with the PROMPT command. You have been using the PROMPT command, so you did not always need to key in CD. However, there are many options to the PROMPT command that we will explore.

9.10 The PROMPT Command

The system prompt is a letter of the alphabet designating the default or assigned disk drive, followed by the greater than sign, such as **A>** or **C>**. This prompt is always displayed when you first boot the system. However, the prompt can be changed to reflect what you want displayed because all you are changing is the way the prompt looks. The new display does not limit the function of the prompt. The new display will function just like the prompt you are accustomed to (**A>**, **B>** or **C>**). You can do this because PROMPT is an internal command. The syntax is:

PROMPT [*prompt-text*]

The PROMPT command also has some special characters that mean specific things. These are called **metastrings**. When you include one of these metastrings, it establishes a specific value for its meaning. Metastrings always have the syntax $c where c represents any of the following values:

$	The dollar sign
t	The time
d	The date
p	The current directory of the default drive
v	The version number

n	The default drive letter
g	The greater than sign, >
l	The less than sign, <
b	The pipe sign, |
q	The equal sign, =
h	The backspace; the previous character is erased
e	The escape character
_	The underscore, which is a CR-LF sequence (carriage return-line feed) meaning go to the beginning of a new line on the screen.

The following activity allows you to change the prompt and use text data as well as metastrings. PROMPT when keyed in without any parameters returns the displayed prompt to the default value (**A>**, **B>**, or **C>**).

Activity 9.11 Changing the Prompt

Note: The DATA disk is in Drive A. The default drive is drive A. The default subdirectory is **POLY-SCI**. The **A:\POLY-SCI>** is displayed.

STEP 1: Key in the following:
A:\POLY-SCI>**PROMPT HELLO $g** <Enter>

```
A:\POLY-SCI>PROMPT HELLO $g

HELLO >_
```

WHAT'S HAPPENING? You changed the way the prompt looks. You no longer see **A:\POLY-SCI>** but instead the text you supplied, **HELLO**. The greater than sign, >, appeared because you keyed in $g. Every time DOS sees $g, it returns the metastring value for g which is the >. The function of the prompt has not changed, only its appearance. The new prompt works just as if **A>** or **B>** or **C>** were displayed. Any command keyed in works the same way. Remember to key in what appears after the >.

STEP 2: Key in the following:
HELLO >**VOL** <Enter>

```
HELLO >VOL

   Volume in drive A is DATA DISK
   Volume Serial Number is 3839-0EC8

HELLO >_
```

WHAT'S HAPPENING? As you can see, the VOL command works the same way. What if you change drives?

STEP 3: Key in the following:
HELLO >**C:** <Enter>

```
HELLO >C:

HELLO >_
```

WHAT'S HAPPENING? You changed the default drive to C; but, by looking at the screen, there is no way to tell what the default drive is.

STEP 4: Key in the following:
HELLO >**VOL** <Enter>

```
HELLO >VOL

   Volume in drive C is MS-DOS_5
   Volume Serial Number is 16D1-68D4

HELLO >_
```

WHAT'S HAPPENING? You changed the designated drive. You can see, however, that having the default drive letter displayed on the screen is very important. You can always return the prompt to the default value by keying in the command with no parameters.

STEP 5: Key in the following:
HELLO >**PROMPT** <Enter>

```
HELLO >PROMPT

C>_
```

WHAT'S HAPPENING? Now you know what drive you are in. You can see the default drive, which is Drive C, displayed in the prompt.

STEP 6: Key in the following:
C>**A:** <Enter>

```
C>A:

A>_
```

WHAT'S HAPPENING? You know what drive you are in, but what subdirectory are you in? Knowing what subdirectory is the default is as important as knowing what the default drive is.

STEP 7: Key in the following:
A>**PROMPT pg** <Enter>

```
A>PROMPT $p$g

A:\POLY-SCI>_
```

WHAT'S HAPPENING? You changed the prompt to display not only the default disk drive but also the default subdirectory (pg). The metastring $p returns the value of the path and the metastring $g returns the value of the greater than sign. Notice how DOS returned you to the last subdirectory you were in. DOS keeps track of where you are. Some of you may always get this **customized prompt**, because someone placed this command in the **AUTOEXEC.BAT** file. We will learn about this file in Chapter 12. For the rest of the text, if you do not automatically begin with the customized prompt, you will continue to key in **PROMPT pg**.

9.12 Subdirectory Markers

The single . (one period) in a subdirectory is the specific subdirectory name. The .. (two periods) is the parent directory of the current subdirectory. The parent directory is the one immediately above the current subdirectory. You can use the .. as a shorthand version of the parent directory name to move up the subdirectory tree structure. You can move up the hierarchy because a child always has one parent. However, you cannot use the .. to move down the hierarchy because a parent can have many children.

Activity 9.13 Using the Subdirectory Markers

Note: The DATA disk is in Drive A. The default drive is Drive A. The default subdirectory is **POLY-SCI**. The **A:\POLY-SCI>** is displayed.

STEP 1: Key in the following:
A:\POLY-SCI>**CD ..** <Enter>

```
A:\POLY-SCI>CD ..

A:\>_
```

WHAT'S HAPPENING? You used the .. to move up to the root or main directory. The root directory is the parent of the subdirectory **\POLY-SCI**.

9.14 Completing Your Tree

To exemplify a disk with many subdirectories, you are going to create more subdirectories and then copy files into the subdirectories.

Activity 9.15 Making More Subdirectories

Note: The DATA disk is in Drive A with the **A:\>** displayed on the screen.

STEP 1: Key in the following:
A:\>**MD \PHYS-ED\GOLF** <Enter>

```
A:\>MD \PHYS-ED\GOLF

A:\>_
```

WHAT'S HAPPENING? You created a subdirectory called **GOLF** under the subdirectory called **PHYS-ED**. Since you were at the root directory, you needed to include the entire path name, **\PHYS-ED\GOLF**. Had you keyed in **MD \GOLF**, the **GOLF** subdirectory would have been created in the root directory because the root directory is the default directory. However, you do not need to include the path name if you change directories and make the **\PHYS-ED** the default directory.

STEP 2: Key in the following:
A:\>**CD PHYS-ED** <Enter>

```
A:\>CD PHYS-ED

A:\PHYS-ED>_
```

WHAT'S HAPPENING? **PHYS-ED** is now the default directory. Any activity that occurs will automatically default to this directory, unless otherwise specified.

STEP 3: Key in the following:
A:\PHYS-ED>**MD DANCE** <Enter>

STEP 4: Key in the following:
A:\PHYS-ED>**MD CYCLING** <Enter>

```
A:\PHYS-ED>MD DANCE

A:\PHYS-ED>MD CYCLING

A:\PHYS-ED>_
```

WHAT'S HAPPENING? You created two more subdirectories, **DANCE** and **CYCLING**, in the parent subdirectory, **PHYS-ED**. You did not need to include the entire path name (**A:\PHYS-ED\DANCE**) since **PHYS-ED** is the default subdirectory. In fact, if you had keyed in **MD \DANCE** you would have placed **DANCE** in the root directory. If you had keyed in **MD \CYCLING**, you would have placed **CYCLING** in the root directory. Since **PHYS-ED** is the default subdirectory, DOS always assumes the default and thus builds subdirectories down the tree, unless you specify otherwise. You can see the new subdirectories by using the DIR command.

STEP 5: Key in the following:
A:\PHYS-ED>**DIR** <Enter>

```
A:\PHYS-ED>DIR

   Volume in drive A is DATA DISK
   Volume Serial Number is 3839-0EC8
   Directory of A:\PHYS-ED

.              <DIR>     11-16-93   9:47p
..             <DIR>     11-16-93   9:47p
CLASS     NAM      44    11-23-92   7:07a
TENNIS         <DIR>     11-16-93  10:10p
GOLF           <DIR>     11-16-93  10:15p
```

```
DANCE          <DIR>     11-16-93 10:15p
CYCLING        <DIR>     11-16-93 10:15p
       7 file(s)            44 bytes
                        205824 bytes free

A:\PHYS-ED>
```

WHAT'S HAPPENING? You created the directories **DANCE** and **CYCLING** in the directory, **PHYS-ED**. Of the seven files in the subdirectory **\PHYS-ED**, six are subdirectories. You know they are subdirectories because they have **<DIR>** after the file names. The entry **CLASS.NAM** is a "regular" file because it does not have **<DIR>** after its file name. You have now created nine subdirectories. Each subdirectory can be used as if it were a separate disk. A pictorial representation would look like Figure 9.10.

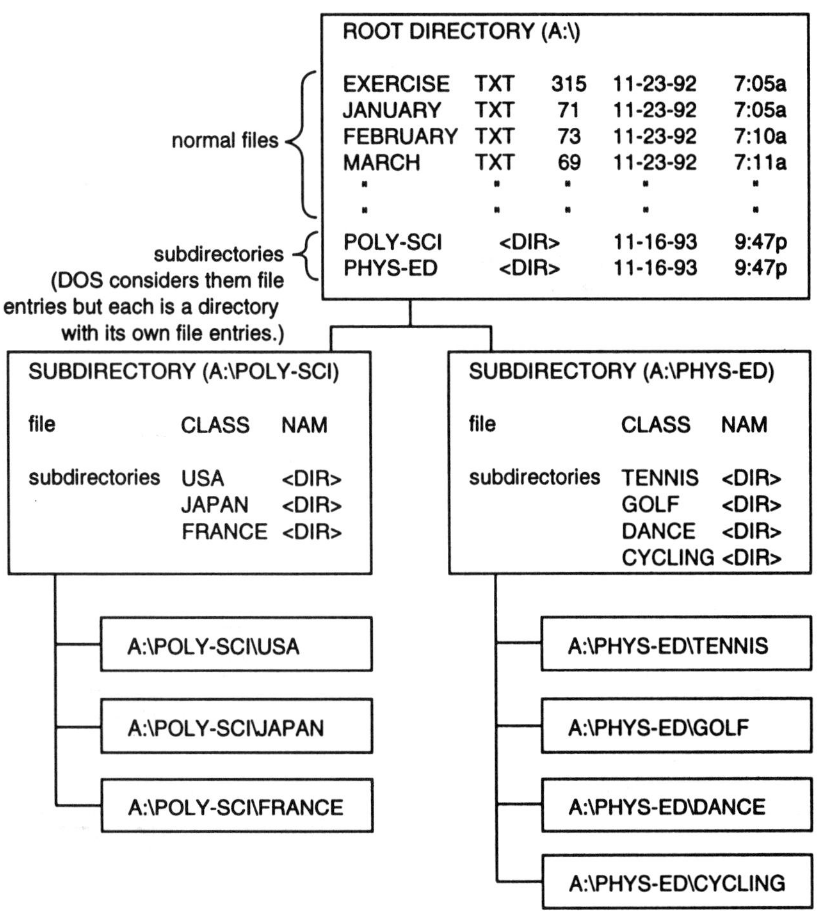

Figure 9.10 Structure of the DATA Disk

Another way to illustrate pictorially the subdirectory structure is:

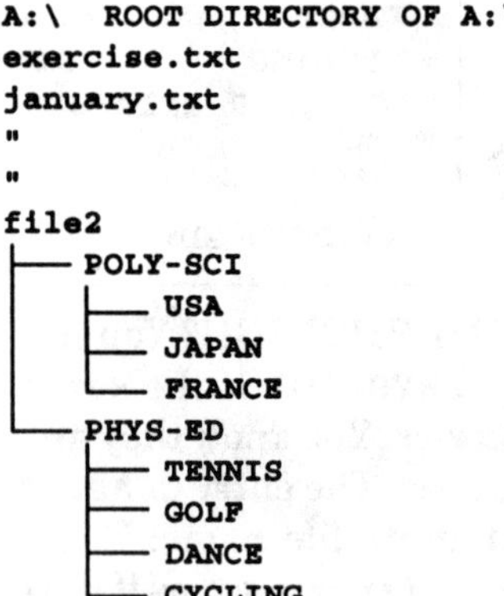

Figure 9.11 Subdirectories: Another View

9.16 Using Commands with Subdirectories

The subdirectories that you created can be used as if they were separate disks. The DOS commands work as usual, but you must include the *path* name to tell DOS what you want done with the files. These subdirectories are currently empty of files. You are going to see how the DOS commands work with subdirectories, by using the COPY command to place files in the subdirectories.

The final tree structure when you complete the next activity will look like Figure 9.12.

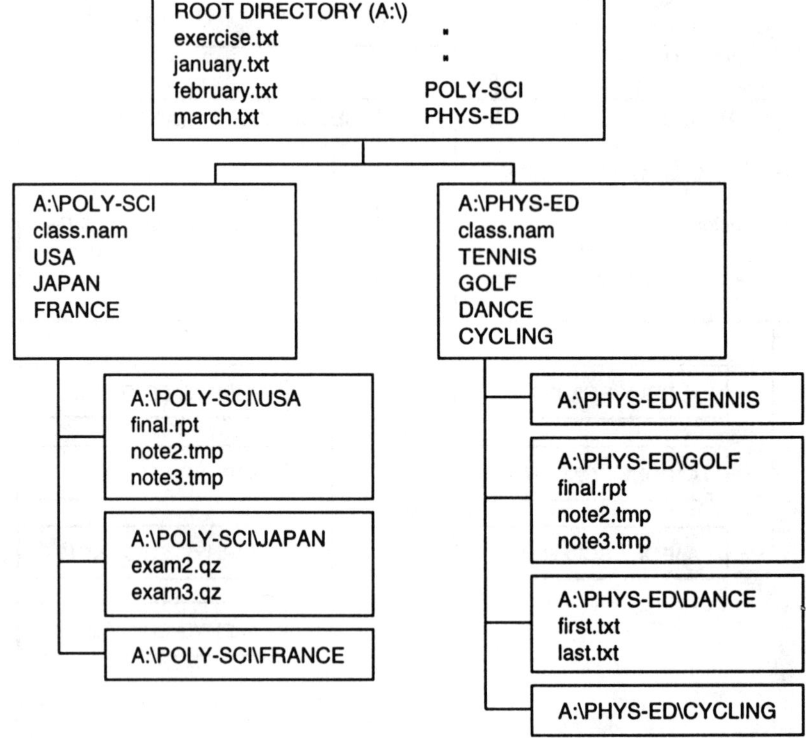

Figure 9.12 Final Tree Structure

Activity 9.17 Using COPY with Subdirectories

Note: You have the DATA disk in Drive A with the **A:\PHYS-ED>** displayed on the screen.

STEP 1: Key in the following:
A:\PHYS-ED>**CD GOLF** <Enter>

```
A:\PHYS-ED>CD GOLF

A:\PHYS-ED\GOLF>_
```

WHAT'S HAPPENING? The prompt should display **A:\PHYS-ED\GOLF>** as the default drive and subdirectory. The prompt is quite lengthy because it shows you the default drive as well as the default subdirectory. All activities will occur in the subdirectory **\PHYS-ED\GOLF**, unless you specify another path. As you will see, the command lines become long when you include the customized prompt as well as the command.

STEP 2: Key in the following:
A:\PHYS-ED\GOLF>**COPY \POLY-SCI\CLASS.NAM FINAL.RPT** <Enter>

```
A:\PHYS-ED\GOLF>COPY \POLY-SCI\CLASS.NAM FINAL.RPT
        1 file(s) copied

A:\PHYS-ED\GOLF>_
```

WHAT'S HAPPENING? Spacing is very important in the above command. COPY comes first; then, a space separates the command from the first parameter. The next parameter, **\POLY-SCI\CLASS.NAM**, has no spaces. There is space before the last parameter, **FINAL.RPT**. The file called **CLASS.NAM** that is in the subdirectory **\POLY-SCI** was successfully copied to the subdirectory **\PHYS-ED\GOLF** but is now called **FINAL.RPT**. The syntax of the COPY command remained the same—COPY *source destination*. First, you issued the command, COPY, but it was not enough to list just the file name **CLASS.NAM** as the source. You had to include the path so that DOS would know in which subdirectory the file was located; hence, the source was **\POLY-SCI\CLASS.NAM**. Users often get confused when using the \. Here is a simple rule: The first \ in any command line always means the root directory. Any other \ in the command is simply a delimiter. Thus, in our example, the first \ tells DOS to go to the root and then, go down to **POLY-SCI**. The second \ is the delimiter between the subdirectory name and the file name, **CLASS.NAM**. The destination is a file called **FINAL.RPT**. You did not have to key in the path for destination because the default (**\PHYS-ED\GOLF**) was assumed. The longhand version of the command is:

```
COPY  A:\POLY-SCI\CLASS.NAM  A:\PHYS-ED\GOLF\FINAL.RPT
```

You did not need to key in the drive letter because the default drive is assumed. If you had keyed in **COPY CLASS.NAM FINAL.RPT**, you would have gotten the error message, "File not found," because DOS would have looked in the current directory (**\PHYS-ED\GOLF**) for the file and would not have found it. Next, you are going to make a copy in the current directory, so you do not need to include the path.

STEP 3: Key in the following:
A:\PHYS-ED\GOLF>**COPY FINAL.RPT NOTE2.TMP** <Enter>

STEP 4: Key in the following:
A:\PHYS-ED\GOLF>**COPY FINAL.RPT NOTE3.TMP** <Enter>

```
A:\PHYS-ED\GOLF>COPY FINAL.RPT NOTE2.TMP
        1 file(s) copied

A:\PHYS-ED\GOLF>COPY FINAL.RPT NOTE3.TMP
        1 file(s) copied

A:\PHYS-ED\GOLF>_
```

WHAT'S HAPPENING? You copied two files. You did not have to include the path because the default was assumed. DOS always assumes the default drive and subdirectory, unless you tell it otherwise. Technically, the commands looked like this:

COPY A:\PHYS-ED\GOLF\FINAL.RPT A:\PHYS-ED\GOLF\NOTE2.TMP

STEP 5: Key in the following:
A:\PHYS-ED\GOLF>**DIR** <Enter>

```
A:\PHYS-ED\GOLF>DIR

   Volume in drive A is DATA DISK
   Volume Serial Number is 3839-0EC8
   Directory of A:\PHYS-ED\GOLF

.            <DIR>     11-16-93 10:15p
..           <DIR>     11-16-93 10:15p
FINAL    RPT       44  11-23-92  7:07a
NOTE2    TMP       44  11-23-92  7:07a
NOTE3    TMP       44  11-23-92  7:07a
        5 file(s)        132 bytes
                      202752 bytes free

A:\PHYS-ED\GOLF>_
```

WHAT'S HAPPENING? You see only the files that are in the default subdirectory. You can also use wildcards with subdirectories.

STEP 6: Key in the following:
A:\PHYS-ED\GOLF>**COPY *.* \POLY-SCI\USA** <Enter>

```
A:\PHYS-ED\GOLF>COPY *.* \POLY-SCI\USA
FINAL.RPT
NOTE2.TMP
NOTE3.TMP
        3 file(s) copied

A:\PHYS-ED\GOLF>_
```

WHAT'S HAPPENING? As the files were copied to the **\POLY-SCI\USA** subdirectory, they were listed on the screen. Again, the syntax is the same, the command, COPY, the *source*, *.* (all the files in the default subdirectory **\PHYS-ED\GOLF**), to the *destination*, **\POLY-SCI\USA**. You had to include the path name in the destination. The first \ in the destination is very important because it tells DOS to go to the top of the tree and then go down to the **POLY-SCI\USA** subdirectory. If you had not included that first backslash, DOS would have looked under the subdirectory **\PHYS-ED\GOLF**. Since you wanted to have the files with the same name in the subdirectory, **\POLY-SCI\USA**, you did not have to specify new file names. DOS used or defaulted to the current file names.

STEP 7: Key in the following:
A:\PHYS-ED\GOLF>**DIR \POLY-SCI\USA** <Enter>

```
A:\PHYS-ED\GOLF>DIR \POLY-SCI\USA

   Volume in drive A is DATA DISK
   Volume Serial Number is 3839-0EC8
   Directory of A:\POLY-SCI\USA

.            <DIR>     11-16-93 10:03p
..           <DIR>     11-16-93 10:03p
FINAL    RPT       44  11-23-92  7:07a
NOTE2    TMP       44  11-23-92  7:07a
NOTE3    TMP       44  11-23-92  7:07a
        5 file(s)         132 bytes
                       199680 bytes free

A:\PHYS-ED\GOLF>_
```

WHAT'S HAPPENING? You can copy files from anywhere to anywhere provided you give the path. Be aware of the default subdirectory, the path.

STEP 8: Key in the following:
A:\PHYS-ED\GOLF>**COPY \POLY-SCI\USA\NOTE?.TMP \POLY-SCI\JAPAN\EXAM?.QZ** <Enter>

```
A:\PHYS-ED\GOLF>COPY \POLY-SCI\USA\NOTE?.TMP \POLY-SCI\JAPAN\EXAM?.QZ
A:\POLY-SCI\USA\NOTE2.TMP
A:\POLY-SCI\USA\NOTE3.TMP
        2 file(s) copied

A:\PHYS-ED\GOLF>_
```

WHAT'S HAPPENING? DOS displayed the entire path name as it copied the files. Here, you copied all the **.TMP** files from the subdirectory **\POLY-SCI\USA** to the subdirectory **\POLY-SCI\JAPAN** with new file names **EXAM?.QZ**. To see that the files were copied correctly, you can use the DIR command.

STEP 9: Key in the following:
A:\PHYS-ED\GOLF>**DIR \POLY-SCI\JAPAN** <Enter>

```
A:\PHYS-ED\GOLF>DIR \POLY-SCI\JAPAN

   Volume in drive A is DATA DISK
   Volume Serial Number is 3839-0EC8
   Directory of A:\POLY-SCI\JAPAN

.             <DIR>     11-16-93 10:03p
..            <DIR>     11-16-93 10:03p
EXAM2     QZ        44  11-23-92  7:07a
EXAM3     QZ        44  11-23-92  7:07a
        4 file(s)          88 bytes
                       199680 bytes free

A:\PHYS-ED\GOLF>_
```

WHAT'S HAPPENING? You successfully copied the files because you used the proper path name. You have been using the COPY and DIR commands to exemplify how to use the path. Any DOS command will work if you use the proper syntax and the proper path.

STEP 10: Key in the following:
A:\PHYS-ED\GOLF>**C:** <Enter>

```
A:\PHYS-ED\GOLF>C:

C:\>_
```

WHAT'S HAPPENING? You changed the default drive to C. In this example, you are in the root directory of C.

STEP 11: Key in the following:
C:\>**CD \JUNK** <Enter>

```
C:\>CD \JUNK

C:\JUNK>_
```

WHAT'S HAPPENING? You changed the default subdirectory to **JUNK** on Drive C.

STEP 12: Key in the following:
C:\JUNK>**COPY DRESS.UP A:** <Enter>

```
C:\JUNK>COPY DRESS.UP A:
        1 file(s) copied

C:\JUNK>_
```

WHAT'S HAPPENING? You executed a simple COPY command. You asked that DOS copy the file called **DRESS.UP** from **\JUNK** to the DATA disk. But where on the DATA disk? Since the last place you were on the DATA disk was the **GOLF** subdirectory, that is where the file was copied. If you wanted the file copied to the root directory of the DATA disk, you would have had to key in **COPY DRESS.UP A:**.

STEP 13: Key in the following:
C:\JUNK>**DIR A:DRESS.UP** <Enter>

STEP 14: Key in the following:
C:\JUNK>**DIR A:\DRESS.UP** <Enter>

```
C:\JUNK>DIR A:DRESS.UP

   Volume in drive A is DATA DISK
   Volume Serial Number is 3839-0EC8
   Directory of A:\PHYS-ED\GOLF

DRESS     UP       25   05-07-92 11:15a
        1 file(s)          25 bytes
                       196608 bytes free

C:\JUNK>DIR A:\DRESS.UP

   Volume in drive A is DATA DISK
   Volume Serial Number is 3839-0EC8
   Directory of A:\

File not found

C:\JUNK>_
```

WHAT'S HAPPENING? The last place you were on the DATA disk was in the subdirectory **\PHYS-ED\GOLF**. DOS "remembered" where you last were and copied the file to the **GOLF** subdirectory, not to the root directory. When you asked for a directory of the file **DRESS.UP** and only preceded it by the A:, DOS looked in the last place you were—**\PHYS-ED\GOLF**. In order to look at the root directory, you had to request **A:\DRESS.UP**. The backslash said to go to the root. Now, when you return to the drive that has the DATA disk, you will also be in the last subdirectory.

STEP 15: Key in the following:
C:\JUNK>**A:** <Enter>

```
C:\JUNK>A:

A:\PHYS-ED\GOLF>_
```

WHAT'S HAPPENING? You are now back on the DATA disk in the **GOLF** subdirectory that is under the **PHYS-ED** subdirectory that is under the root directory. If you change drives during various activities, DOS will remember the last default subdirectory. On Drive C, you are still logged into the **\JUNK** subdirectory.

9.18 Using Subdirectory Markers with the COPY Command

As you can see, the command line can get unwieldy. This situation is another reason for using the **subdirectory markers, dot** and **double dot,** as a shorthand way of writing the commands. The .. represents the parent of a directory. The only directory that does not have a parent is the root directory. We are going to use COPY as an example, but any DOS command works.

Activity 9.19 Using Shortcuts: The Subdirectory Markers

Note: You have the DATA disk in Drive A with the **A:\PHYS-ED\GOLF>** displayed on the screen.

You are going to copy the **FINAL.RPT** file located in the **PHYS-ED** subdirectory to the **DANCE** subdirectory while you are in the **GOLF** subdirectory, **\PHYS-ED\GOLF**. The prompt is quite lengthy because it is showing you the default drive as well as the default subdirectory. All activities will occur in the subdirectory **\PHYS-ED\GOLF**, unless you specify another path. As you will see, the command lines become long when you include the custom prompt as well as the command.

STEP 1: Key in the following:

A:\PHYS-ED\GOLF>**COPY \PHYS-ED\CLASS.NAM \PHYS-ED\DANCE\FIRST.TST** <Enter>

```
A:\PHYS-ED\GOLF>COPY \PHYS-ED\CLASS.NAM \PHYS-ED\DANCE\FIRST.TST
        1 file(s) copied

A:\PHYS-ED\GOLF>_
```

WHAT'S HAPPENING? You copied the file called **CLASS.NAM** from the **PHYS-ED** subdirectory to the **DANCE** subdirectory. You had to include the first backslash because DOS had to go to the top of the hierarchical tree and then back down. However, there is an easier way to issue this command. Since **PHYS-ED** is the parent of **DANCE** and **GOLF** (Refer to Figure 9.12 to see the structure), you can use the subdirectory markers.

STEP 2: Key in the following:

A:\PHYS-ED\GOLF>**COPY ..\CLASS.NAM ..\DANCE\LAST.TST** <Enter>

```
A:\PHYS-ED\GOLF>COPY  ..\CLASS.NAM  ..\DANCE\LAST.TST
        1 file(s) copied

A:\PHYS-ED\GOLF>_
```

WHAT'S HAPPENING? The first .. represented the parent of **GOLF**. You did not have to key in **\PHYS-ED**. However, you did need to key in the \ preceding the file name. This \ is a delimiter. The second .. is **PHYS-ED**, the parent of **DANCE**. You did need to key in the \ preceding **DANCE** and the \ preceding **LAST.TST** because they were needed as delimiters to separate subdirectory names and file names. You can use subdirectory markers to save keystrokes. You can now prove the files are in the **DANCE** subdirectory.

STEP 3: Key in the following:
A:\PHYS-ED\GOLF>**DIR ..\DANCE** <Enter>

```
A:\PHYS-ED\GOLF>DIR ..\DANCE

   Volume in drive A is DATA DISK
   Volume Serial Number is 3839-0EC8
   Directory of A:\PHYS-ED\DANCE

.             <DIR>     11-16-93 10:15p
..            <DIR>     11-16-93 10:15p
FIRST     TST       44  11-23-92  7:07a
LAST      TST       44  11-23-92  7:07a
        4 file(s)           88 bytes
                        194560 bytes free

A:\PHYS-ED\GOLF>_
```

WHAT'S HAPPENING? You successfully copied the files using the subdirectory markers.

9.20 Removing Directories

In the same way a disk can be cluttered with files, so it can be even more cluttered with subdirectories. The ERASE or DEL commands are used to eliminate files, but you cannot use these commands to eliminate subdirectories. Removing subdirectories requires a special command, the remove directory command (RD or RMDIR). If a subdirectory has files in it, you cannot remove the subdirectory until the subdirectory is empty of files. This two-step process prevents you from accidentally wiping out not only a directory but also the files inside. Thus, if a subdirectory has files in it, you must delete (DEL) the file(s) first, then remove the subdirectory. You cannot delete a directory that has hidden or system files in it. In addition, you cannot remove the default subdirectory. In order to remove a subdirectory, you must be in another directory. The command syntax is:

RMDIR [*drive:*]*path*
or RD [*drive:*]*path*

If you do not include the drive designator, DOS will use the default drive. The remove directory command will not remove the directory you are currently in (the current directory), nor will it ever remove the root directory.

Activity 9.21 Using the RD Command

Note: You have the DATA disk in Drive A with the **A:\PHYS-ED\GOLF>** displayed on the screen.

STEP 1: Key in the following:
A:\PHYS-ED\GOLF>**RD \POLY-SCI\JAPAN** <Enter>

```
A:\PHYS-ED\GOLF>RD \POLY-SCI\JAPAN
Invalid path, not directory,
or directory not empty

A:\PHYS-ED\GOLF>_
```

WHAT'S HAPPENING? RD did not remove the directory, **\POLY-SCI\JAPAN**, because the directory was *not* empty. It has the files **EXAM2.QZ** and **EXAM3.QZ** in it. Thus, to remove the directory, you must first delete the files in the directory. ERASE or DEL is for eliminating files; RD is for eliminating directories.

STEP 2: Key in the following:
A:\PHYS-ED\GOLF>**DEL \POLY-SCI\JAPAN*.*** <Enter>

```
A:\PHYS-ED\GOLF>DEL \POLY-SCI\JAPAN\*.*
All files in directory will be deleted!
Are you sure (Y/N)?_
```

WHAT'S HAPPENING? Since you asked DOS to delete *all* the files (*.*), DOS is confirming that you really want to delete all the files. You could have also keyed in the command as **DEL \POLY-SCI\JAPAN** and DOS would have assumed *.* or all the files. Earlier versions of DOS only gave the message, "Are you sure (Y/N)?" Remember, you are deleting only the files in the subdirectory, **\POLY-SCI\JAPAN**, not all the files on the DATA disk.

STEP 3: Key in the following:
Y <Enter>

```
A:\PHYS-ED\GOLF>DEL \POLY-SCI\JAPAN\*.*
All files in directory will be deleted!
Are you sure (Y/N)?Y

A:\PHYS-ED\GOLF>_
```

WHAT'S HAPPENING? Since you responded Y for yes, the files were deleted. By looking at the directory of the **POLY-SCI** subdirectory, you can see that the **JAPAN** subdirectory is still there, but is now empty.

STEP 4: Key in the following:
A:\PHYS-ED\GOLF>**DIR \POLY-SCI** <Enter>

```
A:\PHYS-ED\GOLF>DIR \POLY-SCI

   Volume in drive A is DATA DISK
   Volume Serial Number is 3839-0EC8
   Directory of A:\POLY-SCI

.              <DIR>     11-16-93   9:47p
..             <DIR>     11-16-93   9:47p
CLASS     NAM       44   11-23-92   7:07a
USA            <DIR>     11-16-93  10:03p
JAPAN          <DIR>     11-16-93  10:03p
FRANCE         <DIR>     11-16-93  10:03p
       6 file(s)             44 bytes
                         196608 bytes free

A:\PHYS-ED\GOLF>_
```

WHAT'S HAPPENING? The subdirectory **JAPAN** is still there. But now that the subdirectory **\POLY-SCI\JAPAN** is empty of files, you can remove the directory with the RD command.

STEP 5: Key in the following:
A:\PHYS-ED\GOLF>**RD \POLY-SCI\JAPAN** <Enter>

```
A:\PHYS-ED\GOLF>RD \POLY-SCI\JAPAN

A:\PHYS-ED\GOLF>_
```

WHAT'S HAPPENING? You removed the directory, but you see no message to confirm that it is gone.

STEP 6: Key in the following:
A:\PHYS-ED\GOLF>**DIR \POLY-SCI** <Enter>

```
A:\PHYS-ED\GOLF>DIR \POLY-SCI

   Volume in drive A is DATA DISK
   Volume Serial Number is 3839-0EC8
   Directory of A:\POLY-SCI

.              <DIR>     11-16-93   9:47p
..             <DIR>     11-16-93   9:47p
CLASS     NAM       44   11-23-92   7:07a
USA            <DIR>     11-16-93  10:03p
FRANCE         <DIR>     11-16-93  10:03p
       5 file(s)             44 bytes
                         197632 bytes free

A:\PHYS-ED\GOLF>_
```

WHAT'S HAPPENING? The subdirectory **JAPAN <DIR>** is not displayed. You did indeed remove it. But remember as you created the directories in a hierarchical fashion, top-down, you must remove them bottom-up. So if **JAPAN** had a subdirectory beneath it such as **\POLY-SCI\JAPAN\INDUSTRY**, you would have needed to remove the **INDUSTRY** subdirectory before you could remove the **JAPAN** subdirectory.

9.22 Setting the Path

When you use subdirectories, you will be changing the current or default subdirectory as you go. Often, you will also need or want to use the DOS external commands or have DOS look for programs in other than the current subdirectory. When you try to execute a command that is not in the current subdirectory, DOS will give you the message "Bad command or file name." DOS will look nowhere but in the current subdirectory. In the past, you have copied the needed file to the disk or changed the directory and drive to **C:\DOS**. However, you typically do not want duplicate program files and/or DOS external commands for every subdirectory. To eliminate this problem, there is a PATH command. Although somewhat different from the path to the various subdirectories, the PATH command (an internal command) tells DOS where to look for a command file if it is not in the current directory. In this case, the PATH command means the search path. However, PATH only looks for program files that can be executed —**.COM**, **.EXE** or **.BAT**. All this means is that, when you key in a command and if you have set the PATH, DOS will search for the program in the subdirectories you have selected and, when it finds it, will load and execute it. DOS will not locate files with any other file extensions. You can set the path for command files to another subdirectory or disk drive.

To set the path, the command syntax is:
PATH [[*drive:*]*path*[;...]]

To "unset" the path, the command syntax is:
PATH ;

To see the current path, the command syntax is:
PATH

PATH is the command. PATH with no parameters displays the current path. *drive:* indicates which drive designator you want the path to follow. If you omit the drive designator, DOS will use the default drive. [*path*] is the path name of the subdirectory that contains the command files. You can have DOS search more than one subdirectory, but you use the semicolon ; to indicate another drive and subdirectory with no spaces between the semicolon and the paths. The semicolon ; used without the drive or path cancels any paths you have set.

Activity 9.23 Using the PATH Command

Note: You have the DATA disk in Drive A with the **A:\PHYS-ED\GOLF>** displayed on the screen.

STEP 1: Key in the following:
A:\PHYS-ED\GOLF>**CD ..** <Enter>

```
A:\PHYS-ED\GOLF>CD ..

A:\PHYS-ED>_
```

WHAT'S HAPPENING? You used the subdirectory marker (..) to move to the parent of **GOLF** which is **PHYS-ED**. You could have keyed in **CD \PHYS-ED**, but CD .. is shorter.

STEP 2: Key in the following:
A:\PHYS-ED>**PATH ;** <Enter>

```
A:\PHYS-ED>PATH ;

A:\PHYS-ED>_
```

WHAT'S HAPPENING? You undid all possible existing paths.

STEP 3: Key in the following:
A:\PHYS-ED>**CHKDSK** <Enter>

```
A:\PHYS-ED>CHKDSK
Bad command or file name

A:\PHYS-ED>_
```

WHAT'S HAPPENING? DOS could not execute the external command because **CHKDSK.EXE** is not stored as file in the subdirectory **\PHYS-ED**. Rather than having to copy the file **CHKDSK.EXE** to the subdirectory, you can use the PATH command, which tells DOS that if it does not find CHKDSK in the current subdirectory, it should look for that file in the subdirectory to which the path directed.

STEP 4: Key in the following:
A:\PHYS-ED>**PATH C:\DOS** <Enter>

Note: If the DOS utility programs are in a subdirectory on the hard disk other than **\DOS**, you must key in the appropriate path name, i.e., **PATH C:\BIN**.

```
A:\PHYS-ED>PATH C:\DOS

A:\PHYS-ED>_
```

WHAT'S HAPPENING? It appears that nothing has happened. But it has. You have set a path DOS will search. If it does not find the command in the default drive and subdirectory—in this case **A:\PHYS-ED**—it will go to the path set, the subdirectory called **\DOS** under the root directory of Drive C. There DOS will find the file called **CHKDSK.EXE**.

STEP 5: Key in the following:
A:\PHYS-ED>**CHKDSK** <Enter>

```
A:\PHYS-ED>CHKDSK

Volume DATA DISK   created 11-23-1992 7:00a
Volume Serial Number is 3839-0EC8

    362496 bytes total disk space
     14336 bytes in 14 directories
    151552 bytes in 101 user files
    196680 bytes available on disk

      1024 bytes in each allocation unit
       354 total allocation units on disk
       192 available allocation units on disk

    651264 total bytes memory
    565776 bytes free

A:\PHYS-ED>_
```

WHAT'S HAPPENING? You did not get "Bad command or file name" this time. When DOS could not find the file **CHKDSK.EXE** in the subdirectory, **\PHYS-ED**, it searched the path that was set, found the file on the hard disk in the subdirectory **\DOS**, loaded it into memory, and executed it.

STEP 6: Key in the following:
A:\PHYS-ED>**PATH** <Enter>

```
A:\PHYS-ED>PATH
PATH=C:\DOS

A:\PHYS-ED>_
```

WHAT'S HAPPENING? PATH keyed in by itself displays the current path. You can set more than one search path.

STEP 7: Key in the following:
A:\PHYS-ED>**ADDRESS** <Enter>

```
A:\PHYS-ED>ADDRESS
Bad command or file name

A:\PHYS-ED>_
```

WHAT'S HAPPENING? ADDRESS is an application program, but it is not located in the **\DOS** subdirectory. So even though the path is set, it is set only to one place, **C:\DOS**. That is not where the ADDRESS program is located. In Chapter 6, you copied the file **ADDRESS.EXE** from **\JUNK** to the subdirectory called **USERS** on the DATA disk. (Note: If you did not copy it, do so now.) You do not want to change the default subdirectory to use this program. With the PATH command, you do not have to.

STEP 8: Key in the following:
A:\PHYS-ED>**PATH A:\USERS** <Enter>

STEP 9: Key in the following:
A:\PHYS-ED>**PATH** <Enter>

```
A:\PHYS-ED>PATH A:\USERS

A:\PHYS-ED>PATH
PATH=A:\USERS

A:\PHYS-ED>_
```

WHAT'S HAPPENING? You set the search path to the **USERS** subdirectory on the DATA disk, but by doing so, you canceled the path to the **\DOS** subdirectory. In this example, you wanted to keep both search paths. In order to have more than one search path, you must list all the paths you want, separated by semicolons.

STEP 10: Key in the following:
A:\PHYS-ED>**PATH A:\USERS;C:\DOS** <Enter>

STEP 11: Key in the following:
A:\PHYS-ED>**PATH** <Enter>

```
A:\PHYS-ED>PATH A:\USERS;C:\DOS

A:\PHYS-ED>PATH
PATH=A:\USERS;C:\DOS

A:\PHYS-ED>_
```

WHAT'S HAPPENING? You set the path so that if DOS does not find the program you wish to execute in the default subdirectory, **A:\PHYS-ED**, it will next look in the **USERS** subdirectory on the DATA disk (**A:\USERS**), and if DOS does not find it there, DOS will last look on Drive C in the subdirectory **DOS** (**C:\DOS**). Although it was not mandatory in this case to include the drive letter preceding the **USERS** subdirectory, it is usually a good idea to do so. Thus, if you change drives, DOS will still know which drive to look on. In this example, the path was set to **C:\DOS**. If your setup is different, change the command to reflect your configuration.

STEP 12: Key in the following:
A:\PHYS-ED>**ADDRESS** <Enter>

```
Enter the name of the data file:_
```

WHAT'S HAPPENING? DOS still did not find the ADDRESS program in the default subdirectory **PHYS-ED** on the DATA disk. However, since you set the search path to the **USERS** subdirectory where the ADDRESS program is located,

DOS did not stop looking but continued on the path that was set. DOS looked in the **USERS** subdirectory and found the program ADDRESS. Once DOS found it, it could load it. Since we do not want to execute this program, we will break out of it.

STEP 13: Press the <Ctrl> key and the <Break> key. Do not use <Ctrl>+C. This is an example of an application program that does not recognize <Ctrl>+C but does recognize <Ctrl>+<Break>.

```
Enter the name of the data file: ^C

A:\PHYS-ED>_
```

WHAT'S HAPPENING? You are back at the system level. What if you want to cancel all the paths you set?

STEP 14: Key in the following, the PATH command, followed by a space and a semicolon:

A:\PHYS-ED>**PATH ;** <Enter>

STEP 15: Key in the following:

A:\PHYS-ED>**PATH** <Enter>

```
A:\PHYS-ED>PATH ;

A:\PHYS-ED>PATH
No Path

A:\PHYS-ED>_
```

WHAT'S HAPPENING? The PATH command followed by a space then a semicolon cancels currently set paths. DOS responded with "No Path" telling you that DOS will only look in the default drive and subdirectory for executable programs. As you can see, the PATH command saves you the trouble of copying program files from disk to disk or from subdirectory to subdirectory. Instead, you can set the path.

9.24 The TREE Command

You have been creating subdirectories, copying files, and performing other tasks with subdirectories. How do you keep track of what is on the disk? DOS has a solution to this problem: the TREE command. It shows you the structure of the tree-shaped directory on any disk. The syntax for this external command is:

TREE [*drive:*] [/F] [/A]

The /F parameter will show you all the files in the subdirectories. The /A in DOS 4.0 or above allows you to use an alternate graphic character set. There are some other differences between the 4.0 and above TREE command and earlier DOS versions. First, in the DOS versions above 4.0 the TREE command displays its output in a graphical manner, whereas earlier DOS versions displayed the output in a text manner. Second, any version of the TREE command prior to 4.0 always shows you the entire tree from the root level down. The 4.0 and above versions allow you to select a subdirectory and look only at that subtree.

Activity 9.25 Using the TREE Command

Note: You have the DATA disk in Drive A. The default subdirectory is `A:\PHYS-ED`.

STEP 1: Key in the following:
A:\PHYS-ED>**CD ** <Enter>

STEP 2: Key in the following:
A:\>**PATH C:\DOS** <Enter>

```
A:\PHYS-ED>CD \

A:\>PATH C:\DOS

A:\>_
```

WHAT'S HAPPENING? You have set the path to `C:\DOS` so that you can use the external command, TREE.

STEP 3: Key in the following:
A:\>**TREE** <Enter>

Screen Display DOS 4.0 and 5.0

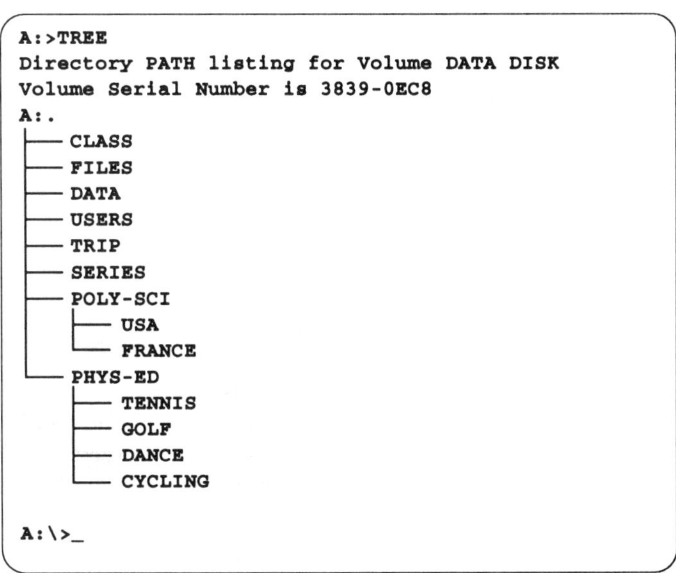

```
A:>TREE
Directory PATH listing for Volume DATA DISK
Volume Serial Number is 3839-0EC8
A:.
├──── CLASS
├──── FILES
├──── DATA
├──── USERS
├──── TRIP
├──── SERIES
├──── POLY-SCI
│     ├──── USA
│     └──── FRANCE
└──── PHYS-ED
      ├──── TENNIS
      ├──── GOLF
      ├──── DANCE
      └──── CYCLING

A:\>_
```

Screen Display
DOS 3.3 and below

```
Path: \PHYS-ED

Subdirectories:  CYCLING

Path:  \PHYS-ED\CYCLING

Subdirectories:  None

A:\>_
```

WHAT'S HAPPENING? The TREE command displayed this information in the shape of a tree. The command started with the root directory and listed the subdirectories beneath the root, including any subdirectories that had subdirectories of their own. The only difference between the versions of DOS is the way the output is displayed. The problem with the screen display of the versions of DOS below 4.0 is that often the display does not fit on one screen. Users who have a version of DOS that is less than 4.0 can use <Pause>, <Ctrl>+S, or <Ctrl>+<NumLock> to stop the screen display from scrolling.

STEP 4: Key in the following:
A:\>**TREE /F** <Enter>

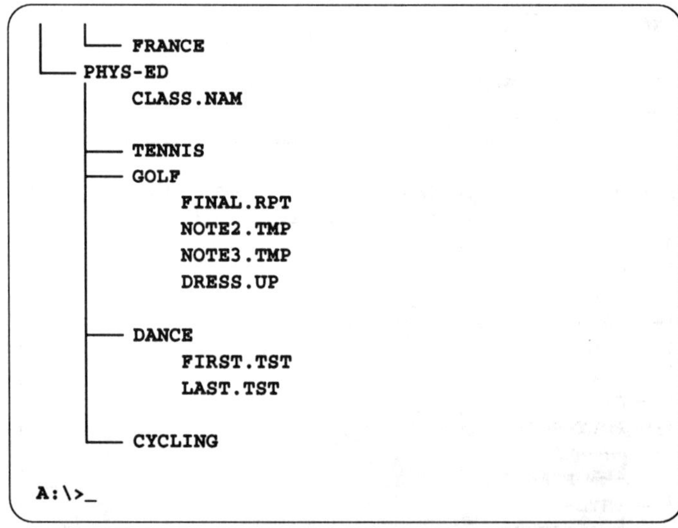

WHAT'S HAPPENING? This time the /F parameter showed not only the subdirectories but also all the files inside each subdirectory. Again, the only difference between versions of DOS is the way the output is displayed. In this case, all DOS users could use <Pause>, the <Ctrl>+S, or <Ctrl>+<NumLock> to stop the screen display from scrolling. One nice feature of DOS 4.0 and above is the ability to use the TREE command with an individual directory. On a large hard disk looking at all the files can be endless. Most often, the user is only interested in a specific subdirectory. Users of DOS below 3.3 have no choice. They must look at the entire structure from the root down. DOS 4.0 and above gives the user the ability to choose a specific subdirectory.

STEP 5: Key in the following:
A:\>**TREE \PHYS-ED /F** <Enter>

```
A:\>TREE \PHYS-ED /F
Directory PATH listing for Volume DATA DISK
Volume Serial Number is 3839-0EC8
A:\PHYS-ED
│   CLASS.NAM
│
├───TENNIS
├───GOLF
│       FINAL.RPT
│       NOTE2.TMP
│       NOTE3.TMP
│       DRESS.UP
│
├───DANCE
│       FIRST.TST
│       LAST.TST
│
└───CYCLING

A:\>_
```

WHAT'S HAPPENING? When you specified the path DOS 4.0 and above displayed only the tree structure for the specific subdirectory you asked for.

STEP 6: Key in the following:
A:\>**C:** <Enter>

STEP 7: Key in the following:
C:\JUNK>**CD ** <Enter>

```
A:\>C:

C:\JUNK>CD \

C:\>_
```

WHAT'S HAPPENING? You returned to the root directory of Drive C.

Chapter Summary

1. Subdirectories are created to help organize a disk as well as to defeat the file limitation of the root directory.
2. MD is an internal command that allows the user to create a subdirectory.
3. Subdirectory-naming conventions follow DOS file-naming conventions, i.e., a limit of 8 characters in the file-name and 3 characters in the file extension.
4. A **<DIR>** following a file name indicates that it is a subdirectory.

5. CD is an internal command that when keyed in by itself will show the user the current or default subdirectory.
6. CD followed by a subdirectory name will change the current directory to the named directory.
7. RD is an internal command that allows users to eliminate subdirectories.
8. Subdirectories must be empty of files prior to using the RD command.
9. Whenever a disk is formatted, one directory is always created. It is called the root directory.
10. The root directory can never be eliminated.
11. When using subdirectories and file names, the backslash (\)is the delimiter that separates subdirectory and/or file names.
12. PATH is an internal command that allows the user to tell DOS on what disk and in what subdirectory to search for command files.
13. DOS will only search the path for executable files, those having a file extension of **.EXE**, **.COM**, or **.BAT**.
14. PATH keyed in by itself will display the current path.
15. PATH keyed in followed by a semicolon will cancel the path.
16. You can have multiple search paths. They are separated by semicolons.
17. Subdirectory markers are shortcuts to using subdirectories. The single dot (.) represents the directory itself. The double dot (..) represents the name of the parent directory.
18. You can only move up the tree with subdirectory markers, not down the tree.
19. The way the prompt looks can be changed with the PROMPT command. The PROMPT command followed by a text string will reflect that text.
20. The PROMPT command also has metastrings. When included following the PROMPT command, the metastrings will return a value. For instance, the metastrings pg will set the prompt to display the default drive and subdirectory. To return the prompt to the default value, key in PROMPT with no parameters.
21. The TREE command displays the structure of a disk. If you have DOS 4.0 or above, the display is graphic.
22. The /F parameter used with the TREE command displays all the files on the disk. If you have DOS 4.0 or above, you can specify a single subdirectory with the /F parameter.
23. The /A parameter used with the TREE command allows the output to be displayed as text characters.

Key Terms

Child directory	Double dot ..	Root directory
Current directory	Hierarchical structure	Subdirectory markers
Customized prompt	Metastring	Tree structure
Dot .	Parent directory	

Discussion Questions

1. What is the directory that is always created when a disk is formatted?
2. What is the root directory?
3. What is a subdirectory?
4. Why would you want to create a subdirectory?
5. When naming subdirectories what naming conventions must be followed?
6. Give the syntax for creating a subdirectory.
7. There are only three file extensions that a program file can have. What are they?
8. What is the purpose and function of the PATH command?
9. Give the syntax for the CD command.
10. What is the path?
11. How can you verify that you have created a subdirectory?
12. What is the difference between keying in **DIR \PHYS-ED** and **DIR PHYS-ED**?
13. What does the TREE command do? When and how would you use it?
14. What is the syntax of the TREE command?
15. What are metastrings?
16. How can you return the prompt to the default value?
17. What is the parent directory?
18. If you wanted to create a subdirectory called **JAIL** under the subdirectory called **COURT** on the disk in Drive A, would you get the same result by keying in either **MD A:\COURT\JAIL** or **MD A:\JAIL**?
19. Is there any way to create a subdirectory under another subdirectory and not include the entire path name?
20. What is the syntax for the remove directory command?
21. Why will the RD command not remove a directory if there is a file in it?
22. What steps must be followed in removing a directory?
23. How can you eliminate the need to copy program files to every subdirectory?
24. What is the PATH command syntax?
25. How can you undo the path?
26. How can you set a multiple search path?
27. What are subdirectory markers? How can they be used?
28. What is the difference between the path to a file and using the PATH command?
29. How can you find out the structure of a disk?
30. How can you find out the structure of a subdirectory?

Application Assignments

1. For the following assignment:
   a. Create a subdirectory called **NEW** under the root directory of the DATA disk.
   b. Make **NEW** the default directory.
   c. Prove that **NEW** is the default subdirectory. Print the screen.
   d. Remove the directory **NEW**. Prove it is gone. Print the screen.

2. For the following assignment:
   a. Change the prompt to **HELLO THERE** drive letter. For drive letter, use the proper metastring to display the current drive. Print the screen with the new prompt command you used.
   b. Return the prompt to the default value. Print the screen with the command you used.
3. For the following assignment:
   a. Change the prompt so that it displays the default drive and default subdirectory.
   b. Make **DATA** the default subdirectory. Print the screen with the new prompt. Note: If you do not have the **DATA** subdirectory on the DATA disk, create it.
   c. Make the root directory the default drive and directory.
4. For the following assignment:
   a. Change the prompt so that it displays the default drive and directory.
   b. Create a subdirectory called **OLD**.
   c. Make **OLD** the default directory.
   d. **OLD** is the default subdirectory. Create a subdirectory called **LETTERS** under the **\POLY-SCI\USA** subdirectory. Print the command you used.
   e. **OLD** is the default subdirectory. Remove the **LETTERS** subdirectory. Print the command you used.
   f. Remove the **OLD** subdirectory. Print the screen to prove it is gone.
5. For the following assignment:
   a. Be sure the prompt displays the default drive and directory. Be sure the root directory is the default.
   b. Create a subdirectory called **PHONE** under the root directory. Display the directory of **PHONE**. Print the screen.
   c. Create two subdirectories under the **PHONE** subdirectory called **PERSONAL** and **BUSINESS**. Display the directory of the subdirectory **PHONE** and print this screen.
   d. Copy any file in the root directory with an extension **.TXT** to the subdirectory **PERSONAL**. Keep the file names the same. When the files have been copied, print the screen, including the COPY command you used.
   e. Copy all the files from the subdirectory **\PHYS-ED\GOLF** to the subdirectory called **BUSINESS**. When the files have been copied, print the screen.
   f. Make **BUSINESS** the default subdirectory. Prove that you have done so by printing the screen.
   g. Use the subdirectory markers to move to the parent of **BUSINESS**. Print the screen with the command you used.
   h. Remove the subdirectories **PHONE**, **BUSINESS**, and **PERSONAL**. Print the screen that proves that they are gone.
6. Display the current path. Print the screen.

7. Change the path to the **\DOS** subdirectory. Print the screen with the new path.
8. For the following assignment:
   a. Be sure the path is set to **\DOS**. Do not worry if your screen print is not a true copy of the screen. Graphics characters do not print correctly.
   b. Use the TREE command to display the structure of the DATA disk. Print the screen.
   c. Use the TREE command to display all the files on the DATA disk. If the output fills more than one screen, wait until the display has stopped scrolling. Print the screen.

Challenge Assignment

9. For the following assignment:
   a. Be sure the prompt displays the default drive and directory.
   b. Create a subdirectory on the DATA disk called **TEAMS** in the root directory. Be sure you are not in a subdirectory. Display this subdirectory on the screen and print it.
   c. On the DATA disk create three subdirectories under **TEAMS** called **BASEBALL**, **FOOTBALL**, and **BASKETBL**. Display the subdirectory **FOOTBALL** on the screen and print it.
   d. Copy the files from **C:\JUNK\SAMPLE** called **COLLEGE.TMS** and **PRO.TMS** to the subdirectory called **FOOTBALL** on the DATA disk. Display the contents of the **FOOTBALL** subdirectory and print it.
   e. Copy the files from **C:\JUNK\SAMPLE** called **AMERICAN.TMS** and **NATIONAL.TMS** to the subdirectory called **BASEBALL** on the DATA disk. Display the contents of the **BASEBALL** subdirectory and print it.
   f. Copy the file from **C:\JUNK\SAMPLE** called **BASKETBL.TMS** to the subdirectory called **BASKETBL** on the DATA disk. Display the contents of the **BASKETBL** subdirectory and print it.
   g. Make **BASEBALL** the default subdirectory. Using subdirectory markers, while **BASEBALL** is the default directory, display the contents of the **COLLEGE.TMS** file, which is in the **FOOTBALL** subdirectory. Print the screen.
   h. Create a path that looks first in the **TEAMS** subdirectory, then the **BASEBALL** subdirectory, then the **FOOTBALL** subdirectory, then the **BASKETBL** subdirectory and last in **C:\DOS**. Display and print the path.
   i. Change the path so that it is not set to any drive or subdirectory. Display and print the path.
   j. Make **BASEBALL** the default subdirectory. While **BASEBALL** is the default subdirectory, remove the subdirectory **BASKETBL** using subdirectory markers. Print the screen that proves that it is gone.
   k. Change the path to **C:\DOS**.
   l. Return to the root directory of the DATA disk.

10

Chapter

Organizing the Hard Disk

After completing this chapter, you will be able to:

1. Organize the hard disk to meet your specific needs.
2. List criteria for organizing a hard disk efficiently and logically.
3. Understand the APPEND command.
4. Compare and contrast the APPEND command with the PATH command and determine when each should be used.
5. Use the APPEND and PATH commands.
6. Explain what a logical disk drive is.
7. Understand and be able to use the SUBST, JOIN, and ASSIGN commands.
8. Explain the function of the XCOPY command.
9. Use the XCOPY command to copy files.
10. Explain the function of the REPLACE command.
11. Use the REPLACE command to update and add files to subdirectories.
12. Explain the functions of utility programs and use a utility program.

Chapter Overview

The more efficiently and logically the disk is organized the easier it becomes to decide where to store a new file or to access an existing file so that it can be used, modified, or deleted. As discussed previously, subdirectories (which are lists of files that have been grouped together under one heading) were developed as a means to help organize the disk so that the user could easily locate a specific file among the thousands that can be listed.

An inefficient but typical hard disk organizational scheme is to divide the disk into major application programs (i.e., word processing program, spreadsheet program, etc.) and to place the data files being used in the same subdirectory. This organizational scheme can create problems in locating a specific data file. To locate a specific file it would be necessary to remember under which program the data file was listed. It also makes more sense never to place program files and data files in the same subdirectory because program files rarely change and data files are always changing.

A more efficient organizational scheme for the disk is needed. Since the majority of people using a computer are working on projects and are utilizing application programs to help them do their work more easily and efficiently, it makes more sense to organize the disk the way most people work—by project, not by software application programs.

This chapter demonstrates ways to use the hard disk efficiently. You will learn how to organize a hard disk to serve your specific needs, use the directory to keep track of the files on your disk, determine the best command to use to locate a specific file, and learn what a logical disk is and the commands that can be used with a logical disk. In addition, you will learn some useful commands to manage the hard disk.

10.0 Why Organize a Hard Disk?

The initial response of users who acquire a hard disk is to load all programs and data into the root directory. When you use the DIR command, the many, many files in the root directory scroll by endlessly. In fact, it becomes very difficult to know which file belongs to which program, and which data files belong to which programs. Furthermore, the root directory on a hard disk can only hold a maximum of 512 file entries, so eventually there is no more room for files. When you consider that an application program like WordPerfect 5.1 comes on eleven 5 1/4-inch disks, you can see how quickly the user runs out of space.

Thus, subdirectories become mandatory. However, once again, when users discover subdirectories, the norm is to create "lump" subdirectories by dividing the disk into major applications, i.e., a word processing subdirectory holding programs and below that a subdirectory holding the data for that application. (It is very important *never* to place program files and data files in the same subdirectory. Programs do not change; data always changes.) For instance, a typical user might have a word processing program (WordPerfect 5.1), a spreadsheet program (Excel), a database program (dBASE IV), DOS, and a desktop publishing program (PageMaker). Thus, the user would create a subdirectory for each application program and beneath each application program, the user would create as many subdirectories as necessary to hold the data files created by the application program. An example of an inefficient but typical hard disk organizational scheme with these programs might look like Figure 10.1 (the ellipses represent all the files for that application program).

This scheme is inefficient. There are too many repeated subdirectory names. In addition, every time the user wants a data file, the user will have to remember not only what application he or she is working on but also where the appropriate file is located. Furthermore, at this point the user must key in long path names. For example, when wanting to retrieve an old chapter in WordPerfect, the user would need to key in `C:\WP51\MYBOOK\OLD\CHAP1.0`. In addition, when the user needs to find a file four levels down the hierarchical tree, DOS must look at every subdirectory on the way down. The heads on the disk drive are constantly going back and forth reading the entries and looking for the files.

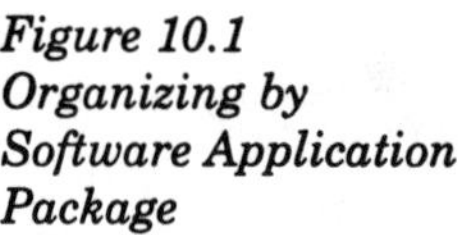

Figure 10.1 Organizing by Software Application Package

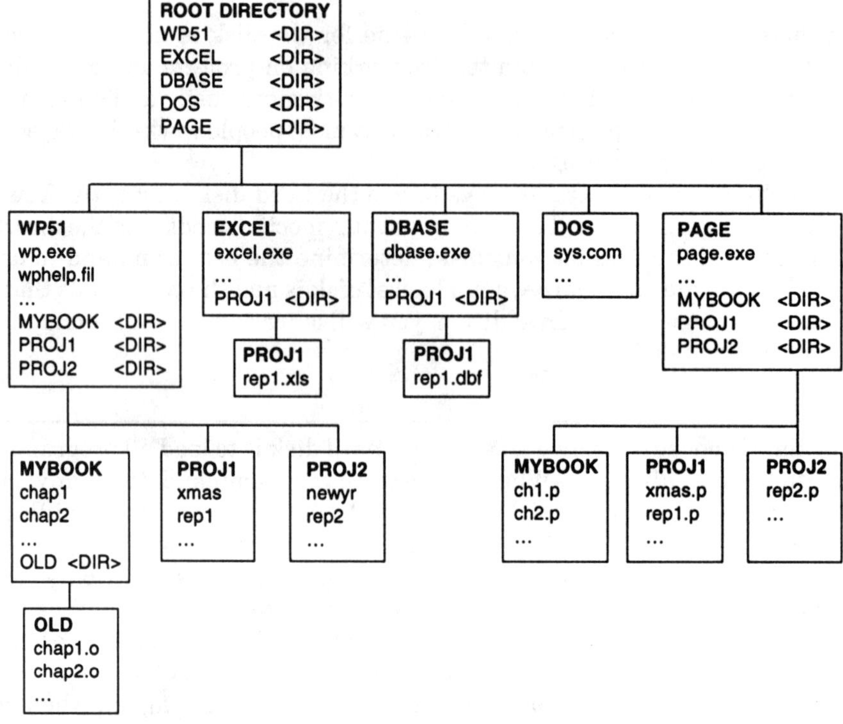

If the user has any data files that are used with more than one package—such as using dBASE IV to generate a mailing list that is going to be used with WordPerfect 5.1—the user ends up with data in two places: the word processing subdirectory and the database subdirectory. More importantly, when the user wants to add or delete software and/or add or delete projects, it becomes a logistic nightmare finding out where the files are located and deciding what data files should be kept.

Generally, people do not work by software package; they work by projects. Software is a tool to help do work more easily and more efficiently. Hence, it makes much more sense to organize a hard disk by the way most people work rather than by application package. In addition, with an efficient organizational scheme, it is easier to add and delete projects and software.

10.1 Methods of Organizing a Hard Disk

Certain criteria can give a hard disk an efficient and logical organization. These include the following suggestions:

1. The root directory should be a map to the rest of the disk. The only files that should be in the root directory are **COMMAND.COM**, **AUTOEXEC.BAT**, and **CONFIG.SYS**. All other files in the root directory should be subdirectory listings.
2. Create subdirectories that are shallow and wide instead of compact and

deep. The reason is that it is easier for DOS to find files that are not buried several levels down. Also, it is much easier for the user to keep track of the subdirectories when the organizational scheme is simple. Remember the old programmer's principle: KISS—Keep It Simple, Stupid. Short path names are easier to key in than long path names.

3. Plan the organization of the hard disk prior to installing software. Create as many subdirectories as you need *before* copying files into subdirectories.
4. Do not place data files in the same subdirectory as program files. Although you are constantly creating and deleting data files, you rarely, if ever, create or delete program files.
5. Many small subdirectories with few files are better than a large subdirectory with many files. It is easier to manage and update a subdirectory with a limited number of files because there is less likelihood of having to determine on a file-by-file basis which file belong where.
6. Keep subdirectory names short but descriptive. The shorter the name, the less there is to key in. For instance, using the subdirectory name PROG for all the software application programs is helpful because PROG is short but descriptive. P, on the other hand, is short but too cryptic for you to remember easily what the P subdirectory holds.
7. Create a separate subdirectory containing all the application software you will be using. This program subdirectory will be a map to all the software application programs on the disk.
8. Create separate subdirectories for the DOS files and for any batch files you might have. Place them under the root directory or under the program directory.
9. Create a separate master subdirectory under the root directory for utility programs mapping the direction that you need to take. Every utility software package should have its own subdirectory under the master utility subdirectory. As you work with computers, you start collecting utility software. Utility software programs provide commonly needed services. Examples of these include Norton Utilities, PC Tools, Nick's DOS Utilities, and shareware that you might receive. (**Shareware** is software that is free to try. If you like it, you pay a registration fee to the software's author.) Furthermore, in many instances software utility and shareware packages have similar names, making it imperative that each has its own separate and readily identifiable subdirectory.
10. Learn how to use the application package and also learn how the application package works. For instance, find out if the application package assigns a file extension. dBASE assigns an extension of .DBF for data base files; WordPerfect 5.1 does not assign a file extension. Find out how the application package works with subdirectories. For instance, does it recognize subdirectories for data files? WordPerfect does but dBASE III does not. Although we are going to learn some DOS tricks to force applications to recognize subdirectories, there are application packages that insist on being directly off the root directory.

An organizational scheme following this logic could look something like Figure 10.2.

Figure 10.2
Organization by Project

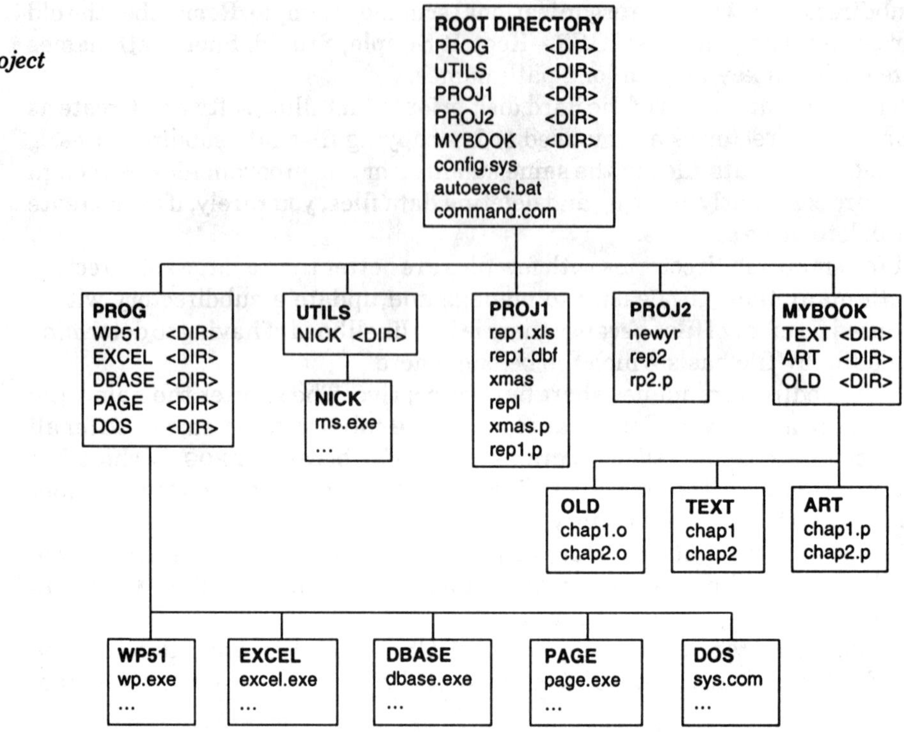

In this organizational scheme, the user knows where all software application programs are located. In addition, it is much easier to add a new software package or to update an existing software package because all the program files are located in one place. Also, since this scheme is organized by project, it is easy to know what data files belong to what project. Again, it is easy to add a new project or delete an old one. Looking at the subdirectory called **PROJ1**, the user knows what data file belongs to what program because in this example **REP1.DBF** belongs to the application program dBASE, whereas **REP1.XLS** belongs to EXCEL. However, in the subdirectory called **MYBOOK**, the user chose to place the WordPerfect data files in a subdirectory called **TEXT**, the desktop publishing data files in a subdirectory called **ART**, and the old chapters in a subdirectory called **OLD**.

This, of course, is not the only way to organize a hard disk. You can organize your hard disk any way you wish, but there should be some organization. Although it may take some time in the beginning, ultimately organization will make more effective use of the hard disk. The two major considerations for any organizational scheme are first, how does the user work, and second, how do the application programs work?

10.2 Organizing a Disk

Most users do not begin with a organized hard disk. Either they have added programs as they received them or another individual has set up the hard disk. What may seem organized to one user is chaos to another. In this instance the user needs to reorganize the hard disk, a process that can be done without reformatting the hard disk. To master this process, you are going to take the ACTIVITIES disk and reorganize it. This exercise will give you some idea of how the process works without having to worry about inadvertently deleting files from the hard disk. Prior to reorganizing it, however, you will make a backup copy of the ACTIVITIES disk.

Activity 10.3 Making a Copy of the Activities Disk

Note 1: The **C:\>** is displayed and the ACTIVITIES disk is in Drive A. Then, if the path is not set to **C:\DOS**, do so now by keying in **PATH C:\DOS**. Remember that if the DOS files are in a subdirectory with a different name, you will have to substitute your subdirectory name for **\DOS**, i.e., **PATH C:\BIN**. You will also have a blank floppy disk.

Note 2: Remember, with DISKCOPY you must use identical media. If you have a 5 1/4-inch disk drive, you must have a blank 360 KB disk. If you have a 3 1/2-inch disk drive, you must have a blank 720 KB disk.

STEP 1: Key in the following:
C:\>**DISKCOPY A: A:** <Enter>

```
C:\>DISKCOPY A: A:

Insert SOURCE diskette in drive A:

Press any key to continue . . .
```

WHAT'S HAPPENING? Since the ACTIVITIES disk is the SOURCE disk, it is already in the proper drive. If it is not, place it there.

STEP 2: Press <Enter>.

```
C:\>DISKCOPY A: A:

Insert SOURCE diskette in drive A:

Press any key to continue . . .

Copying 40 tracks
9 sectors per track, 2 side(s)

Insert TARGET diskette in drive A:

Press any key to continue . . .
```

STEP 3: Remove the ACTIVITIES disk from Drive A. Get a blank disk. Write on the label Organized ACTIVITIES disk. Apply the label to the disk. Insert this blank disk in Drive A. Press any key.

```
Insert TARGET diskette in drive A:

Press any key to continue . . .

Volume Serial Number is 1CF4-2D57

Copy another diskette (Y/N)? _
```

STEP 4: Key in **N**.

```
Copy another diskette (Y/N)? N

C:\>_
```

WHAT'S HAPPENING? You made a backup of the ACTIVITIES disk. You are working on the copy of the ACTIVITIES disk which is why you did not remove the copy from the disk drive. You are going to work on this copy of the ACTIVITIES disk labeled Organized ACTIVITIES disk. Remember, that if you are using a 3 1/2-inch disk, you will have to swap disks.

10.4 Organizing the Activities Disk

The Organized ACTIVITIES disk has minimal organization. The ... represents file names. Its structure is as follows:

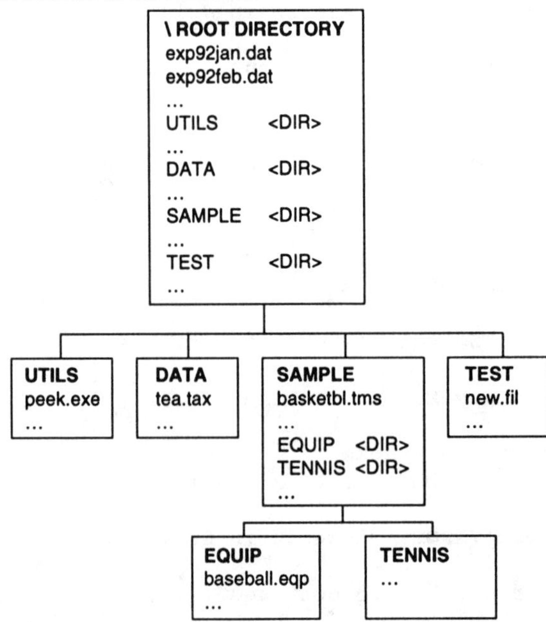

There are programs as well as data files on this disk. You, the user, really cannot tell what is on this disk. In addition, there are so many files in the root directory that when you key in DIR, you see many, many files scrolling by on the screen. Therefore, you are going to reorganize the disk so that it will be easier to manage. When complete, the new structure will look as follows:

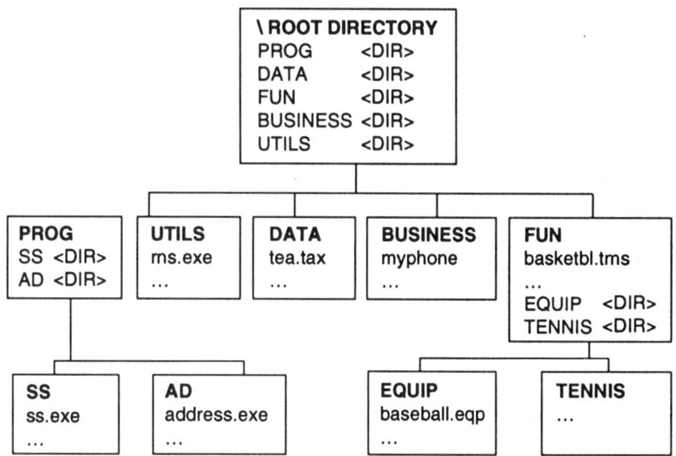

You are going to create the necessary subdirectories and copy the appropriate files to the correct subdirectories. The **PROG** subdirectory will be the map to the programs on the Organized ACTIVITIES disk. In the **PROG** subdirectory you will have the subdirectory **SS** for the spreadsheet program and **AD** for the address program. You will copy the application programs into the proper subdirectories and delete the files from their original locations.

Activity 10.5 Setting up the PROG Subdirectory

Note: You have the Organized ACTIVITIES disk in Drive A and the path set to **C:\DOS**. The default subdirectory is the root directory of the Organized ACTIVITIES disk.

STEP 1: Key in the following:
C:\>**A:** <Enter>

STEP 2: Key in the following:
A:\>**MD PROG** <Enter>

STEP 3: Key in the following:
A:\>**MD PROG\SS** <Enter>

STEP 4: Key in the following:
A:\>**MD PROG\AD** <Enter>

```
A:\>MD PROG

A:\>MD PROG\SS

A:\>MD PROG\AD

A:\>_
```

WHAT'S HAPPENING? You created a generic program subdirectory and identified the specific subdirectories that reflect the programs on the Organized ACTIVITIES disk. Now you need to copy the proper files to the proper subdirectory and delete them from their original location. In addition, you are going to delete some unnecessary files to free up some disk space.

STEP 5: Key in the following:
A:\>**DEL *.BAC** <Enter>

STEP 6: Key in the following:
A:\>**DEL UTILS\ROB.EXE** <Enter>

STEP 7: Key in the following:
A:\>**COPY ADDRESS.EXE PROG\AD** <Enter>

STEP 8: Key in the following:
A:\>**DEL ADDRESS.EXE** <Enter>

```
A:\>DEL *.BAC

A:\>DEL UTILS\ROB.EXE

A:\>COPY ADDRESS.EXE PROG\AD
        1 file(s) copied

A:\>DEL ADDRESS.EXE

A:\>_
```

WHAT'S HAPPENING? You copied the address program to the **PROG\AD** subdirectory. You deleted **ADDRESS.EXE** from the root directory and eliminated the **.BAC** files and the **ROB.EXE** file because they are unnecessary files.

STEP 9: Key in the following:
A:\>**COPY UTILS\SS*.* PROG\SS** <Enter>

STEP 10: Key in the following:
A:\>**DEL UTILS\SS*.*** <Enter>

```
A:\>COPY UTILS\SS*.* PROG\SS
UTILS\SS.EXE
UTILS\SS.DOC
```

```
UTILS\SS.HLP
         3 file(s) copied

A:\>DEL UTILS\SS*.*

A:\>_
```

WHAT'S HAPPENING? You copied the spreadsheet programs to the **PROG\SS** subdirectory and deleted the spreadsheet programs from the subdirectory called **UTILS**, which was under the root directory.

STEP 11: Key in the following:
A:\>**COPY *.TXT \DATA** <Enter>

STEP 12: Key in the following:
A:\>**DEL *.TXT** <Enter>

STEP 13: Key in the following:
A:\>**COPY *.TMP \DATA** <Enter>

STEP 14: Key in the following:
A:\>**DEL *.TMP** <Enter>

STEP 15: Key in the following:
A:\>**COPY *.NEW \DATA** <Enter>

STEP 16: Key in the following:
A:\>**DEL *.NEW** <Enter>

STEP 17: Key in the following:
A:\>**COPY *.DAT \DATA** <Enter>

STEP 18: Key in the following:
A:\>**DEL *.DAT** <Enter>

```
A:\>COPY *.TXT \DATA
EXERCISE.TXT
JANUARY.TXT
FEBRUARY.TXT
MARCH.TXT
APRIL.TXT
HELLO.TXT
TEST.TXT
BYE.TXT
GOODBYE.TXT
         9 file(s) copied

A:\>DEL *.TXT
```

```
A:\>COPY *.TMP \DATA
JAN.TMP
FEB.TMP
MAR.TMP
APR.TMP
        4 file(s) copied

A:\>DEL *.TMP

A:\>COPY *.NEW \DATA
JAN.NEW
FEB.NEW
MAR.NEW
APR.NEW
        4 file(s) copied

A:\>DEL *.NEW

A:\>COPY *.DAT \DATA
EXP92JAN.DAT
EXP92FEB.DAT
EXP92MAR.DAT
EXP93JAN.DAT
EXP93FEB.DAT
EXP93MAR.DAT
EXP94JAN.DAT
EXP94FEB.DAT
EXP94MAR.DAT
        9 file(s) copied

A:\>DEL *.DAT

A:\>_
```

WHAT'S HAPPENING? You copied existing files (***.TXT**; ***.TMP**; ***.NEW**; ***.DAT**) to an existing subdirectory called **DATA**. Then you deleted the files (***.TXT**; ***.TMP**; ***.NEW**; ***.DAT**) from the root directory of the Organized ACTIVITIES disk.

STEP 19: Key in the following:
A:\>**COPY BUSINESS TEST** <Enter>

STEP 20: Key in the following:
A:\>**COPY FRIENDS TEST** <Enter>

STEP 21: Key in the following:
A:\>**COPY MYPHONE TEST** <Enter>

STEP 22: Key in the following:
A:\>**COPY UTILS\BUDGET.SS TEST** <Enter>

STEP 23: Key in the following:
A:\>**DEL BUSINESS** <Enter>

STEP 24: Key in the following:
A:\>**DEL FRIENDS** <Enter>

STEP 25: Key in the following:
A:\>**DEL MYPHONE** <Enter>

STEP 26: Key in the following:
A:\>**DEL UTILS\BUDGET.SS** <Enter>

```
A:\>COPY BUSINESS TEST
        1 file(s) copied

A:\>COPY FRIENDS TEST
        1 file(s) copied

A:\>COPY MYPHONE TEST
        1 file(s) copied

A:\>COPY UTILS\BUDGET.SS TEST
        1 file(s) copied

A:\>DEL BUSINESS

A:\>DEL FRIENDS

A:\>DEL MYPHONE

A:\>DEL UTILS\BUDGET.SS

A:\>_
```

WHAT'S HAPPENING? You copied the files that belong to certain application programs to the **TEST** subdirectory. You then deleted these files from the root directory and eliminated the **BUDGET.SS** file from the subdirectory **UTILS**.

10.6 The XCOPY Command

Although COPY is a useful internal command it has some drawbacks, so when DOS 3.2 was released the XCOPY command was added to the DOS utility programs. Unlike COPY, XCOPY is an external command that allows you to copy files that exist in different subdirectories as well as copy the contents of a subdirectory including both files and subdirectories beneath the parent subdirectory. It allows you to specify a drive as a source and assumes all files on the drive. With XCOPY you can copy files created on or before a certain date. Furthermore, XCOPY can operate faster than the COPY command. The COPY command reads and copies one file at a time, even if you use wildcards. XCOPY first reads all the source files into memory and subsequently copies them to the target as a group of files. XCOPY will not copy system or hidden files. Remember that XCOPY is an external command. The syntax is:

XCOPY *source* [*destination*] [/A ¦ /M] [/D:*date*] [/P] [/S [/E]] [/V] [/W]

The parameters include the following definitions:

source Specifies the file(s) to copy.
destination Specifies the location and/or name of new files.
/A Copies files with the archive attribute bit set to 1 and does not change the attribute of the source files. These are files that have been either created or modified since the last backup.
/M Copies files with the archive attribute set. Most often the archive bit is set by the program being run. If the archive bit is set to 0, it means that the file has already been backed up and has not been changed since the last backup.
/D:*date* Copies files changed on or after the specified date. The *date* parameter is entered as: /D:mm-dd-yy. A specific date such as November 23, 1992 would look like: /D:11-23-92.
/P Prompts you before creating each destination file with a Y or N.
/S Copies directories and subdirectories, except empty ones. Copies files in the source directory and in all subdirectories beneath the starting directory maintaining the same tree structure of the parent. If you do not include the /S parameter, DOS stops copying after the first subdirectory. If you wish to include any empty subdirectories, you must also include the /E parameter.
/E Creates a subdirectory on the target disk even if there are no files in it.
/V Verifies each new file.
/W Prompts you to press any key before copying.

Activity 10.7

Using the XCOPY Command

Note: You have the Organized ACTIVITIES disk in Drive A with the **A:\>** displayed. The default subdirectory is the root directory of the Organized ACTIVITIES disk and the path is set to **C:\DOS**.

STEP 1: Key in the following:
A:\>**DIR \SAMPLE** <Enter>

```
A:\>DIR \SAMPLE

   Volume in drive A is ACTIVITIES
   Volume Serial Number is 1CF4-2D57
   Directory of A:\SAMPLE
```

```
.            <DIR>       05-14-92 11:03a
..           <DIR>       05-14-92 11:03a
BASKETBL  TMS      220   05-14-92 11:03a
PRO       TMS      207   05-14-92 11:04a
COLLEGE   TMS      226   05-14-92 11:04a
AMERICAN  TMS      207   05-14-92 11:04a
NATIONAL  TMS      221   05-14-92 11:04a
EQUIP        <DIR>       05-14-92 11:03a
TENNIS       <DIR>       05-14-92 11:03a
          9 file(s)       1081 bytes
                         63488 bytes free

A:\>_
```

WHAT'S HAPPENING? As you can see, in addition to all the ***.TMS** files, there are two subdirectories, **EQUIP** and **TENNIS**, in the subdirectory **SAMPLE**. If you were going to use the COPY command, you would have to copy the files in the **SAMPLE** subdirectory as well as the files in the subdirectories, **EQUIP** and **TENNIS**. Furthermore, you would have to create the two new subdirectories. XCOPY can do all this work for you. Remember that XCOPY is an external command, so you *must* have the path set to the **C:\DOS**.

STEP 2: Key in the following:
A:\>**XCOPY \SAMPLE \FUN/S/E** <Enter>

```
A:\>XCOPY \SAMPLE \FUN/S/E
Does FUN specify a file name
or directory name on the target
(F = file, D = directory)?_
```

WHAT'S HAPPENING? You asked XCOPY to copy all the files from the **SAMPLE** subdirectory (**\SAMPLE**) to the **\FUN** subdirectory under the root directory of the Organized ACTIVITIES disk. In this case, XCOPY is a smart command. It asks you if you want to place all these files in one file or to create a subdirectory structure. In this case, you want to create the subdirectory structure. The /S parameter means to include *all* the subdirectories and their files under the **SAMPLE** subdirectory. The /E parameter told DOS to create any empty subdirectories (subdirectories with no files in them) on the newly copied disk. Without the /E parameter DOS would not create empty subdirectories.

STEP 3: Key in the following:
D <Enter>

```
A:\>XCOPY \SAMPLE \FUN/S/E
Does FUN specify a file name
or directory name on the target
(F = file, D = directory)?D
Reading source file(s) . . .
```

```
\SAMPLE\BASKETBL.TMS
\SAMPLE\PRO.TMS
\SAMPLE\COLLEGE.TMS
\SAMPLE\AMERICAN.TMS
\SAMPLE\NATIONAL.TMS
\SAMPLE\EQUIP\BASEBALL.EQP
\SAMPLE\EQUIP\FOOTBALL.EQP
        7 file(s) copied

A:\>_
```

WHAT'S HAPPENING? Since you included the /S parameter, XCOPY copied all the files from the subdirectory **SAMPLE**, including the subdirectory called **EQUIP** with its files, **BASEBALL.EQP** and **FOOTBALL.EQP**. What about the subdirectory called **TENNIS**?

STEP 4: Key in the following:
A:\>**DIR \FUN** <Enter>

```
A:\>DIR \FUN

   Volume in drive A is ACTIVITIES
   Volume Serial Number is 1CF4-2D57
   Directory of A:\FUN

.            <DIR>       06-17-93 10:41p
..           <DIR>       06-17-93 10:41p
BASKETBL  TMS      220   05-14-92 11:03a
PRO       TMS      207   05-14-92 11:04a
COLLEGE   TMS      226   05-14-92 11:04a
AMERICAN  TMS      207   05-14-92 11:04a
NATIONAL  TMS      221   05-14-92 11:04a
EQUIP        <DIR>       06-17-93 10:41p
TENNIS       <DIR>       06-17-93 10:41p
        9 file(s)         1081 bytes
                         53248 bytes free

A:\>_
```

WHAT'S HAPPENING? Not only were all the files and subdirectories copied, but the empty subdirectory called **TENNIS** was also created. Only the order is different.

STEP 5: Key in the following:
A:\>**DEL SAMPLE\EQUIP** <Enter>

```
A:\>DEL SAMPLE\EQUIP
All file in directory will be deleted!
Are you sure (Y/N)?_
```

STEP 6: Key in the following:
Y <Enter>

```
A:\>DEL SAMPLE\EQUIP
All file in directory will be deleted!
Are you sure (Y/N)?Y

A:\>_
```

WHAT'S HAPPENING? You deleted the files in the subdirectory **EQUIP**.

STEP 7: Key in the following:
A:\>**DEL SAMPLE*.*** <Enter>

```
A:\>DEL SAMPLE\*.*
All file in directory will be deleted!
Are you sure (Y/N)?_
```

STEP 8: Key in the following:
Y <Enter>

```
A:\>DEL SAMPLE\EQUIP
All file in directory will be deleted!
Are you sure (Y/N)?Y

A:\>_
```

WHAT'S HAPPENING? You removed the files in the subdirectory **SAMPLE**.

STEP 9: Key in the following:
A:\>**RD SAMPLE\TENNIS** <Enter>

STEP 10: Key in the following:
A:\>**RD SAMPLE\EQUIP** <Enter>

STEP 11: Key in the following:
A:\>**RD SAMPLE** <Enter>

```
A:\>RD SAMPLE\TENNIS

A:\>RD SAMPLE\EQUIP

A:\>RD SAMPLE

A:\>_
```

WHAT'S HAPPENING? You eliminated the subdirectory **SAMPLE** and all the subdirectories and files beneath **SAMPLE**.

10.8 The REPLACE Command

You have used the XCOPY command to copy files and subdirectories. There is another command called REPLACE, an external command that also copies files. However, you have more choices when you use REPLACE. Often, you keep multiple copies of files, so that you have both the original files and backup files in case anything happens to the original. These backup files can be on a floppy disk or even in another subdirectory on the hard disk. One of the dilemmas with backup files is that you want to keep them current. The REPLACE command, with no parameters, allows you to replace an entire set of old files with the new files. It also lets you add a new file and/or replace a file that has been changed since the last time you backed up the files. The syntax for REPLACE is:

REPLACE [*drive1:*][*path1*]*filename* [*drive2:*][*path2*] [/A] [/P] [/R] [/W]
REPLACE [*drive1:*][*path1*]*filename* [*drive2:*][*path2*] [/P] [/R] [/S] [/W] [/U]

The syntax is given twice to indicate which parameters cannot be used with one another. The parameters are as follows:

[*drive1:*][*path1*]*filename*	Specifies the source file or files.
[*drive2:*][*path2*]	Specifies the directory where files are to be replaced.
/A	Adds new files to destination directory. Cannot be used with /S or /U switches.
/P	Prompts for confirmation before replacing a file or adding a source file.
/R	Replaces read-only files as well as unprotected files.
/S	Replaces files in all subdirectories of the destination directory. Cannot be used with the /A switch.
/W	Waits for you to insert a disk before beginning.
/U	Replaces (updates) only files that are older than source files. Cannot be used with the /A switch.

Activity 10.9 Using the REPLACE Command

Note: You have the Organized ACTIVITIES disk in Drive A with the `A:\>` displayed. The path is set to `C:\DOS`.

STEP 1: Key in the following:
A:\>`COPY *.MOV \FUN` <Enter>

STEP 2: Key in the following:
A:\>`DIR \FUN\*.MOV` <Enter>

```
A:\>COPY *.MOV \FUN
MUSIC.MOV
DRAMA.MOV
OTHER.MOV
        3 file(s) copied
```

```
A:\>DIR \FUN\*.MOV

   Volume in drive A is ACTIVITIES
   Volume Serial Number is 1CF4-2D57
   Directory of A:\FUN

MUSIC      MOV     225   11-23-92   7:10a
DRAMA      MOV     221   11-23-92   7:11a
OTHER      MOV     211   11-23-92   7:12a
        3 file(s)          657 bytes
                         60416 bytes free

A:\>_
```

WHAT'S HAPPENING? You copied the files with the extension **.MOV** to the **FUN** subdirectory. You then confirmed that they were copied successfully to that directory. Now you are going to use the REPLACE command.

STEP 3: Key in the following:
A:\>**REPLACE *.MOV \FUN** <Enter>

STEP 4: Key in the following:
A:\>**DIR \FUN*.MOV** <Enter>

```
A:\>REPLACE *.MOV \FUN

Replacing A:\FUN\MUSIC.MOV

Replacing A:\FUN\DRAMA.MOV

Replacing A:\FUN\OTHER.MOV

3 file(s) replaced

A:\>DIR \FUN\*.MOV

   Volume in drive A is ACTIVITIES
   Volume Serial Number is 1CF4-2D57
   Directory of A:\FUN

MUSIC      MOV     225   11-23-92   7:10a
DRAMA      MOV     221   11-23-92   7:11a
OTHER      MOV     211   11-23-92   7:12a
        3 file(s)          657 bytes
                         60416 bytes free

A:\>_
```

WHAT'S HAPPENING? As you can see from the messages, each **.MOV** file was replaced in the **FUN** subdirectory. Thus, the REPLACE command globally replaced all the .MOV files in the FUN subdirectory with those .MOV files from the root directory. But it does not seem to be different from simply copying files. In the next step, you will see the difference when you create a new file with COPY CON and only add it to the subdirectory. In the next step, key in the entire series of lines. Remember, <F6> means to press the F6 key, not key it in.

STEP 5: Key in the following:

A:\>**COPY CON AWARD.MOV** <Enter>
Rain Man <Enter>
Dances With Wolves <Enter>
Platoon <Enter>
<F6> <Enter>

STEP 6: Key in the following:

A:\>**TYPE AWARD.MOV** <Enter>

```
A:\>COPY CON AWARD.MOV
Rain Man
Dances With Wolves
Platoon
^Z
         1 file(s) copied

A:\>TYPE AWARD.MOV
Rain Man
Dances With Wolves
Platoon

A:\>_
```

WHAT'S HAPPENING? You created a simple text file of Academy Award-winning films. You then displayed it on the screen. Now you will see how the REPLACE command will add only the newly created file.

STEP 7: Key in the following:

A:\>**REPLACE *.MOV \FUN /A** <Enter>

STEP 8: Key in the following:

A:\>**DIR \FUN*.MOV** <Enter>

```
A:\>REPLACE *.MOV \FUN /A

Adding A:\FUN\AWARD.MOV

1 file(s) added

A:\>DIR \FUN\*.MOV
```

```
   Volume in drive A is ACTIVITIES
   Volume Serial Number is 1CF4-2D57
   Directory of A:\FUN

MUSIC      MOV     225   11-23-92   7:10a
DRAMA      MOV     221   11-23-92   7:10a
OTHER      MOV     211   11-23-92   7:10a
AWARD      MOV      39   06-17-93 10:45p
        4 file(s)          696 bytes
                         58368 bytes free

A:\>_
```

WHAT'S HAPPENING? In this case, because you included the /A parameter for add, the REPLACE command looked at the files in the **\FUN** subdirectory and realized that only **AWARD.MOV** was missing. Thus, it added only that file rather than copying all the **.MOV** files. The REPLACE command is also very useful if you change a file and only want to replace the amended file.

STEP 9: Key in the following:

A:\>**COPY CON AWARD.MOV** <Enter>
Driving Miss Daisy <Enter>
Out of Africa <Enter>
The Last Emperor <Enter>
<F6> <Enter>

STEP 10: Key in the following:

A:\>**TYPE AWARD.MOV** <Enter>

```
A:\>COPY CON AWARD.MOV
Driving Miss Daisy
Out of Africa
The Last Emperor
        1 file(s) copied

A:\>TYPE AWARD.MOV
Driving Miss Daisy
Out of Africa
The Last Emperor

A:\>_
```

WHAT'S HAPPENING? You changed the contents of the file **AWARD.MOV**. Now you are going to use the REPLACE command to update the **\FUN** subdirectory using the /U parameter with the newly edited file.

STEP 11: Key in the following:

A:\>**REPLACE *.MOV \FUN /U** <Enter>

STEP 12: Key in the following:
A:\>**TYPE \FUN\AWARD.MOV** <Enter>

```
A:\>REPLACE *.MOV \FUN /U

Replacing A:\FUN\AWARD.MOV

1 file(s) replaced

A:\>TYPE \FUN\AWARD.MOV
Driving Miss Daisy
Out of Africa
The Last Emperor

A:\>_
```

WHAT'S HAPPENING? Again, the REPLACE command selectively replaced only the file that was updated. When you use the TYPE command, you can see that the correct file was updated in the **\FUN** subdirectory. Thus, the REPLACE command gives you much more flexibility than the COPY command.

10.10 A Utility Program from Nick's DOS Utilities

Many utility programs come with DOS. These include all the external commands such as XCOPY and REPLACE. As you may have noticed, each new edition of DOS comes with more utility programs. XCOPY, for instance, was not available when DOS 1.0 was introduced, primarily because XCOPY is most useful with subdirectories and the ability to create and use subdirectories did not exist in DOS 1.0. In addition to all the new commands that DOS introduces, there are also other commands that DOS has *not* included. Thus, a market has developed for commands not yet available within the standard DOS programs. Some of these programs are given away; others are released as shareware, and others are commercially packaged and sold. Some of the better known commercial software includes Norton Utilities and PC Tools. Why do computer users buy these utility programs? Each program does something useful that DOS does not yet allow you to do.

Nick's DOS Utilities is an educational package that includes various DOS utility programs. Several of these programs, extracted from the complete set, are included on the ACTIVITIES disk to demonstrate the use of utility programs that are not available in DOS.

Activity 10.11 Using RNS, The Rename Subdirectory Utility from Nick's DOS Utilities

Note: The Organized ACTIVITIES disk is in Drive A with the **A:\>** displayed.

STEP 1: Key in the following:
A:\>**DIR UTILS** <Enter>

```
A:\>DIR UTILS

   Volume in drive A is ACTIVITIES
   Volume Serial Number is 1CF4-2D57
   Directory of A:\UTILS

.            <DIR>      12-06-92 10:00a
..           <DIR>      12-06-92 10:00a
PEEK      EXE   69476   02-20-88 12:44p
DEMOS     EXE    5197   02-20-88  4:27p
README    NIK     693   02-24-88  3:24p
README    BAT      28   02-24-88  3:12p
DEMOS     TXT    3577   02-24-88  3:20p
RNS       EXE    7269   11-22-89 10:35p
        8 file(s)       86240 bytes
                        59392 bytes free

A:\>_
```

WHAT'S HAPPENING? The **UTILS** subdirectory contains several files. Every file with an **.EXE** extension is a program. Anything with a **.BAT** file extension is a batch file, a special kind of program. When you get new software, it is very common to see files called **README**. The **README** file name is self-explanatory. In this case, if you wanted to know about Nick's DOS Utilities, you would key in **README**. The program that we are interested in, however, is the one called **RNS.EXE**. When you were cleaning up the Organized ACTIVITIES disk, some of the activities included creating a subdirectory and then copying the appropriate files into the new subdirectory. Some of you may have thought that this was an awful lot of work when, in reality, all you were doing was changing the name of the subdirectory. If you want to change the name of a file, it is very easy. You use the RENAME command. However, DOS provides no equivalent command for renaming subdirectories. Hence, your only choice is to create a new subdirectory or several subdirectories and copy files into the new subdirectory or subdirectories. Nick's DOS Utilities has a program that renames subdirectories just like the DOS command RENAME that renames files.

STEP 2: Key in the following:
A:\>**PATH A:\UTILS** <Enter>

STEP 3: Key in the following:
A:\>**DIR \TEST** <Enter>

```
A:\>PATH A:\UTILS

A:\>DIR \TEST

   Volume in drive A is ACTIVITIES
   Volume Serial Number is 1CF4-2D57
   Directory of A:\TEST
```

```
.            <DIR>        11-16-93  7:05a
..           <DIR>        11-16-93  7:05a
NEW        FIL       31   11-16-93  7:05a
SAMPLE     FIL       23   11-16-93  7:05a
MYPHONE             851   12-06-92  9:11a
LIST                851   12-06-92  9:11a
BUSINESS           1622   10-12-92  9:00p
FRIENDS            3162   10-12-92  9:00p
BUDGET     SS     22281   12-06-92 10:01a
        9 file(s)         28821 bytes
                          59392 bytes free

A:\>_
```

WHAT'S HAPPENING? The first thing you did was to change the path to where the program **RNS.EXE** is located so that you can execute it. The second thing you did was look at the contents of the subdirectory called **TEST**. You decided that **TEST** was not a descriptive name for the subdirectory, and you want to change the subdirectory name from **TEST** to **BUSINESS**. With DOS, you would have to take four steps. First, you would key in **MD \BUSINESS**, and second, you would key in **COPY \TEST \BUSINESS**. Then, you would key in **DEL \TEST*.***. The last step to remove the subdirectory **TEST** would be keying in **RD \TEST.** Instead of taking these four steps, you are going to use the utility program RNS.

STEP 4: Key in the following:
A:\>**RNS \TEST \BUSINESS** <Enter>

```
A:\>RNS \TEST \BUSINESS
RNS    VER. 1.05

A:\>_
```

WHAT'S HAPPENING? This seemed easy enough. Did it work?

STEP 5: Key in the following:
A:\>**DIR \TEST** <Enter>

STEP 6: Key in the following:
A:\>**DIR \BUSINESS** <Enter>

```
A:\>DIR \TEST

   Volume in drive A is ACTIVITIES
   Volume Serial Number is 1CF4-2D57
   Directory of A:\

File not found

A:\>DIR \BUSINESS
```

```
   Volume in drive A is ACTIVITIES
   Volume Serial Number is 1CF4-2D57
   Directory of A:\BUSINESS

.             <DIR>       11-16-93  7:05a
..            <DIR>       11-16-93  7:05a
NEW       FIL        31   11-16-93  7:05a
SAMPLE    FIL        23   11-16-93  7:05a
MYPHONE             851   12-06-92  9:11a
LIST                851   12-06-92  9:11a
BUSINESS           1622   10-12-92  9:00p
FRIENDS            3162   10-12-92  9:00p
BUDGET    SS      22281   12-06-92 10:01a
         9 file(s)        28821 bytes
                          59392 bytes free

A:\>_
```

WHAT'S HAPPENING? The RNS command did rename the subdirectory **\TEST** to **\BUSINESS**. It was much easier to use this command then to have to make and delete a subdirectory and copy and delete files. This is why people write utility programs that extend the power of DOS. Although utility application programs often have overlapping commands, users still purchase more than one utility program because each one has certain useful functions not yet available in DOS.

STEP 7: Key in the following:
A:\>**PATH C:\DOS** <Enter>

```
A:\>PATH C:\DOS

A:\>_
```

WHAT'S HAPPENING? You returned the path to **C:\DOS**, the **DOS** subdirectory.

10.12 The APPEND Command

Although the PATH command is very useful, it has shortcomings. One of the major shortcomings is that the PATH command only looks for program files—those files that are executable. Executable files always have the file extensions of **.COM**, **.EXE** or **.BAT**. Thus, even though you set the path, DOS will not search for any data files. Today most application programs have auxiliary files that the program uses, often called **overlay** files. To see how this process works (Figure 10.3) let's assume that you are working on a report for a class. Your default directory, from the organizational scheme you designed, is the subdirectory called **SCHOOL**. You set the path to **PATH=C:\PROG\WORD**. You key in **WORD**. Because the path is set to **\PROG\WORD** and WORD is an executable file (**WORD.EXE**), the WORD program is loaded. Then the WORD program asks you what file you want to work on. You key in **REPORT.FIL**. Since the default subdirectory is `SCHOOL` and that is where the `REPORT.FIL` is located, the WORD program, through DOS, can find the data file when it looks in the default subdirectory.

Figure 10.3 Shortcomings of the Path Command

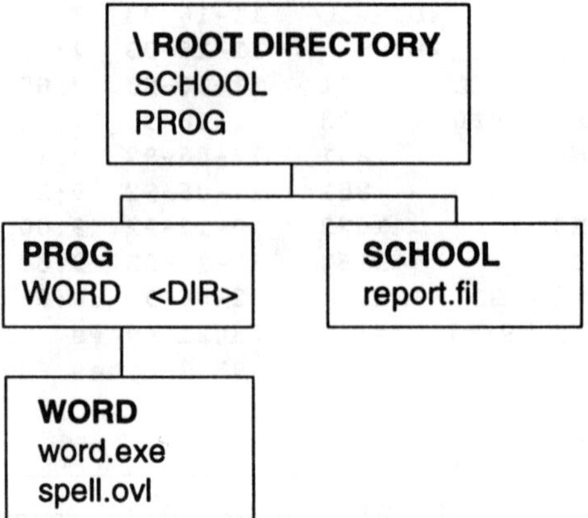

So far, everything is working fine. However, you decide that you want to use the spell checker to look for any typographical errors. You instruct the word processing program to "spell check," but instead of the word processor spell checking your document, you get a message, "File not found." Why? The spell checker is an overlay file. Overlay files are used to keep the maximum amount of memory free. Thus, when you loaded the word processing program, it only placed in memory the part of the program it needed. Now, you want to do another task, so the word processing program must load the spell checker program. Unfortunately, the word processing program cannot find it.

Remember, the word processing program turns to DOS to get what it needs. The word processing program tells DOS to get the overlay file. Because the overlay file does not have the appropriate file extension, DOS tells the word processor that it cannot find the spell checker file. Even though the path is set to `\PROG\WORD`, that only works for the executable file—`WORD.EXE`, not `WORD.OVL`.

To solve these kinds of problems the APPEND command was introduced in DOS 3.3. The APPEND command works much like the PATH command. However, the APPEND command will search for other data files. Although the APPEND command is an external command, once it is loaded, it remains resident in memory until the computer is turned off. In other words, once loaded APPEND becomes an internal command. Hence, you can change your appends during your work session without having to reload the APPEND command. The syntax for DOS 3.3 when first loading APPEND is:

[*d:*][*path*]APPEND *d:path*[;[*d:*]*path*...]
or
[*d:*][*path*]APPEND [/X][/E]

Once APPEND has been loaded, the syntax is:

APPEND *d:path*[;[*d:*]*path*...]
or
APPEND [;]

In later versions of DOS, the syntax is:
APPEND [[*drive:*]*path*[;...]] [/X[:ON ¦ :OFF]] [/PATH:ON ¦ /PATH:OFF] [/E]
APPEND ;

Where the parameters are:

[*drive:*]*path*	Specifies a drive and directory to append.
/X:ON	Applies appended directories to file searches and application execution.
/X:OFF	Applies appended directories only to requests to open files. /X:OFF is the default setting.
/PATH:ON	Applies appended directories to file requests that already specify a path. /PATH:ON is the default setting.
/PATH:OFF	Turns off the effect of /PATH:ON.
/E	Stores a copy of the appended directory list in an environment variable named APPEND. /E may only be used the first time you use APPEND after starting your system.
;	Separates the APPEND paths, or if the semicolon is the only parameter used, cancels all appends.
APPEND	with no parameters displays the appended directory list.

There are some warnings about using APPEND. Data files are always written to the current default subdirectory. Thus, looking at Figure 10.3, if you made **\PROG\WORD** the default subdirectory and used APPEND to append the data subdirectory **SCHOOL** in order to access **REPORT.FIL**, the process would work correctly. However, when you wanted to save the edited **REPORT.FIL** to disk, it would be saved to the default directory—**\PROG\WORD**. Therefore, you would have your original file in **\SCHOOL** and the edited copy in **\PROG\WORD**. See Figure 10.4 on the next page for a graphic example of the differences in using APPEND.

As you can see, it is usually better to be in a data subdirectory and APPEND program files than to be in a program subdirectory and APPEND data files. In addition, there are some application programs that will ignore APPEND or will not work properly when APPEND is invoked. Thus, if an application program begins to act "funny," undo the APPEND to see if that solves the problem. However, in spite of these warnings, APPEND is still a very useful command.

Figure 10.4 Differences in Using APPEND

beginning with **\SCHOOL** as the default subdirectory

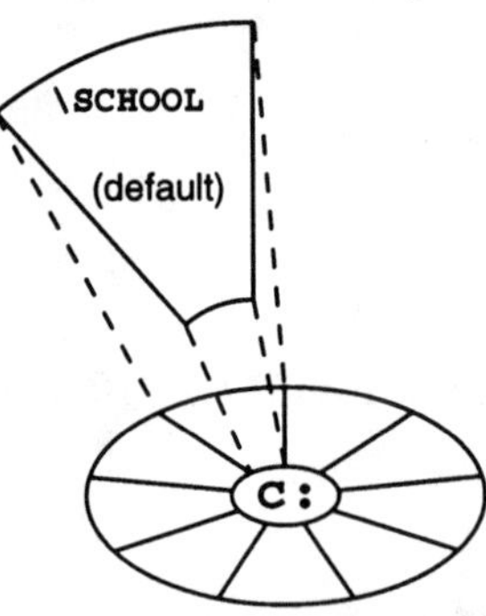

beginning with **\PROG\WORD** as the default subdirectory

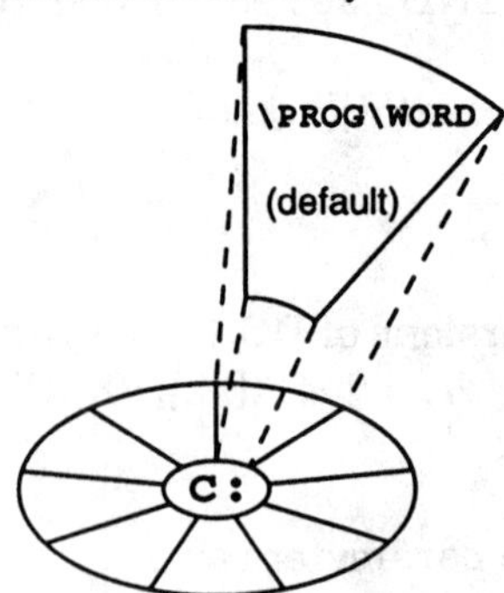

if we append the **\PROG\WORD** subdirectory
C:\SCHOOL>APPEND \PROG\WORD

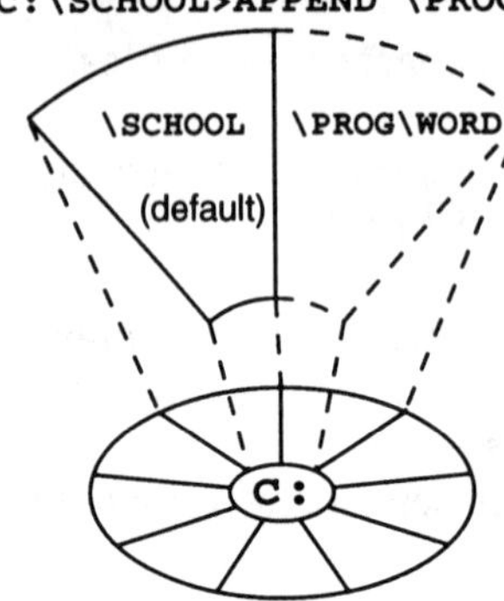

if we append the **\SCHOOL** subdirectory
C:\PROG\WORD>APPEND \SCHOOL

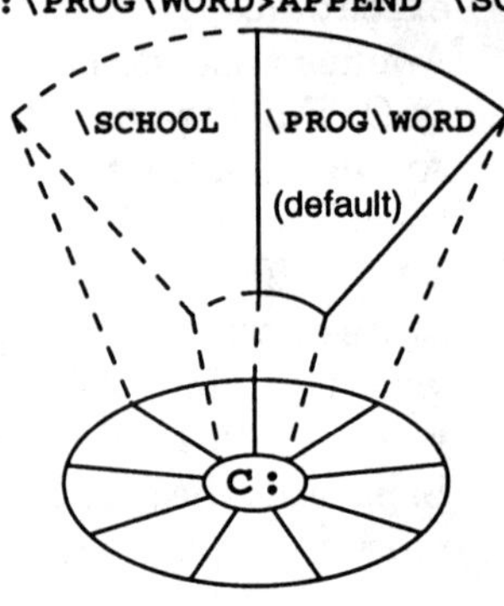

and edit **REPORT.FIL**

C:\SCHOOL>WORD REPORT.FIL

C:\PROG\WORD>WORD REPORT.FIL

DOS retrieves the **WORD** program from **\PROG\WORD**, and retrieves **REPORT.FIL** from **\SCHOOL**

when ready to save, DOS will save **REPORT.FIL** back into the *default* subdirectory, **\SCHOOL**

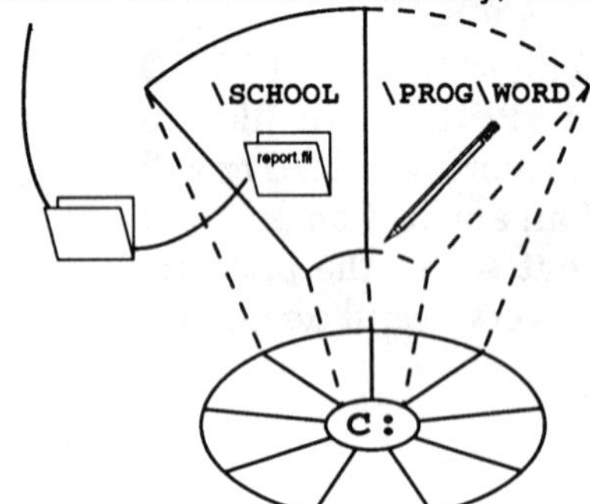

when ready to save, DOS will save **REPORT.FIL** back into the *default* subdirectory, **\PROG\WORD**

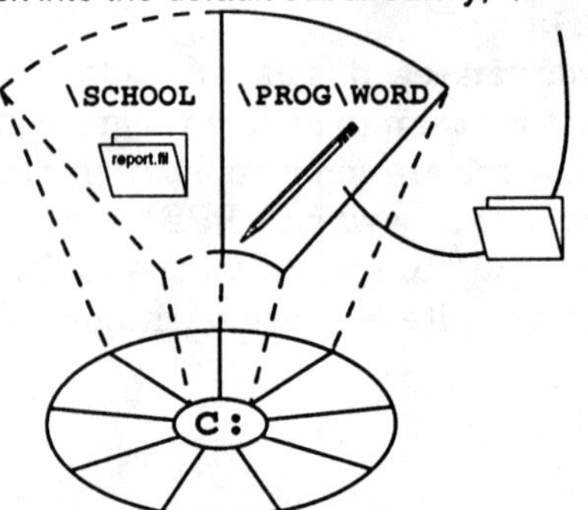

Activity 10.13 Using APPEND and PATH

Note: You have the Organized ACTIVITIES disk in Drive A with the **A:\>** displayed. The default subdirectory is the root of the Organized ACTIVITIES disk and the path is set to **C:\DOS**.

STEP 1: Key in the following:
A:\>**DIR SAMPLE.FIL** <Enter>

STEP 2: Key in the following:
A:\>**DIR \BUSINESS\SAMPLE.FIL** <Enter>

STEP 3: Key in the following:
A:\>**PATH A:\BUSINESS** <Enter>

```
A:\>DIR SAMPLE.FIL

   Volume in drive A is ACTIVITIES
   Volume Serial Number is 1CF4-2D57
   Directory of A:\

File not found

A:\>DIR \BUSINESS\SAMPLE.FIL

   Volume in drive A is ACTIVITIES
   Volume Serial Number is 1CF4-2D57
   Directory of A:\

SAMPLE    FIL      23   11-16-93  7:05a
        1 file(s)         23 bytes
                       63488 bytes free

A:\>PATH A:\BUSINESS

A:\>_
```

WHAT'S HAPPENING? You demonstrated that the file called **SAMPLE.FIL** is in the subdirectory **\BUSINESS** and not in the root directory. You then changed the path to the **BUSINESS** subdirectory.

STEP 4: Key in the following:
A:\>**TYPE SAMPLE.FIL** <Enter>

```
A:\>TYPE SAMPLE.FIL
File not found - SAMPLE.FIL

A:\>_
```

WHAT'S HAPPENING? Even though the path is set to the **BUSINESS** subdirectory, DOS tells you that it cannot find the file **SAMPLE.FIL**. The problem is that PATH is for executable program files. The file called **SAMPLE.FIL** is a data file.

STEP 5: Key in the following:
A:\>**PATH C:\DOS** <Enter>

STEP 6: Key in the following:
A:\>**APPEND /E/X** <Enter>

```
A:\>PATH C:\DOS

A:\>APPEND /E/X

A:\>_
```

WHAT'S HAPPENING? You had to reset the path to **C:\DOS** in order to use the APPEND command. Since this is the first time you are using APPEND, you included the /E and /X parameters. The /E parameter places the APPEND command in the environment. The environment is an area in RAM where information can be placed. You use the /E so that later you will be able to use the SET command to see the append. The /X is a switch that sets an extended search, which allows the APPEND to also search for **.COM**, **.EXE** and **.BAT** files. This process will increase the number of commands that will support APPEND. The /X and /E can *only* be used the first time you invoke APPEND.

STEP 7: Key in the following:
A:\>**APPEND \BUSINESS** <Enter>

STEP 8: Key in the following:
A:\>**TYPE SAMPLE.FIL** <Enter>

```
A:\>APPEND \BUSINESS

A:\>TYPE SAMPLE.FIL
This is a sample.fil

A:\>_
```

WHAT'S HAPPENING? You "appended" a data search path for the **BUSINESS** subdirectory. When you keyed in **TYPE SAMPLE.FIL**, DOS still could not find the file in the root directory of the DATA disk, but DOS did not give up. It checked the APPEND, saw that it also could search the subdirectory **BUSINESS** that you specified, and finally found **SAMPLE.FIL**.

STEP 9: Key in the following:
A:\>**CD BUSINESS** <Enter>

STEP 10: Key in the following:
A:\BUSINESS>**DIR BUDGET.SS** <Enter>

```
A:\>CD BUSINESS

A:\BUSINESS>DIR BUDGET.SS

   Volume in drive A is ACTIVITIES
   Volume Serial Number is 1CF4-2D57
   Directory of A:\BUSINESS

BUDGET    SS    22281   12-06-92 10:01a
        1 file(s)       22281 bytes
                        63488 bytes free

A:\BUSINESS>_
```

WHAT'S HAPPENING? You changed the default subdirectory to **BUSINESS** on the Organized ACTIVITIES disk. You then looked to see if the data file called **BUDGET.SS** was in this subdirectory. The file **BUDGET.SS** is a data file that was generated by the program called **SS.EXE**. However, in order to look at **BUDGET.SS**, you first have to load the SS program.

STEP 11: Key in the following:
A:\BUSINESS>**SS** <Enter>

```
A:\BUSINESS>SS
Bad command or file name

A:\BUSINESS>_
```

WHAT'S HAPPENING? The path is still set to the **\DOS** subdirectory. The search path needs to be set to the **PROG\SS** subdirectory in order to access the **SS.EXE** program.

STEP 12: Key in the following:
A:\BUSINESS>**PATH A:\PROG\SS** <Enter>

STEP 13: Key in the following:
A:\BUSINESS>**SS** <Enter>

```
|  A   |  B   |  C   |  D   |  E   |  F   |  G   |
 1|
 2|
 3|
 4|
 5|
 6|
 7|
 8|
 9|
10|
11|
12|
13|
14|
15|
16|
17|
18|
19|
20|

 %
 F1 - Help     F2 - Erase Line     F3 - Quit
```

WHAT'S HAPPENING? Because you set the search path to the **\PROG\SS** subdirectory, DOS can find the **SS.EXE** program and load it. However, you now want some help, so you are going to press the F1 key.

STEP 14: Press the F1 key.

```
Sorry, file SS.HLP could not be found in current directory
    Press any key to continue
```

WHAT'S HAPPENING? This program, like many other programs, has a help file, but the help file is not a directly executable program. **SS.EXE** needs the **SS.HLP** file, but when **SS.EXE** asked DOS to get the **SS.HLP** file, the only place DOS looked was in the current subdirectory, **BUSINESS**. The path that is set to **\PROG\SS** only looks for a file with an **.EXE**, **.COM** or **.BAT** file extension—executable programs. The PATH command will not look for a file with the **.HLP** extension.

STEP 15: Press <Enter>.

```
|   A   |   B   |   C   |   D   |   E   |   F   |   G   |
  1|
  2|
  3|
  4|
  5|
  6|
  7|
  8|
  9|
 10|
 11|
 12|
 13|
 14|
 15|
 16|
 17|
 18|
 19|
 20|

  %
 F1 - Help      F2 - Erase Line      F3 - Quit
```

WHAT'S HAPPENING? You are back at the main screen. You are going to exit this program and use the APPEND command so that you can access the help file.

STEP 16: Press the F3 key.

```
A:\BUSINESS>_
```

WHAT'S HAPPENING? You are back at the system level.

STEP 17: Key in the following:
A:\BUSINESS>**PATH C:\DOS;A:\PROG\SS** <Enter>

STEP 18: Key in the following:
A:\BUSINESS>**APPEND A:\PROG\SS** <Enter>

```
A:\BUSINESS>PATH C:\DOS;A:\PROG\SS

A:\BUSINESS>APPEND A:\PROG\SS

A:\BUSINESS>_
```

WHAT'S HAPPENING? You set a multiple search path—first to `\DOS` so that you could use the APPEND command and then, separated by a semicolon, to the `\PROG\SS` subdirectory. If DOS does not find the program you are looking for in the default subdirectory, it will look in the subdirectory `\DOS`; then it will look in the subdirectory `\PROG\SS`. You appended the `\PROG\SS` subdirectory so that DOS could look for more than just program files.

STEP 19: Key in the following:
A:\BUSINESS>`ss` <Enter>

```
|   A   |   B   |   C   |   D   |   E   |   F   |   G   |
 1|
 2|
 3|
 4|
 5|
 6|
 7|
 8|
 9|
10|
11|
12|
13|
14|
15|
16|
17|
18|
19|
20|

 %
 F1 - Help      F2 - Erase Line      F3 - Quit
```

WHAT'S HAPPENING? You successfully loaded SS. Let's see if help is now available.

STEP 20: Press the F1 key.

```
Loading help file (SS.HLP), Please wait
```

WHAT'S HAPPENING? This screen appears briefly. However, as you will see, DOS could find the `SS.HLP` file because you appended the `\PROG\SS` subdirectory. Note: Because not all computer configurations are the same, this command will sometimes not work and you might be returned to the DOS prompt. If this does happen to you, don't worry about it and just proceed to step 23.

```
      Help for Example Spreadsheet Program

      Section    Description
        1        Cell definitions (Text and Formulas)
        2        Commands
        3        Glossary

  Press <ESC> to end help.  Press any other key for next page.
```

WHAT'S HAPPENING? Help is indeed available.

STEP 21: Press the <Esc> key.

```
 |    A    |    B    |    C    |    D    |    E    |    F    |    G    |
  1|
  2|
  3|
  4|
  5|
  6|
  7|
  8|
  9|
 10|
 11|
 12|
 13|
 14|
 15|
 16|
 17|
 18|
 19|
 20|

  %
  F1 - Help      F2 - Erase Line      F3 - Quit
```

WHAT'S HAPPENING? You returned to the main screen of the spreadsheet program.

STEP 22: Press the F3 key.

```
A:\BUSINESS>_
```

WHAT'S HAPPENING? You are back at the system level.

STEP 23: Key in the following:

A:\BUSINESS>CD \ <Enter>

```
A:\BUSINESS>CD \

A:\>_
```

WHAT'S HAPPENING? You returned to the root directory of the Organized ACTIVITIES disk.

STEP 24: Key in the following:
A:\>**APPEND ;** <Enter>

```
A:\>APPEND ;

A:\>_
```

WHAT'S HAPPENING? You have undone the APPEND command.

STEP 25: Key in the following:
A:\>**PATH C:\DOS** <Enter>

```
A:\>PATH C:\DOS

A:\>_
```

WHAT'S HAPPENING? You have set the path to C:\DOS, the DOS subdirectory.

10.14 The Pretender Commands, SUBST, ASSIGN and JOIN

Throughout this textbook, we have been accessing actual physical disk drives. When we talked about Drive A, B, or C, we were discussing devices that are physically attached to the computer via cables. These are peripheral hardware. You, the user, perceive these as physical entities. DOS views peripherals in a much more generic way. DOS treats all devices (keyboard, monitor, disk drives, etc.) as logical devices. DOS relies on what are called **device drivers** to handle the input/output to the peripheral hardware in a way that the device can understand. These devices are a part of DOS—the BIOS that users do not see. Since DOS views physical disk drives as logical devices, the user can manipulate disk drives. Thus, in addition to physical disk drives, there are **logical disk drives**. Logical disk drives are not necessarily physically attached to the computer. However, DOS treats a logical drive in the same way it treats a physical drive. DOS can read and write to a logical disk drive, and therefore application programs can read and write to logical drives.

A logical disk drive can provide benefits to the user. You can use an alias for another disk drive or you can use a disk drive letter for a subdirectory name. DOS has three commands to take advantage of logical drives. The SUBST command allows you to treat a subdirectory as a disk drive or, in other words, to "pretend" that a subdirectory is a disk drive. The ASSIGN command reroutes requests for one disk drive to another disk drive or, in other words, "pretends" that one disk drive is another. Last, the JOIN command allows you to make two disk drives one disk drive or, in other words, to "pretend" that two disk drives are really one disk drive. These can be grouped as the **pretender commands**.

There are several reasons for these commands. Some older application programs know *only* about physical Drives A and/or physical Drive B and do not recognize the subdirectories on a hard disk or even the hard disk itself. You need some way to use your hard disk with these older programs. In addition, you can use these commands as shortcuts to avoid having to key in long path names. Sometimes, older programs know about Drives A and B and a hard drive but do not recognize any other drives. Today, it is not unusual to have a computer with two 3 1/2-inch internal floppy drives (Drives A and B) and one hard drive (Drive C). However, some users have one 5 1/4-inch external floppy disk drive (Drive D) for all those older 360 KB disks. If your application program cannot recognize Drive D, you have a real problem. At times, if you have a laptop computer with two 3 1/2-inch floppy drives and no hard drive and you have a very large program, you may want the two disk drives to appear as one disk drive.

Although these pretender commands can assist you in solving these problems, there are pitfalls. For instance, some application programs do what is called **direct read** and **direct write** to a disk drive. In this case, you cannot fool the application program with DOS; you are just out of luck. A direct read and a direct write will bypass DOS. This situation is particularly true with copy-protected programs. Sometimes, you can fool not only DOS but yourself by not remembering which drive is which. If you create logical drives with SUBST or ASSIGN and then try to JOIN them together, not only is this incorrect, but DOS will behave in a confusing and unpredictable manner. Also, you may not use either ASSIGN or JOIN on a network to create logical drives. There are also other commands that cannot be used when SUBST, JOIN, or ASSIGN are in effect, but, in general, these commands are useful.

10.15 The SUBST Command

SUBST is an external command that allows you to substitute a drive letter for a path name. This command can be used to shorten typing in a long path name or with programs that do not recognize a subdirectory but do recognize a disk drive. However, never use SUBST with a network drive. While a substitution is in effect, be very careful when using CD, MD, RD, PATH, APPEND, and LABEL. Furthermore, do not use the commands CHKDSK, FORMAT, DISKCOPY, DISKCOMP, FDISK, PRINT, BACKUP, or RESTORE while a substitution is in effect. The syntax for the SUBST command is:

SUBST [*drive1:* [*drive2:*]*path*]

or to undo a substitution:

SUBST *drive1:* /D

and to see what you have substituted:

SUBST

Activity 10.16 Using SUBST

Note: You have the Organized ACTIVITIES disk in Drive A with the `A:\>` displayed. The path is set to `C:\DOS`.

STEP 1: Key in the following:
A:\>**TYPE \FUN\EQUIP\FOOTBALL.EQP** <Enter>

```
A:\>TYPE \FUN\EQUIP\FOOTBALL.EQP
FOOTBALL EQUIPMENT

Football
Helmet
Mouthpiece
Padding

A:\>_
```

WHAT'S HAPPENING? You displayed the contents of the file called **FOOTBALL.EQP** in the subdirectory called **EQUIP** under the subdirectory called **FUN** in the root directory. Even though you could leave off the first backslash, since the default directory is the root, you still have a lot of keying in to do. If you use the SUBST command, you only need to key in the logical drive letter. In this example, E: is selected. Be sure you use a drive letter that is not on your system.

STEP 2: Key in the following:
A:\>**SUBST E: \FUN\EQUIP** <Enter>

STEP 3: Key in the following:
A:\>**TYPE E:FOOTBALL.EQP** <Enter>

```
A:\>SUBST E: \FUN\EQUIP

A:\>TYPE E:FOOTBALL.EQP
FOOTBALL EQUIPMENT

Football
Helmet
Mouthpiece
Padding

A:\>_
```

WHAT'S HAPPENING? You first set up the substitution. Then, the SUBST command could be executed because the path was set to **C:\DOS**. You said "substitute" the letter E for the path name **\FUN\EQUIP**. Now, every time you want to refer to the subdirectory called **\FUN\EQUIP**, you can just use the letter **E:**, which refers to logical Drive E:. You can use this logical drive just like a physical drive. You can use the DIR command, the COPY command, the DEL command, and any other DOS command you wish.

STEP 4: Key in the following:
A:\>**SUBST** <Enter>

```
A:\>SUBST
E: => A:\FUN\EQUIP

A:\>_
```

WHAT'S HAPPENING? SUBST, when used alone, tells you what substitution you have used. If you are using DOS 4.0 or above, there is an additional command that will indicate the same information—the internal command called TRUENAME. It is what is called an "undocumented" command. An **undocumented command** is one that exists but is not listed in the DOS manual. It is not unusual for software to have undocumented features. The programmers may have decided that the new feature was not quite ready or not quite perfect. It can be used, but there are no guarantees that it will work properly. TRUENAME does exactly what it says. It gives you the actual drive and/or path name of whatever you have substituted, assigned, or joined.

STEP 5: Key in the following:
A:\>**TRUENAME E:** <Enter>

```
A:\>TRUENAME E:

A:\FUN\EQUIP

A:\>_
```

WHAT'S HAPPENING? As you can see, the TRUENAME command did indeed tell us the true name of **E:**. Perhaps in the next version of DOS, TRUENAME will be a documented command.

STEP 6: Key in the following:
A:\>**SUBST E: /D** <Enter>

STEP 7: Key in the following:
A:\>**SUBST** <Enter>

```
A:\>SUBST E: /D

A:\>SUBST

A:\>_
```

WHAT'S HAPPENING? The /D parameter disabled or undid the SUBST command so that logical Drive E no longer refers to the subdirectory **\FUN\EQUIP**. The SUBST that was keyed in with no parameters showed that no substitution was in effect.

10.17 The ASSIGN Command

ASSIGN, an external command, allows you to assign one disk drive to another disk drive. ASSIGN works only with physical disk drives. Thus, both drives must physically exist. Logical drives cannot be assigned. When you assign Drive A to Drive C, every time DOS or an application program wants to access Drive A, it will instead look to Drive C. This command is extremely useful for older programs that do not recognize a hard drive. They want to look only on a floppy disk drive. Thus, by using the command ASSIGN A=C, every time the program looks for a file on Drive A, it will instead look on Drive C. ASSIGN refers to drive letters only and cannot specify a drive and a subdirectory. Do not assign the drive letter of the hard disk to another drive. If possible, use SUBST instead of ASSIGN. If you use both APPEND and ASSIGN, you must use APPEND first, even if the commands will affect different drives. While an assignment is in effect, be very careful using CD, MD, RD, PATH, or APPEND. Do not use the commands FORMAT, DISKCOPY, DISKCOMP, FDISK, FORMAT, PRINT, BACKUP, RESTORE, LABEL, JOIN or SUBST while an assignment is in effect. Furthermore, be very careful with the ASSIGN command. If you assign an application disk to C:, you will not be able to get back to **\DOS**. DOS will not recognize the ASSIGN because it will look only on the application disk. The only way to resolve this problem is to reboot the system. When you reboot the system, all assignments will be canceled. The syntax for the ASSIGN command is:

ASSIGN [*x*[:]=*y*[:][...]]
ASSIGN /STATUS

The parameters are as follows:

x	Specifies the drive letter to reassign and represents the drive that currently gets the I/O requests.
y	Specifies the drive that *x:* will be assigned to and represents the drive letter where you want the I/O requests to be sent.
/STATUS	Displays current drive assignments. This can be abbreviated as /S or /STA. This is new to DOS 5.0.

Key in **ASSIGN** with no parameters to reset all drive letters to the original and undo the assignments.

You may have more than one assignment on the command line, i.e.,
ASSIGN A=C B=C

This command would send all request for information on Drives A or B to Drive C.

Activity 10.18 Using ASSIGN

Note: You have the Organized ACTIVITIES disk in Drive A with the **A:\>** displayed. The path is set to **C:\DOS**. Remember, you may not use ASSIGN on a network. If you are on a network, you should skip this activity.

STEP 1: Key in the following:
A:\>**C:** <Enter>

STEP 2: Key in the following:
C:\>**CD \DOS** <Enter>

```
A:\>C:

C:\>CD \DOS

C:\DOS>_
```

WHAT'S HAPPENING? You changed the default drive and the default subdirectory to **\DOS**.

STEP 3: Key in the following:
C:\DOS>**DIR A:CHKDSK.EXE** <Enter>

```
C:\DOS>DIR A:CHKDSK.EXE

   Volume in drive A is ACTIVITIES
   Volume Serial Number is 1CF4-2D57
   Directory of A:\

File not found

C:\DOS>_
```

WHAT'S HAPPENING? The file called **CHKDSK.EXE** is not on the Organized ACTIVITIES disk. (Note: The file could be called **CHKDSK.COM**.) The next thing we are going to do is assign the drive that holds the ACTIVITIES disk to the drive and subdirectory that holds the DOS system files.

STEP 4: Key in the following:
C:\DOS>**ASSIGN A=C** <Enter>

STEP 5: Key in the following:
C:\DOS>**DIR A:CHKDSK.EXE** <Enter>

```
C:\DOS>ASSIGN A=C

C:\DOS>DIR A:CHKDSK.EXE

   Volume in drive A is HARD DISK
   Volume Serial Number is 16FD-4EA9
   Directory of A:\DOS

CHKDSK    EXE  16200   04-09-91  5:00a
         1 file(s)     16200 bytes
                     3534848 bytes free

C:\DOS>_
```

WHAT'S HAPPENING? The file called **CHKDSK.EXE** is still not on the Organized ACTIVITIES disk. Since you assigned all requests for Drive A to Drive C,

DOS no longer went to the physical disk Drive A but to the assigned disk drive. Now you have no way to access Drive A. Every time DOS sees a request for Drive A, it will only look on Drive C. For those using DOS 4.0 and above, you can use the TRUENAME command here. For those using DOS 5.0, you can use the parameter /STATUS.

STEP 6: Key in the following:
C:\DOS>**TRUENAME A:** <Enter>

STEP 7: Key in the following:
C:\DOS>**ASSIGN /STATUS** <Enter>

```
C:\DOS>TRUENAME A:

C:\DOS

C:\DOS>ASSIGN /STATUS
Original A: set to C:

C:\DOS>_
```

WHAT'S HAPPENING? When you used the TRUENAME command, it reported to you that the real name of Drive A is actually **C:\DOS**. When you used the /STATUS parameter, it told you that "real" Drive A has been set to Drive C. To undo an assignment, you key in ASSIGN with no parameters.

STEP 8: Key in the following:
C:\DOS>**ASSIGN** <Enter>

STEP 9: Key in the following:
C:\DOS>**DIR A:CHKDSK.EXE** <Enter>

STEP 10: Key in the following:
C:\DOS>**ASSIGN /S** <Enter>

```
C:\DOS>ASSIGN

C:\DOS>DIR A:CHKDSK.EXE

   Volume in drive A is ACTIVITIES
   Volume Serial Number is 1CF4-2D57
   Directory of A:\

File not found

C:\DOS>ASSIGN /S

C:\DOS>_
```

WHAT'S HAPPENING? Since you "undid" the assignment, the information on the disks is reported accurately. You are really looking at the Organized ACTIVITIES disk, not a phantom. When you used the /S parameter, DOS just showed the prompt, indicating that there are no assignments.

10.19 The JOIN Command

JOIN, an external command, allows you to make two separate disks appear to be one disk. Thus, a disk will seem to be a subdirectory on another drive. However, unless you have DOS 4.0 or above, JOIN can only be used for root directories and the first level of subdirectories. You cannot go deep into a hierarchical tree. JOIN can be useful when you have software that does not let you work easily between two disk drives. If you have any disk management utilities, such as Norton Utilities, these utilities can work on two disks at once. The same is true of certain DOS utilities. A graphic example is helpful here. Assume that Drive C is structured as follows:

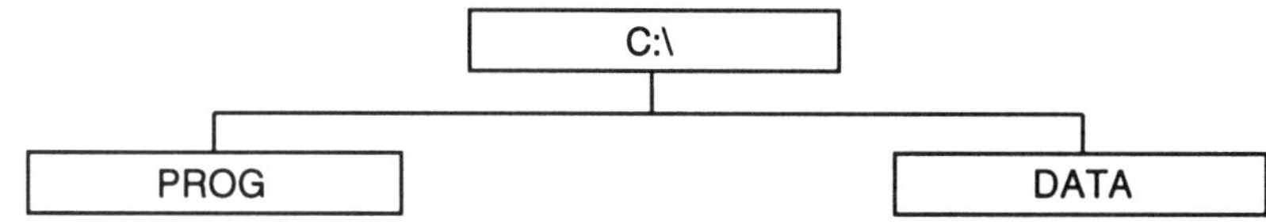

After you join Drive A to Drive C, your structure looks as follows:

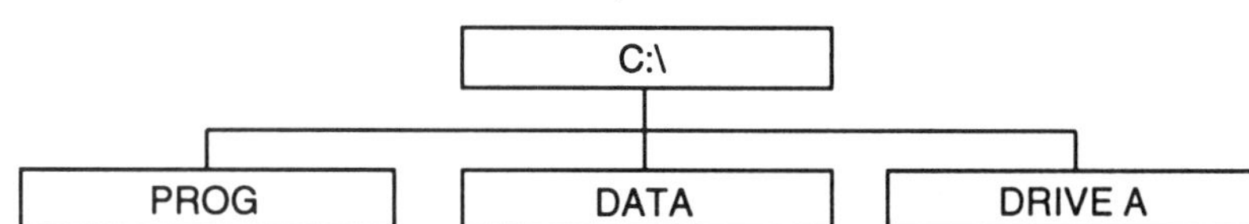

While a JOIN is in effect, be very careful using CD, MD, RD, PATH or APPEND. Do not use the commands ASSIGN, CHKDSK, FORMAT, DISKCOPY, DISKCOMP, FDISK, MIRROR, RECOVER, SYS, PRINT, BACKUP, RESTORE, or LABEL while a JOIN is in effect. Furthermore, if you join an application disk to C:, you will not be able to get back to DOS. DOS will not recognize the JOIN because it will only look on the application disk. The only way to resolve this problem is to reboot the system. When you reboot the system, all joins will be canceled. In order to use the JOIN command, you must first create an empty directory on the disk you intend to use. The syntax of JOIN is:

JOIN [*drive1:* [*drive2:*]*path*]

with the parameters as follows:

drive1:	Specifies a disk drive that will appear as a directory on *drive2*.
drive2:	Specifies a drive to which you want to join *drive1*.
path	Specifies the directory to which you want to join *drive1*. It must be empty and cannot be the root directory.

JOIN	with no parameters will show any joins in effect.
JOIN *drive1:* /D	disables the JOIN.

Activity 10.20 Using JOIN

Note: You have the Organized ACTIVITIES disk in Drive A. The default drive and subdirectory is **C:\DOS**. The path is **C:\DOS**. Remember, you may not use JOIN on a network. If you are on a network, you should skip this activity.

STEP 1: Key in the following:
C:\DOS>**CD ** <Enter>

```
C:\DOS>CD \

C:\>_
```

WHAT'S HAPPENING? You changed the default subdirectory to the root directory of Drive C.

STEP 2: Key in the following:
C:\>**MD \TEST** <Enter>

STEP 3: Key in the following:
C:\>**DIR \TEST** <Enter>

STEP 4: Key in the following:
C:\>**DIR A:\BLUE.JAZ** <Enter>

```
C:\>MD \TEST

C:\>DIR \TEST

   Volume in drive C is HARD DISK
   Volume Serial Number is 16FD-4EA9
   Directory of C:\TEST

.         <DIR>          06-17-93 10:40p
..        <DIR>          06-17-93 10:40p
           2 file(s)            0 bytes
                          3528704 bytes free

C:\>DIR A:BLUE.JAZ

   Volume in drive A is ACTIVITIES
   Volume Serial Number is 1CF4-2D57
   Directory of A:\

BLUE      JAZ       18   10-12-92  9:00p
           1 file(s)           18 bytes
                            63488 bytes free

C:\>_
```

WHAT'S HAPPENING? You proved that you have created an empty directory on Drive C in the root directory. In addition, you saw that the file called **BLUE.JAZ** is on the Organized ACTIVITIES disk. Now, you are going to join the

Organized ACTIVITIES disk to the current default drive so that the contents of the **\TEST** subdirectory will actually be the contents of the Organized ACTIVITIES disk.

STEP 5: Key in the following:
C:\>**JOIN A: C:\TEST** <Enter>

STEP 6: Key in the following:
C:\>**DIR A:\BLUE.JAZ** <Enter>

STEP 7: Key in the following:
C:\>**DIR C:\TEST\BLUE.JAZ** <Enter>

```
C:\>JOIN A: C:\TEST

C:\>DIR A:\BLUE.JAZ
Invalid drive specification

C:\>DIR C:\TEST\BLUE.JAZ

   Volume in drive C is HARD DISK
   Volume Serial Number is 16FD-4EA9
   Directory of C:\TEST

BLUE     JAZ      18   10-12-92  9:00p
        1 file(s)         18 bytes
                     3526656 bytes free

C:\>_
```

WHAT'S HAPPENING? After you joined the Organized ACTIVITIES disk which was in Drive A to Drive C, Drive A no longer exists for DOS. However, when you asked for a display of the file **BLUE.JAZ** that is on the ACTIVITIES disk and prefaced your request with **C:\TEST**, DOS could find it for you because DOS thinks that the disk in Drive A is really the subdirectory called **TEST** in Drive C. You have no way to access Drive A directly because it is *joined* to Drive C. To see what your joined drive is, you can use JOIN with no parameters or you can use the TRUENAME command.

STEP 8: Key in the following:
C:\>**JOIN** <Enter>

STEP 9: Key in the following:
C:\>**TRUENAME C:\TEST** <Enter>

```
C:\>JOIN
A: => C:\TEST

C:\>TRUENAME C:\TEST

A:\

C:\>_
```

WHAT'S HAPPENING? Using JOIN with no parameters displayed what you had joined together. It showed that **C:\TEST** was really Drive A. When you keyed in **TRUENAME C:\TEST**, DOS reported back **A:**. To undo a JOIN assignment, you key in JOIN with the /D parameter.

STEP 10: Key in the following:
C:\>**JOIN A: /D** <Enter>

STEP 11: Key in the following:
C:\>**JOIN** <Enter>

```
C:\>JOIN A: /D

C:\>JOIN

C:\>_
```

WHAT'S HAPPENING? You separated the disk drive from the subdirectory. Now you can access Drive A directly.

STEP 12: Key in the following:
C:\>**DIR C:\TEST** <Enter>

STEP 13: Key in the following:
C:\>**DIR A:\BLUE.JAZ** <Enter>

STEP 14: Key in the following:
C:\>**RD \TEST** <Enter>

```
C:\>DIR C:\TEST

   Volume in drive C is HARD DISK
   Volume Serial Number is 16FD-4EA9
   Directory of C:\TEST

.          <DIR>         06-17-93 10:40p
..         <DIR>         06-17-93 10:40p
           2 file(s)            0 bytes
                         3526656 bytes free

C:\>DIR A:BLUE.JAZ

   Volume in drive A is ACTIVITIES
   Volume Serial Number is 1CF4-2D57
   Directory of A:\

BLUE       JAZ      18   10-12-92  9:00p
           1 file(s)           18 bytes
                           63488 bytes free

C:\>RD \TEST

C:\>_
```

WHAT'S HAPPENING? As you can see, the **TEST** subdirectory is empty of files because you *unjoined* it. You can also access the Organized ACTIVITIES disk directly. Last, you removed the subdirectory **TEST**.

Chapter Summary

1. All disks should be organized. All programs and data should not be in the root directory.
2. The root directory of a hard disk holds only 512 files.
3. Many users inefficiently organize their disk by application program. Too often it becomes a repetition of subdirectory names. Users must remember where they placed their files and must key in long path names. DOS must search every subdirectory. It is difficult to add and delete new application programs and add or delete data files.
4. Most people work by project, and the disk should be organized that way.
5. Some guidelines to organizing a disk:
   a. The root directory is a map to the rest of the disk.
   b. Subdirectories should be shallow and wide.
   c. Plan the organization prior to installing software.
   d. Do not place data files in program subdirectories.
   e. It is better to have small subdirectories with fewer files.
   f. Keep subdirectory names short but descriptive.
   g. Create a separate subdirectory that will contain all software packages.
   h. Create a separate subdirectory for DOS and batch files.
   i. Learn how the application program works.
6. If a disk is not organized, you can organize it by planning it—creating the new organizational scheme, copying files to the new subdirectories, and deleting them from the old subdirectories.
7. The XCOPY command allows you to copy files and the subdirectories beneath them. You may choose:
   a. to be prompted (/P)
   b. to copy by date (/D)
   c. to be instructed to insert another disk (/W)
   d. to copy subdirectories and the files in them (/S)
   e. to create an empty subdirectory (/E)
   f. to verify that sectors are written correctly (/V)
   g. to copy files whose archive bit is set (/M)
   h. to copy only files that have been created or modified since the last backup (/A)
8. The REPLACE command is similar to the COPY and XCOPY command in that it copies files. However, it is much more flexible than COPY. It allows you to keep files updated and to copy selected files as a group. You may choose to:
   a. Update only files that have been changed by using the /U parameter.
   b. Add only new files by using the /A parameter.
   c. Be prompted for a confirmation prior to replacing a file using the /P

parameter.

d. Also replace read-only files by using the /R parameter.
e. Search all subdirectories for replacement files using the /S parameter.
f. Be prompted to insert a disk if you are copying to a floppy disk by using the /W parameter.

9. Utility programs include the ones that come with DOS such as all DOS external commands. Each new release of DOS comes enhanced with utility programs commensurate with advances.
10. There are commercial software packages that add enhancements to DOS. These are either given away, sold or are shareware. Shareware is software that is free on a trial basis. If the user likes it, he or she then pays a fee for it.
11. RNS (rename subdirectory) from Nick's DOS Utilities is an example of a commercial series of DOS utilities.
12. The APPEND command allows DOS to search for other than program files. PATH searches for program files (`.EXE`, `.COM`, and `.BAT`). Many application files have auxiliary data files, often called overlay files, that the PATH command cannot locate. APPEND will look for these files.
13. APPEND is external until loaded for the first time. Thereafter, it is internal. The /X and /E parameters should be included with APPEND the first time it is used. /X will expand APPEND's search capabilities. /E will place the APPEND values in the environment. Even though you APPEND a subdirectory, a data file will always be written back to the default subdirectory. Not all programs will work successfully with APPEND.
14. Physical disk drives are attached to the computer. Logical disk drives are "imaginary" drives that act exactly like real disk drives. DOS looks at peripheral devices as logical devices.
15. The pretender commands are JOIN, ASSIGN and SUBST.
16. The pretender commands help you work with older application programs that do not recognize subdirectories. They let you do things like abbreviate path names.
17. The SUBST command allows you to treat a subdirectory as a disk drive.
18. The ASSIGN command reroutes requests from one disk drive to another.
19. The JOIN command allows you to make two disk drives one disk drive.
20. TRUENAME is an internal, undocumented command that will let you see the actual name of the drive in question.
21. An undocumented command is a command that is provided with software, but is not officially included in the list of commands. There are no guarantees that the undocumented command may work correctly.

Key Terms

Device drivers	Logical disk drives	Shareware
Direct read	Overlay files	Undocumented command
Direct write	Pretender commands	

Discussion Questions

1. Why would you want to organize a hard disk?
2. What are the advantages/disadvantages of organizing a hard disk by application program or by project?
3. Name three criteria that should be used in organizing a hard disk.
4. What should you know about your application programs?
5. In what ways can you organize a hard disk?
6. What are the differences between the COPY command and the XCOPY command?
7. Would you use XCOPY or COPY to copy the parent directory, files and subdirectories from a hard disk to a floppy disk? Why?
8. What are the differences between COPY, XCOPY and REPLACE?
9. What is the syntax of the REPLACE command?
10. When would you use the REPLACE command?
11. Why would you want to own utility programs that do not come with DOS?
12. How do the PATH and APPEND commands differ? When should you use PATH? When should you use APPEND?
13. What are overlay files? How do they affect application programs?
14. What are pretender commands? Why are they used?
15. Describe the purpose of the SUBST command. When should it be used?
16. What is the syntax of the SUBST command?
17. Describe the purpose of the JOIN command. When should it be used?
18. What is the syntax of the JOIN command?
19. Describe the purpose of the ASSIGN command. When should it be used?
20. What is the syntax of the ASSIGN command?
21. What kinds of problems can you have with pretender commands?
22. What is an undocumented command?
23. Give an example of an undocumented command.

Application Assignments

Note 1: Unless otherwise specified, use the Organized ACTIVITIES disk that was created in this chapter. In addition, be sure the prompt is set to `$p$g` and the path is set to `C:\DOS`.

Note 2: These applications are intended to be stand-alone problems. However, if you are missing a subdirectory and/or file, it may have been created in the chapter or in a previous problem. If this is so, simply create the subdirectory and/or copy the appropriate file. Refer to Section 10.4, for the structure of the directories on this Organized ACTIVITIES disk.

Note 3: Because the pretender commands can conflict with one another, be sure to “undo” the SUBST, ASSIGN, APPEND, JOIN or whatever command you used when you finish a problem. If you decide to repeat a problem, also “undo” any command you used.

1. For the following assignment:
   a. Display the current path.

   b. Display the current append.
   c. Print the screen.
2. For the following assignment:
   a. Create a directory called **WILD** under the subdirectory called **DATA**.
   b. Using the XCOPY command, copy the all the files in the root directory that begin with "w" to the subdirectory called **WILD** that you just created.
   c. Print the screen with the command just executed.
   d. Do a directory listing of the **WILD** subdirectory and print the screen.
   e. Delete all the files that begin with "w" in the root directory and print the screen to prove that they are gone.
3. For the following assignment:
   a. Create a directory called **FILES** under the subdirectory called **DATA**.
   b. Using the XCOPY command, copy all the files in the root directory that begin with "f" to the subdirectory called **FILES** under the subdirectory called **DATA** that you just created. Print the screen with the command just executed.
   c. Use the XCOPY command and copy all the files that have a file extension of **.FIL** to the **\DATA\FILES** subdirectory. Print the screen with the executed command.
   d. Delete all the files that begin with "f" in the root directory. Print the screen to prove that they are gone.
   e. Delete all the files that have the file extension **.FIL** in the root directory. Print the screen to prove that they are gone.
4. For the following assignment:
   a. Copy all the files with a **.RED** extension to the **\DATA\FILES** subdirectory created in problem 3. If you do not have such a directory, create it now.
   b. Create a new file in the root directory called **DOWN.RED**. The contents will be:
      ```
      This is a new red file.
      I like the color red.
      ```
   c. Add only the **DOWN.RED** file to the **\DATA\FILES** subdirectory. Do not use the COPY command. Print the screen that shows the command you used.
   d. Change the contents of the **DOWN.RED** file in the root directory to the following:
      ```
      This is the last red file.
      I am not so sure I like the color red.
      ```
   e. Update all the **.RED** files in the **\DATA\FILES** subdirectory. Do not use the COPY or XCOPY command. Print the screen that shows the command you used.
5. For the following assignment:
   a. Rename the subdirectory **DATA** to **STUFF**. Display the command line that you used to make this change and print the screen.
   b. Display only the name of the **STUFF** subdirectory. Print the screen.

c. Rename the **STUFF** subdirectory to **DATA**.
d. Display only the name of the **DATA** subdirectory. Print the screen.

6. For the following assignment:
   a. Make **BUSINESS** the default subdirectory. If you do not have a **BUSINESS** subdirectory, create it now.
   b. Set the path to **C:\DOS** and **A:\PROG\AD**. Display and print the screen that shows the path.
   c. Load the ADDRESS program. Prove that it executes. Use **FRIENDS** as the name of the data file.
   d. Undo the path. Display and print the screen that shows the path.
7. For the following assignment:
   a. Make **BUSINESS** the default subdirectory.
   b. Append both the **FUN** subdirectory and the **DATA** subdirectory. Display and print the screen that shows the append.
   c. Display the contents of the **COLLEGE.TMS** file without using the path to the file. Print the screen.
   d. Display the contents of the **THANK.YOU** file without using the path to the file. Print the screen.
   e. Undo the path. Display and print the screen that shows the path.
   f. Undo the append. Display and print the screen that shows the append.
8. For the following assignment:
   a. Make **BUSINESS** the default subdirectory. If you do not have this subdirectory, create it now.
   b. Set the path to **C:\DOS**.
   c. Indicate the current status of the SUBST command. Print the screen.
   d. Substitute the drive letter E (or whatever drive letter is appropriate on your system) for the subdirectory **\DATA\FILES** created in problem 3. Print the screen with the command line.
   e. Using the drive letter that you substituted, display the contents of **FRANK.FIL**. If the **FRANK.FIL** is not in **\DATA\FILES**, copy it there. Print the screen.
   f. If you are using DOS 4.0 or higher, display the true name of the substituted drive. Print the screen.
   g. Undo the substitution. Print the screen that proves that it is gone.
9. For the following assignment:
   a. Make **FUN** the default subdirectory.
   b. Set the path to the **C:\DOS**.
   c. Indicate the current status of the SUBST command. Print the screen.
   d. Substitute the drive letter E (or whatever drive letter is appropriate on your system) for the subdirectory **\BUSINESS**. Print the screen with the command line.
   e. Using the drive letter that you substituted, display the contents of **NEW.FIL**. If you do not have this file in the **\BUSINESS** subdirectory, copy it there. Print the screen.

f. If you are using DOS 4.0 or higher, display the true name of the substituted drive. Print the screen.
g. Undo the substitution. Print the screen that proves that it is gone.
h. Make the root of the Organized ACTIVITIES disk the default.

10. For the following assignment:
    a. Make **C:\DOS** the default drive and subdirectory. Print the screen that proves that this is so.
    b. Print the screen that proves **FORMAT.COM** is not on the Organized ACTIVITIES disk.
    c. Assign Drive A to Drive C.
    d. Key in **DIR A:FORMAT.COM**. Print the screen.
    e. If you are using DOS 4.0 or higher, display the true name of Drive A. Print the screen.
    f. Undo the ASSIGN. Print the screen that proves that it is gone.
11. For the following assignment:
    a. Make the root directory of C: the default drive and subdirectory.
    b. Create a subdirectory called **SAMPLE** in the root directory of Drive C.
    c. Join the Organized ACTIVITIES disk to the **SAMPLE** subdirectory.
    d. Display the files with the extension **.MOV** in the **SAMPLE** subdirectory. Print the screen.
    e. If you are using DOS 4.0 or higher, display the true name of the **SAMPLE** subdirectory. Print the screen.
    f. Undo the JOIN. Print the screen that proves that it is gone.
    g. Remove the subdirectory **SAMPLE**. Print the screen that proves that it is gone.

Challenge Assignments

12. For the following assignment:
    a. Plan and organize the DATA disk on paper.
    b. Justify your organizational scheme.
    c. If your instructor approves of your plan, take the necessary steps to organize the DATA disk.
13. For the following assignment:
    a. Complete the organization of the Organized ACTIVITIES disk.
    b. Use the TREE command to print the subdirectory structure of this disk.
14. If you have your own computer and hard disk:
    a. Identify the software you own.
    b. Identify how your software works with the data files it generates.
    c. Describe how the hard disk is currently organized.
    d. Plan how your hard disk should be organized on paper.
    e. Justify your organizational scheme.
    f. If your instructor approves of your plan, and you wish, take the necessary steps to organize the hard disk. *Be sure to back up your hard disk prior to organizing it.*

Chapter 11

EDIT, The Text Editor

After completing this chapter you will be able to:

1. Explain the function of a line editor and compare it to a full-screen editor.
2. Explain the reasons for using EDIT instead of a word processor.
3. Create a new file using EDIT.
4. Use EDIT to make corrections in an existing file.
5. Use the EDIT keys or mouse to make corrections to an existing file.
6. Print a file created in EDIT.
7. Exit from EDIT with or without changes to a file.
8. Use the `Search`, `Replace`, `Copy`, and `Move` commands while editing a file.

Chapter Overview

Text files can be created with the COPY command (COPY CON *d:filename*), but there are disadvantages. There is no way either to go back to correct errors or to edit an existing file. To solve these problems a special application program is included with DOS which can be used to create and edit files. This utility program, new to DOS 5.0, is called EDIT, a text editor. In previous versions of DOS, the text editor was EDLIN, and EDLIN still comes with DOS 5.0.

EDIT is a text editor. Editors are used to create new files, to add to, delete, or modify existing files, and to move text around within a file. An editor is different from a word processor. A word processor has features such as wordwrap, formatting, spell-checking, and cursor keys that move up and down the screen for full-screen editing. Word processing programs are software programs that must be purchased, and different people choose different word processors, such as WordPerfect or Word. All word processors take time to load and do not generate pure text files.

There are two types of editors: full-screen editors and line editors. The full-screen editor, although not having the power of a full-fledged word processor, does allow full-screen editing and some other word processing features. A

line editor allows you to edit only one line at a time. EDIT is a full-screen editor, unlike EDLIN, which is a line editor.

Anyone who has DOS 5.0 has EDIT. Since EDIT is a text editor, it is possible to add, delete, or change text. Because EDIT is an application program, it has its own commands and syntax which must be learned. In this chapter you will learn to use the utility program EDIT that comes with DOS 5.0 to create and edit text files, no matter how they were created.

11.0 A Text Editor

DOS contains many utility programs called external commands, such as FORMAT or CHKDSK, which you studied in previous chapters. These commands have been oriented to one task. You keyed in the command name, the program executed one task and brought you back to the system prompt. In addition, you have worked with some application programs such as the spreadsheet program and the address program. EDIT is another utility program supplied with DOS that can be used by anyone working at the system level. Prior to DOS 5.0, EDLIN was the supplied line editor. However, EDIT is an application program. When you load EDIT, it takes you into a separate program with its own commands and syntax. EDIT is a text editor, and that is all it is. It is *not* a full-blown word processor. However, since it is a **full-screen editor**, you can use the cursor keys and/or mouse to move up and down the screen for full-screen editing. You use menus to select commands that work with EDIT. There are three major reasons why you would want to use EDIT instead of a word processor:

1. Word processors vary from user to user. One user could have WordPerfect, another Word for Windows, a third, Ami. Anyone who has DOS 5.0 has EDIT.
2. Word processing programs are large and take time to load. For instance, WordPerfect comes on eleven 5 1/4-inch disks or six 3 1/2-inch disks. The time and effort it takes to load them is just too much for writing a short memo.
3. While most word processing programs use special characters for purposes of underlining or setting margins, EDIT generates pure text files called ASCII files that have none of these special characters. Pure text files in EDIT are **unformatted text files**. The unformatted text feature is extremely important for writing batch files. If you have a version of DOS prior to 5.0, you must use EDLIN. In the next chapters, you will learn how to write batch files and how to write a `CONFIG.SYS` file, both of which must be unformatted ASCII text files. A `CONFIG.SYS` file, among other things, allows you to add devices such as a mouse to your computer system.

11.1 Using EDIT

You have already created text files with the COPY command (COPY CON *d:filename*), but there are disadvantages to this method. You could neither go back to correct any lines that had errors nor could you edit an existing file. With EDIT, you can create and edit documents. Indeed, it will edit any text file, no matter how it was created. You can also use EDIT to create and change files that consist of text data. You use a series of commands that work only with EDIT. DOS commands do not work in EDIT.

When you are in EDIT, you key in lines of data and press <Enter> after each line. EDIT will save a file, if you wish. If you do save a file, you can return to it later to make any necessary changes.

EDIT has its own commands. You will no longer see the DOS prompt, **A>** or **B>** or **C>**. Remember, EDIT is an external program or command. In addition, in order to run EDIT, DOS must have access to **QBASIC.EXE**, which should be in the **DOS** subdirectory. The syntax is:

EDIT [[*drive:*][*path*]*filename*] [/B] [/G] [/H] [/NOHI]
[*drive:*][*path*]*filename* Specifies the file to edit.
/B Allows use of a monochrome monitor with a color graphics card.
/G Provides the fastest update of a CGA screen.
/H Displays the maximum number of lines possible for your hardware.
/NOHI Allows the use of a monitor without high-intensity support.

Activity 11.2 Creating a New File with EDIT and Correcting Errors

---

Note: The **C:\>** is displayed and the DATA disk is in Drive A. The path is set to **C:\DOS**. Remember that if the DOS system files are in a subdirectory with a different name, you will have to substitute your subdirectory name for **\DOS**, i.e., **PATH C:\BIN**. The program EDIT must have access via the path command to the program called **QBASIC.EXE**. It should be in the **DOS** subdirectory. If you have deleted **QBASIC.EXE** to save space on the hard disk, EDIT will not work.

STEP 1: Key in the following:
C:\>**A:** <Enter>

```
C:\>A:

A:\>_
```

WHAT'S HAPPENING? You changed the default drive to the DATA disk.

STEP 2: Key in the following:
A:\>**EDIT** <Enter>

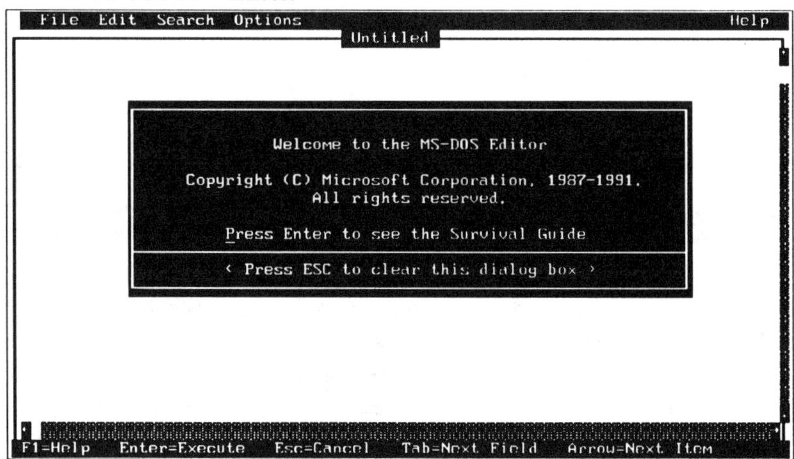

WHAT'S HAPPENING? EDIT is an external program and, therefore, not on the DATA disk. You set the path to where EDIT and QBASIC are located. The DOS prompt is gone and in its place is the opening screen to the EDIT program.

STEP 3: Press <Esc>.

WHAT'S HAPPENING? You have cleared the opening screen and are ready to work. The cursor is blinking on the screen.

STEP 4: Key in the following:
`CLS` <Enter>

WHAT'S HAPPENING? CLS is a DOS internal command that clears the screen, but no action occurred when you pressed <Enter> other than the cursor moving to the next line. DOS commands, internal or external, do not work in EDIT. EDIT has its own set of commands. As far as EDIT is concerned, CLS is simply textual data. EDIT has another feature. You use the arrow keys either on the numeric key pad or on a separate set of keys with arrows on them.

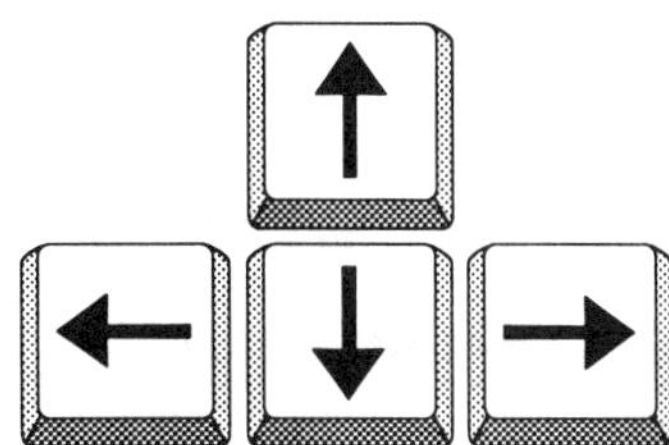

If you have a mouse, you can use the mouse to move around the screen. A mouse is an external device that is attached to the system unit by a cable. The cable is considered the "tail" of the mouse.

The mouse has a ball that rotates. You move the mouse around on a flat surface. That movement on the flat surface correspondingly moves the mouse pointer, a small arrow on the screen. Wherever the mouse pointer is, the cursor is. Some people have a **trackball** instead of a mouse. A trackball is a mouse turned upside down. The trackball device remains stationary and you rotate the ball with your fingers. In the next set of activities, you will be shown how to use either the keys or the mouse, depending on your configuration. The instructions for using the keyboard are in the left-hand column. The instructions for using the mouse are in the right-hand column.

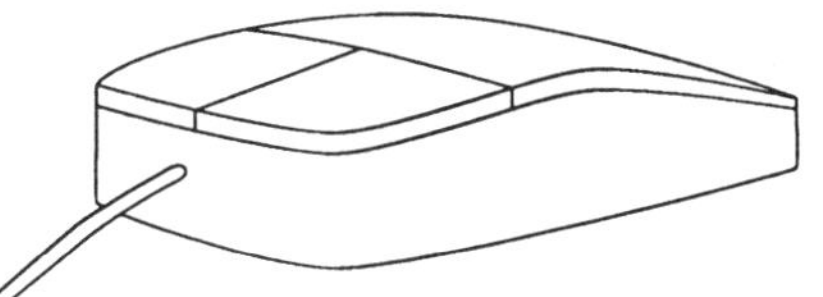

Keyboard	Mouse
STEP 5: Press the <Up arrow> key to move the cursor to the space immediately after the "S" in CLS.	STEP 5: Move the mouse pointer to the space immediately following the letter "S" in CLS.
STEP 6: Holding down the <Shift> key, move the <Left arrow> key until "CLS" is highlighted. Release the <Shift> key.	STEP 6: Holding down the left mouse button, drag the mouse pointer to the left until "CLS" is highlighted. Then release the left mouse button.

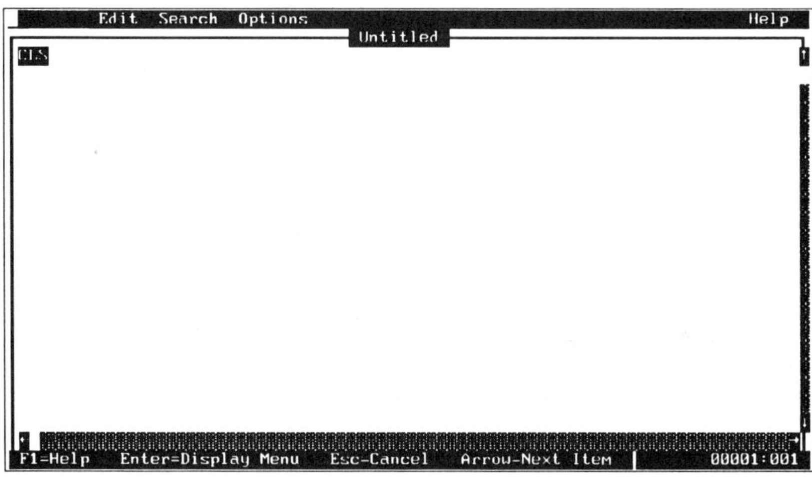

WHAT'S HAPPENING? You selected text to manipulate. Now you can manipulate this text.

STEP 7: Press the <Del> key. STEP 7: Press the <Del> key.

WHAT'S HAPPENING? You deleted the text, "CLS." EDIT has many key commands that allow you to move around the screen. That is why EDIT is called a full-screen editor. When you have a mouse, you can also move around the screen. There is special terminology for mouse users. Moving the mouse around on a flat surface controls the movement of the mouse pointer on the screen. When the instructions say to **click**, that means to hold down and then release the left-mouse button quickly. To **double-click** is to hold down and then release the left mouse button twice quickly. To **drag** means to place the mouse pointer on the desired text, hold down the left mouse button, and move the mouse until you are in the new location. Once you are satisfied with the highlighting or movement of the text, you release the left mouse button.

Moving the cursor means placing the cursor where you next want to do work. With the mouse, moving the cursor is placing the mouse pointer where you want the cursor to be and clicking the left-mouse button once quickly. To move the cursor with keys, you can use the following shortcuts with the directional keys, which include numeric key pad as well as arrow keys.

<Ctrl>+<Left arrow>	Move the cursor one word to the left.
<Ctrl>+<Right arrow>	Move the cursor one word to the right.
<Home>	Moves cursor to the beginning of the line.
<End>	Moves the cursor to the end of the line.
<Ctrl>+<Enter>	Moves the cursor to the beginning of the next line.
<Ctrl>+Q+E	Moves the cursor to the top of the screen.
<Ctrl>+Q+X	Moves the cursor to the bottom of the screen.

You can also use the mouse or keystroke combination to scroll through text. Scrolling allows you to move around the document without changing the location of the cursor. When you use the mouse, you may use the scroll bar.

There is a vertical scroll bar on the right of the screen and a horizontal scroll bar on the bottom of the screen. If you click the up or down arrow in the vertical scroll bar, you will scroll up or down through the document. If you drag the slider box in the scroll bar, or click in the shaded area of the scroll bar, you will also move up or down through the document. The horizontal scroll bar works in the same fashion, but you move left to right instead of up and down.

If you are using the keyboard, you can use the following key combinations.

Keys	Action
<Ctrl>+<Up arrow> or <Ctrl>+W	Scrolls up one line.
<Ctrl>+<Down arrow> or <Ctrl>+Z	Scrolls down one line.
<Page Up>	Scrolls up one screen.
<Page Down>	Scrolls down one screen.
<Ctrl>+<Home> or <Ctrl>+Q+R	Moves the cursor to the beginning of a file.
<Ctrl>+<End> or <Ctrl>+Q+C	Moves the cursor to the end of the file.
<Ctrl>+<Page Up>	Scrolls left one screen.
<Ctrl>+<Page Down>	Scrolls right one screen.

STEP 8: Key in the following lines. Include the errors. You will learn how to correct them later.

STEP 8: Key in the following lines. Include the errors. You will learn how to correct them later.

I am using the editor called EDIT <Enter>
this is the sexxond line of this gile. <Enter>
this is the third line of my gile. <Enter>
Tis is the fourth line of my file. <Enter>

WHAT'S HAPPENING? So far, you have entered data with errors in it. The advantage of using an editor is that you can correct or edit errors in the text.

STEP 9: Press the <Up arrow> key three times to move the cursor to the second line, "this is the sexxond line of my gile." Press the <Home> key to move to the beginning of the line.

STEP 9: Click the mouse pointer on the letter "t" in the second line of text, "this is the sexxond line of my gile."

WHAT'S HAPPENING? You are placing the cursor where you want a change to occur. You want to change the "t" to a "T." In the EDIT program, there are two modes of operation. The default is **insert mode** which will place characters where the cursor is and push the remaining characters to the right. The other mode is **overstrike mode**, also called overtype, which replaces a character and does not push the remaining characters to the right. The two modes are toggled by using the <Ins> key. In insert mode, the cursor is an underscore; in overstrike mode, the cursor is a box.

STEP 10: Press the <Ins> key.

STEP 10: Press the <Ins> key.

STEP 11: Press the <Shift> key, then the letter "T."

STEP 11: Press the <Shift> key then the letter "T."

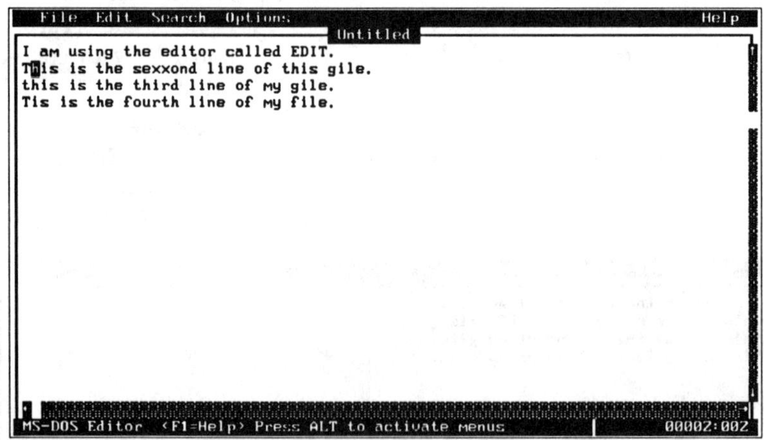

WHAT'S HAPPENING? The "t" was replaced by a "T." Now you are going to move to the word "sexxond" and change it to "second." You are still in the overstrike mode in the second line.

STEP 12: Press <Ctrl>+<Right arrow> key three times. Press the <Right arrow> key until the cursor is under the first "x" in "sexxond."

STEP 12: Click the first "x" in "sexxond."

STEP 13: Press the letter "c."

STEP 13: Press the letter "c."

STEP 14: Press the <Del> key to remove the next "x."

STEP 14: Press the <Del> key to remove the next "x."

WHAT'S HAPPENING? You changed the first "x" in "sexxond" to a "c." You then deleted the second "x" so that the word now reads "second." Next, you want to change the "g" in "gile" in the second line to "f" for "file." You are still in the overstrike mode.

STEP 15: Press the <Ctrl>+<Right arrow> key four times to move to the "g" in "gile."

STEP 15: Click the "g" in "gile."

STEP 16: Press the letter "f."

STEP 16: Press the letter "f."

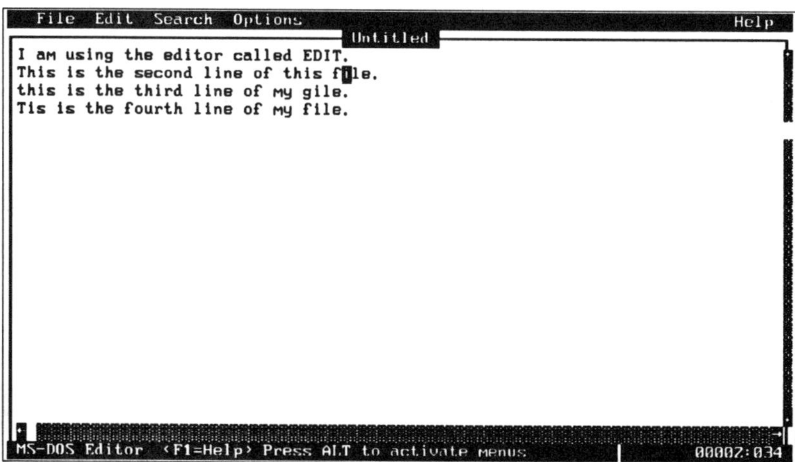

WHAT'S HAPPENING? You changed "gile" to "file" in the second line. Now you want to change the third line "this" to "This."

STEP 17: Press <Ctrl>+<Enter> to move to the beginning of the third line.

STEP 17: Click the first "t" in the third line.

STEP 18: Press the <Shift> key, then the letter "t."

STEP 18: Press the <Shift> key, then the letter "t."

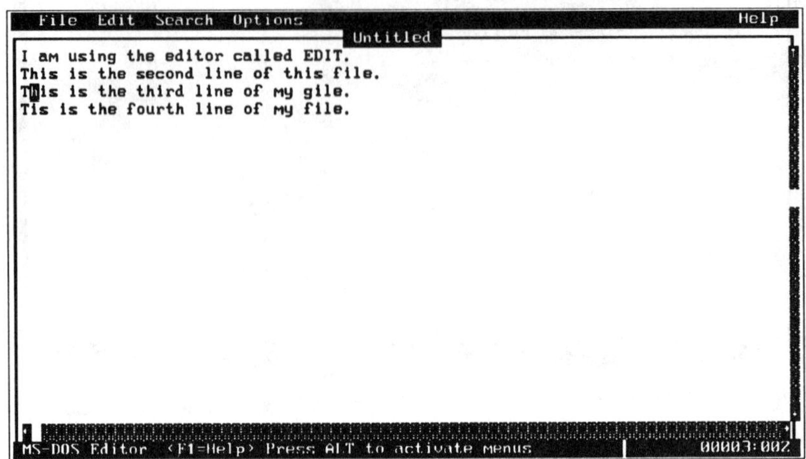

WHAT'S HAPPENING? You changed the "t" in "this" to "T" so that it reads "This." Now you want to move to the "g" in "gile" to change it to "f" for "file" in the third line. Again, you are still in the overstrike mode.

STEP 19: Press the <End> key. Then press the <Left arrow> key five times to position the cursor under "g" in "gile."

STEP 19: Click the "g" in "gile" in the third line.

STEP 20: Press the letter "f."

STEP 20: Press the letter "f."

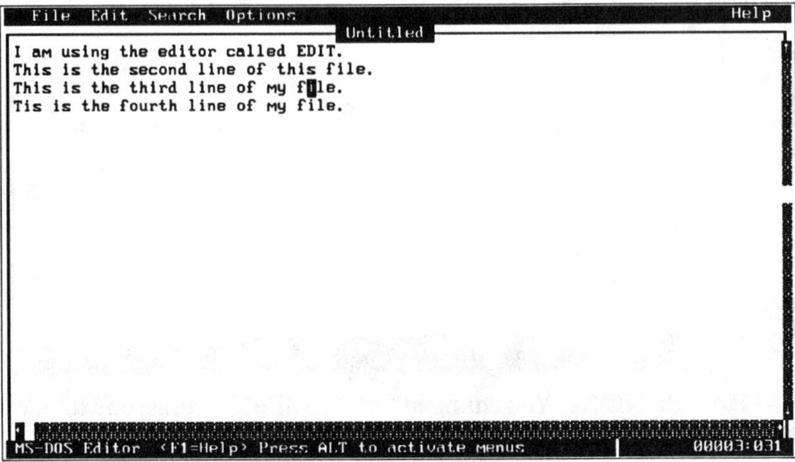

WHAT'S HAPPENING? You corrected the third line of text. Now you want to change the "Tis" in the fourth line to "This." However, you no longer want to be in the overstrike mode. If you were in the overstrike mode, positioned the cursor on "i" in "Tis," and pressed "h," the word would read "Ths." You want to insert the letter "h" and push the letters "i" and "s" to the right. Thus, you need to be in the insert mode. Use the <Ins> key to toggle to the insert mode.

STEP 21: Press <Ctrl>+<Enter> to move to the beginning of the fourth line. Press the <Right arrow> key once to position the cursor under the "i" in "Tis."

STEP 21: Click the "i" in "Tis" on the fourth line.

STEP 22: Press the <Ins> key.

STEP 22: Press the <Ins> key.

STEP 23: Press "h."

STEP 23: Press "h."

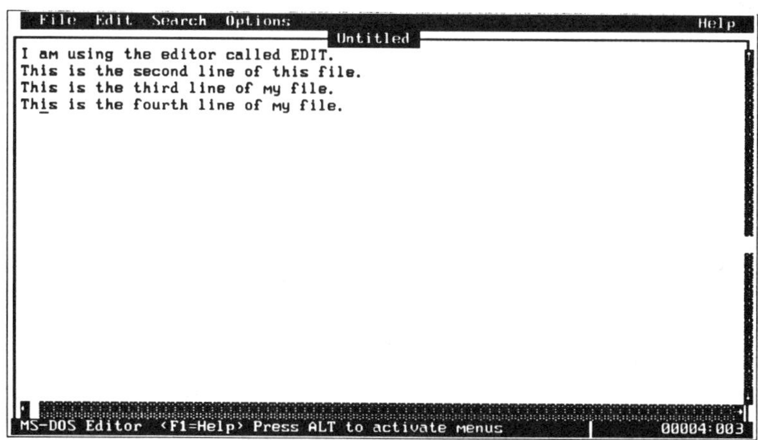

WHAT'S HAPPENING? Because you toggled to the insert mode, the "h" was inserted between the "T" and the "i." Now that you have edited this file, you want to save it.

11.3 Working with Menus and Exiting from a Program

You have been working in a program called EDIT and writing your data lines to memory. So far, nothing has been saved permanently. If you want the file you just created to be stored on the disk, you must exit from the program and return to the prompt or the DOS system level. You must exit properly. If you just turned off your computer without exiting in the proper manner, you would lose what is in memory and, hence, you would lose the file.

All programs have unique ways to end the work session or leave the program. To exit from EDIT you use the menu commands. To perform different operations or tasks in EDIT, you select commands from menus on the **menu bar**. The menu bar is located at the top of the screen with menu selections such as **File** or **Edit**. You "drop-down" the menu and then select the command you wish. You can use either keys or the mouse to select items.

Activity 11.4 Exiting from EDIT

Note: You should still be working with the text from the last activity on the DATA disk.

STEP 1: Press <Alt>+F.

STEP 1: Click the word **File** on the menu bar at the top of the screen.

WHAT'S HAPPENING? You dropped down the **File** menu. If you used keystrokes, you pressed <Alt> and then the first letter of the menu you wanted. If you used the mouse, you clicked the word **File** and dropped down the menu. The **File** menu offers several choices. The word **New** is highlighted. The first item is always highlighted in drop-down menus. Usually, the first item is the one most commonly used. If you wanted to create a new file you would select this command. In this case, however, you want to save the file you just created.

STEP 2: Press the <Down arrow> key until **Save** is highlighted. Press <Enter>.

STEP 2: Click **Save**.

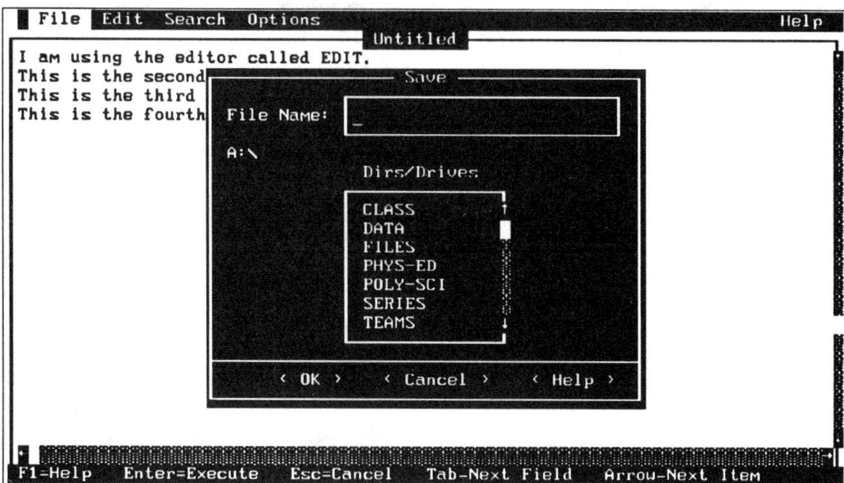

WHAT'S HAPPENING? When you choose some commands from the menu, you are sometimes presented with a **dialog box**. You either key in the requested information or make choices from the options that are presented. In this case, the dialog box is asking you what you wish the file name to be.

STEP 3: Key in the following:
MYLETTER.TXT

STEP 3: Key in the following:
MYLETTER.TXT

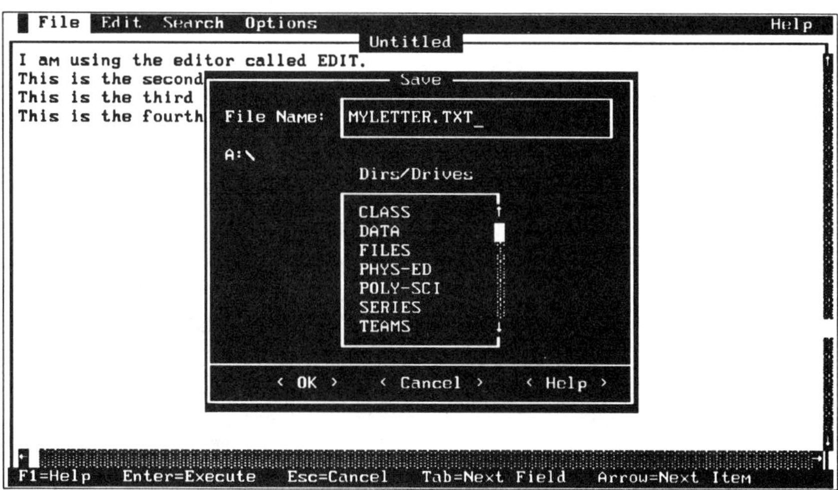

WHAT'S HAPPENING? You selected the name **MYLETTER.TXT** for this file. In order to save it you must press <Enter> or click the OK box.

STEP 4: Press <Enter>.

STEP 4: Click OK.

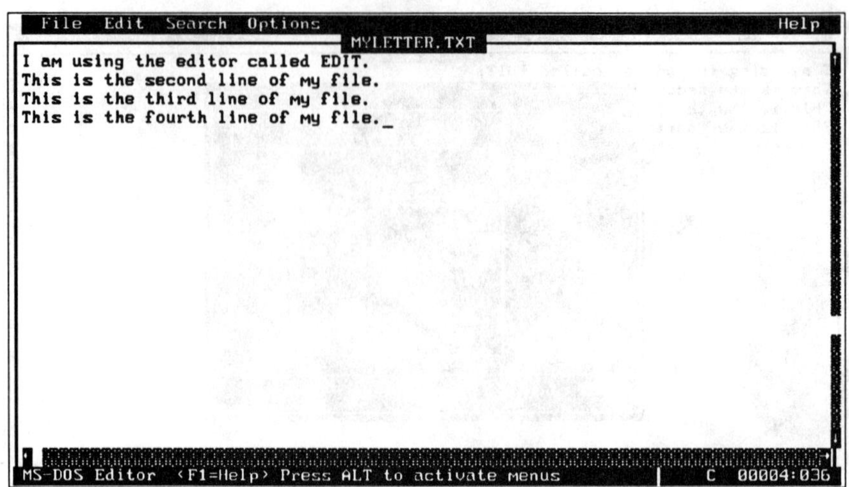

WHAT'S HAPPENING? You saved the file you just created to the DATA disk as **MYLETTER.TXT**. Now you need to exit the EDIT program. This is another choice from the menu.

STEP 5: Press <Alt>+F.	STEP 5: Click **File** on the menu bar.
STEP 6: Press the <Down arrow> until **Exit** is highlighted. Press <Enter>.	STEP 6: Click **Exit** in the **File** menu.

WHAT'S HAPPENING? You have created, edited, and saved the file called **MYLETTER.TXT**. You have now returned to the system level.

11.5 Editing an Existing File

One of the advantages of an editor is that you can always return to a file you created to make changes. When you first saved the file, you named it. Now you have to remember what you named it so that you can retrieve it into the editor. You created the file **MYLETTER.TXT**. With the editor, EDIT, not only can you change existing lines in the file, but you can also add new lines or more data to the file.

Activity 11.6 Editing an Existing EDIT File

Note: The DATA disk is in Drive A with the **A:\>** displayed. Be sure the path is set to **C:\DOS**.

STEP 1: Key in the following: **EDIT MYLETTER.TXT** <Enter>	STEP 1: Key in the following: **EDIT MYLETTER.TXT** <Enter>

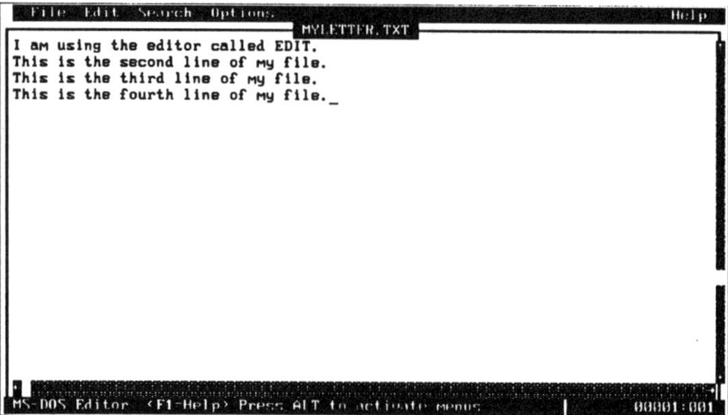

File Edit Search Options
Help
MYLETTER.TXT
I am using the editor called EDIT.
This is the second line of my file.
This is the third line of my file.
This is the fourth line of my file._
MS-DOS Editor <F1=Help> Press ALT to activate menus
00001:001

WHAT'S HAPPENING? You issued the command **`EDIT MYLETTER.TXT`** at the system level prompt so that the file **`MYLETTER.TXT`** is displayed. You have loaded the EDIT program because you see the file you created in the last activity. In addition, you know that this is not a new file because you see the text you keyed in. If you thought that you had asked for an existing file and you got a blank edit screen, the chances are that you probably made a typographical error. If even one character is different, for example **`MILETTER.TXT`** instead of **`MYLETTER.TXT`**, EDIT will think that it is a new file and will treat it as such.

STEP 2: Press <Ctrl>+<End>. Press the <Backspace> key once.

STEP 2: Click the mouse below the "T" on the fifth line.

WHAT'S HAPPENING? You placed the cursor at the end of the file where you wish to add new data. You had an extra blank line so you deleted it with the <Backspace> key. Since the default for EDIT is insert, you can start adding data.

STEP 3: Key in the following:

`This is my fifth line.` <Enter>
`This is my sixth line.` <Enter>
`This is my seventh line.` <Enter>

STEP 3: Key in the following:

`This is my fifth line.` <Enter>
`This is my sixth line.` <Enter>
`This is my seventh line.` <Enter>

File Edit Search Options
Help
MYLETTER.TXT
I am using the editor called EDIT.
This is the second line of my file.
This is the third line of my file.
This is the fourth line of my file.
This is my fifth line.
This is my sixth line.
This is my seventh line.
_
MS-DOS Editor <F1=Help> Press ALT to activate menus
00008:001

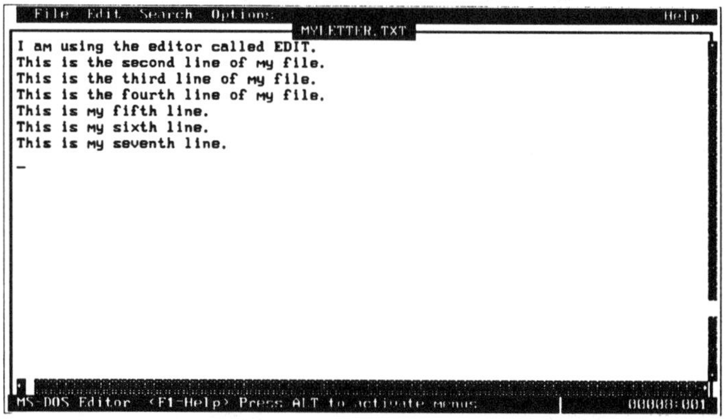

WHAT'S HAPPENING? The original four lines of text are still there and new text lines 5, 6, and 7 have been added. You are not limited to adding new lines of text at the end of a file. You can insert them any place you choose.

STEP 4:	Press <Ctrl>+<Home>. Press the <Down arrow> key once.	STEP 4:	Click the mouse directly on the second line, under the word "I" in the first line.

WHAT'S HAPPENING? You moved the cursor to where you wanted the new data. Now you can key in your new data. Remember, you are in insert mode so everything will be pushed to the right.

STEP 5:	Key in the following: `THIS IS MY NEW LINE 2.`	STEP 5:	Key in the following: `THIS IS MY NEW LINE 2.`

```
 File  Edit  Search  Options                                   Help
                          MYLETTER.TXT
I am using the editor called EDIT.
THIS IS MY NEW LINE 2.This is the second line of my file.
This is the third line of my file.
This is the fourth line of my file.
This is my fifth line.
This is my sixth line.
This is my seventh line.

MS-DOS Editor  <F1=Help> Press ALT to activate menus    00002:023
```

WHAT'S HAPPENING? Because you were in insert mode, the data that was already on line 2 got pushed to the right as you keyed in the new data. You added a new line of text to the file. Now you can press <Enter> to move to the next line.

STEP 6:	Press <Enter>.	STEP 6:	Press <Enter>.

```
 File  Edit  Search  Options                                   Help
                          MYLETTER.TXT
I am using the editor called EDIT.
THIS IS MY NEW LINE 2.
This is the second line of my file.
This is the third line of my file.
This is the fourth line of my file.
This is my fifth line.
This is my sixth line.
This is my seventh line.

MS-DOS Editor  <F1=Help> Press ALT to activate menus    00003:001
```

WHAT'S HAPPENING? You added a new line to the file under line 1. EDIT lets you add a line wherever you like.

Sometimes, users wish to add a blank line, but this can cause confusion. A "blank" line is really not blank. When you want a blank line using a typewriter, you press the carriage return and the paper rolls up one line. The same thing is true for a line editor or word processor. Carriage return is a special signal indicating that the line is over, so move down one line (CR-LF or carriage return, line feed). Thus, to get a blank line, you press the <Enter> key.

STEP 7: Press <Enter>.

STEP 7: Press <Enter>.

```
 File  Edit  Search  Options                                      Help
                              MYLETTER.TXT
I am using the editor called EDIT.
THIS IS MY NEW LINE 2.

This is the second line of my file.
This is the third line of my file.
This is the fourth line of my file.
This is my fifth line.
This is my sixth line.
This is my seventh line.

MS-DOS Editor  <F1=Help> Press ALT to activate menus         00004:001
```

WHAT'S HAPPENING? By pressing the <Enter> key, you marked this line with a "carriage return, line feed." A "blank" line was inserted on line 3. It is not really blank; it has a carriage return, line feed signal for that line. Whenever you wish to stop working on the activities you want to remember to save the file at the last change. Now that you have edited an existing file, the editor will ask you some additional questions.

STEP 8: Press <Alt>+F.

STEP 8: Click `File` on the menu bar.

STEP 9: Press the <Down arrow> key until `Save` is highlighted. Press <Enter>.

STEP 9: Click `Save`.

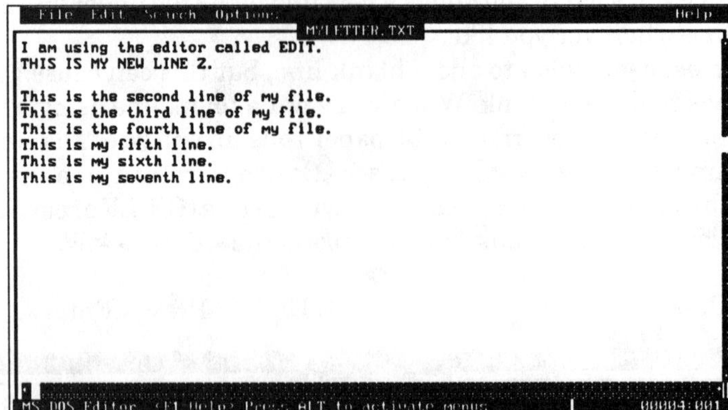

WHAT'S HAPPENING? Nothing apparently happened, but your file was saved with the corrections that you made. Thus, if you want to stop working now, you may because you have saved the file. If you want to leave the program, you pull down the **`File`** menu and select **`Exit`** as you did previously.

11.7 Deleting Text in a File

You can delete words, lines, or any amount of text using EDIT. You select the text and then press the <Del> key or select **`Clear`** from the **`Edit`** menu.

Activity 11.8 Deleting Lines

Note: You should still be in the **`EDIT MYLETTER.TXT`** on the DATA disk. You should see the lines of data. If you see the **`A:\>`** or **`C:\>`**, you should key in **`EDIT MYLETTER.TXT`** at the system prompt.

STEP 1:	Place the cursor at the beginning of line 3, the "blank" line.	STEP 1:	Click at the beginning of line 3, the "blank" line.
STEP 2:	Press the <Del> key.	STEP 2:	Press the <Del> key.

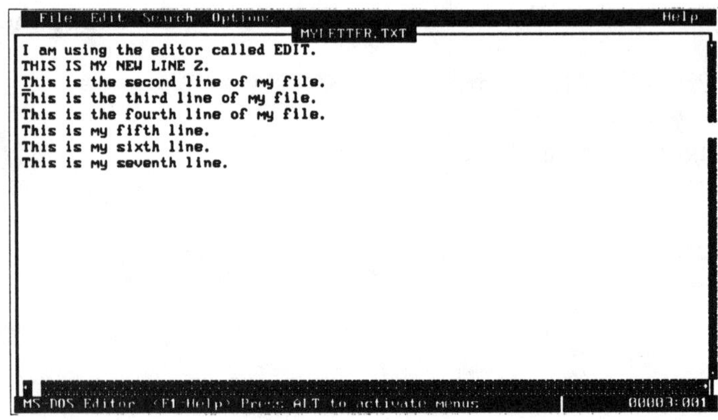

WHAT'S HAPPENING? You removed the signal for the carriage return and the third line was deleted. However, if you want to eliminate a larger block of text, you can do so by selecting the text and choosing `Clear` from the `Edit` menu. You are going to delete the text line, "THIS IS MY NEW LINE 2."

STEP 3: Press the <Up arrow> one time.

STEP 3: Click the first "T" on the second line.

STEP 4: Press <Ctrl> + <Shift> + <Right arrow> key six times until the entire line is highlighted.

STEP 4: Point to the first character on the line. Drag the mouse while holding down the left mouse button until the entire line is highlighted. Release the left mouse button.

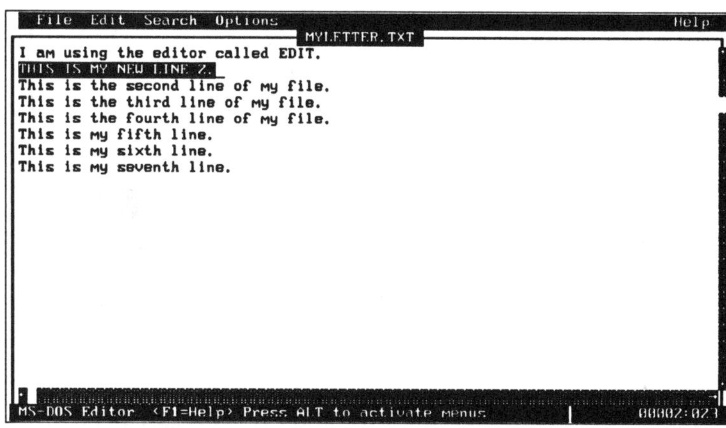

WHAT'S HAPPENING? You selected the text you wish to manipulate. In this case you want to delete it.

STEP 5: Press <Alt>+E.

STEP 5: Click `Edit` on the menu bar.

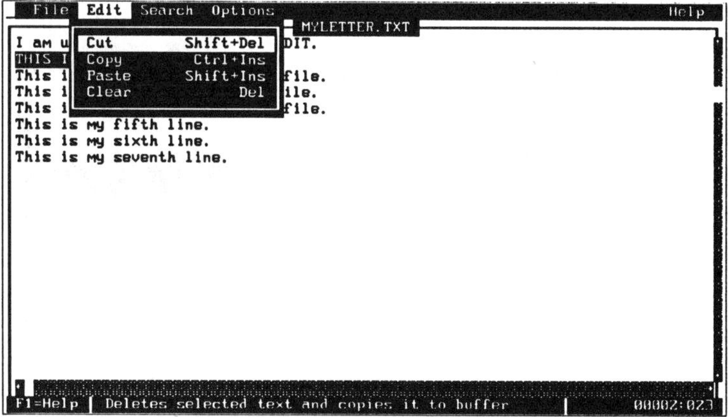

WHAT'S HAPPENING? You dropped down the `Edit` menu. You have several choices—`Cut`, `Copy`, `Paste`, and `Clear`. The drop-down menu also gives the keystrokes that can accomplish the task. In this case, you are going to use `Clear` to delete line 2.

STEP 6: Press the <Down arrow> key until `Clear` is highlighted. Press <Enter>.	STEP 6: Click `Clear`.

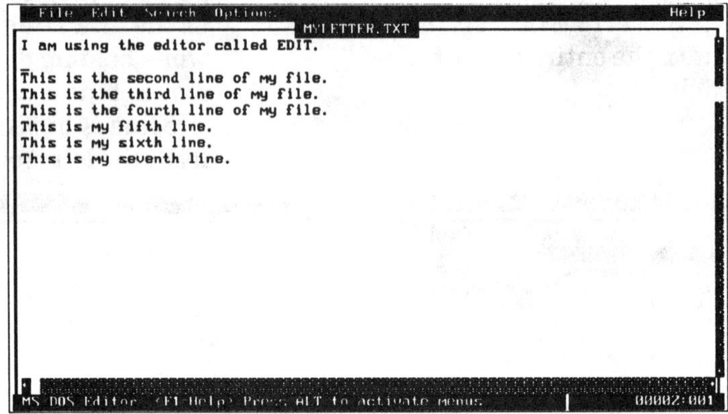

WHAT'S HAPPENING? The second line was indeed cleared, but a blank line space remains. You cleared the line of data, but you did not delete the line. You are next going to eliminate the blank line as well as the last three lines.

STEP 7: Press the <Del> key.	STEP 7: Press the <Del> key.
STEP 8: Press <Ctrl>+<Enter> three times.	STEP 8: Click the beginning of the line "This is my fifth line."
STEP 9: Holding down the <Shift> key, press <Ctrl>+<Enter> three times until the last three lines are highlighted.	STEP 9: Holding down the left mouse button, drag the cursor until the last three lines are highlighted.

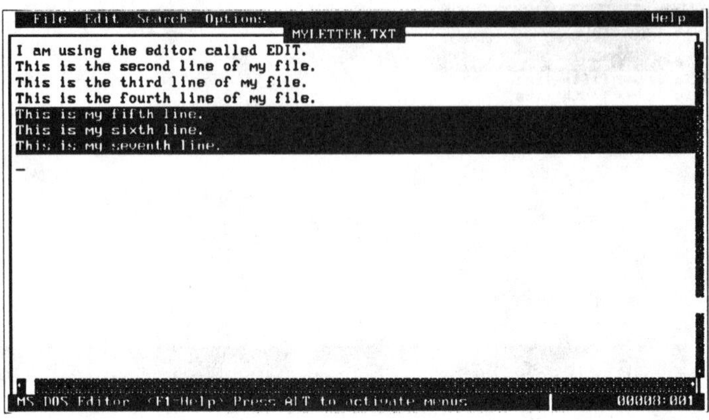

WHAT'S HAPPENING? You highlighted the lines you wish to delete.

STEP 10: Press the <Del> key. STEP 10: Press the <Del> key.

File Edit Search Options
Help
MYLETTER.TXT
I am using the editor called EDIT.
This is the second line of my file.
This is the third line of my file.
This is the fourth line of my file.
MS-DOS Editor <F1=Help> Press ALT to activate menus
00005:001

WHAT'S HAPPENING? You deleted lines 5, 6, and 7 completely. First you had to select the lines prior to manipulating them. In this case, manipulating the lines was deleting them.

STEP 11: Press <Alt>+F. STEP 11: Click **File** on the menu bar.

STEP 12: Select **Save**. STEP 12: Click **Save**.

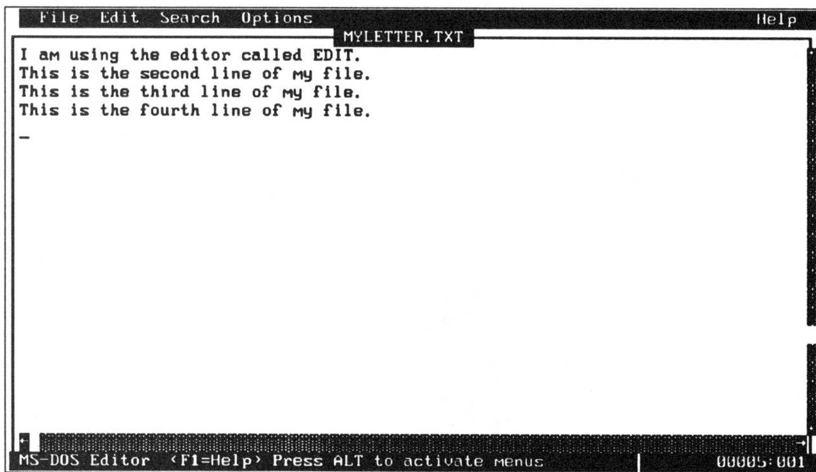
File Edit Search Options
Help
MYLETTER.TXT
I am using the editor called EDIT.
This is the second line of my file.
This is the third line of my file.
This is the fourth line of my file.
MS-DOS Editor <F1=Help> Press ALT to activate menus
00005:001

WHAT'S HAPPENING? You saved the file **MYLETTER.TXT** with the corrections you made.

11.9 Printing a File with EDIT

After you create and edit a file, you typically want a printed copy. EDIT has a print command that allows you to print the file from within the program. In addition, since this is an ASCII file, or an unformatted text file, you can also print the file from the DOS command line using the COPY *file* PRN command.

Activity 11.10 Printing the File

Note: You should still be in **EDIT MYLETTER.TXT** on the DATA disk.

STEP 1: Press <Alt>+F.

STEP 1: Click **File** on the menu bar.

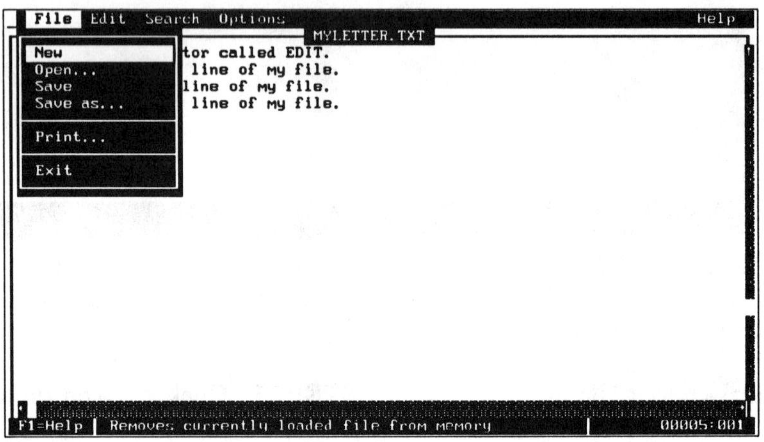

WHAT'S HAPPENING? You selected the **File** menu. Now you are going to select the "Print" option.

STEP 2: Press the <Down arrow> key until **Print** is highlighted. Press <Enter>.

STEP 2: Click **Print**.

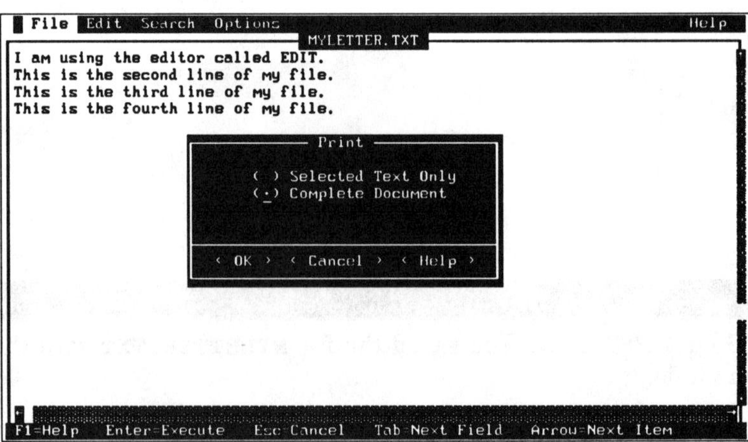

WHAT'S HAPPENING? You are presented with the `Print` dialog box that offers two choices: Print selected text only or print the complete document. The `Complete Document`, the default, is already chosen for you. In this case, you are going to print the entire document. Be sure the printer is turned on.

STEP 3: Press <Enter>.	STEP 3: Click `OK`.

WHAT'S HAPPENING? The file should be printing. The printed copy has no formatting features. You cannot set margin spacing or eject the page in EDIT. The copy looks as follows:

Note: Remember laser printer users must take additional steps.

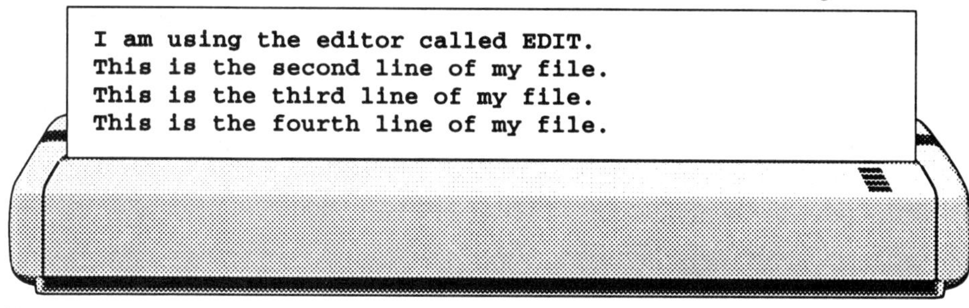
I am using the editor called EDIT.
This is the second line of my file.
This is the third line of my file.
This is the fourth line of my file.

STEP 4: Press <Alt>+F.	STEP 4: Click `File`.
STEP 5: Select `Exit`.	STEP 5: Click `Exit`.

```
A:\>_
```

WHAT'S HAPPENING? You returned to the DOS prompt. Since this is an unformatted text file, you can also print it from the system prompt. Be sure the printer is turned on. To print the file, use the COPY command.

STEP 6: Key in the following: `COPY MYLETTER.TXT PRN` <Enter>	STEP 6: Key in the following: `COPY MYLETTER.TXT PRN` <Enter>

WHAT'S HAPPENING? The file should be printing. The printed copy looks as follows:

Note: Remember laser printer users must take additional steps.

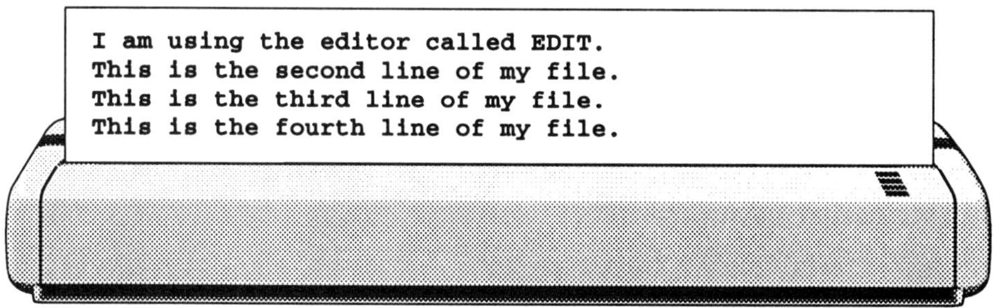
I am using the editor called EDIT.
This is the second line of my file.
This is the third line of my file.
This is the fourth line of my file.

11.11 Editing Text Files

So far EDIT has been used to create files and edit them. You can edit any text file with EDIT; if the file was created with a COPY CON *filename* or with a COPY *filename.one filename.two*, you can still use EDIT to edit the file. The following activity will demonstrate that any text file can be edited with EDIT. Remember, however, you use EDIT with ASCII or unformatted text files. For instance, if you created a data file with a word processing program (like WordPerfect 5.1) the data file is not an ASCII file and can only be edited by the word processing program, because the data file has special symbols that only the word processing program can interpret.

Activity 11.12 Editing Existing Files with EDIT

Note 1: The DATA disk is in Drive A with the **A:\>** displayed.

Note 2: If the files that are needed are not on your DATA disk, you can copy them from **C:\JUNK** or a subdirectory under **\JUNK** to the DATA disk.

STEP 1: Key in the following:
A:\>**DIR *.TMP** <Enter>

```
A:\>DIR *.TMP

  Volume in drive A is DATA DISK
  Volume Serial Number is 3839-0EC8
  Directory of A:\

JAN      TMP      72   11-23-92  7:04a
FEB      TMP      74   11-23-92  7:05a
MAR      TMP      70   11-23-92  7:06a
APR      TMP      71   11-23-92  7:07a
        4 file(s)        287 bytes
                      189440 bytes free

A:\>_
```

WHAT'S HAPPENING? These files were not created with EDIT, but you can edit them with EDIT.

STEP 2: Key in the following:
A:\>**EDIT FEB.TMP** <Enter>

WHAT'S HAPPENING? EDIT allows you to edit any text file no matter how it was created. You know this is an existing file because the data appeared on the screen.

STEP 3: Press <Ctrl>+<End>.

STEP 3: Click the beginning of the fourth line.

STEP 4: Key in the following:
`I am adding a new line to` <Enter>
`this file to change or` <Enter>
`edit it.` <Enter>

STEP 4: Key in the following:
`I am adding a new line to` <Enter>
`this file to change or` <Enter>
`edit it.` <Enter>

WHAT'S HAPPENING? You have added some text to the **`FEB.TMP`** file.

STEP 5: Press <Alt>+F.

STEP 5: Click **`File`** on the menu bar.

STEP 6: Use the <Down arrow> key to highlight **Save As**. Press <Enter>.	STEP 6: Click **Save As**.

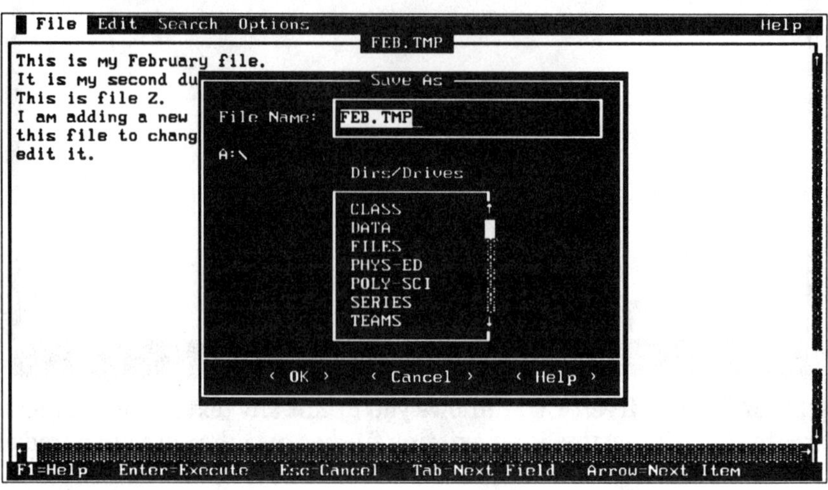

WHAT'S HAPPENING? You have a file called **FEB.TMP**. When you select **Save As**, you are given the opportunity to save the file under a different name and keep the original file as it is.

STEP 7: Key in the following: **FEB.BAK**	STEP 7: Key in the following: **FEB.BAK**

WHAT'S HAPPENING? You gave the edited file a new name, **FEB.BAK**.

STEP 8: Press <Enter>.	STEP 8: Click **OK**.

WHAT'S HAPPENING? You are going to add more data to this file.

STEP 9: You should be at the bottom of the file. If not, press the <Down arrow> key until the cursor is on the first character immediately below "edit" in the sixth line.

STEP 9: You should be at the bottom of the file. If you are not, click the first character immediately below "edit" in the sixth line.

STEP 10: Key in the following:
This is my latest change. <Enter>
That's all folks! <Enter>

STEP 10: Key in the following:
This is my latest change. <Enter>
That's all folks! <Enter>

```
 File  Edit  Search  Options                                  Help
                            FEB.BAK
This is my February file.
It is my second dummy file.
This is file 2.
I am adding a new line to
this file to change or
edit it.
This is my latest change.
That's all folks!
_

MS-DOS Editor  <F1=Help> Press ALT to activate menus    00009:001
```

WHAT'S HAPPENING? You added data and are at the end of the file. Now, you are going to save this file under another name and end the editing session.

STEP 11: Press <Alt>+F.

STEP 11: Click **File**.

STEP 12: Use the <Down arrow> to highlight **Save As**. Press <Enter>.	STEP 12: Click **Save As**.
STEP 13: At **File Name**, key in the following: **FEB.TMP**	STEP 13: At **File Name**, key in the following: **FEB.TMP**

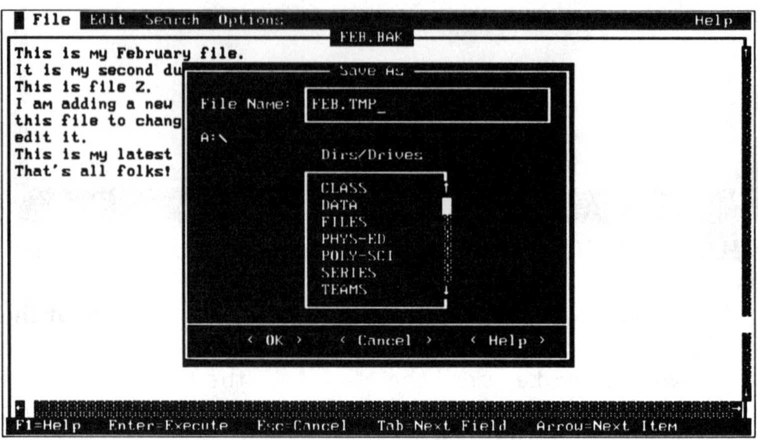

WHAT'S HAPPENING? You pulled down the **Save As** dialog box so that you can save the file. You will have two files, one called **FEB.BAK** and one called **FEB.TMP**.

STEP 14: Press <Enter>.	STEP 14: Click **OK**.

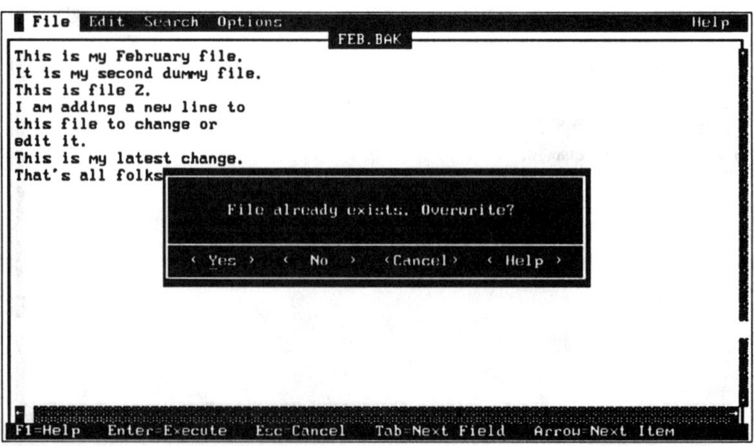

WHAT'S HAPPENING? You see another dialog box. EDIT is telling you that you already have a file by this name. If you save it under **FEB.TMP**, the original file with four lines of data will be overwritten by the new file with eight lines of data.

STEP 15: Press <Enter>.

STEP 15: Click **Yes**.

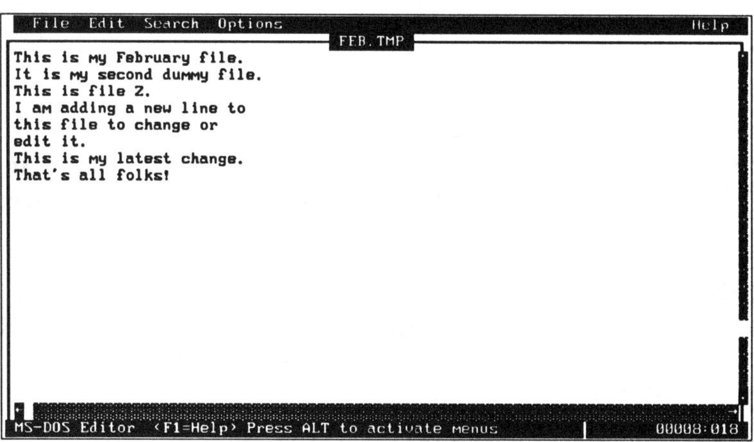

WHAT'S HAPPENING? You saved the file. Notice how the file name under the menu bar has changed from **FEB.BAK** to **FEB.TMP**.

STEP 16: Press <Alt>+F.

STEP 16: Click **File**.

STEP 17: Press X.

STEP 17: Click **Exit**.

```
A:\>_
```

WHAT'S HAPPENING? You returned to the DOS prompt. When you are using keystrokes, you also have a shortcut which you used in this example. "X" was highlighted in **Exit**, indicating that to exit, you could simply press the letter X.

STEP 18: Key in the following:
A:\>**TYPE FEB.TMP** <Enter>

STEP 19: Key in the following:
A:\>**TYPE FEB.BAK** <Enter>

```
A:\>TYPE FEB.TMP
This is my February file.
It is my second dummy file.
This is file 2.
I am adding a new line to
this file to change or
edit it.
This is my latest change.
That's all folks!

A:\>TYPE FEB.BAK
This is my February file.
It is my second dummy file.
```

```
This is file 2.
I am adding a new line to
this file to change or
edit it.

A:\>_
```

WHAT'S HAPPENING? You now have two files, one called **FEB.TMP** and one called **FEB.BAK**. You could retain two versions of the file because when you saved the file, you used **Save As** which does not overwrite an existing file.

11.13 Leaving EDIT without Making Changes

You have been exiting from EDIT with **Exit** after you saved the file. However, if you wish, you can cancel your changes and retain the uncorrected file without having to use **Save As**.

Activity 11.14 Quitting a File in EDIT

Note: You have the DATA disk in Drive A with the **A:\>** displayed

STEP 1: Key in the following:
A:\>**EDIT FEB.TMP** <Enter>

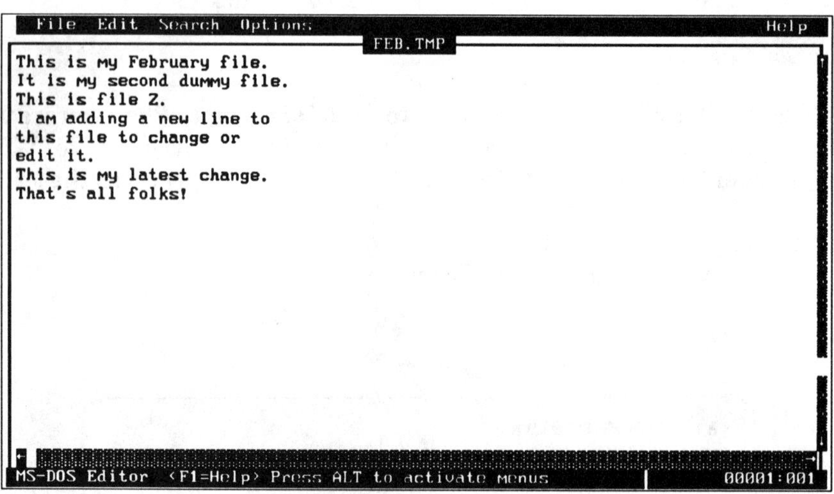

WHAT'S HAPPENING? You loaded the file **FEB.TMP** so that it can be edited.

STEP 2: Press <Ctrl>+<Shift>+<End>.

STEP 2: Holding down the left mouse button, drag the mouse until all the lines of text are highlighted.

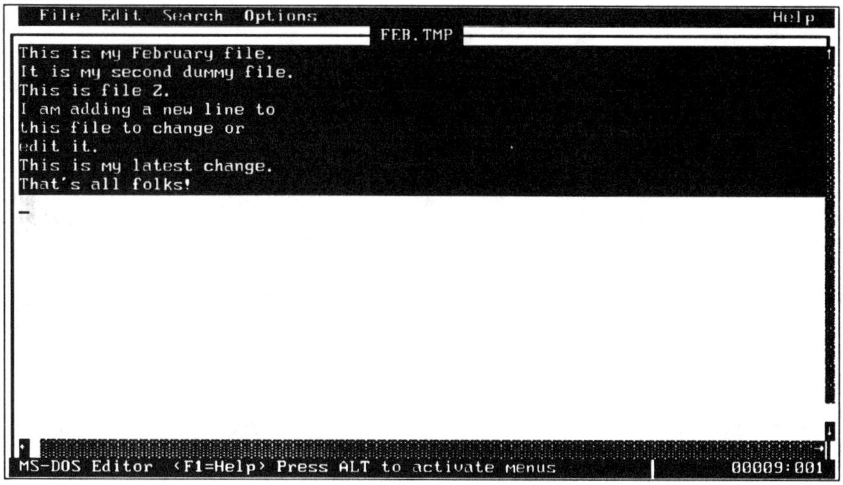

File Edit Search Options Help
FEB.TMP
This is my February file.
It is my second dummy file.
This is file 2.
I am adding a new line to
this file to change or
edit it.
This is my latest change.
That's all folks!
MS-DOS Editor <F1=Help> Press ALT to activate menus 00009:001

WHAT'S HAPPENING? You selected all the text in the file.

STEP 3: Press the <Del> key.

STEP 3: Press the <Del> key.

File Edit Search Options Help
FEB.TMP
MS DOS Editor <F1=Help> Press ALT to activate menus 00001:001

WHAT'S HAPPENING? You deleted all the text in the file.

STEP 4: Press <Alt>+F.

STEP 4: Click **`File`**.

STEP 5: Press X.

STEP 5: Click **`Exit`**.

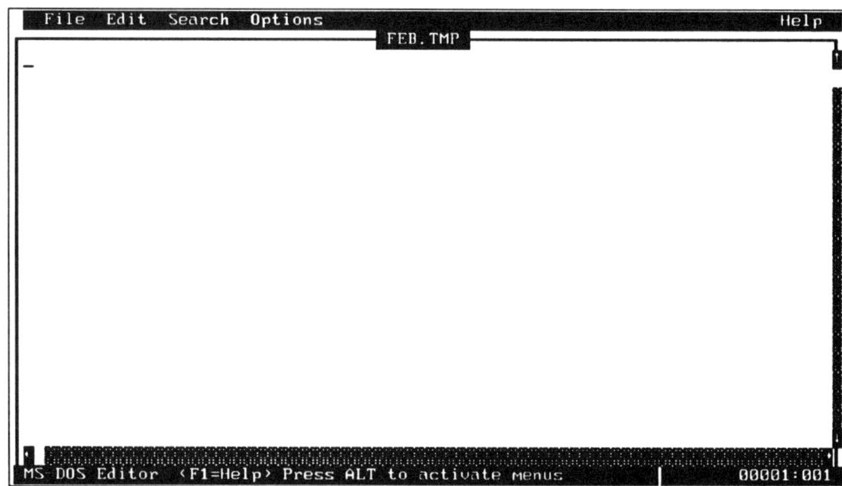

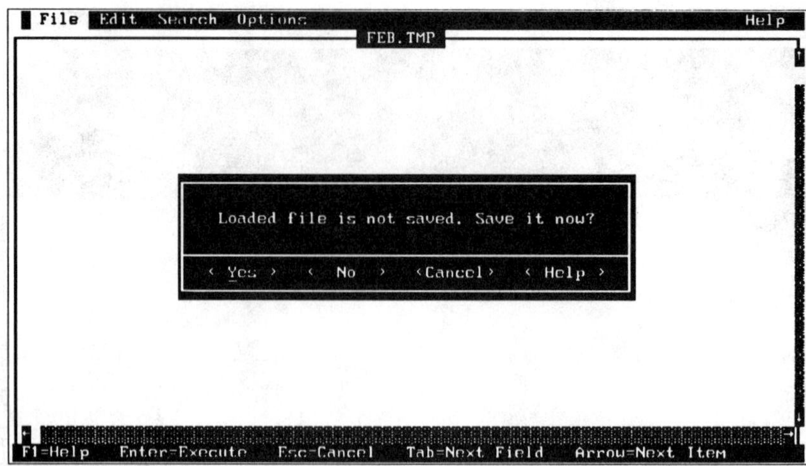

WHAT'S HAPPENING? EDIT is warning you, with a dialog box, that the file is not going to be saved, but your intention is not to save this file.

STEP 6: Press N. STEP 6: Click **No**.

STEP 7: Key in the following:
A:\>**TYPE FEB.TMP** <Enter>

```
A:\>TYPE FEB.TMP
This is my February file.
It is my second dummy file.
This is file 2.
I am adding a new line to
this file to change or
edit it.
This is my latest change.
That's all folks!

A:\>_
```

WHAT'S HAPPENING? You returned to the DOS prompt. Then you looked at the file. You can see that your file is the same as it was prior to the deletion of the lines. When you selected "No," the changes were not written to the disk. No data was lost. You aborted the editing session. Thus, if you end an EDIT editing session and answer "N" to "Loaded file not saved," no changes will be made to the file. If you said "Y" for yes, the changes would have been written to the file.

11.15 Using Editing Keys in EDIT

So far, when you have been working in EDIT, you have been working with entire lines. You have learned about the differences between the insert mode and the overstrike mode. Although EDIT is not a word processor, it does have some editing features that you can use to save keystrokes.

Activity 11.16 Text Editing

Note: You have the DATA disk in Drive A with the **A:\>** displayed.

STEP 1: Key in the following:

A:\>**EDIT SALES.LET** <Enter>

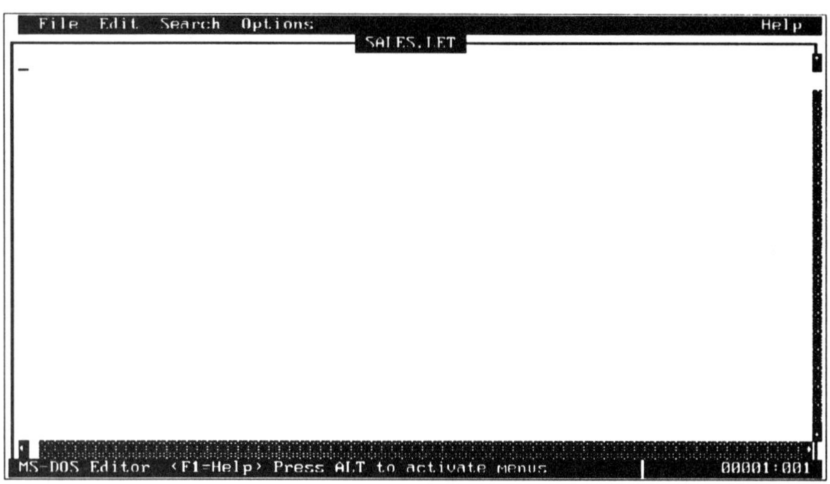

WHAT'S HAPPENING? You have a blank screen, but under the menu bar, EDIT tells you that this file is called **SALES.LET**.

STEP 2: Key in the following text including the errors because you are going to learn how to correct them.

```
Today's date <Enter>
<Enter>
TO: John Jones, Sales Manager <Enter>
FROM: Your name <Enter>
<Enter>
I am interested in setting up a meetin <Enter>
with your staff. I have developed a new software product <Enter>
that I think you <Enter>
will finx of interest. <Enter>
<Enter>
I have developed anew operation system <Enter>
for the microcomputer. It is even <Enter>
easier to run than DOS. I would like <Enter>
to show it off to your staff. <Enter>
I think you will be really <Enter>
impressed. James Smith would be <Enter>
happy to give me a recommendation. <Enter>
I can be reached at (714) 582-8888. <Enter>
I look forward to hearing from you. <Enter>
```

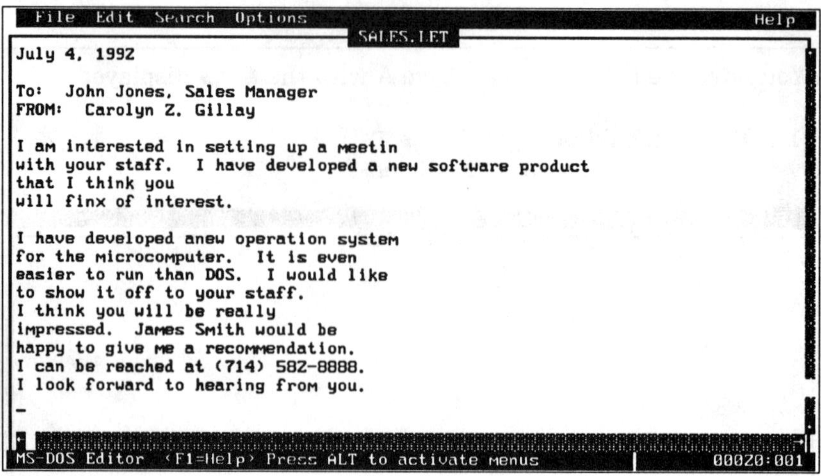

WHAT'S HAPPENING? You created a text file that you are going to edit.

STEP 3: Press <Ctrl>+<Home> to move to the top of the file. Press <Ctrl>+<Enter> eight times. Press <Ctrl>+<Right arrow> once. Press the <Right arrow> until the cursor is under the "x" in "finx."

STEP 3: Click the "x" in "finx."

STEP 4: Press the <Ins> key so you are in overstrike mode.

STEP 4: Press the <Ins> key so you are in overstrike mode.

STEP 5: Press d.

STEP 5: Press d.

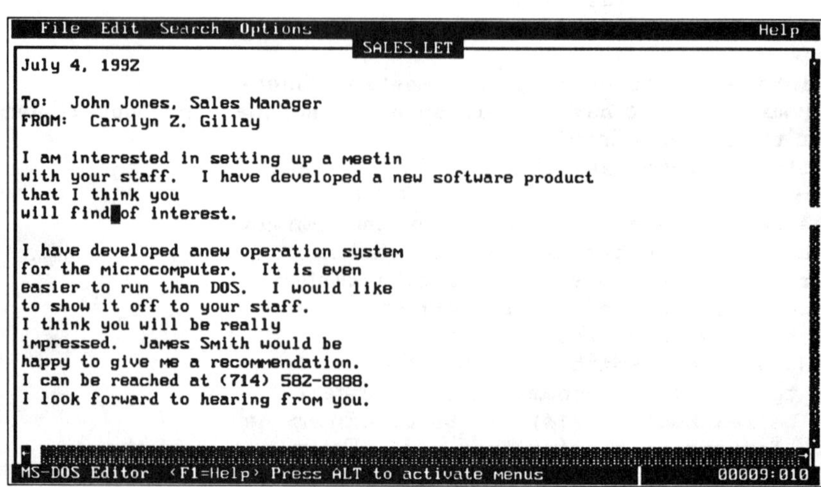

WHAT'S HAPPENING? You changed "finx" to "find."

STEP 6: Press <Ctrl>+<Enter> three times. Press <Ctrl> + the <Right arrow> three times until the cursor is under the "a" in "anew." Press the <Right arrow> until the cursor is under the "n" in "anew."	STEP 6: Click the "n" in "anew."
STEP 7: Press the <Ins> key so you are in insert mode.	STEP 7: Press the <Ins> key so you are in insert mode.
STEP 8: Press the <Spacebar> once.	STEP 8: Press the <Spacebar> once.

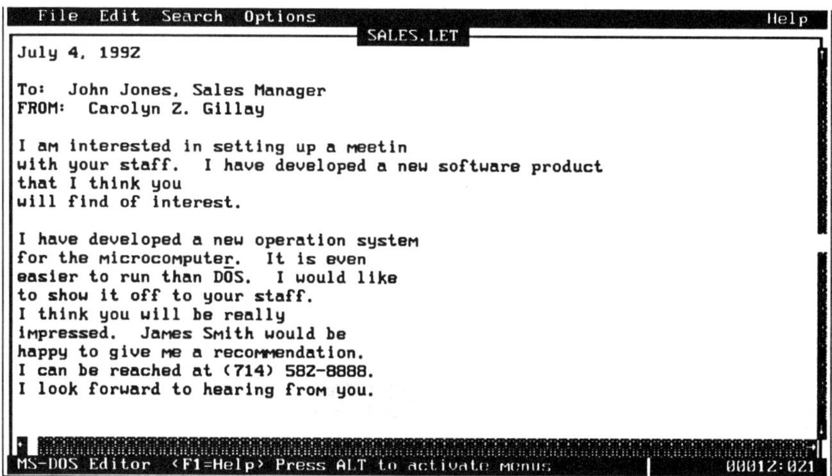

WHAT'S HAPPENING? Because you changed to insert mode, you inserted a space between "a" and "new" and moved "new" to the right. Had you been in overstrike mode you would have overwritten the "n" with a space. You now want to add a "g" at the end of "meetin." To make this correction, you need to move to that location.

STEP 9: Press the <Up arrow> five times. Press the <End> key. The cursor should be immediately following "meetin."	STEP 9: Place the cursor immediately following "meetin."
STEP 10: Press "g".	STEP 10: Press "g".

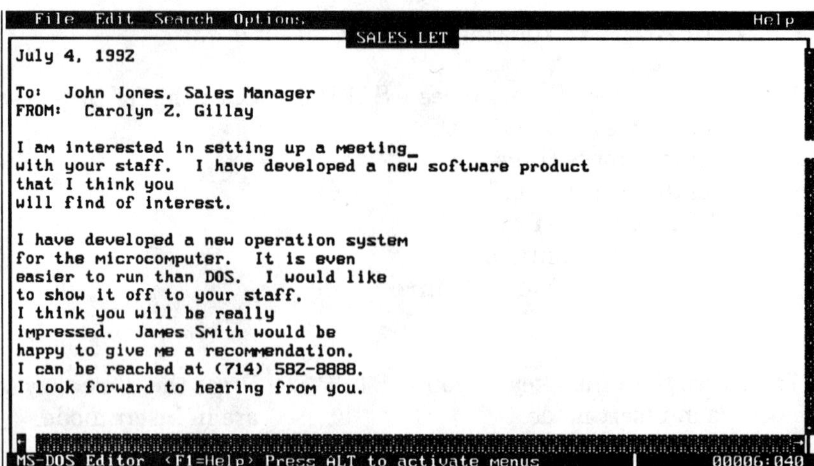

WHAT'S HAPPENING? Because you were still in insert mode, you could add the letter "g" at the end of the line. You next want to insert the word "sales" before "staff" so that the line reads "with your sales staff."

STEP 11: Press <Ctrl>+<Enter> one time. Press <Ctrl>+<Right arrow> two times so that the cursor is under the "s" in "staff."

STEP 11: Click the "s" in "staff."

STEP 12: Key in the following:
sales <Spacebar>

STEP 12: Key in the following:
sales <Spacebar>

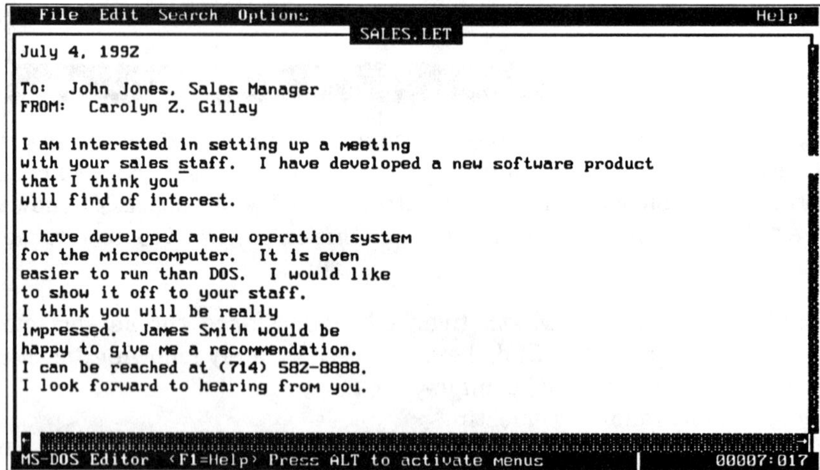

WHAT'S HAPPENING? Here you inserted the word "sales" and pushed the rest of the line to the right to make room for the word. You now wish to change "operation" to "operating."

STEP 13: Press <Ctrl>+<Enter> four times. Press the <End> key. Press the <Left arrow> nine times until the cursor is under the second "o" in "operation."

STEP 13: Click the second "o" in "operation."

STEP 14: Press the <Del> key. Press the <Right arrow> key one time. Key in "g".

STEP 14: Press the <Del> key. Press the <Right arrow> key one time. Key in "g".

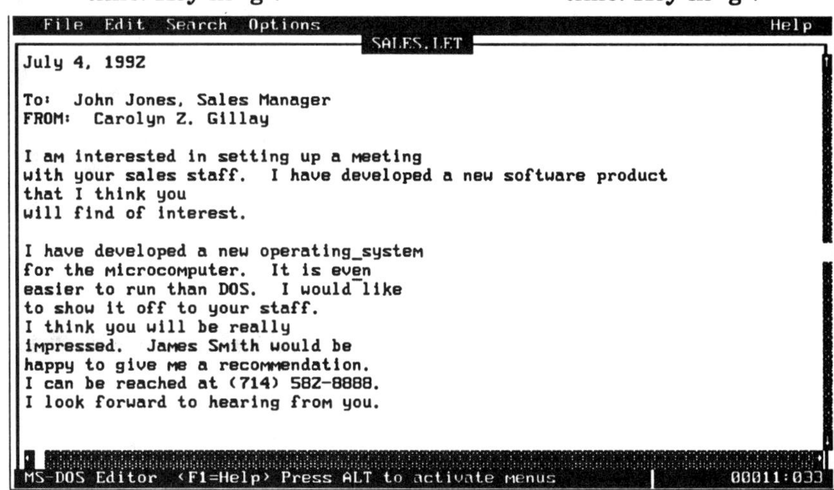

WHAT'S HAPPENING? You changed "operation" to "operating." You next want to remove the word "new" from the same line. You could place the cursor on the "n" in "new" and press the <Del> key four times, but there is an easier way to accomplish this task. You can highlight or select the word "new" and then press the <Del> key only one time.

STEP 15: Press <Ctrl>+<Left arrow> twice. Press <Ctrl>+<Shift> +<Right arrow>. Press <Shift> and <Right arrow> once.

STEP 15: Point at the "n" in "new." Holding down the left mouse button, highlight "new." Be sure to include the space following "new." When it is highlighted, release the mouse button.

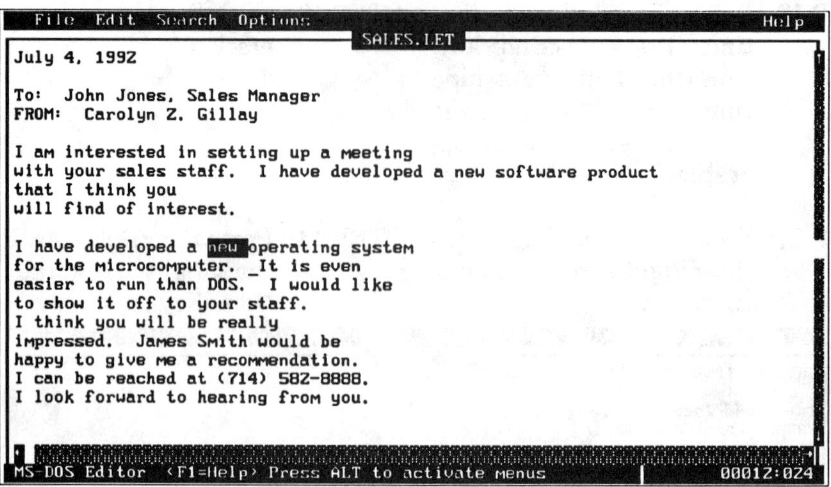

WHAT'S HAPPENING You highlighted the word "new" and the space following it.

STEP 16: Press the <Del> key. STEP 16: Press the <Del> key.

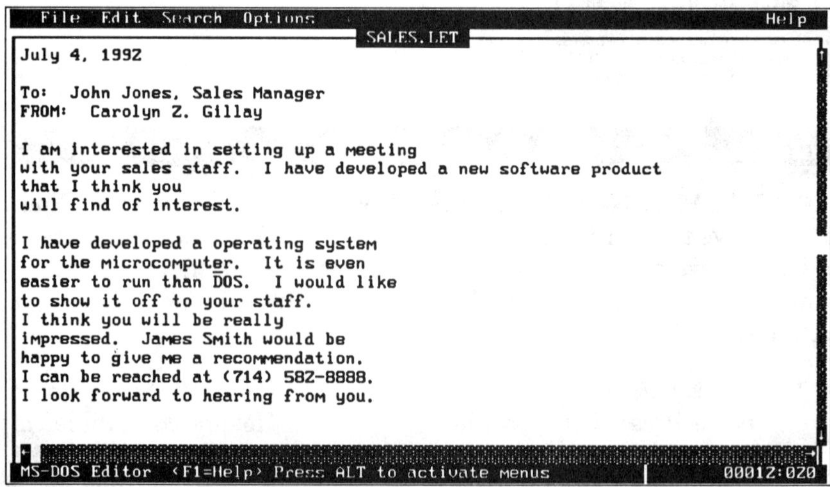

WHAT'S HAPPENING? You deleted the word "new." However, you now need an "n" so that it reads "an" instead of "a."

STEP 17: Press the <Left arrow> key once. Press "n." STEP 17: Press the <Left arrow> key once. Press "n."

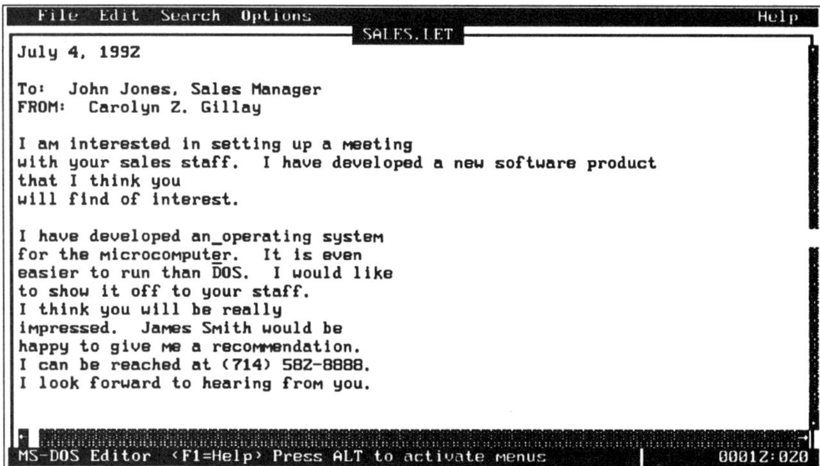

WHAT'S HAPPENING? You changed "a" to "an." You are now going to delete the word "software."

STEP 18: Press the <Up arrow> four times. Press <Ctrl>+<Right arrow> four times. When the cursor is under the "a," press the <Right arrow> once.

STEP 18: Click the space following "a" that follows "developed."

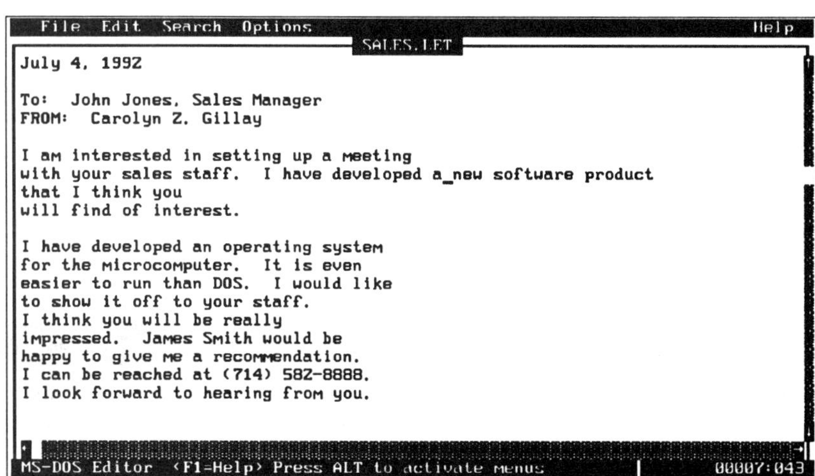

WHAT'S HAPPENING? You positioned the cursor. Now you can select the text and delete it.

STEP 19: Holding down the <Shift> key, press the <Ctrl>+<Right arrow> key once.

STEP 19: Holding down the left mouse button, drag the cursor so that " new" and the space before it are highlighted.

```
 File  Edit  Search  Options                                        Help
                                SALES.LET
July 4, 1992

To:  John Jones, Sales Manager
FROM:  Carolyn Z. Gillay

I am interested in setting up a meeting
with your sales staff.  I have developed a new software product
that I think you
will find of interest.

I have developed an operating system
for the microcomputer.  It is even
easier to run than DOS.  I would like
to show it off to your staff.
I think you will be really
impressed.  James Smith would be
happy to give me a recommendation.
I can be reached at (714) 582-8888.
I look forward to hearing from you.

MS-DOS Editor  <F1=Help> Press ALT to activate menus          00007:047
```

WHAT'S HAPPENING? You selected both the space and the word "new."

STEP 20: Press the <Del> key. STEP 20: Press the <Del> key.

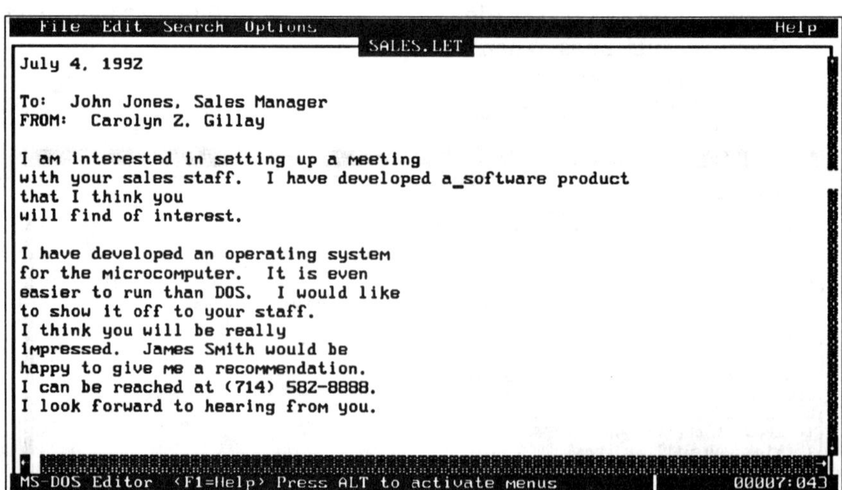

```
 File  Edit  Search  Options                                        Help
                                SALES.LET
July 4, 1992

To:  John Jones, Sales Manager
FROM:  Carolyn Z. Gillay

I am interested in setting up a meeting
with your sales staff.  I have developed a_software product
that I think you
will find of interest.

I have developed an operating system
for the microcomputer.  It is even
easier to run than DOS.  I would like
to show it off to your staff.
I think you will be really
impressed.  James Smith would be
happy to give me a recommendation.
I can be reached at (714) 582-8888.
I look forward to hearing from you.

MS-DOS Editor  <F1=Help> Press ALT to activate menus          00007:043
```

WHAT'S HAPPENING? You eliminated both the space preceding "new" and the word "new."

11.17 Cutting and Pasting in EDIT

You can move blocks of text from one place to another with EDIT. This process is called cutting and pasting. Cutting and pasting is exactly what it says. You take text from one place and "cut" it out electronically instead of using scissors. Pasting the "cut" text to another part of the file is also done electronically. You perform this function by using the drop-down `Edit` menu. However, you must select the text you wish to manipulate before using cut and paste.

Activity 11.18 Using Cut and Paste

Note: You should still be in the file **SALES.LET** on the DATA disk. The cursor should be positioned between "a" and "software."

STEP 1: While pressing the <Shift> key, press the <End> key.

STEP 1: Click the left mouse button and drag the mouse so that "software product" is highlighted.

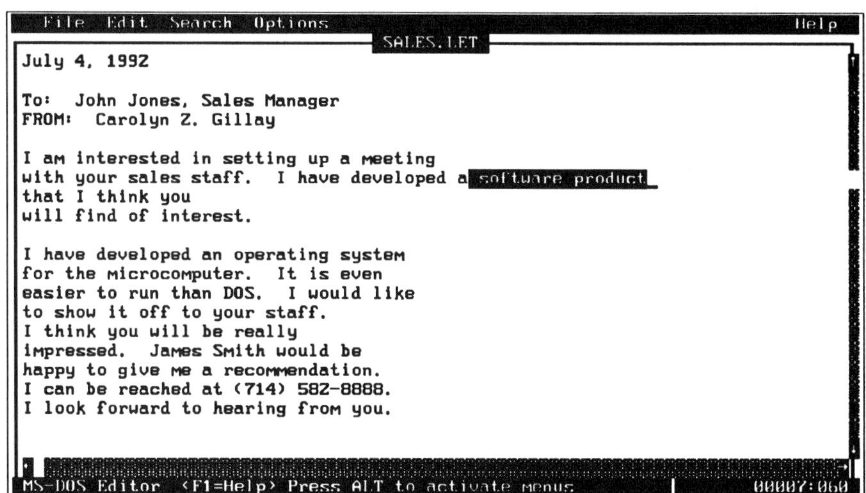

WHAT'S HAPPENING? You selected "software product" and are going to cut this from its current location and paste it at the beginning of the next line.

STEP 2: Press <Alt>+E. Press "t."

STEP 2: Click **Edit**. Click **Cut**.

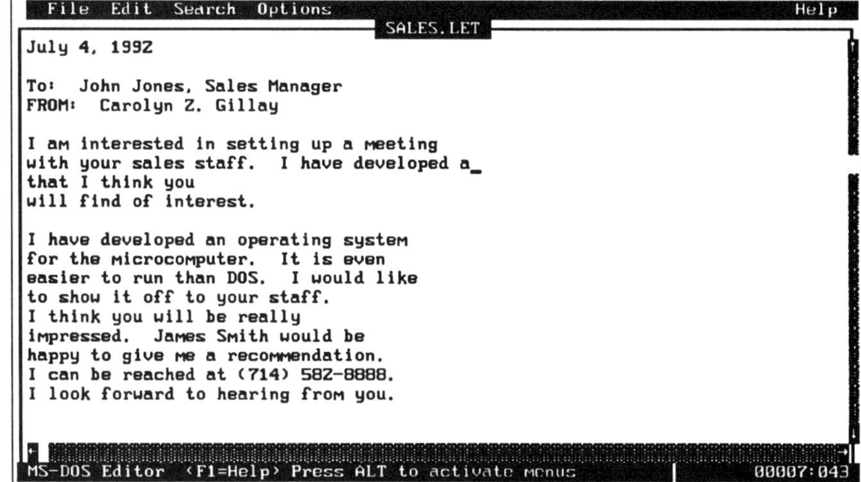

WHAT'S HAPPENING? You cut out the words "software product." However, you have not deleted them. This information remains in a buffer. A **buffer** is a temporary data storage area in memory. There are different kinds of buffers. For instance, a print buffer is used to compensate for differences in rates of the flow of data. The printer, a mechanical device, is much slower than a computer. The computer prepares all the data at once, then places it in the print buffer, and doles it out to the printer at a speed the printer can accept. In this case, the temporary storage area is functioning as an **input buffer**. After you cut the data, it was placed in this type of buffer. It remains there until you replace it either by cutting out other text, which will replace what is in the buffer, or by exiting the program.

STEP 3: Press <Ctrl>+<Enter>. Press <Alt>+E. Press "P" for paste. Press the <Del> key once to remove the space.

STEP 3: Click the beginning of the next line. Click **Edit**. Click **Paste**. Press the <Del> key once.

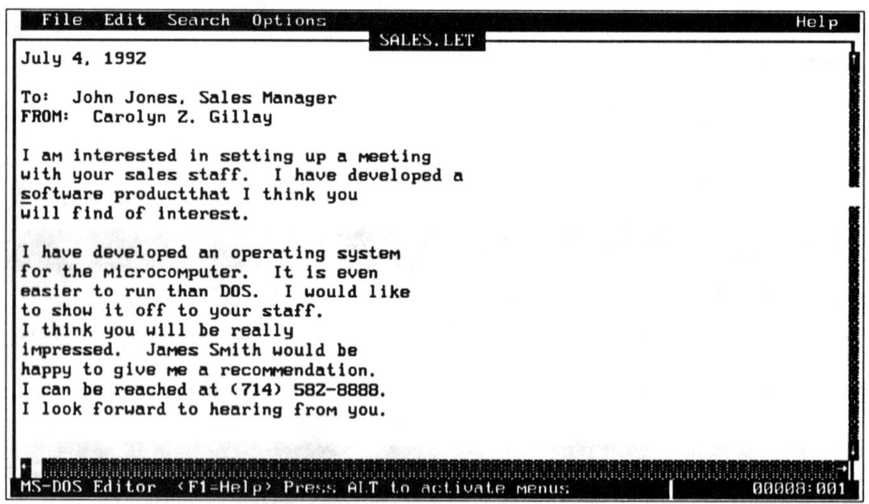

WHAT'S HAPPENING? You pasted the text at the beginning of the line. However, "product" and "that" need proper spacing.

STEP 4: Press the <Right arrow> key until the cursor is on the "t" of "that." Press the <Spacebar> once.

STEP 4: Position the cursor on the first "t" of "that." Press the <Spacebar> once.

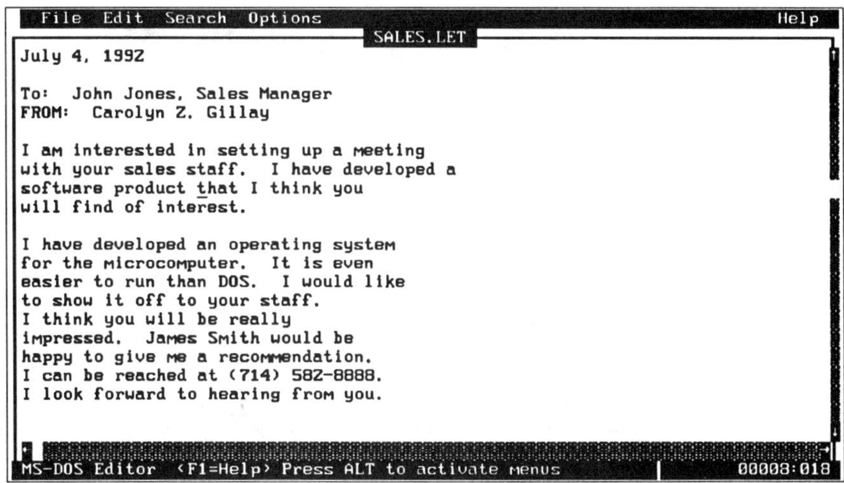

WHAT'S HAPPENING? You added a space.

STEP 5: Move the cursor to the end of the line reading "to show it off to your staff." Press <Enter> two times.

STEP 5: Move the cursor to the end of the line reading "to show it off to your staff." Press <Enter> two times.

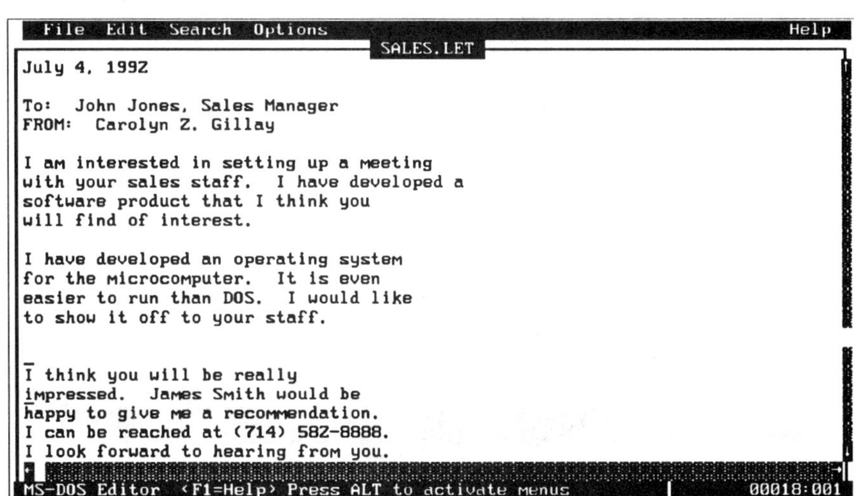

WHAT'S HAPPENING? You are going to add more data to this file.

STEP 6: Key in the following:

STEP 6: Key in the following:

Please let me know when we could get <Enter>
together so I may demonstrate this <Enter>
product.

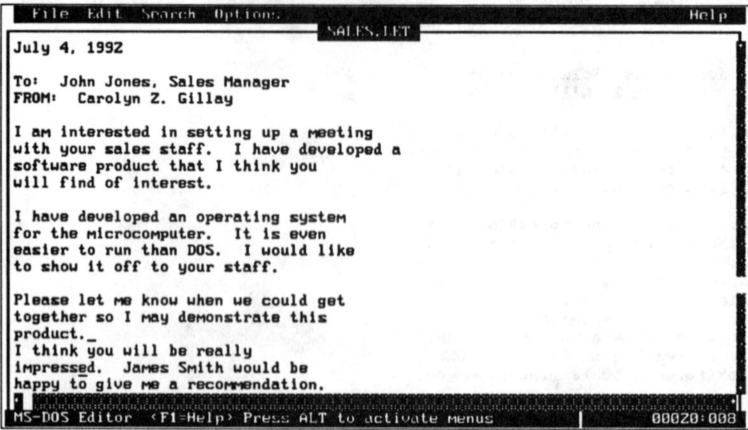

WHAT'S HAPPENING? You keyed in new text. You are going to cut the next line, "I think you will be really" and paste it to the word following "product."

STEP 7: Press <Ctrl>+<Enter>. Press <Shift>+<End>.

STEP 7: Click "I" and, holding down the left mouse button, drag the cursor to the end of the line.

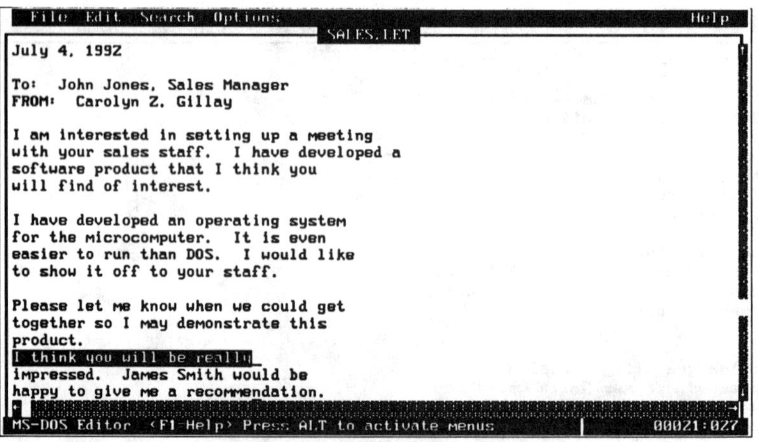

WHAT'S HAPPENING? You highlighted "I think you will be really."

STEP 8: Press <Alt>+E. Press "t" to select `Cut`. Move the cursor to the space following the period in "product" in the preceding line. Press <Alt>+E. Press "P" for `Paste`.

STEP 8: Click `Edit`. Click `Cut`. Click the cursor on the space following the period in "product." Click `Edit`. Click `Paste`.

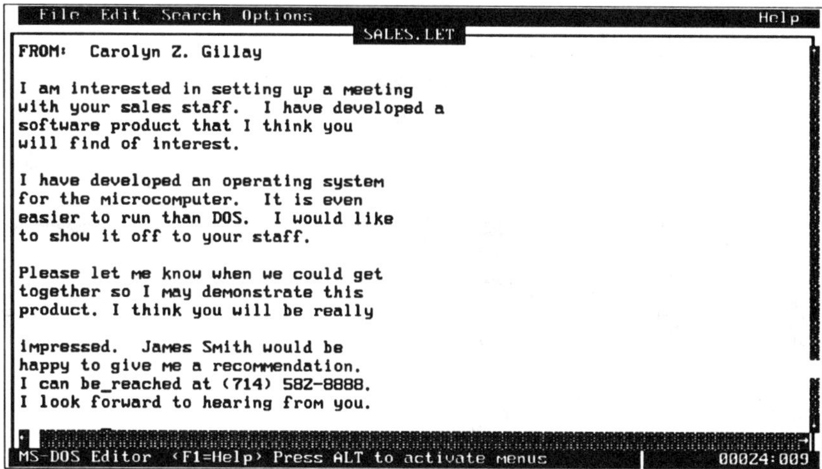

WHAT'S HAPPENING? You pasted in the text. Now you need to eliminate the blank line.

STEP 9: Press <Ctrl>+<Enter>.
Press <Del>.

STEP 9: Click the blank line.
Press <Del>.

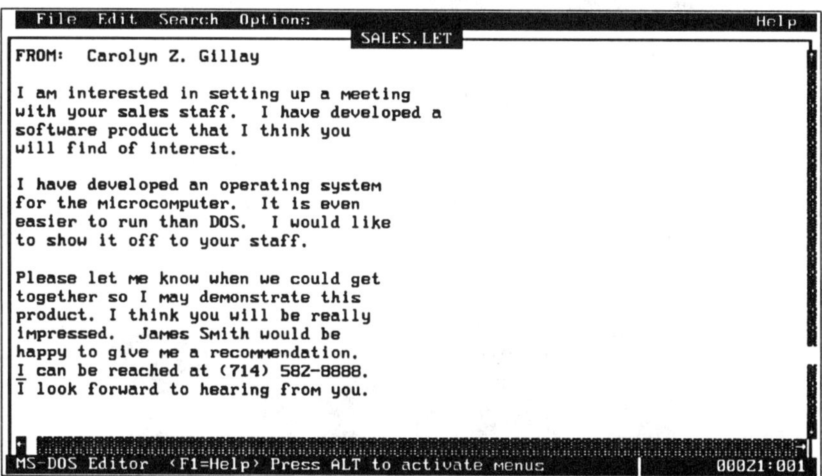

WHAT'S HAPPENING? You removed the blank line.

11.19 Searching a File in EDIT

You can search through any EDIT file by using the `Search` option on the menu bar. `Search` will give you different choices including simply searching a file or searching and replacing within a file. **Search** locates a specific place in a file. **Replace** searches for a specific character string and replaces it with another character string.

Activity 11.20

Using the Search Command in EDIT

Note: You should still be in the file **SALES.LET** on the DATA disk. The cursor should be positioned on the "i" in "impressed."

STEP 1: Press <Alt>+S.

STEP 1: Click **Search**.

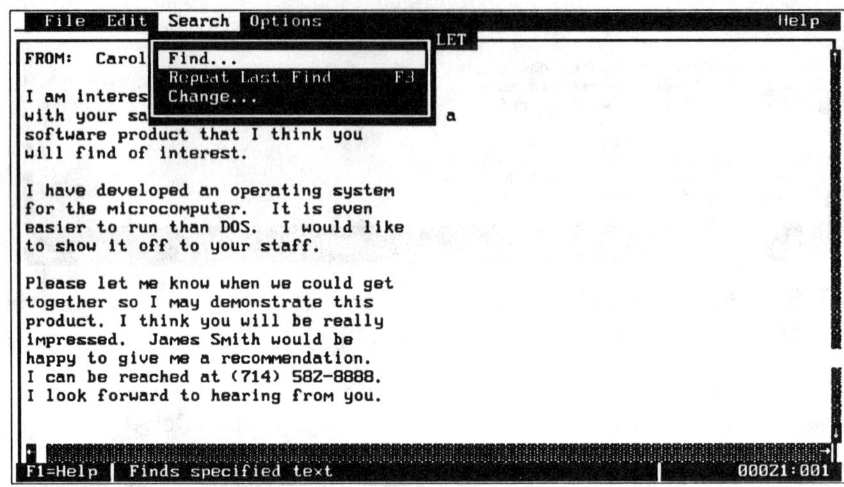

WHAT'S HAPPENING? You have a new menu to choose from. **Find** means search the file to find what is specified.

STEP 2: Press "F."

STEP 2: Click **Find**.

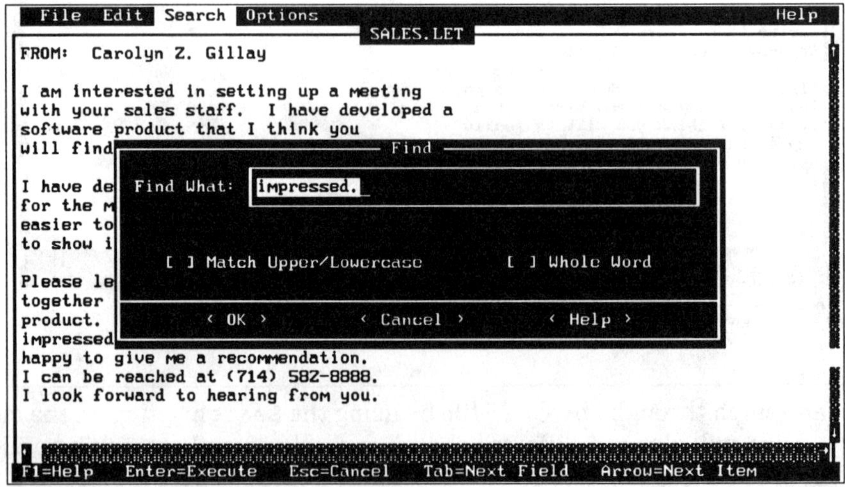

WHAT'S HAPPENING? You see the **Find** dialog box that asks you what to search for. The word "impressed," the last place you were, is in the **Find What** box.

STEP 3: In the **Find What** box, key in the following:
meeting

STEP 3: In the **Find What** box, key in the following:
meeting

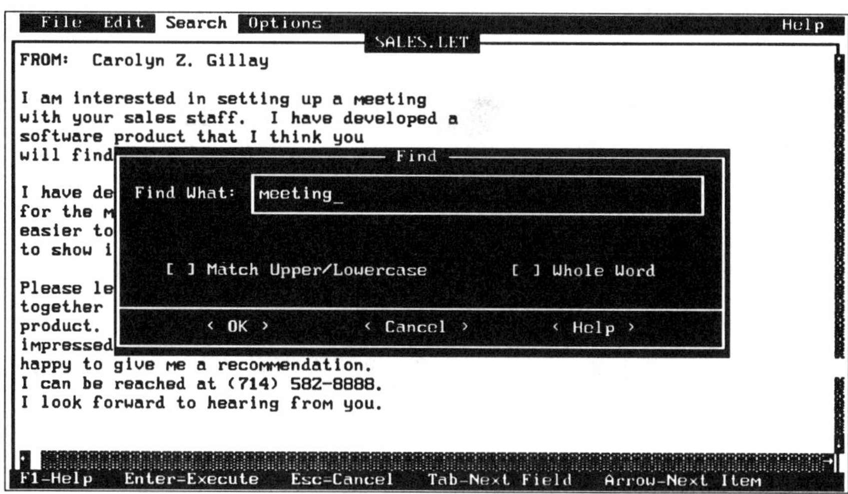

WHAT'S HAPPENING? You keyed in what you want **Find** to find.

STEP 4: Press <Enter>.

STEP 4: Click **OK**.

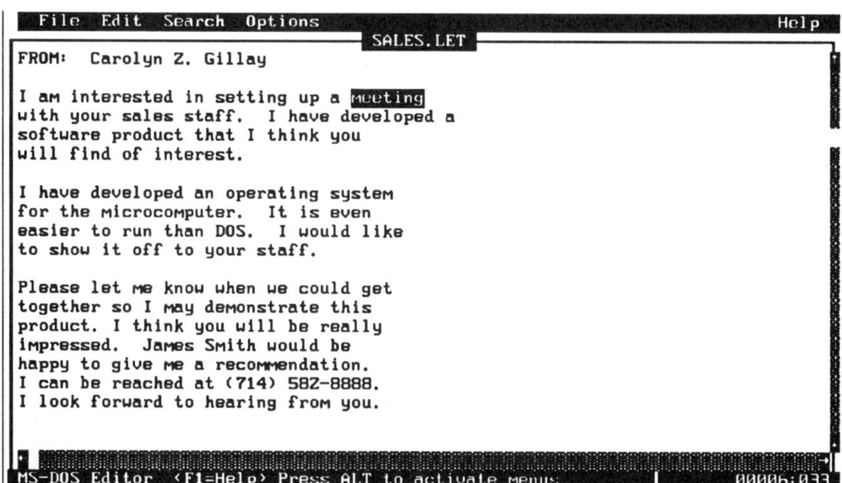

WHAT'S HAPPENING? The first occurrence that matched "meeting" was displayed. In this example, there is only one occurrence of "meeting." **Find** is not useful if you key in the letter "a" or a common word like "the" without specifying **Whole Word** in the **Find** dialog box. If you do not specify the whole word, you will find too many occurrences.

STEP 5: Press <Alt>+S. Press "F." Key in "I" in the **Find What** dialog box. Press the <Tab> key until the cursor is in the **Whole Word** box. Press "W" for whole word.

STEP 5: Click **Search**. Key in "I" in the **Find What** dialog box. Click **Whole Word**.

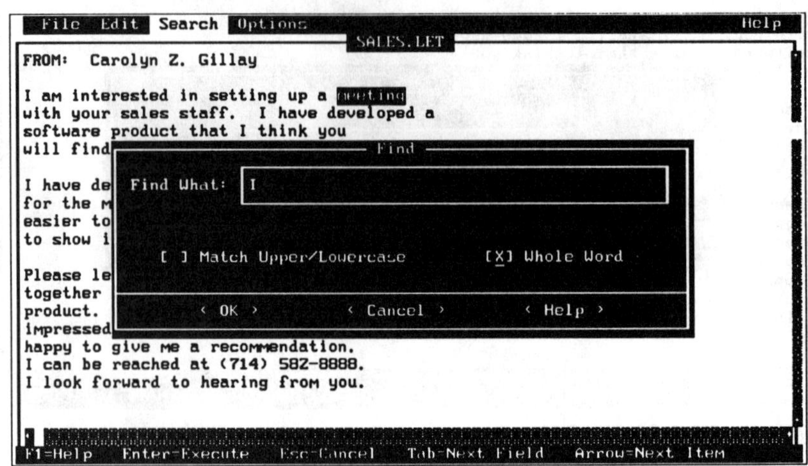

WHAT'S HAPPENING? You wish to search for the word "I," but you only want the whole word.

STEP 6: Press <Enter>.

STEP 6: Click **OK**.

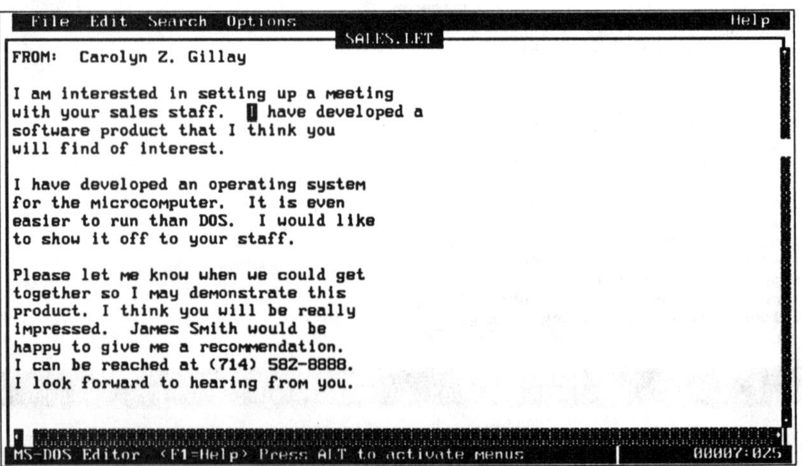

WHAT'S HAPPENING? You are asking to find any occurrence of the capital letter "I." Since you specified whole word, your criterion was very specific. Search is **case sensitive**. If you ask for lowercase "i," it will not stop at an upper case "I" unless you checked the **Match Upper/Lowercase** box. If you want to continue the search, you select another choice from the **Search** menu.

STEP 7: Press <Alt>+S.

STEP 7: Click **Search** on the menu bar.

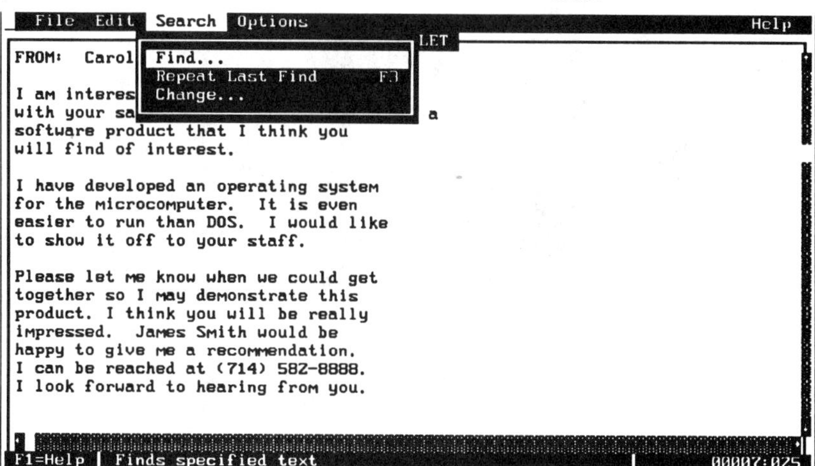

WHAT'S HAPPENING? The menu selection **Repeat Last Find** will continue looking for whatever you last specified.

STEP 8: Press "R."

STEP 8: Click **Repeat Last Find.**

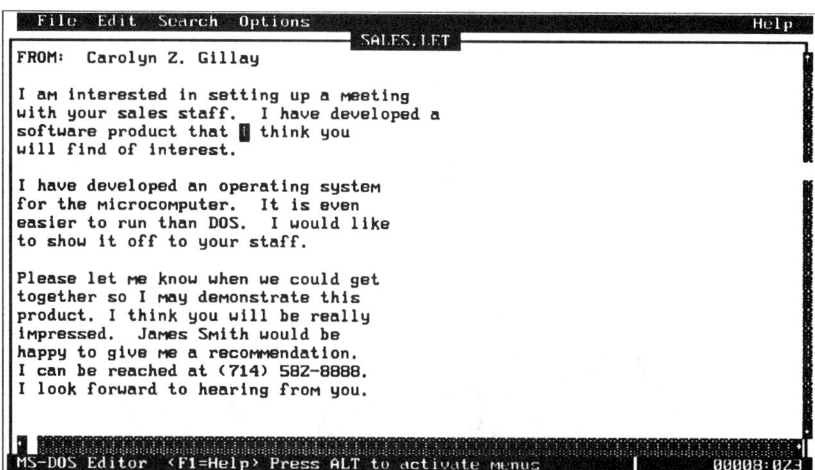

WHAT'S HAPPENING? You saw the next occurrence of "I" without having to key in anything in the dialog box. You can not only find text, but you can also replace it with other text. This edit feature is also selected from the **Search** menu. In this case, you are going to change "Smith" to "Samuels."

STEP 9: Press <Alt>+S.

STEP 9: Click **Search**.

STEP 10: Press C.

STEP 10: Click **Change**.

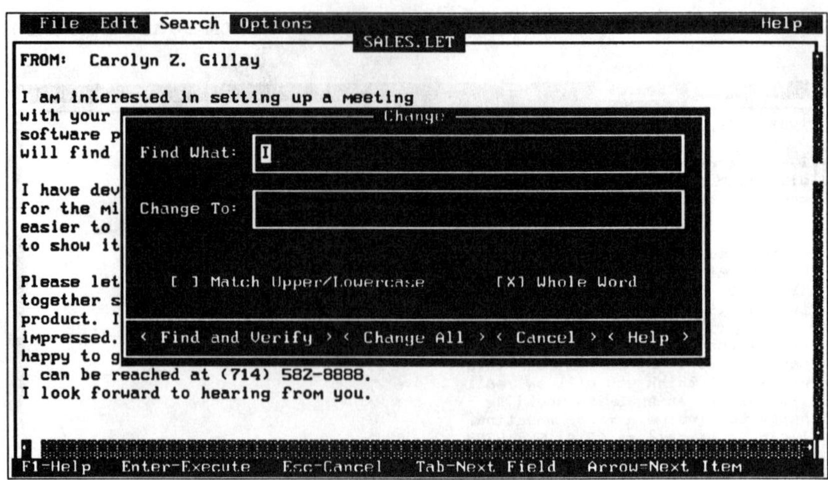

WHAT'S HAPPENING? You see the **Change** dialog box that asks you the questions **Find What** and **Change To**.

STEP 11: In the **Find What** box, key in the following: **Smith.**	STEP 11: In the **Find What** box, key in the following: **Smith.**
STEP 12: Press the <Tab> key once to move to the **Change To** box. Key in the following: **Samuels**	STEP 12: Click the **Change To** box. Key in the following: **Samuels**

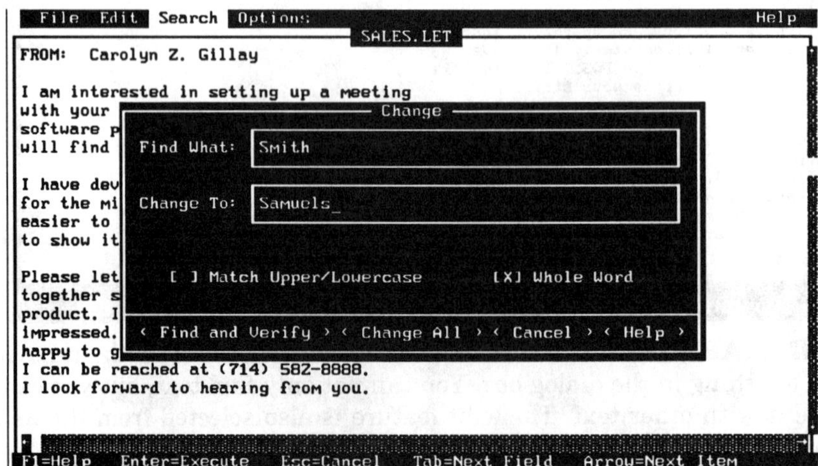

WHAT'S HAPPENING? You told **Find** to find "Smith" and replace it with "Samuels."

STEP 13: Press <Enter>.	STEP 13: Click **OK**.

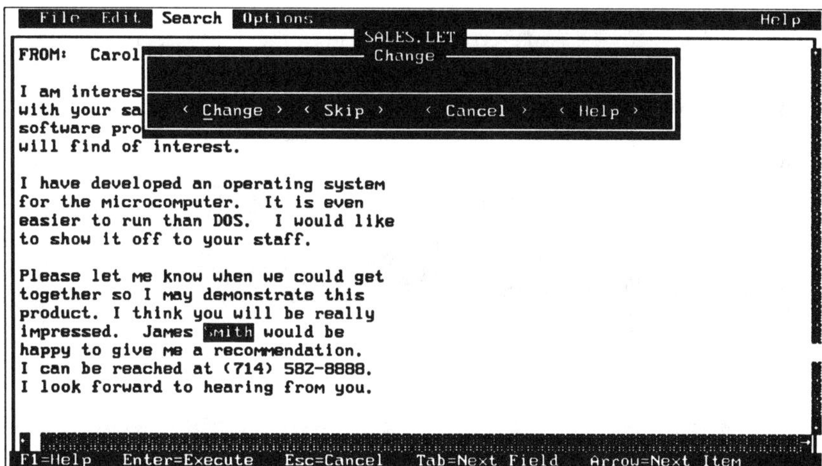

WHAT'S HAPPENING? "Smith" is highlighted. Because you did not specify **Change All** in the dialog box, you are presented with an opportunity to verify your change.

STEP 14: Press <Enter>. STEP 14: Click **Change**.

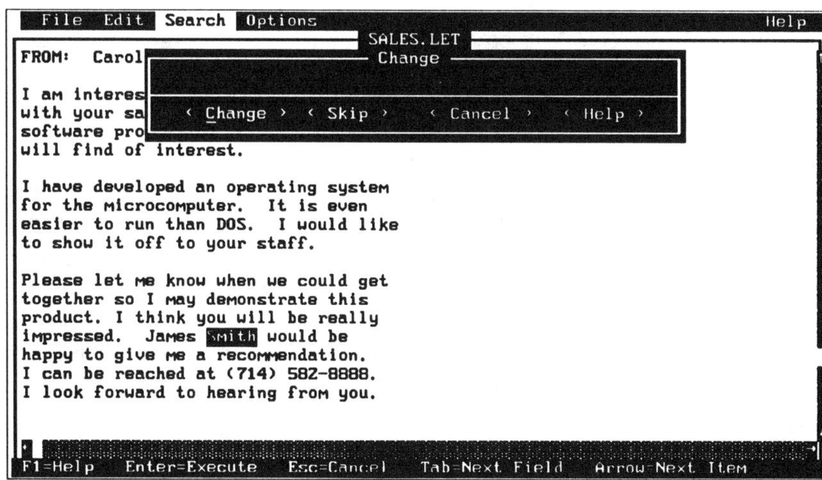

WHAT'S HAPPENING? You receive a message that the change is complete.

STEP 15: Press <Enter>. STEP 15: Click **OK**.

STEP 16: Press <Alt>+F. STEP 16: Click **File**.

STEP 17: Press X. STEP 17: Click **Exit**.

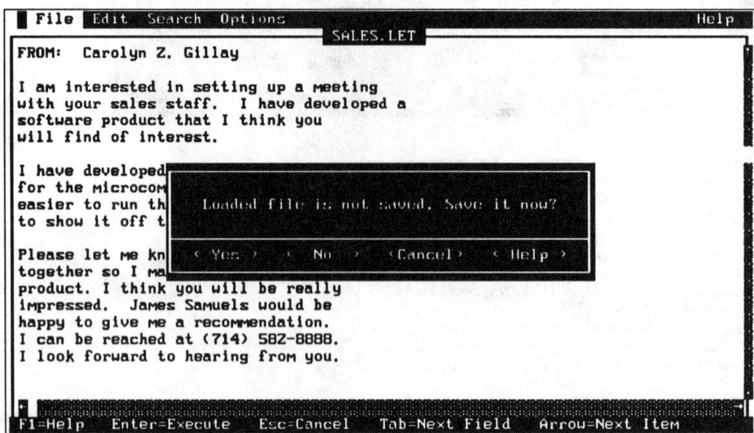

WHAT'S HAPPENING? Because you made changes to the file, EDIT is asking you if you want to save those changes.

STEP 18: Press Y. STEP 18: Click **Yes**.

```
A:\>_
```

WHAT'S HAPPENING? You saved the file with the changes you made. You exited EDIT and are back at the system prompt.

Chapter Summary

1. EDIT is a program that comes with DOS. It is a utility program.
2. The path must be set to where **QBASIC.EXE** is located so that EDIT can work.
3. Both EDLIN and EDIT are text editors. EDLIN is a line editor that allows you to work with only one line at a time. EDIT is a full-screen editor that allows you to work with both the mouse and the keyboard.
4. Both EDLIN and EDIT create ASCII text files or unfromatted text files with no special characters in them. Batch files and **CONFIG.SYS** must be text files.
5. DOS commands, internal or external, do not work once you are in the EDIT program.
6. EDIT allows the user to edit any text file.
7. Because EDIT is a full-screen editor, you may use the mouse or keystroke commands.
8. EDIT has drop-down menus so that the user can select commands with either the mouse or keystrokes.
9. The major EDIT commands from the menu bar include **File**, which allows you to manipulate files by opening, closing, and printing them; **Edit**, which allows you to cut, copy, and paste selected text within a file; and **Search**, which allows you to find selected text and change selected text within a file. It also has **Options**, which allow you to change the colors of the screen display as well as set the search path for help.

10. Some selected commands present you with a dialog box which either gives you information or requests you to key in needed information.
11. In order to manipulate text you must first select text. You may select different increments of text such as a line, word, or sentence.
12. The <Ins> key toggles you between insert mode and overstrike mode. Insert mode is the default mode and allows you to insert text, pushing other text to the right. The overstrike mode replaces characters without moving text.
13. Cutting and pasting text allows you to select text from one section of a document and copy it to another section of the document.
14. The `Search` menu allows you to find a text selection within a document. You also have the option of replacing one selection of text with another.

Key Terms

Buffer
Case sensitive
Click
Dialog box
Double-click
Drag
Full-screen editor
Input buffer
Insert mode
Line editor
Menu bar
Overstrike mode
Search and replace
Text file
Trackball
Unformatted text files

Discussion Questions

1. What is EDIT?
2. What is the difference between EDIT and a word processor?
3. What is the difference between EDLIN and EDIT?
4. Give the syntax for EDIT.
5. Why would you need a text editor such as EDIT? How would you use it?
6. Why is EDIT not on the DATA disk?
7. What is the difference between overstrike and insert mode? Once in the insert mode, what do you have to do to use the overstrike mode?
8. If you wanted to save a file under a new name, how would you accomplish that task?
9. Name two ways you can delete text.
10. How do you end an editing session when you have been using EDIT?
11. How would you print a file in EDIT?
12. Compare and contrast `Save`, `Save As`, and `Exit`.
13. What is a buffer? Why is a buffer necessary?
14. What will `Search` and `Replace` allow you to do?
15. Describe how you would change "Mrs." to "Ms." in a text file.
16. The following is displayed on the screen:

```
Microcomputers are very powerful tools.
They are used in many business applications.

_
```

How would you place a blank line between these lines?

17. Compare and contrast `Cut` and `Paste` from the `Edit` menu.
18. What is the difference between `Clear` from the `Edit` menu and pressing the <Del> key?
19. Before you manipulate text, what must you first do?
20. If you wanted to locate the word "auto," how could you be sure that only "auto" was selected and not such words as "automatic" or "automobile?"

Application Assignments

Place all the applications on the DATA disk.

1. Edit the file called **MYLETTER.TXT** created in the chapter and make the following changes:
    a. Change "second" to "nicest."
    b. Insert a new line 2 that will read "I like DOS."
    c. Add a line at the end of the file that will read "Using a computer is lots of fun."
    d. Save this corrected file.
    e. Print this file with the corrections. Do not use <Shift>+<PrtSc>.
2. Edit the file called **SALES.LET** created in the chapter and make the following changes:
    a. Locate the line "to show it off to your staff" and change it to "to demonstrate it to your staff."
    b. Change "James Samuels" to "James Smythe."
    c. Make the last lines, starting with "I can be reached at" a new or fourth paragraph.
    d. Save this file.
    e. Print this file with the corrections.
3. For the following assignment:
    a. Using EDIT, create a new file called **COMPUTER.APP**. Key in the following text.

```
Your name (use your own name) <Enter>
Your street address <Enter>
Your city, state, and zip code <Enter>
<Enter>
Micro Computer Store <Enter>
15000 Marguerite Parkway <Enter>
Mission Viejo, California 92692 <Enter>
<Enter>
Dear Sir: <Enter>
<Enter>
I purchased an IBM clone from your store last <Enter>
week. I was told that it would run any software <Enter>
application that would run on an IBM. It does not. <Enter>
<Enter>
I am going to return the computer I bought <Enter>
from your store. I need to bxx another computer<Enter>
that works with the software I have. <Enter>
```

<Enter>
Sincerely, <Enter>
<Enter>
<Enter>
<Enter>
Your name <Enter>

b. Save this file.
c. Print this file. Do not use <Shift>+<PrtSc>.
d. Edit the file **COMPUTER.APP** that you just created. Make the following corrections:
   1. Change the name of the company to "New Age, Inc."
   2. In the address block above "New Age, Inc.," insert "Mr. Bill Jones, President."
   3. Correct "bxx" to "buy."
   4. Add a new last paragraph that reads, "If I am not fully satisfied, I will report you to the Better Business Bureau."
   5. Save this file as **COMPUTER.AP2**.
e. Print this file. Do not use <Shift>+<PrtSc>.

4. For the following assignment:
   a. Use EDIT to create a new file called **DOS-PUNS.TXT**.

      You either like puns or you don't. <Enter>
      There are many puns that can be made using <Enter>
      the word DOS. These include: <Enter>
      <Enter>
      Doing the DOSONOVA—a new dance. <Enter>
      DOSOSIS—a fear of DOS. <Enter>
      DOS with the Wind—a famous historical novel. <Enter>
      GENERAL DOSPITAL—a popular daytime soap opera. <Enter>

   b. Save this file.
   c. Print this file. Do not use <Shift>+<PrtSc>.
   d. Edit the file **DOS-PUNS.TXT**. Make the following correction:
      1. At the end of the file, add the line:
         DOSITIS—an inflammation of the DOS.
      2. Add a new line 5:
         MY PUNS
      3. If you can think of any puns, add them to the file.
   e. Save this file.
   f. Print this file. Do not use <Shift>+<PrtSc>.

5. For the following assignment:
   a. Make a copy of the file **PERSONAL.FIL** (in **C:\JUNK** if you do not have it on the DATA disk) and call the new copy **PERSON.FIL**.
   b. Edit this file.
   c. Change "CA" to "California." Print the file.
   d. Change "AZ" to "ARIZONA." Print the file.

   e. Change "ARIZONA" to "AZ." Change "California" to "CA." Print the file.
6. For the following assignment:
   a. Create a new file called **LINE.FIL** with the following contents:

```
This is line A.
This is line B.
This is line C.
This is line D.
This is line E.
This is line F.
This is line G.
```

   b. Copy the second line to the end of the file.
   c. Copy lines 2 through 5 and place them at the beginning of the file.
   d. Move the first two lines to the end of the file.
   e. Save the file.
   f. Print this file. Do not use <Shift>+<PrtSc>.

Challenge Assignment

7. Write a short essay called **ESSAY.TXT** in EDIT describing what you like best and what you like least about DOS. Save and print the file.

Chapter 12

Introduction to Batch Files

After completing this chapter you will be able to:

1. Compare and contrast batch and interactive processing.
2. Explain how batch files work.
3. Use EDIT to write batch files.
4. Write a simple batch file.
5. Execute a simple batch file.
6. Write a batch file to load an application program.
7. Explain the function of an `AUTOEXEC.BAT` file.
8. Write and use an `AUTOEXEC.BAT` file.
9. Explain and use the REM, PAUSE, and ECHO commands in batch files.
10. Terminate a batch file while it is executing.
11. Explain the function and use of replaceable parameters in batch files.
12. Write batch files using replaceable parameters.
13. Explain the function and use of menu systems.
14. Write a menu system using batch files.

Chapter Overview

We have used DOS commands throughout the text. Many of these commands are used repeatedly in the same sequence, which means that if more than one command is needed to execute a program, you have to key in each command at the system prompt. This process is repetitive, time consuming, and increases the possibility of human error.

Creating a batch file enables the computer to execute a series of commands with a minimum number of keystrokes. A batch file is a text file that contains a series of commands stored in the order in which the user wants them carried out. By using batch files it is possible to automate a DOS process and at the same time create a more powerful command, which increases the productivity of the computer user.

In this chapter you will learn to create batch files to automate the sequence of DOS commands, to write and execute an **AUTOEXEC.BAT** file for start-up routines, to write and use batch files for complex tasks, to use batch file subcommands, to stop executing a batch file, to write batch files using replaceable parameters, and to create your own menu system using batch files.

12.0 Concepts of Batch and Interactive Processing

DOS commands are programs that are executed or run when you key in the command name. If you wish to run more than one command, you need to key in each command at the system prompt. You can customize or automate the sequence of DOS commands by writing a command sequence that DOS will execute with a minimum number of keystrokes. This process is called a **batch file**, batch commands, or in application software a macro. Any command that can be entered at the system prompt can be included in a batch file, including application software.

A batch file contains one or more commands. To create this file of commands, you write a text file using EDIT or any text editor. The file that you write and name will run any command that DOS can execute. This file must have the file extension .BAT. Once you have written this command file, you execute or run it by simply keying in the name of the batch file, just as you key in the name of a DOS command such as CHKDSK. DOS reads and executes each line of the command file. It is as if you sat in front of the terminal and separately keyed in each command line. Once you start running a batch file, DOS does not need your attention or input until the batch file is finished executing.

Batch files are used for several reasons. They allow you to minimize keystrokes. They also allow you the freedom to walk away from your computer when it runs a long series of commands. Batch files are used to put together a complex sequence of commands and store them under an easily remembered name. They automate any frequent and/or consistent procedures that you always want to do in the same manner. In addition, you can execute your application programs by calling them with a batch file.

Batch is an old data processing term. In the early days of computing, all work was done by submitting a job (or all the instructions needed to run the job successfully) to the data processing department, which would run these jobs in batches. There was no chance for anyone to interact with the program. The job was run, and the output was delivered. Thus, when you run a batch job, you are running a computer routine without interruption. Batch jobs are still run today. An example of a batch job would be running a payroll—issuing paychecks. The computer program that calculates and prints paychecks is run all at once, without interruption. The output or results are the paychecks. This job can be run at any time. If a company decides that payday will be Friday, the data processing department can run the payroll Thursday night. If the company decides payday will be Monday, the data processing department can run the payroll Sunday night. This is **batch processing**.

Batch files are in contrast to an interactive mode of data processing.

Interactive means that you are interacting directly with the computer. An example of this would be the automatic teller machines (ATM), the money machines that banks use so that you can withdraw or deposit money without human intervention. A bank needs instant updating of its records. It cannot wait until next week to run a batch job to find out how much money you have deposited or withdrawn. If you withdraw $100, the bank first wants to be sure that you have $100 in your account and then it wants the $100 subtracted immediately from your balance. You are dealing with the computer in an interactive, real-time mode. Real-time means timeliness. The information has to be processed as it occurs.

In the DOS world, you can work in an interactive mode, but this usually requires a connection to another computer, often over phone lines. Commercial services called bulletin boards allow you to communicate directly with other computers and perform such functions as reviewing airline flight schedules. However, most of the time, you are working one-on-one with your computer. Hence, the batch mode is the area we will concentrate on.

12.1 How DOS Batch Files Work

You will be creating and executing batch files in this chapter. By now you should know that everything, data and programs, is stored as files. How does DOS know the difference between a data file and a program file? It knows the difference based on the file extension. When you key in something at the prompt, DOS first checks in RAM to see if what you keyed in is an internal command. It compares what you keyed in to the internal table of commands. If it finds a match, DOS executes that program. If what you keyed in does not match an internal command, DOS next "guesses" that what you keyed in has the file extension **.COM**. It looks on the default drive and directory for what you keyed in plus the file extension **.COM**. If it finds a match, it loads the program and runs it. If not, DOS goes through the same process but "guesses" that the file extension is **.EXE**. This is how you load and execute not only the DOS utility programs but also most application software. Application software usually has the file extension **.EXE**, such as **LOTUS.EXE**. If what you keyed in does not match these scenarios, DOS's last "guess" is the file extension **.BAT**. It looks on the default drive and directory for what you keyed in plus the file extension **.BAT**. If it finds a match, it loads and executes the batch file, one line at a time. If what you keyed in does not match any of the above criteria, DOS sends back the message, "Bad command or file name."

An example of this process is the CHKDSK command that is stored as a file called **CHKDSK.EXE**. At the **A>** or **C>** prompt, you key in **CHKDSK**. DOS does not find CHKDSK in the internal table of commands. It then "guesses" that the file is called **CHKDSK.COM**, which in some versions of DOS it is. DOS can find the program on the disk, load it, and execute it. The Microsoft versions of DOS call the file **CHKDSK.EXE**. In this case, DOS would not stop its search at **CHKDSK.COM**. If DOS did not find **CHKDSK.COM**, it would then "guess" that the file is called **CHKDSK.EXE**, which it is. DOS then can find the program on the disk, load it and execute it. What if you had files on a disk called (which you should never do) **CHKDSK.COM**, **CHKDSK.EXE**, and **CHKDSK.BAT**? How would DOS know which program to load and execute? DOS follows the rules. It would find and load the program with the .COM file extension first and would never get to the other files.

Remember that the **.BAT** file must be either on the default drive and directory or the path set to the disk or subdirectory where the batch file is when you invoke it. In addition, any programs, DOS or otherwise, that you wish to use must also be on the default or the path set to where the program is located or you will get an error message. Most importantly, each line in a batch file must contain only *one* command.

12.2 EDIT as a Tool to Write Batch Files

You need a mechanism to write or create batch files. A batch file is an ASCII text file. ASCII is a code used by DOS so that it knows the letters, numbers, and punctuation marks that you key in. In simple terms, if you can read a file with the TYPE command it is an ASCII text file. You could use COPY CON *filename.bat*, but you cannot correct errors or edit a file created in this manner. You could also use a word processing program if it has a nondocument or text mode. However, most word processing programs are quite large and often need their own separate disks or area on the hard disk. Having a small, simple text editor is so important that DOS has always included a text editor as part of the utility programs. Prior to DOS 5.0, the text editor was EDLIN. As of DOS 5.0, although EDLIN is also included, the text editor of choice is EDIT because EDIT is a full-screen editor. The advantage of EDIT is that it is simple to use and universal. Everyone who has DOS 5.0 has EDIT.

You are going to write some batch files using EDIT. Remember, EDIT is only a tool to create the file; it does not run or execute it. You will execute the file when you key in the file name at the DOS command prompt. A batch file must be named with **.BAT** as the file extension.

Activity 12.3 Writing and Executing a Batch File

Note: You have the DATA disk in Drive A with the **A:\>** displayed. Be sure the path is set to **C:\DOS**. Remember that to use EDIT, DOS must be able to find QBASIC, which usually is in the **DOS** subdirectory. If you are working with an earlier version of DOS, you may use EDLIN since EDIT is not available to you.

STEP 1: Key in the following:

A:\>**EDIT EXAMPLE.BAT** <Enter>

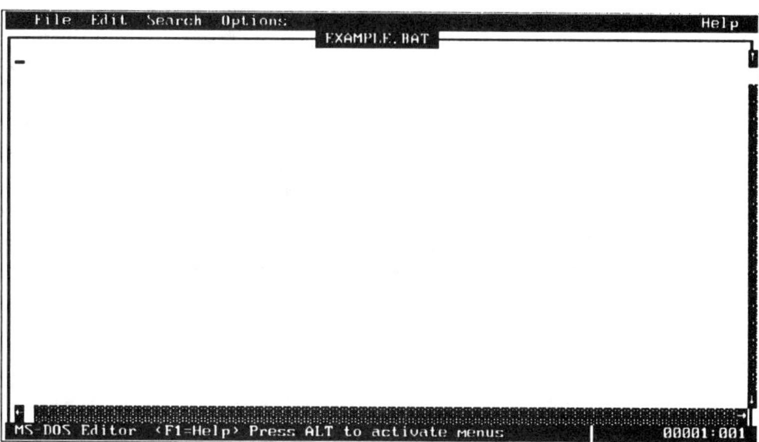

WHAT'S HAPPENING? You are now using EDIT. You are going to create a batch file named **EXAMPLE**. The file extension is **.BAT**.

STEP 2: Key in the following:

DIR *.DOS <Enter>
DIR C:*.DOS

WHAT'S HAPPENING? Look at this file line by line. Each line is a legitimate and separate DOS command that could be keyed in at the prompt. Each command is on a separate line. The first line asks for a listing of all the files on the disk in the default drive that have the file extension **.DOS**. The second line asks for all the files in the root directory of C: that have the file extension **.DOS**. At this point, all that has been done is to write or create the batch file. You need to exit EDIT and save the file to disk.

STEP 3: Press <Alt>+F.

STEP 4: Press X.

WHAT'S HAPPENING? Since you have not saved this file, EDIT reminds you that if you want this file on the disk, you must save it.

STEP 5: Press Y.

```
A:\>EDIT EXAMPLE.BAT

A:\>_
```

WHAT'S HAPPENING? You returned to the system prompt.

STEP 6: Key in the following:
A:\>**DIR EXAMPLE.BAT** <Enter>

```
A:\>DIR EXAMPLE.BAT

   Volume in drive A is DATA DISK
   Volume Serial Number is 3839-0EC8
   Directory of A:\

EXAMPLE   BAT      25   01-24-92 10:06a
       1 file(s)          25 bytes
                      182272 bytes free

A:\>_
```

WHAT'S HAPPENING? You exited the EDIT program and returned to the system prompt. The **DIR EXAMPLE.BAT** command shows that there is a file on the DATA disk called **EXAMPLE.BAT**. It is like any other file. How do you make DOS treat it like a program so that you can execute this file? To run or execute this batch file, you key in the name of the file at the prompt. DOS then looks for a file in its internal table called **EXAMPLE**. It does not find it. It looks for a file called **EXAMPLE.COM** on the default disk, the DATA disk. No file exists called **EXAMPLE.COM**. DOS looks for a file on the default disk called **EXAMPLE.EXE**. No file exists called **EXAMPLE.EXE**. DOS then looks for a file called **EXAMPLE.BAT** on the default disk. It does find a file by this name. It loads it into memory and executes each line, one at a time. Thus, to execute the batch file called **EXAMPLE**, key in the name of the file at the prompt. Watch what happens on the screen after you key in the file name. The display scrolls by.

STEP 7: Key in the following:
A:\>**EXAMPLE** <Enter>

```
A:\>EXAMPLE

A:\>DIR *.DOS

   Volume in drive A is DATA DISK
   Volume Serial Number is 3839-0EC8
   Directory of A:\

WILDONE  DOS     180   05-07-93   9:02a
WILDTWO  DOS     181   05-07-93   9:03a
WILDTHR  DOS     180   05-07-93   9:03a
        3 file(s)         541 bytes
                       182272 bytes free

A:\>DIR C:\*.DOS

   Volume in drive C is HARD DISK
   Volume Serial Number is 1708-78AC
   Directory of C:\

File not found

A:\>
A:\>_
```

WHAT'S HAPPENING? DOS read and executed each line of the batch file you wrote, one line at a time. The screen displayed each command line and the results of the command line as it executed. Each line executed as if you had sat in front of the keyboard and keyed in each command individually. You did key in the commands when you wrote the batch file, but you only had to key them in once. By keying in **EXAMPLE** at the prompt, each command was executed automatically. The first line was **DIR *.DOS**. When DOS read that line, it executed it and showed on the screen all three files on the DATA disk with the file extension **.DOS**. It read the next line of the batch file and looked in the root directory of Drive C: for any file that had the file extension **.DOS**. Since there were no files on that drive with the extension **.DOS**, it gave the message, "File not found." Now that you have written the file **EXAMPLE.BAT**, you can execute this batch file over and over again by keying in **EXAMPLE** at the prompt. By keying in one command, you can execute two DOS commands.

12.4 Writing and Executing a Batch File to Save Keystrokes

The previous example showed you how to write and execute a batch file. However, that file is not especially useful. The next batch file to be written will allow you to key in only one keystroke instead of nine. The command **DIR A:*.** will quickly show you any subdirectories on the DATA disk. The star (*) followed by a period (.) will only show you file names that have no extension. Most subdirectories do not have extensions. But that command is nine keystrokes, and you have to use the shift key to access the colon. With a batch file, you can do the same task by pressing only one key. In addition, DOS 5.0 has some new parameters that are very useful. One of these is O for order. There are many kinds of order you can achieve, but one that is useful is to group directories together at the end of the file list. The command line would be **DIR A:/o-g**. The "o" is for order, the hyphen is for reverse order, placing the grouping of directories at the end of the listing, and the "g" is for grouping directories. This command would take ten keystrokes. You can reduce it to one.

Activity 12.5 Writing and Executing a One-Letter Batch File

Note 1: The DATA disk is in Drive A with the **A:\>** displayed.

Note 2: You may use any text editor you wish for creating the batch files. It is assumed that you know how to use the editor of your choice. The EDIT instructions for keyboard use will be shown.

STEP 1: Key in the following:

A:\>**EDIT D.BAT** <Enter>

STEP 2: Key in the following:

DIR A:*.

STEP 3: Press <Alt>+F.

STEP 4: Press X.

STEP 5: Press Y.

STEP 6: Key in the following:
A:\>**TYPE D.BAT** <Enter>

```
A:\>TYPE D.BAT
DIR A:\*.

A:\>_
```

WHAT'S HAPPENING? You wrote a one-line batch file named **D.BAT** in EDIT. You exited the EDIT program by dropping down the **File** menu (<Alt>+F), pressing X (**Exit** on the **File** Menu in EDIT), then answering Y to the EDIT question of saving the file **D.BAT** to disk. Once you returned to the DOS system prompt, you displayed the contents of **D.BAT** with the TYPE command. However, all EDIT did was allow you to create the file and TYPE merely displayed what is inside the file. To execute the file, you must key in the file name. Now, whenever you want to see the subdirectories on the DATA disk in Drive A, you only have to key in one letter to execute this command.

STEP 7: Key in the following:
A:\>**D** <Enter>

```
A:\>D
A:\>DIR A:\*.

   Volume in drive A is DATA DISK
   Volume Serial Number is 3839-0EC8
   Directory of A:\

CLASS        <DIR>      12-06-92   9:03a
DISKFILE          44    12-06-92   9:04a
DATA         <DIR>      12-06-92   9:05a
USERS        <DIR>      05-07-93  10:05a
WILDONE           92    05-07-93   9:04a
TRIP         <DIR>      06-17-92   9:00p
POLY-SCI     <DIR>      11-16-93   9:47p
PHYS-ED      <DIR>      11-16-93   9:47p
SERIES       <DIR>      05-14-92   3:10p
TEAMS        <DIR>      08-01-92   1:51a
        12 file(s)        152 bytes
                        181248 bytes free

A:\>
A:\>_
```

WHAT'S HAPPENING? Your display may vary based on what subdirectories are on the DATA disk and in what order they were created. As you can see, you set up a command sequence in a batch file called **D.BAT**. You can run this batch file over and over again, simply by keying in the name of the batch file at the system prompt. However, in this display, you also had files displayed that had no extensions. In DOS 5.0, with the new parameters, you can group all the subdirectories together.

STEP 8: Key in the following:
A:\>**EDIT G.BAT** <Enter>
DIR A:\/o-g

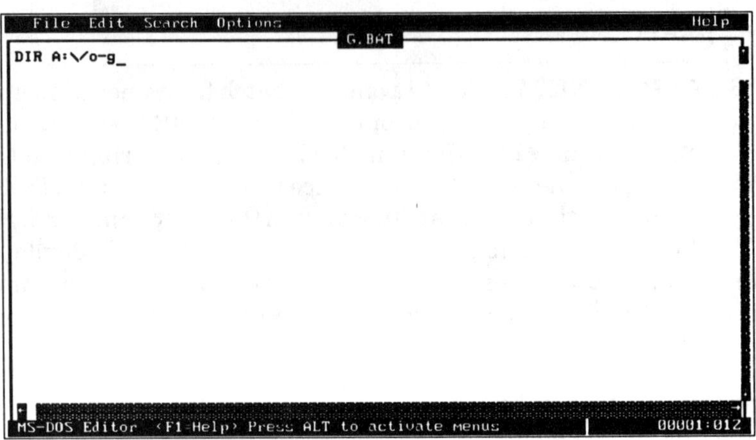

STEP 9: Press <Alt>+F.

STEP 10: Press X.

STEP 11: Press Y.

STEP 12: Key in the following:
A:\>**TYPE G.BAT** <Enter>

```
A:\>EDIT G.BAT

A:\>TYPE G.BAT
DIR A:\/o-g

A:\>_
```

WHAT'S HAPPENING? You created another batch file called **G.BAT** in EDIT. The purpose of the batch file is to group the directories at the end of the directory listing. You then saved the file to disk and looked at its contents with the TYPE command. However, to execute the batch file, you must key in the batch file name (**G**) at the DOS system prompt.

STEP 13: Key in the following:
A:\>**G** <Enter>

```
BYE       TXT       44   11-23-92  7:07a
MYLETTER  TXT      189   07-04-92 11:51p
FEB       BAK      136   07-04-92 11:00p
SALES     LET      637   07-04-92 11:53p
COMPUTER  APP      573   07-04-92 11:58p
DOS-PUNS  TXT      317   07-05-92 12:02a
LINE      FIL      208   07-05-92 12:05a
ESSAY     TXT       93   07-05-92 12:06a
EXAMPLE   BAT       25   01-24-92 10:06a
D         BAT       11   01-24-92 10:10a
G         BAT       13   02-14-93  9:52p
CLASS        <DIR>       11-23-92  7:46a
FILES        <DIR>       12-06-92  9:03a
DATA         <DIR>       12-06-92  9:05a
USERS        <DIR>       05-07-93 10:05a
TRIP         <DIR>       06-17-92  9:00p
POLY-SCI     <DIR>       11-16-93  9:47p
PHYS-ED      <DIR>       11-16-93  9:47p
SERIES       <DIR>       05-14-92  3:10p
TEAMS        <DIR>       08-01-92  1:51a
       82 file(s)         29302 bytes
                         180224 bytes free

A:\>
A:\>_
```

WHAT'S HAPPENING? As you can see, all the subdirectories are indeed grouped at the bottom of the display.

12.6 Loading Application Software

One of the common uses of batch files is to load application software, particularly on a hard disk. Usually, programs are stored in a subdirectory. When you want to use a program, you have to change the directory to the proper subdirectory, load the program, and, when finished using the application program, return to the system level. You usually want to change the default subdirectory to the root directory. This process can be easier with a batch file.

Activity 12.7 Using an Application Package, SS

Note: The DATA disk is in Drive A with the A:\> displayed.

STEP 1: Remove the DATA disk from Drive A. Insert the ACTIVITIES disk in Drive A.

STEP 2: Key in the following:
A:\>**CD \UTILS** <Enter>

STEP 3: Key in the following:
A:\UTILS>**DIR SS.EXE** <Enter>

STEP 4: Key in the following:
A:\UTILS>**DIR BUDGET.SS** <Enter>

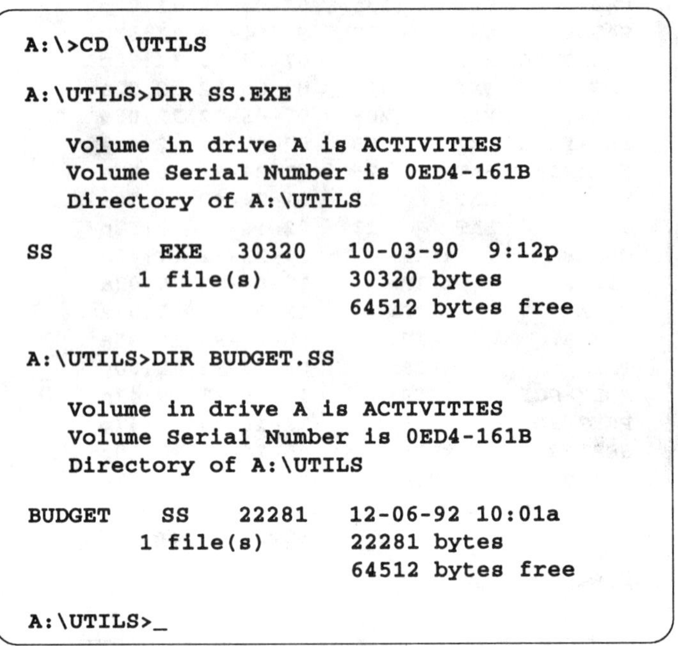

```
A:\>CD \UTILS

A:\UTILS>DIR SS.EXE

   Volume in drive A is ACTIVITIES
   Volume Serial Number is 0ED4-161B
   Directory of A:\UTILS

SS         EXE   30320    10-03-90   9:12p
        1 file(s)         30320 bytes
                          64512 bytes free

A:\UTILS>DIR BUDGET.SS

   Volume in drive A is ACTIVITIES
   Volume Serial Number is 0ED4-161B
   Directory of A:\UTILS

BUDGET     SS    22281    12-06-92 10:01a
        1 file(s)         22281 bytes
                          64512 bytes free

A:\UTILS>_
```

WHAT'S HAPPENING? You are looking at the file **SS.EXE** in the subdirectory **UTILS** on the ACTIVITIES disk. You are going to load the program called **SS.EXE** that simulates a spreadsheet program such as Lotus or VisiCalc, used for financial applications. You are going to use the data file called **BUDGET.SS**, also in the subdirectory **UTILS**.

STEP 5: Key in the following:
A:\UTILS>**SS** <Enter>

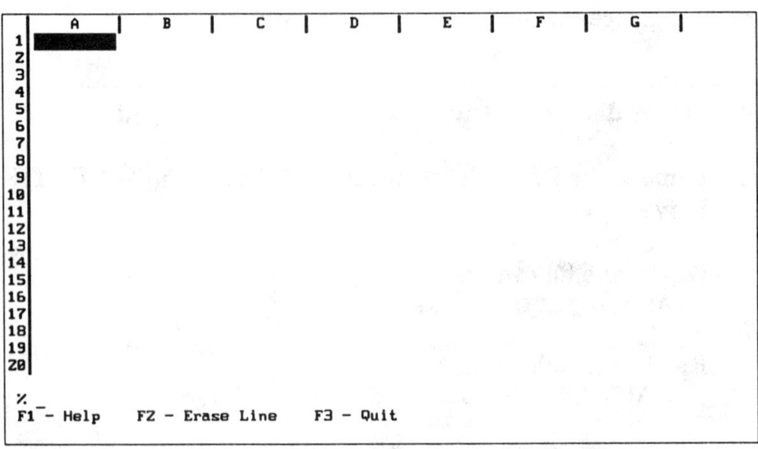

WHAT'S HAPPENING? This is the spreadsheet program SS. Across the top of the screen are letters—columns. Down the side of the screen are numbers—rows. You can pinpoint any location on the grid, e.g. A1—column A, row 1. These locations are called cells. In cells you may place labels—to name a column or a row. You may place values—numbers like 1 or 40. Lastly, you may place formulas—A1+A2 to sum the values in location A1 and A2. The % sign is the prompt for the program.

STEP 6: Key in the following:
`/L,BUDGET` <Enter>

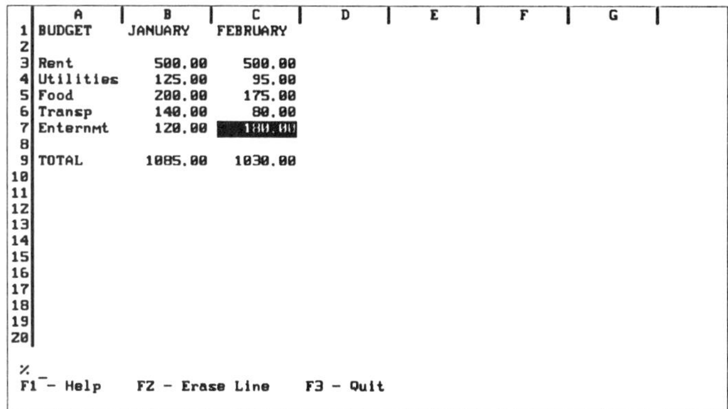

WHAT'S HAPPENING? You loaded the data file **BUDGET**. The words like BUDGET and Rent are labels. The other cell entries are numbers except for cells B9 and C9, which contain formulas. You can use your arrow keys to move around the screen. Try pressing the arrow keys to see how they move. The cell that is highlighted is where you are.

STEP 7: Move the arrow key until cell B9 is highlighted.

STEP 8: At the % prompt, key in the following:
`/E` <Enter>

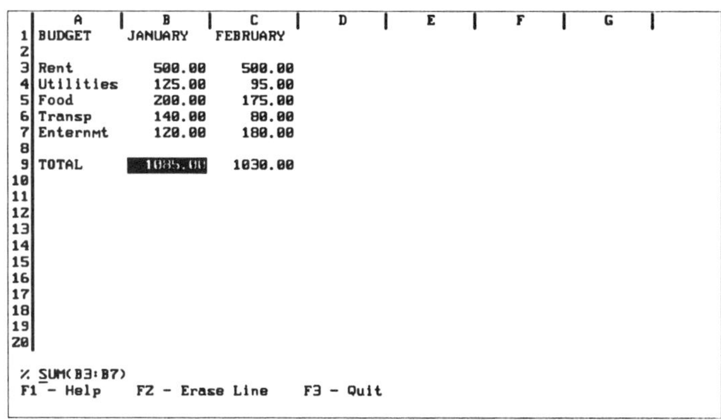

WHAT'S HAPPENING? The /E is a command that allows you to edit the cell. SUM(B3:B7) is a function. It is a formula that adds up or sums the values of cells B3 through B7. You could have keyed in B3 + B4 + B5 +B6 + B7 which would sum these cells, but instead you used a function that is a shortcut to the addition.

STEP 9: Move the arrow key until cell B7 is highlighted. Then, at the % prompt, key in the following:

`5000` <Enter>

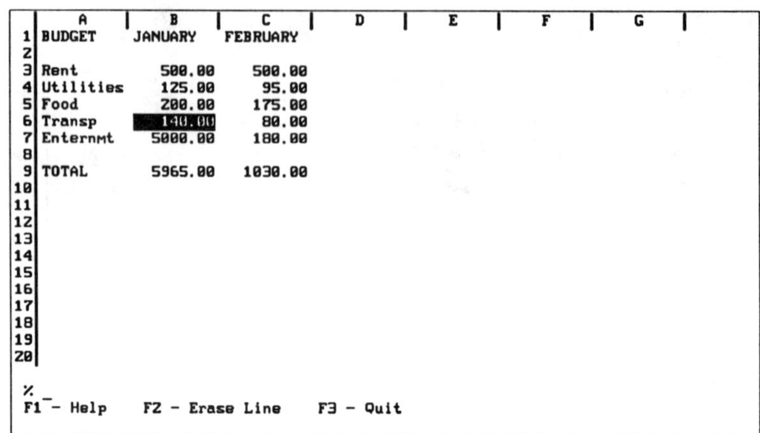

```
  |    A      |    B     |    C     |    D    |    E    |    F    |    G    |
 1 BUDGET      JANUARY    FEBRUARY
 2
 3 Rent           500.00     500.00
 4 Utilities      125.00      95.00
 5 Food           200.00     175.00
 6 Transp         140.00      80.00
 7 Enternmt      5000.00     180.00
 8
 9 TOTAL         5965.00    1030.00
10
11
12
13
14
15
16
17
18
19
20

 % _
 F1 - Help     F2 - Erase Line     F3 - Quit
```

WHAT'S HAPPENING? Other than the fact that you had a really good time in January, notice how the TOTAL changed to 5965.00 because it is a formula. When you change values, any cell that has a formula is affected.

STEP 10: With the arrow key, move the cursor so that cell B7 is highlighted. Key in the following:

`120` <Enter>

```
  |    A      |    B     |    C     |    D    |    E    |    F    |    G    |
 1 BUDGET      JANUARY    FEBRUARY
 2
 3 Rent           500.00     500.00
 4 Utilities      125.00      95.00
 5 Food           200.00     175.00
 6 Transp         140.00      80.00
 7 Enternmt       120.00     180.00
 8
 9 TOTAL         1085.00    1030.00
10
11
12
13
14
15
16
17
18
19
20

 % _
 F1 - Help     F2 - Erase Line     F3 - Quit
```

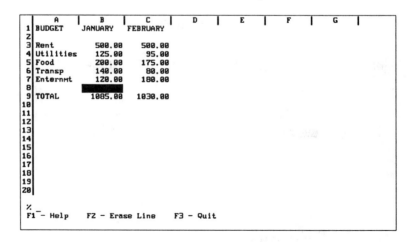

WHAT'S HAPPENING? You corrected the entry.

STEP 11: Move the cursor to cell D1. At the %, key in the following:
"MARCH <Enter>

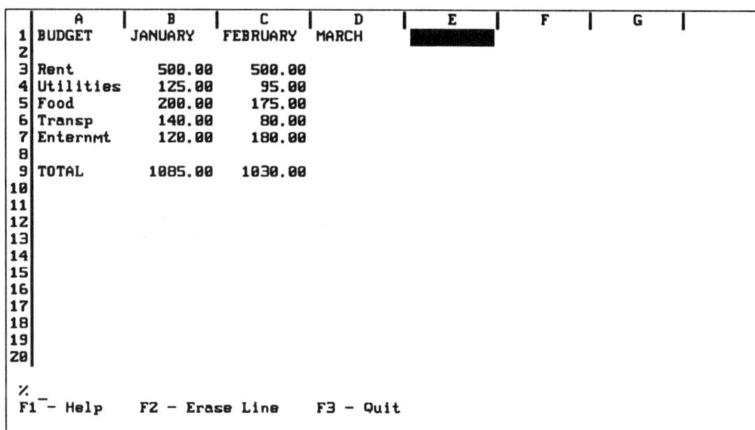

WHAT'S HAPPENING? You use the quotation mark before you key in a title, so that this program knows that MARCH is to be treated as a label, not a number.

STEP 12: Press the F3 key.

```
A:\UTILS>_
```

WHAT'S HAPPENING? You quit the program SS and returned to the DOS system level. However, you are still in the subdirectory UTILS.

STEP 13: Key in the following:
A:\UTILS>CD \ <Enter>

```
A:\UTILS>CD \

A:\>_
```

WHAT'S HAPPENING? You returned to the root directory of the ACTIVITIES disk so that you can do other work, i.e., run another application program.

12.8 Writing a Batch File to Load an Application Program

In the previous activity, in order to execute the spreadsheet program called SS, you needed to take three steps. First you needed to go from the root directory to the subdirectory called UTILS. Then you had to load SS. When you exited SS, you wanted to return to the root directory. A batch file is an ideal place to put all of these commands.

Activity 12.9

Writing a Batch File to Execute SS

Note: The ACTIVITIES disk is still in Drive A with the **A:\>** displayed.

STEP 1: Key in the following:
A:\>**EDIT SS.BAT** <Enter>

STEP 2: Key in the following:
CD \UTILS <Enter>
SS <Enter>
**CD **

WHAT'S HAPPENING? You have just written a batch file to load the **SS** application program automatically. Earlier we said that a batch file should never have the name of a program. Did we violate this rule? No, we did not. Since **SS.BAT** is in the root directory and **SS.EXE** is in a subdirectory, the two files will not conflict.

STEP 3: Press <Alt>+F.

STEP 4: Press X.

STEP 5: Press Y.

STEP 6: Key in the following:
A:\>**TYPE SS.BAT** <Enter>

```
A:\>EDIT SS.BAT

A:\>TYPE SS.BAT
CD \UTILS
SS
CD \

A:\>_
```

WHAT'S HAPPENING? You created the batch file **SS.BAT** in EDIT and then returned to the system prompt. Now you can execute this file.

STEP 7: Key in the following:
A:\>**SS** <Enter>

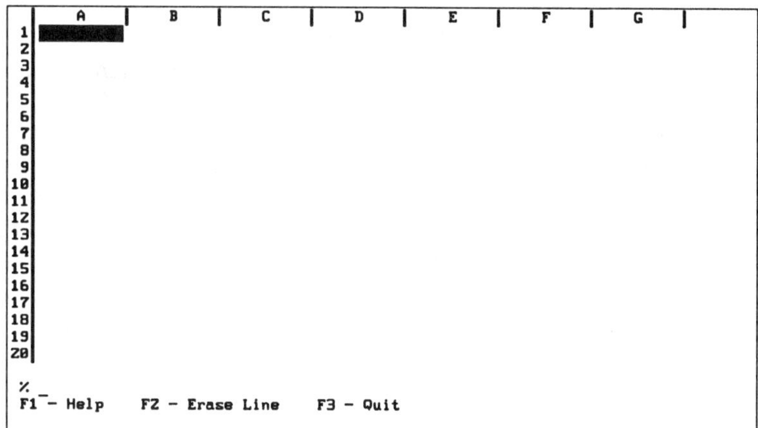

WHAT'S HAPPENING? When you keyed in **SS** at the root directory, DOS first looked in its internal table of commands and could not find **SS**. It next looked in the root directory of the default drive and looked first for **SS.COM**, then **SS.EXE**. It could find neither of these files, so it looked for **SS.BAT** and found it. It read the first line, which said to change the directory to the **UTILS** subdirectory. DOS did that. It then read the second line which said look for a program called **SS** and load it. It then loaded **SS**. You then got the program **SS** on the screen.

STEP 8: Press F3.

```
A:\UTILS>CD \

A:\>
A:\>_
```

WHAT'S HAPPENING? It does not matter if you are in the application program one minute, one hour, or one day. Whenever you exit the application program, which you did by pressing the F3 key, DOS just reads the next line in the batch file. DOS finished executing your batch file. It changed the directory to the root.

12.10 Understanding AUTOEXEC.BAT Files

One unique batch file has a special name: **AUTOEXEC.BAT**, which means automatically execute. When the system is booted and the operating system is loaded into memory, one of the last things DOS does, prior to displaying the date/time prompt, is to look for a file called **AUTOEXEC.BAT** on the booting disk. If DOS finds it, this file takes precedence and DOS automatically runs it. If you do not include the DATE and/or TIME command in **AUTOEXEC.BAT**, DOS will not prompt you for it. The **AUTOEXEC.BAT** file is just a batch file. The only thing special about it is the time it is run. It always runs when you boot the system. Thus, only one **AUTOEXEC.BAT** file can be on any one booting disk. In order for **AUTOEXEC.BAT** to be automatic, it must be on the booting disk, Drive A or Drive C.

This file is typically used for start-up routines. An **AUTOEXEC.BAT** file contains specific commands that a user is interested in having run. In other words, it is a custom program designed by the user.

You are going to create an **AUTOEXEC.BAT** file on a newly formatted floppy disk and then boot from Drive A with that disk in Drive A. You are going to create the **AUTOEXEC.BAT** file on a floppy disk because you may already have an **AUTOEXEC.BAT** file on the hard disk and will not want to overwrite that file. The **AUTOEXEC.BAT** file is going to be written on the new disk and you will use it to boot the system. The **AUTOEXEC.BAT** file is going to change the prompt, set the path, see if you have any files in the DOS subdirectory that begin with the letter **F**, and indicate the version of DOS you are working with.

Activity 12.11 Writing and Using an AUTOEXEC.BAT File

Note 1: If you formatted the DATA disk with the /S parameter in Chapter 4, you already have an operating system on the DATA disk. You may use the DATA disk if you wish, instead of formatting a new disk. If you do, skip to Step 8.

Note 2: The ACTIVITIES disk is in Drive A.

STEP 1: Remove the ACTIVITIES disk from Drive A. Label a new blank disk or a disk you no longer want, "Bootable DOS System Disk." Insert this "Bootable DOS System Disk" in Drive A. Remember that the blank disk must be compatible with your disk drive.

STEP 2: Key in the following:
A:\>**C:** <Enter>

STEP 3: Key in the following:
C:\>**FORMAT A:/S** <Enter>

```
C:\>FORMAT A:/S
Insert new diskette for drive A:
and press ENTER when ready...
```

WHAT'S HAPPENING? You are going to format a disk with an operating system.

STEP 4: Press <Enter>.

```
C:\>FORMAT A:/S
Insert new diskette for drive A:
and press ENTER when ready...
```

```
Checking existing disk format.
Formatting 1.44M
Format complete.
System transferred

Volume label (11 characters, ENTER for none)?_
```

WHAT'S HAPPENING? You transferred the operating system to the disk in Drive A. You do not want a volume label.

STEP 5: Press <Enter>.

```
C:\>FORMAT A:/S
Insert new diskette for drive A:
and press ENTER when ready...

Checking existing disk format.
Saving UNFORMAT information.
Verifying 1.44M
Format complete.
System transferred

Volume label (11 characters, ENTER for none)?

 1457664 bytes total disk space
  119808 bytes used by system
 1337856 bytes available on disk

     512 bytes in each allocation unit.
    2613 allocation units available on disk.

Volume Serial Number is 3D6D-1AD4

Format another (Y/N)?_
```

STEP 6: Press N.

```
Volume Serial Number is 3D6D-1AD4

Format another (Y/N)?N

C:\>_
```

WHAT'S HAPPENING? Now that you have formatted a disk with an operating system on it, you are ready to write an **AUTOEXEC.BAT** file.

STEP 7: Key in the following:

C:\>**A:** <Enter>

STEP 8: Key in the following:

A:\>**COPY CON AUTOEXEC.BAT** <Enter>
PROMPT pg <Enter>
PATH C:\DOS <Enter>
DIR C:\DOS\F*.* <Enter>
VER <Enter>
<Ctrl>+Z <Enter>

```
A:\>COPY CON AUTOEXEC.BAT
PROMPT $p$g
PATH C:\DOS
DIR C:\DOS\F*.*
VER
^Z
    1 file(s) copied

A:\>_
```

WHAT'S HAPPENING? You have written a batch file named **AUTOEXEC.BAT** using COPY CON. You used COPY CON since the file is very short. When you completed writing the batch file, you exited COPY CON and returned to the system prompt. This file, when executed, will not run the date or time command. An **AUTOEXEC.BAT** file will bypass the date and time command if they are not expressly in the **AUTOEXEC.BAT** file. It will then execute the first line which asks for changes in the prompt so that it will reflect the current drive and subdirectory. Furthermore, it will set the path to **C:\DOS**. It will then display all file names in the **DOS** subdirectory that begin with the letter **F**. Last, it will show you the version of DOS you are working with. What makes **AUTOEXEC.BAT** unique is that it executes automatically when you boot the system.

STEP 9: Reboot the system by pressing the <Ctrl>, <Alt>, and <Del> keys. You see the following display.

```
A:\>PROMPT $P$G

A:\>PATH C:\DOS

A:\>DIR C:\DOS\F*.*

   Volume in drive C is HARD DISK
   Volume Serial Number is 1708-78AC
   Directory of C:\DOS

FORMAT    COM   32911   04-09-91   5:00a
FASTOPEN  EXE   12050   04-09-91   5:00a
FDISK     EXE   57224   04-09-91   5:00a
FC        EXE   18650   04-09-91   5:00a
FIND      EXE    6770   04-09-91   5:00a
        5 file(s)      127605 bytes
                      6836224 bytes free
```

```
A:\>VER

MS-DOS Version 5.00

A:\>
A:\>_
```

WHAT'S HAPPENING? You did not have to key in the file name to execute this batch file because it is called **AUTOEXEC.BAT**. This file, **AUTOEXEC.BAT**, always automatically executes when you boot the system. It followed the instructions you included in it. It changed the prompt, set the path, ran the command **DIR C:\DOS\F*.***, and indicated what version of DOS you are running. Since the last command in **AUTOEXEC.BAT** was VER, DOS returns control from the batch file to DOS, ready for the next command.

STEP 10: Key in the following:
A:\>**REN AUTOEXEC.BAT AUTO.BAT** <Enter>

```
A:\>REN AUTOEXEC.BAT AUTO.BAT

A:\>_
```

WHAT'S HAPPENING? You renamed the **AUTOEXEC.BAT** file **AUTO.BAT**. Now, **AUTO.BAT** is just another batch file and will *not* automatically execute when the system is booted from the DATA disk. Remember that the name of the file that automatically executes when you boot the system is **AUTOEXEC.BAT**, not **AUTO.BAT**.

STEP 11: Remove the disk in Drive A.

STEP 12: Reboot the system.

WHAT'S HAPPENING? You have rebooted the system from the hard drive.

12.12 Special Batch File Commands

There are more commands that are specifically designed to be used in batch files. These commands can make batch files extremely versatile. They include REM, ECHO, and PAUSE.

12.13 The REM Command

The REM command, which stands for remarks, is a special command that allows the user to key in explanatory text that will be displayed on the screen. Nothing else happens. REM does not cause DOS to take any action, but it is very useful. When DOS sees REM, it knows that anything following the REM is not a command and, thus, is not supposed to be executed, just displayed on the screen. REM allows a batch file to be **documented**. In a data processing environment, "to document" means to give an explanation about the purpose of the batch file.

This process can be very important when there are many batch files on a disk, especially when someone who did not write the batch file would like to use it. The REM statements should tell anyone what the purpose of the batch file is.

Activity 12.14 Using the REM Command in a Batch File

Note: Be sure the path is set to **C:\DOS**.

STEP 1: Insert the DATA disk in Drive A. Key in the following:
C:\>**A:** <Enter>

```
C:\>A:

A:\>_
```

WHAT'S HAPPENING? You changed the default drive to A:.

STEP 2: Key in the following:
A:\>**EDIT TEST.BAT** <Enter>

REM This is a test file <Enter>
REM to see how the REM <Enter>
REM command works. <Enter>
TYPE EXAMPLE.BAT <Enter>
COPY EXAMPLE.BAT TEST.CAS

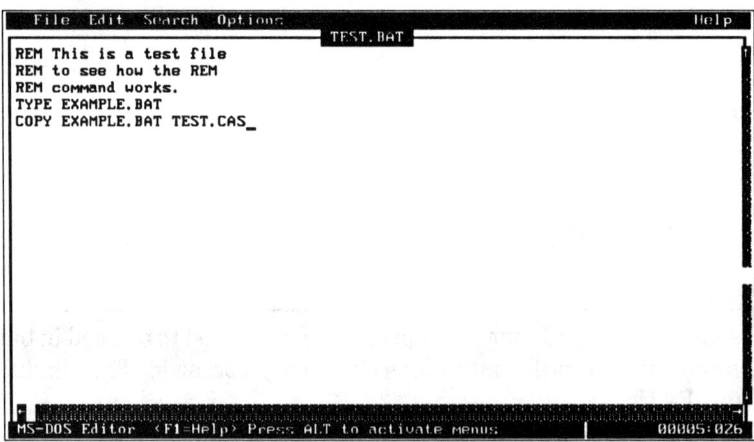

File Edit Search Options Help
TEST.BAT
REM This is a test file
REM to see how the REM
REM command works.
TYPE EXAMPLE.BAT
COPY EXAMPLE.BAT TEST.CAS_
MS-DOS Editor <F1=Help> Press ALT to activate menus
00005:026

WHAT'S HAPPENING? You are writing another batch file called **TEST.BAT** in EDIT. You have inserted some text with REM preceding each line. Then, you keyed in two DOS commands, TYPE and COPY. Now you want to save this file to disk and return to the DOS system level.

STEP 3: Press <Alt>+F.

STEP 4: Press X.

STEP 5: Press Y.

STEP 6: Key in the following:
A:\>**TYPE TEST.BAT** <Enter>

```
A:\>TYPE TEST.BAT
REM This is a test file
REM to see how the REM
REM command works.
TYPE EXAMPLE.BAT
COPY EXAMPLE.BAT TEST.CAS

A:\>_
```

WHAT'S HAPPENING? This batch file was created to be used as a test case. The remarks just keyed in explain the purpose of this batch file. You created **TEST.BAT** in EDIT and returned to the system prompt. You then displayed **TEST.BAT** with the TYPE command. However, to execute **TEST.BAT** batch file, you must call it.

STEP 7: Key in the following:
A:\>**TEST** <Enter>

```
A:\>TEST

A:\>REM This is a test file

A:\>REM to see how the REM

A:\>REM command works.

A:\>TYPE EXAMPLE.BAT
DIR *.DOS
DIR C:\*.DOS

A:\>COPY EXAMPLE.BAT TEST.CAS
    1 file(s) copied

A:\>
A:\>_
```

WHAT'S HAPPENING? When you keyed in **TEST**, the batch file was executed. DOS read the first line of the batch file, "REM This is a test file." DOS knew that it was supposed to do nothing but display the text following REM on the screen. DOS then read the next line in the batch file, "REM to see how the REM" and did the same. DOS kept reading and displaying the REM lines until it got to the line that had the command TYPE. To DOS, TYPE is a command, so it executed or ran the TYPE command with the parameter **EXAMPLE.BAT**. DOS read the next line, which was another command, COPY and copied the file **EXAMPLE.BAT** to a new file called **TEST.CAS**. Then, DOS looked for another line in the batch file but could find no more lines so it returned to the system level. The purpose of REM is to provide explanatory remarks about the batch file, not to execute commands.

12.15 The ECHO Command

Usually a command is displayed and then the results of that command are displayed. ECHO is a command that means "ECHO" or display the command and the output of the command to the screen. The default value for ECHO is "on." The ECHO command is normally *always* on. The only time it is off is if you turn it off. In a batch file, you can turn off the display of the command and see only the output of a command. For instance, **COPY THIS.FIL THAT.FIL** is a command. The output of the command is "1 File(s) copied." The work of the command is the actual copying of the file. Thus:

	ECHO ON SCREEN DISPLAY	ECHO OFF SCREEN DISPLAY
COMMAND	COPY THIS.FIL THAT.FIL	
OUTPUT	1 File(s) copied	1 File(s) copied

If the purpose of the REM command is to document a batch file, what is the purpose of the ECHO command? The ECHO command is a way to not clutter up a screen display with unnecessary verbiage. For instance, although you want to use the REM command to document your batch file, you really do not need to see your documentation every time you run the batch file. ECHO OFF allows you to suppress the display of the commands.

Activity 12.16 Using ECHO

Note: The DATA disk is in Drive A with the **A:\>** displayed.

STEP 1: Key in the following:
A:\>**COPY TEST.BAT TEST1.BAT** <Enter>

```
A:\>COPY TEST.BAT TEST1.BAT
    1 file(s) copied

A:\>_
```

WHAT'S HAPPENING? You made a copy of the file **TEST.BAT**.

STEP 2: Key in the following:
A:\>**EDIT TEST1.BAT** <Enter>
ECHO OFF <Enter>

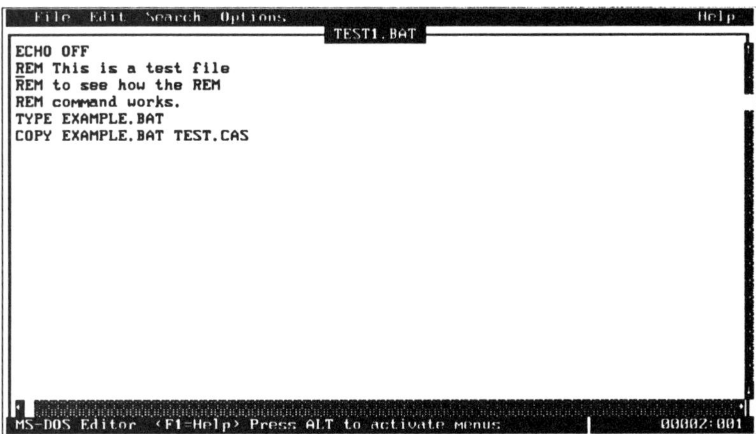

WHAT'S HAPPENING? You are using a copy of the batch file used in the previous activity. The only difference is that you added one line at the top of the file to turn ECHO OFF. Now, you are going to run the batch file so that only the output of each command is displayed, not the actual commands themselves. However, first you must exit EDIT and save the file to disk.

STEP 3: Press <Alt>+F.

STEP 4: Press X.

STEP 5: Press Y.

STEP 6: Key in the following:
A:\>**TYPE TEST1.BAT** <Enter>

```
A:\>TYPE TEST1.BAT
ECHO OFF
REM This is a test file
REM to see how the rem
REM command works.
TYPE EXAMPLE.BAT
COPY EXAMPLE.BAT TEST.CAS

A:\>_
```

WHAT'S HAPPENING? You saved the file as **TEST1.BAT** and displayed the contents on the screen. Now, you wish to execute the file.

STEP 7: Key in the following:
A:\>**TEST1** <Enter>

```
A:\>TEST1

A:\>ECHO OFF
DIR *.DOS
DIR C:\*.DOS
    1 file(s) copied
A:\>_
```

WHAT'S HAPPENING? The batch file **TEST1.BAT** has the same commands as **TEST.BAT**. However, as you can see, you only saw the output of the commands, not the actual commands themselves. For instance, you saw the ECHO OFF command on the screen, but then you did not see the REM command displayed on the screen. You saw the results of the **TYPE EXAMPLE.BAT** command, the contents of the file on the screen, but you never saw the **TYPE EXAMPLE.BAT** command on the screen. You also did not see the **COPY EXAMPLE.BAT TEST.CAS** command, only the results of the command which is the message, "1 File(s) copied." The differences are exemplified below.

	TEST.BAT ECHO ON SCREEN DISPLAY	TEST1.BAT ECHO OFF SCREEN DISPLAY
COMMAND	ECHO ON	ECHO OFF
COMMAND	REM This is a test file	
COMMAND	REM to see how the REM	
COMMAND	REM command works	
COMMAND	TYPE EXAMPLE.BAT	
OUTPUT	DIR *.DOS DIR C:*.DOS	DIR *.DOS DIR C:*.DOS
COMMAND	COPY EXAMPLE.BAT TEST.CAS	
OUTPUT	1 File(s) copied	1 File(s) copied

WHAT'S HAPPENING? The batch file **TEST.BAT** and **TEST1.BAT** executed the same commands. The only difference is that when ECHO was on, which it was for **TEST.BAT**, you saw the remarks as well as the commands. When you executed **TEST1.BAT**, you only saw the output of the commands displayed on the screen, not the actual commands because ECHO was off.

12.17 The PAUSE Command

Another batch file command is PAUSE. PAUSE does exactly what it says: it tells the batch file to stop executing until the user takes some action. No other batch command will be executed until a key is pressed. PAUSE requires user intervention. The PAUSE command will wait forever until the user takes some action.

Activity
12.18
Using the PAUSE Command in a Batch File

Note: The DATA disk is in Drive A with the **A:\>** displayed.

STEP 1: Key in the following:
A:\>**EDIT TEST.BAT** <Enter>

STEP 2: Press <Ctrl>+<End>.

STEP 3: Key in the following:
PAUSE Is the printer on? <Enter>
COPY TEST.CAS PRN <Enter>
DEL TEST.CAS

File Edit Search Options
Help
TEST.BAT
REM This is a test file
REM to see how the REM
REM command works.
TYPE EXAMPLE.BAT
COPY EXAMPLE.BAT TEST.CAS
PAUSE Is the printer on?
COPY TEST.CAS PRN
DEL TEST.CAS_
MS-DOS Editor <F1=Help> Press ALT to activate menus
00008:013

WHAT'S HAPPENING? You edited the batch file **TEST.BAT**. When the file is executed, the first three lines of the file, the REM statements, tell the purpose of the file; **TEST.BAT** then displays the contents of **EXAMPLE.BAT** (**TYPE EXAMPLE.BAT**) on the screen and copies the file **EXAMPLE.BAT** to a new file, **TEST.CAS** (**COPY EXAMPLE.BAT TEST.CAS**). The PAUSE statement gives the user a chance to make sure the printer is turned on before sending output to it. However, it does not make the user turn on the printer; the pause only asks a question. After the user takes action by pressing a key, the file **TEST.CAS** is copied to the printer (**COPY TEST.CAS PRN**). Then, the file **TEST.CAS** is erased **(DEL TEST.CAS)**.

STEP 4: Press <Alt>+F.

STEP 5: Press X.

STEP 6: Press Y.

STEP 7: Key in the following:
A:\>**TYPE TEST.BAT** <Enter>

```
A:\>TYPE TEST.BAT
REM This is a test file
REM to see how the REM
REM command works.
TYPE EXAMPLE.BAT
COPY EXAMPLE.BAT TEST.CAS
PAUSE Is the printer on?
COPY TEST.CAS PRN
DEL TEST.CAS

A:\>_
```

WHAT'S HAPPENING? You saved the file to disk with the changes you made. You then looked at the contents of the file with the TYPE command. To execute `TEST.BAT`, you must key in `TEST` at the prompt.

STEP 8: Key in the following:
A:\>**TEST** <Enter>

```
A:\>TEST

A:\>REM This is a test file

A:\>REM to see how the REM

A:\>REM command works.

A:\>TYPE EXAMPLE.BAT
DIR *.DOS
DIR C:\*.DOS

A:\>COPY EXAMPLE.BAT TEST.CAS
    1 file(s) copied

A:\>PAUSE Is the printer on?
Press any key to continue . . .
```

WHAT'S HAPPENING? If you have a version of DOS less than 4.0, the message will read "Strike a key when ready...". The batch file TEST has stopped running or "paused." It has halted execution until some action is taken. At this point there is a reminder to see if the printer is on. However, if you do not check to see if the printer is on and you press any key, DOS will just read the next line of the batch file. PAUSE is a suggestion reminding you to check the status of the printer, not an order.

STEP 9: Press any key.

```
A:\>PAUSE Is the printer on?
Press any key to continue . . .
```

```
A:\>COPY TEST.CAS PRN
    1 file(s) copied

A:\>DEL TEST.CAS

A:\>
A:\>_
```

WHAT'S HAPPENING? The batch file continued executing all the steps. There should be a printout of the file called **TEST.CAS**. Moreover, since **TEST.CAS** was deleted, it should not be on the directory of the DATA disk. Note: Remember laser printer users must take additional steps.

STEP 10: Key in the following:
A:\>**DIR TEST.CAS** <Enter>

```
A:\>DIR TEST.CAS

 Volume in drive A is DATA DISK
 Volume Serial Number is 3839-0EC8
 Directory of A:\

File not found

A:\>_
```

WHAT'S HAPPENING? The file **TEST.CAS** has been deleted.

12.19 Stopping a Batch File from Executing

In the above activity, you pressed a key after the PAUSE command was displayed so the batch file continued to execute. What if you wanted to stop running the batch file? You can interrupt or exit from a batch file. You do this by pressing the Control key and while pressing the <Ctrl> key, press the letter C (<Ctrl>+C or <Ctrl>+<Break>). At whatever point <Ctrl>+C is pressed, the user leaves the batch file and returns to the system prompt. The rest of the lines in the batch file do not execute.

Activity 12.20 Quitting a Batch File

Note: The DATA disk is in Drive A with the **A:\>** displayed.

STEP 1: Key in the following:
A:\>**EDIT TEST.BAT** <Enter>

STEP 2: Press <Ctrl>+<Enter> 3 times.

STEP 3: Press <Ctrl>+<Shift>+ the <Right arrow> key 3 times.

STEP 4: Press <Del>.

STEP 5: Press the <Down arrow> key once.

STEP 6: Press <Ctrl>+<Right arrow> once.

STEP 7: Press the <Ins> key once.

STEP 8: Key in the following:

Bye test.cas!

STEP 9: Holding the <Ctrl> and <Shift> keys down, press the <Right arrow> key twice. Hold the <Shift> key and press the <Right arrow> key once. Press the <Del> key.

STEP 10: Press the <Ins> key once. Press <Ctrl>+<Enter> once.

STEP 11: Holding the <Ctrl> and <Shift> keys down, press the <Right arrow> three times. Press <Del> twice.

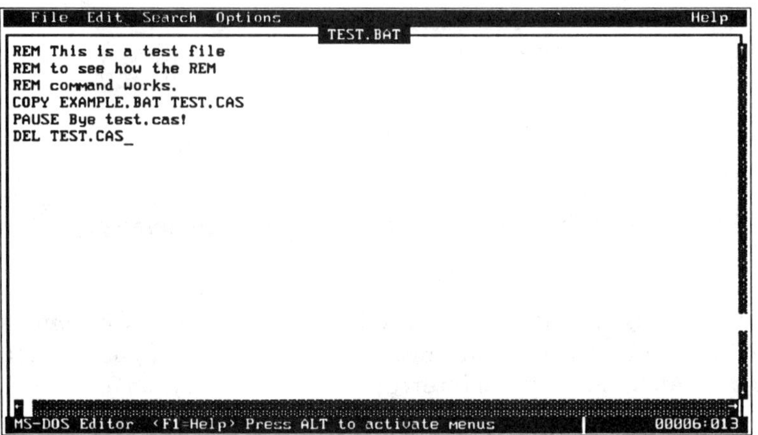
File Edit Search Options
Help
TEST.BAT
REM This is a test file
REM to see how the REM
REM command works.
COPY EXAMPLE.BAT TEST.CAS
PAUSE Bye test.cas!
DEL TEST.CAS_
MS-DOS Editor <F1=Help> Press ALT to activate menus
00006:013

WHAT'S HAPPENING? If your batch file does not look like this, make the appropriate corrections. In this edited batch file, the first three lines tell what this file is about—the REM statements. Line 4 copies the file **EXAMPLE.BAT** to a new file called **TEST.CAS**. The line 5 PAUSE statement allows the user an opportunity not to erase the file **TEST.CAS**. Line 6 erases the file **TEST.CAS**.

STEP 12: Press <Alt>+F.

STEP 13: Press X.

STEP 14: Press Y.

STEP 15: Key in the following:

A:\>**TYPE TEST.BAT** <Enter>

```
A:\>TYPE TEST.BAT
REM This is a test file
REM to see how the REM
REM command works.
COPY EXAMPLE.BAT TEST.CAS
PAUSE Bye test.cas!
DEL TEST.CAS

A:\>
```

WHAT'S HAPPENING? You have saved the edited **TEST.BAT** to disk. You then displayed it on the screen with the TYPE command. Now, to execute it, you must key in **TEST** at the prompt.

STEP 16: Key in the following:
A:\>**TEST** <Enter>

```
A:\>TEST

A:\>REM This is a test file

A:\>REM to see how the REM

A:\>REM command works.

A:\>COPY EXAMPLE.BAT TEST.CAS
    1 file(s) copied

A:\>PAUSE Bye test.cas!
Press any key to continue . . .
```

WHAT'S HAPPENING? The batch file reached the PAUSE command. It stopped running. You do not want to erase **TEST.CAS**. You want the batch file to cease operation. Previous experience with the PAUSE command showed that pressing any key would continue running the program. If any key were pressed here, the next line in the file, **DEL TEST.CAS** would execute and the file **TEST.CAS** would be erased. To stop this from happening, another action must be taken to interrupt the batch file process.

STEP 17: Press the <Ctrl> key. While pressing the <Ctrl> key, press the letter C.

```
A:\>PAUSE Bye test.cas!
Press any key to continue . . .
^C

Terminate batch job (Y/N)?_
```

WHAT'S HAPPENING? The message is giving you a choice: stop the batch file from running (Y for yes) or continue with the batch file (N for no). If you key in Y for yes, the last line in the batch file, **DEL TEST.CAS**, will not execute.

STEP 18: Press Y.

```
A:\>PAUSE Bye test.cas!
Press any key to continue . . .
^C

Terminate batch job (Y/N)?Y

A:\>_
```

WHAT'S HAPPENING? The system prompt is displayed. If the batch job was interrupted properly, **TEST.CAS** should not have been deleted because the line **DEL TEST.CAS** should not have executed.

STEP 19: Key in the following:
A:\>**DIR TEST.CAS** <Enter>

```
A:\>DIR TEST.CAS

 Volume in drive A is DATA DISK
 Volume Serial Number is 3839-0EC8
 Directory of A:\

TEST     CAS       25   01-24-92 10:06a
         1 file(s)           25 bytes
                         177152 bytes free

A:\>_
```

WHAT'S HAPPENING? The file **TEST.CAS** is still on the DATA disk. Pressing <Ctrl>+C at the line **PAUSE Bye test.cas!** broke into the batch file **TEST.BAT** and stopped it from running. Since **TEST.BAT** stopped executing and returned you to the system prompt, it never got to the command line **DEL TEST.CAS**. That is why the file **TEST.CAS** is still on the DATA disk. Although you broke into the batch file at the PAUSE statement, you can press <Ctrl>+C any time during the execution of a batch file. The batch file will stop the first chance it gets.

12.21 Replaceable Parameters in Batch Files

Parameters are used in many DOS commands. Parameters are information that you want the command to have. The commands or programs use the information in the parameter. For instance, look at the command, **DIR A:/W**.

DIR	A: /W
Command	Command line parameter

In the above example, the space, : and / are all delimiters. DIR is the command. A and W are parameters that tell DOS that you want a directory of A and that you want it displayed in a wide mode. Parameters tell DIR what to do. When you use the DIR command as used above, the /W parameter is fixed; you cannot choose another letter.

DOS commands also use variable or replaceable parameters. An example of where a replaceable parameter can be used is with TYPE. TYPE requires one parameter, file name. The command, TYPE, remains the same, but the file name you use will vary; hence, it is a variable parameter. TYPE uses the parameter that you keyed in to choose the file to display on the screen. You can key in **`TYPE THIS.FIL`** or **`TYPE TEST.TXT`** or whatever file name you want. You replace the file name for the parameter.

TYPE	THIS.FIL
Command	Replaceable command line parameter

or

TYPE	TEST.TXT
Command	Replaceable command line parameter

Batch files can also use **replaceable parameters**, also called **dummy parameters**, **substitute parameters** or **positional parameters**. When you key in the name of the batch file to execute, you can also key in additional information that your batch file can use. When you write the batch file, you supply the markers or placeholders to let the batch file know that something, a variable, will be keyed in with the batch file name. The placeholder, marker, or blank parameter used in a batch file is the percent sign (%) followed by a number from 0 through 9. The % sign is the signal to DOS that a parameter is coming. The numbers indicate what position the parameter is. The command itself is always %0.

TYPE	TEST.TXT
%0	%1

COPY	THIS.ONE	THAT.ONE
%0	%1	%2

The batch files that you have written so far deal with specific commands and specific file names, but the real power of batch files is their ability to use replaceable parameters. You are going to write a batch file in the usual way with specific file names and then change the batch file to see how replaceable parameters work.

Activity 12.22 Using Replaceable Parameters in Batch Files

Note: The DATA disk is in Drive A with the **`A:\>`** displayed.

STEP 1: Key in the following:

A:\>**EDIT PRACTICE.BAT** <Enter>
DIR MARCH.TXT <Enter>
TYPE MARCH.TXT <Enter>
COPY MARCH.TXT PRN

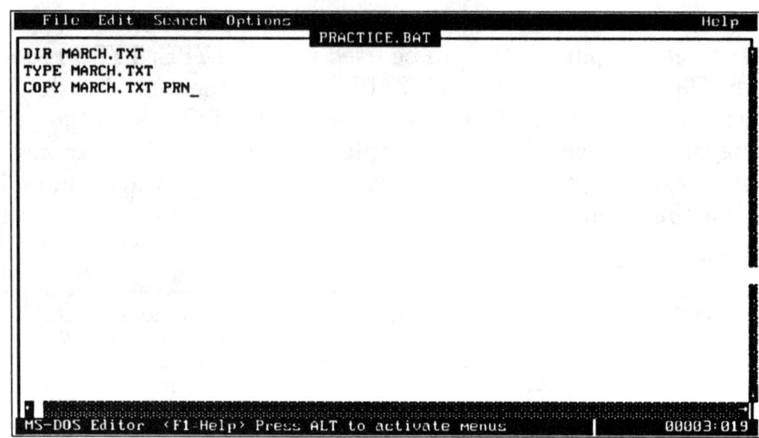

WHAT'S HAPPENING? You created a simple batch file that shows you that the file **MARCH.TXT** is on the DATA disk. Then, you look at the contents of the file called **MARCH.TXT** on the screen with the TYPE command, and you copy **MARCH.TXT** to the printer. Remember that EDIT is the tool to write a batch file. You must save **PRACTICE.BAT** to disk before you can execute it.

STEP 2: Press <Alt>+F.

STEP 3: Press X.

STEP 4: Press Y.

STEP 5: Key in the following:

A:\>**TYPE PRACTICE.BAT** <Enter>

```
A:\>TYPE PRACTICE.BAT
DIR MARCH.TXT
TYPE MARCH.TXT
COPY MARCH.TXT PRN

A:\>_
```

WHAT'S HAPPENING? You saved the file to disk. If **MARCH.TXT** is not on the DATA disk, you can copy it from **C:\JUNK** to the DATA disk. Be sure the printer is on before you execute the batch file. To execute this batch file, you must call it.

STEP 6: Key in the following:

A:\>**PRACTICE** <Enter>

```
A:\>PRACTICE

A:\>DIR MARCH.TXT

 Volume in drive A is DATA DISK
 Volume Serial Number is 3839-0EC8
 Directory of A:\

MARCH    TXT      69   11-23-92   7:11a
        1 file(s)          69 bytes
                       176128 bytes free

A:\>TYPE MARCH.TXT
This is my March file.
It is my third dummy file.
This is file 3.

A:\>COPY MARCH.TXT PRN
    1 file(s) copied

A:\>
A:\>_
```

WHAT'S HAPPENING? The batch file called **PRACTICE** ran successfully. However, it can only be used for the file called **MARCH.TXT**. What if you wanted to do the same sequence of commands for a file called **JAN.TMP** or **PERSONAL.FIL** or any other file on the disk? Until now, you would create another batch file using **JAN.TMP** instead of **MARCH.TXT**. For **PERSONAL.FIL**, you would write another batch file using **PERSONAL.FIL**. As you can see, you can quickly clutter up your disks with many batch files, all doing the same thing but using different file names. An easier way is to have one batch file that does the same steps—a generic batch file. When you execute it, you supply the specific parameter or file name that interests you.

You are going to write a batch file with the same commands as **PRACTICE.BAT**, only this time you will use replacable parameters. Be sure to use the percent sign (%), then the number 1. There is no space between the % and the number 1. Be sure you use the number 1, not the letter l.

STEP 7: Key in the following:

A:\>**EDIT PRAC.BAT** <Enter>
DIR %1 <Enter>
TYPE %1 <Enter>
COPY %1 PRN

STEP 8: Press <Alt>+F.

STEP 9: Press X.

STEP 10: Press Y.

STEP 11: Key in the following:

A:\>**TYPE PRAC.BAT** <Enter>

```
A:\>TYPE PRAC.BAT
DIR %1
TYPE %1
COPY %1 PRN

A:\>_
```

WHAT'S HAPPENING? You created a batch file called **PRAC.BAT** in EDIT. You then saved it to disk. You displayed the contents of the file on the screen. The contents of the batch file **PRAC.BAT** are different from those of the batch file **PRACTICE.BAT**. By using the placeholder %1, instead of a specific file name, you are saying that you do not yet know what file name (%1) you want these commands to apply to. When you run the batch file PRAC, you will provide a value or parameter on the command line that the batch file will substitute for %1. For instance, if you keyed in **PRAC MY**, **PRAC** is the 0 parameter and **MY** is the first parameter. These are called positional parameters. DOS gets the information or knows what to substitute by the position on the command line. The first item is always 0, the second 1, the third 2, and so on. Be sure the printer is turned on.

STEP 12: Key in the following:

A:\>**PRAC DRAMA.TV** <Enter>

```
A:\>PRAC DRAMA.TV

A:\>DIR DRAMA.TV

 Volume in drive A is DATA DISK
 Volume Serial Number is 3839-0EC8
 Directory of A:\

DRAMA     TV       183   11-23-92 10:16a
        1 file(s)          183 bytes
                        174080 bytes free

A:\>TYPE DRAMA.TV
DRAMATIC TELEVISION SERIES

L.A. Law
Playhouse 90
Murder, She Wrote
Dallas
I, Claudius
Upstairs, Downstairs
Falcon Crest
Beauty and the Beast
Columbo
Hill Street Blues
```

```
A:\>COPY DRAMA.TV PRN
    1 file(s) copied

A:\>
A:\>_
```

WHAT'S HAPPENING? In the command line **PRAC DRAMA.TV**, **PRAC** is position 0 and **DRAMA.TV** is position 1. The batch file **PRAC** executed each command line. However, when it found %1 in the batch file, it looked for the first position after **PRAC** on the command line, which was **DRAMA.TV**. It substituted **DRAMA.TV** every time it found %1. As you can see, you have written a generic or "plain wrap" batch file that allows you to use the same batch file over and over. All you have to supply is a value or parameter after the batch file name on the command line. Thus, you could key in **PRAC BUSINESS.APP**, **PRAC SALES.LET**, **PRAC FEB.99**, **PRAC TELE.SET** or any other file name. The batch file will execute the same commands over and over, using the position 1 value (the file name) you keyed in after the batch file name.

12.23 Multiple Replaceable Parameters in Batch Files

In the above example, you used one replaceable parameter. What happens if you need more than one parameter? For instance, if you want to include the COPY command in a batch file, COPY needs two parameters, *source* and *destination*. Many commands require more than one parameter. You may also use multiple parameters in batch files. You can have up to ten dummy parameters (%0 through %9). Replaceable parameters are sometimes called positional parameters, because DOS uses the position number in the command line to determine which parameter to use. The parameters are placed in order from left to right. For example, if you had the command line:

```
COPY MYFILE.TXT YOUR.FIL
```

COPY is in position one, %0 (computers always start with 0, not 1). **MYFILE.TXT** is in position two, %1, and **YOUR.FIL** is in position three, %2.

The next activity will allow you to create a batch file with multiple replaceable parameters. This batch file allows you to create a command that DOS does not have. It will "move" a file from one place to another—copy it to a new location and then delete the file from the original location.

Activity 12.24 Using Replaceable Parameters: Writing Your Own Commands

Note: The DATA disk is in Drive A with the **A:\>** displayed.

STEP 1: Key in the following:

```
A:\>EDIT MOVE.BAT <Enter>
DIR %1 <Enter>
COPY %1 %2 <Enter>
DIR %2 <Enter>
REM If you DO NOT want to delete %1, <Enter>
REM Press Ctrl+C NOW. Otherwise, press any <Enter>
PAUSE key to erase %1 <Enter>
DEL %1
```

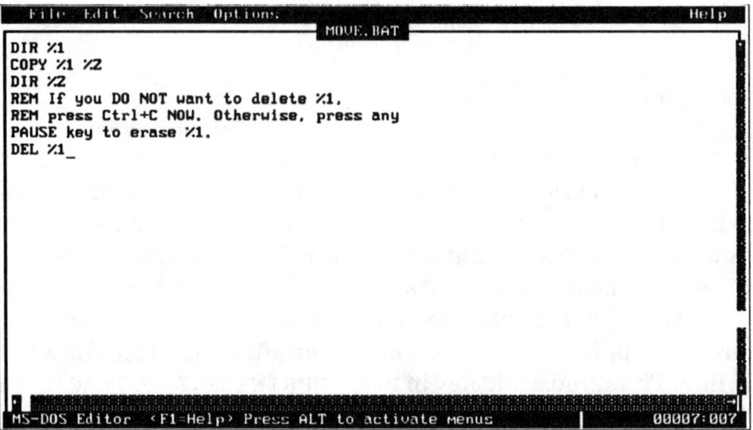

WHAT'S HAPPENING? You created a batch file called **MOVE.BAT** using multiple positional parameters. This is a command that DOS does not have. It copies a file from one location to another and deletes the first file from its original location. Now, you must save the file to disk.

STEP 2: Press <Alt>+F.

STEP 3: Press X.

STEP 4: Press Y.

STEP 5: Key in the following:
A:\>**TYPE MOVE.BAT** <Enter>

```
A:\>TYPE MOVE.BAT
DIR %1
COPY %1 %2
DIR %2
REM If you DO NOT want to delete %1,
REM Press Ctrl+C NOW. Otherwise, press any
PAUSE key to erase %1.
DEL %1

A:\>_
```

WHAT'S HAPPENING? You are displaying the contents of **MOVE.BAT**. To execute it you must not only key in the command name—**MOVE**—but also provide the command with the positional parameters.

STEP 6: Key in the following:
A:\>**MOVE JAN.TMP NOV.TST** <Enter>

```
A:\>MOVE JAN.TMP NOV.TST

A:\>DIR JAN.TMP

 Volume in drive A is DATA DISK
 Volume Serial Number is 3839-0EC8
 Directory of A:\

JAN      TMP      72   11-23-92   7:04a
        1 file(s)         72 bytes
                      172032 bytes free

A:\>COPY JAN.TMP NOV.TST
    1 file(s) copied

A:\>DIR NOV.TST

 Volume in drive A is DATA DISK
 Volume Serial Number is 3839-0EC8
 Directory of A:\

NOV      TST      72   11-23-92   7:04a
        1 file(s)         72 bytes
                      172032 bytes free

A:\>REM If you DO NOT want to delete JAN.TMP,

A:\>REM Press <Ctrl>+C NOW. Otherwise, press any

A:\>PAUSE key to erase JAN.TMP.
Press any key to continue . . .
```

WHAT'S HAPPENING? Earlier versions of DOS have the message, "Strike a key when ready..." The batch file is following the instructions. Since the command line read **MOVE JAN.TMP NOV.TST**., **MOVE** is %0; **JAN.TMP** is %1, and **NOV.TST** is %2. Whenever DOS needed a value in the batch file for %1 or %2, it looked to the command line position to get it. Since you do want to erase the file, you need to press a key so that the batch file will continue executing.

STEP 7: Press any key.

```
A:\>COPY JAN.TMP NOV.TST
    1 file(s) copied

A:\>DIR NOV.TST

 Volume in drive A is DATA DISK
 Volume Serial Number is 3839-0EC8
 Directory of A:\

NOV      TST      72   11-23-92   7:04a
        1 file(s)         72 bytes
                      172032 bytes free
```

```
A:\>REM If you DO NOT want to delete JAN.TMP,

A:\>REM Press Ctrl+C NOW. Otherwise, press any

A:\>PAUSE key to erase JAN.TMP.
Press any key to continue . . .

A:\>DEL JAN.TMP

A:\>
A:\>_
```

WHAT'S HAPPENING? When you pressed any key, the batch file read the next line, which was **DEL JAN.TMP**. It deleted **JAN.TMP**. You ran the batch file called **MOVE**. You substituted or provided the values, **JAN.TMP** (%1) and **NOV.TST** (%2), when you ran the batch file because **JAN.TMP** was in position 1 and **NOV.TST** was in position 2, e.g., **MOVE** (**MOVE JAN.TMP NOV.TST**). To DOS, the command sequence or string of commands looked like this:

```
DIR JAN.TMP
COPY JAN.TMP NOV.TST
DIR NOV.TST
REM If you DO NOT want to delete JAN.TMP,
REM Press Ctrl+C NOW. Otherwise, press any
PAUSE key to erase JAN.TMP.
DEL JAN.TMP
```

Let's explain this command line by command line. When you keyed in **MOVE JAN.TMP NOV.TST**, you asked DOS to load the batch file called **MOVE.BAT**. The first position after **MOVE** has the value of **JAN.TMP** and the second position has the value of **NOV.TST**. DOS then executed the first line, which is:

1. **DIR JAN.TMP**
   This line asked DOS to see if a file called **JAN.TMP** was in the default directory. DOS knew it should substitute **JAN.TMP** for %1 because **JAN.TMP** is in the first position after **MOVE**.
2. **COPY JAN.TMP NOV.TST**
   This line tells DOS to copy the file named **JAN.TMP** (%1) to a new file to be called **NOV.TST** (%2). DOS knew which file was %1 and could substitute **JAN.TMP** for %1 because **JAN.TMP** held the first position after the command **MOVE**. It also knew what file was %2 and could substitute **NOV.TST** for %2 because **NOV.TST** was in the second position after **MOVE**.
3. **DIR NOV.TST**
   This line tells DOS to do a directory search for the file called **NOV.TST** (%2). Again, DOS knew which file was %2 because **NOV.TST** was in the second position. The reason that you included a directory search is to ensure that the file **JAN.TMP** was copied to a new file called **NOV.TST** *before* you erased **JAN.TMP**.
4. **REM If you DO NOT want to delete JAN.TMP,**
   This line is the beginning of the remarks to let you know what is going to happen. It is telling you that **JAN.TMP** (%1) is about to be erased.

5. **REM Press Ctrl+C NOW. Otherwise, press any**
   This remark lets you know what to do if you do not wish to delete the file **JAN.TMP**.
6. **PAUSE key to erase JAN.TMP.**
   This command line allows you to take action. PAUSE stops the batch file from executing until you press a key. DOS knew what file name to substitute for %1. This line is in the batch file, so preventive action can be taken if the file (%1, or **JAN.TMP**) was not copied to a file (%2, or **NOV.TST**), or if you did not, after all, want to erase the file (%1, or **JAN.TMP**). By pressing the <Ctrl> key and the letter C, the batch file is terminated and will not execute the last line of the file.
7. **DEL JAN.TMP**
   Since you pressed a key, DOS read the next line in the batch file which was **DEL JAN.TMP**. This command line will erase the file called **JAN.TMP** (%1). Again, DOS knew which file to substitute for %1. The file %1 or **JAN.TMP** is now deleted.

This command, which you just wrote as a batch file with replaceable parameters, can be very useful. You can use it to copy files from one disk to another and then erase the file from the source disk so that you do not end up with multiple files on multiple disks. You do not need to take separate steps because all the steps are included in the batch file. If you are copying from drive to drive, you must include the drive designator and the path. For example, if you wanted to move a file from the disk in Drive A to the disk in Drive B and then delete it from Drive A, you would key in the following:

A:\>**MOVE AUG.OLD B:AUGUST.NEW**

If you wanted to move a file from Drive C to Drive A, you would key in the following:

A:\>**MOVE C:AUGUST.OLD AUGUST.NEW**

If you wanted to move a file from Drive C in the subdirectory **\JUNK** to Drive A, you would key in the following:

A:\>**MOVE C:\JUNK\AUGUST.OLD AUGUST.NEW**

If you wanted to move a file from one subdirectory to another, you would key in the following:

C:\>**MOVE \JUNK\AUGUST.OLD \SAMPLE\AUGUST.NEW**

12.25 Creating Menus with Batch Files

One of the creative things you can do with batch files is creating menus that relate to your applications. A menu is exactly what it sounds like. In a restaurant, you look at a menu and then pick your selection. In this case, instead of picking out something to eat, you are picking a task to do. A menu system presents a "main menu" with choices on it. Each choice has a corresponding batch file. On the ACTIVITIES disk there are two application programs, the spreadsheet program, SS and the Rolodex program, ADDRESS. In the next activity, you are going to create a menu system to access either of these programs. In addition, you will have a choice of exiting back to DOS.

Activity 12.26 Writing Menus

Note: The DATA disk is in Drive A with the **A:\>** displayed.

STEP 1: Remove the DATA disk from Drive A. Insert the ACTIVITIES disk in Drive A.

STEP 2: Key in the following:
A:\>**MD \BATCH** <Enter>

STEP 3: Key in the following:
A:\>**CD \BATCH** <Enter>

```
A:\>MD \BATCH

A:\>CD \BATCH

A:\BATCH>_
```

WHAT'S HAPPENING? You created a subdirectory on the ACTIVITIES disk called **BATCH** where you will keep all your batch files and any associated files. It is always wise to keep like files together. You then changed the default directory to **BATCH** where you are going to write the necessary files.

STEP 4: Note: When you see <Enter>, press the <Enter> key. When you see <Tab>, press the <Tab> key. Key in the following:
A:\BATCH>**EDIT MENU.TXT** <Enter>
MY MENU SYSTEM <Enter>
<Enter>
<Enter>
A.<Tab>**MY SPREADSHEET PROGRAM** <Enter>
B.<Tab>**MY ADDRESS PROGRAM** <Enter>
E.<Tab>**EXIT TO DOS** <Enter>
<Enter>
<Enter>

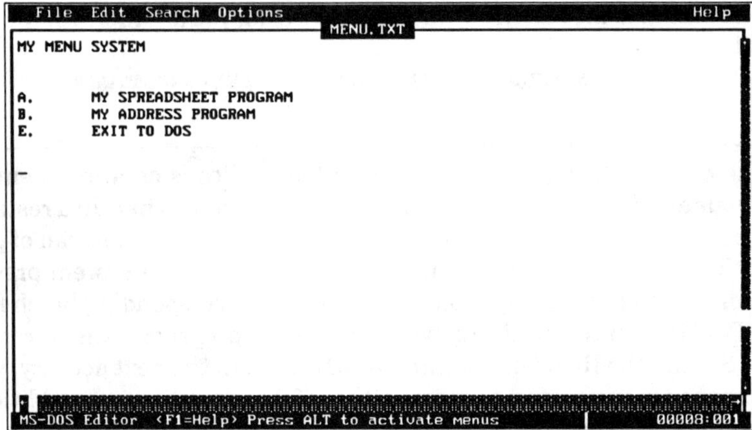

WHAT'S HAPPENING? You are using EDIT to write a text file that will be used in the batch file. You must now save this file to disk.

STEP 5: Press <Alt>+F.

STEP 6: Press X.

STEP 7: Press Y.

STEP 8: Key in the following:
A:\BATCH>**TYPE MENU.TXT** <Enter>

```
A:\BATCH>TYPE MENU.TXT
MY MENU SYSTEM


A.    MY SPREADSHEET PROGRAM
B.    MY ADDRESS PROGRAM
E.    EXIT TO DOS



A:\BATCH>_
```

WHAT'S HAPPENING? The file you just created is not a batch file. It is simply a text file. This text file will display the choices the user can make. It will be displayed in the menu batch file with the TYPE command. It is easier to create a separate text file than it is to put these text lines in a batch file. If you put text lines in a batch file, every line would have to be preceded by a REM so that DOS would not try to execute the line. The next step is to create the **MENU.BAT** file.

STEP 9: Key in the following:
A:\BATCH>**EDIT MENU.BAT** <Enter>
TYPE MENU.TXT <Enter>
PROMPT Select a letter. <Spacebar> <Spacebar>

WHAT'S HAPPENING? This is a two-line batch file. The first command line will display the contents of the **MENU.TXT** file. The **MENU.TXT** file simply tells the user what the choices are. The second command line changes the way the prompt looks. Instead of the prompt being a drive letter such as **A>** or **A:\BATCH>** or **C:\>**, it will now read "**Select a letter.**" You press the <Spacebar> twice after "**Select a letter**" so that you have a visually pleasing prompt. Since it is the command line prompt, any command issued at this prompt will perform in the same way. The prompt just looks different. You must save the file. The next step is to test the menu system.

STEP 10: Press <Alt>+F.

STEP 11: Press X.

STEP 12: Press Y.

STEP 13: Key in the following:
A:\BATCH>**TYPE MENU.BAT** <Enter>

```
A:\BATCH>TYPE MENU.BAT
TYPE MENU.TXT
PROMPT Select a letter.

A:\BATCH>_
```

WHAT'S HAPPENING? You saved the file to disk. The next step is to execute it.

STEP 14: Key in the following:
A:\BATCH>**MENU** <Enter>

```
A:\BATCH>MENU

A:\BATCH>TYPE MENU.TXT
MY MENU SYSTEM


A.   MY SPREADSHEET PROGRAM
B.   MY ADDRESS PROGRAM
E.   EXIT TO DOS



A:\BATCH>PROMPT Select a letter.

Select a letter.
Select a letter._
```

WHAT'S HAPPENING? DOS read and executed each line of the batch file. Notice that the prompt looks different. It will behave the same as any prompt.

However, if you try to select one of the choices from the menu by keying in **A** or **B** or **E**, all that will happen is that you will get a "Bad command or file name" message. When you key something in at the command line prompt, DOS is looking for a program to execute. Thus, if you key in "A," it will be to no purpose since as of yet you have no program called **A.COM**, **A.EXE**, or **A.BAT**. If DOS cannot find a program, it cannot execute it. In the next step you can prove this.

STEP 15: Key in the following:
A <Enter>

```
A:\BATCH>MENU

A:\BATCH>TYPE MENU.TXT
MY MENU SYSTEM


A.    MY SPREADSHEET PROGRAM
B.    MY ADDRESS PROGRAM
E.    EXIT TO DOS



A:\BATCH>PROMPT Select a letter.

Select a letter.
Select a letter. A
Bad command or file name

Select a letter. _
```

WHAT'S HAPPENING? When you keyed in **A** at the prompt "Select a letter," DOS looked for a file called **A.COM**, then **A.EXE** and, last, **A.BAT**. There is no program by that name. You must write a batch file called **A.BAT**, **B.BAT** and **E.BAT** in order to be able to select the choices.

STEP 16: Key in the following:
PROMPT pg <Enter>

```
Select a letter. PROMPT $p$g

A:\BATCH>_
```

WHAT'S HAPPENING? The prompt has been changed from "Select a letter" to a prompt that identifies the default drive and subdirectory. Now you are going to write some other batch files. Each of the batch files will contain the steps necessary to accomplish running the application programs. For instance, you know that on this disk the spreadsheet program, **SS**, is in the subdirectory **\UTILS**. Thus, it will be necessary to change directories prior to issuing the **SS** command. In addition, when you have finished using the spreadsheet program, not only do you want to return to DOS, but you want to return to the menu system. You are, in essence, **chaining batch files** together.

STEP 17: Key in the following:

A:\BATCH>**EDIT A.BAT** <Enter>
PROMPT <Enter>
CD \UTILS <Enter>
SS <Enter>
CD \BATCH <Enter>
MENU

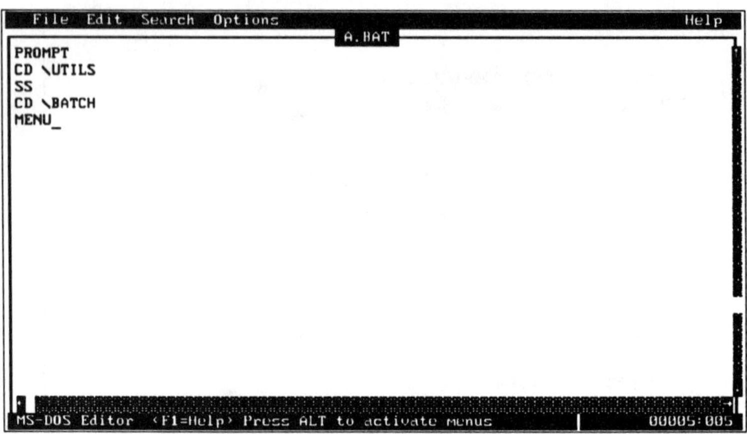

WHAT'S HAPPENING? Each line in the **A.BAT** file takes you through the steps that you need to access the spreadsheet program. First you change the prompt so that it reflects the current drive and subdirectory. Then you change the default directory to the **\UTILS** subdirectory. You next issue the **SS** command that will execute the spreadsheet program. You then can do work in the spreadsheet for an hour, a minute, or a day. Time does not matter. When you exit the spreadsheet program, DOS returns to the next line in the batch file, which returns you to the **\BATCH** subdirectory. It then calls the menu program. You must save this file to disk.

STEP 18: Press <Alt>+F.

STEP 19: Press X.

STEP 20: Press Y.

STEP 21: Key in the following:

A:\BATCH>**TYPE A.BAT** <Enter>

```
A:\BATCH>TYPE A.BAT
PROMPT
CD \UTILS
```

```
SS
CD \BATCH
MENU

A:\BATCH>_
```

WHAT'S HAPPENING? You now have saved the file. To see both **MENU.BAT** and **A.BAT** in action, you must begin with **MENU**.

STEP 22: Key in the following:
A:\BATCH>**MENU** <Enter>

```
A:\BATCH>MENU

A:\BATCH>TYPE MENU.TXT
MY MENU SYSTEM


A.   MY SPREADSHEET PROGRAM
B.   MY ADDRESS PROGRAM
E.   EXIT TO DOS



A:\BATCH>PROMPT Select a letter.

Select a letter.
Select a letter._
```

WHAT'S HAPPENING? The menu system looks the same. However, now that you have written the batch file called **A.BAT**, when you key in "a" at the "Select a letter" prompt, DOS will find **A.BAT** and execute it. Watch the screen closely in the next step. Notice how quickly you will be in the spreadsheet program.

STEP 23: Key in the following:
A <Enter>

```
A:\BATCH>MENU

A:\BATCH>TYPE MENU.TXT
MY MENU SYSTEM


A.   MY SPREADSHEET PROGRAM
B.   MY ADDRESS PROGRAM
E.   EXIT TO DOS



A:\BATCH>PROMPT Select a letter.

Select a letter.
```

```
Select a letter. A

Select a letter. PROMPT

A>CD \UTILS

A>SS
```

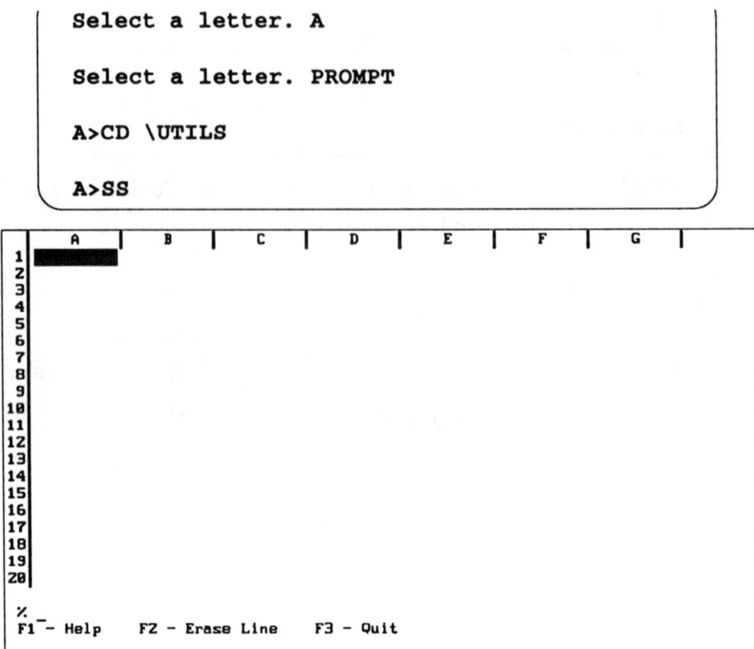

WHAT'S HAPPENING? By selecting the letter "a," you ended up in the application program, **SS**. You could stay here and do your budget or whatever work you planned to do in the spreadsheet program. However, sooner or later you would be finished working and would want to exit the program. The batch file, **MENU.BAT**, is still poised on the line **SS**. The minute you exit the spreadsheet program, DOS will read the next line **CD \BATCH**. Again, watch the screen carefully in the next step because the screen display will execute very quickly.

STEP 24: Press the F3 key.

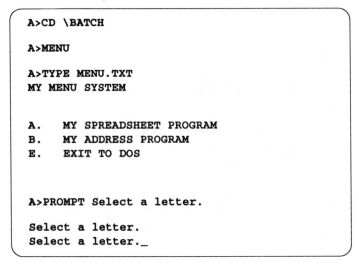

```
A>CD \BATCH

A>MENU

A>TYPE MENU.TXT
MY MENU SYSTEM


A.   MY SPREADSHEET PROGRAM
B.   MY ADDRESS PROGRAM
E.   EXIT TO DOS



A>PROMPT Select a letter.

Select a letter.
Select a letter._
```

WHAT'S HAPPENING? You exited the spreadsheet program. The next line in the batch file was read and executed (**CD \BATCH**), and then the next line was read and executed (**MENU**). Now, you are ready for the next step.

Activity 12.27 Completing the Menu

Note: The ACTIVITIES disk is in Drive A with "Select a letter _" displayed.

STEP 1: Key in the following:
PROMPT pg <Enter>

```
A>CD \BATCH

A>MENU

A>TYPE MENU.TXT
MY MENU SYSTEM


A.    MY SPREADSHEET PROGRAM
B.    MY ADDRESS PROGRAM
E.    EXIT TO DOS



A>PROMPT Select a letter.

Select a letter.
Select a letter. PROMPT $p$g

A:\BATCH>_
```

WHAT'S HAPPENING? You changed the prompt so that it again displays the default drive and subdirectory. Be sure you are in the **BATCH** subdirectory on the ACTIVITIES disk. You are going to write the **E.BAT** file as well as discover how to make the menu system more aesthetically pleasing.

STEP 2: Key in the following:
A:\BATCH>**EDIT END.TXT** <Enter>
You have exited the MENU system. If you wish <Enter>
to return to the MENU system, key in MENU at <Enter>
the prompt.

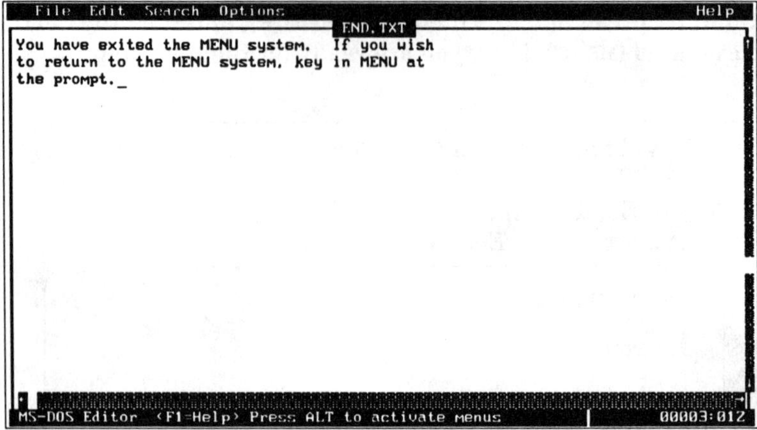

WHAT'S HAPPENING? You wrote a text file that will be displayed in the **E.BAT** file. You must now save this file to disk.

STEP 3: Press <Alt>+F.

STEP 4: Press X.

STEP 5: Press Y.

STEP 6: Key in the following:

A:\BATCH>**EDIT E.BAT** <Enter>
PROMPT pg <Enter>
TYPE END.TXT <Enter>
**CD **

WHAT'S HAPPENING? You have now written the **E.BAT** file. You changed the prompt so it no longer reads "Select a letter" and, instead, displays the default drive and subdirectory. In addition, you gave a message about how to return to the menu system. Last, you moved the user back to the root directory. Now before you test this part of the menu system, you must save the **E.BAT** file to disk.

STEP 7: Press <Alt>+F.

STEP 8: Press X.

STEP 9: Press Y.

STEP 10: Key in the following:
A:\BATCH>**MENU** <Enter>

```
A:\BATCH>MENU

A:\BATCH>TYPE MENU.TXT
MY MENU SYSTEM


A.    MY SPREADSHEET PROGRAM
B.    MY ADDRESS PROGRAM
E.    EXIT TO DOS



A:\BATCH>PROMPT Select a letter.

Select a letter.
Select a letter._
```

WHAT'S HAPPENING? You are back in the menu system. Now, you are going to use your new "Exit to DOS" command, by keying in **E** at the prompt.

STEP 11: Key in the following:
E <Enter>

```
MY MENU SYSTEM


A.    MY SPREADSHEET PROGRAM
B.    MY ADDRESS PROGRAM
E.    EXIT TO DOS



A:\BATCH>PROMPT Select a letter.

Select a letter.
Select a letter. E

Select a letter. PROMPT $p$g

A:\BATCH>TYPE END.TXT
You have exited the MENU system. If you wish
```

```
to return to the MENU system, key in MENU at
the prompt.

A:\BATCH>CD \

A:\>
A:\>_
```

WHAT'S HAPPENING? As you can see, when you selected "E" from the menu, DOS ran the **E.BAT** program and followed the commands in that file. Those commands changed the prompt and returned you to the root directory. You also provided information on how to return to the MENU program by means of the command **TYPE END.TXT**. If you wanted to be able to return to the menu system, you would need to have a PATH statement with **\BATCH** as part of the path so you would not get the "File not found" message. One other thing you can do to make the batch file more attractive is to use commands like CLS that clear the screen and move the cursor to the upper left-hand corner of the screen. In addition, you can get rid of the clutter of commands by turning ECHO OFF.

STEP 12: Key in the following:
A:\>**CD \BATCH** <Enter>

STEP 13: Key in the following:
A:\BATCH>**EDIT MENU.BAT** <Enter>

WHAT'S HAPPENING? You are going to add some lines to the **MENU.BAT** file.

STEP 14: In the EDIT program, key in the following:
ECHO OFF <Enter>
CLS <Enter>

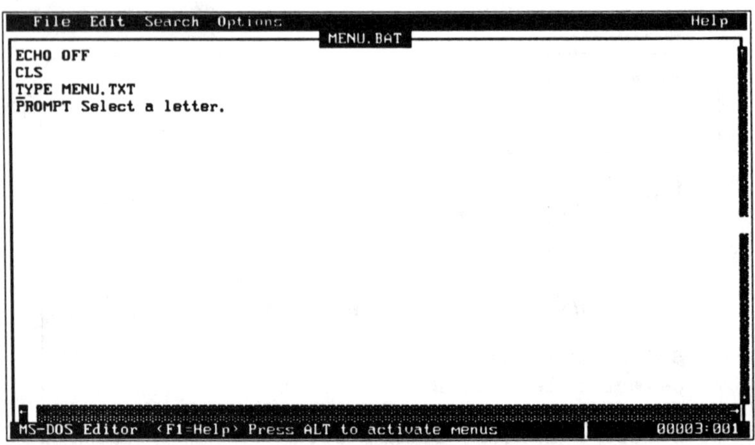

WHAT'S HAPPENING? By adding ECHO OFF, you are turning off the display of commands. By adding CLS, you clear the screen. Now, you must save this file to disk.

STEP 15: Press <Alt>+F.

STEP 16: Press X.

STEP 17: Press Y.

STEP 18: Key in the following:
A:\BATCH>**MENU** <Enter>

```
MY MENU SYSTEM

A.    MY SPREADSHEET PROGRAM
B.    MY ADDRESS PROGRAM
E.    EXIT TO DOS


Select a letter. _
```

WHAT'S HAPPENING? You can see how much neater the menu system is when you do not have to see the commands. You can add designs and center the menu and create many visually pleasing operations.

STEP 19: At the prompt, key in the following:
E <Enter>

```
MY MENU SYSTEM


A.    MY SPREADSHEET PROGRAM
B.    MY ADDRESS PROGRAM
E.    EXIT TO DOS


Select a letter. E

Select a letter. PROMPT $p$g

A:\BATCH>TYPE END.TXT
You have exited the MENU system. If you wish
to return to the MENU system, key in MENU at
the prompt.

A:\BATCH>CD \

A:\>
A:\>_
```

WHAT'S HAPPENING? You exited the menu system and are back at the root directory of the ACTIVITIES disk. Since you did not include ECHO OFF in the **E.BAT** file, you still see the commands. Thus, you could go back and add ECHO OFF to **E.BAT** and **A.BAT**. To complete the menu system, you would also need to write **B.BAT**. That activity will be covered in one of the application assignments.

Chapter Summary

1. Batch processing means running a series of instructions without interruption.
2. Interactive processing allows the user to interface directly with the computer and update records immediately.
3. Batch files allow a user to put together a string of commands and execute them with one command.
4. Batch files must have the **.BAT** file extension.
5. DOS first looks internally for a command, then a **.COM** file extension, then an **.EXE** file extension, and finally a **.BAT** file extension.
6. The PROMPT command, an internal command, allows the prompt to be changed to suit the user.
7. EDIT is a full-screen text editor used to write batch files.
8. A word processor, if it outputs in ASCII, can be used to write batch files. ASCII files are also referred to as unformatted text files.
9. Batch files must be in ASCII.
10. Batch files are executed from the system prompt by keying in the batch file name.
11. A batch file called **AUTOEXEC.BAT** can be created.
12. An **AUTOEXEC.BAT** file will execute automatically when the system is booted.
13. There can only be one **AUTOEXEC.BAT** file per booting disk.
14. There are special commands only used in batch files.
15. REM allows the user to document a batch file.
16. To document means to explain the purpose a file serves.
17. ECHO OFF turns off the display of commands. Only the messages from the commands are displayed on the screen.
18. When DOS sees REM, it displays on the screen whatever text follows the REM but does not execute it as a command.
19. PAUSE allows the user to take some action before the batch file continues to execute.
20. PAUSE does not force the user to do anything. The batch file just stops running until the user presses a key.
21. Replaceable parameters allow the user to write batch files that can be used with many different parameters. The replaceable parameters act as placeholders for values that the user will substitute when executing the batch file.
22. Replaceable parameters are sometimes called dummy, positional, or substitute parameters.
23. The percent (%) sign followed immediately by a numerical value, 0 to 9, indicates a replaceable parameter in a batch file.
24. To stop a batch file from executing, press the <Ctrl> key and the letter C (<Ctrl>+C).
25. You can create a menu system using batch files.
26. A batch file menu system is an on-screen display that lists available choices. When you choose an option, you are actually choosing to run another batch file.

27. In essence, when writing a batch file menu system, you are chaining together batch files.
28. Using ECHO OFF in a batch file menu system allows the screen display to be uncluttered and more aesthetically pleasing.

Key Terms

Batch file	Documented	Positional parameters
Batch processing	Dummy parameters	Replaceable parameters
Chaining batch files	Interactive processing	Substitute parameters

Discussion Questions

1. What is a batch file?
2. Explain batch processing.
3. Explain interactive processing.
4. Give two reasons for writing a batch file.
5. Describe the differences between batch and interactive data processing.
6. How can a batch file be created?
7. When a command is keyed in at the prompt, DOS first checks memory. Why?
8. How does DOS determine if a file is a data file or a program file?
9. You have a batch file called **CHECK.BAT**. You key in **CHECK** at the prompt. What does DOS do? Where does it look for the file?
10. How can a batch file be executed?
11. What is ASCII? Why is it important in batch file processing?
12. Give two reasons for writing batch files with EDIT.
13. When can a word processor be used to write batch files?
14. How is **AUTOEXEC.BAT** used?
15. When is an **AUTOEXEC.BAT** file run?
16. How many **AUTOEXEC.BAT** files can be on a disk?
17. What commands can be put in a batch file?
18. How can you stop running a batch file and return to the system prompt?
19. In a data processing environment, what does it mean to document a batch file?
20. Why would it be important to document a batch file?
21. What happens when DOS sees REM in a file?
22. What will happen when the ECHO command is in the on mode?
23. When is the PAUSE command used in a batch file?
24. Once you have used the PAUSE command, how can you resume the execution of the batch file?
25. What is a replaceable parameter? Describe how it might be used.
26. Is there any limit to the number of replaceable parameters that can be used in a batch file?
27. What indicates to DOS that there is a replaceable parameter in a file?
28. What advantages are there to using replaceable parameters in a batch file?
29. What is a menu system?
30. How can you create a menu system using batch files?

Application Assignments

Note 1: For these assignments, do not print the screen. Do not hand in any output as the result of executing a batch file. All that is needed is the actual batch file itself. Thus, if the batch file is called **ONE.BAT**, for assignment purposes, you would key in:

COPY ONE.BAT PRN

The print out is all that is necessary to turn in.

Note 2: Use the DATA disk for the assignments, unless otherwise stated.

1. Edit the batch file you created in this chapter called **D.BAT**. Document this file. Print it.
2. For the following assignment:
   a. Create a batch file named **EXTRA.BAT** with the following commands:
      (1) Clear the screen.
      (2) Display the root directory of the DATA disk for any file that has **.TXT** as a file extension.
      (3) Make a copy of the file called **WILDONE** and call the copy **TV.CAT**.
      (4) Copy the file called **TV.CAT** to the printer.
      (5) Erase the file called **TV.CAT**.
   b. Execute or run your batch file to be sure it works.
   c. Copy the batch file **EXTRA.BAT** to the printer. Do not print the screen. Do not turn in any output from running the batch file, just the actual contents of the batch file.
   d. Write this batch file using replaceable parameters. Test it and print it.
3. For the following assignment:
   a. Write an **AUTOEXEC.BAT** file that gives a wide display of the default directory and then checks the disk. Copy the contents of the **AUTOEXEC.BAT** file to the printer. Note: Do not place this **AUTOEXEC.BAT** file on the hard disk or on the DOS System Disk unless approved by the instructor.
   b. Print the contents of this file. Do not use the <PrtSc> key.
   c. Write an **AUTOEXEC.BAT** file that could be used on the booting disk. Include a path statement to **C:\DOS**; display the version number of DOS you are using, and change the prompt so that it displays the default drive and default directory. Call the file **AUTO.BAT**. You do not need to test this file. Print the **AUTO.BAT** file.
4. For the following assignment:
   a. Write a batch file called **P.BAT** to change the prompt. In the file, change the prompt to **GOOD MORNING**. Include a metastring so that the prompt will always reflect the current drive.
   b. Execute this batch file. Write down what the prompt looks like.
   c. Write another batch file called **P1.BAT** to change the prompt. In the file, change the prompt so it always displays/reflects the current drive and subdirectory. Be sure that you use a delimiter to identify the prompt. You may use the metastring for >.

   d. Execute this batch file. Write down what the prompt looks like on the screen.
   e. Print both of these batch files. Do not use the <PrtSc> key.
5. For the following assignment:
   a. Write a batch file called **RID.BAT** to delete any file with a **.BAK** file extension.
   b. Document the file.
   c. Execute the batch file.
   d. Print the batch file.
6. For the following assignment:
   a. Do a directory display of all the batch files on the DATA disk.
   b. Print the screen.
7. For the following assignment:
   a. Using replaceable parameters where appropriate write a batch file called **CHECK.BAT** that will:
      (1) check the disk in the default drive.
      (2) do a wide display of the default directory.
      (3) copy a file to the printer.
   b. Include remarks to explain to the user what is going on.
   c. Include an opportunity for the user to ensure the printer is on.
   d. Copy the batch file **CHECK.BAT** to the printer. Do not use the <PrtSc> key.
8. For the following assignment, write a batch file called **PRT.BAT** using replaceable parameters.
   a. The batch file should include the following commands:
      (1) Clear the screen.
      (2) Display the file name of the file to be copied.
      (3) Copy one file to another file name.
      (4) Have the batch file pause prior to printing so that the user can see if the printer is turned on.
      (5) Copy the new file to the printer.
   b. Copy the batch file **PRT.BAT** to the printer.
9. For the following assignment:
   a. Write a batch file called **LIST.BAT**.
   b. Use replaceable parameters so that you can display the contents of three files instead of only one file, which the TYPE command normally allows.
   c. Copy the batch file **LIST.BAT** to the printer.
10. For the following assignment:
   a. If **ADDRESS.EXE** is not in the **USERS** subdirectory on the DATA disk, copy **ADDRESS.EXE** from **C:\JUNK** to the subdirectory called **USERS**. If you do not have a subdirectory called **USERS** on the DATA disk, create it.
   b. Write a batch file called **AD.BAT** that will begin in the root directory, change the directory to **USERS**, load the **ADDRESS** program, and, when completed using **ADDRESS**, will return you to the root directory and clear the screen.

c. Document the batch file.
d. Suppress the display of commands.
e. Print the batch file you just created.

11. In this chapter, you wrote a menu system on the ACTIVITIES disk. The following steps need to be taken on the ACTIVITIES disk to complete the menu system.
    a. Write a batch file called **B.BAT** for the menu system.
    b. Edit the **MENU.TXT** file so that the user knows how to access the menu system.
    c. Edit **A.BAT**, **E.BAT**, and **B.BAT** so that all the files are aesthetically pleasing.
    d. Document the menu system.
    e. Print all the menu files.
12. On the DATA disk there should be a subdirectory called **TEAMS** which has two subdirectories, **BASEBALL** and **FOOTBALL**. If not, create them. The necessary files are in **C:\JUNK\SAMPLE**.
    a. Write a menu system in the **TEAMS** subdirectory that will allow the user to choose to see the contents of **PRO.TMS**, **COLLEGE.TMS**, **AMERICAN.TMS**, or **NATIONAL.TMS**. Be sure the user has enough time to read the files on the screen.
    b. Be sure there is a way to exit to DOS.
    c. Document the menu system.
    d. Make it aesthetically pleasing.
    e. Print the files you created.

Challenge Assignments

13. For the following assignment:
    a. Create a subdirectory on the DATA disk called **BATCH**.
    b. Copy all your batch files in the root directory to the **BATCH** subdirectory.
    c. Delete all your batch files from the root directory.
    d. Make sure that all your batch files are only in the subdirectory **BATCH**.
    e. Print the screen that proves that there are no batch files left in the root directory.
    f. Copy the menu system for **TEAMS** to the **BATCH** subdirectory. Make sure that you adapt the batch files so that they work. Be sure to copy any necessary files that are associated with the **TEAMS** menu system.
    g. Print the files with the editing changes you made.
14. If you have other applications:
    a. Create a batch file(s) to execute these applications and after existing the application will return you to the root directory.
    b. Print these batch files.
15. For the following assignment:
    a. Write a batch file that you will find useful.
    b. Print it.

Chapter

Pipes, Filters, and Redirection

After completing this chapter you will be able to:

1. List the standard input and output devices.
2. Explain redirection.
3. Use the >, <, and >> to redirect standard input and standard output.
4. Explain what filters are and when they are used.
5. Formulate and explain the syntax of the filter commands SORT, FIND, and MORE.
6. Explain when and how to use the SORT, FIND, and MORE commands.
7. Explain what pipes are and how they are used.
8. Combine commands using pipes, filters, and redirection.
9. Explain how batch files can be written using pipes, filters, and redirection.
10. Write a batch file using pipes and filters.

Chapter Overview

DOS usually expects to read information from the keyboard, a standard input device. DOS usually expects to write to the display screen, a standard output device. However, there are times when it is desirable to redirect input and output. It is possible to tell DOS to use devices other than the standard input/output devices. This process is known as redirection. DOS also has three external commands called filters which allow the user to manipulate data. Pipes, used with redirection, allow the user to link commands. Pipes, filters, and redirection give the user choices in determining where information is read from (input) and written to (output). Learning to use pipe, filter, and redirection management commands makes your use of DOS more powerful.

In this chapter you will learn how to command DOS to redirect where information is read from (input) and where it is written to (output). You will also learn to use pipes to connect programs and to use filters to manipulate data. You will write batch files using pipes, filters, and redirection.

13.0 Redirection of Standard I/O (Input/Output)

You use **input** and **output** when working with DOS. When you key in something DOS recognizes it as input. You use an input device such as a keyboard to input data. After DOS processes the input, it writes it to an output device—the most common being the screen. Something written to the screen is called output. In other words, if you key in **TYPE MYFILE.TXT**, the input is what you keyed in. The output is the content of the file that is displayed on the screen. (See Figure 13.1.)

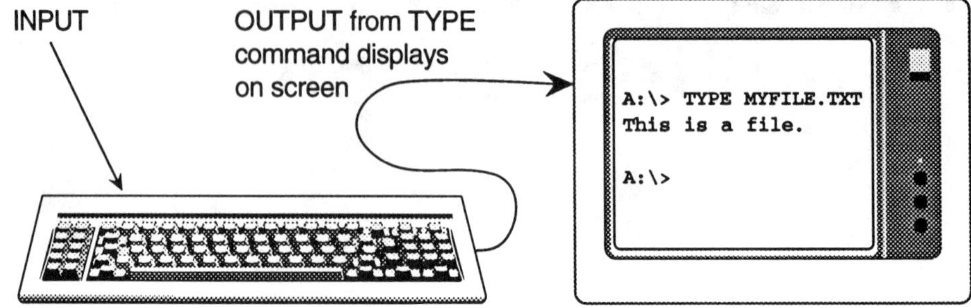

Figure 13.1 Input and Output Devices

In the data processing world, this input/output process is commonly referred to as **I/O**.

DOS gets information from or sends information to three places: **standard input**, **standard output,** and **standard error**. Standard input is the keyboard where DOS (and programs that you use) expect to get data from. Standard output is the display screen where DOS (and programs) expect to write to. Standard error is where DOS writes to the screen any error messages, e.g. "File not found."

Not all commands deal with standard input and standard output. For instance, the result or output of many of the DOS commands you have used has been some action that occurred such as copying a file with the COPY command. There is no standard input or output except the messages written to the screen. (See Figure 13.2.)

Figure 13.2 Results of COPY Command

```
A:\> COPY MY.TXT ONE.FIL   ←— INPUT from user
     1 file(s) copied      ←— OUTPUT from COPY command

A:\>
```

However, the output of other commands such as DIR has been a screen display of all the files on the disk. DOS received information from the standard input device, the keyboard, and sent the results of the DIR command to the standard output device, the screen. DOS wrote to standard output. I/O **redirection** means that you are going to tell DOS that you want information read from or written to a device other than the standard ones. Thus, with the DIR command, you can write the output to some other device like a printer or to another file. This process is called redirecting the output of a command (see Figure 13.3).

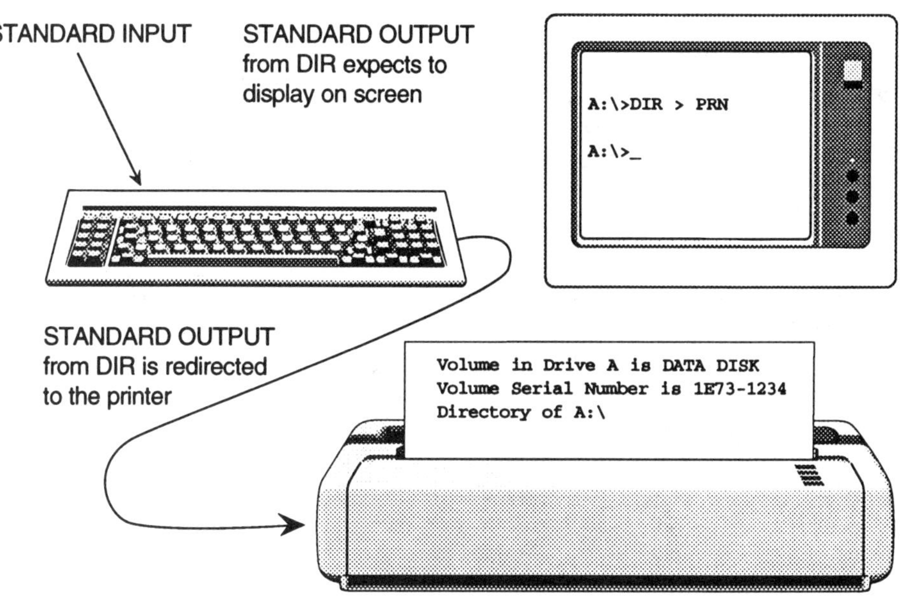

Figure 13.3 Redirecting Standard Output

Redirection only works when the command expects to send its output to standard devices or receive the information from standard input.

The symbols that are used are:

\> The greater than symbol redirects the output of a command to some other device or file.

< The less than symbol tells DOS to get its input from somewhere other than the keyboard, standard input.

\>> The double greater than symbol redirects the output of a command but does not overwrite. It appends to an existing file.

Activity 13.1 Using the > to Redirect Standard Output

Note: The ACTIVITIES disk is in Drive A with the **A:\>** displayed. Be sure the path is set to **C:\DOS**.

STEP 1: Key in the following:
A:\>**DIR *.TXT** <Enter>

```
A:\>DIR *.TXT

 Volume in drive A is ACTIVITIES
 Volume Serial Number is 0ED4-161B
 Directory of A:\

EXERCISE TXT     316   11-23-92   7:03a
JANUARY  TXT      72   11-23-92   7:04a
FEBRUARY TXT      74   11-23-92   7:05a
```

```
MARCH      TXT       70   11-23-92   7:06a
APRIL      TXT       71   11-23-92   7:07a
HELLO      TXT       52   11-23-92   7:07a
TEST       TXT       64   11-23-92   7:07a
BYE        TXT       44   11-23-92   7:07a
GOODBYE    TXT       33   11-23-92   7:07a
          9 file(s)         796 bytes
                          17408 bytes free

A:\>_
```

WHAT'S HAPPENING? This command behaved in the "normal" way. You asked for a display of all the files on the ACTIVITIES disk that had **.TXT** as a file extension. The selected files were displayed on the screen. Since the DIR command writes the results to the screen, it uses standard output. Thus, redirection can be used with this command.

STEP 2: Be sure the printer is turned on. Key in the following:
A:\>**DIR *.TXT > PRN** <Enter>

Note: If you have a laser printer, you must take the following steps to print the output.

1. Take the printer offline by pressing the online button.
2. Press FF (Form Feed).
3. Place the printer back online by pressing the online button.

WHAT'S HAPPENING? The printer should be printing. Nothing appears on the screen. When you key in **DIR *.TXT**, you normally see displayed on the screen the directory listing of all the ***.TXT** files as you did in the display following Step 1. The > sign tells DOS that instead of sending the standard output to the screen, you want to redirect that output to somewhere else. PRN, a device, tells DOS where to redirect the output. Thus, instead of standard output being written to the screen, you redirected the output to a device, the printer. Redirection is very useful. For example, if you wanted a hard copy of the directory of a disk, you *could not* key in **COPY DIR PRN** because DIR is a command, not a file. You cannot copy a command to the printer. COPY is for files only. You can also redirect standard output to a file.

Activity 13.2

Using the < to Redirect Standard Input

Note: The ACTIVITIES disk is in Drive A with the **A:\>** displayed.

STEP 1: Key in the following:
A:\>**DIR TEST** <Enter>

```
A:\>DIR TEST

 Volume in drive A is ACTIVITIES
 Volume Serial Number is 0ED4-161B
 Directory of A:\TEST

.              <DIR>      11-16-93  7:05a
..             <DIR>      11-16-93  7:05a
NEW       FIL        31   11-16-93  7:05a
SAMPLE    FIL        23   11-16-93  7:05a
MYPHONE             851   12-06-92  9:11a
LIST                851   12-06-92  9:11a
         6 file(s)         1756 bytes
                          17408 bytes free

A:\>_
```

WHAT'S HAPPENING? You have a subdirectory called **TEST** with four files in it on the ACTIVITIES disk.

STEP 2: Key in the following:
A:\>**DEL TEST*.*** <Enter>

```
A:\>DEL \TEST\*.*
All files in directory will be deleted!
Are you sure (Y/N)?_
```

WHAT'S HAPPENING? You asked DOS to delete all the files in the subdirectory called **TEST**. DOS is asking you if you are really sure that you want to delete these files. (If you have an earlier version of DOS the message is "Are you sure?(Y/N)_".) DOS is expecting input from its standard input, the keyboard.

STEP 3: Key in the following:
N <Enter>

```
A:\>DEL TEST\*.*
All files in directory will be deleted!
Are you sure (Y/N)?n
A:\>_
```

WHAT'S HAPPENING? DOS returned you to the system prompt without deleting the files in the **TEST** subdirectory because you answered **N** for "no, don't delete." As you can see, DOS took no action until it received input from you via the keyboard. The input was **N**. You can prove that the files are still there by keying in **DIR TEST**.

STEP 4: Key in the following:
A:\>**TYPE Y.FIL** <Enter>

```
A:\>TYPE Y.FIL
Y

A:\>_
```

WHAT'S HAPPENING? The Y.FIL file is a very simple file whose contents are the letter Y followed by a carriage return (<Enter>).

STEP 5: Key in the following:
A:\>**DEL TEST*.* < Y.FIL** <Enter>

```
A:\>DEL TEST\*.* < Y.FIL
All files in directory will be deleted!
Are you sure (Y/N)?Y

A:\>_
```

WHAT'S HAPPENING? This time you told DOS, instead of getting the input it needed from the standard input device, the keyboard, to get the input from a file called Y.FIL (< Y.FIL). Then, when DOS executed DEL TEST*.TXT and displayed the message "Are you sure (Y/N)?," it still needed input, a "Y" or "N" followed by <Enter>. Since you redirected the input, you told DOS not to look to the keyboard for the answer, instead to look to the file Y.FIL. DOS found the file, which had the "Y <Enter>" answer. Since DOS got a response to its question, it could proceed to delete the files in the subdirectory TEST. You must be very careful with redirection of input. If you tell DOS to take input from a file, you are telling DOS to ignore any input from the keyboard. In this example, if the file contents were "X," this would not be a valid answer to the question DOS posed, "Are you sure (Y/N)." DOS only wants "Y" or "N." Any other letter is unacceptable. DOS will keep asking the same question over and over. You could not correct the problem by keying in "Y" or "N" because DOS will never look to the keyboard. You told it not to—you told it to look to the file. If you ever get into this situation, you cannot even use <Ctrl>+<Break> or <Ctrl>+C because DOS will not recognize any input from the keyboard. Thus, your only recourse is to reboot.

STEP 6: Key in the following:
A:\>**DIR TEST** <Enter>

```
A:\>DIR TEST

 Volume in drive A is ACTIVITIES
 Volume Serial Number is 0ED4-161B
 Directory of A:\TEST

.            <DIR>      11-16-93   7:05a
..           <DIR>      11-16-93   7:05a
        2 file(s)            0 bytes
                        21504 bytes free

A:\>_
```

WHAT'S HAPPENING? The files were deleted. You did it with one command line, and you did not have to key in the "Y." The "Y" came from the file **Y.FIL**.

Activity 13.3 Using the >> to Add Redirected Output to a File

Note: The ACTIVITIES disk is in Drive A with the **A:\>** displayed.

STEP 1: Key in the following:
A:\>**TYPE JANUARY.TXT** <Enter>

STEP 2: Key in the following:
A:\>**TYPE FEBRUARY.TXT** <Enter>

```
A:\>TYPE JANUARY.TXT
This is my January file.
It is my first dummy file.
This is file 1.

A:\>TYPE FEBRUARY.TXT
This is my February file.
It is my second dummy file.
This is file 2.

A:\>_
```

WHAT'S HAPPENING? You have two files. You want to add **FEBRUARY.TXT** to the end of **JANUARY.TXT**. If you keyed in **TYPE FEBRUARY.TXT > JANUARY.TXT**, you would overwrite the contents of **JANUARY.TXT** with the contents of **FEBRUARY.TXT**. To append to the end of an existing file, you use the double >>.

STEP 3: Key in the following:
A:\>**TYPE FEBRUARY.TXT >> JANUARY.TXT** <Enter>

STEP 4: Key in the following:
A:\>**TYPE JANUARY.TXT** <Enter>

```
A:\>TYPE FEBRUARY.TXT >> JANUARY.TXT

A:\>TYPE JANUARY.TXT
This is my January file.
It is my first dummy file.
This is file 1.
This is my February file.
It is my second dummy file.
This is file 2.

A:\>_
```

WHAT'S HAPPENING? Instead of writing over the contents of **JANUARY.TXT** with the contents of **FEBRUARY.TXT**, the contents of **FEBRUARY.TXT** were added to the end of the **JANUARY.TXT** file.

13.4 Filters

Filter commands manipulate information. **Filters** read information from the keyboard (standard input), change the input in some way, and write the results to the screen (standard output). Filters work like filters in a water system taking incoming water, purifying it, and sending it along the system. There are three DOS filters, which are external commands:

SORT arranges lines in ascending or descending order.
FIND searches for a particular group of characters, commonly called a character string.
MORE temporarily halts the screen display after each screenful.

These filters are external commands. DOS creates temporary files in the process of "filtering" the data and, thus, during this process, DOS reads and writes to the disk. It is important that DOS have access to the disk and the filters. The user must not only set the path to **C:\DOS** but also must make sure that the floppy disk is not write-protected. If a disk is write-protected, DOS cannot execute the command.

13.5 The SORT Command

The SORT filter command arranges or sorts lines of input text and sends them to the standard output (the screen), unless you redirect it. The default SORT is in ascending order (A to Z or lowest to highest numbers), starting in the first column. The syntax for the command is:

SORT [/R] [/+*n*] The *n* represents any number.

Activity 13.6 Using SORT

Note: The ACTIVITIES disk is in Drive A with the **A:\>** displayed.

STEP 1: Key in the following:

A:\>**SORT** <Enter>
beta <Enter>
omega <Enter>
chi <Enter>
alpha <Enter>
<Ctrl>+Z <Enter>

```
A:\>SORT
beta
omega
chi
alpha
^Z
alpha
beta
chi
omega

A:\>_
```

WHAT'S HAPPENING? As you can see, the SORT command took input from the keyboard. When you pressed <Ctrl>+Z, you told the SORT command that you were finished entering data. Then, the SORT command "filtered" the data and wrote the keyboard input alphabetically. See Figure 13.4 for a graphical representation of this filter.

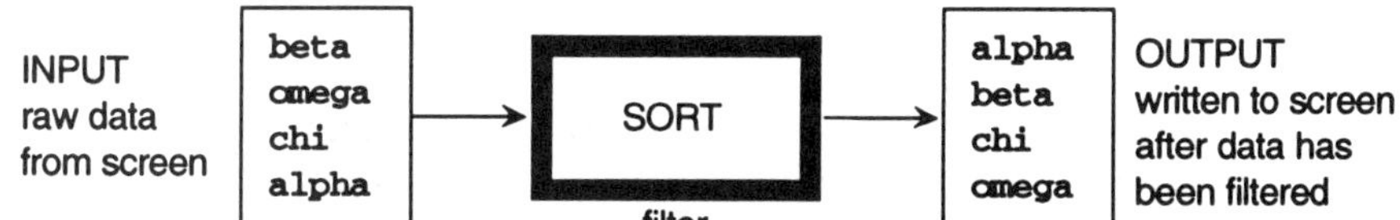

Figure 13.4
Filtering Data

STEP 2: Key in the following:

A:\>**SORT** <Enter>
333 <Enter>
3 <Enter>
23 <Enter>
124 <Enter>
<Ctrl>+Z <Enter>

```
A:\>SORT
333
3
23
124
^Z
124
23
3
333

A:\>_
```

WHAT'S HAPPENING? The SORT command does not seem very smart because these numbers are not in order. When you sort character data, you actually sort the characters from left to right. This is called left-justified. When you sort numeric data, you actually sort the numbers from right to left. This is called right-justified. Thus, if you look at "Smith" and "Smythe," you read character data from left to right and would place "Smith" before "Smythe." Conversely, if you look at "12" and "13," you read numeric data from right to left and would place "12" before "13" because the rightmost "2" comes before the rightmost "3." A human *knows* that "12" comes before "13" because a person has learned how numbers work. DOS is different. DOS relies on something called the **ASCII sort sequence**. ASCII is a standard code for representing characters as binary numbers. A decimal number is assigned to all the punctuation marks, numbers, capitals, and lowercase letters. The sort order is punctuation marks, including the space, then numbers, then uppercase letters, and last lowercase letters. Thus, if you had a series of characters such as BB, aa, #, 123, bb, 13, and AA, the ASCII sort order would be:

123 13 AA aa BB bb

Although DOS, and hence the SORT command, follows the ASCII sort sequence, there is one exception when using DOS 4.0 and above. These DOS versions equate lowercase and uppercase letters so that the sort would look like this:

123 13 aa AA BB bb

There is another point about using the SORT command. Not only does it follow the ASCII sort sequence, but it also sorts the entire lines from left to right. Thus, if you had two names, "Carolyn Smith" and "Robert Nesler," the sort sequence would be:

Carolyn Smith
Robert Nesler

Because the SORT command is looking at the entire line, "Carolyn" comes before "Robert."

In our numeric example, SORT looked at the entire line and since the "1" in "124" preceded the "2" in "23," it placed the "124" before the "23." You force DOS to sort numbers correctly by the following technique.

STEP 3: Key in the following:

A:\>**SORT** <Enter>
333 <Enter>
<space><space>**3** <Enter>
<space>**23** <Enter>
124 <Enter>
<Ctrl>+Z <Enter>

```
A:\>SORT
333
  3
 23
124
^Z
  3
 23
124
333

A:\>_
```

WHAT'S HAPPENING? By entering spaces, you forced the lines to be the same length. Spaces precede numbers. Now, the SORT command could sort the entire line and place it in proper numeric order. Indeed, you made numeric data character data. Essentially, you left-justify character data and right-justify numeric data.

13.7 Filters and Redirection

The standard output of filters is a screen display. Hence, you can redirect both the output and input of these filter commands. The filter commands are not usually used with actual keyboard input but with the input redirected to a file, device, or another command.

Activity 13.8 Using the SORT Command with Redirection

Note: The ACTIVITIES disk is in Drive A with the **A:\>** displayed.

STEP 1: Key in the following:
A:\>**SORT < PERSONAL.FIL** <Enter>

```
JONES     JERRY     244 East      Mission Viejo  CA  Systems Analyst
Jones     Steven    32 North      Phoenix        AZ  Buyer
Low       Ophelia   1213 Wick     Phoenix        AZ  Writer
Markiw    Emily     10 Zion       Sun City West  AZ  Retired
Markiw    Nicholas  12 Fifth      Glendale       AZ  Engineer
Markiw    Nicholas  354 Bell      Phoenix        AZ  Engineer
Markiw    Nick      10 Zion       Sun City West  AZ  Retired
Maurdeff  Kathryn   550 Traver    Ann Arbor      MI  Teacher
Maurdeff  Sonia     550 Traver    Ann Arbor      MI  Student
Moselle   Carolyn   567 Abbey     Rochester      MI  Day Care Teacher
Nyles     John      12 Brooks     Sun City West  AZ  Retired
Nyles     Sophie    12 Brooks     Sun City West  CA  Retired
Panezich  Frank     689 Lake      Orange         CA  Teacher
Papay     Fred      345 Newport   Orange         CA  Manager
Richards  James     56 Twin Leaf  Orange         CA  Artist
Smith     Carolyn   311 Orchard   Ann Arbor      MI  Housewife
Smith     David     120 Collins   Orange         CA  Chef
Smith     Gregory   311 Orchard   Ann Arbor      MI  Engineer
Smith     Henry     40 Northern   Ontario        CA  Engineer
Tally     William   15 Fourth     Santa Cruz     CA  Banker
Tuttle    Steven    356 Embassy   Mission Viejo  CA  Juggler
Winter    Jim       333 Pick      Garden Grove   CA  Key Grip
Winter    Linda     333 Pick      Garden Grove   CA  Teacher

A:\>_
```

WHAT'S HAPPENING? You keyed in the SORT command. You then used the symbol (<) for taking data from other than the keyboard. You are telling SORT to take its input from the file called **PERSONAL.FIL** and feed it into the SORT command. Displayed on your screen (the standard output) is the **PERSONAL.FIL** file arranged in alphabetical order, with "JONES," "JERRY" at the top. You also have the /R parameter, which allows you to sort in reverse or descending order (Z to A or highest to the lowest numbers).

STEP 2: Key in the following:
A:\>**SORT /R < PERSONAL.FIL** <Enter>

```
Maurdeff   Sonia      550 Traver     Ann Arbor        MI   Student
Maurdeff   Kathryn    550 Traver     Ann Arbor        MI   Teacher
Markiw     Nick       10 Zion        Sun City West    AZ   Retired
Markiw     Nicholas   354 Bell       Phoenix          AZ   Engineer
Markiw     Nicholas   12 Fifth       Glendale         AZ   Engineer
Markiw     Emily      10 Zion        Sun City West    AZ   Retired
Low        Ophelia    1213 Wick      Phoenix          AZ   Writer
Jones      Steven     32 North       Phoenix          AZ   Buyer
JONES      JERRY      244 East       Mission Viejo    CA   Systems Analyst
Jones      Cleo       355 Second     Ann Arbor        MI   Clerk
Helm       Milton     333 Meadow     Sherman Oaks     CA   Consultant
Golden     Jane       345 Lakeview   Orange           CA   Nurse
Golden     Herbert    345 Lakeview   Orange           CA   Doctor
Gillay     Carolyn    699 Lemon      Orange           CA   Professor
Gibbs      Michael    134 Seventh    Ann Arbor        MI   Editor
Brogan     Sally      111 Miller     Santa Cruz       CA   Account Manager
Brogan     Lloyd      111 Miller     Santa Cruz       CA   Vice-President
Brent      Wendy      356 Edgewood   Ann Arbor        MI   Librarian
Begg       Leroy      20 Elm         Ontario          CA   Systems Analyst
Babchuk    Walter     12 View        Thousand Oaks    CA   President
Babchuk    Nicholas   13 Stratford   Sun City West    AZ   Professor
Babchuk    Deana      12 View        Thousand Oaks    CA   Housewife
Babchuk    Bianca     13 Stratford   Sun City West    AZ   Professor

A:\>_
```

WHAT'S HAPPENING? The file `PERSONAL.FIL` that the SORT command took as input is displayed on the screen in reverse alphabetical order. The standard output, the results of the SORT command, is written to the screen. The other parameter you can use to sort is a column number (/+*n*).

STEP 3: Key in the following:
A:\>`SORT /+33 < PERSONAL.FIL` <Enter>

```
Richards   James      56 Twin Leaf   Orange           CA   Artist
Smith      David      120 Collins    Orange           CA   Chef
Golden     Herbert    345 Lakeview   Orange           CA   Doctor
Papay      Fred       345 Newport    Orange           CA   Manager
Golden     Jane       345 Lakeview   Orange           CA   Nurse
Gillay     Carolyn    699 Lemon      Orange           CA   Professor
Panezich   Frank      689 Lake       Orange           CA   Teacher
Jones      Steven     32 North       Phoenix          AZ   Buyer
Markiw     Nicholas   354 Bell       Phoenix          AZ   Engineer
Low        Ophelia    1213 Wick      Phoenix          AZ   Writer
Moselle    Carolyn    567 Abbey      Rochester        MI   Day Care Teacher
Brogan     Sally      111 Miller     Santa Cruz       CA   Account Manager
Tally      William    15 Fourth      Santa Cruz       CA   Banker
Brogan     Lloyd      111 Miller     Santa Cruz       CA   Vice-President
Helm       Milton     333 Meadow     Sherman Oaks     CA   Consultant
Babchuk    Nicholas   13 Stratford   Sun City West    AZ   Professor
Babchuk    Bianca     13 Stratford   Sun City West    AZ   Professor
Markiw     Emily      10 Zion        Sun City West    AZ   Retired
Nyles      John       12 Brooks      Sun City West    AZ   Retired
Markiw     Nick       10 Zion        Sun City West    AZ   Retired
Nyles      Sophie     12 Brooks      Sun City West    CA   Retired
```

```
Babchuk   Deana     12 View        Thousand Oaks  CA   Housewife
Babchuk   Walter    12 View        Thousand Oaks  CA   President

A:\>_
```

WHAT'S HAPPENING? This time you sorted by column number, the 33rd position in the list in this example. The file is now ordered by the city names rather than by surnames. Thus, you are now in city order. An important point is that the SORT command does not mean columns in the usual sense. A person would say that the "city column" is the fourth column of columns traditionally numbered from left to right. Column with the SORT command means counting each character (letters and spaces) from left to right, not each column. Thus, "city" is located by literally counting over the number of characters to the ones you want to sort, including the spaces between the characters.

STEP 4: Remove the ACTIVITIES disk from Drive A. Insert the DATA disk in Drive A.

Note: If the file **PERSONAL.FIL** is not on the DATA disk, copy it from **C:\JUNK** to the DATA disk.

STEP 5: Key in the following:
A:\>**SORT < PERSONAL.FIL > SORTED.PER** <Enter>

STEP 6: Key in the following:
A:\>**TYPE SORTED.PER** <Enter>

```
JONES     JERRY     244 East       Mission Viejo  CA   Systems Analyst
Jones     Steven    32 North       Phoenix        AZ   Buyer
Low       Ophelia   1213 Wick      Phoenix        AZ   Writer
Markiw    Emily     10 Zion        Sun City West  AZ   Retired
Markiw    Nicholas  12 Fifth       Glendale       AZ   Engineer
Markiw    Nicholas  354 Bell       Phoenix        AZ   Engineer
Markiw    Nick      10 Zion        Sun City West  AZ   Retired
Maurdeff  Kathryn   550 Traver     Ann Arbor      MI   Teacher
Maurdeff  Sonia     550 Traver     Ann Arbor      MI   Student
Moselle   Carolyn   567 Abbey      Rochester      MI   Day Care Teacher
Nyles     John      12 Brooks      Sun City West  AZ   Retired
Nyles     Sophie    12 Brooks      Sun City West  CA   Retired
Panezich  Frank     689 Lake       Orange         CA   Teacher
Papay     Fred      345 Newport    Orange         CA   Manager
Richards  James     56 Twin Leaf   Orange         CA   Artist
Smith     Carolyn   311 Orchard    Ann Arbor      MI   Housewife
Smith     David     120 Collins    Orange         CA   Chef
Smith     Gregory   311 Orchard    Ann Arbor      MI   Engineer
Smith     Henry     40 Northern    Ontario        CA   Engineer
Tally     William   15 Fourth      Santa Cruz     CA   Banker
Tuttle    Steven    356 Embassy    Mission Viejo  CA   Juggler
Winter    Jim       333 Pick       Garden Grove   CA   Key Grip
Winter    Linda     333 Pick       Garden Grove   CA   Teacher

A:\>_
```

WHAT'S HAPPENING? You saved the sorted output to a file called **SORTED.PER**. The standard output of the command **SORT < PERSONAL.FIL** will normally be written to the screen (standard output). Since standard output is written to the screen, you can redirect it to a file called **SORTED.PER**, or the command line **SORT < PERSONAL.FIL > SORTED.PER**. If you did not want a permanent copy of it but wanted a printed copy of the file, you could have written the command as **SORT < PERSONAL.FIL > PRN**.

13.9 The FIND Filter

The FIND command allows the user to search for a specific **character string** in a file. What is looked for is a literal string of characters enclosed in quotation marks. This command is also **case sensitive** prior to DOS 5.0. In DOS 5.0, there is a new parameter /I which means ignore case. The syntax is:

FIND [/V] [/C] [/N] [/I] "string" [[*drive:*][*path*]*filename*[...]]

The parameters are as follows:

/V Displays all lines *not* containing the specified string.
/C Displays only the count of lines containing the string.
/N Displays line numbers with the displayed lines.
/I Ignores the case of characters when searching for the string.

Activity 13.10 Using the FIND Filter

Note: The DATA disk is in Drive A with the **A:\>** displayed.

STEP 1: Key in the following:
A:\>**FIND "Smith" PERSONAL.FIL** <Enter>

```
A:\>FIND "Smith" PERSONAL.FIL

------ PERSONAL.FIL
Smith     Gregory   311 Orchard    Ann Arbor     MI   Engineer
Smith     Carolyn   311 Orchard    Ann Arbor     MI   Housewife
Smith     David     120 Collins    Orange        CA   Chef
Smith     Henry     40 Northern    Ontario       CA   Engineer

A:\>_
```

WHAT'S HAPPENING? The FIND command found every occurrence of the character string "Smith" in the file **PERSONAL.FIL** located on the DATA disk. A character string *must* be enclosed in quotation marks. Since it is case sensitive, you must key in exactly how it appears in the file. If you had keyed in "SMITH," it would not find any "Smiths" because FIND would be looking for uppercase letters. If you have DOS 5.0 and you wanted to ignore the case, you would use the parameter /I. The FIND command "filtered" the file **PERSONAL.FIL** to extract the character string that matched the specification. With the use of the /V parameter, you can search a file for anything *except* what is in quotation marks.

STEP 2: Key in the following:
A:\>**FIND /V "Smith" PERSONAL.FIL** <Enter>

```
Brogan    Lloyd     111 Miller    Santa Cruz      CA  Vice-President
Brogan    Sally     111 Miller    Santa Cruz      CA  Account Manager
Babchuk   Nicholas  13 Stratford  Sun City West   AZ  Professor
Babchuk   Bianca    13 Stratford  Sun City West   AZ  Professor
Begg      Leroy     20 Elm        Ontario         CA  Systems Analyst
Helm      Milton    333 Meadow    Sherman Oaks    CA  Consultant
Moselle   Carolyn   567 Abbey     Rochester       MI  Day Care Teacher
Markiw    Nicholas  354 Bell      Phoenix         AZ  Engineer
Markiw    Emily     10 Zion       Sun City West   AZ  Retired
Nyles     John      12 Brooks     Sun City West   AZ  Retired
Nyles     Sophie    12 Brooks     Sun City West   CA  Retired
Markiw    Nick      10 Zion       Sun City West   AZ  Retired
Papay     Fred      345 Newport   Orange          CA  Manager
Jones     Steven    32 North      Phoenix         AZ  Buyer
Babchuk   Walter    12 View       Thousand Oaks   CA  President
Babchuk   Deana     12 View       Thousand Oaks   CA  Housewife
Jones     Cleo      355 Second    Ann Arbor       MI  Clerk
JONES     JERRY     244 East      Mission Viejo   CA  Systems Analyst
Low       Ophelia   1213 Wick     Phoenix         AZ  Writer
Tally     William   15 Fourth     Santa Cruz      CA  Banker
Gibbs     Michael   134 Seventh   Ann Arbor       MI  Editor
Richards  James     56 Twin Leaf  Orange          CA  Artist
Markiw    Nicholas  12 Fifth      Glendale        AZ  Engineer

A:\>_
```

WHAT'S HAPPENING? FIND located everyone except "Smith." Furthermore, you can find the specific line number of each occurrence by using the /N parameter.

STEP 3: Key in the following:
A:\>**FIND /N "Smith" PERSONAL.FIL** <Enter>

```
A:\>FIND /N "Smith" PERSONAL.FIL

------ PERSONAL.FIL
[6]Smith  Gregory   311 Orchard   Ann Arbor       MI  Engineer
[7]Smith  Carolyn   311 Orchard   Ann Arbor       MI  Housewife
[27]Smith David     120 Collins   Orange          CA  Chef
[31]Smith Henry     40 Northern   Ontario         CA  Engineer

A:\>_
```

WHAT'S HAPPENING? Displayed on the screen are not only all the "Smiths" but also the line numbers in the file where their names appear. You can also have a numeric count of the number of times a specific character string appears in a file. The FIND command will not display the actual lines, but it will tell you how many occurrences there are of that specific string.

STEP 4: Key in the following:
A:\>**FIND /C "Smith" PERSONAL.FIL** <Enter>

```
A:\>FIND /C "Smith" PERSONAL.FIL

------ PERSONAL.FIL: 4

A:\>_
```

WHAT'S HAPPENING? The number 4 follows the file name. Four is how many times the name "Smith" appears in the file **PERSONAL.FIL**. If you have DOS 5.0, you can tell the FIND command to ignore case.

STEP 5: Key in the following:
A:\>**FIND /I "Jones" PERSONAL.FIL** <Enter>

```
A:\>FIND /I "Jones" PERSONAL.FIL

------ PERSONAL.FIL
Jones     Steven    32 North      Phoenix         AZ   Buyer
Jones     Cleo      355 Second    Ann Arbor       MI   Clerk
JONES     JERRY     244 East      Mission Viejo   CA   Systems Analyst

A:\>_
```

WHAT'S HAPPENING? By using the /I parameter, which told the FIND command to ignore the case, it found both "Jones" and "JONES."

13.11 Pipes

Pipes are used in DOS as a way of stringing two or more programs together so that the output of one of them is fed to the other as input. Thus, you can chain several commands together with the pipe. The term "pipe" reflects the flow of information from one place to another, much like water in a pipe. In the same way that the water department "filters" water, you can filter information. You tell DOS to take the output of one command and make it the input for the next command. The command is what "filters" or changes the data.

The pipe symbol is the vertical broken bar ¦ used between two commands. DOS takes the output from a command and writes it to a temporary file. Then the next command in the pipeline reads the temporary file as input. (See Figure 13.5.)

Figure 13.5
Piping Commands

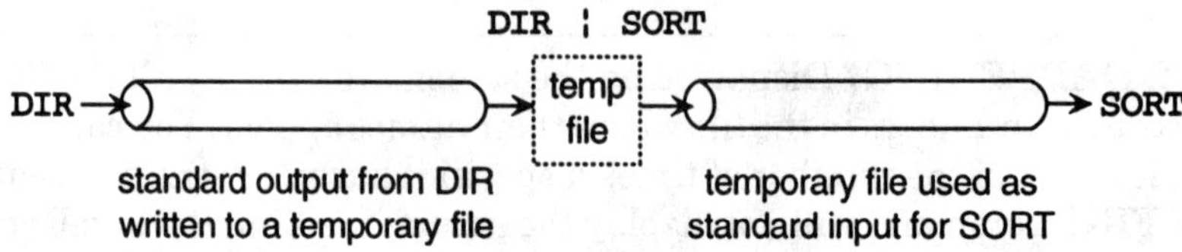

On the original IBM PC keyboard, the pipe symbol is located between the <Shift> and the letter Z. The new IBM PS/2 has the pipe symbol located above the backslash. Other keyboards may have the ¦ symbol in another location. The symbol ¦ is the connection between the two commands, like a "pipe" in a water system. Since the filters are external commands, DOS must be able to access the commands. If a disk is write-protected, the filter commands will not work because these commands read and write temporary files to the disk.

After using pipes with filters, you may see some "strange" files on the directory labeled:

```
%PIPE1.$$$
%PIPE2.$$$
%PIPE3.$$$
```

or

```
11002649
1100274E
```

All files must be named, even temporary files. These are the names that DOS gives for the files that DOS creates when you use piping. These temporary files "hold" the data until the next command can process it. These temporary files are automatically deleted by DOS when you have finished your chain of commands.

13.12 The MORE Filter

The MORE command displays one screenful of data at a time with a prompt that says `-- More --`. The MORE command pauses after the screen is full. When any key is pressed, the display screen continues to scroll. The syntax is:

MORE < [*drive:*][*path*]*filename*
command-name ¦ MORE

The syntax diagram is indicating that MORE can be both redirected and used with a pipe.

Activity 13.13 Using the MORE Filter

Note: The DATA disk is in Drive A with the **A:\>** displayed.

STEP 1: You will use the pipe symbol ¦, so be sure you can locate it on the keyboard. Key in the following:
A:\>**DIR ¦ MORE** <Enter>

```
 Volume in drive A is DATA DISK
 Volume Serial Number is 3839-0EC8
 Directory of A:\

EXERCISE TXT     315   11-23-92  7:05a
JANUARY  TXT      71   11-23-92  7:05a
FEBRUARY TXT      73   11-23-92  7:10a
MARCH    TXT      69   11-23-92  7:11a
APR      TST      70   11-23-92  7:11a
DRAMA    TV      183   11-23-92 10:16a
FUNNY    TV      170   11-23-92 10:17a
```

```
SORTED   PER     2305   02-14-93  8:54p
FEB      TMP      182   07-04-92 11:00p
CLASS        <DIR>      11-23-92  7:46a
JAN      BUD       71   11-23-92  7:05a
FEB      BUD       73   11-23-92  7:10a
MAR      BUD       69   11-23-92  7:11a
APR      BUD       70   11-23-92  7:11a
HOMEWORK DAT      302   12-06-92  9:00a
NAME     FIL       19   12-06-92  9:01a
RESIDENC FIL       18   12-06-92  9:02a
BIRTH    FIL       21   12-06-92  9:02a
NAME     OLD       19   12-06-92  9:01a
-- More --
```

WHAT'S HAPPENING? Your files may vary based on what assignment you did and what files you copied to the DATA disk. By using the pipe symbol, you asked that the output of the DIR command be used as input to the MORE command. The `-- More --` on the bottom of the screen tells you that there are "more" screens of data. Press any key and the next screen of data will display.

STEP 2: Press any key until you are back at the system prompt. You may have to press several times until you are returned to the system prompt.

```
FRANK    FIL       43   11-23-92  7:13a
THIS     ONE       45   11-23-92  7:13a
PERSONAL FIL     2306   11-23-92  7:14a
Y        FIL        4   05-14-92 11:00a
SERIES       <DIR>      05-14-92  3:10p
BYE      TXT       44   11-23-92  7:07a
TEAMS        <DIR>      08-01-92  1:51a
-- More --

MYLETTER TXT      189   07-04-92 11:51p
SALES    LET      637   07-04-92 11:53p
COMPUTER APP      573   07-04-92 11:58p
DOS-PUNS          317   07-05-92 12:02a
LINE     FIL      208   07-05-92 12:05a
ESSAY    TXT       93   07-05-92 12:06a
BGABBLAD            0   09-21-91 10:01p
TEST     CAS       25   01-24-92 10:06a
PRT               183   11-23-92 10:16a
NOV      TST       72   11-23-92  7:04a
BATCH        <DIR>      12-06-93 10:20p
        79 file(s)       28210 bytes
                        138240 bytes free

A:\>_
```

WHAT'S HAPPENING? You returned to the system level. You may ask yourself, why do this when you get the same effect by using DIR /P? There are two reasons for this. The first is that you can connect several commands with pipes and filters. The second is that /P only works with the DIR command.

STEP 3: Key in the following:
A:\>**DIR ¦ SORT ¦ MORE** <Enter>

```
                              138240 bytes free
         79 file(s)            28210 bytes
  Directory of A:\
  Volume in drive A is DATA DISK
  Volume Serial Number is 3839-0EC8

 APR      BUD        70    11-23-92   7:11a
 APR      KKK        71    11-23-92   7:07a
 APR      TMP        71    11-23-92   7:07a
 APR      TST        70    11-23-92   7:11a
 BATCH        <DIR>        12-06-93  10:20p
 BGAFAKDE             0    09-21-91  10:05p
 BGAFAMEI             0    09-21-91  10:05p
 BIRTH    FIL        21    12-06-92   9:02a
 BIRTH    OLD        21    12-06-92   9:02a
 BOOK     BAC        67    12-06-92   9:03a
 BOOK     DBF        67    12-06-92   9:03a
 BYE      TXT        44    11-23-92   7:07a
 CAROLYN  FIL        46    11-23-92   7:13a
 CHKDSK   EXE     16200    04-09-91   5:00a
 CLASS        <DIR>        11-23-92   7:46a
 COMPUTER APP       573    07-04-92  11:58p
 DATA         <DIR>        12-06-92   9:05a
 -- More --
```

WHAT'S HAPPENING? You now have a sorted directory, in this instance sorted alphabetically. If you have a version of DOS earlier than DOS 5.0, this was the only way you could get a sorted directory. The reason the volume label, files, and numbers are at the top is that, as we discussed, in the ASCII sort sequence, spaces come first, then numbers. The files with the strange names, **BGAFAKDE** and **BGAFAMEI**, are the temporary files that DOS created.

STEP 4: Continue pressing any key until you have returned to the system prompt.

```
 STEVEN   FIL        45    11-23-92   7:13a
 TEAMS        <DIR>        08-01-92   1:51a
 TEST     CAS        25    01-24-92  10:06a
 TEST     TXT        63    05-07-93  10:05a
 TESTING             19    12-06-92   9:01a
 THIS     ONE        45    11-23-92   7:13a
 -- More --
```

```
TRIP             <DIR>     06-17-92  9:00p
TV        BAC       44     12-06-92  9:04a
TV        DBF       44     12-06-92  9:04a
USERS            <DIR>     05-07-93 10:05a
WILD1     XXX       63     05-07-93  9:03a
WILD2     YYY       63     05-07-93  9:03a
WILD3     ZZZ       63     05-07-93  9:03a
WILDONE             92     05-07-93  9:04a
WILDONE   DOS      180     05-07-93  9:02a
WILDTHR   AAA      180     05-07-93  9:03a
WILDTHR   DOS      180     05-07-93  9:03a
WILDTWO   DOS      181     05-07-93  9:03a
Y         FIL        4     05-14-92 11:00a
YOURC     LAB       41     05-14-92 11:00a

A:\>_
```

WHAT'S HAPPENING? You returned to the system prompt. Using pipes is also useful with long text files. If you have a text file that is more than one screenful of data, you cannot use TYPE /P *filename.ext* because /P is not a valid switch or parameter that can be used with the TYPE command. However, you can use the MORE command with a file as input. You can either redirect the input of any file to the MORE command, or you can pipe it. Here redirection will be used first.

STEP 5: Key in the following:
A:\>**MORE < PERSONAL.FIL** <Enter>

```
Gillay    Carolyn   699 Lemon      Orange          CA   Professor
Panezich  Frank     689 Lake       Orange          CA   Teacher
Tuttle    Steven    356 Embassy    Mission Viejo   CA   Juggler
Maurdeff  Kathryn   550 Traver     Ann Arbor       MI   Teacher
Maurdeff  Sonia     550 Traver     Ann Arbor       MI   Student
Smith     Gregory   311 Orchard    Ann Arbor       MI   Engineer
Smith     Carolyn   311 Orchard    Ann Arbor       MI   Housewife
Winter    Jim       333 Pick       Garden Grove    CA   Key Grip
Winter    Linda     333 Pick       Garden Grove    CA   Teacher
Golden    Herbert   345 Lakeview   Orange          CA   Doctor
Golden    Jane      345 Lakeview   Orange          CA   Nurse
Brent     Wendy     356 Edgewood   Ann Arbor       MI   Librarian
Brogan    Lloyd     111 Miller     Santa Cruz      CA   Vice-President
Brogan    Sally     111 Miller     Santa Cruz      CA   Account Manager
Babchuk   Nicholas  13 Stratford   Sun City West   AZ   Professor
Babchuk   Bianca    13 Stratford   Sun City West   AZ   Professor
Begg      Leroy     20 Elm         Ontario         CA   Systems Analyst
Helm      Milton    333 Meadow     Sherman Oaks    CA   Consultant
Moselle   Carolyn   567 Abbey      Rochester       MI   Day Care Teacher
Markiw    Nicholas  354 Bell       Phoenix         AZ   Engineer
Markiw    Emily     10 Zion        Sun City West   AZ   Retired
Nyles     John      12 Brooks      Sun City West   AZ   Retired
Nyles     Sophie    12 Brooks      Sun City West   CA   Retired
Markiw    Nick      10 Zion        Sun City West   AZ   Retired
-- More --
```

WHAT'S HAPPENING? You asked that the file from the DATA disk called **PERSONAL.FIL** be redirected as input into (<) the command MORE. The MORE command then displayed a screenful of this file.

STEP 6: Continue to press any key until you have returned to the system prompt.

```
A:\>_
```

WHAT'S HAPPENING? You returned to the system prompt. There is an alternative way to accomplish the same results. You can pipe the output of the file to the MORE command.

STEP 7: Key in the following:
A:\>**TYPE PERSONAL.FIL ¦ MORE** <Enter>

```
Gillay     Carolyn   699 Lemon      Orange         CA   Professor
Panezich   Frank     689 Lake       Orange         CA   Teacher
Tuttle     Steven    356 Embassy    Mission Viejo  CA   Juggler
Maurdeff   Kathryn   550 Traver     Ann Arbor      MI   Teacher
Maurdeff   Sonia     550 Traver     Ann Arbor      MI   Student
Smith      Gregory   311 Orchard    Ann Arbor      MI   Engineer
Smith      Carolyn   311 Orchard    Ann Arbor      MI   Housewife
Winter     Jim       333 Pick       Garden Grove   CA   Key Grip
Winter     Linda     333 Pick       Garden Grove   CA   Teacher
Golden     Herbert   345 Lakeview   Orange         CA   Doctor
Golden     Jane      345 Lakeview   Orange         CA   Nurse
Brent      Wendy     356 Edgewood   Ann Arbor      MI   Librarian
Brogan     Lloyd     111 Miller     Santa Cruz     CA   Vice-President
Brogan     Sally     111 Miller     Santa Cruz     CA   Account Manager
Babchuk    Nicholas  13 Stratford   Sun City West  AZ   Professor
Babchuk    Bianca    13 Stratford   Sun City West  AZ   Professor
Begg       Leroy     20 Elm         Ontario        CA   Systems Analyst
Helm       Milton    333 Meadow     Sherman Oaks   CA   Consultant
Moselle    Carolyn   567 Abbey      Rochester      MI   Day Care Teacher
Markiw     Nicholas  354 Bell       Phoenix        AZ   Engineer
Markiw     Emily     10 Zion        Sun City West  AZ   Retired
Nyles      John      12 Brooks      Sun City West  AZ   Retired
Nyles      Sophie    12 Brooks      Sun City West  CA   Retired
Markiw     Nick      10 Zion        Sun City West  AZ   Retired
-- More --
```

WHAT'S HAPPENING? You took the output from the TYPE command, which is normally a screen display, and piped it as input to the MORE command. The MORE command then displayed a screenful of this file. Remember that there must be a command on either side of the pipe. You could not key in **A:\>PERSONAL.FIL ¦ MORE** because **PERSONAL.FIL** is a file and not a command.

STEP 8: Continue to press any key until you have returned to the system prompt.

```
A:\>_
```

WHAT'S HAPPENING? You returned to the system prompt.

13.14 Combining Commands with Pipes and Filters

You can join commands together just like a pipeline where the standard output of one command is the standard input of the next command. Just use the pipe symbol as the connector. Usually, when you redirect the output and use the >, that becomes the end of the pipeline. Remember that there must be a command on either side of the pipe.

Activity 13.15 Combining the Commands

Note: The DATA disk is in Drive A. The **A:\>** is displayed.

STEP 1: Key in the following:
A:\>**FIND "Smith" PERSONAL.FIL ¦ FIND "Engineer"** <Enter>

```
A:\>FIND "Smith" PERSONAL.FIL ¦ FIND "Engineer"
Smith     Gregory   311 Orchard    Ann Arbor      MI   Engineer
Smith     Henry     40 Northern    Ontario        CA   Engineer

A:\>_
```

WHAT'S HAPPENING? You see displayed only the "Smiths" who are engineers. You asked DOS first to find or locate all the "Smiths" in the file called **PERSONAL.FIL** located on the DATA disk. Then out of that group or subset of "Smiths", you wanted displayed only those "Smiths" who were engineers.

STEP 2: Be sure the printer is on. Key in the following:
A:\>**FIND "Jones" PERSONAL.FIL ¦ SORT > PRN** <Enter>

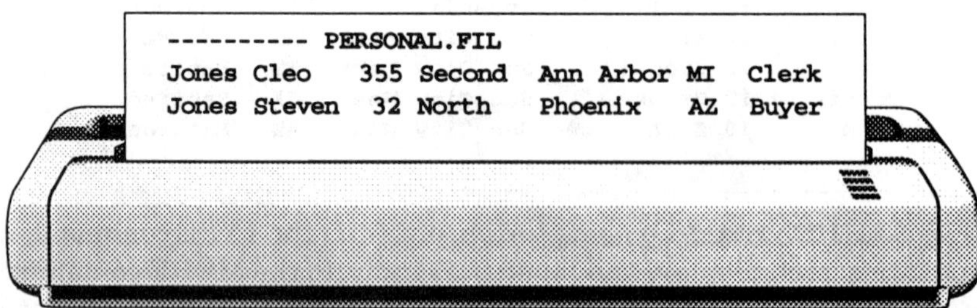

---------- PERSONAL.FIL
Jones Cleo   355 Second Ann Arbor MI Clerk
Jones Steven 32 North   Phoenix   AZ Buyer

WHAT'S HAPPENING? You asked DOS to FIND all the "Joneses." You sent the output or subset of the file **PERSONAL.FIL** as input to the SORT command. You then asked DOS to redirect this subset of sorted "Joneses" to a device, the printer. If you wanted to save a copy of any subset, you could redirect the output from the SORT command to a file instead of to the printer.

STEP 3: Key in the following:
A:\>**FIND "Carolyn" PERSONAL.FIL ¦ SORT > CAROLYN.REP** <Enter>

WHAT'S HAPPENING? Only the system prompt is displayed on the screen. You asked the DOS command FIND to find all the occurrences of "Carolyn" in the file called **PERSONAL.FIL**. You then piped or had the standard output sent to the command SORT because you wanted all the people named "Carolyn" in alphabetical order. Since you wanted a permanent copy of this list, you redirected the standard output (normally displayed on the screen) to a file you named **CAROLYN.REP**.

STEP 4: Key in the following:
A:\>**TYPE CAROLYN.REP** <Enter>

```
A:\>TYPE CAROLYN.REP

------ PERSONAL.FIL
Gillay    Carolyn   699 Lemon     Orange      CA   Professor
Moselle   Carolyn   567 Abbey     Rochester   MI   Day Care Teacher
Smith     Carolyn   311 Orchard   Ann Arbor   MI   Housewife

A:\>_
```

WHAT'S HAPPENING? You see displayed on your screen in alphabetical order only people with the name "Carolyn." The file called **CAROLYN.REP** is a subset of the file **PERSONAL.FIL**. All you have done is extracted information from the file—you have not changed the original file in any way.

STEP 5: Key in the following:
A:\>**DIR ¦ SORT /+9 ¦ MORE** <Enter>

Note: Your screen display will vary based on the work you did as well as the date and time you created the files.

```
                        137216 bytes free
BFCFBKCH             0   09-22-91   9:37p
BFCFBMDF             0   09-22-91   9:37p
TESTING             19   12-06-92   9:01a
DISKFILE            44   12-06-92   9:04a
WILDONE             92   05-07-93   9:04a
PRT                183   11-23-92  10:16a
DOS-PUNS           317   07-05-92  12:02a
USERS           <DIR>    05-07-93  10:05a
SERIES          <DIR>    05-14-92   3:10p
TRIP            <DIR>    06-17-92   9:00p
TEAMS           <DIR>    08-01-92   1:51a
POLY-SCI        <DIR>    11-16-93   9:47p
PHYS-ED         <DIR>    11-16-93   9:47p
CLASS           <DIR>    11-23-92   7:46a
```

```
FILES              <DIR>     12-06-92  9:03a
DATA               <DIR>     12-06-92  9:05a
BATCH              <DIR>     12-06-93 10:20p
WILDTHR   AAA        180     05-07-93  9:03a
EXTRA     ABC         18     10-12-92  9:00p
COMPUTER  APP        573     07-04-92 11:58p
MOVIE     BAC         39     12-06-92  9:04a
-- More --
```

WHAT'S HAPPENING? You took the directory display and piped the output to the SORT command. However, you sorted by the file extension. How did you know that the file extension was in the ninth column? Since you know that all files can have no more than eight character, the extension must start at 9. You then piped the output to the MORE command so that you could see the output one screenful at a time.

STEP 6: Continue pressing <Enter> until you have returned to the system prompt.

STEP 7: Key in the following:
A:\>**DIR ¦ SORT /+24 ¦ MORE** <Enter>

Note: Your screen display will vary based on the work you did as well as the date and time you created the files.

```
 Directory of A:\

TEST      CAS         25     01-24-92 10:06a
SORTED    PER       2305     02-14-93  8:54p
CAROLYN   REP        223     02-14-93  9:34p
CHKDSK    EXE      16200     04-09-91  5:00a
WILDONE   DOS        180     05-07-93  9:02a
WILDTWO   DOS        181     05-07-93  9:03a
WILDTHR   DOS        180     05-07-93  9:03a
WILD1     XXX         63     05-07-93  9:03a
WILD2     YYY         63     05-07-93  9:03a
WILD3     ZZZ         63     05-07-93  9:03a
WILDTHR   AAA        180     05-07-93  9:03a
WILDONE               92     05-07-93  9:04a
USERS              <DIR>     05-07-93 10:05a
TEST      TXT         63     05-07-93 10:05a
MOVIES    LST        655     05-14-92  3:09p
SERIES             <DIR>     05-14-92  3:10p
NOFILE    XYZ         39     05-14-92 11:00a
NOTHING   XYZ         44     05-14-92 11:00a
YOURC     LAB         41     05-14-92 11:00a
Y         FIL          4     05-14-92 11:00a
TRIP               <DIR>     06-17-92  9:00p
-- More --
```

WHAT'S HAPPENING? In this case you piped the output of the directory command to the SORT command, but this time you wanted it sorted by date. You then piped the output to the MORE command so that you could see one screenful at a time. However, in this example, this display is not being sorted by date because the SORT command sorts the entire line. Thus, it read 01-24-92 before it read 04-09-91 because 01 comes before 04. That is how a computer sorts. However, when people sort dates, they usually mean sort the year first, then the month and day. If you have DOS 5.0, you can request this type of sort by keying in **DIR /OD**, but no matter which version of DOS you have, you can always do this in the following way.

STEP 8: Press <Enter> until you have returned to the system prompt.

STEP 9: Presuming that you want to sort from the earliest date to the latest date, you will have to determine the earliest and latest dates on your DATA disk. In this example, the earliest year is 1991 and the latest is 1993. Key in the following:

A:\>**DIR ¦ SORT /+24 ¦ FIND "-91" > YEARS.FIL** <Enter>
A:\>**DIR ¦ SORT /+24 ¦ FIND "-92" >> YEARS.FIL** <Enter>
A:\>**DIR ¦ SORT /+24 ¦ FIND "-93" >> YEARS.FIL** <Enter>
A:\>**TYPE YEARS.FIL ¦ MORE** <Enter>

```
CHKDSK    EXE   16200   04-09-91   5:00a
JOINED    SAM     104   06-22-91   2:15p
MONTHS    SAM     284   06-22-91   2:26p
TEST      CAS      25   01-24-92  10:06a
MOVIES    LST     655   05-14-92   3:09p
SERIES        <DIR>     05-14-92   3:10p
NOFILE    XYZ      39   05-14-92  11:00a
NOTHING   XYZ      44   05-14-92  11:00a
YOURC     LAB      41   05-14-92  11:00a
Y         FIL       4   05-14-92  11:00a
TRIP          <DIR>     06-17-92   9:00p
FEB       TMP     182   07-04-92  11:00p
MYLETTER  TXT     189   07-04-92  11:51p
SALES     LET     637   07-04-92  11:53p
COMPUTER  APP     573   07-04-92  11:58p
DOS-PUNS          317   07-05-92  12:02a
LINE      FIL     208   07-05-92  12:05a
ESSAY     TXT      93   07-05-92  12:06a
TEAMS         <DIR>     08-01-92   1:51a
EXTRA     ABC      18   10-12-92   9:00p
JAN       KKK      72   11-23-92   7:04a
NOV       TST      72   11-23-92   7:04a
EXERCISE  TXT     315   11-23-92   7:05a
JANUARY   TXT      71   11-23-92   7:05a
-- More --
```

WHAT'S HAPPENING? You took the DIR and you sent the output to the SORT command to sort on the 24th column. You then took the output from the SORT command and sent it to the FIND command looking only for lines that had "91" in them or your earliest year. You filtered the data. You then sent the output to a file called **YEARS.FIL**. The next command line looked for "92," but instead of redirecting the output to the file **YEARS.FIL**, which would overwrite it, you used the double >>, which appended the data to the end of the existing file. You did this until you had no more dates. You then used the TYPE command using MORE to see the results.

STEP 10: Press <Enter> until you have returned to the system prompt.

STEP 11: Key in the following:
A:\>**DIR ¦ FIND "<DIR>" ¦ SORT** <Enter>

```
A:\>DIR ¦ FIND "<DIR>" ¦ SORT
BATCH          <DIR>     12-06-93 10:20p
CLASS          <DIR>     11-23-92  7:46a
DATA           <DIR>     12-06-92  9:05a
FILES          <DIR>     12-06-92  9:03a
PHYS-ED        <DIR>     11-16-93  9:47p
POLY-SCI       <DIR>     11-16-93  9:47p
SERIES         <DIR>     05-14-92  3:10p
TEAMS          <DIR>     08-01-92  1:51a
TRIP           <DIR>     06-17-92  9:00p
USERS          <DIR>     05-07-93 10:05a

A:\>_
```

WHAT'S HAPPENING? You sent the output of DIR to FIND. You were looking for any file that had <DIR> in it. You used uppercase letters since everything in the directory is in uppercase. You then sent that output to the SORT command. Now you have an alphabetical list of the subdirectories on your DATA disk.

13.16 Batch Files with Pipes and Filters

You can use batch files to automate these processes. Thus, instead of having to key in the commands, you can save them in an easily remembered batch file name.

Activity 13.17 Writing a Batch File with Pipes and Filters

Note: The DATA disk is in Drive A with the **A:\>** displayed.

STEP 1: Key in the following:
A:\>**EDIT SDIR.BAT** <Enter>
DIR ¦ FIND "<DIR>" ¦ SORT <Enter>

WHAT'S HAPPENING? You created a batch file so that anytime you want a sorted list of the subdirectories on a disk, you just have to key in SDIR. You named it SDIR so that it is not the same name as the DIR command. You must now save the file to disk before you can execute it.

STEP 2: Press <Alt>+F.

STEP 3: Press X.

STEP 4: Press Y.

STEP 5: Key in the following:
A:\>**SDIR** <Enter>

```
A:\>SDIR

A:\>DIR ¦ FIND "<DIR>" ¦ SORT
BATCH          <DIR>     12-06-93 10:20p
CLASS          <DIR>     11-23-92  7:46a
DATA           <DIR>     12-06-92  9:05a
FILES          <DIR>     12-06-92  9:03a
PHYS-ED        <DIR>     11-16-93  9:47p
POLY-SCI       <DIR>     11-16-93  9:47p
SERIES         <DIR>     05-14-92  3:10p
TEAMS          <DIR>     08-01-92  1:51a
TRIP           <DIR>     06-17-92  9:00p
USERS          <DIR>     05-07-93 10:05a

A:\>
A:\>_
```

WHAT'S HAPPENING? You automated the process of seeing a sorted list of the subdirectories. Because this listing was short, you did not need any other command. However, if you thought you might have a long list, you could have piped it to the MORE command. When you have a long list, the MORE command is useful.

STEP 6: When the instructions say <Tab>-8, that means to press the tab key as many times as the number following <Tab>. In addition, the screen will scroll to the right. Key in the following:

A:\>**EDIT NAME.BAT** <Enter>
ECHO OFF <Enter>
ECHO <Tab>-8 **Your name > PRN** <Enter>
ECHO <Tab>-8 **Chapter %1 > PRN** <Enter>

WHAT'S HAPPENING? You wrote a batch file that will automatically print your name and the chapter you are currently working on in the upper right-hand corner of your paper. Remember, though, you must save the file to disk.

STEP 7: Press <Alt>+F.

STEP 8: Press X.

STEP 9: Press Y.

STEP 10: Be sure the printer is on. Key in the following:

A:\>**NAME 13** <Enter>

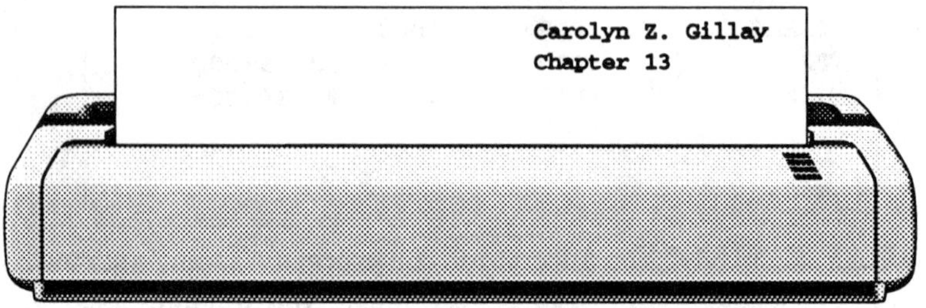

WHAT'S HAPPENING? Since ECHO is a command that "echoes" to the screen, the output can be redirected to the printer. The %1 allows you to key in any number so that the batch file can be used with any chapter.

Chapter Summary

1. The redirection symbols are the >, the <, and the >>.
2. The >> appends output to the end of a file.
3. Redirection, pipes, and filters have to do with standard input and standard output.
4. Any command that expects its input from the keyboard has standard input.
5. Any command that normally displays its output on the screen has standard output.
6. Standard error means that DOS writes error messages to the screen.
7. You can redirect standard input and output to and from devices or files.
8. The pipe symbol is the ¦.
9. The pipe takes standard output from one command and uses it as standard input into the next command.
10. You can pipe many programs together.
11. Filters take data, change it in some fashion, and send the output to the screen.
12. The three DOS filters are SORT, FIND, and MORE.
13. SORT has two parameters, /R for reverse order and /+*n* for column number.
14. FIND has three parameters, /V for everything except, /C for counting occurrences of the item, and /N for line number where the item appears in the file. DOS 5.0 also has the parameter /I for ignore case.
15. MORE lets you look at any text file one screenful at a time. It has no parameters.
16. You can use pipes and filters in batch files.
17. You can redirect the ECHO command to the printer.

Key Terms

ASCII sort sequence	Input/output	Standard error
Filters	Pipes	Standard input
I/O	Redirection	Standard output

Discussion Questions

1. Explain redirection.
2. Explain the terms standard input, standa rd output, and standard error.
3. Does every DOS command use standard input and standard output? If not, why not?
4. What is the difference between > and >> when redirecting output?
5. Explain how the symbol < is used.
6. Keying in `COPY DIR PRN` will not give you a printout of the directory. Why?
7. What are filters?
8. Give the syntax of the SORT command.
9. What do the parameters in the SORT syntax represent?

10. Explain how the SORT command works. Describe any limitations of the SORT command.
11. Identify one place that standard output can be written.
12. Give the syntax for the FIND command.
13. What is the purpose of the FIND command?
14. What are the three parameters that are used with the FIND command and what do they represent?
15. Why must the character string be enclosed in quotation marks when using the FIND command?
16. What are pipes?
17. Are there any restrictions on the use of pipes? If so, what are they?
18. How is the MORE command used?
19. Give the syntax of the MORE command.
20. How may pipes, filters, and redirection be used in batch files?

Application Assignments

Note 1: All exercises should be placed on your DATA disk.

Note 2: Remember that if you are using a laser printer, you must take the necessary steps to print.

1. Take the printer offline by pressing the online button.
2. Press FF (Form Feed).
3. Place the printer back online by pressing the online button.

Note 3: If you do not have the appropriate subdirectories for the assignments, you will need to create them. If you do not have the appropriate files, you will either need to copy them from `C:\JUNK` or the subdirectories under `\JUNK` or create them.

1. For the following assignment:
   a. Sort the file `PERSONAL.FIL` in alphabetical order and place it in a new file called `ORDERED.REP`.
   b. Print `ORDERED.REP`.
2. For the following assignment:
   a. Using the file `PERSONAL.FIL`, create a file called `CALIF.FIL` of the people who live in California.
   b. Print the file.
   c. Sort `CALIF.FIL` in alphabetical order and print it without saving the sorted data to a file.
3. For the following assignment:
   a. Find all the teachers in the file `PERSONAL.FIL`. Extract only those who live in Michigan and then sort and print it without saving the data to a file.
4. For the following assignment:
   a. Using the file `PERSONAL.FIL`, create a new file composed of the people who live in Orange and sort them in descending order. Call the file `ORANGE.FIL`.

b. Print **ORANGE.FIL**.
5. Sort and print the root directory of the DATA disk. Do not save the output to a file.
6. Sort the subdirectory called **BATCH** on the DATA disk and send the output to the printer. Do not save the output to a file. Do not use <Shift>+<PrtSc>.
7. For the following assignment:
   a. Sort the **USERS** directory of the DATA disk and place it in a file called **FILES.DIR**.
   b. Sort the **DATA** directory of the DATA disk and append it to the above file, **FILES.DIR**.
   c. Print the combined file.
   d. Use **FILES.DIR**. Extract only the file names—eliminating such extra information such as Volume Label—sort the output and send it to the printer.
   e. Delete the file called **FILES.DIR**.

Challenge Assignments

8. For the following assignment:
   a. Write a batch file that will allow you to print any file name with only the file name, extension, size, date, and time, followed by the contents of the file. Call it **CONTENT.BAT**.
   b. Be sure the batch file works correctly.
   c. Copy it to the **BATCH** subdirectory and delete it from the root directory.
   d. Document **CONTENT.BAT** and make it visually pleasing.
   e. Print **CONTENT.BAT**.
9. For the following assignment:
   a. Write a batch file that will let you find any file name or extension on a disk, and display the results one screenful at a time. Call it **FINDFILE.BAT**. Use replaceable parameters.
   b. Document it and make it visually pleasing. Print the file.
   c. Copy it to the **BATCH** subdirectory and delete it from the root directory.
   d. Edit **FINDFILE.BAT** so that the output is sorted.
   e. Print **FINDFILE.BAT**.
10. For the following assignment:
   a. Write a batch file in the **BATCH** subdirectory called **ASSN.BAT** that will print your name, class, class time and meeting date, and chapter number in the upper right-hand corner of any assignment. Use replaceable parameters for the chapter number.
   b. Create another batch file in the **BATCH** subdirectory called **ASSN1.BAT** that will print your name, class, class day and time, chapter number, and problem number on any page. Use replaceable parameters for the chapter and problem numbers.
   c. Print both of these batch files.
   d. These two batch files can now be used for your homework assignments and will identify each problem you do.

14

Chapter

Configuring the System

After completing this chapter you will be able to:

1. Explain the importance of a `CONFIG.SYS` file.
2. Explain how a `CONFIG.SYS` file works.
3. List and explain the major commands that can be used in `CONFIG.SYS`.
4. List and explain the system configuration commands.
5. Explain what BUFFERS and FILES statements do in a `CONFIG.SYS` file.
6. Explain the function of device drivers.
7. Explain the function of a virtual disk.
8. Compare and contrast extended and expanded memory.
9. Explain the need for using LASTDRIVE in the `CONFIG.SYS` file.
10. Explain how SHELL can be used to change the computer environment.
11. Explain when the SWITCHES command is needed in the `CONFIG.SYS` file.
12. Write and use a `CONFIG.SYS` file that installs files, buffers, and virtual disks, increases the last drive, and expands the environment.

Chapter Overview

In previous chapters you used DOS commands to manage disks and files. Each command was used in a specific manner and guaranteed certain results. However, a great deal of flexibility has been built into DOS. It is possible to maximize the use of hardware by the use of configuration commands and to improve the performance and flexibility of the computer system by altering the internal environment in which DOS operates. By using the configuration file to change certain characteristics of the operating system it is possible to customize the operating system to meet specific needs.

In this chapter you will learn to maximize the performance and flexibility of your computer system by writing a `CONFIG.SYS` file that configures the computer system.

14.0 Customizing DOS

To date, you have used the DOS commands in specific ways. You key in the command and get certain results, based on the work of the command, including the batch file subcommands. These commands tell DOS what to do. However, in addition, you have the capability of customizing or tailoring DOS for your specific computer configuration. Customizing allows you to install such devices as a mouse, an external drive, or other hardware you may purchase. In addition, you can "tweak the system" or use configuration commands to maximize the use of your hardware. There are also application programs that require hardware settings other than the default settings that come with DOS. The configuration process is similar to setting up your own office environment to your specifications. You can also adjust DOS internally by setting up a **CONFIG.SYS** file, which will alter the environment in which DOS works. These internal adjustments will significantly improve the performance and flexibility of your computer system.

14.1 The CONFIG.SYS File

When you first power-on the computer, the microprocessor goes to the ROM-BIOS chip to do a self-test of memory and hardware. Then it checks for a disk in Drive A. If it finds a disk in Drive A, BIOS reads the first sector on the disk. If it is a DOS System Disk, the system files are loaded. If there is no disk in Drive A, BIOS looks in Drive C. When it finds the system files, it loads them. After loading the system files, it looks for a file called **CONFIG.SYS** in the root directory of the booting disk. If it finds it, it follows the instructions in the **CONFIG.SYS** file. If it does not find this file, it initializes your computer based on the DOS default values. It loads **COMMAND.COM** and then looks for **AUTOEXEC.BAT**. If there is no **AUTOEXEC.BAT** file, DOS displays the date and time prompts and last the **A>** or **C>**. Figure 14.1 demonstrates this process.

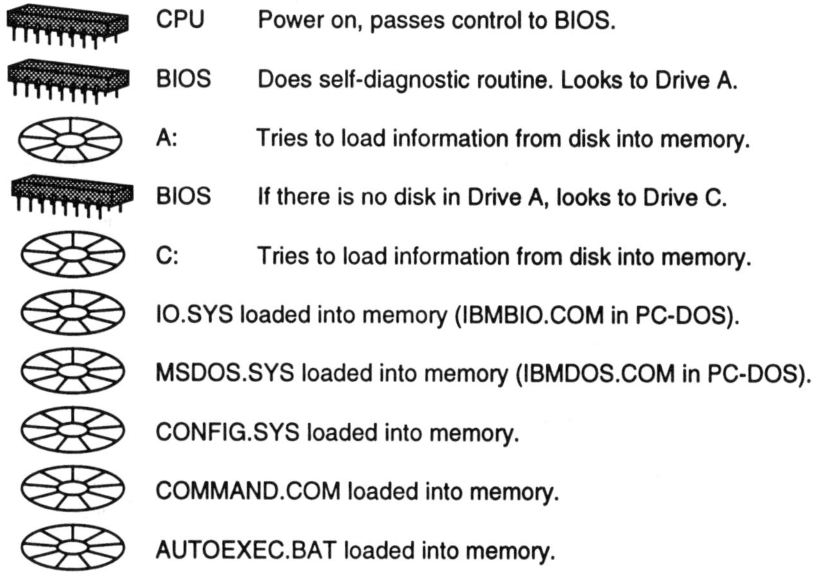

Figure 14.1 Order of Installation

CPU Power on, passes control to BIOS.

BIOS Does self-diagnostic routine. Looks to Drive A.

A: Tries to load information from disk into memory.

BIOS If there is no disk in Drive A, looks to Drive C.

C: Tries to load information from disk into memory.

IO.SYS loaded into memory (IBMBIO.COM in PC-DOS).

MSDOS.SYS loaded into memory (IBMDOS.COM in PC-DOS).

CONFIG.SYS loaded into memory.

COMMAND.COM loaded into memory.

AUTOEXEC.BAT loaded into memory.

The **CONFIG.SYS** file is the mechanism that DOS uses to change the default settings or to add settings. DOS has certain default values it uses when there is no **CONFIG.SYS** file. The only way to alter these defaults is to use a special set of commands that are stored in the **CONFIG.SYS** file. A **CONFIG.SYS** file does not come on a DOS System Disk. It is something that a user creates. If you use the SELECT program with DOS 3.3 or 4.0 or SETUP with DOS 5.0, the programs will create a **CONFIG.SYS** file.

Another way a **CONFIG.SYS** file can be created is by certain application program installation routines. Sometimes, these application programs either add a line to the existing **CONFIG.SYS** file or replace the **CONFIG.SYS** file with the application **CONFIG.SYS** file. The **CONFIG.SYS** file is always a standard ASCII text file, which contains a list of statements that define to DOS the values that the user needs to define a nonstandard configuration. A **CONFIG.SYS** file can alter the internal environment of DOS with a specific but limited set of commands, but it is *only* read or activated when the system is booted or rebooted. All the **CONFIG.SYS** commands, also called **directives**, are listed in Table 14.1.

Table 14.1 System Configuration Commands

Command	Description
BREAK	Checks the keyboard to see if the user has pressed <Ctrl>+C or <Ctrl>+<Break> to cancel a command.
BUFFERS	Tells DOS how much memory to use for holding data. Sets number of disk buffers.
COUNTRY	Tells country's date, time, and number formats DOS will use.
DEVICE	Loads special drivers that tell DOS how to handle I/O devices such as a mouse or external drives.
DEVICEHIGH	Loads device drivers into upper memory area. New to DOS 5.0.
DOS	Sets area of RAM where DOS will be located and whether or not to use upper memory area. New to DOS 5.0.
DRIVPARM	Sets characteristics of a disk drive (non-IBM releases above 3.2).
FCBS	Tells DOS how many file control blocks that DOS can open concurrently.
FILES	Tells DOS the maximum number of files that can be open at one time.
INSTALL	Allows you to install specific memory-resident program such as SHARE and FASTOPEN, new to DOS 4.0.
LASTDRIVE	Tells DOS which drive letter is the last drive letter that can be used.
REM	Lets you document your **CONFIG.SYS** file. DOS ignores any statement with REM in front of it.
SHELL	Tells DOS the location of the command processor, usually **COMMAND.COM**, and also can change the size of the environment.
STACKS	Tells DOS to increase the number and size of stacks that handle hardware interrupts.
SWITCHES	Lets an enhanced keyboard be treated like an old-style keyboard for those older applications that do not recognize the enhanced keyboard, also new to DOS 4.0.

Some of these **CONFIG.SYS** commands are rather esoteric and will be summarized in Appendix H. However, many **CONFIG.SYS** commands are essential to run certain application programs and/or to fine-tune your computer system.

14.2 Files

One of the functions of an operating system is to keep track of open files as well as devices being used. As an operating system, DOS also needs a way to track information in memory about which files are open as well as which devices are to be used. For instance, when you use the COPY command, DOS is actually keeping track of two open files, the source file and the destination file. When you use an application program, the program gives DOS the name of the file or the device it is planning to use. DOS returns to the application program a **file handle**, a two-byte number, which the program then uses to manipulate the file or device. An application program like dBASE III Plus allows the user a maximum of fifteen files open. Although the application program can have fifteen files open at one time and track them, there is a problem with DOS. DOS's default value is eight files. In other words, DOS can keep track of only eight open files at a time. Furthermore, DOS needs five files for its own use. Application programs can use the remaining three files (see Table 14.2).

Table 14.2
DOS Files

stdin	Standard input; source of input.
stdout	Standard output; where DOS is going to write information.
stderr	Standard error; where DOS is going to write error messages.
stdprn	Standard printer; where DOS recognizes the printer.
stdaux	Standard auxiliary; where DOS recognizes the communication port.

Thus, an application program has the use of only three files. Hence, if you are running an application program and get the error message "Too many files open" or "Not enough file handles," it means that the three remaining unassigned default file values were not enough for the application program. In a **CONFIG.SYS** file you can change the number of allowable open files with the FILES command. The FILES command permits a minimum of eight and a maximum of 255 files open. The default value is eight. Each additional file you open after eight takes additional space in memory. The syntax is:

FILES=*x*
where *x* represents a numerical value between 8 and 255.

Many application programs recommend a specific number of files open. If you use several application programs and each recommends a different number of files open, use the highest number. If there are no file recommendations in your software applications, use at least 20. If you run database programs, spreadsheet programs, or Windows, use at least 30. You can have only one FILES statement per booting disk. The reason that you do not use the maximum number of files available is that you pay a price. The price is memory. The more open files you have, the less memory you have available. Thus, you must try to maximize performance without wasting memory.

14.3 Buffers

The buffers in a `CONFIG.SYS` file tell DOS how many disk buffers to use. What is a **disk buffer**? Buffers act as the go-betweens for the disk and RAM. Since a disk drive is a mechanical device, it is slower for DOS to use than RAM. DOS has to go to the disk and read the information into memory. DOS reads into memory a minimum of one sector or 512 bytes at a time. For the sake of efficiency, DOS sets up a reserved area in RAM it can read and write to prior to reading or writing to the disk. This process is called **caching**, pronounced "cashing." When the program makes a request for information from a disk, DOS reads the disk and places the entire 512-byte sector in the buffer, even if the information you need is less than 512 bytes. When you need the next group of information, DOS reads the disk buffer in memory first and, if the information is there, it places it in working memory. Thus, DOS does not have to "read" the disk again.

This go-between process also occurs when you write information to a disk. DOS collects the information in a buffer until it is a full sector, 512 bytes. Only then will DOS write the information to the disk. When a buffer is full and DOS begins writing the information to a disk, DOS is **flushing the buffer**. When you are using an application program and you exit it properly, part of this process is telling DOS the application program is finished. At that time DOS flushes the buffer to indicate that the information is no longer needed and frees up memory.

When you are done working with an application program, do not just turn off the computer because you could still have information in the buffer that would *not* be written to the disk. For example, if you are working with an application package like ADDRESS (a database), each record (name and address) is 128 bytes long. When you want to look at the first name and address (record) that must be loaded into memory, DOS does not just read the first 128 bytes; it reads the entire 512-byte sector. You not only get the first record but also the next three. Then, when you need the second record, DOS does not have to go back to the disk. It just looks in the buffer and, in this case, finds the next record that the application program needs. When there are no more records in the disk buffer, DOS goes to the disk. In this example, instead of having to access the disk four times, DOS only needs to access the disk once. Figure 14.2 demonstrates this process.

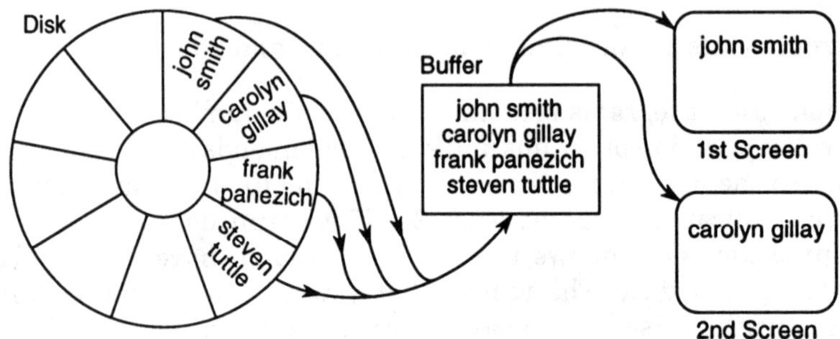

Figure 14.2 Disk Buffers and Application Programs

Remember, DOS reads the *entire* sector into the disk buffer. Then, when the application needs to read the first record and display it on the screen, DOS gets it from the disk buffer. When the application needs the second record to display on the screen, DOS does not have to return to the disk. It checks the disk buffer, finds the record, and passes it to the program.

What DOS is doing, in order to improve performance, is reducing the number of times it has to access the disk. You can have a minimum of 1 to a maximum of 99 buffers. If you have IBM PC-DOS 4.0 and expanded memory, the maximum number of buffers can be 10,000, if you use the /X parameter; that is a lot of go-betweens! The default value of the buffers ranges from 2 to 15, depending on the number of disk drives and memory (see Table 14.3).

Table 14.3 Default Buffers

	Buffers	**Bytes**
Default setting	2	
If any disk drive is greater than 360 KB but memory is less than 128 KB	3	
If memory size is between 128 KB and 255 KB	5	2672
If memory size is between 256 KB and 511 KB	10	5328
If memory size is between 512 KB and 640 KB	15	7984

The syntax is: BUFFERS=*n*[,*m*]

where *n* specifies the numbers of disk buffers and *m* specifies the number of buffers in the secondary cache, called **look-ahead buffers**. Introduced in DOS 4.0, a look-ahead buffer allows DOS to read a number of sectors in advance. Also, if you have DOS 4.0 and expanded memory, you can include the /X parameter and place buffers in expanded memory. The value can go to 10,000. This parameter is only available in IBM PC-DOS 4.0.

However, there is a catch to the go-between process. When working with computers, you always have trade-offs. The trade-off with buffers is that the more buffers you have, the more time DOS must spend looking through them. DOS must read the buffers sequentially prior to reading the disk. If there are too many buffers, it could be faster to go directly to the disk. A buffer also takes about 532 bytes of RAM, reducing the amount of memory available for programs. DOS uses the extra bytes above 512 for overhead. **Overhead** is what DOS needs internally to manage these buffers.

In addition, not all programs make use of buffering. When an application program works by reading an entire file into memory, working on it, and then writing the entire file back to disk, it does not use buffers. Typically, word processing programs and spreadsheet programs are examples of these kinds of applications. Conversely, data base programs usually do read and write information in pieces and, hence, use buffers. Referred to as **disk-intensive**, these types of programs go to the disk repeatedly and need buffers to improve their overall operating performance. However, to further complicate things, more and more software, including word processing software, is becoming more and more powerful and thus makes greater use of overlay or auxiliary files, which benefit by having many buffers. The best advice is to set the number of buffers by the guidelines found in your software application packages. If you have no software guidelines, you may use the following values based on you hard disk size:

Hard Disk Size	Buffers
Less than 40 MB	20
40 – 79 MB	30
80 – 119 MB	40
120 MB or over	50

14.4 Working with CONFIG.SYS and AUTOEXEC.BAT Files

When you begin working with the **CONFIG.SYS** file and the **AUTOEXEC.BAT** file, you want to have a way to recover in case something goes wrong. You do not want to be locked out of your hard disk and/or device drivers that control devices on your particular computer system. Please check with your instructor for the procedures in your laboratory environment. If you are working on your own computer system, there are some important steps to take prior to working on these files.

1. On the hard disk, create a subdirectory called **BACK** or some other appropriate name. Into this subdirectory, copy the **CONFIG.SYS** file and the **AUTOEXEC.BAT** file. In addition, copy any drivers (files that have a **.SYS** extension) that reside in the root directory into the **BACK** subdirectory.
2. Create a bootable floppy disk that can be booted off Drive A—the bootable disk drive. In addition, copy any device drivers to this floppy disk. You may want to rename the **AUTOEXEC.BAT** file on the floppy disk to **AUTOEXEC.BAK**. You want a simple, basic booting disk.
3. If you wish to work on the **CONFIG.SYS** that is on your hard disk, copy the original **CONFIG.SYS** file to some other name such as using your initials as a file extension. In my case, for example, I would "**COPY CONFIG.SYS CONFIG.CZG**." The name **CONFIG.CZG** is chosen because, particularly when you install software, the software installation program will often name the current **CONFIG.SYS** file **CONFIG.BAK** or **CONFIG.OLD**.

If you take these steps, you will always have a way to recover in case disaster strikes.

14.5 The Bootable DOS System Disk

In Chapter 12, you created a bootable floppy disk labeled "Bootable DOS System Disk." You will use this disk for the remainder of this chapter, unless otherwise stated. If your DATA disk was a bootable disk, you may use that disk. Again, please check with your lab instructor if procedures are different in your lab environment. If you are using your own computer system and wish to use the hard disk, be sure to rename and/or save both the **CONFIG.SYS** and **AUTOEXEC.BAT** files.

Activity 14.6 Writing a CONFIG.SYS File with FILES and BUFFERS

Note: No disk is in Drive A. The Bootable DOS System Disk is available. The **C:\>** is displayed. Be sure the path is set to **C:\DOS**. Again, remember that if your DOS system files are in a location other the **C:\DOS**, you must specify that location.

STEP 1: Be sure you have booted from Drive C. Place the Bootable DOS System Disk in Drive A.

STEP 2: Key in the following:
C:\>**A:** <Enter>

STEP 3: Key in the following:
A:\>**EDIT A:AUTOEXEC.BAT** <Enter>
PROMPT pg <Enter>
PATH C:\DOS

WHAT'S HAPPENING? You are creating an **AUTOEXEC.BAT** file on the Bootable DOS System Disk that will change the look of the prompt and also set the path to the subdirectory on the hard disk where the DOS system files are kept. This way you will not have to set the path when you reboot off Drive A. Now, you must save the file to disk.

STEP 4: Press <Alt>+F.

STEP 5: Press X.

STEP 6: Press Y.

STEP 7: Be sure the Bootable DOS System Disk is in Drive A with the drive door shut or latched. Reboot the system.

STEP 8: Key in the following:
A:\>**CHKDSK** <Enter>

```
A:\>CHKDSK

 Volume Serial Number is 07F9-1C19

    362496 bytes total disk space
     71680 bytes in 2 hidden files
     50176 bytes in 3 user files
    240640 bytes available on disk

      1024 bytes in each allocation unit
       354 total allocation units on disk
       235 available allocation units on disk

    652288 total bytes memory
    590080 bytes free

A:\>_
```

WHAT'S HAPPENING? Your numbers will vary, depending on what you have on your disk. Look at the number of bytes free. In this example, it is 590080 bytes free. Make a note of your bytes free.

STEP 9: Key in the following:
A:\>**COPY CON CONFIG.SYS** <Enter>
FILES=20 <Enter>
<Ctrl>+Z <Enter>

```
A:\>COPY CON CONFIG.SYS
FILES=20
^Z
  1 file(s) copied

A:\>_
```

WHAT'S HAPPENING? You used COPY CON to write a simple **CONFIG.SYS** file. Since the **CONFIG.SYS** file must be an ASCII file, you used COPY CON, which writes files in ASCII. You could have used either EDIT or EDLIN, which are both ASCII editors, to create the file. This **CONFIG.SYS** file sets the maximum number of open FILES at 20. However, DOS does not know this yet because DOS only reads the **CONFIG.SYS** file at time of bootup.

STEP 10: Reboot the system.

STEP 11: Key in the following:
A:\>**CHKDSK** <Enter>

```
A:\>CHKDSK

 Volume Serial Number is 07F9-1C19

    362496 bytes total disk space
     71680 bytes in 2 hidden files
     51280 bytes in 4 user files
    238616 bytes available on disk

      1024 bytes in each allocation unit
       354 total allocation units on disk
       234 available allocation units on disk

    652288 total bytes memory
    589376 bytes free

A:\>_
```

WHAT'S HAPPENING? Your numbers will vary, depending on what files you have on the disk. Look at the number of available bytes. In this example, it is 589376 bytes free. You have lost some bytes available for the system to use because they were used for the FILES directive, or statement, in the **CONFIG.SYS** file. You are going to add a line to the **CONFIG.SYS** file. Because you want to add a line, it will be easier to use an editor to edit the existing file.

STEP 12: Edit your **CONFIG.SYS** file and add the line at the end of the file:
BUFFERS=30

STEP 13: Key in the following:
A:\>**TYPE CONFIG.SYS** <Enter>

```
A:\>TYPE CONFIG.SYS
FILES=20
BUFFERS=30

A:\>_
```

WHAT'S HAPPENING? You edited **CONFIG.SYS** with the editor of your choice. You added the line **BUFFERS=30**. You have now changed the buffers so that DOS will no longer use the default value but the value that you substituted, which is 30. However, once again, DOS cannot act unless you reboot the system.

STEP 14: Reboot the system.

STEP 15: Key in the following:
A:\>**CHKDSK** <Enter>

```
A:\>CHKDSK

 Volume Serial Number is 07F9-1C19

    362496 bytes total disk space
     71680 bytes in 2 hidden files
     51200 bytes in 4 user files
    239616 bytes available on disk

      1024 bytes in each allocation unit
       354 total allocation units on disk
       234 available allocation units on disk

    652288 total bytes memory
    581392 bytes free

A:\>_
```

WHAT'S HAPPENING? Your numbers will vary, depending on the files on your disk. Look at the number of available bytes. In this example, it is 581392 bytes free. You have lost some bytes available in RAM because you have used them for the FILES and the BUFFERS statements in the **CONFIG.SYS** file, which took effect when you rebooted the system. You may have noticed a slightly faster performance when DOS executed the CHKDSK command.

14.7 Device Drivers

DOS has built-in software routines to handle certain specific hardware. It knows how to read the keyboard, write to the screen and read and write to standard disk drives, print files and communicate through the serial port. If you have additional nonstandard hardware devices such as a mouse or expanded memory, you have to provide DOS with the proper software (device drivers) and use the DEVICE command in the **CONFIG.SYS** file to load them. Generally, hardware manufacturers provide this software with the hardware.

Thus, another function of **CONFIG.SYS** is to load additional software drivers into memory. Device drivers remain in memory. They are programs that go between the physical device and DOS. A device driver is a software program that controls specific peripheral devices. Since DOS cannot know all the codes or programming instructions for the variety of devices available, it looks for a special driver program to handle the specific device. These device drivers can perform many tasks such as enhancing the keyboard, the display screen, and/or the disk drives.

An example of a device is a mouse. A mouse is an add-on device that allows the user to move the cursor around on the screen by rolling the mouse on a flat surface (see page 369). You can use the mouse instead of the keyboard or in addition to the keyboard. Many tasks are easier with a mouse such as drawing a circle or editing a document. However, the mouse can only be used with specific application programs designed to work with a mouse. The mouse is not yet a standard I/O device (although with newer computers it is becoming almost standard). DOS needs a special program to handle the I/O of the mouse because DOS does not know how to translate movement on a flat surface to movement of the cursor on the screen. When you purchase a mouse, you receive two items—the physical device and the software. The software is called the mouse device driver and must be loaded into memory. Only after the device driver is loaded can the physical device—the mouse—be used.

Actually, when you add additional hardware, you need to do two things. One is to install the piece of hardware physically, which can be as simple as plugging a cable into the back of the system unit or as complex as installing a circuit board within the system unit. Regardless, DOS will not know how to use the hardware unless you also install the software that drives the hardware (device drivers). DOS itself comes with some built-in device drivers for standard devices. In addition, DOS provides additional device drivers that may be installed if you wish to use them (see Table 14.4).

Table 14.4 DOS-Provided Device Drivers

Driver Name	DOS Version	Purpose
`ANSI.SYS`	2.0	Defines functions that change display graphics, controls cursor movement, and reassigns keys.
`DISPLAY.SYS`	3.3	Allows you to use code page switching. (Primarily used for international keyboards—rarely used in the U.S.)
`DRIVER.SYS`	3.2	Allows you to assign logical drive letters and specifies parameters for a drive not supported by your hardware.
`EGA.SYS`	5.0	Allows restoration of EGA screen when using DOS 5.0 Shell–Task Swapper.
`EMM386.EXE`	5.0	Simulates expanded memory by using extended memory. Also provides access to upper memory on a 386 or higher microprocessor. Must have extended memory.
`HIMEM.SYS`	5.0	Memory manager that manages extended memory on a 286 or higher computer with extended memory.
`PRINTER.SYS`	3.3	Allows you to use code page switching for printers. (Primarily used for international printing—rarely used in the U.S.)
`RAMDRIVE.SYS`	3.2	Allows you to create a virtual disk in memory to simulate a hard drive. IBM's DOS version is called `VDISK.SYS`.
`SETVER.EXE`	5.0	Table of DOS versions loaded into memory needed by some application programs.
`SMARTDRV.SYS`	4.0	Creates a disk cache in extended or expanded memory.

Table 14.4 DOS-Provided Device Drivers (continued)

VDISK.SYS	IBM 3.0	Allows you to create a virtual disk in memory to simulate a hard drive. MS-DOS version is called RAMDRIVE.SYS.
XMAEM.SYS	IBM 4.0 only	Emulates expanded memory. Must have a 80386 machine.
XMA2EMS.SYS	IBM 4.0 only	Supports Lotus, Intel, and Microsoft (LIM) Expanded Memory Specification (EMS) 4.0 under DOS 4.0.

You may have other device drivers, depending on what pieces of hardware you have installed. One easy way to find out what device drivers you have is to use the DIR command with the .SYS file extension. Most standard and non-standard drivers have a .SYS file extension. For instance, if you added a nonstandard external 5 1/4-inch high-capacity disk drive to your system, you would need to let DOS know by means of a file called $FDD5.SYS This file name is specific to this disk drive *only*. Without the device drive file $FDD5.SYS installed, even though the disk drive is physically connected to the system unit, DOS would not recognize the drive so it could not be used.

14.8 Virtual Disks

DOS 3.0 and above in PC-DOS and 3.2 in MS-DOS include a driver to create a **RAM** or **virtual disk**. The RAM disk is a logical disk drive, not a physical disk drive. One of the reasons it is called a virtual disk is that it appears to DOS to be a "real" physical disk drive. It is actually an area carved out of RAM that emulates a disk. Since accessing RAM is much faster than accessing an actual physical disk drive, processing speed increases. After you create a virtual disk and place files and/or programs in the virtual drive, DOS can retrieve these "RAM" files in micro- or nanoseconds, instead of the milliseconds that a physical disk drive requires. The danger is, of course, that anything in RAM is volatile, and if there is a power failure or if the user forgets to write files back to a real disk, the information will be lost.

The program to create a virtual disk drive is called VDISK.SYS (PC-DOS) or RAMDRIVE.SYS (MS-DOS). This device driver must be included in the CONFIG.SYS file. You can have more than one virtual disk, but each virtual disk must have a drive letter. DOS normally assigns the next available drive letter. Therefore, if you had Drive A and Drive B and installed a virtual disk, it would be Drive C. If you had a hard disk Drive C and one floppy Drive A, the RAM disk would be Drive D. The syntax is:

DEVICE=[*d:*][*path*]RAMDRIVE.SYS [*DiskSize SectorSize*] [/E ¦ /A]
or
DEVICE=[*d:*][*path*]RAMDRIVE.SYS [*DiskSize SectorSize NumEntries*] [/E ¦ /A]

where:

[*d:*][*path*]	Specifies the location of the `RAMDRIVE.SYS` file.
DiskSize	Specifies the size in KB. Valid ranges are 16 through 4096. Default value is 64.
SectorSize	Specifies sector size in bytes. Valid values are 128, 256, and 512. Default value is 512.
NumEntries	Specifies number of files and directories in RAM disk root directory. Valid values are 2 through 1024. Default value is 64.
/E	Creates RAM drive in extended memory instead of conventional memory.
/A	Creates RAM drive in expanded memory instead of conventional memory.

If you are using `VDISK.SYS`, the syntax is:

DEVICE=[*d:*][*path*]VDISK.SYS [*bbb*] [*sss*] [*ddd*] [/E[:*m*]] [/X[:*m*]]

where:

[*d:*][*path*]	Specifies the location of the `VDISK.SYS` file.
bbb	Specifies size of the virtual disk in KB. Valid values range from 64 KB to maximum amount of RAM available. Default is 64 KB.
sss	Specifies size of the sectors on the virtual disk in bytes. Valid values are 128, 256, or 512. Default value is 128.
ddd	Specifies the number of directory entries on the virtual disk and ranges from 2 to 512. Default value is 64 directory entries.
[/E[:*m*]]	Places a virtual disk in extended memory. The *m* represents the maximum number of sectors that VDISK transfers at one time. The values are 1 through 8 with 8 as the default.
[/X[:*m*]]	Only available in PC-DOS 4.0. Places the virtual disk in expanded memory. The *m* represents the maximum number of sectors that VDISK transfers at one time. The values are 1 through 8. Default value is 8.

Since virtual disks are temporary, it is often wise to store programs on a virtual disk, particularly programs that use overlay files, because if you have a power failure, you can recover your programs from the hard disk or your application program installation disks. Remember, if you place data files on a virtual disk, you risk losing the most current information. However, if you are using an application program that has a lot of disk access, for instance, a large database file, the risks of losing data is outweighed by the quickness of retrieving data.

Activity 14.9 Writing a CONFIG.SYS File Using RAMDRIVE.SYS

Note: The Bootable DOS System Disk is in Drive A.

STEP 1: You must know whether the file is called **VDISK.SYS** or **RAMDRIVE.SYS** on your system. You must also know the location of this file. If it is different from the following step, make the appropriate changes. Using an editor, edit the **CONFIG.SYS** file on the Bootable DOS System Disk. Add the following line at the end of the file:

DEVICE=C:\DOS\RAMDRIVE.SYS

STEP 2: Key in the following:

A:\>**TYPE CONFIG.SYS** <Enter>

```
A:\>TYPE CONFIG.SYS
FILES=20
BUFFERS=30
DEVICE=C:\DOS\RAMDRIVE.SYS

A:\>_
```

WHAT'S HAPPENING? You have now added a device driver to create a virtual disk for your system. Once again, DOS cannot act until you reboot the system.

STEP 3: Reboot the system.

```
Microsoft RAMDrive version 3.06 virtual disk D:
    Disk size: 64K
    Sector size: 512 bytes
    Allocation unit: 1 sectors
    Directory entries: 64

A>PROMPT $p$g

A:\>PATH C:\DOS

A:\>
A:\>_
```

WHAT'S HAPPENING? DOS is indicating that it has created a virtual disk. In this example, the logical drive is D, although it could be a different letter on your system. If you are using **VDISK.SYS**, the message will be slightly different. However, the important issue is that the virtual drive will act exactly like any other drive. Be sure to use the assigned RAM drive letter.

STEP 4: Key in the following (using the appropriate drive letter):

A:\>**DIR D:** <Enter>

```
A:\>DIR D:

Volume in drive D is MS-RAMDRIVE
Directory of D:\

 File not found

A:\>_
```

WHAT'S HAPPENING? As you can see, DOS treats this drive like any other disk drive. Drive D is the assigned letter in this activity. Your assigned drive letter does not have to be D, but what is important is that you *remember* what drive letter was assigned to your virtual drive. You can change the default to D, make subdirectories, or whatever else you do with a physical disk drive except format it or use DISKCOPY with it. Pay attention to how long it takes to run **CHKDSK.EXE** in the next step.

STEP 5: Key in the following:
A:\>**CHKDSK** <Enter>

```
A:\>CHKDSK

 Volume Serial Number is 07F9-1C19

    362496 bytes total disk space
     71680 bytes in 2 hidden files
     51200 bytes in 4 user files
    239616 bytes available on disk

      1024 bytes in each allocation unit
       354 total allocation units on disk
       234 available allocation units on disk

      652288 total bytes memory
      514656 bytes free

A:\>_
```

WHAT'S HAPPENING? Your numbers will vary depending on what is installed on your computer system. Again, the number of available bytes for programs and data in RAM is lower. In this example, it is 514656 bytes free. You have lost some bytes available for the system to use, because you have used them for the FILES statement and the BUFFERS statement, but now you have an installed virtual disk. To see how fast a virtual disk operates, you are going to work with the new disk drive, but be sure you use the drive letter that was assigned to your virtual disk.

STEP 6: Key in the following:
A:\>**D:** <Enter>

STEP 7: Key in the following:

D:\>**COPY C:\DOS\CHKDSK.EXE** <Enter>

(If you receive the message "File not found," use **CHKDSK.COM** for **CHKDSK.EXE**.)

STEP 8: Key in the following:

D:\>**CHKDSK** <Enter>

```
A:\>D:

D:\>COPY C:\DOS\CHKDSK.EXE
        1 file(s) copied

D:\>CHKDSK

 Volume MS-RAMDRIVE created 2-14-93 12:00a

     62464 bytes total disk space
     16384 bytes in 1 user files
     46080 bytes available on disk

       512 bytes in each allocation unit
       122 total allocation units on disk
        90 available allocation units on disk

    652288 total bytes memory
    514656 bytes free

D:\>_
```

WHAT'S HAPPENING? You changed your default to D, the virtual disk. You then copied the **CHKDSK.EXE** or **CHKDSK.COM** program to the virtual drive. You executed the CHKDSK command from the virtual disk. Do you see how fast the command executed? If you wanted to add more than one virtual disk to your system, you must have two or more device statements in your **CONFIG.SYS**, as in:

```
DEVICE=C:\DOS\RAMDRIVE.SYS
DEVICE=C:\DOS\RAMDRIVE.SYS 360
```

This entry would create two virtual drives, one 64 KB in size and the other 360 KB in size, exactly like a double-sided, double-density disk. However, if you used 424 KB (360 + 64) for virtual disks, only 180 KB would remain of RAM to run other programs. This is why users want to have extended and/or expanded memory so that devices such as virtual disks can be placed in extended or expanded memory and not take up room in conventional memory. Remember, conventional memory is where application programs must execute.

14.10 Memory

Memory is organized so that it is addressable. It is much like a bank of mail boxes at the post office. Each box has a unique address. You do not know if there is anything in the mail boxes, but you can locate any mail box by its address. The same is true with memory. It also has addresses that are specific locations. Thus, memory is mapped.

The processor on which the personal computer world is based has different microprocessor chips that are identified by number. Early personal computers used the 8086 or 8088 Intel chip, which had 20 address pins. These address pins connect electrically to whatever else is out there on the system. Each one of these address pins when combined with other pins could "map" or look to many addresses. Since all work in a computer is based on the binary system, with 20 address pins, the largest area that this chip could address is 2^{20}, 1,048,576 unique addresses or 1 MB of address space. Newer chips add more address pins. The 80286 Intel chip can address up to 16 MB of memory. The Intel 80386 chip can address 4 gigabytes (1 gigabyte is 2^{30} bytes, or 1 billion bytes). The addresses are expressed in hexadecimal notation, hexadecimal meaning a base 16 number system. One of the reasons that hexadecimal notation is used is that binary numbers become extremely cumbersome. Base 16 uses the digits 0 through 9 and the letters A through F to represent numbers. Hence, memory addresses start at 0000.

Why should you care about this "technogeek" discussion? Memory is your work area. The larger the work area, the more you can place there to work. More memory could mean an enormous spreadsheet or a large document. It can mean larger and much more powerful application programs. It can mean multitasking. **Multitasking** means that the computer can perform more than one task at a time, such as printing a document while you are updating your address file. In the early days of computing, 256 KB was a lot of memory. Today, people want more memory—4 MB, 8 MB or more. However, there is an enormous catch to this. DOS and most application programs running under DOS do not recognize any memory above 640 KB.

Memory comes in three flavors—**conventional**, **extended** and **expanded**. Conventional memory is the first 640 KB of memory on the computer. All DOS application programs must run in conventional memory. Here is where programs and data are located when you are working. Figure 14.3 shows a graphic example.

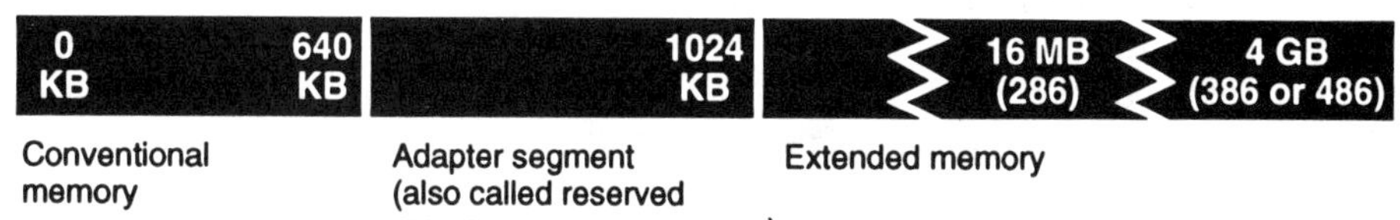

Figure 14.3 Conventional and Extended Memory

Conventional memory cannot exceed 640 KB although the PC can address addresses up to 1 MB. This area of memory, which begins at the end of conventional memory and ends at the beginning of extended memory, is called the **adapter segment** (see Figure 14.4).

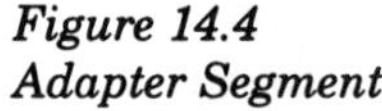

Figure 14.4
Adapter Segment

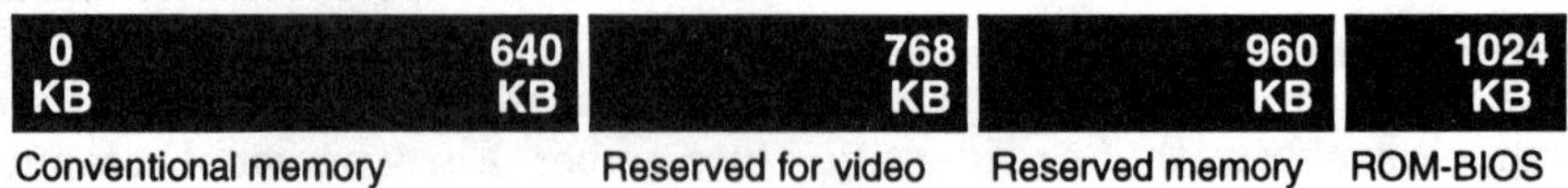

The adapter segment contains room for such things as ROM-BIOS routines, display adapters, and network adapters. The adapter segment is also mapped. It is always located in the same area of the computer's address space—from 640 KB to 1024 KB. There are no exceptions. Thus, when you purchase a computer with 640 KB of memory, it could have 1 MB of address space. It does not mean that you have one megabyte of memory available to you. Adapter segment address space is reserved. However, prior to DOS 5.0, DOS could not recognize anything above 1 MB of memory.

14.11 Extended Memory

Extended memory is a memory board or memory chips on the system board. Extended memory is memory above 1 MB. It is directly addressable but not by DOS below 4.0. Extended memory can only be used on a computer with an 80286, 80386, or 80486 processor. A 286 can use up to 16 MB of extended memory. A 386 or 486 can use up to 4 GB (1 gigabyte=1 billion bytes) of extended memory. An 8086 or 8088 cannot have extended memory. Extended memory can only be used by special, uncommon applications that know about extended memory. Programs that do use extended memory need special instructions to recognize the higher addresses in extended memory. Extended memory is fast and efficient for programs that can use it. DOS 4.0 and above lets you make use of this extended memory with some commands like **RAMDRIVE.SYS** or **VDISK.SYS**, used previously. If you use the /E parameter and if you have extended memory, DOS will place the virtual disk in extended memory, saving conventional memory for the application programs that need it. DOS 5.0 can run in extended memory, leaving more conventional memory available for programs. Windows 3.0 also works in extended memory. Currently, programs that are written to use extended memory run program instructions in conventional memory but can load data in extended memory. To use extended memory most efficiently, certain rules are followed that are set out in the Extended Memory Specification (**XMS**). This means that a special device driver must be installed to manage that memory (see Figure 14.5). In DOS 5.0, this manager is **HIMEM.SYS**.

Figure 14.5
Programs Written for Extended Memory

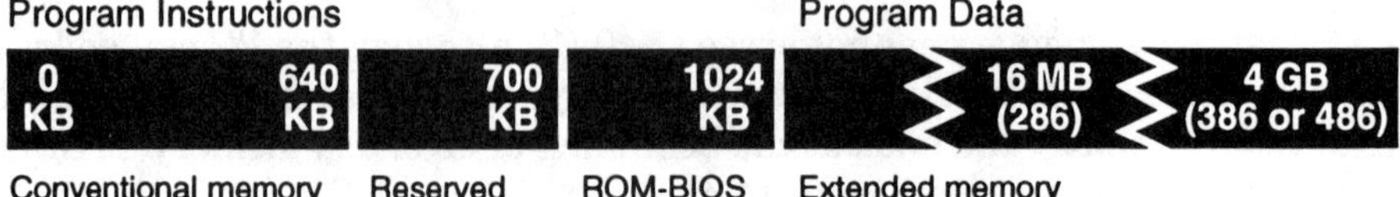

14.12 Expanded Memory

Expanded memory can be used in almost any computer system. You can purchase an expanded memory card that contains more memory. In order to use this memory, you must load a device driver called an **Expanded Memory Manager (EMM)**. The EMM establishes a **page frame** in an empty area of the adapter segment. Each 16 KB is called a **page**, and the area of memory that receives the page is called a page frame. The page frame is the place where the EMM maps information in and out of the RAM of the expanded memory card. The needed information is not physically copied from the card to memory. The device driver changes the page register to make the page frame point to the data on the expanded memory card. The data appears in the page frame so that DOS can access it. This process is called **bank switching** (see Figure 14.6).

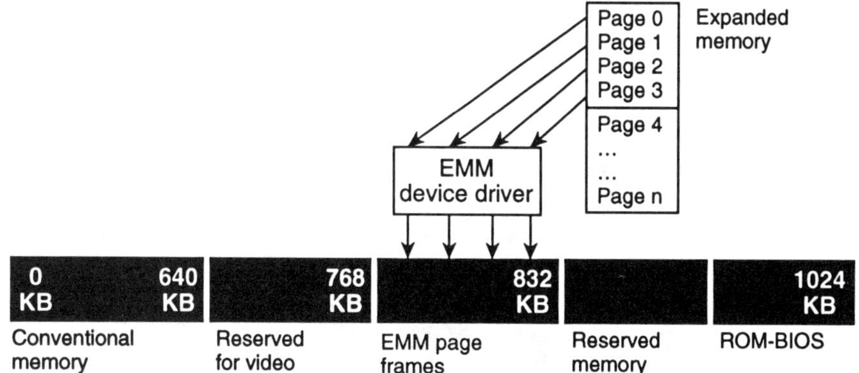

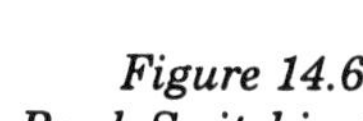

Figure 14.6 Bank Switching

The number and locations vary from machine to machine. The standard is the **LIM** (Lotus Intel Microsoft) **EMS** (Expanded Memory Specification) 3.2 and 4.0, which a software manufacturer can use when writing programs. Lotus is an example of an application program that can directly manipulate expanded memory to handle large spreadsheets. LIM 3.2 supported only four fixed-size 16 KB page frames. Thus, the maximum amount of expanded memory that could be accessed is 8 MB. The page frames have to map to a memory location above 640 KB and below 1024 KB. LIM standard 4.0, to be compatible with LIM 3.2, also requires four 16 KB page frames, but it has more flexibility and allows for any number of additional page frames of any size in any memory location. The maximum amount of memory that can be addressed is 32 MB. However, remember that a program must be written to know about expanded memory in order to use it. Programs that use expanded memory may run more slowly because of all the bank switching.

DOS above 4.0 can use expanded memory. You can place buffers in expanded memory with the /X parameter (PC-DOS 4.0 only), and you can place virtual disks in expanded memory with the /A parameter for `RAMDRIVE.SYS` and the /X parameter with `VDISK.SYS`. Again, however, you are maximizing your use of conventional memory.

If you purchase a third party expanded memory board, you must tell DOS by way of the DEVICE directive or statement in the **CONFIG.SYS** file, the device driver for that expanded memory, so that DOS can turn control over to the software memory manager. You need to know the file name, the file location, and the parameters for that file of the device driver in order to install it in your **CONFIG.SYS** file. To make this more confusing, on 80386 machines, you can configure the extended memory as expanded memory with special device drivers that are placed in the **CONFIG.SYS** file. The reason you must turn extended memory into expanded memory is that more programs can address expanded memory than extended memory.

14.13 Upper Memory Area

Another kind of memory becomes important when using DOS 5.0. It is called the **upper memory area**, the area immediately adjacent to the 640 KB of conventional memory. This area in reserved memory is not considered part of conventional memory. It is normally reserved for running hardware such as the monitor. However, information can be mapped from another kind of memory to the upper memory areas that are unused by your system. The unused portions are called **upper memory blocks (UMB)**. If you have a 386 or above and DOS 5.0, you can use the upper memory area for device drivers and memory resident programs with the assistance of the device driver provided with DOS 5.0, **EMM386.EXE**. This will free conventional memory (see Figure 14.7).

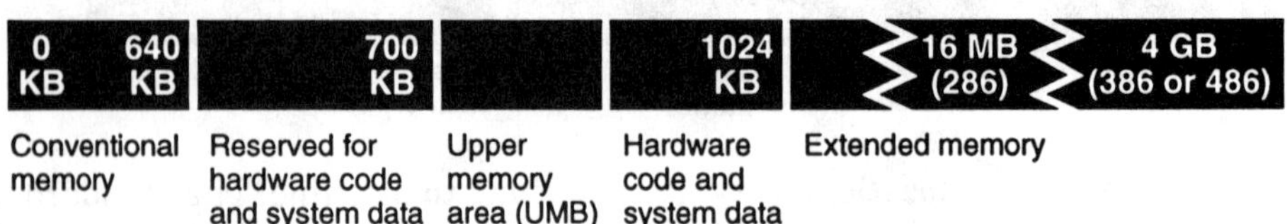

Figure 14.7
Upper Memory Area

14.14 High Memory Area

If you have extended memory, you can run DOS 5.0 in the **high memory area (HMA)**. The high memory area is the first 64 KB of extended memory. Very few programs use this area, so it is a good location for DOS 5.0. If you used the DOS 5.0 SETUP program, it will normally install DOS in the HMA (see Figure 14.8).

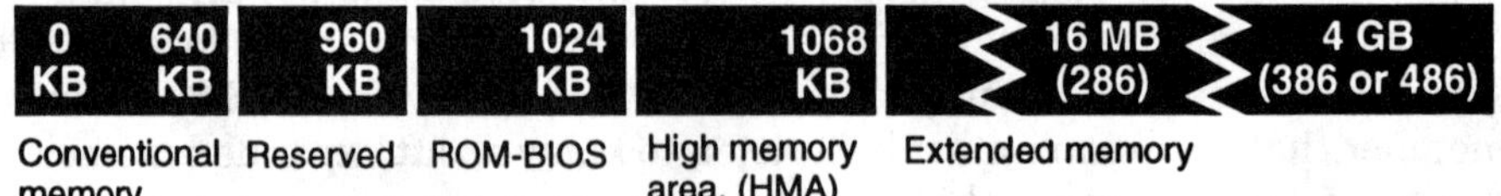

Figure 14.8
High Memory Area

14.15 Using Extended and Expanded Memory

Although all these techniques allow DOS, and hence programs that take advantage of it, the ability to break the 640 KB barrier, they still have limitations. Most of the time, only the data from a program can be stored in either extended or expanded memory. The actual program instructions still must be stored below 1024 KB. The microprocessors above the 286 have two modes of operation—**real** mode and **protected** mode. DOS runs in real mode. Real mode means that program instructions must run under 1024 KB. Other operating systems such as UNIX or other operating environments such as Windows 3.0 (running in 386 enhanced mode) can run in what is called protected mode. Protected mode allows both programs and data to reside above 1024 KB because the processor can form higher-numbered addresses, which means it can reach beyond 1 MB. Since many programs and DOS prior to 4.0 cannot use extended or expanded memory, one of the most common uses for extended and/or expanded memory is for certain configuration commands, placing virtual drives and large disk buffers called disk caches in expanded or extended memory.

How do you know if you have expanded and/or extended memory? Check the documentation for your computer system; it will tell you what you have. There is also an external command with DOS 4.0 and above that will tell you what you have.

14.16 The MEM Command

DOS 4.0 and above

The CHKDSK command gives you a report about disks and conventional memory. Today, users need more information about memory. Thus, the MEM command was introduced in DOS 4.0. The MEM command reports the amount of used and unused memory. This command will report extended memory if memory above 1 MB is installed and will report expanded memory if the memory device drive is installed. The syntax for DOS 4.0 is:

MEM [/PROGRAM ¦ /DEBUG]

where

/PROGRAM Displays all programs presently loaded into memory with a summary of used and unused memory.

/DEBUG Displays complete summary of information, including system device drivers, installed device drivers, all programs presently in memory, and all used and unused memory.

The DOS 5.0 syntax is:

MEM [/PROGRAM ¦ /DEBUG ¦ /CLASSIFY]

where

/PROGRAM Displays status of programs currently loaded in memory. May also use /P.

/DEBUG Displays status of programs, internal drivers, and other information. May also use /D.

/CLASSIFY Classifies programs by memory usage. Lists the size of programs, provides a summary of memory in use, and lists largest memory block available. May also use /C.

Activity 14.17

Using the MEM Command

DOS 4.0 and above

Note: The Bootable DOS System Disk is in Drive A with the **A:\>** displayed.

STEP 1: Key in the following:
A:\>**MEM** <Enter>

```
A:\>MEM

    655360 bytes total conventional memory
    655360 bytes available to MS-DOS
    516576 largest executable program size

   1622016 bytes total EMS memory
    507904 bytes free EMS memory

   3407872 bytes total contiguous extended memory

A:\>_
```

WHAT'S HAPPENING? Your display will vary if you are using DOS 4.0 or 5.0. In addition, the numbers will vary depending on how much, if any, extended memory you have installed on your computer system or if you have installed expanded memory. The **CONFIG.SYS** file did not include any device drivers that were specific for your system, including memory drivers. If you wanted to place the **RAMDRIVE.SYS** file in extended memory prior to rebooting, you would have to modify your **CONFIG.SYS** file to include the following statement:

DEVICE=C:\DOS\RAMDRIVE.SYS /E

To place the virtual disk in expanded memory you would have to take two steps. Order is important. First, you have to install your expanded memory manager with a device directive or statement. Then, you follow it with the **RAMDRIVE.SYS** directive or statement. For example, if your EMM was called **WONDER.SYS**, the directive in the **CONFIG.SYS** file would look as follows:

DEVICE=C:\WONDER.SYS
DEVICE=C:\DOS\RAMDRIVE.SYS /A

To place the buffers in expanded memory (IBM PC-DOS 4.0 only) you would also install your EMM first. Then, you would write the BUFFERS statement as follows:

BUFFERS=20,/X

These device statements allow you to place RAM disks in extended or expanded memory and to place buffers in expanded memory. You get the advantage of RAM disks and more buffers without losing conventional memory for the programs you want to execute.

14.18

Understanding LASTDRIVE

DOS allows you to have more than one virtual disk. However, once again, there is a catch. DOS, as you know, recognizes disk drives by letters of the alphabet.

The first floppy drive is *always* Drive A. The first hard disk is *always* Drive C. If you have only one floppy drive and one hard drive, you have a **logical** Drive B. That is, you can treat the single floppy drive as one logical drive so that you can issue a command such as **COPY A:MYFILE.TXT B:MYFILE.TXT**. DOS will then prompt you to swap disks. DOS knows you have only one floppy disk drive but is letting you pretend that you have two.

You can have all kinds of drive configurations. You can have one floppy disk and one hard drive or one hard drive and two floppy drives. When you initially install DOS, you can divide the hard drive into smaller logical drives, a process called **partitioning**. You can partition your hard drive so that it is two, three, or more logical drives, i.e., Drives C, D, and E. For example, if you had two floppy drives, A and B, and a fixed disk that was logically partitioned into logical drives C and D, and you wanted to have three virtual drives, E, F, and G, you would have a problem. The default value that DOS has for drive letters is A through E. Earlier DOS versions do not recognize any drive letter above E. In DOS 5.0, the last default drive is one more than the number of your physical drives. Thus, if you had Drives A through F, DOS would default to Drive G as the last drive on your system. To solve the problem, DOS permits you to place a LASTDRIVE statement in the **CONFIG.SYS** file to tell DOS how many drive letters you want recognized.

Activity 14.19 Using LASTDRIVE and Virtual Disks

Note: The Bootable DOS System Disk is in Drive A with the **A:\>** displayed.

STEP 1: Using an editor, edit the **CONFIG.SYS** file on the Bootable DOS System Disk. Add the following lines to the end of the file:

```
DEVICE=C:\DOS\RAMDRIVE.SYS 360 512 112
LASTDRIVE=H
```

STEP 2: Key in the following:

A:\>**TYPE CONFIG.SYS** <Enter>

```
A:\>TYPE CONFIG.SYS
FILES=20
BUFFERS=30
DEVICE=C:\DOS\RAMDRIVE.SYS
DEVICE=C:\DOS\RAMDRIVE.SYS 360 512 112
LASTDRIVE=H

A:\>_
```

WHAT'S HAPPENING? If your virtual disk file name is different from the one used here, use the correct file name. Also, if the **RAMDRIVE.SYS** file is in a different subdirectory, add the path, i.e., **DEVICE=C:\BIN\VDISK.SYS**. You have now expanded the drives that DOS will recognize, and you have two device drivers, which will create two virtual disks for your system. The second virtual disk emulates a double-sided, double-density disk of 360 KB; sector size is 512, and directory size is 112 file entries. In addition, you have changed the number of drives that DOS can recognize to Drive H. Once again, DOS cannot act until you reboot the system.

STEP 3: Reboot the system.

```
Microsoft RAMDrive version 3.06 virtual disk D:
    Disk size: 64K
    Sector size: 512 bytes
    Allocation unit: 1 sectors
    Directory entries: 64

Microsoft RAMDrive version 3.06 virtual disk E:
    Disk size: 360L
    Sector size: 512 bytes
    Allocation unit: 1 sectors
    Directory entries: 112


A>PROMPT $p$g

A:\>PATH C:\DOS

A:\>
A:\>_
```

WHAT'S HAPPENING? DOS indicates that it has created two virtual disks. In this example, the logical virtual drives are D and E, although the drive letters could be different on your system.

STEP 4: Key in the following:
A:\>**CHKDSK** <Enter>

```
A:\>CHKDSK

 Volume Serial Number is 07F9-1C19

   362496 bytes total disk space
    71680 bytes in 2 hidden files
    51200 bytes in 4 user files
   239616 bytes available on disk

     1024 bytes in each allocation unit
      354 total allocation units on disk
      234 available allocation units on disk

     652288 total bytes memory
     144560 bytes free

A:\>_
```

WHAT'S HAPPENING? Although you indeed have two virtual disks, you have only 144560 bytes free of conventional memory to run a program. In most cases, this is not enough memory to do anything. It is also possible that you got the message "Insufficient memory" which would tell you that you do not even have enough memory to run CHKDSK. However, these virtual drives are very, very fast. In the next steps, notice the difference in response time between a physical disk drive and a virtual disk drive.

STEP 5: Be sure to use the correct logical drive letter that was assigned when you booted the system. Key in the following:
A:\>**D:** <Enter>

STEP 6: Key in the following:
D:\>**COPY C:\JUNK*.TXT** <Enter>

STEP 7: Key in the following:
D:\>**COPY *.TXT E:** <Enter>

```
D:\>COPY C:\JUNK\*.TXT
C:\JUNK\EXERCISE.TXT
C:\JUNK\JANUARY.TXT
C:\JUNK\FEBRUARY.TXT
C:\JUNK\MARCH.TXT
C:\JUNK\APRIL.TXT
C:\JUNK\HELLO.TXT
C:\JUNK\TEST.TXT
C:\JUNK\BYE.TXT
C:\JUNK\GOODBYE.TXT
  9 file(s) copied

D:\>COPY *.TXT E:
EXERCISE.TXT
JANUARY.TXT
FEBRUARY.TXT
MARCH.TXT
APRIL.TXT
HELLO.TXT
TEST.TXT
BYE.TXT
GOODBYE.TXT
  9 file(s) copied

D:\>_
```

WHAT'S HAPPENING? You should be able to see the significant increase in speed between copying files from a physical disk (Drive C) to a virtual disk (Drive D) and copying between two virtual disks (Drive D and Drive E). Here is the true reason why computer users like virtual disks. However, they are most effective when they are placed in extended or expanded memory, because you can have full use of conventional memory for application programs. That way you get the advantages of virtual disks without having to sacrifice conventional memory.

STEP 8: Key in the following:
D:\>**A:** <Enter>

WHAT'S HAPPENING? You changed the default drive to A where the Bootable DOS System Disk is located.

STEP 9: Key in the following:
A:\>**EDIT CONFIG.SYS** <Enter>

```
A:\>EDIT CONFIG.SYS
Out of memory
A:\>_
```

WHAT'S HAPPENING? You have used so much memory for the virtual disks, that you do not have enough memory to run the EDIT program.

STEP 10: Key in the following:
A:\>**COPY CON CONFIG.SYS** <Enter>
FILES=20 <Enter>
BUFFERS=30 <Enter>
LASTDRIVE=H <Enter>
<Ctrl>+Z <Enter>

STEP 11: Key in the following:
A:\>**TYPE CONFIG.SYS** <Enter>

```
A:\>COPY CON CONFIG.SYS
FILES=20
BUFFERS=30
LASTDRIVE=H
^Z
  1 file(s) copied

A:\>TYPE CONFIG.SYS
FILES=20
BUFFERS=30
LASTDRIVE=H

A:\>_
```

WHAT'S HAPPENING? You overwrote the **CONFIG.SYS** file on the Bootable DOS System Disk so that you have enough conventional memory to do work. However, the virtual disks will not go away until you reboot the system.

STEP 12: Reboot the system with the Bootable DOS System Disk in Drive A.

14.20 The Shell and the Environment

The SHELL configuration command is available only with DOS 2.0 and above. It is another command you can place in the CONFIG.SYS file. It was originally designed so that programmers could use command processors other than COMMAND.COM. However, for people who do not want to write their own command processor, which includes most of us, this directive serves two useful purposes. One is to allow the user to place COMMAND.COM in any subdirectory, and the second is to expand the size of the environment.

The **environment** is an area that DOS sets aside in memory. It is like a scratch pad where DOS keeps a list of specifications that DOS and other application programs can read. (We can also leave messages there *vis-a-vis* batch files.) Application programs can use this environment for their own messages. DOS keeps the location of the command processor in the environment; the path, if one is set; the prompt, if it is changed; and append directions, if append is used. Most of the time, you are only concerned about the environment when you get the message "Out of environment space." If you have DOS 3.1 or above, you can increase the environment size. The default environment size is 127 bytes for DOS 3.0 and 3.1 and 160 bytes for 3.2 and above.

COMMAND.COM, usually located in the root directory of the booting disk, is essentially divided into two parts—the resident portion and the transient portion. The transient part is the area of DOS that holds the internal commands such as DIR, COPY, and so on. When an application program needs the memory that the transient portion of DOS uses, it overwrites this portion of DOS in memory. When the program is completed and turns control back to DOS, it is turning control back to the resident part of DOS. This resident portion of DOS reloads COMMAND.COM into memory. If you ever receive the message, "Insert disk with \COMMAND.COM in Drive A and press any key to continue...," it means that DOS went to reload COMMAND.COM and could not find it on the disk. DOS maintains the location of COMMAND.COM in the environment.

The question is why would you want to place COMMAND.COM in another location? There are several reasons. One reason could be that you are working with more than one version of DOS. Often, before you upgrade DOS, you want to test your programs prior to installing the new version of DOS permanently. Remember, DOS loads into memory the version of DOS it finds on the booting disk. Thus, if DOS 4.0 was on the hard disk and you placed a booting system disk in Drive A with DOS 5.0, DOS 5.0 would be the version of DOS installed in memory. Another reason for placing COMMAND.COM in another location is that it makes the root directory look neater. A more important reason is to protect yourself from losing COMMAND.COM, which can happen. Some programs you use will write a different version of COMMAND.COM to your disk or you could accidentally delete COMMAND.COM. These occurrences can make your system unusable. If you hide COMMAND.COM in a subdirectory, no other programs can overwrite it, nor can you accidentally delete it.

DOS has an internal command called SET that allows you to display what is currently in the environment, set environmental variables, or delete environmental variables. The SET syntax is:

SET [*variable*=[*string*]]

where
variable Specifies the variable you want to set or modify.
string Specifies the string you want to associate with the specified variable.

The syntax for the SHELL command is:

SHELL=*d:\path*\COMMAND.COM *d:\path* /P /E:*size*

The first *d:\path* tells DOS where **COMMAND.COM** is located. The next item is the name of the command processor itself. If you had another command processor, you would tell DOS its name here. The next *d:\path* tells DOS the path to the command processor. DOS uses it to set the COMSPEC variable. **COMSPEC** stands for command processor specification (location). You *must* use the /P variable because it means to *stay* permanent. This statement instructs DOS to load and keep resident a copy of **COMMAND.COM**. Without the /P, DOS would load **COMMAND.COM**, execute any **AUTOEXEC.BAT** file, and immediately exit, leaving you without a command processor. With no command processor, you cannot use any commands. To recover the command processor, you will have to reboot the system with another booting disk.

With DOS versions above 4.0, you can increase the size of the environment. In 3.1, to increase the environment size, you may use the numbers 11 (176 bytes) through 62 (992 bytes). In 3.2 and above the size can be set from 160 to 32,767.

Activity 14.21 Using SET and SHELL

Note: The Bootable DOS System Disk is in Drive A.

STEP 1: Key in the following:
A:\>**SET** <Enter>

```
A:\>SET
COMSPEC=A:\COMMAND.COM
PROMPT=$p$g
PATH C:\DOS

A:\>_
```

WHAT'S HAPPENING? The environment has the location of **COMMAND.COM** in the root directory of A. The default value of COMSPEC is always the root directory of the booting disk. In addition, since this disk has an **AUTOEXEC.BAT** file that tells DOS to change the prompt and to set the path to the **\DOS**

subdirectory on Drive C, DOS leaves a reminder to itself in the environmental scratch pad of what the values for prompt and path are. In the next steps, you are going to tell DOS that even though you are booting from Drive A, you want it to reload **COMMAND.COM** from the hard disk. *You must know the location of COMMAND.COM.* You are also going to increase the size of the environment.

STEP 2: Key in the following:
A:\>**DIR C:\COMMAND.COM** <Enter>

```
A:\>DIR C:\COMMAND.COM

 Volume in drive C is HARD DISK
 Volume Serial Number is 1708-78AC
 Directory of C:\

COMMAND  COM  47845   04-09-91  5:00a
         1 file(s)     47845 bytes
                     5990400 bytes free

A:\>_
```

WHAT'S HAPPENING? You are verifying the location of **COMMAND.COM**. If it is not in the root directory of C, do not continue with the next steps until you can specifically locate it. It could be in the **C:\DOS** subdirectory.

STEP 3: Using an editor, edit the **CONFIG.SYS** file on the Bootable DOS System Disk. Add the following line at the end of the file, and do *not* leave a space between **E:** and **256**.
SHELL=C:\COMMAND.COM C:\ /P /E:256

STEP 4: Key in the following:
A:\>**TYPE CONFIG.SYS** <Enter>

```
A:\>TYPE CONFIG.SYS
FILES=20
BUFFERS=30
LASTDRIVE=H
SHELL=C:\COMMAND.COM C:\ /P /E:256

A:\>_
```

WHAT'S HAPPENING? You are confirming that the **CONFIG.SYS** file has the correct commands in it. You are going to tell DOS to find **COMMAND.COM** in a location other than the root directory of the booting disk (Drive A). Instead of looking there, you are directing DOS to reload **COMMAND.COM** from the root directory of C. In addition, you are increasing the size of the environment. Be sure that the spacing is identical to the example. Also, remember that if **COMMAND.COM** is in another location, you *must* specify that location. For example, if **COMMAND.COM** was in the DOS subdirectory, the **CONFIG.SYS** file would look as follows:

```
FILES=20
BUFFERS=30
LASTDRIVE=H
SHELL=C:\DOS\COMMAND.COM C:\DOS /P /E:256
```

STEP 5: Reboot the system.

STEP 6: Key in the following:
A:\>SET <Enter>

```
A:\>SET
COMSPEC=C:\COMMAND.COM
PROMPT=$p$g
PATH C:\DOS

A:\>_
```

WHAT'S HAPPENING? The environment now has the location of COMMAND.COM in the root directory of C, even though you booted from Drive A. You changed the default value of COMSPEC. You can now remove the disk from Drive A and DOS can still reload COMMAND.COM. In addition, since this disk has an AUTOEXEC.BAT file that tells DOS to change the prompt and to set the path to the \DOS subdirectory on Drive C, DOS leaves a reminder to itself in the environmental scratch pad of what the values for prompt and path are.

14.22 The SWITCHES Command

DOS 4.0 and above

The SWITCHES command is another new DOS command introduced in IBM PC-DOS 4.0 and MS-DOS 5.0. Its purpose is to help you with programs that only recognize the old-style keyboard. The old-style keyboard had the function keys at the left side. Today, the most common keyboard sold is the enhanced keyboard which has the function keys across the top as well as 101 keys. Often, software programs assign functions to certain keys. The key assignments vary from program to program. For example, when using WordPerfect 5.1, pressing the F3 key brings you help while pressing <Shift>+F7 gives you a print menu. These key assignments are made by keyboard drivers. Some older programs cannot use or recognize the placement of the new keyboard locations, making the program unusable. Thus, if you have an older program, you can prevent DOS from using the new keyboard. This command in the CONFIG.SYS file forces DOS to use the old-style conventional keyboard. You need to place this in your CONFIG.SYS file only if you have an older program that will not operate with the new keyboard.

The syntax is:
SWITCHES=/K

It would go into the CONFIG.SYS file exactly as above.

Chapter Summary

1. DOS allows you to customize your system by writing a special file called `CONFIG.SYS`.
2. When you boot the computer, the ROM-BIOS does a self-test and checks for the DOS system files on Drive A. If there is no disk in Drive A, it looks to Drive C, then looks for and loads `CONFIG.SYS`, then loads `COMMAND.COM`, and last looks for and loads `AUTOEXEC.BAT`.
3. The `CONFIG.SYS` file is the mechanism DOS uses to change default settings or add settings for different devices.
4. The `CONFIG.SYS` file does not come with DOS. It is created by the user or by certain programs. Some later versions of DOS will create a `CONFIG.SYS` file when you use the DOS installation program.
5. The `CONFIG.SYS` file is always an ASCII file.
6. The `CONFIG.SYS` file contains a list of statements that define the values that the user needs to define a nonstandard configuration. (See Table 14.1 on page 512.)
7. The only time the commands are read in `CONFIG.SYS` is at the time the system is booted.
8. DOS keeps track of the number of open files. The default value for open files is 8.
9. DOS uses 5 of the 8 files for tracking standard input, standard output, standard error, standard printer and standard auxiliary.
10. In `CONFIG.SYS` you can change the values for the FILES from 8 to 255.
11. The syntax is: FILES=*x*.
12. The BUFFERS statement or directive tells DOS how many disk buffers to use. The minimum value is 2.
13. Disk buffers act as disk and RAM go-betweens.
14. DOS reads and writes a minimum of one sector at a time.
15. The reserved area of RAM where DOS reads and writes prior to reading the disk is the disk buffer area. This process is called caching.
16. If you do not exit an application properly, DOS does not flush the buffers, leaving information in memory that is not written to disk.
17. DOS uses buffers to reduce the time it needs to access the disk to improve performance.
18. Buffers can range from a minimum of 2 to a maximum of 99. If you have IBM PC-DOS 4.0 and expanded memory, you can increase the buffers to 10,000.
19. The syntax is: BUFFERS=*n*[,*m*]
20. If you have too many buffers or files open, you use conventional memory and have less memory for applications.
21. Not all application programs use buffering.
22. You should always have a floppy DOS disk that you can boot from.
23. Before you begin to alter the `CONFIG.SYS` file and/or `AUTOEXEC.BAT`, you should always back them up. You should also back up any device driver files.
24. If you have nonstandard devices, you must provide DOS with software called device drivers that must be loaded into memory prior to using the device.

25. Device drivers are installed in the **CONFIG.SYS** file by means of the DEVICE= statement.
26. Device drivers are special software programs that you provide to DOS so that DOS can let the devices drivers handle the nonstandard I/O.
27. DOS comes with some device drivers. (See DOS-Provided Device Drivers, Table 14.4, page 521.) Other device drivers are dependent on the specific system hardware.
28. Virtual disks are logical disk drives that are placed in RAM.
29. Virtual disks are much faster than physical drives.
30. The device driver to install a virtual disk is called **VDISK.SYS** or **RAMDISK.SYS**.
31. You can have several virtual disk drives.
32. The syntax is:
    DEVICE=[*d:*][*path*]RAMDRIVE.SYS [*DiskSize SectorSize*] [/E] [/A]
    or DEVICE=[*d:*][*path*]VDISK.SYS [*bbb sss ddd*] [/E[:*m*]] [/A[:*m*]]
33. If you have extended or expanded memory you can place virtual drives there.
34. Virtual disks are volatile.
35. Memory is addressable.
36. DOS below 5.0 cannot recognize any memory above 640 KB.
37. Memory comes in three flavors: conventional, expanded, and extended.
38. Conventional memory is the first 640 KB of memory.
39. The adapter segment is the area between 640 KB and 1 MB which is reserved for such information as display adapters and network adapters.
40. Extended memory must be on a 286 machine or above.
41. Extended memory is memory above 1 MB.
42. Most application programs cannot directly use extended memory, although if you have DOS 4.0 and above you can place virtual disks there.
43. Expanded memory can be used in any computer system. An expanded memory card must be purchased and installed.
44. You must use a device driver to make expanded memory work.
45. The expanded memory driver makes use of the adapter segment area to create a page frame. The EMM (expanded memory manager) pages information in and out of the page frame from the expanded memory board. This process is called bank switching.
46. Extended memory can be turned into expanded memory by means of software drivers. This is done because more programs can recognize expanded memory than extended memory.
47. The upper memory area becomes important if you use DOS 5.0. Upper memory is the area immediately adjacent to the first 640 KB of conventional memory. Unused portions are called upper memory blocks (UMB), and if you have DOS 5.0, you can place memory resident programs and device drivers in upper memory with the assistance of the **EMM386.EXE** memory driver provided with DOS 5.0. The **EMM386.EXE** can also use extended memory to emulate expanded memory.
48. The high memory area is the first 64 KB of extended memory. If you have DOS 5.0, you can run DOS in high memory.

49. Real mode means that programs must run in the first 1 MB of memory. Protected mode means that both programs and data can use extended memory. DOS runs in real mode.
50. Buffers in IBM PC-DOS can be placed in expanded memory. Virtual disks in any version of DOS can be placed in expanded memory.
51. The MEM command, introduced in DOS 4.0, gives information on extended and expanded memory. The syntax is:
    MEM [/PROGRAM ¦ /DEBUG ¦ /CLASSIFY]
52. The default value for the last drive DOS recognizes is Drive E or one more drive than you have installed physically. By means of the LASTDRIVE statement, you can increase the number of drives DOS can recognize up to Drive Z. The syntax is: LASTDRIVE=*x*
53. The SHELL statement or directive allows you to place `COMMAND.COM` in other than the root directory.
54. The SHELL statement or directive allows you to expand the size of the environment.
55. The environment is an area of memory that DOS sets aside to keep a list of system specifications.
56. DOS must keep track of `COMMAND.COM`. `COMMAND.COM` has two parts, resident and transient. When application programs need memory, DOS allows them to overwrite the transient part of DOS. When the application finishes, DOS must reload `COMMAND.COM` and, hence, must know its location.
57. The syntax for SHELL is:
    SHELL=[*d:*][*path*]COMMAND.COM *d:*[*path*] /P /E:*size*
58. The SET command tells you what is in the environment.
59. The SWITCHES statement or directive forces DOS to use the old-style keyboard.
60. The syntax for SWITCHES is: SWITCHES /K.

Key Terms

Adapter segment
Bank switching
Caching
COMSPEC
Conventional memory
Directives
Disk buffers
Disk intensive
EMM—Expanded memory manager
Environment
Expanded memory
Extended memory
File handle
Flushing the buffer
High memory area
LIM EMS standard
Look-ahead buffers
Multitasking
Overhead
Page
Page frame
Partitioning
Protected mode
RAM disk
Real mode
UMB
Upper memory area
Upper memory blocks
Virtual disk
XMS—Extended memory specification

Discussion Questions

1. What is the function of a `CONFIG.SYS` file?
2. Before you alter the `CONFIG.SYS` or `AUTOEXEC.BAT` files, what steps should you take and why?

3. If DOS cannot find the **CONFIG.SYS** file how will it initialize the computer?
4. List the five open files that DOS uses.
5. Explain the function of two of the five open files that DOS uses.
6. What is a disk buffer?
7. What is the function of disk buffers?
8. When you are working with an application program, why is it important to exit the program rather than just turn off the computer?
9. What are device drivers?
10. When additional hardware is purchased for the computer, what must you do to have the hardware become operational?
11. What is a virtual disk?
12. Why would a user want to create a virtual disk?
13. What problems can occur when using a virtual disk?
14. Why do users want to have expanded or extended memory installed on their computers?
15. Describe each kind of memory.
16. Identify the purpose of each kind of memory.
17. Explain bank switching.
18. When is bank switching used?
19. What is high memory? When is it used?
20. What is upper memory? When is it used?
21. Why would you turn extended memory into expanded memory?
22. What is the value of placing RAM disks and buffers in expanded memory?
23. Explain the function of the LASTDRIVE command.
24. How can you maximize the use of virtual disks?
25. What is the purpose of the SHELL command?
26. Why is the /P variable such an important part of the SHELL command?
27. Give two reasons for moving **COMMAND.COM** from the root directory.
28. When would you use the SWITCHES command?
29. What purpose does the SET command provide?
30. What is the environment and how does DOS use it?

Application Assignments

You are going to write different **CONFIG.SYS** files. Be sure not to use your real **CONFIG.SYS** file. Write the file to the Bootable DOS System Disk you have been using in this chapter. All activities occur on the Bootable DOS System Disk, unless otherwise stated.

1. For the following assignment:
   a. Write a **CONFIG.SYS** file that has 15 files, 25 buffers, and a 120 KB virtual disk.
   b. Reboot your system to activate your new **CONFIG.SYS** file.
   c. Print the **CONFIG.SYS** file just created.
2. For the following assignment:
   a. Write a **CONFIG.SYS** file that has 20 files, 25 buffers, a 64 KB virtual disk and will allow DOS to recognize up to Drive M.

b. Reboot your system to activate this new **CONFIG.SYS** file.
c. Print the **CONFIG.SYS** file.
d. Write a batch file that will:
   (1) Create a subdirectory called **CLASS** on the virtual disk drive.
   (2) Copy all the **.FIL** files from **C:\JUNK** to the virtual drive subdirectory, **CLASS**.
   (3) Print a copy of this batch file.

3. For the following assignment:
   a. Write a **CONFIG.SYS** file that has:
      (1) 25 files.
      (2) 25 buffers.
      (3) Two virtual disks, one 64 KB and the other 120 KB.
      (4) Reboot your system to activate this new **CONFIG.SYS** file.
      (5) Print the **CONFIG.SYS** file.
      (6) Copy CHKDSK, SORT, MORE, and FIND commands to the first virtual disk.
      (7) Print the screen that proves that they are there.
   b. Write a batch file that will:
      (1) Create a subdirectory called **TEXT** on the second virtual drive.
      (2) Copy all the **.TXT** files from **C:\JUNK** to the virtual drive subdirectory.
      (3) Print a copy of this batch file.
4. For the following assignment:
   a. Print what is in the environment.
   b. Identify each item and describe its purpose in the environment.
5. Identify how much memory you computer has and what kind it is.

Challenge Assignments

6. For the following assignment:
   a. Use the **CONFIG.SYS** file developed in question 3 and write a batch file that will:
      (1) Create a subdirectory on the first virtual disk drive for data files from the ADDRESS program.
      (2) Create a subdirectory for the ADDRESS program on the second virtual disk drive.
      (3) Copy the ADDRESS program from **C:\JUNK** to the appropriate subdirectory on the virtual drive.
      (4) Load the ADDRESS program.
      (5) Return to the root directory of the hard disk when you are done with the ADDRESS program.
   b. Print this batch file.
7. For the following assignment:
   a. Print a copy of the real **CONFIG.SYS** file that exists on the computer system you are using.
   b. Identify the purpose of each statement in the **CONFIG.SYS** file.
   c. Make any recommendations for improving the **CONFIG.SYS** file.

15 Chapter

Managing Devices with PRINT and MODE

After completing this chapter you will be able to:

1. Print text files using three methods.
2. Compare and contrast the differences between the printing methods.
3. Understand differences between hardware and software solutions to common problems.
4. Compare and contrast internal, external, and memory-resident commands.
5. Identify at least two memory-resident commands.
6. Explain how devices are controlled.
7. Compare and contrast serial and parallel communication.
8. Identify and define the purpose of device names.
9. Print using the PRINT command.
10. Use the MODE command to change the characteristics of the printer, the typematic rate, and the monitor and be able to check the status of devices attached to the system.

Chapter Overview

This chapter reviews ways to print text files. In addition, it introduces the PRINT command that allows you to print files. It demonstrates the differences between hardware and software solutions. A new category of command is introduced, the memory-resident command. In order to control devices, DOS provides the MODE command. The differences between parallel and serial communication are discussed as well as different device names. Different parameters of the MODE command are introduced.

15.0

Printing Techniques: Hardware and Software Solutions

You have learned four techniques for printing text files. One is to press the <Shift> key and the <PrtSc> key, and get a printed snapshot of what is on the screen at a specific moment. Another term for this process is **screen dump** because you are dumping data from the screen to the printer. A second technique is to toggle the printer on by pressing the <Ctrl> key and the <PrtSc> key. This method of printing allows you to have a running dialogue with the computer. Everything that is displayed on the screen is printed simultaneously. However, if you are using a laser printer, this technique will not work. The third method is to use the COPY command to copy files to a device, the printer. This method prints a hard copy of the contents of a file. The fourth technique involves using redirection. You can redirect the output of a command to the printer. Thus, you can key DIR > PRN to print the directory of a disk or you can key in TYPE *filename.ext* > PRN to print the contents of a file. The command is expecting to display the output on the screen. By means of the redirection symbol, >, you can tell the command to send the output to some other location.

However, all these printing methods have at least one disadvantage. Every time you want a file to begin printing on a new page, you must manually advance the paper in the printer. If you have a laser printer, you must take certain hardware steps—taking the printer off-line, pressing form feed, and then placing the printer back on-line. What you are doing is manually ejecting the page. In other words, since the printer does not know that you want a "page" printed, you are telling it so by either moving the knob for the platen on a dot-matrix printer or by pressing the appropriate buttons on a laser printer. These steps are hardware solutions. You are resolving the problem by manipulating the hardware. Instead, you can have a software solution. In other words, you want to be able to send a signal to the printer from the computer to tell it to "print a page" or **eject** the current page. Such a software signal is <Ctrl>+L. This combination of keys sends a software signal to the printer to eject a page. <Ctrl>+L means **form-feed**, or eject a page by means of a software command.

Activity 15.1 Ejecting a Page Through a Software Command

Note: The ACTIVITIES disk is in Drive A with the **A:\>** displayed. Be sure the path is set to **C:\DOS**.

STEP 1: Turn on the printer.

STEP 2: Key in the following:
A:\>**TYPE JANUARY.TXT** <Enter>

STEP 3: Press the <Shift> key. While pressing <Shift>, press the <PrtSc> key. Remember, newer computers only require you to press the <PrtSc> key.

WHAT'S HAPPENING? If you have a dot-matrix printer, you see the cursor moving along the screen and hear the printer printing those lines of text on the screen. If you have a laser printer, nothing has printed yet. When you use the <Shift> and <PrtSc> combination, you get a snapshot of whatever is on your screen at a specific time which can be valuable for diagnostic purposes. If something went wrong and you want a hard copy of the message displayed on the screen, you can use this technique. If you have a laser printer, you should be familiar with the hardware steps you must take to print this page. Dot-matrix printer users have to turn the knob manually for the platen to have this screen dump on a page. Instead, both types of printer users are going to send a software control message to the printer to eject the page.

STEP 4: Note: When you see the notation <Ctrl>+L, it means to hold down the <Ctrl> key and press the L key at the same time. Key in the following:
A:\>**ECHO** <Ctrl>+L **> PRN** <Enter>

```
A:\>TYPE JANUARY.TXT
This is my January file.
It is my first dummy file.
This is file 1.
This is my February file.
It is my second dummy file.
This is file 2.

A:\>ECHO ^L > PRN

A:\>_
```

WHAT'S HAPPENING? The printer should have ejected the page for both dot-matrix and laser printer users. When you keyed in ECHO at the command line, you were issuing a command. <Ctrl>+L is the software signal for form-feed or eject a page. Since ECHO normally echoes to the screen, you redirected the output to the printer. As you can see, you can solve problems either by manipulating the hardware or using software solutions. Usually, it is easier to solve problems using software solutions instead of hardware solutions. Since this technique is so useful, it is a perfect candidate for a batch file.

STEP 5: Remove the ACTIVITIES disk from Drive A. Insert the DATA disk in Drive A.

STEP 6: Key in the following:
A:\>**CD \BATCH** <Enter>

STEP 7: Note: When you see the notation <Ctrl>+P, it means to press the <Ctrl> key and while holding the <Ctrl> key, press the letter P. When you see the notation <Alt>+012, it means to hold down the <Alt> key and while holding it down, press the numbers 0, 1, and 2 located on the numeric key pad. Do not use the numbers across the top of the keyboard. When you see the notation <Spacebar>, it means to press the spacebar once.

Key in the following:
A:\BATCH>**EDIT EJECT.BAT** <Enter>
ECHO OFF <Enter>
REM This file is to eject a page from the printer. <Enter>
ECHO<Spacebar><Ctrl>+P<Alt>+012 **> PRN**

WHAT'S HAPPENING? You created a batch file consisting of the same commands you keyed in at the command line. However, the reason that you had to press <Ctrl>+P was that you needed to disable the <Alt> key functions in the EDIT program. Pressing just <Ctrl>+L issues the command to EDIT to **Repeat Last Find**. You cannot press the <Ctrl> key in EDIT and get the same meaning. Instead, you used the ASCII equivalent of <Ctrl>+L which is 012. However, on the screen, <Ctrl>+L is represented as the female symbol (♀). Then, you redirected the output to the printer. Now, you must save the file to disk.

STEP 8: Press <Alt>+F.

STEP 9: Press X.

STEP 10: Press Y.

WHAT'S HAPPENING? You saved the file to disk. Now, you are ready to test it. Look at the printout from the previous activity. You will see that when you print the screen, you see everything—the prompt, the TYPE command, as well as all the blank lines. Thus, if you only wanted the contents of a file and not the prompt or the command, you would not choose to print with <Shift>+<PrtSc>. You also have only the capability of printing what is on the screen which means that if the text of a file were longer than a screenful, you could not print it using <Shift>+<PrtSc>.

STEP 11: Key in the following:
A:\BATCH>**TYPE \PERSONAL.FIL** <Enter>

```
Babchuk    Nicholas  13 Stratford  Sun City West  AZ   Professor
Babchuk    Bianca    13 Stratford  Sun City West  AZ   Professor
Begg       Leroy     20 Elm        Ontario        CA   Systems Analyst
Helm       Milton    333 Meadow    Sherman Oaks   CA   Consultant
Moselle    Carolyn   567 Abbey     Rochester      MI   Day Care Teacher
Markiw     Nicholas  354 Bell      Phoenix        AZ   Engineer
Markiw     Emily     10 Zion       Sun City West  AZ   Retired
Nyles      John      12 Brooks     Sun City West  AZ   Retired
Nyles      Sophie    12 Brooks     Sun City West  CA   Retired
Markiw     Nick      10 Zion       Sun City West  AZ   Retired
Papay      Fred      345 Newport   Orange         CA   Manager
Jones      Steven    32 North      Phoenix        AZ   Buyer
Smith      David     120 Collins   Orange         CA   Chef
Babchuk    Walter    12 View       Thousand Oaks  CA   President
Babchuk    Deana     12 View       Thousand Oaks  CA   Housewife
Jones      Cleo      355 Second    Ann Arbor      MI   Clerk
Smith      Henry     40 Northern   Ontario        CA   Engineer
JONES      JERRY     244 East      Mission Viejo  CA   Systems Analyst
Low        Ophelia   1213 Wick     Phoenix        AZ   Writer
Tally      William   15 Fourth     Santa Cruz     CA   Banker
Gibbs      Michael   134 Seventh   Ann Arbor      MI   Editor
Richards   James     56 Twin Leaf  Orange         CA   Artist
Markiw     Nicholas  12 Fifth      Glendale       AZ   Engineer

A:\BATCH>_
```

WHAT'S HAPPENING? This list, which is longer than a screen, scrolls rapidly. You cannot see the entire file on the screen. If you are only interested in the contents of the file, not the prompts and commands, using the <Shift> key and the <PrtSc> key would not print the entire list. To print a hard copy or printout, you need another command.

STEP 12: Key in the following:
A:\BATCH>**COPY \PERSONAL.FIL PRN** <Enter>

STEP 13: Key in the following:
A:\BATCH>**EJECT** <Enter>

```
A:\BATCH>COPY \PERSONAL.FIL PRN
    1 file(s) copied

A:\BATCH>EJECT

A:\BATCH>ECHO OFF
A:\BATCH>_
```

WHAT'S HAPPENING? With this command, you asked DOS to COPY the contents of the file called **PERSONAL.FIL** located in the root directory of the DATA disk (source) to a device, PRN (destination). You then executed the batch file EJECT, which should have ejected the page. You now have a hard copy of this text file on one page. You printed the file and ejected the page via a software solution. The printout you should get is shown below. You only get one page and only the contents of the file, not the prompt or any of the commands.

```
Gillay    Carolyn  699 Lemon     Orange        CA Professor
Panezich  Frank    688 Lake      Orange        CA Teacher
Tuttle    Steven   356 Embassy   Mission Viejo CA Golf Pro
Maurdeff  Kathryn  550 Traver    Ann Arbor     MI Teacher
Maurdeff  Sonia    550 Traver    Ann Arbor     MI Student
Smith     Gregory  311 Orchard   Ann Arbor     MI Engineer
Smith     Carolyn  311 Orchard   Ann Arbor     MI Housewife
Winter    Jim      333 Pick      Garden Grove  CA Key Grip
Winter    Linda    333 Pick      Garden Grove  CA Teacher
Golden    Herbert  345 Lakeview  Orange        CA Doctor
Golden    Jane     345 Lakeview  Orange        CA Nurse
Brent     Wendy    356 Edgewood  Ann Arbor     MI Librarian
Brogan    Lloyd    111 Miller    Santa Cruz    CA Vice-President
Brogan    Sally    111 Miller    Santa Cruz    CA Account Manager
Babchuk   Nicholas 13 Stratford  Sun City West AZ Professor
Babchuk   Bianca   13 Stratford  Sun City West AZ Professor
Begg      Leroy    20 Elm        Ontario       CA Systems Analyst
Helm      Milton   333 Meadow    Sherman Oaks  CA Consultant
Moselle   Carolyn  567 Abbey     Rochester     MI Day Care Teacher
Markiw    Nicholas 354 Bell      Phoenix       AZ Engineer
Markiw    Emily    10 Zion       Sun City West AZ Retired
Nyles     John     12 Brooks     Sun City West AZ Retired
Nyles     Sophie   12 Brooks     Sun City West CA Retired
Markiw    Nick     10 Zion       Sun City West AZ Retired
Papay     Fred     345 Newport   Orange        CA Manager
Jones     Steven   32 North      Phoenix       AZ Buyer
Smith     David    120 Collins   Orange        CA Chef
Babchuk   Walter   12 View       Thousand Oaks CA President
Babchuk   Deana    12 View       Thousand Oaks CA Housewife
Jones     Cleo     355 Second    Ann Arbor     MI Clerk
Smith     Henry    40 Northern   Ontario       CA Engineer
JONES     JERRY    244 East      Mission Viejo CA Systems Analyst
Low       Ophelia  1213 Wick     Phoenix       AZ Writer
Tally     William  15 Fourth     Santa Cruz    CA Banker
Gibbs     Michael  134 Seventh   Ann Arbor     MI Editor
Richards  James    56 Twin       Orange        CA Artist
Markiw    Nicholas 12 Fifth      Glendale      AZ Engineer
```

You now have a complete page printed. Using COPY *filename* PRN prints the contents of files. But what if you want to print the directory of your disk? You know that you cannot use the <Shift>+<PrtSc> keys if the directory is longer than a screenful. Nor can you use the COPY command because DIR is a command, not a file. What you can do is redirect the output of the DIR command to the printer, then use the EJECT batch file to eject the page.

STEP 14: Key in the following:
A:\BATCH>**DIR ¦ SORT > PRN** <Enter>

STEP 15: Key in the following:
A:\BATCH>**EJECT** <Enter>

WHAT'S HAPPENING? You should have a sorted printout on one page of the **BATCH** file subdirectory. Remember that you cannot key in **COPY DIR PRN** because DIR is not a file but a command.

15.2 Resident Programs

We have discussed two categories of programs, internal commands and external commands. Internal commands are those programs that remain resident in memory once the system is booted and can be used until the power is turned off. They are automatically loaded when the system is booted, as part of the file **COMMAND.COM**. External programs reside on a disk and are called into memory and executed each time they are used. When an external command is finished executing, DOS again takes control of memory. When another external command is called, DOS uses that same area of memory to run the new program.

Application programs are external commands. When you wish to use them, they also must be called into memory so that they can be executed. All programs must be in memory before they can run. A graphic example of the process is in Figure 15.1.

Thus, you start with DOS.

Figure 15.1 Running Programs in Memory

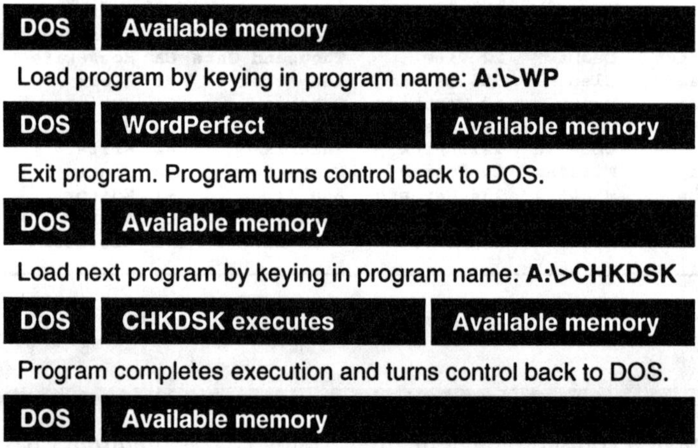

DOS	Available memory	

Load program by keying in program name: **A:\>WP**

DOS	WordPerfect	Available memory

Exit program. Program turns control back to DOS.

DOS	Available memory	

Load next program by keying in program name: **A:\>CHKDSK**

DOS	CHKDSK executes	Available memory

Program completes execution and turns control back to DOS.

DOS	Available memory	

A third category of programs is called **memory-resident** commands. Memory-resident commands are also called **TSRs** for Terminate and Stay Resident. These programs still have to be called into memory from the disk. However, when the memory-resident command is finished executing or completing its job, after turning control back to DOS, it tells DOS not to reuse the memory area where it is located. It is temporarily inactive which means that the next time you wish to use a resident program it is still in memory. It does not have to be reloaded from the disk as external commands do. The TSR, once called into memory, remains there until the power is turned off. There are different ways of reactivating the TSR depending on the specific program. See Figure 15.2 for a graphic example of this process.

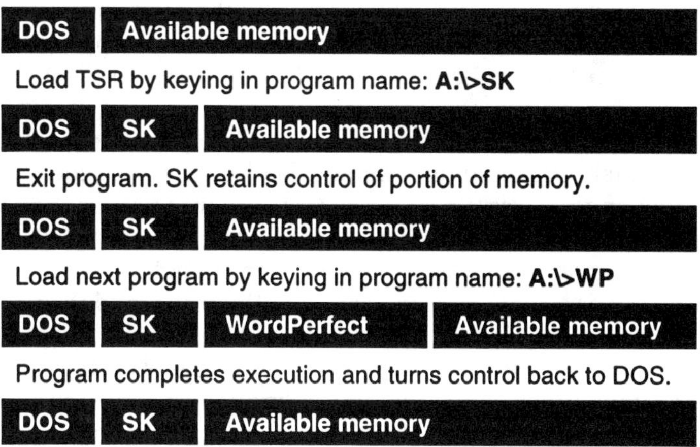

Figure 15.2 Running TSR'S Programs in Memory

Commercially available memory-resident programs include those such as SideKick and PC Tools. SideKick is a TSR that includes such programs as a text editor, a calculator, a calendar, and an appointment book. Thus, you could be working on a document in WordPerfect and interrupt WordPerfect and activate SideKick by pressing some key combination that allows SideKick to "pop up" so that you could use the calculator. You would suspend use of WordPerfect, but you would not have to exit it just to use the calculator. There are many types of TSRs available. DOS also includes some TSRs as part of the DOS utilities. One of these is the PRINT command.

15.3 The PRINT Command

There are disadvantages to each of the printing techniques you have learned. The <Shift> and <PrtSc> keys only allow you to print one screenful at a time and also print the commands and messages. Printing with COPY *filename* PRN prints only the contents of the file, but while files are printing, the computer (and hence you) can do nothing else. In addition, the contents of more than one file print one right after another. COPY *filename* PRN does not advance to the top of the form or a start a new page when a new file begins to print. This shortcoming is also true when using redirection to print. Even after having written the `EJECT.BAT` file, you must remember to use it so that you eject a page. Another disadvantage is that if the file names have nothing in common, a wildcard cannot be used to print many files, so each file requires a separate COPY *filename* PRN command.

There is another way to print the contents of files: by using the PRINT command. This is an external, memory-resident command or TSR. The program is stored in `C:\DOS` as `PRINT.EXE`. (Earlier versions used `PRINT.COM`.) This program acts as a **print spooler**. Spool is an acronym for simultaneous peripheral operations on-line. A printer works much more slowly than the CPU, because it is a mechanical device that cannot print as fast as the computer can send the data to be printed. However, a print spooler can print without tying up the entire CPU. A print spooler intercepts data that is going to the printer. It holds it or "buffers" it in a portion of memory and then the spooler sends it to the printer at a rate the printer can accept. To any program, it appears that the data is being printed much faster because a spooler can accept data much faster than a real printer.

This process is a form of multitasking. The CPU processes tasks. Printing a document is a task. Working on a spreadsheet or a word processor are other tasks. Thus, when the computer is doing two or more tasks at the same time, it is multitasking. When a system is multitasking, it does not perform the tasks at the same time. Instead, it pays attention to one task for a short period of time (usually less than a second), then it goes to another task, and then another until it returns to the first task. This task switching is so quick that it appears that the system is doing tasks simultaneously when in reality it is taking care of business one task at a time. A task can be run in the **background** which means it has a lower priority and uses less of the CPU time than the primary task, which runs in the foreground. The PRINT command is a background program or **background printing** which means that the computer can be doing another task while printing, usually running another program. The other program takes most of the computer's time and is in the **foreground.** A background program gets less of the computer's time.

At this time, microcomputers running under DOS are not true multitasking machines. If they were, you would not need TSRs because you could truly run two or more programs at a time. DOS-based computers can do only one thing at a time. The PRINT program takes turns with whatever else is happening on the computer. The computer appears to be multitasking because it is so fast. DOS can switch tasks about 18 times per second. To the user, this is so quick it seems as if the computer is doing two things at the same time.

The PRINT command is more a print queue than a true print spooler. **Queue**, a word commonly used in England for lining up, means the same thing in computerese. Queuing means keeping a list of files or "lining up" the files to be printed. PRINT keeps track of the list of files and prints them from the disk instead of from memory. One advantage to using PRINT is that more than one file at a time can be printed regardless of their names. Another advantage is that files can be queued to print while you do other things. In addition, each time the PRINT command prints a new file, it will start on a new page or at the top of the form even with a laser printer.

Only ASCII text files should be printed. Programs or non-ASCII data files have control characters. These characters appear as nonsense and can make the printer behave erratically. If you are unsure of what an ASCII file is, a very simple test is to use the TYPE command. If the file displays on the screen in plain English, it can be printed with the PRINT command. Many application programs have a way to output their files in ASCII, sometimes called text mode or unformatted text file. If you can do this with your application program, you can use the PRINT command.

The syntax is of the PRINT command is:

PRINT [/D:*device*] [/B:*size*] [/U:*ticks1*] [/M:*ticks2*] [/S:*ticks3*]
[/Q:*qsize*] [/T] [[*drive:*][*path*]*filename*[...]] [/C] [/P]

where:

/D:*device*	Specifies a print device.
/B:*size*	Sets the internal buffer size in bytes.
/U:*ticks1*	Waits the specified maximum number of clock ticks for the printer to be available.
/M:*ticks2*	Specifies the maximum number of clock ticks it takes to print a character.
/S:*ticks3*	Allocates to the scheduler the specified number of clock ticks for background printing.
/Q:*qsize*	Specifies the maximum number of files allowed in the print queue.
/T	Removes all files from the print queue.
/C	Cancels printing of the preceding file name and subsequent file names.
/P	Adds the preceding file name and subsequent file names to the print queue.

PRINT without parameters will display the contents of the print queue. *filename* represents any file name. The ellipsis points represent any other files that would be queued to print. Up to 10 files can be queued to print. Ten files is the default value for the queue. The command is loaded when it is first keyed in and does not have to be loaded into memory again. It remains in memory until the computer is turned off or rebooted. PRINT uses about 3 KB of memory. You are going to use the PRINT command; however, you will not use all the parameters.

Activity 15.4 Using the PRINT Command

Note: The DATA disk is in Drive A with the **A:\BATCH>** displayed.

STEP 1: Key in the following:
A:\BATCH>**CD ** <Enter>

STEP 2: Key in the following:
A:\>**COPY \BATCH\EJECT.BAT C:\JUNK** <Enter>

STEP 3: Key in the following:
A:\>**C:** <Enter>

STEP 4: Key in the following:
C:\>**CD \JUNK** <Enter>

```
A:\BATCH>CD \

A:\>COPY \BATCH\EJECT.BAT C:\JUNK
    1 file(s) copied

A:\>C:

C:\>CD \JUNK

C:\JUNK>_
```

WHAT'S HAPPENING? You copied the EJECT program to the **JUNK** subdirectory on the hard disk so that you may use it. In addition, you changed the default disk and subdirectory to **C:\JUNK** so that the files to be printed can be located.

STEP 5: Key in the following:
C:\JUNK>**COPY *.99 PRN** <Enter>

STEP 6: Key in the following:
C:\JUNK>**EJECT** <Enter>

```
C:\JUNK>COPY *.99 PRN
JAN.99
FEB.99
MAR.99
APR.99
    1 file(s) copied

C:\JUNK>EJECT

C:\JUNK>ECHO OFF
C:\JUNK>_
```

WHAT'S HAPPENING? You used the COPY command and asked DOS to print all the files in the **\JUNK** subdirectory that have **.99** as a file extension. You then used the EJECT command to eject the page. After the page has ejected, you looked at the printout, which looked like the following:

```
This is my January file.
It is my first dummy file.
This is file 1.
This is my February file.
It is my second dummy file.
This is file 2.
This is my March file.
It is my third dummy file.
This is file 3.
This is my April file.
It is my fourth dummy file.
This is file 4.
```

WHAT'S HAPPENING? These four separate files were printed one after another. The printout looks like one file. Even using the EJECT command did not solve the problem. To print the four files on separate pieces of paper, you would have to issue the COPY and EJECT commands four separate times.

STEP 7: Key in the following:
C:\JUNK>`PRINT *.99` <Enter>

```
C:\JUNK>PRINT *.99
Name of list device [PRN]:_
```

WHAT'S HAPPENING? This is the first time that you have used the PRINT command. It is loaded into memory, as are all external commands. This command is asking for the name of the device that the output should be sent to. Once the command has this information, it will not ask for it again. The device you select will remain in memory. You cannot change the selected device unless you reboot the system. PRN is synonymous with LPT1. You do not have to worry about other devices unless you have other devices on your system such as another printer (LPT2:) or a communications port (COM1:). Never assign a device that is not on your system. In this activity, it is assumed that there is only one printer attached to your system.

STEP 8: Press <Enter>.

```
C:\JUNK>PRINT *.99
Name of list device [PRN]:
Resident part of PRINT installed


 C:\JUNK\JAN.99 is currently being printed
 C:\JUNK\FEB.99 is in queue
 C:\JUNK\MAR.99 is in queue
 C:\JUNK\APR.99 is in queue

C:\JUNK>_
```

WHAT'S HAPPENING? Compare the difference between this command and `COPY *.99 PRN`. When you used `COPY *.99 PRN`, the prompt did not appear until everything was printed. However, when using the PRINT command, you were immediately returned to the default prompt `C:\JUNK>`. The printer is working in background so that you can perform another task in foreground. After the printer has ceased printing, you looked at the printout. Instead of all the file contents being printed as one file, the PRINT command ejected a page after it printed each file. Each file gets a separate page as it starts to print.

STEP 9: Key in the following:
C:\JUNK>`PRINT PERSONAL.FIL MUSIC.MOV *.99` <Enter>

```
C:\JUNK>PRINT PERSONAL.FIL MUSIC.MOV *.99

 C:\JUNK\PERSONAL.FIL is currently being printed
 C:\JUNK\MUSIC.MOV is in queue
 C:\JUNK\JAN.99 is in queue
 C:\JUNK\FEB.99 is in queue
 C:\JUNK\MAR.99 is in queue
 C:\JUNK\APR.99 is in queue

C:\JUNK>_
```

WHAT'S HAPPENING? Since this is a memory-resident program, it does not need to be read into memory again from `C:\DOS`. You did not get the message "Name of list device [PRN]:" because it was established when you first loaded the program. You were immediately returned to the system prompt after the PRINT command listed the files it was going to print. To prove that you can do two tasks almost simultaneously, you are going to execute another command while the printer is printing the listed file. However, you may not be able to do this. If you are working with a laser printer and/or a fast computer such as a 386 33Mhz computer, by the time you read this, the files will already be printed. The files that you are using as examples are very small and do not take much time to print. Thus, check the printer to see the status of the print job.

STEP 10: Key in the following:
C:\JUNK>`TYPE DRAMA.MOV` <Enter>

```
C:\JUNK>TYPE DRAMA.MOV
CAROLYN'S FAVORITE MOVIE DRAMAS

Citizen Kane
The African Queen
Gone With the Wind
Flame and the Arrow
The Caine Mutiny
Stalag 17
Chinatown
The Bridge on the River Kwai
The Women
An Officer and a Gentleman

C:\JUNK>_
```

WHAT'S HAPPENING? If the files have not all printed yet, note how the printer pauses as the TYPE command is being executed. Although the system will respond more slowly to commands, it is both printing the files and displaying the contents of the file `DRAMA.MOV`. You could not do this using the COPY command. In addition, you could print several files with different names. You can see the ability to multitask more clearly when you are printing files that are much longer.

15.5 Viewing and Terminating the Print Queue

You have been queuing up files to print with the PRINT command. However, there are some parameters you should be aware of. You should be able to see what is in the print queue, and be able to stop printing all the files, and be able to cancel a single file from printing. If you key in PRINT by itself, it will display on the screen the files that are still in the queue. Some parameters allow you to interrupt the print queue. If you wish to stop or cancel the print job, you use the PRINT /T parameter (/T means to terminate). If you wish to terminate a specific file, you use PRINT *filename* /C. Please read the following activity before doing it so you know what you are going to do. If you are too slow in keying in the information, the printer will print all the files prior to your keying anything in. Also, some printers will not accept the /T command, i.e., the printer will not stop printing. However, the best way to find out is to try. Again, if you are using a fast printer and/or fast computer, with the short files, by the time you try to terminate the print queue, all the files will have been printed.

Activity 15.6 Using the PRINT Command Parameters

Note: You are logged into the `\JUNK` subdirectory on Drive C with `C:\JUNK>` displayed.

STEP 1: Key in the following:
C:\JUNK>`PRINT *.TXT` <Enter>

```
C:\JUNK>PRINT *.TXT

 C:\JUNK\EXERCISE.TXT is currently being printed
 C:\JUNK\JANUARY.TXT is in queue
 C:\JUNK\FEBRUARY.TXT is in queue
 C:\JUNK\MARCH.TXT is in queue
 C:\JUNK\APRIL.TXT is in queue
 C:\JUNK\HELLO.TXT is in queue
 C:\JUNK\TEST.TXT is in queue
 C:\JUNK\BYE.TXT is in queue
 C:\JUNK\GOODBYE.TXT is in queue

C:\JUNK>_
```

STEP 2: Key in the following:
C:\JUNK>`CLS` <Enter>

STEP 3: Key in the following:
C:\JUNK>`PRINT` <Enter>

STEP 4: Key in the following:
C:\JUNK>`PRINT /T` <Enter>

```
 C:\JUNK\APRIL.TXT is currently being printed
 C:\JUNK\HELLO.TXT is in queue
```

```
 C:\JUNK\TEST.TXT is in queue
 C:\JUNK\BYE.TXT is in queue
 C:\JUNK\GOODBYE.TXT is in queue

C:\JUNK>PRINT /T
PRINT queue is empty

C:\JUNK>_
```

WHAT'S HAPPENING? Your screen may display fewer files, depending on the time when you keyed in the PRINT command. In fact, it could display no files depending on how fast your system is. However, you could execute the CLS command and then display what was currently in line to print. The **EXERCISE.TXT**, **JANUARY.TXT**, **FEBRUARY.TXT**, and **MARCH.TXT** files are no longer displayed since they have already been printed. When you keyed in **PRINT /T**, it could take a little time for the system to respond. The printer will continue to print for a few seconds until it completes the current print job. In fact, you will not see your command displayed on the screen for a few seconds even though you keyed it in. Some printers will beep when they cease printing. You will have printed about four or five files, depending on when you terminated the print job and if your printer will accept the /T parameter.

STEP 5: Key in the following:
C:\JUNK>**PRINT *.FIL *.TXT** <Enter>

STEP 6: Key in the following:
C:\JUNK>**PRINT /T** <Enter>

```
C:\JUNK>PRINT *.FIL *.TXT
PRINT queue is full


 C:\JUNK\CAROLYN.FIL is currently being printed
 C:\JUNK\FRANK.FIL is in queue
 C:\JUNK\STEVEN.FIL is in queue
 C:\JUNK\PERSONAL.FIL is in queue
 C:\JUNK\Y.FIL is in queue
 C:\JUNK\EXERCISE.TXT is in queue
 C:\JUNK\JANUARY.TXT is in queue
 C:\JUNK\FEBRUARY.TXT is in queue
 C:\JUNK\MARCH.TXT is in queue
 C:\JUNK\APRIL.TXT is in queue

C:\JUNK>PRINT/T
PRINT queue is empty

C:\JUNK>_
```

WHAT'S HAPPENING? You received a "PRINT queue is full" message on the screen. The queue's default value is 10 files. There are more than 10 files, but all the PRINT command could do is queue 10 files. The rest of the ***.TXT** files will not be printed because they did not get into the queue. You then immediately "killed the queue," or stopped the printing. However, PRINT /T cancels the entire print job. What if you wanted to print all the files but one? You can selectively remove a file from the print queue with the /C parameter. The syntax is PRINT *filename.ext* /C. In the next steps, you are going to cancel printing the files **BYE.TXT** and **GOODBYE.TXT**. Be sure to read through the following steps before you begin working.

STEP 7: Key in the following:
C:\JUNK>**PRINT *.TXT** <Enter>

```
C:\JUNK>PRINT *.TXT

 C:\JUNK\EXERCISE.TXT is currently being printed
 C:\JUNK\JANUARY.TXT is in queue
 C:\JUNK\FEBRUARY.TXT is in queue
 C:\JUNK\MARCH.TXT is in queue
 C:\JUNK\APRIL.TXT is in queue
 C:\JUNK\HELLO.TXT is in queue
 C:\JUNK\TEST.TXT is in queue
 C:\JUNK\BYE.TXT is in queue
 C:\JUNK\GOODBYE.TXT is in queue

C:\JUNK>_
```

STEP 8: Key in the following:
C:\JUNK>**PRINT BYE.TXT /C** <Enter>

```
C:\JUNK>PRINT BYE.TXT /C

 C:\JUNK\FEBRUARY.TXT is currently being printed
 C:\JUNK\MARCH.TXT is in queue
 C:\JUNK\APRIL.TXT is in queue
 C:\JUNK\HELLO.TXT is in queue
 C:\JUNK\TEST.TXT is in queue
 C:\JUNK\GOODBYE.TXT is in queue

C:\JUNK>_
```

STEP 9: Key in the following:
C:\JUNK>**PRINT GOODBYE.TXT /C** <Enter>

```
C:\JUNK>PRINT GOODBYE.TXT /C

 C:\JUNK\APRIL.TXT is currently being printed
 C:\JUNK\HELLO.TXT is in queue
 C:\JUNK\TEST.TXT is in queue

C:\JUNK>_
```

WHAT'S HAPPENING? After you keyed in PRINT *filename.ext* /C for **BYE.TXT** and **GOODBYE.TXT**, the screen display listing the queued files no longer displayed **BYE.TXT** or **GOODBYE.TXT** because you removed them from the queue.

STEP 10: Key in the following:
C:\JUNK>**PRINT /T** <Enter>

```
C:\JUNK>PRINT/T
PRINT queue is empty

C:\JUNK>_
```

WHAT'S HAPPENING? You terminated the print job.

15.7 Controlling Devices

In order to control peripheral devices, special software is needed called device drivers. Usually, a **controller**, which is a piece of hardware, takes care of the hardware portion of communicating with a peripheral device. DOS groups physical devices into two basic categories: **character devices** and **block devices**. Character devices are those that handle data as individual characters such as keyboards, the screen, serial ports, and parallel ports. Block devices handle data as "chunks" or blocks of data such as disk drives.

Character devices are attached to the computer via a cable attached to a port on the system unit. A **port** is simply an input/output connection, like a plug, where you can connect devices to a computer. Devices include such things as the console, printers, a mouse, a light pen (a device to point to things or draw designs on a special display screen), a fax board (a board that allows the transmission of facsimiles), or a modem (a device that allows computers to communicate over phone lines). There are other devices. DOS is not concerned with the actual device but with the method of interface. **Interface** means the hardware and/or software necessary to connect one system or device to another so that they can transmit and receive information. Thus, DOS defines an interface as either **serial** or **parallel** and calls the plugs serial or parallel ports.

A serial or **asynchronous** port can transfer data at the rate of one bit at a time. It is called asynchronous because the transmission of data is not synchronized by a clock signal. The devices communicating must take turns receiving and sending data; they cannot send data simultaneously or synchronized. The data is sent as bits one after another with a start bit at the beginning and a stop bit at the end to mark the beginning and end of the data. For instance, the word "DOS" in binary is 01000100 (D) 01001111 (O) 01010011 (S).

If you sent it serially, it would travel as in Figure 15.3.

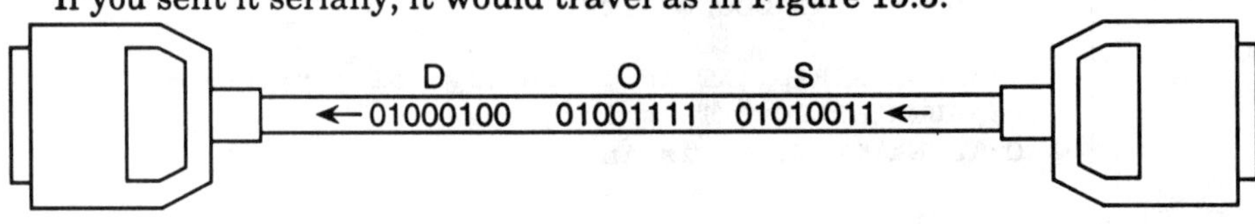

Computer Cable Plug

Figure 15.3 Serial Communication

You can think of it as eight cars parading down the highway, one following the other, with a police car at the beginning and at the end of the parade.

A parallel port, on the other hand, transfers data at the rate of one byte at a time (eight bits). The transfer of eight bits must be concurrent so that the byte (eight bits) looks the same on the receiving end as on the sending end. Thus, sending the word "DOS" in parallel fashion would look like Figure 15.4.

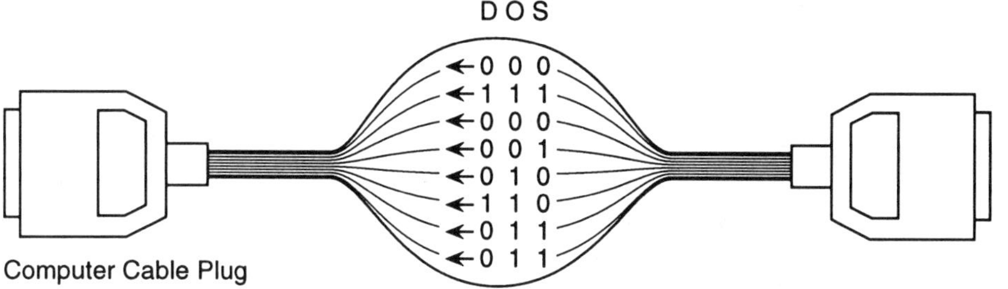

Figure 15.4 Parallel Communication

You can think of it as eight cars going down the highway side by side. Parallel communication is faster than serial communication.

Most computers have at least one parallel port and one serial port. You can add, or upgrade, the hardware to include more ports. You can have up to four serial ports (prior to DOS 3.3, the limitation was two serial ports) and three parallel ports. Different computers can have varying numbers of serial and parallel ports. Most printers are generally parallel printers, but there are serial printers. A parallel printer can have a cable no more than 25 feet from the system unit; any length beyond that can present problems in the printer receiving data. Serial printers do not have this problem and can be more than 50 feet away from the system unit. Devices such as modems are serial devices and are "plugged" into the serial or communication port. The operating system or DOS has reserved names for each standard device. They are shown in Table 15.1.

Table 15.1 Reserved Names for Standard Devices

Port Name	DOS Device Name	Alias	Meaning
Parallel port 1	LPT1:	PRN	Line Printer 1
Parallel port 2	LPT2:		Line Printer 2
Parallel port 3	LPT3:		Line Printer 3
Serial port 1	COM1:	AUX	Communications port 1 Auxiliary device
Serial port 2	COM2:		Communications port 2
Serial port 3	COM3:		Communications port 3 (DOS 3.3 and above)
Serial port 4	COM4:		Communications port 4 (DOS 3.3 and above)

The MODE command in DOS performs several tasks that relate to controlling devices.

15.8 The MODE Command

The MODE command is actually several commands in one. It is used for configuring devices. You can use it to change the number of characters per inch and lines per inch for IBM-compatible dot-matrix printers; to set the characteristics for a serial port; to display the status of one or more devices; to redirect output from a parallel port to a communications port; to prepare, select, and display code pages; and to set the number of rows and columns on a monitor. You can also use it to set the rate at which DOS repeats a character when you hold down a key on the keyboard (**typematic rate**) new to DOS 4.0 and above. Many of these options you will rarely use. For instance, code page setting has to do with character sets for foreign countries. Unless you are working in a language other than English, you will not deal with this setting at all. You will use MODE for other configurations, depending on what hardware you have. If, for instance, you have a serial printer or modem, you will have to set the characteristics for it to be able to communicate.

Serial devices, such as a serial printer or modem, have to agree on the **communication protocol**. Communication protocol means that the computer and device have to agree on how fast they will communicate and how many bits of information they will exchange at one time. These values include the baud rate, parity, data bits, stop bits, and retry value. **Baud rate** is the speed the devices will communicate in bits per second. **Parity** helps the computer and the device know when there is a bit error. An extra "parity" bit is often sent immediately following the data bits. When the device or computer receives the data, it counts the number of binary digits that had the value of 1. The results will be either an odd number or an even number. If the computer and the device agreed on even parity and if the sum is odd, a transmission error has occurred. The default value is even parity. In order to tell when the transmission is complete, one or more **stop bits** are sent. Again, the communication protocol establishes this number. Last, the **retry** parameter tells MODE what to do when it gets a "busy" signal from the device. In addition to setting the communication protocol, if you have a serial printer, you must redirect the output from the parallel port to the serial port. In other words, every time DOS sees output going to PRN, it will redirect it to COM1 or COM2.

Each one of these options of the MODE command has its own syntax and parameters. It is beyond the scope of this text to cover all of these details because MODE is so hardware-dependent. Today, modern software will automatically set up or "configure" the ports as needed. Also, when you do need to use MODE to configure a device, you can check the device's documentation for the appropriate values. Follow the instructions in the documentation to set up MODE with the proper values. Then place it in the `AUTOEXEC.BAT` file and don't worry about it again.

The MODE command is also a TSR external command. In the following activity, you are going to be using the MODE command in conjunction with the printer to change the style of the print. The MODE command works with the IBM and/or Epson FX/MX series of printers or one that acts like the Epson printer.

If you do not have one of these IBM-like printers or a laser printer, this use of the MODE command will not work. You will also change the way the display looks. If you have DOS 4.0 or above, you will also look at the status of your devices and change the typematic rate.

15.9 Setting the Printer Characteristics with the MODE Command

With this command, you can customize your printing. MODE provides the opportunity to use one of three printers. The default printer settings are 80 characters per line (CPL) and 6 lines per inch (LPI). You can also print in a smaller or condensed mode where there are 132 characters per line. In addition, you can print 8 lines per inch.

MODE is an external memory-resident command. When you set the MODE for the printer, it remains set at the parameters that you specified until you change the mode, turn off the printer, or turn off the computer. The syntax is:

MODE LPT*n*[:] [COLS=*c*] [LINES=*l*] [RETRY=*r*]

where:

LPT*n*	Specifies the parallel port the printer is attached to. Valid values for *n* are 1 through 3.
[COLS=*c*]	Specifies characters (columns) per line. The valid values are 80 or 132.
[LINES=*l*]	Specifies lines per inch. The valid values are 6 or 8.
[RETRY=*r*]	Specifies the retry action to take if the printer is busy.

Since MODE is an external command, DOS has to be able to access it initially to load it. However, once the printing characteristics for the printer are set, they remain set regardless of which disk you print from. They remain set at this value until you either change it again with MODE or reboot the system.

Activity 15.10 Printing Using the MODE Command

Note: You are logged into the `\JUNK` subdirectory on Drive C with `C:\JUNK>` displayed. REMEMBER: If you have a laser printer or a noncompatible IBM printer, you will not be able to do this activity.

STEP 1: Be sure that the printer is on. Key in the following:
C:\JUNK>**`MODE LPT1: 132,8`** <Enter>

```
C:\JUNK>MODE LPT1: 132,8

LPT1: not rerouted

LPT1: set for 132

Printer lines per inch set

No retry on parallel printer time-out

C:\JUNK>_
```

WHAT'S HAPPENING? You set the printer so that it will print data condensed, giving 132 characters per line and 8 lines to the inch. Time-outs have to do with the computer looping internally to wait for the printer to be ready. You set your printer mode. Any text file that you print will be printed in a condensed or small mode until you reset the printer mode.

STEP 2: Key in the following:
C:\JUNK>**COPY PERSONAL.FIL PRN** <Enter>

STEP 3: Key in the following:
C:\JUNK>**EJECT** <Enter>

```
Gillay    Carolyn  699 Lemon     Orange       CA Professor
Panezich  Frank    688 Lake      Orange       CA Teacher
Tuttle    Steven   356 Embassy   Mission Viejo CA Golf Pro
Maurdeff  Kathryn  550 Traver    Ann Arbor    MI Teacher
Maurdeff  Sonia    550 Traver    Ann Arbor    MI Student
Smith     Gregory  311 Orchard   Ann Arbor    MI Engineer
Smith     Carolyn  311 Orchard   Ann Arbor    MI Housewife
Winter    Jim      333 Pick      Garden Grove CA Key Grip
Winter    Linda    333 Pick      Garden Grove CA Teacher
Golden    Herbert  345 Lakeview  Orange       CA Doctor
Golden    Jane     345 Lakeview  Orange       CA Nurse
Brent     Wendy    356 Edgewood  Ann Arbor    MI Librarian
Brogan    Lloyd    111 Miller    Santa Cruz   CA Vice-President
Brogan    Sally    111 Miller    Santa Cruz   CA Account Manager
Babchuk   Nicholas 13 Stratford  Sun City West AZ Professor
Babchuk   Bianca   13 Stratford  Sun City West AZ Professor
Begg      Leroy    20 Elm        Ontario      CA Systems Analyst
Helm      Milton   333 Meadow    Sherman Oaks CA Consultant
Moselle   Carolyn  567 Abbey     Rochester    MI Day Care Teacher
Markiw    Nicholas 354 Bell      Phoenix      AZ Engineer
Markiw    Emily    10 Zion       Sun City West AZ Retired
Nyles     John     12 Brooks     Sun City West AZ Retired
Nyles     Sophie   12 Brooks     Sun City West CA Retired
Markiw    Nick     10 Zion       Sun City West AZ Retired
Papay     Fred     345 Newport   Orange       CA Manager
Jones     Steven   32 North      Phoenix      AZ Buyer
Smith     David    120 Collins   Orange       CA Chef
Babchuk   Walter   12 View       Thousand Oaks CA President
Babchuk   Deana    12 View       Thousand Oaks CA Housewife
Jones     Cleo     355 Second    Ann Arbor    MI Clerk
Smith     Henry    40 Northern   Ontario      CA Engineer
JONES     JERRY    244 East      Mission Viejo CA Systems Analyst
Low       Ophelia  1213 Wick     Phoenix      AZ Writer
Tally     William  15 Fourth     Santa Cruz   CA Banker
Gibbs     Michael  134 Seventh   Ann Arbor    MI Editor
Richards  James    56 Twin       Orange       CA Artist
Markiw    Nicholas 12 Fifth      Glendale     AZ Engineer
```

WHAT'S HAPPENING? The file called **PERSONAL.FIL** printed in a much smaller type style. You can have it print a little bigger.

STEP 4: Key in the following:
C:\JUNK>**MODE LPT1: 132,6** <Enter>

```
C:\JUNK>MODE LPT1:132,8

LPT1: not rerouted

LPT1: set for 132

Printer lines per inch set

No retry on parallel printer time-out

C:\JUNK>_
```

WHAT'S HAPPENING? The printer is now set to print 132 characters per line but 6 lines per inch instead of 8, so it will not be as condensed.

STEP 5: Key in the following:
C:\JUNK>**COPY PERSONAL.FIL PRN** <Enter>

STEP 6: Key in the following:
C:\JUNK>**EJECT** <Enter>

```
Gillay    Carolyn  699 Lemon     Orange        CA  Professor
Panezich  Frank    688 Lake      Orange        CA  Teacher
Tuttle    Steven   356 Embassy   Mission Viejo CA  Golf Pro
Maurdeff  Kathryn  550 Traver    Ann Arbor     MI  Teacher
Maurdeff  Sonia    550 Traver    Ann Arbor     MI  Student
Smith     Gregory  311 Orchard   Ann Arbor     MI  Engineer
Smith     Carolyn  311 Orchard   Ann Arbor     MI  Housewife
Winter    Jim      333 Pick      Garden Grove  CA  Key Grip
Winter    Linda    333 Pick      Garden Grove  CA  Teacher
Golden    Herbert  345 Lakeview  Orange        CA  Doctor
Golden    Jane     345 Lakeview  Orange        CA  Nurse
Brent     Wendy    356 Edgewood  Ann Arbor     MI  Librarian
Brogan    Lloyd    111 Miller    Santa Cruz    CA  Vice-President
Brogan    Sally    111 Miller    Santa Cruz    CA  Account Manager
Babchuk   Nicholas 13 Stratford  Sun City West AZ  Professor
Babchuk   Bianca   13 Stratford  Sun City West AZ  Professor
Begg      Leroy    20 Elm        Ontario       CA  Systems Analyst
Helm      Milton   333 Meadow    Sherman Oaks  CA  Consultant
Moselle   Carolyn  567 Abbey     Rochester     MI  Day Care Teacher
Markiw    Nicholas 354 Bell      Phoenix       AZ  Engineer
Markiw    Emily    10 Zion       Sun City West AZ  Retired
Nyles     John     12 Brooks     Sun City West AZ  Retired
Nyles     Sophie   12 Brooks     Sun City West CA  Retired
Markiw    Nick     10 Zion       Sun City West AZ  Retired
Papay     Fred     345 Newport   Orange        CA  Manager
Jones     Steven   32 North      Phoenix       AZ  Buyer
Smith     David    120 Collins   Orange        CA  Chef
Babchuk   Walter   12 View       Thousand Oaks CA  President
Babchuk   Deana    12 View       Thousand Oaks CA  Housewife
Jones     Cleo     355 Second    Ann Arbor     MI  Clerk
Smith     Henry    40 Northern   Ontario       CA  Engineer
JONES     JERRY    244 East      Mission Viejo CA  Systems Analyst
Low       Ophelia  1213 Wick     Phoenix       AZ  Writer
Tally     William  15 Fourth     Santa Cruz    CA  Banker
Gibbs     Michael  134 Seventh   Ann Arbor     MI  Editor
Richards  James    56 Twin       Orange        CA  Artist
Markiw    Nicholas 12 Fifth      Glendale      AZ  Engineer
```

WHAT'S HAPPENING? Compare how this printout differs in size from the previous printout.

STEP 7: Key in the following:
C:\JUNK>**MODE LPT1: 80,6** <Enter>

```
C:\JUNK>MODE LPT1: 80,6

LPT1: not rerouted

LPT1: set for 80

Printer lines per inch set

No retry on parallel printer time-out

C:\JUNK>_
```

WHAT'S HAPPENING? You set the printer back to the default values. Thus, your choices for printing styles are limited to mode LPT1: 132,8; 132,6; 80,6; or 80,8.

15.11 Using MODE with the Display Monitor

You can specify with the MODE command how many characters you want displayed in a row of data on the monitor. You can also specify how many rows you want displayed on the monitor. The changes you can make depend on the type of monitor you have and the version of DOS you have. Prior to DOS 4.0, the syntax was:

MODE [*n*],*m*[,T]

where *n* is

40	Allows you to display 40 characters per row
80	Allows 80 characters per row.
BW40	Disables color on color adapter, 40 characters per row.
BW80	Disables color on a color adapter, 80 characters per row.
CO40	Enables color on a color adapter, 40 characters per row.
CO80	Enables color on a color adapter, 80 characters per row.
MONO	Monochrome display adapter, 80 characters per row.

m	R or L allows you to shift the display right or left.
T	Requires a test pattern used to align the display.

In DOS 4.0 and above, you can also specify the number of columns and rows.

MODE CON [:] [COLS=*c*] [LINES=*n*]

The *c* is a value for columns and can be either 40 or 80. The *n* is a value of lines. For CGA systems the value can be 25; for EGA systems the values can be 25 or 43; and for a VGA system the values can be 25, 43, or 50.

Activity 15.12 Using MODE to Change the Display

Note: You are logged into the **\JUNK** subdirectory on Drive C with **C:\JUNK>** displayed.

STEP 1: Key in the following:
C:\JUNK>**MODE 40** <Enter>

```
C:\JUNK>_
```

WHAT'S HAPPENING? You changed the display so that it is displaying 40 characters instead of 80 characters in a row. In essence, it makes the display twice as large. However, this only works in DOS. Most application packages will not work if the MODE is set to 40.

STEP 2: Key in the following:
C:\JUNK>**MODE 80** <Enter>

```
C:\JUNK>_
```

WHAT'S HAPPENING? You returned the display to the default value.

15.13 Using MODE to Change the Response Rate of the Keyboard

If you have DOS 4.0 or above, you can alter the keyboard typematic rate, the rate at which DOS repeats a character when you press a key. You can increase the value and DOS will increase the speed of the typematic rate. Not all keyboards support this feature. There are two parts to the syntax, the rate and time delay. The rate refers to the rate that the character is repeated on the screen when you hold down a key. Valid values include 2 to 32 characters per second. The default value is 20 for IBM-AT style keyboards and 21 for IBM PS/2 keyboards. If you set the rate you must also set the other component, the delay. The delay sets the amount of time that must elapse after you press and hold down a key before DOS starts to repeat the characters. The valid values include 1, 2, 3, and 4 which represent .25, .50, .75, and 1 seconds. The default value is 2. If you set the delay, you must also set the rate. The syntax is:

MODE CON[:] [RATE=*r* DELAY=*d*]

Activity 15.14 Setting the Quickest Typematic Rate

Note: You are logged into the **\JUNK** subdirectory on Drive C with **C:\JUNK>** displayed.

STEP 1: Hold down the letter x for a few seconds.

```
C:\JUNK>xxxxxxxxxxxxxxxxxx_
```

WHAT'S HAPPENING? Note the speed at which the letter x repeats.

STEP 2: Press <Esc>.

STEP 3: Key in the following:
C:\JUNK>**MODE CON: RATE=32 DELAY=1** <Enter>

```
C:\JUNK>MODE CON: RATE=32 DELAY=1

C:\JUNK>_
```

WHAT'S HAPPENING? You set the rate to the fastest keyboard response. This means that when you hold down a letter on the keyboard, it will repeat 32 times a second.

STEP 4: Hold down the letter x for a few seconds.

```
C:\JUNK>xxxxxxxxxxxxxxxxxx_
```

WHAT'S HAPPENING? You should see the speed of the keyboard increase. If the keyboard seems to be too quick, try to adjust the delay value first so you have a little more time to release the key.

STEP 5: Press <Esc>.

STEP 6: Key in the following:
C:\JUNK>**MODE CON: RATE=21 DELAY=2** <Enter>

```
C:\JUNK>MODE CON: RATE=21 DELAY=2

C:\JUNK>_
```

WHAT'S HAPPENING? You returned the values to their defaults.

15.15 Checking the Status of Devices

If you have DOS 4.0 or above you can check the status of different devices. Using MODE with no parameters will display the status of all devices. If you use the switch, /STATUS, or /STA parameters with the MODE command, it will request the status of any redirected printer. If you specify a device name, it will display the status of the device. You can check either a specific device or all the devices. The syntax is:

MODE [*device*] [/STATUS]

Activity 15.16 Checking the Status of Devices With MODE

Note: You are logged into the **\JUNK** subdirectory on Drive C with **C:\JUNK>** displayed.

STEP 1: Key in the following:
C:\JUNK>**MODE CON:/STATUS** <Enter>

```
C:\JUNK>MODE CON:/STATUS

Status for device CON:
----------------------
Columns=80
Lines=25

Code page operation not supported on this device

C:\JUNK>_
```

WHAT'S HAPPENING? The /STATUS switch gives the information that this monitor is set to 80 characters per column with 25 lines that can be displayed.

STEP 2: Key in the following:
C:\JUNK>**MODE ¦ MORE** <Enter>

```
Status for device LPT1:
-----------------------
LPT1: not rerouted
Retry=NONE

Code page operation not supported on this device

Status for device LPT2:
-----------------------
LPT2: not rerouted

Status for device LPT3:
-----------------------
LPT3: not rerouted

Status for device CON:
----------------------
Columns=80
Lines=25

Code page operation not supported on this device

Status for device COM1:
-- More --
```

WHAT'S HAPPENING? As you can see, the MODE command is reporting the status of all the devices on this system. Your screen display can vary based on what peripherals are on your system. Also note that since MODE writes to the screen—standard output, the output can be redirected to the MORE command.

STEP 3: Press <Enter> until you have returned to the system prompt.

STEP 4: Key in the following:
C:\JUNK>CD \ <Enter>

STEP 5: Key in the following:
C:\>A: <Enter>

```
C:\JUNK>CD \

C:\>A:

A:\>_
```

WHAT'S HAPPENING? You changed the default subdirectory to the root of C. Then you changed the default drive to A.

Chapter Summary

1. Printing the screen can be accomplished by using the <Shift> key and the <PrtSc> key.
2. Printing all the dialogue between the user and the computer can be accomplished by using the <Ctrl> key and the <PrtSc> key as a toggle switch. This technique cannot be used with a laser printer.
3. Text files can be printed using the COPY *filename.ext* PRN command.
4. Another method of printing involves using redirection. You can redirect the output of a command to the printer.
5. All these methods have disadvantages. A primary disadvantage is that you must manually adjust the printer to start a new file on a new page. This is called ejecting the page.
6. Instead of manipulating the hardware manually, you can manipulate it with software by sending <Ctrl>+L to the printer. This signal means eject the current page.
7. You can either send the software command directly from the command line or write a batch file to accomplish the same task.
8. There are three categories of commands, internal, external, and memory-resident. Internal commands remain in memory until the system is turned off. Both external and memory-resident commands must be called from the disk into memory. The difference is that external commands, when finished executing, release the memory they use. Memory-resident commands do not turn back the memory they use. The memory-resident command is available to be used without reloading it from the disk.
9. Memory-resident commands are also called TSRs—Terminate and Stay Resident commands.
10. PRINT is a memory-resident command provided by DOS that, once loaded into memory, remains there until the computer is turned off.
11. The PRINT command acts as a spooler. Since a printer is much slower than memory, a print spooler intercepts data that is going to the printer and holds it until the printer can accept it.
12. The PRINT command is useful for queuing or lining up files to print.

13. The PRINT command is a program that can perform in the background, allowing the user to accomplish some other task while files are being printed.
14. Printing a file while you are running another command is called background printing.
15. Running the program that takes most of the computer's time is putting it in the foreground.
16. Only ASCII text files should be printed with any of the above techniques.
17. ASCII text files are those that, when using the TYPE command, print English characters.
18. The PRINT command will print each new file on a new page.
19. To control devices, special software is needed called device drivers.
20. DOS groups devices into two categories, character and block devices.
21. Character devices are attached to the computer by a cable attached to a port.
22. A port is a connection for an I/O device.
23. A serial port transfers data one bit at a time.
24. A parallel port transfers data one byte (eight bits) at a time.
25. Nearly all computers have at least one parallel and one serial port although there can be more. You can have up to 4 serial ports and 3 parallel ports.
26. DOS has reserved names for standard devices.
27. The MODE command is used for configuring devices attached to the system.
28. The MODE command can be used to alter the type style of an IBM-type printer.
29. The MODE command can be used to set the characteristics of a serial port or the communications protocol. This means that the device and the computer have to agree on how fast they will communicate and how many bits of information they will exchange. You can set the baud rate, parity, stop bit, and retry rate.
30. You can redirect the output of a parallel port to a serial port by means of the MODE command.
31. You can change the characteristics of a display monitor with the MODE command.
32. You can change the rate of speed of the keyboard response time—the typematic—rate with the MODE command.
33. You can request a status report on the devices attached to your system.

Key Terms

Asynchronous
Baud rate
Background
Background printing
Block devices
Character devices
Communication protocol
Controller
Eject
Foreground
Form feed
Interface
Memory-resident
Parallel
Parity
Port
Print spooler
Queue
Retry
Screen dump
Serial
Stop bit
TSR
Typematic rate

Discussion Questions

1. What is a screen dump?
2. How can you manipulate the software to print or eject a page?
3. What are two techniques for printing text files?
4. What is a major drawback of printing text files by dumping the screen to the printer?
5. How can you print the directory of a disk when the directory is longer than a screenful?
6. What are the three categories of commands?
7. Compare and contrast the three categories of commands.
8. How does a TSR operate?
9. What advantages does the PRINT command offer compared to other methods of printing?
10. What is a print spooler?
11. How does a print spooler work?
12. Why is it important that only ASCII files be printed when using the PRINT command?
13. What is multitasking?
14. How can a print job be canceled?
15. Parallel communication is faster than serial communication. Why?
16. If you wanted to hook up a printer to a computer but logistics require that the printer be 30 feet from the system unit, what type of printer would you recommend? Why?
17. What is a port and what is its function?
18. What is the difference between a serial port and a parallel port?
19. Name two functions of the MODE command.
20. Why would it be important to alter the typematic rate?
21. Describe the difference between foreground and background programs.
22. Describe an interface.
23. Name two standard DOS devices.
24. What does queue mean?
25. Why does DOS have reserved names for devices?

Application Assignments

Use the DATA disk unless otherwise specified.

Note 1: The following exercises are not a test in typing. Don't worry if you make typographical errors or if the format is not quite perfect. You are creating the files in order to be able to print them.

Note 2: If your equipment does not allow you to perform the activities, write the command that would accomplish the task if your hardware would allow it.

1. For the following assignment:
   a. Create a new text file on the DATA disk called **LEXICON1.ABC**. In EDIT, using the <Tab> key and pressing <Enter> where the text ends will allow the files to print neatly. Remember, EDIT does not have word wrap. The contents are as follows:

      ANALOG Hors d'oeuvre usually made from cheese and served at staff parties.
      BINARY Possessing the ability to have friends of both sexes.
      BUG Small creeping thing that small boys throw on small girls.
      CPU A juvenile way of telling your dog that it missed the paper.
      CHIP Small, crunchy object often served with onion dip.
      COMMAND Statement presented by a human and accepted by a computer in such a manner as to make the human feel that he or she is in control.
      CURSOR An expert in four-letter words.

   b. Create a new text file on the DATA disk called **LEXICON2.DEF**. The contents are as follows:

      DEBUG The act of placing shoe leather against a small creeping creature.
      DOWNTIME Mental coffee breaks, lunches, or Fridays in the office or school.
      ERROR Something that only humans can commit.
      K A term used in employment ads to disguise how much they are really willing to pay.

   c. Create a new text file on the DATA disk called **LEXICON3.MOR**. The contents are as follows:

      NETWORK The occupation of a fisherperson.
      OUTPUT What people who talk backwards do with their cat.
      RAM A male sheep.
      RAM DRIVE A sheep who has learned to drive.

   d. Display the contents of the file called **LEXICON1.ABC** on the screen. Print the screen and eject the page.
   e. Combine all three lexicon files into one new file on the DATA disk called **DICTNRY.TOT**.
   f. Print all the lexicon files and the **DICTNRY.TOT** file with one command.
   g. After the files have been printed, print the screen with the command you used.

2. For the following assignment:
   a. Print all the files in the **\JUNK** subdirectory that have the **.DAT** file extension and all the files on the DATA disk that have the file extension **.TV** with one command line.
   b. After the files have been printed, print the screen with the command you used.
3. Print a sorted directory of the root directory of DATA disk. Do not use the <Shift> and <PrtSc> keys.
4. If possible on your equipment:
   a. Change the mode to 132 CPL and 8 LPI.
   b. Print the **LEXICON3.MOR** file.
   c. Return the printer to its default settings.
5. If possible on your equipment:
   a. Print all the file on the DATA disk with **.TXT** as a file extension. As soon as you enter the command, cancel the print job.
   b. Print the screen that shows the termination of the command.
6. For the following assignment:
   a. Print a status report of all the devices on your system. Do not use <Shift>+<PrtSc>.
   b. Print the status of the monitor you are using. Do not use <Shift>+<PrtSc>.
7. If possible on your equipment:
   a. Change the typematic rate to a delay of 1 second and a rate of 15.
   b. Print the screen with the command you used to make this change.
   c. Test this typematic rate and write a brief report on the results of this test.
   d. Reset the typematic rate to the default settings.
   e. Print the screen with the command you used to make this change.

Challenge Assignment

8. For the following assignment:
   a. Review the **AUTOEXEC.BAT** and **CONFIG.SYS** files on the system you are using.
   b. Report any statements in these files that relate to configuring devices with the MODE command.
   c. Describe the purpose and meaning of these statements.

Chapter 16

Using Shells: MS-DOS Shell

After completing this chapter you will be able to:

1. Explain what a shell is and how it functions.
2. Install DOS Shell.
3. Once the shell has been installed, use the mouse and/or keyboard to execute commands.
4. Access the command prompt within DOS Shell.
5. Receive online help within DOS Shell.
6. Explain and use the file system.
7. Perform DOS functions within DOS Shell.
8. Compare and contrast the way commands operate in DOS Shell and at the command line prompt.

Chapter Overview

Up to this point we used the command processor COMMAND.COM to communicate with the operating system. At the DOS prompt we entered a command from the keyboard and pressed the <Enter> key to execute the command. The command processor accepted the command, interpreted it, and then executed it. Once the command was executed, the DOS prompt was again displayed on the screen. Although this process certainly works, it is very cryptic.

To make using DOS easier, commercial programs called shells have been developed that provide a different user interface from the command line prompt. A shell surrounds DOS, covering its details and making DOS more "user friendly." One such shell called MS-DOS Shell, is included with Microsoft DOS 4.0 and above. A comparable shell is included in IBM's DOS 4.0 and above and titled simply DOS Shell. Unlike the cryptic system prompt, both MS-DOS Shell and IBM-DOS Shell provide a menulike system that allows the user to communicate with the operating system. In addition, both allow the use of a mouse and provide graphic displays, if the user has the appropriate hardware. Because this chapter is based on Microsoft DOS Shell, we will refer to MS-DOS Shell for all activities with the understanding that MS-DOS Shell and IBM's PC-DOS Shell are virtually the same. In this chapter you will learn how to install and use MS-DOS Shell as an alternative to the command line prompt.

16.0 Shells

Software developers are always looking for ways to make using computer software easier, not only to encourage novice computer users but also to let more sophisticated users take advantage of the power of the new hardware and software. This is especially true when it comes to operating systems. However, in the DOS world, there are new options that reach beyond the command line prompt to make using DOS easier. You can purchase innovative menu systems. You can write menu systems with batch files, as you did in Chapter 12, to make program access easier. In addition, commercial programs called **shells** provide a user interface different from the command line prompt. These programs are called shells because they surround DOS, covering its details. A shell is a program for using DOS. Shells differ from menus in that menus are just lists of options and suboptions. A shell is a complete operating system environment. A shell can contain menus, but menus alone do not make a shell. MS-DOS 4.0 and above comes with a shell called DOS Shell (see Figure 16.1).

Figure 16.1 Layers of Operating Environments

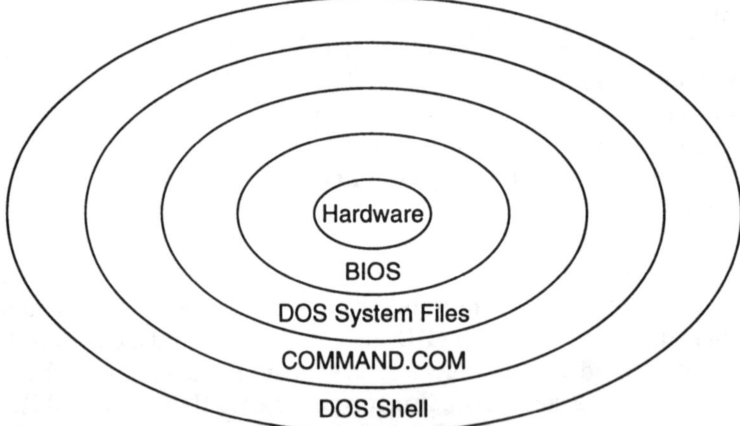

Indeed, the direction in the computer industry is away from command-driven text-based programs like DOS to what is called a graphical user interface (**GUI**, pronounced "gooey"). GUIs let you use the keyboard, as well as a mouse. In addition to text, GUIs provide pictures called **icons** that represent the functions of the program. GUIs are not limited to application programs; they can also be used with operating systems and provide icons for operating system functions. For instance, to access a file, a user would "point and shoot" with the mouse at an icon of a file cabinet. GUIs enhance DOS.

A product called Windows 3.0, endorsed and written by Microsoft, is a shell with many more powerful features such as multitasking and memory managers. Thus, it is more an operating environment rather than just a shell. However,

Windows requires powerful hardware. In order to meet the needs of less powerful systems and to make DOS more "user friendly," Microsoft released a product called MS-DOS Shell to utilize some of the features of a graphical environment for those without the hardware power that is needed for Windows. In addition, MS-DOS Shell comes free with DOS 4.0 and above. In this chapter we will look at MS-DOS Shell, which comes with MS-DOS 5.0. If you are running IBM-PC DOS 5.0, the shell is called DOS Shell but is virtually identical to MS-DOS Shell. Although in the text, we will refer to MS-DOS Shell, it will also mean DOS Shell from IBM. If you are running DOS 4.0, DOS Shell or MS-DOS Shell are very similar to MS-DOS Shell or DOS Shell in DOS 5.0. In Chapter 18, we will look at Windows 3.0.

16.1 MS-DOS Shell

MS-DOS Shell is a user interface that replaces the usual command line interface with a menulike system. MS-DOS Shell allows the user to select DOS commands from a list instead of keying them in at the system prompt. However, the user still has access to the system prompt. Depending on the hardware MS-DOS Shell is also somewhat graphical. For instance, a mouse can be used with MS-DOS Shell. You can also use the keyboard, in addition or instead of the mouse.

MS-DOS Shell provides easy access to programs and DOS commands. You can install your own programs into the menu system. You can have password protection. You can use MS-DOS Shell to manage the files and use drop-down menus, a feature that DOS does not have at the command line. You can only use MS-DOS Shell with DOS 4.0 or above. MS-DOS Shell is included as part of DOS 4.0 and 5.0. MS-DOS Shell is a relatively small program and does not take up much memory. Therefore, you can run it on older computers. Another advantage of MS-DOS Shell is that you can use it even if you do not have a graphics monitor.

In the next activities you are going to take a look at some of the functions of MS-DOS Shell and explore some of the different options. Once you see how it works, you will see that it is fairly easy to utilize. Since we are only sampling MS-DOS Shell, once you are comfortable with it, feel free to explore some of its other areas.

Activity 16.2 Installing MS-DOS Shell

Note: You have booted the system. The default drive is C: and the prompt displayed is **C:\>**. The DATA disk is in Drive A.

STEP 1: Key in the following:

C:\>**DOSSHELL** <Enter>

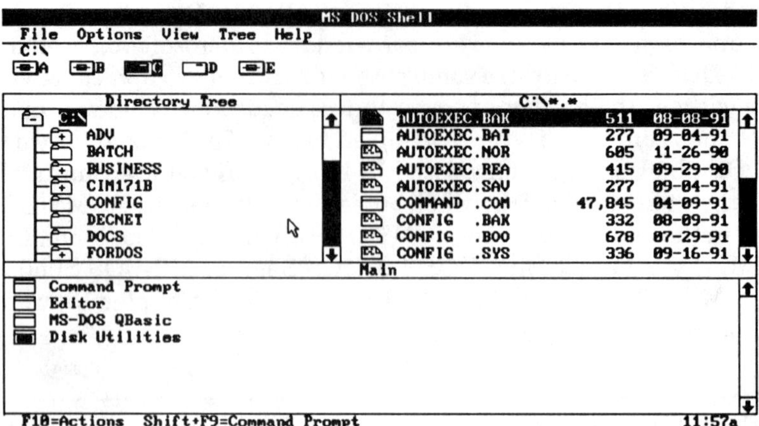

WHAT'S HAPPENING? You installed MS-DOS Shell. If you have a color monitor, the display will be in color. If you have a monitor that does not support graphics, your screen will look as follows.

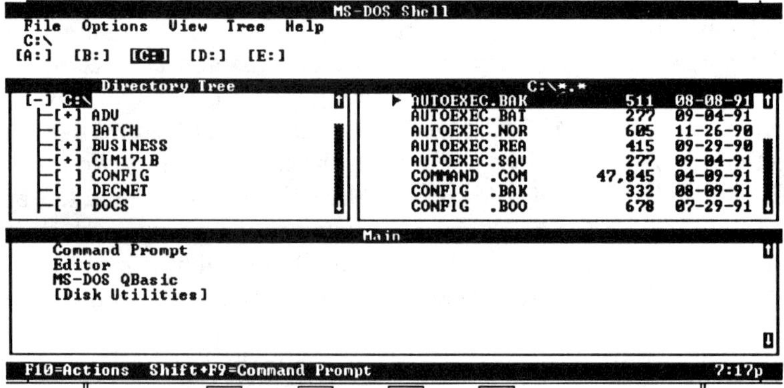

WHAT'S HAPPENING? The nongraphics display is different because it does not show the icons, which are pictures that represent items. For instance, next to each file name is a picture or icon of a file folder. The remainder of this chapter will use the graphics monitor display. Note: If this is not the display you see, take the following steps.

STEP 2: Press <Alt>+V.

STEP 3: Press the <Down arrow> key until `Programs\Files List` is highlighted.

STEP 4: Press <Enter>.

16.3 Explaining MS-DOS Shell

This screen display looks very different from the **`C:\>`** or **`A:\>`**. Although certainly not as cryptic as the system prompt you have been using, the display still needs some explanations. Figure 16.2 outlines some of the major parts of the screen display.

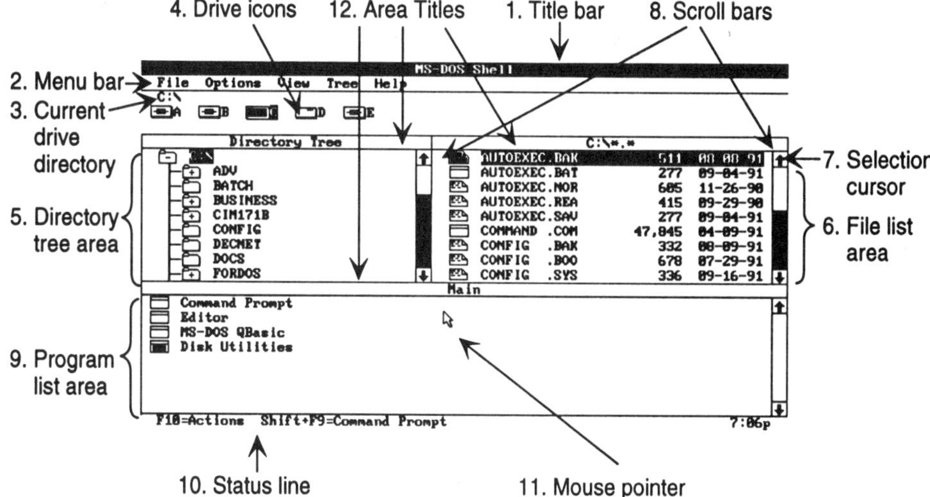

Figure 16.2 The MS-DOS Shell Screen

The delineated portions of the screen are the following:

1. The **title bar** of the screen you are in. In this case it is MS-DOS Shell.
2. The **menu bar** which lists the choices of the available menus. When you choose an item from the menu, the menu bar will display a further list of commands you can use. In this case, your choices are **`File`**, **`Options`**, **`View`**, **`Tree`**, and **`Help`**.
3. The default drive and directory. In this case, it is the root directory of Drive C.
4. The drive icons and/or drive letters available on your specific computer system. In this example, there are Drives A, B, C, D, and E. When you select one of these drive letters, you make it the default drive.
5. The **Directory Tree area**. MS-DOS Shell provides areas. The Directory Tree area displays the structure of the directories of the current disk drive. If you select another disk drive, then the `Directory Tree` would change to reflect the new disk drive structure.
6. The **file list area** shows a list of the files in the default directory. The default directory is the one selected in the `Directory Tree` area.
7. The selection cursor. When an item is in a different color or the colors are inverted, it has been "highlighted" or selected. This tells you what selection you have chosen. In this case, C:\ is highlighted, which informs you that you are looking at the root directory of Drive C. In the file list area, **`AUTOEXEC.BAK`** is in inverse video or "highlighted" and is therefore the file selected.
8. If you have a mouse and a graphic monitor, you will see the vertical scroll bar.

The scroll bar is an easy mechanism to "scroll" or page through the displayed information when it does not fit on one screen.

9. The **program list area,** considered the `Main` program list group, contains programs that you can execute directly from the shell. It includes two programs that you can start from this location, the `Editor` that you worked with in Chapter 11 and the programming language `MS-DOS QBasic` that comes with MS-DOS 5.0. If you select the `Command Prompt`, it allows you to leave MS-DOS Shell and go directly to the DOS command line prompt. The `Disk Utilities` contains several of the DOS programs to maintain disks such as FORMAT and DISKCOPY.
10. The status line displays the time and informs you of some function key options. F10 allows you to take an action, and <Shift>+F9 returns you to the DOS command prompt.
11. The mouse pointer—look closely for it because it is very mobile.
12. The **area titles** tell you the name of the area you are in. When you select an area, it is indicated by a color change or inverse colors on the monitor. The area titles on this screen are `Directory Tree`, `C:\*.*`, and `Main`.

You always work in an "area." However, before you can work in an area, you must select it. If you have a color monitor, the title bar of the area you select will change. If you have a monochrome monitor, the area you select will have a small arrow to the left of an item in the area you selected.

MS-DOS Shell allows you to select items from what are called **drop-down menus**. For example, if you select `File`, `File` then provides you with more choices via the drop-down menu. Here is where you perform such functions as copying or deleting a file. The drop-down menu remains on the screen until you either close it or select another menu item.

16.4 Using the Mouse and Keyboard

When using MS-DOS Shell, you can use either the keyboard or the mouse or a combination of both. Obviously, if you do not have a mouse, you can only use the keyboard. It is useful to understand how you move within MS-DOS Shell using either the mouse or the keyboard. You also need to review some of the terminology.

If you have a mouse, it is attached to the system unit. It is called a mouse because it resembles a mouse with a tail. The mouse has two or three buttons on it. The **mouse pointer** is the arrow-shaped icon on the screen that indicates where you are (see Figure 16.3).

Figure 16.3 Mouse and Mouse Pointer

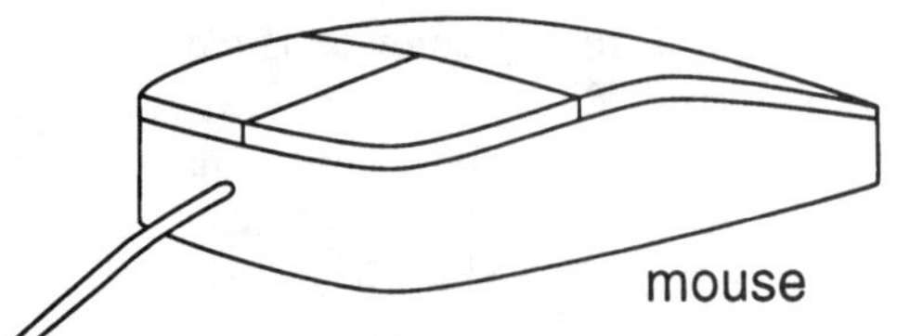

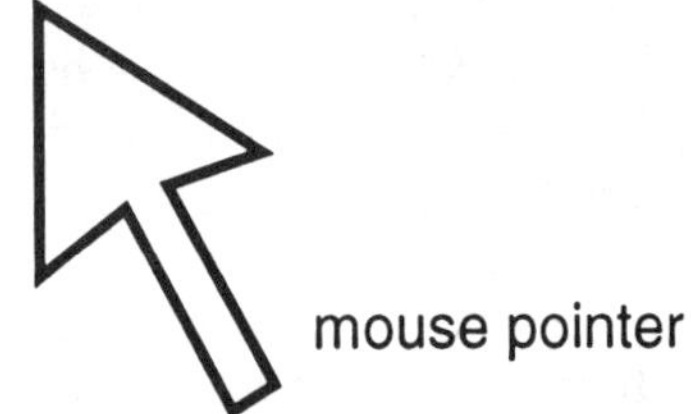

The arrow is the cursor. To use the mouse, move it around on a flat surface next to the computer, usually the table on which your keyboard is placed. That movement on the surface correspondingly moves the pointer on the screen. When you wish to select an item with the mouse, move the mouse pointer to the icon or text phrase that you wish to choose and click the mouse. Click means pressing the left mouse button once. To activate or run your selection, you double-click the mouse. Double-click means to press the left mouse button twice, quickly. This process is also called point and shoot. To drag the mouse means to place the mouse pointer on an item, press and hold down the left mouse button, move the mouse pointer to the new location (i.e., drag the item), and then release the left mouse button. You will need to practice the necessary finger pressure to click, double-click, and drag the mouse. You will also find the pressure varies from mouse to mouse. In MS-DOS Shell, the right mouse button has no functions.

If you do not have a mouse, you can still use MS-DOS Shell with keyboard commands. In general, when you use the keyboard instead of the mouse, you select an item by the use of the <Tab> key, the <Alt> key, the F10 key and/or the arrow keys. As we work with MS-DOS Shell, the keys used will be specified.

Activity 16.5 Getting to the Command Prompt and Using Help

Note 1: You are in MS-DOS Shell. If you are not in MS-DOS Shell, key in **DOSSHELL** at the **C:\>**. The DATA disk is in Drive A.

Note 2: **Highlighting** refers to differentiating choices. If you have a color monitor, highlighted choices will be displayed in different colors. If you have a black and white monitor, the highlighted choices will be in reversed shades.

Note 3: If you wish to use the keyboard, follow the instructions in the left-hand column. If you wish to use the mouse, follow the instructions in the right-hand column.

STEP 1: Press the <Tab> key until `Command Prompt` is highlighted.

STEP 1: Click `Command Prompt` in the `Main` area.

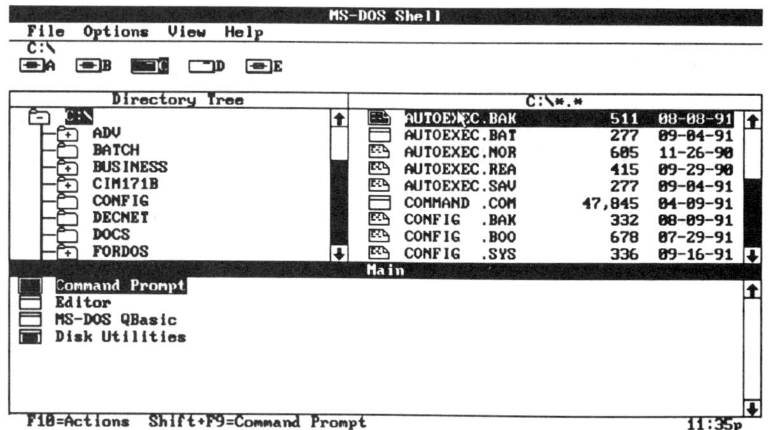

WHAT'S HAPPENING? You highlighted the `Command Prompt`. The command prompt will take you to the DOS system level.

STEP 2: Press <Enter>.

STEP 2: With the mouse pointer on `Command Prompt`, double-click the left mouse button.

```
Microsoft(R) MS-DOS(R) Version 5.00
    (C)Copyright Microsoft Corp 1981-1991.

C:\>_
```

WHAT'S HAPPENING? As you can see, you returned temporarily to the `C:\>` prompt. However, MS-DOS Shell is still there waiting to be used. The `C:\>` prompt works as usual. You can execute any program or command you want. You can always return to MS-DOS Shell by keying in **`EXIT`**, which means that you are "exiting" the command line prompt and returning to MS-DOS Shell.

STEP 3: Key in the following:
C:\>**`EXIT`** <Enter>

STEP 3: Key in the following:
C:\>**`EXIT`** <Enter>

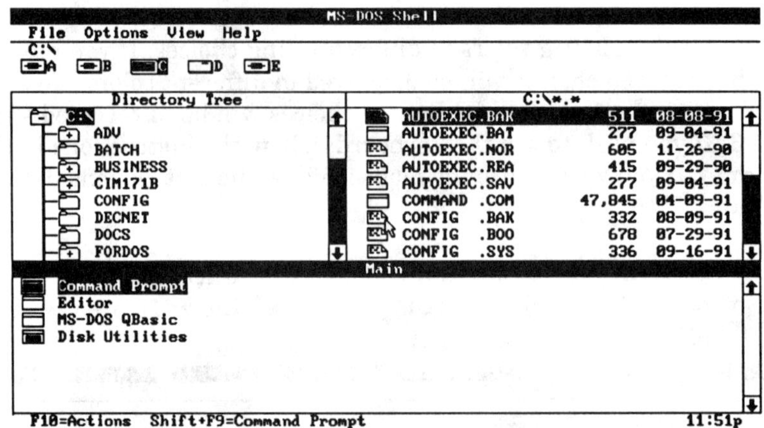

WHAT'S HAPPENING? You returned to MS-DOS Shell. MS-DOS Shell also provides online help. You access help by selecting **`Help`** from the menu bar.

STEP 4: Press <Alt>+H.

STEP 4: Click **`Help`** on the menu bar.

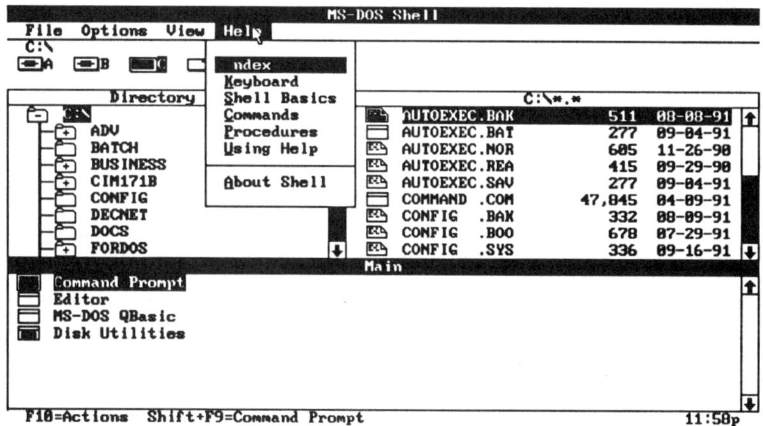

WHAT'S HAPPENING? The online `Help` menu dropped down to assist you. The choice `Index` is highlighted. If you prefer another selection such as `Keyboard`, you would either use the <Down arrow> key to highlight it or move the mouse pointer and click `Keyboard` to highlight it. `Index` is a good choice to begin with since it is an "index" to `Help` on the menu bar.

STEP 5: Press <Enter>. STEP 5: Click **`Index`**.

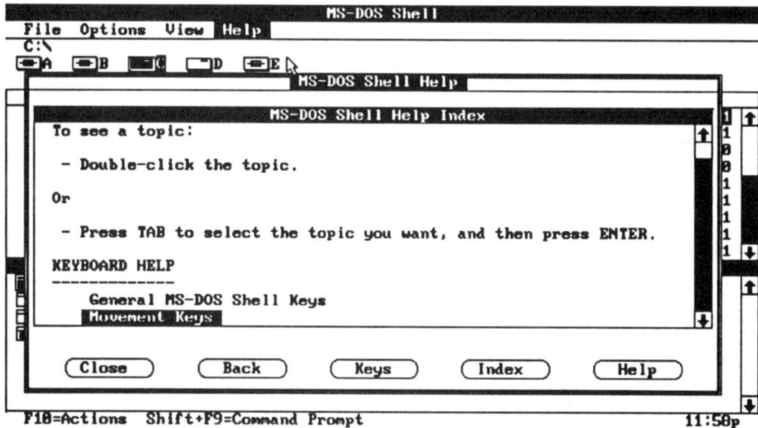

WHAT'S HAPPENING? You have an index to `Help`. Since there is more than one screenful of information, you can scroll through this screen by using the <PgUp>, <PgDn>, <Up arrow> or <Down arrow> keys. You will also use the <Tab> key. If you have a graphics monitor and a mouse, you can use the scroll bar. (see Figure 16.4).

Figure 16.4
The Scroll Bar

The **scroll bar** is designed to be used with a mouse. The arrow symbols tell you how it works. If you place the mouse pointer on the up or down arrow and click once, the display moves up or down one line at a time. If you place the mouse pointer above or below the slider box, you move up or down a page at a time.

The **slider box** is also designed to be used with the mouse. To use the slider box, place the mouse pointer on the slider box, press and hold the left mouse button, and drag the slider box up or down. When you release the left mouse button, the list scrolls to the position nearest to the mouse pointer. You can move around the help screen by using the **`Help Index`**.

WHAT'S HAPPENING? You have an index to all the help available.

STEP 6: Press the <PgDn> key once.

STEP 6: Click the down arrow on the scroll bar a few times until you see the line **`Drive Selection Keys`**.

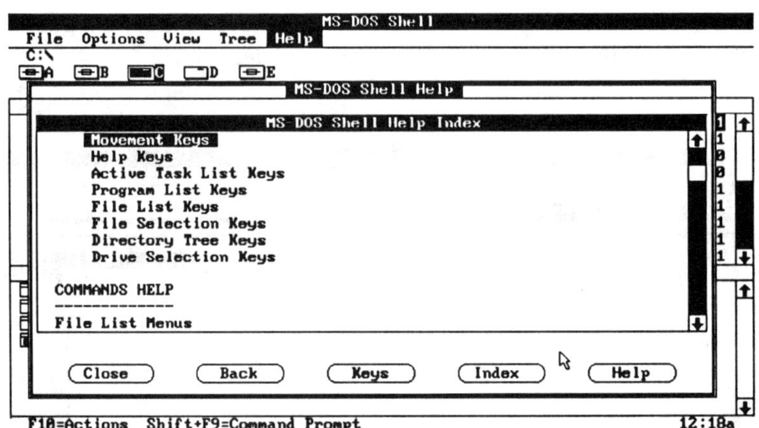

WHAT'S HAPPENING? You scrolled through the index until you saw what you were interested in. You are interested in **`Drive Selection Keys`**. Now you must select it.

STEP 7: Press the <Tab> key until **`Drive Selection Keys`** is highlighted. Press <Enter>.

STEP 7: Double-click **`Drive Selection Keys`**.

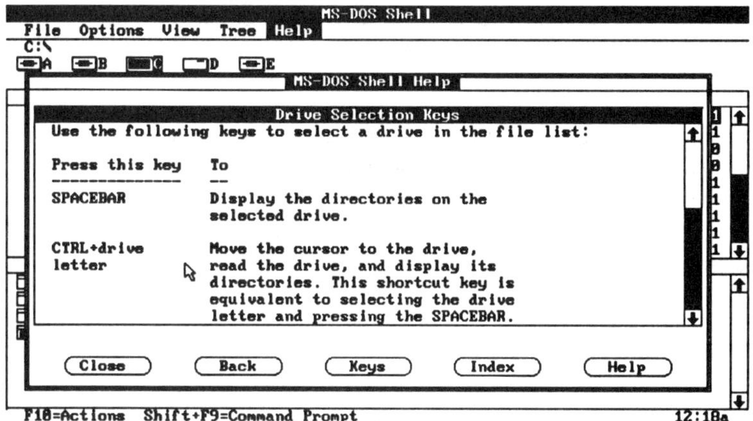

WHAT'S HAPPENING? You got specific help for selecting another disk drive. This help screen is more than one screenful so you will need to scroll through the screens for all the help information. You can use the <PgDn>, <PgUp>, <Up arrow> or <Down arrow> if you wish to use the keyboard to scroll through the pages. If you have a mouse, you can use the scroll bar. Notice that at the bottom of the screen there are five choices. These choices will always be presented to you in `Help`. Selecting `Close` ends `Help`, returning you to what you were last doing. `Back` returns you to the previous help screen, if there is one. `Keys` displays help relating to using the keyboard. `Index` displays the index to `Help`. `Help` displays help on using `Help`. If you have a mouse, click on the selection you wish to choose. If you have a keyboard, use the <Tab> key to select your choice and then press <Enter>.

STEP 8: Press the <Tab> key until you see the cursor in the `Close` box. Press <Enter>.

STEP 8: Click `Close`.

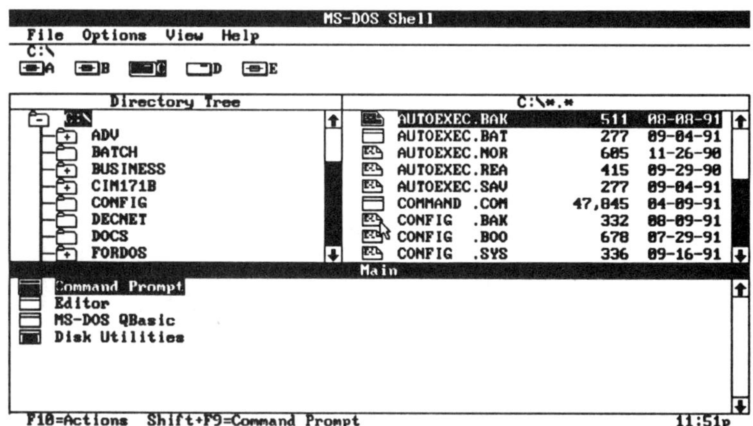

WHAT'S HAPPENING? You returned to the beginning screen of MS-DOS Shell.

16.6 Returning to DOS

When you highlighted the `Command Prompt` and exited to the system level, you were merely suspending the use of MS-DOS Shell. It was still waiting to be used. This is why you could key in **EXIT** and return to the shell. However, you also want to know how to quit the shell and not have it running in the background. The next activity demonstrates this process.

Activity 16.7 Quitting MS-DOS Shell

Note: You are in MS-DOS Shell.

STEP 1: Press F3. STEP 1: Press F3.

```
C:\>_
```

WHAT'S HAPPENING? You returned to the system level. Now you have quit the shell. It is not in the background. You can prove this by attempting to use **EXIT**.

STEP 2: Key in the following: STEP 2: Key in the following:
C:\>**EXIT** <Enter> C:\>**EXIT** <Enter>

```
C:\>EXIT

C:\>_
```

WHAT'S HAPPENING? Since there was no program running in the background, there was nothing to exit.

16.8 Managing Files and Directories with MS-DOS Shell

MS-DOS Shell allows you to manage your files and directories. It allows you to use many of the standard DOS commands you have already learned to accomplish such tasks as copying files, deleting files, and managing files.

Activity 16.9 Managing Directories

Note: You are at the **C:\>**. The DATA disk is in Drive A.

STEP 1: Key in the following: STEP 1: Key in the following:
C:\>**DOSSHELL** <Enter> C:\>**DOSSHELL** <Enter>

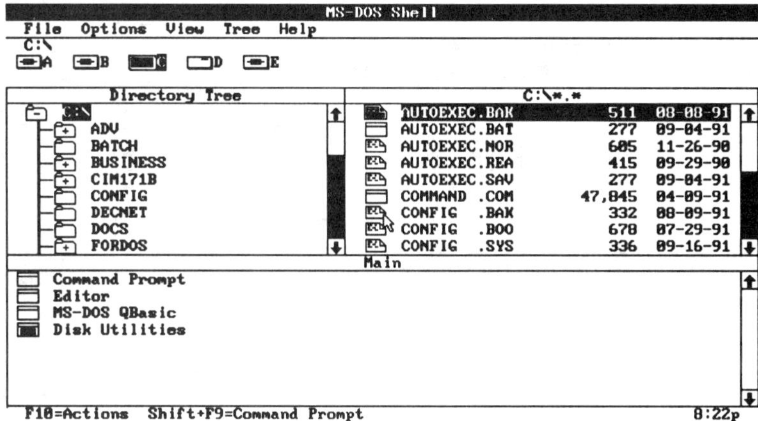

WHAT'S HAPPENING? You loaded to MS-DOS Shell.

STEP 2: Press the <Tab> key until the `Directory Tree` title bar is highlighted.

STEP 2: Click the `Directory Tree` title bar.

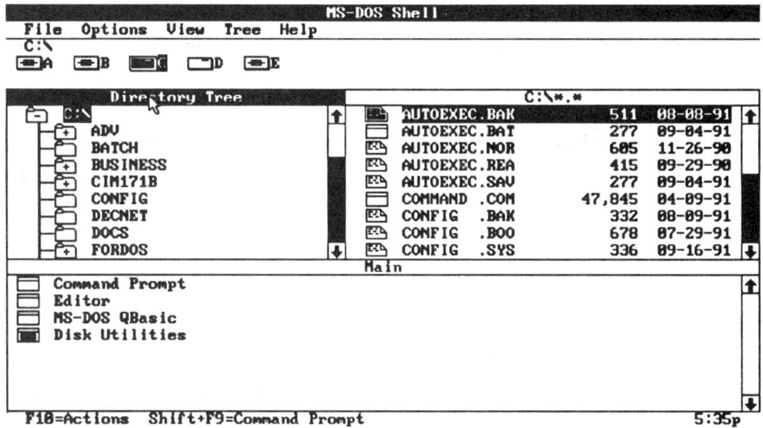

WHAT'S HAPPENING? When you loaded MS-DOS Shell, it read the information on the disk in Drive C. The display will vary based on what directories are on the hard disk. The default drive is C because the C icon is highlighted. You are looking at the root directory of C with its subdirectories. The subdirectories are in alphabetical order. It is important to recognize how you navigate the `Directory Tree` area.

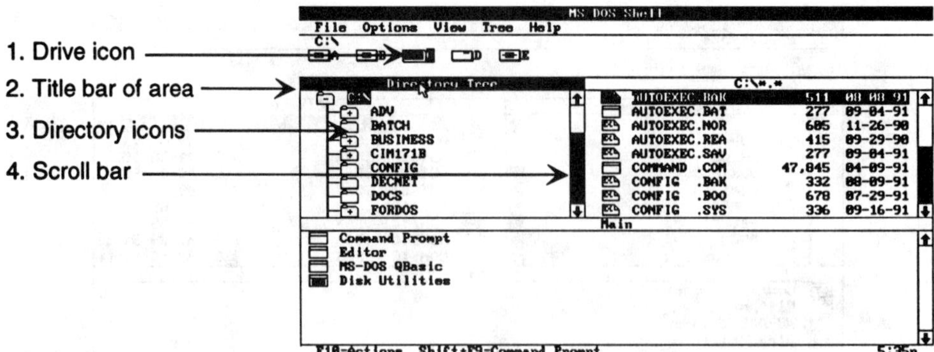

1. The drive icon identifies the default disk drive. If you have a nongraphic monitor, it will be displayed as [C:].
2. Because the `Directory Tree` area title bar is highlighted, it tells you that this is the active area.
3. The subdirectory icons are file folders. They have either a plus sign (+), a minus sign (-), or are blank. If a file folder has a plus sign in it, it means that it is expandable—that there are other subdirectories beneath it. If it has a minus sign, it means that it can be collapsed to a higher level so that you are only looking at the level you are interested in. If it has neither a plus sign or a minus sign, it means there are no more levels. If you have a nongraphical display, instead of a picture of a file folder, you see [+], [-], or [ ] which serve the same functions.
4. To navigate the `Directory Tree`, you may use either the mouse or the keyboard. If you use the mouse, you use the scroll bar. If you use the keyboard, you can use the <PgUp> or <PgDn> key to move a screen at a time. You can use the <Up arrow> or <Down arrow> to move one line at a time. You can also key in the first letter of the directory you are interested in.

STEP 3: Press the <Minus> key on the numeric key pad. (Note: If the file folder icon already has a minus sign in it, press the plus sign. Then press the minus sign.)

STEP 3: Click the minus sign in the file folder icon for C:\. (Note: If the file folder icon already has a minus sign in it, click on the plus sign. Then click on the minus sign.)

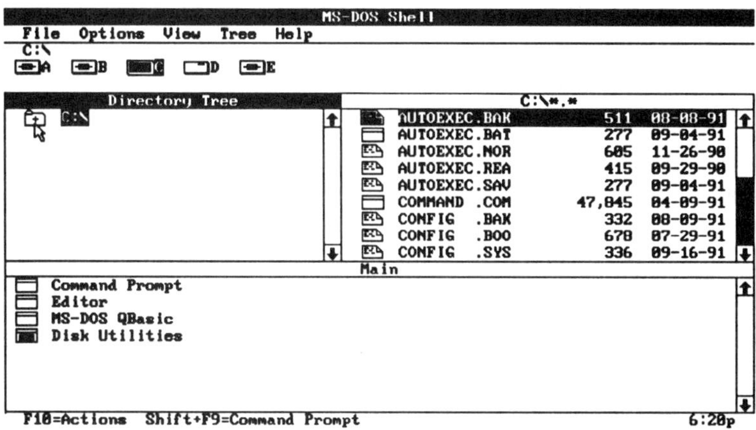

WHAT'S HAPPENING? You collapsed the root directory of C to its highest level. Because it now has a plus sign, you know that you can expand it.

STEP 4: Press the <Plus> key on the numeric key pad.

STEP 4: Click the plus sign in the file folder icon for C:\.

STEP 5: Press the <Down arrow> key once.

STEP 5: Click once on the first file folder name under the C:\.

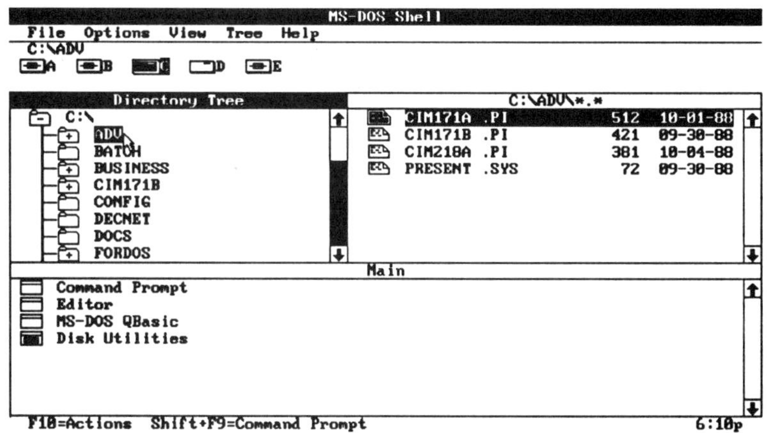

WHAT'S HAPPENING? You expanded the root directory and highlighted the first subdirectory under the root. In this example, you highlighted a subdirectory named **ADV**. On the right-hand area, the files displayed are the ones in the subdirectory **ADV**. In this example, **ADV** has a plus sign which means **ADV** has subdirectories of its own. Your display will be different, depending on what subdirectories are on your hard disk.

STEP 6: Press the letter J.

STEP 6: Click the scroll bar until you see the subdirectory **JUNK**. Click the **JUNK** subdirectory file name.

WHAT'S HAPPENING? Because the JUNK subdirectory has a plus sign, you know it has lower level directories.

STEP 7: Be sure JUNK is highlighted. Press the <Plus> key.

STEP 7: Be sure JUNK is highlighted. Click once on the plus sign in the file folder icon.

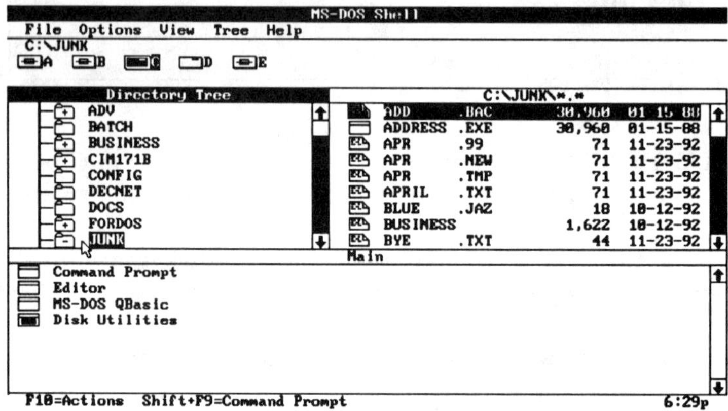

WHAT'S HAPPENING? The plus sign changed to a minus sign. The file list area shows all the files in the JUNK subdirectory. You may not be able to see all the subdirectories under JUNK.

STEP 8: Press the <Down arrow> key until you can see all the subdirectories under JUNK.

STEP 8: Click the down arrow on the scroll bar until you can see all the subdirectories under JUNK.

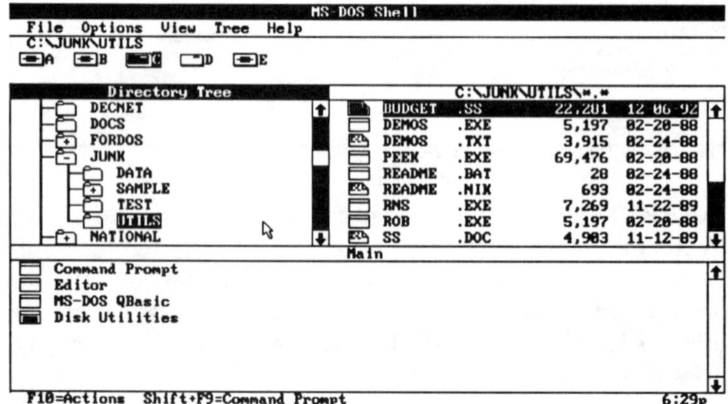

WHAT'S HAPPENING? There are four subdirectories under **JUNK—DATA, SAMPLE, TEST** and **UTILS**. **SAMPLE** has a plus sign in it which means that it can be expanded.

STEP 9: Press the <Up arrow> key until **SAMPLE** is highlighted. Then press the <Plus> key.

STEP 9: Click the plus sign in the **SAMPLE** file folder icon.

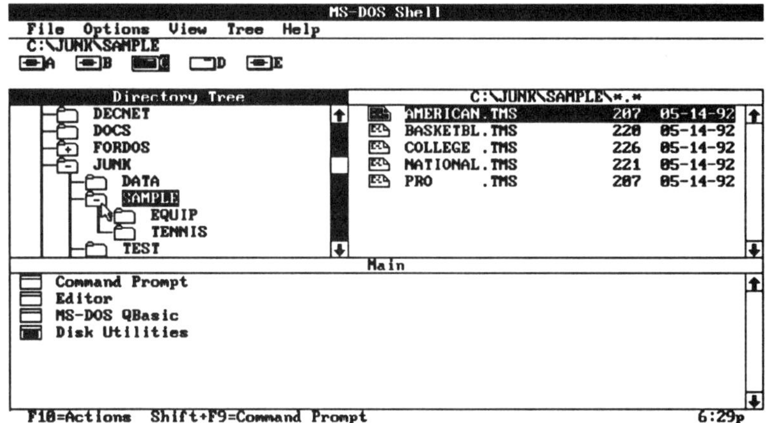

WHAT'S HAPPENING? You expanded the subdirectory called **SAMPLE**. It has two subdirectories called **EQUIP** and **TENNIS**. Look at the file list area. It shows you the files in the **SAMPLE** subdirectory. Because **JUNK** has a minus sign in it and **SAMPLE** has a minus sign in it, each can be collapsed.

STEP 10: Move the <Up arrow> key until **JUNK** is highlighted. Then press the <Minus> key.

STEP 10: Click the minus sign in the **JUNK** file folder icon.

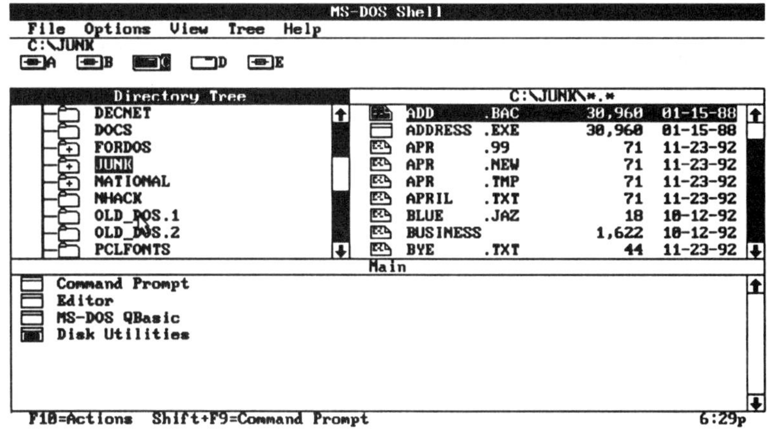

WHAT'S HAPPENING? You collapsed **JUNK** to its highest level so you do not see the subdirectories that are beneath **JUNK**. Be sure **JUNK** is highlighted. You can use the menu bar to accomplish the same tasks.

STEP 11: Press <Alt>+T.

STEP 11: Click **Tree** on the menu bar.

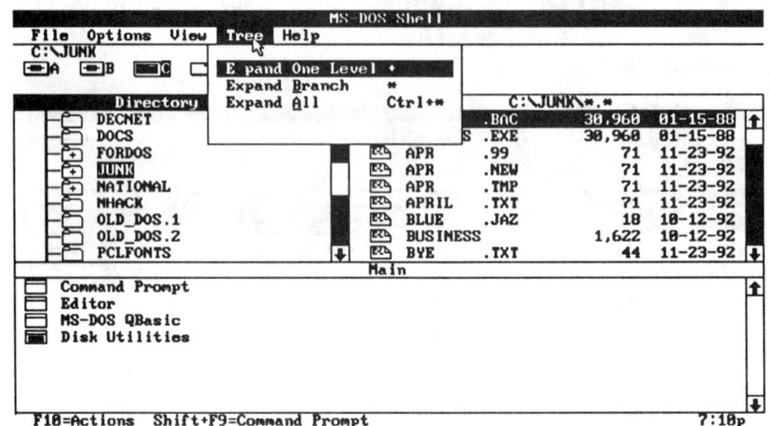

WHAT'S HAPPENING? You have dropped down the **Tree** menu. Listed on it are choices you can make. **Expand One Level** should be highlighted.

STEP 12: Press <Enter>.

STEP 12: Click **Expand One Level**.

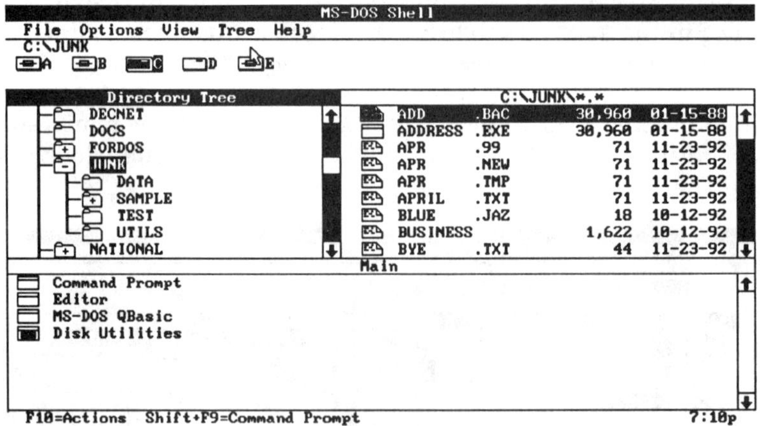

WHAT'S HAPPENING? By selecting **Expand One Level**, you expanded **JUNK** one level.

STEP 13: Press <Alt>+T.

STEP 13: Click **Tree** on the menu bar.

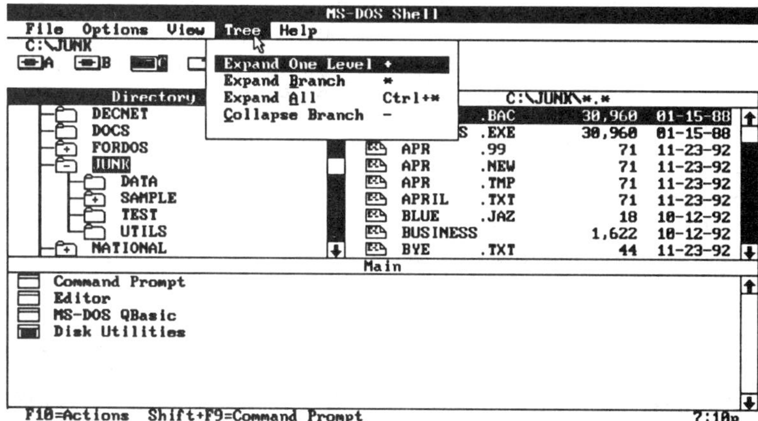

WHAT'S HAPPENING? Once again the drop-down menu is displayed.

STEP 14: Press the <Down arrow> key until `Collapse Branch` is highlighted. Press <Enter>.

STEP 14: Click `Collapse Branch`.

```
                              MS-DOS Shell
File  Options  View  Tree  Help
C:\JUNK
A  B  C  D  E
        Directory Tree                         C:\JUNK\*.*
   DECNET                          ADD      .BAC    30,960  01-15-88
   DOCS                            ADDRESS  .EXE    30,960  01-15-88
   FORDOS                          APR      .99         71  11-23-92
   JUNK                            APR      .NEW        71  11-23-92
   NATIONAL                        APR      .TMP        71  11-23-92
   NHACK                           APRIL    .TXT        71  11-23-92
   OLD_DOS.1                       BLUE     .JAZ        18  10-12-92
   OLD_DOS.2                       BUSINESS          1,622  10-12-92
   PCLFONTS                        BYE      .TXT        44  11-23-92
                                Main
   Command Prompt
   Editor
   MS-DOS QBasic
   Disk Utilities

F10=Actions  Shift+F9=Command Prompt                            7:10p
```

WHAT'S HAPPENING? You collapsed the `JUNK` subdirectory to its highest level.

16.10 Managing Files

MS-DOS Shell also allows you to manage the files on any disk. However, you must tell the Shell which files you are interested in. You do this by selecting a file or a group of files. You have selected files when working from the system level by keying in a command, then typing in the file name. When you work in MS-DOS Shell, first you select a file, then you perform an action. You pick a file with the mouse by clicking the file name. When you use the keyboard, you use the <Tab>

key to move to the file list area, then use the <Up arrow> and <Down arrow> keys to highlight the file you want. At the system level, you can use wildcards to select a group of similarly named files. In the Shell, you can also select groups of files. However, they do not need to have similar names. In the next activity, you will learn how to work with files.

Activity 16.11 Copying a File Using MS-DOS Shell

Note: You are still in MS-DOS Shell. The `Directory Tree` area title is highlighted. The `JUNK` subdirectory in the `Directory Tree` area is highlighted. The DATA disk is in Drive A.

STEP 1:	Press <Alt>+F.	STEP 1:	Click `File` on the menu bar.

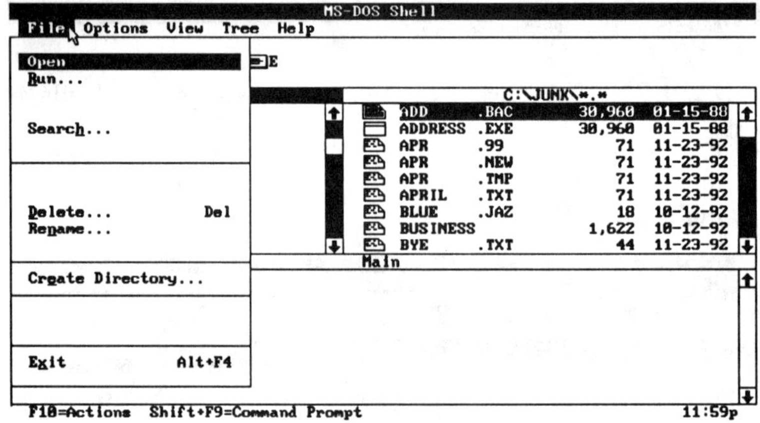

WHAT'S HAPPENING? You dropped down the `File` menu. Listed are many of the DOS commands that you have used at the system prompt. Each command that has an **ellipsis** after it means that a dialog box will appear when the command is selected. If a command is "greyed out" or dim, it means that the command is not available at this time. If you are using a monochrome monitor, you will not see the commands that are not available. You must select a file in order to take action. Here you are going to cancel the menu.

STEP 2:	Press <Esc>.	STEP 2:	Click the mouse someplace outside of the menu.

WHAT'S HAPPENING? You are out of the `File` menu.

STEP 3:	Press the <Tab> key until the file list title bar is highlighted.	STEP 3:	Click the file list title bar.

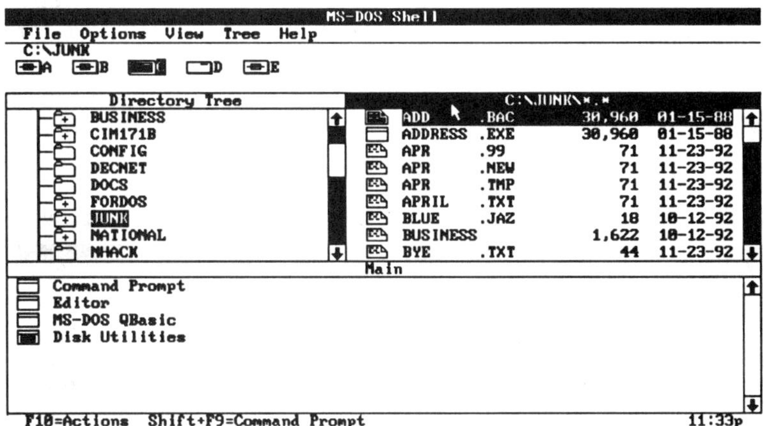

WHAT'S HAPPENING? You selected the file list area of the JUNK subdirectory. If you look at the title bar above the file list, it states which subdirectory files you are looking at: `C:\JUNK\*.*`. (If this is not what is on your screen, return to the `Directory Tree` area and highlight the JUNK icon.) As you can see, the files are listed alphabetically. Now that you have selected the file list area, you must then select a file to manipulate.

STEP 4: Press M. Then press the <Down arrow> key 6 times until **MUSIC.MOV** is highlighted.

STEP 4: Use the scroll bar until you locate the file called **MUSIC.MOV**. Click **MUSIC.MOV**.

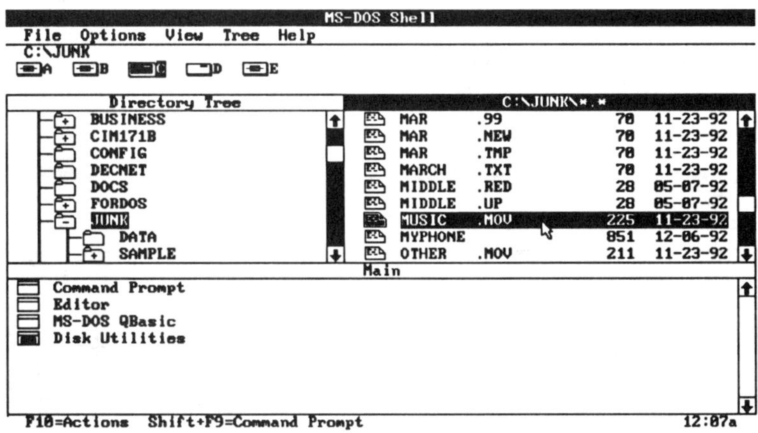

WHAT'S HAPPENING? If you are using the keyboard, you pressed the letter M to take you to files that began with the letter M. You then used the <Down arrow> key to select the specific file. The <Home> key always takes you to the top of the file list and the <End> key takes you to the last file in the list. If you are using a mouse, you used the scroll bar to move to the area you wanted. Then you clicked the file name to select it. If you have a nongraphics monitor, the file name has an arrow and a triangle next to it. Now that you have selected a file, you can manipulate it with commands from the `File` menu. You are going to copy the file `MUSIC.MOV` from the `JUNK` directory on Drive C to the DATA disk on Drive A.

STEP 5: Press <Alt>+F. STEP 5: Click `File` on the menu bar.

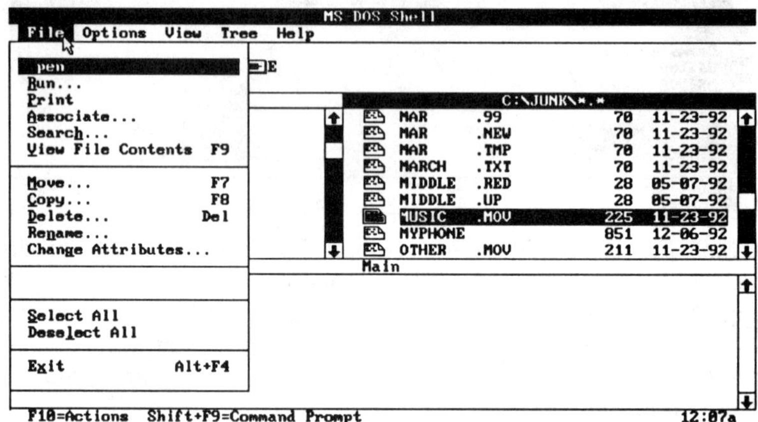

WHAT'S HAPPENING? Now that you have selected a file, the `File` menu presents you with choices you did not have before. Either you can see commands like `Copy` or `Rename` or they are no longer greyed out. If you are using the keyboard, you can use the <Up arrow> and <Down arrow> keys to move down the file list. In addition, you can select the underlined letter in the command such as C in `Copy` or D in `Delete`. Some commands have a key name next to it such as F8 which is a keyboard shortcut you can use to select the command. If you have a mouse, you only need to click the menu selection.

STEP 6: Press F8. STEP 6: Click `Copy`.

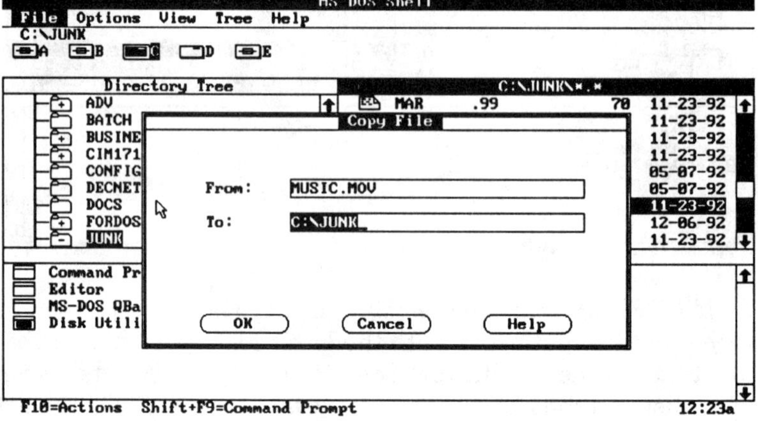

WHAT'S HAPPENING? You are presented with a dialog box. A dialog box requests more information from the user. In this case, the dialog box has to do with the **Copy** command. It is providing the source information, the file name **MUSIC.MOV** in the **From:** box, but it wants you to provide the destination information. It assumed that you want to copy the file to the default drive and directory. That is why in the **To:** box, **C:\JUNK** is already there. Since you want to copy it to the A drive, you must change the destination in the **To:** box.

STEP 7: Press the <Backspace> key until **C:\JUNK** is erased. Then key in **A:** and press <Enter>.

STEP 7: Press the <Backspace> key until **C:\JUNK** is erased. Then key in **A:** and press <Enter>.

WHAT'S HAPPENING? You saw a brief message that 1 file was being copied. Then you were returned to the file list area. How do you know that the file was copied? One way is to look at the disk in Drive A.

STEP 8: Press <Ctrl>+A.

STEP 8: Double-click the Drive A icon.

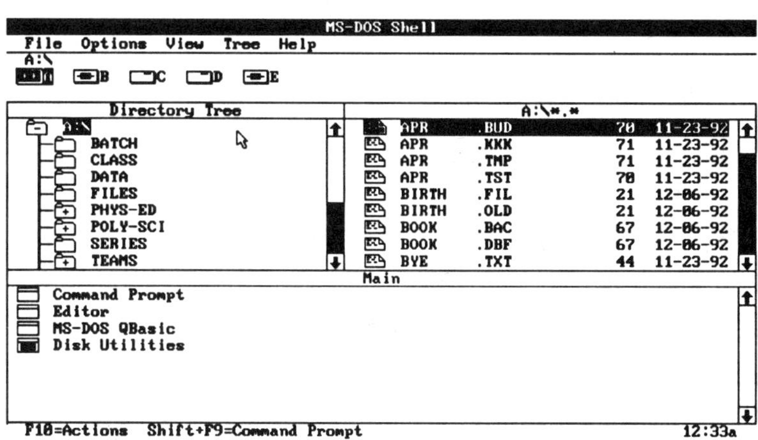

WHAT'S HAPPENING? By pressing <Ctrl>+A or clicking the Drive A icon, you told MS-DOS Shell to read the disk in Drive A. Now the default is Drive A. The file list title now says **A:*.*.** You can use the scroll bar or arrow keys to confirm that **MUSIC.MOV** was indeed copied to Drive A.

STEP 9: Press <Ctrl>+C.

STEP 9: Click the Drive C disk drive icon.

STEP 10: Select the **JUNK** subdirectory. Select the file **MUSIC.MOV** in the file list area.

STEP 10: Select the **JUNK** subdirectory. Select the file **MUSIC.MOV** in the file list area.

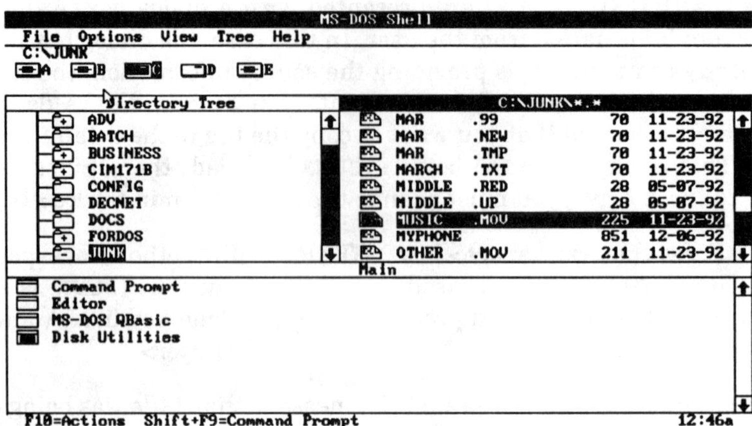

WHAT'S HAPPENING? You made Drive C the default drive. You made **JUNK** the default subdirectory. You then selected the file **MUSIC.MOV**.

STEP 11: Press <Alt>+F.

STEP 12: Press F8 for **Copy**.

STEP 13: When the dialog box appears, in the **To:** box, replace **C:\JUNK** with **A:**. Then press <Enter>.

STEP 11: Click **File** on the menu bar.

STEP 12: Click **Copy**.

STEP 13: When the dialog box appears, in the **To:** box, replace **C:\JUNK** with **A:**. Then press <Enter>.

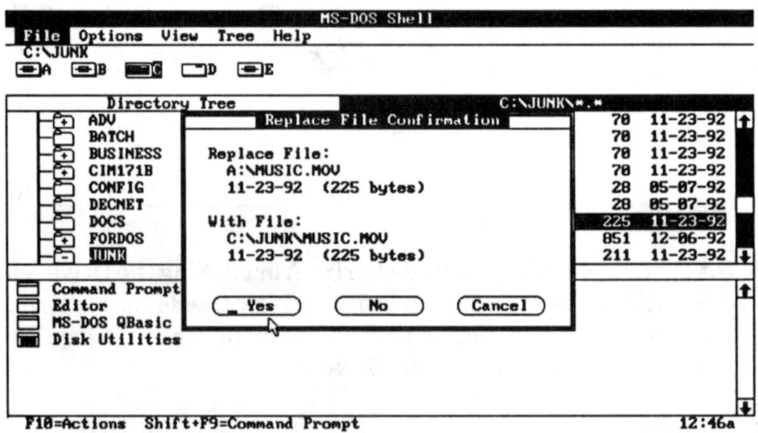

WHAT'S HAPPENING? The MS-DOS Shell informs you that the file **MUSIC.MOV** already exists on Drive A and is asking your confirmation to overwrite the file. The confirmation feature is not available at the DOS system level so DOS would overwrite it. In MS-DOS Shell you are protected from accidently overwriting a file.

STEP 14: Press the <Tab> key until Cancel is selected. Press <Enter>.

STEP 14: Click **Cancel**.

WHAT'S HAPPENING? You canceled **Copy** since you did not want to replace a file that is already on Drive A.

16.12 Manipulating Many Files

When you are at the DOS system level and you wish to manipulate more than one file, you can use wildcards if the files have some part of their name in common. When using MS-DOS Shell, you can accomplish the same goal as well as select files that have no commonality in names. However, remember that if a command cannot be used with more than one file—such as TYPE—it cannot be used with more than one file in MS-DOS Shell.

Activity 16.13 Selecting Files

Note: You are still in MS-DOS Shell. The file list area title bar is highlighted. The **JUNK** subdirectory in the **Directory Tree** area should be the selected subdirectory. The DATA disk is in Drive A.

STEP 1: Press E.

STEP 1: Press E.

STEP 2: Press the <Down arrow> key 6 times.

STEP 2: Click the down arrow on the file list scroll bar until you can see the file **EXP92JAN.DAT**.

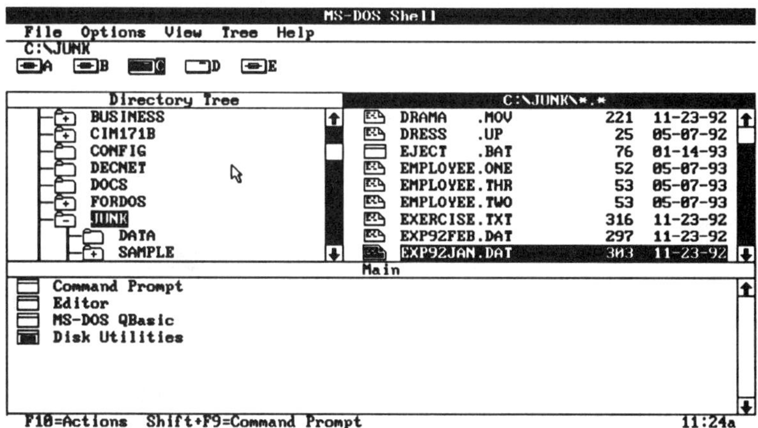

WHAT'S HAPPENING? You can see both the **EXP92JAN.DAT** and **EXP92FEB.DAT** files. You want to copy them to the DATA disk. The file called **EXP92JAN.DAT** is highlighted if you used the keyboard.

STEP 3:	Hold down the <Shift> key and press the <Up arrow> key once.	STEP 3:	Click **`EXP92JAN.DAT`**. Hold down the <Shift> key and click **`EXP92FEB.DAT`**.

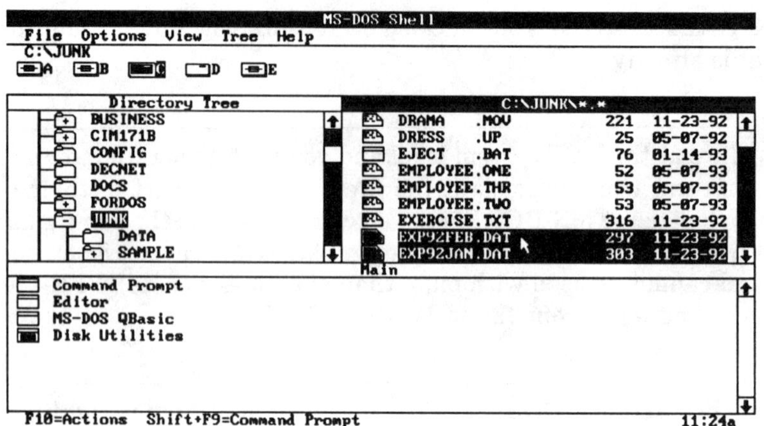

WHAT'S HAPPENING? You selected two adjacent files.

STEP 4:	Press <Alt>+F.	STEP 4:	Click **`File`** on the menu bar.
STEP 5:	Press F8.	STEP 5:	Click **`Copy`**.

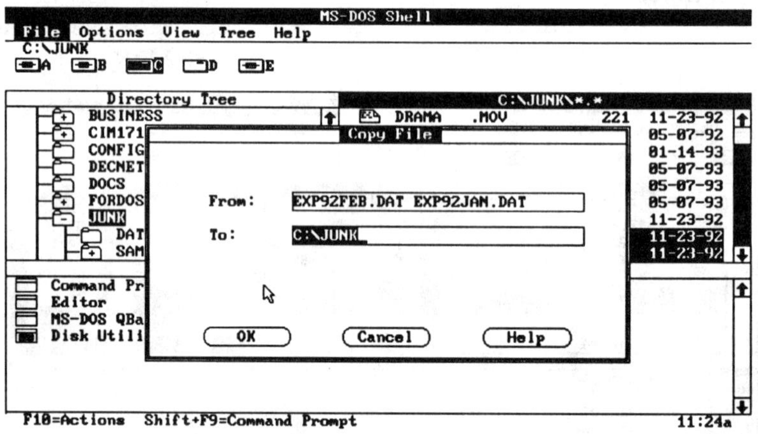

WHAT'S HAPPENING? You see the dialog box for the **`Copy File`**. Both the selected files are in the **`From:`** box.

STEP 6:	Change the **`C:\JUNK`** in the **`To:`** box to **`A:\`**.	STEP 6:	Change the **`C:\JUNK`** in the **`To:`** box to **`A:\`**.
STEP 7:	Press <Enter>.	STEP 7:	Click **`OK`**.

WHAT'S HAPPENING? You see a message which tells you that the files are being copied one file at a time. Then you are returned to the file list area with the same two files highlighted. However, what if you wanted to perform some action on files that were not adjacent to each other?

STEP 8: Press F.

STEP 8: Press F.

STEP 9: Press the <Down arrow> key 9 times.

STEP 9: Click the down arrow on the file list scroll bar 9 times.

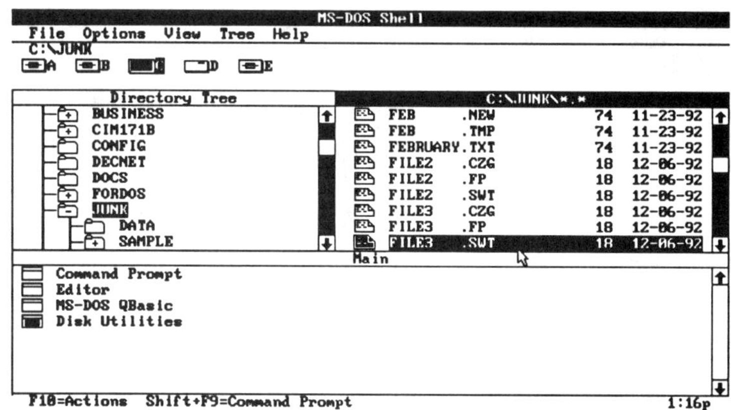

WHAT'S HAPPENING? You want to copy `FILE3.SWT` and `FILE2.SWT` to the DATA disk. However, they are not next to each other.

STEP 10: Press <Shift>+F8.

STEP 10: Click `FILE3.SWT.`

STEP 11: Press the <Up arrow> key 3 times. When `FILE2.SWT` is highlighted, press the <Spacebar>.

STEP 11: Hold down the <Ctrl> key and click `FILE2.SWT.`

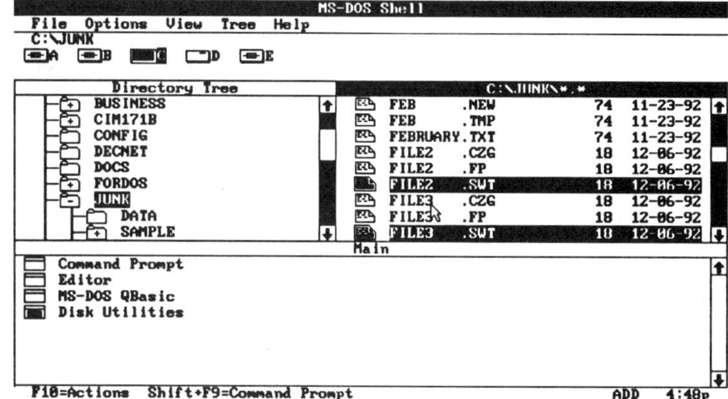

WHAT'S HAPPENING? If you were using the keyboard, you saw `ADD` appear on the status bar when you pressed <Shift>+F8. You selected two nonadjacent files. Now that you have selected them, you can work with them. However, you are now going to cancel your selection.

STEP 12: Press <Alt>+F.	STEP 12: Click `File` on the menu bar.
STEP 13: Press the letter L for `Deselect All`.	STEP 13: Click `Deselect All`.

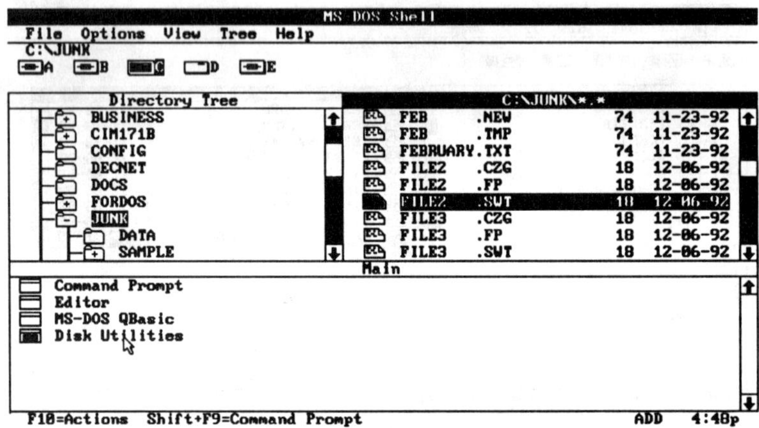

WHAT'S HAPPENING? You quickly unselected all the files.

16.14 Printing Files with MS-DOS Shell

If you want to print a file using MS-DOS Shell, you may. However, MS-DOS Shell does not have a print command of its own. You must first load the PRINT command into memory. You can either do it before loading MS-DOS Shell or from within MS-DOS Shell. If you do it from MS-DOS Shell, you can temporarily exit MS-DOS Shell or you can execute the PRINT program from MS-DOS Shell.

Activity 16.15 Using PRINT in MS-DOS Shell

Note: You are still in MS-DOS Shell. The file list area is highlighted. The `JUNK` subdirectory in the `Directory Tree` area is the selected subdirectory. The DATA disk is in Drive A.

STEP 1: Use the <Tab> key to highlight the `Directory Tree` title bar.	STEP 1: Click the `Directory Tree` title bar.
STEP 2: Use the <Tab> key to highlight the `DOS` subdirectory.	STEP 2: Click the `DOS` subdirectory.

Note: If your DOS programs are in another subdirectory, you must use that subdirectory name. **PRINT.EXE** is sometimes called **PRINT.COM**.

STEP 3:	Use the <Tab> key to highlight the file list area.	STEP 3:	Click the file list area title bar.
STEP 4:	Select the file **PRINT.EXE**.	STEP 4:	Select the file **PRINT.EXE**.

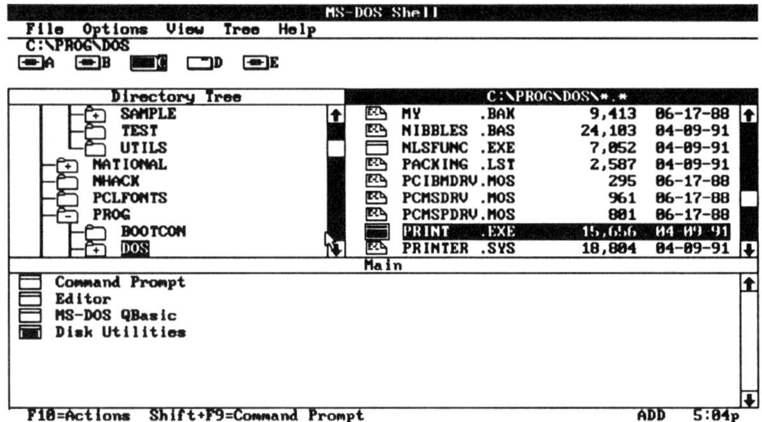

WHAT'S HAPPENING? You selected the **PRINT.EXE** (**.COM**) file. However, this time, instead of manipulating a file by copying it, you want to execute or run it. You still use the **File** menu but you select **Run**. Be sure the printer is on.

STEP 5:	Press <Alt>+F.	STEP 5:	Click **File**.
STEP 6:	Press R.	STEP 6:	Click **Run**.

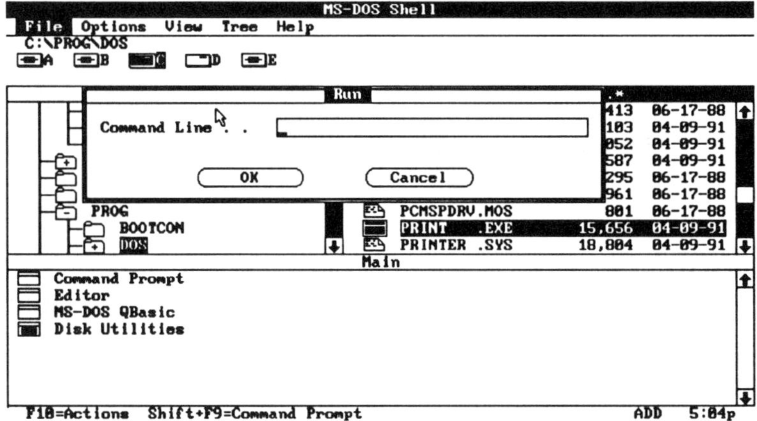

WHAT'S HAPPENING? You see a dialog box asking you what program you wish to execute. If you wanted to, when you selected PRINT in the file list area, you could have double-clicked the file name **PRINT.EXE**. If you were a keyboard user, you could have pressed <Enter> after you selected **PRINT.EXE**.

STEP 7: In the **Command Line:** box key in **PRINT**. Then press <Enter>.	STEP 7: In the **Command Line:** box key in **PRINT**. Then click **OK**.

```
Name of list device [PRN]:
```

WHAT'S HAPPENING? You temporarily exited MS-DOS Shell. The command line prompt wants to know the name of your printer. If PRINT has already been loaded, you will not see this message.

STEP 8: Press <Enter>.	STEP 8: Press <Enter>.

```
Name of list device [PRN]:
Resident part of PRINT installed
PRINT queue is empty


Press any key to return to MS-DOS Shell....
```

WHAT'S HAPPENING? The memory-resident program PRINT was loaded into memory. It will remain in memory until you turn off the system. You can print from within MS-DOS Shell by selecting a file and then choosing **Print** from the **File** menu. Now that you have loaded PRINT, you need to return to the Shell to continue using it. The Shell tells you to press any key, which is equivalent to keying in **EXIT** when you temporarily left the Shell by selecting **Command Prompt** earlier in the chapter.

STEP 9: Press any key.	STEP 9: Press any key.

WHAT'S HAPPENING? You returned to MS-DOS Shell ready to print a file.

STEP 10: Press <Ctrl>+A.	STEP 10: Double-click the Drive A icon.
STEP 11: Use the <Tab> key to highlight the file list title bar.	STEP 11: Click the file list title bar.
STEP 12: Press M.	STEP 12: Press M.
STEP 13: Select the file **MUSIC.MOV**.	STEP 13: Select the file **MUSIC.MOV**.

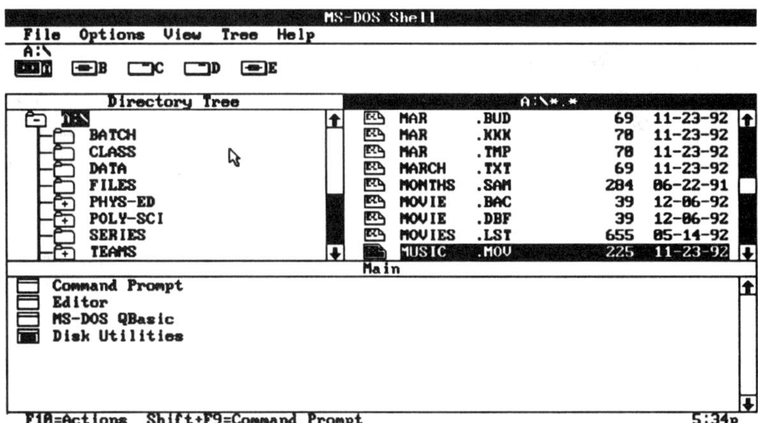

WHAT'S HAPPENING? You chose to look at the disk in Drive A. You then went to the file list area and selected the file called `MUSIC.MOV`. Once the file has been selected, you can manipulate it. In this case, you want to print it. You can print it because the PRINT command is resident in memory.

STEP 14: Press <Alt>+F.

STEP 14: Click **`File`**.

STEP 15: Press P.

STEP 15: Click **`Print`**.

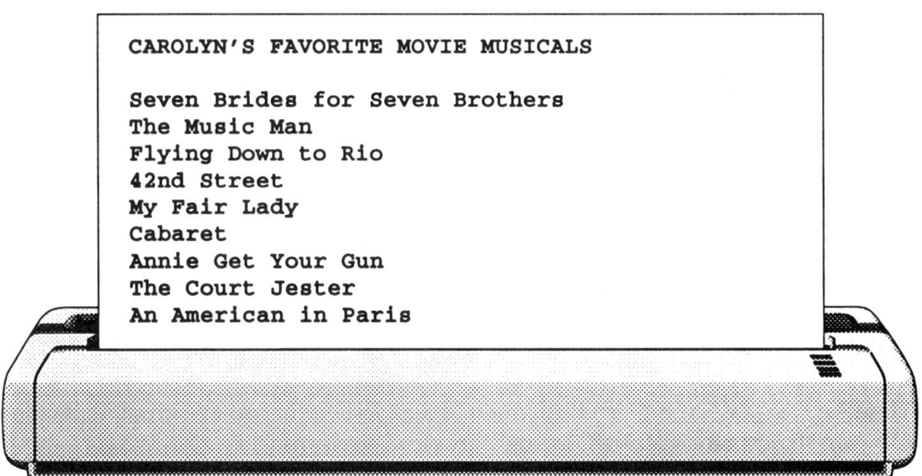
CAROLYN'S FAVORITE MOVIE MUSICALS

Seven Brides for Seven Brothers
The Music Man
Flying Down to Rio
42nd Street
My Fair Lady
Cabaret
Annie Get Your Gun
The Court Jester
An American in Paris

WHAT'S HAPPENING? You have a printout of this file. You also returned to MS-DOS Shell.

STEP 16: Press <Alt>+F.

STEP 16: Click **`File`**.

STEP 17: Press X.

STEP 17: Click **`Exit`**.

```
A:\>_
```

WHAT'S HAPPENING? You left MS-DOS Shell and returned to the system level prompt. The last time you were in MS-DOS Shell, you selected Drive A. When you exited MS-DOS Shell, DOS remembered which drive you had previously used and returned to it. You can do many things with MS-DOS Shell. It is another way to use DOS commands.

16.16 The Disk Utilities

MS-DOS Shell provides some commonly used DOS disk manipulation commands on its **Main** screen. These include DISKCOPY, BACKUP, RESTORE, FORMAT, QUICK FORMAT and UNDELETE.

Activity 16.17 Looking at the Utilities

Note: You are in Drive A with the **A:\>** displayed.

STEP 1: Key in the following: A:\>**C:** <Enter>	STEP 1: Key in the following: A:\>**C:** <Enter>
STEP 2: Key in the following: C:\>**DOSSHELL** <Enter>	STEP 2: Key in the following: C:\>**DOSSHELL** <Enter>

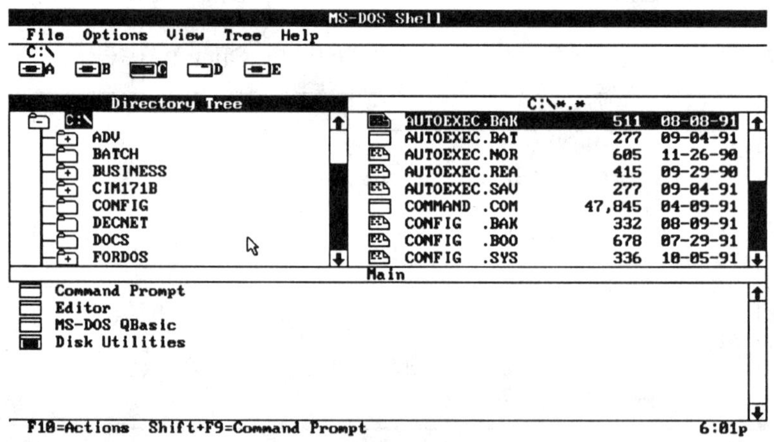

WHAT'S HAPPENING? You reloaded MS-DOS Shell. You are going to look at the **Disk Utilities** MS-DOS Shell provides for you.

STEP 3: Press the <Tab> key until the **Main** title bar is highlighted. Then press the <Down arrow> key 3 times until **Disk Utilities** is highlighted. Then press <Enter>.	STEP 3: Double-click **Disk Utilities** in **Main**.

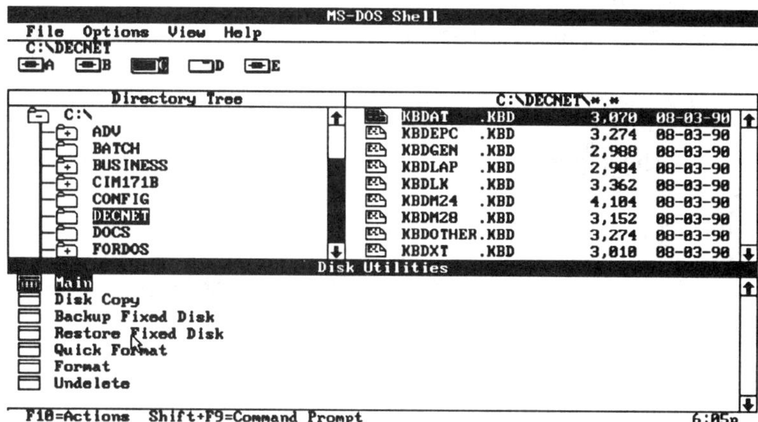

WHAT'S HAPPENING? MS-DOS Shell provides you with some disk functions on this menu. If you wanted to use one of them, you would select it. If you have a mouse, you would double-click your selection. If you are using the keyboard, you would <Tab> to your selection and press <Enter>. You could also execute any of these commands by selecting `Run` from the `File` menu and keying in the command name.

STEP 4: Press <Esc>.

STEP 4: Press <Esc>.

STEP 5: Press <Alt>+F4.

STEP 5: Press <Alt>+F4.

```
C:\>_
```

WHAT'S HAPPENING? You canceled the `Disk Utilities` selection and quit MS-DOS Shell which returned you to the root directory of C:\.

Chapter Summary

1. Shells provide a different user interface from the command line prompt.
2. Shells surround DOS and cover the details of the operating system from the user.
3. Shells differ from menu systems in that menus are lists of choices whereas shells provide an operating system environment.
4. A GUI is a graphical user interface.
5. A shell may have menus, but a menu system is not necessarily a shell.
6. Microsoft has a powerful operating environment called Windows that runs best with powerful hardware.
7. DOS 4.0 and above provides a free shell called DOS Shell or MS-DOS Shell.
8. MS-DOS Shell does not require any special hardware.
9. You can use a mouse with MS-DOS Shell. A mouse is an input device that is rolled on a flat surface. Any mouse movement on the flat surface correspondingly moves the cursor on the screen.

10. When using a mouse, click means to press the left mouse button once. Double-click means to press the left mouse button twice, quickly. To drag an item on the screen means to place the cursor on the selected item and then press and hold the left button while you move the mouse. When you reach the location you want, release the left mouse button.
11. When using the keyboard in MS-DOS Shell, you select items by use of the <Tab> key, the F10 key, and/or the arrow keys.
12. If you have a graphics monitor, MS-DOS Shell will display pictures called icons. Icons represent items.
13. To install MS-DOS Shell or DOS Shell, key in **DOSSHELL** at the system prompt.
14. The initial installation of MS-DOS Shell provides you with a menu bar, a `Directory Tree` area, a file list area, a status line, and a `Main` area that includes the `Command Prompt`, `Editor`, `QBasic`, and `Disk Utilities`.
15. You move within the areas by clicking the title bar of the area or using the <Tab> key.
16. DOS Shell provides online help.
17. Many of the selections provide drop-down menus. Drop-down menus are not visible until you select them. You then make a choice from the menu.
18. Drop-down menus are activated by clicking the word `File` on the menu bar or by using <Alt>+F to drop the menu down.
19. When the `Command Prompt` is selected, you are returned to the DOS system prompt temporarily. It operates as it normally does. To return to MS-DOS Shell, key in **EXIT**.
20. MS-DOS Shell allows you to manage directories by using the `Directory Tree`.
21. If a directory has a plus sign preceding it, it can be expanded. This means it has subdirectories beneath it.
22. If a directory has a minus sign preceding it, it can be collapsed. This means you can close it to its highest level.
23. You can collapse and expand directories by using the mouse, the keyboard, or selecting from the menu.
24. The file list allows you to manipulate files using such DOS commands as COPY and RENAME. You must first select a file before you can manipulate it.
25. If you drop down the `File` menu and commands are greyed out or not visible, they are not available to use.
26. You may select more than one file to manipulate. However, the rules of DOS still apply. If you cannot use wildcards with the command (such as TYPE), then you cannot select more than one file in the file list area.
27. Dialog boxes are presented by MS-DOS Shell when it needs more information.
28. To print files in MS-DOS Shell, you must first load the PRINT command. PRINT can be placed in the **AUTOEXEC.BAT** file or it may be loaded from the shell.

29. You may execute programs by double-clicking the mouse on the selected program name or selecting the file name and then pressing <Enter>. You may also choose the `Run` command from the `File` menu.
30. The `Disk Utilities` in the `Main` area provide some commonly used disk management commands such as FORMAT and DISKCOPY.

Command and Key Summary

<Alt>+F4	Quits MS-DOS Shell.
<Alt>+letter	Selects item from menu bar.
<Ctrl>+drive letter	Changes disk drive.
DOSSHELL	Loads DOS Shell or MS-DOS Shell.
<End>	Scrolls to end of list.
Exit	Returns you to MS-DOS Shell from the command line prompt.
<Home>	Scrolls to beginning of list.
<PgUp> or <PgDn>	Moves you up or down one window.
<Shift>+F9	Leaves MS-DOS Shell temporarily.
<Tab>	Moves you from area to area.

Key Terms

Area titles
Directory tree
Drop-down menu
Ellipsis
File list area
GUI (graphical user interface)
Highlighting
Icons
Mouse pointer
Program list area
Scroll bars
Shell
Slider box
Title bar

Discussion Questions

1. What are shells?
2. What is a mouse?
3. What are icons?
4. What is MS-DOS Shell?
5. Describe the difference between shells and menu programs.
6. What is a GUI?
7. How do you start MS-DOS Shell from the system prompt?
8. Describe the purpose and operation of the `Command Prompt` in MS-DOS Shell.
9. What is the `Directory Tree` area?
10. How would you use the `Directory Tree` area?
11. What does a plus sign (+) mean preceding a directory name?
12. What does a minus sign (-) mean preceding a directory name?
13. What is the file list area?
14. How can it be used?
15. If you wish to manipulate a file, what is one of the most important things you must first do?
16. Identify the purpose of two choices available on the drop-down `File` menu.

17. How do you change disk drives using MS-DOS Shell?
18. Name two ways to execute programs within MS-DOS Shell.
19. What is the first task you must do prior to printing a file within MS-DOS Shell?
20. What does the EXIT command do? When do you use it?
21. What is the difference between quitting DOS Shell and exiting MS-DOS Shell?
22. What are drop-down menus? What is their function?
23. What is a dialog box? What is its function?
24. Why must you select a file prior to performing an operation on it?
25. Explain any differences in the COPY command in MS-DOS Shell and at the system prompt.

Application Assignments

Note: All files are written to the DATA disk. Use MS-DOS Shell, unless otherwise indicated. If you do not have a necessary file on the DATA disk, copy it from `C:\JUNK` or a subdirectory under `\JUNK`.

1. For the following assignment:
   a. Number from 1 to 14 on a separate piece of paper.
   b. Using the list below, identify by letter each numbered item on the screen display on the next page.

   A. Current drive-directory
   B. `Directory Tree` area
   C. `Directory Tree` title bar
   D. Drive icons
   E. File list area
   F. File list title bar
   G. Menu bar
   H. Mouse pointer
   I. Program list area
   J. Program list title bar
   K. Scroll bar(s)
   L. Selection cursor
   M. Subdirectory icon
   N. Status bar

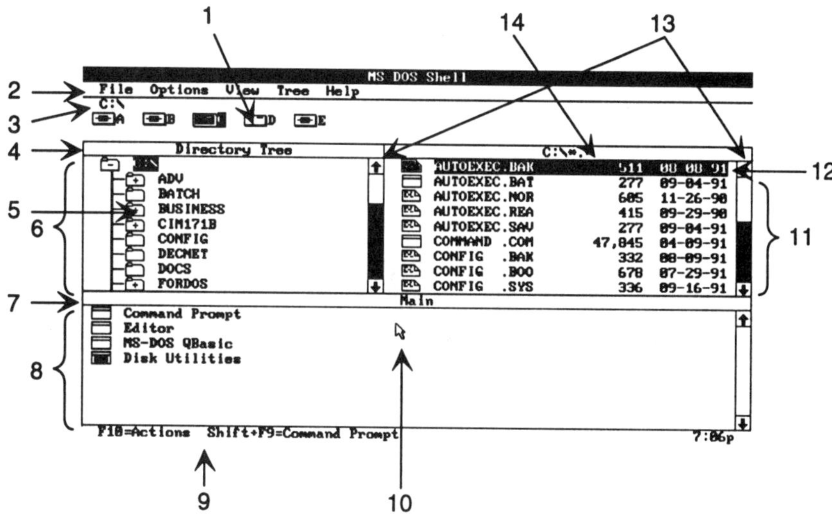

2. For the following assignment:
   a. Use Help to find informaton on the "Run Command." (Hint: You must locate "File List Menus," and then "File Menus.")
   b. On a separate piece of paper, write down what you found about out the "Run Command."
3. For the following activity:
   a. Locate the file called `FRANK.FIL` in the subdirectory `JUNK`.
   b. Copy it to a new file called `FRANK.YOU` on the DATA disk.
   c. Describe each step you took.
   d. Delete the file called `FRANK.YOU` on the DATA disk.
   e. Describe each step you took.
4. For the following assignment:
   a. Check the disk in Drive A with CHKDSK while in MS-DOS Shell.
   b. Describe the steps you took to accomplish the task.
5. For the following assignment:
   a. Locate the file called `OTHER.MOV` in the subdirectory `JUNK`.
   b. Copy it to a new file called `FILMS.MOV` on the DATA disk.
   c. Describe each step you took.
   d. Print the file called `FILMS.MOV`.
   e. Delete the file called `FILMS.MOV` on the DATA disk.
   f. Describe each step you took.

Challenge Assignments

6. For the following assignment:
   a. Using the `Options` on the menu bar, sort the DATA disk by file extension in descending order.
   b. On a piece of paper write the names of the first and last files listed.
7. For the following assignment, use `View` on the menu bar.
   a. Change the view to `Program List`.
   b. Change the view back to `Program/File Lists`.
   c. Describe on paper the different views.

17 Chapter

Utility Programs:
Norton Utilities and PC Tools

After completing this chapter you will be able to:

1. Compare and contrast utility programs to application programs.
2. Name some common functions of utility programs.
3. Describe sources of utility programs.
4. Use selected Norton Utilities programs.
5. Display information about your computer hardware using Norton Utilities.
6. Describe why you can recover a deleted file.
7. Unerase a file using Norton Utilities.
8. Use selected PC Tools utility programs.
9. Unerase a file using PC Tools and DOS 5.0.
10. Explain a fragmented disk.
11. Compress a disk using the COMPRESS program of PC Tools.

Chapter Overview

This chapter introduces DOS utility programs. You will learn what a utility program is and how to use it. Two major utility programs will be introduced, Norton Utilities and PC Tools. You will use some utilities from each program. In addition, you will use the UNDELETE command found in the latest version of DOS.

17.0

Utility Programs

In the preceding chapters, you used DOS commands. As you worked, you may have noticed that there were tasks you could not accomplish with DOS commands. Other people have also noticed some of the absent features of DOS. They wrote utility programs to accomplish nonstandard DOS tasks. Indeed, utility programs can be written for many different kinds of software application programs, making the applications easier to use. Typically, utility programs are too small and too specific to be considered application programs.

Many of these programs are available to you. If you know how to program, you can write a utility program for yourself. You can get them from such sources as an **electronic bulletin board**. These bulletin boards include a forum where people exchange ideas or solve computer problems. They can also be the place where programmers leave programs for anyone who wants them. Electronic bulletin boards usually belong to a service such as Prodigy or CompuServe and are available to you through the use of a modem. Sometimes, these programs are free; sometimes they are shareware. Since most of these utility programs were written for programmers by programmers, utilities can be cryptic and complex.

You can also purchase utility programs. There are literally thousands of commercial utility programs available. Two of the most popular are Norton Utilities and PC Tools. Both of these programs almost move into the application area, because they provide many utilities and have user-friendly menus. Both of these utility programs provide many powerful additions to DOS.

It is not uncommon for users to purchase more than one utility program. Although there are overlaps, there are also differences. For instance, Norton Utilities, PC Tools, and DOS 5.0 have an "unerase" feature. Norton Utilities has a batch file enhancer that allows you to write more powerful batch files, whereas PC Tools does not. PC Tools includes a hard disk backup option which is not included in Norton Utilities. In this chapter we are going to take a look at some of the features of both PC Tools and Norton Utilities along with the most important utility features of the latest version of DOS.

17.1 Norton Utilities

Peter Norton almost single-handedly began the DOS utilities industry. His first version of Norton Utilities was comprised of only six programs—one of which, UNERASE, built his empire. UNERASE does what it sounds like. It allows a user to retrieve a file that was accidently erased—something not available in DOS until DOS 5.0. Norton Utilities prior to version 6.01 came in two flavors, Standard Edition and Advanced Edition. The Advanced Edition had more commands than the Standard Edition. Version 6.01, the latest release of Norton Utilities, combines the Standard and Advanced Editions as well as introducing some new features. We will look at version 6.01 in this chapter.

Norton Utilities version 6.01 is a complex set of utilities that can be divided into several general categories. These include data recovery and disk repair, speed and performance enhancements, security, other miscellaneous tools, and command line utilities including a new command processor.

Data recovery and disk repair programs include:

Norton Disk Doctor Repairs most logical and physical disk drive problems.
Unerase Unerases files.
Unformat Recovers the hard disk if you accidentally format it.
Erase protect Protects deleted files from being overwritten so that they can be more rapidly recovered.

Image Stores a picture of the structure of a disk and assists in recovering data.
File fix Repairs corrupted Lotus and dBase files.
Disk editor Allows you to edit data at any location on the hard disk.
Disk tools Assists you in such tasks as making a disk bootable or marking clusters.

Speed and performance enhancement programs include:

Speed disk Optimizes the hard disk.
Calibrat Provides such tasks as low-level formatting and performs many system tests.
Norton cache Provides a better and faster cache than DOS.

Security programs include:

Disk monitor Provides read/write protection, parks heads, and informs you whenever disk drives are being accessed.
Diskreet Encrypts and decrypts files for data protection and provides password protection.
Wipeinfo Deletes files so that they can never be recovered.

Tool programs include:

Safe format Protects you against accidentally formatting a disk.
File find Searches all directories for files and allows different search criteria.
Norton change directory Allows you to move among your directories quickly while providing graphical displays of directories.
Norton Control Center Allows you to modify your hardware settings.
System information Reports on your hardware, memory usage, and more.
Batch enhancer Provides commands to make batch files even more powerful.

The following command line utilities allow you to use Norton Utilities from the DOS prompt without having to be in a full-screen version of Norton Utilities. The command line utilities include:

Directory sort Sorts files in directories.
File attributes Allows you to change the attributes of files.
File date Allows you to change the date and time of a file.
File locate Allows you to locate any file quickly.
File size Shows you the exact size of a file.
Line print Allows you to print text files from the command line.
Text search Allows you to search for some specified text that is in a file.

In addition, NDOS is a replacement for `COMMAND.COM`. NDOS is also a command processor but is more powerful than `COMMAND.COM`.

Norton Utilities can be run from a menu system or you can run individual utility programs from the DOS prompt. Norton Utilities 6.01 comes on either four 5 1/4-inch high-density or four 3 1/2-inch disks. Both types of disks are included in the package.

The instructions for installing Norton Utilities are beyond the scope of this textbook. You can follow the instructions in the manual that comes with Norton Utilities. However, installation is fairly easy. You place the disk labeled INSTALL and at the DOS prompt key in **INSTALL**. Often, users purchase Norton Utilities because they have just erased an important file. Hence, the general instructions include special instructions that allow you to recover a file prior to installing Norton Utilities. You may not simply copy the files to a subdirectory. The files are large and come in a **compressed** or **archived** format that must be uncompressed or unarchived. This process is common with newer software application packages.

As you can see, mastering Norton Utilities would take a lot of time. Hence, we are going to sample utilities from Norton Utilities, using them with or without menus.

17.2 System Information

The system information portion of Norton Utilities gives you a plethora of facts about your system. You will get information about your hardware and memory and a benchmark test that will tell you how fast your system is. This command will even print reports for you. In the next activity, you will look at the menu and select the system information.

Activity 17.3 Loading Norton Utilities and Using System Information

Note: You have installed Norton Utilities on a hard disk and the path is set to the subdirectory where Norton Utilities is installed. Although some utilities can be run from a floppy disk, these utilities are really most effective on a hard disk.

STEP 1: Key in the following:
C:\>**NORTON** <Enter>

```
 Menu   Configuration   Advise   Quit!                         F1=Help

                    Norton Utilities
                      Version 6.0
           A Product of Symantec Corporation
                   Carolyn Z. Gillay
                     THE BOOK BIZ

                                                      Norton Utilities
```

WHAT'S HAPPENING? You see this screen briefly before the next screen appears.

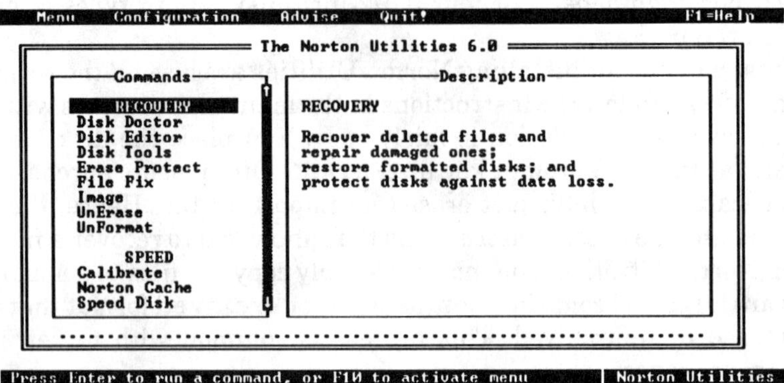

WHAT'S HAPPENING? You see the first menu of Norton Utilities. `Recovery` is highlighted. On the right-hand side of the display, you see a capsule description of what is displayed on the left-hand side.

If you are using keystrokes, use the instructional steps in the left column. If you are using a mouse, use the instructional steps in the right column.

STEP 2: Use the <Down arrow> key to highlight `Disk Doctor`.

STEP 2: Click `Disk Doctor`.

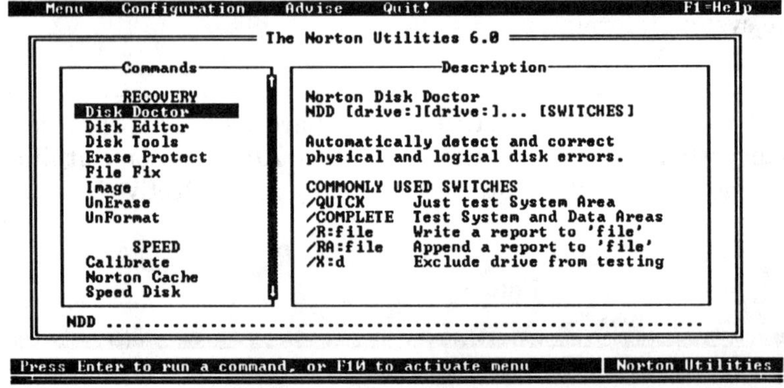

WHAT'S HAPPENING? As you highlighted the item labeled `Disk Doctor`, the purpose of the command appeared on the right-hand side of the screen. In addition, the syntax and all the parameters with their purposes are displayed. On the bottom of the screen is `NDD`. If you wanted to use this command from the DOS prompt, you would key in `NDD`.

STEP 3: Use the <Down arrow> key until `System Info` is highlighted. It is listed under the major heading `TOOLS`.

STEP 3: Click the scroll bar until `System Info` is highlighted.

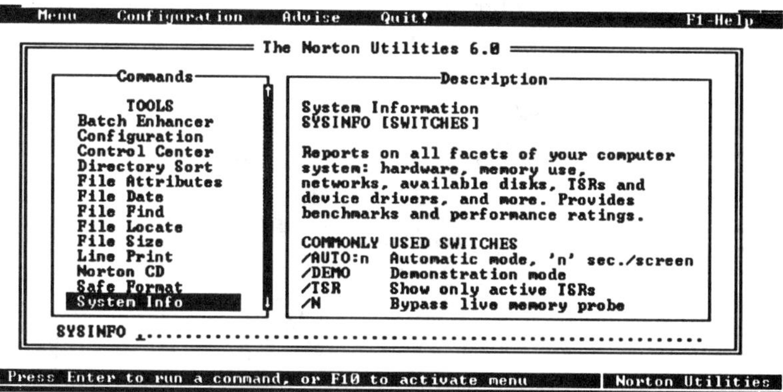

WHAT'S HAPPENING? The description tells you that by using this command, you will get a report on your hardware and software. It provides the syntax and the parameters. Again, if you wanted to use this command at the DOS prompt, you could. Look at the bottom of the screen. It displays SYSINFO. SYSINFO is the non-menu DOS command.

STEP 4: Press <Enter>. STEP 4: Double-click `System Info`.

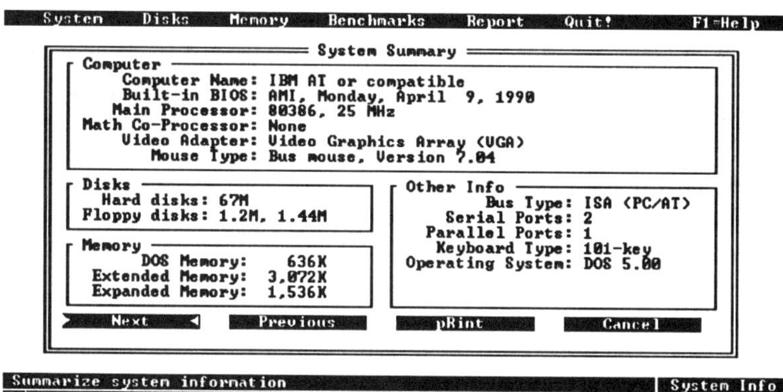

WHAT'S HAPPENING? Your report will vary based on your hardware. The screen is divided into four report areas: the `Computer` itself, the `Disks`, `Memory`, and `Other Info`. Most of the items are self-explanatory. However, there are some interesting things to notice. One is the `Built-in BIOS`, which could be important information if you ever have difficulty running programs. Being able to know the BIOS manufacturer and the date of manufacture can be important tools in diagnosing problems. Common BIOS are AMI—the one listed here—and Phoenix. By looking at this report, you see that this computer is a 386 that runs at 25 megahertz. You see that there is a 67 MB hard disk drive, one floppy 1.2 MB floppy disk drive and one 1.44 MB floppy disk drive. In addition, the report indicates that there is a VGA monitor, a bus mouse, 1 parallel and 2 serial ports. One fun exercise is to run a **benchmark** test to see how quickly your system operates.

STEP 5: Use the F10 key to highlight the menu bar. Highlight **Benchmarks** by pressing the <Right arrow> key.

STEP 5: Click **Benchmarks** on the menu bar.

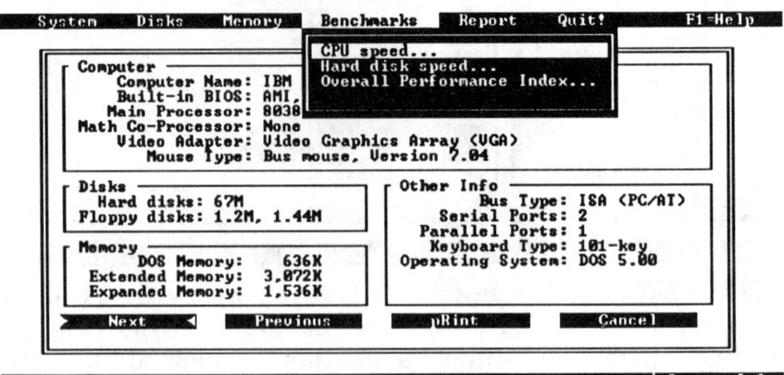

WHAT'S HAPPENING? As you move along the menu bar with the arrow keys, drop-down menus indicating further choices appear for each item on the menu. The `CPU speed` line is highlighted.

STEP 6: Press <Enter>.

STEP 6: Click `CPU speed`.

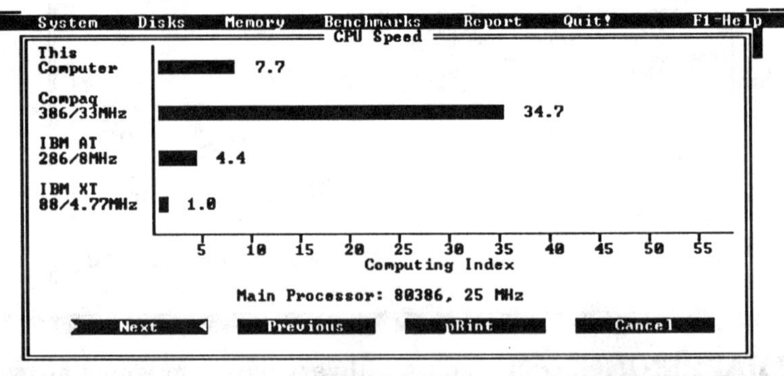

WHAT'S HAPPENING? Norton Utilities uses three computers and compares them to the unit being tested. The first is the Compaq 386 at 33 MHz, which is a very fast, relatively high-technology machine. The next computer benchmark is the IBM AT 286/8 MHz machine. This computer is older and not nearly as fast as the Compaq. In fact, the Compaq runs more than 34 times the speed of the IBM AT class computer. The last benchmark is an IBM XT machine with the old 8088/4.77 MHz performance level. It is quite slow. This particular machine runs almost twice as fast as the AT 286 but not nearly as fast as the Compaq 386.

STEP 7:	Use the F10 key to highlight the menu bar. Move until **`Benchmarks`** is highlighted. Use the <Down arrow> key to highlight **`Overall Performance Index`**.	STEP 7:	Click **`Benchmarks`**.

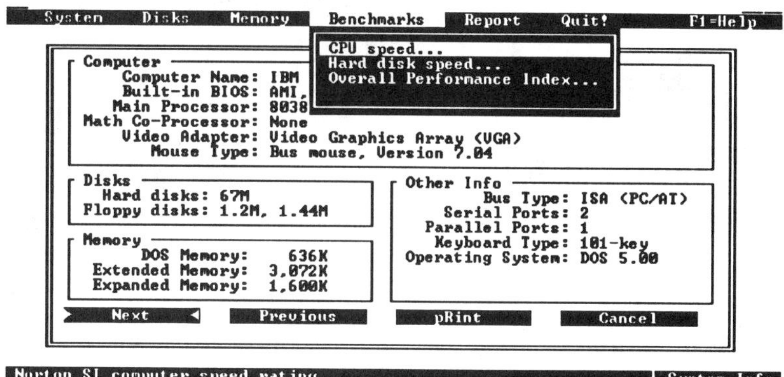

WHAT'S HAPPENING? **`Network performance speed`** is greyed out because this computer is not hooked up to a network.

STEP 8:	Press <Enter>.	STEP 8:	Click **`Overall Performance Index`**.

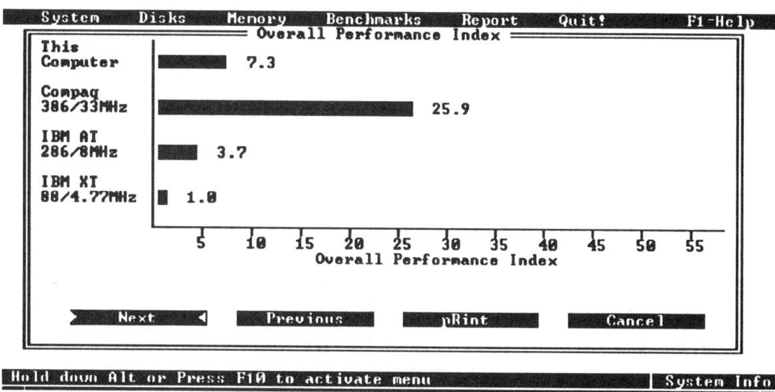

WHAT'S HAPPENING? Again, the benchmark compares a Compaq, IBM AT, and IBM XT to the computer you are testing. The Compaq is definitely the fastest. This computer's overall performance is much faster than either of the IBM computers. You are going to exit **`Benchmarks`**.

STEP 9:	Use the F10 and <Right arrow> keys to highlight **`Quit!`** on the menu bar. Press <Enter>.	STEP 9:	Click **`Quit!`**.

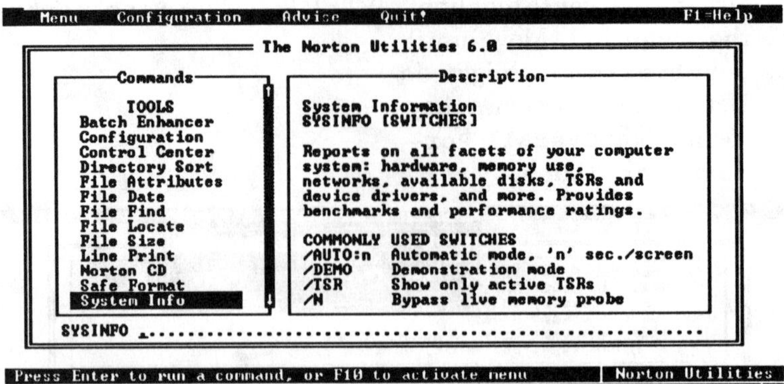

WHAT'S HAPPENING? You returned to the main menu. You can either highlight `Quit!` to return to DOS, or you can use the <Esc> key to return to DOS.

STEP 10: Press <Esc>. STEP 10: Click `Quit!`

```
C:\>_
```

WHAT'S HAPPENING? You returned to the system prompt.

17.4 UNERASE in Norton Utilities

Who among us has not accidentally deleted a file or group of files? It always seems that the files you accidentally delete are the most important. When you are using the DOS command prompt, DOS Shell, or even Windows and delete a file, your file is gone from the disk. This tragedy means untold work recreating the file. This tragic event is one of the reasons why Norton Utilities is so popular. It has a utility program called UNERASE that allows you to recover a deleted file.

As mentioned in Chapter 7, when you delete a file, DOS does not eliminate the data. It simply changes the first character in the file's directory entry to the extended ASCII character σ which indicates to DOS that there is an available directory entry. DOS then adjusts the clusters in the FAT to indicate an available disk cluster. Because DOS does not actually erase the data or the cluster numbers, Norton Utilities can allow you to recover a deleted file.

The best time to unerase a file is immediately after you deleted it. Remember, if DOS indicates that the clusters and directory entry are available, the next time you write a file to disk, DOS will overwrite that area. Once that is done, you cannot be sure of recovering all the data. However, the UNERASE program is very sophisticated, and it may be able to save part of the overwritten file, sometimes, depending on how many files you have written to the disk.

In the next activity, you will unerase a file without using the menu. Although you do not choose the program from the menu, when you key in the command at the DOS prompt, it will bring up a menu for that specific program. Each Norton Utility has a menu.

Activity 17.5 Using UNERASE

Note: You have Norton Utilities installed on a hard disk and the path is set to the subdirectory where Norton Utilities is installed. The **C:\>** is displayed and the DATA disk is in Drive A. If the specified files are not on the DATA disk, they can be copied from **C:\JUNK**.

STEP 1: Key in the following:
C:\>**DIR A:WILD3.ZZZ** <Enter>

```
C:\>DIR A:WILD3.ZZZ

 Volume in drive A is DATA DISK
 Volume Serial Number is 3D4F-0EC7
 Directory of A:\

WILD3     ZZZ      63   11-23-91   7:42a
         1 file(s)     14336 bytes free

C:\>_
```

WHAT'S HAPPENING? The file called **WILD3.ZZZ** is on the DATA disk.

STEP 2: Key in the following:
C:\>**TYPE A:WILD3.ZZZ** <Enter>

STEP 3: Key in the following:
C:\>**DEL A:WILD3.ZZZ** <Enter>

STEP 4: Key in the following:
C:\>**DIR A:WILD3.ZZZ** <Enter>

```
C:\>TYPE A:WILD3.ZZZ
This is another wildcard file
with a file extension of zzz.

C:\>DEL A:WILD3.ZZZ

C:\>DIR A:WILD3.ZZZ

 Volume in drive A is DATA DISK
 Volume Serial Number is 3D4F-0EC7
 Directory of A:\

File not found

C:\>_
```

WHAT'S HAPPENING? You displayed the contents of the file **WILD3.ZZZ**, then deleted it. When you used the DIR command, DOS told you the file was gone.

STEP 5: Key in the following:
C:\>**UNERASE** <Enter>

```
 File   Search   Options   Quit!                                  F1-Help
        ──────────────── Erased files in C:\ ───────────────────
           Name           Size       Date       Time     Prognosis
        ─────────────────────────────────────────────────────────
         DECNET            DIR      2-14-91    9:18 pm   SUB-DIR
         DONEBOOK          DIR      4-19-91    1:58 pm   SUB-DIR
         JUNK              DIR     11-23-92    7:00 am   SUB-DIR
         LETTERS           DIR      5-27-91    9:07 pm   SUB-DIR
         NATIONAL          DIR      2-17-91    6:19 pm   SUB-DIR
         PCLFONTS          DIR      4-27-91    6:20 pm   SUB-DIR
         POOLRAD           DIR      7-17-91    9:28 pm   SUB-DIR
         PROG              DIR      7-28-90    4:11 pm   SUB-DIR
         SCREEN            DIR      4-22-93   10:10 am   SUB-DIR
         TEMP              DIR      8-06-90   11:07 pm   SUB-DIR
         WORDBOOK          DIR      2-17-91    6:19 pm   SUB-DIR
         WPBOOK            DIR      2-14-91   11:59 pm   SUB-DIR
        ─────────────────────────────────────────────────────────
               Info          View          UnErase

 Select files to UnErase                                           UnErase
```

WHAT'S HAPPENING? Displayed on the screen is a list of the subdirectories in the root directory of C as well as any files that were erased. However, you are interested in Drive A.

STEP 6: Use the F10 key to highlight **File** on the menu bar.

STEP 6: Click **File**.

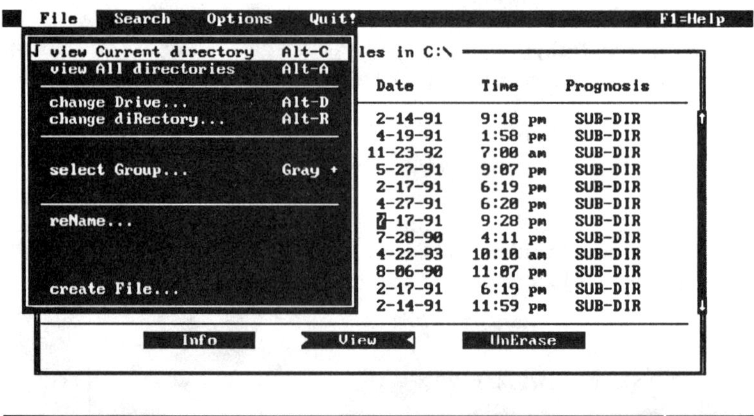

WHAT'S HAPPENING? You see a menu that allows you to perform tasks such as selecting a directory or changing directories.

STEP 7: Use the <Down arrow> key and highlight **change Drive**. Press <Enter>.

STEP 7: Click **change Drive**.

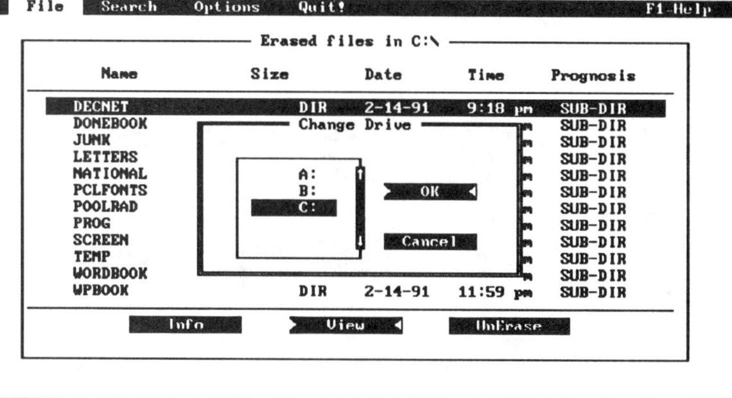

WHAT'S HAPPENING? Displayed on the screen are the disk drives that are installed on your system.

STEP 8: Highlight Drive A and press <Enter>.

STEP 8: Double-click the Drive A icon.

```
 File   Search   Options   Quit!                              F1=Help

 ================== Erased files in A:\ ==================
      Name          Size        Date      Time       Prognosis

    BATCH                   DIR   11-25-91  10:14 am   SUB-DIR
    CLASS                   DIR   10-30-91   6:54 pm   SUB-DIR
    DATA                    DIR   10-30-91   7:39 pm   SUB-DIR
    FILES                   DIR   10-30-91   7:35 pm   SUB-DIR
    PHYS-ED                 DIR   11-08-91   5:59 pm   SUB-DIR
    POLY-SCI                DIR   11-08-91   5:59 pm   SUB-DIR
    SERIES                  DIR   1[illegible]-30-91   9:48 pm   SUB-DIR
    TEAMS                   DIR   11-10-91   6:55 pm   SUB-DIR
    TRIP                    DIR   11-01-91   8:20 pm   SUB-DIR
    USERS                   DIR   10-30-91   8:15 pm   SUB-DIR
    ?d          bat          92   11-24-91   7:50 pm   good
    ?ild3       zzz          63    5-07-93   9:03 am   good

            Info           View           UnErase

 Select files to UnErase                                    UnErase
```

WHAT'S HAPPENING? You selected Drive A. The UNERASE command shows you the directories and all the files you recently deleted. It also displays on the right-hand side its expectations of being able to recover a specific file.

STEP 9: Use the <Down arrow> key to highlight `?ILD3.ZZZ`.

STEP 9: Click `?ILD3.ZZZ`.

STEP 10: On the bottom of the screen are three boxes: `Info`, `View`, and `UnErase`. Use the <Right arrow> key to highlight `UnErase` and then press <Enter>.

STEP 10: Click `UnErase`.

WHAT'S HAPPENING? `Info` tells you the prognosis for recovering the file. `View` lets you look at the contents of the file. You selected `UnErase`. `UnErase` presents you with a dialog box, which tells you that DOS has overwritten the first letter of the file. `UnErase` asks you to supply a new first letter.

STEP 11: At the cursor, key in the following:
`W` <Enter>

STEP 11: At the cursor, key in the following:
`W` <Enter>

```
 File   Search   Options   Quit!                                    F1=Help
                         Erased files in A:\
       Name             Size       Date        Time       Prognosis

       BATCH             DIR    11-25-91    10:14 am    SUB-DIR
       CLASS             DIR    10-30-91     6:54 pm    SUB-DIR
       DATA              DIR    10-30-91     7:39 pm    SUB-DIR
       FILES             DIR    10-30-91     7:35 pm    SUB-DIR
       PHYS-ED           DIR    11-08-91     5:59 pm    SUB-DIR
       POLY-SCI          DIR    11-08-91     5:59 pm    SUB-DIR
       SERIES            DIR    10-30-91     9:48 pm    SUB-DIR
       TEAMS             DIR    11-10-91     6:55 pm    SUB-DIR
       TRIP              DIR    11-01-91     8:28 pm    SUB-DIR
       USERS             DIR    10-30-91     8:15 pm    SUB-DIR
       ?d        bat      92    11-24-91     7:50 pm    good
       wild3     zzz      63     5-07-93     9:03 am    RECOVERED

              Info            View            UnErase

 Select files to UnErase                                            UnErase
```

WHAT'S HAPPENING? The UNERASE command screen display tells you that it recovered the file called `WILD3.ZZZ`.

STEP 12: Press <Esc>.

STEP 12: Click `Quit!`

```
C:\>_
```

WHAT'S HAPPENING? You returned to the system prompt. You are now going to verify that the file `WILD3.ZZZ` has indeed been unerased.

STEP 13: Key in the following:
C:\>**DIR A:WILD3.ZZZ** <Enter>

```
C:\>DIR A:WILD3.ZZZ

 Volume in drive A is DATA DISK
 Volume Serial Number is 3D4F-0EC7
 Directory of A:\

WILD3    ZZZ      63   05-07-93  9:03a
        1 File(s)    113664 bytes free

C:\>_
```

WHAT'S HAPPENING? The file **WILD3.ZZZ** is still on the DATA disk. Has the information in the file changed at all?

STEP 14: Key in the following:
C:\>**TYPE A:WILD3.ZZZ** <Enter>

```
C:\>TYPE A:WILD3.ZZZ
This is another wildcard file
with a file extension of zzz.

C:\>_
```

WHAT'S HAPPENING? The file contents are identical. However, if the file was in a subdirectory that had been deleted, you would first have to unerase the subdirectory before unerasing the file.

17.6 PC Tools

PC Tools Deluxe, version 7.1 written by Central Point Software is a set of utilities that can be divided into several general categories. These include data recovery, data protection and security, a fast hard disk backup and restore, performance and system information, a complete communications program, a shell, a complete desktop manager and also some of its applications which are Windows specific.

PC Shell is a utility program that provides the critical DOS maintenance commands in a windowed environment with a complete menuing system. It can be run as a memory-resident program or as a stand-alone application. It includes functions to copy a file, move a file, edit files and manage subdirectories through its prune and graft feature.

Commute is a full communications program which runs another computer by remote control—either using modems or a **Novell LAN** (**Local Area Network**).

Data recovery utilities include:

Undelete Allows the user to recover deleted files.
DiskFix Repairs problems like a disk that will not boot or corrupted directories that can occur on hard or floppy disks.
Unformat Unformats disks that have been accidently formatted.
FileFix Recovers damaged Lotus and dBase files.

Data protection and security utilities include:

Mirror Provides protection against accidental erasure or formatting of the hard disk by keeping a "mirror" image of your disk.
Data monitor A memory-resident program that has various options to protect against data loss, protect confidential files and provide such enhancements as a screen blanker which prevents screen burn-in and a write protection which prevents critical files from being overwritten, deleted, or damaged.
Wipe Deletes files so that they may not be recovered.
PC Secure Encrypts programs and data. It can encrypt, decrypt, compress, and hide files on a disk.
VDefend Detects and protects the hard disk from over 500 viruses.
PCFormat Replaces the DOS format command so that UNDELETE and UNFORMAT can recover data.
CP Backup Allows the user to back up data on the hard disk to any format media including tape backup systems. It provides unattended backups and has a "smart" restore command.

Performance and system utilities include:

Compress Unfragments or rearranges files on a hard or floppy disk to enhance disk performance, known as optimizing the disk.
PC-Cache Speeds up disk performance by creating and managing a cache. A cache stores in memory the most frequently used disk information.
System information Provides information about your computer such as how it is configured and how its memory is being used.
Filefind Locates any file on a disk.
Directory maintenance Provides an easy means to manipulate directories with deleting, moving, and renaming commands.
View Allows you to see data files in their native formats without having to load the application program.

Desktop Manager is a complete desktop manager that has full keyboard or mouse support, drop-down menus, moveable and sizeable windows, and color control. It can be run as a resident program or as a stand-alone DOS application.

The desktop manager includes eleven programs. They are:

Notepads A simple word processor.
Outlines Allows you to create outlines, expand and collapse them, and edit them.
Databases A simple data base, including an automatic phone dialer.
Appointment scheduler A calendaring function. You use it like a standard calendar, but it also can run programs at night when the user is not present.
Telecommunications-Modem Allows the user to send and receive data and program files easily.
Electronic mail Allows the user to access electronic mail using MCI Mail, CompuServe, or Easylink.
Telecommunications-Fax Allows the user to send and receive faxes but only if the user has an internal fax board or is on a network that has a computer with an internal fax board.
Macro editor Allows the user to record and save commonly used sequences that can be replaced by one keystroke.
Clipboard A temporary storage place for cutting and pasting data among applications.
Calculators Allow the user to accomplish mathematical functions. These include algebraic, financial, scientific, and programmers calculators.
Utilities Allow the user to modify different PC Tools settings including removing PC Tools from memory.

Windows Included is a Windows 3.0 version of certain PC Tools utilities. These include CP Backup, Scheduler, CP Launcher (lets you begin any program from a menu), and Undelete.

PC Tools can be run from a shell—the menu interface. However, the user can choose not to install the shell and run individual programs from the DOS prompt. When you purchase PC Tools, you receive both 5 1/4- and 3 1/2-inch disks.

The instructions for installing PC Tools Version 7.1 are beyond the scope of this textbook. You can follow the instructions in the PC Tools manual. However, installation is easy. You place the disk labeled INSTALL (Disk 1) into Drive A and key in `INSTALL`. Often, the first time a user wants to use PC Tools is to recover a deleted file. Thus, there are special directions that allow the user to recover a file prior to installing PC Tools. When installing PC Tools, the user may not create a subdirectory and copy the files to it. The files supplied with PC Tools are large and compressed. They must be uncompressed by PC Tools, which happens during the installation process.

PC Tools is a complex program to master. Thus, we are going to look at a sampling. We will use one utility with the menu and another without the menu. You may choose to use PCShell (the menu interface) or run the utilities from the DOS prompt, but remember, each utility within PC Tools has a specific menu.

17.7 Recovering an Erased File in PC Tools

Accidentally deleting a file is so common that most utility programs have a facility for recovering those files. PC Tools has an unerase feature called UNDEL which can be executed from the DOS prompt or UNDELETE in the PC Tools Shell.

As mentioned previously in this chapter, when you delete a file, DOS does not eliminate the data. Because DOS does not erase the data or the cluster numbers, PC Tools can allow you to recover the deleted file.

Even though you will be using a different unerase utility, the rules have not changed. The best time to unerase a file is just after it has been deleted. Next, you will unerase a file first by using PC Tools from the DOS prompt and then by using PC Tools Shell.

Activity 17.8 Using UNDEL from the DOS Prompt

Note: You have PC Tools installed on the hard disk and the path set to the subdirectory where PC Tools is located. You are at the root directory of Drive C. The DATA disk is in Drive A. Although some utilities can be run from a floppy disk, these utilities are most effective when using a hard disk.

STEP 1: Key in the following:
C:\>**DIR A:\FUNNY.TV** <Enter>

Note: If this file is not on the DATA disk, you may copy it from **C:\JUNK\DATA** and it is called **COMEDY.TV**.

```
C:\>DIR A:FUNNY.TV

 Volume in drive A is DATA DISK
 Volume Serial Number is 3D4F-0EC7
 Directory of A:\

FUNNY    TV      170   11-23-92 10:17a
        1 File(s)    112640 bytes free

C:\>_
```

WHAT'S HAPPENING? The file called **FUNNY.TV** is on the DATA disk.

STEP 2: Key in the following:
C:\>**TYPE A:FUNNY.TV** <Enter>

```
C:\>TYPE A:FUNNY.TV
COMEDY TELEVISION SERIES

Cheers
Family Ties
SOAP
```

```
Head of the Class
Perfect Strangers
I Love Lucy
Roseanne
TAXI
The Mary Tyler Moore Show
The Wonder Years

C:\>_
```

STEP 3: Key in the following:
C:\>**DEL A:FUNNY.TV** <Enter>

STEP 4: Key in the following:
C:\>**DIR A:FUNNY.TV** <Enter>

```
C:\>DEL A:FUNNY.TV

C:\>DIR A:FUNNY.TV

 Volume in drive A is DATA DISK
 Volume Serial Number is 3D4F-0EC7
 Directory of A:\

File not found

C:\>_
```

WHAT'S HAPPENING? The file **FUNNY.TV** has been deleted from the DATA disk.

STEP 5: Key in the following:
C:\>**UNDEL A:*.*** <Enter>

```
C:\>UNDEL A:\*.*

Undelete V7.1 (c)1990-1991 Central Point Software, Inc.

Directory: A:\

       3 deleted files.
       3 recorded by DOS.

?UNNY    .TV         170 11/23/92 10:17a Excellent
Do you want to recover this file? (Y/N)_
```

WHAT'S HAPPENING? You are executing the PC Tools **stand-alone** version of UNDELETE. It is showing you that on this disk there are three deleted files that have been recorded by DOS (your display may vary). It is asking you if you want to undelete the first deleted file, **?UNNY.TV**.

STEP 6: Key in the following:
Y <Enter>

```
?UNNY    .TV          170 11/23/92 10:17a Excellent
Do you want to recover this file? (Y/N)Y


Enter the first letter for this file. (ESC will Cancel)_
```

WHAT'S HAPPENING? The UNDEL program has located the last file deleted, **FUNNY.TV**. It is asking you to enter the first letter of the file name to replace the ? that DOS substituted when you deleted **FUNNY.TV**.

STEP 7: Key in the following:
F <Enter>

```
?UNNY    .TV          170 11/23/92 10:17a Excellent
Do you want to recover this file? (Y/N)Y


Enter the first letter for this file. (ESC will Cancel)
FUNNY    .TV  Recovered

?IST     .BAT          29 11/24/91  7:49p Excellent
Do you want to recover this file? (Y/N)_
```

WHAT'S HAPPENING? The file was successfully recovered. PC Tools is now showing you the next deleted file it can recover.

STEP 8: Press <Esc>.

```
?IST     .BAT          29 11/24/91  7:49p Excellent
Do you want to recover this file? (Y/N)
C:\>_
```

WHAT'S HAPPENING? You have returned to the DOS prompt. Is the file really there and is the data the same?

STEP 9: Key in the following:
C:\>**DIR A:FUNNY.TV** <Enter>

STEP 10: Key in the following:
C:\>**TYPE A:FUNNY.TV** <Enter>

```
C:\>DIR A:FUNNY.TV

 Volume in drive A is DATA DISK
 Volume Serial Number is 3D4F-0EC7
 Directory of A:\

FUNNY     TV      175   11-23-92 10:17a
         1 File(s)      14336 bytes free
```

```
C:\>TYPE A:FUNNY.TV
COMEDY TELEVISION SERIES

Cheers
Family Ties
SOAP
Head of the Class
Perfect Strangers
I Love Lucy
Roseanne
TAXI
The Mary Tyler Moore Show
The Wonder Years

C:\>_
```

WHAT'S HAPPENING? The file `FUNNY.TV` is on the DATA disk. The data inside the file has not changed.

17.9 UNDELETE in PC Tools Using PC Tools Shell

You just executed the UNDEL program from the DOS prompt. In addition, PC Tools has a file management capability. It is a shell, much like DOS Shell discussed in Chapter 15. Norton also has a file management capability shell. However, it is not in Norton Utilities. It is in a separate program called Norton Commander. PC Tools Shell has more powerful features than DOS Shell. In the next activity, you are going to use PC Tools Shell to both delete and recover a file.

Activity 17.10 Using PC TOOLS Shell

Note: You have PC Tools installed on the hard disk and the path set to the subdirectory where PC Tools is located. The `C:\>` is displayed. The DATA disk is in Drive A.

STEP 1: Key in the following:
C:\>`PCSHELL` <Enter>

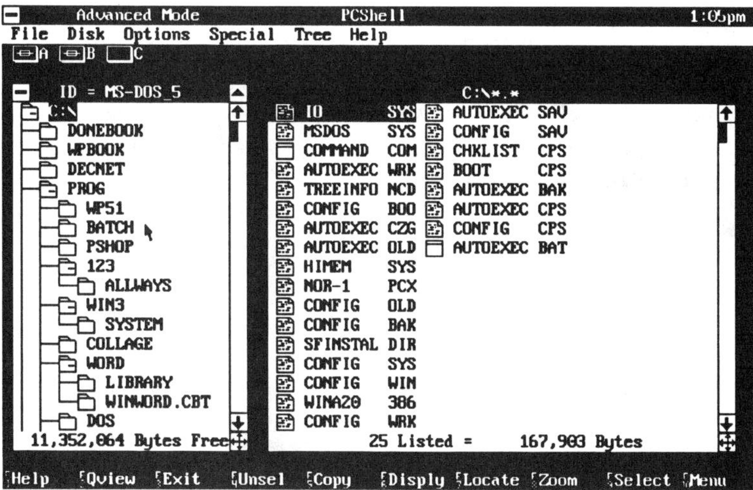

WHAT'S HAPPENING? You are looking at the first screen of PC Tools Shell. To the left is the directory tree of Drive C. To the right are the files that are located in the root directory of Drive C. At the bottom of the screen is the message bar. Each number refers to pressing a function key. For example, $^F_1$`Help` means that pressing F1 will provide help, and $^F_3$`Exit` means pressing the F3 key to quit the program. If you have a mouse, you may accomplish the same tasks by placing the mouse pointer on the "buttons" and clicking. Across the top is the horizontal menu bar. Each entry provides a further drop-down menu having to do with that topic. Again, if you have a mouse, you can click on the word you want.

STEP 2: Press <Ctrl>+A. STEP 2: Click the Drive A icon.

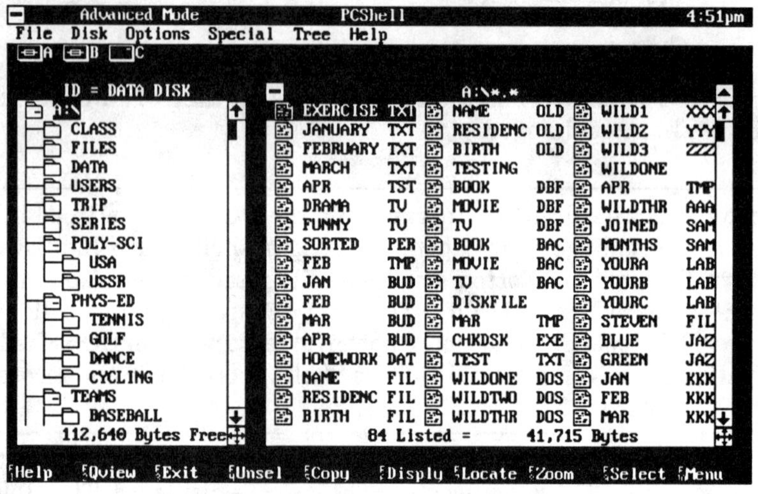

WHAT'S HAPPENING? You are looking at the DATA disk. Pressing <Ctrl>+A or clicking the Drive A icon allowed you to select Drive A.

STEP 3: If the cursor is not on the right-hand side of the display, use the <Tab> key to place the cursor there. Then, using the <Down arrow> key, highlight the file called **FEB.BUD**. STEP 3: Click **FEB.BUD**.

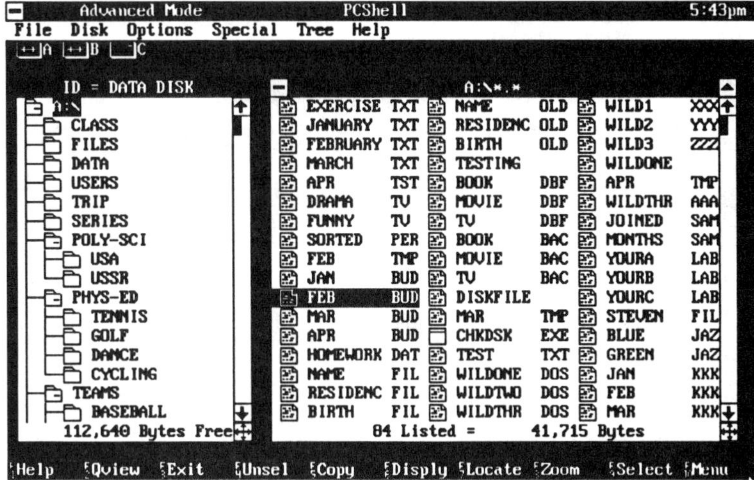

STEP 4: Press <Alt>+F to select the **File** menu.

STEP 4: Click **File** on the menu bar.

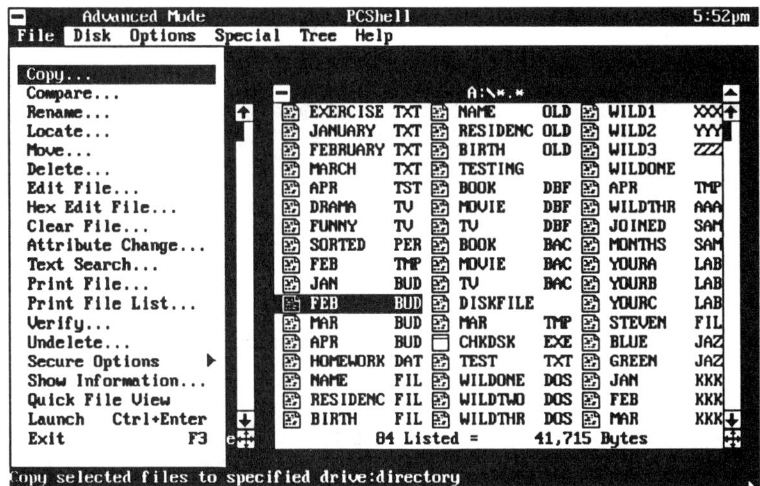

WHAT'S HAPPENING? You are presented with the drop-down menu giving you choices for file management options.

STEP 5: Use the <Down arrow> key and highlight **Delete**. Press <Enter>.

STEP 5: Click **Delete**.

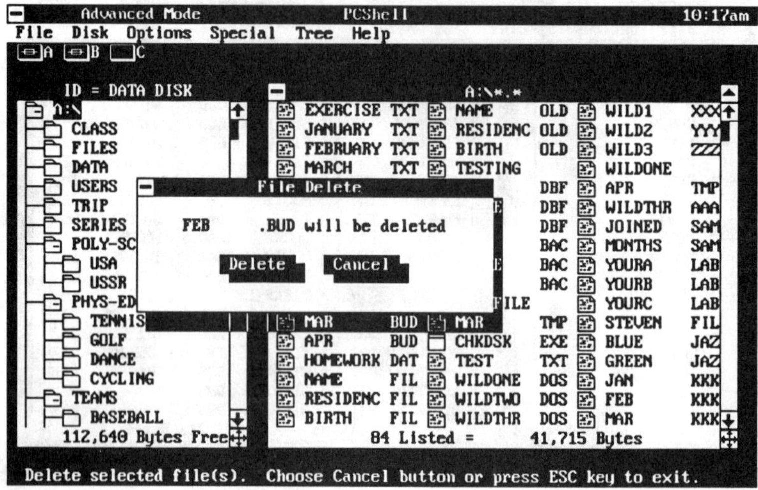

WHAT'S HAPPENING? You are presented with a dialog box asking you to confirm the deletion of the file called `FEB.BUD`.

STEP 6: Press D. STEP 6: Click `Delete`.

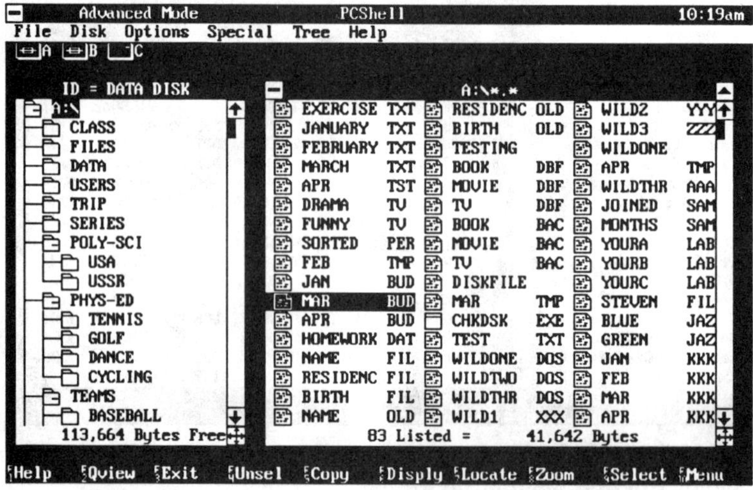

WHAT'S HAPPENING? The file `FEB.BUD` has been deleted.

STEP 7: Press <Alt>+F. STEP 7: Click `File` on the menu bar.

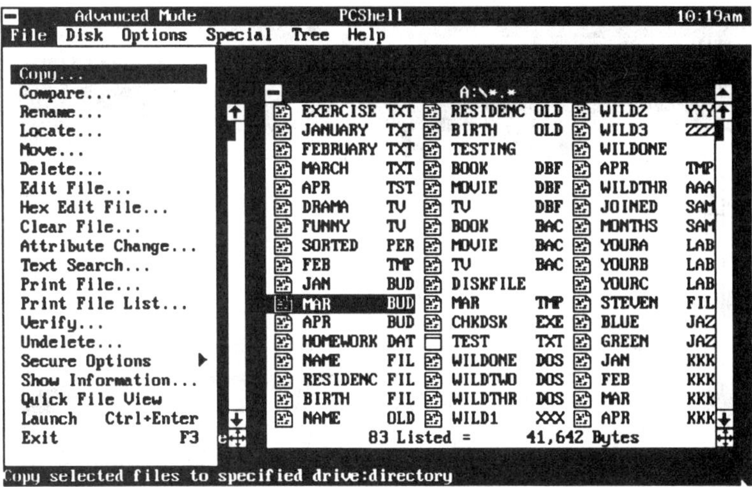

WHAT'S HAPPENING? You pulled down the `File` menu.

STEP 8: Highlight `Undelete` and press <Enter>.

STEP 8: Click `Undelete`.

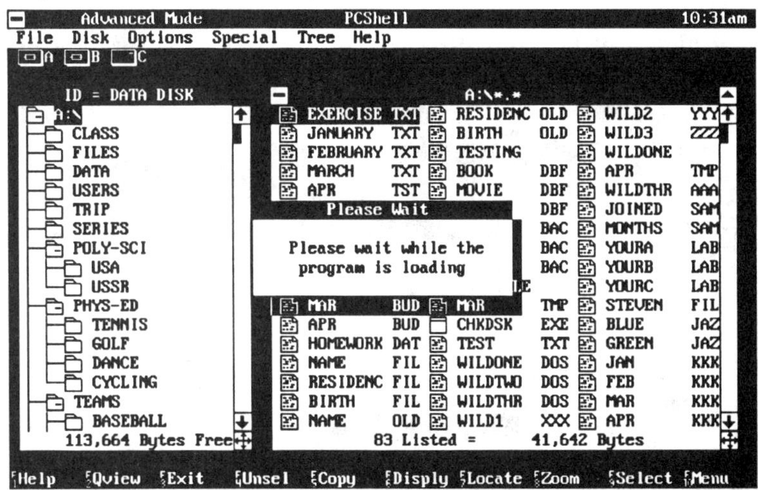

WHAT'S HAPPENING? You see a momentary message indicating that the program is loading and another indicating that PC Tools is reading the directory information on Drive A.

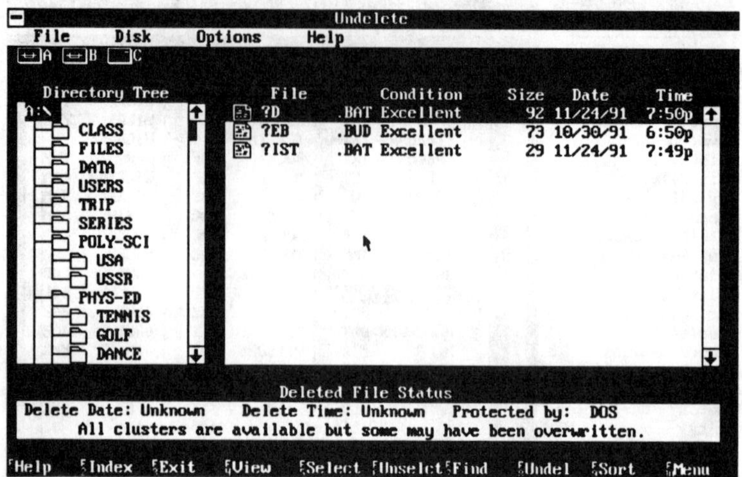

WHAT'S HAPPENING? On the right-hand side of the screen, you are presented with an alphabetic list of files that were recently deleted. The chance to recover the **FEB.BUD** file is excellent.

STEP 9: Use the <Down arrow> key to highlight **?EB.BUD**. Press F8.

STEP 9: Click **?EB.BUD**. Then click the F8 **Undel** icon at the bottom of the screen.

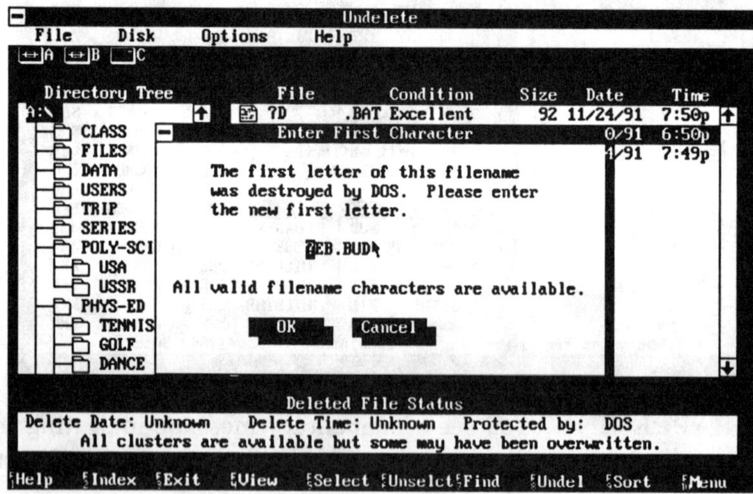

WHAT'S HAPPENING? Again, the UNDELETE command is asking for the first letter of the deleted file.

STEP 10: Key in F. Press O for OK. Press O for OK.

STEP 10: Key in F. Click OK.

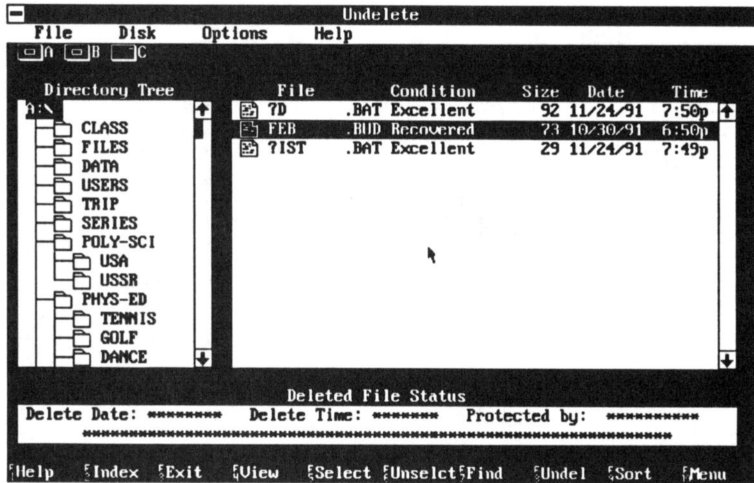

WHAT'S HAPPENING? The file `FEB.BUD` was successfully recovered.

STEP 11: Press F3.

STEP 11: Click the F3 `Exit` icon at the bottom of the screen.

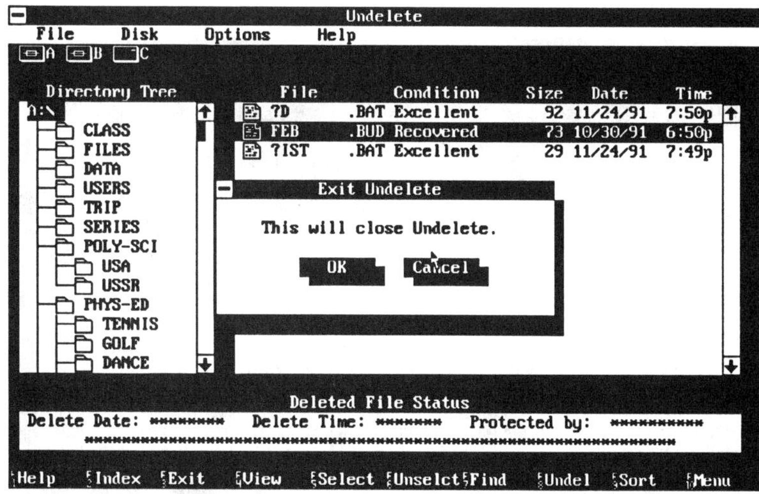

WHAT'S HAPPENING? PC Tools is asking you if you want to close the UNDELETE program.

STEP 12: Press O.

STEP 12: Click **OK**.

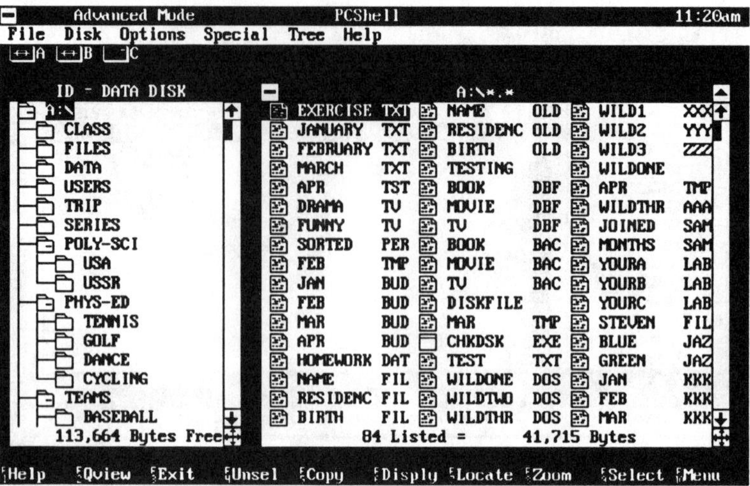

WHAT'S HAPPENING? You have returned to the PC Tools opening screen. You can now exit PC Tools.

STEP 13: Press F3.

STEP 13: Click the `Exit` icon at the bottom of the screen.

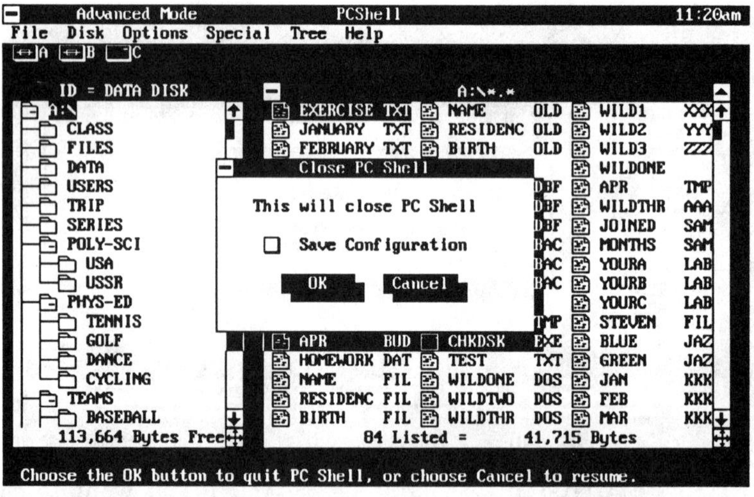

WHAT'S HAPPENING? You are asked to confirm exiting the program.

STEP 14: Press O.

STEP 14: Click OK.

```
A:\>_
```

WHAT'S HAPPENING? You returned to the system level prompt. You were returned to the root of the disk in Drive A since that was where you were when you exited PC Tools. You have now used PC Tools Shell to delete and recover a file.

17.11 Compressing the Disk

As you write files to a disk, DOS writes them contiguously, or all the parts next to one another, as discussed in Chapter 8. As you add information to files, delete files, and add new files, each file becomes fragmented or noncontiguous. Parts of the file are scattered over the disk. There are two consequences of this fragmentation. First, files become much slower to access because they are physically scattered over the disk. Second, it is much harder to recover deleted files with utility programs. One solution to the problem is to reformat a disk and then copy all the files from the old disk to the newly formatted one. However, since this is an ongoing problem, it will continue to occur. Also, although newly formatting a disk and copying files may not be a bad solution when working with floppy disks, it is not a practical solution when working with a hard disk, because the problem becomes more acute with hard disks.

The solution for this problem cannot be found in DOS, but utility programs do solve it. This process is called **optimizing the disk, compressing the disk,** or **unfragmenting the disk**. Compressing the disk is the least correct name because the data on the disk are not actually compressed. Instead, the disk is reorganized. Unfragmenting programs optimizes the disk by reorganizing it: storing each file's data in a single group of contiguous clusters. This rearrangement allows a disk drive to locate all the data in a file very quickly. Optimization moves all the files near the front of the disk because that is the area that the disk drive can access the fastest. In addition, all the unused clusters are moved to the back of the disk, minimizing future fragmentation. This process needs to be done on a regular basis because disks eventually become fragmented.

Both PC Tools and Norton Utilities have an optimization tool. In Norton Utilities, the program is called SPEEDISK; in PC Tools it is called COMPRESS. Each utility has different options, which can include sorting directories or analyzing disk surface defects. In the next activity, you are going to compress the DATA disk.

Prior to proceeding, read these important warnings—regardless of which optimization tool you use.

1. Be sure that you have no memory-resident programs in memory other than the optimization tool you are using.
2. If there are any deleted files or subdirectories you wish to recover, recover them prior to using any optimization program. An optimization program, in the process of reading and writing to the disk, will destroy all deleted files and subdirectories.
3. **Back up the hard disk!** The hard disk should always be backed up regularly. However, it is particularly crucial prior to running an optimization program. First, you never know when a program is not going to work correctly. If this happens while you are running an optimization program, you could totally destroy all data on the hard disk with little chance of recovering it. Second, the optimization process involves memory. These programs read and write to the disk using memory as the storage area. If there is a power outage or a power surge during this process, all data could be destroyed.

With these warnings in mind, you are going to optimize the DATA disk. Using the DATA disk as a test case is safe, particularly since you can use DISKCOPY to back up the DATA disk before you run the program. Remember that DISKCOPY makes an identical copy of a disk, including the fragmentation. Although the instructions do not tell you to back up the DATA disk, you may want to take this step.

Activity 17.12 Using COMPRESS in PC Tools

Note: You have PC Tools installed on a hard disk and the path set to the subdirectory where PC Tools is located. The **C:\>** is displayed and the DATA disk is in Drive A. Remember, if you want to repeat this activity, use DISKCOPY to make a copy of the DATA disk.

STEP 1: Key in the following:

C:\>**COMPRESS A:** <Enter>

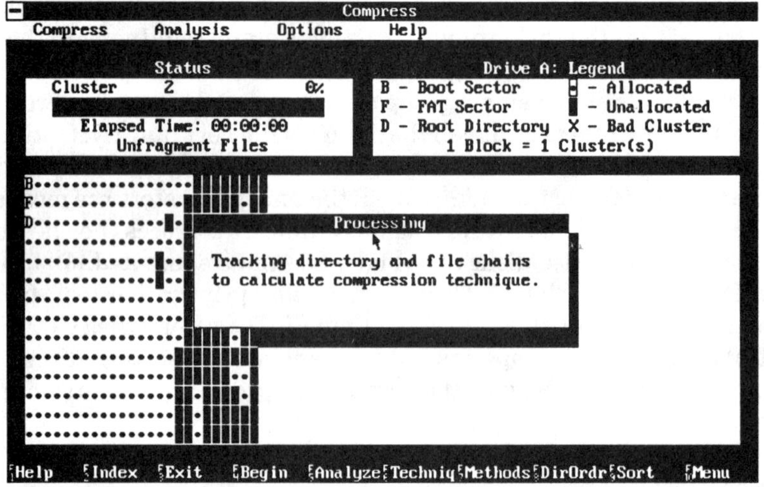

WHAT'S HAPPENING? You see several screens as PC Tools rapidly analyzes the disk in Drive A. The COMPRESS program is showing you what the disk looks like. This disk, like all disks, has a B which indicates the boot sector. The F is the File Allocation Table (FAT). The D is the root directory of the disk. The horizontal menu bar across the top of the screen indicates the drop-down menus. The graphical disk map represents all the files on your disk. Different colors and patterns represent the different files on the disk, free space, and any bad blocks. The more fragmented the display looks, the more fragmented the disk is. The message bar at the bottom of the screen provides more information, keystroke options, and help suggestions. When COMPRESS is finished, it makes a diagnosis.

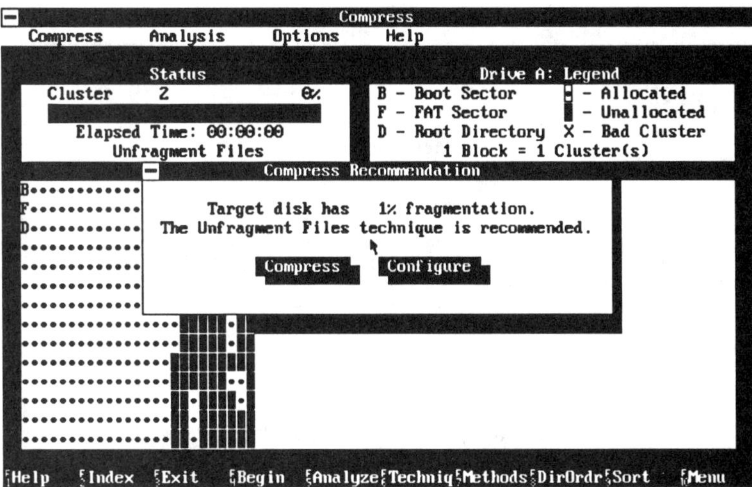

WHAT'S HAPPENING? COMPRESS is recommending that you compress the DATA disk.

STEP 2: Press <Esc>. Press <Alt>+A.

STEP 2: Press <Esc>. Click **`Analysis`** on the menu bar.

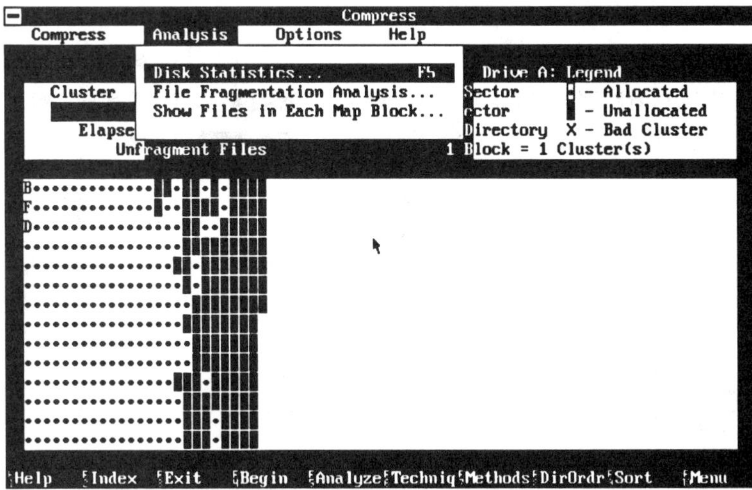

WHAT'S HAPPENING? You are given some choices. **`Disk Statistics`** analyzes the disk for such items as allocated and unallocated clusters. The next item, **`File Fragmentation Analysis`**, checks individual files for fragmentation. Last, **`Show Files in Each Map Block`** means that each symbol may represent more than one file. This option lets you examine the clusters and files.

STEP 3: Be sure **`Disk Statistics`** is highlighted. Press <Enter>.

STEP 3: Click **`Disk Statistics`**.

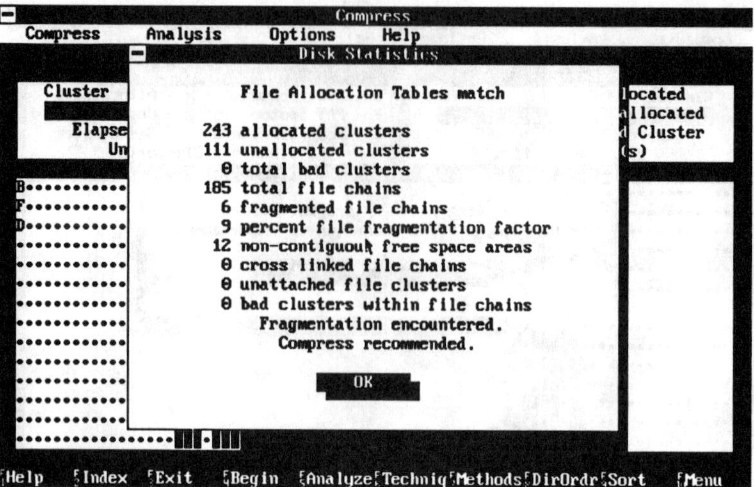

WHAT'S HAPPENING? You received a report about the DATA disk. The COMPRESS program believes that there are enough fragmented files to justify compressing the disk.

STEP 4: Press <Esc>.	STEP 4: Press <Esc>.
STEP 5: Press F4.	STEP 5: Click the **Begin** icon at the bottom of the screen.

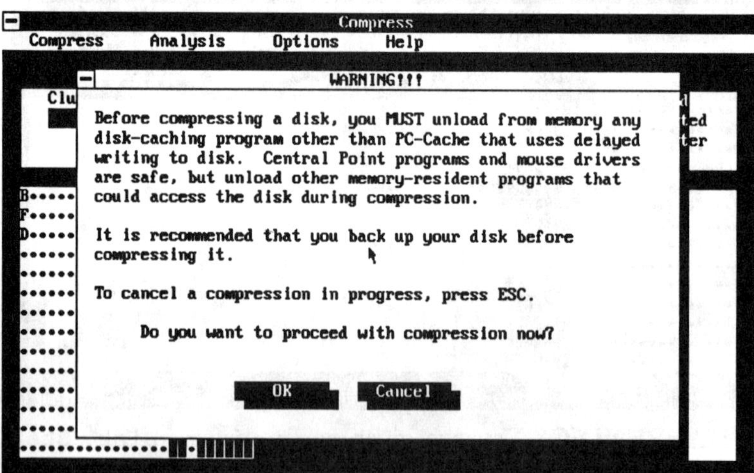

WHAT'S HAPPENING? Pressing or clicking F4 brought up COMPRESS. The COMPRESS program is warning you to back up your disk and to be sure that there are no memory-resident programs running before it begins compressing.

STEP 6: Press O.	STEP 6: Click OK.

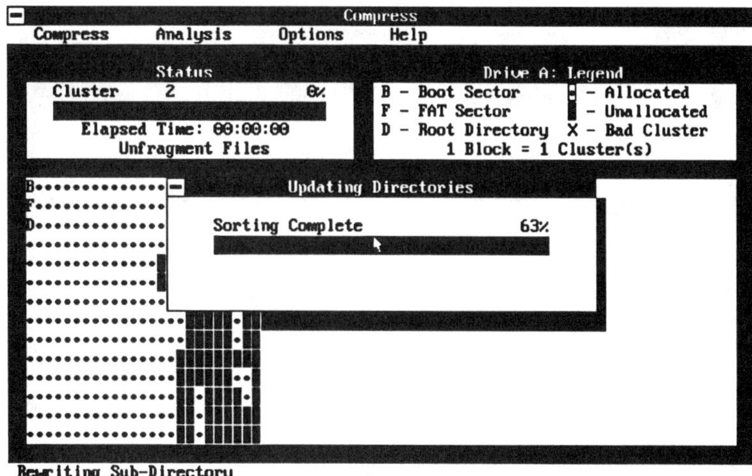

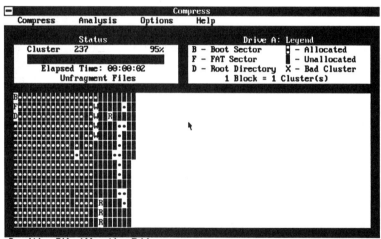

Compress
Compress Analysis Options Help
Status
Cluster 237 95%
Elapsed Time: 00:00:02
Unfragment Files
Drive A: Legend
B - Boot Sector
F - FAT Sector
D - Root Directory
- Allocated
- Unallocated
X - Bad Cluster
1 Block = 1 Cluster(s)
Rewriting File Allocation Tables

WHAT'S HAPPENING? First, COMPRESS updates the directories. Then as the files are being compressed, you see an R for read and a W for write. The COMPRESS program tells you which file it is moving and where it is moving to. When it has completed compressing the files, you see the following message.

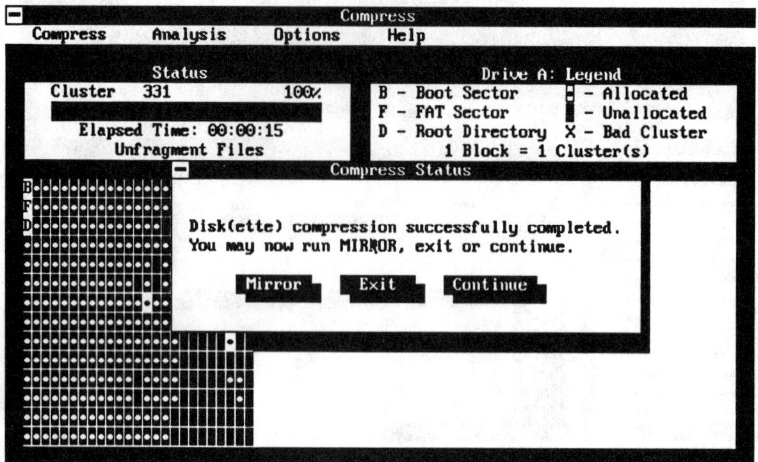

STEP 7: Press X. STEP 7: Click **Exit**.

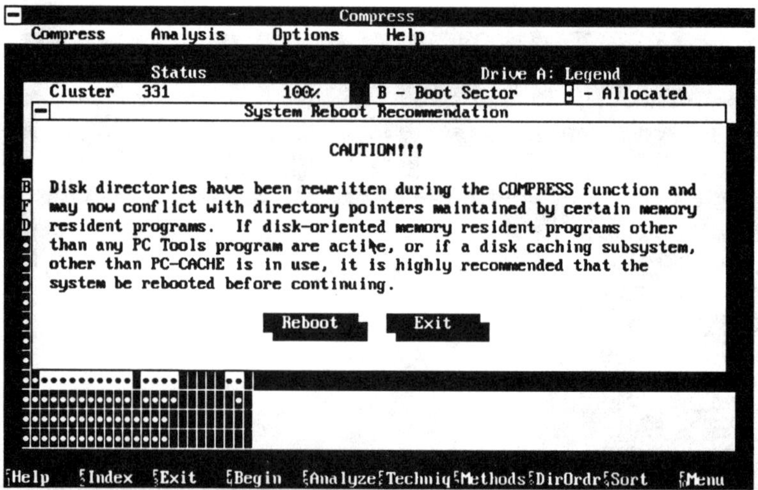

WHAT'S HAPPENING? It is good advice to reboot after compression to ensure that you will not lose any data. However, since you compressed the DATA disk, not the hard disk, it is unnecessary to reboot, especially in a laboratory environment.

STEP 8: Press X. STEP 8: Click **Exit**.

```
C:\>_
```

WHAT'S HAPPENING? You exited COMPRESS. Your DATA disk is no longer fragmented.

17.13 UNDELETE in DOS 5.0

Since accidentally deleting a file is so common, DOS 5.0 also includes a utility for unerase. It is a command that executes from the DOS system level. If the command looks like the undelete from PC Tools, it is for good reason. MS-DOS 5.0 licensed UNDELETE, UNFORMAT and MIRROR from Central Point Software, the manufacturer of PC Tools.

Even though you will be using a different unerase utility, the rules have not changed. The best time to unerase a file is just after it has been deleted. In the next activity, you will unerase a file by using the DOS 5.0 command UNDELETE.

Activity 17.14 Using UNDELETE in DOS 5.0

Note: Be sure you are at the DOS system level and not in any of the utility subdirectories. You should be at the root directory of Drive C with the path set to **C:\DOS**.

STEP 1: Key in the following:
C:\>**DIR A:\FUNNY.TV** <Enter>

Note: If this file is not on the DATA disk, you may copy it from **C:\JUNK\DATA**. It is called **COMEDY.TV**.

```
C:\>DIR A:FUNNY.TV

 Volume in drive A is DATA DISK
 Volume Serial Number is 3839-0EC8
 Directory of A:\

FUNNY     TV      170   11-23-92 10:17a
        1 file(s)         170 bytes
                       113664 bytes free

C:\>_
```

WHAT'S HAPPENING? The file called **FUNNY.TV** is on the DATA disk.

STEP 2: Key in the following:
C:\>**TYPE A:\FUNNY.TV** <Enter>

```
C:\>TYPE A:\FUNNY.TV
COMEDY TELEVISION SERIES

Cheers
Family Ties
SOAP
Head of the Class
Perfect Strangers
I Love Lucy
Roseanne
TAXI
```

```
The Mary Tyler Moore Show
The Wonder Years

C:\>_
```

STEP 3: Key in the following:
C:\>**DEL A:\FUNNY.TV** <Enter>

STEP 4: Key in the following:
C:\>**DIR A:\FUNNY.TV** <Enter>

```
C:\>DEL A:\FUNNY.TV

C:\>DIR A:\FUNNY.TV

 Volume in drive A is DATA DISK
 Volume Serial Number is 3839-0EC8
 Directory of A:\

File not found

C:\>_
```

WHAT'S HAPPENING? The file **FUNNY.TV** has been deleted from the DATA disk.

STEP 5: Key in the following:
C:\>**CD \DOS** <Enter>

STEP 6: Key in the following:
C:\DOS>**UNDELETE A:\FUNNY.TV** <Enter>

```
C:\>CD \DOS

C:\DOS>UNDELETE A:\FUNNY.TV

Directory: A:\
File Specifications: FUNNY.TV

 Deletion-tracking file not found.

 MS-DOS directory contains 1 deleted files.
 Of those, 1 files may be recovered.

Using the MS-DOS directory.

 ?UNNY    TV   170   11-23-92 10:17a   ...A Undelete (Y/N)?_
```

WHAT'S HAPPENING? You are executing the DOS version of UNDELETE. To be sure of that, you moved to the DOS subdirectory. It is no surprise that it looks very similar to the PC Tools stand-alone UNDEL command since Microsoft licensed it from Central Point Software. The DOS UNDELETE is asking you if you want to undelete this file.

STEP 7: Key in the following:
Y <Enter>

```
C:\DOS>UNDELETE A:\FUNNY.TV

Directory: A:\
File Specifications: FUNNY.TV

 Deletion-tracking file not found.

 MS-DOS directory contains 1 deleted files.
 Of those, 1 files may be recovered.

Using the MS-DOS directory.

  ?UNNY    TV    170   11-23-92   10:17a ...A Undelete (Y/N)?Y
  Please type the first character for ?UNNY .TV : _
```

WHAT'S HAPPENING? The UNDELETE program has located the file **FUNNY.TV**. MIRROR is another program that DOS licensed from PC Tools. It creates a "mirror" image of the disk. Thus, if you run the MIRROR program, DOS has a better chance of recovering files. Because the MIRROR program was not run, DOS cannot find the special file track. Nonetheless, it still can help you. It is asking you to enter the first letter of the file name to replace the ? that DOS substituted when you deleted **FUNNY.TV**.

STEP 8: Key in the following:
F

```
 Please type the first character for ?UNNY .TV : F

File successfully undeleted.

C:\DOS>_
```

WHAT'S HAPPENING? The file was successfully recovered. Is the file really there and is the data the same?

STEP 9: Key in the following:
C:\DOS>**CD ** <Enter>

STEP 10: Key in the following:
C:\>**DIR A:\FUNNY.TV** <Enter>

STEP 11: Key in the following:
C:\>**TYPE A:\FUNNY.TV** <Enter>

```
C:\DOS>CD \

C:\>DIR A:FUNNY.TV

 Volume in drive A is DATA DISK
 Volume Serial Number is 3839-0EC8
 Directory of A:\

FUNNY    TV       170   11-23-92 10:17a
        1 file(s)          170 bytes
                        113664 bytes free

C:\>TYPE A:\FUNNY.TV
COMEDY TELEVISION SERIES

Cheers
Family Ties
SOAP
Head of the Class
Perfect Strangers
I Love Lucy
Roseanne
TAXI
The Mary Tyler Moore Show
The Wonder Years

C:\>_
```

WHAT'S HAPPENING? The file FUNNY.TV was recovered on the DATA disk. The data inside the file has not changed.

Chapter Summary

1. A utility is a program that accomplishes one task.
2. Utility programs fill in the gaps in DOS and provide commands that DOS does not have.
3. A person who knows how to program can write a utility program.
4. Utility programs are available from electronic bulletin boards, which is one means of exchanging programs and information.
5. To use an electronic bulletin board, you must have a modem and usually belong to a computer service.
6. DOS utility programs can be purchased.
7. Two of the most popular utility programs are Norton Utilities and PC Tools.
8. These commercial utility programs are actually a group of utility programs that can be used with a menu or can be run individually.
9. Norton Utilities prior to version 6.01 came in both a Standard Edition and an Advanced Edition. The new version includes both Standard Edition and Advanced Edition features.

10. Norton Utilities can be divided into some general categories—data recovery and disk repair, speed and performance embracements, security and tools.
11. Two interesting commands from Norton Utilities are UNERASE and SYSINFO.
12. UNERASE allows you to recover deleted files, because DOS does not remove the data from the disk. DOS only changes the entry in the directory to indicate that the file has been erased.
13. SYSINFO gives you information about your hardware. You can perform a benchmark test to compare your computer to a Compaq, IBM AT, or IBM XT.
14. PC Tools includes data recovery and protection programs, a shell, a hard disk backup, and a desktop manager and other related programs.
15. PC Tools can be run from the shell or, if the user chooses, can be run from the command line prompt.
16. The UNERASE program in PC Tools is called UNDEL.
17. The best time to recover a deleted file is immediately after deleting it. Otherwise, DOS allocates the space as unused, and other files will be written in that space.
18. A program run from the DOS prompt is considered a stand-alone program.
19. The PC Tools shell is called PC Shell. It has complete file management capabilities. Norton Utilities does not include a shell. Norton has a separate program called Norton Commander that provides a shell.
20. PC Shell works with drop-down menus. Either the keyboard or a mouse may be used.
21. DOS always attempts to write files contiguously to a disk. However, as a user adds information to files, adds new files, and deletes files, the disk becomes fragmented and files are scattered over the disk.
22. A fragmented disk is slow and can prevent the successful recovery of deleted files.
23. A user can "unfragment" a disk by formatting a new disk and copying files from the fragmented disk to the newly formatted disk, but this process is inefficient. DOS has no program to solve this problem. However, there are utility programs that accomplish this task. They are called optimization programs.
24. Both PC Tools and Norton Utilities have such optimization programs.
25. SPEEDISK is Norton Utilities' optimization program, and COMPRESS is PC Tools' optimization program.
26. DOS 5.0 includes a file recovery utility called UNDELETE.
27. DOS licensed UNDELETE, UNFORMAT, and MIRROR from PC Tools.
28. Each of these DOS commands runs from the command line prompt.

Key Terms

Archived files
Benchmark
Compressed files
Compressing the disk
Electronic bulletin board
Fragmented disk
Optimizing the disk
Stand-alone program
Unfragmenting the disk

Discussion Questions

1. What are utility programs?
2. Why would you want to use utility programs?
3. What is the difference between utility programs and application programs?
4. Where can you get utility programs?
5. What is an electronic bulletin board? How can it be used?
6. What is Peter Norton known for?
7. When and why would you use an unerase command?
8. How can a utility program recover a deleted file when DOS prior to version 5.0 cannot?
9. What kind of information does SYSINFO in Norton Utilities provide?
10. What are benchmark tests?
11. Why would a user want to purchase more than one utility program?
12. What is PC Shell? What does it provide a user?
13. Name two ways you can unerase a file with PC Tools.
14. What is the purpose of the MIRROR program in PC Tools?
15. When you unerase a file in either PC Tools or Norton Utilities, what does each program need from the user before proceeding?
16. Can deleted files always be recovered? Why or why not?
17. Why does a disk become fragmented? Is there any way to prevent this from happening?
18. How can DOS help prevent a disk from becoming fragmented?
19. What are optimization programs?
20. What benefits does a user receive from running an optimization program?
21. Do PC Tools and/or Norton Utilities provide an optimization program? If so, what are the programs called?
22. Are there any steps that should be taken prior to optimizing a disk?
23. Does any version of DOS allow you to unerase a file?

Application Assignments

Note: All assignments will occur on the DATA disk.

1. For the following assignment:
   a. Delete the file called **SALES.LET** from the DATA disk.
   b. Print the screen that proves that it has been deleted.
   c. Recover the deleted file.
   d. Print the screen that proves that the file has been recovered.
2. For the following assignment:
   a. Delete the file called **WILDONE.DOS** from the DATA disk.
   b. Print the screen that proves that it has been deleted.
   c. Recover the deleted file.
   d. Print the screen that proves that the file has been recovered.
3. For the following assignment:
   a. Delete the file called **MOVE.BAT** in the **BATCH** subdirectory on the DATA disk.

   b. Print the screen that proves that it has been deleted.
   c. Recover the deleted file.
   d. Print the screen that proves that the file has been recovered.
4. For the following assignment:
   a. Delete the file called **RED.JAZ** in the **TRIP** subdirectory on the DATA disk.
   b. Print the screen that proves that it has been deleted.
   c. Recover the deleted file.
   d. Print the screen that proves that the file has been recovered.
5. For the following assignment:
   a. Delete all the files that begin with **WILD** on the DATA disk.
   b. Print the screen that proves that they have been deleted.
   c. Recover the deleted files.
   d. Print the screen that proves that the files have been recovered.
6. For the following assignment:
   a. Delete all the files in the **BATCH** subdirectory on the DATA disk.
   b. Print the screen that proves that they have been deleted.
   c. Recover the deleted files.
   d. Print the screen that proves that the files have been recovered.
7. Find the CPU speed of your computer. Write down the answer.
8. Find the hard disk speed of your computer. Write down the answer.
9. What is the date and type of your BIOS? Write down the answer.
10. How many serial ports does your computer have? How many parallel ports does your computer have? Write down the answers.
11. Optimize the ACTIVITIES disk. Describe how you accomplished it.
12. If you could only purchase either PC Tools or Norton Utilities, which would you choose? Defend your selection.

18 Chapter

Windows

After completing this chapter you will be able to:

1. Explain Windows as an example of a graphical user interface.
2. List and explain hardware requirements for the different operating modes of Windows.
3. Explain the components of the Windows screens and manipulate the appearance of windows available to the user.
4. Explain the function of foreground and background windows.
5. Load and use foreground and background programs.
6. Access and use online help.
7. Explain the function of the `File Manager`.
8. Use the `File Manager` to perform file management functions.
9. Explain which DOS commands can be used with Windows.
10. Compare and contrast command line DOS and Windows.
11. Select and print files using `File Manager`.

Chapter Overview

In earlier chapters, we used **COMMAND.COM** as the command processor. To perform operating system tasks required the user to know commands and issue them at the command line prompt. DOS Shell is another means of performing operating system tasks. DOS Shell surrounds DOS, covering its details and providing the user with menus to communicate with DOS.

Windows 3.0 is another, more powerful means of interfacing with the operating system. Windows 3.0 is a complete operating environment. Windows provides a graphic user interface, allows multitasking, improves memory management, and, in general, utilizes the computer's capacity and versatility more fully. In addition, Windows comes with several application programs such as NOTEPAD, a text editor, and WRITE, a word processor.

Although Windows replaces the DOS command line, it does not replace DOS but instead works hand in hand with DOS. All DOS-based applications can be run in Windows as well as programs written specifically for Windows.

In this chapter you will learn how to use Windows and how to use some different functions that Windows provides.

18.0 About Windows 3.0

Windows 3.0 is a true graphical user interface (GUI) and is also considered an operating environment. It replaces the DOS command line, but it does not replace DOS (see Figure 18.1).

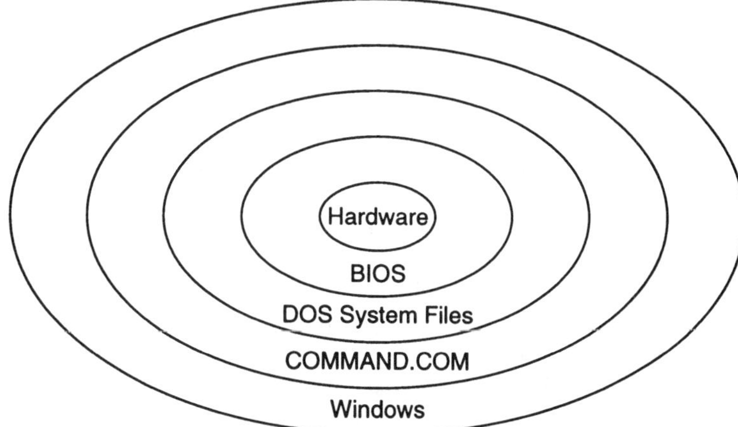

Figure 18.1 The Operating Environment

Windows works hand-in-hand with DOS. However, the user has a totally different interface using icons and drop-down menus in conjunction with the mouse. An icon is a tiny symbol on the screen representing a program, file, or task. For instance, a tiny picture of a wastebasket could represent the command to delete a file. You would activate deleting a file by dragging the file name to the icon and clicking the mouse.

One significant advantage of Windows 3.0 is the ability to run more than one program at a time. Each application can run in a "window." The contents of several windows can appear at one time. Thus, the user can be looking at the data in a spreadsheet and at the same time be writing a report about that data in the word processing application window. You can work on one document while printing another. Windows has a standard method for copying or moving data from one application to another. Thus, you can copy the data from a spreadsheet directly into the word processing document by means of the CLIPBOARD program. You can switch from running one application to running another just by clicking the mouse. The `Program Manager`—the Windows program execution shell—allows you to see your applications as icons. Application programs can be organized into groups. Programs can be executed by clicking the mouse or using keyboard commands. Windows has a `File Manager` that performs such operating system tasks as copying or deleting a file. Additionally, there is consistency among commands. Applications also use drop-down menus, dialog boxes, and the mouse. Thus, learning a new application requires less time. Windows also has a built-in memory manager that makes efficient use of the memory of the computer. Most importantly, programs that have been written for Windows can "break" the memory barrier to take advantage of memory beyond 640 KB.

Using Windows does not mean that you must give up all your non-Windows applications. You can still run all the DOS-based applications in Windows. In addition, Windows comes with some applications. These include the CLOCK, the CALCULATOR, a CARDFILE, and a CALENDAR for scheduling events. There is even an alarm in CALENDAR to remind you of meetings. NOTEPAD is an editor, much more powerful than EDIT. You also get a true word processor (WRITE), a drawing program (PAINTBRUSH), and a communication program (TERMINAL).

18.1 Hardware Requirements for Windows 3.0

Because Windows is such a powerful package, it needs powerful hardware and software to run successfully. You must have at least DOS 3.1 to run Windows. In addition, Windows has three modes of operating, real mode, standard mode, and 386 enhanced mode. These modes are dependent on hardware.

Real mode allows you to run Windows on a microcomputer with an 8086 or 8088 microprocessor. You must have at least 640 KB of RAM and 6 to 8 MB free on a hard disk. You *must* have a hard disk. You cannot run Windows on a floppy-based computer system. If you run in real mode, you do not have access to RAM beyond 640 KB.

Standard mode allows you to run on a microcomputer with a 80286 microprocessor and 1 MB of RAM. Again, you must have a hard disk with 6 to 8 MB free for Windows. In standard mode, you can use RAM above 640 KB. You can run Windows and non-Windows applications. However, each non-Windows application will take the entire screen, running in foreground only. This means that you suspend one program to run another.

The **386 enhanced mode** allows you to run on a microcomputer that has an 80386 or 80386SX or above microprocessor. You must have at least 2 MB of RAM as well as a hard disk with 6 to 8 MB free. It is better if you have 4 MB of RAM to take advantage of Windows. Enhanced mode is really the way that you want to run Windows. In enhanced mode, Windows can use what is called **virtual memory**. When you run out of RAM, Windows can write data to and from the hard disk temporarily, allowing almost limitless space to run application programs. In addition, you can not only run non-Windows applications as full screens in foreground but can actually place these non-Windows applications in windows and continue to run them in foreground or background.

To use Windows most effectively, it is best to have a color VGA monitor. Although you can run Windows with other types of monitors, you do not get the high-resolution benefits of the graphics and icons. In addition, you should have a mouse. Again, the advantages of GUIs cannot be fully exploited without a mouse.

Activity 18.2 Loading Windows and Working with Windows

Note 1: No disk needs to be in a drive at this time. You need to be at the root directory of C. Be sure the path is set to whatever subdirectory that Windows is located in. Some common subdirectory names are **\WINDOWS** or **\WIN3**.

Note 2: Instructions for keyboard users are in the left column. Instructions for mouse users are in the right column.

Note 3: All screen displays in this chapter are based on the default Windows installation.

STEP 1: Key in the following: C:\>**WIN** <Enter>	STEP 1: Key in the following: C:\>**WIN** <Enter>

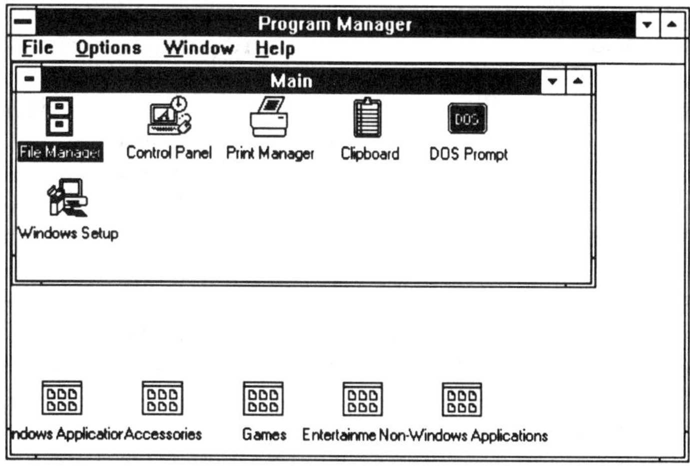

WHAT'S HAPPENING? This screen is the default installation of Windows. In order to understand how Windows operates, you must know the terminology. Look at the following screen display:

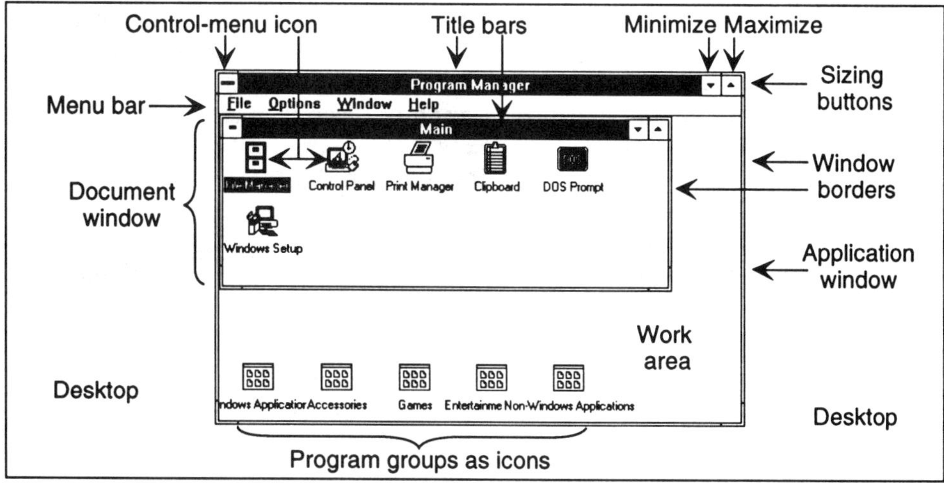

Document window. These windows appear only with applications that can open two or more documents at a time inside the same workspace. The **`Main`** window is an example of a document window. The document window can also be called the active window or the group window.

Application window. An application window contains any running application. **`Program Manager`** is an example of an application window.

Window borders. These are the edges that define the windows.

Title bar. The title bar contains the name of the window.

Control-menu icon. This box is an icon that can be "opened." When opened, it provides a drop-down menu with more commands. It can also be called the control-menu box, the system menu, or the control-menu button.

Sizing buttons. There are two arrows in the sizing box. One arrow points up, the other down. The up arrow is called the maximize button and the down arrow is called the minimize button. The upward pointing arrow allows you to maximize the window. In other words, you can make the window or the application in the window fill the entire screen. If you want to devote all your attention to a program, you can maximize it. The downward pointing arrow allows you to minimize the window. In other words, you can make the window or application in the window shrink to an icon. Thus, by minimizing an application, you can get it out of your way yet still keep it on the desktop (screen).

Menu bar. The menu bar allows you access to most of the commands of a specific application. The commands can vary from application to application, but if it is a Windows application, the commands will usually be the same.

Work area. The area within the window is the place where you work on the application.

Desktop. The desktop is analogous to your desk. You can treat it as a desk by stacking programs on it, limited only by the memory of your computer.

Program groups. Program groups have icons that allow you to start applications. They can contain similar types of applications. For instance, the icon named **`Games`** contains two programs that are games. In addition, a program group can contain documents related to a specific application. If you had a word processing program group, it could contain not only the actual application program but also all those documents associated with the application.

In the previous screen, **`Program Manager`** has one open window and five minimized windows. **`Program Manager`** is both the application and the parent window. The five internal minimized windows at the bottom of the screen can be called child windows.

STEP 2:	Press <Alt>+<Spacebar>+X.	STEP 2:	Click the upward pointing arrow (maximize button) on the **`Program Manager`** title bar.

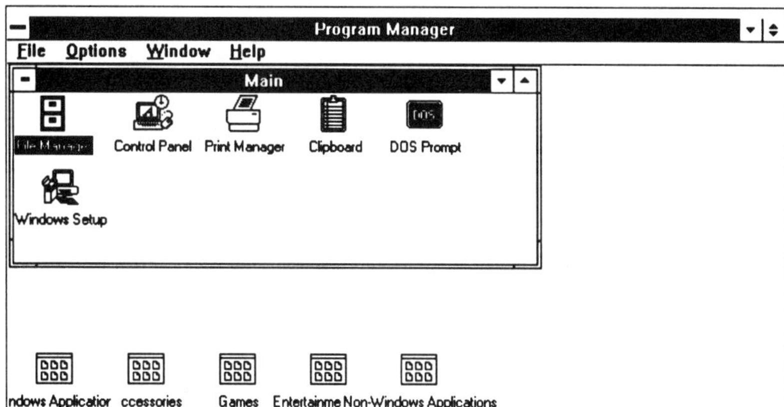

WHAT'S HAPPENING? You have maximized the window. It now fills the screen completely. If you look at the sizing buttons, you will see that you still have the downward pointing arrow, but instead of the upward pointing arrow, you now have a double-headed arrow. This arrow is known as the "restore button" which restores the window to its previous size.

STEP 3:	Press <Alt>+<Spacebar>+R.	STEP 3:	Click the restore button.

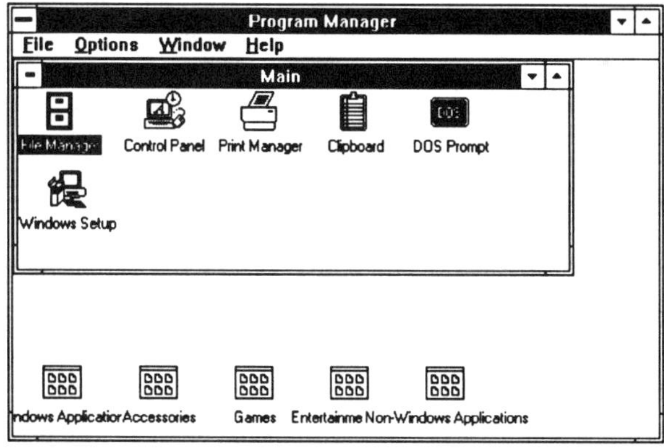

WHAT'S HAPPENING? You restored the window to the default size.

STEP 4:	Press <Alt>+<Spacebar>+N.	STEP 4:	Click the downward pointing arrow (minimize button).

WHAT'S HAPPENING? You minimized **`Program Manager`**, which appears in its icon form in the lower part of the screen. Remember that each Windows application has a unique icon that is recognizable. **`Program Manager`** is still open and on the desktop, but it is out of the way.

STEP 5: Press <Alt>+<Spacebar>+R to restore the window.

STEP 5: Double-click **`Program Manager`** icon to restore it.

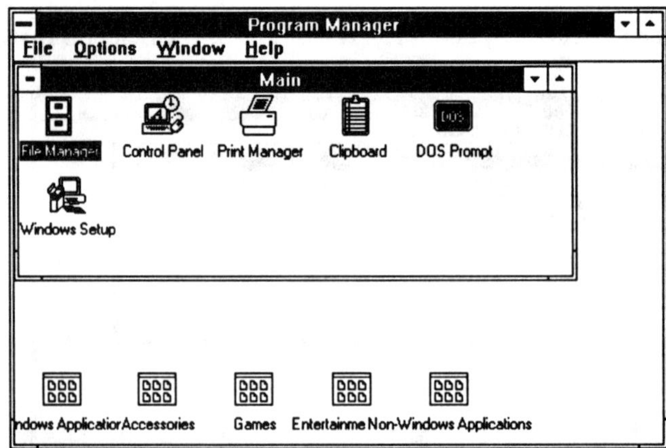

WHAT'S HAPPENING? The Program Manager window is restored.

STEP 6: Press <Alt>+<Hyphen>+M. A new pointer shape appears, the four-headed arrow (✥). Press the <Right arrow> key 8 times and press the <Down arrow> key 15 times to move the **`Main`** window. Once you are in position, press <Enter>.

STEP 6: Place the mouse pointer on the title bar labeled **`Main`**. Hold down the left mouse button and move the mouse in a downward and rightward direction. The entire **`Main`** window should move down and to the right. When you have moved the window, release the left mouse button.

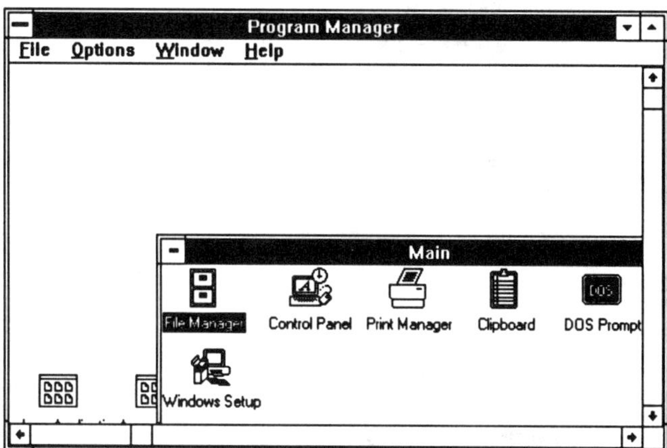

WHAT'S HAPPENING? As you can see, you can move the **Main** window around. You can move all windows using the same technique.

STEP 7: Press <Alt>+<Hyphen>+M. Press the <Up arrow> key 15 times. Press the <Left arrow> key 8 times. When the **Main** window is in its original position, press <Enter>.	STEP 7: Place the mouse pointer on the title bar labeled **Main** and return the **Main** window to its original position.
STEP 8: Press <Alt>+<Spacebar> +S. You will see a double-headed arrow (⇔). Press the <Right arrow> key once which will move you to the border of the **Program Manager**. Press the <Left arrow> key 15 times. Press <Enter>.	STEP 8: Place the mouse pointer on the right **Program Manager** window border. The arrow should become double-headed (⇔). Now press and hold the left mouse button while moving to the left on the border. The border of **Program Manager** should contract because you are pushing in.

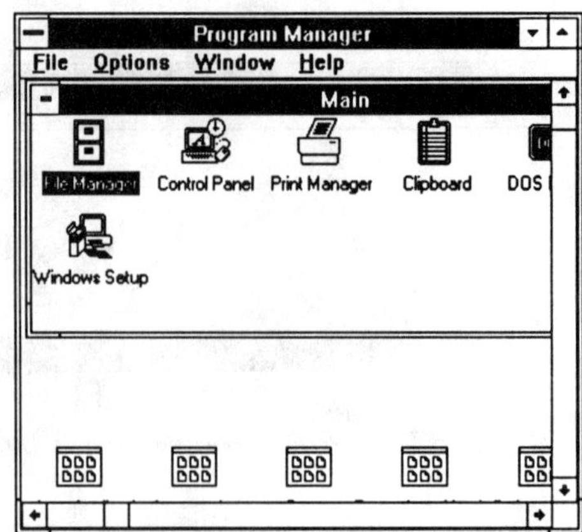

WHAT'S HAPPENING? Your screen will look something like the above display, depending on how you moved the borders.

STEP 9: Press <Alt>+<Spacebar> +S. Press the <Right arrow> key once. Press the <Right arrow> key fifteen times. Press <Enter>.

STEP 9: Place the mouse pointer on the right border of **`Program Manager`**. Press and hold the left mouse button and move the mouse to the right, expanding the border to its original position.

18.3 Using Windows

In the above exercises, you were manipulating the appearance of the different windows. In the next series of activities, you will learn how to start a program in Windows and also how to have more than one program running at a time. When you have only one application program open, it is in the foreground. The foreground application is the one that Windows treats as the application you are working on. The foreground application is also known as the foreground window, the active window, or the current window. If you have more than one application open, only one application is in the foreground; the rest of the applications are in the background. The active window is always on the top of the desktop with its title bar highlighted.

Activity 18.4 Loading Foreground and Background Programs

Note: You are in Windows. The **`Program Manager`** window is displayed with the **`Main`** window inside **`Program Manager`**. If **`Program Manager`** fills the entire screen, restore it to its default size by clicking the restore button on the title bar or by pressing <Alt>+<Spacebar>+R. If **`Program Manager`** is an icon, restore it by double-clicking the **`Program Manager`** icon or pressing <Alt>+<Spacebar>+R.

STEP 1: Press <Alt>+W.

STEP 1: Click the word **`Window`** on the **`Program Manager`** title bar.

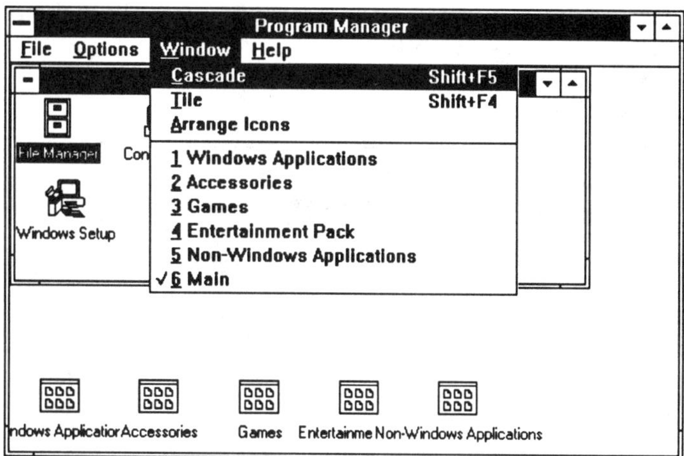

WHAT'S HAPPENING? You opened **Program Manager**'s **Window** menu. **Main** has a check mark by it indicating that it is the open window. You have several choices to select from. Each choice indicates a group of programs. The selection may differ on your computer, depending on what programs have been installed. In this case, you are going to select **Games**. In this example, **Games** is number 3. On your system, it could be a different number.

STEP 2: Move the <Down arrow> key until **Games** is highlighted. Then, press <Enter>.

STEP 2: Click **Games**.

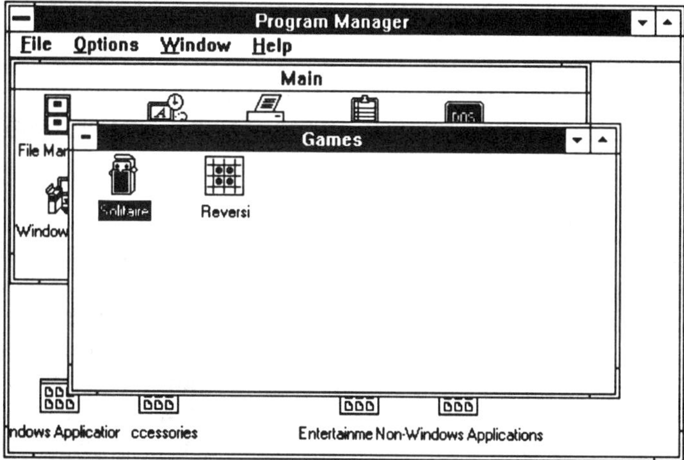

WHAT'S HAPPENING? You selected the **Games** program group. Windows comes with two games, **Solitaire** and **Reversi**. Each game is represented by an icon. If you had other games, you could add them to this program group. If you have a mouse, you could have gone directly to this window by double-clicking the **Games** icon, bypassing the menu.

STEP 3: Use the arrow key to highlight **Reversi**. When **Reversi** is highlighted, press <Enter>.	STEP 3: Double-click **Reversi**.

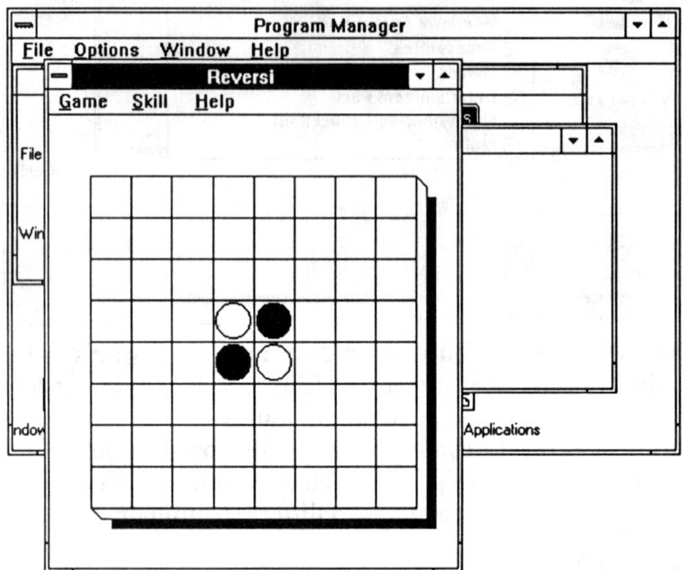

WHAT'S HAPPENING? `Reversi` is now in the foreground and is the active application. If you wanted to, you could play this game. `Program Manager` is in the background. You can tell which is the active application not only because `Reversi` is lying on top of `Program Manager` but also because the title bar for `Reversi` is highlighted. You now have two open windows, `Program Manager` and `Reversi`. However, only `Reversi` is the active or current window. You can switch windows or switch programs since both are open. You can even open other applications.

STEP 4: Press <Alt>+<Tab>.	STEP 4: `Program Manager` should still be visible in the background. Click the `Program Manager` title bar or anywhere in the `Program Manager` window. If you cannot see `Program Manager` window, press <Alt>+<Tab>.

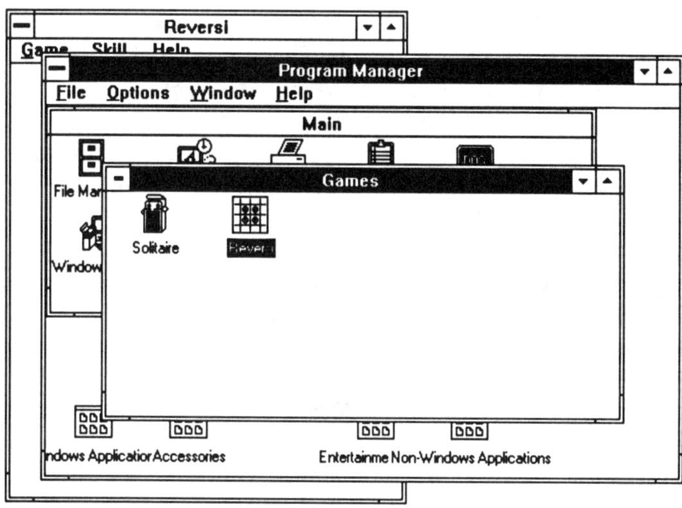

WHAT'S HAPPENING? **`Program Manager`** is now the **active window**. You should still be able to see **`Reversi`** in the background, but its title bar should not be highlighted.

STEP 5: Press <Alt>+<Esc>. **`Reversi`** will be in the foreground.

STEP 6: Press <Alt>+<Tab> so that the **`Games`** window is in the foreground.

STEP 7: Use the arrow keys to highlight **`Solitaire`**. Then press <Enter>.

STEP 5: Press <Alt>+<Esc>. **`Reversi`** will be in the foreground.

STEP 6: Press <Alt>+<Tab> so that the **`Games`** window is in the foreground.

STEP 7: Double-click the **`Solitaire`** icon.

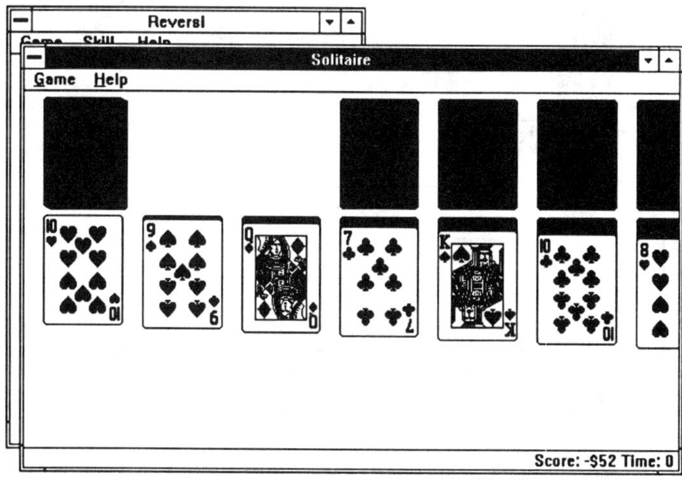

WHAT'S HAPPENING? You now have three windows open, `Reversi`, `Program Manager`, and `Solitaire`. Because `Solitaire` is on top, it is the active window. You could play solitaire now if you wanted. It is the foreground window that takes the majority of the computer's processing time. `Reversi` and `Program Manager` are open but not active. They are in the background and therefore get a smaller share of the computer's processing time. If you have a mouse, you can always click the window you want active.

If you cannot see the window you wish to use or you do not have a mouse, you can use <Alt>+<Tab> or <Alt>+<Esc>. If you hold down the <Alt> key and press the <Tab> key several times they will cycle though the open windows without drawing the inside of the window on the screen. You will see only the title bar and the border of the window. The <Alt>+<Esc> key combination shows not only the title bar and borders but also draws the window contents. Because graphics takes so much time, the <Alt>+<Tab> key combination is much quicker to use than the <Alt>+<Esc> key combination.

STEP 8: Try the <Alt>+<Esc> and <Alt>+<Tab> key combinations a few times to see how differently they work. Be sure to end with `Solitaire` as the active window.

STEP 8: Try the <Alt>+<Esc> and <Alt>+<Tab> key combinations a few times to see how differently they work. Be sure to end with `Solitaire` as the active window.

STEP 9: Press <Ctrl>+<Esc>.

STEP 9: Double-click the mouse anywhere on the desktop and outside of any window. If you cannot see the desktop, press <Ctrl>+<Esc>.

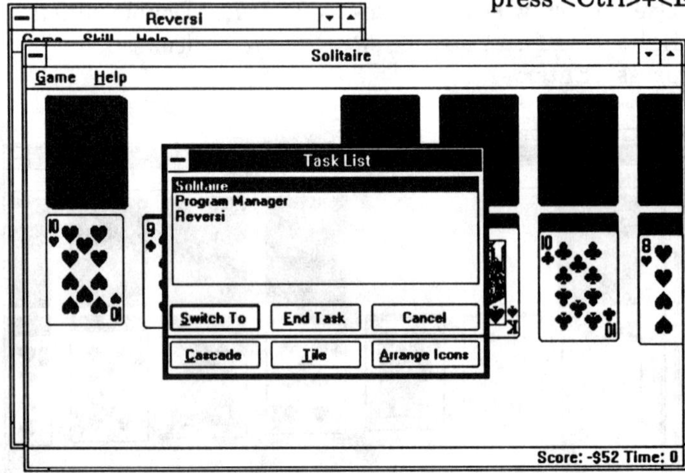

WHAT'S HAPPENING? You opened the `Task List` window. In it are lists of all the programs that are presently open. In addition, it has some command buttons at the bottom. These buttons allow you to switch (`Switch To`) or close applications (`End Task`). You may take no action and leave this window (`Cancel`). You may order the icons (`Arrange Icons`). You may also change the appearance of the windows. First, you are going to switch to the `Reversi` window.

STEP 10: Use the arrow key to highlight `Reversi`. Then press <Alt>+S.

STEP 10: Click `Reversi`. Click `Switch To`. You can also double-click `Reversi` to make it active in one step.

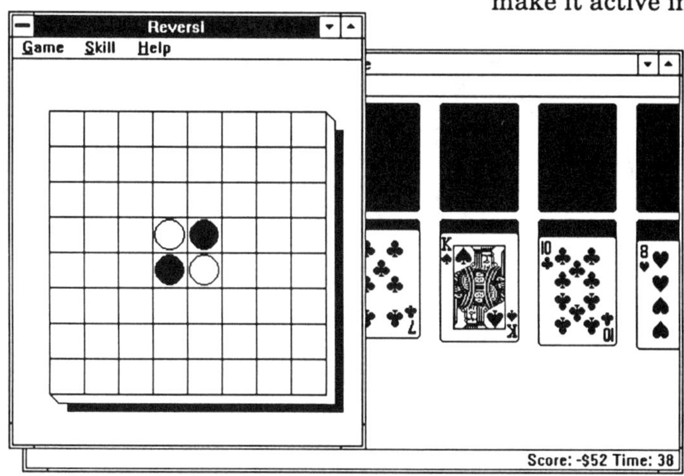

WHAT'S HAPPENING? You switched programs and made `Reversi` the active and foreground window. `Program Manager` and `Solitaire` are still open, but they are not active and therefore in the background.

STEP 11: Press <Ctrl>+<Esc>.

STEP 11: Double-click the mouse on the desktop or anywhere outside the windows. If you cannot see the desktop, press <Ctrl>+<Esc>.

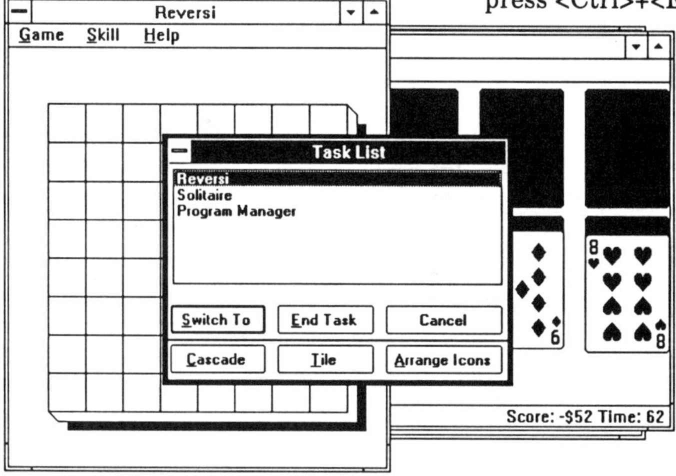

WHAT'S HAPPENING? You are now back at the `Task List` window.

STEP 12: Press <Alt>+T.

STEP 12: Click **`Tile`**.

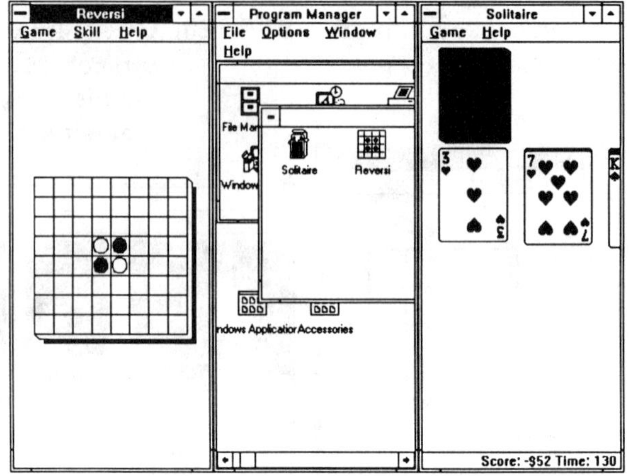

WHAT'S HAPPENING? Your open windows are now displayed side by side. The title bar of the active window is highlighted. In this case, the title bar of Reversi is highlighted. You can work in any of the open windows, once you make them active.

STEP 13: Press <Alt>+<Esc> to highlight the different title bars. Finish by having the **`Reversi`** highlighted.

STEP 13: Click the title bar of **`Solitaire`**. Then click **`Program Manager`**. Last, click **`Reversi`**.

STEP 14: You cannot see the desktop. Thus, to return to **`Task List`**, press <Ctrl>+<Esc>.

STEP 14: You cannot see the desktop. Thus, to return to **`Task List`**, press <Ctrl>+<Esc>.

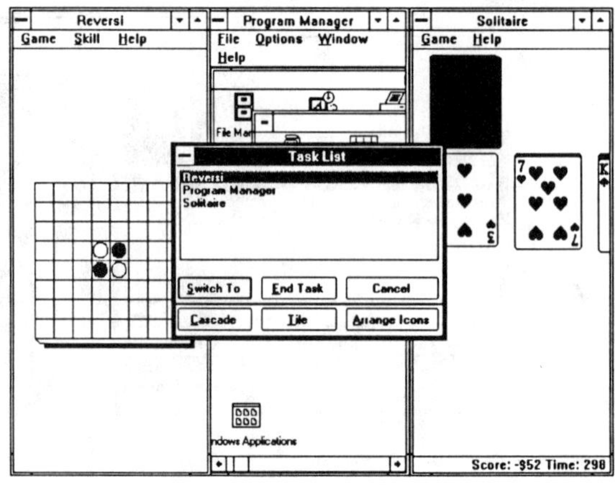

WHAT'S HAPPENING? You returned to `Task List`.

STEP 15: Press <Alt>+C.

STEP 15: Click `Cascade`.

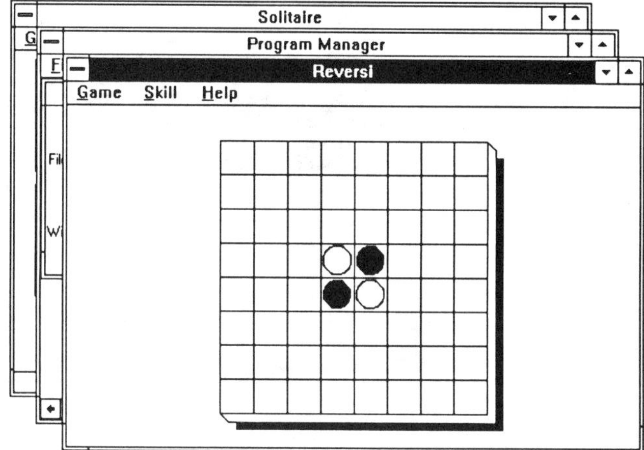

WHAT'S HAPPENING? Now the open windows are stacked on top of each other. Once again, the active window title bar is highlighted. In this case, it is `Reversi`.

STEP 16: Press <Alt>+F4.

STEP 16: Double-click the control menu icon of `Reversi`. It is the box in the left corner of the `Reversi` title bar.

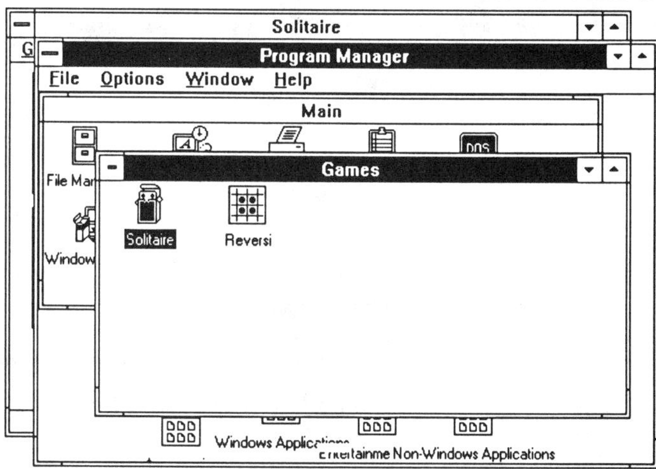

WHAT'S HAPPENING? You closed `Reversi` and are at the `Games` window. You can also close an application by using `Task List`.

STEP 17: Press <Ctrl>+<Esc>.

STEP 17: Click on the desktop anywhere outside a window.

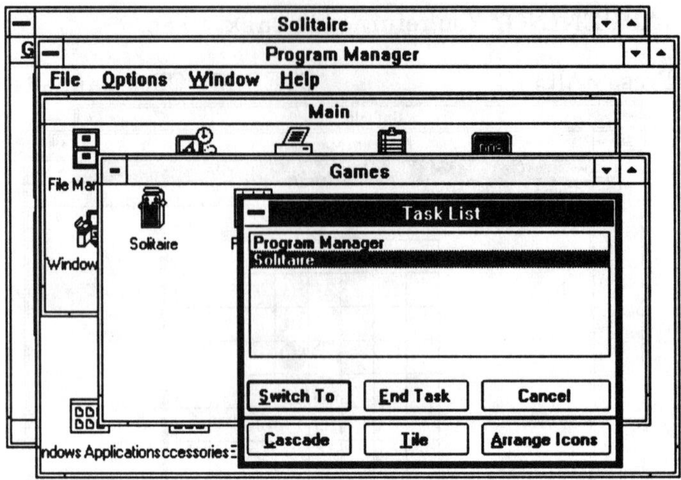

WHAT'S HAPPENING? You returned to **Task List**.

STEP 18: Use the arrow key to highlight **Solitaire**. Then press <Alt>+E.	STEP 18: Click **Solitaire**. Click **End Task**.

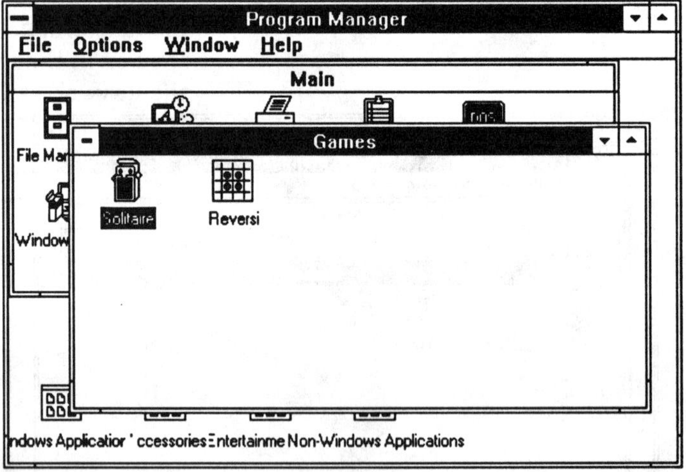

WHAT'S HAPPENING? You closed both **Reversi** and **Solitaire**. Next, you need to close **Games**.

STEP 19: Press <Alt>+<Hyphen>+N.	STEP 19: Double-click the control menu icon on the **Games** title bar.

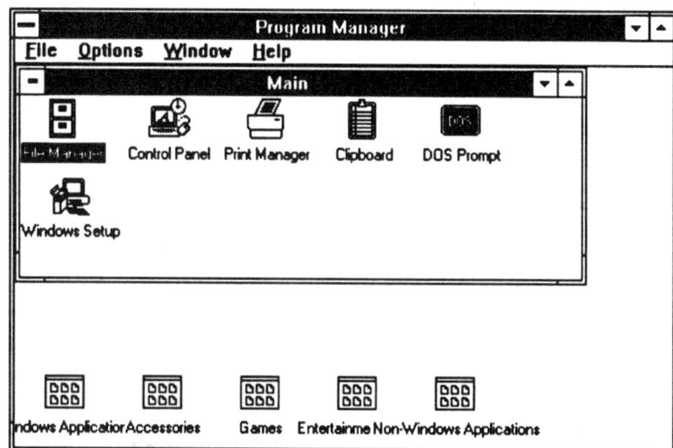

WHAT'S HAPPENING? You returned to the `Program Manager` window. Since all your application windows are closed, you can now exit Windows.

STEP 20: Press <Alt>+F4.

STEP 20: Double-click the control menu icon for `Program Manager`.

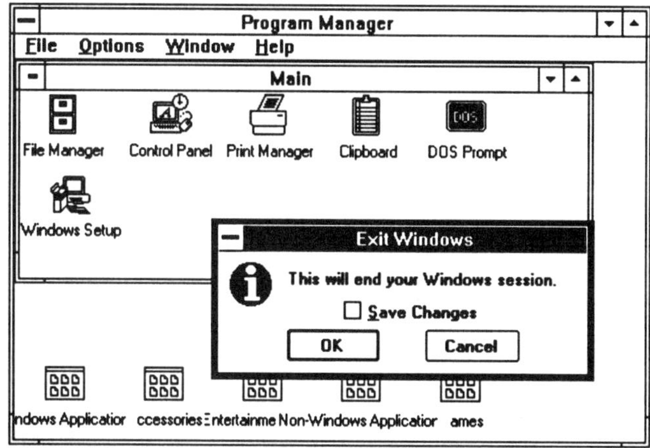

WHAT'S HAPPENING? Before you exit Windows, it gives you one chance to change your mind. You can "unquit" by clicking `Cancel` or pressing <Esc>.

STEP 21: Press <Enter>.

STEP 21: Click `OK`.

```
C>_
```

WHAT'S HAPPENING? You returned to DOS.

18.5 Working with Help

Windows provides an online help facility. An online help capability lets you access help directly from the screen rather than from a manual.

Activity 18.6 Using Help

	Keyboard		Mouse
STEP 1:	Key in the following: C:\>**WIN** <Enter>	STEP 1:	Key in the following: C:\>**WIN** <Enter>

WHAT'S HAPPENING? The **Program Manager** window is displayed with the **Main** window within.

STEP 2:	Press <Alt>+H.	STEP 2:	Click **Help** on the **Program Manager** menu bar.

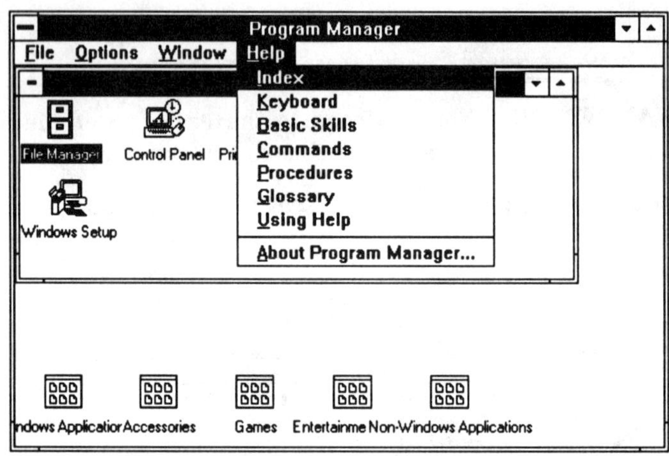

WHAT'S HAPPENING? You selected the **Help** menu, which gives you help with the **Program Manager**.

STEP 3:	Use the arrow keys to highlight **About Program Manager** and then press <Enter>.	STEP 3:	Click **About Program Manager**.

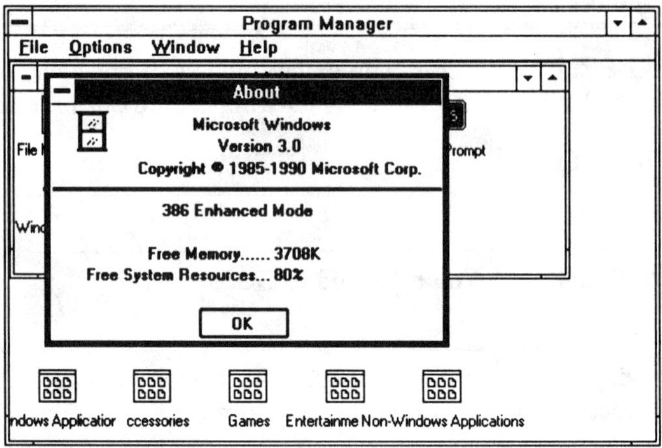

WHAT'S HAPPENING? Selecting `About` identifies the mode of Windows you are running: standard, real, or enhanced and supplies other details about your hardware operating environment.

STEP 4: Press <Alt>+F4.

STEP 4: Click `OK`.

WHAT'S HAPPENING? You returned to the `Program Manager` window.

STEP 5: Press F1.

STEP 5: Press F1.

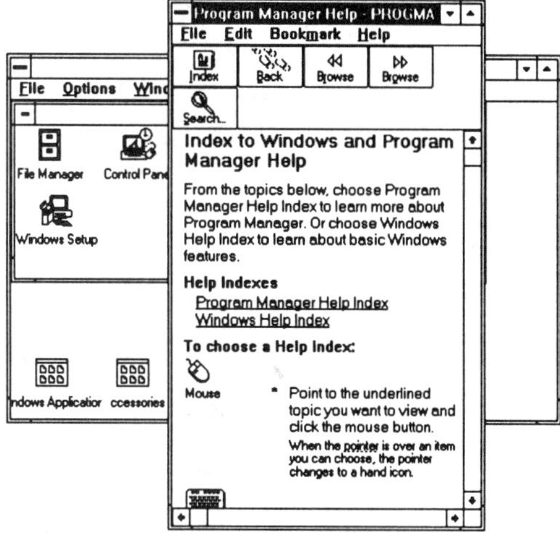

WHAT'S HAPPENING? F1 is another way to get help.

STEP 6: Press the <Tab> key until `Pointer` is highlighted.

STEP 6: Move the mouse to `Pointer`, which has a dotted underline.

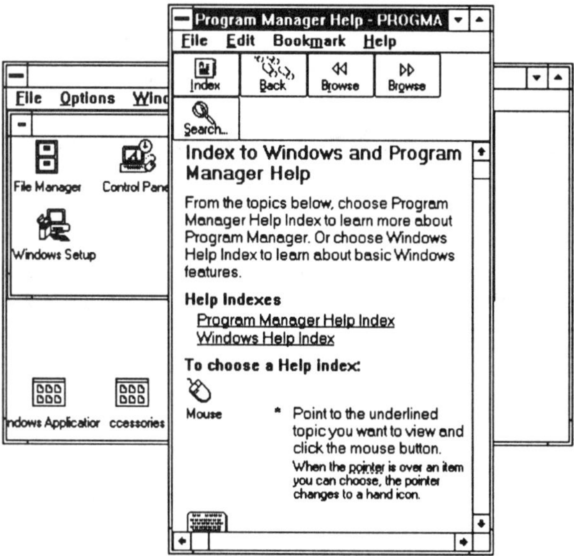

WHAT'S HAPPENING? If you have a mouse, the arrow changed to a little hand pointing at the word `Pointer`. If you have a color monitor, `Pointer` will be in a different color. If you are using keyboard commands, `Pointer` will be highlighted. The words that have a dotted underline are key terms. A key term gives you a brief capsule description of the highlighted item.

STEP 7: Press and hold <Enter> while `Pointer` is highlighted.	STEP 7: Hold down the left mouse button while the little hand is on `Pointer`.

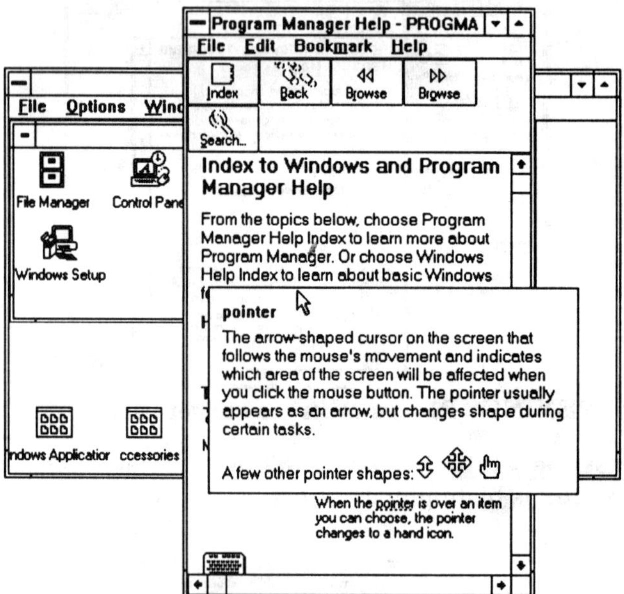

WHAT'S HAPPENING? You got a brief description of the term `Pointer`.

STEP 8: Release the <Enter> key.	STEP 8: Release the left mouse button.
STEP 9: Press the <Tab> key until `Window Help Index` is highlighted.	STEP 9: Move the mouse to `Window Help Index` until the arrow changes to a little hand.

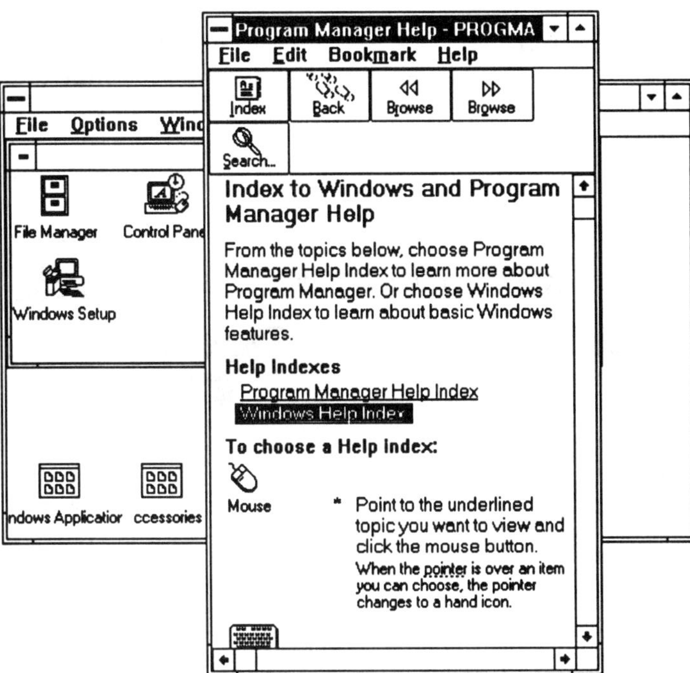

WHAT'S HAPPENING? You highlighted a solidly underlined item. If you have a color monitor, it will be in a different color. Solidly underlined items are key words. A key word calls up a major help screen to assist you.

STEP 10: Press <Enter> while **`Windows Help Index`** is highlighted.

STEP 10: Click **`Windows Help Index`**.

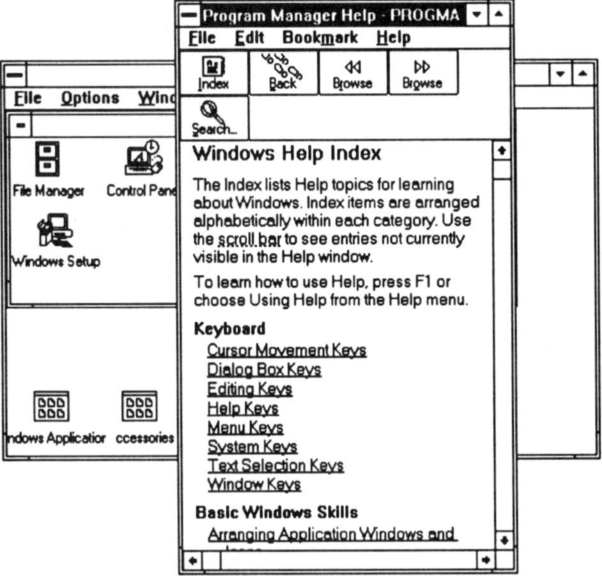

WHAT'S HAPPENING? You now have an index to all the help topics. Again, anything that is underscored gives you a full description of the command. The dotted underscore gives you a brief description of the item you selected.

STEP 11: Press <Alt>+F4.

STEP 11: Double-click the control menu icon on the **Program Manager Help** title bar.

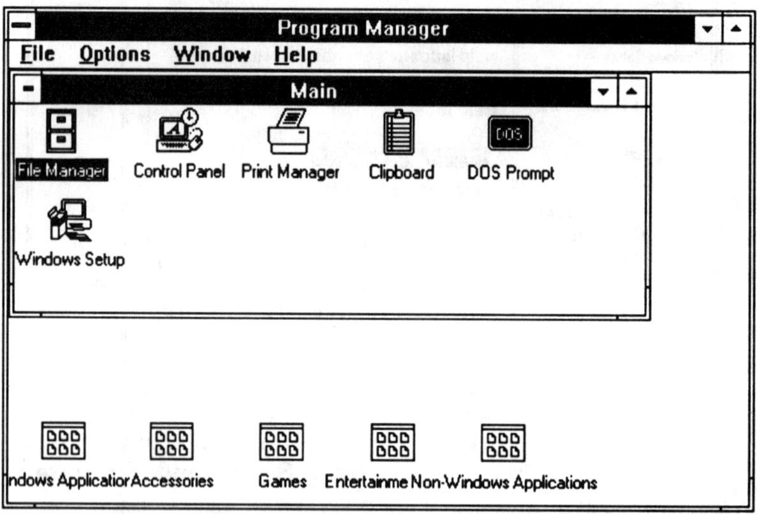

WHAT'S HAPPENING? You returned to **Program Manager**.

18.7 File Manager

File Manager allows you to accomplish many of the tasks you accomplished at the DOS command line prompt. You can perform such tasks as copying files, deleting files, creating subdirectories, formatting floppy disks, and executing programs. In addition, **File Manager** also gives you capabilities not available in DOS such as the ability to rename a subdirectory or move a file.

Activity 18.8 Using File Manager

Note: The DATA disk is in Drive A. You are in Windows. The **Program Manager** window should be displayed with the **Main** window within the **Program Manager** window.

STEP 1: Press an arrow key to highlight the **File Manager** icon. Then press <Enter>.

STEP 1: Double-click the **File Manager** icon.

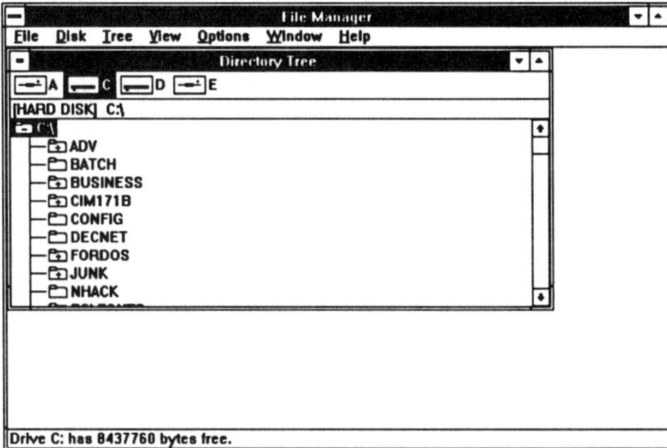

WHAT'S HAPPENING? Your display will be different depending on the hardware, software, subdirectories, and files you have. What you see is the `Directory Tree` window for Drive C. It shows you the structure of the directories on the hard disk. A further description of the items on the `Directory Tree` window follows.

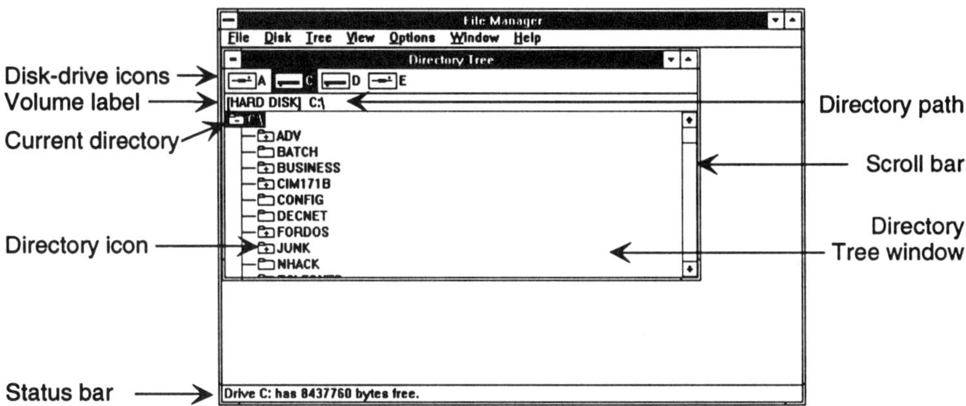

Volume label. The volume label of the disk.

Disk-drive icons. The disk drives on your computer system. A drive letter follows each icon. The icon that is highlighted is the default disk drive.

Directory path. The path of the currently highlighted drive. In this case, it is the root directory of C. As you select different subdirectories, this line will change, indicating what the path is.

Current directory. The default directory.

Directory icons. Represented by a file folder. Each one represents a directory, and the list is alphabetical. If a directory contains other directories, it is indicated by a plus sign (+) within the file folder icon.

Scroll bar. If there are more directories or data than can be shown vertically in the window, a vertical bar called the vertical scroll bar is added to the right side of the window. If there are more directories or data than can be shown horizontally in the window, a horizontal bar is added on the bottom of the window. A scroll bar is a way to move the screen display with the mouse. The scroll bar also indicates your current position in the document or display window. To use the scroll bar, click the vertical scroll bar up or down arrow to move up or down one line. To use the horizontal scroll bar, click the left or right arrow to move right or left. To move quickly, locate the slider box within the scroll bar and drag the slider box either up or down or left or right. To jump windows, click above or below the slider box.

STEP 2: Use the <Down arrow> key to highlight **JUNK**. Then press the <Plus> key on the numeric key pad.

STEP 2: Click once on the plus sign next to the icon named **JUNK**.

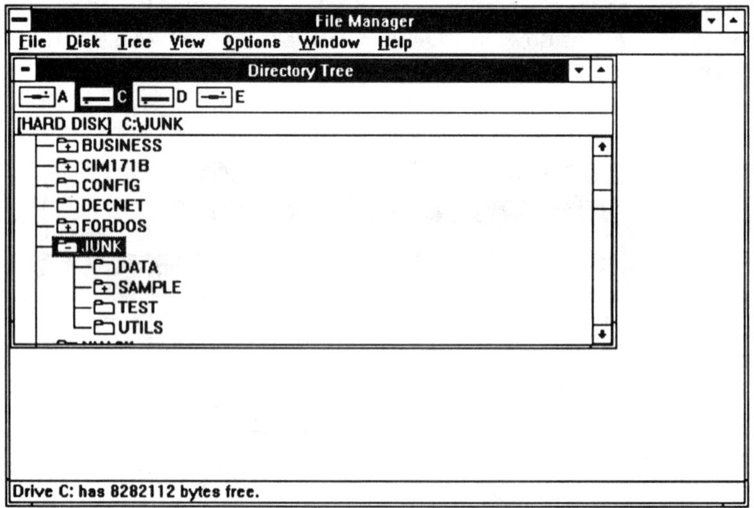

WHAT'S HAPPENING? By clicking on the plus sign in the folder, you see the next level of detail within the **JUNK** subdirectory. The display is still the **Directory Tree** window. In this instance, it shows you the subdirectories that are presently in **JUNK**. The plus sign in the file folder icon has changed to a minus sign. The plus sign means that you can expand a directory listing. The minus sign means that you can collapse the directory listing. You can see that the subdirectory called **SAMPLE** has a plus sign in its folder which indicates that there are more directories within.

STEP 3: Highlight **SAMPLE** and press the <Asterisk> key on the numeric key pad.

STEP 3: Click once on the plus sign next to the icon called **SAMPLE**.

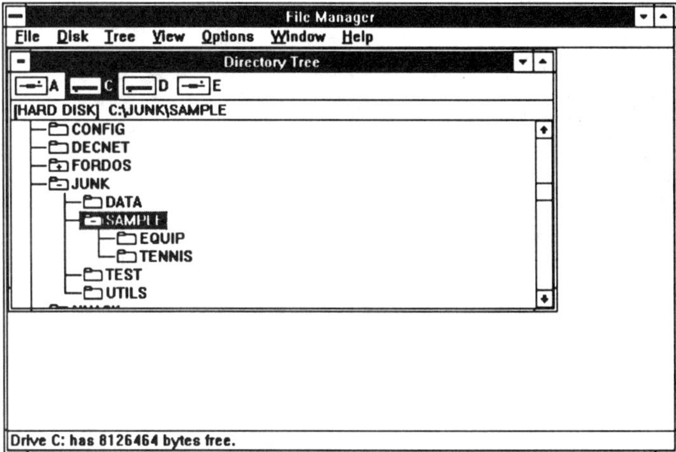

WHAT'S HAPPENING? You expanded the **SAMPLE** subdirectory listing, and you see that there are subdirectories called **EQUIP** and **TENNIS** under **SAMPLE**. Since there is neither a plus nor a minus sign in the file folder icon, there are no more subdirectories under **SAMPLE**. In order to see the files that are in a directory, you must take another step.

STEP 4: Highlight **EQUIP** and press <Enter>.

STEP 4: Double-click **EQUIP**.

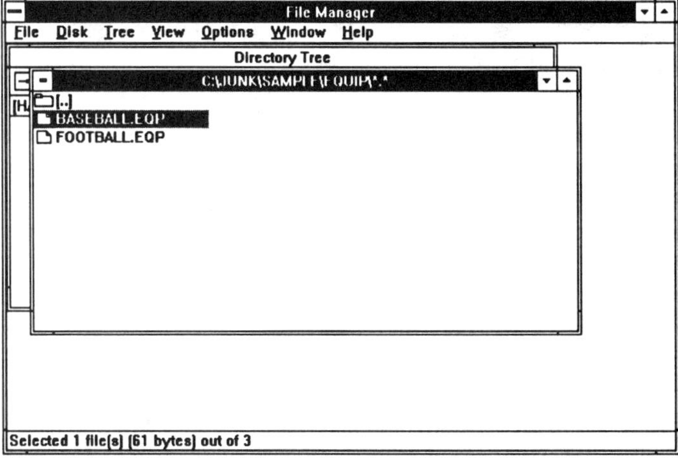

WHAT'S HAPPENING? You displayed the files in the subdirectory called **EQUIP**. Next, you are going to return to the previous screen.

STEP 5: Press <Ctrl>+F4.

STEP 5: Double-click the control menu icon of the **JUNK\SAMPLE\EQUIP** window.

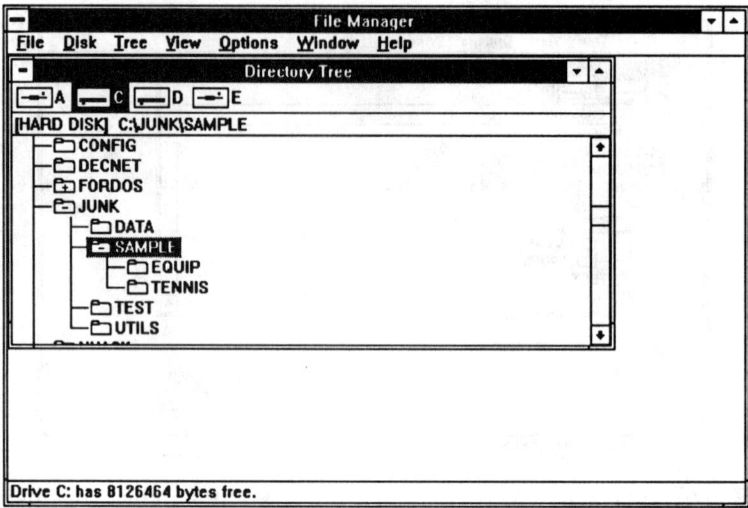

WHAT'S HAPPENING? You returned to the previous screen. When you double-clicked, you bypassed the control menu. If you had clicked only once you would see a drop-down menu. You could have then clicked `Close` in the drop-down menu. If you do not have a mouse and want to use the control menu, press <Alt>+<Hyphen>, move the cursor down to `Close`, and then press <Enter>.

STEP 6: Press <Ctrl>+A.

STEP 6: Click the Drive A icon.

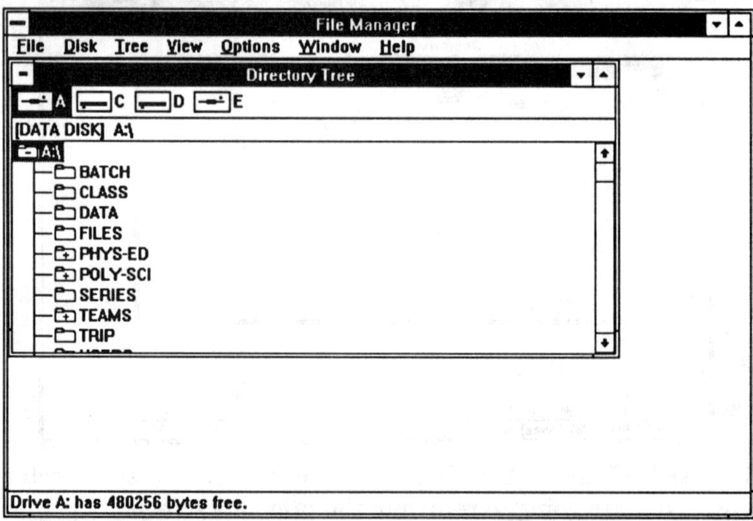

WHAT'S HAPPENING? You are displaying the directories on the DATA disk. You may have already noticed that Windows automatically alphabetizes the entries.

STEP 7: Press <Ctrl>+C.

STEP 7: Click the Drive C icon.

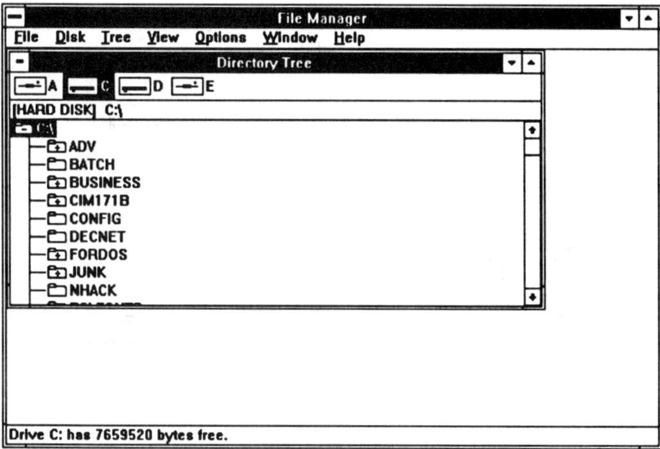

WHAT'S HAPPENING? You returned to the screen display of Drive C where you can look at several subdirectories at one time.

STEP 8: Highlight the **JUNK** icon and press the <Asterisk> key.

STEP 8: Click on the plus sign in the **JUNK** icon.

STEP 9: Use the arrow key to highlight **SAMPLE**. Press <Enter>.

STEP 9: Double-click the **SAMPLE** icon.

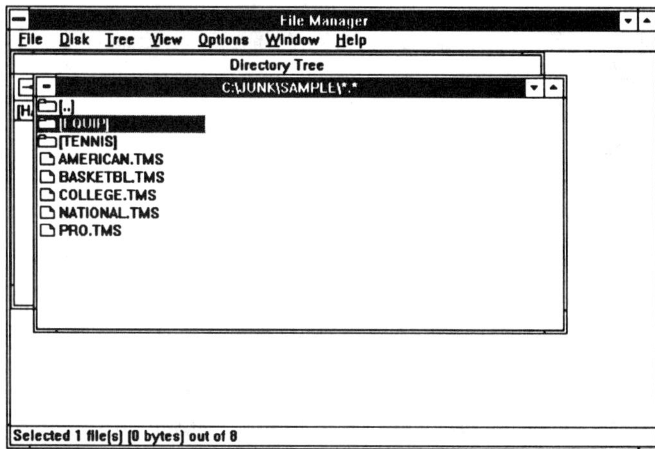

WHAT'S HAPPENING? You are displaying all the files, arranged alphabetically, in the subdirectory **SAMPLE**. The subdirectories are listed first. An advantage of Windows is that you can have more than one directory window open at a time.

STEP 10: Press <Ctrl>+F6.

STEP 10: Click once on the window behind the current window. If you cannot see it, press <Ctrl>+F6.

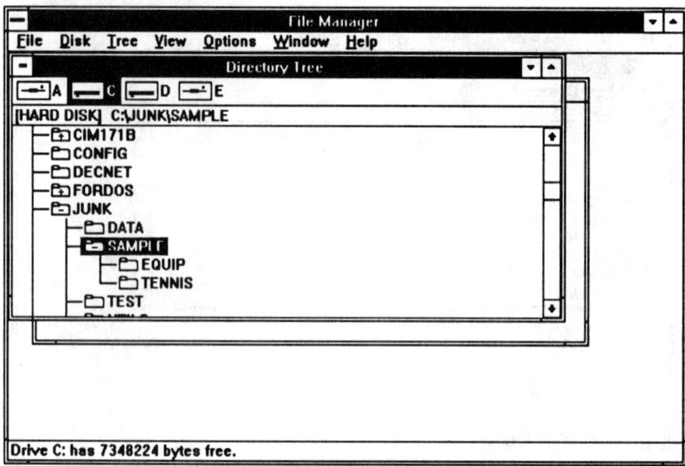

WHAT'S HAPPENING? You returned to the **`Directory Tree`** window of Drive C.

STEP 11: Highlight the **`DATA`** icon and press <Enter>.

STEP 11: Double-click **`DATA`**.

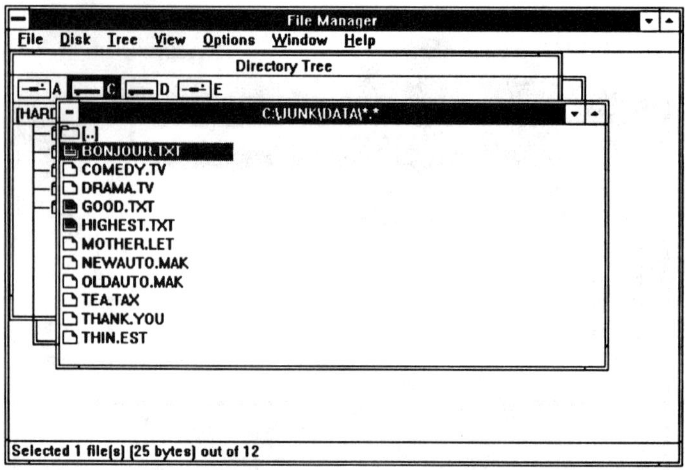

WHAT'S HAPPENING? You now have two directory windows open. You can look at both of these open windows at the same time.

STEP 12: Press the F10 key so that the **`File Manager`** title bar is highlighted; then use the arrow keys to highlight **`Window`** and press <Enter>.

STEP 12: Click **`Window`** on the **`File Manager`** title bar.

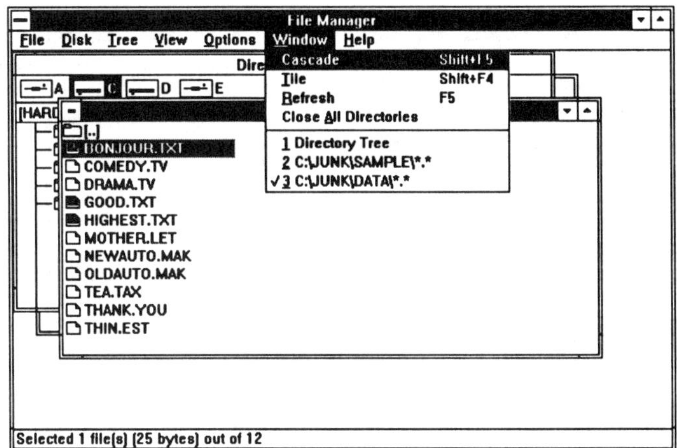

WHAT'S HAPPENING? You opened the drop-down menu `Window`.

STEP 13: Highlight `Tile` and press <Enter>.

STEP 13: Click on `Tile`.

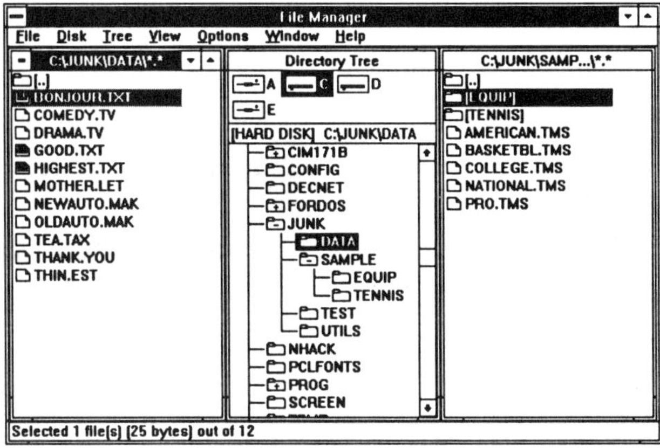

WHAT'S HAPPENING? You see three open directory windows. These windows are **tiled**, arranged side by side. You can open more directory windows. You are going to open the `UTILS` subdirectory in the `JUNK` subdirectory on Drive C.

STEP 14: Press <Ctrl>+F6 to change the active window to the `Directory Tree` window. In this case it is the window in the middle. You can tell which window is active by a different color or shade on the title bar.

STEP 14: Click the `Directory Tree` window. In this case it is the window in the middle. You can tell which window is active by a different color or shade on the title bar.

STEP 15: Highlight `UTILS` and press <Enter>.

STEP 15: Double-click `UTILS`.

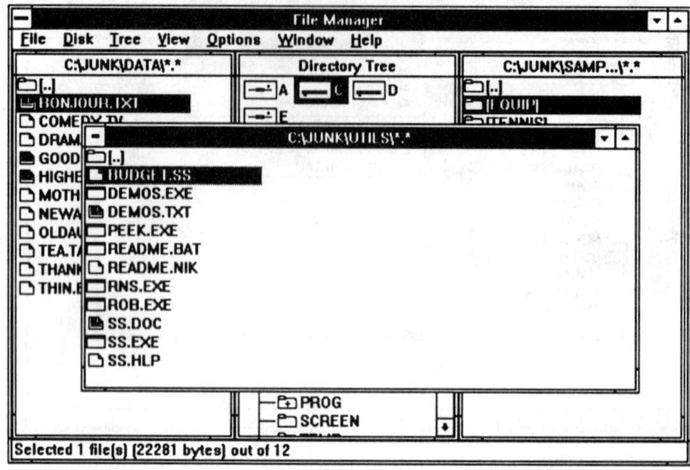

WHAT'S HAPPENING? You opened a directory window for the `UTILS` subdirectory on Drive C. You can also include this window in the tiled display.

STEP 16: Press the F10 key and use the arrow key to highlight `Window` on the menu bar.	STEP 16: Click `Window` on the menu bar.
STEP 17: Highlight `Tile` and press <Enter>.	STEP 17: Click `Tile`.

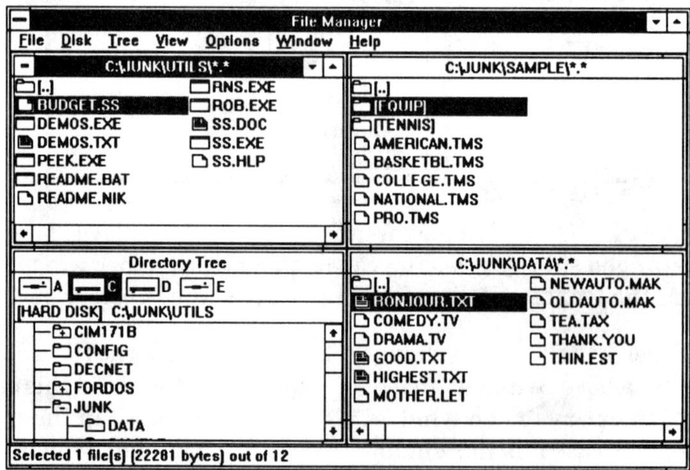

WHAT'S HAPPENING? The tiled display shows all four of the directory windows you opened. You know which is active by which bar is highlighted. The directory windows uses four different kinds of file icons to distinguish different file types.

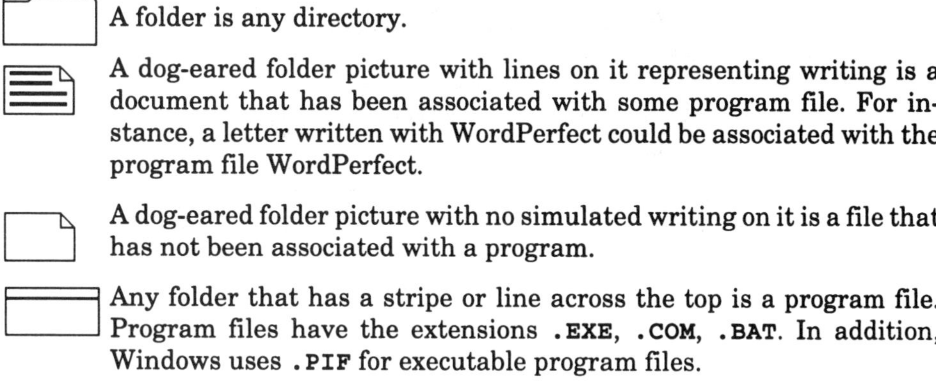

A folder is any directory.

A dog-eared folder picture with lines on it representing writing is a document that has been associated with some program file. For instance, a letter written with WordPerfect could be associated with the program file WordPerfect.

A dog-eared folder picture with no simulated writing on it is a file that has not been associated with a program.

Any folder that has a stripe or line across the top is a program file. Program files have the extensions `.EXE`, `.COM`, `.BAT`. In addition, Windows uses `.PIF` for executable program files.

STEP 18: Press F10, highlight `Window`, and then press <Enter>.

STEP 18: Click `Window`.

STEP 19: Highlight `Cascade` and press <Enter>.

STEP 19: Click `Cascade`.

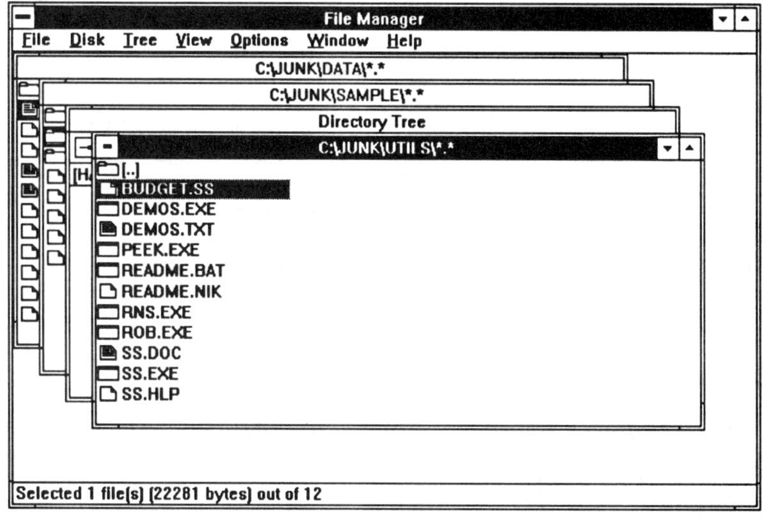

WHAT'S HAPPENING? The directory windows are stacked, or **cascaded**, one on top of the other. You can move through them by clicking on the title bar of the window you are interested in. If you do not have a mouse, you can use <Ctrl>+F6 to move among the windows. `File Manager` can be minimized or maximized.

STEP 20: Press <Ctrl>+F4.

STEP 20: Double-click the control menu icon on the title bar labeled `\JUNK\UTILS`.

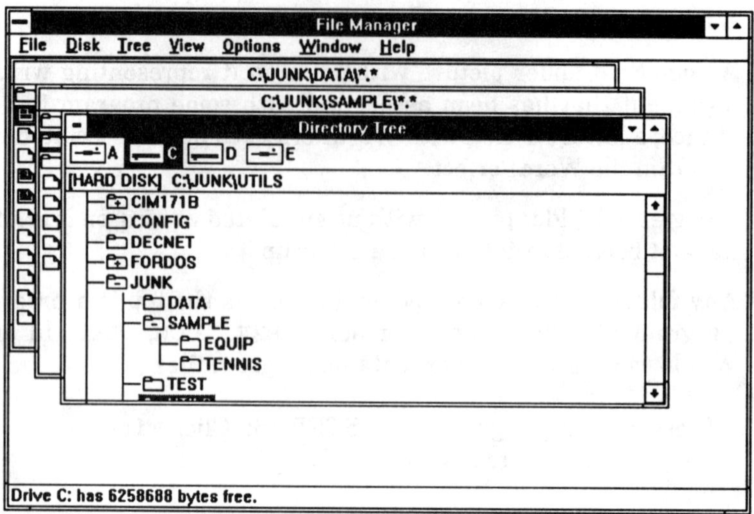

WHAT'S HAPPENING? You closed the directory window labeled **`UTILS`**. You could close each directory window individually, but you can exit and close all the directory windows with one command.

STEP 21: Press <Alt>+F4.

STEP 21: Double-click the control menu icon on the **`File Manager`** title bar.

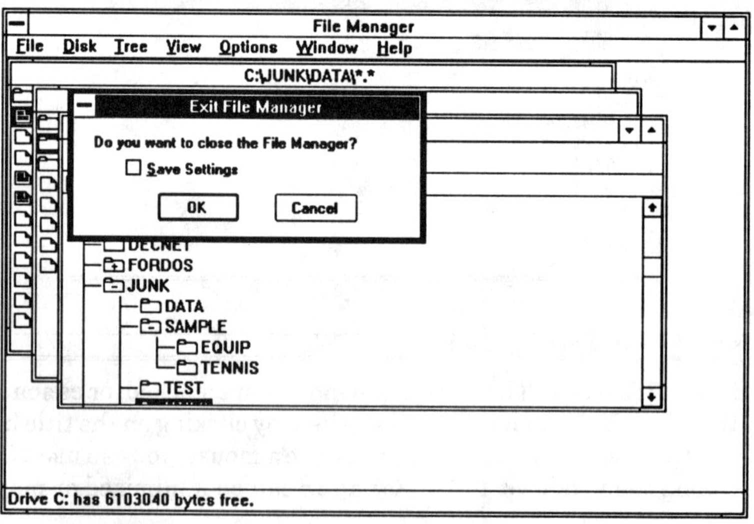

WHAT'S HAPPENING? You see a dialog box asking you if you want to exit **`File Manager`**.

STEP 22: Press <Enter>.

STEP 22: Click **OK**.

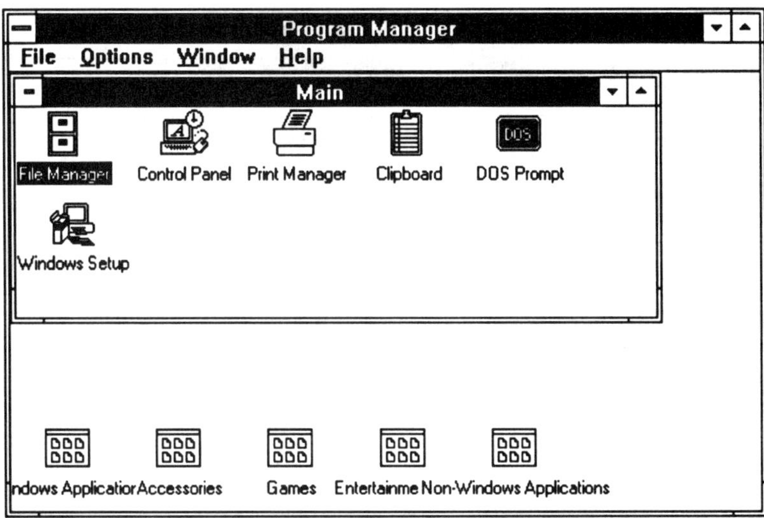

WHAT'S HAPPENING? You exited `File Manager` and returned to `Program Manager`.

18.9 DOS Commands in File Manager

`File Manager` is designed to help you manipulate your files. Thus, the commands you learned in DOS work the same way in `File Manager`. You will also see similarities to DOS Shell. The difference is that in Windows you will get menus and prompts to assist in file management chores. Furthermore, there are some tasks that you will be able to do in `File Manager` that you were unable to do in either the command line prompt or DOS Shell. However, there are some things that you cannot do in Windows. Do not run CHKDSK /F. It can be dangerous to your data. Windows does not like the pretender commands, APPEND, ASSIGN, JOIN, and SUBST, so avoid them when using Windows.

Activity 18.10 Using DOS Commands in File Manager

Note: You are in Windows. The `Program Manager` window should be displayed with the `Main` window inside the `Program Manager`.

STEP 1: Remove the DATA disk from Drive A. Insert the ACTIVITIES disk in Drive A.	STEP 1: Remove the DATA disk from Drive A. Insert the ACTIVITIES disk in Drive A.
STEP 2: Highlight the `File Manager` icon with the arrow keys and then press <Enter>.	STEP 2: Double-click `File Manager`.

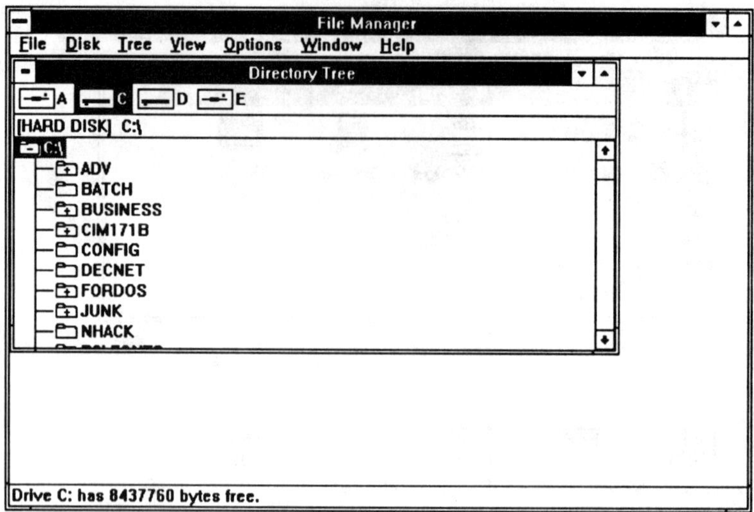

WHAT'S HAPPENING? The `Directory Tree` window of Drive C is displayed.

STEP 3: Press <Ctrl>+A.

STEP 3: Click the Drive A disk drive icon.

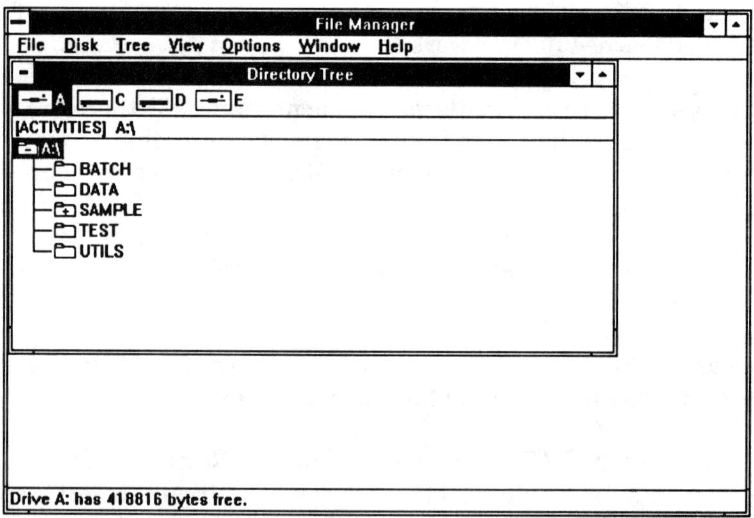

WHAT'S HAPPENING? You are looking at the `Directory Tree` window of Drive A. One important point is that when you change floppy disks during a `File Manager` session, `File Manager` does not update the directory tree windows. You will be looking at the directory of the old disk, not the new one you placed in Drive A. To resolve this problem, you can use the `Refresh` command.

STEP 4: Press <Alt>+W.

STEP 4: Click `Window`.

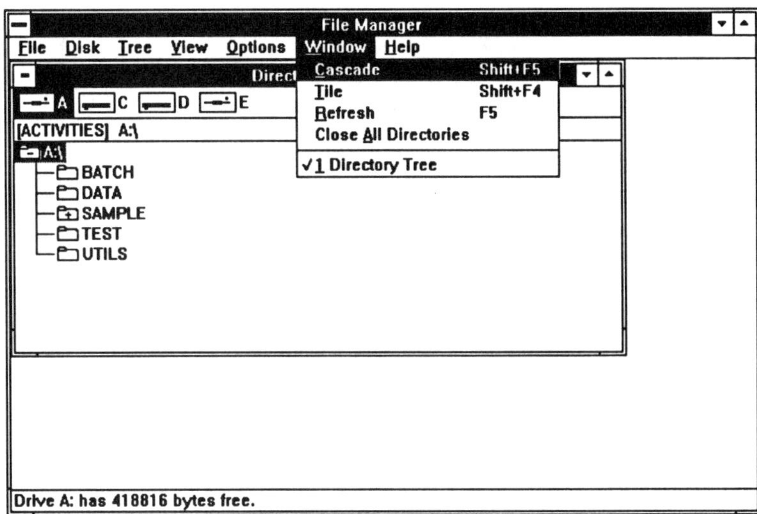

WHAT'S HAPPENING? To ensure that `File Manager` is reading the correct disk, choose the `Refresh` option.

STEP 5: Highlight `Refresh` and press <Enter>.

STEP 5: Click `Refresh`.

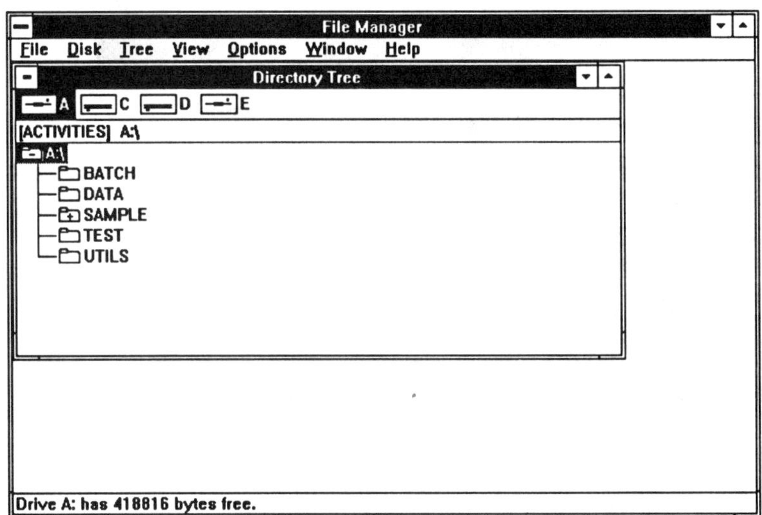

WHAT'S HAPPENING? You ensured that the Drive A directory window has read the correct disk information.

STEP 6: Press <Alt>+F.

STEP 6: Click `File`.

File Manager
File Disk Tree View Options Window Help
Open Enter
Run...
Search...
Move... F7
Copy... F8
Delete... Del
Rename...
Create Directory...
Exit
Directory Tree
Drive A: has 418816 bytes free.

WHAT'S HAPPENING? You selected the file management commands. As you can see, they are the same DOS file management commands you have used in the past. However, some commands are unreadable or greyed out because they cannot be used. For instance, `Select All` is not readable because you have yet to select any files.

STEP 7: Highlight `Open` in the menu and then press <Enter>.

STEP 7: Click `Open`.

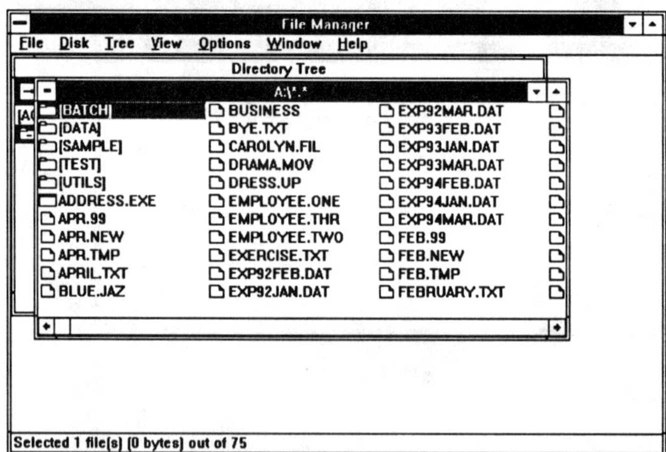

WHAT'S HAPPENING? `File Manager` opened the directory window for the root directory of the ACTIVITIES disk. The subdirectories are listed first, alphabetically. The subdirectory names have brackets around them. Then, all the files follow, again arranged alphabetically.

STEP 8: Highlight the file name **APR.NEW** and then press <Enter>.

STEP 8: Double-click **APR.NEW**.

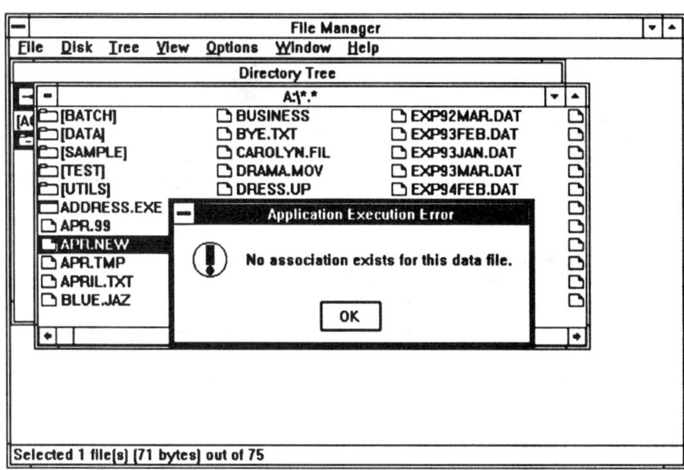

WHAT'S HAPPENING? Since **APR.NEW** is not a program, **File Manager** cannot execute it. This process is no different from keying in **APR.NEW** at the command line prompt and expecting DOS to execute it. **APR.NEW** is a file, not a program. DOS and **File Manager** execute only programs.

STEP 9: Press <Enter>. STEP 9: Click **OK**.

STEP 10: Press <Alt>+F. STEP 10: Click **File**.

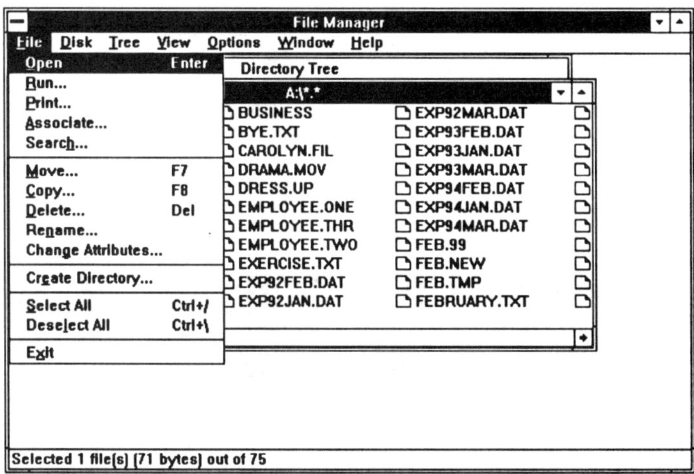

WHAT'S HAPPENING? Since you selected a file, all the options on the **File** menu are now available.

STEP 11: Highlight **Copy** in the menu and press <Enter>. STEP 11: Click **Copy**.

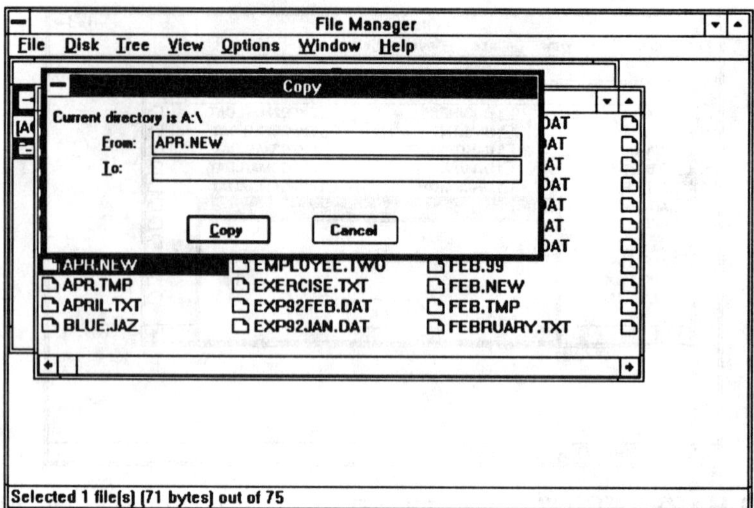

WHAT'S HAPPENING? `File Manager` presented you with a dialog box. Since you already selected **APR.NEW**, it places that file in the **From:** box. However, since it does not know where or how you want the file copied, it placed the cursor in the **To:** box.

STEP 12: Key in the following:
APR.ONE <Enter>

STEP 12: Key in the following:
APR.ONE <Enter>

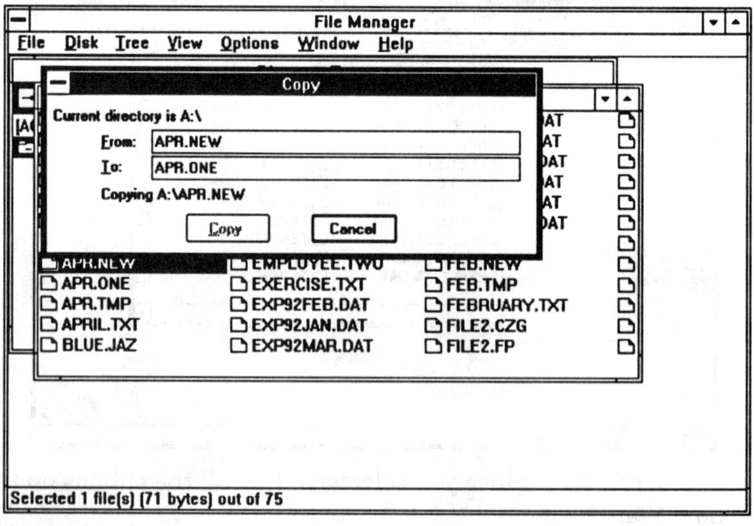

WHAT'S HAPPENING? You receive a quick message that the file is being copied. You then see the next screen.

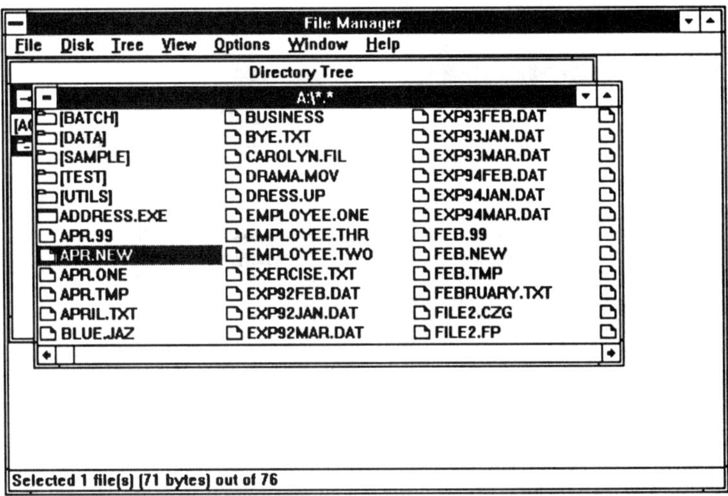

WHAT'S HAPPENING? You successfully copied the file. You can see **APR.ONE** listed alphabetically underneath **APR.NEW**.

STEP 13: Highlight **APR.ONE**.

STEP 13: Click **APR.ONE**.

STEP 14: Press <Alt>+F, highlight **Move**, and press <Enter>.

STEP 14: Click **File**. Click **Move**.

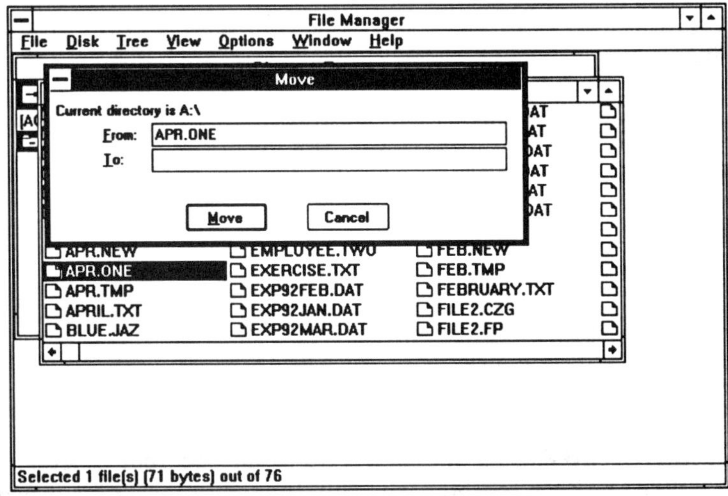

WHAT'S HAPPENING? **Move** is a new command not available in DOS. **Move** relocates a file from its original location to a new location.

STEP 15: Key the following in the **To:** box:

\TEST\APR.XYZ <Enter>

STEP 15: Key the following in the **To:** box:

\TEST\APR.XYZ <Enter>

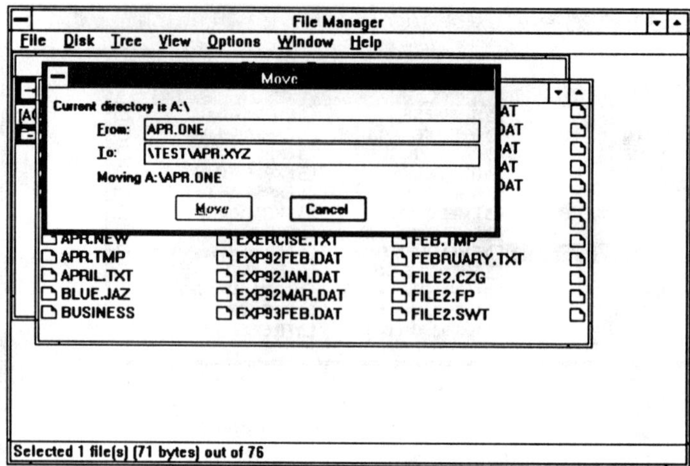

WHAT'S HAPPENING? You see a quick message that the file **APR.ONE** is being moved to the subdirectory **TEST** and has acquired a new name—**APR.XYZ**. You then returned to the directory window. The top line in the directory window is highlighted because **APR.ONE** is no longer in the root directory of A.

STEP 16: Highlight the **TEST** subdirectory and press <Enter>.

STEP 16: Double-click the **TEST** subdirectory.

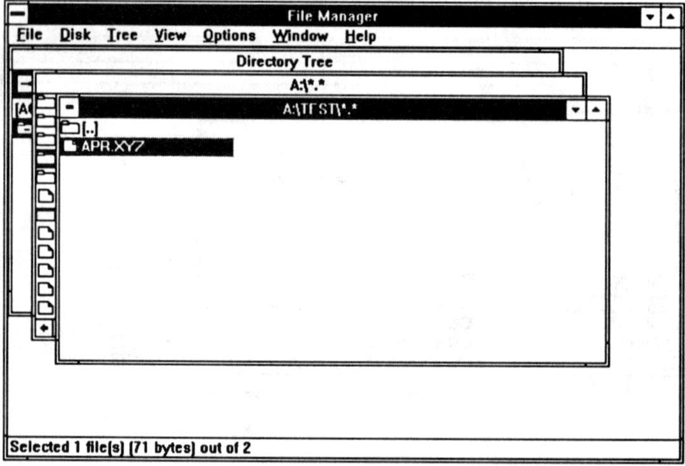

WHAT'S HAPPENING? The file **APR.ONE** from the root directory of the ACTIVITIES disk has been moved to the subdirectory **TEST** and has acquired a new file name—**APR.XYZ**. Furthermore, the file **APR.ONE** has been deleted from the root directory.

STEP 17: Press <Alt>+O.

STEP 17: Click **Options**.

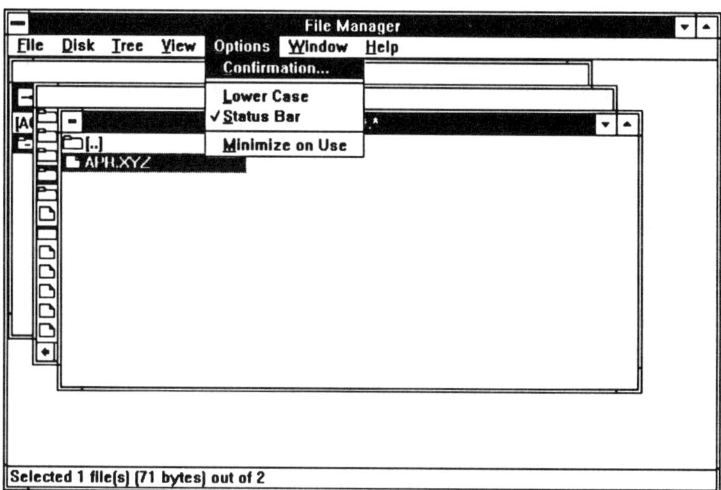

WHAT'S HAPPENING? `File Manager` is giving you a choice of options. In this case, you are interested in `Confirmation`.

STEP 18: Highlight `Confirmation` and press <Enter>.	STEP 18: Click `Confirmation`.

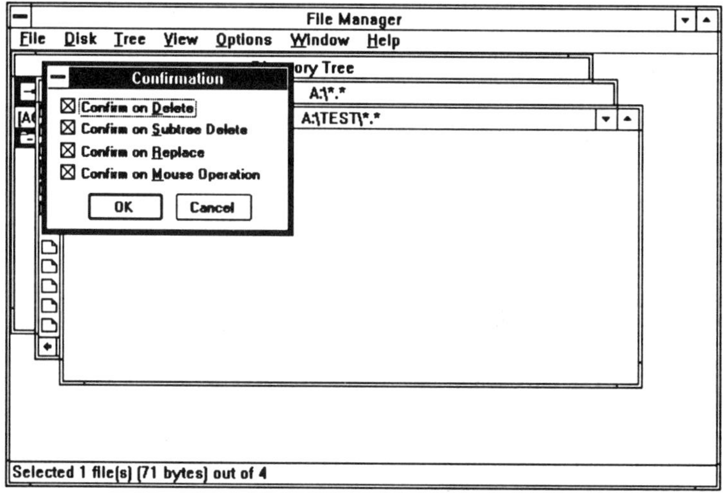

WHAT'S HAPPENING? `File Manager` is querying you to confirm whether or not you want to be asked prior to a file or subdirectory deletion. If you want to be queried before a deletion, the appropriate box must have an X in it. If there is no X, you will not be queried.

STEP 19: Be sure the `Confirm on Delete` box is checked. Press <Enter>.	STEP 19: Be sure the `Confirm on Delete` box is checked. Click `OK`.

STEP 20: Be sure that **APR.XYZ** is highlighted. Press <Alt>+F, highlight **Delete**, and then press <Enter>.

STEP 20: Be sure that **APR.XYZ** is highlighted. Click **File**. Click **Delete**.

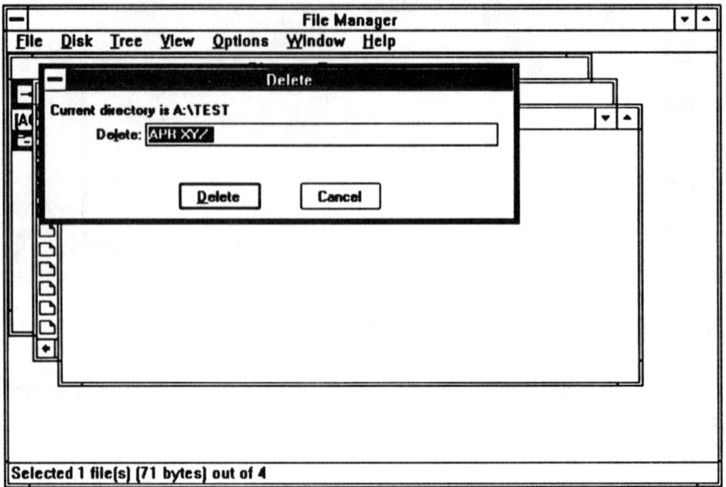

WHAT'S HAPPENING? The **Delete** dialog box on the screen displays the file name to be deleted and gives you a chance to cancel the deletion.

STEP 21: Press <Enter>.

STEP 21: Click **Delete**.

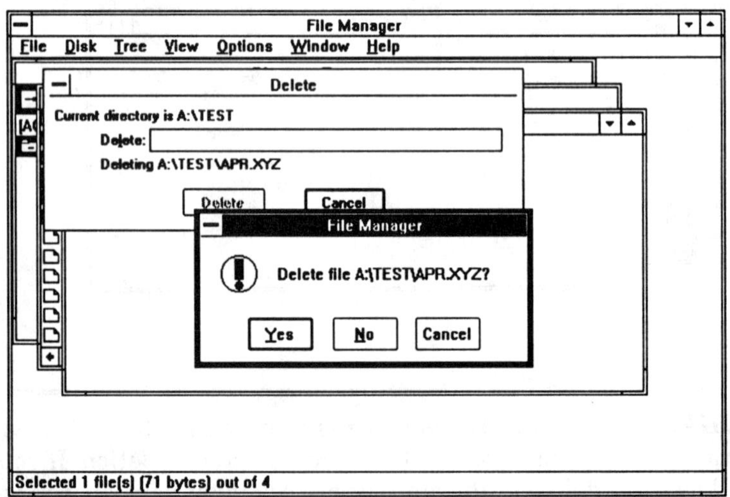

WHAT'S HAPPENING? DOS does not confirm a file deletion; the **File Manager** does because the option was set to **Confirm on Delete**.

STEP 22: Press <Enter>.

STEP 22: Click **Yes**.

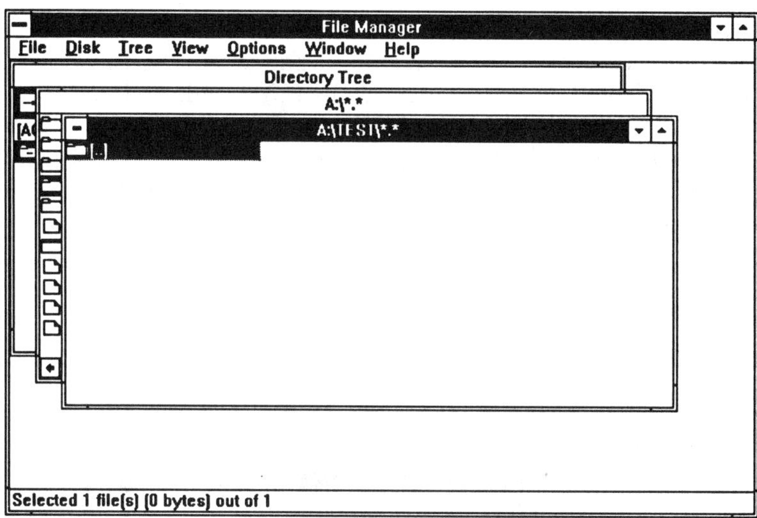

WHAT'S HAPPENING? You received a quick message that the file was deleted. You then returned to the directory window of **`TEST`**.

STEP 23: Press <Alt>+F4.

STEP 23: Double-click the control menu icon on the **`File Manager`** title bar.

STEP 24: Press <Enter>.

STEP 24: Click **`OK`**.

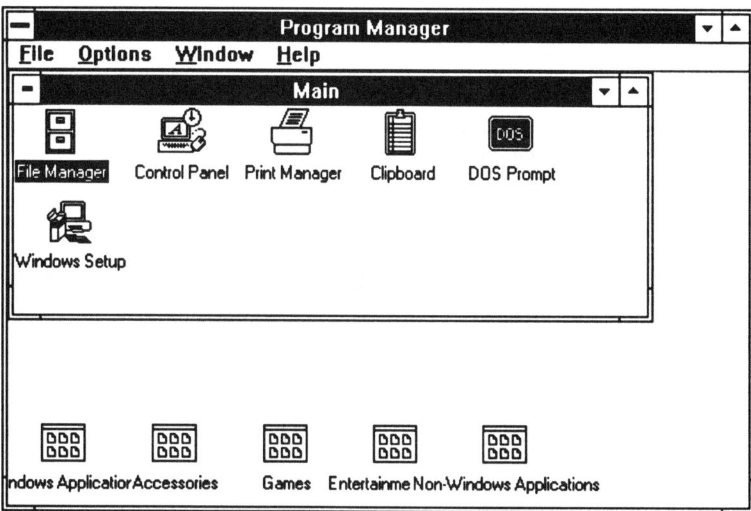

WHAT'S HAPPENING? You returned to **`Program Manager`**. As you can see, most of the DOS commands in Windows work the same way they did at the command prompt.

18.11 Selecting and Printing Files

Printing text files is easy in **File Manager**. You select the file(s) you want to print and use the drop-down menu to print them. You will find that the print file utility in **File Manager** is more sophisticated than printing files at the DOS prompt. **File Manager** will eject a page after printing, which means that when a page or a file is finished printing, the printer will advance to the top of the next clean sheet of paper.

Activity 18.12 Printing Files with File Manager

Note: The ACTIVITIES disk is in Drive A. You are in Windows. The **Program Manager** window is displayed with the **Main** window inside **Program Manager**.

STEP 1: Highlight **File Manager** and then press <Enter>.

STEP 1: Double-click **File Manager**.

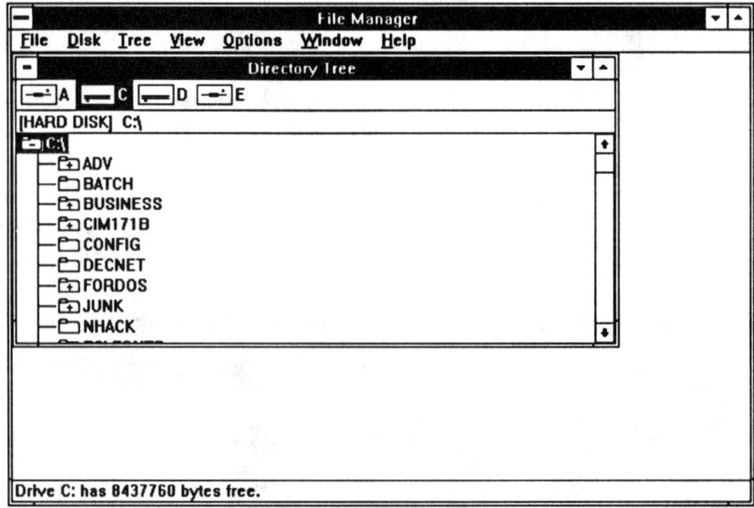

WHAT'S HAPPENING? You are looking at the **Directory Tree** window for Drive C.

STEP 2: Press <Ctrl>+A. If you do not have the ACTIVITIES disk window displayed, use the **Refresh** option.

STEP 2: Click the Drive A icon. If you do not have the ACTIVITIES disk window displayed, use the **Refresh** option.

STEP 3: Press <Enter>.

STEP 3: Double-click the root directory icon.

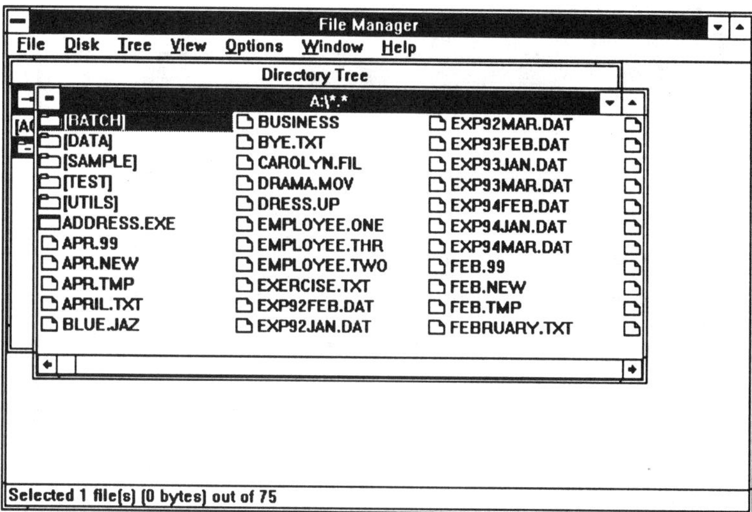

WHAT'S HAPPENING? You are looking at the directory window of the ACTIVITIES disk which displays the directories and files in the root directory.

STEP 4: Highlight the file called **EMPLOYEE.ONE**.

STEP 4: Click **EMPLOYEE.ONE**.

STEP 5: Press <Alt>+F.

STEP 5: Click **File**.

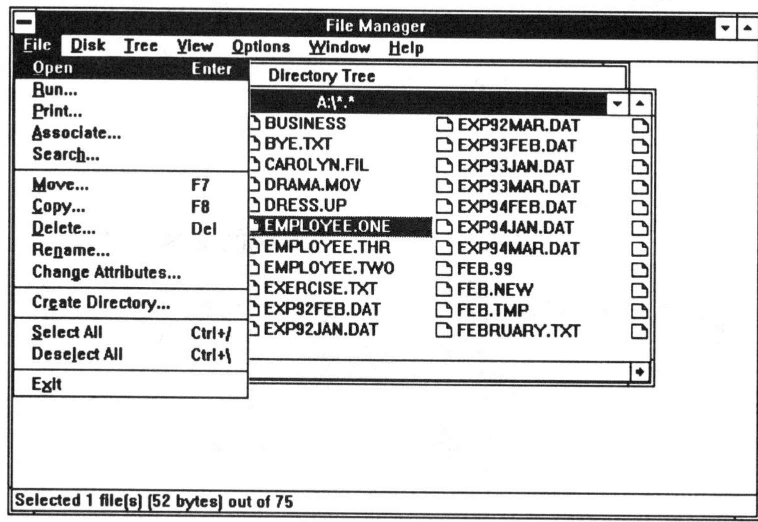

WHAT'S HAPPENING? The drop-down menu for file commands is on the screen.

STEP 6: Highlight **Print** and press <Enter>.

STEP 6: Click **Print**.

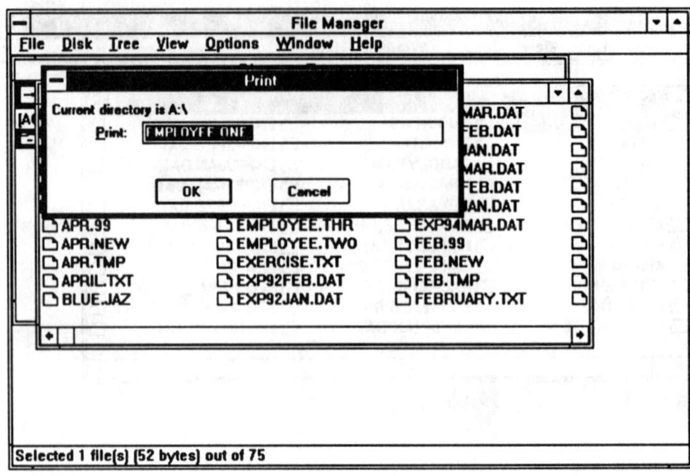

WHAT'S HAPPENING? You see a dialog box. It is asking if you want to print this file.

STEP 7: Press <Enter>.

STEP 7: Click **OK**.

WHAT'S HAPPENING? The file should print. Notice how the printer ejects the page when it finishes printing the file. You can also print more than one file at a time, but first you must choose which ones you want printed. You are going to print three files that are next to each other, or contiguous—the employee files.

STEP 8: Highlight **EMPLOYEE.ONE** and then hold down the <Shift> key while you are moving the <Down arrow> key to **EMPLOYEE.TWO**.

STEP 8: Click **EMPLOYEE.ONE**. Hold down the <Shift> key and click **EMPLOYEE.TWO**.

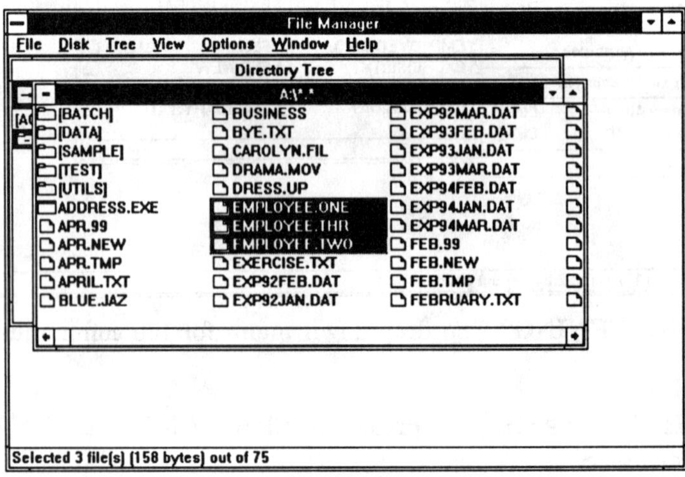

WHAT'S HAPPENING? All three files that are in sequence (contiguous) have been selected.

STEP 9: Press <Alt>+F.

STEP 9: Click **File**.

STEP 10: Highlight **Print** and press <Enter>.

STEP 10: Click **Print**.

STEP 11: Press <Enter>.

STEP 11: Click **OK**.

WHAT'S HAPPENING? The three files should be printing. Again, notice that each file prints on a new page. If you want to select files that are noncontiguous, you must use a different technique.

STEP 12: If you do not have a mouse, the procedure is more complicated.

a. Press and release <Shift>+F8. The cursor will become a blinking rectangular box.
b. Press the <Spacebar> to unselect **EMPLOYEE.TWO**. Press the direction key to highlight **EMPLOYEE.THR** and then press the <Spacebar> to unselect it. Do the same for **EMPLOYEE.ONE**.
c. Press the direction key to highlight **APRIL.TXT**. Press the <Spacebar> to select it.
d. Press the direction key to highlight **CAROLYN.FIL**. Press the <Spacebar> to select it.
e. Press the direction key to highlight **FEB.NEW**. Press the <Spacebar> to select it.
f. Press <Shift>+F8. This completes the selection process.

STEP 12: Click **APRIL.TXT**. Then hold down the <Ctrl> key and click on **CAROLYN.FIL**. Continue to hold down the <Ctrl> key and click on **FEB.NEW**.

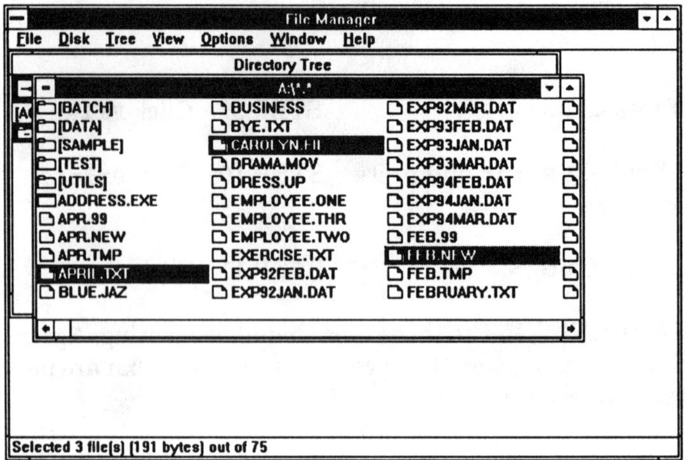

WHAT'S HAPPENING? You selected files that are out of sequence (noncontiguous). Once you have chosen files, you are not limited to printing them. You can copy them, rename them, or use any of the other choices on the `File` menu.

STEP 13: Press <Alt>+F4.

STEP 13: Double-click the control menu icon on the `File Manager` title bar.

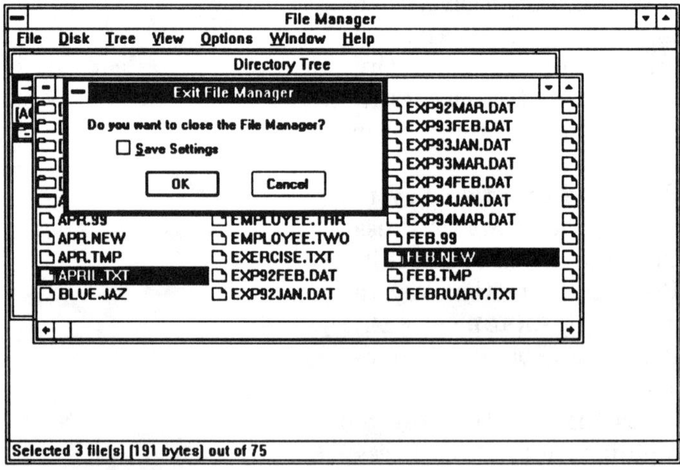

WHAT'S HAPPENING? You are closing `File Manager`.

STEP 14: Press <Enter>.

STEP 14: Click `OK`.

WHAT'S HAPPENING? You closed `File Manager` and returned to `Program Manager`.

STEP 15: Press <Alt>+F4.

STEP 15: Double-click the control menu icon on the **Program Manager** title bar.

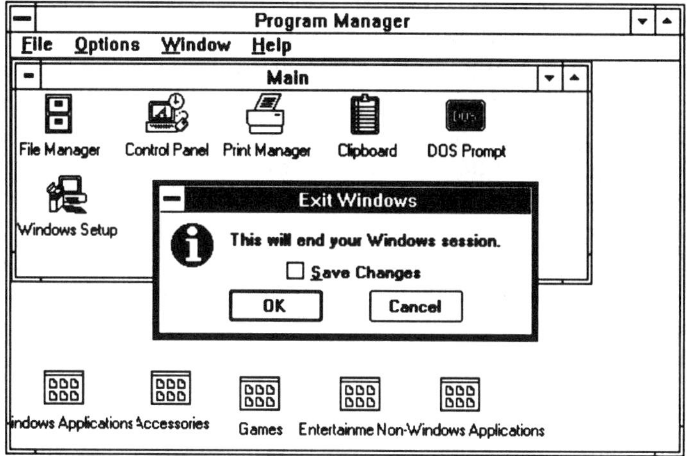

WHAT'S HAPPENING? You are asked if you want to exit Windows.

STEP 16: Press <Enter>.

STEP 16: Click **OK**.

```
C:\>_
```

WHAT'S HAPPENING? You exited Windows and returned to DOS. Your introduction to Windows is complete.

Chapter Summary

1. Windows is a graphical user interface (GUI).
2. Windows works with DOS and is considered an operating environment.
3. Instead of the command line prompt that you see with DOS, you use icons and drop-down menus to maneuver in Windows.
4. Windows can run more than one application program at a time.
5. Applications, even those not designed for Windows, can run in a window.
6. Windows allows the user to perform more than one task at a time.
7. **Program Manager** is the Windows program execution shell.
8. Windows has a **File Manager** that allows you to perform operating system tasks.
9. In applications written expressly for Windows, there is a consistency among the commands that makes learning new applications easier.
10. Windows has a memory manager that makes efficient use of computer memory. In addition, programs written for Windows can break the memory barrier of 640 KB.
11. You can use application programs that were not written expressly for Windows in Windows.

12. Windows comes with built-in application programs such as WRITE and PAINTBRUSH.
13. Windows runs in three modes—real, standard and enhanced. The mode depends on the hardware that you have.
14. You must have a hard disk with at least 6-8 MB free to run Windows.
15. To take advantage of the power of Windows, it is best to run in enhanced mode, which requires a 386 or better processor. It is also advantageous to have at least 4 MB of memory, a mouse, and a color VGA monitor.
16. When running in enhanced mode, Windows uses virtual memory, which allows Windows to write information to and from the hard disk when it runs out of memory.
17. The initial Windows screen includes window borders, the title bar, the control menu icon, sizing buttons, the menu bar, program groups, the work area, and the desktop.
18. Minimizing and maximizing the window allows you to enlarge the window or to have a window reduced to an icon.
19. You can move a window around the screen by dragging it with the mouse or using the keyboard.
20. You can change the size of a window.
21. A foreground program is the one that is currently open and active. It can also be called the active window or the current window. The foreground program takes the majority of the processor's time.
22. Only one program can be active at a time, although many programs can be open. The active program lies on top of the other application programs. Its title bar is highlighted.
23. A background program is open but not active. It takes less of the processor's resources.
24. To open other applications, you may use `Window` on the `Program Manager` title bar to select any other program listed or you can double-click on the application you wish to open.
25. The <Alt>+<Tab> and <Alt>+<Esc> key combinations allow you to cycle through the open windows. The former does not draw the windows whereas the latter does.
26. The <Ctrl>+<Esc> key combination opens `Task List`, which lists all the open programs.
27. `Task List`, in addition to listing all the open programs, allows you to switch among the open applications, close applications, or even change the appearance of a window.
28. The windows can appear either tiled, side by side, or as a cascade—layered one on top of another.
29. Windows provides online help, which can be accessed either by pressing the F1 key or by clicking the mouse on `Help`. The help facility includes an index, key terms that provide capsule descriptions, and key words that call up major help screens.

30. `File Manager` allows you to accomplish operating system tasks. It is a file manager.
31. When you activate `File Manager`, it provides a `Directory Tree` window that displays the structure of a disk.
32. Directory icons are indicated by file folders. Each one represents a directory. If a directory icon contains a plus sign, it can be expanded. If a directory icon contains a minus sign, it can be collapsed into its parent directory. If it has neither a plus or minus, clicking the icon will present the files in the directory.
33. Scroll bars allow the user to move about the display screen when there is more than one screenful of information.
34. `File Manager` automatically arranges its listings alphabetically.
35. You can open and look at more than one directory window at a time.
36. Four types of icons are used to distinguish among file types. A plain folder is a directory window. A dog-eared folder with lines on it is a document associated with a program. A dog-eared folder with no lines on it is an unassociated file. A folder with a stripe on it is an executable program.
37. `File Manager` can either be minimized or maximized.
38. DOS commands can be used in `File Manager`.
39. DOS commands in `File Manager` are presented with menus and dialog boxes.
40. Do not run CHKDSK/F or the pretender commands SUBST, ASSIGN, APPEND, and JOIN while in Windows.
41. The rules of DOS do not change even though you are in `File Manager`.
42. `File Manager` has options and commands not available at the DOS command line. For instance, you can arrange the directory display by file size and can use new commands.
43. Printing text files in `File Manager` is accomplished by using the `Print` menu.
44. `Print Manager` is more sophisticated in Windows than in DOS. The Windows `Print Manager` will start each file on a new page.
45. Files must be selected to accomplish work such as printing or copying. You may select more than one file at a time, either in sequence or out of sequence.

Key Terms

386 enhanced mode
Active window
Cascade
Control menu icon
Program groups
Real mode
Sizing buttons
Standard mode
Tiled
Virtual memory
Window borders

Discussion Questions

1. What is Windows?
2. What are some of the advantages of using Windows?
3. What is an icon?
4. What is a drop-down menu?
5. What are the three modes of operating in Windows?
6. How does the user determine which mode to utilize with Windows?
7. What is virtual memory?
8. Why would you maximize or minimize a window?
9. What happens to an application program that is not active?
10. What is `Task List`?
11. How can you access online help?
12. What is the advantage of having online capability?
13. What will be found in the `Help` facility?
14. What is `File Manager`?
15. How can `File Manager` be accessed?
16. What is the function of a scroll bar?
17. What does a plus or minus sign mean in a directory icon?
18. List the four types of icons that are used to distinguish among file types.
19. What command(s) should not be run when using Windows?
20. How can you make an application program active?
21. When using the `Help Index`, what information will you receive for command terms that are underscored?
22. When using the `Help Index`, what information will you receive for terms that are dotted line underscored?
23. What does it mean if a directory icon has neither a plus nor a minus sign?
24. How are DOS commands presented in `File Manager`?
25. What is the function of the `Refresh` command?

Application Assignments

Note 1: All activities will be placed on the DATA disk, unless otherwise stated. All activities will occur in Windows unless otherwise stated.

Note 2: If you are missing any needed files and/or subdirectories, create them and/or copy them from `C:\JUNK` to the DATA disk.

1. For the following assignment, identify by letter the following items on the Windows screen shown below.
   a. Application window
   b. Sizing buttons
   c. Program groups
   d. Desktop
   e. Control menu icon
   f. Menu bar
   g. Title bar
   h. Window borders

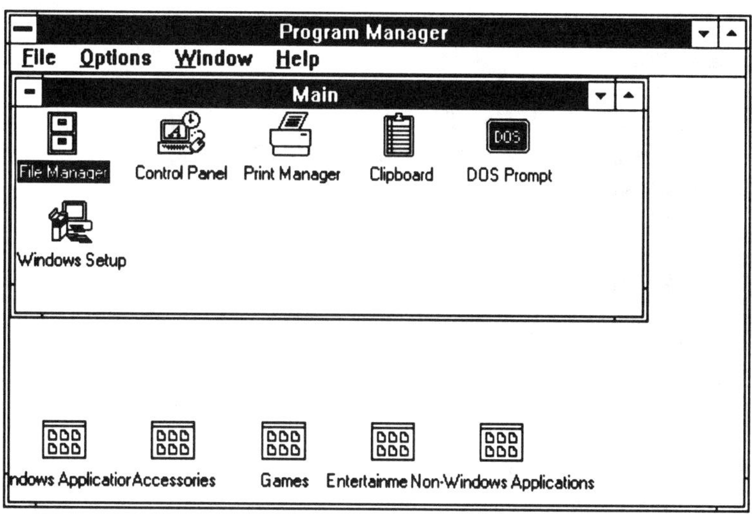

2. For the following assignment, respond to the following questions based on the system you are using.
   a. What mode are you running in?
      Mode ____________
   b. How much free memory do you have?
      Memory ___________
3. For the following assignment:
   a. Use **Help**.
   b. Select **Index**.
   c. Select **Program Manager Help Index**.
   d. Select **File Menu Commands**.
   e. Locate **Exit Windows**.
   f. Write below the first three words under **Exit Windows**.

      ____
4. For the following assignment:
   a. Use **Help**.
   b. Select **Glossary**.
   c. Locate **dialog box**.
   d. Write the first three words of the definition for **dialog box**.

      ____
   e. Write the term that immediately precedes **dialog box**.

      ____
5. For the following assignment:
   a. Open the **Games** window.
   b. Launch **Solitaire**.
   c. Maximize **Solitaire**.
   d. Access **Help** in **Solitaire**.
   e. Access **Commands**.
   f. Print the **Game Menu Commands** in **Help**. To print the help topic, press

<Alt>+F or click **`File`** on the **`Solitaire Help`** menu bar. Then select **`Print Topic`**.

   g. Label the print-out with your name and class information.
   h. Play **`Solitaire`**. (Note: If you have a mouse, please use it to play the game. This exercise will give you the "feel" of dragging, clicking, and double-clicking.)
   i. Close **`Solitaire`**.
   j. Close the **`Games`** window.

6. For the following assignment:
   a. Open the **`Games`** window.
   b. Open **`Reversi`**.
   c. Minimize **`Reversi`**.
   d. Describe the first two steps you took to accomplish this task.
   e. Close **`Reversi`**.
   f. Close the **`Games`** window.
7. For the following assignment:
   a. Move the **`Program Manager`** window into each of three positions labeled Screen 7.1, Screen 7.2, and Screen 7.3.

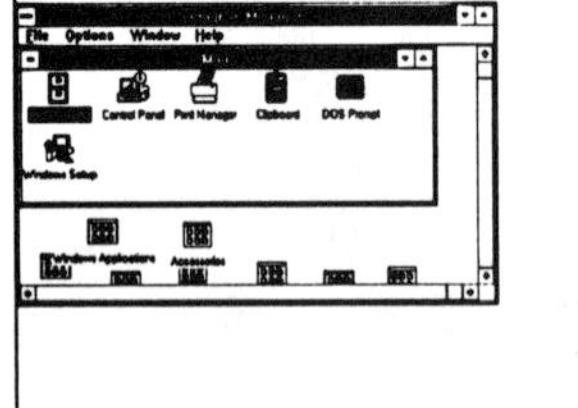

Screen 7.1

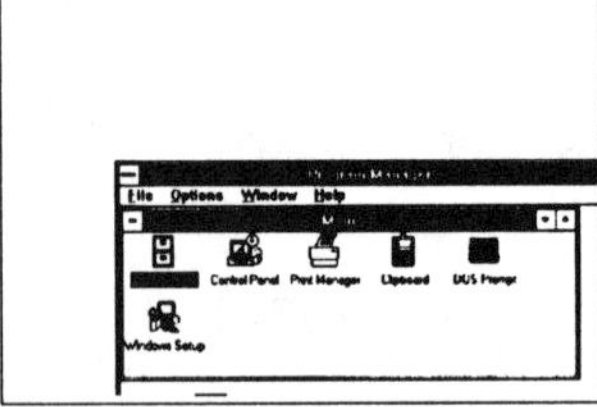

Screen 7.2

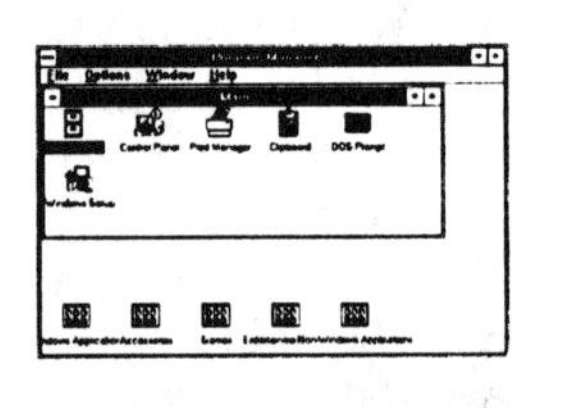

Screen 7.3

   b. Describe the last step you took to move:
      1. Screen 7.1.
      2. Screen 7.2.
      3. Screen 7.3.
8. For the following assignment:
   a. Open the **`Games`** window.
   b. Size the **`Games`** window to the size indicated by Screen 8.1 below. Then return the **`Games`** window to its default size indicated by Screen 8.2.

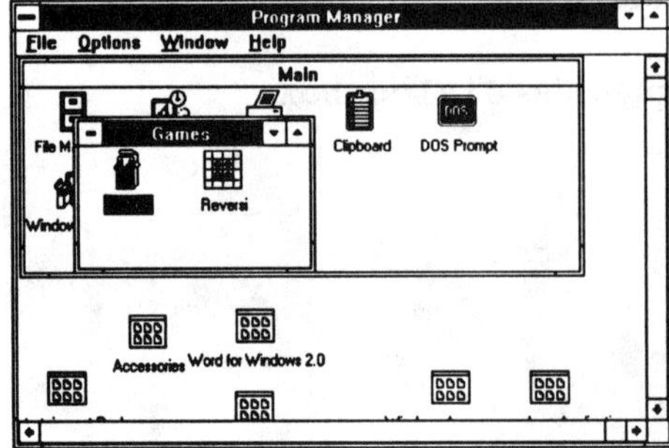

Screen 8.1

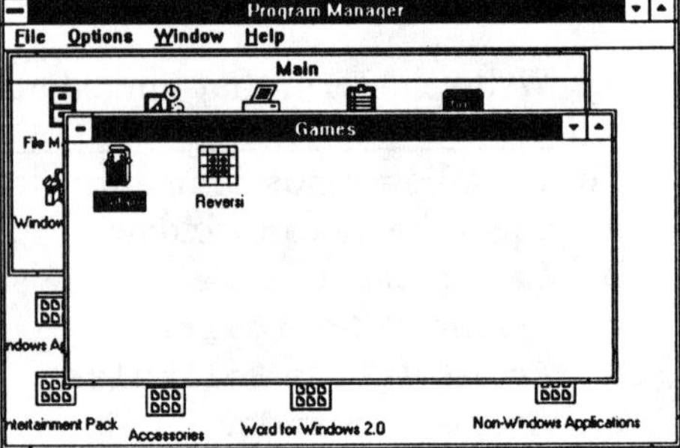

Screen 8.2

   c. Describe the steps you took to size:
      1. Screen 8.1.
      2. Screen 8.2.
   d. Close the **`Games`** window.
9. For the following assignment, use Screen 9.1 to answer the questions.
   a. What is the default directory?
   b. Name the disk drives on this system.
   c. Identify the volume label.

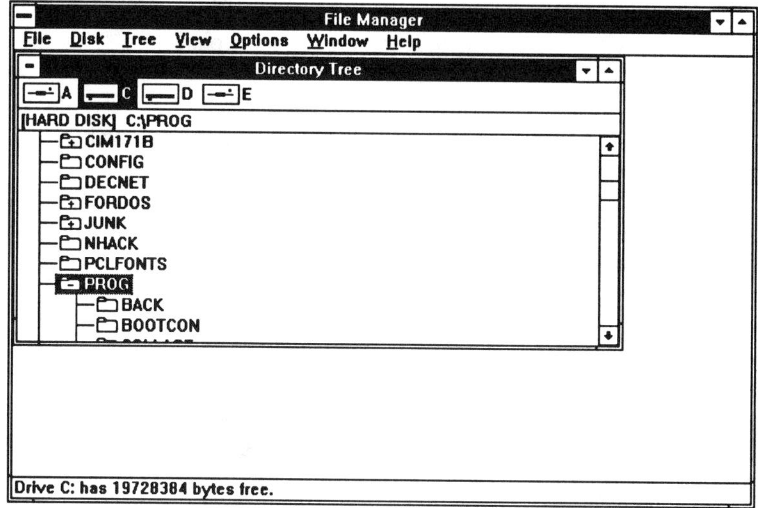

Screen 9.1

10. For the following assignment, use **`C:\JUNK>`**.
    a. Open **`File Manager`**.
    b. Expand **`JUNK`** and display all the files in **`JUNK`**.
    c. Expand **`TEST`** and display all the files in **`TEST`**.
    d. Expand **`UTILS`** and display all the files in **`UTILS`**.
    e. Expand **`SAMPLE`** and display all the files in **`SAMPLE`**.
    f. What is the first file listed in **`SAMPLE`**? What kind of file is it?
    g. What is the first directory listed in **`SAMPLE`**?
    h. Tile the display.
    i. How many open windows are there (including the **`Directory Tree`** window)?
    j. Which is the active window?
    k. Expand **`DATA`** and display all the files in **`DATA`**.
    l. Cascade the windows.
    m. Which is the top window?
    n. Exit **`File Manager`** the quickest way.
    o. Describe the first step you took to exit **`File Manager`**.

11. For the following assignment:
    a. Make two directories in the root directory of the DATA disk.
    b. Name them **NOTES** and **PROJECT**.
    c. Copy all the files from Drive C in the **\JUNK\DATA** subdirectory with the file extension **.TV** to the **PROJECT** subdirectory on the disk in Drive A.
    d. Describe the first three steps you took to accomplish this task.
12. For the following assignment:
    a. Copy the files from Drive C in the **\JUNK** subdirectory called **FRANK.FIL**, **MIDDLE.RED**, and **HELLO.TXT** to the root directory of the DATA disk.
    b. Describe the steps you took to select the files.
    c. Print the three files you copied.

Challenge Assignments

13. This assignment requires that you completed Assignment 11.
    For the following assignment:
    a. Open all the directories on the DATA disk.
    b. Tile the display.
    c. List all the open windows.
    d. Which is the active window?
    e. Copy the file called **FRANK.FIL** to the **NOTES** subdirectory. Call the file **SAMPLE.FIL** in the **NOTES** subdirectory.
    f. Move the file called **MIDDLE.RED** to the **NOTES** subdirectory.
    g. Rename the file called **MIDDLE.RED** to **FASHION.PNK**.
    h. Describe the steps you took to accomplish the above tasks.
    i. Cascade the windows.
    j. Which window is on top?
    k. Close all the directory windows on Drive A and return to **File Manager** on Drive C.
14. This assignment requires that you completed Assignments 11, 12, and 13.
    For the following assignment:
    a. Copy the files with the **.TV** extension from the **PROJECT** subdirectory to the **NOTES** subdirectory on the DATA disk.
    b. Delete the files **COMEDY.TV** and **FASHION.PNK** in the **NOTES** subdirectory.
    c. Describe the steps you took to accomplish the above tasks.

Appendix

Making a System Disk

DOS 3.3, 4.0 and 5.0 come on several disks. To make it easier to follow the beginning chapters, the user will work with a single DOS System Disk, which will include the major commands covered in this text. This book is designed to be used with DOS 5.0 with a system configuration of one hard disk and one floppy disk. However, a user who has only two floppy disk drives and an earlier version of DOS can still follow the text. That user will substitute **`A:\>`** for `C:\>` and **`B:\>`** for **`A:\>`**.

The selected files were designed to fit on a single 360 KB floppy disk. A user who has a larger disk size will simply have more room on the disk. A user who is working with a 360 KB DOS System Disk may not have sufficient room on the working DOS System Disk to add files as specified in later chapters; that user will have to delete the file **`DISKCOMP.COM`**. A user who is working with other disk formats will find enough room on the disks to include the appropriate files.

Two disk drive users must have a single floppy DOS System Disk. Hard disk users, although primarily using DOS on the hard disk, will still, on occasion, need a single floppy DOS System Disk. Once a master DOS System Disk has been created, the user can make other copies with the DISKCOPY command.

Instructions for creating a single DOS System Disk from the original DOS disks follow the list of files. Instructions are for both two disk drive and hard disk drive users.

Users must also know what kind of disk drives they have. The media types must match. A user with a 5 1/4-inch 360 KB disk drive (double-sided, double-density disk drive) should use a blank 360 KB double-sided, double-density disk. A user with a 5 1/4-inch 1.2 MB disk drive (double-sided, high-density or high-capacity disk drive) should use a blank 1.2 MB high-density disk. Someone who has a 3 1/2-inch 720 KB disk drive (double-sided, double-density disk drive) should use a blank 720 KB disk, and someone with a 3 1/2-inch 1.44 MB disk drive (high-density or high-capacity disk drive) should use a blank 1.44 MB high-density disk.

A.1 Selected DOS System Disk Files

The following is a list of files that should be on the DOS 3.3 single floppy System Disk:

```
COMMAND   COM   25307    03-17-87 12:00p
ANSI      SYS    1678    03-17-87 12:00p
APPEND    EXE    5825    03-17-87 12:00p
ATTRIB    EXE    9529    03-17-87 12:00p
CHKDSK    COM    9850    03-18-87 12:00p
COMP      COM    4214    03-17-87 12:00p
DISKCOMP  COM    5879    03-17-87 12:00p
DISKCOPY  COM    6295    03-17-87 12:00p
EDLIN     COM    7526    03-17-87 12:00p
FIND      EXE    6434    03-17-87 12:00p
FORMAT    COM   11616    03-18-87 12:00p
JOIN      EXE    8969    03-17-87 12:00p
LABEL     COM    2377    03-17-87 12:00p
MODE      COM   15487    03-17-87 12:00p
MORE      COM     313    03-17-87 12:00p
PRINT     COM    9026    03-17-87 12:00p
SORT      EXE    1977    03-17-87 12:00p
SUBST     EXE    9909    03-17-87 12:00p
TREE      COM    3571    03-17-87 12:00p
VDISK     SYS    3455    03-17-87 12:00p
XCOPY     EXE   11247    03-17-87 12:00p
        21 File(s)      138240 bytes free
```

bytes left on a 360 KB disk

Files that should be on the DOS 4.0 single floppy System Disk:

```
COMMAND   COM   37652    11-11-88 12:00p
ANSI      SYS    9172    03-29-89 12:00p
APPEND    EXE   11186    08-03-88 12:00p
ASSIGN    COM    5785    06-17-88 12:00p
CHKDSK    COM   17771    06-17-88 12:00p
COMP      COM    9491    06-17-88 12:00p
DISKCOMP  COM    9889    06-17-88 12:00p
DISKCOPY  COM   10428    06-17-88 12:00p
EDLIN     COM   14249    06-17-88 12:00p
FIND      EXE    5983    06-17-88 12:00p
FORMAT    COM   22923    06-17-88 12:00p
JOIN      EXE   17457    06-17-88 12:00p
LABEL     COM    4490    06-17-88 12:00p
MODE      COM   23120    11-11-88 12:00p
MORE      COM    2166    06-17-88 12:00p
PRINT     COM   14024    08-03-88 12:00p
SORT      EXE    5914    06-17-88 12:00p
SUBST     EXE   18143    06-17-88 12:00p
TREE      COM    6334    06-17-88 12:00p
VDISK     SYS    7446    04-06-89 12:00p
XCOPY     EXE   17087    06-17-88 12:00p
        21 File(s)        9216 bytes free
```

bytes left on a 360 KB disk

Files that should be on the DOS 5.0 single floppy DOS System Disk.

```
COMMAND  COM   47845   04-09-91  5:00a
APPEND   EXE   10774   04-09-91  5:00a
ASSIGN   COM    6399   04-09-91  5:00a
CHKDSK   EXE   16200   04-09-91  5:00a
COMP     EXE   14282   04-09-91  5:00a
DISKCOMP COM   10652   04-09-91  5:00a
DISKCOPY COM   11793   04-09-91  5:00a
FIND     EXE    6770   04-09-91  5:00a
FORMAT   COM   32911   04-09-91  5:00a
JOIN     EXE   17870   04-09-91  5:00a
LABEL    EXE    9390   04-09-91  5:00a
MODE     COM   23537   04-09-91  5:00a
MORE     COM    2618   04-09-91  5:00a
PRINT    EXE   15656   04-09-91  5:00a
RAMDRIVE SYS    5873   04-09-91  5:00a
SORT     EXE    6938   04-09-91  5:00a
SUBST    EXE   18478   04-09-91  5:00a
TREE     COM    6901   04-09-91  5:00a
XCOPY    EXE   15804   04-09-91  5:00a
        19 file(s)     280691 bytes
                         1024 bytes free
```

bytes left on a 360 KB disk

Activity A.2 Making a DOS System Disk with DOS 3.3

Two Disk Drive Users Only

STEP 1: Place the disk labeled "DOS Start-up Diskette" in Drive A. Be sure the drive door is shut. Note: If you are working with 720 KB disk drives, there will be only one disk labeled "DOS Start-Up/Operating Diskette."

STEP 2: Boot the system.

STEP 3: Enter the current time and date.

STEP 4: Key in the following:
A:\>**FORMAT B:/S** <Enter>

```
Insert new diskette for Drive B:
and strike ENTER when ready...
```

WHAT'S HAPPENING? You entered the FORMAT command.

STEP 5: Place a blank disk in Drive B.

STEP 6: Press any key.

```
Head h Cylinder c
```

WHAT'S HAPPENING? DOS is formatting the disk in Drive B. When the formatting is completed, you see the following screen display:

```
Format complete
System Transferred

Volume label (11 characters, ENTER for none)?_
```

STEP 7: Press <Enter>.

```
xxxxxx bytes total disk space
 xxxxx bytes used by system
xxxxxx bytes available on disk

Format another (Y/N)?_
```

STEP 8: Key in the following:
`N` <Enter>

```
A>_
```

Note: The next step is a continuing series of COPY commands. As soon as you see the message "1 file(s) copied" and return to the `A>` prompt, key in the next COPY command.

STEP 9: Key in the following:

```
COPY A*.* B: <Enter>
COPY M*.* B: <Enter>
COPY V*.* B: <Enter>
```

STEP 10: Remove the disk labeled "DOS Start-Up/Operating Diskette" from Drive A. Insert the disk labeled "DOS Operating Diskette" in Drive A. Note: If you have a 720 KB diskette, you do not need to change disks.

Note: The next step is a continuing series of COPY commands.

STEP 11: Key in the following:

```
COPY A*.EXE B: <Enter>
COPY C*.* B: <Enter>
COPY DISK*.* B: <Enter>
COPY E*.* B: <Enter>
COPY F*.* B: <Enter>
COPY J*.* B: <Enter>
COPY L*.* B: <Enter>
COPY MORE.COM B: <Enter>
COPY P*.* B: <Enter>
COPY SORT.EXE B: <Enter>
COPY SUBST.EXE B: <Enter>
COPY T*.* B: <Enter>
COPY X*.* B: <Enter>
```

STEP 12: Remove the disk just created from Drive B and insert it in Drive A. Place a new disk in Drive B and label it "DOS Master System Disk."

STEP 13: Key in the following:
FORMAT B:/S <Enter>

```
Insert new diskette for Drive B:
and strike ENTER when ready...
```

WHAT'S HAPPENING? You entered the FORMAT command.

STEP 14: Press any key.

```
Head h Cylinder c
```

WHAT'S HAPPENING? DOS is formatting the disk in Drive B. When the formatting is completed, you see the following screen display:

```
Format complete
System Transferred

Volume label (11 characters, ENTER for none)?_
```

STEP 15: Press <Enter>.

```
xxxxxx bytes total disk space
 xxxxx bytes used by system
xxxxxx bytes available on disk

Format another (Y/N)?_
```

STEP 16: Key in the following:
N <Enter>

```
A>_
```

Note: The next step is a continuing series of COPY commands.

STEP 17: Key in the following:
COPY A*.* B: <Enter>
COPY C*.* B: <Enter>
COPY D*.* B: <Enter>
COPY E*.* B: <Enter>
COPY F*.* B: <Enter>
COPY J*.* B: <Enter>
COPY L*.* B: <Enter>
COPY M*.* B: <Enter>
COPY P*.* B: <Enter>
COPY S*.* B: <Enter>
COPY T*.* B: <Enter>
COPY V*.* B: <Enter>
COPY X*.* B: <Enter>

WHAT'S HAPPENING? The disk in Drive B is now the master DOS System Disk.

STEP 18: Remove the disk from Drive B. Label this disk "Master DOS System Disk."

STEP 19: Remove the disk from Drive A and turn off the computer.

Activity A.3

Making a DOS System Disk with DOS 3.3

Hard Disk Users Only

At this point, DOS should have been installed on the hard disk. If not, please refer to Appendix B.

STEP 1: Boot the system. You will be at the `C>`.

STEP 2: Enter the current time and date.

STEP 3: Key in the following:
C>**FORMAT A:/S** <Enter>

```
Insert new diskette for Drive A:
and strike ENTER when ready...
```

Note: If, instead of the above message, you receive a message that states "Bad command or file name," your DOS programs are in a subdirectory. Typically this subdirectory is called **\DOS**. If it is not, you will have to locate the subdirectory that holds the DOS system files and use it instead of **\DOS**. You will have an additional step prior to Step 3. It is:
C>**CD \DOS** <Enter>

WHAT'S HAPPENING? You entered the FORMAT command.

STEP 4: Place a blank disk in Drive A.

STEP 5: Press any key.

```
Head h Cylinder c
```

WHAT'S HAPPENING? DOS is formatting the disk in Drive A. When the formatting is completed, you see the following screen display:

```
Format complete
System Transferred

Volume label (11 characters, ENTER for none)?_
```

STEP 6: Press <Enter>.

```
xxxxxx bytes total disk space
 xxxxx bytes used by system
xxxxxx bytes available on disk

Format another (Y/N)?_
```

STEP 7: Key in the following:

N <Enter>

```
C>_
```

Note 1: The chances are that the DOS files you need will be in a subdirectory. Typically the subdirectory is called **\DOS**. This entry is assumed for the next series of steps. If the DOS files are in a different subdirectory, you will have to substitute that subdirectory name for **\DOS**.

Note 2: The file names listed are those for IBM PC-DOS. If you are using MS-DOS, some file names may have the **.EXE** file extension instead of the **.COM** file extension. If you get the message "File not found," try substituting **.EXE** for **.COM**. In addition, the **COMP.COM** is called **FC.EXE**; **CHKDSK.COM** is called **CHKDSK.EXE**; and **VDISK.SYS** is called **RAMDRIVE.SYS** in MS-DOS.

Note 3: The next step is a continuing series of COPY commands. As soon as you see the message "1 file(s) copied" and return to the **C>** prompt, key in the next COPY command.

STEP 8: Key in the following:

```
COPY C:\DOS\ANSI.SYS A: <Enter>
COPY C:\DOS\APPEND.EXE A: <Enter>
COPY C:\DOS\ATTRIB.EXE A: <Enter>
COPY C:\DOS\CHKDSK.COM A: <Enter>
COPY C:\DOS\COMP.EXE A: <Enter>
COPY C:\DOS\DISKCOMP.COM A: <Enter>
COPY C:\DOS\DISKCOPY.COM A: <Enter>
COPY C:\DOS\EDLIN.COM A: <Enter>
COPY C:\DOS\FIND.EXE A: <Enter>
COPY C:\DOS\FORMAT.COM A: <Enter>
COPY C:\DOS\JOIN.EXE A: <Enter>
COPY C:\DOS\LABEL.COM A: <Enter>
COPY C:\DOS\MODE.COM A: <Enter>
COPY C:\DOS\MORE.COM A: <Enter>
COPY C:\DOS\PRINT.COM A: <Enter>
COPY C:\DOS\SORT.EXE A: <Enter>
COPY C:\DOS\SUBST.EXE A: <Enter>
COPY C:\DOS\TREE.COM A: <Enter>
COPY C:\DOS\VDISK.SYS A: <Enter>
COPY C:\DOS\XCOPY.EXE A: <Enter>
```

WHAT'S HAPPENING? The disk in Drive A is now the master DOS System Disk.

STEP 9: Remove the disk from Drive A. Label this disk "Master DOS System Disk."

STEP 10: Remove the disk from Drive A and turn off the computer.

Activity A.4

Making a DOS System Disk with DOS 4.0

Two Disk Drive Users Only

STEP 1: Place the disk labeled "Install" in Drive A. Be sure the drive door is shut. Note: If you are working with 720 KB disk drives, there will be only two disks, one labeled "Install" and the other labeled "Operating." If you are working with a 360 KB disk drive, there will be five disks, labeled "Install," "Select," "Operating 1," "Operating 2," and "Operating 3."

STEP 2: Boot the system.

STEP 3: Key in the following:
FORMAT B: <Enter>

```
Insert new diskette for Drive B:
and press ENTER when ready...
```

WHAT'S HAPPENING? You entered the FORMAT command.

STEP 4: Place a blank disk in Drive B.

STEP 5: Press any key.

```
xx percent of disk formatted.
```

WHAT'S HAPPENING? DOS is formatting the disk in Drive B. The **xx** represents a percentage that changes as the disk is being formatted. When the formatting is completed, you see the following screen display.

```
Format complete

Volume label (11 characters, ENTER for none)?_
```

STEP 6: Press <Enter>.

```
362496 bytes total disk space
362496 bytes available on disk

1024 bytes in each allocation unit
 354 allocation units available on disk

Volume Serial Number is 1636-17E5

Format another (Y/N)?_
```

STEP 7: Key in the following:
N <Enter>

STEP 8: Key in the following:
COPY DISK*.* B: <Enter>
COPY FOR*.* B: <Enter>

STEP 9: Remove the disk labeled "Install" from Drive A. Place the disk labeled "Operating 1" in Drive A.

STEP 10: Key in the following. (Note: The following is a series of steps to key in as each file is copied.)

COPY A*.EXE B: <Enter>
COPY COMP.* B: <Enter>
COPY DISK*.* B: <Enter>
COPY E*.* B: <Enter>
COPY FIND*.* B: <Enter>
COPY J*.* B: <Enter>
COPY L*.* B: <Enter>
COPY M*.COM B: <Enter>
COPY SORT.EXE B: <Enter>
COPY SUBST.EXE B: <Enter>
COPY T*.* B: <Enter>
COPY X*.* B: <Enter>

STEP 11: Remove the disk labeled "Install" from Drive A. Place the disk labeled "Operating 2" in Drive A. (Note: If you are working with a 720 KB disk, you will not have to remove any disks at this time.)

STEP 12: Key in the following. (Note: The following is a series of steps to key in as each file is copied.)

COPY CH*.* B: <Enter>
COPY PRINT*.* B: <Enter>

STEP 13: Remove the disk labeled "Operating 2" from Drive A. Place the disk labeled "Operating 3" in Drive A. (Note: If you are working with a 720 KB disk, you will not have to remove any disks at this time.)

STEP 14: Key in the following. (Note: The following is a series of steps to key in as each file is copied.)

COPY A*.* B: <Enter>
COPY V*.* B: <Enter>

STEP 15: Remove the disk from Drive B and place it Drive A. Place a new, blank disk in Drive B and label it "DOS System Disk."

STEP 16: Key in the following:

FORMAT B:/S <Enter>

```
Insert new diskette for Drive B:
and press ENTER when ready...
```

WHAT'S HAPPENING? You entered the FORMAT command. Since you already have a disk in Drive B, you may continue.

STEP 17: Press any key.

```
xx percent of disk formatted.
```

WHAT'S HAPPENING? DOS is formatting the disk in Drive B. When the formatting is completed, you see the following screen display.

```
Format complete
System transferred

Volume label (11 characters, ENTER for none)?_
```

STEP 18: Press <Enter>.

```
362496 bytes total disk space
109568 bytes used by system
252928 bytes available on disk

  1024 bytes in each allocation unit
   247 allocation units available on disk

Volume Serial Number is 0F4C-17F3

Format another (Y/N)?_
```

STEP 19: Key in the following:

```
N <Enter>
```

STEP 20: Key in the following. (Note: The following is a series of commands to key in.)

```
COPY ANSI.SYS B: <Enter>
COPY APPEND.EXE B: <Enter>
COPY ATTRIB.EXE B: <Enter>
COPY CHKDSK.* B: <Enter>
COPY COMP.COM B: <Enter>
COPY DISKCOMP.COM B: <Enter>
COPY DISKCOPY.COM B: <Enter>
COPY E*.* B: <Enter>
COPY FIND.EXE B: <Enter>
COPY FORMAT.COM B: <Enter>
COPY J*.* B: <Enter>
COPY L*.* B: <Enter>
COPY M*.* B: <Enter>
COPY P*.* B: <Enter>
COPY S*.* B: <Enter>
COPY T*.* B: <Enter>
COPY V*.* B: <Enter>
COPY X*.* B: <Enter>
```

WHAT'S HAPPENING? The disk in Drive B is now the master DOS System Disk.

STEP 21: Remove the disk from Drive B. Label this disk "Master DOS System Disk."

STEP 22: Remove the disk from Drive A and turn off the computer.

Activity A.5 Making a DOS System Disk with DOS 4.0

Hard Disk Users Only

At this point, DOS has been installed on the hard disk. If not, please refer to Appendix B.

STEP 1: Boot the system. You will be at the C>.

STEP 2: Enter the current time and date, if necessary.

STEP 3: Key in the following:
C>**FORMAT A:/S** <Enter>

```
Insert new diskette for Drive A:
and press ENTER when ready...
```

Note: If, instead of the above message, you receive a message that states "Bad command or file name," your DOS programs are in a subdirectory. Typically this subdirectory is called \DOS. If it is not, you will have to locate the subdirectory that holds the DOS system files and use it instead of \DOS. You will have an additional step prior to taking Step 3. It is:
C>**CD \DOS** <Enter>

WHAT'S HAPPENING? You entered the FORMAT command.

STEP 4: Place a blank disk in Drive A and press any key.

```
xx percent of disk formatted.
```

WHAT'S HAPPENING? DOS is formatting the disk in Drive A. When the formatting is completed, you see the following screen display.

```
Format complete
System transferred

Volume label (11 characters, ENTER for none)?_
```

STEP 5: Press <Enter>.

```
362496 bytes total disk space
109568 bytes used by system
252928 bytes available on disk

  1024 bytes in each allocation unit
   247 allocation units available on disk

Volume Serial Number is 0F4C-17F3

Format another (Y/N)?_
```

STEP 6: Key in the following:
N <Enter>

```
C>_
```

Note 1: The chances are that the DOS files you need will be in a subdirectory. Typically the subdirectory is called **\DOS**. This entry is assumed for the next series of steps. If the DOS files are in a different subdirectory, you will have to substitute that subdirectory name for **\DOS**.

Note 2: The file names listed are those for IBM PC-DOS. If you are using MS-DOS, some file names may have the **.EXE** file extension instead of the **.COM** file extension. If you get the message "File not found," try substituting **.EXE** for **.COM**. In addition, the **COMP.COM** is called **FC.EXE**; **CHKDSK.COM** is called **CHKDSK.EXE**; and **VDISK.SYS** is called **RAMDRIVE.SYS** in MS-DOS.

Note 3: The next step is a continuing series of COPY commands. As soon as you see the message "1 file(s) copied" and return to the **C>** prompt, key in the next COPY command.

STEP 7: Key in the following:

```
COPY C:\DOS\ANSI.SYS A: <Enter>
COPY C:\DOS\APPEND.EXE A: <Enter>
COPY C:\DOS\ATTRIB.EXE A: <Enter>
COPY C:\DOS\CHKDSK.COM A: <Enter>
COPY C:\DOS\COMP.EXE A: <Enter>
COPY C:\DOS\DISKCOMP.COM A: <Enter>
COPY C:\DOS\DISKCOPY.COM A: <Enter>
COPY C:\DOS\EDLIN.COM A: <Enter>
COPY C:\DOS\FIND.EXE A: <Enter>
COPY C:\DOS\FORMAT.COM A: <Enter>
COPY C:\DOS\JOIN.EXE A: <Enter>
COPY C:\DOS\LABEL.COM A: <Enter>
COPY C:\DOS\MODE.COM A: <Enter>
COPY C:\DOS\MORE.COM A: <Enter>
COPY C:\DOS\PRINT.COM A: <Enter>
COPY C:\DOS\SORT.EXE A: <Enter>
COPY C:\DOS\SUBST.EXE A: <Enter>
COPY C:\DOS\TREE.COM A: <Enter>
COPY C:\DOS\VDISK.SYS A: <Enter>
COPY C:\DOS\XCOPY.EXE A: <Enter>
```

WHAT'S HAPPENING? The disk in Drive A is now the master DOS System Disk.

STEP 8: Remove the disk from Drive A. Label this disk "Master DOS System Disk."

STEP 9: Remove the disk from Drive A and turn off the computer.

Activity A.6 Making a DOS System Disk with DOS 5.0

Hard Disk Users Only

At this point, DOS has been installed on the hard disk. If not, please refer to Appendix B. In addition, if you have only two floppy disks, refer to Appendix B for installing DOS on floppy disks.

STEP 1: Boot the system. You will be at the `C>`.

STEP 2: Enter the current time and date, if necessary.

STEP 3: Key in the following:

C>**FORMAT A:/S** <Enter>

```
Insert new diskette for Drive A:
and press ENTER when ready...
```

Note: If, instead of the above message, you receive a message that states "Bad command or file name," your DOS programs are in a subdirectory. Typically this subdirectory is called `\DOS`. If it is not, you will have to locate the subdirectory that holds the DOS system files and use it instead of `\DOS`. You will have an additional step prior to taking Step 3. It is:

C>`CD \DOS` <Enter>

WHAT'S HAPPENING? You entered the FORMAT command.

STEP 4: Place a blank disk in drive A and press any key.

```
xx percent of disk formatted.
```

WHAT'S HAPPENING? DOS is formatting the disk in Drive A. When the formatting is completed, you see the following screen display.

```
Checking existing disk format.
Saving UNFORMAT information.
Verifying 360K
Format complete.
System transferred

Volume label (11 characters, ENTER for none)?_
```

STEP 5: Press <Enter>.

```
 362496 bytes total disk space
 119808 bytes used by system
 242688 bytes available on disk

   1024 bytes in each allocation unit.
    237 allocation units available on disk.

Volume Serial Number is 3C20-07F7

Format another (Y/N)?_
```

STEP 6: Key in the following:

```
N <Enter>
```

```
C>_
```

Note 1: The chances are that the DOS files you need will be in a subdirectory. Typically the subdirectory is called **\DOS**. This entry is assumed for the next series of steps. If the DOS files are in a different subdirectory, you will have to substitute that subdirectory name for **\DOS**.

Note 2: The file names listed are those for MS-DOS. If you are using IBM PC-DOS, some file names may have the **.COM** file extension instead of the **.EXE** file extension. If you get the message "File not found," try substituting **.COM** for **.EXE**. In addition, the **COMP.EXE** is called **COMP.COM**; **CHKDSK.EXE** is called **CHKDSK.COM**; and **RAMDRIVE.SYS** is called **VDISK.SYS** in IBM PC-DOS.

Note 3: The next step is a continuing series of COPY commands. As soon as you see the message "1 file(s) copied" and return to the **C>** prompt, key in the next COPY command.

STEP 7: Key in the following:

```
COPY C:\DOS\APPEND.EXE A: <Enter>
COPY C:\DOS\ASSIGN.COM A: <Enter>
COPY C:\DOS\CHKDSK.EXE A: <Enter>
COPY C:\DOS\COMP.EXE A: <Enter>
COPY C:\DOS\DISKCOMP.COM A: <Enter>
COPY C:\DOS\DISKCOPY.COM A: <Enter>
COPY C:\DOS\FIND.EXE A: <Enter>
COPY C:\DOS\FORMAT.COM A: <Enter>
COPY C:\DOS\JOIN.EXE A: <Enter>
COPY C:\DOS\LABEL.EXE A: <Enter>
COPY C:\DOS\MODE.COM A: <Enter>
COPY C:\DOS\MORE.COM A: <Enter>
COPY C:\DOS\PRINT.EXE A: <Enter>
COPY C:\DOS\RAMDRIVE.SYS <Enter>
COPY C:\DOS\SORT.EXE A: <Enter>
COPY C:\DOS\SUBST.EXE A: <Enter>
COPY C:\DOS\TREE.COM A: <Enter>
COPY C:\DOS\XCOPY.EXE A: <Enter>
```

WHAT'S HAPPENING? The disk in Drive A is now the master DOS System Disk.

STEP 8: Remove the disk from Drive A. Label this disk "Master DOS System Disk."

STEP 9: Remove the disk from Drive A and turn off the computer.

Appendix

Installing DOS to the Hard Disk

In order to use the hard disk, three things must occur. The disk must be low-level formatted. It must be partitioned and then formatted, sometimes called high-level formatting. If you wish to boot off the hard disk, which most users do, you must install the DOS system files on the hard disk. Usually, when a person purchases a computer system, the low-level formatting, partitioning, formatting and installation of DOS is done by the computer store or the computer manufacturer. This is not always true. Sometimes the hard disk will be partitioned, but DOS will not be installed. Sometimes neither the hard disk is partitioned nor DOS is installed. In addition, prior to DOS 4.0, a hard disk could be no larger than 32 MB. Hence, if you had a hard disk larger than 32 MB, it was partitioned into two or more logical drives. If you are upgrading to DOS 5.0 and now wish to have only one logical drive, you will need to repartition the hard disk. In either case you will have to partition the hard disk and install DOS or, if the disk is partitioned, you will have to install DOS.

With DOS 3.3, 4.0, and 5.0 you are provided with a program that automates the process. As you become more sophisticated, you may choose to install DOS in a different location or by a different process. However, for beginners, it is best to use the installation program and let it do the work for you.

B.1 Low-level Formatting

A hard disk is comprised of many disks called drive platters. Each platter is divided into concentric rings (cylinders) and each cylinder is divided into sectors. On a floppy disk, cylinders are referred to as tracks. The term heads refers to the number of heads on the drive itself, but since there is a direct relationship between the drive heads and recording surfaces, the term heads usually refers to both the drive mechanism and the number of surfaces where data may be stored. On floppy disks, heads are referred to as sides.

Low-level formatting tells where the cylinders and sectors lie on the disk. This process creates the sectors and cylinders by writing to the disk surface the

ID numbers of the sectors that tell where each sector is located. This identification or address tells the hard-disk controller where the requested information is on the disk.

The numbering of each sector provides two primary benefits (besides the obvious one of giving the controller a place to find the information on the disk): the sector interleave and marking the bad sectors on a disk. The sector interleave matches the rotation of the disk to the rate at which the disk controller can physically process data passing underneath the drive head. Thus, sectors may not be consecutively numbered on the disk, because not all computers can read a sector, write it to RAM, and get ready to read the next sector by the time the next consecutively numbered sector appears. Rather than having to wait for an entire revolution of the disk for the next sector, the sectors are spaced so that when the head is ready to read the next sector, the next consecutively numbered sector is under the drive head. The example to the right show a 3:1 interleave ratio. The sectors are spaced two apart. Thus, when the controller is ready to read the next consecutive sector, it is in the proper place and performance improves.

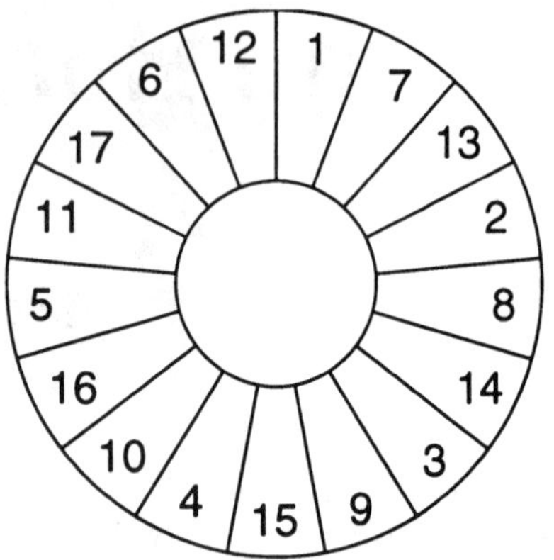

Newer computers, including most 386 computers, can handle a 1:1 interleave factor where the sectors are consecutively numbered.

Low-level formatting also marks any bad sectors on the disk so that they will not be written to. This marking is usually done at the place of manufacture or by the other equipment manufacturer (OEM), which receives a "defect" list supplied by the drive manufacturer.

Usually a disk only needs low-level formatting once. If you wish to do this, you must have your own utility program because low-level formatting is not a function of DOS. Some hard disks come with a low-level formatter and some have a low-level formatter that can be used with DEBUG. Some hard disks can only be formatted at the factory. Commercially available utilities such as SpinRite II from Gibson Research allow you to low-level format a disk. In general, however, unless you are having problems, it is unnecessary.

B.2 Partitioning a Hard Disk

A hard disk must be partitioned prior to installing DOS. Partitioning assigns parts of the disk to different operating systems. A partition defines what part of the hard disk belongs to which operating system. You may choose to have more than one operating system on the hard disk. For instance, you could have both DOS and UNIX on the hard disk. However, only one of these operating systems can be used at one time. You cannot run both at the same time.

DOS has three partition types: the primary DOS partition, the extended DOS partition, and the non-DOS partition. If you wish to use DOS on a hard disk, at least one partition is required and is called the primary DOS partition. The primary DOS partition must exist in order to boot from the hard disk. It is the first partition on the disk. In DOS 3.3, this partition size is limited to 32 MB. In DOS 4.0 and above there is no limitation.

The extended DOS partition can be any size within your hard disk size and can be subdivided into logical disk drives. Each logical disk drive is assigned a drive letter and acts like any other disk drive. The maximum number of partitions that DOS supports is four.

If you are using DOS 3.3, the hard disk must first be partitioned using the FDISK command. If you are using DOS 4.0, SELECT will automatically execute FDISK for you. Whichever version of DOS you are using, you should back up the original DOS disk before beginning (see Chapter 2, DISKCOPY), and you should carefully read the manual on how to install DOS.

Remember that partitioning a disk removes or destroys all the data on the disk. Thus, if you are partitioning a disk with data, first back up your data and programs.

B.3 Formatting a Hard Disk

In order for a disk to be used, it must first be formatted. This is also true of a hard disk. Formatting is the process of laying out the tracks and sectors DOS needs to keep track of files. If you wish to be able to boot off the hard disk, the DOS system files must be installed. For a complete discussion of the FORMAT command, see Chapter 4.

B.4 Identifying the Need for Installing DOS

If you do not know if your hard disk has been partitioned and/or formatted with DOS as the operating system, there is a simple way to find out.

1. Be sure there is no disk in any drive.
2. Find the switch to power on the computer and monitor. Some monitors do not have a separate switch.
3. If you see `C>`, the hard disk has been partitioned and formatted with DOS. You do not need to continue with this Appendix.
4. If you see the message "Non-system disk or disk error, replace and strike key when ready," the hard disk has been partitioned but DOS has not been installed. You only need to install DOS.
5. If you see a message such as "Invalid partition table" or "Invalid drive" or "Drive not ready," the hard disk has not been partitioned or formatted and you must follow all the steps indicated.

Activity B.5 Partitioning the Disk with FDISK—DOS 3.3

WARNING: DURING THE FOLLOWING STEPS, THE HARD DISK WILL BE PARTITIONED. THIS PROCESS WILL DESTROY ANY DATA ON THE DISK.

DOS 3.3 comes on either two 5 1/4-inch disks or one 3 1/2-inch disk.

STEP 1: Place the disk labeled "Start-up" in Drive A.

STEP 2: Find the switch to power on the computer and monitor. Some monitors do not have a separate switch.

STEP 3: Make backup copies of all disks that come with your system. See Chapter 2 on how to use DISKCOPY.

STEP 4: You should have the `A>` displayed. With the DOS Start-up disk in Drive A, key in the following:

`FDISK` <Enter>

```
  IBM Personal Computer
Fixed Disk Setup Program Version 3.30
(C)Copyright IBM Corp. 1983, 1987

FDISK Options

    Current fixed disk drive: 1

    Choose one of the following:

    1. Create DOS Partition
    2. Change Active Partition.
    3. Delete DOS Partition
    4. Display Partition Information
    5. Select Next Fixed Disk Drive

    Enter choice: [1]

    Press Esc to exit FDISK
```

WHAT'S HAPPENING? DOS is ready to partition the disk. "Enter choice: [1]" is the default choice.

STEP 5: Press <Enter>.

```
Create DOS Partition

Current Fixed Disk Drive: 1

     1. Create Primary DOS partition
     2. Created Extended DOS partition

Enter choice: [1]

Press ESC to return to FDISK Options
```

WHAT'S HAPPENING? You are ready to create the primary DOS partition. If you have a 32 MB hard disk or less, this is the only step you will have to take. If you have a hard disk larger than 32 MB, you will have to create an extended partition in order to use the remainder of the hard disk.

STEP 6: Press <Enter>.

```
Create Primary DOS Partition

Current Fixed Disk Drive : 1

Do you wish to use the maximum size
for a DOS partition and make the DOS
partition active (Y/N).............? [Y]

Press ESC to return to FDISK Options
```

WHAT'S HAPPENING? Since you want DOS to be the only operating system with the largest possible space and you want to be able to boot from Drive C, you are going to accept the default value of yes [Y].

STEP 7: Press <Enter>.

```
System will now restart

Insert DOS diskette in drive A:
Press any key when ready....
```

WHAT'S HAPPENING? The DOS Start-Up Diskette is in Drive A. When the system restarts and you are presented with the date and time prompt, the hard disk has been partitioned. However, prior to being able to use it, you still need to format the hard disk and install DOS on it.

WARNING: DURING THE FOLLOWING STEPS, THE HARD DISK WILL BE FORMATTED. THIS PROCESS WILL DESTROY ANY DATA ON THE DISK. FOLLOW THESE STEPS ONLY IF YOU ARE SURE THE HARD DISK HAS NOT BEEN FORMATTED.

STEP 1: Place the disk labeled "Start-up" in Drive A.

STEP 2: Find the switch to power on the computer and monitor.

STEP 3: Key in the following:
A>**SELECT C:\DOS 001 US** <Enter>

```
SELECT is used to install DOS the first
time. SELECT erases everything on the
specified target and then installs DOS.
Do you want to continue (Y/N) Y
```

WHAT'S HAPPENING? You are going to install DOS and place the DOS files in a subdirectory called **DOS**. The 001 and US are the country and keyboard codes that will be used. They determine the date format, the time format, the currency symbol, and the decimal separator.

STEP 4: Press <Enter>.

```
WARNING, ALL DATA ON NON-REMOVABLE DISK
DRIVE C: WILL BE LOST!
Proceed with Format (Y/N)?_
```

WHAT'S HAPPENING? You are getting one more chance to change your mind.

STEP 5: Key in the following:
`Y` <Enter>

WHAT'S HAPPENING? The disk begins to be formatted. As it is being formatted, you see a message that shows you the head and cylinder numbers, which change as the formatting process continues. When formatting is complete, you see the following message.

```
Format complete
System transferred

Volume labeled (11 characters, ENTER for none)?_
```

WHAT'S HAPPENING? The hard disk has been formatted. A volume label identifies the hard disk, an optional action.

STEP 6: Press <Enter>.

```
xxxxxx bytes total disk space
 xxxxx bytes used by system
xxxxx bytes in bad sectors
xxxxx bytes available on disk

Reading source file(s)...
```

WHAT'S HAPPENING? The names of the DOS files appear on the screen as they are copied to the hard disk. When the `A>` appears, the process is complete. DOS is installed on the hard disk. You may boot off the hard disk. When you look for your DOS files, you will find them in the subdirectory called `DOS`.

B.7 Installing DOS—DOS 4.0

DOS 4.0 comes on either two 3 1/2-inch disks labeled "Install" and "Operating" or five 5 1/4-inch diskettes labeled "Install," "Select," "Operating 1," "Operating 2," and "Operating 3." DOS 4.0 comes with an easy-to-use installation program called INSTALL. This program takes care of partitioning the disk, formatting the disk, and installing both the DOS system files and the DOS files on the disk. If you are a beginner, it is easiest for you to use this program. You must have several blank floppy disks of your system size. The manual labeled "Getting Started" has very clear instructions and should be used.

Activity
B.8
Installing DOS with INSTALL —DOS 4.0

STEP 1: Place the disk labeled "Install" in Drive A.

STEP 2: Find the switch to power on the computer and monitor. Some monitors do not have a separate switch.

Note: If you are working with 5 1/4-inch disks, remove the disk labeled "Install" and insert the disk labeled "Select"; then press <Enter>.

```
                    IBM
                DOS SELECT
                 DOS 4.00
      (C) Copyright IBM Corp. 1988
           All rights reserved

     Press Enter (<-|) or Esc to Cancel
```

WHAT'S HAPPENING? This screen tells you that it is going to start installing DOS. You will change disks several times during the installation process. The messages on the screen will instruct you when and which disks to change. At this point, always accept the highlighted defaults on the screen, especially when the disk is partitioned.

STEP 3: Press <Enter> and follow the instructions.

WHAT'S HAPPENING? You will be given instructions on what to do. During the installation process, you will see the following screen:

```
Select Installation Drive

Choose the drive to install DOS on:

     1.  C
     2.  A

Enter     Esc=Cancel  F1=Help
```

WHAT'S HAPPENING? Drive C or choice 1 should be highlighted.

STEP 4: Press <Enter>.

```
Specify DOS Location
You can accept the DOS directory name shown or type a new
directory name.

DOS Directory.... C:\[DOS   ]

To select option 1 below, press Enter. To change your
option, press the tab key, highlight your choice and then
press Enter.
```

```
     1.            Update all DOS files on fixed disk
     2.            Copy non-system files to directory specified.

 Enter             Esc=Cancel  F1=Help
```

WHAT'S HAPPENING? Choice 1 should be highlighted because it is the choice you want.

STEP 5: Press <Enter> and continue following the instructions on the screen. (Note: Be sure to let the SELECT program partition the disk.)

WHAT'S HAPPENING? When the installation is complete, you will get a screen message that says "Installation of IBM DOS 4.0 is complete" with additional information depending on your particular installation. The installation process is complete. DOS is installed on the hard disk. You may boot off the hard disk. When you look for your DOS files, you will find them in the subdirectory called DOS.

B.9 Upgrading to DOS 5.0

The upgrade kit from Microsoft does not have a bootable disk. You must have a version of DOS later than 2.11 already installed on your current computer system in order to upgrade to DOS 5.0. You must have at least 512 KB of memory and at least 2.8 MB of space free on the hard disk in order to place DOS 5.0 on the hard disk. It is a good idea to make a set of floppy disks for backup purposes. You can also use DISKCOPY with the original upgrade disks. The next set of instructions will lead you through making a set of floppy disks for DOS 5.0. If you have a new computer that has no operating system on it, see Appendix B.15 and Activity B.16. If you just wish to upgrade the hard disk to DOS 5.0, see Appendix B.11 and Activity B.12.

Activity B.10 Installing DOS 5.0 on Floppy Disks

STEP 1: Remove any memory-resident programs from **AUTOEXEC.BAT**.

STEP 2: Reboot the system with the current version of DOS.

STEP 3: Insert Disk 1 from the MS-DOS 5.0 upgrade kit in Drive A.

STEP 4: Prepare and label disks as follows: Seven 5 1/4-inch disks labeled "Startup," "Support," "Shell," "Help," "Basic/Edit," "Utility," and "Supplemental." Four 3 1/2-inch disks labeled "Startup/Support," "Shell/Help," "Basic/Edit/Utility," and "Supplemental."

STEP 5: Key in the following:
C:\>**A:SETUP /F** <Enter>

```
Microsoft (R) MS-DOS (R) Version 5.0
************************************
Welcome to Setup
```

```
Setup will help you create a set of working disks of MS-DOS
version 5.0. During Setup, MS-DOS files will be copied onto
floppy disks that you provide and label as shown below:
These disks can be formatted or unformatted.

STARTUP/SUPPORT
SHELL/HELP
BASIC/EDIT/UTILITY
SUPPLEMENTAL

If you want additional information or instructions about a
screen or option during Setup, press the Help key, F1. To
continue Setup, press ENTER. To exit Setup without creating
a set of MS-DOS working disks, press F3.

ENTER=Continue  F1=Help  F3=Exit  F5=Remove Color
```

WHAT'S HAPPENING? If you have different hardware and/or a 5 1/4-inch disk drive, you will see information reflecting those differences.

STEP 6: Press <Enter>.

```
Setup has gathered the following information about
your system.

     *****************************
     *Install to Drive    : A
     *Display Type        : VGA
     *
     *Continue Setup      : The information is correct.
     *****************************

If all the items in the list are correct, press ENTER to
continue Setup. If you want to change an item in the
list, use the UP ARROW or DOWN ARROW key to select it.
Then press ENTER to see some alternatives for that item.

ENTER=Continue  F1=Help  F3=Exit
```

WHAT'S HAPPENING? Again, if you have different hardware or want to make other choices, you are instructed on how to do so.

STEP 7: Press <Enter>.

```
MS-DOS version 5.0 is now being set up.

Setup installs a basic MS-DOS System. See the 'Microsoft
MS-DOS User's Guide and Reference' to learn about
additional features.

You may want to read the chapter on optimizing your system
in the manual. This chapter describes how to fine-tune
MS-DOS to achieve maximum performance.
```

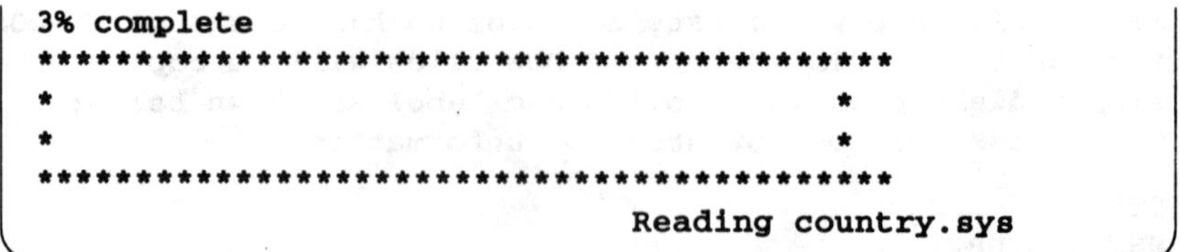

```
3% complete
*******************************************
*                                         *
*                                         *
*******************************************
                        Reading country.sys
```

WHAT'S HAPPENING? As the SETUP program works, it shows a bar graph filling as it completes its tasks. At the bottom of the screen, it tells you what file it is reading into memory. When it needs a disk, you see a message in the center of the screen as follows:

```
      Label a floppy disk
        STARTUP/SUPPORT
    and insert it into drive
              A:
     When ready, press ENTER.

    WARNING: All existing files
    on this disk will be deleted.
```

WHAT'S HAPPENING? The messages prompt you on the steps to take. Continue following the steps on the screen. Remove and insert disks only when you are instructed to do so. When you receive a message that SETUP is complete, the message will tell you to insert the Startup disk in Drive A and reboot. If you want to install DOS 5.0 on the hard disk, see Appendix B.11 and Activity B.12.

B.11

Upgrading to DOS 5.0 on the Hard Disk

The upgrade kit from Microsoft does not have a bootable disk. You must have a version of DOS later than 2.11 already installed on your current computer system in order to upgrade to DOS 5.0. You must have at least 512 KB of memory and at least 2.8 MB of space free on the hard disk in order to place DOS 5.0 on the hard disk. It is a good idea to make a set of floppy disks for backup purposes. See Appendix B.10 for instructions. You can also use DISKCOPY with the original upgrade disks. If you have a new computer that has no operating system on it, see Appendix B.15. If you have already made a backup copy of the floppy disks and now want to proceed to installing DOS 5.0 on the hard disk, continue with the next activity. If you want to repartition your hard disk, see Appendix B.13 and Activity B.14.

Activity B.12

Upgrading to DOS 5.0 on the Hard Disk

STEP 1: Remove any memory-resident programs from **AUTOEXEC.BAT**.

STEP 2: Reboot the system with the current version of DOS.

STEP 3: Insert Disk 1 from the MS-DOS 5.0 upgrade kit in Drive A.

Note: Use the next step only if you wish to back up the entire hard disk. If you only have a few files you wish to save, just copy those files to a floppy disk. Installing DOS 5.0 on the hard disk should not affect the files already on the disk. This step is not necessary other than the fact that it is always appropriate to have backed up important data files to floppies.

STEP 4: Key in the following:
C:\>**A:HDBKUP** <Enter>

WHAT'S HAPPENING? SETUP will estimate how many floppy disks you need to back up the files and then will step you through the process.

STEP 5: Key in the following:
C:\>**A:SETUP** <Enter>

```
Microsoft (R) MS-DOS (R) Version 5.0

Welcome to Setup

Setup upgrades your original DOS files to MS-DOS version 5.0.
During Setup you need to provide a floppy disk (or disks).
Setup will use the disk(s) to store your original DOS files.

Label the disks as follows.

                UNINSTALL #1
                UNINSTALL #2 (if needed)

The disk(s), which can be formatted or newly formatted,
must be used in Drive A.

Setup copies some files to the Uninstall disk(s) and
others to a directory on your hard disk called OLD_DOS.x.
Using these files, you can restore the original DOS on your
hard disk if you need to.

ENTER=Continue  F1=Help  F3=Exit  F5=Remove Color
```

WHAT'S HAPPENING? SETUP is getting ready to install DOS. Be sure to have one or two floppy disks.

STEP 6: Press <Enter>.

```
If you use a network, you will probably
need to complete a few additional steps
before installing MS-DOS version 5.0.

If you use a network, press Y.
If you do not use a network, press N.
```

WHAT'S HAPPENING? Since you are not installing to a network, select N.

STEP 7: Press N and <Enter>.

```
Before upgrading to MS-DOS version 5.0, Setup can back up
your hard disk.

Use the UP ARROW or DOWN ARROW key to select the option
you want and press ENTER

Do not back up hard disk(s).
Back up hard disk(s).
```

WHAT'S HAPPENING? "Do not back up hard disk(s)" should be highlighted. In this case, you are not going to back up the hard disk.

STEP 8: Press <Enter>.

```
Setup has determined that your system includes the
following hardware and software components.

DOS Type            :MS-DOS
DOS Path            :C:\DOS
MS-DOS Shell     :Do not run MS-DOS Shell on Startup.
Display Type     :VGA

Continue Setup   :The information above is correct.

If all the items in the list are correct, press ENTER.
If you want to change an item in the list, use the UP
ARROW or DOWN ARROW key to select it. Then press ENTER
to see alternatives for that item.
```

WHAT'S HAPPENING? You see a correct list of your hardware. Again, if you want to make changes, follow the instructions on the screen.

```
Setup is ready to upgrade to MS-DOS 5.0. If you
continue, you may not be able to interrupt Setup until it
has completed installing MS-DOS on your system.

To upgrade to MS-DOS version 5.0 now, press Y.

To exit Setup without upgrading, press F3.

To review your configuration, press any other key.
```

WHAT'S HAPPENING? You are now ready to install DOS 5.0.

STEP 9: Press Y.

```
       Label a floppy disk
          UNINSTALL #1
     and insert it into drive
               A:
      When ready, press ENTER.

     WARNING: All existing files
    on this disk will be deleted.
```

WHAT'S HAPPENING? If the floppy disk you insert is not formatted, SETUP will prompt you to select high-density or low-density format. As SETUP continues, it will prompt you when and which disk to insert into Drive A. Follow the instructions on the screen. You will see a horizontal bar graph at the bottom of the screen as it completes its tasks.

```
3% complete
*******************************************
*                                         *
*                                         *
*******************************************
```

When SETUP is complete, you will see the following screen:

```
Setup is now complete. Please remove any floppy
disks from your drives and then press ENTER to
start MS-DOS 5.0.

Note:
     Your original AUTOEXEC.BAT and CONFIG.SYS
     (if any) were saved as AUTOEXEC.DAT and
     CONFIG.DAT on the Uninstall disk.
```

WHAT'S HAPPENING? DOS 5.0 is now installed on the hard disk.

STEP 10: Remove any disks from the drives and press <Enter>.

WHAT'S HAPPENING? The system should now reboot. You should always have a floppy DOS System Disk so you can start your computer if the hard disk fails.

STEP 11: Insert a blank disk in drive A.

STEP 12: Key in the following:
C:\>**FORMAT A:/S** <Enter>

```
C:\>FORMAT A:/S
Insert new diskette for drive A:
and press ENTER when ready...
```

STEP 13: Press <Enter>.

```
Format complete
System transferred

Volume labeled (11 characters, ENTER for none)?_
```

STEP 14: Press <Enter>.

```
xxxxxx bytes total disk space
 xxxxx bytes used by system
xxxxx bytes in bad sectors
xxxxx bytes available on disk

Do you wish to format another disk (Y/N)?_
```

STEP 15: Press N and <Enter>.

WHAT'S HAPPENING? You have created an emergency booting disk. Label it and place it in a safe place. You have installed DOS 5.0.

B.13 Upgrading to DOS 5.0 and Repartitioning the Hard Disk

The upgrade kit from Microsoft does not have a bootable disk. You must have a version of DOS already installed in order to upgrade to DOS 5.0. If you simply wish to upgrade, go to Appendix B.12. If you want to repartition your hard disk, you should do so only if

1. the primary DOS partition is too small,
2. the size of the clusters or sectors are incompatible with DOS 5.0,
3. there are more than four partitions,
4. the primary DOS partition is inaccessible,
5. a disk-partitioning program is not compatible with the SETUP program (see the **README.TXT** file on Disk 5 (5 1/4-inch) or Disk 3 (3 1/2-inch)), or
6. you have a hard disk larger than 32 MB and in earlier versions of DOS you were forced to have logical disk drives.

To repartition the hard disk, take the following steps:

1. Remove any memory-resident programs from the **AUTOEXEC.BAT** file.
2. Back up the files on your hard disk. You may use any commercial program such as Fastback or PC Tools Backup. You may also use the HDBKUP utility on Disk 1 in the MS-DOS 5.0 upgrade.
3. Install DOS 5.0 to floppy disks using the SETUP /F parameter so you can boot from floppies. You will need seven 5 1/4-inch disks or three 3 1/2-inch disks.
4. Remove the partitions from the hard disk using the program that created them. If you used MS-DOS FDISK to partition the hard disk originally, you may use the FDISK program on the MS-DOS 5.0 disk.
5. Place the Startup or Startup/Support disk in Drive A.
6. Reboot the computer.
7. Use the FDISK command to remove the old partitions and logical drives.
8. Partition the hard disk.
9. Format the hard disk with the /S parameter.
10. Restore your files to the hard disk.
11. Proceed with the hard disk installation as you normally would.

Remember that to install DOS 5.0, you need MS-DOS 2.11 or later, at least 512 KB of memory, and at least 2.8 MB of free space on the hard disk.

Activity B.14 Repartitioning the Hard Disk with DOS 5.0

WARNING: THIS IS FATAL TO DATA ON THE HARD DISK.

STEP 1: Remove any memory-resident programs from **AUTOEXEC.BAT**.

STEP 2: Reboot the system with the current version of DOS.

STEP 3: Insert Disk 1 from the MS-DOS 5.0 upgrade kit in Drive A.

Note: Use the next step only if you wish to back up the entire hard disk. If you only have a few files you wish to save, just copy those files to a floppy disk.

STEP 4: Key in the following:
A:HDBKUP <Enter>

WHAT'S HAPPENING? SETUP will estimate how many floppy disks you need to back up the files and then will step you through the process. You will next create a set of DOS 5.0 disks on floppies—a set of working disks.

STEP 5: Prepare and label disks as follows: Seven 5 1/4-inch disks labeled "Startup," "Support," "Shell," "Help," "Basic/Edit," "Utility," and "Supplemental." Four 3 1/2-inch disks labeled "Startup/Support," "Shell/Help," "Basic/Edit/Utility," and "Supplemental."

STEP 6: Key in the following:
A:SETUP /F <Enter>

```
Microsoft (R) MS-DOS (R) Version 5.0
***********************************

Welcome to Setup

Setup will help you create a set of working disks of MS-DOS
version 5.0. During Setup, MS-DOS files will be copied onto
floppy disks that you provide and label as shown below:
These disks can be formatted or unformatted.

STARTUP/SUPPORT
SHELL/HELP
BASIC/EDIT/UTILITY
SUPPLEMENTAL

If you want additional information or instructions about a
screen or option during Setup, press the Help key, F1. To
continue Setup, press ENTER. To exit Setup without creating
a set of MS-DOS working disks, press F3.

ENTER=Continue  F1=Help  F3=Exit  F5=Remove Color
```

WHAT'S HAPPENING? If you have different hardware and/or a 5 1/4-inch disk drive, you will see information reflecting those differences.

STEP 7: Press <Enter>.

```
Setup has gathered the following information about
your system.

     ******************************
     *Install to Drive    : A
     *Display Type        : VGA
     *
     *Continue Setup      : The information is correct.
     ******************************

If all the items in the list are correct, press ENTER to
continue Setup. If you want to change an item in the
list, use the UP ARROW or DOWN ARROW key to select it.
Then press ENTER to see some alternatives for that item.

ENTER=Continue  F1=Help  F3=Exit
```

WHAT'S HAPPENING? Again, if you have different hardware or wanted to make other choices, you are instructed on how to do so.

STEP 8: Press <Enter>.

```
MS-DOS version 5.0 is now being set up.

Setup installs a basic MS-DOS System. See the 'Microsoft
MS-DOS User's Guide and Reference' to learn about
additional features.

You may want to read the chapter on optimizing your system
in the manual. This chapter describes how to fine-tune
MS-DOS to achieve maximum performance.

3% complete
********************************************
*                                          *
*                                          *
********************************************
                          Reading country.sys
```

WHAT'S HAPPENING? As the SETUP program works, it shows a bar graph filling as it completes its tasks. At the bottom of the screen, it tells you what file it is reading into memory. When it needs a disk, you see a message in the center of the screen as follows:

```
        Label a floppy disk
          STARTUP/SUPPORT
      and insert it into drive
                A:
       When ready, press ENTER.

      WARNING: All existing files
     on this disk will be deleted.
```

WHAT'S HAPPENING? As you can see, the messages prompt you on the steps to take. Continue following the steps on the screen. Remove and insert disks only when you are instructed to do so. When you receive a message that SETUP is complete, the message will tell you to insert the Startup disk in Drive A and reboot.

STEP 9: Insert the newly created Startup/Support disk in Drive A and reboot the system. (If you have 5 1/4-inch disks, it is labeled Startup.)

Note: If you partitioned the hard disk with any other program than FDISK, you must use *that* program to delete the partitions. *Do not take the next step.*

STEP 10: Key in `FDISK`. (Note: If you are working with 5 1/4-inch disks, you will need to insert the disk labeled "Support.")

```
                       MS-DOS Version 5.00
                        Fixed Disk Setup Program
                 (C)Copyright Microsoft Corp.1983-1991

                              FDISK Options

Current fixed disk drive: 1

Choose one of the following:

1. Create DOS partition or Logical DOS Drive
2. Set active partition
3. Delete partition or Logical DOS Drive
4. Display partition information

Enter choice: [1]


Press Esc to exit FDISK
```

WHAT'S HAPPENING? This is the partitioning utility. Before you can repartition the hard disk, you must delete the current partitions and/or any logical drives. It is also useful to see what you already have. You can choose choice 4 to display the partition information on your system. This choice is particularly useful because you will need to know the volume label, the partition number, and any other logical disk drives you have on your system.

STEP 11: Select 4 and press <Enter>.

```
Display Partition Information

Current fixed disk drive: 1

Partition  Status  Type  Volume Label  Mbytes  System Usage
C: 1          A   PRI DOS HARD DISK       70    FAT16   64%
   2              EXT DOS                 40            36%

 Total disk space is 110 Mbytes (1 Mbyte = 1048576 bytes)
```

```
The Extended DOS Partition contains Logical DOS Drives.
Do you want to display the logical drive information
(Y/N)......?[Y]

    Press Esc to return to FDISK Options
```

WHAT'S HAPPENING? This displays shows that there is an extended DOS partition. To see it, press Y for yes.

STEP 12: If you do not have an extended DOS partition, press <Esc>, otherwise press Y.

```
Display Logical DOS Drive Information

Drv  Volume Label  Mbytes  System  Usage
D:                     40  FAT16    100%

Total Extended DOS Partition size is 40 Mbytes
(1 MByte = 1048576 bytes)

    Press Esc to continue
```

WHAT'S HAPPENING? The drive letter and size of the extended DOS partition are displayed.

STEP 13: Press <Esc> twice to return to the FDISK main menu.

STEP 14: Select 3 and press <Enter>.

```
Delete DOS Partition or Logical DOS Drive

Current fixed disk drive: 1

Choose one of the following:

1.    Delete Primary DOS Partition
2.    Delete Extended DOS Partition
3.    Delete Logical DOS Drive(s) in the Extended Partition
4.    Delete Non-DOS Partition

Enter choice:    [ ]
```

WHAT'S HAPPENING? Your system information could be different depending on how the hard disk was partitioned. You must delete each logical drive, then the extended partition, and last the primary DOS partition. You must delete in the following order: first choice 4, any non-DOS partitions—this is new to DOS 5.0. Then choice 3, any logical DOS drives. The program will ask you for the drive letter that you wish to delete. Next choose 2, delete the extended DOS partition. Last, choose 1, delete primary DOS partition. FDISK will ask you for the volume label prior to deleting the primary DOS partition. When you have deleted all the partitions, return to the main menu of FDISK.

```
                    MS-DOS Version 5.00
                     Fixed Disk Setup Program
              (C)Copyright Microsoft Corp.1983-1991

                          FDISK Options

Current fixed disk drive: 1

Choose one of the following:

1. Create DOS partition or Logical DOS Drive
2. Set active partition
3. Delete partition or Logical DOS Drive
4. Display partition information

Enter choice: [1]


Press Esc to exit FDISK
```

WHAT'S HAPPENING? You returned to the main menu of FDISK.

STEP 15: Be sure 1 is in the Enter Choice box. If not, key in the following:
1 <Enter>

```
Create DOS Partition

Current Fixed Disk Drive: 1
     1. Create Primary DOS partition
     2. Create Extended DOS partition
     3. Create logical DOS Drive(s) in the
        Extended DOS Partition

Enter choice: [1]

Press ESC to return to FDISK Options
```

WHAT'S HAPPENING? You are ready to create the primary DOS partition. The [1] should be selected.

STEP 16: Press <Enter>.

```
Create Primary DOS Partition

Current Fixed Disk Drive : 1

Do you wish to use the maximum size
for a DOS partition and make the DOS
partition active (Y/N).............? [Y]

Press ESC to return to FDISK Options
```

WHAT'S HAPPENING? Since you want DOS to be the only operating system with the largest possible space and you want to be able to boot from Drive C, you are going to accept the default value of yes [Y].

STEP 17: Press <Enter>.

WHAT'S HAPPENING? You receive this message: "Primary DOS Partition created, drive letters changed or added." Then the next screen appears.

```
System will now restart

Insert DOS diskette in drive A:
Press any key when ready....
```

WHAT'S HAPPENING? The DOS Start-Up Diskette should still be in Drive A. If not, place it in Drive A. When the system restarts and you are presented with the date and time prompt, the hard disk has been partitioned. However, before being able to use it, you need to format the hard disk and install DOS. The Startup disk is still in Drive A.

STEP 18: Key in the following:
A:\>`FORMAT C:/S` <Enter>

```
WARNING, ALL DATA ON NON-REMOVEABLE DISK
DRIVE C: WILL BE LOST:
PROCEED WITH FORMAT (Y/N)?_
```

STEP 19: Press Y and <Enter>.

```
Format complete
System transferred

Volume labeled (11 characters, ENTER for none)?_
```

WHAT'S HAPPENING? The hard disk has been formatted. A volume label identifies the hard disk, an optional action.

STEP 20: If you want to have a volume label, enter it now or just press <Enter>.

```
xxxxxx bytes total disk space
 xxxxx bytes used by system
xxxxx bytes in bad sectors
xxxxx bytes available on disk
```

WHAT'S HAPPENING? You have formatted the hard disk. You can now restore any files that you backed up. Use the utility program or copy the file back to the hard disk if you did not use the utility program HDBKUP. If you used HDBKUP, take the next step.

STEP 21: If you have 5 1/4-inch disks, insert Disk 3 into Drive A. If you have 3 1/2-inch disks insert Disk 2 in Drive A, then key in the following:
A:\>`A:HDRSTOR` <Enter>

WHAT'S HAPPENING? Follow the instructions on the screen to restore your files. If you backed up multiple drives, repeat this step for each drive you backed up. Now you can proceed to installing DOS 5.0 on the hard disk. See Appendix B.12 for the instructions.

B.15 Installing DOS 5.0 on a New Computer

Usually when you purchase a new computer, the hard disk has been partitioned and DOS 5.0 is installed. If you have purchased a new computer that has no operating system on it, the manufacturer should have provided you with the appropriate disks to partition the hard disk and install their version of DOS. The process should be fairly simple. The OEM DOS disks should automatically partition the disk and install DOS with a minimum of user effort. You must be sure you have at least 256 KB of memory prior to proceeding. However, be sure to check your documentation.

Activity B.16 Installing DOS on a New Computer with Partitioning

Note: This activity is only for those users who have a new computer that has no version of DOS installed on it and is not partitioned.

STEP 1: Insert the disk labeled Disk 1 into Drive A.

STEP 2: Turn on the power switch.

WHAT'S HAPPENING? After the computer performs any built-in tests, it should start the installation program SETUP. You see the following message.

```
Please wait
Setup is determining your system configuration
```

WHAT'S HAPPENING? The SETUP program determines what hardware you have. You then receive the next message.

```
Welcome to Setup
Setup prepares MS-DOS Version 5.0 to run
on your system. Each screen has basic instructions for
completing a step of the installation. If you want
additional information and instructions about a
screen or option, press the Help key, F1.
To continue Setup, press Enter.
```

WHAT'S HAPPENING? The message tells you what to do to continue.

STEP 3: Press <Enter>.

WHAT'S HAPPENING? You see a screen display that shows the following lines: Date/Time; the Country, the Keyboard, and Install To:. These are usually correct and do not need to be changed unless you have a unique setup problem such as wanting to use a different country keyboard. Use the up and down arrows to highlight the area you wish to change, then make the change and press <Enter>. Continue to do this until all changes you wish to make are complete.

STEP 4: Press <Enter>.

WHAT'S HAPPENING? You see another box asking Setup To:. The default value is **C:\DOS**. You also see this choice:

```
Run the Shell on startup
Do not run the Shell on startup.
```

WHAT'S HAPPENING? The first line is highlighted. If you leave this highlighted, every time you boot DOS, the Shell will be the default and you will not see the DOS prompt. In this case, you do not wish the Shell to run on booting the system.

STEP 5: Highlight the line "Do not run the Shell on startup" and press <Enter>.

STEP 6: Highlight the line "The listed options are correct" and press <Enter>.

```
Your system has one or more hard disks with free space
that can be used by MS-DOS Version 5.0. This space
needs to be set up before MS-DOS can use it.
```

WHAT'S HAPPENING? The SETUP program is preparing to partition the hard disk. You see the following choices:

```
Partition all free space for MS-DOS.
Partition some of the free space for MS-DOS.
Do not partition free space for MS-DOS.
```

WHAT'S HAPPENING? "Partition all free space for MS-DOS" should be highlighted. Use this default value. If you plan on installing an additional operating system like UNIX selected "Partition some of the free space." Do not choose "Do not partition free space for MS-DOS." If you do, you will only be able to install DOS to floppy disks and *will not* be able to use DOS or any DOS application on the hard disk.

STEP 7: Be sure "Partition all free space for MS-DOS" is highlighted and then press <Enter>.

WHAT'S HAPPENING? SETUP creates the partition, then reboots the system. It then begins to format the hard disk. You see the following messages.

```
Formatting Hard Disk Partition.
You have set up some or all of the disk space for use
with MS-DOS. This space is being formatted now.

MS-DOS Version 5.0 is now being set up. Setup
installs a basic MS-DOS system. See the 'MS-DOS
User's Guide and Reference" to learn about
additional features. You may want to read the
chapter on optimizing your system. This chapter
describes how to fine-tune MS-DOS to achieve
maximum performance.
```

WHAT'S HAPPENING? SETUP copies files to the hard disk. You will be instructed on the screen which disks to insert into which drive at what time. SETUP displays a bar graph that indicates by percentage where it is in the installation process. SETUP will tell you when it is done. At that time, remove the last disk and reboot the system.

C Appendix

BACKUP and RESTORE

C.0 Understanding BACKUP and RESTORE

Backing up data and programs is extremely important. A hard disk cannot be backed up with the DISKCOPY or COPY commands. Instead, DOS provides two utility programs, BACKUP and RESTORE, which are specifically designed to back up the hard disk files and then restore the files when needed. The BACKUP command is different from the COPY or DISKCOPY commands because BACKUP will prompt you to insert disks so that all of the hard disk can be copied to many floppy disks.

Backing up the hard disk is not a trivial task. In versions prior to DOS 4.0, it requires formatted disks. Also, to back up a 10 MB hard disk entirely takes about 30 360 KB floppy disks. A 20 MB hard disk takes about 60 disks. Table C.1 gives the approximate number of floppy disks you need depending on your media.

Table C.1 Disks Required to Back Up a Hard Disk

Hard Disk	**Floppy Disks Required**			
	360 KB	720 KB	1.2 MB	1.44 MB
10 MB	29	13	9	8
20 MB	59	29	18	15
30 MB	83	44	27	22
40 MB	116	38	35	29
70 MB	200	100	60	50

By the number of disks required, you can see that backing up the hard disk takes time. You sit in front of the computer and insert each floppy disk when DOS instructs you to do so. DOS automatically numbers the disks in the proper order, but it is a good idea to prenumber the disks by hand on paste-on labels before getting started.

These floppies that hold the backup are not usable by themselves. If you wish to use them, you must use the RESTORE command, which will again prompt you to insert disks.

Backups are insurance. You back up the hard disk for archival purposes or for storing the files just in case. In other words, you usually do not need the backups unless there is a problem with the hard disk. Something unexpected may occur, such as the hard disk crashing or you may lose an important data file and need to restore it. However, it is extremely important and prudent to make backing up the hard disk a regular routine. In addition, it is wise to have more than one backup. How often you back up depends on how long it would take you to "rekey in" or recover the information. Usually, if you update files daily, you probably want to back them up daily. If you update files weekly, you probably want to back them up weekly. You can see that you will need lots of floppy disks, which is one reason why many people go to a tape-based backup system or use a faster backup program such as the backup program from PC Tools.

The major reason you back up so often relates to the following scenario. It is Friday. The hard disk crashes. You go to restore the hard disk from Thursday's floppy backup disks. Thursday's disks are bad. Because you only had one day's backup, you are out of luck, but you have prepared and go to Wednesday's floppy disks. All you have lost is Thursday's work instead of the whole week's work.

You should have at least two sets of backup floppy disks. If there is a power failure or a hardware problem prior to the completion of the backup routine, all the backup files will be useless because BACKUP deletes everything from the floppy disks. Thus if BACKUP is interrupted, the previous backup is destroyed before the new backup can be completed.

C.1 Backing up a Hard Disk with BACKUP

If you have a version of DOS less than 3.3, be sure you have enough formatted floppy disks. You cannot interrupt the BACKUP program to format disks. However, if you have DOS version 3.3, you can add a switch to format the backup disks. DOS 4.0 or above will automatically format target disks for you. Version 2.x only allows you to back up the hard disk to floppies. Version 3.x and above allows you to back up from or to any valid DOS medium. The source disk must not be write-protected, and, if you are on a network, BACKUP will not archive programs you do not have access to. The syntax for the command is:

BACKUP *source destination*

or *d:\path*\BACKUP *ds:*[*path*][*filename.ext*] *dd:* [/S] [/M] [/A] [/D:*mm-dd-yy*] [/T:*hh:mm:ss*] [/F] [/L:*drive path filename*]

where the switches are:

/S	Backs up subdirectories files and the files in the specified or current directory.
/M	Backs up only files that have been modified since the last BACKUP by checking the archive bit of the file.
/A	Adds the files to be backed up to the files already present on the backup disk.

/D:*mm-dd-yy*	Backs up files that have been modified on or after the specified date.
/T:*hh:mm:ss*	Backs up files that have been modified on or after the specified time.
/F	Formats the target floppy disk, if not already formatted. *Version 3.3 only.*
/L:*filename*	Creates a log file in the file specified. If no file name is given, the name `BACKUP.LOG` is placed in the root directory of the source drive. If a log file exists, the new information is appended to the end of that file.

Activity C.2 Doing a Full Backup

Note: Do not do this unless you have enough floppy disks and are prepared to back up your entire hard disk. If you have a large hard disk, it can take an enormous amount of time. In addition, if you have any copy-protected programs on the hard disk, read the documentation for each application package first. Sometimes you must uninstall an application package before using the BACKUP command.

STEP 1: Key in the following:
C>`BACKUP C:\*.* A:/S` <Enter>

```
C>BACKUP C:*.* A:/S

Insert backup diskette 01 in drive A:
WARNING! Files in the target drive
A:\ root directory will be erased
Press any key to continue...
```

WHAT'S HAPPENING? You are asking to back up all the files from Drive C in the root directory (C:*.*) and all the subdirectory files on the hard disk (/S) to the disk in Drive A. Note that the /S parameter for subdirectories comes *after* the destination or A:.

STEP 2: Insert a disk you no longer want or a newly formatted disk in Drive A. Press <Enter> to begin backing up the hard disk.

```
***Backing up files to drive A:***
Diskette number: 01
\JANUARY.TXT
\FEBRUARY.TXT
......
......
```

WHAT'S HAPPENING? ...... represents all the files as they are found. Each file is listed on the screen as it is copied from the hard disk to the disk in Drive A. If one disk will not take all the files, the following message appears:

```
Insert backup diskette 02 in drive A:
WARNING! Files in the target drive
A:\ root directory will be erased
Press any key to continue...
```

WHAT'S HAPPENING? Continue to insert disks until the hard disk is backed up. Each disk is numbered sequentially by DOS, but it is still important to number them yourself. When you have completed the process, look at the directory on A:. If you have a version of DOS prior to 3.3, you see a file named **BACKUPID.@@@**. This file is on each disk you back up. It supplies the backup identification number.

If you have DOS 3.3 or above, the backup is handled differently. Only two files are placed on the backup disk, a control file and a data file. The control file has the housekeeping information about the data files. The single data file holds the backup files. This new technique for backing up disks is 40 percent faster than the older version of BACKUP.

C.3 Incremental Backups

You can back up the hard disk in increments. For example, you can back up individual files, a subdirectory, only those files that have been modified since the last backup, and files that have been created or modified since a certain date. Remember that whenever you use a disk for backup, whatever was on that disk is lost. The following activities can be done using the subdirectory **\JUNK** that you created in the text.

Activity C.4 Backing Up a File

STEP 1: Key in the following:
C>**BACKUP C:\JUNK\JAN.TMP A:** <Enter>

```
C>BACKUP C:\JUNK\JAN.TMP A:

Insert backup diskette 01 in drive A:
WARNING! Files in the target drive
A:\ root directory will be erased
Press any key to continue...
```

WHAT'S HAPPENING? You are going to back up one file from the subdirectory **\JUNK** on Drive C called **JAN.TMP** to the disk in Drive A.

STEP 2: Insert a disk you no longer want or a newly formatted disk in Drive A. Press <Enter>.

```
***Backing up files to drive A:***
Diskette number: 01
\JUNK\JAN.TMP

C>_
```

WHAT'S HAPPENING? Since you only backed up one file, the process is complete.

Activity C.5 Backing Up a Subdirectory

STEP 1: Key in the following:
C>**BACKUP C:\JUNK\SAMPLE A:** <Enter>

```
C>BACKUP C:\JUNK\SAMPLE A:

Insert backup diskette 01 in drive A:
WARNING! Files in the target drive
A:\ root directory will be erased
Press any key to continue...
```

WHAT'S HAPPENING? You are asking the system to back up all the files from Drive C in the subdirectory called **\JUNK\SAMPLE** to the disk in Drive A.

STEP 2: Insert a disk you no longer want or a newly formatted disk in Drive A. Press <Enter> to begin backing up the hard disk.

```
          ***Backing up files to drive A:***
Diskette number: 01
\JUNK\SAMPLE\BASKETBL.TMS
\JUNK\SAMPLE\PRO.TMS
\JUNK\SAMPLE\COLLEGE.TMS
\JUNK\SAMPLE\AMERICAN.TMS
\JUNK\SAMPLE\NATIONAL.TMS

C>_
```

WHAT'S HAPPENING? Each file is listed on the screen as it is copied from the hard disk to the disk in Drive A. If one disk will not take all the files, you are prompted to insert disks until all the files in the subdirectory are backed up.

Activity C.6 Backing Up Selected Files in a Subdirectory

STEP 1: Key in the following:
C>**BACKUP C:\JUNK*.99 A:**

```
C>BACKUP C:\JUNK\*.99 A:

Insert backup diskette 01 in drive A:
WARNING! Files in the target drive
A:\ root directory will be erased
Press any key to continue...
```

WHAT'S HAPPENING? You are asking the system to back up from Drive C only the files that have the file extension **.99** in the subdirectory called **\JUNK** to the disk in Drive A.

STEP 2: Insert a disk you no longer want or a newly formatted disk in Drive A. Press <Enter>.

```
            ***Backing up files to drive A:***
Diskette number: 01
\JUNK\JAN.99
\JUNK\FEB.99
\JUNK\MAR.99
\JUNK\APR.99

C>_
```

WHAT'S HAPPENING? There were only four files with the extension **.99** in the subdirectory **\JUNK**. Each file was listed on the screen as it was copied from the hard disk to the disk in Drive A. In this case, all the files fit on one disk. However, if one disk would not take all the files, you would be asked to insert additional disks until all the files are backed up. When you have completed the process, you can look at the directory on Drive A to see the backups.

STEP 3: Key in the following:
C>**DIR A:** <Enter>

```
C>DIR A:

 Volume in drive A is BACKUP 001
 Volume Serial Number is 2343-13D7
 Directory of A:\

BACKUP    001     287   05-13-91   6:46p
CONTROL   001     345   05-13-91   6:46p
        2 File(s)    1212928 bytes free

C>_
```

WHAT'S HAPPENING? You can see the **BACKUP.001** and the **CONTROL.001** files that you backed up.

Activity C.7 Backing Up Files Modified Since the Last Backup

STEP 1: Key in the following:
C>**COPY CON C:\JUNK\CHANGE.99** <Enter>
This is my change document to <Enter>
demonstrate how the /M parameter works. <Enter>
<Ctrl>+Z <Enter>

```
C>COPY CON C:\JUNK\CHANGE.99
This is my change document to
demonstrate how the /M parameter works.
^Z

C>_
```

WHAT'S HAPPENING? You created a file that has been changed.

STEP 2: Key in the following:
C>**BACKUP C:\JUNK*.99 A:/M** <Enter>

```
C>BACKUP C:\JUNK\*.99 A:/M

Insert backup diskette 01 in drive A:
WARNING! Files in the target drive
A:\ root directory will be erased
Press any key to continue...
```

WHAT'S HAPPENING? You first created a new file, one that was modified since the last backup. You then asked the system to back up from Drive C only the files that have the file extension **.99** in the subdirectory called **\JUNK** to the disk in Drive A.

STEP 3: Insert the disk you used in Activity C.6. Press <Enter>.

```
          ***Backing up files to drive A:***
Diskette number: 01
\JUNK\CHANGE.99

C>_
```

WHAT'S HAPPENING? As it is copied from the hard disk to the disk in Drive A the file is listed on the screen. Since only one file has changed since the last backup, only the file **CHANGE.99** is backed up to the disk in Drive A.

STEP 4: Key in the following:
C>DIR A: <Enter>

```
C>DIR A:

 Volume in drive A is BACKUP 001
 Volume Serial Number is 2343-13D7
 Directory of A:\

BACKUP    001      73   05-13-91  7:06p
CONTROL   001     243   05-13-91  7:06p
        2 File(s)    1212928 bytes free

C>_
```

WHAT'S HAPPENING? The same files are on the disk, **BACKUP.001** and **CONTROL.001**, but only the new file was backed up to the disk in Drive A. All the other files are gone. If you wanted to add the files to the ones that were there, you should have used the /A parameter.

Activity C.8

Backing Up Selected Files by Date

STEP 1: Key in the following:
C>DATE 11/23/95 <Enter>

STEP 2: Key in the following:
C>COPY CON \JUNK\NEW.99 <Enter>
This is a new file to <Enter>

show how the BACKUP command will <Enter>
backup by a certain date. <Enter>
<Ctrl>+Z <Enter>

```
C>DATE 11/23/95

C>COPY CON NEW.99
This is a new file to
show how the BACKUP command will
backup by a certain date.
^Z

1 file(s) copied

C>_
```

WHAT'S HAPPENING? You first changed the date to a date in the future. You then created a file based on that date so that you could test the /M option of the BACKUP command.

STEP 3: Key in the following:
C>BACKUP C:\JUNK*.99 A:/D:11/23/95 <Enter>

```
C>BACKUP C:\JUNK\*.99 A:/D:11/23/95

Insert backup diskette 01 in drive A:
WARNING! Files in the target drive
A:\ root directory will be erased
Press any key to continue...
```

WHAT'S HAPPENING? You are asking the system to back up from Drive C only the files with the extension .99 that have been created or modified on or after November 23, 1995 in the subdirectory \JUNK to the disk in Drive A. The /D: parameter follows the destination drive.

STEP 4: Insert the disk you used in Activity C.7. Press <Enter>.

```
          ***Backing up files to drive A:***
Diskette number: 01
\JUNK\NEW.99

C>_
```

WHAT'S HAPPENING? Only \JUNK\NEW.99 was modified or created on or after November 23, 1995 in the subdirectory \JUNK. It was listed on the screen as it was copied from the hard disk to the disk in Drive A.

STEP 5: Key in the following:
C>DIR A: <Enter>

```
C>DIR A:

 Volume in drive A is BACKUP 001
 Volume Serial Number is 2343-13D7
 Directory of A:\

BACKUP    001       85   11-23-95  7:54p
CONTROL   001      243   11-23-95  7:54p
        2 File(s)    1212928 bytes free

C>_
```

WHAT'S HAPPENING? The backup and control files have the 1995 date.

STEP 6: Key in the following:
C>TYPE A:BACKUP.001 <Enter>

```
C>TYPE A:BACKUP.001
This is a new file to
show how the BACKUP command will
backup by a specific date.

C>_
```

WHAT'S HAPPENING? You are looking at the file you just created.

STEP 7: Change the date back to the current date by using the DATE command.

Activity C.9

Adding Files to a Backup Disk

STEP 1: Insert the disk you used in Activity C.8 into Drive A.

STEP 2: Key in the following:
C>BACKUP C:\JUNK*.99 A:/A <Enter>

```
C>BACKUP \JUNK\*.99 A:/A

Insert last backup diskette in drive A:
Press any key to continue . . .
```

WHAT'S HAPPENING? You did not get a warning that the data would be destroyed on Drive A because the files will be added to the backup.

STEP 3: Press <Enter>.

```
*** Backing up files to drive A: ***
Diskette Number: 01

\JUNK\JAN.99
\JUNK\FEB.99
\JUNK\MAR.99
\JUNK\APR.99
```

```
\JUNK\CHANGE.99
\JUNK\NEW.99

C>_
```

WHAT'S HAPPENING? The files were added to the disk in Drive A. Each was listed as it was copied.

STEP 4: Key in the following:
C>**DIR A:** <Enter>

STEP 5: Key in the following:
C>**TYPE A:BACKUP.001** <Enter>

```
C>DIR A:

 Volume in drive A is BACKUP 001
 Volume Serial Number is 2343-13D7
 Directory of A:\

BACKUP   001     530   05-13-91  8:07p
CONTROL  001     517   05-13-91  8:07p
        2 File(s)    1211904 bytes free

C>TYPE A:BACKUP.001
This is a new file to
show how the BACKUP command will
backup by a specific date.
This is my January file.
It is my first dummy file.
This is file 1.

C>_
```

WHAT'S HAPPENING? The file dates reflect the current system date. In addition, the file contents have changed.

C.10 Restoring a Hard Disk Using RESTORE

You restore the hard disk by using the disks with which you backed up the file to with the RESTORE command. The syntax for the command is:

RESTORE *source destination*
or [*d:*][*path*]RESTORE *source drive d:* [*target drive*][*path*][*filename*][*ext*] [/P] [/M] [/S] [/B:*mm-dd-yy*] [/A:*mm-dd-yy*] [/E:*hh:mm:ss*] [/N]

The first *d:* represents the source drive, usually Drive A. The second *drive* and *path* represent where you want the files restored to. The *filename* means you can select individual files to restore. The other switches are:

/S Restores all files in subdirectories and files in specified subdirectories.
/P Prompts you before restoring files that have been changed since the last backup.
/B Restores all files modified on or before the date specified.
/A Restores all files modified on or after the date specified.
/M Restores files modified or deleted since last back up.
/N Restores files that no longer exist on target disk.
/L Restores only files that were modified at or later than the given time.
/E Restores only files that were modified at or earlier than the given time.

RESTORE will not restore the system files. The files being restored must have been placed on the source disk with the BACKUP command. Files must be restored to the same directory they were in when BACKUP copied them. If you try to restore them to a different subdirectory, you will receive an error message.

Activity C.11 Doing a Full Restore

DANGER: Do not attempt this process unless you really want to restore the hard disk and you are sure there are no copy-protected programs on the hard disk. Before you do a complete restore, read the instructions of the software you have installed on the hard disk. Be sure you have all the floppy disks that you used with the BACKUP command. RESTORE will only restore the files on the BACKUP disks. Hence, if you did not do a full backup, RESTORE will erase the files on the hard disk before copying backup files from the floppy disks.

STEP 1: Key in the following:
C>RESTORE A: C:\S <Enter>

```
C>RESTORE A: C:\S

Insert backup disk 01 in drive A:
Press any key to continue ...
```

STEP 2: Insert the properly numbered disk. Press <Enter>.

```
*** Files were backed up 11/23/1991 ***

*** Restoring files from drive A: ***
Diskette: 01
\JUNK\NEW.99
......
......
```

WHAT'S HAPPENING? ...... represents all the files as they were found. Each file was listed on the screen as it was copied from the floppy disk to the hard disk. If more than one floppy disk was required for the BACKUP, the following message appeared:

```
Insert backup disk 02 in drive A:
Press any key to continue ...
```

WHAT'S HAPPENING? Continue to insert disks in the proper order until the hard disk is restored.

C.12 Incremental Restores

You can restore from backup floppy disks to the hard disk in increments. You can restore individual files, a group of files or a subdirectory. In the next activity, you are going to restore files you backed up in Activity C.11.

Activity C.13 Restoring Selected Files in a Subdirectory

STEP 1: Key in the following:
C>**RESTORE A: C:\JUNK*.99** <Enter>

```
C>RESTORE A: C:\JUNK\*.99

Insert backup diskette 01 in drive A:
Press any key to continue . . .
```

STEP 2: Insert the backup disk from Activity C.11 in Drive A. Press <Enter>.

```
*** Files were backed up 05-13-1991 ***

*** Restoring files from drive A: ***
Diskette: 01
\JUNK\NEW.99
\JUNK\JAN.99
\JUNK\FEB.99
\JUNK\MAR.99
\JUNK\APR.99
\JUNK\CHANGE.99
\JUNK\NEW.99

C>_
```

WHAT'S HAPPENING? Each file was restored to the hard disk as it was found on the backup disk. If the backup required more than one disk, DOS prompted you to insert the next numbered disk.

C.14 Restoring a File with the /P Parameter

Sometimes you will update a file on the hard disk but you do not back it up. Therefore, when you restore the hard disk, you do not want to restore the old version of the file. The /P parameter will prompt you and ask if you want this file restored.

Activity C.15 Changing a File and then Restoring It

STEP 1: Key in the following:
C>**COPY CON \JUNK\CHANGE.99** <Enter>
This is the changed file. <Enter>
<Ctrl>+Z <Enter>

```
C>COPY CON \JUNK\CHANGE.99
This is the changed file.
^Z
  1 File(s) copied
```

WHAT'S HAPPENING? The file **CHANGE.99** is now different from the one that is on the floppy disk.

STEP 2: Key in the following:
C>**RESTORE A: C:\JUNK\CHANGE.99 /P** <Enter>

```
C>RESTORE A: C:\JUNK\CHANGE.99 /P

Insert backup diskette 01 in drive A:
Press any key to continue . . .
```

STEP 3: Press <Enter>.

```
*** Files were backed up 05-13-1991 ***

*** Restoring files from drive A: ***
Diskette: 01

WARNING! File CHANGE.99
was changed after it was backed up
Replace the file (Y/N)?_
```

WHAT'S HAPPENING? Now you have the option of restoring the older file or keeping the new version.

STEP 4: Press N. Press <Enter>.

```
WARNING! No files were found to restore

C:\>_
```

WHAT'S HAPPENING? Because you requested only one file to be restored, RESTORE had no more work to do. You did not restore the file **CHANGE.99**. If you had keyed in Y for yes, the file on the floppy disk would have replaced the file on the hard disk.

Appendix

Transferring System Files

When you formatted a disk with the /S option (FORMAT [*d:*] /S), you made the disk bootable. You put the operating system, comprised of the two hidden files `IO.SYS` and `MSDOS.SYS` (`IBMBIO.COM` and `IBMDOS.COM`) and the `COMMAND.COM` files, on the first sectors and tracks of the disk. The FORMAT command with the /S parameter, however, not only put the system files on the disk; it also erased everything else that was on the disk. Formatting a disk always removes all the data on the disk. If you wish to preserve the data but still place an operating system on a disk, an external command called SYS allows you to transfer only the hidden system files without formatting the disk. However, the disk you wish to transfer the system files to must already have the space available to transfer the files or must be "preformatted." Thus, if you had formatted a disk without the /S option and placed various files on it, you could not go back and add the operating system to make it bootable. If you tried it, you would get an error message that said "No room for system on destination disk." You would get this message regardless of how many bytes were available on the disk because the hidden system files *must* occupy the first tracks and sectors on the disk. Sounds a little circular? You cannot put the system files on a disk unless it has been preformatted with the /S option. When you format a disk with the /S option, you are putting the system files on it, but you are also erasing the disk. The SYS command allows you to place the system files on a disk without removing the data on the disk. In DOS 5.0, you do not need to preformat before using the SYS command. It does it for you. Why do you need to know about this apparently useless command? There are two major reasons.

First, if you purchased an application package that you wanted to make bootable and the package you purchased was copy-protected (copy-protected means that the manufacturer of the application package has a "lock" on the disk and you cannot use ordinary DOS commands to make a backup copy of the disk), you could not use FORMAT /S to put the operating system on the application disk. FORMAT /S would, indeed, place the operating system on the application disk, but at the same time it would erase all the other application programs that were on that disk. You need a special command that puts the operating system on the application disk but does not erase the program files. Here is the primary value of the SYS command. SYS is designed to transfer the operating system's hidden files `IO.SYS` and `MSDOS.SYS` (`IBMBIO.COM` and `IBMDOS.COM`) to the proper tracks and sectors of the disk. SYS will let you transfer these system files to an application program disk that is meant to use DOS but sold without the operating system. The space required on the disk for the DOS files has already been reserved for these files. (Note: The application package instructions will tell you if you can use this command. Be sure to read the installation instructions for any package before using this or any other command.)

The second reason for using the SYS command occurs when DOS is updated and a new version is released. You can overwrite all the old DOS programs by using the COPY command which replaces the old files with the new ones. However, you cannot use the COPY command to copy the hidden system files. You must copy the operating system files. You do not need or want to reformat the disk. You want to overwrite the current operating system files with the new version. The hidden system files must always occupy the proper place on the disk for it to be bootable.

SYS is designed to copy or transfer the two hidden system files from one disk to another. It does not work on network drives. SYS does not transfer or copy the third system file, `COMMAND.COM`. Thus, using the SYS command is a two-part process. After you finish executing the SYS command, you COPY `COMMAND.COM`. However, in DOS 5.0, the SYS command will copy all three system files making the transfer a one-step process. The syntax of the command is:

SYS [*d:*]

SYS is an external command. *d:* stands for "designated drive," but you do not use the letter *d*. You substitute the correct letter of the drive to which you want the files copied. If you wished to transfer the system files to the disk in Drive B, you would substitute B: for *d:*.

Activity D.1

Using the SYS Command

STEP 1: Boot the system. You should have the path set to `C:\DOS` and the prompt set to `PROMPT $p$g`.

```
C:\>_
```

STEP 2: Place a blank formatted disk in Drive A.

STEP 3: Key in the following:
C:\>`SYS A:` <Enter>

```
C:\>SYS A:
System transferred

C:\>_
```

WHAT'S HAPPENING? You transferred the hidden files to the blank disk. You can do this because this disk was blank. There was no information on the disk. The message "System transferred" tells you that those hidden files were copied to the blank disk. If you used a disk that already had files on it, you would get the message "No room for system on destination disk" and you could not add the system files to the disk. Remember, DOS writes to the first available sectors on the disk. The operating system hidden files *must* be in the first track and sectors of a disk on versions of DOS less than 5.0.

There is one more step to this process. SYS copied the hidden files **IO.SYS** and **MSDOS.SYS** (**IBMBIO.COM** and **IBMDOS.COM**), but it did not copy **COMMAND.COM**. Remember, these *three* files make up the operating system, and in DOS 5.0 all of these files would be transferred. Thus, you want to be sure to copy **COMMAND.COM**, and the **COMMAND.COM** file must be from the same version of DOS. Since **COMMAND.COM** is not a hidden file, you just use the COPY command.

STEP 4: Key in the following:
C:\>**COPY \COMMAND.COM A:**<Enter>

```
C:\>COPY \COMMAND.COM A:
        1 File(s) copied

C:\>_
```

WHAT'S HAPPENING? You completed the process for transferring the DOS operating system to the blank disk. The benefit of DOS 5.0 is that this step was not necessary.

Note: Before you attempt any procedures when dealing with application packages, you must read and understand the installation instructions. These instructions come with the application packages you purchase. Often, this process includes more than just upgrading the operating system to a higher version. Other important files can be affected, especially printer driver files. Thus, if you do not understand the installation instructions and/or the ramifications, *do not do anything* until you understand the installation process or until you get professional assistance from the store where you purchased the package.

You are now aware of the SYS command and how to use it. Knowing when to use it depends on the specific applications that could be affected.

E Appendix

Data Representation, Bits and Bytes

How do you measure the capacity of RAM or a disk? How much will it hold? A computer does not understand actual words, letters, or numbers. Its integrated circuits are a series of switches that are either on or off. The CPU controls the electronic states of RAM, with 0 representing an off state and 1 representing an on state. How does this translate into working with a computer?

Humans use a decimal counting system, which is comprised of 10 digits that range from 0 to 9 and is called base 10. We can represent any number with a combination of these digits. However, a decimal system is not the only way to represent counting. The binary system consists of only two digits (base 2) which represent all numerical values. If you were asked to write the number 245, you would quickly write down the three digits, 2, 4, and 5. Here is what you are really doing:

Every number has a position value; in other words, its relative position determines its value. In any numbering system the rightmost position has a value of the base to the zero power, or one (in a decimal system, $10^0 = 1$). The second position is the base to the first power (in a decimal system, $10^1 = 10$). The third position is the base to the second power, or the base squared (in a decimal system, $10^2 = 100$). The third position is the base to the third power or cubed, and so forth. These values are then summed (see Table E.1).

Table E.1 The Decimal System

Position number:	5	4	3	2	1	
Position value:	10^4	10^3	10^2	10^1	10^0	
Represented as:	10000	1000	100	10	1	
Totals by position:	_	_	2	_	_	2 x 100 = 200
	_	_	_	4	_	4 x 10 = 40
	_	_	_	_	5	5 x 1 = 5
Cumulative total:	_	_	2	4	5	245

The binary numbering system works the same way, except that you have only two digits to represent any number. Table E.2 shows how to write 245 in the binary system.

Table E.2
The Binary System

Position Number:	8	7	6	5	4	3	2	1	
Position Value:	2^7	2^6	2^5	2^4	2^3	2^2	2^1	2^0	
Decimal as:	128	64	32	16	8	4	2	1	
Totals by position:	1	_	_	_	_	_	_	_	1 x 128 = 128
	_	1	_	_	_	_	_	_	1 x 64 = 64
	_	_	1	_	_	_	_	_	1 x 32 = 32
	_	_	_	1	_	_	_	_	1 x 16 = 16
	_	_	_	_	0	_	_	_	0 x 8 = 0
	_	_	_	_	_	1	_	_	1 x 4 = 4
	_	_	_	_	_	_	0	_	0 x 2 = 0
	_	_	_	_	_	_	_	1	1 x 1 = 1
Cumulative total:	1	1	1	1	0	1	0	1	245

Thus, to represent the number 245 in decimal requires 3 digits. In binary, the number 245 is 11110101. Binary numbers take many more places to represent numbers. However, the binary numbering scheme is perfect for computers because it is easy to translate 1 for an on state and 0 for an off state. Remember, all a computer can do is indicate on or off.

The word bit comes from binary digit. A bit is the smallest unit a computer can recognize, an on or off state. However, while a bit may be meaningful to a computer, it is not meaningful to humans. What we want represented are letters, numbers, and symbols. Thus, bits are combined in meaningful groups, much as letters of the alphabet are combined to make words. The most common grouping is eight bits. A pattern of eight bits makes one byte:

```
0 0 0 0 0 0 0 0   All bits off
0 0 0 0 0 0 0 1   All bits off except 1 on
0 0 0 0 0 0 1 1   All bits off except 2 on
```

Rather than showing each pattern manually, the total number of patterns can be calculated mathematically by the rules of permutation and combinations: 2^8 calculates to 256 separate patterns into which a 1 and a 0 can be combined. Thus, a byte can be thought of as a singular letter or number.

However, there is more to a byte than that. There has to be a commonly agreed meaning for these patterns. For instance, *jour* meaning "day" is a valid combination of letters but only if you speak French. In English, to communicate *jour*, you combine a different pattern of letters, *day*. These are arbitrary assignments. The same is true with computers. The most common coding scheme for microcomputers is ASCII (pronounced as-key). ASCII stands for American Standard Code for Information Interchange. When you press the letter M on the keyboard, it is encoded to a bit configuration (pattern of 1s and 0s—0100 1101) on input so the computer can interpret it. Then, in output it is decoded so we can understand it as the letter M. If the lowercase letter m is keyed in, it has a completely different bit configuration (0110 1101) because to the computer there is no relationship between uppercase M and lowercase m.

RAM, ROM, and disk capacities are measured in bytes, typically in thousands of bytes or KB (kilobytes). K is the symbol for 2^{10} or 1024. If your computer has 64 KB of memory, its actual memory size is 64 x 1024 or 65,546 bytes. For simplification, the KB is rounded off to 1000 so that 64 KB of memory means 64,000 bytes. You should know the capacity of the memory of your computer because it determines how big a program and/or data the computer can hold. For instance, if you had a 64 KB computer and a program that required 256 KB, your computer could not hold that program. Disk capacity is also measured in bytes. A single-sided disk holds 180 KB of data (180,000 bytes); a double-sided disk holds 360 KB (360,000). Because a hard disk holds so much more than a floppy disk, hard disks are measured in millions of bytes. This is known as megabytes or referred to as meg. Typical hard disks hold 60 meg (sixty million bytes) and up. Today, floppy disks also have increased capacity. These disks are the high-capacity disks. A high-capacity 5 1/4-inch disk stores 1.2 MB of data. A 3 1/2-inch floppy disk holds 1.44 MB of information.

Appendix

Special Keys in DOS

Key	Function
<Backspace>	Deletes any characters to left of cursor.
<Ctrl>	When pressed in conjunction with another key, gives the other key an additional meaning. The symbol ^ represents pressing the Ctrl key.
<Ctrl>+<Alt>+<Del>	Reboots the system.
<Ctrl>+<Break>	Interrupts function and returns to default prompt.
<Ctrl>+C	Interrupts and stops a command from executing.
<Ctrl>+<NumLock>	Freezes and halts whatever is displayed on the screen. Pressing any key releases the freeze.
<Ctrl>+<PrtSc>	Toggles the printer on or off.
<Ctrl>+Z	Terminates the COPY CON function.
<Del>	Deletes character in current command line. One character is deleted each time the <Del> key is pressed.
<Enter>	Causes command to be executed.
<Esc>	An abbreviation for Escape. Cancels the previously keyed-in line. DOS ignores the previously keyed-in line.
<F1>	Replaces a previously entered command one character per press.
<F2>	Displays all characters in command line up to character keyed in after pressing <F2>.
<F3>	Repeats previously entered command line.
<F4>	Deletes all characters in a command line before the character you key in after pressing <F4>.
<F6>	Identical to pressing <Ctrl>+Z.
<Ins>	Allows insertion of characters within the current line.
<Pause>	On many computers, freezes and halts whatever is displayed on the screen. Pressing <Pause> releases the freeze. Same as <Ctrl>+<NumLock>.
<PrtSc>	Prints the screen. On newer keyboards, it is labeled <Print Screen>.
<Shift>	In conjunction with another letter, changes the case of the letter to uppercase. If <Caps Lock> key is toggled on, changes the case of the letter to lowercase. The <Shift> key must always be pressed to display the special characters above the number keys.
<Shift>+<PrtSc>	Prints whatever is displayed on the screen.

Appendix

EDIT Command and Key Summary

Moving the Cursor

Arrow keys	Moves the cursor one character or one line.
<Ctrl>+<Left arrow>	Moves the cursor one word to the left.
<Ctrl>+<Right arrow>	Moves the cursor one word to the right.
<Home>	Moves cursor to the beginning of the line.
<End>	Moves the cursor to end of the line.
<Ctrl>+<Enter>	Moves the cursor to the beginning of the next line.
<Ctrl>+Q+E	Moves the cursor to the top of the window.
<Ctrl>+Q+X	Moves the cursor to the bottom of the window.

Scrolling through Text

<Ctrl>+<Up arrow> or <Ctrl>+W	Scrolls up one line.
<Ctrl>+<Down arrow> or <Ctrl>+Z	Scrolls down one line.
<Page Up>	Scrolls up one screen.
<Page Down>	Scrolls down one screen.
<Ctrl>+<Home> or <Ctrl>+Q+R	Moves the cursor to the beginning of a file.
<Ctrl>+<End> or <Ctrl>+Q+C	Moves the cursor to the end of a file.
<Ctrl>+<Page Up>	Scrolls left one screen.
<Ctrl>+<Page Down>	Scrolls right one screen.

Appendix

System Configuration Commands

BREAK	Checks the keyboard to see if the user has pressed <Ctrl>+C or <Ctrl>+<Break> to cancel a command.
BUFFERS	Tells DOS how much memory to use for holding data. Sets number of disk buffers.
COUNTRY	Tells country's date, time, and number formats DOS will use.
DEVICE	Loads special drivers that tell DOS how to handle I/O devices such as a mouse or external drives.
DEVICEHIGH	Loads device drivers into upper memory area. New to DOS 5.0.
DOS	Sets area of RAM where DOS will be located and whether or not to use upper memory area. New to DOS 5.0.
DRIVPARM	Sets characteristics of a disk drive (non-IBM releases above 3.2).
FCBS	Tells DOS how many file control blocks that DOS can open concurrently.
FILES	Tells DOS the maximum number of files that can be open at one time.
INSTALL	Allows you to install specific memory-resident program such as SHARE and FASTOPEN, new to DOS 4.0.
LASTDRIVE	Tells DOS which drive letter is the last drive letter that can be used.
REM	Lets you document your `CONFIG.SYS` file. DOS ignores any statement with REM in front of it.
SHELL	Tells DOS the location of the command processor, usually `COMMAND.COM`, and also can change the size of the environment.
STACKS	Tells DOS to increase the number and size of stacks that handle hardware interrupts.
SWITCHES	Lets an enhanced keyboard be treated like an old-style keyboard for those older applications that do not recognize the enhanced keyboard, new to DOS 4.0.

Appendix I

DOS Supplied Device Drivers

Name	DOS Version	Purpose
ANSI.SYS	2.0	Defines functions that change display graphics, controls cursor movement, and reassigns keys.
DISPLAY.SYS	3.3	Allows you to use code page switching. (Primarily used for international keyboards—rarely used in the U.S.)
DRIVER.SYS	3.2	Allows you to assign logical drive letters and specifies parameter for a drive not supported by your hardware.
EGA.SYS	5.0	Allows restoration of EGA screen when using DOS 5.0 Shell–Task Swapper.
EMM386.EXE	5.0	Simulates expanded memory by using extended memory. Also provides access to upper memory on a 386 or higher microprocessor. Must have extended memory.
HIMEM.SYS	5.0	Memory manager that manages extended memory on a 286 or higher computer with extended memory.
PRINTER.SYS	3.3	Allows you to use code page switching for printers. (Primarily used for international printing—rarely used in the U.S.)
RAMDRIVE.SYS	3.2	Allows you to create a virtual disk in memory to simulate a hard drive. IBM's DOS version is called VDISK.SYS.
SETVER.EXE	5.0	Table of DOS versions loaded into memory needed by some application programs.
SMARTDRV.SYS	4.0	Creates a disk cache in extended or expanded memory.
VDISK.SYS	IBM 3.0	Allows you to create a virtual disk in memory to simulate a hard drive. MS-DOS version is called RAMDRIVE.SYS.
XMAEM.SYS	IBM 4.0 only	Emulates expanded memory. Must have a 80386 machine.
XMA2EMS.SYS	IBM 4.0 only	Supports Lotus, Intel, and Microsoft (LIM) Expanded Memory Specification (EMS) 4.0 under DOS 4.0.

Appendix

Batch File Commands

Command	Format	Explanation
@	@ *command*	Supresses echoing of the command on screen.
CALL	CALL [*drive:*][*path*]*filename* [*parameters*]	Calls one batch program from inside another.
ECHO	ECHO [ON ¦ OFF]	Turns command echoing on or off.
FOR	FOR *%variable* IN (*set*) DO *command* [*parameters*]	Repeats the specified command for each file in the specified set of files.
GOTO	GOTO *label*	Jumps within a batch file to a previously labeled line.
IF	IF [NOT] ERRORLEVEL *number command*	Executes the command if errors were (not) avoided.
	IF [NOT] *string1==string2 command*	Executes the command if the two strings are (not) equal.
	IF [NOT] EXIST *filename command*	Executes the command if the specified file does (not) exist.
PAUSE	PAUSE	Halts execution of the batch file and asks the user to "Press any key to continue . . ."
REM	REM *statement*	Tells DOS to ignore the following statement. Primarily used to document a batch file.
SHIFT	SHIFT	Shifts parameter positions within a batch file by one position (%2 becomes %1).

Appendix K

Command Summary

Command	Syntax	Description
<	*command* < *command*	Redirection symbol that tells DOS to get input from somewhere besides the standard input.
>	*command* > *command*	Redirection symbol that tells DOS to redirect standard output of a command to a device or a file.
>>	*command* >> *command*	Redirection symbol that also redirects standard output of a command to a device or a file but appends to the file instead of overwriting it.
¦	*command* ¦ *command*	Pipe symbol that allows the standard output of one command to be the standard input of the next command.
A:	A:	Switches the current drive to Drive A.
ADDRESS	ADDRESS	Not a DOS program. A toy database program included with the ACTIVITIES disk.
APPEND	APPEND [[*drive:*]*path*[;...]] [/X:ON ¦ /X:OFF] [/PATH:ON ¦ /PATH:OFF] [/E]	Accesses files in other directories as if they existed in the current directory.
	APPEND ;	Undo all appended paths.
ASSIGN	ASSIGN [*x*[:]=*y*[:][...]]	Assigns disk drive *x* to disk drive *y*.
	ASSIGN /STATUS	Displays all current assignments.
	ASSIGN	Undo all current assignments.
ATTRIB	ATTRIB [±A] [±H] [±R] [±S] [*drive:*][*path*]*filename* [/S]	Displays or changes the attributes of a file. A plus sign (+) turns the attribute on. A minus sign (-) turns the attribute off.

Command	Syntax	Description
	±A	Turns on/off the archive attribute.
	±H	Turns on/off the hidden file attribute.
	±R	Turns on/off the read-only attribute.
	±S	Turns on/off the system file attribute.
	/S	Processes all files in any subdirectory.
B:	B:	Switches the current drive to Drive B.
BACKUP	BACKUP *source destination* *d:**path*\\BACKUP *ds:*[*path*][*filename.ext*] *dd:* [/S] [/M] [/A] [/D:*mm-dd-yy*] [/T:*hh:mm:ss*] [/F] [/L:*drive path filename*]	Primarily used to backup a hard disk. Used in conjuction with RESTORE command.
	/S	Backs up subdirectories' files and the files in the specified or current directory.
	/M	Backs up only files that have been modified since the last BACKUP by checking the archive bit of the file.
	/A	Adds the files to be backed up to the files already present on the backup disk.
	/D:*mm-dd-yy*	Backs up files that have been modified on or after the specified date.
	/T:*hh:mm:ss*	Backs up files that have been modified on or after the specified time.
	/F	Formats the target floppy disk, if not already formatted. Version 3.3 only.
	/L:*filename*	Creates a log file in the file specified. Default file name is `BACKUP.LOG`.
BREAK	BREAK [ON ¦ OFF]	Enables or disenables display status of <Ctrl>+<Break> keys. Default is OFF. See also System Configuration Commands, Appendix H.
C:	C:	Switches the current drive to Drive C.
CD	CD	Displays the current directory and path.
	CD [*path*]	Changes the current directory to *path*.
CHDIR	CHDIR [*path*]	Same as CD.
CHKDSK	CHKDSK [*drive:*] [[*path*]*filename*] [/F] [/V]	Examines and reports the status of the specified drive or file.
	CHKDSK /F	Fixes any errors found.
	CHKDSK /V	Displays filenames as they are checked.
CLS	CLS	Clears the screen.
COMMAND	COMMAND [[*drive:*]*path*] [*device*] [/E:*nnnnn*] [/P] [/C *string*] [/MSG]	Starts a new instance of `COMMAND.COM`.

Command	Syntax	Description
	COMMAND A:\DOS /E:8192	Starts new COMMAND.COM from A:\DOS with an environment size of 8192 bytes.
COMP	COMP *file1 file2* [/D] [/A] [/L] [/N=*number*] [/C]	Compares the contents of two files byte by byte.
	/D	Displays differences in decimal format.
	/A	Displays differences as ASCII characters.
	/L	Displays the line numbers of any differences.
	/C	Ignores differences between upper and lowercase letters.
	/N=*number*	Compares only the first *number* lines.
COMPRESS	COMPRESS	A utility from PC Tools that optimizes a disk.
COPY	COPY *source destination*	Copy from the *source* file to the *destination* file.
	COPY [*d:*][*path*]*oldfile.ext* [*d:*][*path*]*newfile.ext*	Copy from the *oldfile* to the *newfile*.
COPY CON	COPY CON *filename*	Copy all data entered into the keyboard to *filename* until a <Ctrl>+Z is entered.
DATE	DATE [*mm-dd-yy*]	Changes the current date setting. DATE without parameters displays the current date.
DEL	DEL [*drive:*][*path*]*filename* [/P]	Deletes the specified file.
	/P	Prompts the user for confirmation before deleting the file.
DIR	DIR [*drive:*][*path*][*filename*] [/P] [/W] [/A[[:]*attributes*]] [/O[[:]*sortorder*]] [/S] [/B] [/L]	Displays a list of a directory's files and subdirectories.
	/P	Pauses between screenfuls.
	/W	Displays filenames in a wide format.
	/A:H	Displays files ATTRIButed as hidden.
	/A:S	Displays system files.
	/A:D	Displays only names of directories.
	/A:A	Displays files ATTRIButed as archived.
	/A:R	Displays files ATTRIButed as read-only.
	/O:N	Displays alphabetically (A-Z) by filename
	/O:E	Displays alphabetically (A-Z) by extension.
	/O:D	Displays in date order, from oldest to newest.
	/O:S	Displays in size order, from smallest to largest.
	/O:G	Displays directories before files.
	/S	Searches through all subdirectories.
	/L	Displays in lowercase letters.
	/B	Displays only filenames and extension.
DISKCOMP	DISKCOMP [*drive1:* [*drive2:*]]	Compares the contents of two floppy disks.
DISKCOPY	DISKCOPY [*drive1:* [*drive2:*]]	Copies the contents of the floppy disk in *drive1* to the floppy disk in *drive2*.

DOSKEY	DOSKEY [/H] [/M]	Starts the DOSKEY program to recall commands, edit command lines, or create macros.
	/H	Displays list of all commands stored in memory.
	/M	Displays list of all DOSKEY macros.
DOSSHELL	DOSSHELL [/T] [/B] [/G]	Starts DOSSHELL, a graphical interface to DOS.
	/T	Starts DOSSHELL in text mode
	/B	Starts DOSSHELL in black-and-white.
	/G	Starts DOSSHELL in graphics mode.
ECHO	ECHO [ON ¦ OFF] ECHO [*message*]	Turns command echoing feature on or off, or displays a message.
EDIT	EDIT [[*drive:*][*path*]*filename*]	Starts MS-DOS Editor. See Appendix G for commands within Editor.
EDLIN	EDLIN [[*drive:*][*path*]*filename*]	Starts EDLIN.
EMM386	EMM386 [ON ¦ OFF ¦ AUTO]	Enables or disenables expanded-memory support on 386 or higher systems. EMM386 without parameters displays current status.
ERASE	ERASE [*drive:*][*path*]*filename* [/P]	Erases the specified file.
	/P	Prompts the user for confirmation before erasing the file.
EXIT	EXIT	Quits command processor and returns to the program that started COMMAND.COM.
EXPAND	EXPAND [*drive:*][*path*]*filename* [...] *destination*	Expands a compressed MS-DOS version 5.0 file.
FASTOPEN	FASTOPEN *drive:*[[=]*n*] [...] [/X]	Starts the FASTOPEN program, which decreases the time needed to open files used often.
	n	Specifies the number of files FASTOPEN can open.
	/X	Creates the name cache in expanded memory.
FC	FC [/A] [/C] [/L] [/LB*n*] [/N] [/T] [/W] [/*nnnn*] *filename1 filename2*	Compares and displays differences between two ASCII files.
	/C	Ignores upper vs. lowercase.
	/L	Compares files in ASCII mode.
	/W	Ignores white space in the files.
	/N	Displays line numbers.
	FC /B *filename1 filename2*	Compares and displays differences between two binary files.
FDISK	FDISK	Configures and/or partitions a hard disk for use with MS-DOS.

FIND	FIND [/V] [/C] [/N] *"string"*[*filename*]		Searches for character strings within a file.
		/V	Locates every occurence of the string except the one selected.
		/C	Counts every occurence of the string.
		/N	Locates and displays line numbers of each occurence of the string.
FORMAT	FORMAT *drive:* [/V[:*label*]] [/Q] [/U] [/F:*size*] [/B ¦ /S] FORMAT *drive:* [/V[:*label*]] [/Q] [/U] [/T:*tracks* /N:*sectors*] [/B ¦ /S] FORMAT *drive:* [/V[:*label*]] [/Q] [/U] [/1] [/4] [/B ¦ /S] FORMAT *drive:* [/Q] [/U] [/1] [/4] [/8] [/B ¦ /S]		Prepares a floppy disk for use with DOS.
		/V:*label*	Specifies a volume label.
		/Q	Deletes any previous file allocation table or root directory.
		/U	Unconditional format.
		/F:*size*	Specifies the disk size.
		/B	Reserves space for system files.
		/S	Copies system files onto formatted disk.
		/T:*tracks*	Specifies number of tracks on the disk.
		/N:*sectors*	Specifies number of sectors on the disk.
		/1	Formats on side of the disk only.
		/4	Formats a 5 1/4-inch double-density disk on a high-density disk drive.
		/8	Formats a 5 1/4-inch floppy disk to be compatible with MS-DOS version prior to 2.0.
GRAFTABL	GRAFTABL[*nnn*]		Displays extended characters for a specified graphics mode. Default is the U.S. character set.
GRAPHICS	GRAPHICS [*type*] [*filename*] [/R] [/B] [/LCD] [/PRINTBOX:STD ¦ /PRINTBOX:LCD]		Allows printing of graphics screens.
		[*type*]	Specifies type of printer.
		[/R]	Prints the image in reverse.
		[/B]	Prints the background in color.
		[/LCD]	Prints LCD screens.
		[/PRINTBOX:STD ¦ /PRINTBOX:LCD]	Selects the print-box size.
HELP	HELP [*command*] *command* /?		Accesses online help about any MS-DOS command.
JOIN	JOIN [*drive1:* [*drive2:*]*path*]		Joins a disk drive to a directory on another disk drive. JOIN without parameters displays all JOINs in effect.
	JOIN *drive:* /D		Cancels the JOIN for this drive.
LABEL	LABEL [*drive:*] [*label*]		Updates the volume label of any disk.

LOADHIGH LOADHIGH [*drive:*][*path*]*filename* [*parameters*]
Loads a program into the upper memory area.
LH [*drive:*][*path*]*filename* [*parameters*] Alternate shorthand.

MD MD [*drive:*]*path* Creates a directory. Same as MKDIR.

MEM MEM [/PROGRAM ¦ /DEBUG ¦ /CLASSIFY]
Displays current status of a system's used and free memory.

/PROGRAM	Displays status of currently loaded programs. May also use /P
/DEBUG	Displays status of programs and drivers. May also use /D
/CLASSIFY	Displays status of programs loaded into conventional and upper memory areas. May also use /C.

MIRROR MIRROR [*drive:*[...]] [/1] [/T*drive*]
Records information about one or more disks so that lost data may be recovered. Originally only available in PC Tools but now also available in DOS 5.0.

/1	Records only the latest information.
/T*drive*	Loads a deletion-tracking program to be used by the UNDELETE command.

MIRROR /U Unloads deletion-tracking program.
MIRROR /PARTN Records hard disk partitioning information to be used by the UNFORMAT command.

MKDIR MKDIR [*drive:*]*path* Creates a directory. Same as MD.

MODE MODE [*device*] [/STATUS] Displays the status of all or any devices.
MODE [*display*] [*shift*[,T]] Sets the monitor characteristics. Values for *display* are:

40	40 characters per row.
80	80 characters per row.
BW40	Black-and-white, 40 characters per row.
BW80	Black-and-white, 80 characters per row.
CO40	Color, 40 characters per row.
CO80	Color, 80 characters per row.
MONO	Monochrome, 80 characters per row.
shift	L or R shifts display left or right.
T	Aligns display with a test pattern.

MODE CON[:] [COLS=*c*] [LINES=*n*] Sets other characteristics for the monitor (CON).

COLS=*c*	Number of columns.
LINES=*n*	Number of lines.

MODE LPT*n*[:] [COLS=*c*] [LINES=*l*] [RETRY=*r*]
Sets characteristics for the printer (LPT*n*).

Command	Syntax / Option	Description
	COLS=*c*	Characters per line (80 or 132 only).
	LINES=*l*	Lines per inch (6 or 8 only).
	RETRY=*r*	Specifies retry action if printer is busy.
	MODE CON[:] [RATE=*r* DELAY=*d*]	Sets the typematic rate for keyboards.
MORE	MORE < [*drive:*][*path*]*filename*	
	command ¦ MORE	Displays one screenful of output at a time.
PATH	PATH [[*drive:*]*path*[;...]]	Sets the path that DOS follows when searching for a file.
	PATH ;	Undoes all current paths.
	PATH	Displays all current paths.
PRINT	PRINT [/D:*device*] [/B:*size*] [/U:*ticks1*] [/M:*ticks2*] [/S:*ticks3*] [/Q:*qsize*] [/T]*filename*[...] [/C] [/P]	
	/D:*device*	Specifies a print device.
	/B:*size*	Sets the internal buffer size in bytes.
	/U:*ticks1*	Specifies the maximum number of clock ticks to wait for the printer to be available.
	/M:*ticks2*	Specifies the maximum number of clock ticks it takes to print a character.
	/S:*ticks3*	Specifies the number of clock ticks to allocate to the scheduler for background printing.
	/Q:*qsize*	Specifies the maximum number of files allowed in the print queue.
	/T	Terminates all print jobs waiting in the print queue.
	/C	Cancels printing of the preceding *filename*.
	/P	Adds the preceding *filename* to the print queue.
	PRINT	Displays the contents of the print queue.
PROMPT	PROMPT [*text*]	Changes the current prompt display. Common values for *text* are:
	$p	Current drive and path.
	$v	Current version number.
	$t	Current time.
	$d	Current date.
	$g	> (greater-than sign).
QBASIC	QBASIC [/B] [/EDITOR] [/G] [/H] [[/RUN] [*drive:*][*path*]*filename*]	Starts the QBasic programming environment.
	/B	Displays QBasic in black-and-white.
	/EDITOR	Invokes the MS-DOS Editor.
	/G	Displays QBasic in graphics mode.
	/H	Displays the maximum lines possible on a screen.
	/RUN	Runs program before displaying it.

RD	RD [*drive:*]*path*	Removes a subdirectory. A subdirectory may not be removed if it is the root, the default, or if there are still files in it. Same as RMDIR.
RECOVER	RECOVER [*drive:*][*path*] *filename*	Recovers readable data from a defective disk.
REN	REN [*drive:*][*path*] *oldname*[*.ext*] *newname*[*.ext*]	Changes a file's name from *oldname.ext* to *newname.ext*. Same as RENAME.
RENAME	RENAME [*drive:*][*path*] *oldname*[*.ext*] *newname*[*.ext*]	See REN.
REPLACE	REPLACE [*drive1:*][*path1*]*filename* [*drive2:*][*path2*] [/A] [/P] [/R] [/S] [/U] [/W]	Replaces files in the destination directory with identically named files in the source directory.
	/A	Adds new files to the destination directory. Cannot be used with /S or /U.
	/P	Prompts user for confirmtion before each replace.
	/R	Replaces read-only files as well as unprotected files.
	/S	Replaces files in all subdirectories of the destination directory. Cannot be used with /A.
	/U	Updates (replaces) only files that are older than source files. Cannot be used with /A.
	/W	Waits for the user to insert a disk.
RESTORE	RESTORE *source destination*	Restores files archived by the BACKUP command.
	[*d:*][*path*]RESTORE *source drive d:*[*target drive*][*path*][*filename*][*ext*] [/P] [/M] [/S] [/B:*mm-dd-yy*] [/A:*mm-dd-yy*] [/L:*hh:mm:ss*] [/E:*hh:mm:ss*] [/N]	
	/S	Restores all files in subdirectories and files in specified subdirectories.
	/P	Prompts you before restoring files that have been changed since the last backup.
	/B	Restores all files modified on or before given date.
	/A	Restores all files modified on or after given date.
	/M	Restores files modified or deleted since last backup.
	/N	Restores files that no longer exist on target disk.
	/L	Restores files modified at or later than given time.
	/E	Restores files modified at or earlier than given time.
RMDIR	RMDIR [*drive:*]*path*	See RD.
RNS	RNS [*drive:*][*path*]*oldname* [*drive:*][*path*]*newname*	Not a DOS program. A utility program from Nick's DOS Utilities that renames subdirectories.
SELECT	SELECT	The installation program from DOS 4.0.
SET	SET [*variable*=[*string*]]	Sets or updates variables in the DOS environment.
	SET	Displays current environment settings.

SETVER SETVER [*drive:path*] *filename n.nn* [/D]
Sets the version number (*n.nn*) that DOS reports to *filename*. Used primarily for older applications that require a specific version of DOS to run correctly.
/D — Deletes the version table entry for the specified file.
n.nn — Specifies the MS-DOS version (i.e., 3.3 or 4.01).

SHARE SHARE [/F:*space*] [/L:*locks*] — Installs file-sharing and locking capabilities on a hard disk.

SORT SORT [/R] [/+*n*] [<] *filename1* [> *filename2*]
Sorts the data in *filename1* in ASCII order, and optionally sends the output to *filename2*.
[*command* ¦] SORT [/R] [/+*n*] [> *filename2*]
Sorts the output from *command* and sends it to *filename2*.
/R — Reverses the sorting order.
/+*n* — Sorts from the character in column *n*.

SUBST SUBST [*drive1:* [*drive2:*]*path*] — Substitutes the single letter *drive1:* for [*drive2:*]*path*.
SUBST *drive1:* /D — Undoes any substitutions for *drive1:*.
SUBST — Displays all current substitutions.

SYS SYS [*drive1:*][*path*] *drive2:* — Copies system files from *drive1:* to *drive2:*.

SYSINFO SYSINFO — A utility from Norton's Utilities that gives user information about computer hardware.

TIME TIME [*hh:mm:ss*] — Sets or displays the current time.

TREE TREE [*drive:*][*path*] [/F] [/A] — Displays the tree structure of a disk.
/F — Displays filenames as well.
/A — Displays in text characters instead of graphics.

TRUENAME TRUENAME — An undocumented command that displays the actual physical drive name of any assigned, substituted, or joined drives.

TYPE TYPE [*drive:*][*path*]*filename* — Displays the contents of *filename*.

UNDELETE UNDELETE [[*drive:*][*path*]*filename*] [/LIST ¦ /ALL] [/DOS ¦ /DT]
Recovers files deleted by the DEL command. Originally only available in PC Tools but now also available in DOS 5.0.
/LIST — Lists the deleted files available for recovery.
/ALL — Recovers all deleted files without prompting for confirmation.
/DOS — Recovers only files listed internally by MS-DOS as deleted. Prompts for confirmation on each file.

		/DT	Recovers only files listed as deleted by the MIRROR's deletion-tracking program. Prompts for confirmation.
UNERASE	UNERASE		A utility from Norton's Utilities that recovers one or more deleted files.
UNFORMAT	UNFORMAT *drive:* [/U] [/L] [/TEST] [/P]		Restores a disk erased by FORMAT.
	UNFORMAT *drive:* [/J]		Originally only available in PC Tools but now also
	UNFORMAT [/PARTN] [/L]		available in DOS 5.0.
		drive:	Specifies the drive where to recover files.
		/J	Verifies that information created by the MIRROR command agrees with the system information.
		/U	Unformats a disk without using the mirror file.
		/L	When used with /PARTN, lists every file and subdirectory found by UNFORMAT. When used without /PARTN, UNFORMAT displays the partition table.
		/TEST	Simulates recovery before actual recovery.
		/P	Sends output messages to the printer.
		/PARTN	Restores corrupted partition table.
VER	VER		Displays the current version of DOS.
VOL	VOL [*drive:*]		Displays the volume label of a disk.
WIN	WIN		Begins Windows, the graphical user interface that works with DOS.
XCOPY	XCOPY *oldfile newfile* [/A ¦ /M] [/D:*date*] [/P] [/S [/E]] [/V] [/W]		Copies files, subdirectories, and directories
		/A	Copies files ATTRIButed as archived without changing the archive attribute.
		/M	Copies files ATTRIButed as archived and turns off the archive attribute.
		/D:*date*	Copies files changed on or after the specified *date*.
		/P	Prompts you before creating each *newfile*.
		/S	Copies directories and subdirectories, except empty ones.
		/E	Copies directories and subdirectories, including empty ones.
		/V	Verifies each new file.
		/W	Prompts you to press a key before copying.

Glossary

386 enhanced mode A mode of running Windows that provides access to the virtual memory capabilities of the 80386 processor.

Active window Window currently in use when multiple windows are displayed in Windows.

Adapter cards Printed circuit board that is installed in a computer to control some type of a device such as a printer.

Adapter segment Area between the end of conventional memory and the beginning of extended memory. *See also* upper memory area.

Alphanumeric keys The keys on the keyboard that include letters (A to Z), the digits from 0 to 9, and other characters such as the punctuation characters.

Application packages *See* application software.

Application program *See* application software.

Application software Computer program that is user-oriented, usually for a specific job such as word processing. Application software are also called packages, off-the-shelf or canned software.

Archival backup Backup procedure in which all files on the hard disk are backed up by copying them to floppy disks or some other backup medium.

Archival data Information that is stored in archive files.

Archive bit A file attribute that gives the backup history of a file which tells whether or not file has been backed up.

Archiving To "save" a file. Usually refers to long-term storage. Sometimes used to refer to compressed or compressing files in order to conserve space on disk.

Area title Used in MS-DOS Shell to refer to a specific area on the screen.

ASCII Acronym for American Standard Code for Information Interchange. A coding scheme used for transmitting text data between computers and peripherals. Each character has its own numerical equivalent in ASCII.

ASCII sort sequence The order in which data is sorted based on the assigned decimal number.

Associate Method of saving time by "associating" a set of files that are generated by a specific program. A feature of MS-DOS Shell and Windows.

Asynchronous Not synchronized or not happening at regular time intervals.

Asynchronous communication Form of data transmission which comes into play when only two wires are used for communication between computers (generally used for communicating via modems). Data is transmitted by sending one character at a time with variable time intervals between characters with a start bit and a stop bit to mark the beginning and end of the data.

AUTOEXEC.BAT A batch file (set of specific commands) that automatically executes every time the system is booted.

Background program A background program refers to a program that is being executed in the back at the same time that the user is working with another program in the foreground. For example printing one document (background program) while at the same time editing another document (foreground program).

Background printing Printing a document in the background while another program is being worked on in the foreground.

Backup Process in which a user makes a copy of an original file or files for safekeeping.

Bank switching Method of expanding an operating system's memory by switching rapidly between two banks of memory chips.

Batch files A text file of DOS commands. When its name is keyed in at the DOS system level, the commands in the batch file are executed sequentially.

Batch processing Manner of running programs without interruption. Programs to be executed are collected and placed into prioritized batches and then the programs are then processed one after another without user interaction or intervention.

Baud rate Measure of how fast a modem can transmit data. Named after the French telegrapher and engineer Jean-Maurice-Emile Baudot.

Benchmark A test used to measure hardware or software performance.

Beta-test Formal process of pretesting hardware and software that is still under development with selected "typical" users to see whether any operational or utilization errors (bugs) still exist in the program before the product is released to the general public.

BIOS Acronym for Basic Input/Output System. Program that controls Input/Output devices.

Bit Smallest unit of information that the computer can measure and is expressed in binary numbers, 0 or 1. Eight bits make a byte.

Block Group of data (words, characters, or digits) that are handled as a unit.

Block device Any device (such as a disk drive) that moves information from one part of the text to another as blocks of information rather than one character at a time.

Boot Starting up the computer by loading the operating system into memory.

Boot record If the disk is a system disk this will contain the bootstrap routine used for loading. Otherwise, will present a message to user that it is not a bootable disk.

Bootable disk Disk containing the operating system files.

Booting the system Process of "Powering On" the computer and loading the operating system into memory.

Buffer Temporary holding area for data in memory.

Bug Error(s) in software which cause programs to malfunction or to produce incorrect results.

Business Resumption Plan Disaster and recovery plan that includes the entire business spectrum in addition to data processing.

Byte Unit of measure which represents one character (a letter, number, or punctuation symbol). A byte is comprised of eight bits. Computer memory and disk storage are measured in bytes.

Cache Place in memory where data can be stored for quick access.

Caching Process where DOS sets up a reserved area in RAM where it can read and write frequently used data quickly prior to reading or writing to the disk.

Cascade Windows layered one on top of another. Used in Windows.

Case-sensitive When a program distinguishes between characters that are keyed in as upper or lower case.

Cells In a spreadsheet, the rectangle formed where a row and column intersect.

Chaining Used with the File Allocation Table to point to the next segment of a file.

Chaining batch files Linking together two or more batch files.

Character device Computer device (i.e., keyboard or printer) that receives or sends information one character at a time.

Character strings Set of letters, symbols and/or control characters that are treated as a unit.

Child directory Analogous title given to offshoots (subdirectories) of any root or subdirectory.

Click Pressing and releasing the mouse button once.

Cluster Smallest unit of disk space that DOS can write to or read from. It is comprised of one or more sectors.

Command An instruction, which is a program, that the user keys in at the DOS prompt. This instruction then executes the selected program.

COMMAND.COM That part of DOS that the user actually communicates and interacts with. It processes and interprets what has been keyed in. Also known as the command processor or command interpreter.

Command processor That portion of an operating system that interprets what the user keys in.

Command specification (COMSPEC) The location of `COMMAND.COM` so that DOS can reload the transient portion of `COMMAND.COM`. The default is the root directory of the booting disk unless altered by the user in `CONFIG.SYS`.

Command syntax Proper order of command, parameters and punctuation necessary to execute a command.

Communication protocol Set of communication rules that enable computers to exchange information.

Compressed files File written (utilizing a file compression utility) to a special disk format that minimizes the storage space needed.

Compressing a disk *See* optimizing the disk.

CON Device name that is reserved by DOS for the keyboard and monitor.

Concatenate files To combine the contents of two or more text files into a new file.

Contiguous files Files that are written to adjacent clusters on a disk.

Control key Key labeled <Ctrl> on the keyboard that, when held down with another key, causes that key to have another meaning.

Control-menu icon In Windows, the icon that can be opened to provide a drop-down menu with additional commands.

Controller Board that goes into the computer and is needed to operate a peripheral device.

Conventional memory First 640 KB of memory where programs and data are located while the user is working.

Copy protected Disks which cannot be "backed up" with regular DOS commands.

CPU Acronym for Central Processing Unit. The CPU is the brains of the computer which carries out the instructions or commands given to it by a program.

Cross-linked files Two files which claim the same sectors in the File Allocation Table (FAT).

CRT Cathode Ray Tube. Another name for the monitor.

Current directory The default directory.

Cursor Location where the user can key in information.

Customized prompt Modifying the prompt to suit the needs or preferences of the user.

Cylinder The vertical measurement of two or more disk platters that have the tracks aligned. Used in referring to hard disks.

Daisy-wheel printer Computer printer that uses a rotating plastic wheel as a printing element. The quality of print is comparable to that of a carbon-ribbon typewriter. Daisy wheel printers were considered high quality printers until laser printers became available.

Data Information in the widest possible sense. Usually it refers to the numbers and text used by the computer to do the work wanted by the user.

Data bits Group of bits used to represent a single character for transmission over a modem. A start bit and stop bit must be used in transmitting a group of data.

Data file Usually composed of related data created by the user with an application program, organized in a specific manner, and which can be used only by this program.

Database Collection of related information (data) stored on a computer, organized and structured so that the information can be easily manipulated.

Database Management Program Application program that allows for manipulation of information in a database.

Default What the computer system "falls back to" if no other specific instructions are given.

Default drive Disk drive that DOS looks on to locate commands or files if no other instructions are given.

Default subdirectory Subdirectory that the computer "falls back to" when no other specific instructions are given.

Delimiter A special character that is used to separate information so that DOS can recognize where one part of the parameter ends and the next begins.

Designated drive *See* default drive.

Desktop In Windows, an on-screen work area that simulates the top of a desk.

Destination file The file to which data is copied.

Device Piece of computer equipment that does one specific job such as a disk drive or a printer.

Device drivers Software necessary for the use of additional hardware devices. The program controls the specific peripheral devices.

Device name Reserved name that DOS assigns to a device such as PRN for printer.

Dialog box In a graphic user interface, a box that either conveys or requests information from the user. Used in MS-DOS Shell and Windows.

Direct read When an application program reads the information directly from a disk bypassing DOS.

Direct write When an application program writes the information directly to a disk bypassing DOS.

Directional keys Keys used to move the cursor in various directions.

Directory Index or list of files that DOS maintains on each disk. The DIR command displays this list.

Directory sectors A table that tracks all the files and records certain specific information about a file. The DIR command reads this table to display the files on a disk.

Directive Used in the `CONFIG.SYS` file to refer to the acailable commands.

Directory tree The structure of the current disk drive.

Disaster and recovery plan Backing up data files in case something happens to the original data.

Disk Magnetically coated mylar disk that allows permanent storage of computer data.

Disk file Related information stored on a disk in a file with a unique name.

Disk buffer Acts as the go-between for the disk and RAM.

Disk drive A device that rotates the disk so that the computer can read and write information to the disk.

Disk intensive Programs that are constantly reading and writing records to a disk

Documentation Written instructions that inform a user how to use hardware and/or software.

Documented The process of writing the purpose and any instructions for a computer program.

DOS Acronym for Disk Operating System which refers to the most common operating system used on microcomputers.

Dot A subdirectory marker, a shorthand name, the . for the specific subdirectory name.

Dot-matrix printer Printer that produces text characters and graphs by creating them with a series of closely spaced dots.

Double-click Pressing and releasing the mouse button twice in rapid succession.

Double dot A subdirectory marker, a shorthand name, the .. for the parent directory of the current subdirectory.

Drive letter Letter of the alphabet that identifies a specific disk drive.

Drag To move or manipulate objects on the screen by holding down the left mouse button.

Drop-down menus Menus that present choices which drop down from the menu bar when requested and remain open on the screen until the user chooses a menu item or closes the menu.

Dummy files Files without particular meaning usually created for test purposes.

Dummy parameters *See* replaceable parameters.

Edit To alter the contents of a file. Also the editor that comes with DOS 5.0.

Eject The process where a printer will eject a page so that the next blank page is at the top of that page.

Electronic bulletin board Forum where people exchange ideas or solve computer problems. Usually accessed by a modem.

Ellipsis Used in menus in such programs as Windows and DOS Shell to indicate that there are more choices available.

Enhancement To increase the capabilities of a computer by adding or updating hardware and/or software.

Environment Area in memory where DOS keeps a list of specifications that itself and other application programs can read.

EOF (end of file) Symbol that alerts DOS when the file has finished.

Executing a program Process where instructions are placed in memory and then followed by the computer.

Expanded memory Additional hardware added to the computer that makes available more memory. Only programs that are designed to use expanded memory can take advantage of it.

Expanded memory manager (EMM) A software program that must be installed in order to use expanded memory.

Expansion slots Empty slots or spaces inside the main computer housing that can be used for adding new boards to expand the capabilities of the computer.

Extended memory Memory above 1 MB. Most programs do not know how to access extended memory.

Extended memory specification (XMS) A specification developed by Lotus, Intel and Microsoft that defines the necessary software interface to allow an application to use extended memory. Must be installed prior to using extended memory.

Extension *See* file extension.

External commands Program that resides on a disk and must be read into RAM before it can be used.

FAT Acronym for File Allocation Table. Map of the disk which keeps track of all of the spaces (tracks, sectors, and clusters) on the disk.

File Program or a collection of related information stored on a disk.

File attributes Attributes are stored as part of the file's directory entry and describes and/or gives other information about the file.

File extension Up to three characters that can be added to a file name to extend the file name or to help identify a file. Usually file extensions describe the type of data in the file.

File handle Two-byte number DOS uses in referring to an open file or device.

File name Label used to identify a file. Technically, it is the name of the file made up of no more than eight characters. However, when most users refer to the file name they are actually referring to the file specifications.

File specification Complete name of the file, including the file name and the file extension.

Filters Commands that redirect input through the process of reading information, changing the input and writing the results to the screen.

Firmware Software and hardware designed for a specific task that has been permanently stored in ROM (Read-Only Memory) rather than on a disk. Firmware cannot be modified by the user.

Fixed disk *See* hard disk.

Fixed parameters Parameters where DOS supplies the value.

Fixes *See* Bug.

Floppy disk *See* disk.

Floppy disk drive *See* disk drive.

Flushing the buffer A process where DOS writes information to a disk after a buffer has been filled

Foreground Application or window on which the user is currently working.

Form feed Operation that advances the hard copy on the printer to the next page.

Format To prepare a disk so that it can be used by the computer.

Fragmented disks Disk that has many noncontiguous files on it.

Fragmented files *See* noncontiguous files.

Full screen editing To alter text by being able to move the cursor keys around the screen.

Function keys Programmable keys on a keyboard. F1 and F2 are examples of function keys. Function keys are program dependent.

Global file specifications *See* wildcards.

Graphics Pictures and drawings that can be produced on the screen or printer.

GUI Acronym for Graphical User Interface. Display format that allows the user to interact with the computer by using pictorial representations and menus choices to manage the computer resources and work with application programs.

Hard copy Refers to the printed paper copy of information created using the computer. Also referred to as printouts.

Hard disk Disk that is permanently installed in a computer and that has a larger capacity to store files and programs than a floppy disk. Its capacity is measured in megabytes.

Hard disk drive *See* hard disk.

Hardware Physical components of a computer.

Head slot Exposes the disk surface to the read/write heads via an opening in the jacket of a floppy disk.

Help Form of on-screen assistance provided by many computer programs that a user can turn to when a question arises or the user needs additional information on how the system or program works. Available in DOS 5.0, MS-DOS Shell and Windows.

Hexadecimal A numbering system that uses a base of 16 consisting of the digits 0-9 and the letters A-F.

Hidden attribute Prevents MS-DOS from displaying a file in a directory list.

Hidden files Files that are not displayed when the DIR command is used. In MS-DOS, the two hidden files are `IO.SYS` and `MSDOS.SYS`. In IBM PC-DOS, the two hidden files are `IBMBIO.COM` and `IBMDOS.COM`.

Hierarchical structure The logical grouping of files and programs based on pathways between root directories and their subsequent directories. Also called tree-structured directories.

High-capacity disks Disks that can store up to 1.2 MB on a 5 1/4-inch floppy disk or 1.44 MB on a 3 1/2-inch floppy disk Also called high-density disks.

High-density disks *See* high-capacity disks.

Highlighting Used to select characters, files or other information that the user wishes to act upon such as copying or deleting.

High memory area (HMA) High memory is the first 64 KB of extended memory. DOS 5.0 can be installed in HMA.

IBMBIO.COM One of the hidden system files that make-up the operating system of IBM PC-DOS. This file manages the input/output devices.

IBMDOS.COM Hidden system file that is one of the files that makes up the operating system of IBM PC-DOS. This file manages the disks.

Icon Symbol that represents a more simple access to a program file or task.

Impact printer Type of printer where the image is transferred onto paper through the process of a printing mechanism striking the paper ribbon and character simultaneously. Similar to the process of a typewriter.

Ink jet printer A printer that sprays drops of ink through a print head to shape characters and graphics.

Input Refers to data or information entered into the computer.

Input buffer Portion of computer memory that has been set aside to store keyed in data arriving for processing.

Input/Output The process of data and program instructions going into and out of the CPU (Central Processing Unit). Also referred to as I/O.

Insert mode Program mode used to enter data in which inserted text is entered at the cursor pushing all text that follows right and down.

Integrated circuit Electronic device that combines thousands of transistors on a small wafer of silicon (chip). Such devices are the building blocks of computers.

Interactive The ability to update data within the computer system instantaneously.

Interface Hardware and/or software needed to connect computer components. Also used as a synonym when the user interacts with the computer.

Internal commands A part of the third operating system file, COMMAND.COM, that includes commands that are loaded into memory when the operating system is booted and remain resident in memory until the computer is turned off.

I/O *See* Input/Output.

IO.SYS One of the hidden system files that make-up the operating system of MS-DOS. This file manages the input/output devices.

Keyboard Major device used for entering data into a computer consisting of typewriter-like collection of labeled keys.

Keyboard buffer *See* Input buffer.

Key term A device used in Help feature of Windows that gives a brief capsule description of the highlighted term.

LAN Acronym for Local Area Network. Network of computer equipment located in one room or building and connected by a communication link that enables any device to interact with any other in the network making it possible for users to exchange information, share peripherals, and draw on common resources.

Laser printer High resolution nonimpact printer that provides letter quality output of text and graphics. Based on advanced technology in which characters are formed by a laser and made visible by the same technology used by photocopy machines.

LIM EMS Standard An acronym for Lotus Intel Microsoft Expanded Memory Specifications. Standards designed for adding memory to DOS based-systems. Called LIM EMS because it was developed by a Lotus/Intel/ Microsoft Collaboration.

Light pen Pointing device (connected to the computer by a cable and resembling a pen) that is used to provide input to the computer by writing, sketching, or selecting commands on a special CRT screen which has been sensitized to respond to it.

Line editor Text editing program that numbers each line of text and then allows the user to edit the text only one line at a time. EDLIN is a line editor included with DOS.

Line feed Operation that advances the hard copy to the next line of text whether or not the line is full.

Logged drive *See* Default drive.

Logical devices Device named by the logic of a software system regardless of its physical relationship to the system.

Logical disk drives "Imaginary drives" that act exactly like real disk drives.

Look-ahead buffers A secondary buffer cache used to store contents of files that programs are using.

Lost clusters Sectors which have no directory entry and do not belong to any file that DOS knows about. They are debris resulting from incomplete data and should be cleaned up periodically to open up space on the disk.

Macro Short key code command which stands for a sequence of saved instructions that when retrieved will execute the commands to accomplish a given task.

Meg *See* Megabyte.

Megabyte Unit of measure that is roughly equal to one million bytes. Abbreviated MB.

Mega-string Symbol used with the PROMPT command that returns a value for the symbol. For example, using the mega-string "d" will return the system date.

Memory Commonly used to mean temporary workspace of the computer where data and programs are kept while they are being worked on. Also referred to as RAM, (Random access memory). Information in RAM is lost when the computer is turned off.

Memory manager Utility program that controls and allocates memory resources.

Memory-resident program Program that remains in the computer memory after being loaded from disk. *See also* Terminate and Stay Resident (TSR).

Menu List of choices/selections (within a program) that are displayed on the screen from which the user selects a course of action.

Menu bar A rectangular bar (usually at the top of the screen) in program in which the names of the available menus are shown. The user chooses one of the menus and by using the keyboard or mouse can cause the list of options in that menu to be displayed. Available in MS-DOS Shell and Windows.

Menu-driven Program Programs that make extensive use of menus to present choices of commands and available options.

Message Text that appears on the screen and which provide information to assist the user in completing a task, suggesting an action, or informing the user of an error.

Microfloppy disk 3 1/2-inch disk encased in a hard protective shell.

Microcomputer Personal computer usually used by one person.

Minicomputer Midlevel computer larger than a microcomputer but smaller than a mainframe computer. Usually used to meet the needs of a small company or department.

Minifloppy disk A 5 1/4-inch floppy disk.

Modem Short for Modulator-demodulator. Provides communication capabilities between computers utilizing telephone lines. Often used to access-on-line information services.

Monitor Device similar to a television screen that displays the input and output of the computer Also called display screen, screen, CRT (cathode-ray tube), or VDT (video display terminal).

Mouse Small input device equipped with two or more control buttons housed in a palm-sized case, and used to control cursor movement.

Mouse pointer On-screen pointer that is controlled by the mouse.

MS-DOS Abbreviation for Microsoft Disk Operating System which is an operating system for computers that use the 8086 (or above) microprocessor.

MSDOS.SYS Hidden system file that is one of the files that makes up the operating system of MS-DOS. This file manages the disks.

Multitasking Mode of operation in which the operating system of a computer allows the user to work on more than one task or application program at one time.

Non-bootable disk Disk that does not contain the operating system files and the computer cannot boot from it.

Noncontiguous files Files that are written to the disk in nonadjacent sectors.

Non-impact printers Type of printer where the image is transferred onto paper by means of ink-jet sprayers, melting ink, or through the use of lasers.

Norton Utilities Popular commercial utility program with programs that extend the capabilities of DOS.

Notepad Text editor available in Windows.

Numeric keypad Separate set of keys next to the main keyboard that contain the digits 0 through 9. Also includes alternate set of commands that can be toggled such as <PgUp> and the arrow keys. These functions are program dependent.

Online Indicates that the printer is not only attached to the computer but also activated and ready for operation.

Online help On-screen assistance consisting of advice or instructions on utilizing the program's features that can be accessed without interrupting the work in progress.

Operating system Master control program (set of programs) that manages the operation of all the parts of a computer. Loaded into memory when the computer is booted and known as system software. Must be loaded prior to any application software.

Optimizing the disk Making files contiguous on the disk. Function of utility programs. (Not included with DOS.)

Optional parameters Parameters that may be used with a command but are not mandatory.

Overhead Information that provides support to a computing process but often adds processing time that cause performance of a program or peripheral to be slower than usual.

Overlay files Segments of a large program that get loaded into memory as the program needs it. This allows a large program to fit into a limited amount of memory.

Overwrite Process of erasing data by writing over it. Usually by copying over another file.

Overwrite mode Newly typed characters replace existing characters to the left of the cursor.

Page The section of expanded memory that can be swapped in and out of the page frame.

Page frame Physical address in conventional memory where a page of expanded memory may be stored.

Parallel In data transmission refers to sending one byte (eight bits) at one time.

Parameters A qualifier or modifier that can be added to a command that will specify the action to be taken.

Parent directory The subdirectory above the current subdirectory. The parent directory is always one step closer to the root than the child.

Parity Parity bit is a simple method used to check for transmission errors. An extra bit is added to be sure that there is always either an even or an odd number of bits.

Partitioning Process of physically dividing a section of the hard disk from the other sections of the disk and then having the operating system treat that section as if it were a separate unit.

Path Tells DOS where to look for the programs and files on a disk that has more than one directory.

Pause Temporarily stopping the execution of a program or a command by pressing the pause key on the keyboard. Also a batch file subcommand.

PC-DOS A disk operating system that manages computer resources and allows the user to manage the files and devices of a computer. Developed for IBM Personal Computer by Microsoft. Virtually identical to MS-DOS.

PC Tools Popular utility program that includes data recovery and protection programs.

Peripheral devices Any device connected to and controlled by the CPU such as a keyboard, monitor, printer, etc.

Pipes A method of stringing two or more programs together so that the output of one program becomes the input of another program.

Pixels Smallest element (a picture cell) on the display screen grid that can be stored or displayed and is used in creating and/or printing letters, numbers, or graphics. The more pixels there are, the higher the resolution.

Port A location or place on the CPU to connect other devices to a computer. It allows the computer to send information to and from the device.

Position parameters *See* replaceable parameters.

Pretender commands Commands that allow the user to manipulate disk drives and directories. Usually, the JOIN, SUBST and ASSIGN commands are considered the pretender commands.

Print buffer Section of memory where print output is sent for temporary storage until the printer is ready to print. Compensates for differences in rates of the flow of data by taking print output at high speed from the computer and passing it along at the much slower rate required by the printer thus freeing the computer for other tasks.

Print spooler Program that compensates for differences in rates of the flow of data by temporarily storing data in memory and then dolling it out to the printer at the proper speed.

Printer Computer peripheral that produces hard copies of text or graphics on paper.

Program A set of step-by-step instructions that tell the computer what to do.

Program files Files containing executable computer programs. *See also* application program.

Program list area In MS-DOS Shell, the area on the screen where programs are listed that can be directly launched from MS-DOS Shell.

Program groups In Windows, the windows that contain icons that can start applications. Usually, similar types of applications are in the same group.

Program Manager The Windows program execution shell that enables user to view the applications as icons.

Programming language processors Tool for writing programs so that users can communicate with computers.

Prompt *See* system prompt.

Protected mode Operating mode in which different parts of memory are allocated to different programs so that when programs are running simultaneously they cannot invade each other's memory space and can only access their own memory space.

Queue A line-up of items waiting for processing.

RAM (Random access memory) *See* memory.

RAM drive Creates a disk drive in memory to emulate a disk drive.

Read-only A file or disk that may only be read and not written to or altered in any way.

Read-only attributes Prevents a file from being changed or deleted.

Real mode Enables user to run Windows on a microcomputer with an 8086 or 8088 microprocessor.

Real time Actual amount of time a computer uses to complete an operation.

Rebooting Reloading the operating system from the disk.

Redirection Process where DOS is told to take input or output from other than standard input or standard output and send to other than standard input/output.

Replace The process of placing new data in the place of other data usually after a search for the data to be replaced.

Replaceable parameters Act as place holders for values. Allows user to write batch files that can be used with many different parameters.

Resident commands *See* Internal commands.

Releases *See* Version.

ROM (Read only memory) Acronym for Read-Only-Memory. Memory that contains programs that are written on ROM chips and are retained when the computer is turned off. Often contain the start-up routines of the computer.

ROM-BIOS (read-only memory-basic input/output system) Chip built into the hardware of the system unit. Its functions include running the self-diagnostics, loading the boot record, and handling low-level system tasks.

Root directory The directory that DOS creates on each disk when the disk is formatted. The backslash (\) is the symbol used to represent the root directory.

Scanners Device that enables a computer to read a handwritten or printed page.

Screen dump Transferring the data on the monitor to a printer or another hard-copy device.

Scroll bar Used to move part of the list into view on the monitor when the entire list won't fit on the screen. Used in MS-DOS Shell and Windows.

Scrolling Vertical movement of text.

Search To seek the location of a file or to search a file for specific data.

Search path The set search path for program files.

Sector Data is stored on disks in concentric circles (tracks) that are divided. A sector is a portion of the track. Every sector is 512 bytes long.

Serial port The communications port to which a device, such as a modem or a serial printer, can be attached. The data is transmitted and/or received one bit at a time.

Shareware Process where the software is initially free on a trial basis with the option to either purchase or return it.

Shell A program that surrounds DOS and presents menus or graphics for executing programs and managing files.

Sizing buttons Allows the user to minimize or maximize a window in Windows.

Slider box A box located in a scroll bar that by dragging it with a mouse will move the user up or down in the document.

Software Programs that tell the computer what to do.

Source file What information is to be copied.

Spreadsheet programs Programs that allow for budget management and financial projections.

Stand alone programs Program run from the DOS prompt.

Standard error Where DOS writes error messages to the screen.

Standard input Where DOS expects to receive information, usually the keyboard. Keyboard from which DOS receives data.

Standard mode A mode of running in Windows that requires a minimum of a 80286 processor and 1 MB of memory.

Standard output Command that normally writes its output to the screen.

Stop bit Indicates the end of asynchronous serial transmission.

Subdirectories A hierarchical filing system that allows the user to divide a disk into manageable portions. Subdirectories have names and are files.

Subdirectory markers Symbols used to move through the hierarchical structure easily. *See also* dot and double-dot.

Substitute parameters *See* replaceable parameters.

Switch The forward slash (/) used as a delimiter with a parameter.

Syntax Proper order or sequence of the computer language and/or command.

Syntax diagram Graphic representation of a command and its syntax.

System attibute Marks a file as a system file.

System configuration The components that make a specific computer system.

System date The current date kept by the computer system.

System level When you are not in an application program and you see the C:\> or A:\> or B:\>, you are at the system level.

System prompt A symbol on the screen that tells the user that the computer is ready for the next command. The prompt consists of the letter of the current drive followed by a greater than sign (A>, B>, C>).

System software Set of programs that coordinate the operations of the hardware components.

System time The current time kept by the computer.

System utilities *See* utility programs.

Terminate and stay resident (TSR) programs Program that remains in memory after it has been initially loaded from disk. *See also* memory resident programs.

Text files File that contains text as opposed to a program. It consists of data that can be read, such as letters and numbers, with the TYPE command. Text files do not contain any special symbols. Also referred to as unformatted text files.

Thermal printers Nonimpact printer that prints by using heat to melt wire particles that contain ink and printing on heat sensitive paper.

Tiled A display mode in Windows that will divide the screen equally among open applications.

Title bar Contains the name of the program that the user is working on. Used in MS-DOS Shell and Windows.

Toggle switch Turns function on and off.

Trackball Device used to move cursor around on monitor. Usually consists of box with in which sits a ball. Cursor is moved by rotating ball.

Tracks A concentric circle on the disk where data is stored. Each track is further divided into sectors. All tracts and sectors are numbered so that computer can quickly locate information.

Transient commands *See* external commands.

Tree structure *See* Hierarchical Structure.

Typematic rate Rate or speed at which MS-DOS repeats a character when the key for that character is held down on the keyboard.

Undocumented command Command that exists but is not listed in the DOS manual.

Unfragmenting the disk *See* optimizing the disk.

Unformatted text files *See* text files.

Upper memory area Area reserved for running system's hardware. Programs cannot store information in this area. Also called adapter area and reserved area.

Upper memory blocks (UMB) Unused parts of upper memory area. Can be used for device drivers and TSR's if the computer is a 386 and you have DOS 5.0.

Utility programs Programs whose purpose is to carry out specific, vital functions that assist in the operation of a computer or software. DOS utility programs include such programs as FORMAT and CHKDSK. There are also commercial utility programs such as PCTools and Norton Utilities. *See also* external commands.

Variable parameters Value/information provided by the user.

Verbose Parameter used in conjunction with CHKDSK that gives both the status report and lists every file on the disk, including hidden ones.

Verify Command which "double-checks" a file or program and insures that sectors have been recorded correctly.

Version The numbering scheme which indicates the progressive enhancements and improvement of software.

Virtual disk drive *See* RAM drive.

Virtual memory Method of extending the size of commuter memory by using a disk to simulate memory space.

Volume label The electronic label for a disk that a user can assign at the time of formatting a disk.

Wildcards The symbols, * and ?, also called global file specifications, used to represent a character (?) or a group of characters (*) in a file name.

Window borders Edges that define the window in Windows.

Word processing programs Software that allows the user to write, edit, and print any type of text and facilitates writing.

Write-protect notch Cutout on the side of a 5 1/4-inch floppy disk that when covered keeps programs and data from being written to the disk. On a 3 1/2-inch floppy disk, the write-protect is a slider.

Write protected disk Floppy disk that can only be read-from, not written to.

XMS *See* Extended memory specification.

Index

G

H

I

J

K

L

M

Q

R

S

T